# CATALOGUE

OF THE

# PUBLIC LIBRARY

OF

# CINCINNATI.

---

CINCINNATI:
PRESS OF WILSTACH, BALDWIN & CO.
1871.

# HISTORICAL SKETCH.

---

THE PUBLIC LIBRARY OF CINCINNATI had its origin in a statute passed by the Legislature of Ohio, May 4, 1853, which provided that a state tax of one-tenth of one mill on the dollar valuation be levied, and expended under the direction of the state commissioner of common schools, for furnishing school libraries and apparatus. In conformity with this statute, small libraries comprising the same books, were distributed through the county officers to the school districts of the state. In 1854, sixteen such libraries, one for each district of the city, and each the precise duplicate of the others, were sent to Cincinnati. The Board of Education objected to this method of receiving its quota of the state tax, and asked to be supplied with books appropriate for the formation of a single library, or the means for purchasing the same. The state commissioner consented to this arrangement, and the following year a list of books recommended by a committee of the Board of Education was purchased.

In 1856 a contract was made between the Board of Education and the Ohio Mechanics' Institute, by which, in consideration of city bonds to the amount of $10,000, the Institute gave a perpetual lease of the second story of its building on the corner of Vine and Sixth streets, and the use of its library. It was provided that, in case the premises were vacated after due notice, the $10,000 should be refunded.

The "OHIO SCHOOL LIBRARY," as it was then called, was opened in the Mechanics' Institute building in July, 1856, with 11,630 volumes. Of these 6,583 volumes belonged to the Institute, and 5,047 volumes, costing $7,541.92, were purchased with funds coming from the state, though more than double that amount had been levied from the city for the purchase of school libraries. The number of accounts opened the first year was 2,400, and the circulation was 20,179. A catalogue (114 pages, octavo), constructed, it is said, by boys from the Hughes High School, and with entire innocence of any knowledge on the subject, was printed soon after.

The imprint on the title page is 1856, but the preface is dated January 12, 1857.

The state tax for libraries was suspended for the years 1856 and 1857, was again imposed in 1858 and 1859, and, in 1860, the statute of 1853, so far as it sustained libraries, was repealed. For the year ending June, 1858, the number of readers reported was 4,251, and the circulation 47,866. In 1859 the readers were 5,453, the circulation 61,787; and a fund amounting to $6,285 was in the hands of the state commissioner for the increase of the library. There is no record during these years of the number of books purchased, or of their cost. The school report for 1860 states that "the present contents of the library number 22,648 volumes, besides the books of the Ohio Historical Society, over 3,000 volumes." This indicates that the library proper then contained 16,065 volumes. The only other statistics of 1860 are thus given: "The circulation of the past year was nearly 8,000 volumes monthly. Nearly that number of readers are now registered on the roll."

The second catalogue of the library, 204 pages, double columns, octavo, was printed in 1860.

For seven years after the repeal of the state tax in 1860, the library had no public funds available for its increase. The accessions in 1861 were 86 volumes, all by donation; in 1862, 115, all by donation; in 1863, 65 purchased by subscription and 100 by donation; in 1864, 373 by donation, of which 300 were given by Mr. E. M. Shield to be used for reference only; in 1865, 500 purchased by subscription, and 28 by donation. In 1866 there is no record of the accessions, of the number of readers, or of the circulation. During the seven years of famine the library greatly deteriorated, and while the nominal enrollment of readers increased, the circulation fell off, and the books disappeared.

In 1866, the gentleman who had filled the position of librarian for ten years died, and his successor reported the library as being in a wretched condition. He says: "So little care was exercised in the entry and receipt of books, so many erasures of accounts before a careful examination, and so much laxity in the observance of rules, that the recovery of missing volumes is now impossible. The library altogether exhibits signs of decay of such a character as to alarm those who are conversant with its past usefulness." He reports the number of volumes in the library as 16,200—about the same number as six years before.

In 1867, a subscription for the purchase of books, amounting to $4,760.15, was made; and Mrs. Sarah Lewis bequeathed to the library a legacy of $5,000, the annual income of which was to be expended for books. The same year the Library Committee, supported by the Board of Education and the City Council, petitioned the Legislature to permit the Board of Education to levy a tax for the support of the library; and March 10, 1867, a statute was enacted authorizing boards of education in cities of the first and second class to levy a tax of one-tenth of a mill on the dollar valuation of the city, for the purchase books for the school library. This tax gave an annual income of $13,500 for the purchase of books, but was not available till the following year. A month later (April 3) the Legislature passed an act authorizing a board of education having custody of a public library in a city of 20,000 or more inhabitans, to constitute a board of seven managers of said library, of whom the president of the board of education should *ex-officio* be one. Such a Board of Managers was appointed in July, 1867, and the institution received the name of the "PUBLIC LIBRARY OF CINCINNATI."

The amount expended for books in 1867 was $1,683.49, but the number of volumes added is not stated. The exact number of volumes belonging to the library proper was reported to be 12,483. This large diminution from previous estimates is not accounted for; and probably resulted from the losses, the rejection of worn-out copies, and most likely an over-estimate in previous reports.

In 1868, 3,686 volumes were added by purchase at a cost of $7,089.77, and 352 volumes by donation. In 1869, 5,113 volumes were added by purchase at a cost of $11,089.64, and 279 by donation. The number of volumes reported was 21,588. The accessions in 1870 were 1,070 volumes by purchase, at a cost of $1,164.19, and 107 volumes by donation. The number of volumes in the library proper ascertained by actual count was 22,537. The accessions for the year ending in June, 1871, was 7,901 volumes by purchase at a cost of $13,791.92. Deducting 132 volumes, condemned the past year as worn out, the total number of volumes now in the library, and included in this catalogue, is 30,306.

In July, 1866, a new registration of readers was commenced. The old registration, not having been renewed for ten years, had reached the number 16,101. In July, 1867, the number of readers registered was 2,120; in 1868, 3,505; in 1869, 5,111; in 1870, 6,773; in 1871, 11 231.

In August, 1868, the city of Cincinnati purchased, for the location of a Public Library building, a lot on the west side of Vine street, between Sixth and Seventh streets, for the sum of $83,000. The lot is 80 feet front and 190 feet deep, running through to College street. The previous owner had commenced to build an opera house upon it, and had expended $50,000 in that enterprise, chiefly in the erection of a free-stone structure upon the front of the lot. Mr. James W. McLaughlin was employed as architect to prepare plans for remodeling the front structure, and for erecting the main library building in the rear, which should cover the whole lot. His plans were accepted, and the work of remodeling the front building has been completed, at a cost of $65,000. The library was removed from the Ohio Mechanics' Institute building, and opened to the public, in the new building, December 9, 1870. The same month contracts, amounting to $131,788, were made by the Board of Education, and subsequently confirmed by both branches of the city government, for erecting the main building. Of the sum above-named $105,500 was for the iron work, which is the best indication that the building is to be wholly fire-proof. The contractors are rapidly pushing on the work with the purpose of having the building under cover during the coming winter. The whole structure is estimated to have a capacity of containing 250,000 volumes.

Messrs. Louis Ballauf, Joseph P. Carbery, Henry Mack, John Richardson, and G. W. Gladden are the present members of the Building Committee. Mr. Ballauf and Mr. Mack have served, the former as chairman of the committee, from the inception of the enterprise.

The Theological and Religious Library, containing 3,291 volumes, has recently been deposited in the Public Library, but its books are not contained in this catalogue. Arrangements have also been made with the Ohio Medical College, the Academy of Medicine, and Cincinnati Hospital Trustees, by which a large medical department of the library will be built up. In the reading rooms, 353 different periodicals are on file.

The present income of the library for the purchase of books, according to the recent valuation of the city, is $17,500. The current expenses of the library are paid by the Board of Education from the general educational funds of the city.

PUBLIC LIBRARY OF CINCINNATI, August 10, 1871.

# REGULATIONS

OF THE

# PUBLIC LIBRARY OF CINCINNATI.

---

The Librarian shall, under the direction of the Board of Managers, have the charge and superintendence of the rooms of the Library, and shall be responsible for the care and safety of all books and other public property contained in them, as well as for the orderly deportment of readers.

## READING ROOMS.

Any person of good deportment and habits may use the Reading Rooms.

Ample arrangements having been made for washing, the attendants are instructed to deliver no periodical or book into unclean hands.

Persons desiring books for consultation in the building will apply to the attendants in the Reading Rooms.

## LIBRARY.

Any resident of Cincinnati may draw books from the Library by registering his or her name and residence, and complying with either of the following conditions:

1. By furnishing satisfactory security, in the form prescribed by the Board of Managers, to remain in force not more than three years.
2. By depositing with the Librarian three dollars, or the value of the work desired.

The following persons shall be exempt from making a deposit or giving security:

The Mayor and members of the Boards of Aldermen and Council;

The members and officers of the Board of Education; the Board of Managers of the Public Library; the Union Board of High Schools; and the Board of Examiners;

The teachers of the Public Schools;

Ordained clergymen and city missionaries regularly officiating in the city;

Benefactors of the Library to the amount of one hundred dollars;

Other persons to whom the Board of Managers may, for special reasons, and for a period of not more than one year, accord this privilege.

Non-residents may draw books from the Library by making a deposit of three dollars and an annual payment in advance of five dollars.

## RULES FOR THE CIRCULATION OF BOOKS.

One volume only can be taken on one account, unless the work be in duodecimo, or smaller volumes, when two volumes may be taken.

Books may be retained two weeks, and may be renewed for the same period. They can not be re-issued to the same person until they have been on the shelves twenty-four hours.

Books of recent purchase, which are labeled "Seven-Day Book," shall not be retained more than one week, and can not be renewed.

Encyclopædias, dictionaries, and other works of reference, rare and illustrated books, and such works as, for any reason, are restricted from circulation by the Board of Managers, can be consulted only in the building.

All injuries to books beyond reasonable wear, and all losses, shall promptly be made good to the satisfaction of the Librarian.

A fine of three cents a day shall be paid on each volume which is not returned according to the provisions of the preceding rules. To this fine shall be added the expense of collection and of serving notice.

If any book be not returned within one month after serving a notice, the Librarian shall proceed to collect, through the City Solicitor, the value of the book, with accrued fines and other charges to the date of payment.

Any person abusing the privileges of the Library or violating these rules, shall be temporarily suspended from its privileges; and the case shall be reported to the Board of Managers for such action as the Board may deem proper.

The Library and Reading Rooms shall be open from 8 o'clock A. M. to 10 o'clock P. M. on all secular days, and on Sundays, for reference only, between the same hours; Provided, that said rooms may be closed on holidays at the discretion of the Board of Managers.

These Regulations, or any of them, may be repealed or amended at any regular meeting of the Board of Education, a majority of the whole Board concurring.

APPROVED, February 25, 1871.

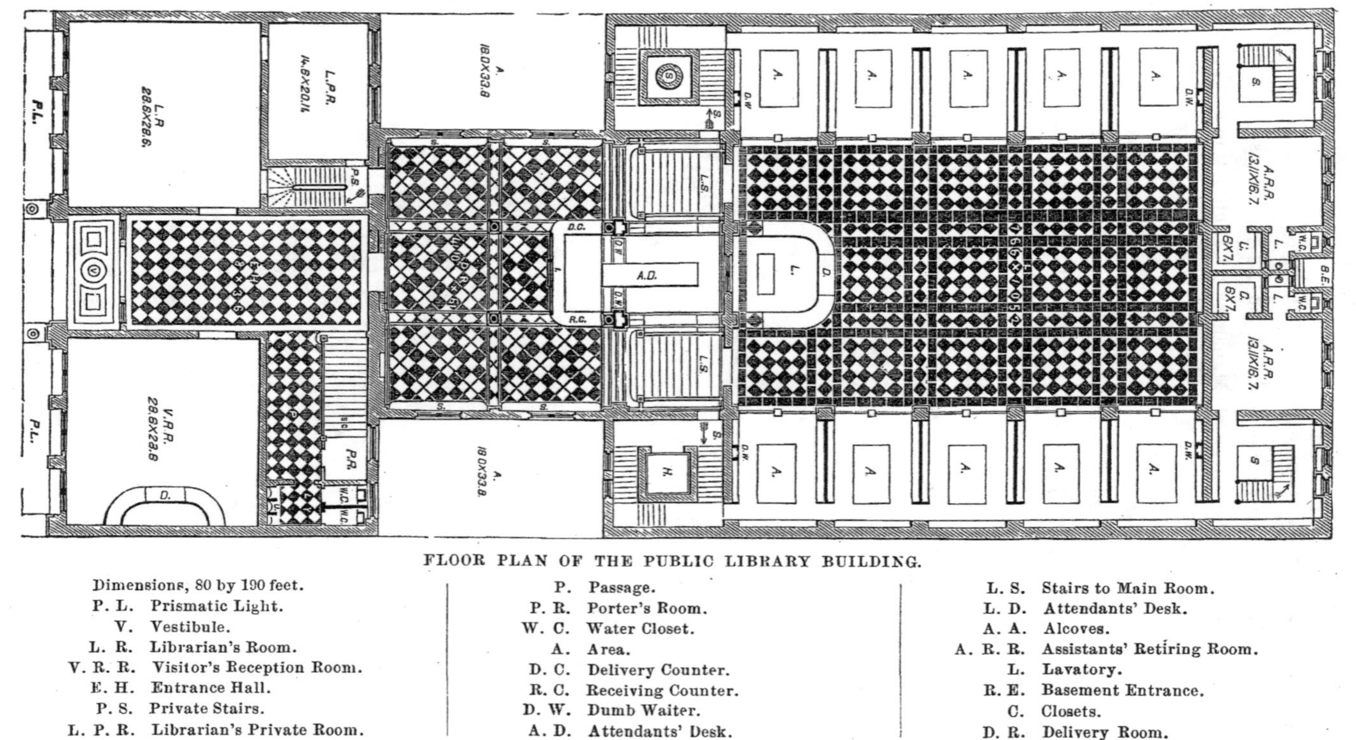


FLOOR PLAN OF THE PUBLIC LIBRARY BUILDING.

Dimensions, 80 by 190 feet.

| | |
|---|---|
| P. L. | Prismatic Light. |
| V. | Vestibule. |
| L. R. | Librarian's Room. |
| V. R. R. | Visitor's Reception Room. |
| E. H. | Entrance Hall. |
| P. S. | Private Stairs. |
| L. P. R. | Librarian's Private Room. |
| P. | Passage. |
| P. R. | Porter's Room. |
| W. C. | Water Closet. |
| A. | Area. |
| D. C. | Delivery Counter. |
| R. C. | Receiving Counter. |
| D. W. | Dumb Waiter. |
| A. D. | Attendants' Desk. |
| L. S. | Stairs to Main Room. |
| L. D. | Attendants' Desk. |
| A. A. | Alcoves. |
| A. R. R. | Assistants' Retiring Room. |
| L. | Lavatory. |
| R. E. | Basement Entrance. |
| C. | Closets. |
| D. R. | Delivery Room. |

# EXPLANATIONS.

The plan of this Catalogue is very simple. Each work in the library is catalogued under its *author* and under its *subject.* Works of fiction, and those having arbitrary titles which do not admit of being placed under subjects, are catalogued under *authors* and *titles.* Anonymous works are placed under *titles* and *subjects.* The imprint of the work is given as well under the subject as the author. The titles are brief, and usually take but one line. The whole is arranged in one alphabetical series. A work can therefore readily be found by referring, as in a dictionary, to its author, subject, or title.

The shelf-marks are given in the right-hand margin. The small capital indicates the *case,* and the figures following indicate the *number* of the work in the case. The work may comprise more than one volume. Particular volumes of the set are referred to by additional figures, thus: C,860,11 denotes the 11th volume of C,860, or the 11th volume of Sparks's American Biography. L,175,7, the shelf-mark of Homer's Iliad translated by Cowper, denotes the 7th volume of Cowper's Works, L,175.

A star (*) prefixed to a shelf-mark shows that the work can not be taken from the Library. L.R. indicates Librarian's Room; P.D. Public Document Room; R.R. Reading Room; and S.C. Shield Collection. The books thus marked belong to the reference department, and can not be taken from the Library.

It will be for the convenience of readers and of the attendants, that books be called for by their shelf-marks, rather than by their titles. The attendants will furnish cards on which readers will copy from the Catalogue the shelf-marks of the books they desire.

# CATALOGUE.

---

Abbot, The. Sir W. Scott. Boston, 1868. 16°. . . . . . . K,924
The same. Philadelphia, n. d. 12°. . . . . . . K,954
The same. Philadelphia, 1869. 8°. . . . . . K,1109
The same. Leipzig, 1860. 16°. . . . . . . . J,437

Abbott, C. *Lord Tenderden.* Law of Merchant Ships. Boston, 1854. 8°. U,531

Abbott, J. American History. New York, n. d. 8 v. 16°. . . J,1696

Vol. 1. Aboriginal America.
2. Discovery of America.
3. The Southern Colonies.
4. The Northern Colonies.
Vol. 5. Wars of the Colonies.
6. Revolt of the Colonies.
7. War of the Revolution.
8. Washington.

Florence Stories. New York, 1867. 6 v. 16°. . . . J,1382

Vol. 1. Florence and John.
2. Grimkie.
3. Orkney Islands.
Vol. 4. English Channel.
5. Isle of Wight.
6. Florence's Return.

Fire-side Piety. New York, 1835. 16°. . . . . . . J,1313

Harper's Story Books. New York, 1870. 12 v. 12°. . . J,1629

Vol. 1. Bruno; Willie and the Mortgage; Strait Gate.
2. Little Louvre; Frank; Emma;
3. Virginia; Timboo and Joliba; Timboo and Fanny.
4. Harper Establishment; Franklin; The Studio.
5. Story of Ancient History; English History; American History.
6. John True; Elfred; Museum.
7. Engineer; Rambles among the Alps; Three Gold Dollars.
8. Gibraltar Gallery; Alcove; Dialogues.
9. The Great Elm; Aunt Margaret; Vernon.
10. Carl and Jocko; Lapstone; Orkney.
11. Judge Justin; Minigo; Jasper.
12. Congo; Viola; Little Paul.

History of Alexander the Great. New York, 1848. 16°. . J,1315
History of Alfred, King of England. New York, 1854. 16°. J,1396
History of King Charles I. New York, 1865. 16°. . . J,1412
History of King Charles II. New York, 1864. 16°. . . J,1401
History of Cleopatra. New York, 1851. 16°. . . . J,1409
History of Cyrus the Great. New York, 1867. 16°. . . J,1393
History of Darius the Great. New York, 1864. 16°. . . J,1410
History of Queen Elizabeth. New York, 1849. 16°. . . J,1389
History of Genghis Khan. New York, 1860. 16°. . . J,1392
History of Hannibal. New York, 1868. 16°. . . . J,1402
History of Julius Cæsar. New York, 1864. 16°. . . . J,1414
History of Margaret of Anjou. New York, 1861. 16°. . . J,1417
History of Mary, Queen of Scots. New York, 1848. 16°. . J,1407
History of Nero. New York, 1864. 16°. . . . . . J,1386
History of Peter the Great. New York, 1865. 16°. . . J,1394

Abbott, J. History of Pyrrhus. New York, 1854. 16°. . . . . J,1421
History of King Richard I. New York, 1858. . . . . . J,1418
History of King Richard II. New York, 1858. 16°. . . J,1387
History of King Richard III. New York, 1858. 16°. . . J,1379
History of Romulus. New York, 1865. 16°. . . . . . J,1419
History of William the Conqueror. New York, 1864. 16°. . . J,1405
History of Xerxes the Great. New York, 1850. 16°. . . J,1415
Jonas Stories. New York, n. d. 6 v. 18°. . . . . . J,1714

Vol. 1. Jonas's Stories.
2. Jonas a Judge.
3. Jonas on a Farm—Winter.
Vol. 4. Jonas on a Farm—Summer.
5. Caleb in Town.
6. Caleb in the Country.

Marco Paul's Voyages and Travels. New York, 1852-3. 6 v. 16°. J,1380

Vol. 1. In New York
2. On the Erie Canal.
3. In Maine.
Vol. 4. In Vermont.
5. In Boston.
6. At Springfield Armory.

Rainbow and Lucky Stories. New York, 1860. 5 v. 16°. . J,1381

Vol. 1. Handie.
2. Rainbow's Journey.
Vol. 3. Three Pines.
4. Selling Lucky.
Vol. 5. Up the River.

Rollo Series. New York, 1869. 14 v. 18°. . . . . . J,1390

Vol. 1. Rollo Learning to Talk.
2. Rollo Learning to Read.
3. Rollo at Work.
4. Rollo at Play.
5. Rollo at School.
6. Rollo's Vacation.
7. Rollo's Experiments.
Vol. 8. Rollo's Museum.
9. Rollo's Travels.
10. Rollo's Correspondence.
11. Rollo's Philosophy—Water.
12. Rollo's Philosophy—Air.
13. Rollo's Philosophy—Fire.
14. Rollo's Philosophy—Sky.

Rollo's Tour in Europe. New York, 1869. 10 v. 16°. . . J,1391

Vol. 1. Rollo on the Atlantic.
2. Rollo in Paris.
3. Rollo in Switzerland.
4. Rollo in London.
5. Rollo on the Rhine.
Vol. 6. Rollo in Scotland.
7. Rollo in Geneva.
8. Rollo in Holland.
9. Rollo in Naples.
10. Rollo in Europe.

The Teacher. New York, 1856. 12°. . . . . . . . O,941
Young Christian Series. New York, 1860. 4 v. 12°. . . . P,281

Vol. 1. Young Christian.
2. Corner-Stone.
Vol. 3. Way to do Good.
4. Hoaryhead and M'Donner.

Abbott, J. Hand-Book of Idiotcy. London, 1857. 12°. . . . . O,914
Abbott, J. S. C. Correspondence of Napoleon and Josephine. N.Y. 1856. 12°. D,604
Empire of Austria. New York, 1859. 12°. . . . . . B,526
Empire of Russia. New York, 1860. 12°. . . . . . B,539
French Revolution of 1789. New York, 1859. 8°. . . . . B,257
History of the Civil War in America. Springfield, 1866. 2 v. 8°. B,918
History of Hernando Cortez. New York, 1855. 16°. . . J,1717
History of Henry IV, of France. Boston, 1856. 16°. . . J,1416
History of Hortense. New York, 1870. 16°. . . . . J,1403
History of Joseph Bonaparte. New York, 1869. 16°. . . J,1716
History of Josephine. New York, 1867. 16°. . . . J,1411
History of Marie Antoinette. New York, 1849. 16°. . . J,1384
History of Mary, Queen of Scots. New York, 1868. 16°. . J,1407
History of Napoleon Bonaparte. New York, 1867. 2 v. 8°. . D,564
Kings and Queens; Life in the Palaces. New York, 1855. 12°. J,1397
Mother at Home. New York, 1855. 16°. . . . . . J,1398
The same. New York, n. d. 18°. . . . . . . P,746,24
Napoleon I. at St. Helena. New York, 1855. 8°. . . . . D,565
Napoleon III. Boston, 1869. 8°. . . . . . . . . D,584
History of King Philip of the Wampanoags. New York, 1857. 16°. J,1406

Abbott, J. S. C. History of Madame Roland. New York, 1867. 16°. J,1404
Romance of Spanish History. New York, 1869. 12°. . . . B,453
South and North. New York, 1860. 12°. . . . . . . V,90
Abbott, L. Jesus of Nazareth; his Life and Teachings. N. Y. 1869. 8°. P,379
Abdallah; or, the Four-leaved Shamrock. E. Laboulaye. London, 1868. 16°. I,566
Abel, A. Aus der Natur. Leipzig, 1852–61. 16 v. in 5. 8°. . . . G,671
Abel, C. D. Principles of Machinery. London, 1860–68. 12°. . . M,825
Atlas to the same. London, 1860. 4°. . . . . . . Q,359
Abel, F. A., and Bloxam, C. L. Handbook of Chemistry. Phil. 1854. 8°. N,202
Abell, L. G. Skillful Housewife's Book. New York, 1858. 12°. . M,533,4
Abeokuta and Camaroon Mountains. R. F. Burton. Lond. 1863. 2 v. 8°. V,798
Abercrombie, J. Essays. New York, 1845. 18°. . . . . . . P,343
Inquiries concerning the Intellectual Powers. New York, 1852. 18°. L,368
Philosophy of the Moral Feelings. New York, 1854. 18°. . . L,380
Aberdeen, History of. J. Gordon. See *Spalding Club Publications*, v. 9.
and Banff, Records of Shires of. See *Spalding Club Pub.* v. 12–15.
Burgh Records, 1398–1625. See *Spalding Club Publications*, v. 18, 19.
Fasti Aberdonenses, 1494–1854. See *Spalding Club Publications*, v. 28.
Records of Kirk Session, etc. See *Spalding Club Publications*, v. 22.
Registrum Episcopatus Aberdonenses. See *Spald. Club Pub.* v. 20, 21.
Earl of, Letters to, 1681–84. See *Spalding Club Publications*, v. 26.
Earl of. See *Gordon, G. H.*
Abergavenny, Sanitary Condition of. S. H. Steel. Abergavenny, 1847. 8°. N,252,29
Abernethy, J. Memoirs of G. Macilwain. New York, 1853. 12°. . . D,161
About, E. Germaine. Boston, 1860. 12°. . . . . . . . . H,966
Greece and the Greeks. New York, 1857. 12°. . . . . V,538
King of the Mountains. Boston, 1861. 12°. . . . . . H,971
Roman Question. New York, 1859. 12°. . . . . . . V,497
Abrantes, Duchess d'. See *Junot, L. P.*
Abyssinia, Captivity in. H. Blanc. London, 1868. 12°. . . . . V,804
Life in. M. Parkyns. New York, 1854. 2 v. 12°. . . . V,790
New Tributaries of. Sir S. W. Baker. Philadelphia, 1868. 12°. . V,781
Story of the Captives in. H. Blanc. London, 1868. 16°. . . V,787
Travels in Southern. C. Johnston. London, 1844. 2 v. 8°. . V,806
Academic Unity. G. Dyer. London, 1827. 8°. . . . . . O,1251,3
Acetaria; a Discourse of Sallets. J. Evelyn. London, 1706. f°. . . Q,121
Acheta, *pseud.* See *Budgen, L. M.*
Achilles Tatius. Greek Romances; trans. by R. Smith. London, 1855. 12°. L,58
Achilli, G. Dealings with the Inquisition. London, 1851. 12°. . . P,822
Acids and Bases, Heat developed in. T. Andrews. Dublin, 1841. 4°. N,252,42
Ackermann, R. Manual of Colours. London, 1844. 16°. . . . M,2
Picturesque Tour of the English Lakes. London, 1821. 4°. . *Q,207
Acoustics in Public Buildings. T. R. Smith. London, n. d. 12°. . . M,858
Wonders of. R. Radau. New York, 1870. 12°. . . . M,1060
Across America and Asia. R. Pumpelly. New York, 1870. 8°. . V,1084
Acrostics. R. Blackwell. St. Louis, 1869. 12°. . . . . . . I,288
Acting Charades. H. and A. Mayhew. London, n. d. 12°. . . . . I,710
Acton Bell, *pseud.* See *Brontë, Anna.*
Ad Clerum: Advices to a Young Preacher. J. Parker. Boston, 1871. 12°. H,511
Ad Fidem; or, Parish Evidences of the Bible. E. F. Burr. Bost. 1871. 12°. P,282

Adalbert, H. W. Travels in South of Europe and Brazil. Lon. 1849. 2 v. 8°. v,1071
Adam and the Adamite. D. M'Causland. London, 1864. 12°. . . P,915
Adam, A. Roman Antiquities. New York, 1842. 8°. . . . . . A,165
Summary of Geography and History. Edinburgh, 1794. 8°. . v,1109
Adam Bede. M. J. Lewes. New York, 1868. 12°. . . . . . . K,792
The same. Leipzig, 1859. 2 v. in 1. 16°. . . . . . J,295
Adam Blair. J. G. Lockhart. Edinburgh, 1849. 16°. . . . . . K,805
Adam of Murimuth. Chronica sui temporis; ed. T. Hog. Lond. 1846. 8°. U,630
Adams, Abagail. Journal and Correspondence. New York, 1841. 12°. . C,731
Adams, A. L. Naturalist in India and Cashmere. Edinburgh, 1867. 8°. . V,613
Adams, C. Boys at Home. New York, 1870. 12°. . . . . . J,1640
Edgar Clifton; or, Right and Wrong. New York, 1870. 12°. J,1645
Adams, D. Agricultural Reader. Boston, 1824. 12°. . . . . . O,769
Adams, C. B. Elements of Geology. New York, 1854. 12°. . . . N,605
Report on the Geology of Vermont. Burlington, 1846. 8° . . N,878
Adams, H. G. Life and Adventures of Dr. Livingston. London, n. d. 12°. D,366
Adams, F. C. Manuel Pereira; Sov. Rule of South Carolina. Wash. 1853. 12°. K.1
Adams, J., Life of. J. Q. and C. F. Adams. Phil. 1871. 2 v. 12°. C,1012
Memoirs of the Administration of. G. Gibbs. N. Y. 1846. 2 v. 8°. B,811
Suppressed History of Administration of. J. Wood. Phil. 1846. 12°. B,852
Works; ed. with Life by C. F. Adams. Boston, 1850–56. 10 v. 8°. U,63
and Cunningham, W. Correspondence. Boston, 1823. 8°. . . H,836
Review of the same. T. Pickering. Salem, 1824. 8°. . . H,836
Adams, J. Q., Discourse on the Death of. E. E. Magoon. Cincinnati, 1848. T,19,2
Documents relating to the Negotiation at Ghent. Wash. 1822. 8°. . B,702
Lectures on Rhetoric and Oratory. Cambridge, 1810. 2 v. 8°. . L,551
Letters and Opinions of the Masonic Institution. Cin'ti, 1851. 8°. O,381
Life of. J. Quincy. Boston, 1858. 8°. . . . . . . C,1089
Life of. W. H. Seward. Auburn, 1849. 12°. . . . . . . C,977
Lives of James Madison and James Munroe. Buffalo, 1850. 12°. . C,918
Poems of Religion and Society. New York, 1850. 12°. . . . I,5
Report upon Weights and Measures. Washington, 1821. 8°. . . O,502
and C. F. Life of John Adams. Philadelphia, 1871. 2 v. 12°. C,1012
Adams, Nehemiah. Broadcast. Boston, 1863. 16°. . . . . . P,146
Evenings with the Doctrines. Boston, 1866. 12°. . . . . P,112
Friends of Christ in the New Testament. Boston, 1864. 12°. . . P,147
Life of John Eliot. Boston, 1870. 12°. . . . . . . . D,8,3
Sable Cloud; a Southern Tale. Boston, 1866. 12°. . . . . K,294
South-Side View of Slavery. Boston, 1860. 12°. . . . . O,406
Adams, S., Life of. W. V. Wells. Boston, 1865. 3 v. 8°. . . C,1067
Adams, W. Sacred Allegories. Leipzig, 1864. 16°. . . . . . J,1
Three Gardens; Eden, Gethsemene, Paradise. New York, 1868. 12°. P,95
Adams, W. H. D. Buried Cities of Campania. London, 1868. 12°. . B,499
Lighthouses and Lightships. New York, 1870. 12°. . . . M,1054
Neptune's Heroes; or, Sea-Kings of England. London, 1861. 16°. C,1242
Queen of the Adriatic; Venice. London, 1869. 12°. . . . B,500
Records of Noble Lives. London, 1870. 12°. . . . . . C,1243
Adams, W. T. Army and Navy Stories. Boston, 1869. 6 v. 16°. . J,1536

Vol. 1. Soldier Boy. Vol. 4. Yankee Middy.
2. Sailor Boy. 5. Fighting Joe.
3. Young Lieutenant. 6. Brave Old Salt.

Adams, W. T. Boat Club Series. Boston, 1870. 6 v. 16°. . . J,1435

Vol. 1. Boat Club.
2. All Aboard.
3. Now or Never.
Vol. 4. Little by Little.
5. Try Again.
6. Poor and Proud.

Lake Shore Series. Boston, 1870. 6 v. 16°. . . . . . J,1537

Vol. 1. Through by Daylight.
2. Lightning Express.
3. On Time.
Vol. 4. Switch-Off.
5. Brake Up.
6. Bear and Forbear.

Starry Flag Series. Boston, 1870. 6 v. 16°. . . . . . J,1534

Vol. 1. Starry Flag.
2. Freaks of Fortune.
3. Breaking Away.
Vol. 4. Seek and Find.
5. Make or Break.
6. Down the River.

Upward and Onward Series. Boston, 1871. 3 v. 16°. . . J,1468

Vol. 1. Field and Forest.
Vol. 2. Plane and Plank.
Vol. 3. Desk and Debit.

Woodville Stories. Boston, 1870. 6 v. 16°. . . . . . J,1467

Vol. 1. Rich and Humble.
2. In School and Out.
3. Watch and Wait.
Vol. 4. Work and Win.
5. Hope and Have.
6. Haste and Waste.

Young America Abroad. Boston, 1870. 6 v. 16°. . . J,1535

Vol. 1. Outward Bound.
2. Shamrock and Thistle.
3. Red Cross.
Vol. 4. Dikes and Ditches.
5. Palace and Cottage.
6. Down the Rhine.

Addington, H., Life of. G. Pellew. New York, 1857. 8°. . . C,1253

Addison, J. Sir Roger de Coverley. London, 1865. p. 8°. . . I,664,2

Life of. L. Aikin. Philadelphia, 1846. 8°. . . . . . D,201

Works; edited by G. W. Green. New York, 1854. 6 v. 12°. . U,170

Vol. 1. Life; Translations; Poems; Dramas.
2. Dialogues on Ancient Medals; Travels; Virgil's Georgics; Ancient and Modern Learning; Christian Religion; Letters; Political Writings.
3. Freeholder; Plebeian; Lover.
4. Tatler; Guardian.
5, 6. Spectator.

The same. New York, 1853. 5 v. 12°. . . . . . S.C.

Vol. 1. Life; Translations; Poems; Dramas.
2. Dialogues on Ancient Medals; Travels; Virgil's Georgics; Ancient and Modern Learning; Christian Religion; Letters; Political Writings.
3. Freeholder; Plebeian; Tatler; Guardian; Lover.
4, 5. Spectator.

The same; edited by R. Hurd. London, 1854. v. 1–3. p. 8°. L,259

Vol. 1. Poems; Dialogues on Ancient Medals; Remarks on Italy.
2, 3. Tatler; Spectator.

and Sir R. Steele. Spectator. Cincinnati, 1851. 2 v. 8°. . . H,459

Selections from Spectator, Tatler, etc. Lond. 1849. 2 v. 12°. H,530

Adèle. J. Kavanagh. New York, 1867. 12°. . . . . . . . K,739

The same. Leipzig, 1858. 3 v. 16°. . . . . . . J,226

Adela Cathcart. G. Mac Donald. London, 1864. 3 v. 12°. . . . J,571

Adirondack; or, Life in the Woods. J. T. Headley. New York, 1869. 12°. V,25

Adirondacks, Adventures in the. W. H. H. Murray. Boston, 1869. 12°. V,98

Forest Arcadia of Northern New York. Boston, 1864. 16°. . . V,147

Adler, J. G. German and English Dictionary. New York, 1869. 8°. . L.R.

The same. New York, 1869. 8°. . . . . . . . . R.R.

Admirals, Lives of British. R. Southey. London, 1833–40. 5 v. 12°. M,1009

Adolphus, J. History of England, 1773–1804. London, 1840–45. 7 v. 8°. A,413

History of France. London, 1803. 2 v. 8°. . . . . . . B,333

Royal Exile; Memoirs of Queen Caroline. Lond. 1820–21. 4 v. 8°. D,113

Adopted Heir. J. Pardoe. Philadelphia, n. d. 12°. . . . . . K,587

Adornments, Rustic, for Homes of Taste. S. Hibberd. London, 1870. 4°. M,160

Adrianni, A. Gutta Percha; or Caoutchouc. Utrecht, 1850. 8°. . N,252,50

Adriatic Sea, Islands of the. A. A. Paton. London, 1849. 2 v. 8°. . V,435

Adrift in Dixie; a Yankee among the Rebels. J. R. Gilmore. N.Y. 1866. 12°. K,301
Adulterations in Food and Medicine. A. H. Hassall. London, 1857. 8°. L,905
Verfälschungen der Nahrungsmittel. F.H. Walchner. Carlsr.'40. 16°. N,252,37
Adventure, American, by Land and Sea. New York, 1841. 16°. . J.1307
Adventurer, The. Boston, 1866. 3 v. 8°. . . . . . H,536,19-21
Adventures in Wilds of America. C. Lanman. London, 1863. p. 8°. I,659,2
of British Seamen. Edinburgh, 1817. 16°. . . . . . . I,493
of a Marquis. A. Dumas. Philadelphia, n. d. 8°. . . . H,979
of a Young Naturalist. L. Biart. New York, 1871. 12°. . . J,1311
of Philip. W. M. Thackeray. Leipzig, 1862. 2 v. in 1. 16°. . J,478
of Mr. Ledbury. A. Smith. London, n. d. 16°. . . . . . J,651
on the Great Hunting Grounds of the World. New York, 1870. 12°. M,1064
Advice to the Clergy. Dublin, 1790. 8°. . . . . . . . . H,630
to Young Ladies. T. S. Arthur. Philadelphia, n. d. 16°. . . H,15
to Young Men. T. S. Arthur. Philadelphia, n. d. 16°. . . H,16
Æschines. Oration against Ctesiphon; ed. by J. T. Chaplin. Camb. 1850. 12°. U,401
Æschylus, Agamemnon; edited by C. C. Felton. Boston, 1847. 12°. . U,402
New Readings in Hermann's edition. London, 1853. 12°. . . L,34,2
Prometheus; edited by T. D. Woolsey. Boston, 1856. 12°. . . U,406
Septem Contra Thebas; edited by A. Sachtleben. Boston, 1853. 12°. U,403
Tragedies; translated by R. Potter. Norwich, 1777. 4°. . . U,593
The same; translated by R. Potter. New York, 1852°. 16°. U,371
The same; translated by T. A. Buckley. London, 1870. p. 8°. L,34
The same; trans. by T. A. Buckley. New York, 1856. 12°. . U,383
The same; trans. by C. H. Plumptre. Lond. 1868. 2 v. 12°. U,382
Compositions from Tragedies of. J. Flaxman. London, 1831. 4°. . Q,235
Æsopus. Fables of Æsop. New York, 1869. 16°. . . . . . . G,1
Æsthetics. Æsthetische Forschungen. A. Zeising. Frankfurt, 1855. 8°. G,576
Introduction to the Study of. J. C. Moffat. Cincinnati, 1856. 12°. O,615
Letters on. J. C. F. von Schiller; tr. by J. Weiss. Boston, 1845. 12°. O,614
Afflicted, Companion for the. T. Walker. New York, 1851. 12°. . . P,292
Afghanistan, War in. J. W. Kaye. London, 1857-8. 3 v. 8°. . . B,78
Afloat and Ashore. J. F. Cooper. New York, 1867. 12°. . . . K,24
The same. New York, 1861. 8°. . . . . . . . . K,57
Afloat in the Forest. M. Reid. Boston, 1868. 12°. . . . . J,1589
Afraja. T. Mügge. Frankfurt, 1857. 12°. . . . . . . G,354
Africa and America Described. M. Banim. New York, 1854. 12°. . V,771
and the American Flag. A. H. Foote. New York, 1854. 12°. . V,828
and Europe, Travels in. M. M. Noah. New York, 1819. 8°. . V,1087
Arabia, and Madagascar. W. F. W. Owen. N.Y. 1833. 2 v. 12°. V,1079
Africa, Central, Inner Africa laid open. W. D. Cooley. London, 1852. 8°. V,835
Journal in Interior of, 1805. M. Park. London, 1815. 4°. . V,718
Journey to. B. Taylor. Philadelphia, 1870. 12°. . . V,776
Lake Regions of. R. F. Burton. New York, 1860. 8°. . V,853
Travels in Interior of, 1795-7. M. Park. London, 1799. 4°. V,719
Travels through, 1824-28. R. Caillie. Lond. 1830. 2 v. 8°. V,834
and North, Travels in. H. Barth. N. Y. 1857-59. 3 v. 8°. V,870
Die Erdkunde. C. Ritter. Berlin, 1822. 8°. . . . . . . E,153
Discovery and Adventure in. R. Jameson, etc. N. Y. 1855. 18°. . L,349
Eastern, Travels in. J. L. Krapf. Boston, 1860. 8°. . . . V,801

Africa, Explorations and Adventures in. P. B. Du Chaillu. N.Y. 1862. 8°. v,869
Hunter's Life in South. R. G. Cumming. N. Y. 1864. 2 v. 12°. . v,802
Hunting in South. W. C. Baldwin. New York, 1863. 12°. . . . v,803
Kru Coast, Cape Palmas, and Niger. W. Durrant. Lond. 1862. 8°. v,1086,2
Niger Expedition. W. Allen & T. R. H. Thomson. Lond. 1848. 2 v. 8°. v,837
Journal of Niger Expedition. R. and J. Lander. Lond. 1832. 16°. I,611
The same. New York, 1854. 2 v. 16°. . . . . . L,367
Niger, Tshadda, & Binue Expedition. T. J. Hutchinson. Lon.'65. p. 8°. I,658,1
Reisen in Afrika, 1835–41. J. Russegger. Stutt. 1841–48. 4 v. in 7. 8°. E,161
Second Expedition into. H. Clapperton. Philadelphia, 1829. 8°. v,832
Savage. W. W. Reade. New York, 1864. 8°. . . . . . v,866
South, Letters from the Cape. Lady Duff-Gordon. Lond. 1864. 8°. v,1086,3
Missionary Travels in. D. Livingstone. N. Y. 1858. 8°. . v,864
Missionsreisen in. D. Livingstone. Leip. 1858. 2 v. in 1. 8°. E,229
Travels in. J. Chapman. London, 1868. 2 v. 8°. . . v,816
Southwestern. Lake Ngami. J. C. Andersson. N. Y. 1861. 12°. . v,800
Reisen in. C. J. Andersson. Leipzig, n. d. 2 v. in 1. . 8°. E,230
Travels in. E. D. Clarke. New York, 1813–14. 2 v. 12°. . v,1035
Travels of Mungo Park in. Edinburgh, n. d. 12°. . . . . v,772
Western. J. L. Wilson. New York, 1856. 12°. . . . . . v,793
Colonization on Western Coast. A. Alexander. Phil. 1849. 8°. C,437
Navigation a la Côte. C. P. Kerhallet. Paris, 1852. 4°. Q,425,2
Wanderings in. R. F. Burton. London, 1863. 2 v. 8°. . v,796
African Crusoes. Mrs. R. Lee. Boston, 1871. 16°. . . . . . J,1552
African Wanderings. F. Werne. London, 1852. 12°. . . . . v,766
The same. London, 1854. p. 8°. . . . . . . . I,658,2
After Dark. W. Collins. Leipzig, 1856. 16°. . . . . . . . . J,72
After Icebergs with a Painter. L. L. Noble. New York, 1861. 12°. . v,171
After Life; sequel to Home Life. E. M. Sewell. Leip. 1868. 2 v. in 1. 16°. J,453
After the Storm. T. S. Arthur. Philadelphia, n. d. 16°. . . . . J,606
After the War; a Southern Tour. W. Reid. Cincinnati, 1866. 12°. . v,148
Afternoon Lectures on Literature, etc., Dublin, 1863–8. Lond. 1863–69. 5 v. 16°. H,566
Agassiz, E. C. First Lesson in Natural History. Boston, 1859. 16°. . N,494
and A. Seaside Studies in Natural History. Boston, 1865. 8°. . O,63
Agassiz, L. Bibliographia Zoologiæ et Geologiæ. Lond. 1848–54. 4 v. 8°. O,300
Echinodermes Fossiles de la Suisse. Paris, n. d. 4°. . . . N,750
Geological Sketches. Boston, 1866. 12°. . . . . . . . . N,608
Lake Superior; Narrative by J. E. Cabot. Boston, 1850. 8°. . v,1115
Methods of Study in Natural History. Boston, 1866. 12°. . . N,644
Natural History of the United States. Boston, 1857. 2 v. 4°. . Q,115
Structure of Animal Life. New York, 1866. 8°. . . . . N,540
and E. C. Journey to Brazil. Boston, 1868. 8°. . . . . . v,255
and Gould, A. A. Comparative Physiology. London, 1870. p. 8°. . L,271
Principles of Zoölogy. Boston, 1854. 12°. . . . . N,650
Agatha's Husband. D. M. Craik. New York, 1868. 8°. . . . . . K,641
The same. Leipzig, 1860. 16°. . . . . . . . . J,82
Age, The; a Colloquial Satire. P. J. Bailey. Boston, 1858. 16°. . . I,282
Age of Reason. T. Paine. No imprint. 12°. . . . . . . . P,37
Agincourt. G. P. R. James. Leipzig, 1844. 16°. . . . . . . J,199
Agincourt, History of the Battle of. Sir H. Nicolas. London, 1833. 8°. . B,97

Agincourt. See *Séroux d' Agincourt, J. B. L. G.*
Agnes; a Novel. M. Oliphant. New York, 1867. 8°. . . . . . K,861
The same. Leipzig, 1865. 2 v. in 1. 16°. . . . . . J,396
Agnes Grey. A. and E. Brontë. Leipzig, 1851. 2 v. in 1. 16°. . . . J,46
Agnes of Sorrento. H. B. Stowe. Boston, 1867. 12°. . . . . . K,281
Agnew, D. H. Practical Anatomy. Philadelphia, 1868. . . . . L,882
Agricultural and Literary Essays. J. C. Gray. Boston, 1856. 12°. . . H,266
Agricultural Chemistry, Address on. J. Locke. Lebanon, O., 1854. 8°. . T,19,2
Essay on. T. Graham. Newcastle-on-Tyne, 1842. 12°. pp. 32. N,252,23
Jahresbericht über. R. Hoffmann. Berlin, 1860–65. 6 v. 8°. . G,755
and Geology, Elements of. J. F. W. Johnston. N. Y. 1855. 12°. M,514
Lectures on. J. F. W. Johnston. Edinburgh, 1847. 8°. . M,573
Agricultural Essays. J. Taylor. Georgetown, 1814. 12°. . . . . . M,486
Agricultural Improvement by Education. W. Evans. Montreal, 1837. 16°. M,433
Agricultural Society, English, Journal of. Lond. 1839–64. 1st ser. v. 1–25. 8°. R,18
The same. London, 1865–68. 2d ser. 4 v. 8°. . . . . R,18
Agriculture. Bodenkunde. C. Sprengel. Leipzig, 1844. 8°. . . . . G,660
Canadian, Theory and Practice of. W. Evans. Mont. 1835–36. 2 v. 8°. M,434
Chemische Untersuchung des Bodens. F. v. Babo. Frank. 1843. 8°. N,252,24
Chemistry of. D. Christy. Cincinnati, 1852. 8°. . . . . . M,554
J. A. Stöckhardt. London, 1855. 12°. . . . . . . L,320
Chemistry and Geology applied to. J. F. W. Johnston. N.Y. n. d. 12°. M,515
Elements of. G. E. Waring. New York, 1855. 12°. . . . M,484
Elements of Scientific. J. P. Norton. New York, 1855. . . . M,513
Encyclopædia of. J. C. Loudon. London, 1844. 8°. . . . . M,574
Landwirthschaftliche Erfahrungen. H.W. v. Pabst. Stuttgart, 1849. 8°. G,658
Landwirthschaft in Beziehungen zur Chemie, Physik und Meteorologie. J. B. J. D. Boussingault. Halle, 1851–56. 4 v. 8°. . G,656
Landwirthschaft in Ober-Italien. J. Burger. Wien, 1851. 2 v. 12°. G,655
Liebig's Ackerbautheorie. F. G. Schulze. Jena, 1846. 8°. . N,252,24
Principles of. A. D. Thaër. New York, 1846. 8°. . . . . . M,563
Recreations in. J. Anderson. London, 1799–1802. 6 v. 8°. . H,615
Relation which Science bears to. J. F. W. Johnston. N. Y. 1850. 12°. M,496
Scientific and Practical. J. L. Campbell. Philadelphia, 1859. 16°. M,510
State and Prospects of British. W. Hutt. London, 1837. 8°. N,252,6
Végétation appliquée à. A. Bouchardat. Paris, 1846. 16°. . N,252,26
What can be done for English? J. F. W. Johnston. Lond. 1842. 8°. N,252,6
Agriculturist's Assistant. J. Ewart. Glasgow, 1857. 16°. . . . M,439
Agrippina; the Great Empress. S. De Vere. Philadelphia, 1870. 12°. . K,220
Aguecheek. C. B. Fairbanks. Boston, 1859. 12°. . . . . . . H,125
Aguilar, G. Days of Bruce. New York, 1868. 2 v. 12°. . . . K,578
Essays and Miscellanies. Philadelphia, 1853. 12°. . . . . . H,568
Home Influence. New York, 1868. 12°. . . . . . . . K,579
The same. Leipzig, 1859. 2 v. in 1. 16°. . . . . . J,2
Home Scenes and Heart Studies. New York, 1864. 12°. . . K,580
Mother's Recompense. New York, 1868. 12°. . . . . . . K,581
The same. Leipzig, 1859. 2 v. in 1. 16°. . . . . . J,3
Vale of Cedars. New York, 1868. 12°. . . . . . . . K,583
Woman's Friendship. New York, 1867. 12°. . . . . . . K,582
Women of Israel. New York, 1864. 2 v. 12°. . . . . . D,766

Ahiman Rezon; History and Polity of Free Masonry. Philad. 1825. 8°. . o,382
Ahn, F. Method of Learning German. New York, 1870. 8°. . . L,553
Aïdé, H. Carr of Carrlyon; a Novel. Leipzig, 1862. 2 v. in 1. 16°. . J,4
Marstons; a Novel. Leipzig, 1868. 2 v. in 1. 16°. . . . J,5
Rita; an Autobiography. Leipzig, 1859. 16°. . . . . J,6
Aids to Reflection. S. T. Coleridge. New York, 1863. 12°. . . . H,450
Aikin, J. Select Works of the British Poets. Phila. 1845. 3 v. 8°. . S.C.
and A. L. Barbauld. Evenings at Home. Edinburgh, n. d. 16°. . J,1439
Annals of the Reign of George III. London, 1816. 2 v. 8°. . A,540
England Described. London, 1818. 8°. . . . . . . . V,267
Aikin, L. Life of Joseph Addison. Philadelphia, 1846. 8°. . . . D,201
Memoirs of the Court of Charles I. London, 1833. 2 v. 8°. . . A,503
Memoirs of the Court of Queen Elizabeth. London, 1819. 2 v. 8°. A,501
Memoirs of the Court of James I. London, 1822. 2 v. 8°. . . A,502
Aikman, J. History of Scotland. Edinburgh, 1856. 6 v. 8°. . . . S.C.
Aimwell Stories. W. Simonds. Boston, 1865–70. 7 v. 16°. . . J,1431
Vol. 1. Oscar. 2. Clinton. Vol. 3. Ella. 4. Whistler. 5. Marcus. Vol. 6. Jessie. 7. Jerry.
Ainslee Stories. H. C. Weeks. New York, 1869. 16°. . . . J,1618
Ainsworth, W. H. Cardinal Pole; a Romance. Leip. 1863. 2 v. in 1. 16°. J,11
Constable de Bourbon. Leipzig, 1866. 2 v. in 1. 16°. . . . J,7
Constable of the Tower. Leipzig, 1861. 16°. . . . . . J,8
Flitch of Bacon. Leipzig, 1854. 16°. . . . . . . . J,9
Hilary St. Ives. Leipzig, 1869. 2 v. in 1. 16°. . . . . J,10
Jack Sheppard; a Romance. Leipzig, 1846. 16°. . . . . J,12
John Law, the Projector. Leipzig, 1864. 2 v. in 1. 16°. . . J,13
Lancashire Witches. Leipzig, 1849. 2 v. in 1. 16°. . . . J,14
Lord Mayor of London. Leipzig, 1862. 2 v. in 1. 16°. . . . J,15
The same. London, n. d. 12°. . . . . . . . J,560
Mervyn Clithroe. Leipzig, 1858. 2 v. in 1. 16°. . . . . J,16
Myddleton Pomfret; a Novel. Leipzig, 1868. 2 v. in 1. 16°. . J,17
Old Court; a Novel. Leipzig, 1867. 2 v. in 1. 16°. . . . J,18
Ovingdean Grange. Leipzig, 1860. 16°. . . . . . . . J,19
Saint James. Leipzig, 1844. 16°. . . . . . . . . J,20
South-Sea Bubble. Leipzig, 1868. 2 v. in 1. 16°. . . . . J,21
Spanish Match. Leipzig, 1865. 2 v. in 1. 16°. . . . . J,22
Spendthrift; a Tale. Leipzig, 1856. 16°. . . . . . J,23
Star Chamber. Leipzig, 1854. 2 v. in 1. 16°. . . . . J,24
Talbot Harland. Leipzig, 1870. 16°. . . . . . . . J,26
Windsor Castle; a Romance. Leipzig, 1844. 16°. . . . . J,25
Air, Uses and Abuses of. J. H. Griscom. New York, 1850. 12°. . . L,883
Air-Pump, Early History of the. G. Wilson. Edinburgh, 1849. . N,252,33
Airy, G. B. Popular Astronomy. London, 1866. 16°. . . . . N,254
Treatise on Trigonometry. London, 1855. p. 8°. . . . M,1141
Undulatory Theory of Optics. London, 1866. 12°. . . . . N,23
Aitken, W. Science and Practice of Medicine. London, 1858. 8°. . . L,873
Akenside, M. Poetical Works. Boston, 1854. 16°. . . . . . . I,195
and J. Dyer. Poetical Works. London, 1855. 16°. . . . . I,274
Akerman, J. Y. Study of Ancient and Modern Coins. London, 1848. 16°. M,385
Alabama and Sumter, Cruise of. R. Semmes. London, 1864. 2 v. 12°. . B,954

Alaska and its Resources. W. H. Dall. Boston, 1870. 8°. . . . . v,131
Travels in. F. Whymper. London, 1868. 8°. . . . . . v,82
Albania, Travels in. T. S. Hughes. London, 1830. 2 v. 8°. . . . v,569
Albany, Random Recollections of. G. A. Worth. . . . . . . c,121
Albemarle, Earl of. See *Keppel, G. T.*
Albert, Prince. Addresses on different Occasions. London, 1857. 4°. N,252,52
Early Years of. C. Grey. New York, 1867. 12°. . . . . . D,315
Speeches and Addresses. Leipzig, 1866. 16°. . . . . . . J,27
Albert Nyanza, The. Sir S. W. Baker. Philadelphia, 1866. 8°. . . . v,814
Alberti di Villanova, F.de. Dictionnaire François-Ital. Bassano, 1811. 2 v. 4°. L.R.
Albion, Perlen Britischer Lyrik. A. Böttger. Leipzig, n. d. 24°. . . E,258
Albrechtsberger, J. G. Thorough-Bass, Harmony, etc. Lond. 1855. 8°. M,421,2
Albro, J. A. Life of Thos. Shepard. Boston, 1870. 12°. . . . . . D,8,4
Alcobaça and Batalha, Monasteries of. W. Beckford. London, 1835. 8°. v,474
Alcock, Sir R. Capital of the Tycoon; 3 years in Japan. N.Y. 1868. 2 v. 12°. v,617
Alcohol and the Constitution of Man. E. L. Youmans. N. Y. 1854. 12°. L,875
and Tobacco. J. Fiske. New York, 1869. 16°. . . . . . H,222
Alcoholic Liquors, Use and Abuse of. W. B. Carpenter. Phila. 1854. 12°. L,859
Alcott, A. B. Record of his School by a Teacher. Boston, 1835. 12°. O,1176
Tablets. Boston, 1868. 16°. . . . . . . . . . . . H,188
Alcott, L. M. Hospital Sketches. Boston, 1869. 16°. . . . . . K,2
Little Women. Boston, 1870. 2 v. 16°. . . . . . . . . K,3
Moods. Boston, 1865. 12°. . . . . . . . . . . K,4
Old-Fashioned Girl. Boston, 1870. 16°. . . . . . . . . K,5
Three Proverb Stories. Boston, 1871. 16°. . . . . . . K,19
Alcott, W. A. First Public School in Hartford. Hartford, 1832. 18°. . O,993
Gift Book for Young Men. Auburn, 1853. 12°. . . . . . H,254
Laws of Health. Boston, 1860. 12°. . . . . . . . . . L,864
Lectures on Life and Health. Boston, 1853. 12°. . . . . . L,847
Moral Philosophy of Courtship and Marriage. Boston, 1857. 12°. . L,911
Physiology of Marriage. Boston, 1868. 12°. . . . . . . . L,918
Alden, J. Science of Government. New York, 1867. 12°. . . . . O,478
Alden T. American Epitaphs and Inscriptions. N. Y. 1814. 5 v. 18°. *C,830
Alder, J. and H., A. British Nudibranchiate Mollusca. Lon. 1845-55. p. 1-7. 4°. *Q,67
Alderbrook. E. Chubbuck. Boston, 1847. 2 v. 12°. . . . . . . H,272
Aldrich, T. B. Poems. Boston, 1865. 24°. . . . . . . . . I,1
Story of a Bad Boy. Boston, 1870. 16°. . . . . . . . J,1713
Alec Forbes of Howglen. G. Mac Donald. Leipzig, 1865. 2 v. in 1. 16°. J,340
Alembert, J. le R. d'. Œuvres. Paris, 1821-22. 5 v. 8°. . . . H,1008
Aleppo to Jerusalem; a Journey. H. Maundrel. Oxford, 1707. 8°. . . v,639
Alexander the Great, Geschichte der. J. G. Droysen. Berlin, 1833. 8°. . E,13
History of. J. Abbott. New York, 1848. 16°. . . . . J,1315
Life of. J. Williams. London, 1829. 16°. . . . . . . I,623
Q. Curtius Rufus. New York, 1858. 12°. . . . . . U,415
Alexander, A. Colonization on Western Coast of Africa. Philad. 1849. 8°. C,437
History of the Israelitish Nation. Philadelphia, 1853. 8°. . . . A,218
Outlines of Moral Science. New York, 1855. 12°. . . . . . O,713
Alexander, J. E. L'Acadie; or, Explo. in Brit. America. Lon. 1849. 2 v. 12°. v,174
Alexander, J. H. Dictionary of Weights and Measures. Baltimore, 1850. 8°. L.R.
Alfieri. V. Life and Adventures of. E. Copping. London. 1857. 8°. . D,702

Alford, H. Letters from Abroad. London. 1865. 8°. . . . . . v,487
Plea for the Queen's English. New York, n. d. 16°. . . . . L,563
Poetical Works. Boston, 1853. 16°. . . . . . . . . . I,275
Alfred, King, the Great. T. Hughes. London, n. d. 12°. . . . . A,491
Anglo-Saxon Version of Boethius. London, 1864. p. 8°. . . L,2
of Gregory's Pastoral Care; part 1. London, 1871. 8°. L,605,45
History of. J. Abbott. New York, 1849. 16°. . . . J,1396
Life of. J. A. Giles. Oxford, 1854. 8°. . . . . . . . A,494
R. Pauli. London, 1853. 12°. . . . . . . . L,23
Algæ, British Marine. W. H. Harvey. London, 1849. 8°. . . N,1005
of the Southern Ocean. W. H. Harvey. London, 1847-49. 8°. N,1005
Diatoms, etc., Handy-Book to Collection. J. Nave. Lond. 1867. 16°. N,936
Algebra. Haddon, J. London, 1855. 12°. . . . . . . . M,926
Kirkman, T. P. London, 1852. 12°. . . . . . . . M,942
J. Ryan. New York, 1843. 12°. . . . . . . . M,1100
Eleméns d'. A. C. Clairaut. Paris, 1768. 12°. . . . M,1104
J. G. Garnier. Paris, 1811. 8°. . . . . . . M,1116
S. F. La Croix. Paris, 1818. 8°. . . . . . . M,1117
Elements of. J. W. Colenso. London, 1855. 18°. . . M,1083
The same. London, 1854-55. 2 v. 12°. . . . M,1096
for Beginners, and Key. I. Todhunter. London, 1869. 2 v. 8°. M,1109
for Schools, and Key. I. Todhunter. London, 1870. 2 v. 8°. M,1098
Higher and Key. J. Ray. Cincinnati, 1866. 12°. . . . M,1099
Key to Intellectual. D. B. Tower. New York, 1845. 16°. . O,1098
made Easy. T. Tate. London, 1856. 16°. . . . . . M,1092
Treatise on. J. W. McGauley. Dublin, 1854. 16°. . . . M,1097
G. Peacock. Cambridge, 1842-45. 2 v. 8°. . . . M,1120
H. N. Robinson. New York, 1863. 8°. . . . . . M,1118
Algebraical Problems. M. Bland. London, 1849. 8°. . . . M,1122
Alger, H. Charlie Codman's Cruise. Boston, 1867. 16°. . . . J,1594
Frank's Campaign. Boston, 1871. 16°. . . . . . . J,1592
Luck and Pluck. Boston, 1871. 16°. . . . . . . J,1595
Paul Prescott's Charge. Boston, 1871. 16°. . . . . . J,1593
Ragged Dick Series. Boston, n. d. 6 v. 16°. . . . . . J,1430

Vol. 1. Ragged Dick.
2. Fame and Fortune.
3. Mark, the Match Boy.
Vol. 4. Rough and Ready.
5. Ben, the Luggage Boy.
6. Rufus and Rose.

Sink or Swim. Boston, 1871. 16°. . . . . . . . J,1596
Tattered Tom. Boston, 1871. 16°. . . . . . . . J,1598
Alger, W. R. Friendships of Women. Boston, 1868. 12°. . . . H,282
Doctrine of a Future Life. New York, 1866. 8°. . . . . P,106
Poetry of the Orient. Boston, 1866. 12°. . . . . . . . I,6
Solitudes of Nature and Man. Boston, 1869. 16°. . . . . H,236
Algeria, Tales of. A. Dumas. Philadelphia, 1868. 12°. . . . . H,973
Algiers; Artists and Arabs. H. Blackburn. Lond. 1868. 8°. . . . V,805
L'Algérie. A. J. C. A. Dureau De La Malle. Paris, 1852. 12°. . V,807
Description Nautiques des Côtes de. M. A. Bérard. Paris, 1839. 8°. V,1113
Topography and History of. J. R. Morell. London, 1854. 8°. . V,812
Alhambra. W. Irving. New York, 1868. 16°. . . . . . . . U,3
The same. New York, 1867. 12°. . . . . . . . U,30
Ali Bey. Travels in Morocco, Tripoli, etc. Philadelphia, 1816. 2 v. 8°. V,1082

Ali Pasha, Life of. R. A. Davenport. London, 1837. 16°. . . . . I,627
Alice; or, the Mysteries. Sir E. Bulwer Lytton. Philadelphia, 1868. 12°. K,806
The same. Leipzig, 1842. 16°. . . . . . . . . J,303
Alice Franklin. M. Howitt. New York, 1867. 24°. . . . . . J,1154
Alimentary Substances, Composition of. W. Proute. London, 1827. 4 °. N,252,42
Alison, A. Essays on the Nature and Principles of Taste. N.Y. 1854. 12°. O,624
Alison, Sir A. History of Europe, 1789–1815. Edinb. 1849–50. 14 v. 8°. A,341
The same. New York, 1854. 4 v. 8°. . . . . . . A,339
History of Europe, 1815–52, v. 1–5. Edinburgh, 1854–6. 5 v. 8°. . A,342
Life of John, Duke of Marlborough. New York, 1848. 12°. . . D,160
Miscellaneous Essays. Boston, 1857. 8°. . . . . . . H,621
Alkali, L'Extraction de, et Fabrication des Savons. Paris, n. d. 4°. . N,252, 41
Alken, H. Art and Practice of Etching. London, 1849. 8°. . . . M,36
National Sports of Great Britain. London, 1825. f°. . . . M,342
All Aboard; or, Life on the Lake. W. T. Adams. Boston, 1870. 16°. J,1435,1
All for Greed. Leipzig, 1868. 16°. . . . . . . . . . . J,28
All's not Gold that Glitters. A. B. Haven. New York, 1867. 16°. . J,1330
Alleghany Mountains, Letters from. C. Lanman. New York, 1849. 12°. V,59
Allegories, Sacred. W. Adams. Leipzig, 1864. 16°. . . . . . . J,1
Allelein-Horn, The. L. Stephen. London, 1861. 8°. . . . . V,1086,1
Allen, C. B. Cottage Building. London, 1857. 12°. . . . . . . M,887
Allen, E. A. H. Means of Mental Development. Boston, 1854. 12°. O,820,21
Allen, D. O. Ancient and Modern India. Boston, 1856. 8°. . . . V,757
Allen, E. Reason the only Oracle of Man. New York, 1836. 12°. . . P,227
Life of. J. Sparks. New York, 1860. 16°. . . . . . C,860,1
Allen, I. J. The American Merchant; an Address. Columbus, 1855. 12°. T,19,1,2
Allen, Joseph. Battles of the British Navy. London, 1852–3. 2 v. p. 8°. L.19
Allen, Julian. Autocracy in Poland and Russia. New York, 1854. 12°. . V,532
Allen, J. F. Culture and Treatment of the Grape Vine. N. Y. 1857. 12°. M,534
Allen, L. F. Rural Architecture. New York, 1869. 12°. . . . . . M,181
Allen, P. Lewis and Clarke's Expedition. New York, 1855. 2 v. 18°. . L,441
Allen, R. L. American Farm Book. New York, 1856. 12°. . . . M,487
Domestic Animals. New York, 1855. 12°. . . . . . . M,465
Allen, W., and T. R. H. Thomson. Niger Expedition. Lond. 1848. 2 v. 8°. V,837
Allen, W. American Biographical Dictionary. Boston, 1857. 8°. . *C,1018
Allen, Z. Philosophy of the Mechanics of Nature. New York, 1852. 8°. N,85
Allen House, The. T. S. Arthur. Philadelphia, n. d. 16°. . . . . J,607
Alleyn, E., Memoirs of. J. P. Collier. London, 1841. 8°. . . I,885,1
Alleyn Papers. J. P. Collier. London, 1843. 8°. . . . . . I,885,17
Allman, G. J. Monograph of Fresh-Water Polyzoa. London, 1856. 4°. . *Q,66
Almost a Priest. J. McN. Wright. Philadelphia, 1870. 12°. . . . K,408
Allibone, S. A. Dictionary of Authors. Philadelphia, 1858–71. 3 v. 8°. . L.R.
Allom, T. Chinese Empire Illustrated. London, n. d. 2 v. 4°. . . F,220
Allston, W. Lectures on Art, and Poems. New York, 1850. 12°. . . M,42
Monaldi; a Tale. Boston, 1856. 12°. . . . . . . . K,289
Outlines and Sketches. Boston, 1850. f°. . . . . . . *Q,454
Works and Genius of. W. Ware. Boston, 1852. 12°. . . . . M,50
Allworth Abbey. E. D. E. N. Southworth. Philadelphia, 1870. 12°. . K,412
Almanac, American, 1830–61. Boston, 1830–61. 32 v. 12°. . . . . T,51
National, 1863–4. Philadelphia, 1863–4. 2 v. 8°. . . . . T,52

Almanac, Tribune. New York. 1838–68. 2 v. 12°. . . . . . T,50
United States, 1844. Philadelphia, 1844. 2 v. 12°. . . . . T,49
Almon, J. Anecdotes of William Pitt. London, 1810. 3 v. 8°. . . . D,385
Almoran and Hamet. J. Hawkesworth. London, 1820. 12°. . . . K,537
Almost a Nun. J. McN. Wright. Philadelphia, 1868. 16°. . . . K,407
A. L. O. E. See *Tucker, C.*
Aloes, Monographia generum. J. v. S.-R. Dyck. Bonnae, 1836–63. 7 v. 4°. *Q,124
Alone. M. V. Terhune. New York, 1869. 12°. . . . . . . . K,315
Alphabet, Standard, for Unwritten Languages. C. R. Lepsius. Lond.1863. 8°. L,525
Alphabets, Harmony of Primeval. C. Foster. London, n. d. 8°. . . L,533
Alps, The, Allelein-Horn. L. Stephen. London, 1861. 8°. . . V,1086,1
Ascent of the Matterhorn. F. V. Hawkins. London, 1861. 8°. V,1086,1
Die Deutschen. E. A. Schaubach. Jena, 1845–47. 5 v. in 3. 8°. . E,202
From Lauterbrunnen to Æggisshorn. J. Tyndall. Lond. 1861. 8°. V,1086,1
Glaciers of the. J. Tyndall. Boston, 1861. 8°. . . . . . N,785
Graian, and Mount Iseran. J. J. Cowell. London, 1861. 8°. . V,1086,1
in Natur-und Lebensbildern. H. A. Berlepsch. Leipzig, 1862. 8°. E,185
Journals of Excursions in. W. Brockedon. London, 1833. 12°. . V,502
Physikalische Geographie der. H. and A. Schlagintweit. Leip. 1850. 8°. E,206
Sketches of Nature in. J. Auldjo. London, 1864. p. 8°. . I,656,1
Thierleben der Alpenwelt. F. von Tschudi. Leipzig, 1865. 8°. . G,935
Alroy; a Novel. B. Disraeli. London, 1868. 12°. . . . . . . K,673
The same. Leipzig, 1846. 16°. . . . . . . . J,139
Alston, R. H. Seamanship and Duties in Royal Navy. London, 1860. 8°. M,755
Alte Dessauer, Der; Historischer Roman. F. Carion. Leip. 1867. 4 v. 16°. G,274
Althaus, J. Treatise on Medical Electricity. London, 1859. 8°. . . L,921
Alton Locke. C. Kingsley. New York, 1867. 16°. . . . . . . K,748
The same. Leipzig, 1857. 16°. . . . . . . . J,241
Alton, Narrative of Riots at. E. Beecher. Alton, 1838. 12°. . . . C,158
Amari, M. War of the Sicilian Vespers. London, 1850. 3 v. 12°. . B,509
Amateur Mechanics' Workshop. London, 1870. 8°. . . . . . . M,661
Amazon, The. F. Dingelstedt. New York, 1868. 12°. . . . . . G,187
and the Andes. J. Orton. New York, 1870. 8°. . . . . . V,244
and Rio Madeira. C. Young. London, 1862. 8°. . . . V,1086,2
Naturalist on. H. W. Bates. London, 1863. 2 v. 8°. . . . V,243
Palm Trees of. A. R. Wallace. London, 1853. 8°. . . . N,954
Valley of. W.L.Herndon and L.Gibbon, with maps. Wash. 1854. 4 v. 8°. V,263
Amber Gods, and other Stories. H. E. Spofford. Boston, 1869. 12°. . K,246
Ambros, A. W. Geschichte der Musik. Breslau, 1862–68. 3 v. 8°. . G,636
Die Grenzen der Musik und Poesie. Leipzig, 1855. 12°. . . G,637
Amelia. H. Fielding. New York, 1850. 12°. . . . . . . . K,699
America, Ancient Inhabitants of. A. v. Humboldt. London, 1814. 2 v. 8°. V,258
Adventures in the Wilds of. C. Lanman. London, 1863. p. 8°. I,659,2
and American Methodism. New York, 1857. 8°. . . . . . V,63
and the American People. F. L. G. von Raumer. N. Y. 1846. 8°. V,126
and Europe. A. G. de Gurowski. New York, 1857. 12°. . . . O,489
and the West Indies. H. C. Carey and J. Lea. London, 1823. 8°. . B,621
British Empire in. J. H. Wynne. London, 1770. 2 v. 8°. . . B,696
Civilized. T. C. Grattan. London, 1859. 2 v. 8°. . . . . V,129
Discoverers and Pioneers of. H. F. Parker. New York, 1856. 12°. C,1047

America, Discovery of by Northmen. J. T. Smith. London, 1839. 12°. . B,698
Divers Voyages to. R. Hakluyt. London, 1850. 8°. . . . V,994
Future Civil Policy of. J. W. Draper. New York, 1865. 8°. . B,857
The same. New York, 1866. 8°. . . . . . . . S.C.
Geography, History, and Statistics of. H. C. Carey. Lond. 1823. 8°. B,621
General History of. A. de Herrera. London, 1725-6. 6 v. 8°. . B,582
Historical, Statistic, Descriptive. J.S.Buckingham. N.Y.1841. 2 v. 8°. V,120
The same. J. S. Buckingham. London, n. d. 3 v. 8°. . V,121
History of. W. Robertson. London, 1818. 3 v. 18°. . . . B,683
The same, abridged. New York, 1854. 18°. . . L,466
Empire in. J. H. Wynne. London, 1770. 2 v. 8°. . . B,696
Impressions of. F. Bremer. New York, 1853. 2 v. 12°. . . V,53
T. Power. London, 1836. 2 v. 8°. . . . . . V,146
Institutions of Ancient. A. von Humboldt. London, 1814. 2 v. 8°. V,256
Jenseits des Oceans. G. Byam. Dresden, 1852. 8°. . . . E,170
Kolonisation und Unabhängigkeit. H. Handelmann. Kiel, 1856. 8°. E,123
Letters from. J. Flint. Edinburgh, 1822. 8°. . . . . V,107
Men and Manners in. T. Hamilton. Philadelphia, 1833. 8°. . V,79
New. W. H. Dixon. Leipzig, 1867. 2 v. in 1. 16°. . . . J,151
an Ode; and other Poems. N. W. Coffin. Boston, 1843. 12°. . I,42
Pilgrimage in, and Europe. J. C. Beltrami. London, 1828. 2 v. 8°. V,1074
Pre-Columbian Discovery of. B. F. De Costa. Albany, 1868. 8°. . B,625
Progress of. J. Macgregor. London, 1847. 2 v. 8°. . . . B,828
Discovery on Northern Coasts of. P. F. Tytler. N.Y.1833. 18°. L,376
Rare Documents concerning. E. G. Squier. Albany, 1860. 4°. . F,62
Religion in. R. Baird. New York, 1856. 8°. . . . . . P,582
Religion and Education in. J. D. Lang. London, 1840. 12°. . O,822
Remarkable Events in History of. J. Frost. Phila. 1848. 2 v. 8°. B,703
Resources and Prospects of. Sir S. M. Peto. New York, 1866. 16°. V,102
Spanish Conquest in. A. Helps. New York, 1856. 2 v. 12°. . C,369
Things as they are in. W. Chambers. London, 1857. 8°. . . V,58
Travels to Equinoctial. A. von Humboldt. Lond. 1852-3. 3 v. p. 8°. L,296
The same. London, 1818-29. 8 v. in 7. 8°. . . . . . V,257
Views in. T. Nelson. London, 1857. 16°. . . . . . V,1029,1
Voyage to. G. Clarke. Albany, 1867. 4°. . . . . . . C,103
West Coast of. H. W. Baxley. New York, 1865. 8°. . . . V,127
American Aboriginal Languages, Literature of. H.E.Ludewig. Lond.1858. 8°. H,666
American Adventure by Land and Sea. New York, 1859. 2 v. 18°. . L,457
American Agriculturist, v. 21-24. O. Judd. New York, 1863-65. 4 v. 4°. Q,266
American Almanac. Boston, 1830-61. 32 v. 12°. . . . . . T,51
American Annals of Education and Instruction, v. 2-5. Bost. 1832-35. 8°. O,1259
American Annals of the Deaf and Dumb. Hartford, 1848-49. 8°. . O,1236
American Annual Cyclopædia. New York, 1864-70. 9 v. 8°. . . . L.R.
American Antiquarian Soc. Archælogia Americana, v. 1. Worcester, 1820. 8°. B,605
American Antiquities; History of Red Race. A.W. Bradford. N.Y.1841. 8°. B,606
American Architect. J. W. Ritch. New York, n. d. 4°. . . . . M,296
American Association for the Advancement of Science. Proceedings of 1st-16th meeting. Philad., Cambridge, etc., 1849-68. 16 v. in 12. 8°. R,22
American Authors, Homes of. New York, 1857. 4°. . . . . . . H,664
American Bards. G. A. Worth. 1819. 12°. . . . . . . . . I,156

American Bible Society, History of. W. P. Strickland. New York, 1856. 8°. P,645
American Biography. J. Belknap. Boston, 1794-98. 2 v. 8°. . . . C,769
The same; ed. by F. M. Hubbard. New York, 1855. 3 v. 16°. L,447
American Biographical Dictionary. W. Allen. Boston, 1857. 8°. . *C,1018
American Boy's Book of Sports and Games. New York, 1864. 12°. . J,1326
American Catalogue for 1871. F. Leypoldt. New York, 1871. 8°. . . L.R.
American Citizens, Duties of. B. P. Aydelott. Cincinnati, 1840. 8°. . H,302
American Civil War, History of the. J. W. Draper. N. Y. 1867-70. 3 v. 8°. B,919
See also *United States, Southern Rebellion.*
American Coinage, Historical Account of. J. H. Hickox. Albany, 1858. 8°. M,390
American Colonies previous to Independence. London, 1869. 8°. . . . B,626
American Colleges and American Public. N. Porter. New Haven, 1870. 12°. O,810
American Conflict, The. H. Greeley. Hartford, 1864-66. 2 v. 8°. . B,920
American Cottage Building. J. Bullock. Philadelphia, 1868. 8°. . . M,192
American Cyclopædia; ed. by G. Ripley and C. A. Dana. N. Y. 1871. 16 v. 8°. R.R.
The same. New York, 1863. 16 v. 8°. . . . . . S.C.
American Debater. J. N. McElligott. New York, 1870. 12°. . . . O,558
American Eclectic Medical Register. New York, 1868. 8°. . . . L,944
American Education. E. D. Mansfield. New York, 1851. 8°. . . . O,954
American Educational Year-Book, 1857. A. R. Pope. Boston, 1857. 12°. O,1250
American Eloquence; edited by F. Moore. New York, 1857. 2 v. 8°. . H,824
American Ephemeris, 1855. Washington, 1855. 8°. . . . . . . N,303
American Family in Germany. J. R. Browne. New York, 1867. 12°. . V,418
American Farm Book. R. L. Allen. New York, 1856. 12°. . . . M,487
American Farmer in England. F. L. Olmsted. New York, 1852. 2 v. 12°. V,335
The same. Columbus, 1859. 8°. . . . . . . . M,516
American First-Class Book. J. Pierpont. New York, 1835. 12°. . . O,882
American Government, Thirty Years' View. T. H. Benton. N. Y. 1856-58. 2 v. 8°. B,665
American Guide Book. Philadelphia, 1846. 12°. . . . . . . V,7
American Historical and Literary Curiosities. J. J. Smith and J. F. Watson. Philadelphia, 1861. 4°. . . . . . . . . . *Q,227
The same. New York, 1852. f°. . . . . . . . S.C.
American History. J. Abbott. New York, n. d. 8 v. 16°. . . . J,1696

| | |
|---|---|
| Vol. 1. Aboriginal America. | Vol. 5. Wars of the Colonies. |
| 2. Discovery of America. | 6. Revolt of the Colonies. |
| 3. The Southern Colonies. | 7. War of the Revolution. |
| 4. The Northern Colonies. | 8. Washington. |

M. Willson. New York, 1847. 8°. . . . . . . . . B,701
Incidents in. J. W. Barber. Boston, n. d. . . . . . B,694
Library of. Cincinnati, 1846. 8°. . . . . . . . . B,829
List of Books on. J. Sparks. Boston, 1855. 8°. . . . . A,321
Remarkable Events in. J. Frost. Philadelphia, 1848. 2 v. 8°. . B,703
Tales from. New York, 1830-52. 3 v. 18°. . . . . . J,1218
American Institute of Instruction, Lectures, 1830-58. Bos.'31-59. 29 v. 8° & 12°. O,820
American Journal of Education; ed. by H. Barnard. Hartf. 1855-62. 12 v. 8°. S,26
American Journal of Science; ed. B. Silliman and others. 1st ser. v. 1-7, 13-49. 2d ser. 1. 1-9, 26. New Haven, 1819-58. 54 v. 8°. . S,31
American Literary Gazette. Philadelphia, 1863-68. 11 v. 8°. . . . S,46
American Law, Commentaries on. J. Kent. Boston, 1867. 4 v. 8°. . U,421
American Life Underwriter's Convention, Proceedings. N. Y. 1859. 8°. B,809,1
American Literature, Compendium of. C. D. Cleveland. Phila. 1859. 12°. H,663

American Literature, Guide to. N. Trübner. London, 1859. 8°. . . . L.R.
Hand-Book of. Philadelphia, n. d. 18°. . . . . . . . . H,659
Sketch of. H. T. Tuckerman. Philadelphia, 1854. 12°. . . H,694
Views and Reviews in. W. G. Simms. New York, 1845. 8°. . H,660
American Loyalists. L. Sabine. Boston, 1847. 8°. . . . . . C,1091
American Merchant, The; an Address. I. J. Allen. Columbus, 1855. 12°. T,19,2
American Nations. C. S. Rafinesque. Philadelphia, 1836. 2 v. in 1. 12°. B,693
American Naturalist, The. Salem, Mass, 1868. v. 1. 8°. . . . . N,539
American Note Books, Passages from. N. Hawthorne. Bost. 1868. 2 v. 16°. H,235
The same. 12°. . . . . . . . . . . U,40,15,16
American Notes. C. Dickens. New York, 1871. 12°. . . . K,1126
The same. Leipzig, 1842. 16°. . . . . . . . . J,113
and Picnic Papers. C. Dickens and others. Philadelphia, n. d. 8°. V,123
American Orator's Own Book. Philadelphia, 1854. 18°. . . . . L,582
American Oratory. Philadelphia, 1853. 12°. . . . . . . . H,819
American Ornithology. See *Ornithology* and *Birds*.
American Pharmaceutical Association, Proceedings. Phila. 1866–69. 2 v. 8°. L,946
American Philosophical Society; Transactions, v. 3. Philadelphia, 1843. 8°. H,220
American Phonetic Journal, v. 2, 4, 5. Cincinnati, 1855–57–58. 8°. . . L,727
American Phonographic Journal, v. 1, 2. Philadelphia, 1848–49. 18°. . L,717
American Pioneer. Chillicothe, 1842–43, v. 1, 2. 8°. . . . . . . T,20
American Plants, Catalogus. H. Muhlenberg. Lancaster, Penn. 1813. 8°. N,1022
American Poets, Selections from. W. C. Bryant. New York, 1854. 18°. . L,414
American Portrait Gallery. J. B. Longacre & J. Herring. Phil. 1836–9. 4 v. 4°. L.R.
American Privateers in 1812–14. G. Coggeshall. New York, 1861. 8°. . B,856
American Publishers' Circular. Philadelphia, 1863–68. 11 v. 8°. . . S,46
American Pulpit. H. Fowler. New York, 1856. 8°. . . . . . C,946
American Repertory of Arts, Sciences, etc. New York, 1840–42. 4 v. 8°. T,26
American Review of History and Politics. R. Walsh. Phil. 1811–2. 4 v. 8°. T,43
American Revolution, Anecdotes of. A. Garden. Brooklyn, 1865. 3 v. 4°. F,59,1–3
Border Wars of. W. L. Stone. New York, 1864. 2 v. 18°. . . L,451
Camp-Fires of. New York, 1865. 8°. . . . . . . . B,752
Colored Patriots of. W. C. Nell. Boston, 1855. 12°. . . . B,740
Correspondence of; edited by J. Sparks. Boston, 1853. 4 v. 8°. . S.C.
The same; edited by J. Sparks, v. 1, 3, 4. Boston, 1853. 8°. . B,749
Diary of. F. Moore. New York, 1863. 2 v. 8°. . . . . B,750
Diplomacy of. W. H. Trescot. New York, 1852. 12°. . . . B,743
Diplomatic Correspondence of. Boston, 1829–30. 12 v. 8°. . . B,678
Documentary History of. R. W. Gibbes. N. Y. 1853–57. 2 v. 8°. . B,746
Domestic History of. E. F. Ellet. New York, 1851. 12°. . . B,744
Field-Book of. B. J. Lossing. New York, 1860. 2 v. 8°. . . B,751
History of. D. Ramsay. London, 1791. 2 v. 8°. . . . . B,739
the American War. C. Stedman. London, 1794. 2 v. 4°. . B,830
the War of Independence. C. Botta. Phila. 1820–21. 3 v. 8°. B,745
Journal and Letters of S. Curwen, 1775–83. Boston, 1864. 12°. . C,779
Memoirs and Reminiscences of. E. Watson. New York, 1856. 8°. C,723
Men and Times of. E. Watson. New York, 1857. 12°. . . C,1014
Military Heroes of. C. J. Peterson. Philadelphia, 1848. 8°. . . C,686
Orators of. E. L. Magoon. New York, 1848–50. 12°. . . . C,1026
Orders issued during. G. Washington. New York, 1844. 8°. . B,747

American Revolution, Personal Recollections of. S. Barclay. N.Y. 1859. 12°. B,754
Public Men of. W. Sullivan. Philadelphia, 1847. 8°. . . . . C,882
Records of. W. T. R. Saffell. New York, 1858. 12°. . . . B,755
Tracts on. London, 1769-76. 8°. . . . . . . . . *B,753

1. Controversy between Great Britain and her Colonies Reviewed, 1769.
2. American Independence the Interest and Glory of Great Britain, 1774.
3. Address to Protestant Dissenters of all Denominations on the approaching election of Members of Parliament, 1774.
4. Bernard, Gov. Select Letters on the Trade and Government of America, 1764.
5. Rights of the Colonies and the extent of the Legislative Authority of Great Britain, 1769.
6. Considerations on certain Political Transactions of the Province of South Carolina, 1774.
7. Appeal to the Public, stating the objections to the Quebec Bill, 1774.
8. Paine, T. Common Sense; addressed to the Inhabitants of America. 2d edition. 1776.
9. Plain Truth; containing Remarks on a late Pamphlet intitled Common Sense, 1776.
10. Pownall, T. Administration of the British Colonies, part ii. 1774.

View of. G. W. Green. Boston, 1865. 12°. . . . . . . B,742
Women of. E. F. Ellet. New York, 1852-54. v. 2, 3. 12°. . . C,653
American Rose Culturist. New York, 1856. 12°. . . . . M,533,2
American Socialisms, History of. J. H. Noyes. Philadelphia, 1870. 8°. . O,378
American State Papers. Washington, 1832-61. 33 v. f°. . . . P.D.
American Statesmen. A. Young. New York, 1855. 8°. . . . . O,592
American Temperance Magazine. New York, 1851. 8°. . . . . T,33
American Theater, History of. W. Dunlap. New York, 1832. 12°. . . I,712
American Tract Society, Publications of. New York, n. d. 12 v. 12°. P,746,34-45
American Travel, Appleton's Hand-Book of. E. H. Hall. N. Y. 1869. 8°. V,119
American Whig Society, Catalogue. Princeton, N. J. 1845. 8°. . B,809,1
American Woman's Home. C. E. Beecher and H. B. Stowe. N. Y. 1869. 8°. O,366
American Year Book and National Register, 1869. Hartford, 1869. 8°. . *T,48
Americanisms, Dictionary of. J. R. Bartlett. Boston, 1859. 8°. . . L.R.
Glossary of Supposed. A. L. Elwyn. Philadelphia, 1859. 12°. . L.R.
Americans, Famous, of Recent Times. J. Parton. Boston, 1869. 8°. . C,910
Amerikanischer Leser, Zweites Buch. Cincinnati, n. d. 16°. . . . G,545
Ames, F. Works; with Selections from Speeches. Boston, 1854. 2 v. 8°. C,1086
Ames, J. Typographical Antiquities. London, 1785-1819. 4 v. 4°. . . L.R.
Ames, W. Works. London, 1643. 4°. . . . . . . . . . P,98
Amherst College, Reminiscences of. E. Hitchcock. Northampton, 1863. 12°. O,808
Ammianus Marcellinus. Roman Hist.; tr. C. D. Yonge. London, 1862. p. 8°. L,35
Ammonia, Nature of the Compounds of. R. Kane. Dublin, 1839. 4°. N,252,42
Among My Books. J. R. Lowell. Boston, 1870. 12°. . . . . H,239
Among the Hills. J. G. Whittier. Boston, 1869. 16°. . . . . I,152
Among the Pines. J. R. Gilmore. New York, 1862. 12°. . . . K,302
Amoor, Upper and Lower. T. W. Atkinson. New York, 1860. 8°. . . V,683
Voyage Down the. P. Mc. D. Collins. New York, 1860. 12°. . V,614
Amos, A. Trial of Earl of Somerset for Poisoning. London, 1846. 8°. . B,30
Amouroux, Practical Draughtman's Book. New York, 1854. 4°. . . Q,169
Amy Herbert. E. M. Sewell. New York, 1866. 12°. . . . . K,1058
The same. Leipzig, 1857. 2 v. in 1. 16°. . . . . . J,454
Amyot, T. (Ed.) Old Taming of a Shrew. London, 1844. 8°. . . I,885,23
Anacharsis's Travels in Greece. J. J. Barthélmy. London, 1806. 8 v. 8°, 4°. V,572
The same. London, 1817. 6 v. 8°. . . . . . . V,573

Anacharsis, Voyage en Grece. J. J. Barthélemy. Paris, 1817. 7 v. 8°. . v,571
Atlas to the Same. Paris, 1817. f°. . . . . . . Q,388
Anacreon; translated by T. Bourn. New York, 1844. 18°. . . . . U,370
Analecta Ante-Nicæna. C. C. J. Bunsen. London, 1854. 3 v. 8°. . . P,123
Analogy of Religion and Sermons. J. Butler. London, 1868. p. 8°. . . L,170
Analyse der Thierischen Concretionen. Altona, 1837. 8°. . . . N,252,1
Analysis, Introductio in Analysin Infinitorum. L. Euler. Lausan. 1748. 2 v. 4°. M,1186
Manual of Technical. P. A. Bolley. London, 1857. 12°. . . L,274
Tables for Qualitative. F. T. Conington. London, 1864. 8°. . . N,201
Anatomical Atlas of the Human Body. H. H. Smith. Philadelphia, 1851. 8°. L,1036
Anatomical Memoirs. J. Goodsir. Edinburgh, 1868. 2 v. 8°. . . L,1005
Anatomico-Physiological Lectures. C. N. Jenty. v. 3. London, 1757. 8°. L,857,3
Anatomy, Atlas of. J. Fau. London, 1849. 4°. . . . . . . . Q,194
and Philosophy of Expression. Sir C. Bell. London, 1865. 8°. . M,140
and Physiology. E. Hitchcock and E. Hitchcock, Jr. N.Y. 1863. 12°. . L,885
Cyclopædia of. R. B. Todd. Lond. 1859. 5 v. in 6. 8°. . L,1034
of the Human Body. J. and C. Bell. London, 1829. v. 2, 3. 8°. L,974
Lectures on. M. S. Gore. New York, 1846. 12°. . . . L,869
Comparative, Lectures on. T. H. Huxley. London, 1864. 8°. . . L,989
W. Lawrence. London, 1848. 12°. . . . . . . . L,897
of Invertebrate Animals. R. Owen. London, 1855. . 8°. L,988
R. Wagner. Philadelphia, 1845. 8°. . . . . . L,990
of Vertebrates. R. Owen. London, 1866. 3 v. 8°. . . L,986
Descriptive and Surgical. H. Gray. Philadelphia, 1867. 8°. . L,1035
Essays on. J. Hunter. London, 1861. 2 v. 8°. . . . . . N,720
Hand-Atlas der Anatomie. C. E. Bock. Berlin, 1860. f°. . . Q,292
Human, Principles of. E. or W. J. E. Wilson. Philad. 1866. 8°. L,1021
Introductory Lecture on. J. P. Judkins. Cincinnati, 1846. 8°. . H,302
Manual of Human Microscopic. A. Kölliker. London, 1860. . . L,972
of the External Forms of Man. J. Fau. Lond. 1849. 8°. Atlas, 4°. L,975
of the Human Body. J. Cruveilhier. New York, 1853. 8°. . L,1006
A. H. Hassall. New York, 1851. 2 v. 8°. . . . . L,973
of the Human Body; and Plates. Appleton's. N. Y. 1856. 2v. 8°. & 4°. Q,257
Outlines of. F. Hollick. Philadelphia, 1846. 4°. . . . . . Q,289
Physiology, and Hygiene. C. Cutter. New York, 1852. 12°. . . L,871
J. R. Loomis. New York, 1860. 12°. . . . . . . L,874
Practical. D. H. Agnew. Philadelphia, 1868. . . . . . . L,882
Special and Histology. W. E. Horner. Philadelphia, 1851. 2 v. 8°. L,1007
Anatomy of Melancholy. R. Burton. Philadelphia, 1854. 8°. . . . H,629
Ancestors, Our British. S. Lysons. Oxford, 1865. p. 8°. . . . . N,439
Ancient Books, Transmission of, to Modern Times. I. Taylor. Lond. 1859. 8°. H,722
Ancient Cities, Ruins of. C. Bucke. New York, 1854. v. 1. 18°. . . L,428
Ancient Monuments of the Mississippi Valley. E. G. Squier and E. H. Davis.
Washington, 1847. 4°. . . . . . . . . . . . Q,324,1
Ancient Philosophers. Lives of the. F. de S. de La M. Fénélon. N.Y. 1854. 18°. L,432
Ancient States and Empires. J. Lord. New York, 1869. 8°. . . . A,12
Ancient World, The. D. T. Ansted. London, 1847. 12°. . . . . N,782
Andersen, H. C. Danish Fairy Legends and Tales. London, 1861. p. 8°. L,92
Danish Story Book. New York, 1869. 16°. . . . . . . J,1488
Fairy Tales. New York, 1869. 16°. . . . . . . . J,1660

Andersen, H. C. The Improvisatore. New York, 1867. 8°. . . . . G,182
In Spain and Portugal. New York, 1870. 12°. . . . . . V,464
Only a Fiddler! and O. T. New York, 1862. 8°. . . . . . G,181
Sand-Hills of Jutland. Boston, 1865. 16°. . . . . . J,1489
Stories and Tales. New York, 1871. 12°. . . . . . J,1519
Story Book. New York, 1869. 16°. . . . . . . J,1437
Story of my Life. New York, 1871. 12°. . . . . . D,533
The Two Baronesses; a Romance. New York, 1869. 12°. . . G,227
True Story of my Life. Boston, 1847. 16°. . . . . . D,533
Wonder Stories told for Children. New York, 1870. 12°. . . J,1492
Wonderful Tales from Denmark. New York, 1869. 16°. . . J,1661
Anderson, C. Annals of the English Bible. London, 1845. 2 v. 8°. . . P,447
Anderson, James. Constitution of the Fraternity of Freemasons. Lond.1767.4°. O,383
Anderson, James. Ladies of the Reformation. London, 1857. 12°. . . C,516
Anderson, James. Recreations in Agriculture. London, 1799–1802. 6 v. 8°. H,615
Anderson, John. Course of Creation. Cincinnati, 1851. 12°. . . . N,868
Anderson, John. History of Edinburgh. Edinburgh, 1856. 8°. . . B,130
Anderson, Rufus. Hawaiian Islands. Boston, 1865. 8°. . . . . V,883
Andersonville Prison. A. C. Hamlin. Boston, 1866. 12°. . . . . B,895
Andersson, C. J. Lake Ngami, South-western Africa. New York, 1861. 12°. V,800
Okavango River; a Narrative. New York, 1861. 8°. . . . V,850
Reisen in Süd-west Afrika. 1850–1854. Leipzig, n. d. 2 v. in 1. 8°. E,230
Andersson, N. T. Weltumsegelung mit der Fregatte Eugenie. Leip. 1854. 12°. E,160
Andes and the Amazon. J. Orton. New York, 1870. 8°. . . . . V,244
Andrée de Taverney. A. Dumas. Philadelphia, n. d. 8°. . . . . H,980
Andral, G. Essai d' Hématologie Pathologique. Paris, 1845. 8°. . N,252,14
et Gavarret, J. Analyses du Sang. Paris, 1842. 8°. . . N,252,14
André, J. Arnold and André. G. H. Calvert. Boston, 1864. 16°. . . I,27
Life and Career of. W. Sargent. Boston, 1861. 8°. . . . C,1265
Vindication of the Captors of. E. Benson. New York, 1865. 8°. . C,908
Andreas Hofer. C. Mundt. New York, 1868. 12°. . . . . . G,194
Andresen, K. G. Deutsche Orthographie. Mainz, 1855. 8°. . . . G,592
Andrew, J. A. Sketch of Life of. A. G. Browne, Jr. New York, 1868. 16°. C,735
Andrews, E. A. Latin-English Lexicon. New York, 1856. 8°. . . L.R.
and Stoddard, S. Latin Grammar. Boston, 1864. 12°. . . . L,753
Andrews, G. H. Agricultural Engineering. London, 1852. 3 v. in 1. 16°. M,888
Andrews, I. D. Trade of British-American Colonies. Washington, 1854. 8°. P.D.
Andrews, J. The Art of Flower Painting. London, n. d. 8°. . . . M,141
Andrews, J. P. History of Great Britain. London, 1796. 2 v. 8°. . . A,464
Andrews, S. P. and Boyle, A. F. Phonographic Class-Book. N. Y. 1848. 12°. L,690
Phonographic Reader. New York, 1848. 12°. . . . . . L,691
Andrews, T. Heat developed by Acids and Bases. Dublin, 1841. 4°. N,252,42
Voltaic Circles with Sulphuric Acid as Conductor. Dublin, 1838. 4°. N,252,57
Andriveau-Goujon, G. G. Atlas Universel de Geographie. Paris, 1835. f°. Q,446
Andromeda; and other Poems. C. Kingsley. Boston, 1858. 16°. . . I,362
Andros, Sir E. Commission of James II. to, 1686. See *Force's Tracts*, v. 4.
Anecdotes of Literature and Art, Cyclopædia of. K. Arvine. Bost. 1870. 8°. H,670
Moral and Religious, Cyclopædia of. K. Arvine. New York, 1855. 8°. P,107
of the American Revolution. A. Garden. Brooklyn, 1865. 3 v. 4°. . F,59
of the English Language. S. Pegge, Jr. London, 1844. 8°. . . L,617

Anecdotes of Habits and Instincts of Animals. R. Lee. Boston, 1871. 16°. J,1553
of Habits of Birds, Reptiles, etc. R. Lee. Boston, 1871. 16°. . J,1554
of Literature and Scarce Books. W. Beloe. Lond. 1807-12. 6 v. 8°. H,737
of Painters, Engravers, Sculptors, etc. S. Spooner. N.Y. 1865. 3 v. 12°. M,52
Percy. T. Bryerley and J. C. Robertson. London, 1868. 2 v. 12°. I,541
Zoological Notes and Anecdotes. London, 1852. 12°. . . . N,651
Anemometer, Osler's Registering. J. Newman. London, 1840. 8°. . N,252,33
Angel and the Demon. T. S. Arthur. Philadelphia, n. d. 16°. . . . J,608
in the House; the Betrothal. C. Patmore. Boston, 1856. 16°. . I,93
the Espousals. C. Patmore. Boston, 1856. 16°. . . . I,92
of the Household. T. S. Arthur. Philadelphia, n. d. 16°. . . J,609
Angels, Good and Evil, Scripture Revelations on. R. Whately. Lon. 1855. 12°. P,265
Angelic Wisdom concerning Divine Love. E. Swedenborg. N. Y. 1863. 8°. P,855
concerning Divine Providence. New York, 1857. 8°. . . . P,856
Angelina. M. Edgeworth. New York, 1860. 12°. . . . . . . K,678
Angelo, Michael. See *Buonarotti, M. A.*
Angler and his Friend. J. Davy. London, 1855. 16°. . . . . . M,344
The Complete. I. Walton and C. Colton. London, 1853. 12°. . M,309
The same. London, 1870. p. 8°. . . . . . . . . L,153
in the Lake District. J. Davy. London, 1857. 16°. . . . . M,322
Angler's Guide, American. J. J. Brown. New York, 1845. 16°. . . M,299
The same. New York, 1850. 8°. . . . . . . . M,313
Angling Literature of all Nations. R. Blakey. London, 1856. 12°. . . M,303
Anglo-American Literature and Manners. P. Chasles. N. Y. 1852. 12°. . H,656
Anglo-German Vocabulary, Symbolic. London, n. d. 8°. . . . . . L.R.
Anglo-Saxon and Early English Psalter. London, 1843. v. 1. 8°. . F,126,16
Anglo-Saxon and English Dictionary. J. Bosworth. London, 1855. 8°. . L.R.
Anglo-Saxon Chronicle. London, 1861. 2 v. 8°. . . . . . . W,173
Anglo-Saxon Church, Antiquities of. J. Lingard. Philadelphia, 1848. 8°. P,609
Latin Hymns of the. Durham, 1851. 8°. . . . . . . F,126,23
Anglo-Saxon Language, Grammar of. L. F. Klipstein. N. Y. 1857. 12°. . L,579
Hand-Book of Anglo-Saxon Derivatives. N. Y. 1855. 12°. . . L,542
Hand-Book of Root-Words. New York, 1857. 12°. . . . L,541
Literature, Historical Sketches of. J. Petheram. London, 1840. 8°. H,744
Selections from. L. F. Klipstein. New York, 1849. 12°. . H,743
Anglo-Saxons, Codex Diplomaticus. J. M. Kemble. Lond. 1839-48. 6 v. 8°. U,616
History of. T. Miller. London, 1856. 12°. . . . . . . L,127
F. Palgrave. London, 1867. 12°. . . . . . . A,441
S. Turner. London, 1823. 3 v. 8°. . . . . . . . A,434
The same. Paris, 1840. 3 v. 8°. . . . . . . A,492
Aniline Colors, Manufacture of. M. Reimann. New York, 1868. 8°. . N,191
Animal Body, Motion of the Juices in. J. Liebig. London, 1848. 8°. . L,936
Animal Biography. W. Bingley. London, 1813. 3 v. 8°. . . . N,657
Animal Chemistry. W. Odling. London, 1866. 8°. . . . . . . N,176
J. F. Simon. London, 1845-46. 2 v. 8°. . . . . . . N,189
Grundrisz der. H. K. Geubel. Frankfurt-a-M. 1845. 8°. . N,252,17
Letter to J. von Liebig concerning. G. Kemp. London, 1844. 8°. N,252,14
Thier-Chemie. J. von Liebig. Braunschweig, 1846. 8°. . . G,758
Verhältniss der. J. von Liebig. Heidelberg, 1844. 8°. . . N,252,7
Animal Kingdom. Baron G. Cuvier. London, 1851. 8°. . . . . . N,559

Animal Kingdom. Baron G. Cuvier and P. A. Latrielle. Lond.1837. 4 v. 8°. N,663
Analyse der Thierischen Concretionen. Altona, 1837. 8°. . N,252,1
Anat.-Phys. Uebersicht. C. Bergmann and R. Leuckart. Stutt. 1851. 8°. E,422
Atlas des Thierreichs. Breslau, n. d. 4°. . . . . . . . G,938
Facts connected with. J. C. Hall. London, 1841. 8°. . . . N,445
Fossil Remains of the. E. Pidgeon. London, n. d. 8°. . . . N,802
Manual of the. J. R. Greene. London, 1861, 1863. 2 p. 16°. . O,2
Organization of the. T. R. Jones. London, 1861. 8°. . . . N,554
Thierische Organisation. H. Burmeister. Leipzig, 1856. 2 v. 8°. G,917
Verzeichnisz aller Säugethiere. H. Schinz. Solothurn, 1844. 3v. in 1. 8°. G,923
Animal Life. Bilder aus dem Thierleben. C. Vogt. Frankfurt-a-M. 1852. 8°. G,915
Sketches of. J. G. Wood. London, 1854. 8°. . . . . . . N,621
Structure of. L. J. R. Agassiz. New York, 1866. 8°. . . . N,540
Studies of. G. H. Lewes. New York, 1860. 12°. . . . . . N,648
Thierleben der Alpenwelt. F. von Tschudi. Leipzig, 1865. 8°. . G,935
Animal Magnetism, Letters on. W. Gregory. Philadelphia, 1851. 12°. . L,877
Manual of. A. Teste. Philadelphia, 1844. 12°. . . . . . L,879
Animal Mechanism and Physiology. J. H. Griscom. New York, 1855. 18°. L,399
Animal Physiology. W. B. Carpenter. London, 1859. p. 8°. . . . L,285
and Vegetable Physiology. P. M. Roget. London, 1867. 2 v. p. 8°. L,281
Animal Traits and Characteristics. J. G. Wood. London, 1860. 16°. . N,627
Animal World. Die Thierwelt. H. Masius. Essen, 1862. 8°. . . . G,930
Studium der Thierwelt. E. A. Rosmäszler. Leipzig, 1856. 8°. . G,931
Skizzen aus der Pflanzen und Thierwelt. H. Masius. Leip. 1852. 8°. G,702
Animalcules, General History of. A. Pritchard. London, 1843. 8°. . O,64
Animals, Anecdotes of Habits of. R. Lee. Boston, 1871. 16°. . . J,1553
and Plants, Geographical Distribution of. C. Pickering. Bost.1854. 4°. Q,282
under Domestication. C. Darwin. New York, 1868. 2 v. 12°. N,504
Architecture in Typical Forms of. G. Ogilvie. London, 1858. 12°. N,645
Bible. J. G. Wood. London, 1869. 8°. . . . . . . . N,690
Creation, History, Habits, and Instincts of. W. Kirby. Lon.1852. 2v. p.8°. L,275
Das Thier-Reich. H.G. Bronn and W. Keferstein. Leip.'59–66. 3v. in 4. 8°. G,937
des Waldes. A. E. Brehm and E. A. Rossmäszler. Leip. 1864–67. 2v. 8°. G,936
Domestic. R. L. Allen. New York, 1855. 12°. . . . . . M,465
Geog. Verbreitung der Thiere. L.K. Schmarda. Wien, 1853. 3v. in 1. 8°. G,921
Geography and Classification of. W. Swainson. London, 1835. 12°. M,1030
Habits and Instincts of. W. Swainson. London, 1840. 12°. . M,1037
History of. Aristotle; trans. by R. Creswell. London, 1862. p. 8°. L,41
J. Hill. London, 1752. f°. . . . . . . . . . Q,111
Habits, and Instincts of. W. Kirby. Philadelphia, 1836. 8°. N,686
Intelligence of. E. Menault. New York, 1869. 12°. . . M,1047
in Menageries. W. Swainson. London, 1838. 12°. . . . M,1032
Leben der Hausthiere. H. Pösche. Glogau, 1864. 8°. . . . G,933
Natural History of. J. Bigland. Philadelphia, 1849. 12°. . . N,630
S. and A. A. Tenney. New York, 1866. 12°. . . N,654
Naturgeschichte der Thiere. C. Vogt. Frankfurt-a-M. 1851. 2 v. 8°. G,929
Nützliche und Schädliche Thiere. C. Vogt. Leipzig, 1864. 16°. . G,912
of Scotland, Rare. Sir J. G. Dalyell. London, 1847–48. 2 v. 4°. . Q,7
Phénomènes Electriques des Animaux. C. Matteucci. Paris, 1840. 8°. N,252,8
Physiologie der Pflanzen und Thiere. M.J. Schleiden. Brschw.1850. 8°. G,659

Animals, Studies of. F. N. Otis. New York, 1866. 8°. . . . . . Q,198
Zug- und Wander-Thiere. C. Cornelius. Berlin, 1865. 16°. . . G,913
Annals and Magazine of Natural History. London, 1838–68. 66 v. 8°. . R,40
of a Quiet Neighborhood. G. Mac Donald. New York, 1867. 12°. K,837
The same. Leipzig, 1867. 2 v. in 1. 16°. . . . . . J,341
of the Parish. J. Galt. Edinburgh, 1844. 16°. . . . . K,703
The same. London, 1841. 16°. . . . . . . K,1154
Anne, Queen of England, History of Reign of. A. Boyer. Lond. 1703–8. 6 v. 8°. A,481
Reign of. P. H. Stanhope. London, 1870. 8°. . . . . A,433
Anne of Austria, Regency of. M. W. Freer. London, 1866. 2 v. 8°. . B,528
Anne Hereford. H. Wood. Leipzig, 1869. 2 v. in 1. 16°. . . . J,517
Anne of Geierstein. Sir W. Scott. Boston, 1859. 2 v. 12°. . . . K,925
The same. Philadelphia, 1869. 8°. . . . . . K,1115
The same. Philadelphia, 1853. 8°. . . . . . . K,955
Anners, H. F. The Gem; a Christmas Present for 1840. Phila. 1839. 18°. H,29
Annuaire des Marées des Côtes de France. Paris, 1850, '52, '54, '57–62. 9 v. 24°. S,7
du Bureau des Longitudes. Paris, 1836, 1851. 2 v. 24°. . . S,6
Annual Biography and Obituary. London, 1817–37. 21 v. 8°. . . C,568
of Scientific Discovery; ed. D. A. Wells and others. Bos. 1850–71. 21 v. 12°. M,766
Register, 1758–1858; index 1758–1819. Lond. 1759–1859. 101 v. 8°. Q,1
Anonymes et Pseudonymes Ouvrages, Dictionaire des. A. A. Barbier. Paris, 1822–27. 4 v. 8°. . . . . . . . . . . L.R.
Anquetil, L. P. Histoire du France. Paris, 1832. 13 v. 8°. . . . B,329
Anson, G., *Lord*. Voyage Round the World, 1740–44. London, 1748. 4°. Q,432
The same, abridged. London, 1853. 8°. . . . . N,252,45
Ansted, D. T. Ancient World. London, 1847. 12°. . . . . . . N,782
Elementary Course of Geology. Edinburgh, 1859. 8°. . . . N,610
Geological Gossip. London, 1860. 16°. . . . . . . . N,600
Geologist's Text-Book. London, 1845. 12°. . . . . . N,601
Geology, Introductory and Practical. London, 1844. 2 v. 8°. . N,806
Great Stone Book of Nature. Philadelphia, 1863. 12°. . . . N,767
Physical Geography. Philadelphia, 1867.p. 8°. . . . . V,1118
Anstie, F. E. Notes on Epidemics. London, 1866. 16°. . . . . . L,840
Anstis, J. Observations on the Knighthood of the Bath. London, 1725. 4°. A,498
Antediluvian World, Remains of an. J. Parkinson. Lond. 1804–11. 3 v. 4°. N,748
Anthems, Fifty Metrical; adapted by J. P. Metcalfe. London, 1858. 8°. . M,422
Twenty; Morning and Evening Service. J. Kent. Lond. n. d. 2 v. M,426
Anthon, C. Ancient and Mediæval Geography. New York, 1850. 8°. V,1116
Classical Dictionary. New York, 1869. 8°. . . . . . . L.R.
The same. New York, 1854. 8°. . . . . . . . R.R.
First Greek Lessons. New York, 1852. 12°. . . . . . . L,734
Grammar of the Greek Language. New York, 1856. 12°. . . L.733
Greek Lessons; part second. New York, 1846. 12°. . . . L,732
Manual of Grecian Antiquities. New York, 1852. 12°. . . . A,76
Greek Literature. New York, 1853. 12°. . . . . H,724
Roman Antiquities. New York, 1854. 12°. . . . . . A,138
Anthony Waymouth. W. H. G. Kingston. Boston, 1865. 12°. . . J,1501
Antioch College, Dedication of. Yellow Springs, 1854. 12°. . . O,1117
Antique Gems. C. W. King. London, 1866. 8°. . . . . . . M,100
Antique Vases, etc., Collection of. H. Moses. London, 1814. 4°. . . . M,98

Antiquary, The. Sir W. Scott. Boston, 1852. 2 v. 16°. . . . . . K,926
The same. Philadelphia, 1864. 8°. . . . . . . K,956
The same. Philadelphia, 1869. 8°. . . . . K,1104
The same. Leipzig, 1845. 16°. . . . . . . . J,438
Antiquities, Baronial and Eccles., of Scotland. R.W.Billings. Edin.1855. 4v. 4°. Q,142
Book of Days; edited by R. Chambers. Edinb. 1863-4. 2 v. 8°. . I,591
Catalogue of, Archæological Institute, etc. Edinburgh, 1859. 8°. . M,123
Greek and Roman, Dictionary of. A. Rich, Jr. London, 1860. 8°. A,79
Dictionary of. W. Smith. New York, 1850. 8°. . . . L.R.
Hebrew, Hand-Book of. H. Browne. London, 1852. 12°. . . A,200
Northern. P. H. Mallet. London, 1847. 12°. . . . . . . L,17
Illustrations of. H. Weber and R. Jameson. Edinb. 1814. 4°. F,232
of the Anglo-Saxon Church. J. Lingard. Philadelphia, 1848. 8°. P,609
of Athens. J. Stuart and N. Revett. London, 1837. 16°. . . A,61
of Great Britain. J. Brand. London, 1849. 3 v. p. 8°. . . L,3
of Herculaneum; tr. by T. Martyn and J. Lettice. London, 1773. 4°. Q,371
of the State of New York. E. G. Squier. Buffalo, 1851. 8°. . . C,91
Roman. A. Adam. New York, 1842. 8°. . . . . . . A,165
J. D. Fuss. Oxford, 1840. 8°. . . . . . . . A,166
Antiquity explained in Scriptures. B. de Montfaucon. Lond. 1721-22. 7v. f°. Q,314
Antisell, T. Cyclopædia of Useful Arts. New York, 1855. 12°. . . M,632
Manufacture of Hydro-Carbon Oils. New York, 1859. 8°. . . N,195
Anti-Slavery Associations, Apology for Ladies'. London, 1828. 8°. . . O,396
Anti-Slavery Conflict, Recollections of. S. J. May. Boston, 1869. 12°. . O,390
Anti-Slavery Measures in Congress, History of. H. Wilson. Bost. 1865. 12°. O,430
Antommarchi, F. Last Days of Napoleon I. London, 1826. 2 v. in 1. 8°. D,580
Antonia. Mad. Dudevant. Boston, 1870. 12°. . . . . . . K,1117
Antonina; or, the Fall of Rome. W. W. Collins. New York, 1868. 8°. . K,633
The same. Leipzig, 1863. 2 v. in 1. 16°. . . . . . J,73
Antonio Perez and Philip II. F. A. A. Mignet. London, 1846. 12°. . D.704
Antrobus, J. Parental Wisdom. London, 1849. 8°. . . . . . . O,928
Auvergne, Geological Notes on. A. Geikie. London, 1862. 8°. . V,1086,2
Anxious Inquirer after Salvation. J. A. James. New York, n. d. 18°. P,746,21
Apache Country, Adventures in. J. R. Browne. New York, 1869. 12°. . V,116
Aphorisms and Reflections. W. B. Clulow. London, 1843. 8°. . . H,448
Apocalypse Revealed. E. Swedenborg. New York, 1862. 2 v. 8°. . . P,850
Apocalyptic Sketches. J. Cumming. Philadelphia, 1858. 2 v. 12°. . P,255
Apostles, The. E. Renan. New York, 1867. 12°. . . . . . . P,145
Apostolic Church, History of. M. Baumgarten. Edinburgh, 1854. 3 v. 8°. P,403
History of. Philip Schaff. New York, 1856. 8°. . . . . P,405
Apostolic Era of Christianity. E. de Pressensé. New York, 1870. 12°. . P,575
Apparitions, Second Sight, etc., Treatises on. See *Miscellanea Scotica*, v. 3.
Appeal on the behalf of Cameria. Cincinnati, 1868. 8°. . . . . C,237
Appert, C. L'Art de Conserver toutes les Substances. Paris, 1831. 8°. N,252,13
Appianus Alexandrinus. Romanæ Historiæ. Paris, 1840. 8°. . . . U,550
Apples, American Pomology. J. A. Warder. New York, 1867. 12°. . M,553
Appleton's (D.&Co.) Anatomy of Human Body, and Plates. N. Y. 1856. 2v. 8°. Q,257
Art of Building, Ancient and Modern, and Plates. N.Y.1856. 2 v. 8°. Q,254
Countries and Cities of the World. New York, 1856. 8°. . . Q,260
Customs and Costumes of People. New York, 1856. 8°. . . . . Q,261

Appleton's (D.&Co.) Cyclopædia of Drawing; ed.W.E.Worthen. N.Y.1866. 8°. M,230
Dictionary of Machines, Mechanics, etc. New York, 1852. 2 v. 8°. *M,802
Fine Arts illustrated. New York, 1856. 8°. . . . . . . Q,252
Hand-Book of American Travel. E. H. Hall. New York, 1869. 8°. V,119
Illustrations to Architecture, Plates. New York, 1856. 8°. . Q,254,2
to the Fine Arts, Plates. New York, 1856. 8°. . . Q,252,2
to History and Ethnology, Plates. New York, 1856. 8°. Q,258,2
to Mathematics and Astronomy, Plates. New York, 1856. 8°. Q,259,2
to Military Sciences, Plates. New York, 1856. 8°. . . Q,256,2
to Naval Sciences, Plates. New York, 1856. 8°. . . Q,255,2
Laws of Nature. New York, 1856. 8°. . . . . . . Q,259,2
Library Manual. New York, 1852. 8°. . . . . . . . *L.R.
Modern Atlas of the Earth. New York. 8°. . . . . . V,1145
Navigation of all Ages. New York, 1856. 8°. . . . . . . Q,255
Religions and Mythology, and Plates. New York, 1856. 2 v. 8°. . Q,253
Sciences Illustrated, and Plates. New York, 1856. 2 v. 8°. . . Q,250
Short-Trip Guide to Europe. H. Morford. New York, 1868. 16°. . V,295
Technology Illustrated, and Plates. New York, 1856. 2 v. 8°. . Q,251
Warfare of all Ages, and Plates. New York, 1856. 2 v. 8°. . . Q,256
Appleton, E. Early Education. London, 1821. 12°. . . . O,1171
Private Education. London, 1816. 12°. . . . . . . O,1025
Appleton, William, Memoir of. C. Robbins. Boston, 1863. 8°. . . C,757
Apuleius. Works translated. London, 1853. p. 8°. . . . . . . L,36
Aquarium, Fresh and Salt-Water. J. G. Wood. London, 1868. 16°. . N,473
Objects of the Sea Shore. J. G. Wood. London, 1859. 16°. . . N,475
Popular History of. G. B. Sowerby. London, 1857. 16°. . . N,477
Arabella Stuart. G. P. R. James. Leipzig, 1844. 16°. . . . . . J,200
Arabia, Central and Eastern, Journey thro'. W.G.Palgrave. Lond.1865. 2v. 8°. V,750
History of. A. Crichton. New York, 1855. 2 v. 18°. . . . L,387
Travels in. J. L. Burckhardt. London, 1829. 2 v. 8°. . . V,755
J. Griffith. London, 1805. 4°. . . . . . . V,1144
Petræa, Travels in. S. Olin. New York, 1851. 2 v. 12°. . V,1057
See also *Egypt, Arabia, Petræa, etc.*
Arabian Days' Entertainments. W. Hauff. Boston, 1868. 12°. . . J,1343
Arabian Nights' Entertainments. Boston, 1867. 12°. . . . . . J,1441
The same. London, 1841. 3 v. 8°.. . . . . . K,1095
Arabic Grammar. n. d. 12°. . . . . . . . . . . . L,777
Arabs in Spain, Dominion of. J. A. Condé. London, 1854. 3 v. p. 8°. . L,174
Arago, F. Astronomie Populaire. Paris, 1854-56. 4 v. 8°. . . . N,284
Biographies of Distinguished Scientific Men. London, 1857. 8°. . C,557
The same. Boston, 1859. 2 v. 12°. . . . . . . C,498
Vol. 1. Bailly; Fourier; W. Herschel; Laplace.
2. Canot; Fresner; Malus; Watt; Young.
History of my Youth. London, 1865. p. 8°. . . . . I,661,4
Meteorological Essays. London, 1855. 8°. . . . . . N,108
Observations Géodésiques, Astronomiques, etc. Paris, 1821. 4°. . N,384
Popular Astronomy. London, 1855. 2 v. 8°. . . . . . . N,358
Sämmtliche Werke. Leipzig, 1854-59. 7 v. 8°. . . . . . E,310
Unterhaltungen aus der Naturkunde. Stuttgart, 1837-38. 3 v. in 1. 8°. G,670
Ararat, Journey to. F. Parrott. New York, 1846. 12°. . . . . V,631

Arator; Agricultural Essays. J. Taylor. Georgetown, 1814. 12°. . . M,486
Araucanians, The; Indians of Chili. E. R. Smith. New York, 1855. 12°. V,251
Arbouin, J. Dissertations on the Regenerate Life. Boston, 1841. 16°. . O,988
Arc of the Meridian, Méthodes Analytiques pour la Determination d'. J. B. J. Delambre. Paris, 1799. 4°. . . . . . . . . M,1175
Arcana, Heavenly. E. Swedenborg. New York, 1854-63. 10 v. 8°. . P,851
Archæologia Americana; Amer. Antiq. Soc. v. 1. Worcester, Mass., 1820. 8°. B,605
Archæological Album. T. Wright. London, n. d. 4°. . . . . B,184
Archæological Institute, Catalogue of Antiquities. Edinburgh, 1859. 8°. . M,123
Archaic and Provincial Words, Dictionary of. J.O.Halliwell. Lon.1855. 2 v. 8°. L.R.
Archbishops of Canterbury. W. F. Hooke. London, 1861-68. 7 v. 8°. . D,215
Archer, J. W. Vestiges of Old London; Etchings. London, 1851. f°. . Q,308
Archer, T. C. Economic Botany. London, 1853. 16°. . . . . N,915
Arches, Piers, etc., Construction of. W. Bland. London, 1867. 12°. . . M,829
Archibald Hamilton. E. W. Baärnhielm. Boston, 1869. 16°. . . . J,1669
Archie Lovell. A. B. Edwards. Leipzig, 1867. 2 v. in 1. 16°. . . J,154
Architect, Model. S. Sloan. Philadelphia, 1860. 2 v. 4°. . . . Q,221
Architects, Lives of British. A. Cunningham. London, 1831. 16°. . . I,640
    Lives of Celebrated. F. Milizia. London, 1826. 2 v. 8°. . . M,204
    Painters and Sculptors, Lives of Eminent. G.Vasari. Lon.1851. 5v. p.8°. L,244
Architectural Criticism, Elements of. J. Gwilt. London, 1837. 8°. . . M,144
Architectural Designs for Country Residences. J. Riddell. Phil. 1861. f°. Q,245
Architectural Magazine; ed. by J. C. Loudon. London, 1834-38. 5 v. 8°. M,265
Architecture and Building, Rudiments of; ed. J. Bullock. N. Y. 1855. 12°. M,152
    Application of Iron to Buildings. W. Fairbairn. London, 1870. 8°. M,665
    Arts connected with. J. B. Waring. London, 1858. f°. . *Q,348
    Baudenkmäler aller Völker. H. Berghaus. Brüssel, 1854. 2 v. 8°. G,735
    Baustyle und Säulen-Ordnungen. Leipzig, 1854. 8°. . . . G,626
    Beauties of Modern. M. Lafever. New York, 1849. 8°. . . M,227
    Building, Masonry, etc. W. Hosking and others. New York, 1852. 4°. M,286
    Chapel and Church. G. Bowler. Boston, 1856. f°. . . *Q,389
    City. M. Field. New York, 1854. 8°. . . . . . . . M,225
        and Suburban. S. Sloan. Philadelphia, n. d. 4°. . *Q,222
    Civil. E. Shaw. Boston, 1852. 4°. . . . . . . . . M,287
    Constructive. S. Sloan. Philadelphia, 1859. 4°. . . . *Q,173
    Cyclopædia of. R. Stuart. New York, 1855. 2 v. in 1. 8°. . . M,168
    Dictionary of Terms used in. London, 1858-59. 12°. . . . M,973
    Domestic of Middle Ages. J. H. Parker. Oxford, 1853-9. 3 v. 8°. M,186
        of Thirteenth Century. T. H. Turner. Oxford, 1851. 8°. . M,159
    Elizabethan. J. Hakewill. London, 1835. 8°. . . . . M,221
    Encyclopædia of. J. C. Loudon. London, 1860. 8°. . . *M,169
        J. Gwilt. London, 1867. 8°. . . . . . . . *M,172
        P. Nicholson; edited by Lomax. London, 1852. 2 v. 4°. *M,264
    English. J. Dallaway. London, 1806. 8°. . . . . . . M,184
    Glossary of Terms used in. J. H. Parker. Oxford, 1850. 3 v. 8°. M,205
    Gothic, Essays on. T. Wharton and others. London, 1808. 8°. . M,208
        Examples of. A. and A. W. Pugin. London, 1850. 3 v. 4°. *Q,345
        Specimens of. W. Caveler. London, 1839. 4°. . . *Q,175
    Grecian. G. H. Gordon, *Earl of Aberdeen*. London, 1860. 12°. . M,843
    Hints on Public. R. D. Owen. New York, 1849. 4°. . . *Q,180

Architecture, History of. J. Fergusson. London, 1862–67. 3 v. 8°. *M,173
J. S. Memes. Edinburgh, 1829. 16°. . . . . . I,515
Home for All. O. S. Fowler. New York, 1854. 12°. . . . M,201
Illustrated, Appleton's. New York, 1856. 2 v. 8°. . . . Q,254
Hand-Book of. J. Fergusson. London, 1855. 2 v. 8°. *M,189
in England. J. Dallaway. London, 1833. 8°. . . . . M,228
Lectures on. J. Ruskin. New York, 1856. 12°. . . . . M,151
Manuel Complet d'. C. J. Toussaint. Paris, 1837. 2 v. 24°. . M,589
Marine and Naval. J. W. Griffiths. New York, 1851. 4°. . . Q,220
M. Vitruvius Pollio; tr. by J. Gwilt. London, 1860. 12°. . . M,860
of Country Houses. A. J. Downing. New York, 1851. 8°. . . M,185
The same. New York, 1866. 8°. . . . . . . . M,190
of the Heavens. J. P. Nichol. London, n. d. 8°. . . . . N,336
Orders of. W. H. Leeds. London, 1854. 12°. . . . . . M,947
Photographs from Pugin's Sketches. S. Ayling. Lond. 1865. 2 v. 4°. M,281
Principles of Design in. E. L. Garbett. London, 1850. 12°. . . M,916
Rudiments of. J. Gwilt. London, 1839. 8°. . . . . . . M,220
Rudiments of Ancient. London, 1804. 8°. . . . . . . M,208
Rural. L. F. Allen. New York, 1869. 12°. . . . . . M,181
E. Shaw. Boston, 1843. 4°. . . . . . . . . M,294
School. H. Barnard. Cincinnati, 1854. 8°. . . . . . M,188
Seven Lamps of. J. Ruskin. New York, 1857. 12°. . . . M,74
Street Fronts, etc. M. F. Cummings and C. C. Miller. Troy, 1865. 4°. *Q,200
Styles of. T. T. Bury. London, 1857. 12°. . . . . . M,899
Wonders of. M. Lefèvre. New York, 1870. 12°. . . . M,1052
Arctic Boat Journey. I. I. Hayes. Boston, 1867. 12°. . . . . V,938
Arctic Crusoe. P. B. St. John. Boston, 1866. 16°. . . . . J,1476
Arctic Explorations, Grinnell Expedition. E. K. Kane. Boston, 1854. 8°. V,940
Second Grinnell Expedition. E. K. Kane. Phil. 1858. 2 v. 8°. . V,939
Journey to the Polar Sea. Sir J. Franklin. London, 1824. 2 v. 8°. V,942
Second Expedition to Polar Sea. Sir J. Franklin. Lond. 1828. 4°. V,1014
Narrative of the Arctic Expedition. G. Back. Philadel. 1837. 8°. V,957
Arctic Ocean, Journey to the, 1833–35. R. King. London, 1836. 2. v. . V,914
Arctic Queen; a Poem. M. V. Fuller. Sandusky, 1856. 12°. . . . T,19,2
Arctic Regions, Voyages to. F. Mayne. London, 1853. p. 8°. . . I,656,7
Voyages within the. Sir J. Barrow. New York, 1846. 12°. . . V,915
Arctic Researches. C. F. Hall. New York, 1866. 8°. . . . . . V,183
Arctic Searching Expedition. Sir J. Richardson. New York, 1852. 12°. . V,912
Arctic Seas, Tidal Observations in. E. K. Kane. Washington, 1863. 4°. Q,324,13
Voyage towards the North Pole, 1818. F.W. Beechey. Lond. 1843. 8°. V,956
Ardvoirlich; a Romantic Tragedy. R. Warden. Cincinnati, 1857. . . H,302
Arendts, C. Naturhistorischer Schulatlas. Leipzig, 1866. 8°. . . . F,91
Arey, H. E. G. Household Songs; and other Poems. N. Y. 1855. 12°. . I,7
Argenson, R. L. de V. de P. de. Mémoires. Paris, 1853. 12°. . . . D,610
Argentine Confederation. LaPlata and Paraguay. T. J. Page. N. Y. 1859. 8°. V,262
Argentine Republic, Life in. D. F. Sarmiento. New York, 1868. 12°. . V,234
Twenty-Four Years in. J. A. King. London, 1846. 8°. . . . V,249
Argyle, Duke of. See *Campbell, G. J. D.*
Arians of the Fourth Century. J. H. Newman. London, 1833. 8°. . . P,614
Ariosto, L. Orlando Furioso. London, 1823–31. 8 v. 8°. . . . . . G,78

Ariosto, L. Orlando Furioso; tr. by W. S. Rose. London, 1864-65. 2 v. p. 8°. L,93
Aristænetus. Love Epistles; tr. by R. B. Sheridan. London, 1854. p. 8°. L,75
Aristophanes. Comedies; tr. by W. J. Hickie. London, 1853. 2 v. p. 8°. . L,37
Aristotle. Ethics and Politics; Life by J. Gillies. London, 1797. 2 v. 4°. O,735
History of Animals; tr. by R. Cresswell. London, 1862. p. 8°. . L,41
Metaphysics; tr. by J. H. M'Mahon. London, 1857. p. 8°. . . L,40
Organon, or Logical Treatise; tr. by O. F. Owen. Lond. 1853. 2 v. p. 8°. L,42
Politics and Economics; tr. by E. Walford. London, 1853. p. 8°. . L,39
Nicomachean Ethics of; tr. by R. W. Browne. London, 1853. p. 8°. L,38
Treatise on Rhetoric; tr. by T. Hobbes. London, 1853. p. 8°. . . L,43
Arithmetic. J. W. Colenso. London, 1856. 12°. . . . . . . M,1084
J. R. Young. London, 1857. 12°. . . . . . . . . M,980
and Geometry, Theoretisch-Praktische. J. E. Vierenklee. Leip. 1822. 8°. E,432
and Key. J. Haddon. London, 1862. 2 v. 12°. . . . . M,844
Arithmetica Universalis. Sir I. Newton. London, 1722. 8°. . M,1105
Child's. J. Ray. Cincinnati, 1853. 16°. . . . . . . O,1094
Course of. J. L. Ellenberger. London, 1854. 8°. . . . M,1089
Disquisitiones Arithmeticæ. C. F. Gauss. Lipsiæ, 1801. 8°. . M,1115
Elementary Intellectual. D. Leach and R. Swan. Bost. 1854. 16°. O,1093
Equational. W. Hipsley. London, 1854. 12°. . . . . M,937
Examples in. S. Newth. London, 1859. 8°. . . . . . M,1101
Exercises in. D. Ring. Philadelphia, 1845. 24°. . . . O,1091
First Book of. Dublin, 1844. 18°. . . . . . . . O,1089
First Lessons in. G. Rae. Edinburgh, n. d. 16°. . . . O,1090
First Principles of. T. Tate. London, 1857. 8°. . . . M,1090
for the Young. J. Cassell. London, 1857. 16°. . . . O,1097
Intellectual. C. Davies. New York, 1854. 16°. . . . O,1095
J. Ray. Cincinnati, 1853. 16°. . . . . . . O,1080
Lehrbuch der Arithmetik. E. G. Fischer. Leipzig, 1842. 8°. . . E,429
Mental; part second. J. Ray. Cincinnati, 1849. 16°. . . O,1094,2
Third book. Cincinnati, n. d. 16°. . . . . . O,1096
Mercantile. R. Nelson. Cincinnati, 1859. 16°. . . . O,1101
Practical. J. B. Thomson. Cincinnati, 1848. 12°. . . . O,1100
Primary. P. A. Towne. Louisville, Ky. 1867. 12°. . . M,1093
Questions in. W. Thrower. London, 1855. 12°. . . . O,1099
Recherches Arithmétiques. C. F. Gauss. Paris, 1807. 4°. . M,1205
Solution to Examples in. J. W. Colenso. London, 1854. 12°. M,1091
Stepping-Stone to. A. Arman. London, 1864. 12°. . . . . M,827
Traité Élémentaire d'. S. F. LaCroix. Paris, 1823. 8°. . . M,1103
Treatise on. D. Lardner. London, 1834. 12°. . . . . M,1019
The same. London, n. d. 16°. . . . . . . M,1095
Arizona and Sonora, Silver Region of. S. Mowry. New York, 1864. 12°. C,246
Arkwright, R., Life of. H. Coleridge. London, 1852. 8°. . . . C,1166,2
Armadale. W. Collins. New York, 1866. 8°. . . . . . . . K,634
The same. Leipzig, 1866. 3 v. 16°. . . . . . . J,74
Arman, A. Ready-Reckoner for Land. London, 1862. 12°. . . . M,826
Stepping-Stone to Arithmetic. London, 1864. 12°. . . . . M,827
Armengaud, J. E. and others. Practical Draughtsman's Book. N. Y. 1854. 4°. Q,169
Armenia, History of. M. Chamich. Calcutta, 1827. 2 v. 8°. . . . A,32
Tour through. H. Southgate. New York, 1840. 2 v. 12°. . . V,646

Armenia, Travels in. R. Curzon. New York, 1854. 12°. . . . . . V,640
Armin, R. Nest of Ninnies. London, 1842. 8°. . . . . . I,885,10
Arminius, J. Works. Auburn, 1853. 3 v. 8°. . . . . . . . . P,736
Armor, Ancient, Critical Inquiry on. R. S. Meyrick. Lond. 1842–3. 3 v. 4°. *Q,372
Illustrations of the Above. J. Skelton. London, 1844. 2 v. 4°. . *Q,373
Arms and Armor. M. P. Lacombe. New York, 1870. 12°. . . . M,760
Armstrong, J. Life of A. Wayne. New York. 12°. . . . . . C,860,4
Life of R. Montgomery. New York, 1848. 12°. . . . C,860,1
Armstrong, R. Steam Boilers. London, 1857. 12°. . . . . . . M,889
Steam without Smoke. London, n. d. 8°. . . . . . . . N,252,30
Armstrong, R. and T. English Composition. London, 1855. 2 v. 16°. . O,775
Key to English Composition. London, 1854. 16°. . . . . . O,776
Armstrong, W. Furnace & Steam Jet as Ventilating Powers. Durham, 1853. 8°. N,252,56
Army and Navy Stories. W. T. Adams. Boston, 1869. 6 v. 16°. . J,1536

Vol. 1. The Soldier Boy. Vol. 4. Yankee Middy.
2. The Sailor Boy. 5. Fighting Joe.
3. Young Lieutenant. 6. Brave Old Salt.

Army Life on the Border, Thirty Years of. R. B. Marcy. N. Y. 1866. 8°. V,108
Army Life in a Black Regiment. T. W. Higginson. Boston, 1870. 12°. . B,892
Army Meteorological Register; 1843–1854. Washington, 1855. 4°. . . P.D.
Army of the Cumberland, Society of, Report. Cincinnati, 1868. 8°. . . B,947
of the Potomac, Medical Recollections of. J. Letterman. N.Y. 1866. 8°. L,943
Re-union at Chicago, 1868. Chicago, 1869. 8°. . . . . . B,948
Arnald, R. Commentary on the Apocrypha. Philadelphia, 1846. 8°. . P,556
Arné; Sketch of Norwegian Country Life. B. Björnson. Lond. 1866. 8°. K,738
Arnold, B. and Major André. G. H. Calvert. Boston, 1864. 16°. . . I,27
Biography of. G. C. Hill. Philadelphia, 1868. 18°. . . . . C,835
Life of. J. Sparks. New York. 12°. . . . . . . . C,860,3
Journal of the Detachment of. R. J. Meigs. Cincinnati, 1852. 8°. C,710
Proceedings of Court-Martial for Trial of. New York, 1865. 4°. . F,37
Arnold, G. Poems, Grave and Gay. Boston, 1867. 16°. . . . . . I,3
Arnold, J. F. Grammatik der Englischen Sprache. Stuttgart, 1834. 12°. L,771
Arnold, M. Essays in Criticism. Boston, 1866. 12°. . . . . . . H,480
Poems. Boston, 1856. 16°. . . . . . . . . . . I,276
New Poems. London, 1867. 8°. . . . . . . . . . I,277
Study of Celtic Literature. London, 1867. 8°. . . . . . . H,765
Arnold, R. Customs of London. London, 1811. 4°. . . . . . . F,154
Arnold, T. History of Rome. New York, 1866. 8°. . . . . . . A,170
Lectures on Modern History. New York, 1847. 12°. . . . . A,318
Life and Correspondence of. A. P. Stanley. Boston, 1860. 2 v. 12°. D,208
The same. London, 1868. 2 v. 8°. . . . . . . . D,209
Life of Hannibal. New York, 1865. 16°. . . . . . . . D,747
Miscellaneous Works. New York, 1846. 8°. . . . . . . P,777
Sermons; the Christian Life. Philadelphia, 1856. 12°. . . . P,57
Arnold, T. Manual of English Literature. London, 1867. 12°. . . H,698
Arnold, T. K. English-Latin Lexicon. New York, 1856. 8°. . . . L.R.
First Latin Book. New York, 1858. 12°. . . . . . . . . L,751
Introduction to Latin Prose Composition. New York, 1854. 12°. . L,752
Arnot, D. H. Gothic Architecture. New York, 1850. 4°. . . . M,295
Arnot, W. Roots and Fruits of the Christian Life. London, 1860. 8°. . P,103

Arnott, G.A.W. and Hooker. Botany of Beechey's Voyage. London, 1841. 4°. Q,113
Arnott, N. Elements of Physics; or, Natural Philosophy. Lon. 1864–5. 2 v. 8°. N,84
Arrah Neil. G. P. R. James. Leipzig, 1844. 16°. . . . . . . J,201
Arrianus. Anabasis et Indica. Paris, 1846. 8°. . . . . . . . U,551
Arrington, A. W., Memorial of. Chicago, 1868. 4°. . . . . . C,1057
Arseniates, Phosphates, and Phosphoric Acid. T. Graham. Lond. 1833. 4°. N,252,57
Arsenic, De l'. F. P. Danger et C. Flandin. Paris, 1844. 8°. . . . N,252,12
Arsenic Poisoning, Recherches Med.-legales. M. J. B. Orfila. Paris, 1842. 8°. N,262,12
Forensisch-Chem. Verfahren. F. Wöhler u. E. v. Siebold. Ber. 1847. 8°. N,252,44
Art, Ancient, and its Remains. C. O. Müller. London, 1852. 8°. . . . M,97
History of. J. J. Winckelmann. Boston, 1856. 2 v. 8°. . M,134
Ancient and Modern. G. Cleghorn. Edinburgh, 1848. 2 v. 16°. . M,7
Ancient Vases. W. Hamilton. Naples, 1791–95. 3 v. f°. . . L.R.
and Nature, Laws of. L. Erckern. London, 1868. f°. . . . Q,294
and Science, Museum of. D. Lardner. Lond. 1854–56. 12 v. in 6. 12°. M,770
Collection of. W. G. Coesvelt; ed. by A. Jameson. London, 1836. 4°. *Q,182
Early Florentine School. W. Y. Ottley. London, 1826. f°. . . L.R.
Elementary. J. D. Harding. London, n. d. 4°. . . . *Q,213
Essays on. J. W. von Goethe. Boston, 1845. 16°. . . . . M,9
F. T. Palgrave. New York, 1867. 16°. . . . . . . M,15
Examples of Stained Glass, Fresco Ornament, Marble and Enamel Inlay, and Wood Inlay. J. B. Waring. London, 1858. f°. *Q,348
Galleries of Great Britain. G. F. Waagen. London, 1857. 8°. . M,59
Geschichte der Deutschen Kunst. E. Förster. Leipzig, 1860. 5 v. in 2. 12°. G,624
Glossary of Ecclesiastical Ornament and Costume, from ancient authorities. A. W. Pugin. London, 1868. 4°. . . . *Q,216
Grammar of Ornament. O. Jones. London, 1856. f°. . . *Q,458
Hand-Book of Pictorial. R. St. J. Tyrwhitt. Oxford, 1868. 8°. . M,95
Handbuch der Archäologie der Kunst. C. O. Müller. Breslau, 1848. 8°. E,455
Hieroglyphica of Merkbeelden. R. de Hooghe. Amsteldam, 1735. 4°. *Q,340
Hints. J. J. Jarves. New York, 1855. 12°. . . . . . . M,153
History of. W. Lübke. London, 1868. 2 v. 8°. . . . . . M,115
J. B. L. G. Séroux d' Agincourt. London, 1847. 3 v. in 1. 4°. *Q,468
Idea; Sculpture, Painting, etc., in America. J. J. Jarves. N.Y. 1866. 16°. M,4
Ideal in. H. Taine. New York, 1869. 16°. . . . . . M,29
Illuminated Ornaments; 6th–17th centuries. H. Shaw. Lond. 1833. 4°. *Q,185
Imitative. F. Howard. London, n. d. 12°. . . . . . M,28
Italian School of Design. W. Y. Ottley. London, 1823. f°. . . L.R.
Kunst und Culturentwickelung. M. Carriere. Leipzig, 1863–8. 4 v. 8°. G,625
Lectures on. J. Ruskin. New York, 1870. 12°. . . . . M,64
W. B. Scott. London 1867. 12°. . . . . . . . M,81
and Poems. W. Allston. New York, 1850. 12°. . . . M,42
on Painting. J. Barry and others. London, 1848. p. 8°. . L,303
Literature, and Character, Sketches of. A. Jameson. Bost. 1866. 16°. M,16
and the Drama. M. F. Ossoli. New York, 1869. 12°. . . U,95
Memoirs and Essays illustrative of. A. Jameson. London, 1846. 12°. H,563
Philosophy of. H. A. Taine. London, 1865. 12°. . . . . M,30
Photographs from Pugin's Sketches. S. Ayling. Lond. 1865. 2 v. 4°. *M,281
Poetry of Christian. A. F. Rio. London, 1854. 12°. . . . M,37
Political Economy of. J. Ruskin. New York, 1858. 12°. . . M,67

Art, pour Tous. Paris, 1861–68. 7 v. f°. . . . . . . . . . L.R.
Princes of; the Old Masters. Boston, 1870. 12°. . . . . M,202
Principles and Practice of. J. D. Harding. London, 1845. 4°. . Q,211
Sacred and Legendary. A. Jameson. London, 1857. 8°. . . M,77
The same. Boston, 1866. 2 v. 16°. . . . . . . M,20
The same. London, 1866. 2 v. 8°. . . . . . *M,116
Sketches of the Progress of. T. J. Gullick. London, 1859. 16°. . M,3
Study of. M. A. Dwight. New York, 1856. 12°. . . . . M,10
Suggestions in Design. L. Limner. London, 1853. 4°. . . . *Q,166
Thoughts about. P. G. Hamerton. Boston, 1871. 12°. . . . M,32
Treasures of, in Great Britain. G. F. Waagen. Lond. 1854. 3 v. 8°. M,59
True and Beautiful in. J. Ruskin. New York, 1859. 12°. . . M,75
Two Paths; Lectures on. J. Ruskin. New York, 1859. 12°. . . M,68
Wonders of Italian. L. Viardot. New York, 1870. 12°. . M,1051
Art Journal. London, 1839–1867. 30 v. 4°. . . . . . . *Q,361
Art Recreations. S. R. Urbino and H. Day. Boston, 1869. 12°. . . M,35
Art Student in Munich. A. M. Howitt. Boston, 1854. 16°. . . . V,413
Art Thoughts. J. J. Jarves. New York, 1870. 16°. . . . . . . M,41
Art Union and Journal. See *Art Journal.*
Artist and Tradesman's Companion. M. L. Byrn. New York, 1867. 12°. M,673
Artist-Life; American Painters. H. T. Tuckerman. New York, 1847. 12°. M,38
Artist's Married Life. L. Schefer. New York, 1867. 16°. . . . . . D,524
Artists and Arabs; Sketching in Sunshine. H. Blackburn. Lond. 1868. 8°. V,805
Book of American. H. T. Tuckerman. New York, 1867. 8°. . M,282
Artemus Ward, his Book. C. F. Browne. New York, 1870. 12°. . . H,46
his Travels. C. F. Browne. New York, 1866. 12°. . . . H,47
in London. C. F. Browne. New York, 1867. 12°. . . . . . H,48
Arthur, La Mort d'; edited by T. Wright. London, 1858. 3 v. 16°. . A,389
Arthur Brown; the Young Captain. E. Kellogg. Boston, 1871. 16°. J,1475,1
Arthur Mervyn; or, Memoirs of 1793. C. B. Brown. Phila. 1857. 2 v. 12°. K,463
Arthur O'Leary. C. Lever. Leipzig, 1847. 2 v. in 1. 16°. . . . J,268
Arthur, T. S. Advice to Young Ladies. Philadelphia, n. d. 16°. . . H,15
Advice to Young Men. Philadelphia, n. d. 16°. . . . . . H,16
After the Storm. Philadelphia, n. d. 16°. . . . . . . J,606
Allen House. Philadelphia, n. d. 16°. . . . . . . . J,607
Angel and the Demon. Philadelphia, n. d. 16°. . . . . . J,608
Angel of the Household. Philadelphia, n. d. 16°. . . . . J,609
Good Time Coming. Philadelphia, n. d. 16°. . . . . . . J,610
Heart-Histories and Life-Pictures. Philadelphia, n. d. 16°. . . J,611
Home; Lights and Shadows. Philadelphia, n. d. 16°. . . . J,612
Home-Heroes, Saints, and Martyrs. Philadelphia, 1865. 12°. . . J,645
Home Stories. New York, 1869. 6 v. 16°. . . . . . . J,1478

Vol. 1. Hidden Wings. Vol. 4. The Peace-Maker.
2. Sowing the Wind. 5. Not Anything for Peace.
3. Sunshine at Home. 6. After a Shadow.

Household Library. Philadelphia, 1859. 12 v. in 6. 12°. . . . J,600

Vol. 1. Married Life; Home Scenes.
2. Seed-Time and Harvest; Off-Hand Sketches.
3. Stories for Young Housekeepers; Stories for Parents.
4. The Two Wives; Lessons in Life.
5. Woman's Trials; Ways of Providence.
6. Words for the Wise; The Tried and the Tempted.

Arthur, T. S. Light on Shadowed Paths. New York, 1864. 12°. . . . K,6
Lights and Shadows of Real Life. Philadelphia, n. d. 16°. . J,613
Nothing but Money. New York, 1866. 12°. . . . . . . K,7
Off-Hand Sketches. Philadelphia, 1858. 18°. . . . . . . J,1302
Sparing to Spend. Philadelphia, n. d. 16°. . . . . . J,614
Stories for Parents. Philadelphia, 1858. 16°. . . . . . J,1196
Ten Nights in a Bar-Room. Philadelphia, n. d. 16°. . . . J,615
Three Eras of a Woman's Life. Philadelphia, n. d. 16°. . . J,616
Trials and Confessions of a Housekeeper. Philadelphia, n. d. 16°. . J,617
True Riches, and other Tales. Philadelphia, n. d. 16°. . . . J,618
Way to Prosper, and other Tales. Philadelphia, n. d. 16°. . . J,619
What can Woman do? Philadelphia, n. d. 16°. . . . . J,620
Withered Heart. Philadelphia, n. d. 16°. . . . . . J,621
Young Lady at Home; Home Stories. Philadelphia, n. d. 16°. . J,622
and W. H. Carpenter. History of Georgia. Philadelphia, 1852. 16°. C,154
History of New Jersey. Philadelphia, 1853. 16°. . . . C,156
of New York. Philadelphia, 1853. 16°. . . . C,155
Arthur W. Italy in Transition. New York, 1860. 12°. . . . . V,510
Arthurian Localities, Essay on. J. S. S. Glennie. London, 1869. 8°. L,605,36
Artis, E. T. Antediluvian Phytology. London, 1838. 4°. . . . . . Q,120
Arts and Manufactures, Novelties in. London, 1853. 16°. . . . . M,598
and Sciences, Introduction to. J. Joyce. London, 1852. 12°. . . M,786
Cyclopædia of Useful. T. Antisell. New York, 1855. 12°. . . M,632
Legendary and Mythological. C. E. Clement. New York, 1871. 12°. M,82
Les Arts au Moyen Age. P. Lacroix. Paris, 1869. 2 v. 4°. . *Q,360
Manufactures, and Mines, Dictionary of. A. Ure. N.Y. 1857. 2 v. 8°. S.C.
The same, 6th edition. London, 1867. 3 v. 8°. . . *M.805
The same, and supplement. New York, 1854–63. 3 v. 8°. *M,804
of the Middle Ages. J. Labarte. London, 1855. 8°. . . . M,96
Sciences, etc., American Repertory of. New York, 1840–42. 4 v. 8°. T,26
Treatise on Soluble Glass. L. Feuchtwanger. New York, 1870. 12°. M,683
Arvine, K. Cyclopædia of Anecdotes of Literature and Art. Bost. 1870. 8°. H,670
of Moral and Religious Anecdotes. New York, 1855–57. 8°. P,107
Arzoomund. M. M. Sherwood. New York, 1856. 12°. . . . K,1008,8
Asbury, F., Life of. W. P. Strickland. New York, 1858. 8°. . . C,1285
Ascham, R., Life of. H. Coleridge. London, 1852. 8°. . . . C,1166,2
Aschbach, J. Geschichte der Ommaijaden in Spanien. Frank.-a-M. 1829. 2 v. 8°. E,95
Gesch. Spaniens und Portugals. Frankfurt-a-M. 1833–7. 2 v. 8°. E,93
der Westgothen. Frankfurt-a-M. 1827. 8°. . . . . . E,24
Ash, J. Art of Double-Counting on the Lathe. London, 1857. 8°. . . M,655
Ash, J. Dictionary of the English Language. London, 1775. 8°. . . L.R.
Ashango-Land, Equatorial Africa, Journey to. P.B. Du Chaillu. Lon. 1867. 8°. V,847
Ashley, A. Art of Etching on Copper. London, n. d. 8°. . . . Q,203
Ashmun, J., Life of. R. R. Gurley. New York, 1839. 8°. . . . C,932
Asia, Across America and. R. Pumpelly. New York, 1870. 8°. . V,1084
American Merchant in. G. F. Train. New York, 1857. 12°. . V,1034
Antenor's Reisen durch. E. F. de Lantier. Hamburg, 1806. 5 v. 16°. E,191
Central, Travels in, 1863. A. Vámbérg. New York, 1865. 8°. . V,680
Eastern, Rambles in. B. C. Ball. Boston, 1865. 12°. . . . V,589
Erdkunde von Asien. C. Ritter. Berlin, 1822–59. 9 v. in 21. 8°. . E,153

Asia, Overland through. T. W. Knox. Hartford, 1870. 8°. . . . . V,670
Reisen in Asien, etc. J. Russeger. Stuttgart, 1841–48. 4 v. in 7. 8°. E,161
Atlas to the same. Portfolio. . . . . . . . . . *Q,459
Travels in. J. Bell. Glasgow, 1763. 2 v. 4°. . . . . . V,536
E. D. Clarke. New York, 1813–14. 2 v. 12°. . . . V,1035
Asia Minor, Description of. J. A. Cramer. Oxford, 1832. 2 v. 8°. . . V,705
Observations in. J. P. Durbin. New York, 1854. 2 v. 12°. . V,1058
Travels in. J. Griffith. London, 1805. 4°. . . . . . V,1144
Asiatic Journal. London, 1830–45. 4 v. 8°. . . . . . . . . S,95
Asiatic Researches. London, 1801–18. 12 v. 8°. . . . . . . . S,70
Assayer's Guide. O. M. Lieber. Philadelphia, 1869. 12°. . . . M,715
Assaying, Manuel de l' Essayeur. L. N. Vauquelin. Paris, 1812. 8°. N,252,15
Practical. J. Mitchell. London, 1854. 8°. . . . . . . N,193
Aspendale. H. W. Preston. Boston, 1871. 12°. . . . . . . K,222
Asser, J. Life of Alfred the Great. London, 1848. p. 8°. . . . . L,26
Assurance, Life, American Manual of. Newark. 18°. . . . . . O,460
Astié, J. F. Louis XIV. and Writers of his Age. Boston, 1855. 12°. . H,758
Astoria. W. Irving. New York, 1868. 16°. . . . . . . . . U,4
The same. New York, 1866. 12°. . . . . . . . . U,24
Astronomer, Practical. T. Dick. New York, 1846. 12°. . . . . N,262
The same. Philadelphia, 1869. 12°. . . . . . U,260,5
Astronomical Discovery, History of. C. P. Weidemann. Lond. 1850. 16°. H,391
Astronomical Investigations. H. F. A. Pratt. London, 1865. 8°. . . N,292
Astronomical Journal; ed. by B. A. Gould. Cambridge, 1851–61. 6 v. 4°. N,385
Astronomy. Sir J. F. W. Herschel. London, 1833. 12°. . . . M,1023
D. Lardner. Philadelphia, 1851. 12°. . . . . . . . . S.C.
The same. Philadelphia, 1864. 8°. . . . . . . M,772
Abrégé d' Astronomie. J. B. J. Delambre. Paris, 1813. 8°. . . N,283
Ancient, Histoire de l'. J. B. J. Delambre. Paris, 1817. 2 v. 4°. . N,383
and Natural Philosophy; 1st course. D. Lardner. Phila. 1854. 12°. N,79,1
The same; 3d course. Philadelphia, 1854. 12°. . . . . N,79,3
Architecture of the Heavens. J. P. Nichol. London, n. d. 8°. . N,336
Astronomische Nachrichten. H. C. Schumacher. Altona, 1854–5. 3 v. 4°. G,849
Celestial Objects for Common Telescopes. T. W. Webb. Lond. 1868. 16°. N,259
Celestial Scenery and Siderial Heavens. T. Dick. Phila. 1869. 12°. U,260,4
Connaisance des Tems. Paris, 1834–39. 7 v. 8°. . . . . . . R,20
Contemplations of the Solar System. J. P. Nichol. Edinb. 1844. 8°. N,335
Descriptive. G. T. Chambers. Oxford, 1867. 8°. . . . . . N,344
Ecce Cœlum. E. F. Burr. Boston, 1869. 16°. . . . . . N,321
Elements of. J. Brocklesby. New York, 1859. 12°. . . . . N,324
J. Davis. Philadelphia, 1868. 12°. . . . . . . N,264
G. H. Peabody. Cincinnati, 1869. 12°. . . . . . . N,331
W. J. Rolfe and J. A. Gillet. Boston, 1868. 12°. . . . N,325
Familiar. H. M. Bouvier. Philadelphia, 1857. 8°. . . . . N,341
Great Architect. M. Ponton. London, 1866. 12°. . . . . . N,269
Half-Hours with the Stars. London, 1870. 4°. . . . . . N,388
Hand-Book of. D. Lardner. Philadelphia, 1854. 12°. . . . M,772,2
Heavens, The. A. Guillemin. 2d ed. London, 1867. 8°. . *N,346
The same, 4th edition. New York, 1871. 8°. . . N,350
Histoire de l'. J. S. Bailly. Paris, 1805. 2 v in 1. 8°. . . . . N,282

Astronomy, Illustrated, Appleton's. New York, 1856. 2 v. 8°. . . . Q,259
Introduction to. J. R. Hind. London, 1863. p. 8°. . . . . L,294
to Practical. E. Loomis. New York, 1855. 8°. . . . . N,359
E. P. Mason. New York, 1841. 8°. . . . . . N,293
Jahrbuch für 1836-43. Stuttgart, 1836–43. 7 v. 12°. . . . . G,799
Lehrbuch der Sphärischen Astronomie. F. Brünnow. Berlin, 1851. 8°. G.779
Lessons in. J. N. Lockyer. London, 1868. 16°. . . . . . N,255
Letters on. D. Olmsted. New York, 1855. 12°. . . . . . N,266
Nautical, Traité des Calculs de l'. E. P. E. de Rossel. Paris, 1810. 8°. N,299,4
Observations Astronomiques. F. Arago. Paris, 1821. 4°. . . . N,384
J. B. Biot. Paris, 1821. 4°. . . . . . . . . . M,817
of the Bible. O. M. Mitchell. New York, 1870. 12°. . . . . N,332
of Middle Ages, Histoire de l'. J. B. J. Delambre. Paris, 1819. . N,382
Outlines of. Sir J. F. W. Herschel. Philadelphia, 1853. 8°. . . N,330
The same. London, 1869. 8°. . . . . . . . . N,349
Physical, History of. R. Grant. London, 1852. 8°. . . . . N,348
Popular. D. Vaughan. Cincinnati, 1858. 8°. . . . . N,290
Traité Elémentaire d'. J. P. Biot. Paris, 1810-11. 3 v. 8°. N,299
Physics, and Natural Theology. W. Whewell. London, 1852. p. 8°. L,277
Populäre. F. T. Schubert. St. Petersburg, 1804–10. 3 v. 8°. . G,798
Populaire. F. Arago. Paris, 1854–56. 4 v. 8°. . . . . N,284
Popular. G. B. Airy. London, 1866. 16°. . . . . . . N,254
F. Arago. London, 1855. 2 v. 8°. . . . . . . N,358
O. M. Mitchell. New York, 1860. 12°. . . . . . . N,320
Practical. L. B. Francœur. Paris, 1830. 8°. . . . . . . N,288
Progress of. E. Loomis. New York, 1851. 12°. . . . . . N,272
Refractors-Beobachtungen der K. Universität. H. Schultz. Ups. 1864. 8°. G,801
Rudimentary. R. Main. London, 1852. 12°. . . . . . . M,948
Solar System. T. Dick. Philadelphia, 1869. 12°. . . . . U,260,5
Spherical and Practical. W. Chauvenet. Philadelphia, 1864. 2 v. 8°. N,360
System of the World. J. P. Nichol. Edinburgh, 1848. 8°. . . N,334
Système du Monde. M. G. de Pontécoulant. Paris, 1829. 3 v. 8°. . N,286
Tabulæ Regiomontanæ, 1750-1850. F. W. Bessel. Regiomonti, 1830. 8°. N,301
Theoretische und Practische. J. J. von Littrow. Wien, 1821-27. 3 v. 8°. G,782
Théorique et Pratique. J. B. J. Delambre. Paris, 1814. 3 v. 4°. . N,381
Traité Eélmentaire d'. L. B. Francœur. Paris, 1837. 8°. . . N,287
Treatise on. W. A. Norton. New York, 1867. 8°. . . . . . N,345
Vorlesungen über die Sternkunde. J. F. Fries. Heidelberg, 1833. 12°. G,780
Atlas to the same. 8°. . . . . . . . . . . . F,88
Wunder des Himmels. J. J. Littrow. Stuttgart, 1837. 8°. . . G,783
The same; 4th edition. Stuttgart, 1854. 8°. . . . . . G,784
Astro-Theology. W. Derham. London, 1726. 8°. . . . . . . P,258
At Home and Abroad. M. F. Ossoli. New York, 1869. 12°. . . . U,93
At Home and Abroad. B. Taylor. New York, 1866. 2 v. 12°. . V,1055
At Odds. I. von Tautphoeus. Philadelphia, 1863. 12°. . . . . . G,237
The same. Leipzig, 1863. 2 v. in 1. 16°. . . . . . J,471
Atala; René; etc. R. F. A. de Chateaubriand. Paris, 1854. 12°. . . H,937
Atalanta in Calydon. A. C. Swinburne. Boston, 1866. 16°. . . . I,436
Atheists, Plato against the. New York, 1855. 12°. . . . . . . U,407
Athelings, The. M. Oliphant. New York, 1857. 8°. . . . . . K,862

Athenæum, The. London, 1831, 1839-66. 33 v. 4°. . . . . . . Q,378
Athenæus. Deipnosophists; tr. by C. D. Yonge. London, 1854. 3 v. p. 8°. L,44
Athenian Letters; ed. P. Yorke, *Earl of Hardwicke.* London, 1798. 2 v. 4°. F,221
Athenians, Public Economy of the. A. Böckh. Boston, 1857. 8°. . . . A,99
- Staatshaushaltung der Athener. A. Böckh. Berlin, 1817. 2 v. 8°. . G,609
  - Tables to the same. 2 v. 4°. . . . . . . . . . G,609

Athens, Antiquities of. J. Stuart and N. Revett. London, 1858. p. 8°. . L,149
- The same; abridged. London, 1837. 16°. . . . . . A,61
- Few Days in. F. Wright. London, 1822. 8°. . . . . . . V,546
- its Rise and Fall. Sir E. L. Bulwer Lytton. New York, 1860. 12°. A,70
  - The same. Leipzig, 1843. 2 v. in 1. 16°. . . . . . J,304
- Views of. W. Colton. New York, 1851. 12°. . . . . . . V,355

Athens Co., Ohio, History of. C. M. Walker. Cincinnati, 1869. 8°. . . C,218
Athletic Sports and Recreations. J. G. Wood. London, 1864. 12°. . . M,302
Athos, Mount, Monks of. H. F. Tozer. London, 1862. 8°. . . V,1086,2
Atkins, M. A. Earl Whiting; or, Career of a Nameless Boy. Bost.1870. 16°. J,1555
- Little Pea-Nut Merchant. Boston, 1869. 16°. . . . . . . J,1657

Atkinson, E. W. Memoirs of the Queens of Prussia. London, 1858. 8°. . D,530
Atkinson, J. C. British Birds' Eggs and Nests. London, 1861. 16°. . . O,84
- Playhours and Half-Holidays. London, 1868. 8°. . . . . J,1378
- Sketches in Natural History. London, 1861. 8°. . . . . N,628
- Walks and Talks of Two Schoolboys. London, 1864. 16°. . . J,1517

Atkinson, T. W. Oriental and Western Siberia. New York, 1865. 12°. . V,685
- Upper and Lower Amoor. New York, 1860. 8°. . . . . V,683

Atlantic, Sea-Bed of the North. G. C. Wallich. London, 1862. 4°. . . Q,109
Atlantic Monthly. Boston, 1859-70. 26 v. 8°. . . . . . . . T,23
Atlantic Telegraph. W. H. Russell. London, n. d. 4°. . . . . Q,268
- History of. C. W. Field. New York, 1866. 12°. . . . . M,693

Atlas, Classical. A. G. Findlay. New York, n. d. 8°. . . . V,1127
- Classique et Universel de Geographie. G.G.A.Goujon. Paris, 1835. f°. *Q,446
- des Pflanzenreichs. Breslau, n. d. 4°. . . . . . . . G,854
- des Thierreichs. Breslau, n. d. 4°. . . . . . . . . G,938
- Family. A. J. Johnston. New York, 1863. 4°. . . . . . R.R.
- General. G. W. Colton. New York, 1870. f°. . . . . . *Q,461
  - A. and C. Black. Edinburgh, 1853. 4°. . . . . . . R.R.
    - The same. Edinburgh, 1870. 4°. . . . . . *Q,469
  - S. A. Mitchell. Philadelphia, 1868. 4°. . . . . . *Q,464
- Modern Historical. W. L. Gage. New York, 1869. 8°. . . *V,1141
- National. A. R. Johnston. Edinburgh, 1851. f°. . . . . *Q,465
- New Reference. S. A. Mitchell. Philadelphia, 1865. 4°. . *Q,370
- of Modern Geography. A. K. Johnston. Edinburgh, 1868. 4°. *Q,368
- of Classical Geography. London, 1861. p. 8°. . . . . . . L,79
- of State of Ohio, and of U.S. H. F. Walling. New York, 1868. 4°. *Q,392
- of the World. A. and C. Black. London, 1870. f°. . . *Q,469
- Physical. A. K. Johnston. Edinburgh, 1849. f°. . . . . *Q,466

At Last; a Novel. M. V. Terhune. New York, 1870. 12°. . . . . K,331
Atmosphere, Respiration and Combustion of. C.T.Coathupe. Bristol,1838. 8°. N,252,2
Atmospheric System and Prognostication. T. B. Butler. Norwalk, 1870. 12°. N,102
Atomic Theory, Supplement to the. C. Dauberry. London, 1840. 8°. N,252,28
Atoms, Theorie des Atomes. F. Ehoron. Paris, 1837. 8°. . . . N,252,4

Atonement and Eternal Judgment. C. Beecher. Boston, 1864. 12°. . P,128

Extent of the. T. W. Jenkyn. Boston, 1846. . . . . . . P,153

Atrocious Judges. R. Hildreth. New York, 1856. 12°. . . . . D,180

Attache; or, Sam Slick in Europe. T. C. Haliburton. London, 1843. 2 v. 12°. K,713

Atterbury, F. and W. Pitt. T. B. Macaulay. Leipzig, 1860. 16°. . . . J,338

Memoirs and Correspondence. F. Williams. London, 1869. 2 v. 8°. D,340

Attic Philosopher in Paris. E. Souvestre. New York, 1868. 12°. . . H,906

The same. London, 1865. p. 8°. . . . . . . . I,664,1

Attorneys and Solicitors, Duties of. S. Warren. New York, 1849. 16°. . U,485

Attractions, Treatise on. J. Pratt. Cambridge, 1868. 12°. . . . N,270

Atwater, C. Essay on Education. Cincinnati, 1841. 8°. . . . O,1199

Tour to Prairie du Chien. Columbus, 1831. 12°. . . . . V,28

Aubrey. A. Marsh-Caldwell. Leipzig, 1853. 2 v. in 1. 16°. . . . J,364

Aubrey, J. Letters by Eminent Persons. London, 1813. 3 v. 8°. . . H,823

Miscellanies. London, 1857. 16°. . . . . . . . . . H,586

Aubuisson de Voisins, J. F. d'. Treatise on Hydraulics. Boston, 1852. 8°. N,131

Auckland Isles, Cast Away on the. T. Musgrave. London, 1866. 8°. . V,540

Audebert, J. B. Histoire Naturelle des Singes et des Makins. Paris, 1800. f°. Q,445

Audelay, J. Poems. London, 1844. 12°. . . . . . . . L,606,14

Audin, J. M. V. Life of Henry VIII. London, 1852. 8°. . . . . D,394

Life of John Calvin. Louisville, n. d. 8°. . . . . . . D,678

Audubon, J. J. Birds of America. London, 1827–38. 4 v. elph. f°. . L.R.

The same. New York, 1856. 7 v. 8°. . . . . . *O,138

Ornithological Biography of Birds of America. Edinb. 1831–9. 5 v. 8°. O,139

Synopsis of the Birds of America. Edinburgh, 1839. 8°. . . . O,108

and J. Bachman. Quadrupeds of North America. N.Y. 1854. 3 v. 8°. *N,467

Audubon, L. Life of J. J. Audubon. New York, 1869. 12°. . . . . C,748

Auerbach, B. Black-Forest Village Stories. New York, 1869. 12°. . . G,178

Edelweiss; a Story. Boston, 1869. 16°. . . . . . . . G,183

Gesammelte Schriften. Stuttgart, 1863–4. 22 v. 12°. . . . . E,311

Vol. 1–8. Schwarzwälder Dorfgeschichten.
9. Barfüszele.
10, 11. Spinoza; ein Denkerleben.
12, 13. Dichter und Kaufmann.
14–16. Neues Leben.
17, 18. Schatzkästlein des Gevattersmann's.
19. Deutsche Abende.
20. Schrift und Volk.
21. Joseph im Schnee.
22. Edelweisz.

On the Heights; a Novel. Boston, 1869. 16°. . . . . . . G,184

The same. Leipzig, 1867. 16°. . . . . . . . G,185

Villa on the Rhine. New York, 1869. 2 v. 16°. . . . . . G,186

Auersperg, A. A., Gesdichte. Leipzig, 1844. 12°. . . . . . . E,257

Auerswald, B. and Rossmäszler, E. A. Botanische Unterhaltungen. Leip. 1858. 8°. G,855

Auf der Düne. F. Spielhagen. Berlin, 1866. 16°. . . . . . . G,451

Auf Deutscher Erde. E. Hoefer. Stuttgart, 1860. 2 v. 16°. . . . . G,323

August der Starke, Jahr aus dem Leben. F. Lubojatzky. Wien, 1863. 2 v. 24°. G,340

Augustinus, St., Life and Labors of. P. Schaff. New York, 1854. 12°. . D,757

Auldjo, J. Ascent of Mont Blanc. London, 1864. p. 8°. . . . . I,656,1

Sketches of Nature in the Alps. London, 1864. p. 8°. . . . I,656,1

Auntient Lere; Aphoristical and Perceptive Passages. London, 1812. 12°. H,479

Aunt Mary's Stories. M. Hughes. New York, n. d. 16°. . . . . . J,1216

Aurelian. W. Ware. New York, 1866. 2 v. 12°. . . . . . . K,352

Auricular Confession, History of. C. P. de Lasteyrie. London, 1848. 12°. P,804
Aurora Floyd. M. E. Braddon. Leipzig, 1863. 2 v. in 1. 16°. . . J,34
Aurora Leigh; and other Poems. E. B. Browning. New York, n. d. 16°. I,290
Aus Alter und Neuer Zeit. L. Schücking. Leipzig, 1865. 24°. . . G,446
Aus den Tagen der groszen Kaiserin. L.Schücking. Prag u. Leipzig, 1858. 24° G,448
Aus der Natur. A. Abel. Leipzig, 1852-61. 12 v. in 4, 12°. & 4 v. in 1, 8°. G,671
Aus Eig'ner Kraft. B. von Guseck. Prag und Leipzig, 1858. 2 v. in 1, 24°. G,283
Auscultation, Clinical Introduction to. H. M. Hughes. Lond. 1845. 12°. . L,855
Austen, J. Emma; a Novel. Boston, 1864. 12°. . . . . . . . K,593
Mansfield Park. Boston, 1864. 12°. . . . . . . . K,594
The same. Leipzig, 1867. 16°. . . . . . . . J,29
Pride and Prejudice. Leipzig, 1879. 16°. . . . . . . . J,30
Northanger Abbey. Boston, 1864. 12°. . . . . . . K,595
Sense and Sensibility. Leipzig, 1864. 16°. . . . . . . . J,31
and Persuasion. Boston, 1864. 12°. . . . . . . . K,596
Austin, H. Report of the Health of Towns Association. Lond. 1847. 8°. N,252,29
Sanitary Condition of Worcester, Eng. Worcester, 1847. 8°. . N,252,29
Austin, J. G. Cipher; a Romance. New York, 1869. 8°. . . . . . K,8
Shadow of Moloch Mountain. New York, 1870. 8°. . . . K,207
Austin, J. M. Golden Steps to Respectability. Auburn, 1853. 12°. . . J,1466
Austin, S. Fragments from German Prose Writers. N. Y. 1841. 12°. . H,746
Austin, T. Recent and Fossil Crinoidea. London, n. d. 4°. . . . Q,39
Austin, W. S., Jr., and R. J. Lives of the Poets-Laureate. Lond. 1853. 8°. D,441
Austin Elliot. H. Kingsley. Boston, 1863. 12°. . . . . . . K,754
The same. Leipzig, 1863. 16°. . . . . . . . J,247
Australia. R. M. Martin. London, 1853. 8°. . . . . . . . F,219
American Merchant in. G. F. Train. New York, 1857. 12°. . V,1034
Beiträge zur Geologie von. L. Leichhardt. Halle, 1855. 4°. . . Q,46
Boys' Adventures in. W. Howitt. London, 1866. 12°. . . J,1232
Present State of. R. Dawson. London, 1831. 8°. . . . . V,895
Three Colonies of. S. Sidney. London, 1853. 8°. . . . . V,892
Australian Almanack for 1829. Sydney, 1829. 8°. . . . . . . T,44
Australian Colonies. W. Hughes. London, 1862. p. 8°. . . . . . I,660
Australian Wanderings. R. Lee. Boston, 1871. 16°. . . . . J,1551
Austria. J. G. Kohl. London, 1843. 8°. . . . . . . . . V,433
Empire of. J. S. C. Abbott. New York, 1859. 12°. . . . B,526
Ferdinand I. and Maximilian II. L. Rauhe. London, 1856. p. 8°. I,661,2
Geschichte von Oestreich. J. G. Mailáth. Hamburg, 1834-50. 5 v. 8°. E,77
History of House of, 1218-1792. W. Coxe. Lond. 1847. 4 v. p. 8°. . L,177
continued by W. K. Kelly. London, 1853. p. 8°. . . L,177,4
in 1848-49. W. H. Stiles. New York, 1852. 2 v. 8°. . . . B,529
Memoirs of the Court of. E. Vehse. London, 1856. 2 v. 12°. . B,525
Travels in. C. B. Elliott. Philadelphia, 1839. 2 v. 12°. . . . V,339
Austrian Lombardy, Tyrol, and Bavaria, Tour in. J. Barrow. Lond. 1841. 12°. V,485
Austrian Revolution, Details of Late. G. L. von Hartig. Lond. 1853. p. 8°. L,177,4
Auteurs Comiques, Chefs-d' Œuvre des. Paris, 1845. 12°. . . . . H,860
Author's Daughter; a Tale. M. Howitt. New York, n. d. 8°. . . . K,727
Authors, Calamities and Quarrels of. I. D'Israeli. London, 1859. 8°. . H,649
Catalogue of Royal and Noble. H. Walpole. Lond. 1806-23. 5 v. 8°. C,1307
Dictionary of British and American. S.A.Allibone. Phil.1858-71. 3v. 8°. L.R.

Autocracy in Poland and Russia. J. Allen. New York, 1854. 12°. . . V,532
Autocrat of the Breakfast-Table. O. W. Holmes. Boston, 1866. 12°. . H.61
Auvergne, Pilgrimage to. L. S. Costello. London, 1842. 2 v. 8°. . . V,478
Ava, Embassy to, in 1795. M. Symes. Edinburgh, 1827. 2 v. 16°. . . I.496
Avillion; and other Tales. D. M. Craik. New York, 1854. 8°. . . . K,640
Awdeley, J. Fraternity of Vacabondes. London, 1869. 8°. . . L,604,9
Axel and Anna. F. Bremer. London, 1853. p. 8°. . . . . . L,169,4
Aydelott, B. P. Church's Duties in the Temperance Cause. Cincin. 1865. 24°. P,10
Duties of American Citizens. Cincinnati, 1840. 8°. . . . . H,302
Ethics for our Country and the Times. Cincinnati, 1866. 12°. . P,345
Incidental Benefits of Denominational Division. Cincinnati, 1846. 12°. P,36
Prejudice against Colored People. Cincinnati, n. d. 24°. . . . P,226
Sceptical Philosophy examined. Cincinnati, 1868. 16°. . . . P,228
Thoughts for the Thoughtful. Cincinnati, 1866. 24°. . . . P,9
Ayling, S. Photographs from Pugin's Architectural Sketches. Lon. 1865. 2 v. 4°. *M,281
Aylmer, J., Life and Acts. J. Strype. Oxford, 1821. 8°. . . . . . P,684
Ayres, J. A. Legends of Montauk. New York, 1849. 8°. . . . . I,15
Ayrshire Legatees. J. Galt. London, 1841. 16°. . . . . . K,1154
Aytoun, W. E. Ballads of Scotland. Edinburgh, 1859. 2 v. 12°. . . I,280
Bothwell; a Poem. Boston, 1856. 16°. . . . . . . . I,279
Lays of the Scottish Cavaliers. New York, 1866. . . . . I,278
Life and Times of Richard I. London, 1840. 16°. . . . . I,625
Memoir of. T. Martin. Edinburgh, 1867. 8°. . . . . . D,449
Azais, P. H. Compensations dans les Destinées Humaines. Paris, 1853. 12°. H,861
Azarian; an Episode. H. E. Spofford. Boston, 1864. 12°. . . . K,144
Azeglio, M. d'. Recollections; tr. by Count Maffel. London, 1868. 2 v. 12°. D,725
Azores, History of the. London, 1813. 4°. . . . . . . . . F,217
Visit to the. C. A. Murray. London, 1854. 2 v. 12°. . . . V,11
Azuni, D. A. Maritime Law of Europe. New York, 1806. 2 v. 8°. . . U,542

Baärnhielm, E. W. Archibald Hamilton. Boston, 1869. 16°. . . . J,1669
Babbage, C. Economy of Machinery and Manufactures. London, 1846. 12°. M,599
Babees Book; edited by F. J. Furnivall. London, 1868. 8°. . . L,605,32
Babes in the Wood. M. M. Sherwood. New York, 1860. 12°. . . K,1008,4
Babington, C. C. Manual of British Botany. London, 1847. 12°. . . N,949
Babo, F. von. Chemische Untersuchung des Bodens. Frank.-a-M. 1843. 8°. N,252,15
Babon, L. von. Spannkraft des Dampfes in Salzlösungen. Freib. 1847. 8°. N,252,33
Babylon, Discoveries at. A. H. Layard. London, 1853. 8°. . . . V,677
Bach, J. S. Leben und Kunst. J. N. Forkel. Leipzig, 1855. 4°. . . G,736
Bachaumont, F. le C. Voyage. Paris, 1851. 8°. . . . . . D,608
Bachaumont, L. P. de, Mémoires, 1762-82. Paris, 1846. 12°. . . . D,602
Bache, A. D. Horizontal Force. London, 1863. 4°. . . . . . Q,324,13
Bache, R. M. Young Wrecker of the Florida Reef. Philadelphia, n. d. 16°. J,1606
Bachelor of the Albany. M. W. Savage. London, 1854. 12°. . . . K,555
Bachelor of Salamanca. A. R. Le Sage. Philadelphia, 1868. 2 v. 16°. . H,961
Bachman, J. Quadrupeds of North America. New York, 1854. 3 v. 8°. N,467
Back, G. Narrative of the Arctic Land Expedition. Philadelphia, 1837. 8°. V,957
Backus, W. and S. D. Village and Farm Cottages. New York, 1856. 8°. M,223

Backwoodsman; Life on Indian Frontier. C. F. L. Wraxall. Bost. 1866. 12°. K,1104
Bacon, D. Philosophy of the Plays of Shakespeare. Boston, 1857. 8°. . I,868
Bacon, F., *Lord.* Essays, Moral, Economical, and Political. N.Y. 1868. 18°. L,454
Letters and Life. London, 1862-68. 4 v. 8°. . . . . . . D,395
Moral and Historical Works. London, 1854. p. 8°. . . . . L,166
New Atlantis. London, 1852. 12°. . . . . . . . . K,690
Personal History of. W. H. Dixon. Leipzig, 1861. 16°. . . . J,148
Physical and Metaphysical Works. London, 1868. p. 8°. . . L,257
Works. London, 1857-59. 7 v. 8°. . . . . . . . . U,219
Bacon, L. Discourse on the Settlement of Tallmadge. Akron, O. 1857. 8°. C,204
Bacon, N., Life of. W. Ware. Boston. 16°. . . . . . . C,860,13
Bacon, O. N. History of Natick, Mass. Boston, 1856. 8°. . . . . C,59
Bacon, R. Opera inedita. London, 1859. 8°. . . . . . . . W,165
Baddington Peerage. G. A. Sala. London, 1861. 3 v. 12°. . . . K,562
Badeau, A. Military History of Gen. U. S. Grant. v. 1. N. Y. 1868. 8°. . B,958
Baedeker, F. W. J. Die Eier der Europäischen Vögel. Leipzig, 1863. f°. Q,89
Baffin's Bay, Voyage of Discovery to. J. Ross. London, 1819. 2 v. 8°. . V,941
Bage, R. Man as he is not. London, 1820. 12°. . . . . . . K,549
Bagster, S. Analytical Greek Lexicon. London, 1852. 4°. . . . L.R.
Bailey, N. Universal English Dictionary. London, 1747. 2 v. 8°. . . L.R.
Bailey, P. J. The Age; a Colloquial Satire. Boston, 1858. 16°. . . I,282
Festus; a Poem. Boston, 1850. 12°. . . . . . . . . I,283
Baillie, J. Dramatic and Poetical Works. London, 1851. 8°. . . . I,752
Bailly, J. S. Histoire de l'Astronomie. Paris, 1805. 2 v. in 1. 8°. . . N,282
Life of. F. Arago. Boston, 1859. 12°. . . . . . . C,498,1
Bain, A. Emotions and the Will. London, 1859. 8°. . . . . . O,687
Mental and Moral Science. London, 1868. 12°. . . . . O,645
Moral Science. New York, 1869. 12°. . . . . . . . O,716
Senses and the Intellect. London, 1855. 8°. . . . . . . O,688
Study of Character. London, 1861. 8°. . . . . . . . O,734
Baines, E. History of Wars of the French Revolution. Phila. 1835. 2 v. 8°. B,288
Baines, E., jr. Cotton Manufacture in Great Britain. London, 1835. 8°. . M,654
Education Promoted by Freedom. London, 1854. 8°. . . O,1251,1
Visit to the Vaudois of Piedmont. London, 1853. p. 8°. . . I,656,7
Baird, H. M. Modern Greece. New York, 1856. 12°. . . . . V,562
Baird, J. Management of Health. London, 1868. 12°. . . . . M,828
Baird, R. Religion in America. New York, 1856. 8°. . . . . P,582
West Indies and North America, 1849. Philadelphia, 1850. 16°. . V,18
Baird, S. F. Mammals of North America. Philadelphia, 1857. 4°. . . *Q,37
and others. Birds of North America. Philadelphia, 1860. 2 v. 4°. *Q,36
Baird, W. Natural History of British Entomostraca. London, 1850. 8°. . O,302
Baked Meats of the Funeral. C. G. Halpine. New York, 1866. 12°. . H,75
Baker, C. Graduated Reading Lessons. London, n. d. 16°. . . . O,756
Baker, C. R. Practical and Scientific Fruit Culture. Boston, 1866. 12°. . M,559
Baker, D. E., and I. Reed. Biographia Dramatica. Lond. 1812. 4 v. 8°. L.R.
Baker, G. E. Life of W. H. Seward. New York, 1855. 12°. . . . C,745
Baker, G. M. Amateur Dramas. Boston, 1870. 12°. . . . . . . I,722
Mimic Stage; Series of Dramas, Comedies, etc. Boston, 1870. 12°. I,721
Baker, H. N. Governor's Pardon; or, Bridge of Sighs. Boston, 1870. 16°. J,1691
Live and Learn. Boston, 1869. 16°. . . . . . . . . J,1694

Baker, H. N. Little Agnes Library. Boston, 1868. 4 v. 16°. . . J,1699
Vol. 1. Little Agnes. Vol. 3. I'll Try.
2. Trying to be Useful. 4. Art and Artlessness.
Paul Barton; or, Drunkard's Son. Boston, 1870. 16°. . . J,1692
Play and Study Series. Boston, 1869. 4 v. 16°. . . . . J,1702
Vol. 1. Play and Study. Vol. 3. Howard and his Teacher.
2. Motherless Children. 4. Jack, the Chimney-Sweeper.
Walter and Frank; or, Lathrop Farm. Boston, 1870. 16°. . J,1693
Baker, L. C. History of the Secret Service. Philadelphia, 1869. 8°. . B,924
Baker, Sir R. Chronicle of the Kings of England. London, 1674. f°. . F,289
Baker, Sir S. W. Albert Nyanza, Great Nile Basin. Phila. 1866. 8°. . V,814
Eight Years' Wanderings in Ceylon. Philadelphia, 1869. 12°. . V,587
Nile Tributaries of Abyssinia. Philadelphia, 1868. 12°. . . . V,781
Baker, T. Land and Engineering Surveying. London, 1859. 12°. . . M,890
Mechanism and Machines. London, 1858-59. 12°. . . . . M,891
Mensuration. London, 1859. 12°. . . . . . . . . M,892
Statics and Dynamics. London, 1851. 12°. . . . . . M,893
Bakewell, F. C. Great Facts; History of Inventions. New York, 1860. 12°. M,623
Bakewell, R. Introduction to Geology. London, 1838. 8°. . . . N,822
Balbo, C. Life of Dante Alighieri. London, 1852. 2 v. 8°. . . . D,734
Baldwin, G. C. Representative Men of the New Testament. N. Y. 1860. 12°. P,99
Baldwin, J. D. Pre-Historic Nations. New York, 1869. 12°. . . A,10
Baldwin, J. G. Sketches of Party Leaders. New York, 1856. 12°. . . C,527
Baldwin, T., and T. J. Lippincott's Gazetteer of the U. S. Phila. 1854. 8°. L.R.
Pronouncing Gazetteer of the World. Philadelphia, 1870. 8°. . . L.R.
Baldwin, W. Reliquiæ Baldwinianæ. W. Darlington. Phila. 1843. 12°. H,98
Baldwin, W. C. Hunting in South Africa. New York, 1863. 12°. . . V,803
Balfour, J. H. Botanical Companion. Edinburgh, 1860. 12°. . . . N,944
Class-Book of Botany. Edinburgh, 1852. 8°. . . . . . N,1007
Manual of Botany. Edinburgh, 1863. 12°. . . . . . . N,975
Outlines of Botany. Edinburgh, 1862. 8°. . . . . . . N,939
Plants of the Bible. London, 1857. 8°. . . . . . . N,1026
Baliol, M. B., *pseud.* See *Manning, A.*
Ball, B. L. Rambles in Eastern Asia. Boston, 1865. 12°. . . . . V,589
Ball, C. History of the Indian Mutiny. London, n. d. 2 v. r. 8°. . . F,263
Ball, S. Cultivation and Manufacture of Tea in China. London, 1848. 8°. M,575
Ballad Stories from the Scandinavian; tr. by R. Buchanan. N. Y. 1869. 16°. I,557
Ballads, Ancient Spanish. J. G. Lockhart. New York, 1842. 8°. . . J,862
Bentley's; ed. by J. Doran. London, 1866. p. 8°. . . . . I,170
Book of British. S. C. Hall. London, 1853. 4°. . . . . J,884
English and Scottish. F. J. Child. Boston, 1857-58. 8 v. 16°. . I,196
from Early Printed Literature; ed. by J. P. Collier. Lond. 1840. 12°. L,606,1
of Ireland. E. Hayes. London, 1855. 2 v. 12°. . . . . I,345
of Scotland. W. E. Aytoun. Edinburgh, 1859. 2 v. 12°. . . I,280
Spanisches Liederbuch. E. Geibel und P. Heyse. Berlin, 1852. 24°. E,265
Old, Historical, and Narrative. T. Evans. London, 1784. 4 v. 12°. I,369
Political. W. W. Wilkins. London, 1860. 2 v. 12°. . . . I,99
Ballantyne, J. R. Christianity contrasted with Hindū Philosophy. Lond.'59. 8°. P,828
Ballantyne, R. M. Coral Island; a Tale of the Pacific Ocean. Lond. 1870. 16°. J,1484
Deep Down. Philadelphia, 1869. 16°. . . . . . . J,1371
Dog Crusoe. Philadelphia, n. d. 16°. . . . . . . J,1272

Ballantyne, R. M. Floating Light of Goodwin Sands. Phila. 1871. 16°. J,1637
Gorilla Hunters. Philadelphia, n. d. 16°. . . . . . J,1614
Martin Rattler. London, 1867. 16°. . . . . . . . J,1518
Red Eric; or, The Whaler's Last Cruise. London, 1861. 16°. . J,1271
Shifting Winds. Philadelphia, 1870. 16°. . . . . . J,1674
Ungava. Boston, 1859. 16°. . . . . . . . . J,1469
World of Ice. London, 1863. 16°. . . . . . . . J,1718
Young Fur Traders. London, n. d. 16°. . . . . . . J,1239
Ballantyne, T. Essays in Mosaic. New York, 1870. 16°. . . . . I 569
Balling, C. J. N. Fortschritte der Zymotechn. Wissenschaft. Prag, 1847. 8°. N,252,40
Balloon Ascents, Wonderful. F. Marion. New York, 1870. 12°. . M,1063
Ballou, M. M. History of Cuba. Boston, 1854. 12°. . . . . . V,190
Balmes, J. Fundamental Philosophy. New York, 1856. 2 v. 12°. . . S.C.
Baltic Sea, Rob Roy on the. J. MacGregor. London, 1867. 16°. . . V,521
Bainbrigge, W. Early Education. London, 1854. 16°. . . . O,1124
Bambus und Comp. A. von Winterfeld. Leipzig, 1865. 3 v. 16°. . . G,519
Bampfylde, J. Poetical Works; illustr. by B. Foster. London, 1855. 16°. I,453
Bancroft, E. Experimental Researches in Colours. London, 1813. 2 v. 8°. M,651
Bancroft, G. History of the United States. Boston, 1848–66. 9 v. 8°. . B,637
Literary and Historical Miscellanies. New York, 1855. 8°. . . H,150
Banditti and Robbers, Lives of. C. Mac Farlane. London, 1837. 16°. . I,649
Bandtke, G. S. Polnisch-Deutsches Wörterbuch. Breslau, 1806. 2 v. 8°. L.R.
Bangs, N. History of the Methodist Episcopal Church. N. Y. 1857. 4 v. 12°. P,841
Banier, A. Mythology and Fables of the Ancients. Lond. 1739–40. 4 v. 8°. P,918
Banim, M. Africa and America. New York, 1854. 12°. . . . . V,771
Banished Son. C. L. Hentz. New York, 1870. 12°. . . . . . K,165
Banking, Capital, and Currency. J. Wilson. London, 1847. 8°. . . O,530
History of. W. J. Lawson. Boston, 1852. 8°. . . . . . O,568
Philosophy of Joint Stock. G. M. Bell. London, 1855. 8°. . . O,590
Practical Treatise on. J. W. Gilbert. London, 1849. 2 v. 8°. . O,567
Theory and Practice of. H. D. Macleod. London, 1866. 2 v. 8°. O,566
Banks of the U. S., Report on Condition of, 1862. Washington, 1862. 8°. . O,587
Banks, N. P.; the Bobbin Boy. W. M. Thayer. Boston, 1863. 16°. . . J,1293
Banvard, J. Adventures of Explorers of North America. Bost. 1853. 12°. B,686
Life of D. Webster. Boston, 1853. 16°. . . . . . . J,1206
Plymouth and the Pilgrims. Boston, 1866. 16°. . . . . . C,17
Romance of American History. Boston, 1860. 16°. . . . . . B,699
Wisdom, Wit, and Whims of Ancient Philosophers. N. Y. 1855. 12°. H,13
Baptist Churches, Principles and Practices of. F. Wayland. N. Y. 1867. 12°. P,805
Baptists of Virginia. R. B. C. Howell. Philadelphia, 1857. 8°. . B,809,2
Barbara's History. A. B. Edwards. New York, 1868. 8°. . . . . K,679
The same. Leipzig, 1864. 2 v. in 1. 16°. . . . . . J,155
Barbary, Travels in. R. F. A. de Chateaubriand. London, 1812. 2 v. 8°. V,1083
Trip to. G. A. Sala. London, 1866. 8°. . . . . . . . V,754
History and Present Condition of. M. Russell. N. Y. 1854. 2 v. 18°. L,391
Barbauld, A. L. British Novelists. London, 1820. 50 v. 12°. . .
Vol. 1–8. Richardson, S. Clarissa Harlowe. . . . . . K,529
9–15. Sir Charles Grandison. . . . . . K,530
16, 17. DeFoe, D. Robinson Crusoe. . . . . . . K,531
18. Fielding, H. Joseph Andrews. . . . . . K,532
19–21. Tom Jones. . . . . . . . . K,533

Barbauld, A. L. British Novelists. *Continued.*

Vol. 22. Reeve, C. Old English Baron.
Walpole, H. Castle of Otranto. . . . . . K,534
23. Coventry, F. Pompey the Little.
Goldsmith, O. Vicar of Wakefield. . . . K,535
24, 25. Lennox, C. Female Quixote. . . . . K,536
26. Johnson, S. Rasselas.
Hawkesworth, J. Almoran and Hamet. . . K,537
27. Brooke, F. M. Julia Mandeville.
Inchbald, E. S. Nature and Art. . . . . K,538
28. Simple Story. . . . . . . . K,539
29. Mackenzie, H. Man of Feeling; Julia de Roubigne. . K,540
30, 31. Smollet, T. Humphrey Clinker. . . . . K,541
32, 33. Graves, R. Spiritual Quixote. . . . . K,542
34, 35. Moore, J. Zeluco. . . . . . . K,543
36, 37. Smith, C. Old Manor House. . . . . K,544
38, 39. D'Arblay, F. Evelina. . . . . . K,545
40–42. Cecilia. . . . . . . . . K,546
43, 44. Radcliffe, A. Romance of the Forest. . . . K,547
45–47. Mysteries of Udolpho. . . . . . K,548
48. Bage, R. Man as he is not. . . . . K,549
49, 50. Edgeworth, M. Belinda; Modern Griselda. . . K,550

Evenings at Home. Edinburgh, n. d. 16°. . . . . . J,1439
Things by their Right Names. New York, 1854. 16°. . . J,1462
Works; with a Memoir. London, 1825. 2 v. 8°. . . . U,193
Barbé-Marbois, F. de. History of Louisiana. Philadelphia, 1830. 8°. . C,187
Barber, J. W. Historical Collections of Massachusetts. Worc. 1840. 8°. . C,54
History of New England and Middle States. Hartford, 1856. 8°. . C,20
Incidents in American History. Boston, n. d. . . . . B,694
and Howe, H. Loyal West in the Rebellion. Cincinnati, 1865. 8°. B,957
Historical Collections of New York State. New York, 1842. 8°. C,94
Barbier, A. A. Dictionnaire des Ouvrages Anonymes et Pseudonymes. Paris, 1822–27. 4 v. 8°. . . . . . . . . . . . L.R.
Barbour, J. The Bruce; Book of Robert de Broyss. London, 1870. 8°. L,604,11
Barchester Towers. A. Trollope. Leipzig, 1859. 2 v. in 1. 16°. . . J,491
Barclay, A. Cytezen and Uplondyshman; an Eclogue. London, 1847. 12°. L,606,22
Barclay, J. M. Digest of Rules of House of Representatives. Wash. 1861. 8°. B,720
Barclay, J. T. City of the Great King. Philadelphia, 1858. 8°. . . V,662
Barclay, S. Personal Recollections of American Revolution. N. Y. 1859. 12°. B,754
Baretti, G. Spanish and English Dictionary. New York, 1852. 8°. . L.R.
Barfüszele. B. Auerbach. Stuttgart, 1864. 12°. . . . . E,311,9
Barham, R. H. Ingoldsby Legends; or, Mirth and Marvels. Lond. 1866. 12°. K,597
Baring-Gould, S. Curious Myths of the Middle Ages. Boston, 1867. 16°. A,227
Iceland; Its Scenes and Sagas. London, 1863. 8°. . . . V,170
In Exitu Israel. New York, 1870. p. 8°. . . . . . K,585
Origin and Development of Religious Belief. New York, 1870. 12°. P,273
Silver Store; Mediæval Poems. London, 1868. 12°. . . . I,281
Barker, W. B. Lares and Penates; or, Cilicia. London, 1853. 8°. . V,674
Barlow, Sir G. H. Administration at Madras. C. Marsh. Lon. 1813. 8°. C,408
Barlow, S. History of Ireland. London, 1814. 2 v. 8°. . . . V,402
Barnaby Rudge. C. Dickens. New York, 1868. 12°. . . . . K,467
The same. Philadelphia, 1841. 8°. . . . . . K,503
The same. New York, 1871. 2 v. 12°. . . . K,1127
The same. Leipzig, 1846. 2 v. 16°. . . . . . J,127

Barnard, C. Tone Masters. Boston, 1871. 3 v. 16°. . . . . . J,1344
Vol. 1. Mozart and Mendelssohn. 2. Handel and Haydn. 3. Bach and Beethoven.
Barnard, G. Drawing from Nature. London, 1865. 8°. . . . . . M,135
Landscape-Painting in Water-Colours. London, 1861. 8°. . . M,137
Trees from Nature. London, 1868. f°. . . . . . . . *Q,452
Barnard, H. American Journal of Education. Hart. 1855-62. 12 v. 8°. S 26
Educational Biography, v. 1. New York, 1859. 8°. . . . O,1057
National Education in Europe. Hartford, 1854. 8°. . . . O,1237
Pestalozzi and Pestalozzianism. New York, 1862. 8°. . . . O,1216
School Architecture. New York, 1854. 8°. . . . . . . M,188
Tribute to Gallaudet. Hartford, 1852. 8°. . . . . . . C,1070
Barnes's Defence of the Berde. London, 1870. 8°. . . . . L,604,10
Barnes, A. Evidences of Christianity. New York, 1861. 12°. . . P,211
Notes on the Book of Job. New York, 1856. 2 v. 12°. . . P,470
Notes on the Book of Psalms. New York, 1869. 3 v. 12°. . . P,480
Notes on the Book of Isaiah. New York, 1855. 2 v. 12°. . . P,469
The same. London, 1867. 3 v. 12°. . . . . . . P,482
Notes on Daniel. London, n. d. 2 v. 12°. . . . . . . P,488
Notes on the Gospels. New York, 1868. 2 v. 12°. . . . P,464
Notes on the Acts. New York, 1855. 12°. . . . . . . P,466
Notes on the Epistle to the Romans. New York, 1869. 12°. . P,467
Notes on First Corinthians. New York, 1870. 12°. . . . P,477
Notes on Second Corinthians and Galatians. New York, 1869. 12°. P,468
Notes on Ephesians, Phillipians, and Colossians. N. Y. 1869. 12°. P,475
Notes on Thessalonians, Timothy, Titus, and Philemon. N.Y. 1869. 12°. P,479
Notes on the Epistle to the Hebrews. New York, 1869. 12°. . P,476
Notes on James, Peter, John, and Jude. New York, 1869. 12°. . P,478
Notes on the Book of Revelation. New York, 1870. 12°. . . P,465
Way of Salvation. Philadelphia, 1863. 12°. . . . . . P,111
Barnes, R. Injunctions, etc., 1575-87. Durham, 1850. 8°. . . F,126,22
Barnes, W. Philological Grammar. London, 1854. 8°. . . . L,527
Barnes, W. Rural Poems. Boston, 1869. 16°. . . . . . . I,75
Barnes, W. H. History of Thirty-Ninth Congress. Indianapolis, 1867. 8°. B,722
Barney, H. H. American System of Free Schools. Cincinnati, 1851. 8°. O,1009
Barnfield, R. Affectionate Shepherd. London, 1845. 12°. . . L,606,20
Barnum, P. T. Humbugs of the World. New York, 1866. 12°. . . H,89
Struggles and Triumphs; or, Forty Years' Recollections. Hart. 1870. 8°. C,755
Barometer, Instructions necessary in using Newman's. Lond. 1841. 8°. N,252,33
Baron Munchausen's Travels. R. E. Raspe. New York, 1869. 12°. . J,1494
Barony, The. A. M. Porter. London, 1830. 3 v. 12°. . . . . . K,557
Barré, L. Herculanum et Pompéi. Paris, 1839-40. 8 v. 8°. . *M,133
Barré, W. L. Life of Millard Fillmore. Buffalo, 1856. 12°. . . C,926
Barrell, G. Pedestrian in France and Switzerland. New York, 1853. 12°. V,456
Barren Honor. G. A. Lawrence. Leipzig, 1862. 16°. . . . . . J,254
Barrera, A. de. Memoirs of Rachel. New York, 1858. 12°. . . . D,641
Barrett, R.A.F. Synopsis of Criticisms on Old Test. Lond. 1847. 3 v. in 5. 8°. P,486
Barrett, S. Principles of Grammar. Boston, 1858. 8°. . . . . . L,552
Barrow, Sir G. Ceylon; Past and Present. London, 1857. 12°. . . V,583
Barrington, Sir J. Rise and Fall of the Irish Nation. Dublin, 1868. 12°. . B,159
Personal Sketches of his own Times. New York, n. d. 12°. . . H,614

Barrington, Sir J. Historic Memoirs of Ireland. London, 1833. 2 v. 4°. F,287
Barrington, G. History of New South Wales. London, n. d. 8°. . . . C,436
Barrington, A. Physical Geography. New York, 1851. 12°. . . . V,1122
Barrington. C. Lever. New York, 1862. 8°. . . . . . . . K,768
The same. London, 1863. 8°. . . . . . . . K,882
The same. Leipzig, 1863. 2 v. in 1. 16°. . . . . . J,269
Barrow, Sir J. Autobiographical Memoir. London, 1847. 8°. . . . D,444
Life of Peter the Great. London, 1861. 16°. . . . . . . I,626
The same. New York, 1856. 18°. . . . . . . . L,386
Life of Richard, Earl Howe. London, 1838. 8°. . . . . . D,277
Mutiny of the Bounty. London, 1831. 16°. . . . . . . I,613
The same. New York, n. d. 16°. . . . . . . . L,364
Voyages within the Arctic Regions. New York, 1846. 12°. . . V,915
Barrow, J. Life of Admiral Sir Wm. S. Smith. London, 1848. 2 v. 8°. D,129
Tour in Austrian Lombardy, Tyrol, and Bavaria. Lond. 1841. 12°. V,485
of the Continent in 1852. London, 1855. p. 8°. . . I,656,2
round Ireland. London, 1836. 12°. . . . . . . V,268
Barrow, W. Essay on Education. London, 1802. 2 v. 12°. . . . O,917
Barrows, W. Twelve Nights in the Hunter's Camp. Boston, 1870. 16°. J,1611
Barruel, A. de. Memoirs illustrating Hist. of Jacobinism. Lond.1798. 4 v. 8°. B,271
Barry, J., and others. Lectures on Painting. London, 1848. p. 8°. . . L,303
Barry, J. S. History of Massachusetts. Boston, 1855-57. 3 v. 8°. . C,67
History of Hanover, Mass. Boston, 1853. 8°. . . . . . . C,72
Barry Lyndon, Memoirs of. W. M. Thackeray. Boston, 1869. 12°. K,1088,1
The same. Leipzig, 1856. 16°. . . . . . . . J,484,6
Barrry Cornwall, *pseud.* See *Procter, B. W.*
Barstow, G. History of New Hampshire. Boston, 1853. 8°. . . . C,25
Bartels,J.M.C. Vorlesungen über Mathematische Analysis. Dorp.1837. 2v. 4°. E,437
Barth, H. Travels in North and Central Africa. New York, 1857-9. 3 v. 8°. V,870
Barthélemy,J.J. Travels of Anacharsis in Greece. London, 1806. 8 v. 8°, 4°. V,572
The same. London, 1817. 6 v. 8°. . . . . . . V,573
Voyage de Anacharsis en Grèce. Paris, 1817. 7 v. 8°. . . . V,571
Atlas to the same. Paris, 1817. f°. . . . . . *Q,388
Barthélemy, J. P. Lessons in French. Dayton, 1858. 8°. . . . . L,807
Barthold,F.W. Geschichte des Groszen Deutschen Krieges. Stutt.1843. 2v. 8°. E,66
Bartholow, R. On Spermatorrhœa. New York, 1866. 12°. . . . L,908
Principles and Practice of Disinfection. Cincinnati, 1867. 12°. . L,909
Bartholomew de Cotton. Historia Anglicana, 449-1298. London, 1859. 8°. W,166
Bartholomew, W. N. Linear Perspective explained. Boston, 1866. 8°. . M,210
Bartlett, D. W. Heroes of the Indian Rebellion. Columbus, 1859. 8°. C,1210
Life of Joan of Arc. Auburn, 1854. 12°. . . . . . . D,595
Bartlett, J. Familiar Quotations; 5th edition. Boston, 1869. 12°. . . I,484
Bartlett, J. R. Dictionary of Americanisms. Boston, 1859. 8°. . . L.R.
Explorations in Texas and New Mexico. New York, 1854. 2 v. 8°. V,124
Bartlett,W.H. Pilgrim Fathers; or, Founders of New England. Lond.1853. 8°. C,74
Nile Boat; or, Glimpses of Egypt. London, n. d. 4°. . . . V,846
Pictures from Sicily. London, 1853. 8°. . . . . . . . V,518
Ports, Harbors, etc., of Great Britain. London, 1841-44. 2 v. 4°. *Q,417
Scripture Sights and Scenes. London, n. d. 12°. . . . V,1038
Bartlett, W. H. C. Elements of Natural Philosophy. New York, 1851. 8°. N,132

Bartol, C. A. Church and Congregation. Boston, 1858. 16°. . . . P,231
Pictures of Europe. Boston, 1855. 12°. . . . . . . . . V,386
Word of the Spirit to the Church. Boston, 1859. 16°. . . . P,229
Bartol, M. Honor May. Boston, 1866. 12°. . . . . . . . K,21
Barton, B. Household Verses. Philadelphia, 1849. 16°. . . . . . I,2
Bary, A. de. Brandpilze und Krankheiten der Pflanzen. Berlin, 1853. 8°. G,856
Bascom, J. Principles of Psychology. New York, 1869. 12°. . . . O,668
Science, Philosophy, and Religion. New York, 1871. 12°. . . P,214
Baskerville, A. The Poetry of Germany. Philadelphia, 1856. 8°. . . G,44
Basil. W. Collins. Leipzig, 1862. 16°. . . . . . . . . . J,75
Bass Rock, Geology of. T. Mac Crie. New York, 1852. 12°. . . . N,612
Bassnett, T. Mechanical Theory of Storms. New York, 1854. 12°. . . N,105
Bastile, History of the. R. A. Davenport. London, 1838. 16°. . . I,618
Bates, J., Memorial of. Boston, 1865. 8°. . . . . . . . . . C,982
Presentation of Bust and Portrait to Boston Pub. Library. Bost.1866. 4°. L.R.
Bates, H. W. Naturalist on the Amazon. London, 1863. 2 v. 8°. . . V,243
Bates, P. Book of Holy and Eternal Wisdom, v. 1. Cant. N.H. 1849. 12°. P,300
Baths, Treatise on. J. Bell. Philadelphia, 1859. 8°. . . . . . L,907
and Wells of Europe. J. Macpherson. London, 1869. 16°. . . L,919
Battle of Agincourt. Sir H. Nicolas. London, 1833. 8°. . . . . . B,97
of Life; and, Haunted Man. C. Dickens. Leipzig, 1856. 16°. . J,115
of Magh Leana; edited by E. Curry. Dublin, 1855. 8°. . . . L,811
of the Books. M. A. Dodge. New York, 1870. 12°. . . . . H,59
Battles of the Rebellion, Twelve Decisive. W. Swinton. New York, 1867. 8°. B,938
Fifteen Decisive, of the World. E. S. Creasy. London, 1856. 8°. . A,326
of the British Army. C. Mac Farlane. London, 1860. 12°. . . B,77
of the British Navy. J. Allen. London, 1852-53. 2 v. p. 8°. . L,91
Baucher, F. Method of Horsemanship. Philadelphia, 1856. 12°. . . M,470
Baudicor, P. de. Le Peintre-Graveur Français continué. Paris,1859-61. 2v. 8°. L.R.
Baudouin, A. Anecdotes Historiques de la Restauration. Paris, 1853. 12°. B,201
Baudrimont, A. Etat de la Chimie Organique. Paris, 1838. 8°. . N,252,1
Bauerman, H. Metallurgy of Iron. New York, 1868. 12°. . . . M,714
Baumgarten, M. History of the Church in Apostolic Age. Edin.1854. 3 v. 8°. P,403
Bautain, M. Art of Extempore Speaking. New York, 1868. 12°. . . L,601
Baxley, H. W. West Coast of America and Hawaiian Islands. N.Y.1865. 8°. V,127
Baxter, R. D. Taxation of the United Kingdom. London, 1869. 8°. . O,555
Baxter, R. Call to the Unconverted. New York, n. d. 18°. . . P,746,6
Jesuit Juggling. New York, 1835. 12°. . . . . . . . . P,812
Practical Works. London, 1845. 4 v. 8°. . . . . . . . P,787
Saints' Everlasting Rest. New York, 1855. 8°. . . . . . P,163
The same. New York, n. d. 18°. . . . . . . . P,746,5
Bayard, Chevalier. See *Du Terrail, P.*
Bayard, J. Exposition of the Constitution of U. S. Philadelphia, 1833. 12°. O,480
Bayle, P. Dictionnaire Historique et Critique. Amsterdam, 1730. 4 v. f°. Q,140
Dictionary Historical and Critical. London, 1734-38. 5 v. f°. *Q,139
Baylee, J. Mysteries of the Kingdom. London, 1852. 16°. . . . P,287
Baylies, F. History of Plymouth Colony. Boston, 1866. 2 v. 8°. . . C,48
Bayne, P. Christian Life; Social and Individual. Boston, 1858. 12°. . P,295
Essays in Biography and Criticism. Boston, 1867. 2 v. 12°. . H,196
Life and Letters of Hugh Miller. Boston, 1871. 2 v. 12°. . . D,210

Baynes, R. H. Lyra Anglicana; Hymns. Leipzig, 1868. 16°. . . . J,32
Bay-Path. J. G. Holland. New York, 1866. 12°. . . . . . . K,178
Beach Rambles in Search of Pebbles. J. G. Francis. London, 1866. 16°. N,472
Beagle, Voyage of the. C. Darwin. London, 1845. 12°. . . . . N,633
Beale, A. Simplicity and Fascination. Boston, 1866. 12°. . . . . K,598
Beale, L. S. How to Work with the Microscope. London, 1868. 8°. . N,13
Microscope applied to Practical Medicine. London, 1858. 8°. . L,971
Beard, J. R. Life of Toussaint L'Ouverture. London, 1853. 8°. . . C,876
Bear Hunters of the Rocky Mountains. A. Bowman. Phil. n. d. 16°. . J,1603
Bèarn and the Pyrenees, Tour to. L. S. Costello. London, 1844. 2 v. 8°. V,477
Beatrice. J. Kavanagh. New York, 1868. 12°. . . . . . . K,656
The same. Leipzig, 1864. 2 v. in 1. 16°. . . . . . J,227
Beatrice Boville. L. de la Rame. Philadelphia, 1867. 12°. . . . K,879
Beatrice Cenci. F. D. Guerrazzi. New York, 1869. 12°. . . . . G,231
Beatson, R. Chronological Register of British Parliament. Lond. 1807. 3 v. 8°. A,462
Political Index to Histories of Great Britain. Lond. 1806–7. 3 v. 8°. A,461
Beattie, J. Dissertations; Moral and Critical. London, 1783. 4°. . . H,634
Poetical Works. Boston, 1854. 16°. . . . . . . . . I,197
with Life by G. Gilfillan. New York, 1854. 8°. . . . J,851
illustrated by B. Foster. London, 1855. 16°. . . . . I,453
Beattie, W. Ports, Harbors, etc., of Great Britain. London, 1841. 2 v. 4° *Q,417
Beauchamp; or, The Error. G. P. R. James. Leipzig, 1846. 16°. . . J,202
Beauchampe; the Kentucky Tragedy. W. G. Simms. New York, 1864. 12°. K,247
Beauchesne, A. de. Life of Louis XVII. New York, 1853. 2 v. 12°. . D,646
Beaufort, M., *Countess of Richmond,* Life of. C. A. Halsted. Lond. 1845. 8°. D,278
Beaumarchais; Historischer Roman. A. E. Brachvogel. Leip. 1865. 4v. 16°. G,263
Beaumarchais, P. A. C. de., and his Times. L. de Loménie. N. Y. 1857. 12°. D,648
The same. London, 1856. 4v. 8°. . . . . . . . D,660
Beaumont, F., and Fletcher, Selections; ed. by L. Hunt. London, 1862. p. 8°. L,167
Works. London, 1843–46. 11 v. 8°. . . . . . . I,715
Beautemps-Beaupré, C. F. Cartes Hydrographiques. Paris, 1811. 4°. . M,819
Reconnaissance Hydrographique des Côtes de France. Paris, 1829. 4°. M,821
Beauties of Nature. C. Bucke. London, 1823. 4v. 8°. . . . . M,367
of the British Poets. G. Croly. New York, n. d. 12°. . . . I,336
Beautiful, The, in Nature, Art and Life. A. J. Symington. Lond. 1857. 2v. 8°. . M,53
Idee des Schönen. A. Kuhn. Berlin, n. d. 12°. . . . . G,566
Beautiful Bertha. L. C. Tuthill. New York, n. d. 16°. . . . J,1346
Beauty in Art, True Principles of. J. Fergusson. London, 1849. 8°. .
Science of. D. R. Hay. Edinburgh, 1856. 8°. . . . . M,111
in Woman. A. Walker. London, 1836. 8°. . . . . . M,106
is Power. New York, 1871. 12°. . . . . . . . . H,496
Beaver, American, and his Works. L. H. Morgan. Philadelphia, 1868. 8°. N,688
Bechstein, J. M. Cage and Chamber Birds. London, 1853. p. 8°. . . O,86
and Scharfenberg, Schädliche Forstinsekten. Leipzig, 1805. 3 v. 4°. G,957
Bechstein L. Wanderung durch Thüringen. Leipzig, n. d. 8°. . E,186,4
The same. Leipzig, n. d. 12°. . . . . . . . E,184
Bechstein R. Altdeutsche Märchen, Sagen und Legenden. Leipzig, 1863. 16°. G,260
Beck, L. C. Botany of Northern United States. New York, 1848. 8°. . N,952
Mineralogy of New York. Albany, 1842. 4°. . . . . Q,101,8
Becker, W. A. Charicles; Private Life of Ancient Greeks. Lond. 1854. 12°. A,152

Becker, W. A. Gallus; Roman Scenes at Time of Augustus. Lond. 1853. 8°. A,153
Becket, A. Dramatic and Prose Miscellanies. London, 1838. 2 v. 8°. . I,741
Becket, G. A. à. Comic Blackstone. Philadelphia, n.d. 12°. . . . U,482
Comic History of England. London, n. d. 8°. . . . . . A,445
of Rome. London, n. d. 8°. . . . . . . . A,150
Beckett, T. à, Life of. Robert of Gloucester. London, 1845. 12°. . L,606,19
Beckford, W. Italy, Spain, and Portugal. London, 1834. 2 v. 12°. . . V,516
Monasteries of Alcobaça and Batalha. London, 1835. 8°. . . V,474
Vathek; an Arabian Tale. New York, 1868. 16°. . . . . K,616
Beckmann, J. History of Inventions and Discoveries. Lond. 1814. 4 v. 8°. M,642
The same. London, 1846. 2 v. p. 8°. . . . . . . L,168
Beckoning Series. P. Cobden. Boston, 1871. 2 v. 16°. . . . J,1546
Vol. 1. Who Will Win. Vol. 2. Going on a Mission.
Beckwith, G. C. Peace Manual. Boston, 1847. 18°. . . . . O,461
Beda Venerabilis. Complete Works. London, 1843-4. 12 v. 8°. . . P,388
Ecclesiastical History of England. London, 1849. 12°. . . . L,1
Historia Ecclesiasticæ; ed. J. Stevenson. London, 1838. 8°. . . U,628
Opera Historica; ed. J. Stevenson. London, 1841. 8°. . . . U,633
Bede, Cuthbert, *pseud.* See *Bradley, E.*
Bedell, G. T., Memoirs. S. H. Tyng. London, 1835. 12°. . . . C,809
Bee, Hive and Honey. L. L. Langstroth. New York, 1859. 12°. . . M,464
Honey. J. Samuelson and J. B. Hicks. London, 1860. 12°. . O,27
Bee-Keeper's Manual. T. B. Miner. New York, 1855. 12°. . . . M,467
Bee-Keeping, Mysteries of, explained. M. Quinby. New York, 1857. 12°. M,468
Beechcroft. C. M. Yonge. New York, 1856. 12°. . . . . . K,1074
Bees, Natural History of. F. Huber. Edinburgh, 1808. 12°. . . . M,444
Sir W. Jardine. Edinburgh, 1852. 16°. . . . N,470,34
Their Habits and Treatment. J. G. Wood. London, n. d. 16. . M,442
Beecher, C. The People Interpreters of the Bible. New York, 1860. 12°. P,296
Redeemer and the Redeemed. Boston, 1864. 12°. . . . . . P,128
Beecher, C. E. Letters on Health and Happiness. New York, 1856. 16°. L,866
Physiology and Calisthenics. New York, 1856. 16°. . . . L,861
Religious Training of Children. New York, 1864. 12°. . . . P,38
Treatise on Domestic Economy. New York, 1854. 12°. . . . H,277
True Remedy for the Wrongs of Women. Boston, 1851. 12°. . O,387
and Stowe, H. B. American Woman's Home. New York, 1869. 8°. O,366
Beecher, E. Concord of Ages. New York, 1860. 12°. . . . . . P,187
Conflict of Ages. Boston, 1854. 12°. . . . . . . . P,188
Narrative of Riots at Alton. Alton, 1838. 12°. . . . . . C,158
Papal Conspiracy Exposed. New York, 1855. 12°. . . . . P,820
Beecher, H. W. Lecture-Room Talks. New York, 1870. 12°. . . . P,237
Lectures to Young Men. Boston, 1869. 12°. . . . . . . H,221
Life Thoughts. New York, 1866. 12°. . . . . . . . P,317
Morning and Evening Exercises. New York, 1871. 8°. . . P,897
New Star-Papers. New York, 1859. 12°. . . . . . . P,86
Norwood. New York, 1868. 12°. . . . . . . . . K,10
Notes from Plymouth Pulpit. New York, 1859. 12°. . . . P,56
Prayers from Plymouth Pulpit. New York, 1868. 12°. . . P,905
Royal Truths. Boston, 1866. 16°. . . . . . . . . P,289
Sermons. New York, 1868. 2 v. 8°. . . . . . . . . P,763

Beecher, H. W. Star-Papers; or, Art and Nature. New York, 1855. 12°. H,231
Talk about Fruit, Flowers, and Farming. New York, 1859. 12°. . H,90
Beecher, L. Autobiography; ed. by C. Beecher. New York, 1864-65. 2 v. 12°. C,704
Plea for the West. Cincinnati, 1835. 12°. . . . . . . O,987
Works. Boston, 1852-53. 3 v. 12°. . . . . . . . . . P,762
Beechey, F. W. Voyage towards the North Pole, 1818. London, 1843. 8°. . V,956
Botany of a Voyage to the Pacific. London, 1841. 4o. . . . Q,113
Zoology of a Voyage to the Pacific. London, 1839. 4° . . . Q,6
Beer, How to Brew Good. J. Pitt. London, 1864. 12°. . . . . M,669
Beethoven, L., von. Letters, 1790-1826. New York, 1867. 2 v. 16°. . G,24
Engedi; David in the Wilderness; ed. by V. Novello. Lond. n. d. 8° . M,425
Mass in C; ed. by V. Novello. London, n. d. 8°. . . . . . M,425
Sonaten für das Pianoforte. Wolfenbüttel, n. d. 2 v. 4°. . . Q,190
Leben und Schaffen. A. B. Marx. Berlin, 1859. 2 v, 8°. . . G,638
Beetles, Natural History of. J. Duncan. Edinburgh, 1852. 16°. . N,470-33
Sacred. J. O. Westwood. London, n. d. 4°. . . . . . . Q,114
Beeton, S. O. Dict. of Universal Information, Geography, etc. Lond. n. d. 8°. L.R.
Before the Footlights, etc. O. Logan. Philadelphia, 1870. 8°. . . I,719
Bégat, P. Opérations Géodésiques. Paris, 1839. 4°. . . . . M,822
Traité de Géodésie à l'Usage des Marins. Paris, 1839. 8°. . . M,707
Beginning Life, Lectures to Young Men. J. Tulloch. London, 1864. 16°. H,565
Beitzke, H. Geschichte der Deutschen Freiheitskriege. Berlin, 1864. 3 v. 8°. E,70
Geschichte des Russischen Krieges, 1812. Berlin, 1862. 8°. . . E,88
Bekehrt Euch. J. F. Fries. Heidelberg, 1814. 24°. . . . . G,532
Belcher, J. Historical Sketches of Hymns. Philadelphia, 1859. 12°. . P,889
Religious Denominations in the U. S. Philadelphia, 1855. 8°. . S. C.
Belden, E. P. New York City; Past, Present, and Future. N. Y. 1850. 12°. C,171
Belforest. A. Manning. London, 1865. 2 v. 12°. . . . . . . J,593
Belgium, Hand-Book for. J. Murray. London, 1852. 16°. . . . V,412
Belief, Restoration of. I. Taylor. Boston, 1867. 12°. . . . . P,75
Believe as You List; a Tragedy. P. Massinger. London, 1849. 12°. L,606,27
Belinda. M. Edgeworth. London, 1820. 2 v. 12°. . . . . . K,550
The same. New York, 1859. 12°. . . . . . . K,678,11,12
Belisle, D. W. History of Independence Hall. Philadelphia, 1859. 12°. . B,848
Belknap, J. American Biography. Boston, 1794-8. 2 v. 8°. . . . C,769
The same; ed. by F.M.Hubbard. New York, 1855. 3 v. 16°. . L,447
Life of. J. Belknap. New York, 1847. 16°. . . . . . . C,837
Bell, A. System of Instruction. London, 1840. 12°. . . . O,1158
Bell, Sir C. Anatomy and Philosophy of Expression. London, 1865. 8°. . M,140
The Hand, its Mechanism, etc. London, 1870. p. 8°. . . . L,311
Bell, Currer, *pseud.* See *Nicholls, C. B.*
Bell, G. M. Philosophy of Joint-Stock Banking. London, 1855. 8°. . O,590
Bell, H. G. Life of Mary Queen of Scots. Edinburgh, 1828. 2 v. 16°. I,507
The same. New York, 1859. 2 v. 8°. . . . . . . L,354
Operations in the Birmese Empire. Edinburgh, 1827. 2 v. 16°. . I,496
Remarkable Phenomena of Nature. Edinburgh, 1827. 16°. . . I,499
Bell, J. British Theatre; English Plays. London, 1776-78. 20 v. 12°. . I,682
Classical Arrangement of Fugitive Poetry. Lond.1789-97. 18v.in 9. 16°. I,194
Bell, J. Travels in Asia. Glasgow, 1763. 2 v. 4°. . . . . . V,536
Bell, J. Water as a Preservative and as a Remedy. Phila., 1859. 8°. . L,907

Bell J., and C. Human Anatomy and Physiology. Lond. 1829. v. 2-3. 8°. L,974
Bell, M. Julia Howard. New York, 1864. 8°. . . . . . . K,599
Bell, R. History of Russia. London, 1836-38. 3 v. 12°. . . . . M1000
Life of George Canning. New York, 1846. 12°. . . . . D,155
Lives of English Poets. London, 1839. 2 v. 12°. . . . M,1015
(Ed.) Ancient Poems, Ballads, and Songs. London, 1857. 16°. . I,244
Songs from the Dramatists. London, 1855. 16°. . . . . I,253
Bell, T. Fossil Reptilia of the London Clay. London, 1849. 4°. . . Q,21
Bell, W. E. Carpentry made Easy. Philadelphia, 1858. 8°. . . . M,196
Bellairs, N. Hardy Ferns. London, 1865. 8°. . . . . . . . N,942
Wayside Flora towards Rome. London, 1866. 16°. . . . N,940
Belles Lettres, Encyclopædia of. S. Maunder. London, 1845. 12°. . L.R.
Method of Teaching and Studying. C. Rollin. London, 1769. 2 v. 8°. H,912
Bellows, A. J. Philosophy of Eating. New York, 1869. 12°. . . L,899
Bellows, H. W. Old World in its New Face. New York, 1868-9. 2 v. 12°. V,369
Beloe, W. Anecdotes of Literature and Scarce Books. Lond. 1807-12. 6 v. 8°. H,737
The Sexegenarian. London, 1817. 2 v. 8°. . . . . . . L.R.
Belsham, W. History of Great Britain, 1688-1802. Lond. 1806-12. 12 v. 8°. A,429
Belton Estate. A. Trollope. Leipzig, 1866. 2 v. in 1. 16°. . . . J,492
The same. New York, 1866. 8°. . . . . . K,1059
Beltrami, J. C. Pilgrimage in Europe and America. Lond. 1828. 2 v. 8°. V,1074
Beltz, G. F. Order of the Garter. London, 1841. 8°. . . . . D,279
Belzoni, G. B. Discoveries in Egypt and Nubia. London, 1821. 4°. . V,873
Bement, C. N. American Poulterer's Companion. New York, 1852. 12. M,451
The same. New York, 1856. 8°. . . . . . M,473
Rabbit Fancier. New York, 1856. 12°. . . . . . . M,533,3
Bemrose, W., jr. Fret-Cutting and Perforated Carving. London, n. d. 4°. . Q,165
Manual of Wood Carving. London, n. d. 4°. . . . . M,677
Ben Brace; Last of Nelson's Agamemnons. F. Chamier. Lon. 1836. 3 v. 12°. J,577
Bench and Bar; Digest of Wit, Humor, etc. L. J. Bigelow. N.Y. 1867. 8°. H,127
Benedict of Peterborough. Chronicle of the Reigns of Henry II. and Richard I. London, 1867. 2 v. 8°. . . . . . . . . . W,199
Benedicite. G. C. Child. London, 1868. 16°. . . . . . . . P,348
Benedictines, Inventories of Jarrow and Monk-Wearmouth. Dur. 1854. 8°. F,126,29
Bengal, Annals of Rural. W. W. Hunter. London, 1868. 8°. . . C,403
Description of Dinájpur. F. Buchanan. Calcutta, 1833. 8°. . V,698
Scenery in. London, 1816. 8°. . . . . . . . . . F,695
Bengel, J. A. Gnomon of New Testament. Edingburgh, 1859. 5 v. 8°. P,487
Benger, E. O. Life of Anne Boleyn. Philadelphia, 1852. 12°. . . . D,380
Life of Mary, Queen of Scots. Philadelphia, 1851. 2 v. 12°. C,1223
Memoirs of the Life of Anne Boleyn. Philadelphia, n. d. 12°. . D,380
Benjamin, A. Builder's Guide. Boston, 1857. 4°. . . . . . M,285
Benjamin, S. G. W. Turk and the Greek. New York, 1867. 16°. . V,539
Bennett, E. T. On a Pteropine Bat. London, n. d. 4°. . . . . Q,114
Bennett, J. H. Winter and Spring on the Mediterranean. N. Y. 1870. 8°. . V,345
Bennett, J. C. Poultry Book. Boston, 1854. 12°. . . . . . M,445
Bennett, J. E. Crime and Education. London, 1846. 8°. . . O,1251,1
Bennett, J. W. Rare and Curious Fishes of Ceylon. London, 1851. 4°. . Q,38
Benson, E. Vindication of the Captors of Major André. N. Y. 1865. 8°. C,908
Benson, J. Life of J. W. de La Flechere. New York, 1855. 12°. . . D,520

Benson, W. Improved Projectiles for Military Purposes. Glas. 1860. 8°. N,252,49
Bent's Literary Advertiser. London, 1856. 4°. . . . . . . Q,377
Bentham, J. Book of Fallacies. London, 1824. 8°. . . . . . O,496
Chrestomathia. London, 1816. 8°. . . . . . . . . . O,1208
Panopticon Penitentiary-House. London, 1791. 16°. . . . O,465
Principles of Legislation. Boston, 1830. 8°. . . . . . O,495
Rationale of Judicial Evidence. London, 1827. 5 v. 8°. . . U,544
Punishment. London, 1830. 8°. . . . . . . . . . O,553
Bentley Ballads; edited by J. Doran. London, 1866. p. 8°. . . . I,170
Bentley, J. Education as it is and ought to be. Cincinnati, 1849. 12°. . O,1143
Bentley, R., Life of. H. Coleridge. London, 1852. 8°. . . . C,1166,1
Benton, T. H. Abridgement of Debates of Congress. N.Y. 1857–9. 12 v. 8°. P.D.
Examination of the Dred Scott Decision. New York, 1858. 8°. . O,424
Thirty Years' View of American Government. N.Y. 1856–8. 2 v. 8°. B,665
Bentz, L. Elements of Agriculture. New York, 1856. 12°. . . M,533,2
Benzoni, G. History of the New World. London, 1857. 8°. . . . V,979
Beppo. T. A. Trollope. Philadelphia, 1870. 12°. . . . . K,1040
Béranger, P. J. de. Lyrical Poems; translated by W. Young. N.Y. 1857. 12°. H,920
Memoirs of, by himself. London, 1858. 8°. . . . . . . D,606
Bérard, M. A. Description Nautique des Côtes de l'Algerie. Paris, 1839. 8°. V,1113
Berg oder Burg. E. Fritze. Hannover, 1863. 16°. . . . . G,277,2
Berghaus, H. Allgemeine Länder-und Völkerkunde. Stutt. 1837–44. 6 v. 8°. E,157
Baudenkmäler aller Völker der Erde. Leipzig, 1854. 2°. . . . G,735
Bergmann, C., and Leuckart, R. Uebersicht des Thierreichs. Stutt. 1851. 8°. E,422
Bergmann, L. Baustyle und Säulen-Ordnungen. Leipzig, 1854. 8°. . G,626
Berkley, C. The Hamiltons. New York, 1856. 18°. . . . J,1193
Berkeley, G. Siris; Virtues of Tar-Water in Disease. London, 1747. 8°. O,648
Works. London, 1843. 2 v. 8°. . . . . . . . . . U,203
Berkeley, M. J. Cryptogamic Botany. London, 1857. 8°. . . N,1000
Berlepsch, H. A. Alpen in Natur-und Lebensbildern. Leipzig, 1862. 8°. E,185
Berlin and Sans-Souci. C. Mundt. New York, 1868. 8°. . . . G,195
and its Treasures. New York, 1867. 4°. . . . . . . L.R.
Secret History of Court of. H. G. R. de Mirabeau. Dublin, 1789. 8°. B,209
Berlioz, H. Modern Instrumentation and Orchestration. Lond. 1858. 8°. M,421,2
Bermuda, Naturalist in. J. M. Jones and others. London, 1859. 12°. N,521
Bernan, W. Art of Warming and Ventilating. London, 1845. 2 v. 16°. L,865
Bernard, F. Wonderful Escapes. New York, 1871. 12°. . . M,1061
Bernardus, St. De Cura Rei Famuliaris, etc. London, 1870. 8°. . L,605,42
Life and Times of. Abbé Ratisbonne. N. Y. 1855. 12°. . . D,635
Bernard, Sir F. American Trade, 1774. See *American Revolution, Tracts*, 4.
Berry, M. Journal and Correspondence. London, 1865. 3 v. 8°. . . D,465
Social Life in England and France. London, 1844. 2 v. 12°. . H,313
Bertha's Journal; Visit to England. London, 1851. 12°. . . . V,320
Bertram, J. G. Fish Culture in France. London, 1864. 8°. . . V,1086,3
Bertram, J. M. St. Helena and the Cape of Good Hope. N. Y. 1852. 12°. V,808
Bertram Noel. E. J. May. New York, 1870. 12°. . . . . J,1644
Bertrams, The. A. Trollope. Leipzig, 1859. 2 v. in 1. 16°. . . J,493
Bertrand de Moleville, A.F. Annals of French Revolution. Lon. 1800. 4 v. 8°. B,285
The same. London, 1800–2. 9 v. 8°. . . . . . . B,332
Private Memoirs of Louis XVI. London, 1797. 8°. . . . D,677

Berzelius, J. J. Lehrbuch der Chemie. Leipzig, 1856. 5 v. 8°. . . . G,750
Untersuchung der Mineral-Wasser von Karlsbad. Leip. 1825. 8°. N,252,27
Use of the Blowpipe. Boston, 1845. 8°. . . . . . . . . N,206
Besant, W. Studies in Early French Poetry. London, 1868. 12°. . . H,757
Bescherelle, L. N. Dict. National de la Langue Française. Paris, '66. 2 v. 4°. L.R.
Beseelte Schatten, Der. G. Höcker. Prag, 1859. 2 v. in 1. 24°. . . G,313
Besenval, P. V. de, Mémoires. Paris, 1855. 12°. . . . . . . D,601
Bessé, A. de. The Turkish Empire. Philadelphia, 1854. 12°. . . V,560
Besse, J. Sufferings of the Quakers. London, 1733-38. 3 v. 8°. . . P,633
Bessel, F. W. Tabulæ Regiomontanæ, 1750-1850. Regiomonti, 1830. 8°. N,301
Best, H. Rural Economy of Yorkshire, 1641. London, 1857. 8°. . F,126,33
Bessy's Money; a Tale. A. Manning. London, 1863. 16°. . . . J,579
Betham, Sir W. Etruscan Literature and Iberno-Celtic. Dub. 1842. 2 v. 8°. H,732
Bethune, G. W. Lectures on Heidelberg Catechism. N. Y. 1864. 2 v. 12°. P,904
Bethune, M. de, *Duc de Sully*, Memoirs. London, 1856. 2 v. 12°. . . L,327
and the Trial of Francis Ravaillac. Edinb. 1770. 5 v. 12°. . D,597
Betrothed, The. Sir W. Scott. Boston, 1858. 2 v. 12°. . . . K,927
The same. Philadelphia, 1857. 8°. . . . . . . K,957
The same. Philadelphia, 1869. 8°. . . . . . K,1113
Better Land. A. C. Thompson. Boston, 1869. 12°. . . . . . . P,50
Beudant, F. S. Composition des Minéraux. Paris, n. d. 8°. . . N,252,42
Beulah. A. J. Wilson. New York, 1868. 12°. . . . . . . . K,105
Bewick, T. History of British Birds. Newcastle, 1797-1804. 2 v. 8°. . O,110
Beyle, H. Lives of Haydn and Mozart. Boston, 1839. 12°. . . . D,495
The same. London, 1817. 8°. . . . . . . . . . D,523
Metastasio and Music in France and Italy. London, 1817. 8°. . D,523
Beyond the Breakers. R. D. Owen. Philadelphia, 1870. 8°. . . . K,229
Beyond the Mississippi. A. D. Richardson. Hartford, 1869. 8°. . . V,130
Bhâgvât Gēētā; translated by C. Wilkins. London, 1785. 4°. . . Q,420
Biart, L. Adventures of a Young Naturalist. New York, 1871. 12°. J,1311
Biber, E. Christian Education. London, 1830. 8°. . . . . . O,1202
Pestalozzi and his Plan of Education. London, 1831. 8°. . . D,527
Bible, The, Anglo-Saxon Metrical Paraphrase by Cædmon. Lond. 1832. 8°. P,437
Celtic. Dublin, 1827. 8°. . . . . . . . . . . . P,433
Commentary on. A. Clarke. London, n. d. 6 v. r. 8°. . . . P,552
J. P. Lange. New York, 1870-1. 12 v. 8°. . . . . P,387
S. Patrick, Lowth, and others. Phila. 1846-48. 4 v. 8°. . . P,556
English, Douay and Rheims edition. New York, 1843. 8°. . . P,422
Large Print Paragraph Bible. London, n. d. 4 v. 8°. . . P,418
Self-Explanatory Reference Bible. New York, 1854. 8°. . S.C.
English Translation, History of. H. C. Conant. N. Y. 1856. 12°. . P,446
French, Sainte Bible; tr. par D. Martin. New York, 1846. 12°. . P,428
German, Polyglotten Bible. Bielefeld, 1854-56. 4 v. in 5. 8°. . E,445
Hebrew, Biblia Hebraica. Novi Eboraci, 1850. 8°. . . . . . P,420
Polyglot, Hebrew, and Greek, Account of. T. F. Dibden. Lon. 1827. 2 v. 8°. L.R.
Spanish, Biblia Sagrada. New York, 1854. 8°. . . . . . P,419
Old Testament, Septuagint Version in Greek. London, n. d. 8°. . P,430
English. London, 1844. 2 v. 8°. . . . . . P,434
*Two Leaves of* Biblia Latina. In Civitate Moguntina. 1462. f°. . L.R.
Introduction to. H. A. C. Hävernick. Edinburgh, 1852. 8°. P,512

Bible, O. T., Pentateuch, and Joshua. W. J. Colenso. N.Y. 1863. 2 v. 12°. P,493
Jewish Reply to Colenso. London, 1865. 8°. . . . . P,158
Introduction to. H. A. C. Hävernick. Edinburgh, 1850. 8°. P,511
Genuineness of. E. W. Hengstenberg. Edinburgh, 1847. 2 v. 8°. P,513
Prophets and Kings of. F. D. Maurice. Boston, 1853. 12°. . P,116
Synopsis of Criticism on. R.A.F.Barrett. Lond.1847. 3v.in5.8°. P,486
Genesis, Notes on. G. Bush. New York, 1868. 2 v. 12°. . . . P,490
Quæstiones Mosaicæ. O. De B. Priaulx. London, 1854. 8°. P,179
Exodus, Notes on. G. Bush. New York, 1867. 2 v. 12°. . . P,489
Joshua, Commentary on. K. F. Keil. Edinburgh, 1857. 8°. . . P,530
Book of Ruth; illustrated by *Lady* A. Cadogan. London, 1850. 8°. . P,435
Kings, Commentary on. K. F. Keil. Edinburgh, 1857. 2 v. 8°. . P,541
Ezra, in Phonetics. London, 1849. 18°. . . . . . . . L,659
Job, Notes on. A. Barnes. New York, 1856. 2 v. 12°. . . . P,470
Psalms, Anglo-Saxon and Early English. London, 1843. 8°. . F,126,16
Commentary on. J. Calvin. Oxford, 1840. 3 v. 8°. . . P,497
E. W. Hengstenberg. Edinburgh, 1851–57. 3 v. 8°. . P,514
in Phonetic Shorthand. London, 1853. 18°. . . . L,670
Literal Translation by J. Jebb. London, 1846. 2 v. 8°. . P,431
New Translation of. G. R. Noyes. New York, 1863. 12°. . P,503
Notes on. A. Barnes. New York, 1869. 3 v. 12°. . . P,480
Te Samz of David in Meter. Lundun, 1850. 32°. . . . P,1
Proverbs, Commentary on. M. Stuart. New York, 1859. 12°. . P,504
Ecclesiastes, and Canticles; tr. by G. R. Noyes. Bost. 1846. 12°. P,502
Ecclesiastes, Commentary on. M. Stuart. Andover, 1864. 12°. . P,536
Lectures on. R. Wardlaw. Philadelphia, 1822. 8°. . . P,471
Isaiah, New Translation by R. Lowth. London, 1848. 8°. . . P,542
Notes on. A. Barnes. New York, 1855. 2 v. 12°. . . P,469
The same. London, 1867. 3 v. 12°. . . . . P,482
Ezekiel, Improved Version by W. Newcome. London, 1836. 8°. . P,545
Daniel, Improved Version by T. Wintle. London, 1836. 8°. . . P,485
Notes on. A. Barnes. London, n. d. 2 v. 12°. . . . P,488
Genuineness of, and Integrity of Zechariah. E. W. Hengstenberg. Edinburgh, 1848. 8°. . . . . . . . P,515
New Testament; edited by C. Tischendorf. Leipzig, 1869. 16°. . J,33
with Analysis by J. Wesley. London, n. d. 18°. . . . P,415
Commentary on. A. Clarke. Philadelphia, 1870. 8°. . . P,520
H. Olshausen. New York, 1858. 6 v. 8°. . . . P,553
English Hexapla; six translations. London, n. d. 4°. . . *Q,145
Wiclif, 1380, Cranmer, 1539, Anglo-Rhemish, 1582,
Tyndale, 1534, Genevan, 1557, Authorized, 1611.
First Translation into English, by W. Tyndale. Lond. 1836. 8°. P,417
German, Das Neue Testament. New York, 1861. 18°. . P,414
Greek, ex Codice Vaticano. New York, 1859. 8°. . . P,438
Hindustani; tr. by Calcutta Baptist Mission. Calcutta, 1839. 8°. P,421
Latin, Novum Testamentum. New York, 1855. 12°. . . P,427
Manual. S. Hawes. Boston, 1871. 16°. . . . . . P,184
Notes on. H. Crosby. New York, 1863. 12°. . . . P,524
Polyglot, Bagster's. London, n. d. 4°. . . . . . *P,463
Græcè; Latinè; Lusitanè; Anglicanè; Gallicè; Italicè; Hispanicè; Germanicè; Syriacè.

Bible, New Testament, Divine Authority of. D. Bogue. New York, n. d. 18°. P,746
Gnomon of. J. A. Bengel. Edinburgh, 1859. 5 v. 8°. . P,487
Grammar to. W. Trollope. London, 1842. 8°. . . . . L,739
Grammar of. G. B. Winer. Philadelphia, 1849. 2 v. 8°. . P,484
of the Idiom of. G. B. Winer. Andover, 1870. 8°. . P,439
Greek Lexicon of. E. Robinson. New York, 1858. 8°. . P,451
Introduction to. S. Davidson. London, 1848–51. 3 v. 8°. . P,498
J. D. Michaelis. Cambridge, 1801. 5 v. 8°. . . . P,543
Notes on the Miracles. R. C. Trench. New York, 1855. 8°. P,517
on the Parables. R. C. Trench. New York, 1855. 8°. P,516
Parables of Our Lord; with Illustrations. London, n. d. 16°. P,367
Authorized Version of. R. C. Trench. New York, 1858. 12°. L,729
Representative Men of. G. C. Baldwin. New York, 1860. 12°. P,99
Studies in the Gospels. R. C. Trench. London, 1867. 8°. . P,279
Synonyms of. R. C. Trench. New York, 1858. 12°. . . L,730
Unity of. F. D. Maurice. London, 1854. 8°. . . . P,522
Gospels, Commentary on. T. Aquinas. Oxford 1841–45. 4 v. in 8. 8°. P,473
Examination of the Four. S. Greenleaf. London, 1847. 8°. P,510
History and Harmony of the. Dublin, 1759. 24°. . . . P,366
Notes on. A. Barnes. New York, 1868. 2 v. 12°. . . P,464
Four Witnesses. I. Da Costa. New York, 1855. 8°. . . P,496
Introduction to Study of. B. F. Westcott. Boston, 1869. 12°. P,505
Lindisfarne and Rushworth. Lond. 1854–63. 3 v. 8°. F,126,28,39,43
Remarks on. W. H. Furness. Philadelphia, 1836. 12°. . P,507
Translation of, with Notes. A. Norton. Boston, 1855. 2 v. 8°. P,546
Unconscious Truth of. W. H. Furness. Philadelphia, 1868. 12°. P,230
with Moral Reflections. P. Quesnel. Philad. 1855. 2 v. 8°. P,547
St. Luke, Commentary on. Cyrillus Alexandrinus. Oxford, 1859. 2 v. 8°. P,495
Acts, Commentary on. H. B. Hackett. Boston, 1870. 8°. . . P,534
Notes on. A. Barnes. New York, 1855. 12°. . . . P,466
M. W. Jacobus. New York, 1863. 12°. . . . P,526
Epistles of St. Paul. W. D. Conybeare and J. S. Howson. N. Y. 1858. 2 v. 8°. P,406
Epistres, Les; interpreted by J. Diodati. Amsterdam, 1667. 12°. . P,416
Romans, Commentary on. M. Stuart. London, 1857. 8°. . . P,533
Lectures on. T. Chalmers. New York, 1868. 12°. . . P,535
Notes on. A. Barnes. New York, 1869. 12°. . . . . P,467
Translated and explained. J. W. Colenso. N. Y. 1863. 12°. P,494
First Corinthians, Notes on. A. Barnes. New York, 1870. 12°. . P,477
Second Corinthians and Galatians, Notes on. A. Barnes. N. Y. 1869. 12°. P,468
Ephesians, Philippians, etc., Notes on. A. Barnes. N. Y. 1869. 12°. P,475
Thessalonians, Timothy, etc., Notes on. A. Barnes. N. Y. 1869. 12°. P,479
Hebrews, Commentary on. M. Stuart; ed. E. Henderson. Lond. 1856. 8°. P,532
Lectures on. F. D. Maurice. London, 1846. 8°. . . . P,537
Notes on. A. Barnes. New York, 1869. 12°. . . . P,476
James, Peter, John, etc., Notes on. A Barnes. New York, 1869. 12°. P,478
Epistles of Peter; Analytical Exposition. W. Ames. Lond. 1641. 4°. P,98
Revelation, Apocalyptic Sketches. J. Cumming. Phila. 1858. 12°. P,255
Epistles to the Seven Churches. London, 1861. 16°. . . P,521
Expounded. E. W. Hengstenberg. Edinburgh, 1851–52. 2 v. 8°. P,529
Lectures on. F. D. Maurice. London, 1861. 12°. . . P,68

Bible, N. T., Revelation, Notes on. A. Barnes. New York, 1870. 12°. . P,465
Ad Fidem; Parish Evidences of. E. F. Burr. Boston, 1871. 12°. . P,282
Animals of. J. G. Wood. London, 1869. 8°. . . . . . . N,690
Annals of the English. C. Anderson. London, 1845. 2 v. 8°. . P,447
Atlas, Explanatory. W. Jenks. Boston, 1847. 4°. . . . . Q,369
Astronomy of. O. M. Mitchell. New York, 1870. 12°. . . . N,332
Bards of. G. Gilfillan. New York, 1855. 12°. . . . . . P,508
Bible Hour; Scripture Lessons. London, 1859. 16°. . . J,1316
Bible Thoughts. H. Melvill. New York, n. d. 18°. . . P,746,19
Christology of the Old Test. E.W. Hengstenberg. Edinb.1858. 4 v. 8°. P,528
Claims of, and of Science. F. D. Maurice. London, 1863. 12°. . P,303
Complete Analysis of. N. West. New York, 1855. 4°. . . . P,558
Concordance of. A. Cruden. New York, 1868. r. 8°. . . . *P,499
Cyclopædia of. J. P. Lawson. Edinburgh, n. d. 3 v. 8°. . . P,460
Dictionary of. W. Smith. Boston, 1863. 3 v. 8°. . . . . *P,450
Divine Authority of. J. Leland. London, 1837. 8°. . . . P,174
Editions of, from 1505 to 1850. H. Cotton. Oxford, 1852. 8°. . . *P,407
printed in America. E. B. O'Callaghan. Albany, 1861. 4°. . L.R.
Errata to the Protestant. T. Ward. Dublin, 1807. 4°. . . . P,461
Evidences of the Truth of. G. Rawlinson. Boston, 1860. 12°. . P,53
Historic Notes on. S. Sharpe. London, 1858. 8°. . . . . P,540
History for Children. London, 1859. 12°. . . . . . J,1191
History of. J. Fleetwood. New York, 1855. 8°. . . . P,449
G. R. Gleig. New York, 1854. 2 v. 18°. . . . . L,345
History of the Books of. C. E. Stowe. Hartford, 1867. 8°. . . P,448
History of the English Translation. H. C. Conant. N. Y. 1856. 12°. P,446
Family Pictures from. E. F. Ellet. New York, 1849. 12°. . . P,136
Horæ Biblicæ. C. Butler. London, 1817. 8°. . . . . . P,483
Hulsean Lectures on. R. C. Trench. Philadelphia, 1854. 12°. . P,48
Illustrations of. G. Bush. Philadelphia, 1850. 8°. . . . . P,500
G. Paxton. Philadelphia, 1822. 2 v. 8°. . . . . P,474
Key to. D. Dobie. New York, 1856. 12°. . . . . . . P,506
in the Counting House. H. A. Boardman. Philadelphia, 1853. 12°. P,210
in the Family. H. A. Boardman. Philadelphia, 1869. 12°. . . P,246
in the Public Schools of Cincinnati. Cincinnati, 1870. 8°. . . O,957
in Spain. G. Borrow. Philadelphia, 1843. 8°. . . . . V,476
in the Workshop. J. W. Mears. New York, 1857. 12°. . . . P,302
Koran and the Talmud. G. Weil. New York, 1855. 16°. . . P,73
Notes on all the Books of. J. Priestley. Northumb. 1803-4. 4 v. 8°. U,294
People Interpreters of. C. Beecher. New York, 1860. 12°. . . P,296
Personal Names in. W. F. Wilkinson. London, 1865. 12°. . . L,557
Plants of. J. H. Balfour. London, 1857. 8°. . . . . . N,1026
Popular Scripture Zoology. M. E. Catlow. London, 1852. 12°. . N,623
Seeds and Sheaves; or, Words of. A. C. Thompson. Boston, 1869. 12°. P,45
Smaller Scripture History. W. Smith. New York, 1871. 16°. . P,579
Typology of. P. Fairbairn. Philadelphia, 1859. 2 v. 8°. . . P,161
Biblia Pauperum, in fac-simile; introd. by J. P. Berjeau. Lond. 1859. f°. *Q,226
Biblical Antiquities. F. A. Cox. London, 1852. p. 8°. . . . . P,256
Biblical Archæology. J. Jahn. New York, 1856. 8°. . . . . A,219
Biblical Geography, Text-Book and Atlas of. L. Coleman. Phila. 1857. 8°. V,1143

Biblical Literature, Cyclopædia of. J. Kitto. Philadelphia, 1866. 3 v. 8°. *P,452
J. Kitto and J. Taylor. Boston, 1854. 8°. . . . . . . . *P,788
Illustrations of. J. Townley. New York, 1842. 2 v. 8°. . . . *P,472
Bibliographer's Manual of English Literature. W. T. Lowndes. London, 1857–60. 5 v. in 10. 12°. . . . . . . . . . . . L.R.
Bibliographia Zoologiæ et Geologiæ. L. Agassiz. London, 1848–54. 4 v. 8°. *O,300
Bibliographical Dictionary. A. Clarke. Liverpool, 1802–4. 6 v. 12°. . L.R.
F. A. Ebert. Oxford, 1837. 4 v. 8°. . . . . . . . . L.R.
Biographical Miscellany. A. Clarke. London, 1806. 2 v. 12°. . . . L.R.
Bibliographical Tour in France and Germany. T.F.Dibdin. Lond.1821. 3v. 8°. L.R.
The same. London, 1829. 3 v. 8°. . . . . . . . M,58
Bibliography, Annalen der Deutschen Literatur bis 1536. G. W. Panzer. Nürnberg, 1788-1803. 2 v. 4°. . . . . . . . . L.R.
Annales Typograph. ad 1536. G.W.Panzer Norimb. 1793–1803. 11v. 4°. L.R
Bibliographie Instructive. G. F. De Bure. Paris, 1763–9. 9 v. 8°. L.R.
Catalogue of Books on, in N. Y. State Library. Albany, 1858. 8°. . L.R.
Introduction to the Study of. T. H. Horne. Lond. 1814. 2 v. 8°. L.R.
Manuel du Libraire. J. C. Brunet. Paris, 1860–65. 6 v. 8°. . L.R.
Travaux de la Société des Philobiblon. O. Delepierre. Lond. 1862. 8°. L.R.
Bibliotheca Americana. C. Leclerc. Paris, 1867. 8°. . . . . . L.R.
1820–52. O. A. Roorbach. New York, 1852. 8°. . . . . . L.R.
The same, 1858–61. New York, 1861. 8°. . . . . . L.R.
Bibliotheca Veterum Patrum. See *Magna Bibliotheca*, etc. . . . .
Bibliotheca Britannica. R. Watt. Edinburgh, 1824. 4 v. 4°. . . . L.R.
Bibliotheca Classica. J. Lempriere. New York, 1853. 8°. . . . L.R.
Bibliotheca Historico-Naturalis, v. 1. W. Engelmann. Leipzig, 1846. 8°. L.R.
Bibliotheca Mejicana; Sale Catalogue of Mexican Books. London, 1869. 8°. L.R.
Bibliothèque Entomologique. Paris, 1833–52. 2 v. 8°. . . . . . O,31
Kirby, J. Centurie d'Insectes.
Eschscholtz, J. F. Œuvres Entomologiques.
Mac Leary, M. W. S. Insectes de Java.
Bibliothèque Portative; Morceaux en Prose et Vers. M. Moysant. Lon. 1800. 4v. 8°. H,1021
Bibra, E. F. von. Chemische Untersuchungen der Eiterarten. Berl. 1842. 8°. N,252,9
Bickersteth, E. H. Yesterday, To-day, and Forever. New York, 1869. 8°. I,284
Bickersteth, H., *Lord Langdale*, Memoirs of. T. D. Hardy. Lond. 1852. 2v. 8°. D,130
Bickham, W. D. Rosecrans' Campaign with 14th Army Corps. Cin. 1863. 12°. B,898
Bickley, G. W. L. Principles of Scientific Botany. Cincinnati, 1853. 8°. N,1038
Bickmore, A. S. Travels in the East Indian Archipelago. Lond. 1868. 8°. V,896
Bierce, L. V. Historical Reminiscences of Summit County. Akron, 1854. 16°. C,153
Bigelow, E. B. Tariff Question. Boston, 1862. 4°. . . . . . . Q,217
Bigelow, J. Modern Inquiries. Boston, 1867. 8°. . . . . . . H,242
Nature in Disease. Boston, 1854. 12°. . . . . . . . L,848
Useful Arts in Connection with Science. New York, 1856. 2 v. 12°. M,612
Bigelow, J. Jamaica in 1850; or, Sixteen Years of Freedom. N. Y. 1851. 12°. V,187
Bigelow, L. J. Bench and Bar; a Digest of Wit, Humor, etc. N.Y. 1867. 8°. H,127
Bigland, J. Natural History of Animals. Philadelphia, 1849. 12°. . N,630
Biglow Papers. J. R. Lowell. 1st and 2d series. Boston, 1848–67. 2 v. 12°. I,8
Bilder aus dem Thierleben. C. Vogt. Frankfurt, 1852. 8°. . . . G,915
Bill Droch's Investment. M. D. Chellis. Boston, 1870. 16°. . . . J,1620
Billiards, Game of. M. Phelan. New York, 1865. 12°. . . . . M,336
Billing A. Science of Gems, Jewels, Coins, and Medals. Lond. 1867. 8°. M,99

Billings, R. W. Baronial Antiquities of Scotland. Edinburgh, n. d. 4 v. 4°. *Q,143
Binding the Sheaves. S. S. Robbins. New York, 1868. 16° . . . . J,1662
Bingham, J. Antiquities of the Christian Church. London, 1840. 9 v. 8°. P,784
Bingley, W. Animal Biography. London, 1813. 3 v. 8° . . . . N,657
History of Animated Nature. Cincinnati, 1868. 8° . . . . . N,557
Binney, T. How to make the best of both Worlds. London, 1856. 12°. . P,183
Binns, J. Recollections of his Life. Philadelphia, 1854. 12° . . . . C,747
Biographia Literaria. S. T. Coleridge. New York, 1852. 8° . . . . H,654
The same. London, 1870. p. 8° . . . . . . . L,173,2
Biographica Britannica Literaria. T. Wright. London, 1846. 8° . . . D,360
Biographical and Critical Miscellanies. W. H. Prescott. New York, 1845. 8°. H,147
Biographical Dictionary. J. L. Blake. Boston, 1854. 8° . . . . *C,622
J. Gorton. London, 1851. 4 v. 8° . . . . . . . . *C,598
American. W. Allen. Boston, 1857. 8° . . . . . *C,1018
T. J. Rogers. Easton, 1824. 8° . . . . . . *C,1029
of Living Authors of Great Britain. London, 1816. 8° . . . . D,276
Biographical Essays. H. T. Tuckerman. Boston, 1857. 8° . . . . C,555
Biographical Index to History of England. S. Y. McMasters. Alton, 1854. 12°. A,392
Biographical Sketch-Book, American. W. Hunt. New York, n. d. 8°. . C,776
Biographical Sketches. H. Martineau. New York, 1869. 12° . . . . C,554
N. W. Senior. London, 1863. 8° . . . . . . . . . C,537
Biographical Studies. G. W. Greene. New York, 1860. 12° . . . . H,267
Biographical Treasury. S. Maunder. London, 1845. 12° . . . . C,488
Biography, American. J. Belknap. Boston, 1794-8. 2 v. 8° . . . C,769
The same; edited by F. M. Hubbard. New York, 1855. 3 v. 16°. L,447
and Criticism, from "The Times." London, 1860. 16° . . . . H,579
and Mythology, Dictionary of. J. Thomas. Phila. 1870-71. 2 v. 8°. L.R.
Annual and Obituary. London, 1817-37. 21 v. 8° . . . . C,568
Appleton's Cyclopædia of; ed. by F. L. Hawkes. New York, 1868. 8°. C,620
Biographia Dramatica. D. E. Baker and I. Reed. London, 1812. 4 v. 8°. L.R.
Biographie Universelle des Contemporains. Paris, 1834. 4 v. 8°. . C,544
Biographies of Good Wives. L. M. Child. New York, 1859. 16°. C,536
Scientific Men. F. Arago. London, 1857. 8° . . . . C,557
The same. Boston, 1859. 2 v. 16° . . . . . C,498
British. London, 1766-68. 4 v. 8° . . . . . . . . D,18
British Admirals. R. Southey. London, 1833-40. 5 v. 12°. M,1009
British Military Commanders. G. R. Gleig. Lond. 1831-32. 3 v. 12°. M,1008
Vol. 1. Sir Walter Manny; Sir Francis De Vere; Oliver Cromwell; Duke of Marlborough.
2. Duke of Marlborough; Charles Mordaunt; Maj.-Gen. James Wolf.
3. Lord Clive; Marquis Cornwallis; Sir Ralph Abercromby; Sir John Moore.
British Public Characters, 1798-1805. London, 1798-1805. 6 v. 8°. C,580
Byepaths of. C. L. Brightwell. London, n. d. 16° . . . . C,497
Celebrated Female Sovereigns. A. Jameson. N. Y. 1862. 2 v. 18°. L,366
Choice English. I. Walton. New York, 1854. 8° . . . . . D,404
Classic and Historic Portraits. J. Bruce. New York, 1854. 12°. . C,503
Ecclesiastical, Essays in. Sir J. Stephen. London, 1860. 8°. . . C,594
Educational, H. Barnard. v. 1. New York, 1859. 8° . . . . O,1057
Eminent British Lawyers. H. Roscoe. London, 1830. 12°. . M,1010

Biography, Eminent British Statesmen. J. Mackintosh, and others. London, 1831–39. 7 v. 12°. . . . . . . . . M,1011

Vol. 1. Sir Thomas More; Cardinal Wolsey; Archbishop Cranmer; Wm. Cecil, Lord Burleigh.
2. Sir John Eliot; Thomas Wentworth, Earl of Stafford.
3. John Pym; John Hampden.
4. Sir Henry Vane, the Younger; Henry Marten.
5. Robt. Cecil, Earl of Salisbury; Thomas Osborn, Earl of Danby.
6. Oliver Cromwell
7. Cromwell and the Republicans.

Eminent Foreign Statesmen. E.E.Crowe and G.P.R.James. Lond.1833. M,1012

Vol. 1. Cardinal Amboise; Ximenes; Leo the Tenth; Cardinal Granvelle, and Maurice of Saxony; Barneveldt; Sully; Duke of Lerma; Duke of Ossuño; Lorenzo de Medici.
2. Cardinal de Richelieu; Count Oxensteirn; Count Olivarez, Duke of San Lucar; Cardinal Mazarin.
3. Cardinal de Retz; Marquis de Seignelai; John De Witt; Marquis de Louvois.
4. Louis de Haro; Cardinal Dubois; Cardinal Alberoni; Duke of Ripperda.
5. Cardinal de Fleury; Count Zinzendorf; Marquis of Pombal; Count of Florida Blanca; Duke of Choiseul; James Necker.

Eminent Men of France. London, 1838-39. 2 v. 12°. . . . M,1014

Vol. 1. Montaigne; Rabelais; Corneille; LaRochefoucauld; Molière; La Fontaine; Pascal; Madame de Sévigné; Boileau; Racine; Fénélon.
2. Voltaire; Rousseau; Condorcet; Mirabeau; Madame Roland; Madame de Staël.

Eminent Men of Italy and Portugal. M. W. Shelley, and others. London, 1835–37. 3 v. 12°. . . . . . M,1013

Vol. 1. Dante; Petrarch; Boccaccio; Lorenzo de Medici; Bojardo; Berni; Ariosto; Machiavelli.
2. Galileo; Guicciardini; Vittoria Colonna; Guarini; Tasso; Chiabrera; Tassoni; Marini; Filicaja; Metastasio; Goldoni; Alfieri; Monti; Ugo Foscolo
3. Boscan; Garcilaso de La Vega; Diego Hurtado de Mendoza; Luis de Leon; Herrera; Ercilla; Cervantes; Lope de Vega; Vicente Espinel; Esteban de Villegas; Gongora; Quevedo; Calderon; Early Poets of Portugal; Camoens.

Epoch Men, and their Results. S. Neil. Edinburgh, n. d. 12°. . C,485
Familiar Sketches of Sculptors. H. F. Lee. Boston, 1854. 2 v. 12°. M,13
Famous London Merchants. H. R. F. Bourne. New York, 1869. 16°. J,1670
Footprints of Famous Men. J. G. Edgar. New York, 1854. 16°. . C,487
Imperial Dict. of Universal. J. Eadie, and others. Lond. 1866. 6 v. 8°. L.R.
Index to. J. Haydn; edited by J. B. Payne. London, 1870. 8°. . C,582
Ladies of the Reformation. J. Anderson. London, 1857. 12°. . C,516
Lives of British Architects. A. Cunningham. London, 1831. 16°. I,640
British Painters. A. Cunningham. Lond. 1830-33. 4 v. 16°. I,638
and Sculptors. A. Cunningham. N. Y. 1845-68. 5 v. 18°. L,352
British Physicians. London, 1830. 16°. . . . . . . I,641
British Sculptors. A. Cunningham. London, 1830. 16°. . I,639
Celebrated Women. S. G. Goodrich. Boston, 1855. 12°. . C,499
Chief Justices of England. J. Campbell. Phila. 1844. 2v. 8°. . D,248
the United States. H. Flanders. Phila. 1855. 8°. . C,816
Eminent Persons. London, n. d. 8°. . . . . . . C,581
Individuals risen from Poverty. London, 1841. 16°. . . I,636
Lord Chancellors of England. J. Campbell. Phila. 1851. 7 v. 8°. D,249
Men of Letters. H. Brougham. Philadelphia, 1845. 2 v. 12°. C,522
Princesses of England. M. A. E. Green. Lond.1850-5. 6 v. 8°. D,338
Scottish Worthies. P. F. Tytler. London, 1832–33. 3 v. 16°. I,642
Nouvelle Biog. Générale. J. C. F. Hoefer. Paris, 1862-66. 46 v. 8°. L.R.
of Self-Taught Men. R. B. Edwards. Boston, n. d. 12°. . . C,515

Biography, Queens of Society. K. B. and J. C. Thomson. Lond. 1870. 12°. C,590
Sacred. H. Hunter. New York, 1852. 8°. . . . . . . P,178
Weltgeschichte in Biographien. K.W. Böttiger. Berl. 1839-40. 3v. 8°. E,7
Wits and Beaux of Society. K. B. and J. C. Thomson. Lond. 1867. 12°. C,589
Biology, Principles of. H. Spencer. New York, 1866-7. 2 v. 12°. . O,657
Bion. Idylls; translated by J. Banks. London, 1853. . . . . L,87
Selections; translated by R. Polwhele. Exeter, 1786. 4°. . . U,480
Biondi, Sir F. History of Civil Warres of England. London, 1641. f°. . F,270
Biot, J. B. Essai de Géométrie Analytique, etc. Paris, 1813. 8°. . M,1127
Traite Elémentaire d'Astronomie Physique. Paris, 1810-11. 4 v. 8°. N,299
and Arago, F. Observations Géodésiques, etc. Paris, 1821. 4°. . N,384
Birch, T. Court and Times of Charles I. London, 1848. 2 v. 8°. . A,507
Court and Times of James I. London, 1849. 2 v. 8°. . . . A,542
Bird, J. and H. Singing-School Companion. Boston, 1852. 16°. . . M,418
Bird, R. M. Nick of the Woods. New York, 1868. 12°. . . . J,1243
Bird, The. J. Michelet; illustrated by Giacomelli. London, 1869. 8°. . O,123
Bird-Fancier, American. D. J. Browne. New York, 1850. 12°. . . O,103
Birds and Bird-Life. F. T. Buckland and others. London, n. d. 12°. . O,102
and Reptiles. L. Figuier. New York, 1870. p. 8°. . . . N,529
Architecture of. J. Rennie. London, 1831. 16°. . . . . L,469
Cage and Chamber. J. M. Bechstein. London, 1853. 12°. . . O,86
Domestic Habits of. J. Rennie. London, 1833. 16°. . . . L,477
Eggs of British. R. Laishley. London, 1858. 16°. . . . O,82
and Nests of British. J. C. Atkinson. London, 1861. 16°. . O,84
Eier der Europæischen Voegel. F.W. J. Baedeker. Leipzig, 1863. f°. *Q,89
Faculties of. J. Rennie. London, 1835. 16°. . . . . . L,476
Fähigkeiten und Kräfte der Vögel. J. Rennie. Leipzig, 1839. 16°. G,910
Familiar History of. E. Stanley. London, 1865. 12°. . . . O,100
Game, of the Northern States. R. B. Roosevelt. New York, 1866. 12°. M,318
History of. T. Bewick. Newcastle, 1797-1804. 2 v. 8°. . . O,110
British. F. O. Morris. London, 1868. 6 v. 8°. . . *O,87
Leben der Hochnordischen Vögel. F. Faber. Leipzig, 1826. 8°. . G,920
Leben der Vögel. A. E. Brehm. Glogau, 1861. 8°. . . . G,934
Lebensweise der Vögel. J. Rennie. Leipzig, 1835. 16°. . . G,911
Natural History of. J. G. Wood. London, 1865. 4°. . . . O,105
J. Rennie. New York, 1855. 18°. . . . . . . L,404
and Classification of. W. Swainson. London, 1836. 2 v. 12°. M,1033
Nests and Eggs of British. F. O. Morris. London, 1867. 3 v. 8°. *O,88
of America. J. J. Audubon. London, 1827-38. 4 v. eleph. f°. . L.R.
The same. New York, 1856. 7 v. 8°. . . . *O,138
of the British Islands. R. Mudie. London, 1854. p. 8°. . . L,129
of California, Illustrations of. J. Cassin. Philadelphia, 1862. 8°. O,312
of Europe, History of. C. R. Bree. London, 1866. 4 v. 8°. . O,124
of Great Britain. W. Lewin. London, 1797-1800. 8 v. in 4. 4°. Q,11
and Ireland. Sir W. Jardine. Edinburgh, n. d. 4 v. 16°. N,470,1-4
of Long Island. J. P. Giraud. New York, 1844. 8°. . . . O,121
of North America. J. J. Audubon. Edinburgh, 1839. 8°. . . O,108
S. F. Baird and others. Philadelphia, 1860. 2 v. 4°. . . Q,36
of the Tanagrine Genus Calliste. P. L. Sclater. London, 1857. 8°. O,107
of Western Africa. W. Swainson. Edinburgh, n. d. 2 v. 16°. N,470,11,12

Birds, Popular History of. A. White. London, 1855. 16°. . . . . o,81
Birmese Empire, Operations in. H. G. Bell. Edinburgh, 1827. 16°. I,496,2
Birmingham and Midland Hardware Dist.; ed. S. Timmons. Lond. 1866. 8°. o,580
Catalogue of Manufacturers' Exhibition. Birmingham, 1839. 8°. N,252,2
Institution of Mechanical Engineers, Report. Birmingham, 1849. 8°. N,252,40
Walks in the Black Country. E. Burritt. London, 1868. 12°. . V,394
Birth and Education. M. S. Schwartz. Boston, 1871. 8°. . . . . G,224
Birthday Present. M. M. Sherwood. New York, 1856. 12°. . . K,1008,8
Bischof, C. G. C. Chemische und Physik. Geologie. Bonn, 1847–51. 3v. 8°. G,844
Chemical and Physical Geology. London, 1854–59. 3 v. 8°. . . N,804
Bischoff, G.W. Botanische Terminologie. Nürnberg, 1830–44. 3 v. in 6. 4°. G,962
Wörterbuch der beschreibenden Botanik. Stuttgart, 1839. 8°. . . G,857
and others. Naturgeschichte der drei Reiche. Stuttgart, 1832–43. 14 v. in 12. 8°. . . . . . . . . . G,812
Vol. 1. Leuckart, F. S. Allgemeine Einleitung in die Naturgeschichte.
Blum, J. R. Lithurgik; oder, Mineralien und Felsarten.
2. Leonhard, K. C. v. Lehrbuch der Geognosie und Geologie.
3-7. Bischoff, G. W. Lehrbuch der Botanik.
8–10. Voigt, B. S. Lehrbuch der Zoologie.
11, 12. Broun, H. G. Handbuch einer Geschichte der Natur.
Bishop, H. E. First Years of Minnesota. New York, 1857. 12°. . . V,76
Bishop, J. L. History of American Manufactures. Phila. 1868. 3 v. 8°. M,676
Bishop, N. P. 1000 Miles Walk across South America. Boston, 1870. 16°. J,1610
Bisset, A. History of Commonwealth of England. London, 1867. 2 v. 8°. . A,509
Bisset, R. History of Reign of George III. Philadelphia, 1828. 3 v. 8°. . A,409
Bismark, O. von, Life of. J. G. L. Hesekiel. New York, 1870. 8°. . D,528
Bitter-Sweet; a Poem. J. G. Holland. New York, 1864. 12°. . . I,58
Bivouac, The; or, Stories of Peninsular War. W. H. Maxwell. Lond. 1857. 16°. K,1155
Bizot, P. Histoire Metallique de Hollande. Amsterdam, 1688–90. 3 v. 8°. . M,386
Björnson, B. Arne; a Sketch of Norwegian Country Life. Lond. 1866. 8°. . K,738
Black, A. and C. General Atlas of the World. Edinburgh, 1853. f°. . R.R.
The same. London, 1870. f°. . . . . . . . . . *Q,469
Black Country, Walks in the. E. Burritt. London, 1868. 8°. . . . V,394
Black, J. System of Teaching Languages, v. 2. London, 1826. 12°. . . L,806
Black, W.A. (Ed.) Enterlude of J. Bon and Mast Person. Lond. 1852. 12°. L,606,30
Blackboard in the Primary School. Boston, 1841. 16°. . . . . . O,932
Black Dwarf. Sir W. Scott. Boston, 1858. 12°. . . . . . . K,928
The same. Philadelphia, 1869. 8°. . . . . . K,1106
The same. Leipzig, 1868. 16°. . . . . . . . J,439
Black-Forest Village Stories. B. Auerbach. New York, 1869. 12°. . G,178
Black Hawk, Life of; edited by J. B. Patterson. Cincinnati, 1833. 12°. . C,917
Black Man, The; his Antecedents, etc. W. W. Brown. Boston, 1863. 12°. . C,534
Black Sea, and Caspian, Nations near. A. von Haxthausen. Lond. 1854. 8°. V,703
Black Sheep. E. Yates. Leipzig, 1867. 2 v. in 1. 16°. . . . . . J,537
Blackburn, H. Artists and Arabs; Sketching in Sunshine. Lond. 1868. 8°. V,805
Blackburn, W. M. W. Farel; and Story of Swiss Reform. Edinb. 1867. 12°. D,698
Blackie, J. S. Homer and the Iliad. Edinburgh, 1866. 4 v. 8°. . . U,436
Blackie, W. G. Imperial Gazetteer. Glasgow, 1855. 2 v. r. 8°. . . L. R.
Blackstone, Sir W. Commentaries; ed. G. Sharswood. Phila. 1869. 2 v. 8°. U,502
edited by J. L. Wendell. New York, 1854. 4 v. 8° . . U,505
Extracts from his Commentaries. S. Warren. London, 1837. . . U,501
Blackstone, The Comic. G. A. à Beckett. Philadelphia, n. d. 12°. . . U,482

Blackwall, J. Spiders of Great Britain and Ireland. Lond. 1861. 2 v. 4°. . Q,75
Blackwell, R. Original Acrostics. St. Louis, 1869. 12°. . . . . I,288
Blackwood, F. T., *Lord Dufferin.* Yacht Voyage to the North. Bost. 1869. 12°. V,322
Reise nach Island und Spitzbergen. Braunschweig, 1860. 8°. . . E,172
Blackwood's Edinburgh Magazine. Edinburgh, 1817-67. 101 v. 8°. . . R.1
Blaikie, W. G. Heads and Hands in World of Labour. London, 1865. 16°. H,468
Blakal, G. Brieffe Narration of Services, etc. See *Spalding Club. Pub.* v 17.
Blaine, D. P. Encyclopædia of Rural Sports. London, 1852. 8°. . *M,316
Blainville, H. M. D. de. Conchyliologie et Malacologie. Paris, 1816-30. 8°. Q,337,6
Vers et Zoophytes. Paris, 1816-30. 2 v. in 1. 8°. . . . . Q,337,11
Blair, H. Lectures on Rhetoric and Belles Lettres. Philadelphia, 1829. 8°. L,597
Blair, J. Chronological Tables. London, 1856. p. 8°. . . . . . L,272
Blair, R. Poetical Works; with Life by G. Gilfillan. New York, 1854. 8°. . J,851
Blake, J. Manners and Customs of all Nations. New York, 1853. 12°. V,1050
Blake, J. L. General Biographical Dictionary. Boston, 1854. 8°. . . *C,622
Family Text-Book for the Country. New York, 1856. 12°. . . M,541
Blake, R., Life of. J. Gorton. London, n. d. 8°. . . . . . . C,581
Blake, W. P. Geological Reconnoissance in California. New York, 1858. 4°. Q,49
Blakely, J. Theology of Inventions. New York, 1856. 12°. . . . P,85
Blakey, R. Angling Literature of all Nations. London, 1856. 12°. . . M,303
History of Philosophy of the Mind. London, 1850. 4 v. 8°. . . O,677
Shooting; Manual of Practical Information. London, n. d. 16°. . M,339
Blameless Prince. E. C. Stedman. Boston, 1869. 16°. . . . . I,144
Blanc, C. Painters of all Nations; illustrated. London, 1855. 4°. . *Q,179
Blanc, H. Captivity in Abyssina. London, 1868. 12°. . . . . . V,804
Blanc, L. Historical Revelations, 1848. London, 1858. 8°. . . . B,245
History of Ten Years, 1830-1840. Philadelphia, 1848. 2 v. 12°. . B,246
The same. London, 1844-45. 2 v. 8°. . . . . . B,371
Bland, M. Algebraical Problems. London, 1849. 8°. . . . M,1122
Geometrical Problems. London, 1842. 8°. . . . . M,1132
Bland, W. Construction of Arches, Piers, etc. London, 1867. 12°. . . M,829
Ships and Boats. London, 1868. 12°. . . . . . . . M,830
Blast Furnaces, Erwärming der Gebläseluft. S.A.W. v. Herder. Freib.'40. 8°. N,252,18
Blasting Rocks and Quarrying. Sir J. Burgoyne. London, 1856. 12°. . M,894
Blaze de Bury, *Baroness.* Germania; Germany as it is. Lond. 1851. 2v. 8°. V,432
Bleaburn, Sickness and Health of People of. Boston, 1853. 16°. . . K,239
Bleachery, Vollständige Bleich-Kunde. J. C. Leuchs. Nürnberg, 1845. 8°. N,252,13
Bleak House. C. Dickens. New York, 1868. 12°. . . . . . . K,468
The same. Philadelphia, 1853. 8°. . . . . . . . K,504
The same. New York, 1871. 2 v. 12°. . . . . . K,1128
The same. Leipzig, 1852. 4 v. 16°. . . . . . . J,114
Blegewyrd. Annales Cambriæ. London, 1860. 8°. . . . . . . W,170
Blenkarn, J. British Timber Trees. London, 1859. 8°. . . . . . N,950
Blennerhassett, H., Life of; and Burr Expedition. W.H.Safford. Cin.1859. 12°. C,746
Blessington, Countess of. See *Gardiner, M.*
Blinn, L. J. Tin, Sheet-Iron, and Copper-Plate Workers. Phil. 1869. 12°. M,671
Bliss, Mrs. Practical Cook-Book. Philadelphia, 1867. 12°. . . . H,296
Blithedale Romance. N. Hawthorne. Boston, 1852. 16°. . . . K,158
The same. Boston, 1868. 12°. . . . . . . . U,40,8
Blodget, L. Climatology of the United States. Philadelphia, 1857. 8°. . N,145

Blomfield, C. J., and others. Greek and Roman Philosophy and Science. London, 1853. 12°. . . . . . . . . . . . . . o,633
Blomfield, E. Lectures on Philosophy of History. London, 1819. 4°. . F,225
Blondel, D. Treatise of the Sibyls. London, 1661. f°. . . . . . Q,264
Blood, Analyse des Blutes. G. Zimmermann. Berlin, 1847. 8°. . N,252,32
Analysis du Sang. G. Andral, et J. Gavarret. Paris, 1842. 8°. . N,252,14
Chemical Composition of Human. T. Richardson. n. t. p. 8°. N,252,1
Etudes Chimiques sur le Humain. R.E. Le Canu. Paris, 1837. 4°. N,252,57
Hématologie Pathologique. G. Andral. Paris, 1845. . . N,252,14
Blot, P. Hand-Book of Practical Cookery. New York, 1868. 12°. . . H,297
Blount, T. Boscobel Tracts; relating to Charles II. Edinburgh, 1857. 8°. . A,518
Blowpipe in Chemistry and Mineralogy. J. J. Berzelius. Boston, 1845. 8°. N,206
Instruction in Practical Use of. New York, 1858. 12°. . . . N,204
Bloxam, C. L. Chemistry, Inorganic and Organic. London, 1867. 8°. . N,213
Hand-Book of Chemistry. Philadelphia, 1854. 8°. . . . . . N,202
Bloxam, T. Sandstones of Craigleith. Edinburgh, 1858. 8°. . . N,252,44
Blue Laws of the Early Colonies. R. R. Hinman. Hartford, 1838. 12°. . C,2
Blücher, G. L. von, Life and Campaigns of. Count Gneisenau. Lond. 1815. 8°. D,517
Blum, J. R. Lithurgik; oder, Mineralien und Felsarten. Stuttgart, 1840. 8°. G,812,1
Pseudomorphosen des Mineralreichs. Stuttgart, 1847. 8°. . N,252,35
Blumenhagen, W. Wanderung durch den Harz. Leipzig, n. d. 12°. . E,183
The same. Leipzig, n. d. 8°. . . . . . . . E,186,5
Blunders, Book of. C. C. Bombaugh. Philadelphia, 1861. 16°. . . H,50
Blunt, C. F. Beauty of the Heavens. London, 1849. 4°. . . . . . N,329
Blunt, I. J. Sketch of the Reformation in England. London, 1832. 16°. I,603
Blunt, J. Shipmasters' Assistant. New York, 1851. 8°. . . . . . U,528
Boardman, H. A. Bible in the Counting-House. Philadelphia, 1853. 12°. P,210
Bible in the Family. Philadelphia, 1869. 12°. . . . . . . P,246
Boardman, W. A. Haps and Mishaps in the Brown Family. Phila. 1870. 16°. J,1708
Mother-in-Law. Philadelphia, 1870. 16°. . . . . . . . J,1710
Nellie Gates. Philadelphia, 1870. 16°. . . . . . . J,1709
Sister's Triumph. Philadelphia, 1870. 16°. . . . . . J,1711
Boat-Club Series. W. T. Adams. Boston, 1870. 6 v. 16°. . . . J,1435

Vol. 1. Boat Club. 2. All Aboard. Vol. 3. Now or Never. 4. Little by Little. Vol. 5. Try Again. 6. Poor and Proud.

Boat-Life in Egypt and Nubia. W. C. Prime. Philadelphia, 1867. 8°. . V,829
Boats, and Coast Scenery, Studies of. S. Prout. London, 1816. 4°. . *Q,195
Bobbin Boy; How Nat got his Learning. W. M. Thayer. Boston, 1863. 16°. J,1293
Boccaccio, G. Decameron; translated by W. K. Kelly. London, 1869. *L,328
Bock, C. E. Hand-Atlas der Anatomie des Menschen. Berlin, 1860. f°. *Q,292
Bode, A. Anleitung zum Torfbetriebe in Ruszland. Mitau, 1846. 16°. N,252,38
Bodily Strength and Skill, Wonders of. G. Depping. New York, 1871. 12°. M,1062
Body and Mind, Reciprocal Influence of. W. Newnham. Lond. 1842. 8°. O,675
Body, Use of, in Relation to the Mind. G. Moore. New York, 1854. 16°. O,652
Boece, H. Metrical Version of his Chronicles of Scotland, v. 1, 2, 3. W. Stewart. London, 1858–63. 3 v. 8°. . . . . . . . . . W,156
Böckh, A. Public Economy of the Athenians. Boston, 1857. 8°. . . A,99
Staatshaushaltung der Athener u. Tafeln. Berl. 1817. 4 v. 8° and 4°. G,609
Boegner, J. Entstehung der Quellen. Frankfurt-a-M. 1843. 16°. . N,252,38
Erdbeben und seine Erscheinungen. Frankfurt, 1847. 8°. . N,252,35

Boelker, B. Constitution of France. Boston, 1848. 12°. . . . . . S.C.
Bölte, A. Franziska von Hohenheim. Hannover, 1863. 2 v. 16°. . . G,261
Frau von Staël. Biographischer Roman. Wien, 1861. 3 v. 24°. . G,262
Boerne, L. Gesammelte Schriften. Milwaukee, Wis. 1858. 5 v. 8°. . E,312
Boethius. De Consolatione Philosophiæ; tr. by Chaucer. Lond. 1868. 8°. L,604,5
Böttger, A. Albion; Perlen Britischer Lyrik. Leipzig, n. d. 16°. . E,258
Gedichte. Leipzig, 1850. 16°. . . . . . . . . . . E,259
Boethius, A. M.S. De Consolatione Philosophiæ; King Alfred's Anglo-Saxon Version; translated by S. Fox. London, 1864. p. 8°. . . . L,2
Böttiger, K. W. Geschichte Sachsens. Hamburg, 1830–31. 2 v. 8°. . E,81
Weltgeschichte in Biographien. Berlin, 1839–40. 3 v. 8°. . . E,7
Bogart, W. H. Daniel Boone and Hunters of Kentucky. Bost. 1870. 16°. C,911
Bogue, D. Divine Authority of the New Testament. New York, n. d. 18°. P,746,18
Bohemia. Geschichte von Böhmen. F. Palacky. Prag, 1844–65. 5 v. in 9. 8°. E,78
Bohn, H. G. Hand-Book of Games. London, 1867. p. 8°. . . . L,292
Modern Geography. London, 1865. p. 8°. . . . . . L,137
Polyglot of Foreign Proverbs. London, 1857. p. 8°. . . . L,24
Pottery, Porcelain, and Objects of Vertu. London, 1857. p. 8°. . L,142
Young Lady's Book. London, 1859. p. 8°. . . . . . . L,165
Bohne, W. Gutta Percha in techn. Bedeutung. Iserlohn, n. d. 16°. N,252,38
Bohny, N. New Picture Book. Edinburgh, 1858. 8°. . . . . Q,199
Boileau, D. Analytical Dictionary of French Nouns. London, 1827. 12°. L,803
Boileau-Despréaux, N. Œuvres. Paris, 1856. 12°. . . . . . . H,992
Œuvres Poetiques. Paris, 1853. 8°. . . . . . . H,1002
Boissy, T. G., *Marquise* de. My Recollections of Lord Byron. N. Y. 1869. 8°. D,75
Boitard, P. Manuel de l'Architecte des Jardins. Paris, 1834. 18°. . . M,593
Boiteau d'Ambly, P. Cartes à Jouer. London, 1859. 16°. . . . M,325
Boker, G. H. Königsmark; Legend of the Hound, etc. Phil. 1869. 12°. I,10
Plays and Poems. Boston, 1857. 2 v. 12°. . . . . . . I,11
Poems of the War. Boston, 1864. 12°. . . . . . . . I,9
Bojesen, E. F. C. Manual of Grecian Antiquities. New York, 1854. 12°. A,72
Bokhara; its Amir and People. Khanikoff. London, 1845. 8°. . . V,700
Mission to, 1843–45. J. Wolff. New York, 1845. 8°. . . . V,702
Boldon, B. Possessions of the See of Durham. Durham, 1852. 8°. . F,126,25
Bolingbroke, *Lord.* See *St. John, H.*
Bolley, P. A. Manual of Technical Analysis. London, 1857. 12°. . . L,274
Bolton, S. Treatises on Religious Subjects. London, 1656. 8°. . . . P,181
Boleyn, Anne, Life of. E. O. Benger. Philadelphia, 1852. 12°. . . D,380
Bombaugh, C. C. Book of Blunders. Philadelphia, 1871. 16°. . . H,45
Bombet, L. A. C., *pseud.* See *Beyle, H.*
Bonaparte, C. L. American Ornithology. Edinburgh, 1831. 4 v. 16°. . O,80
Bonaparte, L. Charlemagne; an Epic Poem. London, 1815. 2 v. 4°. . U,590
Bonaparte, J. Correspondence with Napoleon. New York, 1856. 2 v. 12°. D,671
History of. J. S. C. Abbott. New York, 1869. 16°. . . . J,1716
Bonar, H. Hymns of Faith and Hope. New York, 1868. 3 v. 16°. . I,105
Bond, G. P. Observations on Great Nebula of Orion. Cambridge, 1867. 4°. Q,106,5
Bond, H. Family Memorials of Watertown. Boston, 1855. 2 v. in 1. 8°. C,56
Bond, J. W. Minnesota and its Resources. New York, 1854. 12°. . . C,186
Bond, W. Hand-Book of the Telegraph. London, 1870. 12°. . . . M,831
Boner, C. Forest Creatures. London, 1861. 12°. . . . . . . N,634

Bones, Crushed, as a Manure. C. W. Johnson. London, 1836. 8°. . N,252,25
Diseases of. E. Stanley. London, 1849. 8°. . . . . . . L,931
Bonnechose, E. de. History of France. London, 1868. 2 v. 8°. . . B,342
Bonner, J. Child's History of Greece. New York, n. d. 2 v. 16°. . J,1442
of Rome. New York, 1856. 2 v. 16°. . . . . J,1422
of the United States. New York, 1866. 3 v. 16°. . J,1248
Bonneville, Capt., Adventures of. W. Irving. New York, 1867. 12°. . U,26
Bonnycastle, Sir R. H. Canada; as it was and is. London, 1852. 2 v. 12°. V,178
Newfoundland in 1842. London, 1842. 2 v. 12°. . . . . . V,177
Bononi, J. Nineveh and its Palaces. London, n. d. 8°. . . . . V,676
The same. London, 1857. p. 8°. . . . . . . . . L,95
Bonpland, A., and Humboldt, A. von. See *Humboldt, A. von.* . . . V,257
Book for a Corner. L. Hunt. New York, 1852. 12°. . . . . . H,582
Book of Blunders. C. C. Bombaugh. Philadelphia, 1871. 16°. . . H,45
Book of Common Prayer, History of. T. Lathburg. Oxford and Lond. 1858. 8°. P,900
Illustration of the. C. Wheatley. London, 1857. p. 8°. . L,247
Book of Costume. London, 1847. 8°. . . . . . . . . . M,368
Book of Days; edited by R. Chambers. Edinburgh, 1863-64. 2 v. 8°. . I,591
Book of Deer; edited by J. Stuart. See *Spalding Club Pub.*, v. 36.
Book of Holy Wisdom, v. 1. P. Bates. Canterbury, N. H. 1849. 12°. . P,300
Book of Orm. R. Buchanan. London, 1870. 12°. . . . . . . I,299
Book of Rights. J. O'Donovan. Dublin, 1847. 8°. . . . . . . L,812
Book of Snobs. W. M. Thackeray. Boston, 1869. 12°. . . . K,1038,3
The same. Philadelphia, 1866. 12°. . . . . . K,1087,1
The same. Leipzig, 1849. . . . . . . . . . J,484,1
Book of Trades. J. Wylde. London, 1866. 16°. . . . . . . M,668
Book of the Illustrious Henries. J. Capgrave. London, 1858. 8°. . . B,65
Book-Binding, Art of. J. B. Nicholson. Philadelphia, 1856. 12°. . . M,620
Nouveau Manuel du Relieur. S. Lenormand. Paris, 1840. 18°. . M,595
Book-Hunter. J. H. Burton; ed. by R. G. White. New York, 1863. 8°. . L.R.
Book-Keeping. S. W. Crittenden. Philadelphia, 1866. 8°. . . M,1179
P. Duff. New York, 1868. 8°. . . . . . . . . . M,1171
J. C. Smith. Cincinnati, 1853. 8°. . . . . . . . . M,1170
and Business Manual. H. W. Ellsworth. New York, 1868. 16°. M,1164
Elements of. J. Morrison. London, n. d. 8°. . . . . . M,1169
Practical. J. C. Smith. Cincinnati, 1853. 8°. . . . . . M,1170
Practical System of. I. Mayhew. New York, 1854. 12°. . M,1088
Treatise on. S. W. Crittenden. Philadelphia, 1853. 12°. . M,1167
Books and Men, Anecdotes of. J. Spence. London, 1858. 16°. . . . H,575
and Reading. N. Porter. New York, 1871. 12°. . . . . O,985
Rarest, in the English Language. J. P. Collier. N. Y. 1866. 4 v. 8°. L.R.
Transmission of Ancient. I. Taylor. London, 1859. 8°. . . H,722
Boole, G. Treatise on Differential Equations. Cambridge, 1865. 12°. M,1147
Investigation of the Laws of Thought. London, 1854. 8°. . . O,690
Boone, D., Adventures of. G. Imlay. London, 1793. 8°. . . . . . V,44
and the Hunters of Kentucky. W. H. Bogart. Boston, 1870. 16°. . C,911
Life of. C. B. Hartley. Philadelphia, 1865. 12°. . . . J,1234
Boorde, A. Dyetary of Helth, 1542. London, 1870. 8°. . . . L,604,10
Introduction of Knowledge, 1547. London, 1870. 8°. . . L,604,10
Booth, J. Education and Educational Institutions. London, 1846. 8°. O,1251,2

Booth, J. Theory of Elliptic Integrals. London, 1851. 8°. . . M,1152
Booth, J. B., Life of; by his daughter. New York, 1866. 12°. . . . D,227
Booth, J. C. Phonographic Instructor. Philadelphia, 1850. 18°. . . L,671
Booth, M. L. Clock and Watchmakers' Manual. New York, 1863. 12°. . M,625
Bopp, F. Comparative Grammar of Sanscrit, etc. London, 1862. 3 v. 8°. L,531
Glossarium Comparativum Linguæ Sanscritæ. Berolini, 1866. 4°. . L.R.
Grammaire Comparée des Langues Indo-Europe. Paris, 1869. 4 v. 8°. L,538
Vergleichende Grammatik des Sanskrit, etc. Berlin, 1859–68. 3 v. 8°. G,582
Border Beagles. W. G. Simms. New York, 1864. 12°. . . . . . K,248
Border and Bastile. G. A. Lawrence. Leipzig, 1863. 16°. . . . J,255
Borneo, Expedition to. H. Keppel. New York, 1846. 12°. . . . V,235
Borrow, G. Bible in Spain. Philadelphia, 1843. 8°. . . . . . V,476
Roving Adventures. Cincinnati, 1852. 8°. . . . . . . K,600
Zincali; the Gypsies of Spain. London, 1861. 12°. . . . . D,705
Bosanquet, J. W. Fall of Nineveh. London, 1853. 8°. . . . . . A,328
Boscobel Tracts; relating to Charles II. T. Blount. Edinburgh, 1857. 8°. A,518
Boss, H. R. Early Newspapers in Illinois. Chicago, 1870. 4°. . . . F,172
Bossuet, J. B. Chefs-d'Œuvre Oratoires. Paris, 1855. 2 v. 8°. . H,1003
Discours sur l'Histoire Universelle. Paris, 1855. 12°. . . . P,59
Oraisons Funèbres de. Paris, 1855. 12°. . . . . . . . . P,60
Sermons Choisis. Paris, 1855. 12°. . . . . . . . . . P,58
Variations of the Protestant Churches. New York, 1836–42. 2 v. 12°. P,568
Boston, Board of Trade Reports, 1862–63. Boston, 1862–63. 2 v. 8°. . O,596
Board of Education, Report. Boston, 1848. 8°. . . . O,1262
City Hospital, Report, 1870. Boston, 1870. 8°. . . . L,1022
East, History of. W. H. Sumner. Boston, 1858. 8°. . . . C,81
History and Antiquities of. S. G. Drake. Boston, 1856. 8°. . . C,62
Boston Athenæum. J. Quincy. Cambridge, 1851. 8°. . . O,829
the Second Church. C. Robbins. Boston, 1852. 8°. . . C,83
in Colonial Times; or, Sir C. H. Frankland. E. Nason. Albany, 1865. 8°. C,53
Lectures, 1870. Christianity and Scepticism. Boston, 1870. 12°. . P,151
List of Persons taxed on $10,000. Boston, 1863. 8°. . . . B,809,2
Massacre, March 5, 1770. F. Kidder. Albany, 1870. 8°. . . B,748
Mercantile Library Catalogue. Boston, 1854. 8°. . . . . . L.R.
The same. Boston, 1870. 8°. . . . . . . . . . L.R.
Ministry at Large. J. Tuckerman. Boston, 1838. 12°. . . . P,49
Municipal History of. J. Quincy. Boston, 1852. 8°. . . . C,60
Public Library; Annual Reports, 1852–70. Boston, 1852–70. 2 v. 8°. L.R.
Bulletins, nos. 1–17. Boston, 1867–71. 8°. . . . . . L.R.
Catalogue of Books in Bates Hall. Boston, 1861. 8°. . . L.R.
First Supplement to the same. Boston, 1866. 8°. . . L.R.
Catalogue of Books in Lower Hall. Boston, 1858. 8°. . . L.R.
of the East Boston Branch. Boston, 1871. 8°. . . L.R.
Dedication of the Building. Boston, 1858. 8°. . . . L.R.
Finding Lists. Boston, 1868–71. 8°. . . . . . . L.R.
Memorial of J. Bates. Boston, 1865. 8°. . . . . . C,982
Presentation of Bust and Portrait of J. Bates. Bost. 1866. 4°. L.R.
Prince Library Catalogue. Boston, 1870. 8°. . . . . L.R.
Record of the Boston Stage. W. W. Clapp. Boston, 1853. 12°. . I,714
Schoolmasters' Controversy with H. Mann. Boston, 1844–46. 8°. *O,927

Boston, Siege of, and Battle of Bunker Hill. R. Frothingham. Bost. 1849. 8°. C,43
Watch and Police, History of. E. H. Savage. Boston, 1865. 8°. . O,364
Boston, T., Life of, written by himself. Aberdeen, 1852. 8°. . . . D,442
Boswell, J. Life of Samuel Johnson. New York, 1854. 2 v. 8°. . . D,358
The same. Boston, n. d. . . . . . . . . . . S.C.
The same. New York, 1858. 4 v. 12°. . . . . D,152
Tour to the Hebrides. London, 1852. 8°. . . . . . . V,363
Bosworth, J. Anglo-Saxon and English Dictionary. London, 1855. 8°. . L.R.
Botanical and Physiological Memoirs. A. Henfrey. London, 1853. 8°. O,306
Botanical Companion. J. H. Balfour. Edinburgh, 1860. 12°. . . N,944
Botanical Dictionary. J. Paxton and J. Lindley. London, 1849. 8°. . N,943
Botanical Register. London, 1815–47. 33 v. 8°. . . . . . . R,31
Botanical Text-Book. A. Gray. New York, 1850. 8°. . . . . . N,972
Botanische Zeitung. H. von Mohl. Berlin, 1843–49. 7 v. 4°. . . . G,858
Botany, Æsthetik der Pflanzenwelt. F. T. Bratranek. Leipzig, 1853. 8°. . G,859
Antediluvian Phytology. E. T. Artis. London, 1838. 4°. . . Q,120
Beautiful-Leaved Plants. E. J. Lowe. London, 1865. 8°. . . N,1037
Bericht über Botanik. A. H. R. Grisebach. Berl. 1845–56. 11 v. 8°. G,870
Botanische Terminologie. G. W. Bischoff. Nürnberg, 1830–44. 3 v. 4°. G,962
Botan. Unterhaltungen. B. Auerswald u. Rossmäszler. Leip. 1858. 8°. G,855
Class-Book of. J. H. Balfour. Edinburgh, 1852. 8°. . . N,1007
F. H. Green and J. W. Congdon. New York, 1856. 4°. . N,1033
A. Wood. Claremont, N. H. 1851. 12°. . . . . N,977
Cryptogamic. M. J. Berkeley. London, 1857. 8°. . . N,1000
of Scotland. R. K. Grenville. Edinburgh, 1823–8. 6 v. 8°. N,1032
der Alten Griechen und Römer. H. O. Lenz. Gotha, 1859. 8°. . . G,882
Descriptive and Physiological. J. S. Henslow. London, 1836. 12°. M,1039
Dichalamydeous Plants, History of. G. Don. London, 1831–38. 4 v. 4°. Q,12
Dissertationes Botanicæ. C. v. Linnæus. Lugd. Batav. 1749–85. 9 v. 8°. N,966
Economic. T. C. Archer. London, 1853. 16°. . . . . N,915
Elements of. A. de Jussieu; edited by J. H. Wilson. Lond. 1855. p. 8°. L,301
T. Moore. London, 1765. 16°. . . . . . . . N,928
Field. A. Catlow. London, 1852. 16°. . . . . . . . N,916
for Young People. A. Gray. New York, 1859. 4°. . . . N,948
Fossil. S. R. Pattison. London, 1849. 12°. . . . . N,604
Geschichte der Botanik. E. H. F. Meyer. Königsberg, 1854–57. 4 v. 12°. G,884
Greenhouse. A. Catlow. London, 1857. 16°. . . . . N,917
Grundzüge der Botanik. S. Endlicher und F. Unger. Wein, 1843. 8°. G,866
Icones Anatomico-Botanicæ. H.F.Link. Berlin, 1837–38. 3 v. in 1. f°. Q,86
Introduction to. A. Gray. New York, 1865. 12°. . . . N,991
J. Lindley. London, 1835. 8°. . . . . . . . N,978
Journal of. Sir W. J. Hooker. 1834–42. 4 v. 8°. . . N,1008
Ladies'. J. Lindley. London, n. d. 2 v. 8°. . . . N,1035
Lehrbuch der Botanik. G. W. Bischoff. Stutt. 1834–39. 4 v. in 5. 8°. G,812,3–7
Lessons in Elementary. D. Oliver. London, 1864. 16°. . . N,911
Magazine of Zoölogy and. Edinburgh, 1837-38. 2 v. 8°. . . R,29
Manual of. J. H. Balfour. Edinburgh, 1863. 12°. . . . N,975
of British. C. C. Babington. London, 1847. 12°. . . . N,949
of Structural. M. C. Cooke. London, n. d. 18°. . . . M,909
Medicinisch-Pharmaceutische Botanik. M.J.Schleiden. Leip. 1852. 8°. G,895

Botany, Miscellaneous Works on. R. Brown. London, 1866. 8°. . . . O,310
Natural System of. J. Lindley. London, 1836. 8°. . . N,1019
Nervation der Celastrineen. C. R. von Ettingshausen. Wien, 1857. 4°. F,98
of Captain Beechey's Voyage. Sir W. J. Hooker and G. A. W. Arnott. London, 1841. 4°. . . . . . . . . Q,113
of Northern United States. L. C. Beck. New York, 1848. 8°. . N,952
A. Gray. Boston, 1848. 12°. . . . . . . . N,974
The same. New York, 1856. 8°. . . . . N,973
of United States Expl. Expedition, Atlas. A. Gray. N.Y. 1857. f°. Q,354
Outlines of. J. H. Balfour. Edinburgh, 1862. 8°. . . . N,939
Pflanze und ihr Leben. M. J. Schleiden. Leipzig, 1854. 8°. . G,896
Pflanzendecke der Erde. L. Rudolph. Berlin, 1859. 8°. . . . G,892
Atlas to the same. Berlin, 1864. f°. . . . . . . Q,131
Pflanzenkunde in Populärer Darstellung. M. Seubert. Leip. 1861. 8°. G,900
Pflanzenzelle. H. Schacht. Berlin, 1852. 8°. . . . . G,902
Philosophische Botanik. F. T. Kützing. Leip. 1851–2. 2 v. in 1. 8°. G,878
Popular Economic. T. C. Archer. London, 1853. 16°. . . N,915
Posthumous Papers, parts 2, 3, 4. W. Griffith. Calcutta, 1849.–54. 4°. Q,126
Principles of Scientific. G. W. L. Bickley. Cincinnati, 1853. 8°. N,1038
M. J. Schleiden. London, 1849. 8°. . . . . . . N,1001
Reise des Prinzen Waldemar nach Ceylon. Berlin, 1862. 4°. . Q,127
Reports and Papers on. Ray Society. London, 1846. 8°. . . O,293
The same. London, 1849. 8°. . . . . . . . O,295
Rudiments of. A. Henfrey. London, 1858. 8°. . . . . N,938
Species Plantarum. Vienna, 1764. 2 v. 8°. . . . . N,964
Structur der Jubæa Spectabilis. P. Wossidlo. Jena, 1861. 4°. . Q,117
Sylva Brittanica; Portraits of Forest Trees. J. G. Strutt. Lon. 1826. f°. Q,350
System of. W. Curtis. London, 1777. 4°. . . . . . N,1034
Vermischte Botanische Schriften. R. Brown. Leip. 1825–34. 5 v. 8°. G,861
Wörterbuch der Beschreibenden Botanik. G.W. Bischoff. Stutt.'39. 8°. G,857
The same. Stuttgart, 1839. 8°. . . . . . . I,812,7
See also *Flora*.
Bothie of Toper-na-Fuosich; a Pastoral. A. H. Clough. Camb. 1849. 12°. I,323
Bothwell; a Poem. W. E. Aytoun. Boston, 1856. 16°. . . . . I,279
Both Sides of the Street. M. S. Walker. Boston, 1870. 16°. . . J,1539
Botta, C. Compendio della Storia d'Italia, 1534–1815. Parigi, 1834. 2v. 12°. B,483
War of Independence of the United States. Philad. 1820–1. 3 v. 8°. B,745
Botta, V. Dante as Philosopher, Patriot, and Poet. New York, 1865. 12°. D,727
Bottarelli, F. Pocket Dictionary, v. 2, 3 in 1. Venice, 1791. 8°. . . L.R.
Vol. 2. English, French, and Italian. Vol. 3. Francois, Italian, et Anglois.
Bottom of the Sea. L. Sonrel. New York, 1870. 12°. . . . M,1049
Botts, J. M. The Great Rebellion. New York, 1866. 12°. . . . B,905
Bouchardat, A. Végétation appliquée à l'Agriculture. Paris, 1846. 16°. N,252,26
Boucharlat, J. L. Calcul Différential et Calcul Intégral. Paris, 1838. 8°. M,1149
Boucher, F., Life of. C. Blanc. London, 1855. 4°. . . . . . Q,179
Boulay, C. E. du. Le Thresor des Antiqvitez Romaines. Paris, 1650. f°. F,237
Boulden, J. E. P. An American Among the Orientals. Philad. 1855. 12°. V,558
Boulton, M., Life of. S. Smiles. London, 1865. 8°. . . . . . D,59
Bound to John Company. New York, 1869. 8°. . . . . . . K,602
Bouquet, H. Expedition against Ohio Indians, 1764. Cincinnati, 1868. 8°. C,217

Bourdaloue, L. Sermons. Liege, 1784. 13 v. 12°. . . . . . . H,970
Bourne, A. Guano; Varieties, Analysis, etc. London, 1845. 8°. . N,252,6
Bourne, B. F. Captive in Patagonia. Boston, 1853. 12°. . . . . V,193
Bourne, H. R. F. Famous London Merchants. New York, 1869. 16°. . J,1670
Memoirs of English Merchants. London, 1866. 2 v. 8°. . . D,383
Memoir of Sir Philip Sidney. London, 1862. 8°. . . . . C,1269
Bourne, J. Catechism of the Steam Engine. New York, 1865. 12°. . . M,685
Hand-Book of the Steam Engine. New York, 1865. 12°. . . M,618
Treatise on the Steam Engine. London, 1868. 4°. . . . . *Q,267
Bourne, W. O. Gems from Fable Land. New York, 1853. 12°. . . J,1208
Bourrienne, F. de. Memoirs of Napoleon I. Edinburgh, 1830-31. 4 v. 16°. I,527
The same. Hartford, 1854. 8°. . . . . . . . D,560
Boussingault, J. B. J. D. Amerikanische Amalgamation. n. t. p. . N,252,30
Landwirthschaft in Beziehungen zur Chemie, etc. Halle, 1851-6. 4v. 8°. G,656
Rural Economy; its Relation with Chemistry. New York, 1856. 12°. M,521
Bouterwek, F. History of Spanish Literature; tr. by T. Ross. Lond. 1847. 12°. H,763
and Portuguese Literature. Lond. 1823. 2 v. 8°. . H,766
Boutron-Charlard, A. F. Analyse des Eaux de Paris. Paris, 1848. 8°. N,252,39
Bouton, N. History of Concord, N. H. Concord, 1856. 8°. . . . C,13
Bouverie, F. W. B. Story of Herbert Lovell. London, n. d. 16°. . J,1647
Bouvet, F. Turks in Europe. New York, 1853. 16°. . . . . C,490
Bouvier, H. M. Familiar Astronomy. Philadelphia, 1857. 8°. . . N,341
B. O. W. C. Series. J. De Mille. Boston, 1871. 3 v. 16°. . . J,1505

Vol. 1. The B. O. W. C. Vol. 2. Boys of Grand Pré School.
Vol. 3. Lost in the Fog.

Bowden, J. Norway; its People and Institutions. London, 1867. 8°. . V,544
Bowditch, N. I. Memoir of N. Bowditch. Boston, 1839. 4°. . . Q,104,4
Bowen, C. C. Visit to Peru. London, 1861. 8°. . . . . V,1086,1
Bowen, E. Coal and Coal Oil. Philadelphia, 1865. 8°. . . . . N,759
Bowen, F. American Political Economy. New York, 1870. 12° . . O,513
Life of Benj. Lincoln. Boston, 1860. 16°. . . . . . . C,860,23
of James Otis. Boston, 1860. 16°. . . . . . C,860,12
of Sir William Phips. New York, 1860. 16°. . . C,860,7
of Baron Steuben. New York, 1860. 16°. . . . C,860,9
Lowell Lectures; Metaphysics and Religion. Boston, 1849. 8°. . O,706
Bowen, G. F. Mount Athos, Thessaly, and Epirus. London, 1852. 12°. . V,567
Bowerbank, J. S. Monograph of British Spongiadæ. Lond. 1864-6. 2 v. 8°. O,308
Bowes, G. S. Illustrative Gatherings. Philadelphia, 1864. 12°. . . P,90
Bowes, R. Correspondence as Ambassador to Scotland. Lond. 1842. 8°. F,126,14
Bowler, G. Chapel and Church Architecture. Boston, 1856. f°. . . Q,389
Bowles, S. Across the Continent. Springfield, 1866. 12°. . . . . V,61
Our New West. Hartford, 1869. 8°. . . . . . . . V,111
Switzerland of America. Springfield, Mass. 1869. 16°. . . . V,3
Bowles, W. L. Poetical Works. New York, 1855. 2 v. 8°. . . . J,850
Bowley, M. Universal History on Scriptural Principles. Lond. n.d. 6v. 16°. A,5
Bowman, A. Bear Hunters of the Rocky Mountains. Phila. n. d. 16°. J,1603
Young Yachtsmen. London, n. d. 16°. . . . . . . J,1227
Bowman, J. E. Introduction to Practical Chemistry. Phila. 1864. 12°. . N,178
Bowman, S. M., and Irwin. Sherman and his Campaigns. N. Y. 1865. 8°. . B,931
Bowring, J. Ancient Poetry and Romances of Spain. London, 1824. 12°. I,161

Bowring, J. Matins and Vespers. London, 1823. 12°. . . . . . I,286
Poetry of the Magyars. London, 1830. 12°. . . . . . . I,176
Specimens of Russian Poetry. London, 1821–23. 2 v. in 1. 12°. . I,160
Boy Hunters. M. Reid. Boston, 1869. 16°. . . . . . . J,1561
Boy of Mount Rhigi. C. M. Sedgwick. Philadelphia, 1867. 16°. . J.1687
Boy Slaves. M. Reid. Boston, 1868. 12°. . . . . . . . J,1586
Boy Tar, The. M. Reid. Boston, 1866. 16°. . . . . . . J,1581
Boy's Annual; edited by E. Routledge. London, 1865–70. 6 v. 8°. . J,1350
Boy's Book of Trades. London, 1866. sm. 4°. . . . . . . J,1284
of Modern Travel. M. Johnes. London, n. d. 16°. . . J,1237
of Travel and Adventure. M. Johnes. New York, 1870. 12°. J,1639
Boy's Own Book of Natural History. J. G. Wood. London, 1861. 8°. . N,625
Boy's Play-Book of Science. J. H. Pepper. London, 1862. 8°. . . M,768
Boy's Sports and Pastimes. J. G. Wood. London, 1866. 8°. . . . M,300
Boys at Home. C. Adams. New York, 1870. 12°. . . . . . J,1640
at Dr. Murray's. W. J. Bradley. Boston, 1868. 16°. . . J,1682
of Grand Pré School. J. De Mille. Boston, 1871. 16°. . . J,1505,2
Boyd, A. K. H. Every-Day Philosopher. Boston, 1869. 12°. . . . H,306
Graver Thoughts of a Country Parson. Boston, 1869-65. 2 v. 12°. H,570
Leisure Hours in Town. Boston, 1869. 12°. . . . . . . H,555
Recreations of a Country Parson. Boston, 1869. 2 v. 12°. . . H,569
Boyer, A. Dict. François-Anglois et Anglois-François. Paris, 1797. 2 v. 8°. L.R.
History of the Reign of Queen Anne. London, 1703–8. 6v. 8°. . A,481
Life and Reign of Queen Anne. London, 1722. f°. . . . Q,310
Boyes, J. F. Life and Books. London, 1859. 16°. . . . . . . H,475
Boyhood of Great Men. J. G. Edgar. London, 1864. 8°. . . . J,1515
Boyle, A. F. Phonographic Class-Book. New York, 1848. 12°. . . L,690
Phonographic Reader. New York, 1848. 12°. . . . . . . L,691
Boynton, C. B. History of the Navy during the Rebellion. N.Y.1867–8. 2v. 8°. B,959
and Mason, T. B. Journey through Kansas. Cincinnati, 1855. 12°. V,100
Boynton, E. C. History of West Point. New York, 1864. 8°. . . . C,316
Bozman, J. L. History of Maryland. Baltimore, 1837. 2 v. 8°. . . C,124
Sketch of the History of Maryland. Baltimore, 1811. 8°. . . C,113
Brabrook, E. W. Law of Industrial and Provident Societies. Lond.1869. 12°. O,508
Bracciolini, P., Life of. W. Shepherd. London, 1837. 8°. . . . D,739
Brace, C. L. Home Life in Germany. New York, 1853. 12°. . . . V,417
Hungary in 1851. New York, 1853. 12°. . . . . . . V,427
New West; or, California in 1867–68. New York, 1869. 12°. . . V,153
Norse-Folk; Norway and Sweden. New York, 1859. 12°. . . V,541
Races of the Old World. New York, 1863. 8°. . . . . . N,416
Bracebridge Hall. W. Irving. New York, 1868. 16°. . . . . U,6
The same. New York, 1867. 12°. . . . . . . . . U,22
Brachiopoda, British Carboniferous. T. Davidson. London, 1848. 4°. . Q,32
Brachvogel, A. E. Beaumarchais; Historischer Roman. Leip. 1865. 4 v. 16°. G,263
Hamlet; Roman. Breslau, 1867. 3 v. 16°. . . . . . . G,264
Schubart und seine Zeitgenossen. Leipzig, 1864. 4 v. 16°. . . G,265
Brackenridge, H. M. Persons and Places in the West. Phila. 1834. 12°. V,8
The same; 2d edition. Philadelphia, 1868. 12°. . . . V,95
Whiskey Insurrection in Pennsylvania. Pittsburgh, 1859. 8°. . B,861
Braddock, E. History of his Expedition; ed. by W. Sargent. Phila. 1855. 8°. B,707

Braddock, J. Gunpowder. Madras, 1829. 8°. . . . . . . N,252,50
Braddon, M. E. Aurora Floyd. Leipzig, 1863. 2 v. in 1. 16°. . . . J,34
Dead-Sea Fruit. Leipzig, 1868. 2 v. in 1. 16°. . . . . . J,35
Doctor's Wife. Leipzig, 1864. 2 v. in 1. 16°. . . . . . . J,36
Eleanor's Victory. Leipzig, 1863. 2 v. in 1. 16°. . . . . . J,37
Henry Dunbar. Leipzig, 1864. 2 v. in 1. 16°. . . . . . J,38
John Marchmont's Legacy. Leipzig, 1864. 2 v. in 1. 16°. . . J,39
Lady Audley's Secret. Leipzig, 1862. 2 v. in 1. 16°. . . . J,40
Lady's Mile. Leipzig, 1866. 2 v. in 1. 16°. . . . . . . J,41
Only a Clod. Leipzig, 1865. 2 v. in 1. 16°. . . . . . . J,42
Run to Earth. Leipzig, 1869. 2 v. in 1. 16°. . . . . . . J,43
Rupert Godwin. Leipzig, 1867. 2 v. in 1. 16°. . . . . . J,44
Sir Jasper's Tenant. Leipzig, 1866. 2 v. in 1. 16°. . . . . J,45
Bradford, A. History of Massachusetts. Boston, 1835. 8°. . . . . C,47
of Massachusetts from 1764 to 1765. Boston, 1822. 8°. . C,50
of the Federal Government. Boston, 1840. 8°. . . . B,721
New England Chronology to 1820. Boston, 1843. 12°. . . . C,1
Bradford, A. W. American Antiquities and Red Race. N.Y. 1841. 8°. . B,606
Bradford, S. H. History of Peter the Great. New York, 1865. 16°. J,1357
Story of Columbus. New York, 1857. 12°. . . . . . J,1203
Bradford, W. History of Plymouth Plantation. Boston, 1856. 8°. . . C,61
Bradford, W. J. A. Notes on the North-West. New York, 1846. 12°. . C,164
Bradley, E. Nearer and Dearer. New York, 1864. 12°. . . . . . K,603
Bradley, J. W., and Goodwin, T.G. Manual of Illumination. Lond.1867. 12°. M,26,1
Bradley, M. E. Douglass Farm. New York, 1863. 16°. . . . J,1356
and Neely, K. J. Proverb Series. Boston, 1871. 6 v. 16°. . J,1700

Vol. 1. Birds of a Feather.
2. Fine Feathers do not make fine Birds.
3. Handsome is that handsome does.
4. Wrong confessed is half redressed.
5. One good turn deserves another.
6. Actions speak louder than words.

Bradley T. Geometry; Linear, Perspective, and Projection. Lond. n.d. 8°. M,1131
Bradley, W. J. Boys at Dr. Murray's. Boston, 1868. 16°. . . . J,1682
Donald Deane and his Cross. Boston, 1868. 16°. . . . J,1653
Gilbert Starr and his Lessons. Boston, 1870. 16°. . . . J,1676
Gilbert's Last Summer at Rainsford. Boston, 1870. 16°. . . J,1677
Jack Arcombe; Story of a Waif. Boston, 1870. 16°. . . J,1679
Miss Patience Hathaway. Boston, 1868. 16°. . . . . J,1655
Mr. Pendleton's Cup. Boston, 1868. 16°. . . . . . . J,1654
One-Armed Hugh. Boston, 1870. 16°. . . . . . . J,1680
Wheel of Fortune. Boston, 1870. 16°. . . . . . . . J,1681
Will Rood's Friendship. Boston, 1870. 16°. . . . . . J,1678
Brady, N., and Tate. Psalms of David, fitted to Tunes. Cambridge, 1831. 8°. P,429
Brady, R. Complete History of England. London, 1685–1700. 2 v. f°. F,286
Brage-Beaker with the Swedes. W. B. Jerrold. London, 1854. 12°. . . V,537
Bragelone. A. Dumas. Philadelphia, n. d. 8°. . . . . . . . H,981
Brain and Mind, Obscure Diseases of. F. Winslow. Philadelphia, 1866. 8°. L,930
Brainerd, D. Life from his Diary; edited by J. Edwards. N. Y. n. d. 18°. P,746,7
Life of. W. B. O. Peabody. New York. 16°. . . . . . C,860,8
Brainerd, J. Quartz Pebbles of Sandstone Conglomerate. Cleveland, 1854. 8°. T,19,2
Braithwaite, W. and J. Retrospect of Medicine, v. 1–51. Lond. 1842–65. 12°. L,952

Brambletye House. H. Smith. London, 1826. 3v. 12°. . . . . . J,649
Bramleighs of Bishop's Folly. C. Lever. Leipzig, 1868. 2 v. in 1. 16°. J,270
Brand, J. History of Newcastle-upon-Tyne. London, 1789. 2 v. 4°. . F,288
Popular Antiquities of Great Britain. London, 1849. 3 v. p. 8°. . L,3
Brande, W. T. Dictionary of Science, Literature, and Art. N. Y. 1870. 8°. L.R.
Manual of Chemistry. London, 1819. 8°. . . . . . . N,181
Tables of Definite Proportionals. London, 1828. 8°. . . . M,1160
Brandeburg, Mad. de; Historischer Roman. B. v. Guseck. Wein, 1863. 24°. G,295
Brandely, A. Traité des Manipulations Electro-Chimiques. Paris, 1848. 8°. N,252,34
Brandon, R., and J. A. Open Timber Roofs of Middle Ages. Lond. 1849. 4°. *Q176
Brant, J., Life of. W. L. Stone. Buffalo, 1851. 2 v. 8°. . . . . . C,724
Brassfounder's Manual. W. Graham. London, 1870. 12°. . . . M,842
Bratranek, F. T. Æsthetik der Pflanzenwelt. Leipzig, 1853. 8°. . . G,859
Brave Lady. D. M. Craik. New York, 1870. 8°. . . . . . . K,642
The same. Leipzig, 1870. 2 v. in 1. 16°. . . . . . J,83
Brave Old Salt. W. T. Adams. Boston, 1859. 16°. . . . . . J,1536,6
Bravo, The. J. F. Cooper. New York, 1867. 12°. . . . . . . K,25
The same. New York, 1859. 8°. . . . . . . . . K,79
Bray, C. Philosophy of Necessity. London, 1841. 2 v. 8°. . . . . O,682
Brayley, E. W. Beauties of England and Wales. Lond. 1801–15. 18v. in 25. 8°. *V,271
Londiniana. London, 1829. 4v. 16°. . . . . . . . V,296
Brazil and the Brazilians. J. C. Fletcher and D. P. Kidder. Boston, 1867. 8°. V,254
and La Plata. C. S. Stewart. New York, 1856. 12°. . . . V,238
Amazon, and Rio Madeira. London, 1862. 8°. . . . . V,1086,2
Explorations of the Highlands of. N. F. Burton. London, 1869. 2v. 8°. V,259
Journey to. L. and E. C. Agassiz. Boston, 1868. 8°. . . . V,255
Life in. T. Ewbank. New York, 1856. 8°. . . . . . . V,245
Reise nach Brasilien. H. Burmeister. Berlin, 1853. 12°. . . . E,176
A. P. Maximilian, *Prinz*. Frankfurt-a-M. 1820–21. 2 v. 4°. . Q,434
Atlas to the same. 2 portfolios. . . . . . . . Q,470
J. B. von Spix and C. F. P. Martius. München, 1823–31. 4 v. 4°. Q,427
Atlas to the same. 3 portfolios. . . . . . . . Q,471
Ten months in. J. Codman. Boston, 1867. 16°. . . . . . V,252
through a Naval Glass. E. Wilberforce. London, 1856. p. 8°. . I,659
Travels in. Adalbert, *Prince of Prussia*. London, 1849. 2 v. 8°. V,1071
Bread upon the Waters, etc. D. M. Craik. Leipzig, 1865. 16°. . . J,84
History of a Mouthful of. J. Mace. New York, 1868. 12°. . . L,901
Breakfast in Bed. G. A. Sala. Boston, 1863. 12°. . . . . . H,591
Breaking Away. W. T. Adams. Boston, 1868. 12°. . . . . J,1534,3
Breaking a Butterfly. G. A. Livingston. Leipzig, 1869. 2 v. in 1. 16°. . J,256
Bree, C. R. History of British Birds. London, 1866–67. 4 v. 8°. . . *O,124
Brees, S. C. Railway Practice. London, 1847–56. 3 v. in 1. 4°. . . Q,286
Plates to the same. London, 1849. f°. . . . . . . Q,315
Brehm, A. E. Leben der Vögel. Glogau, 1861. 8°. . . . . . G,934
and E. A. Rossmäszler. Thiere des Waldes. Leipzig, 1864–67. 2 v. 8°. G,936
Brehm, and Zimmermann, T. F. Zoologische Bilder. Hamburg, 1865. . G,932
Bremer, F. Brothers and Sisters. New York, 1867. 8°. . . . . . K,604
Hertha. New York, 1856. 12°. . . . . . . . . K,605
Home. New York, 1843. 8°. . . . . . . . . . . K,606
Homes of the New World. New York, 1853. 2 v. 12°. . . . . V,53

Bremer, F. Life in Sweden; President's Daughters; Nina. N. Y. n. d. 8°. K,584

in the Old World. Philadelphia, 1860. 2 v. 8°. . . . . . V,416

Letters, and Posthumous Works. New York, 1868. 12°. . . . D,767

Midnight Sun; a Pilgrimage. New York, 1860. 8°. . . . K,608

Neighbors. New York, 1842. 8°. . . . . . . . . K,609

Twelve Months with, in Sweden. London, 1866. 2 v. 8°. . . V,542

Gesammelte Schriften. Leipzig, 1857–64. 10 v. 12°. . . . E,313

B. 1. Tochter des Präsidenten.
2, 3. Das Haus.
4, 5. Die Nachbarn.
B. 6. 7. Nina.
8. H—— Familie.
9. Kleinere Erzählungen.
10. Streit und Friede.

Works; translated by M. Howitt. London, 1852. 4 v. 8°. . . L,169

Vol. 1. Neighbors; Hopes; Twins; Solitary; Comforter; Letter about Suppers; Trälinnan.
2. President's Daughters; Nina.
3. Home; Strife and Peace.
4. Diary; H—— Family; Axel and Anna.

Brentano, L. History of Guilds and Trades' Unions. London, 1870. 8°. L,605,40

Brett, W. H. Indian Tribes of Guiana. London, 1868. 8°. . . . V,246

Brettner, H. A. Lehrbuch der Geometrie. Breslau, 1853. 12°. . . E,430

Brewer, Complete Practical. M. L. Byrn. Philadelphia, 1869. 12°. . M,649

Brewer, E. C. Guide to Scientific Knowledge. London, 1869. 18°. . N,16

Sound and its Phenomena. London, 1863. 18°. . . . . . N,17

Brewster, Sir D. Kaleidoscope; its History and Construction. Lond. 1858. 8°. N,25

Letters on Natural Magic. New York, 1855. 18°. . . . . . L,374

The same. London, 1832. 16°. . . . . . . . . I,635

Life of Sir Isaac Newton. New York, 1831. 18°. . . . . . L,359

The same. London, 1831. 16°. . . . . . . . . I,635

Martyrs of Science. London, 1870. p. 8°. . . . . . . C,551

The same. New York, 1854. 16°. . . . . . . . . L,424

Memoirs of Sir Isaac Newton. Edinburgh, 1855. 2 v. 8°. . . D,295

More Worlds than One. New York, 1854. 12°. . . . . . N,260

Optics. London, 1831. 12°. . . . . . . . . . M,1024

Stereoscope; its History and Construction. London, 1856. 8°. . N,24

Brewster, G. Lectures on Education. Columbus, 1833. 8°. . . . . O,926

on the Origin of the Globe. Columbus, 1850. 12°. . . N,602

Brewster, W., Life of. A. Steele. Philadelphia, 1857. 8°. . . . . C,812

Brialmont, A. Life of the Duke of Wellington. London, 1858–60. 4 v. 8°. D,217

Brian O'Linn; Luck is Every-Thing. W. H. Maxwell. Lond. 1849. 3 v. in 1. 12°. K,688

Brick and Marble in the Middle Ages. G. E. Street. London, 1855. 8°. . M,203

Brick-Making and Tile-Making. E. Dobson. London, 1857. 12°. . . M,909

Bridal-Eve. E. D. E. N. Southworth. Philadelphia, 1870. 12°. . . K,413

Bride of Lammermoor. Sir W. Scott. Boston, 1852. 2 v. 16°. . . . K,930

The same. Philadelphia, 1869. 8°. . . . . . K,1108

The same. Leipzig, 1858. 16°. . . . . . . . J,440

of Llewellyn. E. D. E. N. Southworth. Philadelphia, 1870. 12°. . K,415

Bride's Fate. E. D. E. N. Southworth. Philadelphia, 1870. 12°. . . K,414

Bridel-Brideri, S. E. v. Muscologia Recentiorum, 3 pts. Gothæ, 1797–1801. N,895

Bridge Construction, General Theory of. H. Haupt. New York, 1853. 8°. M,701

Bridgeman, T. Young Gardener's Assistant. New York, 1865. 12°. . M,520

Bridges, J. H. France under Richelieu and Colbert. Edinb. 1866. 8°. . B,338

Bridges, Tubular and Girder. G. D. Dempsey. London, 1850. 12°. . M,906

Bridgewater Treatises. London, 1852-70. 10 v. p. 8°.

Bell, Sir C. The Hand. . . . . . . . . . . . L,311
Buckland, W. Geology and Mineralogy. 2 v. . . . . . L,280
Chalmers, T. Adaptation of Nature to Moral Constitution of Man. L,278
Kidd, J. Adaptation of Nature to Physical Condition of Man. . L,276
Kirby, W. History and Instincts of Animals. 2 v. . . . L,275
Prout, W. Chemistry, Meteorology, and Digestion. . . . L,279
Roget, P. M. Animal and Vegetable Physiology. 2 v. . . . L,281
Whewell, W. Astronomy and General Physics. . . . . L,277

Brief Remarker on the Ways of Man. E. Sampson. New York, 1855. 12°. H,210
Brierre de Boismont, A. Hallucinations. Philadelphia, 1853. 8°. . . O,693
Brigand; or, Demon of the North. V. Hugo. Philadelphia, n. d. 8°. . H,944
Brigham, A. Influence of Mental Cultivation on Health. Hartford, 1832. 12°. L,860
Bright, J. Speeches on Questions of Public Policy. London, 1869. 12°. H,772
Bright Days. M. Howitt. Boston, 1869. 12°. . . . . . . J,1667
Brightwell, C. L. Byepaths of Biography. London, n. d. 16°. . . . C,497
Heroes of the Laboratory and Workshop. London, 1859. 8°. . J,1250
Brillat-Savarin, M. Hand-Book of Dining. New York, 1865. 12°. . . H,305
Brine, L. Taeping Rebellion in China. London, 1862. 12°. . . . V,603
Brinley, F. Life of Wm. T. Porter. New York, 1860. 12°. . . . C,737
Brinton, D. G. Myths of the New World. New York, 1868. 8°. . . P,916
Brissot de Warville, J. P. New Travels in the U. S. London, 1792. 8°. . V,106
The same. Paris, 1791. 2 v. 8°. . . . . . . . V,43
Bristed, C. A. Five Years in an English University. N. Y. 1852. 2 v. 12°. O,812
Britain, Invasion of, by Julius Cæsar. T. Lewin. London, 1859. 8°. . A,493
British Admirals, Lives of. R. Southey. London, 1833-40. 5 v. 12°. M,1009
British Agriculture, State and Prospects of. W. Hutt. London, 1837. 8°. N,252,6
British America, L'Acadie; Explor. in. J. E. Alexander. Lond. 1849. 2v. 12°. V,174
Historical Account of. H. Murray. New York, 1848. 2 v. 16°. . L,407
British American Colonies, Trade of. T. D. Andrews. Washington, 1854. 8°. P.D.
British Ancestors, Our. S. Lysons. Oxford, 1865. p. 8°. . . . . N,439
British Assoc. for Advance. of Science, Reports. London, 1831-69. 39 v. 8°. . *R,23
British Biography. London, 1766-68. 4 v. 8°. . . . . . . . D,18
British Cabinet in 1853. Philadelphia, 1853. 16°. . . . . . C,1163
British Churches, Antiquities of. E. Stillingfleet. London, 1865. f°. *Q,304
British Colonies, Plan of Union. W. Kennedy. London, 1856. 12°. . P,563
Twelve Years' Wanderings in the. J. C. Byrne. Lond. 1848. 2 v. 8°. V,893
History, Extent, and Resources. R. M. Martin. London, n. d. 4°. N,252,53
British Eloquence. C. A. Goodrich. New York, 1853. 8°. . . . H,799
British Empire, Constitutional History of. G. Brodie. Lond. 1866. 3 v. 8°. B,54
History of. G. Brodie. Edinburgh, 1822. 4 v. 8°. . . . . . A,465
J. MacGregor. London, 1852. 2 v. 8°. . . . . . . A,412
in America. J. H. Wynne. London, 1770. 2 v. 8°. . . . . B,696
British Guiana, Reisen in, 1840-4. R. Schomburgk. Leip. 1847-8. 3 v. 8°. Q,429
British Heroes in Foreign Wars. J. Grant. London, 1865. 8°. . . . D,436
British Historians, Lives of the. E. Lawrence. New York, 1855. 2 v. 12°. D,406
British History. J. Wade. London, 1847. 8°. . . . . . . . . A,439
Biography, and Manners; ed. by E. Lodge. London, 1838. 3 v. 8°. A,524
Illustrations of. E. Lodge. London, 1791. 3 v. 4°. . . . . F,276
R. Thomson. Edinburgh, 1828. 2 v. 16°. . . . . . I,504
Catalogue of Materials for. T. D. Hardy. London, 1862-65. 3 v. 8°. W,176

British Islands, Gazetteer of. J. A. Sharp. London, 1852. 2 v. 8°. . . L.R.
Geological Maps of. I. A. Knipe. London, 1843. 2 v. 8°. . *N,791
British Legislation, Annals of. L. Levi. London, 1857–59. 4 v. 8°. . B,181
British Military Commanders. G. R. Gleig. London, 1831–32. 3 v. 12°. M,1008
British Museum, Ancient Marbles of. T. Combe. London, 1812–15. 4°. . Q,206
Catalogue of Mazatlan Shells. P. P. Carpenter. London, 1857. 8°. O,17
Elgin and Phigaleian Marbles. Sir H. Ellis. Lond. 1833. 2 v. 16°. L,475
Townley Gallery. London, 1836. 2 v. 16°. . . . . . . L,490
British Navy, Battles of the. J. Allen. London, 1852–53. 2 v. p. 8°. . L,91
History of. C. D. Yonge. London, 1863. 2 v. 8°. . . . . B,94
British Parliament; Chronological Register, 1708–1807. R. Beatson. London, 1807. 3 v. 8°. . . . . . . . . . . . . . A,462
British Plutarch; edited by T. Mortimer London, 1776. 6 v. 12°. . C,1188
Modern. W. C. Taylor. New York, 1846. 12°. . . . . . D,439
British Possessions in N. America, Geograph. View of. M. Smith. Balt. 1814. 24°. V,1027
British Public Characters, 1798–1805. London, 1798–1805. 6 v. 8°. . . C,580
British Spy, Letters of the. W. Wirt. New York, 1848. 12°. . . . H,215
British Statesmen, Lives of. J. Macdiarmid. London, 1807. 4°. . . F,24
Britons, History of the Ancient. J. A. Giles. Oxford, 1854. 2 v. 8°. . A,495
Brittan, S. B. Man and his Relations. New York, 1864. 8°. . . . N,431
Brittany and the Bible. I. Hope. London, 1853. p. 8°. . . . I,656,7
and the Chase. I. Hope. London, 1853. p. 8°. . . . I,656,7
and England; Livere de Reis de. London, 1865. 8°. . . . W,192
and La Vendée. E. Souvestre. New York, 1857. 12°. . . . H,950
Histoire de Bretagne. P. A. N. B. Daru. Paris, 1826. 3 v. 8°. . B,330
Vacation in. C. R. Weld. London, 1856. 12°. . . . . V,461
Britton, J. Public Buildings of London. London, 1823–28. 2 v. 4°. .*Q,344
and Brayley, E. W. Beauties of England and Wales. Lond. 1801–15. 18 v. in 25. 8°. . . . . . . . . . . . *V,271
Broadcast. N. Adams. Boston, 1863. 16°. . . . . . . . . P,146
Broadluck, C., *pseud.* See *Gazlay, A. W.*
Broadus, J. A. Preparation and Delivery of Sermons. Phila. 1870. 12°. . L,602
Brock, W. Biography of Sir Henry Havelock. Leipzig, 1858. 16°. . . J,47
Brockedon, W. Journals of Excursions in the Alps. London, 1833. 12°. V,502
Brocklesby, J. Elements of Astronomy. New York, 1859. 12°. . . N,324
of Meteorology. New York, 1855. 12°. . . . . . . N,106
Views of the Microscopic World. New York, 1851. 12°. . . . N,8
Broderip, W. J. Leaves from the Note-Book of a Naturalist. Lond. 1852. 12°. N,655
Zoological Recreations. London, 1849. 12°. . . . . . . N,656
Brodhead, J. R. History of the State of New York, 1609–1664. N.Y. 1853. 8°. C,98
Brodie, A. Diary, 1680–85. See *Spalding Club Publications*, v. 34.
Brodie, Sir B. C. Mind and Matter; Physiolog. Inquiries. N.Y. 1857. 12°. O,646
Psychological Inquiries. London, 1854–62. 2 v. in 1. 16°. . . O,694
Brodie, G. History of the British Empire. Edinburgh, 1822. 4 v. 8°. . A,465
The same; revised edition. London, 1866. 3 v. 8°. . . B,54
Brodie, P. B. Fossil Insects in Secondary Rocks of England. Lond. 1845. 8°. N,816
Brogden, J. Catholic Safeguards against Romish Errors. Lond. 1851. 3 v. 8°. P,814
Broken Hyacinth. M. M. Sherwood. New York, 1860. 12°. . . K,1008,4
Broken Lights; Inquiry on Religious Faith. F. P. Cobbe. Lond. 1864. 12°. P,261
Broken Pitcher; or, Ways of Providence. Chicago, 1870. 16°. . . J,1672

Broken to Harness. E. Yates. Boston, 1866. 12°. . . . . . K,1073
The same. Leipzig, 1866. 2 v. in 1. 16°. . . . . . J,538
Bromby, C. H. Church and the Working-Classes. London, 1850. 8°. O,1251,3
Bromine, Physiological Properties of. R. M. Glover. Edinb. 1842. 8°. N,252,14
Bromwell, W. J. History of Immigration to the United States. N. Y. 1856. 8. B,862
Brongniart, A. Classification Naturelle des Reptiles. Paris, 1805. 4°. . N,744
Bronn, H. G. Geschichte der Natur. Stuttgart, 1841–3. 2 v. 8°. . G,812,11–12
Gestaltungs-Gesetze der Naturkörper. Leipzig, 1858. 8°. . . . G,719
and Keferstein, W. Das Thier-Reich. Leipzig, 1859–66. 3 v. in 4. 8°. G,937
Bronner, J. P. Weinbau in Süd-Deutschland. Heidelb. 1833–42. 7v. in 2. 8°. G,860
Bronson, H. History of Waterbury, Conn. Waterbury, 1858. 8°. . . C,12
Brontë, A. Poems. London, 1846. 16°. . . . . . . . . . I,285
Tenant of Wildfell Hall. New York, n. d. 12°. . . . . . K,611
Brontë, C. See *Nicholls, C. B.*
Brontë, E. Poems. London, 1846. 16°. . . . . . . . . . I,291
Wuthering Heights. New York, n. d. 12°. . . . . . . K,610
and A. Wuthering Heights and Agnes Grey. Leip.1851. 2 v. in 1. 16°. J,46
Brook, B. Lives of the Puritans. London, 1813. 3 v. 8°. . . . . D,132
Brooke, C. Elements of Natural Philosophy. London, 1867. 8°. . . N,67
Brooke, F. M. Julia Mandeville. London, 1820. 12°. . . . . . K,538
Brooke, H. Fool of Quality. New York, 1860. 2 v. 12°. . . . . K,612
Brooke, S. A. Life and Letters of F. W. Robertson. Boston, 1870. 12°. C,1212
Brooke, W. Julia; a Poem. Boston, 1855. 16°. . . . . . . I,287
Brookes, J. Manners and Customs of the English Nation. Lond. n.d. 8°. A,480
Brookes, S. H. Select Designs for Public Buildings. London, 1842. 4°. . M,297
Brookes of Bridlemere. G. J. W. Melville. Leipzig, 1864. 2 v. in 1. 16°. J,372
Brooks, C. T. German Lyrics. Boston, 1853. 16°. . . . . . . G,45
Brooks, N. C. History of the Mexican War. Philadelphia, 1849. 8°. . B,885
Brooks, S. Russians of the South. London, 1854. p. 8°. . . . . I,656,6
Silver Cord. Leipzig, 1862. 3 v. 16°. . . . . . . . J,48
Sooner or Later. Leipzig, 1868. 3 v. 16°. . . . . . . J,49
Brooks, W. H. Lecture on thorough Teaching. Boston, 1838. 8°. . O,1260,2
Brotherhead, A. P. Himself his Worst Enemy. Philadelphia, 1871. 12°. K,311
Brothers and Sisters. F. Bremer. New York, 1867. 8°. . . . . . K,604
Brougham, H., *Lord*. Discourse of Natural Theology. London, 1836. 12°. P,155
Historical and Political Dissertations. London, 1857. 12°. . . H,407
Life and Times of; by himself, v. 1. New York, 1871. 12°. . . C,532
History of England and France. London, 1861. 8°. . . . . A,529
Men of Letters and Science of Time of George III. Lond. 1855. 12°. . C,541
in Time of George III. Phil. 1846. 2 v. 12°. . . C,522
Miscellanies. Philadelphia, 1841. 2 v. 12°. . . . . . . H,395
Observations on Popular Education. Boston, 1826. 8°. . O,1251,2
Philosophers of the Time of George III. London, 1855. 12°. . C,542
Political Philosophy, v. 2, 3. London, 1853. 2 v. 8°. . . . O,539
Rhetorical and Literary Dissertations and Addresses. Lond.1856. 12°. H,408
Speeches on Social and Political Subjects. London, 1857. 12°. . H,781
The same. Philadelphia, 1841. 2 v. 8°. . . . . . H,792
Statesmen in the Time of George III. Philadelphia, 1854. 2 v. 12°. C,543
The same. Philadelphia, 1840. 2 v. 8°. . . . . . C,556
The same. London, 1855–6. 3 v. 12°. . . . . . . C,540

Brought to Light. T. Speight. New York, 1867. 8°. . . . . K,1017
Broughton, R. Cometh up as a Flower. Leipzig, 1867. 16°. . . . . J,51
Not Wisely, but too Well. Leipzig, 1867. 2 v. in 1. 16°. . . . J,53
Red as a Rose is She. Leipzig, 1870. 2 v. in 1. 16°. . . . . J,52
The same. New York, 1870. 8°. . . . . . . . . . K,607
Brown, A. V. Speeches. Nashville, 1854. 8°. . . . . . . . . H,820
Brown, C. A. Shakespeare's Autobiographical Poems. Lond. 1838. 12°. I,864
Brown, C. B. Arthur Mervyn; or, Memoirs of 1793. Phil. 1857. 2 v. 12°. K,463
Edgar Huntley; or, Memoirs of a Sleep-Walker. Phil. 1857. 12°. . K,464
Jane Talbot. Philadelphia, 1857. 12°. . . . . . . . . K,465
Life of. W. H. Prescott. New York, 1848. 16°. . . . . C,860,1
Ormond and Clara Howard. Philadelphia, 1857. 12°. . . . K,461
Willard; or, the Transformation. Philadelphia, 1870. 12°. . . K,462
Brown, G. English Grammar. New York, 1866. 12°. . . . . . L,540
Grammar of English Grammars. New York, 1858. 8°. . . . . L,539
Brown, J.; Chess Strategy. Collection of Problems. London, 1865. 8°. . M,334
Brown, J. Essays on "Characteristics" of Earl of Shaftesbury. Lond.1752. 8°. P,89
Brown, Capt. J., Life of. J. Redpath. Boston, 1860. 12°. . . . . C,693
Brown, Dr. J. Horæ Subsecivæ; Locke and Sydenham. Edinb. 1858. 8°. H,449
Rab and his Friends, etc. Leipzig, 1862. 16°. . . . . . . J,54
Spare Hours. Boston, 1864-66. 2 v. 12°. . . . . . . H,185
Brown, J. B. Home Life; its Divine Idea. New York, 1867. 12°. . . P,20
Brown, J. J. American Angler's Guide. New York, 1845. 16°. . . M,299
The same; 4th edition. New York, 1850. 8°. . . . . M,313
Brown, J. N. (Ed.) Encyclopædia of Religious Knowledge. Phil. 1859. 8°. P,325
Brown, Richard. History of Cape Breton. London, 1869. 8°. . . . . C,342
Brown, Richard. Principles of Drawing Ornaments. London, 1822. 4°. . Q,172
Brown, Robert. Miscellaneous Botanical Works, v. 1. London, 1866. 8°. O,310
Vermischte Botanische Schriften. Nürnberg, 1825-34. 5 v. 8°. . G,861
Brown, S. G. Memoir of Rufus Choate. Boston, 1862. 2 v. 8°. . . C,964
Brown, Capt. T. Butterflies, Sphinxes, and Moths. Edinb. 1832-4. 3 v. 16°. I,536
Land and Fresh-Water Conchology. London, 1845. 8°. . . . . O,73
Taxidermist's Manual. London, 1870. 16°. . . . . . . N,480
Brown, Dr. T. Philosophy of the Human Mind. Hallowell, 1850. 2 v. 8°. O,699
Brown, T. N. Life and Times of Hugh Miller. New York, 1858. 12°. C,1205
Brown, W. W. The Black Man; his Antecedents, etc. Boston, 1863. 12°. C,534
Browne, A. G., jr. Sketch of Life of John A. Andrew. N. Y. 1868. 16°. C,735
Browne, C. F. Artemus Ward in London. New York, 1867. 12°. . . H,48
his Book. New York, 1870. 12°. . . . . . . . . H,46
his Travels. New York, 1866. 12°. . . . . . . . H,47
Browne, D. J. American Bird-Fancier. New York, 1850. 12°. . . O,103
The same. New York, 1856. 12°. . . . . . . M,533,2
Trees of America. New York, 1846. 8°. . . . . . . N,1024
Browne, H. Hand-Book of Hebrew Antiquities. London, 1852. 12°. . A,200
Browne, J. History of the Highland Clans. Edinburgh, 1852-6. 4 v. 8°. B,128
Browne, J. H. Four Years in Secessia. Hartford, 1865. 8°. . . . . B,908
Great Metropolis; a Mirror of New York. Hartford, 1869. 8°. . C,106
Browne, J. R. Adventures in the Apache Country. New York, 1869. 12°. V,116
American Family in Germany. New York, 1867. 12°. . . . V,418
Crusoe's Island. New York, 1867. 12°. . . . . . . . V,54

Brown, J. R. Land of Thor. New York, 1867. 12°. . . . . . . v,528
Debates in the Convention of California. Washington, 1850. 8°. . o,425
Resources of the Pacific Slope. New York, 1869. 8°. . . . v,125
Yusef; a Crusade in the East. New York, 1865. 12°. . . v,1041
and Taylor, J. W. Mineral Resources of U. S. Wash. 1867. 8°. N,861,1867
Browne, R. W. History of Greek Classical Literature. Phil. 1852. 8°. . H,725
Roman Classical Literature. Philadelphia, 1857. 8°. . . H,726
Browne, Sir T. Works; edited by S. Wilkin. London, 1852. 3 v. p. 8°. . L,4
Vol. 1. Johnson's Life of the Author, and Memoir by Editor; Four Books of Vulgar Errors.
2. Three last Books of Vulgar Errors; Religio Medici; Garden of Cyrus
3. Urn Burial; Christian Morals; Miscellanies, Correspondence, etc.
Brownell, C. De W. Indian Races of America. Cincinnati, 1853. 8°. . S.C.
Brownell, H. H. Poems. New York, 1847. 12°. . . . . . . I,4
Browning, E. B. Aurora Leigh; and other Poems. New York, n. d. 16°. I,290
Poems. New York, 1867. 4 v. 12°. . . . . . . . . . I,289
Browning, R. Dramatis Personæ. Boston, 1864. 12°. . . . . I,294
Poems. Boston, 1856. 2 v. 12°. . . . . . . . . . I,293
Sordello, Strafford, Christmas-Eve and Easter-Day. Bost. 1864. 12°. I,295
Browning, W. S. History of the Huguenots. London, 1842. 8°. . . B,367
Brownlow, W. G. Sketches of Secession; and, Adventures. Phil. 1862. 12°. B,899
and Pryne, A. Debate on American Slavery. Philadelphia, n. d. 12°. o,408
Bruce, G. New-York Type-Foundry Specimens. New York, 1853. 8°. *M,641
Bruce, Life and Adventures of. Sir F. B. Head. New York, 1855. 16°. . L,422
The same. London, 1830. 16°. . . . . . . . . I,634
Travels to Source of the Nile, v. 2–8. Edinburgh, 1804. 7 v. 8° and 4°. v,831
Bruce, J. Classic and Historic Portraits. New York, 1854. 12°. . . C,503
Bruce, John. Annals of the East India Co., 1600–1708. Lond. 1810. 3 v. 4°. F,218
Brummel, G., *Beau*, Life of. W. Jesse. London, 1844. 2 v. 8°. . . D,466
Brünnow, F. Lehrbuch der Sphärischen Astronomie. Berlin, 1851. 8°. . G,779
Bruin; the Grand Bear Hunt. M. Reid. Boston, 1866. 16°. . . J,1582
Brunet, J. C. Manuel du Libraire. Bruxelles, 1838–43. 5 v. 8. . . L.R.
The same. Paris, 1860–65. 6 v. 8°. . . . . . . . L.R.
Brus, The. See *Spalding Club Publications*, v. 31.
Brut y Tywysogion; Chronicle of the Princes of Wales; Annalos Cambriæ. Caradoc of Llancarvan. London, 1860. 8°. . . . . . . W,167
Bryan, M. Dictionary of Painters and Engravers. London, 1853. 8°. *M,138
Bryant, W. C. Discourse on Washington Irving. New York, 1860. 12°. C,847
Letters of a Traveler. New York, 1851. 12°. . . . . . v,1052
from the East. New York, 1869. 12°. . . . . v,1059
Poems. New York, 1866. 2 v. 12°. . . . . . . . . I,12
The same. New York, 1859. 12°. . . . . . . . I,13
Selections from the American Poets. New York, 1854. 16°. . . L,414
Thirty Poems. New York, 1864. 12°. . . . . . . . I,14
Bryce, J. Holy Roman Empire. London, 1871. 12°. . . . . . A,222
Brydges, Sir E. Restituta; Old Books Revived. London, 1814–16. 4 v. 8°. L.R.
Brydges, Sir H. J. Mission to Court of Persia, 1807–11. Lond. 1834. 2 v. 8°. v,753
Brydone, P. Travels in Sicily and Malta. Aberdeen, 1848. 12°. . . v,491
Bryerley, T., and Robertson, J. C. Percy Anecdotes. London, 1868. 2 v. 12°. I,541
Bubbles from the Brunnen of Nassau. Sir F. B. Head. London, 1866. 12°. v,392
of Canada. T. C. Haliburton. London, 1839. 8°. . . . . . C,335

Buccaneers of America. J. Esquemeling. Boston, 1856. 8°. . . . . C,383
History of. J. Burney. London, 1816. 4°. . . . . . . Q,142
Buchan, A. Description of St. Kildu. See *Miscellanea Scotica*, v. 2.
Buchanan, C., Memoir of. H. Pearson. New York, n. d. 18°. . . P,746,16
Buchanan F. Description of Dinajpur in Bengal. Calcutta, 1833. 8°. . V,698
Journey from Madras. London, 1807. 3 v. 4°. . . . . . V,717
Buchanan, G. History of Scotland. Edinburgh, 1821. 3 v. 8°. . . B,125
Life of. D. Irving. Edinburgh, 1817. 8°. . . . . . . D,372
Buchanan, J., Administration of, on Eve of the Rebellion. N. Y. 1866. 8°. B,953
Life of. R. G. Horton. New York, 1859. 12°. . . . . C,701
Buchanan, J. Faith in God and Modern Atheism. Edinb. 1855. 2 v. 8°. P,108
Buchanan, J. R. Journal of Man, v. 5. Cincinnati, 1855. 8°. . . L,985
Society as it is and as it should be. Cincinnati, 1846. 8°. . H,302,4
Buchanan, R. Disruption of Church of Scotland. Glasg. 1857. 2 v. 12°. P,565
Notes of the Holy Land. London, 1859. 8°. . . . . . . V,633
Buchanan, R. Ballad Stories of the Affections. New York, 1869. 16°. . I,557
Book of Orm. London, 1870. 12°. . . . . . . . . I,299
Poems. Boston, 1866. 16°. . . . . . . . . . . I,297
Buchanan, R. Mill-Work and Machinery. London, 1841–2. 3 v. 8°. . M,680
Buchanan, R. Culture of Grape and Wine Making. Cincinnati, 1855. 12°. M,490
Buchanan, W. Ancient Scottish Surnames. See *Miscellanea Scotica*, v. 4.
Bucke, C. Beauties, Harmonies and Sublimities of Nature. Lond. 1823. 4v. 8°. M,367
The same; abridged. New York, 1855. 18°. . . . . L,435
Life of Duke of Marlborough. London, 1839. 16°. . . . . I,631
Ruins of Ancient Cities. London, 1840. 2 v. 16°. . . . . . I,621
The same. New York, 1856. 2 v. 16°. . . . . . L,428
Buckingham, Duke of. See *Villiers, G.*
Buckingham and Chandos, Duke of. See *Grenville, R. P.*
Buckingham, J. S. America; Historical and Descriptive. Lond. n. d. 3v. 8°. V,121
The same. New York, 1841. 2 v. 8°. . . . . . . V,120
Eastern and Western States of America. London, n. d. 3 v. 8°. . V,122
Buckingham, J. T. Memoirs of Editorial Life. Boston, 1852. 2 v. 16°. . C,743
Specimens of Newspaper Literature. Boston, 1852. 2 v. 12°. . C,720
Buckland, F. T. Curiosities of Natural History. London, 1866. 2 v. 12°. N,517
The same. New York, 1859. 12°. . . . . . . . N,516
and others. Birds and Bird Life. London, n. d. 12°. . . . . O,102
Buckle, H. T. History of Civilization in England. New York, 1866. 2 v. 8°. B,33
Essays. New York, 1863. 12°. . . . . . . . . H,486
Buckland, W. Geology and Mineralogy, and plates. Lond. 1869–70. 2 v. p. 8°. L,280
with Reference to Natural Theology. London, 1858. 2 v. 8°. N,805
Buckley, T. A. Boy's Help to Reading. London, 1854. 2 v. 16°. . . O,768
Canons and Decrees of the Council of Trent. London, 1851. 12°. . P,888
Catechism of the Council of Trent. London, 1852. 8°. . . . P,890
Girl's Help to Reading. London, 1854. 2 v. 16°. . . . . O,767
Great Cities of the Ancient World. London, 1864. 16°. . . . A,4
History of the Council of Trent. London, 1852. 12°. . . . P,906
Buckminster, J., Memoir of. E. B. Lee. Boston, 1851. 12°. . . . C,752
Buddhism, New Views of. G. Moore. London, 1861. 8°. . . . N,432
Maháyansi, etc.; sacred books of Ceylon. London, 1833. 3 v. 8°. P,827
Budgen, L. M. Episodes of Insect Life. New York, 1851–2. 3 v. 8°. . O,33

Budgen, L. M. March Winds and April Showers. London, 1854. 16°. . N,497
May Flowers. London, 1855. 8°. . . . . . . . . J,1262
Büchner, A. Lord Byron's letzte Liebe. Liepzig, 1862. 2 v. 12°. . . G,273
Bülau, F. Geschichte Deutschlands, 1806-30. Hamburg, 1842. 8°. . E,69
Bürger, G. A. Sämmtliche Werke. Göttingen, 1844. 4 v. 12°. . . E,315
Buff, H. Physik der Erde. Braunschweig, 1850. 12°. . . . . G,672
Buffon, G. L. L. Natural History. New York, 1853. 2 v. 12°. . . N,498
The same. New York, 1856. 2 v. in 1. 8°. . . . . N,524
Œuvres Choisies, v. 2. Paris, 1855. 12°. . . . . . N,635
Builder, The; a Magazine. London, 1843-68. 26 v. 4°. . . . . Q,334
Builder's Guide. A. Benjamin. Boston, 1857. 4°. . . . . . M,285
Builder's Pocket Companion. A. C. Smeaton. Philadelphia, 1850. 12°. M,145
Builder's Practical Director. Leipzig, n. d. 4°. . . . . . M,298
Building, Art of. Appleton's. New York, 1856. 2 v. 8°. . . . Q,254
E. Dobson. London, 1854. 12°. . . . . . . . M,908
Masonry, etc. W. Hosking and others. New York, 1852. 4°. . M,286
Metropolitan Building Act. London, 1859. 12°. . . . . M,921
Buildings, Application of Iron to. W. Fairbairn. London, 1870. 8°. . M,665
in Towns, Regulation of. W. Hosking. London, 1848. 12°. . M,180
Bulbs, Hardy and Tender. E. S. Rand, jr. Boston, 1866. 12°. . . N,956
Bukarest und Stambul. R. Kunisch. Berlin, 1861. 12°. . . . . E,210
Bulfinch, T. Age of Chivalry. Boston, 1867. 12°. . . . . A,223
Age of Fable. Boston, 1866. 12°. . . . . . . . . P,907
Hebrew Lyrical History. Boston, 1853. 16°. . . . . I,300
Legends of Charlemagne. Boston, 1866. 12°. . . . . A,224
Oregon and El Dorado; or, Romance of the Rivers. Boston, 1866. 8°. C,183
Bullock, W. H. Across Mexico, in 1864-65. London, 1866. 8°. . . V,192
Bullock, J. American Cottage-Builder. Philadelphia, 1868. 8°. . . M,192
Rudiments of Architecture and Building. New York, 1855. 12°. . M,152
of the Art of Building. New York, 1853. 8°. . . M,150
Bullock, T., and F. Popular Education. London, 1849. 12°. . . O,1126
Bulls and the Jonathans. J. K. Paulding. New York, 1868. 8°. . . H,216
Bulwer, Sir E. L. See *Lytton, Sir E. B.*
Bulwer, Sir H. L. Historical Characters. Leipzig, 1868. 2 v. in 1. 16°. J,332
Talleyrand; Cobbett; Mackintosh; Canning.
Life of Viscount Palmerston. Philadelphia, 1871. 2 v. 12°. . C,1213
Bumstead, J. On the Wing; a Book for Sportsmen. Boston, 1869. 12°. M,319
Bunbury, Sir H. Life of Sir T. Hanmer. London, 1838. 8°. . . D,387
Bungalow and the Tent; Visit to Ceylon. E. Sullivan. London, 1854. 12°. V,585
Bungener, L. F. History of the Council of Trent. New York, 1855. 12°. P,811
Priest and the Huguenot, v. 2. Boston, 1856. 12°. . . . H,952
Bunker Hill, Battle of. R. Frothingham. Boston, 1849. 8°. . . C,43
Doubts concerning. C. Hudson. Boston, 1857. 12°. . . . B,741
Bunn, A. Old England and New England. Philadelphia, 1853. 12°. . V,75
Bunner, E. History of Louisiana. New York, 1855. 16°. . . . L,458
Bunon, R. Essai sur les Maladies des Dents. Paris, 1743. 16°. . . L,842
Bunsen, C. C. J. Analecta Ante-Nicæna. London, 1854. 3 v. 8°. . P,123
Egypt's Place in Universal History. London, 1859-66. 5 v. 8°. . V,849
God in History. London, 1868-70. 3 v. 8°. . . . . . . P,121
Hippolytus and his Age. London, 1854. 2 v. 8°. . . . P,402

Bunsen, C. C. J. Life of Martin Luther. New York, 1865. 16°. . . D,491
Memoir of, by his Widow. Philadelphia, 1868. 2 v. 8°. . . D,525
Signs of the Times; Dangers to Religious Liberty. N.Y. 1856. 12°. P,88
Bunsen, R. Untersuchungen über die Kakodylreihe. n. t. p. . . N,252,21
Bunyan, J. The Holy War. Philadelphia, 1841. 12°. . . . . . P,17
Pilgrim's Progress; illustrated by C. Bennett. New York, 1866. 12°. K,615
The same. Leipzig, 1855. 16°. . . . . . . . J,55
Practical Works. Philadelphia, 1852. 8 v. 12°. . . . . . P,706
Buonarroti, M. A., Life of. R. Duppa. London, 1870. p. 8°. . . . L,126
H. Grimm. Boston, 1866. 2 v. 12°. . . . . . . D,728
J. S. Harford. London, 1858. 2 v. 8°. . . . . . . D,761
T. Roscoe. London, n. d. 8°. . . . . . . . C,581
Burckhardt, J. L. Travels in Arabia. London, 1829. 2 v. 8°. . . V,755
Burder, S. Oriental Customs. London, 1808. 2 v. 8°. . . . . . P,481
Burdett, C. Chances and Changes. New York, 1852. 18°. . . . J,1192
Life of Kit Carson. Philadelphia, 1866. 16°. . . . . . C,654
Burdy, S. Life of Philip Skelton. London, 1816. 8°. . . . C,1289
Burger, J. Landwirthschaft in Ober-Italien. Wien, 1851. 2 v. 12°. . G,655
Burges, G. Greek Anthology. London, 1854. p. 8°. . . . . . L,57
Burghley, Lord. See *Cecil, W.*
Burgoyne, Sir, J. Blasting and Quarrying of Stone. London, 1862. 12°. M,894
Buried Alone; a Story. Leipzig, 1869. 16°. . . . . . . . J,56
Buried Cities of the Campania. W. H. D. Adams. London, 1868. 12°. . B,499
Burke, E.; a Historical Study. J. Morley. London, 1867. 8°. . . D,252
Life of. J. Prior. Boston, 1854. 2 v. p. 8°. . . . . . . D,193
The same. London, 1854. p. 8°. . . . . . . . L,262
Life and Times of. T. Macknight. London, 1858–60. 3 v. 8°. . D,251
Speeches; with Memoir by J. Burke. Dublin, 1867. 12°. . . H,773
Works. London, 1855. 2 v. p. 8°. . . . . . . . L,260
The same. Boston, 1866–67. 12 v. 8°. . . . . . U,259
Burke, J. History of Commoners of Great Britain. Lond. 1836–8. 4 v. 8°. B,75
Burke, Sir J. B. Dictionary of the Peerage. London, 1856. 8°. . *C,623
Historic Lands of England. London, 1849. 8°. . . . . . A,466
Burke, W. Virginia Mineral Springs. Richmond, Va. 1853. 12°. . . V,39
Burlamqui, J. J. Principles of Nat. and Polit. Law. London, 1784. 2 v. 8°. U,541
Burleigh, J. B. Legislative Guide. Philadelphia, 1865. 8°. . . . B,719
Burmeister, H. Thierische Organisation. Leipzig, 1856. 2 v. 8°. . G,917
Geschichte der Schöpfung. Leipzig, 1851. 8°. . . . . . . G,827
The same. Leipzig, 1856. 8°. . . . . . . . G,826
Handbuch der Entomologie Berlin, 1832-55. 5 v. 8°. . . . G,944
Atlas to the same. Berlin, n. d. 4°. . . . . . . G,964
Manual of Entomology. London, 1836. 8°. . . . . . . O,37
Organization of Trilobites. London, 1846. f°. . . . . . . Q,63
Reise nach Brasilien. Berlin, 1853. 8°. . . . . . . . E,176
Burn, R. S. Illustrated London Practical Geometry. London, 1853. 8°. M,1125
London Drawing-Book. London, 1853. 8°. . . . . . . M,43
Outlines of Modern Farming. London, 1865–69. 5 v. 12°. . . M,832
Burnaby, A. Middle Settlements in North America, 1759-60. Lond. 1798. 4°. Q,442
Burnap, G. W. Life of Leonard Calvert. Boston, 1860. 16°. . . C,860,19
Burnby, J. Obituary Roll from 1233. . . . . . . . . . F,126,31

Burnell, G. R. Hydraulic Engineering, 2 pts. London, 1858-59. 12°. . M,896
Limes, Cements, Mortars. London, 1857. 12°. . . . . . M,898
Burnes, Sir A. Cabool in 1836-38. Philadelphia, 1843. 8°. . . V,1072
Reisen in Indien und nach Bukhara. Stuttgart, 1835-36. 2 v. 8°. E,218
Burnet, G. History of his own Times. London, 1857. 8°. . . . . A,469
Reformation of the Church of England. New York, 1843. 3 v. 8°. P,661
The same. London, 1850. 2 v. 8°. . . . . . . . P,649
Thoughts on Education. London, 1761. 16°. . . . . . O,1136
Burnet, Jacob. Address before Cincinnati Astronomical Soc. Cin. 1844. 8°. T,19,9
Discourse on. D. K. Este. Cincinnati, 1853. 8°. . . . T,19,9
Early Settlement of Northwestern Territory. Cincinnati, 1847. 8°. C,274
Burnet, James, *Lord Monboddo*. Origin and Progress of Language. London, 1736-1809. 6 v. 8°. . . . . . . . . . . L,523
Burnet, John. Hints on Portrait Painting. London, 1850. 4°. . . Q,161
Landscape Painting in Oil Colours. London, 1849. 4°. . . . Q,168
Treatise on Painting. London, 1850. 4°. . . . . . . . Q,170
Burnett, Sir W. Preservation of Timber, Canvass, etc. Lond. 1848. 8°. N,252,40
Burney, C., Memoirs of. F. D'Arblay. Philadelphia, 1833. 8°. . . D,362
Burney, F. See *D'Arblay, F.*
Burney, J. History of the Buccaneers of America. London, 1816. 4°. . Q,142
Burns, E. V. Cildhud Orz; for Cildren. Sinsinati, 1850. 18°. . . L,667
Burns, J. Mothers of the Wise and Good. Boston, 1854. 12°. . . . C,489
Burns, R., Genius and Character of. J. Wilson. Philadelphia, 1854. 12°. H,703
Land of Burns. J. Wilson. Glasgow, 1846. 4°. . . . . . M,283
Life of. T. Carlyle. New York, 1864. 16°. . . . . . . D,1
J. G. Lockhart. Edinburgh, 1828. 16°. . . . . . . I,506
Poetical Works. Leipzig, 1845. 16°. . . . . . . . J,57
The same. New York, 1868. 16°.. . . . . . . . I,298
Reliques; collected by R. M. Cromek. London, 1817. 8°. . U,194,5
Works; with Life by A. Cunningham. Boston, 1855. 8°. . . J,888
with Life by J. Currie. London, 1820. 4 v. 8°. . . . U,194
Burr, A., Life and Times of. J. Parton. Boston, 1867. 2 v. 12°. . . C,792
Memoirs of. M. L. Davis. New York, 1836-37. 2 v. 8°. . C,1028
Private Journal; edited by M. L. Davis. New York, 1838. 2 v. 8°. C,725
Trial of. D. Robertson. Philadelphia, 1808. 2 v. 8°. . . . U,509
Burr, E. F. Ad Fidem; or, Parish Evidences of the Bible. Bost. 1871. 12°. P,282
Ecce Cœlum; Parish Astronomy. Boston, 1869. 16°. . . . N,321
Pater Mundi; Testimony of Modern Science. Boston, 1870. 12°. . P,129
Burr, F., jr. Garden Vegetables. Boston, 1866. 8°. . . . . . M,511
Burcliff. J. T. Trowbridge. New York, 1869. 16°. . . . . J,1210
Burritt, E. Lectures and Speeches. London, 1869. 12°. . . . . H,782
Sparks from the Anvil. London, n. d. 12°. . . . . . . H,133
Thoughts and Things at Home and Abroad. Boston, 1854. 12°. . P,149
Walk from London to John O'Groat's. London, 1864. 12°. . . V,375
Walk from London to Land's End. London, 1868. 12°. . . V,395
Walks in the Black Country. London, 1868. 8°. . . . . . V,394
Burrow, E. J. Elgin Marbles. London, 1837. 8°. . . . . . . M,79
Burrowes, J. F. Thorough-Bass Primer. Philadelphia, n. d. 12°. . . M,403
Burt, N. C. The Far East. Cincinnati, 1868. 12°. . . . . . . V,638
The Land and its Story. New York, 1869. 8°. . . . . . V,651

Burton, J. H. Book-Hunter; edited by R. G. White. New York, 1863. 8°. L.R.
Criminal Trials in Scotland. London, 1852. 2 v. 12°. . . . U,496
History of Scotland, v. 1-4. Edinburgh, 1867. 8°. . . . . B,117
Letters of Eminent Persons to D. Hume. Edinburgh, 1849. 8°. . H,832
Lives of Simon Lord Lovat and D. Forbes. London, 1847. 8°. . . D,202
Burton, R. Anatomy of Melancholy. Philadelphia, 1859. 8°. . . H,629
Burton, R. F. Abeokuta and Camaroons Mountains. Lond. 1863. 2 v. 8°. V,798
City of the Saints. New York, 1862. 8°. . . . . . . . V,115
Explorations of the Highlands of Brazil. London, 1869. 2 v. 8°. V,259
Lake Regions of Central Africa. New York, 1860. 8°. . . . . V,853
Letters from the Battles of Paraguay. London, 1870. 8°. . . V,247
Pilgrimage to El-Medinah and Meccah. New York, 1856. 12°. . . V,630
Wanderings in West Africa. London, 1863. 2 v. 8°. . . . V,796
Burton, T. Diary. London, 1828. 4 v. 8°. . . . . . . . A,512
Burton, W. District School as it was. Boston, 1850. 16°. . . . O,964
Burton, W. E. Cyclopædia of Wit and Humor. New York, 1866. 2 v. 8°. H,172
Burton, W. W. Religion and Education in New South Wales. Lond. 1840. 8°. P,175
Burty, P. Chefs-d'Œuvre of the Industrial Arts. N. Y. 1869. 8°. . M,120
Bury, T. T. Styles of Architecture. London, 1857. 12°. . . . . M,899
Busch, A. L. Vorschule der Darstellenden Geometrie. Berlin, 1846. 8°. E,434
Bush, G. Life of Mohammed. New York, 1854. 18°. . . . . L,343
Mesmer and Swedenborg. New York, 1847. 12°. . . . . P,842
Notes on Exodus. New York, 1867. 2 v. 12°. . . . . P,489
on Genesis. New York, 1868. 2 v. 12°. . . . . P,490
Illustrations of the Holy Scriptures. Philadelphia, 1850. 8°. . P,500
Bush-Boys. M. Reid. Boston, 1866. 16°. . . . . . . . J,1583
Bushnan, J. S. Animal and Vegetable Physiology. Phil. 1854. 12°. . L,887
Natural History of Fishes. Edinburgh, 1853. 16°. . . . N,470,35
Bushnell, H. Christ and His Salvation. New York, 1869. 12°. . . P,110
Christian Nurture. New York, 1868. 12°. . . . . . . P,41
Moral Uses of Dark Things. New York, 1868. 12°. . . . P,51
Nature and the Supernatural. New York, 1864. 12°. . . . P,52
Sermons for the New Life. New York, 1859. 12°. . . . . P,705
Vicarious Sacrifice. New York, 1866. 8°. . . . . . . P,109
Woman's Suffrage; the Reform against Nature. New York, 1869. 12°. O,371
Work and Play. New York, 1864. 12°. . . . . . . . H,257
Bushrangers; Yankee's Adventures in Australia. W. H. Thomes. Bost. 1870. 12°. K,114
Bushwhacker, Dr., Sayings of. F. C. Cozzens. New York, 1867. 12°. . H,96
Business, Laws of. T. Parsons. Boston, 1857. 8°. . . . . . . U,508
Practical Treatise on. E. P. Freedley. Philadelphia, 1853. 12°. . H,260
Business Meetings, Rules of Order for. B. Matthias. Phil. 1851. 16°. . O,463
Busk, G. Fossil Polyzoa of the Crag. London, 1859. 4°. . . . Q,32
and others. Reports and Papers on Botany. London, 1846. 8°. . O,293
Reports on Zoology, 1843-44. London, 1847. 8°. . . . O,294
Busk, H. Navies of the World. London, 1859. 8°. . . . . . . I,555
Bussey, G. M., and Gaspey, T. History of France. London, 1843. 2 v. 8°. . B,276
Butler, A. Lives of the Saints. Dublin, 1866-67. 12 v. 12°. . . P,794
Moveable Feasts and Fasts of Catholic Church. N. Y. 1852. 12°. . P,823
Butler, B. F. Gen. Butler in New Orleans. J. Parton. N. Y. 1864. 12°. B,928
Butler, C. Horæ Biblicæ. London, 1817. 8°. . . . . . . . P,483

Butler, C. Life of Fénélon. London, 1819. 8°. . . . . . . D,605
Reminiscences of. C. Butler. London, 1822. 8°. . . . . . D,93
Butler, J. Analogy of Religion. New York, 1856. 12°. . . . . P,83
and Sermons. London, 1868. p. 8°. . . . . . . L,170
Butler, J. E. Woman's Work and Culture. London, 1869. 8°. . . O,377
Butler, M. History of Kentucky. Cincinnati, 1836. 12°. . . . C,231
Butler, S. Hudibras. London, 1867. 12°. . . . . . . . . I,301
The same. London, 1859. 2 v. p. 8°. . . . . . . L,96
Poetical Works. Boston, 1854. 2 v. 16°. . . . . . . I,199
The same; edited by G. Gilfillan. New York, 1854. 8°. . J,852
with Memoir; ed. by R. Bell, v. 1, 3. Lond. 1855. 16°. I,245
Butler, S. Atlas of Ancient Geography. Philadelphia, 1851. 8°. . V,1123
Geographia Classica. Philadelphia, 1847. 12°. . . . V,1121
Butler, T. B. Atmospheric System and Prognostication. Norwalk, 1870. 12°. N,102
Philosophy of the Weather. New York, 1856. 12°. . . . N,104
Butler, W. A. History of Ancient Philosophy. Philadelphia, 1857. 2 v. 8°. O,662
Butler County, Ohio, Early Settlers of. J. McBride. Cincinnati, 1869. 8°. C,220
Butt, I. History of Italy. London, 1860. 2 v. 8°. . . . . . . B,489
Butter, H. Gradations in Reading and Spelling. Philadelphia, 1842. 12°. O,759
Butterflies, British. W. S. Coleman. London, 1862. 8°. . . . . . O,3
J. Duncan. Edinburgh, n. d. 16°. . . . . . . N,470,29
Foreign. J. Duncan. Edinburgh, 1852. 16°. . . . . N,470,31
Lepidoptera of Java. T. Horsfield. n. p. n. d. 4°. . . . . Q,114
Manual of European. W. F. Kirby. London, 1862. 8°. . . O,21
Sphinxes and Moths. T. Brown. Edinburgh, 1832-34. 3 v. 16°. I,536
von Europa. F. Ochsenheimer. Leipzig, 1807-35. 10 v. in 17. 8°. G,955
Buttman, P. Greek Grammar; translated by E. Everett. Bost. 1822. 8°. L,737
By the Sea. S. Currier. New York, 1871. 12°. . . . . . . . J,629
Byam, G. Jenseits des Oceans. Dresden, 1852. 8°. . . . . . . E,170
Wanderungen durch Chile und Peru. Dresden, 1852. 8°. . . E,170
Byfield, N. Late Revolution in New England, 1689. See *Force's Tracts*, v. 4.
Byrd, W. History of the Dividing Line. Richmond, 1866. 2 v. 4°. . C,248
Byrn, M. L. Artist and Tradesman's Companion. New York, 1867. 12°. M,673
Complete Practical Brewer. Philadelphia, 1868. 12°. . . . M,649
Practical Distiller. Philadelphia, 1870. 12°. . . . . . . M,650
Byrne, J. C. Twelve Years in the British Colonies. London, 1848. 2 v. 8°. V,893
Byrne, O. Mechanics. New York, 1860. 12°. . . . . . . . M,674
Practical Metal-Worker's Assistant. Philadelphia, 1867. 8°. . . M,721
Model Calculator. Philadelphia, 1851. 8°. . . . . . S.C.
(Ed.) Spon's Dict. of Engineering, v. 1, in 3 div. Lond. 1869-70. 8°. M,731
Byron, G. G. N., *Lord*, and his Contemporaries. J. L. Hunt. Phil. 1828. 8°. D,78
and Shelley, Last Days of. E. J. Trelawny. Boston, 1859. 12°. C,1244
Correspondence with Countess of Blessington. Cincinnati, 1851. 12°. D,76
Dramas. London, 1837. 2 v. 24°. . . . . . . . . . I,311
Finden's Illustrations of; ed. by W. Brockedon. Lond. 1833-4. 3 v. 8°. *J,855
Letzte Liebe. A. Büchner. Leipzig, 1862. 2 v. 12°. . . . . G,273
Life of. J. Galt. London, 1830. 16°. . . . . . . . . D,310
The same. New York, 1830. 18°. . . . . . L,342
T. Moore. Philadelphia, 1869. 2 v. 8°. . . . . . D,82
My Recollections of. *Marquise* T. G. de Boissy. N. Y. 1869. 8°. . D,75

Byron, G. G. N., *Lord.* Poetical Works. Edinburgh, 1868. 8°. . . . I,313
Works. Leipzig, 1866. 5 v. 16°. . . . . . . . . . J,58

Vol. 1. Don Juan.
2. Childe Harold; Giaour; Corsair; Lara; Siege of Corinth; Prisoner of Chillon; Mazeppa; Beppo.
3. Bride of Abydos; Island; Hours of Idleness; English Bards and Scotch Reviewers.
4. Hebrew Melodies; Domestic and Occasional Pieces; Manfred; Cain; Deformed Transformed; Heaven and Earth.
5. Marino Faliero; Two Foscari; Sardanapalus; Werner; Appendix.

The same. Boston, 1868. 10 v. 16°. . . . . . . I,200

Vol. 1. Life; Hours of Idleness; Article from Edinburgh Review; Occasional Pieces.
2. English Bards and Scotch Reviewers; Hints from Horace; Curse of Minerva; Waltz; Ode to Napoleon; Hebrew Melodies; Domestic Pieces; Monody on Sheridan; Dream; Lament of Tasso; Ode on Venice.
3. Beppo; Prophecy of Dante; Francesca of Rimini; Morgante Maggiore of Pulcè; The Blues; Vision of Judgment; Age of Bronze.
4. Childe Harold.
5. Giaour; Bride of Abydos; Corsair; Lara; Siege of Corinth; Parisiana; Prisoner of Chillon; Mazeppa; Island.
6. Manfred; Marino Faliero.
7. Sardanapalus; Two Foscari; Cain.
8. Heaven and Earth; Deformed Transformed; Werner.
9, 10. Don Juan.

Byron, Lady, Vindicated. H. B. Stowe. Boston, 1870. 12°. . . . H,279
Byzantine and Greek Empires. G. Finlay. Edinburgh, 1854–56. 2 v. 8°. A,86

Cabell, J. C. Early History of University of Virginia. Richmond, 1856. 8°. O,817
Cabin on the Prairie. C. H. Pearson. Boston, 1870. 16°. . . J,1609
Cabinet Cyclopædia, Lardner's. See *Lardner, D.*
Cabinet Library. S. G. Goodrich. Boston, 1864. 20 v. 12°. . . J,1493
Cabinet-Maker's and Upholsterer's Companion. J. Stokes. Phil. 1850. 12°. M,147
Cabinet-Maker's Assistant. Glasgow, 1853. r. 4°. . . . . . . S.C.
Cabot, J. C. Narrative of a Tour to Lake Superior. Boston, 1850. 8°. V,1115
Cabot, S., Life of. J. F. Nichols. London, 1869. 8°. . . . . . . D,182
Life of. C. Hayward, jr. New York. 16°. . . . . . C,860,9
Cabul, Account of the Kingdom of. M. Elphinstone. Lond. 1839. 2 v. 8°. C,407
in 1836–38. Sir A. Burnes. Philadelphia, 1843. 8°. . . V,1072
Military Operations at. V. Eyre. Philadelphia, 1843. . V,1072
Cædmon. Anglo-Saxon Paraphrase of the Holy Scriptures. Lond. 1832. 8°. P,437
Cæsar, C. J. Commentaries on Gallic and Civil Wars. N. Y. 1868. 12°. . U,385
The same; literally translated. London, 1870. p. 8°. . . L,45
The same; translated by W. Duncan. N. Y. 1855. 2 v. 18°. U,357
Histoire de. Napoléon III. New York, 1866. 2 v. 8°. . . D,733
History of. Napoleon III. New York, 1866. 2 v. 8°. . . . D,742
Atlas to the same. New York, 1865–66. 2 v. 4°. . . . Q,462
Life of. H. G. Liddell. New York, 1865. 16°. . . . . D,713
Z. Williams. London, 1854. 8°. . . . . . . . D,714
Opera; ed. N.L. Achaintre et N.E. Lemaire. Parisiis, 1819–22. 4 v. 8°. U,311
Werke; übers. von A. Baumstark. Stutt. 1835–40. 8 v. in 2. 24°. E,2
Cæsars, The. T. De Quincy. Boston, 1851. 16°. . . . . . . H,422
The same. Edinburgh, 1863. 12°. . . . . . . H,412,9
Caffraria, Journeys in, 1777–79. W. Paterson. London, 1789. 4°. . . Q,422
Caged Lion. C. M. Yonge. Leipzig, 1870. 2 v. in 1. 16°. . . . J,543

Cahours, A. Thèses de Chimie et de Physique. Paris, 1845. 4°. . N,252,41
Caillie, R. Travels through Central Africa to Morocco. Lond. 1830. 2 v. 8°. V,834
Caird, J. High Farming under Liberal Covenants. Edinburgh 1849. 8°. N,252,31
High Farming vindicated. Edinburgh, 1850. 8°. . . . N,252,31
Prairie Farming in America. New York, 1859. 12°. . . . M,492
Cairnes, J. E. The Slave Power. New York, 1863. 8°. . . . . O,397
Caithness, Pre-Historic Remains of. S. Laing. Edinburgh, 1866. 8°. . N,438
Cajütenbuch, Das. C. Sealsfield. Stuttgart, 1847. 2 v. 24°. . . E,357,14
Cakes and Ale. D. Jerrold. London, 1852. 12°. . . . . . U,178,4
Cakes and Ale at Woodbine. R. B. Coffin. New York, 1868. 12°. . . K,93
Calamy, E. Nonconformist's Memorial. London, 1802-3. 3 v. 8°. . . D,233
Calculating Machine, Description of. J. W. Nystrom. Phil. 1852. 8°. . M,704
Calculator, Practical Model. O. Byrne. Philadelphia, 1851. 8°. . . S.C.
Calculus, Differential. J. Haddon. London, 1851. 12°. . . . . . M,927
Differential. I. Todhunter. London, 1864. 8°. . . . M,1106
W. S. B. Woolhouse. London, 1852. 12°. . . . . M,978
and Integral. A. De Morgan. London, 1842. 8°. . M,1154
Elémens de. J. L. Boucharlat. Paris, 1830. 8°. . M,1149
Théorie des Principes du. J. L. Lagrange. Paris, 1813. 4°. M,1187
Traité élémentaire. S. F. La Croix. Paris, 1806. . . M,1150
Integral. H. Cox. London, 1850. 12°. . . . . . . . M,902
Elements of. J. R. Young. London, 1831. 12°. . . . M,1145
Examples of. J. Hann. London, 1850. 12°. . . . M,929
Infinitesimal, Metaphysique du. L. N. M. Carnot. Paris, 1839. 8°. M,1151
of Probabilities, Traité élémentaire du. S. F. La Croix. Paris, 1822. 8°. M,1148
Calderon de la Barca, Madame. Attaché in Madrid. N. Y. 1858. 12°. . V,468
Calderon, the Courtier. Sir E. B. Lytton. Philadelphia, 1868. 12°. . . K,818
Calderon, S. E. de, Life and Genius of. R. C. Trench. N. Y. 1856. 12°. D,702
Caldwell, C. Autobiography; edited by H. W. Warner. Phil. 1855. 8°. C,1103
Memoirs of Nathaniel Greene. Philadelphia, 1819. 8°. . . . C,771
Thoughts on Physical Education. Boston, 1834. 12°. . . O,1132
Caleb Williams. W. Godwin. London, 1831. 16°. . . . . . . K,524
Calendar of the Seasons, Pictorial. M. Howitt. London, 1854. p. 8°. . L,107
Calhoun, J. C. Works. New York, 1853-5. 6 v. 8°. . . . . . U,101
California and India in Romantic Aspects. J. W. Palmer. N.Y. 1859. 12°. K,295
and Oregon, History of. R. Greenhow. New York, 1845. 8°. . C,250
and the Pacific Slope. J. Todd. Boston, 1870. 16°. . . . V,92
Cincinnati Excursion to, 1869. Cincinnati, 1870. 12°. . . . V,99
Debates on the State Constitution, 1849. Washington, 1850. 8°. . O,425
Eldorado; California and Mexico. B. Taylor. N. Y. 1868. 12°. . V,35
Geological Survey of. San Francisco, 1864-70. 4 v. 4°. . .
Geology, Reports from 1860 to 1864, v. 1. J. D. Whitney. . N,741
Ornithology, Land Birds, v. 1. J. G. Cooper. . . . N,739
Palæontology, F. B. Meek and W. M. Gabb. 2 v. . . . N,740
Geology of. J. D. Graham. Washington, 1851. 8°. . . . N,876
Geological Reconnaissance in. W. P. Blake. New York, 1858. 4°. Q,49
History of. E. S. Capron. Boston, 1854. 12°. . . . . . C,165
M. Venegas. London, 1759. 2 v. 8°. . . . . . . C,245
Natural Wealth of. T. F. Cronise. San Francisco, 1868. 8°. . . C,249
New West; or, California in 1867-68. C. L. Brace. N. Y. 1869. 12°. V,153

California, Overland Journey to, in 1859. H. Greeley. N. Y. 1860. 12°. . V,118
Resources of. J. S. Hittell. San Francisco, 1868. 12°. . . . V,94
Scenes of Wonder and Curiosity in. J. M. Hutchings. N. Y. 1870. 8°. V,113
Caliph Haroun Alraschid. A. Manning. London, 1855. 12°. . . . J,647
Caliphs, Geschichte der Chalifen. G. Weil. Mannheim, 1846–51. 3 v. 8°. E,25
Calisthenic and Hygienic Exercises. R. S. Thomson. London, 1854. 16°. M,304
Calisthenics and Physiology. C. E. Beecher. New York, 1856. 16°. . L,861
Calkins, N. A., and Adams, W. T. Universal Speaker. Boston, 1861. 12°. O,1223
Call to the Unconverted. R. Baxter. New York, n. d. 18°. . . . P,746,6
Called to Account. A. Cudlip. Leipzig, 1867. 2 v. in 1. 16°. . . . J,104
Callery, J. M., and Yvan M. Insurrection in China. New York, 1853. 12°. V,599
Callicot, T. C. Hand-Book of Universal Geography. New York, 1853. 12°. V,1139
Callimachus. Works; translated by J. Banks. London, 1856. 12°. . L,60
Callista; Sketch of the Third Century. J. H. Newman. Leipzig, 1869. 16°. J,386
Caloric, Action sur les Corps Organiques. J. B. Dumas. Paris, 1838. 4°. N,252,57
its Agency in Nature. S. L. Metcalf. Philadelphia, 1859. 2 v. 8°. N,44
Calvert, F. Lectures on Coal-Tar Colours. Philadelphia, n. d. 12°. . M,653
Calvert, F. C. Power of Metals and Alloys to conduct Heat. Lond. 1858. 4°. N,252,52
Calvert, G. H. Benedict Arnold and Major André. Boston, 1864. 16°. . I,27
Introduction to Social Science. New York, 1856. 12°. . . . O,369
Scenes and Thoughts in Europe. Boston, 1863. 2 v. 16°. . . V,306
Calvert, J., and Williams, T. Fiji and the Fijians. N. Y. 1859. 8°. . V,899
Calvert, L., Life of. G. W. Burnap. Boston. 16°. . . . . . C,860,19
Calvin, J., and Saint Louis. F. Guizot. Philadelphia, 1869. 12°. . . D,655
Commentary on the Psalms of David. Oxford, 1840. 3 v. 8°. . . P,497
Letters; edited by J. Bonnet. Edinburgh, 1855. 2 v. 8°. . . P,778
Life of. J. M. V. Audin. Louisville, n. d. 8°. . . . . . D,678
T. H. Dyer. New York, 1855. 12°. . . . . . . D,645
Calvanism; an Address. J. A. Froude. New York, 1871. 12°. . . P,863
Einflusz des Calvinismus. C. B. Hundeshagen. Bern, 1842. 8°. N,252,33
Cambacérès, Prince. E. L. de Lamothe-Langon. London, 1837. 2 v. 8°. B,272
Cambist, Universal, and Commercial Instructor. P. Kelly. London, 1831. . Q,328
Cambrensis Eversus. J. Lynch. Dublin, 1848–52. 3 v. 8°. . . . B,165
Cambridge, Eng., Portfolio; ed. by J. J. Smith. London, 1840. 2 v. 4°. . Q,214
Reminiscences of. H. Gunning. London, 1855. 2 v. 8°. . . B,59
University, History of. G. Dyer. London, 1814. 2 v. 8°. . . O,814
Privileges of the. G. Dyer. London, 1824. 2 v. 8°. . O,1056
Studies at. W. Whewell. London, 1850. 8°. . . . O,910
Cambridge, Mass., High School, Catalogue of Library. Camb. 1853. 8°. L.R.
Camden, W. Britannia; edited by R. Gough. London, 1789. 3 v. f°. . F,121
Camel, Introduction of into United States. Boston, 1856. 12°. . . M,446
Camel-Hunt; a Narrative of Adventure. J. W. Fabens. N. Y. 1853. 12°. K,293
Cameos from English History. C. M. Yonge. New York, 1869. 12°. . A,478
Cameria, Appeal on the behalf of. Cincinnati, 1868. 8°. . . . . . C,237
Cameron, J. (Female Convict). Memoirs of. London, 1864. 2 v. 12°. C,1232
Cameron Pride. M. J. Holmes. Philadelphia, 1870. 12°. . . . K,180
Camilla. F. D'Arblay. London, 1796. 5 v. 16°. . . . . . . K,669
Camille; or, the Coquette. A. Dumas, fils. Philadelphia, n. d. 12°. . H,974
Camoëns, L. de. Lusiad; or, Discovery of India. Oxford, 1776. 4°. . I,389
Camp, D. N. American Year-Book and Register for 1869. Hartf. 1869. 8°. T,48

Camp, G. S. Democracy. New York, 1859. 16°. . . . . . . L,430
Camp-Fire and Cotton-Field. T. W. Knox. New York, 1865. 8°. . . B,910
Camp-Fires of the Revolution. H. C. Watson. New York, 1865. 8°. . B,752
Campan, Mme. de. Mémoires de Marie Antoinette. Paris, 1855. 12°. . D,599
Memoirs of Court of Marie Antoinette. Phil. 1850. 2 v. 12°. . D,621
Campbell, C. History of Virginia. Philadelphia, 1860. 8°. . . . C,116
Scripture Testimony, v. 1. New York, 1863. 12°. . . . P,79
Campbell, D., Life of. D. DeFoe. London, 1720. 8°. . . . . U,249
Campbell, E. W. Biog. Sketches of J. W. Campbell. Columbus, 1838. 8°. C,773
Campbell, G. Dissertation on Miracles. London, 1839. 8°. . . . P,518
Philosophy of Rhetoric. New York, 1854. 12°. . . . . L,593
The same. Boston, 1823. 8°. . . . . . . . L,596
Campbell, G. J. D., *Duke of Argyll.* Primeval Man. N. Y. 1869. 16°. . N,390
Reign of Law. London, 1867. 8°. . . . . . . . . U,539
Campbell, J. Naval History of Great Britain. London, 1818. 8 v. 8°. B,93
Campbell, J., *Lord.* Lives of Chief Justices of England. Phil. 1844. 2 v. 8°. D,248
Lives of Lord Chancellors of England. Philadelphia, 1851. 7 v. 8°. D,249
The same, v. 8–10. London, 1857. 3 v. 12°. . . . D,424
Shakespeare's Legal Acquirements. New York, 1859. 12°. . . I,865
Campbell, J. F. Frost and Fire. Edinburgh, 1865. 2 v. 8°. . . V,1112
Campbell, J. L. Scientific and Practical Agriculture. Phil. 1859. 16°. . M,510
and Hadley, A. M. Teacher's Miscellany. Cincinnati, 1856. 12°. . O,949
Campbell, J. W., Biograph. Sketches of. E. W. Campbell. Columbus, 1838. 8°. C,773
Campbell, Sir N. Napoleon I. at Fontainebleau and Elba. Lond. 1869. 8°. D,581
Campbell, T. Frederick the Great. London, 1845. 2 v. 8°. . . . D,511
Life and Letters; ed. by W. Beattie. N. Y. 1850. 2 v. 12°. . . D,197
Life of Petrarch. Philadelphia, 1841. 8°. . . . . . . D,741
Poetical Works. Boston, 1857. 16°. . . . . . . . I,201
The same. Boston, 1853. 12°. . . . . . . . I,315
Specimens of the British Poets. Philadelphia, 1853. 8°. . . J,856
Campbell, W. W. Life of De Witt Clinton. New York, 1849. 12°. . C,702
Campion, E. Historie of Ireland till 1571. Dublin, 1809. 4°. . . B,182,1
The same. Dublin, 1809. r. 8°. . . . . . . A,565,1
Campin, F. W. Law of Patents. London, 1869. 12°. . . . . M,834
Can You Forgive Her? A. Trollope. New York, n. d. 8°. . . . K,1042
The same. Leipzig. 1865. 3 v. 16°. . . . . . . J,494
Can Wrong be Right? S. C. Hall. Leipzig, 1868. 16°. . . . . J,196
Canada, Agriculture in. W. Evans. Montreal, 1835–36. 2 v. 8°. . . M,434
and United States, Tour in. C. R. Weld. London, 1855. 12°. . V.140
as it was, is, and may be. Sir R. H. Bonnycastle. Lond. 1852. 2v. 12°. V,178
Backwoods of. C. P. Traill. London, 1839. 16°. . . . . L,470
Bubbles of. T. C. Haliburton. London, 1839. 8°. . . . . C,335
Catalogue of Books on America in Assembly's Library. Quebec, 1845. 8°. L.R.
Supplement to same. Montreal, 1848. 8°. . . . . L.R.
Census of, 1851–2. Quebec, 1853–55. 2 v. 8°. . . . . . . P.D.
Conquest of. E. Warburton. New York, 1850. 12°. . . . C,340
Digest of the Criminal Law of. W. C. Peele. Toronto, 1843. 8°. . U,498
Directory for 1857–58. Montreal, 1858. 8°. . . . . . . C,343
Geological Reports; Plans of Lakes and Rivers. Toronto, 1857. 4°. Q,48

Canada, Geological Survey, 1845-49, 1853-56. W. E. Logan. Montreal, 1845-57. 3 v. 8° and 4°. . . . . . . . . . . N,870
Lower, History of. R. Christie. Montreal, 1866. 6 v. 16°. . . C,339
History of the Five Indian Nations. J. C. Colden. London, 1747. 8°. B,584
in 1832-34. Dublin, 1835. 12°. . . . . . . . . . V,150
its Defences, etc. W. H. Russell. London, 1865. 8°. . . . V,22
Journal of Board of Agriculture of, v. 1. Toronto, 1856. 8°. . . P.D.
Letters from. A. M. Murray. New York, 1856. 12°. . . . V,13
Letter from Delta to Senex. Montreal, 1827. 8°. . . . . T,57
Lower, Reports; Seigniorial Questions. Quebec, 1856. 2 v. 8°. . C,344
Maps of. Toronto, 1857. 4°. . . . . . . . . . . Q,103
Nine Weeks in. R. Collinson. London, 1862. 8°. . . . V,1086,2
Past, Present, and Future. W. H. Smith. Toronto, n. d. 2 v. 8°. C,341
Relations des Jésuites. Qu ebec, 1858. 3 v. 8°. . . . . B.653
Rise of, v. 1. C. Roger. Quebec, 1856. 8°. . . . . . C,337
Sketches in. A. Jameson. London, 1863. p. 8°. . . . . I,659,2
Tables of Trade and Navigation for 1854. Quebec, 1855. 8°. . . P.D.
Travels in. F. Hall. London, 1818. 8°. . . . . . . . V,179
I. Weld. London, 1799. 4°. . . . . . . . . V,151
United States and Cuba. A. M. Murray. London, 1855. 2 v. 12°. V,144
Yankee in. A. D. Thoreau. Boston, 1866. 12°. . . . . V,176
Canadian Crusoes. C. P. Traill. Boston, n. d. 16°. . . . . . J,1616
Canadian Forest, Stories of. C. P. Traill. Boston, n. d. 16°. . . . J,1615
Canadian Naturalist. P. H. Gosse. London, 1840. 12°. . . . . N,500
Canadian Review. Incomplete. Montreal. v. y. 8°. . . . . T,57
Canadians, Celebrated, Sketches of. H. J. Morgan. Montreal, 1865. 8°. C,1231
Canal, Considerations on the Great Western. Brooklyn, 1818. 8°. . B,809,2
Canals of New York, Engineer's Report, 1859. Albany, 1860. 2 v. 8°. P. D.
Railways, etc., Reports on. W. Strickland. Philadelphia, 1826. 4°. Q,90
Candid Estimates of the Minister's Abilities. London, 1782. 8°. . . O,565
Candle, Chemical History of a. M. Faraday. New York, 1861. 16°. . N,200
Candles, Art of Manufacturing. A. Ott. Philadelphia, 1867. 12°. . . M,626
Canning, G., Select Speeches. Philadelphia, 1844. 8°. . . . . H,793
and his Times. A. G. Stapleton. London, 1859. 8°. . . . D,61
Life of. R. Bell. New York, 1846. 12°. . . . . . D,155
Memoirs of. New York, 1830. 2 v. 12°. . . . . . C,1207
Canoe and the Saddle. T. Winthrop. Boston, 1863. 12°. . . . . . V,4
Canot, Capt.; or, 20 Years of an African Slaver. B. Mayer. N. Y. 1864. 12°. V,783
Canova, A. Works in Sculpture and Modeling. London, 1824-28. 3 v. 4°. Q,225
Canterbury, Archbishop of. W. F. Hooke. London, 1861-8. 7 v. 8°. . D,215
Canterbury Tales. G. Chaucer; edited by Tyrwhitt. London, 1867. 12°. I,328
The same; edited by T. Wright. London, 1847-51. 3v. 12°. L,606,24
Cantu, C. Histoire Universelle. Paris, 1853-56. 19 v. 8°. . . . A,14
Cape Anne, The Landing at. J. W. Thornton. Boston, 1854. 8°. . . C,49
Cape Breton, History of. R. Brown. London, 1869. 8°. . . . . C,342
Cape Cod. H. D. Thoreau. Boston, 1866. 12°. . . . . . . . V,72
and all along Shore. C. Nordhoff. New York, 1868. 12°. . . K,139
Cape of Good Hope, Letters from. Lady Duff-Gordon. London, 1864. 8°. V,1086,3
Capefigue, B. H. R. Œuvres. Bruxelles. 3 tom. 1840-41. 8°. . . A,370
Capefigue, J. B. H. R. Charlemagne (in French). Brux. 1842. 3 v. 16°. H,1023

Capell Brooke, A. de. Sketches in Spain and Morocco. Lond. 1831. 2 v. 8°. V,475
Capgrave, J. Book of the Illustrious Henries. London, 1858. 8°. . . B,65
Chronicles of England. London, 1858. 8°. . . . . . . W,151
Liber de Illustribus Henricis. London, 1858. 8°. . . . . W,157
Capital, Currency, and Banking. J. Wilson. London, 1847. 8°. . . O,530
Safe Investment of. E. S. Freedley. Philadelphia, 1859. 12°. . H,271
Capron, E. S., History of California. Boston, 1854. 12°. . . . . C,165
Captains of the Roman Republic. H. W. Herbert. New York, 1854. 12°. C,500
Caractères de Théophraste. J. de La Bruyère. Paris, 1853. 8°. . . H,892
The same. Paris, 1856. 12°. . . . . . . . H,869
Caradoc of Llancarvan. Chronicle of Princes of Wales. London, 1860. 8°. W,167
Carafas of Maddaloni. A. de Reumont. London, 1854. 12°. . . . L,171
Caravan Journeys. J. P. Ferrier. London, 1856. 8°. . . . . V,758
Cardiphonia. J. Newton. London, 1857. 16°. . . . . . . . P,19
Cardinal Pole; a Romance. W. H. Ainsworth. Leipzig, 1863. 2 v. in 1. 16°. J,11
Cardinals, English, Lives of. F. Williams. v. 1, 2. London, 1868. 2 v. 8°. D,429
Cards; Cartes à Jouer. P. Boiteau d'Ambly. London, 1859. 16°. . . M,325
Cardwell, E. Metropolitan Gas Inquiry. London, 1850. 8°. . . N,252,39
Reformation of Ecclesiastical Laws. Oxford, 1850. 8°. . . . P,902
Two Books of Common Prayer compared. Oxford, 1852. 8°. . . P,901
Carey, H. C. Slave Trade, Domestic and Foreign. Philadelphia, 1853. 12°. O,407
Past, the Present, and the Future. Philadelphia, 1848. 8°. . . O,549
Principles of Social Science. Philadelphia, 1858–60. 3 v. 8°. . O,548
and Lea, L. Geography and Statistics of America. Lond. 1823. 8°. B,621
Carey, M. Ireland Vindicated. Philadelphia, 1837. 8°. . . . . B,170
Philosophy of Common Sense. Philadelphia, n. d. 18°. . . . O,350
Caribbean Sea, Manuel de la Navigation. C. P. Kerhallett. Paris, 1854. 4°. Q,425,1
Caribbeans, Relation Exacte des Caraibes. M. de la Borde. Leide, 1704. 12°. V,149
Caricature and Grotesque, History of. T. Wright. Lond. 1865. 8°. . M,80
Caricature History of the Georges. T. Wright. London, 1867. 8°. . . A,537
Caricatures, Account of Gillray's. T. Wright and R. H. Evans. Lond. 1851. 8°. L.R.
Works of J. Gillray. London, n. d. 2 v. f°. . . . . . . L.R.
Carion, F. Alte Dessauer; Historischer Roman. Leipzig, 1867. 4 v. 16°. G,274
Carl Bartlett; or, what can I do? D. S. Erickson. Boston, 1869. 16°. . J,1658
Carleton, G. W. Our Artist in Cuba. New York, 1865. 16°. . . . V,169
Carleton, J. W. Recreations in Shooting. London, 1859. 12°. . . L,144
Carleton, W. Tales of the Irish Peasantry. New York, n. d. 16°. . . K,588
Traits and Stories of the Irish Peasantry. London, 1868. 2 v. 8°. K,619
Willy Reilly. Dublin, 1857. 16°. . . . . . . . . K,601
Carlisle, N. Endowed Grammar Schools in England. London, 1818. 2v. 8°. O,813
Carlisle, *Earl* of. See *Howard, G. W. F.*
Carlson, F. F. Geschichte Schwedens. Gotha, 1832–55. 4 v. 8°. . . E,112
Carlyle, A., Autobiography of. Boston, 1861. 12°. . . . . . D,190
Carlyle, T. Ausgewählte Schriften. Leipzig, 1855–66. 6 v. 8°. . . E,316
Critical and Miscellaneous Essays. Boston, 1848. 4 v. 12°. . . H,431
The same. Boston, 1860. 4 v. 8°. . . . . . . H,432
Estimate of Luther's Character. New York, 1865. 16°. . . . D,491
French Revolution. New York, 1851. 2 v. 12°. . . . . B,206
The same. Leipzig, 1851. 3 v. 16°. . . . . . . J,60

Carlyle, T. German Romance; Specimens. Edinburgh, 1827. 4 v. 12°. G,51

Vol. 1. Musæus and La Motte Fouqué. Vol. 3. Jean Paul F. Richter.
2. Tieck and Hoffman. 4. Goethe.

Heroes, Hero-Worship, and the Heroic in History. N. Y. 1859. 12°. H,429
History of Frederick the Great. New York, 1858–66. 6 v. 12°. . D,510
The same. Leipzig, 1858–65. 13 v. 16°. . . . . . J,59
Latter-Day Pamphlets. Boston, 1855. 12°. . . . . . . H,427
Life of R. Burns. New York, 1864. 16°. . . . . . . D,1
of F. Schiller. Leipzig, 1869. 16°. . . . . . . . J,62
of J. Sterling. Boston, 1852. 12°. . . . . . . D,246
of F. Schiller and J. Sterling. London, 1857. 8°. . . . C,523
Oliver Cromwell's Letters and Speeches. Leipzig, 1861. 4 v. 16°. J,61
The same. London, 1857. 3 v. 8°. . . . . . . H,838
Past and Present; Chartism, and Sator Resartus. N. Y. 1852. 12°. H,430
Sartor Resartus; Lectures on Heroes. London, 1858. 8°. . . H,428
Carnot, L. N. M. Geometrie der Stellung. Altona, 1808-10. 2 v. 8°. . E,433
Life of. F. Arago. Boston, 1859. 8°. . . . . . C,498,2
Metaphysique du Calcul Infinitésimal. Paris, 1839. 8°. . M,1151
Principes Fondamentaux de l'Equilibre. Paris, 1803. 8°. . . N,127
Carnation Pink, Culture of. T. Hogg. London, 1839. 12°. . . . N,947
Caroline, Queen, Consort of George IV., Trial of. London, 1820. 8°. . U,532
Memoirs of. J. G. Adolphus. London, 1820–21. 4 v. 8°. . . D,113
Caroline Mordaunt. M. M. Sherwood. New York, 1860. 12°. . K1008,13
Carpani, G., Life of Haydn. Boston, 1839. 12°. . . . . . . . D,495
The same. London, 1817. 8°. . . . . . . . D,523
Carpenter, F. B. Six Months at the White House. New York, 1866. 16°. C,916
Carpenter, J. E. Popular Readings in Prose and Verse. Lond. 1867. 5 v. 12°. H,393
Carpenter, L. Principles of Education. London, 1820. 8°. . . O,1051
Systematic Education. London, 1815. 2 v. 8°. . . . . O,1207
Carpenter, M. Our Convicts. London, 1864. 2 v. in 1. 8°. . . . O,357
Juvenile Delinquents. London, 1853. 12°. . . . . . O,358
Reformatory Schools for Children. London, 1851. 8°. . . . O,922
Carpenter, T. B. Catalogue of Mazatlan Shells in Brit. Mus. Lon. 1857. 8°. O,17
Carpenter, W. Scriptural Natural History. London, 1828. 8°. . . N,523
Carpenter, W. B. Animal Physiology. London, 1859. p. 8°. . . . L,285
Mechanical Philosophy, Horology, Astronomy. London, 1857. p. 8°. L,283
Microscope and its Revelations. Philadelphia, 1856. 8°. . . N,12
Principles of Comparative Physiology. Philadelphia, 1854. . . L,961
Use and Abuse of Alcoholic Liquors. Philadelphia, 1854. 12°. . L,859
Vegetable Physiology and Systematic Botany. London, 1858. p. 8°. L,284
Zoology. London, 1857–58. 2 v. p. 8°. . . . . . . . L,282
and others. Study of the Foraminifera. London, 1862. 4°. . . Q,68
Carpenter, W. H. History of Massachusetts. Philadelphia, 1853. 12°. . C,38
and T. S. Arthur. History of Georgia. Philadelphia, 1852. 12°. . C,154
History of New Jersey. Philadelphia, 1853. 16°. . . C,156
of New York. Philadelphia, 1853. 16°. . . . C,155
of Vermont. Philadelphia, 1865. 16°. . . . C,15
of Virginia. Philadelphia, 1865. 16°. . . . . C,176
Carpenter, W. W. Travels and Adventures in Mexico. New York, 1851. 12°. V,195
Carpenter, American House. R. G. Hatfield. New York, 1857. 8°. . M,206

Carpenters' and Joiners' Assistant. L. D. Gould. New York, 1855. 4°. . M,280
Carpentry and Joinery. J. Robison and T. Tredgold. London, 1859. 12°. M,957
Atlas of the same. London, 1859. 4°. . . . . . . Q,162
Histoire de la. Paris, 1858. 8°. . . . . . . . . . . M,743
made Easy. W. E. Bell. Philadelphia, 1858. 8°. . . . . M,196
Text-Book of Modern. T. W. Silloway. Boston, 1858. 12°. . . M,631
Carr of Carrlyon; a Novel. H. Aïdé. Leipzig, 1862. 2 v. in 1. 16°. . J,4
Carr, W. Dialect of Craven, York. London, 1828. 2 v. 8°. . . . L.R.
Carrel, J. B. N. A. Counter Revolution in England, 1688. Lond. 1846. 12°. A,476
Carrick, J. D. Life of Sir W. Wallace. Edinburgh, 1830. 2 v. 16°. . I,525
Carrier, A. H. Monument to Henry Clay. Cincinnati, 1859. 4°. . . C,705
Carriere, M. Kunst und Culturentwickelung. Leipzig, 1863–8. 4 v. 8°. G,625
Weltanschaung der Reformationszeit. Stuttgart, 1847. 8°. . . E,33
Carroll, B. R. Historical Collections of South Carolina. N. Y. 1836. 2 v. 8°. C,196
Carruthers, R. Life of Alexander Pope. London, 1857. 12°. . . L,141
Carson, Kit, Life of. C. Burdett. Philadelphia, 1866. 16°. . . . C,654
Carter, R. Summer Cruise on Coast of New England. Boston, 1870. 16°. V,49
Carthage and her Remains. N. Davis. New York, 1861. 8°. . . . V,852
Carthaginians, Researches concerning the. A. H. L. Heeren. Lond. 1850. 8°. A,39
Cartwright, P. Autobiography. Cincinnati, 1868. 12°. . . . . . C,684
Carulli, F. Complete Method for the Guitar. Boston, n. d. 4°. . . Q,189
Carus, C. G. King of Saxony in England and Scotland. London, 1846. 8°. V,399
Physis; zur Geschichte des Leiblichen Lebens. Stuttgart, 1851. 8°. E,415
Proportionslehre der Menschlichen Gestalt. Leipzig, 1854. f°. . Q,448
Psyche; Entwicklungs Geschichte der Seele. Stuttgart, 1851. 8°. . G,547
Symbolik der Menschlichen Gestalt. Leipzig, 1858. 8°. . . E,400
Carving, Fret-Cutting and perforated. W. Bemrose, jr. London, n. d. 4°. . Q,165
Manual of Wood. W. Bemrose, jr. London, n. d. 4°. . . . M,677
Carwithen, J. B. S. Hist. of Christian Church to 12th Cent. Lond. 1856. 12°. P,571
Cary, A. Ballads, Lyrics, and Hymns. New York, 1869. 12°. . . I,48
Pictures of Country Life. New York, 1866. 12°. . . . . . K,11
Cary, H. Memoir of Henry F. Cary. London, 1847. 2 v. 12°. . C,1208
Cary, H. F. Early French Poets. London, 1846. 16°. . . . . H,756
Cary, P. Poems and Parodies. Boston, 1854. 16°. . . . . . . I,30
Cash and Character. W. T. Coggeshall. Cincinnati, 1855. 16°. . . H,2
Cashmere, Wanderings in. A. L. Adams. Edinburgh, 1867. 8°. . . V,613
Casimir Maremma. A. Helps. Boston, 1870. 12°. . . . . . K,725
Caspian Sea and Caucasus, Reise auf. E. Eichwald. Stuttgart, 1834–37. 2 v. 8°. E,217
Cassell, J. Arithmetic for the Young. London, 1857. 16°. . . O,1097
Cassin, J. Illustrations of Birds of California. Philadelphia, 1862. 8°. . O,312
Mammalogy and Ornithology of U. S. Ex. Exp. Philad. 1858. 4°. *Q,277
Atlas to the same. Philadelphia, 1858. f°. . . . . . *Q,351
Cast away in the Cold. I. I. Hays. Boston, 1870. 12°. . . . . J,1269
Castell, W. Petition for propagating Gospel, 1641. See *Force's Tracts*, v. 1.
Castle Avon. A. Marsh-Caldwell. Leipzig, 1852. 2 v. in 1. 16°. . J,365
Castle Builders. C. M. Yonge. New York, 1868. 12°. . . . K,1075
Castle Dangerous. Sir W. Scott. Philadelphia, 1869. 8°. . . . K,933
The same. Philadelphia. . . . . . . . . K1116
Castle of Ehrenstein. G. P. R. James. Leipzig, 1847. 16°. . . . J,203
Castle of Otranto. H. Walpole. London, 1820. 12°. . . . . . K,534

Castle Richmond. A. Trollope. New York, 1860. 12°. . . . . K,1043
The same. Leipzig, 1860. 2 v. in 1. 16°. . . . . . J,495
Castlemon, H. *pseud.* Gunboat Series. Cincinnati, 1870. 6 v. 16°. . . J,1520

Vol. 1. Frank, the Young Naturalist. Vol. 4. Frank on the Prairie.
2. Frank on a Gunboat. 5. Frank before Vicksburg.
3. Frank in the Woods. 6. Frank on the Lower Mississippi.

Rolling-Stone Series. Cincinnati, 1871. 3 v. 16°. . . . J,1474

Vol. 1. Tom Newcombe. Vol. 2. Go Ahead. Vol. 3. No Moss.

Castles in the Air. C. G. F. Gore. Leipzig, 1856. 16°. . . . . . J,184
Castlereagh, Viscount. See *Stuart, R.*
Castriot, G., Life of. C. C. Moore. New York, 1850. 12°. . . . . D,759
Castro, Guillen de, Life of. H. R. Fox. London, 1817. 8°. . . . . D,701
Casuistry, Lectures on. F. D. Maurice. London, 1868. 8°. . . . O,720
Catacombs of Rome. W. I. Kip. New York, 1854. 12°. . . . . V,499
Catalogues of Books. . . . . . . . . . . . . . . . L.R.
American, for 1871. F. Leypoldt. New York, 1871. 8°.
American Portion of Canada Legislative Assembly. Quebec, 1845. 8°.
Supplement. Montreal, 1848. 8°.
American Portion of Prince Library. W. H. Whitmore. Boston, 1868. 12°.
American Publications, 1820–52. O. A. Roorbach. New York, 1852. 8°.
Third supplement, 1858–61. New York, 1861. 8°.
Boston Public Library, Bates Hall. Boston, 1861. 8°.
First supplement. Boston, 1866. 8°.
Lower Hall. Boston, 1858. 8°.
Prince Library. Boston, 1870. 8°.
Boston Mercantile Library. Boston, 1854. 8°.
The same. Boston, 1869. 8°.
Cincinnati Educational Library. Cincinnati, 1855. 8°.
Cincinnati Mercantile Library. Cincinnati, 1855. 8°.
The same. Cincinnati, 1869. 8°.
Cincinnati Ohio School Library. Cincinnati, 1856. 8°.
The same. Cincinnati, 1860. 8°.
Cambridge, Mass., High School Library. Cambridge, 1853. 8°.
Canadian Legislative-Assembly Library. Montreal, 1846. 8°.
Congress Library. Washington, 1864. 8°.
Additions, Dec. 1865–Dec. 1866. Washington, 1866. 8°.
Dec. 1866–Dec. 1867. Washington, 1868. 8°.
Dec. 1868–Dec. 1869. Washington, 1870. 8°.
East Hampton, Mass., Public Library. East Hampton, 1871. 8°.
English Catalogue, 1835–62. London, 1863. 8°.
Supplements, 1863–70. London, 1864–71. 8°.
Lambeth Library; Early Printed Books. London, 1843. 8°.
Massachusetts Historical Society, Dowse Library. Boston, 1870. 8°.
Massachusetts State Library. Boston, 1858. 8°.
Milwaukee Young Men's Association. Milwaukee, 1855. 8°.
New-York Mercantile Library. New York, 1866. 8°.
Supplement. New York, 1869. 8°.
New-York-State Library, 1855. Albany, 1856. 8°.
Law Library, 1855. Albany, 1856. 8°.
Bibliography, Typography, etc. Albany, 1858. 8°.
Maps, MSS., Engravings, Coins, etc. Albany, 1857. 8°.

Catalogue of Books. *Continued.*
Original Documents relating to Maine. G. Folsom. N. Y. 1858. 8°.
Philadelphia Mercantile Library. Philadelphia, 1850. 8°.
The same. Philadelphia, 1870. 8°.
Additions from 1850 to 1856. Philadelphia, 1856. 8°.
Royal College of Surgeons' Library. London, 1853. 8°.
Royal Society, of Scientific Papers, v. 1-4. London, 1867-70 4 v. 4°
St. Louis-Public School Library. St. Louis, 1870. 8°.
Syracuse Central Library. Syracuse, 1869. 8°.
Waterbury, Ct., Bronson Library. Waterbury, 1870. 8°.
Catalogues, Sale, Bibliotheca Mejicana. London, 1869. 8°.
H. G. Bohn's Guinea. London, 1841. 8°.
R. Clarke & Co.'s. Cincinnati, 1859. 8°.
R. Heber's, 13 parts. London, 1834-7. 4 v. 8°.
G. H. Holliday's. New York, 1870. 8°.
Z. Hosmer's. Boston, 1861. 8°.
C. Leclerc's. Paris, 1867. 8°.
J. Munsell's. New York, 1865. 8°.
H. W. Poole's. Boston, 1871. 8°.
B. Quaritch's. London, 1868. 8°.
Construction of. C. C. Jewett. Washington, 1853. 8°. . . . . L.R.
Catel, C. S. Treatise on Harmony. London, 1854. 8°. . . . . M,421,1
Cathcart, Sir G. Correspondence on Affairs in Kaffraria. Lond. 1856. 8°. B,84
Cathedral, The. J. R. Lowell. Boston, 1870. 12°. . . . . . . I,51
Cathedral Churches of England and Wales. R. R. Winkles. Lond. 1860. 3v. 8°. *M,143
Catherine. W. M. Thackeray. Leipzig, 1870. 16°. . . . . . . J,479
The same. Boston, 1869. 12°. . . . . . . . . K,1038,5
Catherine II., *of Russia*, Memoirs of; by herself. New York, 1859. 12°. . D,752
S. M. Smucker. New York, 1855. 12°. . . . . . . D,753
Catholic Church. See *Roman Catholic Church.*
Catlin, G. Eight Years in Europe; with Indian Collection. Lond. 1848. 2v. 8°. B,598
Manners and Customs of N. American Indians. Lond. 1851. 2 v. 8°. B,612
The same. London, 1866. 2 v. 8°. . . . . . . S.C.
Catlow, A. Drops of Water seen with the Microscope. London, 1851. 12°. O,13
Field Botany. London, 1852. 16°. . . . . . . . . . N,916
Greenhouse Botany. London, 1857. 16°. . . . . . . . N,917
and Reeve, L. Conchologist's Nomenclator. London, 1845. 8°. . N,718
Catlow, M. E. Popular British Entomology. London, 1852. 16°. . . O,4
Popular Scripture Zoology. London, 1852. 16°. . . . . N,623
Cats and Dogs. H. Miller. London, 1868. 8°. . . . . . . J,1186
Cattermole, G. Evenings at Haddon Hall. London, 1860. p. 8°. . . L,97
Cattermole, R. Book of Raphael's Cartoons. London, 1845. 8°. . . M,92
Cattle; Breeds, Management. W. Youatt and W. C. L. Martin. N. Y. 1858. 12°. M,466
Cattle Doctor, American. G. H. Dadd. New York, 1856. 8°. . . . L,920
Catullus, C. V. Carmina; ex. ed. F. G. Doering, etc. Parisiis, 1826. 8°. . U,312
and Tibullus, A. Poems; tr. by W. K. Kelly. London, 1854. p. 8°. L,46
Caucasus, Country of Schamyl. W. Marshall. London, 1862. 8°. .. V,1086,2
und das Land der Kosaken, 1843-46. M. Wagner. Dresden, 1848. 2v. 16°. E,212
Caucuses, Political, of 1860. M. Halstead. Columbus, 1860. 8°. . . O,526
Caulkins, F. M. Palissy, the Huguenot Potter. Boston, 1858. 16°. . . D,664

Causes of Phenomena, Our Knowledge of. T. H. Huxley. London, 1863. 8°. N,499
Cavalier, The. G. P. R. James. Philadelphia, 1859. 12°. . . . . K,730
Cavaliers of Fortune. J. Grant. London, 1865. 16°. . . . . . . D,436
Cavalry; its History, Management, etc. J. Roemer. New York, 1863. 8°. M,710
Cavé, M. E. Color. New York, 1869. 12°. . . . . . . . . . M,49
Drawing from Memory. New York, 1869. 12°. . . . . . M,24
Cave, W. History of the Lives of the Primitive Fathers. Lond. 1687. 2 v. f°. F,105
Caveler, W. Specimens of Gothic Architecture. London, 1839. 4°. . . Q,175
Cavour, *Count*, Life of. W. de la Rive. London, 1862. 8°. . . . D,745
Cawdor Castle, Historical Papers from. See *Spalding Club Publications*. v. 32.
Caxton, W., Life of. London, n. d. 8°. . . . . . . . . . C,581
Caxtoniana. Sir E. B. Lytton. New York, 1863. 12°. . . . . H,444
The same. Leipzig, 1864. 2 v. in 1. 16°. . . . . J,305
Caxtons, The. Sir E. B. Lytton Philadelphia, 1868. 12°. . . . . K,807
The same. Leipzig, 1849. 2 v. in 1. 16°. . . . . . J,356
Caxton's Book of Curtesye. London, 1868. 8°. . . . . . . L,604,3
Cazin, A. Phenomena and Laws of Heat. London, 1868. 12°. . . M,1058
Cecil, W., *Lord Burleigh*, Life of. J. Macdiarmid. London, 1807. 4°. . F,24
Memoirs of. E. Nares. London, 1828–31. 3 v. 4°. . . . F,22
State Papers, 1542–1596. London, 1740–59. 2 v. f°. . . . F,290
Cecil Castlemaine's Gage. L. de la Rame. Philadelphia, 1867. 12°. . . K,880
Cecil Dreeme. T. Winthrop. Boston, 1868. 16°. . . . . . . K,400
Cecilia; or, The Adventures of an Heiress. F. D'Arblay. Lond. n. d. 12°. K,1153
The same. London, 1820. 3 v. 12°. . . . . . . K,546
Celebrated Friendships. A. T. Thomson. London, 1861. 2 v. 8°. . . C,561
Celebrated Jumping Frog, etc. S. L. Clemens. New York, 1869. 16°. . H,63
Celebrated Travellers. J. A. St. John. New York, 1854. 3 v. 18°. . . L,369
Celestial Bodies, Theoria Motus Corporum Cœlestium. C. F. Gauss. Hamburgi, 1809. 4°. . . . . . . . . . . . . . . . N,386
Celestial Scenery. T. Dick. New York, 1855. 16°. . . . . . . L,398
The same. Philadelphia, 1869. 12°. . . . . . U,260,4
Celibacy, Sacerdotal, Historical Sketch of. H. C. Lea. Phila. 1867. 8°. . P,830
Cellini, B., Memoirs of; by himself. New York, 1851. 8°. . . . . D,721
The same. London, 1850. p. 8°. . . . . . . . L,172
Celnart, Madame. Manuel de la Maitresse de Maison. Paris, 1839. 18°. . M,594
Manuel des Habitans de la Campagne. Paris, 1834. 8°. . . . M,592
Celtic Literature, Study of. M. Arnold. London, 1867. 8°. . . . H,765
Celtic Nations, Eastern Origin of. J. C. Prichard. London, 1857. 8°. . N,434
Celtic Society, Miscellany of; edited by J. O'Donovan. Dublin, 1849. 8°. L,813
Cements, Limes, Mortars. G. R. Burnell. London, 1857. 12°. . . . M,898
Centeola; and other Tales. D. P. Thompson. New York, 1864. 12°. . K,298
Central America, Monograph of Authors on. E. G. Squier. Albany, 1861. 4°. F,63
Staaten von. E. G. Squier. Leipzig, 1865. 8°. . . . . . E,171
States of. E. G. Squier. New York, 1858. 8°. . . . . . . V,202
Travels in. A. Morelet. New York, 1871. 12°. . . . . . V,205
C. Scherzer. London, 1857. 2 v. 12°. . . . . . . V,231
J. L. Stephens. New York, 1853. 2 v. 8°. . . . . . V,199
Voyages in. O. W. Roberts. Edinburgh, 1827. 16°. . . . . I,502
and Mexico, Journey in. G. F. von Tempsky. London, 1858. 8°. . V,204
Central Route to the Pacific. G. H. Heap. Philadelphia, 1854. 8°. . . V,80

Central Society of Education, Publications. London, 1837–39. 3 v. 12°. . O,1191
Cephalopoden. F. A. Quenstedt. Tübingen, 1849. 8°. . . . . . G,837
Cerise; Tale of the Last Century. G. J. W. Melville. Leip. 1866. 2 v. in 1. 16°. J,373
Cervantes Saavedra, M. de. Don Quichotte de la Manche. Paris, 1854. 12°. G,239
Don Quixote of La Mancha. London, 1866. 8°. . . . . . G,233
The same. Boston, 1865. 4 v. 4°. . . . . . . . G,234
The same; illustrated by G. Doré. London, n. d. 4°. . . *Q,239
Life and Writings of. T. Roscoe. London, 1839. 16°. . . . I,629
Story of. A. B. Edwards. London, 1863. 16°. . . . . J,1202
Cervin, Mount (Matterhorn), Ascent of. F. V. Hawkins. Lond. 1861. 8°. V,1086,1
Cessart, L. A. de. Description des Travaux Hydrauliques. Paris, 1806–8. 2 v. 4°. Q,295
Cetacea, Memoirs on the; edited by W. H. Flower. London, 1866. 4°. . Q,73
Ceylon, Botanik der Reise des Prinzen Waldemar nach. Berlin, 1862. 4°. . Q,127
Christianity in. Sir J. Tennent. London, 1850. 8°. . . . P,636
Eight Years' Wanderings in. Sir S. W. Baker. Phila. 1869. 12°. . V,587
Eleven Years in. F. E. Forbes. London, 1841. 2 v. 8°. . . V,696
Notes on. R. Heber. London, 1828. 3 v. 8°. . . . . . V,737
Past and Present. Sir G. Barrow. London, 1857. 12°. . . . V,583
Recollections of. J. Selkirk. London, 1844. 8°. . . . . V,699
Sacred and Historical Books of. London, 1833. 3 v. 8°. . . P,827
Visit to. E. Sullivan. London, 1854. 12°. . . . . . V,585
Chackeray, C. T. Le Fumier de Basse-Cour. Paris, 1847. 8°. . . N,252,25
The same. Paris, 1847. 8°. . . . . . . . N,252,31
Dessèchment et l'Assainissement des Terres. Paris, 1846. 8°. . N,252,31
Chadbourne, P. A. Lectures on Natural Theology. New York, 1869. 12°. P,66
Chadwick, W. Life of D. De Foe. London, 1859. 8°. . . . . . D,296
Chainbearer, The. J. F. Cooper. New York, 1865. 12°. . . . . . K,27
The same. New York, 1860. 8°. . . . . . . . K,58
Chaldee and Hebrew Lexicon. B. Davidson. London, n. d. 4°. . . L.R.
Chaldæa, Travels in. W. K. Loftus. New York, 1857. 8°. . . . V,684
Chalmers, G. Life of Mary, Queen of Scots. London, 1822. 3 v. 8°. . D,128
Chalmers, T. Application of Christianity to Affairs of Life. N. Y. 1853. 12°. P,207
Christian Revelation and Modern Astronomy. N. Y. 1855. 12°. . P,35
Evidences of the Christian Revelation. New York, 1854. 2 v. 12°. P,209
Goodness of God in the Adaptation of Nature to Man. Lond. 1853. 12°. L,278
Lectures on Paul's Epistle to the Romans. New York, 1868. 8°. . P,535
Life of. W. Hanna. New York, 1851–52. 4 v. 12°. . . . D,230
J. C. Moffatt. Cincinnati, 1853. 8°. . . . . . . D,196
Natural Theology. New York, 1845. 2 v. 12°. . . . . . P,208
Posthumous Works. New York, 1848–51. 8 v. 12°. . . . . P,757
Power, Wisdom, and Goodness of God. Glasgow, 1830-39. 2 v. 8°. P,216
Selection from his Correspondence. New York, 1853. 12°. . . H,592
Chalybäus, H. M. Speculative Philosophy from Kant to Hegel. And. 1854. 8°. O,619
Chamberlain, C. A. Poems. Cincinnati, 1853. 12°. . . . . . . I,37
Chamberlain, N. H. Autobiog. of a New-Eng. Farm-House. N.Y. 1865. 12°. K,153
Chambers, G. T. Descriptive Astronomy. Oxford, 1867. 8°. . . . N,344
Chambers, R. Book of Days. Edinburgh, 1863–64. 2 v. 8°. . . . *I,591
Cyclopædia of English Literature. Boston, 1854. 2 v. 8°. . *H,713
The same. Boston, 1855. 2 v. 8°. . . . . . . . S.C.
Dictionary of Eminent Scotsmen. Glasgow, 1855. 5 v. 8°. . . S.C.

Chambers, R. Domestic Annals of Scotland. London, 1858. 2 v. 8°. . B,126
Land of Burns. Glasgow, 1846. 4°. . . . . . . . . . M,283
Life of King James I. Edinburgh, 1830. 2 v. 16°. . . . I,526
Rebellions in Scotland, 1638–60. Edinburgh, 1828. 2 v. 16°. . . I,511
1689 and 1715. Edinburgh, 1829. 16°. . . . . . I,517
1745–46. Edinburgh, 1827. 2 v. 16°. . . . . . I,501
Traditions of Edinburgh. Edinburgh, 1856. 12°. . . . . . B,112
Chambers, T., and Tattersall, G. Metropolitan Building Act. Lond. 1865. 12°. U,486
Chambers, T. W. Memoir of T. Frelinghuysen. New York, 1863. 12°. . C,767
Chambers, W. Things as they are in America. London, 1857. 8°. . . V,58
and R. Edinburgh Journal. Edinburgh, 1844–65. 44 v. 8°. . . T,35
Encyclopædia, v. 1–10. Philadelphia, 1867–68. 8°. . . L.R
Home Book; or, Pocket Miscellany. Boston, 1868. 6 v. 12°. H,554
Infant Education. Edinburgh, 1852. 16°. . . . O,1153
Information for the People. Philadelphia, 1866. 2 v. 8°. . H,633
Miscellany of Entertaining Tracts. Phila. 1857–58. 10 v. 16°. H,556
Moral Class-Book. London, 1856. 16°. . . . . . .
Papers for the People. Edinburgh, 1850–56. 12 v. in 6. 12°. H,558
Repository Instructive and Amusing Tracts. Edinb. n.d. 6 v. 16°. H,557
Chamich, M. History of Armenia. Calcutta, 1827. 2 v. 8°. . . . . A,32
Chamier, F. Ben Brace. London, 1836. 3 v. 12°. . . . . . . J,577
Chamisso, A. von. Werke. Berlin, 1864. 6 v. 12°. . . . . . . E,317
Vol. 1. Der Dichter; Lieder und Lyrisch-Epische Gedichte.
2. Sonnete u. Terzinen; Gelegenheits-Gedichte; Dramatisches; Uebersetzungen; Adelbert's Fabel; Peter Schlemihl; Nachlese zu den Gedichten.
3, 4. Reise um die Welt.
5, 6. Leben und Briefe.
Champagne Country. R. Tomes. New York, 1867. 12°. . . . . . V,460
Champlain, Lake, History of, from 1609–1814. P. S. Palmer. Albany, 1866. 8°. C,90
Champlain Valley, Pioneer History of. H. C. Watson. Albany, 1863. 8°. C,122
Champlin, J. Grammar of the English Language. N. Y. 1850. 16°. . L,558
Chance, H. Manufacture of Crown and Sheet Glass. London, 1856. 4°. N,252,51
Chancery, Practice of the Court of. M. Hoffman. N. Y. 1839–43. 3 v. 8°. U,516
Chances and Changes. C. Burdett. New York, 1852. 18°. . . . J,1192
Chandler, J. R. Common-School Grammar. Philadelphia, 1847. 12°. O,1074
Chandos. L. de la Rame. Philadelphia, 1869. 12°. . . . . . K,887
Changed Brides. E. D. E. N. Southworth. Philadelphia, 1870. 12°. . K,416
Changing Base. W. Everett. Boston, 1870. 16°. . . . . . J,1369
Channing, B. H. Sunny Skies. Boston, 1869. 12°. . . . . . J,1668
Channing, E. T. Lectures in Harvard College. Boston, 1856. 12°. . . L,584
Life of William Ellery. New York. 16°. . . . . . C,860,6
Channing, W. A Summer in Europe. Boston, 1856. 12°. . . . . V,346
Channing, W. E., Memoir of. W. H. Channing. Boston, 1850. 3 v. 12°. C,744
Channing, W. H., Memoir of. Jas. H. Perkin. Cincinnati, 1851. 2 v. 12°. C,846
Works. Boston, 1849–53. 6 v. in 3. 12°. . . . . . . . P,707
Channings, The. Mrs. H. Wood. Leipzig, 1862. 2 v. in 1. 16°. . . J,518
Chap-Books and Fugitive Tracts. J. O. Halliwell. London, 1849. 12°. L,606,29
Chanoine, J. S. Lois d'Instruction Criminelle, v. 2. Paris, 1826. . . U,525
Chapel and Church Architecture. G. Bowler. Boston, 1856. f°. . . Q,389
Chapelle, C. E. L., and Bachaumont, F. le C. Voyage. Paris, 1851. 12°. D,608
Chapin, A. B. Glastenbury for Two Hundred Years. Hartford, 1853. 8°. C,57

Chapin, E. H. Characters in the Gospels. New York, 1852. 12°. . . . P,47
Duties of Young Men. Boston, 1849. 18°. . . . . . . H,247
of Young Women. Boston, 1850. 18°. . . . . . . H,300
Humanity in the City. New York, 1854. . . . . . . . P,46
Moral Aspects of City Life. New York, 1854. 12°. . . . . H,261
Chaplet of Pearls. C. M. Yonge. New York, 1869. 8°. . . . K,1076
The same. Leipzig, 1869. 2 v. in 1. 16°. . . . J,544
Chaplin, J. D. Out of the Wilderness. Boston, 1870. 12°. . . . K,96
Chapman, B. Gustavus Adolphus and Thirty Years' War. Lond. 1856. 8°. D,760
Chapman, H. T. Treatment of Ulcers on the Leg. Cincinnati, 1853. 8°. L,922
Chapman, J. Travels in South Africa. London, 1868. 2 v. 8°. . . V,816
Chapman, J. G. American Drawing-Book. New York, 1864. 4°. . . M,290
Chapman, J. R. Instructions to Young Marksmen. New York, 1848. 12°. M,307
Chappell, W. Popular Music of the Olden Time. London, n. d. 2 v. 8°. M,429
Chapsal, C. P. See *Noel, F. J. M.*, and *Chapsal.*
Character and Characteristic Men. E. P. Whipple. Boston, 1867. 12°. . H,255
Philosophy of. H. Strait. Nashville, 1846. 16°. . . . . O,630
Study of. A. Bain. London, 1861. 8°. . . . . . . . O,734
of the Gentleman. F. Lieber. Philadelphia, 1864. 12°. . . H,228
Characteristics of Women. A. Jameson. London, 1858. 2 v. 8°. . . O,388
of Men, Manners, etc. A. A. Cooper. London, 1732. 3 v. 8°. . H,460
Characters of English Revolutionary Period. E. O. Jones. Lond. 1853. 12°. C,1286
Charades, Acting. H. and A. Mayhew. London, n. d. 12°. . . . I,710
and Proverbs. S. A. Frost. New York, 1866. 16°. . . . I,711
Charicles; Dramatic Poem. J. P. Quincy. Boston, 1856. 16°. . . I,113
Charicles; Private Life of the Ancient Greeks. W. A. Becker. Lond. 1854. 12°. A,152
Charities of Europe, Six Months among. J. De Liefde. Lond. 1666. 2 v. 8°. O,356
Charlemagne (in French). J. B. H. R. Capefigue. Bruxelles, 1842. 3 v. 16°. H,1023
History of. G. P. R. James. New York, n. d. 18°. . . . L,382
The same. New York, 1854. 16°. . . . . . . . B,198
Legends of. T. Bulfinch. Boston, 1866. 12°. . . . . . A,224
Charlemagne; an Epic Poem. L. Bonaparte. London, 1815. 2 v. 4°. . U,590
Charlemont. W. G. Simms. New York, 1866. 12°. . . . . . K,249
Charles and Antoine Lucyon. H. Martineau. Cincinnati, 1853. 18°. J,1052
Charles I. and the English Revolution. F. Guizot. London, 1854. 2 v. 8°. A,508
and Charles II., Sketches of. W. D. Fellowes. London, 1828. 8°. . F,265
and some of the Regicides, Trials of. London, 1832. 16°. . . I,606
Court and Times of. T. Birch. London, 1848. 2 v. 8°. . . A,507
Fairfax Correspondence; ed. by G. W. Johnson. Lond. 1848. 2 v. 8°. A,511,1,2
History of. J. Abbott. New York, 1865. 16°. . . . J,1412
Life of. W. Harris. London, 1772. 8°. . . . . . . . D,31
The same. London, 1814. 8°. . . . . . D,393,2
and Reign of. I. Disraeli. London, 1851. 2 v. 8°. . . D,234
Memoirs of the Court of. L. Aiken. London, 1833. 2 v. 8°. . A,503
Charles II., Beauties of the Court of. A. Jameson. London, 1851. 4°. . D,300
Boscobel Tracts; edited by J. Hughes. Edinburgh, 1857. 8°. . . A,518
Diary of the Times of. H. Sidney. London, 1843. 2 v. 8°. . . A,517
History of. J. Abbott. New York, 1864. 16°. . . . J,1401
in the Channel Islands. S. E. Hoskins. London, 1854. 2 v. 8°. . A,519
Life of. W. Harris. London, 1814. 8°. . . . . . . D,393,4,5

Charles V. *of Germany,* Cloister Life of. W. Stirling. Boston, 1853. 12°. D,515
Correspondence of. London, 1850. 8°. . . . . B,454
History of the Reign of. W. Robertson. New York, 1848. 8°. U,205,2
The same; abridged. New York, 1869. 16°. . . . . L,467
The same; continued by W. H. Prescott. Bost. 1857. 3 v. 8°. B,531
The same; v. 1, 2. Boston, 1857. 2 v. 8°. . . . . . S.C.
Charles XII. *of Sweden,* Histoire de. F. M. A. de Voltaire. N. Y. 1854. 16°. D,592
The same. Paris, 1856. 12°. . . . . . . . . D,749
History of. F. M. A. de Voltaire. N. Y. 1858. 12°. . . . D,751
Charles, John, *of Sweden.* Memorials. W. G. Meredith. Lond. 1829. 8°. D,775
Charles the Bold, *Duke of Burgundy,* Hist. of. J. F. Kirk. Phil. 1864. 3 v. 8°. B,350
Charles, E. Cripple of Antioch. New York, 1866. 16°. . . . . K,620
Diary of Mrs. Kitty Trevylyan. Leipzig, 1869. 16°. . . . J,64
The same. New York, 1864. 12°. . . . . . . . K,621
Early Dawn; England in the Olden Time. New York, 1864. 12°. K,623
Draytons and the Davenants. New York, 1868. 12°. . . . K,622
The same. Leipzig, 1868. 2 v. in 1. 16°. . . . . . J,63
Martyrs of Spain and Liberators of Holland. N. Y. 1865. 12°. . K,624
On Both Sides of the Sea. New York, 1868. 12°. . . . . K,625
The same. Leipzig, 1868. 2 v. in 1. 16°. . . . . . J,65
Schönberg-Cotta Family. New York, 1866. 16°. . . . . K,627
The same. Leipzig, 1867. 2 v. in 1. 16°. . . . . . J,66
Two Vocations. New York, 1865. 12°. . . . . . . K,628
Winifred Bertram. New York, 1866. 12°. . . . . . K,629
The same. Leipzig, 1869. 16°. . . . . . . . J,67
Charles Auchester. E. S. Sheppard. New York, n. d. 8°. . . K,1005
Charles O'Malley. C. Lever. Philadelphia, 1865. 8°. . . . . K,769
The same. Leipzig, 1848. 3 v. 16°. . . . . . . J,271
Charleston, Operations against, 1863. Q. A. Gillmore. N. Y. 1865. 8°. . B,952
Charley Roberts Series. Boston, 1871. 3 v. 16°. . . . . . J,1632
Vol. 1. How Charley Roberts became a man.
2. How Eva Roberts gained her Education.
3. Charley and Eva Roberts's Home in the West.
Charlie Codman's Cruise. H. Alger. Boston, 1867. 16°. . . . J,1594
Charmed Sea, The. H. Martineau. Cincinnati, 1853. 18°. . . . J,1453
Charms and Counter-Charms. M. J. MacIntosh. New York, 1864. 12°. K,212
Chartism. T. Carlyle. New York, 1852. 12°. . . . . . . H,430
Chase, H., and Sanborn, C. W. North and the South. Boston, 1856. 12°. O,394
Chase, S. P. Sketch of the History of Ohio. Cincinnati, 1833. 8°. . C,227
Chasles, P. Anglo-American Literature and Manners. N. Y. 1852. 12°. H,656
Notabilities in France and England. New York, 1853. 12°. . . C,519
Chasseaud, G. W. Druses of the Lebanon. London, 1855. 8°. . . V,681
Chastelard; a Tragedy. A. C. Swinburne. New York, 1866. 16°. . . I,437
Chastellux, F. J. de. Travels in North America, 1780–82. N. Y. 1828. 8°. V,86
Chateaubriand, R. F. A. de. Analyse de l'Histoire de France. Paris, 1853. 12°. B,219
Atala; René; Voyage en Amérique. Paris, 1854. 12°. . . . H,937
Autobiography. London, 1854. 4 v. in 1. 16°. . . . . . D,594
Discours sur la Chute de l'Empire Romain, v. 1–4. Brux. 1831. 16°. A,75
The same. Paris, 1855. 12°. . . . . . . . . . A,164
Génie du Christianisme. Paris, 1852. 2 v. 12°. . . . . . P,132
Genius of Christianity. Baltimore, 1856. 8°. . . . . . . P,138

Chateaubriand, R.F.A.de. Itinéraire de Paris à Jerusalem. Par.1854. 2 v. 12°. V,624
Les Martyrs. Paris, 1855. 12°. . . . . . . . . . H,936
Martyrs; edited by O. W. Wight. New York, 1863. 12°. . . . H,934
Mélanges Politique et Litteraires. Paris, 1854. 12°. . . . H,935
Memoires d' Outre-Tombe. New York, 1848. 2 v. 8°. . . . H,917
Les Natchez. Paris, 1853. 12°. . . . . . . . . H,938
Travels in Greece, Palestine, Egypt, and Barbary. Lond. 1812. 2 v. 8°. V,1083
Chatham Artillery, Historical Sketch of. C. C. Jones. Albany, 1867. 8°. C,65
Chatrian, A. See *Erckmann, E., et Chatrian.*
Chattaway, E. D. Railway Working in Great Britain. Lond. 1855–6. 12°. M,900
Chatterton, T., Life of. G. Gregory. London, 1789. 8°. . . . . . D,386
Poetical Works. Boston, 1857. 2 v. 12°. . . . . . . I,202
Chatto, W. A., and Jackson. Treatise on Wood Engraving. Lond. 1861. *M,139
Chaucer, G. Canterbury Tales; edited by T. Wright. London, 1867. 12°. I,328
The same. London, 1847–51. 3 v. 12°. . . . . L,606,24–26
Illustrations of. H. J. Todd. London, 1810. 8°. . . . . . H,705
Legende of Goode Women; ed. by H. Corson. Philadelphia, 1864. 12°. I,243
Poetical Works, v. 2–6. London, 1852. 16°. . . . . . . I,316
with Life; edited by R. Bell. London, 1854–56. 8 v. 16°. . I,246
Chaudon, L. M., et Delandine. Diction. Historique. Caen, 1804. 13 v. 8°. C,597
Chauvenet, W. Spherical and Practical Astronomy. Phil. 1864. 2 v. 8°. N,360
Cheever, G. B. Hill Difficulty, and other Papers. New York, 1849. 12°. H,462
Journal of the Pilgrims at Plymouth. New York, 1848. 12°. . C,3
Lectures on Cowper. New York, 1856. 12°. . . . . . . D,419
Pilgrim in the Shadow of Jungfrau Alps. New York, 1846. 8°. . V,500
Punishment by Death. New York, 1855. 12°. . . . . . O,355
Winding of the River of the Water of Life. New York, 1849. 12°. P,262
Cheever, H. T. Island World of the Pacific. New York, 1856. 12°. . V,882
Life in the Sandwich Islands. New York, 1856. 12°. . . . V,876
Memoir of Walter Colton. Cincinnati, 1851. 12°. . . . . V,300
Memorials of Obadiah Congar. New York, 1851. 16°. . . . C,842
Reel in a Bottle. New York, 1852. 12°. . . . . . . J,1497
Cheke, Sir J., Life of. J. Strype. Oxford, 1821. 8°. . . . . . . P,686
Chellis, M. D. Bill Droch's Investment. Boston, 1870. 16°. . . . J,1620
Deacon Sims's Prayers. Boston, 1868. 16°. . . . . . . J,1633
Old Doctor's Son. Boston, 1870. 16°. . . . . . . . J,1619
Chelsea Hospital and its Traditions. London, 1838. 3 v. 12°. . . J,570
Cheltenham, Geology of. R. I. Murchison. London, 1845. 8°. . . N,821
Chemical Analysis. H. M. Noad. Philadelphia, 1849. 8°. . . . N,205
Hand-Book of. F. T. Conington. London, 1858. 2 v. 8°. . . N,201
Practische Uebungen in. F. Wöhler. Göttingen, 1853. 8°. . . G,774
Qualitative. C. R. Fresenius. Braunschweig, 1843–45. 8°. . N,252,11
The same; translated. London, 1864. 8°. . . . . . N,207
Quantitative. London, 1865. 8°. . . . . . . . . . N,208
C. F. Rammelsberg. Berlin, 1843–45. 8°. . . . . N,252,16
Traité d'. H. Rose. Paris, 1852. 2 v. 8°. . . . . . . N,179
Chemical Elements, Spectra of the. G. Kirchhoff. Cambridge, 1863. 4°. N,146
Chemical and Pharmaceutical Manipulations. C. and C. Morfit. Phil. 1857. 8°. N,211
Chemical Atlas. E. L. Youmans. New York, 1855. 4°. . . . . Q,326
Chemical Field Lectures. J. A. Stöckhardt. Cambridge, 1853. 12°. . N,174

Chemical History of a Candle. M. Faraday. New York, 1861. 16°. . N,200
Chemical Manipulations. M. Faraday. London, 1842. 8°. . . . N,210
Chemical Method. A. Laurent. London, 1855. 8°. . . . . . N,190
Chemical News and Journal of Physical Science. New York, 1867. 8°. . N,247
Chemical Proportions, Lehrbuch der. C. F. Rammelsberg. Berl. 1842. 8°. N,252,16
Versuch eines Lehrbuchs der. H. Buff. Nürnberg, 1829. 8°. N,252,4
Chemical Students, Lecture Notes for. E. Frankland. Lond. 1866. 12°. N,186
Chemical Technology. E. Ronalds and T. Richardson. Lon. 1855. 3 v. in 4. 8°. N,102
Chemical Theory, History of. A. Wurtz. London, 1869. 8°. . . . N,185
Chemical Wonders, Laboratory of. G. W. S. Piesse. London, 1860. 12°. N,184
Chemistry. M. Donovan. London, 1832. 12°. . . . . . . M,1026
G. Fownes. London, 1857. 12°. . . . . . . . . M,914
Agricultural. C. A. A. Lloyd. Shrewsbury, 1840. 8°. . . N,252,6
Elements of. J. F. W. Johnston. New York, 1855. 12°. . M,514
Jahresbericht über. R. Hoffman. Berlin, 1860–65. 6 v. 8°. G,755
Lectures on. J. F. W. Johnston. Edinburgh, 1847. 8°. . M,573
Lehrbuch der. F. Schulze. Leipzig, 1846. 8°. . . . G,769
Amerikanische Amalgamation. J. P. J. D. Boussingault. . N,252,30
and Natural Theology. W. Prout. London, 1855. p. 8°. . . L,279
and Physics. M. Faraday. London, 1859. 8°. . . . . . M,792
Physiology and Pathology. J. Liebig. London, 1846. 8°. N,252,32
and Religion. J. P. Cooke, jr. New York, 1867. 12°. . . . P,217
and Rural Economy. J. B. Boussingault. New York, 1856. 12°. . M,521
Animal. J. Liebig. Cambridge, 1842. 12°. . . . . . . N,233
Verhältniss der. J. Liebig. Heidelberg, 1844. 8°. . N,252,7
Zoochemie. C. G. Lehmann. Heidelberg, 1858. 8°. . . G,756
applied to Agriculture. J. C. Nesbit. London, 1847. 8° . . N,252,31
and Physiology. J. von Liebig. New York, 1856. 12°. M,540
to the Arts. S. Muspratt. Glasgow, 1869. 2 v. 8°. . . N,253
E. Ronalds and T. Richardson. Lond. 1855. 3 v. in 4. 8°. N,192
to Dyeing. J. Napier. Philadelphia, 1853. 12°. . . . M,652
to Medicine. R. M. Glover. London, 1841. 8°. . . N,252,14
Berzelius Ansichten über. L. Müller. Breslau, 1846. 8°. . N,252,32
Chimie du Fer. J. J. Berzelius. Paris, 1826. 8°. . . . . N,252,18
Chemische Feldpredigten. J. A. Stöckhardt. Leipzig, 1856. 8°. . G,770
Chemisch-Technische Mittheilungen. L. Elsner. Berlin, 1849. 8°. N,252,40
Chemische Untersuchungen. O. B. Kühn. Leipzig, 1842. 8°. N,252,12
Class-Book of. E. L. Youmans. New York, 1865. 12°. . . N,172
Conversations on. T. P. Jones. Philadelphia, 1834. 12°. . . N,171
Dictionary of. H. Watts. London, 1864–68. 5 v. 8°. . . *N,240
Elements of. J. Webster. London, 1811. 8°. . . . . . N,251
M. V. Regnault. Philadelphia, 1853. 2 v. 8°. . . . N,216
T. Graham. London, 1850–58. 2 v. 8°. . . . . N,212
W. A. Miller. London, 1867. 3 v. 8°. . . . . N,238
B. D. Reid. New York, 1849. 12°. . . . . . N,168
W. J. Rolfe and J. A. Gillet. Boston, 1868. 12°. . . . N,228
der Pharmaceutischen. J. W. Döbereiner. Jena, 1816. 8°. G,751
of Medical. B. H. Rand. Philadelphia, 1871. 12°. . . N,217
et Physiologie Végétales. H. Le Docte. Bruxelles, 1849. 8°. . N,252,34
Etudes de Chimie Organique. E. Millon. Lille, 1849. 8°. . N,252,32

Chemistry, Expériences Chimiques. F. Kuhlmann. Paris, 1847. 8°. . N,252,31
Fortschritte der Angewandten. F. L. Stumpf. Berlin, 1853. 8°. . G,772
First Book in. W. Hooker. New York, 1862. 16°. . . . N,166
First Principles of. B. Silliman, jr. Philadelphia, 1867. 12°. . N,229
for the School and Family. W. Hooker. New York, 1864. 12°. . N,226
for Students. A. W. Williamson. Oxford, 1865. 16°. . . . N,167
Gewicht Chem. Verbindungen. H. Kopp. Frank.-a-M. 1844. 8°. N,255,21
Grundlehren der. J. J. Prechtl. Wien, 1817. 2 v. 8°. . . G,760
Grundrisz der. F. F. Runge. Munchen, 1846–47. 2 v. 8°. . . G,765
der Organischen. R. F. Marchand. Leipzig, 1839. 8°. N,252,28
der Unorganischen. F. Wöhler. Berlin, 1837. 8°. . N,252,5
der Zoophysiologischen. H. K. Geubel. Frank.-a M. 1845. 8°. N,252,17
Handbuch der Technischen. E. L. Schubarth. Berlin, 1851. 3 v. 8°. G,768
Altas to the same. Berlin, 1851. 4°. . . . . . . F,94
Hand-Book of. F. A. Abel. Philadelphia, 1854. 8°. . . . N,202
Illustrated, Appleton's, with plates. New York, 1856. 2 v. 8°. . Q,250
Important Facts in. T. Exley. London, 1837. 8°. . . . N,252,2
Inorganic, Manual of. C. W. Eliot and F. H. Storer. N. Y. 1868. 8°. N,221
and Organic. C. L. Bloxam. London, 1867. 8°. . . . N,213
Introduction to Practical. J. E. Bowman. Philadelphia, 1864. 12°. N,178
Laboratorium der Ludwig's Universität. J. P. Hoffman. Heid. 1842. 8°. N,252,7
Lehrbuch der. J. J. Berzelius. Leipzig, 1856. 5 v. 8°. . . G,750
Lessons in Elementary. H. E. Roscoe. London, 1868. 16°. . . N,219
Magnetismus, Elektricität, u. Chemismus. G. F. Pohl. Berl. 1829. 12°. N,252,23
Manual of. W. T. Brande. London, 1819. 8°. . . . . . N,181
J. Johnston. Philadelphia, 1856. 12°. . . . . . . N,231
Elementary. G. Fownes. Philadelphia, 1870. 12°. . . N,223
Introduction to. A. W. Hofmann. London, 1866. 8°. . . . N,225
Neueste Fortschritte in. R. Wagner. Berlin, 1850. 8°. . . N,252,49
of Agriculture. D. Christy. Cincinnati, 1852. 8°. . . . . M,554
J. A. Stöckhardt. London, 1855. 12°. . . . . . . L,320
of Common Life. J. F. W. Johnston. New York, 1855. 2 v. 12°. N,170
of Non-Metalic Elements. J. J. Griffin. London, 1860. 12°. . . N,177
of the Stars. G. Wilson. London, 1862. p. 8°. . . . . . I,666
Organic and Physiological. K. Löwig. Philadelphia, 1853. 8°. . N,194
Thèse sur l'Etat de. A. Baudrimont. Paris, 1838. 8°. . N,252,1
Traité de. C. Gerhardt. Paris, 1860–63. 4 v. 8°. . . N,180
Organische. J. Liebig. Heidelberg, 1843. 8°. . . . . . G,757
J. E. Schlossberger. Leipzig, 1860. 8°. . . . . . . G,767
Outlines of. W. Gregory. Cincinnati, 1851. 8°. . . . . . N,187
The same. New York 1852. 8°. . . . . . . . N,224
Pamphlets on Chemical Subjects. 57 v. 8°. . . . . . . N,252
Philosophie der. C. J. B. Karsten. Berlin, 1843. 8°. . . N,252,7
Physiologie und Pathologie. D. M. Pettenkofer. München, 1848. 4°. N,252,41
Polizeilich-Chemische Skizzen. D. J. Gottlieb. Leipzig, 1853. 8°. G,753
Principles of. A. Naguet. London, 1868. 8°. . . . . . N,214
J. A. Porter. New York, 1865. 12°. . . . . . . N,227
J. A. Stöckhardt. Philadelphia, 1868. 12°. . . . . . N,230
Progress of. J. von Liebig and others. London, 1849–53. 4 v. 8°. N,188
Revenue in jeopardy from Spurious. A. Ure. London, 1843. 8°. N,252,13

Chemistry, Review of. J. C. Murphy. Philadelphia, 1851. 12°. . . . N,175
Rudiments of. D. B. Reid. Philadelphia, 1846. 12°. . . . N,169
Schule der. J. A. Stöckhardt. Braunschweig, 1855. 16°. . . G,771
Solubilities of Chemical Substances. F. H. Storer. 1864. 8°. . . N,246
State of the Schools of. W. Gregory. London, 1842. 8°. . N,252,21
Statique Chimique des Etres Organisés. J. B. Dumas. Paris, 1841. 8°. N,252,7
Text-Book on. H. Draper. New York, 1866. 12°. . . . N,220
Thèses de Chimie et de Physique. A. Cahours. Paris, 1845. 4°. N,252,41
und Experimental Physik. K. W. G. Kastner. Erlangen, 1850. 8°. N,252,33
Untersuchungen des Schildpatts. A. Völcher. Gottingen, 1847. 8°. N,252,40
Cheney, O. A. Sunday-School Speaker. Boston, 1869. 12°. . . . O,824
Chénier, M. J. de. Chefs-d'Œuvre Tragiques. Paris, 1845. 12°. . . H,883
Cherefeddin, A. History of Timur Bec; or, Tamerlain. London, 1723. 2v. 8°. D,769
Cherry and Violet. A. Manning. London, 1870. 12°. . . . . . J,623
Cherry, C. Geological Report, Sonora Mining. Cincinnati, 1866. 8°. . O,501
Cherubini, L. Treatise on Counterpoint and Fugue. London, 1854. 8°. M,421,1
Cheseboro', C. Foe in the Household. Boston, 1871. 8°. . . . K,150
Chesney, F. R. Narrative of the Euphrates Expedition. London, 1868. 8°. V,706
Chess, History of. D. W. Fiske. New York, 1859. 12°. . . . . M,329
Congress of, 1862; edited by J. Löwenthal. London, 1864. p. 8°. . L,286
First American Congress. D. W. Fiske. New York, 1859. 12°. . M,329
Paul Morphy's Games; ed. by J. Löwenthal. London, 1869. p. 8°. L,308
The same. New York, 1860. p. 8°. . . . . . . M,330
and Frère's Problem Tournament. New York, 1859. 18°. M,324
Player's Companion. H. Staunton. London, 1849. 12°. . . M,327
Player's Hand-Book. H. Staunton. London, 1870. . . . . L,315
Praxis; supplement to Hand-Book. H. Staunton. London, 1860. p. 8°. L,316
Science and Art of. J. Monroe. New York, 1859. 12°. . . . M,332
Strategy; Collection of Problems. J. Brown. London, 1865. 8°. . M,334
Tournament, 1851. H. Staunton. London, 1852. p. 8°. . . . L,318
Treatise on. J. H. Sarratt. v. 2. London, 1808. 8°. . . . M,335
Chesterfield, *Earl*. See *Stanhope, P. D.*
Chester Plays at Whitsuntide; ed. by T. Wright. Lond. 1843–7. 2 v. 8°. I,885,33
Chettle, H. Kind-Heart's Dream. London, 1841. 12°. . . . L,606,5
Cheuelere Assigne, Romance of. London, 1868. 8°. . . . . L,604,6
Chevalier, M. Probable Fall in Value of Gold. New York, 1859. 8°. . O,524
Society in the United States. Boston, 1839. 8°. . . . . V,46
Chevalier, The. A. Dumas. Philadelphia, n. d. 8°. . . . . . H,975
Chevaliers of England. H. W. Herbert. New York, 1852. 12°. . . K,190
of France. H. W. Herbert. New York, 1853. 12°. . . . K,189
Chevallier, A. Dissolution de la Gravelle. Paris, 1837. 8°. . . N,252,9
Chevreul, M. E. Principles of Harmony and Colours. Lond. 1859. p. 8°. . L,287
Chicago, Army Reunion at, 1868. Chicago, 1869. 8°. . . . . B,948
History of. J. D. Guyer. Chicago, 1869. 4°. . . . . . C,314
Walks about, and Sketches. F. B. Wilkie. Chicago, 1869. 12°. . H,273
Cheverus, J., *Cardinal de*, Life of. M. Hamond. Philadelphia, 1839. 12°. D,642
Chief Justices of England, Lives of. J. *Lord* Campbell. Phil. 1853. 2 v. 12°. D.248
of the United States, Lives of. H. Flanders. Philadelphia, 1855. 8°. C,816
Lives of. G. Van Santvoord. New York, 1854. 8°. . . . C,817
The same. New York, 1854. 8°. . . . . . . . . S.C.

Child's Book of Nature. W. Hooker. New York, 1869. 12°. . . . N,642
Child, F. J. (Ed.) English and Scottish Ballads. Boston, 1857–58. 8 v. 16°. I,196
Child, G. C. Benedicite; Song of the Three Children. London, 1868. 16°. P,348
Child, J. New-Englands Jonas cast up in London, 1647. Boston, 1869. 8°. C,10
The same. *Force's Tracts*, v. 4.
Child, L. M. Biographies of Good Wives. New York, 1859. 16°. . . C,536
Fact and Fiction. New York, 1854. 12°. . . . . . . . J,1220
Flowers for Children. Boston, 1865. 16°. . . . . . . . J,1433
Freedman's Book. Boston, 1865. 12°. . . . . . . . H,97
Isaac T. Hopper; a True Life. Boston, 1853. 12°. . . . C,1011
Letters from New York. New York, 1850. 2 v. 12°. . . . V,52
Looking towards Sunset. Boston, 1867. 12°. . . . . . . H,294
Memoirs of Mad. de Staël and Mad. Roland. New York, 1854. 16°. D,652
New Flower for Children. Boston, 1865. 16°. . . . . . J,1432
Romance of the Republic. Boston, 1868. 12°. . . . . . . K,23
Children, Education of. J. Witherspoon. Andover, 1817. 12°. . . O,1157
Lytille Childrens' Lytil Boke. London, 1868. 8°. . . . L,605,32
of the Abbey. R. M. Roche. Philadelphia, 1868. 12°. . . . K,911
of the New Forest. F. Maryatt. New York, 1868. 12°. . . . V,840
The same. Leipzig, 1848. 16°. . . . . . . . . J,353
Children's Crusade; Episode of 13th Century. G. Z. Gray. N. Y. 1870. 12°. J,1545
Chili, Araucanians, Indians of Chili. E. R. Smith. New York, 1855. 12°. V,251
Astronomical Expedition to. J. M. Gilliss. Washington, 1855. 2 v. 4°. P.D.
Peru and Mexico, Voyage to. B. Hall. Edinburgh, 1826–27. 2 v. 16°. I,492,2,3
und Peru, Reise in. E. Poeppig. Leipzig, 1835–36. 2 v. . . . Q,287
Atlas to the same. f°. . . . . . . . . . . Q,460
U. S. Astronom. Expedi. to, v. 1–3, 6. J. M. Gilliss. Wash. 1855. 4 v. 4°. Q,271
Wanderungen durch. G. Byam. Dresden, 1852. . . . . . E,170
Chillingworth, W. Religion of Protestants. London, 1854. 12°. . . P,658
Works; with Life by T. Birch. Philadelphia, 1844. 8°. . . P,726
Chimney Corner, The. H. E. B. Stowe. Boston, 1868. 16°. . . . H,276
China and the Chinese. J. L. Nevius. New York, 1869. . . . . V,601
and Japan; Baron Gros's Embassy to. M. de Moges. Lon. 1860. 12°. V,602
Lord Elgin's Mission to. L. Oliphant. Edinb. 1859. 2 v. 8°. V,738
Journey to the Capitals of. R. Fortune. London, 1863. 8°. V,623
Visit to. B. Taylor. New York, 1869. 12°. . . . . V,606
during and since the War. J. F. Davis. London, 1852. 2 v. 12°. V,621
Five Years in. F. E. Forbes. London, 1848. 8°. . . . . V,642
History of. J. G. de Mendoza. London, 1853–54. 2 v. 8°. . . V,980
Insurrection in. J. M. Callery and M. Yvan. New York, 1853. 12°. V,599
its State and Prospects. W. H. Medhurst. London, 1857. 8°. . V,667
Journey to the Tea Countries of. R. Fortune. London, 1852. 8°. V,739
Life in. W. C. Milne. London, 1857. 12°. . . . . . . V,592
Middle Kingdom. S. W. Williams. New York, 1857. 2 v. 12°. . V,618
Observations on. W. L. G. Smith. New York, 1863. . . . . V,597
Pictorial, Descriptive, and Historical. J. Corner. Lond. 1853. p. 8°. L,98
Political, Commercial, and Social. R. M. Martin. Lond. 1847. 2 v. 8°. V,619
Taeping Rebellion. L. Brine. London, 1862. 12°. . . . . V,603
Tartar Conquerors of. P. J. D'Orleans. London, 1854. 8°. . V,997
Tartary and Thibet, Christianity in. E. R. Huc. Lond. 1858. 3 v. 8°. V,622

China, Tartary, and Thibet, Journey in. E. R. Huc. N. Y. 1852. 2 v. 12°. V,588
Times' Correspondent in. G. W. Cooke. London, 1858. 8°. . . V,594
Wanderungen in China. R. Fortune. Göttingen, 1853. 8°. . . E,219
Who is God in? S. C. Malan. London, 1855. 8°. . . . . . L,529
China Seas, Die Expedition in. W. Heine. Leipzig, 1858. 3 v. in 2. 8°. E,232
Kathay; a Cruise in. W. H. Macauley. New York, 1852. 12°. . V,598
Chincha Islands and Melbourne. G. W. Peck. New York, 1854. 12°. V,1064
Chinese, The. J. F. Davis. London, 1836. 2 v. 16°. . . . . . L,487
The same. New York, 1855. 2 v. 16°. . . . . . . L,396
Residence among the. R. Fortune. London, 1857. 8°. . . . . V,604
Social Life of the. J. Doolittle. New York, 1865. 2 v. 12°. . . V,595
Chinese Classics. J. Legge. v. 1. London, 1867. 12°. . . . . . D,774
Confucius and the; ed. by A. W. Loomis. San Francisco, 1867. 12°. G,5
Chinese Emigration; The How and Why. R. H. Conwell. Bost. 1871. 12°. V,605
Chinese Empire, illustrated. T. Allom. London, n. d. 2 v. 4°. . *F,220
Journey Through. E. R. Huc. London, 1855. 2 v. 8°. . . . V,643
The same. New York, 1855. 2 v. 12°. . . . . . . V,596
Chinese Language, Elementary Characters of. J. Hager. London, 1801. f°. Q,247
Chinese Repository, v. 2–4. Canton, 1834–36. 3 v. 8°. . . . . . S,18
Chinigchinick; Indians of California. G. Boscana. New York, 1846. 12°. V,154
Chipman, N. Principles of Government. Burlington, 1833. 8°. . . O,571
Chips from a German Workshop. F. M. Müller. New York, 1869–71. 3v. 12°. G,20
The same; v. 1, 2. London, 1868. 2 v. 8°. . . . . . G,21
Chissold, A. Practical Doctrines of Swedenborg. Boston, 1839. 12°. . P,844
Chittenden, L. E. Constitutional Convention, 1861. New York, 1864. 8°. B,921
Chivalry, Age of. T. Bulfinch. Boston, 1867. 12°. . . . . . . A,223
and the Crusades, History of. H. Stebbing. Edinburgh, 1830. 2 v. 16°. I,523
History of. G. P. R. James. New York, 1855. 16°. . . . . L,353
Choate, R., Works and Memoir of. S. G. Brown. Boston, 1862. 2 v. 8°. . C,964
Reminiscences of. E. G. Parker. New York, 1860. 12°. . . . C,751
Choice Notes from "Notes and Queries." London, 1859. 16°. . . . H,567
Cholera, as it appeared in Cincinnati. O. E. Newton. New York, 1867. 8°. L,928
Treatise on. G. Tinn. Newcastle, 1837. 8°. . . . . . N,252,1
Cholerstearine, De. O. B. Kühn. Lipsiæ, n. d. 4°. . . . . . N,252,41
Choron, A. Dictionary of Musicians. London, 1827. 2 v. 8°. . . . M,409
Choules, J. O. Cruise of the North Star. Boston, 1854. 12°. . . . V,338
Young Americans Abroad. Boston, 1864. 16°. . . . . J,1424
and Smith, T. History of Missions. Boston, 1832. 2 v. 4°. . . Q,265
Chrestomathic Day School. J. Bentham. London, 1816. 8°. . . O,1208
Chris and Otho. J. P. Smith. New York, 1870. 12°. . . . . . J,656
Christ. See *Jesus Christ.*
Christian Character, Young Lady's Guide to. H. Newcomb. Boston, 1843. H,289
Christian Church, Antiquities of. J. Bingham. London, 1840. 9 v. 8°. . P,784
History of. C. Hase. New York, 1855. 8°. . . . . . . P,591
A. Neander. London, 1851. 2 v. p. 8°. . . . . . . L,217
J. Priestley. Northumberland, 1802–3. 6 v. 8°. . . U,294,1–4
H. Stebbing. London, 1833–34. 2 v. 12°. . . . . M,1003
History of in 2d and 3d Centuries. J. A. Jeremie. Lond. 1852. 12°. P,570
from 4th to 12th Century. J. Carwithen. London, 1856. 12°. P,571
from 13th Century. A. Lyall and others. London, 1858. 12°. P,572

Christian Churches and Sects, History of. J. B. Marsden. Lond. 1856. 2 v. 8°. P,604
Christian Doctrine, Development of. J. H. Newman. London, 1845. 8°. . P,615
System of. C. I. Nitzsch. Edinburgh, 1849. 8°. . . . . . P,139
Christian Doctrines, Evenings with the. N. Adams. Boston, 1866. 12°. . . P,112
Christian Dogmas, History of. A. Neander. London, 1866. 2 v. p. 8°. . L,219
Christian Evidences, Introductory Lessons on. London, 1868. 32°. . . P,3
See also *Christianity, Evidences of.*
Christian Iconography, v. 1. A. N. Didron. London, 1851. 12°. . . L,102
Christian Library. New York, n. d. 45 v. 12° and 18°. . . . . P,746

Abbott, J. Young Christian, v. 32.
Abbott, J. S. C. Mother at Home, v. 24.
Child at Home, v. 24.
Amer. Tract Soc. Publications, v. 34–45.
Baxter, R. Call to the Unconverted, v. 6,
Dying Thoughts, and Life, v. 6.
Saint's Everlasting Rest, v. 5.
Bogue, D. Divine Authority of N. T., v. 18.
Brainerd, D., Life of. J. Edwards, v. 7.
Buchanan, C., Memoir of. H. Pearson, v. 16.
Edwards, J. Work of Redemption, v. 9.
Treatise on Religious Affections, v. 3.
Flavel, J. The Fountain of Life, v. 31.
Gallaudet, T. H. History of Josiah, v. 28.
Natural Theology, v. 28.
Repentance, v. 28.
Scripture Biography, v. 25–27.
Harris, J. Mammon, v. 20.
Hawes, J. Life of N. Smith, v. 29.
Hooker, H. Child's Book on Sabbath, v. 29.
James, J. A. Anxious Inquirer, v. 21.
Jenyns, S. Internal Evidence of Christianity, v. 14.
Kilpin, S., Life of, v. 23.
Krummacher, F. W. Elijah, v. 17.
Leslie, C. Short Method with Deists, v. 14.
Lyttleton, G. Conversion of St. Paul, v. 14.
Martyn, H., Memoir of. J. Sargent, v. 8.
Mason, J. Self-Knowledge, v. 21.
Melvill, H. Bible Thoughts, v. 19.
More, H. Practical Piety, v. 30.
Nevins, W. Practical Thoughts, v. 13.
Page, H., Memoir of. W. A. Halleck, v. 23.
Payson, E., Memoir of. A. Cummings, v. 12.
Pike, J. G. Guide for Young Disciples, v. 11.
Persuasives to Early Piety, v. 10.
Taylor, J. B., Memoir of. J. H. Rice, v. 15.
Venn, H. Complete Duty of Man, v. 33.
Watson, R. Reply to Gibbon and Paine, v. 14.
Wilberforce, W. Practical View of Christianity, v. 2.
Winslow, M. Memoir of H. L. Winslow, v. 22.

Christian Life. T. Arnold. Philadelphia, 1856. 12°. . . . . . . P,57
Memorials of. A. Neander. London, 1852. p. 8°. . . . . . L,218
Roots and Fruits of the. W. Arnot. London, 1860. 8°. . . . P,103
Social and Individual. P. Bayne. Boston, 1858. 12°. . . . P,295
Christian Meditation. L. Furlong. London, 1854. 16°. . . . . P,346
Christian Nurture. H. Bushnell. New York, 1868. 12°. . . . . P,41
Christian Philosopher. T. Dick. Philadelphia, 1869. 12°. . . U,260,1
Christian Psalmist. S. W. Leonard and A. D. Fillmore. Cincin. 1847. 16°. P,887
Christian Religion, History of. A. Neander. Lond. 1852–70. 9 v. in 10. p. 8°. L,215
The same. Boston, 1854–55. 5 v. 8°. . . . . . . P,612
Evidences, Doctrines, and Duties of the. O. Gregory. Lond. 1851. 12°. L,189
True. E. Swedenborg. New York, 1858. 8°. . . . . . . P,858
Christian Revelation and Modern Astronomy. T. Chalmers. N. Y. 1855. 12°. P,35
Evidences of the. T. Chalmers. New York, 1854. 2 v. 12°. . P,209
Christian Review, v. 17–20. New York, 1852–55. 4 v. 8°. . . . T,59
Christian Singers of Germany. C. Winkworth. Philadelphia, n. d. p. 8°. H,648
Christian Union, Argument for. B. P. Aydelott. Cincinnati, 1846. 12°. . P,36
Christian Year. J. Keble. Philadelphia, 1854. 24°. . . . . . . I,353
Christian's Mistake. D. M. Craik. New York, 1865. 12°. . . . . K,652
The same. Leipzig, 1865. 16°. . . . . . . . J,85
Christianity and Greek Philosophy. B. F. Cocker. New York, 1870. 8°. P,144
and Positivism. J. McCosh. New York, 1871. 12°. . . . . P,577
and Scepticism; Boston Lectures, 1870. Boston, 1870. 12°. . . P,151
Ancient. L. Coleman. Philadelphia, 1853. 8°. . . . . . P,404
applied to Affairs of Life. T. Chalmers. New York, 1853. 12°. . P,207
contrasted with Hindū Philosophy. J. R. Ballantyne. Lond. 1859. 8°. P,828
Corruptions of. J. Priestley. Birmingham, 1793. 2 v. 8°. . U,294,7,8

Christianity, Early Conflicts of. W. I. Kip. New York, 1850. 12°. . . P,566
Early Years of, Apostolic Era. E. de Pressensé. N. Y. 1870. 12°. . P,575
Essay on. P. B. Shelley. Boston, 1859. 12°. . . . . . C,1169
Evidences of. A. Barnes. New York, 1868. 8°. . . . . P,211
M. Hopkins. Boston, 1870. 12°. . . . . . . . P,165
Lectures on, at University of Virginia. New York, 1856. 8°. P,162
C. P. M'Ilvaine. Philadelphia, 1867. 12°. . . . . P,166
R. Owen and A. Campbell. Cincinnati, 1852. 8°. . . . P,115
J. Priestley. London, 1794-99. 3 v. 8°. . . U,294,10-12
W. Paley. New York, 1843. 18°. . . . . . . . P,344
The same. London, 1845. 8°. . . . . . P,709,1
F. Wrangham. Edinburgh, 1828. 16°. . . . . . . I,508
Internal Evidences of. S. Jenyns. New York, n. d. 18°. . P,746,14
First Historical Transformations of. A. Coquerel. Bost. 1867. 16°. P,347
Génie du. R. F. A. de Chateaubriand. Paris, 1852. 2 v. 12°. . P,132
Genius of. R. F. A. de Chateaubriand. Baltimore, 1856. 8°. . . P,138
History of. H. H. Milman. New York, 1855. 8°. . . . . P,595
in China, Tartary, and Thibet. E. R. Huc. London, 1857-8. 3 v. 8°. V,622
in India. J. W. Kaye. London, 1859. 8°. . . . . . P,593
Latin, History of. H. H. Milman. London, 1854-55. 6 v. 8°. . P,605
Lessons on the Truth of. Dublin, 1850. 24°. . . . . O,1103
the Logic of Creation. H. James. New York, 1857. 12°. . . P,350
Meditations on. F. Guizot. New York, 1865. 8°. . . . . P,84
Practical View of. W. Wilberforce. New York, n. d. 18°. . P,746,2
Republican. E. L. Magoon. Boston, 1849. 12°. . . . . P,194
Rise and Early Progress of. S. Hinds. London, 1854. 12°. . . P,569
Rise and Progress of. R. W. Mackay. London, 1854. 12°. . . P,603
Rise, Progress, and Corruptions of. R. Whately. N. Y. 1860. 12°. P,297
Supernatural Origin of. G. P. Fisher. New York, 1866. 8°. . . P,239
Tracts concerning. A. Norton. Cambridge, 1852. 8°. . . . P,140
without Judaism. B. Powell. London, 1857. 12°. . . . . P,222
Christie Johnstone. C. Reade. Boston, 1866. 16°. . . . . . K,897
Christison, R. Treatise on Poisons. Edinburgh, 1845. 8°. . . . L,968
Christmas, H. Echoes of the Universe. Philadelphia, 1850. 12°. . . O,334
Christmas Carol. C. Dickens. Leipzig, 1846. 16°. . . . . . J,116
Christmas Carols, Specimens of Old. London, 1841. 12°. . . . L,606,4
Christmas Guest. E. D. E. N. Southworth. Philadelphia, 1870. 12°. . K,417
Christmas Holidays in Rome. W. I. Kip. Philadelphia, 1846. 12°. . . V,495
Christmas in Montenegro. London, 1862. 8°. . . . . . . V,1086,2
Christmas Stories. C. Dickens. New York, 1868. 12°. . . . . K,470
The same. Philadelphia, n. d. 8°. . . . . . . . K,505
The same. New York, 1871. 12°. . . . . . . K,1129
The same. Leipzig, 1862. 16°. . . . . . . . J,117
Christy, D. Chemistry of Agriculture. Cincinnati, 1852. 8°. . . . M,554
Christie, R. History of Lower Canada. Montreal, 1866. 6 v. 16°. . . C,339
Chromatics. G. Field. London, 1845. 8°. . . . . . . . . M,109
Darstellung der Farbenlehre. H. W. Dove. Berlin, 1853. 8°. . G,720
Chromatography; a Treatise on Colors. G. Field. London, 1835. 4°. . Q,204
Chronica Monasterii Sancti Albani. London, 1863-9. 7 v. 8°. . . W,178
Chronicle of Ethelfled. A. Manning. London, 1861. 12°. . . . J,585

Chronicle of Florence of Worcester. London, 1854. 12°. . . . . . L,9
of the Abbey of Croyland. Ingulphus and Peter of Blois. Lond.1854. 12°. L,13
of Henry of Huntingdon. London, 1853. 8°. . . . . . . L,12
of the War in the Three Kingdoms. J. Heath. London, 1676. f°. F,275.
Chronicles and Memorials of Great Britain. See *Great Britain.*
of Canongate. Sir W. Scott. Boston, 1859. 12°. . . . . . K,931
The same. Philadelphia, 1852. 8°. . . . . . . K,958
The same. Philadelphia, 1869. 8°. . . . . . . K,1114
of Carlingford. M. Oliphant. New York, 1863. 8°. . . . K,874
The same. Leipzig, 1870. 7 v. in 4. 16°. . . . . .
Rector and Doctor's Family. J,399 Perpetual Curate. 2 v. in 1. J,401
Salem Chapel. 2 v. in 1. . J,400 Miss Marjoribanks. 2 v. in 1. J,402
of the Crusades. London, 1870. p. 8°. . . . . . . . L,5
of England, France, and Spain. Sir J. Froissart. Lond. 1857. 2 v. 8°. A,345
of London Bridge. London, 1839. 16°. . . . . . . . I,619
of the Priory of Hexham. Durham, 1863. 8°. . . . . F,126,44
Six Old English; edited by J. A. Giles. London, 1848. 8°. . . L,26
Chronicon Monasterii de Abingdon, v. 1, 2. London, 1858. 2 v. 8°. . W,152
Monasterii de Melsa, 1150–1406, v. 1–3. T. de Burton. Lon.1866–8. 3v. 8°. W,193
Scotorum. London, 1866. 8°. . . . . . . . . . . W,196
Chronicque de la Träison et Mort de Richart II. London, 1846. 8°. . U,629
Chronographie. M. Hanmer. London, 1607. 4°. . . . . . . P,647
Chronological Tables. J. Blair. London, 1856. p. 8°. . . . . . L,272
Ancient and Medieval History. London, 1857. 2 v. 12°. . . A,304
Chronological Theatre. C. Helvicus. London, 1687. 4°. . . . . . F,233
Chronology of Ancient Kingdoms. Sir I. Newton. London, 1728. 4°. . A,48
Dictionary of. W. Tegg. London, 1854. 8°. . . . . . . A,306
of the Church. H. B. Smith. New York, 1859. f°. . . . . Q,450
of History. Sir H. Nicolas. London, 1833. 12°. . . . . . M,985
Chrysander, F. G. F. Händel. Leipzig, 1858–60. 2 v. 8°. . . . . E,240
Jahrbücher für Musikalische Wissenschaft. Leipzig, 1863–7. 2 v. 8°. G,639
Chrysostom, J., Life of. F. M. Perthes. Boston, 1854. 12°. . . . . D,744
Chubbuck, E. Alderbrook. Boston, 1847. 2 v. 12°. . . . . . H,272
Church, B. History of Philip's War. n. p. n. d. 12°. . . . . . B,685
Church, F. Confessions of Gerald Estcourt. Leipzig, 1867. 2 v. in 1. 16°. J,347
For Ever and Ever. Leipzig, 1866. 2 v. in 1. 16°. . . . . J,348
Love's Conflict. Leipzig, 1865. 2 v. in 1. 16°. . . . . . J,349
Nelly Brooke. Leipzig, 1869. 2 v. in 1. 16°. . . . . . . J,350
Petronel. Leipzig, 1870. 2 v. in 1. 16°. . . . . . . . J,351
Véronique. Leipzig, 1869. 2 v. in 1. 16°. . . . . . . J,352
Church, J. Use of Clay-Retorts for Gas-Making. London, 1858. 8°. N,252,50
Church, The. Collection of Music. Cincinnati, 1855. 8°. . . . . M,417
Ancient. W. D. Killen. New York, 1859. 8°. . . . . . P,401
Popular Preachers of. W. Wilson. London, 1865. 12°. . C,517
and Congregation; Plea for Unity of. C. A. Bartol. Boston, 1858. 16°. P,231
and State. F. D. Maurice. London, 1839. 12°. . . . . O,1029
and Working-Classes. C. H. Bromby. London, 1850. 8°. . O,1251,3
and State in Scotland. R. Keith. Edinburgh, 1844–50. 3 v. 8°. . P,594
Essays on the Union of. B. W. Noël. New York, 1849. 12°. P,114
Early History of. E. M. Sewell. New York, 1867. 16°. . . . . P,600

Church, History of the. J. Milner and T. Haweis. London, 1847. 4 v. . P,574
History of the. H. Stebbing. London, 1842. 3 v. 8°. . . . P,626
The same. London, 1833–34. 2 v. 12°. . . M,1003
G. Waddington. London, 1835. 3 v. 8°. . . . . P,634
Doctrine and Practice of. J. Dunlavy. New York, 1847. 8°. . P,240
of the Apostolic Age. M. Baumgarten. Edinb. 1854. 3 v. 8°. . P,403
of England; an Eirenicon. E. B. Pusey. New York, 1866. 12°. . P,238
Discourses on the Liturgy. M. Hole. Lond. 1837–38. 4 v. 8°. P,899
Faith of the Liturgy. F. D. Maurice. London, 1860. 12°. . P,886
Reformation of the. G. Burnet. London, 1850. 2 v. 8°. . P,649
The same. New York, 1843. 3 v. 8°. . . . P,661
of Scotland, History of. W. M. Hetherington. New York, 1848. 8°. P,592
History of the Sufferings of. R. Wodrow. Glasgow, n. d. 4 v. 8°. P,646
Prophetical Office of. J. H. Newman. London, 1837. 8°. . . P,799
Church Dictionary. W. F. Hook. Philadelphia, 1854. 8°. . . . P,164
Church History, Manual of. H. E. F. Guericke. Andover, 1869. 8°. . P,606
Text-Book of. J. C. L. Gieseler. New York, 1855–58. 3 v. 8°. . P,589
J. H. Kurtz. Philadelphia, 1870. 2 v. 8°. . . . . P,607
Church Memorial. R. D. Harper. Columbus, 1858. 12°. . . . . P,277
Church Principles. W. E. Gladstone. London, 1840. 8°. . . . P,312
Church Schoolmaster. S. Robins. London, 1850. 12°. . . . O,1138
Churches, Designs for Parish. J. C. Hart. New York, 1857. 8°. . . M,229
Variations of the Protestant. J. B. Bossuet. N. Y. 1836–42. 2 v. 12°. P,568
Churchill, C., and De Foe. J. Forster. London, 1806. p. 8°. . . I,661,3
Poetical Works. Boston, 1854. 3 v. 16°. . . . . . . I,203
Churchill, C. H. Druzes and Maronites, 1840–60. London, 1862. 12°. . B,556
Mount Lebanon. London, 1853. 3 v. 8°. . . . . . . V,641
Churchill, J., *Duke of Marlborough*, Life of. A. Alison. N. Y. 1848. 12°. D,160
Life of. C. Bucke. London, 1839. 16°. . . . . . . I,631
C. Mac Farlane. London, 1854. 16°. . . . . . J,1231
Memoirs of. W. Coxe. London, 1847–48. 3 v. p. 8. . . . L,176
Churchill, O., and J. Collection of Voyages. London, 1744–6. 6 v. f°. Q,435,1,2
Churchill, S., *Duchess of Marlborough*, Private Corresp. Lond. 1838. 2 v. 8°. H,840
Church-Yards, Chapters on. C. B. Southey. Edinburgh, 1829. 2 v. 16°. H,585
Churton, E. Gongora; or, Times of Philip III. and IV. of Spain. London, 1862. 2 v. p. 8°. . . . . . . . . . . . B,455
Cibber, C. Dramatic Works. London, 1760. 4 v. 12°. . . . . . I,681
Cicero, M. T. Academic Quest., De Finibus, and Tus. Disp. N. Y. 1853. p. 8°. L,50
Cato and Lælius; Old Age and Friendship. Lond. 1795. 2 v. 8°. U,256,5
De Senectute, De Amicitia, etc; ed. by C. Anthon. N. Y. 1855. p. 8°. U,411
Epistolæ omnes; ex ed. J. V. Leclerc. Parisiis, 1827–8. 3 v. 8°. U,313
Fragmenta; ex editione J. V. Leclerc. Parisiis, 1831. 8°. . . U,314
Letters. London, n. d. 3 v. 8°. . . . . . . . . U,256,2–4
and Life. C. Middleton. London, 1858. 8°. . . . . D,737
to his Friends. Edinburgh, 1808. 5 v. 16°. . . . . H,857
The same; edited by W. Melmoth. London, n. d. 8°. U,256,2
Life of. W. Forsyth. London, 1867. 8°. . . . . . . . D,736
J. F. Hollings. London, 1839. 16°. . . . . . . I,628
Offices, Old Age, Friendship, etc. London, 1855. p. 8°. . . . . L,51
Opera Philosophica; ex ed. J. V. Leclerc. Parisiis, 1828–31. 6 v. 8°. U,316

Cicero, M. T. Opera Rhetorica et Oratorica; ed. J. W. Rinn. Par. 1831-2. 2 v. 8°. U,317
Orationes omnes; ex ed. J. V. Leclerc. Parisiis, 1827-30. 6 v. 8°. U,315
Orations; translated by C. D. Yonge. London, 1851-56. 4 v. p. 8. L,47
Offices, Cato and Lælius. New York, 1855. 3 v. 18°. . . U,359
Oratory and Orators; translated by J. S. Watson. Lond. 1855. p. 8°. L,48
Quinque Indices; ex editione J. V. Leclerc. Parisiis, 1832. 8°. . U,318
Select Orations; translated by C. D. Yonge. New York, 1856. 12°. U,414
Three Dialogues on the Orator; tr. by W. Guthrie. N. Y. 1855. 18°. U,358
Treatises; translated by C. D. Yonge. London, 1853. p. 8°. . . L,49
Tusculan Disputations; edited by C. Anthon. New York, 1852. 12°. U,412
Cid, Chronicle of the. R. Southey. Lowell, 1846. 8°. . . . . . B,478
Cider, Manuel du Fabricant de. L. F. Dubief. Paris, 1834. 24°. . . M,591
Cilicia and its Governors. W. B. Barker. London, 1853. 8°. . . . V,674
Cincinnati, Bible in the Public Schools of. Cincinnati, 1870. 8°. . . O,957
Charter, Amendments, and Ordinances. Cincinnati, 1850. 8°. . . P.D.
City Departments, Annual Reports, 1867-70. Cin. 1869-70. 4 v. 8°. O,594
Common Schools; Reports, 4th to 41st. Cincin. 1830-70. 38 v. 8°. *O,836
Diary and Business Guide. F. W. Hurtt. Cincinnati, 1856-7. 2 v. 24°. C,148
Directory, 1819, 20, 42, 44, 49-70. Cincin. 1819-70. 24 v. 12° and 8°. P.D.
Early Physicians, Scenery, etc., of. D. Drake. Cincin. 1852. 12°. L,830
Excursion to California, 1869. Cincinnati, 1870. 12°. . . . V,99
Hughes High School, Annual of Alumni, 1870. Cincinnati, 1870. 8°. O,834
in 1826. B. Drake and E. D. Mansfield. Cincinnati, 1827. 12°. . *C,208
in 1841, Annals and Prospects of. C. Cist. Cincinnati, 1841. 12°. . C,210
in 1851, Sketches and Statistics of. C. Cist. Cincinnati, 1851. 12°. C,211
in 1859, Sketches and Statistics of. C. Cist. Cincinnati, 1859. 12°. C,212
Lancet and Observer, v. 8. Cincinnati, 1865. 8°. . . . . . L,950
Laws and General Ordinances. Cincinnati, 1853. 8°. . . . . P.D.
The same. Cincinnati, 1854. 8°. . . . . . . . . P.D.
The same. Cincinnati, 1866. 8°. . . . . . . . . P.D.
Supplement. Cincinnati, 1869. 8°. . . . . . . . P.D.
Mercantile Library Association Catalogue. Cincinnati, 1855. 8°. . L.R.
The same. Cincinnati, 1869. 8°. . . . . . . . L.R.
Miscellany, v. 1, 2. C. Cist. Cincinnati, 1845-46. 8°. . . . C,215
Newspapers, Bound.
Atlas, 1843, 44, 48, 49. 3 v. f°. . . . . . . F,81
Chronicle, 1830, 36, 37, 39-50. 21 v. f°. . . . . . F,80
Chronicle and Literary Gazette, 1830. 1 v. . . . . . F,801
Commercial, 1861-65. 10 v. f°. . . . . . . F,300
Ohio School-Library Catalogue. Cincinnati, 1856. 8°. . . . L.R.
The same. Cincinnati, 1860. 8°. . . . . . . . . L.R.
Plants of. T. G. Lea. Philadelphia, 1849. 8°. . . . . N,1010
Position, Duty, and Destiny of. W. Bebb. Cincinnati, 1848. . T,19,2
Queen City in 1869. G. E. Stevens. Cincinnati, 1869. 16°. . . C,209
Schools of. J. P. Foote. Cincinnati, 1855. 8°. . . . . O,1012
Sonora Mining Association, Report. Cincinnati, 1866. 8°. . . O,501
Spring Grove Cemetery. Cincinnati, 1869. 4°. . . . . . F,42
Report for 1857. Cincinnati, 1857. 8°. . . . . . . C,228
Suburbs of. S. D. Maxwell. Cincinnati, 1870. 4°. . . . . . C,226
Type Foundry Specimens. Cincinnati, 1844. 8°. . . . . . M,740
View of. D. Drake. Cincinnati, 1815. 12°. . . . . . . *C,207

Cinnamon and Pearls. H. Martineau. London, 1859. 16°. . . . . K,551
Cipher; a Romance. J. G. Austin. New York, 1869. 8°. . . . K,8
Clarkson, T. Quakerism. Indianapolis, 1870. 8°. . . . . . . P,861
Circassia. G. L. Ditson. New York, 1850. 8°. . . . . . . V,679
Circle of Light. H. P. Malet. London, 1869. p. 8°. . . . . . . H,244
Cirripedia, Monograph on the. C. Darwin. London, 1851–54. 2 v. 8°. . O,304
Cist, C. Cincinnati in 1841. Cincinnati, 1841. 12°. . . . . . . C,210
in 1851. Cincinnati, 1851. 12°. . . . . . . . C,211
in 1859. Cincinnati, 1859. 12°. . . . . . . . C,212
Cincinnati Miscellany, v. 1, 2. Cincinnati, 1845–46. 2 v. in 1. 8°. . *C,215
Cities and Towns of the World. London, 1830. 12°. . . . M,1007
of the Ancient World, Great. T. A. Buckley. London, 1864. 16°. A,4
Ruins of Ancient. C. Bucke. New York, 1856. 2 v. 16°. . . L,428
Citoyenne Jacqueline. S. Tytler. London, 1865–66. 3 v. 16°. . K,1056
City Life, Moral Aspects of. E. H. Chapin. New York, 1854. 12°. . . H,261
City of the Great King. J. T. Barclay. Philadelphia, 1858. 8°. . . V,662
City of the Magyar. J. Pardoe. London, 1840. 3 v. 12°. . . . V,429
City Poems. A. Smith. Boston, 1857. 16°. . . . . . . . . I,424
Civil Code, Pleadings and Practice under. S. Nash. Cincinnati, 1856. 8°. U,515
Civil Engineering. H. Law. London, 1858–59. 3 v. in 1. 12°. . . M,943
Elementary Course of. D. H. Mahan. New York, 1867. 8°. . M,706
Encyclopædia of. E. Cresy. London, 1865. 8°. . . . *M,712
of North America. D. Stevenson. London, 185–. 12°. . . . M,963
Civil Engineers' and Architects' Journal. London, 1837–60. 23 v. 8°. . Q,321
Civil Law, Corpus Juris Civilis. Lipsiæ, 1856. 3 v. 8°. . . . Q,342
The same. Gottingæ, 1776. 2 v. 4°. . . . . . . . Q,147
in its natural order. J. Domat. Philadelphia, 1850. 2 v. 8°. . U,517
Civil Liberty and Self-Government. T. Lieber. Philadelphia, 1859. 8°. . O,551
Civil War, 1861–65. See *United States, Southern Rebellion.*
Civil Wars, Select Tracts on the. London, 1815. 8°. . . . . . A,561
Civilization, History of. F. Guizot. London, 1868–70. 3 v. p. 8°. . . L,192
The same. New York, 1850–52. 4 v. 12°. . . . . . S.C.
en Europe, Historie de. H. Roux-Ferrand. Paris, 1833–41. 6 v. 8°. A,311
in England, History of. H. T. Buckle. New York, 1866. 2 v. 8°. B,33
in Europe, History of. F. Guizot. New York, 1846. 4 v. 12°. . A,301
in the Fifth Century. A. F. Ozanam. London, 1868. 2 v. 12°. . A303
Origin of. Sir J. Lubbock. New York, 1871. 12°. . . . . . O,534
Civilized America. T. C. Grattan. London, 1859. 2 v. 8°. . . . V,129
Claiborne, J. F. H., Life of. J. A. Quitman. New York, 1860. 2 v. 12°. C,929
Clairaut, A. C. Elémens d'Algèbre. Paris, 1768. 12°. . . . . M,1104
Clairon, C. J., Mémoires de; edited by J. F. Barriere. Paris, 1855. 12°. . D,612
Clanny, W. R. Invention of the Safety-Lamp. Gateshead, 1844. 12°. N,252,23
Clapp, W. W. Record of the Boston Stage. Boston, 1853. 12°. . . I,714
Clapperton, H. Second Expedition into Africa. Philadelphia, 1829. 8°. V,832
Clara Stevens. M. M. Sherwood New York, 1860. 12°. . . K,1008,4
Clara Vere. F. Spielhagen. Berlin, 1867. 16°. . . . . . . G,452
Clarendon, Earl of. See *Hyde, E.*
Claret and Olives. A. B. Reach. London, 1852. 8°. . . . . . V,479
Clarissa Harlowe. S. Richardson. London, 1820. 8 v. 12°. . . . K,529
The same. Leipzig, 1862. 4 v. 16°. . . . . . . . J,422

Clark, A. School-Day Dialogues. Philadelphia, n. d. 12°. . . . . o,1224
Clark, B. F. Mirthfulness and its Exciters. Boston, 1870. 12°. . . H,121
Clark, D. K. Railway Machinery. Glasgow, 1855. 2 v. 4°. . . . S.C.
Clark, E. L. Daleth; Egypt Illustrated. Boston, 1864. 8°. . . . V,868
Clark, G. R. Campaign in the Illinois, 1778–79. Cincinnati, 1869. 8°. . C,219
Clark, H. Introduction to Heraldry. London, 1866. p. 8°. . . . L,288
Clark, J. W. Yacht Voyage to Faroe Islands and Iceland. Lond. 1861. 8°. V,1086,1
Clark, H. J. Mind in Nature. New York, 1865. 8°. . . . . N,556
Clark, W. G. Naples and Garibaldi. London, 1861. 8°. . . . V,1086,1
Poland. London, 1864. 8°. . . . . . . . . V,1086,3
Clark, J. H. Sight and Hearing. New York, 1856. 8°. . . . . L,878
Clark, R. S. Dotty Dimple Stories. Boston, 1870. 6 v. 16°. . . . J,1650

Vol. 1. Dotty Dimple at her Grandmother's. Vol. 4. Dotty Dimple at Play.
2. Dotty Dimple at Home. 5. Dotty Dimple at School.
3. Dotty Dimple Out West. 6. Dotty Dimple's Flyaway.

Clark, T. Hot-Blast in Manufacture of Cast-Iron. Edinburgh, 1835. 4°. N,252,57
Difficulty in Isomorphism. Aberdeen, 1836. 8°. . . . N,252,2
Process for Purifying Water. London, 1841. 8°. . . . N,252,22
Clark, W. G. Literary Remains. New York, 1844. 8°. . . . . H,146
Clarke, A. Autobiography. London, 1841. 8°. . . . . . . . D,451
Bibliographical Dictionary. Liverpool, 1802–4. 6 v. 12°. . . L.R.
Bibliographical Miscellany. London, 1806. 2 v. 12°. . . . L.R.
Commentary on the New Testament. Philadelphia, 1870. 8°. . P,520
on the Bible. London, n. d. 6 v. r. 8°. . . . . . P,552
Memoirs of the Wesley Family. New York, 1851. 12°. . . C,1186
Religious and Literary Life of. London, 1841. 8°. . . . . D,451
Clarke, E. D. Travels in Europe, Asia, and Africa. N. Y. 1813–14. 2 v. 12°. V,1035
Clarke, G. Voyage to America. Albany, 1867. 4°. . . . . . . C,103
Clark, J., the Pioneer Preacher. J. M. Peck. New York, 1855. 16°. . C,829
Clarke, J. F. Eleven Weeks in Europe. Boston, 1852. 12°. . . . V,336
Steps in Belief; or, Christianity *vs.* Atheism. Boston, 1870. 12°. . P,71
Ten Great Religions; Comparative Theology. Boston, 1871. 8°. . P,584
Clarke, M. C. Complete Concordance to Shakespeare. Boston, n. d. 8°. . *I,892
Girlhood of Shakespeare's Heroines. London, 1864. 3 v. 12°. . . I,848
Iron Cousin. New York, 1866. 12°. . . . . . . . K,919
Portia, and Stories from Shakespeare. New York, 1868. 12°. . K,1649
Yarns of an Old Mariner. Boston, 1869. 16°. . . . . . . J,1550
Clarke, S. Sermons. London, 1730–44. 10 v. 8°. . . . . . P,671
Classic and Historic Portraits. J. Bruce. New York, 1854. 12°. . . C,503
Classical Bibliography, Manual of. J. W. Moss. London, 1825. 2 v. 8°. L.R.
Classical Dictionary. C. Anthon. New York, 1869. 8°. . . . . . L.R.
The same. New York, 1854. 8°. . . . . . . . R.R.
J. Lempriere. New York, 1825. 8°. . . . . . . . . L.R.
Classical Geography, Atlas of. London, 1861. 8°. . . . . . . L,79
Classical Literature, Manual of. J. J. Eschenburg. Philadelphia, 1852. 8°. H,733
Classical Pronunciation, Key to. J. Walker. Philadelphia, 1808. 8°. . L.R.
Classical Scholarship and Learning. J. W. Donaldson. Camb. 1856. 12°. O,833
Classical Study, Method of. S. H. Taylor. Boston, 1861. 12°. . . . O,974
Classical Studies. B. Sears and others. Boston, 1843. 12°. . . . L,549
Classics, Greek and Latin, Rare editions of. T. F. Dibdin. Lond. 1827. 2 v. 8°. L.R.
Classiques de la Table. Paris, 1855. 2 v. 12°. . . . . . . . H,872

Clater, F., and J. Every Man his own Farrier. London, 1854. 12°. . . M,469
Claude, the Colporteur. A. Manning. London, 1854. 12°. . . . J,584
Claudia. C. Tucker. New York, 1870. 16°. . . . . . . . K,575
Claudianus, C. Opera omnia; recensuit N. L. Artaud. Parisiis, 1824. 2 v. 8°. U,319
Claverings, The. A. Trollope. New York, 1866. 8°. . . . K,1044
The same. Leipzig, 1867. 2 v. in 1. 16°. . . . . J,496
Clavigero, F. S. History of Mexico. Philadelphia, 1804. 3 v. 8°. . . C,371
Clay, C. M. Writings. New York, 1848. 8°. . . . . . . . U,116
Clay, H. Clay Code; Text-Book of Eloquence. New York, 1844. 12°. . O,825
Last Seven Years of. C. Colton. New York, 1856. 8°. . . C,1109
Life of. E. Sargent and H. Greeley. Auburn, 1853. 12°. . . C,703
and Times of. C. Colton. New York, 1846. 2 v. 8°. . . C,1107
Monument to the Memory of. A. H. Carrier. Cincinnati, 1859. 4°. C,705
Speech at Dayton, Sept. 29, 1842. Cincinnati, 1842. 8°. . . H,302,4
Works; edited by C. Colton. New York, n. d. 6 v. 8°. . . U,102
Clay, W. Manufacture of Wrought Steel. London, 1858. 4°. . N,252,51
Water Supply of London. London, 1849. 8°. . . . N,252,39
Clay-Lands and Loamy Soils. J. Donaldson. London, 1852. 12°. . . M,912
Clayton, J. Account of Observables in Virginia, 1688. See *Force's Tracts*, v. 3.
Cleaveland, H. W., and others. Village and Farm Cottages. N. Y. 1856. 8°. M,223
Cleaveland, P. Treatise on Mineralogy and Geology, v. 1. Boston, 1822. 8°. N,858
Cleghorn, G. Ancient and Modern Art. Edinburgh, 1848. 2 v. 16°. . M,7
Cleland, T., Memoirs of. E. P. Humphrey and T. H. Cleland. Cin. 1859. 12°. C,802
Clemens, S. L. Celebrated Jumping Frog, etc. New York, 1869. 16°. . H,63
Innocents Abroad. Hartford, 1870. 8°. . . . . . . . . V,400
Mark Twain's Burlesque Autobiography. New York, 1871. 12°. . K,263
Clement, C. E. Legendary and Mythological Art. New York, 1870. 12°. M,82
Clement, J. Noble Deeds of American Women. New York, 1856. 12°. . C,739
Clementi, M. Sonaten für das Pianoforte. Wolfenbüttel, n. d. 3 v. 4°. . Q,192
Cleopatra, History of. J. Abbott. New York, 1851. 16°. . . . J,1409
Clergyman's Companion in Visiting the Sick. W. Paley. Lond. 1845. 8°. P,709,3
Clergyman's Wife, and other Sketches. A. C. Ritchie. New York, 1867. 12°. K,221
Cléry, J. B. C. H., Mémoires de. Paris, 1855. 12°. . . . . . . D,611
Cleve Hall. E. M. Sewell. New York, 1868. 12°. . . . . . . K,994
Cleveland, Ohio, Early History of. C. Whittlesey. Cleveland, 1867. 8°. . C,224
Cleveland, C. D. Compendium of American Literature. Phila. 1858. 12°. H,663
Compendium of English Literature. Philadelphia, 1859. 12°. . H,682
English Literature of Nineteenth Century. Philadelphia, 1863. 8°. . H,697
Cleveland, H. W. S. Hints to Riflemen. New York. 1864. 8°. . . M,337
Cleveland, H. R. Life of Henry Hudson. New York, 1860. 12°. . C,860,10
Cleveland, J. F. Political Text-Book for 1860. New York, 1860. 8°. . O,527
Clever Woman of the Family. C. M. Yonge. New York, 1868. 8°. . K,1077
The same. Leipzig, 1865. 2 v. in 1. 16°. . . . . J,545
Cliff Climbers. M. Reid. Boston, 1866. 16°. . . . . . . . J,1563
Climatology of the United States. L. Blodget. Philadelphia, 1857. 8°. N,145
Clinton, De W., Life of. W. W. Campbell. New York, 1849. 12°. . . C,702
Life of. J. Renwick. New York, 1854. 16°. . . . . . . L,420
Report on Correspondence with Gov. Williamson. Trent. 1826. 8°. B,809,2
Clinton Bradshaw. F. Thomas. Cincinnati, 1847. 2 v. in 1. 8°. . *T,19,3
Clive, C. Paul Ferroll. Leipzig, 1856. 16°. . . . . . . . J,68

Clive, C. Why Paul Ferroll killed his Wife. Leipzig, 1861. 16°. . . . J,69
Year after Year. Leipzig, 1858. 16°. . . . . . . . J,70
Clock and Watchmakers' Manual. M. L. Booth. New York, 1863. 12°. M,625
Clock and Watchmaking. E. B. Denison. London, 1850. 12°. . . . M,907
Cloister and the Hearth. C. Reade. New York, 1865. 8°. . . . . K,898
The same. Leipzig, 1864. 2 v. in 1. 16°. . . . . J,417
Cloquet, J. Private Life of General Lafayette. London, 1835. 8°. . . D,623
Cloud on the Heart. A. S. Roe. New York, 1869. 12°. . . . . K,269
Clouds and Sunshine. C. Reade. Boston, 1855. 16°. . . . . K,899
Cloudesley; a Tale. W. Godwin. London, 1830. 3 v. 12°. . . . K,526
Clough, A. B. Contractors' and Builders' Manual. Philadelphia, 1855. 18°. M,672
Clough, A. H. Poems; with a Memoir. London, 1863. 16°. . . . . I,319
Bothie of Toper-na-Fuosich. Cambridge, 1849. 12°. . . . . I,323
Poems and Prose Remains. London, 1869. 2 v. 12°. . . . U,265
Club Life of London. J. Timbs. London, 1866. 2 v. 12°. . . . B,58
Clulow, W. B. Aphorisms and Reflections. London, 1843. 8°. . . . H,448
Coal and Coal Oil. E. Bowen. Philadelphia, 1865. 8°. . . . . N,759
Combustion of. C. W. Williams. London, 1858. 12°. . . . M,975
Entstehung der Steinkohlen. H. R. Göppert. Leiden, 1848. 4°. . Q,44
Europa's. H. B. Geinitz. Munchen, 1865. 2 v. and Atlas. 4°. . F,95
Our, and our Coal Pits. London, 1865. p. 8°. . . . . . . I,665
Statistics of. R. C. Taylor. Philadelphia, 1855. 8°. . . . . N,847
Zusammensetzung der. T. Richardson. n. t. p. 8°. . . . N,252,1
Coal Field, Economy of a. J. F. W. Johnston. Durham, 1838. 8°. . N,252,2
Coal Gas. S. Hughes. London, 1853. 12°. . . . . . . . M,939
Coal Mines, Explosions in. M. Dunn. London, 1845. 8°. . . N,252,35
Ventilating by Steam Jet. J. A. Lougridge. Newcastle, 1852. 8°. N,252,56
N. Wood. Newcastle, 1853. 8°. . . . . . . N,252,56
M. Dunn. Newcastle, 1854. 8°. . . . . . . N,252,56
Coal Question, The. W. S. Jevons. London, 1866. 8°. . . . . N,846
Coale, W. E. Hints on Health. Boston, 1852. 18°. . . . . . . L,837
The same. Boston, 1857. 12°. . . . . . . . L,846
Coathupe, C. T. Effects of Respiration on Air. Bristol, 1838. 8°. . N,252,2
Glass Tubes for Eudiometrical Purposes. Bristol, 1840. 4°. . N,252,42
Coats, W. Geography of Hudson's Bay, 1727–51. London, 1852. 8°. . V,993
Cobb, L. New North-American Reader; Fifth Book. New York, 1844. 12°. O,878
New Spelling Book. Cincinnati, 1849. 12°. . . . . . . O,771
Cobb, T. R. R. Law of Negro Slavery in the U. S., v. 1. Phil. 1858. 8°. O,399
Cobbe, F. P. Broken Lights; Inquiry on Religious Faith. Lond. 1864. 12°. P,261
Hours of Work and Play. London, 1867. 12°. . . . . . H,322
Italics; Brief Notes in Italy in 1864. London, 1864. 8°. . . V,503
Pursuits of Women. London, n. d. 12°. . . . . . . . . O,410
Religious Duty. London, 1854. 12°. . . . . . . . P,102
Studies, Ethical and Social. London, 1865. p. 8°. . . . O,557
Cobbett, W. Cottage Economy. London, 1822. 12°. . . . . . . M,670
Little Plain English on the Treaty, etc. Philadelphia, 1795. 8°. . B,859
Paper against Gold. New York, 1854. 18°. . . . . . . O,462
Porcupine's Works, v. 2–12. London, 1801. 11 v. 8°. . . . U,258
Protestant Reformation in England and Ireland. Lond. 1829. 2 v. 8°. P,664
Selections from his Political Works. London, n. d. 6 v. 8°. . . U,226

Cobbett, W., and others. Collection of State Trials. Lond. 1816–28. 34 v. 8°. U,701
Cobden, P. Beckoning Series. Boston, 1871. 2 v. 16°. . . . . J,1546
Vol. 1. Who will Win. Vol. 2. Going on a Mission.
Cobden, R., Biography of. J. Mac Gilchrist. New York, 1865. 16°. . D,3
Cocculus Indicus, Fatty Acid of. W. Crowder. London, 1852. 8°. . N,252,44
Cochin, A. Results of Slavery. Boston, 1863. 12°. . . . . . . O,402
Results of Emancipation. Boston, 1863. 12°. . . . . . . O,391
Cochrane, J. D. Journey through Russia and Tartary. Edinb. 1829. 2 v. 16°. I,513
Cochrane, R., and J. Geometry, with Drawing. Baltimore, 1857. 8°. M,1123
Cochut, A. Le Chili en 1859. Paris, 1860. 8°. . . . . . . N,252,45
Cockayne, T. O. Life of Marshal Turenne. London, 1856. p. 8. . I,661,1
Cockburn, H. T., *Lord*. Life of Francis Jeffrey. Phil. 1856. 2 v. in 1. 12°. D,55
Memorials of his Time. New York, 1859. 12°. . . . . D,291
Cocker, B. F. Christianity and Greek Philosophy. New York, 1870. 8°. P,144
Cockton, H. Percy Effingham. London, 1853. 2 v. 12°. . . . J,563
Sylvester Sound; the Somnambulist. London, 1867. p. 8°. . . K,630
Valentine Vox. Philadelphia, n. d. 8°. . . . . . . . K,632
Code Napoléon. London, n. d. 8°. . . . . . . . . . U,506
Code Correctionnel et de Simple Police. Paris, n. d. 8°. . . . . U,540
Code of Gentoo Laws; translated by N. B. Halbed. London, 1776. 4°. . Q,341
Codman, J. Ten Months in Brazil. Boston, 1867. 16°. . . . . V,252
Coffin, C. C. Following the Flag. Boston, 1865. 16°. . . . J,1500
Four Years of Fighting. Boston, 1866. 8°. . . . . . . B,940
My Days and Nights on the Battle-Field. Boston, 1868. 16°. . J,1236
Our New Way round the World. Boston, 1869. 8°. . . V,1075
Seat of Empire. Boston, 1870. 12°. . . . . . . . . V,51
Winning his Way. Boston, 1866. 16°. . . . . . . J,1270
Coffin, J. History of Newbury and Newburyport. Boston, 1845. 8°. . . C,71
Coffin, N. W. America; an Ode, and other Poems. Boston, 1843. 12°. . I,42
Coffin, R. B. Cakes and Ale at Woodbine. New York, 1868. 12°. . . K,93
Matrimonial Infelicities. New York, 1865. 8°. . . . . . K,12
My Married Life at Hillside. New York, 1865. 12°. . . . K,13
Out of Town; Rural Episode. New York, 1867. 12°. . . . K,109
Coggeshall, G. History American Privateers in 1812–14. N. Y. 1861. 8°. B,856
Coggeshall, W. T. Cash and Character. Cincinnati, 1855. 16°. . . H,2
Chronology of Paper and Paper-Making. Albany, 1856. 8°. . . M,639
Index to the Laws of Ohio. Columbus, 1858. 8°. . . . . . P.D.
Lincoln Memorial. Columbus, 1865. 12°. . . . . . . C,959
Newspaper Record. Philadelphia, 1856. 2 v. 8°. . . . . M,639
Poets and Poetry of the West. New York, 1864. 8°. . . . . I,168
Writing and Spelling Reform. n. t. p. 16°. . . . . . . L,675
Cohn, A. Shakespeare in Germany. London, 1865. 4°. . . . . . I,788
Coin Collector's Manual. H. N. Humphreys. London, 1853. 2 v. 12°. . L,298
Coinage, Account of American. J. H. Hickox. Albany, 1858. 8°. . . M,390
of Great Britain, Annals of. R. Ruding. London, 1840. 3 v. 4°. *Q,269
Coins, Ancient and Modern. J. R. Snowden. Philadelphia, 1860. 8°. *M,389
Study of. J. Y. Akerman. London, 1848. 16°. . . . M,385
Gold and Silver. J. R. Eckfeldt and W. E. Du Bois. Phil. 1842. 4°. *M,391
Coke, Sir E., Life of. E. P. Burke. London, n. d. 8°. . . . . . C,581
Life of C. W. Johnson. London, 1837. 2 v. 8°. . . . . . D,92

Coke, T., Life of. S. Drew. New York, 1847. 12°. . . . . . c,1000
Coke et Charbon de Tourbe, Fabrication du. J. Pelouze. Paris, 1842. 8°. N,252,10
Colburn, Z. Memoir; written by himself. Springfield, 1833. 12°. . . c,741
Colburn, Z., jr. Locomotive Engine. Philadelphia, 1854. 12°. . . M,634
Colchis, Reise nach Kolchis. M. Wagner. Leipzig, 1850. 12°. . . . E,214
Colden, C. History of Five Indian Nations of Canada. London, 1747. 8°. *B,584
Cole M. Frank Warrington. New York, 1864. 12°. . . . . . . K,16
Louie's last Term at St. Mary's. New York, 1864. 12°. . . . K,15
Rutledge. New York, 1868. 12°. . . . . . . . . K,14
St. Philip's. New York, 1865. 12°. . . . . . . . . K,17
Roundhearts, and other Stories. New York, 1867. 12°. . . J,1436
Sutherlands. New York, 1867. 12°. . . . . . . . . K,18
Cole, S. W. American Fruit-Book. New York, 1858. 18°. . . . M,435
Cole, T., Life of. L. L. Noble. New York, 1853. 8°. . . . . D,156
Coleman, L. Ancient Christianity. Philadelphia, 1853. 8°. . . . P,404
Text-Book and Atlas of Biblical Geography. Philadelphia, 1857. 8°. V,1143
British Butterflies. London, 1862. 8°. . . . . . . . O,3
Coleman, W. S. Our Woodlands, Heaths, and Hedges. London, 1859. 16°. N,926
Colenso, J. W. Arithmetic. London, 1856. 12°. . . . . M,1084
Elements of Algebra. London, 1855. 18°. . . . . M,1083
The same, 11th edition. London, 1854–55. 2 v. 12°. . M,1096
Pentateuch and Book of Joshua. New York, 1863. 2 v. 12°. . P,493
St. Paul's Epistle to the Romans. New York, 1863. 12°. . . . P,494
Solution of Examples in Plane Trigonometry. London, 1856. 16°. M,1085
Solutions to Examples in Arithmetic. London, 1854. 12°. . . M,1091
Collegiate System in the United States. F. Wayland. Boston, 1842. 16°. O,961
Coleoptera, Einführung in das Studium der. L. Imhoff. Basel, 1856. 8°. G,947
Coleridge, H. Index to English Literature of 13th Century. Lond. 1859. 8°. L,573
Lives of Northern Worthies. London, 1852. 3 v. 8°. . . C,1166

Vol. 1. A. Marvell; R. Bentley; Thomas, Lord Fairfax; J., Earl of Derby.
2. Lady Anne Clifford; R. Ascham; J. Fisher; W. Mason; R. Arkwright.
3. Wm. Roscoe; Capt. James Cook; Wm. Congreve; John Fothergill.

Coleridge, H. N. Six Months in the West Indies. London, 1832. 16°. . I,614
Coleridge, Sir J. T. Memoir of J. Keble. Oxford, 1869. 8°. . . . D,425
Coleridge, S. T. Aids to Reflection. New York, 1863. 12°. . . . H,450
and Opium-Eating. T. De Quincy. Edinburgh, 1868. 12°. . . H,412
Biographia Literaria. New York, 1852. 8°. . . . . . . H,654
The same. London, 1870. p. 8°. . . . . . . L,173,2
Complete Works. New York, 1854. 7 v. 12°. . . . . U,171

Vol. 1. Aids to Reflection; Statesman's Manual.
2. The Friend; Miscellaneous.
3. Biographia Literaria.
Vol. 4. Shakespeare and the Dramatists.
5. Literary Remains.
6. Church and State.
7. Poetical and Dramatic.

Friend; Essays. London, 1867. p. 8°. . . . . . . L,173,1
Life of. J. Gillman. London, 1838. 8°. . . . . . . C,1255
Method in Mental Science. London, 1855. 8°. . . . . O,726
Poems; with Memoir. Leipzig, 1860. 16°. . . . . . . J,71
Poetical and Dramatic Works. Boston, 1854. 3 v. 12°. . . . I,204
Theory of Life. Philadelphia, 1848. 12°. . . . . . . P,291
Reminiscences of. J. Cottle. New York, 1847. 12°. . . C,1248
Coles, E. History of the Ordinance of 1787. Philadelphia, 1856. 8°. . B,860
The same. Philadelphia, 1856. 8°. . . . . . B,809,2

Colfax, S., Life of. E. D. Mansfield. Cincinnati, 1868. 12°. . . . . C,957
Life of. A. Y. Moore. Philadelphia, 1868. 12°. . . . . . C,680
C. A. Phelps. Boston, 1868. 12°. . . . . . . . C,1001
Coliseum of Rome, Flora of. R. Deakin. London, 1855. 16°. . . . N,937
Collé, C. Le Verité dans le Vin; Comédie. Paris, 1855. 12°. . . . D,601
Collection of Pictures. W. G. Coesvelt; ed. A. Jameson. London, 1836. 4°. *Q,182
of Poems. London, 1765. 6 v. 8°. . . . . . . . . J,834
College, Market, and Court. C. H. Dall. Boston, 1867. 12°. . . . O,386
Colleges, American, and American Public. N. Porter. New Haven, 1870. 12°. O,810
Collegiate System of the United States. F. Wayland. Boston, 1842. 16°. O,961
Colletta, P. History of Kingdom of Naples, 1734–1825. Edinb. 1858. 2 v. 8°. B,495
Collier, J. Ecclesiastical History of Great Britain. Lond. 1852. 9 v. 8°. P,580
Collier, J. P. Memoirs of Edward Alleyn. London, 1841. 8°. . . I,885,1
Notes and Emendations on Shakespeare. New York, 1853. 12°. . I,845
Strictures on. A. Dyce. London, 1859. 8°. . . . . . I,887
Shakespeare vindicated. S. W. Singer. London, 1853. . . I,870
Rarest Books in the English Language. New York, 1866. 4 v. 8°. L.R.
(Ed.) Alleyn Papers. London, 1843. 8°. . . . . . . I,885,17
Ghost of Richard III.; a Poem. London, 1844. 8°. . . I,885,21
Inigo Jones, etc. London, 1848. 8°. . . . . . I,885,36
Lyrical Poems, 1589-1600. London, 1844. 12°. . . L,606,13
Old Ballads. London, 1840. 12°. . . . . . . L,606,1
Registers of Stationers' Co. 1557–70. Lond. 1848–9. 2 v. 8°. I,885,42,43
Collier, W. F. History of England. London, 1868. 12°. . . . . . A,402
History of English Literature. London, 1869. 12°. . . . H,679
Collins, C. A. Cruise upon Wheels in France. London, 1862. 2 v. 8°. . V,453
Collins, L. Historical Sketches of Kentucky. Maysville, Ky. 1847. 8°. C,234
Collins, J. Nature's Aristocracy; Plea for the Oppressed. Bost. 1871. 16°. H,120
Collins, P. McD. Voyage down the Amoor. New York, 1860. 12°. . . V,614
Collins, T. W. Humanics. New York, 1860. 8°. . . . . . . O,673
Collins, Wilkie. After Dark. Leipzig, 1856. 16°. . . . . . . . J,72
Armadale. Leipzig, 1866. 3 v. 16°. . . . . . . . . J,74
The same. New York, 1866. 8°. . . . . . . . . K,634
Antonina; or, Fall of Rome. Leipzig, 1863. 2 v. in 1. 16°. . . J,73
The same. New York, 1868. 8°. . . . . . . . K,633
Basil. Leipzig, 1862. 16°. . . . . . . . . . . . J,75
Dead Secret. Philadelphia, n. d. 12°. . . . . . . . K,639
The same. Leipzig, 1857. 2 v. 16°. . . . . . J,130,4,5
Hide and Seek. Leipzig, 1856. 2 v. in 1. 16°. . . . . . J,76
Man and Wife. New York, 1870. 8°. . . . . . . . K,631
The same. Leipzig, 1870. 3 v. 16°. . . . . . . . J,77
Moonstone; a Novel. Leipzig, 1868. 2 v. in 1. 16°. . . . . J,78
The same. New York, 1868. 8°. . . . . . . . K,635
No Name; a Novel. New York, 1863. 8°. . . . . . . K,636
The same. Leipzig, 1863. 3 v. 16°. . . . . . . J,79
Plot in Private Life. Leipzig, 1859. 12°. . . . . . . . J,80
Queen of Hearts. New York, 1859. 12°. . . . . . . . K,638
Woman in White. New York, 1867. 8°. . . . . . . . K,637
The same. Leipzig, 1860. 2 v. in 1. 16°. . . . . . J,81
Collins, W. Oriental Eclogues. London, n. d. 24°. . . . . . . I,325

Collins, W. Poetical Works. Boston, 1854. 12°. . . . . . . I,205
Collinson, J. Life of Thuanus. London, 1807. 8°. . . . . . . D,665
Collinson, R. Nine weeks in Canada. London, 1862. 8°. . . V,1086,2
Colloquies of Edward Osborne. A. Manning. London, n. d. 12°. . . J,586
Colloquies on Religion and Religious Education. London, 1837. 8°. . P,215
Colman, H. European Agriculture and Rural Economy. Bost. 1850. 2 v. 8°. M,578
European Life and Manners. Boston, 1850. 2 v. 12°. . . . V,344
Colomba. P. Mérimé. Boston, 1856. 16°. . . . . . . . H,967
Colombia, Visit to, in 1822-23. M. Duane. Philadelphia, 1826. 8°. . V,260
Colonel Floyd's Wards. M. V. Terhune. New York, 1866. 12°. . . K,328
Colonization on Western Coast of Africa. A. Alexander. Phil. 1849. 8°. C,437
Color. M. E. Cavé. New York, 1869. 12°. . . . . . . . M,49
and Taste. Sir J. G. Wilkinson. London, 1858. 8°. . . . M,93
Aniline and its Derivatives. M. Reimann. New York, 1868. 8°. . N,191
as a means of Art. F. Howard. London, 1849. 8°. . . . M,47
Color-Guard, The. J. K. Hosmer. Boston, 1864. 12°. . . . . B,951
Colored Patriots of the American Revolution. W. C. Nell. Boston, 1855. 12°. B,740
Colored People, Prejudice against. B. P. Aydelott. Cincinnati, n. d. 24°. P,226
Coloring, Laws of Harmonious. D. R. Hay. Edinburgh, 1847. 16°. . M,11
Coloring Matter, Action of Dry Gases on. G. Wilson. Edin. 1848. 4°. N,252,42
Colors, Manual of. R. Ackermann. London, 1844. 16°. . . . . M,2
Nomenclature of. D. R. Hay. Edinburgh, 1846. 8°. . . . M,54
Permanent, Researches in. E. Bancroft. London, 1813. 2 v. 8°. . M,651
Theory of. J. W. von Goethe. London, 1840. 8°. . . . . M,48
Treatise on. G. Field. London, 1835. 4°. . . . . . . Q,204
Vollständiges Farben-Laboratorium. C.H.Schmidt. Weimar, 1847. 16°. G,627
Colorado; a Summer Trip. B. Taylor. New York, 1867. 8°. . . . V,34
Summer Tour through. J. F. Meline. New York, 1868. 12°. . V,185
Summer Vacation in. S. Bowles. Springfield, 1869. 16°. . . V,3
Colorado River, Explorations of. J. C. Ives. Washington, 1861. 4°. . Q,184
Colquhoun, J. C. Life in Italy and France in Olden Time. Lond. 1868. 8°. D,709
National Education in Ireland. Cheltenham, 1838. 12°. . . O,1140
Colton, C. Four Years in Great Britain. New York, 1836. 12°. . . V,380
Last Seven Years of Henry Clay. New York, 1856. 8°. . . . C,1109
Life and Times of Henry Clay. New York, 1846. 2 v. 8°. . . C,1107
Public Economy for the United States. New York, 1847. 8°. . . O,544
Colton, C. C. Lacon; or, many things in few words. New York, 1866. 8°. . H,123
Colton, G. W. General Atlas. New York, 1870. f°. . . . . *Q,461
and Fitch, G. W. Introductory School Geography. N. Y. 1856. 8°. O,904
Colton, J. H. Map of Indiana. New York, 1854. 24°. . . . . . C,151
Colton, W. Land and Lee in the Bosphorus and Ægean. N. Y. 1851. 12°. V,355
Sea and Sailor; Notes on France and Italy. Cincinnati, 1851. 12°. V,300
Ship and Shore; Madeira, Lisbon, etc. New York, 1851. 12°. . V,311
Columbus, C., and Vespucius, Lives of. New York, 1847. 16°. . . . D,711
Life of. A. Helps. London, 1869. 12°. . . . . . . . D,726
A. de Lamartine. New York, 1865. 16°. . . . . D,712
Life and Voyages of. W. Irving. N. Y. 1868-69. 3 v. 12°. . . U,7
The same, abridged. London, 1830. 16°. . . . . I,616
The same. New York, 1859. 3 v. 12°. . . . . U,21
Select Letters; translated by R. G. Major. London, 1847. 8°. . V,991

Columbus, C., Story of. S. H. Bradford. New York, 1857. 12°. . . J,1203
Voyages of the Companions of. W. Irving. London, 1831. 16°. . I,617
Columna, G. de. "Gest Hystoriale" of Destruction of Troy. Lond. 1869. 8°. L,605-39
Colwell, S. Ways and Means of Payment. Philadelphia, 1859. 8°. . . O,572
Combe, A. Life of. G. Combe. Philadelphia, 1850. 12°. . . . . D,200
Physiology applied to Health and Education. New York, 1851. 16°. L,389
Treatise on the Management of Infancy. New York, 1854, 12°. . L,852
Combe, G. Constitution of Man. Boston, 1854. 12°. . . . . . . L,898
Lectures on Popular Education. Edinburgh, 1848. 8°. . . O,1251,1
Life of Andrew Combe. Philadelphia, 1850. 12°. . . . . D,200
Moral Philosophy. New York, 1840. 18°. . . . . . . O,709
Combe, T. Ancient Marbles in the British Museum. London, 1812-15. 4°. Q,206
Combe, W. Tour of Doctor Syntax. London, 1866. 24°. . . . . . I,326
Combustion of Coal. C. W. Williams. London, 1858. 12°. . . . M,975
Comet. Berchnung der Bahn eines Cometen. Weimar, 1847. 8°. . . G,796
Comets, Differential Formeln für. G. D. E. Weyer. Berlin, 1852. 8°. . G,779
Cometh up as a Flower. R. Broughton. New York, 1868. 8°. . . . K,613
The same. Leipzig, 1867. 16°. . . . . . . . . J,51
Comforter, The. F. Bremer. London, 1852. 12°. . . . . . . L,169
Comic Blackstone. G. A. à Beckett. Philadelphia, n. d. 12°. . . . U,482
Comic History of England. G. A. à Beckett. London, n. d. 8°. . . . A,445
of Rome. G. A. á Becket. London, n. d. 8°. . . . . . . A,150
of the United States. J. D. Sherwood. Boston, 1870. 12°. . . B,697
Comic Sketch-Book. J. Poole. London, 1835. 2 v. 12°. . . . H,91
Comines, P. de. Memoirs; edited by A. R. Scoble. Lond. 1855-56. 2 v. 8°. L,326
Comings, B. N. Preservation of Health. New York, 1854. 12°. . . L,851
Commerce, Cyclopædia of. J. S. Homans. New York, 1858. 8°. . . S.C.
de la Grande-Bretagne. C. Dupin. Paris, 1826. 2 v. 4°. . . M,818
Commerce, The Brig, Loss of. J. Riley. London, 1817. 4°. . . . Q,415
Commercial Dictionary. J. R. McCulloch. London, 1869. 8°. . . *O,611
Commercial Instructor. P. Kelly. London, 1831. 2 v. in 1. 4°. . . L,328
Commercial Law; its Principles. L. Levi. London, 1850-51. 2 v. 4°. . Q,218
Commercial Statistics. J. Macgregor. London, 1850. 5 v. 8°. . . O,607
Commercial Terms in English and French. A. Spiers. Phila. 1847. 12°. L.R.
Common Objects of the Country. J. G. Wood. London, 1866. 12°. . . N,478
Common-Place Book. R. Southey. New York, 1855. 2 v. 8°. . . . H,628
of Thoughts and Memories. A. Jameson. New York, 1855. 12°. . H,508
Common Sense. C. J. Newby. Leipzig, 1866. 2 v. in 1. 16°. . . . J,385
Philosophy of. M. Carey. Philadelphia, n. d. 18°. . . . O,350
Common-School Journal; edited by H. Mann. Boston, 1839-45. 8 v. 8°. O,1267
Common Things explained. D. Lardner. London, 1856. 2 v. 12°. . . H,195
Companion; After-dinner Table-talk. C. Evelyn. New York, 1850. 12°. . H,211
Companions of my Solitude. A. Helps. Boston, 1852. 16°. . . . H,438
Compensationss dans les Destinées Humaines. H. Azaïs. Paris, 1853. 12°. H,861
Compliment and Courtship, Poetry of. J. W. Palmer. Boston, 1868. 12°. I,488
Composer, The Young. J. Cornell. London, 1855. 12°. . . . . O,1067
Composition, Art of English. H. N. Day. New York, 1867. 8°. . . L,594
First Lessons in. G. P. Quackenbos. New York, 1855. 12°. . . O,1076
Practical English. R. Hiley. London, 1855. 16°. . . . O,1061,62
Practical Treatise on. H. Willson. London, 1851. 8°. . . . Q,163

Comstock, J. L. Outlines of Geology. New York, 1837. 12°. . . . . N,603
Comte, A. General View of Positivism; tr. by J. H. Bridges. Lond. 1865. 8°. O,643
Philosophy of the Mathematics. New York, 1851. 8°. . . M,1189
Philosophy of the Sciences; tr. by G. H. Lewes. London, 1853. p. 8°. L,289
Positive Philosophy; tr. by H. Martineau. New York, 1853. 2 v. 12°. O,661
Reviewed. J. S. Mill. Boston, 1866. 8°. . . . . . O,627
Comyn, Sir R. History of the Western Empire. London, 1851. 2 v. 8°. A,246
Conant, H. C. English Bible; History of the Translation. N. Y. 1856. 12°. P,446
Conchological Manual. G. B. Sowerby, jr. London, 1852. 8°. . . O,65
Conchologist's Nomenclature. A. Catlow and L. Reeve. London, 1845. 8°. N,718
Conchologist's Text-Book. W. Macgillivray. London, 1853. . . . . O,19
Conchology, British Marine. C. Thorpe and others. London, 1844. 12°. O,25
General. W. Wood. London, 1835. 8°. . . . . . . . O,69
Handbuch der. R. A. Philippi. Halle, 1853. 8°. . . . . . G,922
Illustrations of. T. Brown. London, 1845. 8°. . . . . . O,73
Introductions to. J. Johnston. London, 1850. 8°. . . . . . N,717
Land and Fresh Water. T. Browne. London, 1845. 8°. . . . O,73
Popular British. G. B. Sowerby, jr. London, 1854. 16°. . . . O,7
Shells of the British Islands. W. Turton. London, 1857. 12°. . O,62
Concord and Merrimack Rivers, Week on. H. D. Thoreau. Boston, 1862. 12°. V,24
Concord (N. H.), History of. N. Bonton. Concord, 1856. 8°. . . . . C,13
Concord of Ages. E. Beecher. New York, 1860. 12°. . . . . . P,187
Con Cregan; the Irish Gil Blas. C. Lever. Philadelphia, n. d. 8°. . K,770
Condé, J. A. History of the Arabs in Spain. London, 1854–55. 3 v. p. 8°. L,174
Condensed Novels. F. B. Harte. London, 1867. 12°. . . . . . K,131
Conduct of Life. R. W. Emerson. Boston, 1861. 16°. . . . . . H,99
Confessio Amantis. J. Gower. London, 1857. 3 v. 8°. . . . . . J.876
Confession, Auricular, History of. C. P. de Lasteyrie. London, 1848. 12°. P,804
Confession of the Blind Heart. W. G. Simms. New York, 1864. 12°. K,250
Confessions. W. H. Ireland. London, 1805. 12°. . . . . . . I,889
J. J. Rousseau. Paris, 1856. 12°. . . . . . . . . . D,628
d'un Ouvier. E. Souvestre. Bruxelles, 1852. 16°. . . . H,1037
of an English Opium-Eater. T. De Quincey. Edinburgh, 1862. 12°. H,412
of a Working-Man. E. Souvestre. London, 1865. p. 8°. . . I,664,1
Confidence-Man. H. Melville. London, 1857. 16°. . . . . . . J,639
Confectioner, Royal. C. E. Francatelli. London, 1866. 8°. . . . H,304
Confidences d'un Joueur de Clarinette. E. Erckmann. Paris, 1861. . . H,1015
Confidential Disclosures. A. de Lamartine. New York, 1857. 12°. . . H,969
Conflict of Ages. E. Beecher. Boston, 1854. 12°. . . . . . . P,188
Confucius and Chinese Classics; ed. by A. W. Loomis. San Franc. 1867. 12°. G,5
Life and Teachings of. J. Legge. Philadelphia, 1867. 12°. . . D,774
Congar, O. Autobiography and Memorials. New York, 1851. 16°. . C,842
Congdon, J. W. Analytical Class-Book of Botany. New York, 1856. 4°. N,1033
Congo River, Exploration, 1816. J. K. Tuckey. New York, 1818. 8°. . V,833
Congregational Churches, Vindication of. J. Hawes. Hartford, 1830. 12°. P,839
Congregationalism; what it is, etc. H. M. Dexter. Boston, 1868. 8°. . P,218
Congress, Abridgement of Debates in. T. H. Benton. N. Y. 1857–59. 12 v. 8°. P,D.
Dictionary of. C. Lanman. Philadelphia, 1859. 12°. . . . . C,777
Eight Years in, 1857–65. S. S. Cox. New York, 1865. 8°. . . O,573
History of, from 1789 to 1793. Philadelphia, 1843. 8°. . . . . B,666

Congress, Library of, Catalogue. Washington, 1864. 8°. . . . . . L.R.
Additions. Dec. 1865–Dec. 1866. Washington, 1866. 8°. . L.R.
Dec. 1866–Dec. 1867. Washington, 1868. 8°. . . L.R.
Dec. 1868–Dec. 1869. Washington, 1870. 8°. . . L.R.
Congressional Globe. Washington, 1833–70. 90 v. 4°. . . . . . P.D.
Congreve, W. Dramatic Works. London, 1866. 8°. . . . . I,728
Life of. H. Coleridge. London, 1852. 8°. . . . . . C,1166,3
Poem to the Memory of. London, 1843. 12°. . . . . . L,606,9
Coningsby; a Novel. B. Disraeli. London, 1868. 12°. . . . . K,671
The same. Leipzig, 1844. 16°. . . . . . . . J,140
Conjugal Love. E. Swedenborg. New York, 1860. 8°. . . . . P,852
Conkling, A. Young Citizen's Manual. Albany, 1836. 18°. . . . O,464
Connecticut Common-School Journal, v 1. Hartford, 1854. 8°. . . O,1265
Geological Survey of. C. U. Shepard. New Haven, 1837. 8°. . N,871
Geology of. J. G. Percival. New Haven, 1842. 8°. . . . N,872
History of. T. Dwight, jr. New York, 1859. 18°. . . . . . L.427
History of the Indians of. J. W. DeForest. Hartford, 1853. 8°. . B,627
Newgate and Wethersfield Prison. R. H. Phelps. Albany, 1860. 4°. C,77
Poets of. C. W. Everest. New York, 1847. 8°. . . . . . J,873
Connoisseur. Boston, 1866. 2 v. 8°. . . . . . . . . . H,536,25,26
Conington, F. T. Chemical Analysis, Tables. London, 1858. 2 v. 12°. N,201
Conquest and Self-Conquest. M. J. McIntosh. New York, 1864. 24°. J,1175
Conscience, H. Summer Evening Tales. New York, n. d. 12°. . K,1023
Conscience, Lectures on. F. D. Maurice. London, 1868. 8°. . . . O,720
Conscript, The. A. Dumas. New York, 1855. 12°. . . . . . . H,972
Consolation, Sermons of. F. W. P. Greenwood. Boston, 1842. 12°. . . P,672
Consolations in Travel. Sir H. Davy. Boston, 1870. 16°. . . . H,453
Conspiracies in European History. J. P. Lawson. Edinburgh, 1829. 2 v. 16°. I,518
Conspiracy of Pontiac. F. Parkman. Boston, 1851. 8°. . . . . . B,600
The same; sixth edition. Boston. 1870. 2 v. 8°. . . . . B,613
Constable, A. Miscellany. Edinburgh, 1826–34. 81 v. 16°. . . I,492,538
Vol. 1–3. Hall, B. Journal of Voyages. 3 v. . . . . . . . . I,492
4. Adventures of British Seamen. . . . . . . . . I,493
5. LaRochejaquelein, M. L. Memoirs. . . . . . . . I,494
6, 7. Crichton, A. Converts from Infidelity. 2 v. . . . . . I,495
8, 9. Symes, M. Embassy to Ava. Bell, H. G. Birmese Empire, 2 v. I,496
10. Table Talk. . . . . . . . . . . . . I,497
11. Perils and Captivity. . . . . . . . . . . I,498
12. Bell, H. G. Phenomena of Nature. . . . . . . . I,499
13, 14. Mariner, W. Tonga Islands. 2 v. . . . . . . . I,500
15, 16. Chambers, R. Rebellion in Scotland, 1745–46. 2 v. . . . I,501
17. Roberts, O. W. Voyages in Central America. . . . . . I,502
18, 19. Schiller, F. Thirty Years' War. 2 v. . . . . . . I,503
20, 21. Thomson, R. Illustrations of British History. . 2 v. . . I,504
22. Register of Politics and Literature for 1827. . . . . I,505
23. Lockhart, J. G. Life of Burns. . . . . . . . . I,506
24, 25. Bell H. G. Mary, Queen of Scots. 2 v. . . . . . . I,507
26. Wrangham, F. The Pleiad; Seven Writers on Christianity. . I,508
27, 28. Memorials of the Late War, 1806–15. 2 v. . . . . . I,509
29, 30. Russell, J. Tour in Germany. 2 v. . . . . . . . I,510
31, 32. Chambers, R. Rebellions in Scotland, 1638–60. 2 v. . . I,511
33–35. Crichton, A. Revolutions in Europe. 3 v. . . . . . I,512
36, 37. Cochrane, J. D. Pedestrian Journey through Russia and Tartary. 2 v. I,513
38. Inglis, H. D. Journey through Norway and Sweden. . . I,514
39. Memes, J. S. Sculpture, Painting, and Architecture. . . I,515

Constable, A. Miscellany. *Continued.*

40,41. Upham E. History of the Ottoman Empire. 2 v. . . . . I,516
42. Chambers, R. Rebellions in Scotland, 1689, 1715. . . . I,517
43,44. Lawson, J. P. Conspiracies in European History. 2 v. . I,518
45. White, G. Natural History of Selborne. . . . . . I,519
46. Sinclair, J. D. Autumn in Italy. . . . . . . . . I,520
47,48. Russell, M. Life of Oliver Cromwell. 2 v. . . . . . I,521
49. Trueba y Cosio, T. de. Life of Hernando Cortez. . . . I,522
50,51. Stebbing, H. History of Chivalry and the Crusades. . . I,523
52. Stafford, W. C. History of Music. . . . . . . . I,524
53,54. Carrick, J. D. Life of Sir William Wallace. 2 v. . . . I,525
55,56. Chambers, R. Life of James I. 2 v. . . . . . . I,526
57–59. Bourrienne, F. de. Memoirs of Napoleon I. 4 v. . . . I,527
60,61. Keightley, T. War of Independence in Greece. 2 v. . . I,528
62. Trueba y Cosio, T. de. Conquest of Peru. . . . . . I,529
63,64. Sutherland, A. Knights of Malta. 2 v. . . . . . I,530
65. St. John, J. A. Residence in Normandy. . . . . . I,531
66,67. Inglis, H. D. Switzerland, France, and Pyrenees. 2 v. . I,532
68–71. Wilson, A. and Bonaparte, C. L. American Ornithology. 4 v. I,533
72. Memes, J. S. Memoirs of Josephine. . . . . . . I,534
73,74. Taylor, W. C. Civil Wars in Ireland. 2 v. . . . . . I,535
75,76,80. Brown, T. Butterflies, Sphinxes, and Moths. 3 v. . . . I,536
77. Mudie, R. Guide to the Observation of Nature. . . . I,537
78,79. History of Shipwrecks and Disasters at Sea. . . . . I,538

Constable de Bourbon. W. H. Ainsworth. Leipzig, 1866. 2 v. in 1. 16°. J,7
Constable of the Tower. W. H. Ainsworth. Leipzig, 1861. 16°. . . J,8
Constance Sherwood. G. Fullerton. Leipzig, 1865. 2 v. in 1. 16°. . . J,166
Constantinople during the Crimean War. E. Hornby. London, 1863. 8°. V,575
Month at. A. Smith. London, 1851. 16°. . . . . . . V,551
Turks of. C. M. Kennedy. London, 1864. 8°. . . . V,1086,3
Views of. W. Colton. New York, 1851. 12°. . . . . . . V,355
Constitution of Man. G. Combe. Boston, 1854. . . . . . . L,898
Constitution of the United States. See *United States.*
Constitutional Convention, 1861. L. E. Chittenden. New York, 1864. 8°. B,921
Consuelo. Mad. Dudevant. Philadelphia, 1861. 8°. . . . . . H,919
Consumption. W. W. Hall. New York, 1857. 12°. . . . . . . L,910
Contarini Fleming. B. Disraeli. London, 1868. 12°. . . . . . K,676
The same. Leipzig, 1846. 16°. . . . . . . . . J,141
Contes des Bords du Rhin. E. Erckmann et A. Chatrian. Paris, 1861. 12°. H,1014
Contes Moraux. J. F. Marmontel. London, 1793. 6 v. 24°. . . . H,853
Contentment better than Wealth. A. B. Haven. New York, 1867. 16°. J,1328
Contractors, Enactment for Guidance of. London, 1858–59. 12°. . . . M,959
Contractor's Manual and Price-Book. A. B. Clough. Philad. 1855. 18°. M,672
Contracts, Law of. D. Gibbons. London, 1857. 12°. . . . . . M,920
Contradiction; or, High Life at Edgerton. Boston, 1869. 16°. . . J,1631
Conversation, Art of. T. De Quincey. Edinburgh, 1863. 12°. . . . H,412,13
New York, 1864. 12°. . . . . . . . . . . . . L,587
Rhetoric of. G. W. Hervey. New York, 1853. 12°. . . . L,586
Conversations-Lexicon; elfte Aufl. Leipzig, 1864–68. 15 v. 8°. . . L.R.
Bilderatlas; Kupfer. Leipzig, 1856. 10 v. in 3. obl. 4°. . . L.R.
Text. Leipzig, 1857. 10 v. in 2. 8°. . . . . . . L.R.
Unsere Zeit; Monatsschrift. Leipzig, 1865–68. 6 v. . . . L.R.
Converts from Infidelity. A. Crichton. Edinburgh, 1727. 2 v. 16°. . I,495
Convict, The. G. P. R. James. Leipzig, 1847. 2 v. in 1. 16°. . . J,204

Convicts, Our. M. Carpenter. London, 1864. 2 v. in 1. 8°. . . . O,357
Conway, Derwent. See *Inglis, H. D.*
Conway, M. D. Earthward Pilgrimage. London, 1870. 8°. . . . . P,44
Rejected Stone. Boston, 1862. 12°. . . . . . . . . H,88
Conwell, R. H. Why and how the Chinese Emigrate. Boston, 1871. 12°. V,605
Conybeare, W. D., and Howson, J. S. Life of St. Paul. N. Y. 1858. 2 v. 8°. P,406
Cooke, G. W. China. London, 1858. 8°. . . . . . . . . V,594
History of Party. London, 1836–37. 8°. . . . . . . . . B,31
Cook, Capt. J. and King. Voyage to Pacific Ocean, 1776–80. Lon. 1784. 3v. 4°. V,1010
Life of. H. Coleridge. London, 1852. 8°. . . . . . C,1166,3
Cooke, J. E. Fairfax; or, Master of Greenway Court. N. Y. 1868. 12°. J,632
Hammer and Rapier. New York, 1870. 12°. . . . . . . J,633
Hilt to Hilt; or, the Shenandoah in 1864. New York, 1869. 12°. . J,630
Mohun; or, the Last Days of Lee. New York, 1869. 12°. . . . J,634
Out of the Foam. New York, 1871. 12°. . . . . . . J,655
Surry of Eagle's-Nest. New York, 1866. 12°. . . . . J,631
Wearing the Gray. New York, 1867. 8°. . . . . . . B,955
Cooke, J. P., jr. Religion and Chemistry. New York, 1867. 12°. . . P,217
Cooke, M. C. Account of British Fungi. London, 1862. 12°. . . . N,925
Manual of Structural Botany. London, n. d. 18°. . . . N,909
Our Reptiles. London, 1865. 12°. . . . . . . . . N,699
Study of Microscopic Fungi. London, 1865. 12°. . . . . N,924
Cooke, W. B. Rome and its Surrounding Scenery. London, 1840. 4°. . V,574
Cook-Book. E. Raffald. London, 1801. 24°. . . . . . . . H,183
Practical. Mrs. Bliss. Philadelphia, 1867. 12°. . . . . H,296
E. Leslie. Philadelphia, 1857. 12°. . . . . . . . H,292
Cookery, Gastronomic Regenerator. A. Soyer. London, 1861. 8°. . H,320
Guide to Domestic. L. G. Abell. New York, 1858. 12°. . . M,533,4
Hand-Book of Practical. P. Blot. New York, 1868. 12°. . . H,297
Modern Housewife. A. Soyer. London, 1861. 12°. . . . H,319
Cooley, W. D. Inner Africa laid open. London, 1852. 8°. . . . V,835
Maritime and Inland Discovery. London, 1830–31. 3 v. 12°. . M,1006
Cooper, A. A., *Earl of Shaftesbury*. Characteristics of Men. Lon. 1732. 3 v. 8°. H,460
Essays on his "Characteristics." J. Brown. London, 1752. 8°. . P,89
Original Letters; edited by T. Forster. London, 1830. 8°. . . H,612
Cooper, Sir A., Life of. B. B. Cooper. London, 1843. 2 v. 8°. . . D,94
Cooper, E. The Crisis. Cincinnati, 1827. 12°. . . . . . P,294
Cooper, J. F. History of United States Navy. N. Y. 1853. 3 v. in 1. 8°. B,855
Leather-Stocking Tales. New York, 1870. 5 v. 12°. . . . . K,20
Vol. 1. Deerslayer. Vol. 3. Pathfinder.
2. Last of the Mohicans. 4. Pioneers.
Vol. 5. Prairie.
Novels. New York, 1867. 33 v. 12°.

| | | | |
|---|---|---|---|
| Afloat and Ashore. | K,24 | Pathfinder. | K,41 |
| Bravo. | K,25 | Pilot. | K,42 |
| Chainbearer. | K,27 | Pioneers. | K,43 |
| Crater. | K,26 | Prairie. | K,44 |
| Deerslayer. | K,28 | Precaution. | K,45 |
| Headsman. | K,29 | Red Rover. | K,46 |
| Heidenmauer. | K,30 | Redskins. | K,47 |
| Home as Found. | K,31 | Satanstoe. | K,48 |
| Homeward Bound. | K,32 | Sea Lions. | K,49 |
| Jack Tier. | K,33 | Spy. | K,50 |

Cooper, J. F. Novels. *Continued.*

| | | | |
|---|---|---|---|
| Last of the Mohicans. | K,37 | Two Admirals. | K,51 |
| Lionel Lincoln. | K,34 | Water Witch. | K,53 |
| Mercedes of Castile. | K,35 | Ways of the Hour. | K,52 |
| Miles Wallingford. | K,36 | Wept of Wish-ton-Wish. | K,55 |
| Monikins. | K,38 | Wing-and-Wing. | K,54 |
| Ned Myers. | K,39 | Wyandotte. | K,56 |
| Oak Openings. | K,40 | | |

The same; illust. by F. O. C. Darley. N. Y. 1859–61. 32 v. 8°.

| | | | |
|---|---|---|---|
| Afloat and Ashore. | K,57 | Pathfinder. | K,69 |
| Bravo. | K,79 | Pilot. | K,70 |
| Chainbearer. | K,58 | Pioneers. | K,71 |
| Crater. | K,59 | Prairie. | K,72 |
| Deerslayer. | K,145 | Precaution. | K,73 |
| Headsman. | K,61 | Red Rover. | K,74 |
| Heidenmauer. | K,146 | Redskins. | K,75 |
| Home as Found. | K,60 | Satanstoe. | K,76 |
| Homeward Bound. | K,62 | Sea Lions. | K,77 |
| Jack Tier. | K,63 | Spy. | K,80 |
| Last of the Mohicans. | K,66 | Two Admirals. | K,78 |
| Lionel Lincoln. | K,64 | Water Witch. | K,83 |
| Mercedes of Castile. | K,147 | Ways of the Hour. | K,84 |
| Miles Wallingford. | K,65 | Wept of Wish-ton-Wish. | K,81 |
| Monikins. | K,67 | Wing-and-Wing. | K,85 |
| Oak Openings. | K,68 | Wyandotte. | K,82 |

Stories of the Prairie. New York, 1868. 12°. . . . J,1374
of the Sea. New York, 1868. 12°. . . . . . J,1373
of the Woods. New York, 1869. 12°. . . . . . J,1375
Cooper, J. G. Ornithology of California; ed. S. F. Baird. San Fran. 1870. 4°. N,739
Cooper, S. F. Mount Vernon. New York, 1859. 16°. . . . . . H,4
Rhyme and Reason of Country Life. New York, 1854. 8°. . . I,44
Rural Hours. New York, 1868. 12°. . . . . . . . H,274
Coopers, The; or, Getting under Way. A. B. Haven. New York, 1866. 12°. K,119
Copenhagen. Mémoires de Soc. Royale des Antiquit. 1845–9. Copen. n. d. 8°. R,32
Copley, E. Early Friendships. New York, 1852. 18°. . . . . . J,1243
Copway, G. Indian Life and Indian History. Boston, 1860. 12°. . . B,628
Coppée, H. Elements of Logic. Philadelphia, 1870. 12°. . . . O,733
Grant and his Campaigns. New York, 1866. 8°. . . . . . B,930
Copper, Metallurgy of. B. Kerl. London, 1868. 8°. . . . M,717,2
Silver and Lead, Metallur. of. R. H. Lamborn. Lon. 1869. 2 v. 12°. M,848
Copper-Plate and Tin-Workers. L. J. Blinn. Philadelphia, 1869. 12°. M,671
Copping, E. Lives of Alfieri and Goldoni. London, 1857. 8°. . . D,720
Coquerel, A. First Transformations of Christianity. Boston, 1867. 16°. . P,347
Coquette; or, Eliza Wharton. H. Foster. Philadelphia, 1866. 12°. . K,154
Coral Islands; Tale of Pacific Ocean. R. M. Ballantyne. Lond. 1870. 16°. J,1484
Coral Reefs and Islands. J. D. Dana. New York, 1853. 8°. . . . N,824
Corbet, R. Poems. London, 1807. 8°. . . . . . . . . I,322
Corda, A. C. J. Beiträge zur Flora der Vorwelt. Prag, 1845. 4°. . . Q,128
Flora Europäischer Schimmelbildungen. Leipzig, 1839. f°. . Q,87
Corinne; ou l'Italie. Mad. de Staël-Holstein. Paris, 1855. 12°. . . H,932
The same; translated. New York, n. d. 12°. . . . H,921
Corkran, J. F. National Constituent Assembly, 1848. New York, 1849. 12°. B,238
Cormenin, L. M. de L. H. History of the Popes. Phil. 1857. 2 v. in 1. 8°. P,815
Corneille, P., and his Times. F. Guizot. New York, 1852. 12°. . . D,658
Chefs-d'Œuvre Dramatiques. Paris, 1855. 2 v. 8°. . . . H,897

Corneille, P. Commentaires sur. F. M. A. de Voltaire. Paris, 1851. 12°. . H,876
P., et T., Théatre de. Paris, 1855–56. 2 v. 12°. . . . . . H,878
Cornelius, C. Zug- und Wander-Thiere aller Thierklassen. Berl. 1865. 16°. G,913
Cornelius, E., Memoir of. B. B. Edwards. Boston, 1834. 12°. . . C,750
Cornelius Nepos. Leben Ausgezeichneter Feldherren. Stuttgart, 1827. 24°. E,237
Lives of Eminent Commanders; tr. J. S. Watson. Lon. 1853. p. 8°. . L,64
Opera; Curante J. B. F. Descuret. Parisiis, 1820. 8°. . . . U,334
Cornell, S. S. Primary Geography. New York, 1854. 4°. . . . O,905
Corner, J. China; Pictorial, Descriptive, etc. London, 1853. p. 8°. . L,98
English Envoy at Court of Nicholas I. New York, 1854. 12°. . K,94
India; Pictorial, Descriptive, and Historical. London, 1857. p. 8°. L,110
Cornhill Magazine. London, 1860–66. 14 v. 8°. . . . . . . R,4
Cornwall, B. *pseud.* See *Procter, B. W.*
Cornwall; its Mines and Miners. London, 1865. p. 8°. . . . . . I,665
Cornwallis, C. F. Juvenile Delinquency. London, 1853. 8°. . . . O,354
Cornwell, J. Young Composer. London, 1845. 12°. . . . . . O,1067
Corpus Juris Canonici; edited by A. L. Richter. Lipsiæ, 1833. 4°. . Q,146
Corse de Leon. G. P. R. James. New York, 1855. 12°. . . . . K,731
Corsica. E. J. Morris. Philadelphia, 1855. 12°. . . . . . . V,492
Picturesque, Social, and Historical. F. Gregorovius. Lond. 1855. p. 8°. I,656,2
Corson, J. W. Loiterings in Europe. New York, 1848. 12°. . . . V,366
Correspondence with a Child. J. W. von Goethe. Boston, 1859. 12°. . G,29
Correspondences from the Word. E. Swedenborg. Boston, 1847. 12°. . P,846
Cortez, H., Adventures of. New York, 1854. 16°. . . . . . J,1306
Dispatches of, to Charles V. New York, 1843. 8°. . . . . . C,386
History of. J. S. C. Abbott. New York, 1855. 16°. . . J,1717
Life of. T. de Trueba y Cosio. Edinburgh, 1829. 16°. . . . I,522
Cosin, J. History of Popish Transubstantiation. Oxford, 1850. 12°. . P,807
Cosmos. A. von Humboldt. Stuttgart and Tübingen, 1845–58. 4 v. 8°. G,686
The same; translated by E. C. Otté. Lond. 1849–58. 5 v. p. 8°. L,295
The same. London, 1860. 5 v. p. 8°. . . . S.C.
Costello, D. Tour through Valley of the Meuse. London, 1846. 12°. . V,393
Costello, L. S. Béarn and the Pyrenees. London, 1844. 2 v. 8°. . . V,477
Pilgrimage to Auvergne. London, 1842. 2 v. 8°. . . . . . V,478
Costume, Book of; or, Annals of Fashion. London, 1847. 8°. . . . M,368
Dresses and Decorations of Middle Ages. H. Shaw. Lond. 1858. 2 v. 8°. *Q,188
History of British. J. R. Planché. London, 1836. 12°. . . . L,472
The same. London, n. d. 12°. . . . . . . . M,365
in England. F. W. Fairholt. London, 1860. 8°. . . . . . M,366
of the Ancients. T. Hope. London, 1812. 2 v. 8°. . . . M,369
Cotsell, G. Ships' Anchors. London, 1856. 12°. . . . . . . M,901
Cotta, B. von. Deutschland's Boden. Leipzig, 1858. 2 v. 8°. . . . G,828
Geologie der Gegenwart. Leipzig, 1866. 8°. . . . . . G,829
Geologische Bilder. Leipzig, 1852. 8°. . . . . . . . G,830
Geology and History. London, 1865. 16°. . . . . . . N,598
and others. Briefe über A. v. Humboldt's Cosmos. Leip. 1848–60. 6 v. 8°. G,700
Cottage Building. C. B. Allen. London, 1857. 12°. . . . . . . M,887
Cottage Economy. W. Cobbett. London, 1822. 12°. . . . . . M,670
Cottages, Views of Rural. S. Prout. London, 1819. 8°. . . . . . Q,209
Village and Farm. H. W. Cleaveland, and others. N. Y. 1856. 8°. M,223

Cottagers of Glenburnie. E. Hamilton. Edinburgh, 1808. 8°. . . . K,718
Cottages, Villas and. C. Vaux. New York, 1857. 8°. . . . . . M,183
Cottin, S. R. Elizabeth; or, Exiles of Siberia. Philadelphia, 1868. 12°. . H,951
Cottle, J. Reminiscences of S. T. Coleridge. New York, 1847. 12°. . C,1248
Cotton, A. Our late Troubles in Virginia, 1676. See *Force's Tracts*, v. 1.
Cotton, H. Editions of Bible, from 1505 to 1850. Oxford, 1852. 8°. . P,407
Rhemes and Doway versions of Bible. Oxford, 1855. 8°. . . P,813
Cotton, J. Abstract of Laws of New-England, 1641. See *Force's Tracts*, v. 3.
Letter to Roger Williams. See *Narragansett Club Publications*, v. 1.
Reply to. R. Williams. See *Narragansett Club Publications*, v. 1.
Reply to Williams. See *Narragansett Club Publications* v. 2.
Life of. A. W. McClure. Boston, 1870. 12°. . . . . . . D,8,1
Queries of the highest consideration. See *Narragansett Club Publications*, v. 2.
Cotton, J. Vocabulary of the Natick Indian Language. Cambridge, 1829. 8°. *L,618
Cotton, Cultivation of. J. W. Mallet. London, 1862. 12°. . . . M,647
is King. E. N. Elliott. Augusta, Ga. 1860. 8°. . . . . . O,609
is King; or, its Culture and Relations. Cincinnati, 1855. 12°. . O,392
Cotton Kingdom; a Traveler's Observ. F. L. Olmsted. N. Y. 1862. 2 v. 12°. V,87
Cotton Manufacture in Great Britain. E. Baines, jr. London, 1835. 8°. . M,654
A. Ure. London, 1861. 2 v. p. 8°. . . . . . . L,321
Rise and Progress of. G. S. White. Philadelphia, 1836. 8°. . . D,363
Cotton-Spinner and Manufacturer. R. Scott. Philadelphia, 1851. 8°. . M,658
Cotton Trade. G. McHenry. London, 1863. 8°. . . . . . . O,523
Couch, J. Fishes of the British Islands. London, 1866-67. 4 v. 8°. . N,704
Illustrations of Instinct. London, 1847. 12°. . . . . . . N,652
Coultas, H. What may be Learned from a Tree. New York, 1863. 8°. N,1023
Count of Monte-Cristo. A. Dumas. Philadelphia, n. d. 8°. . . . H,982
Council of Trent, History of. T. A. Buckley. London, 1852. 12°. . . P,906
History of. L. F. Bungener. New York, 1855. 12°. . . . P,811
Count Mirabeau. T. Mundt. New York, 1868. 8°. . . . . . . G,193
Count Robert of Paris. Sir W. Scott. Boston, 1859. 2 v. 16°. . . K,932
The same. Philadelphia, 1860. 8°. . . . . . . K,959
The same. Philadelphia, 1869. 8°. . . . . . K,1116
Counterparts. E. S. Sheppard. Boston, 1869. 8°. . . . . . K,1006
Counterpoint and Fugue, Treatise on. M. Cherubini. London, 1854. 8°. M,421,1
Countess de Charny. A. Dumas. Philadelphia, n. d. 8°. . . . . H,976
Countess Gisela. E. John. Philadelphia, 1869. 12°. . . . . . G,190
Countess Ida; a Tale of Berlin. T. S. Fay. New York, 1840. 2 v. 12°. K,110
Countess Kate. C. M. Yonge. New York, 1866. 16°. . . . J,1285
Countess of Monte-Cristo. Philadelphia, 1871. 8°. . . . . H,1040
Countess of Pembroke's Arcadia. Sir P. Sidney. London, 1868. 16°. K,1009
Country Homes. F. E. and F. W. Woodward. New York, 1866. 12°. . M,149
Country Houses, Architecture of. A. J. Downing. New York, 1851. 8°. M,185
Country Living and Country Thinking. M. A. Dodge. Boston, 1866. 16°. H,52
Country Margins. S. H. Hammond and L. W. Mansfield. N. Y. 1855. 12°. H,34
Country Quarters. M. Gardiner. Leipzig, 1850. 2 v. in 1. 16°. . . J,192
Country Rambles in England. J. L. Knapp. Buffalo, 1853. 12°. . . N,503
Country Seats. H. H. Holly. New York, 1866. 4°. . . . . . M,195
Country Year-Book. W. Howitt. New York, 1855. 12°. . . . . H,573
T. Miller. London, n. d. 12°. . . . . . . . . . H,564

Courcillon, E. de. Le Curé Manqué; or, Customs in France. N.Y. 1855. 12°. D,667
Courier, P. L. Œuvres. Paris, 1854. 12°. . . . . . . . . H,993
Course of Time. R. Pollok. New York, 1868. 12°. . . . . . . I,376
Court and Society, English, 1558–1702. W. D. Montague. Lond. 1864. 2 v. 8°. A,500
Court of Chancery, Practice of. M. Hoffman. N. Y. 1839–43. 3 v. 8°. U,516
Court Fools, History of. J. Doran. London, 1858. 12°. . . . . H,310
Courtenay, T. P. Life of Sir W. Temple. London, 1836. 2 v. 8°. . . D,80
Courtesy, Principles of. G. W. Hervey. . . . . . . . . . H,283
Courtesy Books, German. W. M. Rossetti. London, 1869. 8°. . . L,604,8
Italian. W. M. Rossetti. London, 1869. 8°. . . . . . L,604,8
Courts and Lawyers, Pleasantries about. C. Edwards. N. Y. 1867. 12°. . H,509
Courtship and Compliment, Poetry of. J. W. Palmer. Boston, 1868. 12°. I,488
and Marriage. C. L. Hentz. Philadelphia, 1870. 12°. . . . K,455
Moral Philosophy of. W. A. Alcott. Boston, 1857. 12°. . L,911
of Momera; translated from Celtic by E. Curry. Dublin, 1855. 8°. L,811
Cousin Alice. See *Haven, A. B.*
Cousin Maude and Rosamond. M. J. Holmes. New York, 1867. 12°. . K,181
Cousin Phillis; and other Tales. E. C. Gaskell. Leipzig, 1867. 16°. . J,174
Cousin, V. Education in Holland. London, 1838. 8°. . . . O,1197
History of Modern Philosophy. New York, 1864. 2 v. 8°. . . O,671
Secret History of the French Court. New York, 1859. 12°. . . B,239
True, the Beautiful, and the Good. New York, 1854. 8°. . . O,629
Youth of Madame de Longueville. New York, 1854. 12°. . . D,625
Coutts, B. Prizes at the Whitelands Institution. London, n. d. 8°. . O,1200
Covell, L. T. Digest of English Grammar. New York, 1853. 12°. . . L,577
Coventry, F. Pompey the Little. London, 1820. 12°. . . . . K,535
Covetousness the Sin of the Church. J. Harris. New York, n. d. 18°. P,746,20
Sin and Evils of. T. Dick. Philadelphia, 1869. 12°. . . U,260,3
Cow, How to choose a good. J. H. Mayne. Glasgow, 1857. 16°. . . M,443
Cowan, F. Curious Facts in the History of Insects. Philadelphia, 1865. 12°. O,23
Cowdery, M. F. Elementary Moral Lessons. Philadelphia, 1856. 12°. . O,785
Cowell, J. J. Graian Alps and Mount Iseran. London, 1861. 8°. . V,1086,1
Cowley, A. Essays; with Life. London, 1868. 16°. . . . . . . I,565
Works. London, 1700. f°. . . . . . . . . . F,169
Cowley, C. Ladies' History of England. London, 1780. f°. . . . Q,309
Cowper, W., Lectures on. G. B. Cheever. New York, 1856. 12°. . . D,419
Life and Works; ed. by W. Hayley and Grimshawe. Lond. 1854. 8 v. 16°. I,329
Poems. Boston, 1866. 12°. . . . . . . . . . . I,332
Poetical Works; with Memoir. Boston, 1853. 3 v. 16°. . . . I,206
The same; edited by R. Bell. London, 1854. 3 v. 16°. . I,247
Task, Table-Talk, etc.; edited by J. R. Boyd. New York, 1854. 12°. I,330
Works; with Life by R. Southey. London, 1853–55. 8 v. p. 8°. . L,175
Vol. 1, 2. Life by R. Southey.
3, 4. Letters; Connoisseur; Commentary on Paradise Lost.
5. Miscellaneous Poems; Hymns; Translations.
6. Task; Tiroconium; Miscellaneous Poems.
7. Homer's Iliad, translated.
8. Homer's Odyssey, translated.
and Thompson, J. Works. Philadelphia, 1848. 8°. . . . . J,857
Cox, F. A. Biblical Antiquities. London, 1852. p. 8°. . . . . . P,256
Sacred History and Biography. London, 1850. 12°. . . . . P,458
Cox, G. W. Manual of Mythology. New York, 1868. 16°. . . . . P,910

Cox, G. W. Tale of the Great Persian War. London, 1861. 16°. . . . A,132
Tales of the Gods and Heroes. London, 1862. 16°. . . . . . P,912
Cox, J. D. Emancipation of Science; an Address. Salem, O. 1853. 8°. . T,19,2
Cox, H. Treatise on Integral Calculus. London, 1852. 12°. . . . . M,902
Cox, S. S. Buckeye Abroad. New York, 1852. 12°. . . . . . . V,321
Eight Years in Congress, 1857–65. New York, 1865. 8°. . . . O,573
Search for Winter Sunbeams. New York, 1870. 8°. . . . V,1070
Coxe, W. History of House of Austria, 1218–1792. Lond. 1847–52. 4 v. p. 8°. L,177
Memoirs of the Duke of Marlborough. London, 1847–48. 3 v. 12°. L,176
Cozzens, F. S. Sayings of Dr. Bushwhacker. New York, 1867. 12°. . H,96
Sparrowgrass Papers. Philadelphia, 1869. 12°. . . . . . H,66
Crabb, G. English Synonyms. New York, 1854. 8°. . . . . L,572
New Pantheon. London, 1854. 18°. . . . . . . . . . P,908
Crabbe, G. Poetical Works. Boston, 1865. 24°. . . . . . . . I,327
The same; with Life by his Son. London, 1854. 8°. . . D,98
Crabbe, G. Outline of Natural Theology. London, 1840. 8°. . . . P,219
Craddock, T. Condensing Steam Engine. London, 1847. 8°. . . N,252,40
Crag Mollusca. S. V. Wood. London, 1848. 2 v. 4°. . . . . Q,30
Craig, A. R. Philosophy of Training. London, 1843. 16°. . . O,1122
Craig, J. Dictionary of the English Language. London, 1856. 2 v. 8°. . L.R.
Craig, N. B. History of Pittsburgh. Pittsburgh, 1851. 12°. . . . C,169
Craik, D. M. *formerly Miss Muloch.* Agatha's Husband. New York, 1868. 8°. K,641
The same. Leipzig, 1860. 16°. . . . . . . . . J,82
Avillion; and other Tales. New York, 1854. 8°. . . . . K,640
Brave Lady. New York, 1870. 8°. . . . . . . . . . K,642
The same. Leipzig, 1870. 2 v. in 1. 16°. . . . . . J,83
Bread upon the Waters, etc. Leipzig, 1865. 16°. . . . . . J,84
Christian's Mistake. New York, 1865. 12°. . . . . . . K,652
The same. Leipzig, 1865. 16°. . . . . . . . . J,85
Domestic Stories. Leipzig, 1862. 16°. . . . . . . . . J,86
Fair France; Impressions of a Traveler. New York, 1871. 12°. . V,449
Fairy Book. New York, 1867. 16°. . . . . . . . . J,1204
Head of the Family. New York, n. d. 8°. . . . . . . K,643
The same. Leipzig, 1858. 2 v. in 1. 16°. . . . . . J,87
John Halifax, Gentleman. New York, 1869. 12°. . . . . . K,659
The same. Leipzig, 1857. 2 v. in 1. 16°. . . . . . J,88
Life for a Life. New York, n. d. 12°. . . . . . . . K,660
The same. Leipzig, 1859. 2 v. in 1. 16°. . . . . . J,89
Lord Erlistoun, etc. Leipzig, 1864. 16°. . . . . . . J,557
Mistress and Maid. New York, n. d. 8°. . . . . . . . K,645
The same. Leipzig, 1862. 16°. . . . . . . . . J,556
Noble Life. New York, 1867. 12°. . . . . . . . . K,661
The same. Leipzig, 1866. 16°. . . . . . . . . J,558
Nothing New; Tales. New York, n. d. 8°. . . . . . . K,650
Ogilvies. New York, n. d. 8°. . . . . . . . . . K,647
The same. Leipzig, 1863. 16°. . . . . . . . . J,90
Olive. New York, 1867. 8°. . . . . . . . . . . K,649
The same. Leipzig, 1866. 2 v. in 1. 16°. . . . . . J,91
Poems. Boston, 1866. 16°. . . . . . . . . . . I,341
The same. Leipzig, 1868. 16°. . . . . . . . . J,92

Craik, D. M. Romantic Tales. Leipzig, 1861. 16°. . . . . . . . J,93
Studies from Life. New York, 1861. 12°. . . . . . . . K,662
The same. Leipzig, 1867. 16°. . . . . . . . . J,94
Two Marriages. New York, 1867. 12°. . . . . . . . K,663
The same. Leipzig, 1867. 16°. . . . . . . . . J,95
Unkind Word; and other Stories. New York, 1870. 12°. . . K,664
The same. Leipzig, 1869. 2 v. in 1. 16°. . . . . . J,101
Woman's Kingdom. New York, 1868. 8°. . . . . . . K,651
The same. Liepzig, 1868. 2 v. in 1. 16°. . . . . . J,102
Woman's Thoughts about Women. New York, 1864. 12°. . . O,409
The same. Leipzig, 1860. 16°. . . . . . . . . J,103
Craik, G. M. Faith Unwin's Ordeal. Leipzig, 1866. 16°. . . . . J,96
Leslie Tyrrell. Leipzig, 1867. 16°. . . . . . . . . J,97
Lost and Won. Leipzig, 1862. 16°. . . . . . . . . J,98
Mildred; a Novel. New York, 1868. 8°. . . . . . . . K,644
The same. Leipzig, 1868. 16°. . . . . . . . . J,99
Winifred's Wooing. Leipzig, 1868. 16°. . . . . . . . J,100
Craik, G. L. English of Shakespeare. Boston, 1867. 12°. . . . I,846
History of English Literature. New York, 1863. 2 v. 8°. . . H,711
and MacFarlane. Pictorial History of England. Lond. 1849. 8 v. 8°. A,418
The same. New York, 1848. 4 v. 8°. . . . . . . A,415
Pursuit of Knowledge under Difficulties. London, 1868. p. 8°. . L,99
The same. London, 1834. 2 v. 16°. . . . . . . L,485
The same. New York, 1868. 2 v. 16°. . . . . . L,402
Romance of the Peerage. London, 1848–50. 4 v. 12°. . . . C,1230
Cramer, J. A. Description of Ancient Greece. Oxford, 1828. 3 v. 8°. . A,97
Description of Asia Minor. Oxford, 1832. 2 v. 8°. . . . V,705
and Wilkham. Passage of Hannibal over Alps. London, 1828. 8°. A,159
Crampton, T., and Turner. Geographical Reading-Book. Lond. 1857. 16°. O,895
Crane, A. M. See *Seemuller, A. M. C.*
Cranes, Construction of. J. Glynn. London, 1854. 12°. . . . . M,923
Cranford. E. C. Gaskell. New York, n. d. 16°. . . . . . K,704
The same. Leipzig, 1867. 16°. . . . . . . . . J,175
Cranmer, T., Life of. C. W. Le Bas. London, 1833. 2 v. 16°. . . D,331
Life of. J. Strype. Oxford, 1840. 2 v. 8°. . . . . . . P,685
Memorials of. J. Strype. London, 1853. 2 v. 12°. . . . D,316
Crashaw, R. Complete Works. London, 1858. 16°. . . . . . . I,333
Crater; or, Vulcan's Peak. J. F. Cooper. New York, 1852. 12°. . . K,26
The same. New York, 1861. 8°. . . . . . . . . K,59
Cratylus, New; Study of Greek Language. J. W. Donaldson. Lond.1859. 8°. L,741
Craven, J. J. Prison Life of Jeff. Davis. New York, 1866. 12°. . . C,931
Crawford, A. W. *Lord Lindsay.* Letters on Egypt. London, 1858. p. 8°. L,115
Crawford, M. S. Life in Tuscany. Columbus, 1859. 8°. . . . . V,512
Crayon Miscellany. W. Irving. New York, 1868. 16°. . . . . U,8
The same. New York, 1867. 12°. . . . . . . . . U,25
Creasy, E. S. Eminent Etonians. London, 1850. 8°. . . . . . D,101
Fifteen Decisive Battles of the World. London, 1856. 8°. . . A,326
History of England. London, 1869. 2 v. 8°. . . . . . A,437
Rise and Progress of the English Constitution. New York, 1856. 12°. B,47
Creation, Cosmogony; or, Mysteries of. T. A. Davis. New York, 1857. 8°. P,177

Creation, Course of. J. Anderson. Cincinnati, 1851. 12°. . . . . . N,868
Epoch of. E. Lord. New York, 1851. 12°. . . . . . . P,134
Geschichte der Schöpfung. H. Burmeister. Leipzig, 1856. 8°. . G,826
Natürliche Geschichte der Schöpfung. C.Vogt. Braunschweig, 1858. 8°. G,839
Philosophy of. B. Powell. London, 1855. 8°. . . . . . O,676
Physics of. H. James. Boston, 1863. 8°. . . . . . . P,167
Plan of the. C. L. Hequembourg. Boston, 1859. 12°. . . . . P,250
Powers Displayed in. Sir J. G. Dalyell. Lond. 1851, 53, 58. 3 v. 4°. Q,8
Sketches of. A. Winchell. New York, 1870. 12°. . . . . . M,771
Vestiges of the Natural History of. New York, 1854. 18°. . . N,441
Credit System, Analysis of. S. Colwell. Philadelphia, 1859. 8°. . . O,572
Credo. L. T. Townsend. Boston, 1870. 16°. . . . . . . . P,40
Creed, Exposition of the. J. Pearson. London, 1869. p. 8°. . . . L,221
Cree Language, Grammar of the. J. House. London, 1844. 8°. . . L,781
Cresap, M., Biographical Sketch of. J. J. Jacob. Cincinnati, 1866. 4°. . C,1054
Crescent and Cross. E. Warburton. New York, 1845. 2 v. in 1. 8°. . V,627
The same. Leipzig, 1852. 2 v. in 1. 16°. . . . . . J,511
Cresy, E. Encyclopædia of Civil Engineering. London, 1865. 8°. . *M,712
Crete, Excursion to. B. Taylor. New York, 1868. 12°. . . . . . V,382
Reise nach Kreta, 1817. F. W. Sieber. Leipzig, 1823. 2 v. 8°. . E,201
Creyton, P. *pseud.* See *Trowbridge, J. T.*
Crichton, A. Converts from Infidelity. Edinburgh, 1827. 2 v. 16°. . I,495
History of Arabia, Ancient and Modern. New York, 1855. 16°. . L,387
Revolutions in Europe. Edinburgh, 1828. 3 v. 16°. . . . . I,512
and Wheaton. Scandinavia; Ancient and Modern. N. Y. 1841. 2v. 16°. L,429
The same. New York, 1856. 2 v. 16°. . . . . . B,574
Crime, Juvenile Delinquents. M. Carpenter. London, 1853. 12°. . . O,358
Crimea, The, Culinary Campaign in. A. Soyer. London, 1857. 12°. . B,89
and Odessa. C. Koch. London, 1855. 12°. . . . . . . V,550
British Expedition to. W. H. Russell. London, 1858. 8°. . . B,82
Fall of. E. Spencer. London, 1854. 12°. . . . . . . B,79
Invasion of. A. W. Kinglake. Leipzig, 1863–68. 8 v. 16°. . . J,240
The same. New York and Edinburgh, 1864–68. 4 v. 12°. and 8°. B,81
Krim und Odessa. C. Koch. Leipzig, 1854. 12°. . . . . . E,198
Crimean War. W. H. Russell. London, 1856. 12°. . . . . . . B,80
Criminal Trials. D. Jardine. London, 1832–35. 2 v. 16°. . . . L,473
in Scotland. J. H. Burton. London, 1852. 2 v. 12°. . . . U,496
Crinoidea, Recent and Fossil. T. and T. Austin. London, n. d. 4°. . Q,39
Cripple of Antioch. E. Charles. New York, 1866. 16°. . . . . K,620
Crisis, The. E. Cooper. Cincinnati, 1827. 12°. . . . . . . P,294
Criterion, The. H. T. Tuckerman. New York, 1866. 12°. . . . H,41
Criticism, Canons of. T. Edwards. London, 1753. 12°. . . . . . I,866
Elements of. H. Home, *Lord Kames;* ed. by J. R. Boyd. N. Y. 1855. 12°. L,595
Essays in. M. Arnold. Boston, 1866. 12°. . . . . . . H,480
Critic of Pure Reason. I. Kant. London, 1838. 8°. . . . . . . . O,672
Crittenden, S. W. Elementary Treatise on Book-Keeping. Phila. 1853. 12°. M,1167
Inductive and Practical Treatise on Book-Keeping. Phila. 1866. 8°. M,1179
Crockett, D., Life of. Philadelphia, n. d. 16°. . . . . . . . C,938
Sketches and Eccentricities of. Louisville, n. d. 16°. . . . C,827
Croke, J. Thirteen Psalms, etc., in English Verse. London, 1844. 12°. L,606,11

Croker, J. W. Essays on the French Revolution. London, 1857. 8°. . B,258
Croker, T. C. Keen of the South of Ireland. London, 1844. 12°. . L,606,13
Memoirs of Joseph Holt. London, 1838. 2 v. 8°. . . . . . D,469
(Ed.) Brittania's Pastorals. London, 1852. 12°. . . . L,606,30
Historical Songs of Ireland. London, 1841. 12°. . . L,606,1
Kerry Pastorals. London, 1843. 12°. . . . . . L,606,7
Songs of the French Invasion of Ireland. Lond. 1845. 12°. L,606,21
Croll, A. A. Domestic Uses of Gas. Cottenham, 1848. 16°. . . N,252,37
Croly, G. Life and Times of George IV. New York, 1855. 16°. . . L,348
Beauties of the British Poets. New York, n. d. 12°. . . . I,336
Poetical Works. London, n. d. 2 v. 12°. . . . . . . I,351
Cromwell, O., and Luther. J. T. Headley. New York, 1850. 12°. . . C,491
and the Protectorate. D. Wilson. London, 1848. 16°. . . . D,377
Letters and Speeches. T. Carlyle. London, 1857. 3 v. 8°. . . H,838
The same. Leipzig, 1861. 4 v. 16°. . . . . . . . J,61
Life of. H. W. Herbert. New York, 1856. 12°. . . . . K,177
M. Russell. Edinburgh, 1829. 2 v. 16°. . . . . I,521
The same. New York, n. d. 2 v. 18°. . . . L,384
W. Harris. London, 1818. 8°. . . . . . . D,393,3
History of. F. Guizot. Philadelphia, 1854. 2 v. 12°. . . . D,402
Sketches of. W. D. Fellowes. London, 1828. 4°. . . . . F,265
Cromwell, R., and the Restoration. F. Guizot. London, 1856. 2 v. 8°. . A,525
Crown of Success; or, Four Heads to furnish. C. Tucker. London, 1870. 16°. J,663
Cronise, T. S. Natural Wealth of California. San Francisco, 1868. 8°. . C.249
Crookes, W., and Röhrig, E. (Editors). See *Kerl, B.* . . . . . .
Crosby, H. Notes on the New Testament. New York, 1863. 12°. . . F,524
Crosland, N. Memorable Women. Boston, 1857. 12°. . . . . C,504
Crotch, W. Thorough-Bass and Theory of Tuning. London, 1856. 8°. M,421,1
Crotia and Hungary, Tour in. G. A. Spottiswoode. London, 1861. 8°. V,1086,1
Croton Aqueduct, Illustrations of. F. B. Tower. New York, 1845. 4°. . Q,270
Crouch, J. Three Successful Girls. New York, 1871. 12°. . . . K,151
Croucher, J. H. Photographs by Calotype and Energiatype. Phila. 1853. 12°. M,613
Crowden, W. Fatty Acid of Cocculus Indicus. London, 1852. 8°. . N,252,44
Crowe, C. Night-Side of Nature. New York, 1850. 12°. . . . . . O,333
Crowe, E. E. Eminent Foreign Statesmen. London, 1833. 5 v. 12°. M,1012
Greek and the Turk. London, 1853. 12°. . . . . . . . V,531
History of France. London, 1830–31. 3 v. 12°. . . . . . M,989
The same. New York, 1854. 3 v. 16°. . . . . . . B,200
The same. London, 1848–68. 5 v. 8°. . . . . . . B,340
Reigns of Louis XVIII. and Charles X. London, 1854. 2 v. 8°. . B,263
Crowe, J. A., and Cavalcaselle. Hist. of Painting in Italy. Lond. 1864. 3v. 8°. M,105
Crowfield, C. *pseud.* See *Stowe, H. B.*
Crowne-Garland of Golden Roses. R. Johnson. London, 1842. 12°. L,606,6
The same; part 2. London, 1845. 12°. . . . . L,606,15
Crown Jewels. E. L. Moffett. New York, 1871. 12°. . . . . J,657
Crown of Wild Olive. J. Ruskin. New York, 1866. 12°. . . . . . M,72
Croyland Abbey, Chronicle of. Ingulphus and Peter of Blois. Lond. 1854. p. 8°. L,13
Cruden, A. Concordance of Holy Scriptures. New York, 1868. r. 8°. *P,499
Cruel as the Grave. E. D. E. N. Southworth. Boston, 1871. 16°. . . K,411
Cruikshank, G. Three Courses and a Dessert. London, 1867. p. 8°. . L,100

Cruise of the Betsey. H. Miller. Boston, 1859. 12°. . . . . . v,357
of the Frolic. W. H. G. Kingston. Boston, 1866. 12°. . . J,1495
Crumbs Swept Up. T. De W. Talmage. Philadelphia, 1870. 12°. . . H,130
Crusades and Chivalry, History of. H. Stebbing. Edinb. 1830. 2 v. 16°. I,523
and the Crusaders. J. G. Edgar. Boston, 1860. 16°. . . J,1513
Chronicles of. London, 1870. p. 8°. . . . . . . . . . L,5
The same. London, 1856. p. 8°. . . . . . . . . A,226
French, and the Crescent. G. L. Ditson. New York, 1859. 12°. . v,774
Gemälde aus dem Zeitalter der. K. W. F. Funck. Leip. 1821-4. 3 v. 8°. E,28
Geschichte der Kreuzzüge. F. Wilken. Leipzig, 1807–32. 7 v. 8°. E,29
History of. J. F. Michaud. New York, 1853. 3 v. 12°. . . A,225
C. Mills. London, 1821. 2 v. 8°. . . . . . . . . A,247
H. Proctor. Philadelphia, 1856. 8°. . . . . . . A,245
Crusoe's Island. J. R. Browne. New York, 1867. 12°. . . . . v,54
Crustacea, British. A. White. London, 1857. 16°. . . . . . O,6
Süd-Afrikanische Crustaceen. F. Krauss. Stuttgart, 1843. 6°. . F,96
Cruveilhier, J. Anatomy of the Human Body. New York, 1854. 8°. L,1006
Cryptogram. J. De Mille. New York, 1871. 8°. . . . . . K,357
Cryptogamia. W. Hofmeister. London, 1862. 8°. . . . . . O,307
Deutschlands Kyrp. Gewäsche. D. Dietrich. v.3,6–9. Jena, 1846–8. 5 v. 8°. G,862
C. Schkuhr. Wittenberg, 1809. 4°. . . . . . . G,903
Supplement. G. Kunze. Leipzig, 1840–47. 2 v. 4°. . . G,963
Lichenes, etc. G. F. Hoffmann. Lipsiæ, 1784. 2 v. in 1. f°. . . Q,76
Cryptogamic Botany of Scotland. M. J. Berkeley. London, 1857. 8°. *N,1000
Crystal Palace, 1851, Description of. J. Tallis. London, n. d. 2 v. 4°. . S.C.
Exhibition at. H. Greeley. New York, 1853. 12°. . . . M,608
Crystalline; Heiress of Fall-Down Castle. F. W. Shelton. N. Y. 1854. 12°. K,297
Crystallization, Ethics of the Dust. J. Ruskin. New York, 1866. 12°. . M,66
Crystallography, Treatise on. H. P. Regnault. London, 1848. 8°. . N,252,33
Csink, J. Grammar of the Hungarian Language. London, 1853. 8°. . L,778
Cuba, and Porto Rico, Travels in. D. Turnbull. London, 1840. 8°. . v,141
Gan-Eden; or, Pictures of. W. H. Hurlbut. Boston, 1854. 12°. . v,189
The same. London, 1855. p. 8°. . . . . . . I,659,1
History of. M. M. Ballou. Boston, 1854. 12°. . . . . v,190
Our Artist in. G. W. Carleton. New York, 1865. 16°. . . . v,169
To Cuba and Back. R. H. Dana, jr. Boston, 1859. 12°. . . v,188
United States and Canada. A. M. Murray. New York, 1856. 12°. v,13
H. A. Murray. London, 1855. 2 v. 12°. . . . v,144
Yankee Travels in. New York, 1856. 12°. . . . . . v,232
Cucumber; its Culture, Uses, and History. W. G. Johnson. Lond. 1847. 16°. N,252,37
Cudjo's Cave. J. T. Trowbridge. Boston, 1869. 12°. . . . . K,351
Cudlip, A. (*formerly A. Thomas.*) Called to Account. Leip. 1867. 2 v. in 1. 16°. J,104
Dennis Donne. Leipzig, 1864. 2 v. in 1. 16°. . . . . . J,105
Married at Last. Philadelphia, n. d. 12°. . . . . K,1147
Only Herself. Leipzig, 1870. 2 v. in 1. 16°. . . . . . J,107
On Guard; a Novel. New York, 1865. . . . . . . . K,665
The same. Leipzig, 1865. 2 v. in 1. 16°. . . . . . J,106
Played Out. Leipzig, 1867. 2 v. in 1. 16°. . . . . . J,108
Theodore Leigh; a Novel. New York, 1865. 8°. . . . . K,666
Walter Goring. Leipzig, 1866. 2 v. in 1. 16°. . . . . J,109

Cudworth, R. Intellectual System of the Universe. London, 1845. 3 v. 8°. P,141
The same. Andover, 1837–38. 2 v. 8°. . . . . . . P,142
Cudworth, W. H. Hist. of First Massachusetts Regiment. Bost. 1866. 12°. B,925
Cuendias, E. von. Spanien und die Spanier. Brüssel, 1851. 8°. . . E,203
Culinary Campaign in the Crimea. A. Soyer. London, 1857. 12°. . . B,89
Cullum, G. W. Register of Academy at West Point. N. Y. 1868. 2 v. 8°. C,1031
Culprit Fay. J. R. Drake. New York, 1864. 12°. . . . . . . I,31
Culture and Religion. J. C. Shairp. New York, 1871. 12°. . . . P,182
and War, Conversations on. A. Helps. Boston, 1871. 12°. . . H,325
demanded by Modern Life. E. L. Youmans. N. Y. 1867. 12°. . M,627
Culverwel, N. Light of Nature, with other Treatises. London, 1654. 4°. . P,311
Cumberland, Army of, Report of First Meeting. Cincinnati, 1868. 8°. . B,947
Cumberland, G. Original Tales. London, 1810. 2 v. 12°. . . . K,667
Cumberland, R. Memoirs; written by himself. Philadelphia, 1856. 8°. . D,60
Observer; Collection of Essays. London, 1798. 6 v. 12°. . . H,524
Cuming, F. Tour to the Western Country. Pittsburgh, 1810. 12°. . . V,96
Cumming, J. Apocalyptic Sketches. Philadelphia, 1858. 12°. . . . P,255
Great Consummation. New York, 1863–64. 2 v. 12°. . . . P,249
Great Tribulation. New York, 1860. 12°. . . . . . . P,253
Sabbath Evening Readings. Boston, 1856. 12°. . . . . . P,456
Cumming, R. G. Hunter's Life in South Africa. N. Y. 1864. 2 v. 12°. V,802
Cummings, A. Memoir of E. Payson. New York, n. d. 18°. . . P,746,12
Cummings, M. F., and Miller, C. C. Architecture. Troy, 1865. 4°. . . Q,200
Cummins, M. S. El Fureidis. Boston, 1861. 12°. . . . . . . K,90
Haunted Hearts. Boston, 1864. 12°. . . . . . . . K,89
Lamplighter. Boston, 1868. 12°. . . . . . . . . K,88
Cundall, J. (Ed.) Examples of Ornament. London, 1855. 4°. . *Q,177
Cunningham, A. Life and Writings of Sir J. Reynolds. N. Y. 1860. 12°. D,244
Life of R. Burns. Boston, 1855. 8°. . . . . . . . . J,888
Lives of British Architects. London, 1831. 16°. . . . . I,640
of British Painters. London, 1830–33. 4 v. 16°. . . . I,638
and Sculptors. New York, 1845–68. 5 v. 18°. . . L,352
of British Sculptors. London, 1830. 16°. . . . . . I,639
Songs of Scotland. London, 1825. 4 v. 8°. . . . . . . I,350
Cunningham, G. G. Lives of Eminent Englishmen. Lond. 1853. 8 v. 8°. C,1270
The same. Glasgow, 1838. 8 v. in 4. 8°. . . . . . S.C.
Cunningham, W., and Adams, J. Correspondence. Boston, 1823. 8°. . H,836
Cupples, G. Driven to Sea. Boston, 1870. 16°. . . . . . J,1324
Curiosities of Civilization. A. Wynter. London, 1860. 8°. . . . H,316
of History. J. Timbs. London, 1849. 16°. . . . . . . I,546
of the Law Reporters. F. F. Heard. Boston, 1871. 12°. . . H,134
of Nature and Art. S. G. Goodrich. Cincinnati, 1857. 8°. . . H,149
of Science. J. Timbs. London, 1849. 2 v. in 1. 16°. . . . I,545
Curran, J. P., and his Contemporaries. C. Phillips. New York, 1854. 12°. D,440
Speeches. London, 1847. 8°. . . . . . . . . . . H,794
The same; edited by T. Davis. Dublin, 1867. 12°. . . H,774
Curran, W. H. Sketches of the Irish Bar. London, 1855. 2 v. 12°. . D,432
Currency, Capital, and Banking. J. Wilson. London, 1847. 8°. . . O,530
History of. J. Maclaren. London, 1858. 8°. . . . . . . O,531
Principles of. B. Price. Oxford, 1869. 8°. . . . . . . O,529

Currents and Counter-Currents in Med. Science. O. W. Holmes. Bost. 1861. 12°. L,862
Currer Bell *pseud.* See *Nicholls, C. B.*
Currie, J. Infant-School Education. Edinburgh, n. d. p. 8°. . . O,1001
Principles and Prac. of Common-School Education. Edinb. 1869. 12°. O,971
Currier, S. By the Sea. New York, 1871. 12°. . . . . . . . J,629
Curse of Clifton. E. D. E. N. Southworth. Philadelphia, 1870. 12°. . K,418
Curse of Gold. A. S. Stephens. Philadelphia, 1870. 12°. . . . K,443
Curtasye, Boke of. London, 1868. 8°. . . . . . . . . . L,605,32
Curtis, G. T., Life of Daniel Webster. New York, 1870. 2 v. 8°. . C,1030
On the Constitution of United States. New York, 1854-59. 2 v. 8°. B,663
Curtis, G. W. Howadji in Syria. New York, 1852. 12°. . . . . V,625
Lotus-Eating. New York, 1852. 12°. . . . . . . . . V,103
Memoir of A. J. Downing. New York, 1853. 8°. . . . . . M,576
Nile Notes of a Howadji. New York, 1862. 12°. . . . . . V,799
Potiphar Papers. New York, 1860. 12°. . . . . . . . . K,92
Prue and I. New York, 1868. 12°. . . . . . . . . . K,91
Trumps; a Novel. New York, 1870. . . . . . . . K,126
Curtis, J. British Entomology. London, 1824-28. 5 v. 8°. . . . O,50
Curtis, J., Memoirs of. C. M. Sedgwick. New York, 1858. 16°. . . C,841
Curtis, T. F. Human Element in Inspiration. New York, 1867. 12°. . P,501
Curtis, W. Linnæus's System of Botany. London, 1777. 4°. . . N,1034
Curtius, E. History of Greece. London, 1868-70. 3 v. 8°. . . . A,88
Curtius, G. Griechische Etymologie. Leipzig, 1858-62. 2 v. in 1. 8°. . G,596
Curtius Rufus, Q. De gestis Alexandri Magni. Parisiis, 1822-24. 2 v. in 3. 8°. U,320
Life of Alexander the Great. New York, 1858. 12°. . . . U,415
Curwen, M. E. Manual on Titles to Real Property. Cincin. 1865. 16°. . U,484
Curwen, S. Journal and Letters from England, 1775-83. Boston, 1864. 8°. C,779
Curzon, R. Armenia; a Year at Erzeroom. New York, 1854. 12°. . V,640
Visits to Monasteries in the Levant. London, 1849. 12°. . V,1060
Cushing, L. S. Law and Practice of Legis. Assemblies. Boston, 1866. 8°. *U,503
Manual of Parliamentary Practice. Boston, 1856. 18°. . . . O,459
Cushing, W., Life of. H. Flanders. Philadelphia, 1855. 8°. . C,816,2
Cust, Sir E. Warriors of the Thirty Years' War. London, 1865. 2 v. 12°. D,512
Custine, A. Russia. New York, 1854. 12°. . . . . . . . V,530
The same. London, 1863. p. 8°. . . . . . . . I,656,5
Custis, G. W. P. Recollections and Memoirs of Washington. N. Y. 1860. 8°. C,1104
Customs and Costumes of People, Appleton's. New York, 1856. 8°. . Q,261
Oriental. S. Burder. London, 1808. 2 v. 8°. . . . . . P,481
Cuthbert, St., Libellus de. London, 1835. 8°. . . . . . . F,126,1
Life of. London, 1838. 8°. . . . . . . . . . F,126,8
Cuthbert Bede *pseud.* See *Bradley, E.*
Cutter, C. Anatomy and Physiology. Boston, 1848. 12°. . . . L,845
Anatomy, Physiology, and Hygiene. New York, 1852. 12°. . . L,871
Cutter, G. W. Poems and Fugitive Pieces. Cincinnati, 1857. 8°. . . I,38
Cutter, W. Life of General Lafayette. Cincinnati, 1854. 12°. . . D,631
Cuvier, G., *Baron.* Animal Kingdom. London, 1851. 8°. . . . N,550
Discours sur les Revolutions du Globe. Paris, 1854. 12°. . . N,476
Essay on the Theory of the Earth. Edinburgh, 1827. 8°. . . N,792
Memoirs of. R. Lee. London, 1833. 8°. . . . . . . D,682

Cuvier, G., *Baron*, and Latreille, P.A. Animal Kingdom. Lon.1834-6. 8v. 8°. *N,663
Vol. 1. Mammalia; Aves.
2. Reptilia; Pisces.
3. Mollusca; Annelides; Crustacea; Arachnides.
4. Insecta; Zoöphytes.
5. Plates—Mammalia; Aves.
6. Plates—Reptilia; Pisces.
7. Plates—Mollusca; Annelides; Crustacea; Arachnides.
8. Plates—Insecta, Zoöphytes.

Cuzco, Ancient Capital of Peru. C. R. Markham. London, 1856. 8°. . V,239
Cyclopædia, American Annual, 1861-69. New York, 1862-70. 9 v. 8°. . L.R.
Bibliographica. J. Darling. London, 1854. 2 v. 8°. . . . L.R.
Subjects; Holy Scriptures. J. Darling. London, 1859. 8°. L.R.
New American; ed. G. Ripley and C. A. Dana. N. Y. 1871. 16 v. 8°. R.R.
of American Literature. E. A. and G. L. Duyckinck. N.Y. 1856. 2 v. 8°. S.C.
The same, and Supplement. New York, 1856. 3 v. 8°. *H,660
of Anecdotes of Literature and Art. K. Arvine. Boston, 1870. 8°. H,670
of Architecture. R. Stuart. New York, 1854. 2 v. in 1. 8°. *M,168
of Biblical Literature. J. Kitto; ed. W.L. Alexander. Phil. '66. 3 v. 8°. *P,452
of Biography, Appleton's. New York, 1868. 8°. . . . . . *C,620
of Commerce and Navigation. J. S. Homans. New York, 1858. 8°. S.C.
of English Literature. R. Chambers. Boston, 1855. 2 v. 8°. . S.C.
of Literary and Scientific Anecdotes. Columbus, 1859. 8°. . . H,620
of Moral and Religious Anecdotes. K. Arvine. N. Y. 1855-57. 8°. P,107
of Physical Sciences. J. P. Nichol. London, 1868. 8°. . . M,793
of Political Knowledge. London, 1849-53. 4 v. p. 8°. . . . L,248
of Useful Arts. T. Antisell. New York, 1855. 12°. . . . M,632
of Wit and Humor. W. E. Burton. New York, 1866. 2 v. 8°. . H,172
See also *Encyclopædia.*

Cyrilla. I. von Tautphoeus. Leipzig, 1853. 2 v. in 1. 16°. . . . J,472
Cyrillus, A., St. Commentary upon St. Luke. Oxford, 1859. 2 v. 8°. . P,495
Cyrus the Great, History of. J. Abbott. New York, 1867. 16°. . . J,1393
Travels of. A. M. Ramsay. London, 1727. 2 v. 8°. . . V,1069
Czar, The, and the Sultan. A. Gilson. New York, 1853. 16°. . . . C,490
his Court and People. J. S. Maxwell. New York, 1854. 12°. . V,527

Dadd, G. H. American Cattle Doctor. New York, 1856. 8°. . . . . L,920
Modern Horse Doctor. New York, 1854. 12°. . . . . M,452
Daguerre, L. J. M. Photogenic Drawing. London, 1839. 16°. . N,252,38
Dahlia, Directions for Treatment of. New York, 1856. 12°. . . M,533,2
Dahlmann, F. C. Geschichte der Englischen Revolution. Leipzig, 1846. 8°. E,43
Französische Revolution. Leipzig. 1847. 8°. . . . . . E,87
von Dänemark. Hamburg, 1840-43. 3 v. 8°. . . . . . E,111
Daily Counsellor. L. H. Sigourney. Hartford, 1859. 8°. . . . . . I,97
Dairy Farming, and Milch Cows. C. L. Flint. Boston, 1868. 12°. . . M,453
Dairyman's Daughter. L. Richmond. Philadelphia, n. d. 24°. . . J,1297
Daisy. S. Warner. Philadelphia, 1869. 2 v. 12°. . . . . . . K,369
Daisy Burns. J. Kavanagh. New York, 1867. 12°. . . . . . . K,740
The same. Leipzig, 1853. 2 v. in 1. 16°. . . . . . J,228
Daisy Chain. C. M. Yonge. New York, 1867. 2 v. 12°. . . K,1078
The same. Leipzig, 1856. 2 v. in 1. 16°. . . . . . J,546

Dakotah; or, Sioux-Indian Mission, History of. Boston, 1841. 16°. . J,1727
Dall, C. H. College, Market and Court. Boston, 1867. 12°. . . . O,386
Patty Gray's Journey to Cotton Islands. Boston, 1870. 3 v. 16°. . J,1701
Vol. 1. From Boston to Baltimore. Vol. 2. From Baltimore to Washington. Vol. 3. On the Way; or, Patty at Mount Vernon.
Dall, W. H. Alaska and its Resources. Boston, 1870. 8°. . . . V,131
Dallas, E. S. The Gay Science. London, 1866. 2 v. 8°. . . . O,796
Dallas, R. C. History of the Maroons. London, 1803. 2 v. 8°. . . C,427
Dallas, W. S. Elements of Entomology. London, 1857. 12°. . . . O,30
Dallaway, J. Discourses on Architecture in England. London, 1833. 8°. M,228
Observations on English Architecture. London, 1806. 8°. . . M,184
Dalmatia and Istria, Voyage Historique de. J. Lavallée. Lond. 1802. f°. *Q,349
and Montenegro. Sir J. G. Wilkinson. London, 1842. 2 v. 8°. V,434
Dalrymple, Sir J. Great Britain and Ireland. London, 1771–73. 2 v. 4°. A,470
Dalton, H. G. History of British Guiana. London, 1855. 2 v. 8°. . V,248
Dalton, J. C. Treaties on Human Physiology. Philadelphia, 1864. 8°. . L,962
Dalton, W. Lost in Ceylon. London, 1861. 16°. . . . . . J,1508
Nest Hunters. London, 1863. 16°. . . . . . . . . J,1719
War Tiger. London, 1869. 16°. . . . . . . . J,1264
White Elephant; or, the Hunters of Ava. London, 1860. 16°. J,1509
Will Adams; the First Englishman in Japan. London, 1861. 12°. J,1510
Wolf-Boy in China. London, n. d. 16°. . . . . . . J,1511
Daltons; or, Three Roads in Life. C. Lever. London, 1865. 2 v. 8°. K,772
The same. Leipzig, 1852. 4 v. 16°. . . . . . . J,272
Daly, R., Trial of J. Magee for Libel against. Dublin, 1790. 8°. . . H,630
Dalyell, Sir J. G. Powers Displayed in Creation. Lond. 1851–58. 3 v. 4°. Q,8
Rare Animals of Scotland. London, 1847–48. 2 v. 4°. . . Q,7
Damascus, Five Years in. J. L. Porter. London, 1855. 2 v. 8°. . . V,658
Dan to Beersheba. J. P. Newman. New York, 1864. 12°. . . . V,644
Dames Vertes, Les. F. Dudevant. Paris, n. d. 12°. . . . H,1026
Dana, C. A. Household Book of Poetry. New York, 1867. 8°. . . I,167
and Wilson, J. H. Life of U. S. Grant. Springfield, 1868. 8°. . C,772
Dana, D. D. Fireman; Fire Departments of U. S. Boston, 1858. 12°. O,348
Dana, J. D. Coral Reefs and Islands. New York, 1853. 8°. . . . N,824
Manual of Geology. Philadelphia, 1864. 8°. . . . . . . N,801
System of Mineralogy. New York, 1850. 8°. . . . . . . N,862
The same. New York, 1868. 8°. . . . . . . . N,863
Text-Book of Geology. Philadelphia, 1864. 8°. . . . . . N,762
Zoöphytes, Report on U. S. Exploring Expedition. Philad. 1848. 4°. *Q,278
Atlas to the same. Philadelphia, 1849. f°. . . . *Q,352
Dana, R. H. Poems and Prose Writings. New York, 1850. 2 v. 8°. . U,90
Dana, R. H., jr. To Cuba and Back. Boston, 1859. 12°. . . . . V,188
Two years before the Mast. Boston, 1869. 12°. . . . . V,157
Dana, S. L. Essay on Manure. New York, 1856. 12°. . . . M,533,2
Dance of Death, Holbein's. F. Douce. London, 1858. p. 8°. . . . L,106
Danger in the Dark. I. Kelso. Cincinnati, 1857. 12°. . . . . K,200
Danger, F. P. et Flandin, C. De l'Arsenic. Paris, 1844. 8°. . . N,252,12
Daniell, T. and W. Oriental Scenery; Views in Hindostan; and Text. London, 1795–1804. 6 v. in 3. elph. f°. Text 1 v. 8°. . L.R.
Picturesque Voyage to India. London, 1810. f°. . . . . *Q,428
Daniel Rock. E. Erckmann et A. Chatrian. Paris, 1861. 12°. . . H,1020

Danish Story Book. H. C. Andersen. New York, 1869. 16°. . . . J,1488
Dasent, G. W. Gisli, the Outlaw; tr. from the Icelandic. Edinb. 1866. 4°. G,6
Dante Alighieri, as Philosopher, etc. V. Botta. New York, 1865. 12°. . D,727
Divine Comedy; tr. by H. W. Longfellow. Boston, 1867. 3 v. r. 8°. I,179
The same; tr. J. C. Wright; illus. by Flaxman. Lon. 1867. p.8°. L,101
The same. London, 1854. p. 8°. . . . . . G,79
Göttliche Komödie; üb. von Kannegieszer. Leip. 1843. 3 v. 16°. E,287
Inferno; illustrated by G. Doré. London. 1866. 4°. . . *Q,240
The same; translated by J. C. Carlyle. New York, 1849. 12°. G,81
The same; trans. by H. F. Cary; with Life. N. Y. 1851. 16°. G,80
Life of. C. Balbo. London, 1852. 2 v. 8°. . . . . . . . D,734
New Life; translated by C. E. Norton. Boston, 1867. r. 8°. . . I,180
Danube, Descent of the. J. R. Planché. London, 1828. 8°. . . . V,431
Danubius Pannonico-Mysicus. L. F. Marsigli. Hagæ Comitum, 1726. 6 v. in 3. f°. . . . . . . . . . . *F,301
Danvers, Mass. Reception of G. Peabody, Oct. 9, 1856. Boston, 1856. 8°. C,64
Danvers Papers; Prince and the Page. C. M. Yonge. Leipzig, 1867. 16°. J,547
D'Arblay, F. (*formerly Miss Burney.*) Camilla. London, 1796. 5 v. 16°. K,669
Cecilia. London, 1820. 3 v. 12°. . . . . . . . . . K,546
The same. London, n. d. 12°. . . . . . . K,1153
Diary and Letters. London, 1854. 7 v. 12°. . . . . . . D,5
Evelina. London, 1850. 16°. . . . . . . . . . . J,50
The same. London, 1820. 2 v. 12°. . . . . . . K,545
The same. Leipzig, 1820. 2 v. 12°. . . . . . . K,645
Memoirs of Doctor Charles Burney. Philadelphia, 1833. 8°. . . D,362
Renunciation; a Romance. Philadelphia, 1840. 2 v. 12°. . . K,670
Darien; or, the Merchant Prince. E. Warburton. Leip. 1853. 2 v. in 1. 16°. J,512
Darius the Great, History of. J. Abbott. New York, 1864. 16°. . . J,1410
Dark Night's Work. E. C. Gaskell. New York, 1863. 8°. . . . K,705
The same. Leipzig, 1863. 16°. . . . . . . . J,176
Darkness and Daylight. M. J. Holmes. New York, 1868. 12°. . . K,182
Darley, F. O. C. Sketches Abroad with Pen and Pencil. N. Y. 1869. 8°. V,403
Darley, J. R. Grecian Drama. Dublin, 1840. 8°. . . . . . . H,731
Darling, J. Cyclopædia Bibliographica. London, 1854. 2 v. 8°. . . L.R.
Subjects; Holy Scriptures. London, 1859. 8°. . . L.R.
Darlington, W. American Weeds and Useful Plants. New York, 1859. 12°. N,953
Reliquiæ Baldwinianæ. Philadelphia, 1843. 12°. . . . . H,98
Darnley. G. P. R. James. Leipzig, 1847. 16°. . . . . . . . J,205
Daru, P. A. N. B. *Comte.* Histoire de Bretagne. Paris, 1826. 3 v. 8°. . B,330
République de Venise. Paris, 1821. 8 v. 8°. . . . . B,527
Darwin, C. Animals and Plants under Domestication. N. Y. 1868. 2 v. 12°. N,504
Darwin'sche Schöpfungstheorie. Leipzig, 1864. 8°. . . . G,816
Descent of Man; Selection in Relation to Sex. N. Y. 1871. 2 v. 8°. N,440
Entstehung der Arten. Stuttgart, 1863. 8°. . . . . . . G,813
Facts and Arguments for. F. Müller. London, 1869. 12°. . . N,519
Fossil Balanidæ and Verrucidæ. London, 1854. 4°. . . . Q,29
Fossil Lepadidæ of Great Britain. London, 1851. 4°. . . . Q,29
Monograph on the Cirripedia. London, 1851–54. 2 v. 8°. . . O,304
Natural History of Voyage of the Beagle. London, 1845. 12°. . N,633
Orchids fertilized by Insects. London, 1862. 8°. . . . . M,557

Darwin, C. Origin of Species. New York, 1860. 12°. . . . . . N,495
Researches in Natural History and Geology. New York, 1852. 2 v. 12°. N,633
Darwin, E. Plan for Female Education. Derby, 1797. 4°. . . . O,1269
Dates, Dictionary of. J. Haydn; edited by B. Vincent. London, 1866. 8°. *A,307
The same; with additions. New York, 1869. 8°. . . *A,308
Index of. J. W. Rosse. London, 1858-59. 2 v. p. 8°. . . . L,273
Daubeny, C. Plants of the World, and where they grow. London, 1865. 16°. N,912
Daubeny, C. G. B. Active and Extinct Volcanoes. London, 1848. 8°. V,1114
Miscellanies. Oxford, 1867. 2 v. 8°. . . . . . . . N,845
Atomic Theory. London, 1840. 8°. . . . . . . N,252,28
Daughter of an Empress. C. Mundt. New York, 1868. 8°. . . . G,197
Daughter of an Egyptian King. G. Ebers. Philadelphia, 1871. 12°. . G,226
Daughters, Education of. F. de S. de La M. Fénélon. Boston, 1820. 24°. O,1110
Daunou, P. C. F. Histoire de la Convention Nationale. Paris, 1848. 12°. D,609,2
Daussy, P. Opérations Géodé. sur les Côtes de France. Paris, 1829. 4°. M,821
Davenport, Iowa; Past and Present. F. B. Wilkie. Davenport, 1858. 8°. C,240
Davenport, J., Life of. A. W. M'Clure. Boston, 1870. 12°. . . . D,8,2
Davenport, R. A. History of the Bastile. London, 1838. 16°. . . . I,618
Life of Ali Pasha. London, 1837. 16°. . . . . . . . I,627
Narratives of Peril and Suffering. London, 1840. 2 v. 16°. . . I,637
Perilous Adventures. New York, 1865. 18°. . . . . . . L,445
Davenport Dunn. C. Lever. London, 1829. 2 v. 8°. . . . . K,773
The same. Leipzig, 1849. 3 v. 16°. . . . . . . J,273
David, King of Israel. F. W. Krummacher. New York, 1868. 12°. . P,280
Repentance of; Lectures. J. W. Hatherell. London, 1847. 12°. . P,254
David, M. Campaigns of Gen. C. Pichegru. London, 1796. 8°. . . B,331
David Copperfield. C. Dickens. New York, 1868. 12°. . . . . K,473
The same. Philadelphia, 1853. 8°. . . . . . . K,506
The same. New York, 1871. 2 v. 12°. . . . . K,1131
The same. Leipzig, 1849-59. 3 v. 16°. . . . . J,118
David Elginbrod. G. Mac Donald. London, 1863. 3 v. 12°. . . . K,803
Davids, A. L. Grammaire Turke. London, 1836. 4°. . . . . L,637
Davidson, B. Hebrew and Chaldee Lexicon. London, n. d. 4°. . . L.R.
Davidson, L. M., Life of. C. M. Sedgwick. New York, 1860. 16°. . C,860,7
Poems. Boston, 1854. 12°. . . . . . . . . . . I,39
Davidson, S. Introduction to New Testament. London, 1848-51. 3 v. 8°. P,498
Davidson, T. British Carboniferous Brachiopoda. London, 1848. 4°. . Q,32
British Fossil Brachiopoda, v. 1. London, 1851-54. 4°. . . . Q,33,1
Davie, W. R., Life of. F. M. Hubbard. Boston. 16°. . . . C,860,25
Davies, C. Elements of Descriptive Geometry. New York, 1866. 8°. M,1124
Intellectual Arithmetic. New York, 1854. 16°. . . . . O,1095
Logic and Utility of Mathematics. New York, 1850. 8°. . M,1172
Shades, Shadows, and Linear Perspective. New York, 1856. 8°. . M,211
and Peck, W. G. Mathematical Dictionary. New York, 1859. 8°. M,1176
Davies, C. M. History of Holland. London, 1851. 3 v. 8°. . . . B,410
Davies, E. Mythology and Rites of the British Druids. London, 1809. 8°. P,831
Davies, T. Preparation of Microscopic Objects. London, n. d. 16°. . N,2
Davies, T. A. Cosmogony; or, Mysteries of Creation. New York, 1857. 8°. P,177
How to make and keep Money New York, 1870. 18°. . . . H,492
Davis, A. J. Great Harmonia. New York, 1850. 5 v. 12°. . . . P,866

Davis, E. Half Century; Changes between 1800 and 1850. Boston, 1851. 12°. B,695
Davis, G. L. L. Day-Star of American Freedom. New York, 1855. 12°. C,168
Davis, Jeff., Prison Life of. J. J. Craven. New York, 1866. 12°. . . C,931
Life of. E. A. Pollard. Philadelphia, 1869. 8°. . . . . . C,756
Davis, John. Elements of Astronomy. Philadelphia, 1868. 12°. . . N,264
Davis, J. F. China, during and since the War. London, 1852. 2 v. 12°. V,621
The Chinese. London, 1836. 2 v. 16°. . . . . . . . . L,487
The same. New York, 1855. 2 v. 16°. . . . . L,396
Davis, E. Teacher Taught. Boston, 1839. 12°. . . . . . O,1173
Davis, M. L. Memoirs of Aaron Burr. New York, 1836-37. 2 v. 8°. . C,1028
(ed.) Private Journal of Aaron Burr. New York, 1858. 2 v. 8°. C,725
Davis, N. Carthage and her Remains. New York, 1861. 8°. . . . V,852
Davis, R. H. Waiting for the Verdict. New York, 1868. 8°. . . . K,100
Davis, W. W. H. El Gringo; or, New Mexico. New York, 1857. 12°. . V,33
Davis, Z. A. Freemason's Monitor. Philadelphia, 1843. 12°. . . O,380
Davison, W., Life of. N. H. Nicolas. London, 1823. 8°. . . . . D,39
Davy, Sir H. Consolations in Travel. Boston, 1870. 16°. . . . H,453
Fragmentary Remains, Literary and Scientific. London, 1858. 8°. H,595
Life of. J. Davy. London, 1836. 2 v. in 1. 8°. . . . . . D,85
H. Mayhew. London, 1856. 16°. . . . . . . . . D,2
Salmonia; or, Days of Fly-Fishing. Boston, 1870. 16°. . . M,301
Works. London, 1839-40. 9 v. 8°. . . . . . . . . . U,289

Vol. 1. Memoirs of his Life by John Davy.
2. Researches on Nitrous Oxide, etc.
3. Early Miscellaneous Papers, 1799-1805.
4. Elements of Chemical Philosophy.
5. Bakerian Lectures, and Miscellaneous Papers, from 1806-15.
6. Researches on the Safety Lamp, and Flame, and Misc. Papers and Researches, 1815-28.
7. Discourses before the Royal Society; Elements of Agricultural Chemistry.
8. Agricultural Chemistry, Part I.; Miscellaneous Lectures.
9. Salmonia; and Consolations in Travel.

Davy, J. Angler in the Lake District. London, 1857. 16°. . . . M,322
Angler and his Friend. London, 1855. 16°. . . . . . . M,344
Life of Sir H. Davy. London, 1836. 2 v. in 1. 8°. . . . D,85
Dawes, R. Miscellanea Critica. Lipsiæ, 1800. 8°. . . . . . . U,420
Suggestive Hints for Teachers. London, 1853. 16°. . . . O,908
Dawson, H. B. Assault on Stony Point. Morrisania, 1863. 8°. . . F,58
and "Selah." Gen. Israel Putnam. Morrisania, 1860. 8°. . . B,814
Dawson, M. Civil and Military Services of W. H. Harrison. Cinn. 1824. 8°. C,797
Dawson, R. The Present State of Australia. London, 1831. 8°. . . V,895
Dawson, S. J. Exploration in Red-River Country. Toronto, 1859. 4°. . Q,59
Day by the Fire; and other Papers. L. Hunt. Boston, 1870. 16°. . . H,583
Day, H. Opium Habit. New York, 1868. 12°. . . . . . . L,868
Day, H. N. Art of English Composition. New York, 1867. 8°. . . L,594
Elements of Logic. New York, 1867. 12°. . . . . . O,728
Introduction to English Literature. New York, 1869. 12°. . . H,693
Day, S. Historical Collections of Pennsylvania. Philadelphia, 1843. 8°. C,111
Day, S. P. Juvenile Crime. London, 1858. 8°. . . . . . . O,352
Day, T. Sandford and Merton. Baltimore, 1801. 16°. . . . . J,1205
The same. Edinburgh, n. d. 16°. . . . . . . . . J,1205
Day Dreams of a Schoolmaster. D. W. Thompson. Edinburgh, 1864. 16°. O,934
Day Star of American Freedom. G. L. L. Davis. New York, 1855. 12°. C,168
Day's Ride; a Life's Romance. C. Lever. London, n. d. 8°. . . . K,771

Day's Ride; a Life's Romance. C. Lever. Leipzig, 1864. 2 v. in 1. 16°. . J,274
Days, Book of; edited by R. Chambers. Edinburgh, 1863-64. 2 v. 8°. . *I,591
Days of Bruce. G. Aquilar. New York, 1868. 2 v. 12°. . . . K,578
Days of Knox; a Tale. London, 1869. 12°. . . . . . . . K,617
Days of my Life. M. Oliphant. New York, 1863. 12°. . . . . K,863
Days of Yore. S. Tytler. London, 1866. 2 v. 8°. . . . . K,1051
Dazincourt, J. J. B. A., Mémoires de. Paris, 1855. 12°. . . . . D,612
Deacon Sims's Prayers. M. D. Chellis. Boston, 1868. 16°. . . . J,1633
Dead Sea, Expedition to. W. F. Lynch. Philadelphia, 1850. 8°. . . V,660
The same, abridged. Philadelphia, 1852. 8°. . . . V,636
Journey round. L. J. F. C. de Saulcy. Philadelphia, 1854. 2 v. 12°. V,647
Dead-Sea Fruit. M. E. Braddon. Leipzig, 1868. 2 v. in 1. 16°. . . J,35
Dead Secret. W. Collins. Philadelphia, n. d. 12°. . . . . . K,639
The same. Leipzig, 1857. 2 v. 16°. . . . . J,130,4,5
Deaf and Dumb, American Annals of. v. 1. Hartford, 1848. 8°. . . O,1236
Vocabulary for. London, 1857. 4°. . . . . . . . O,1268
Deakin, R. Flora of the Coliseum of Rome. London, 1855. 16°. . . N,937
Dealty, W. Laborer; Remedy for his Wrongs. Cincinnati, 1869. 12°. . O,487
Deane, J. Ichnographs from Connecticut River. Boston, 1861. 4°. . . *Q,47
Dean, J. W. Memoir of Nathaniel Ward. Albany, 1868. 8°. . . . C,909
Dean's Daughter. C. G. F. Gore. Leipzig, 1853. 2 v. in 1. 16°. . . J,185
Dean's [Dean Alford's] English. G. W. Moon. London, 1865. 16°. . L,559
Debate between Pride and Loveliness. F. Thynn. London, 1841. 8°. . I,885,5
Debater, American. J. N. McElligott. New York, 1870. 12°. . . O,558
Debates between A. Lincoln and S. A. Douglas. Columbus, 1860. 8°. . O,574
of Congress, 1789 to 1856; abridged. T. H. Benton. N. Y. 1859. 8°. P.D.
of Convention of Virginia, 1788. Richmond, 1805. 8°. . . . O,35
of the Convention of California. J. R. Browne. Washington, 1850. 8°. O,425
on the Federal Constitution. J. Elliot. Philadelphia, 1859. 5 v. 8°. O,427
Debenham's Vow. A. B. Edwards. New York, 1870. 8°. . . .
The same. Leipzig, 1870. 2 v. in 1. 16°. . . . . . J,156
Debit and Credit. G. Freytag. New York, 1858. 12°. . . . . G,188
Deborah's Diary. A. Manning. London, 1860. 16°. . . . . . J,581
De Bow, J. D. B. Industrial Resources of United States. N. Y. 1854. 3 v. 8°. B,705
Statistical View of the United States. Washington, 1854. 8°. . . P.D.
De Bure, G. F. Bibliographie Instructive et Supp. Paris, 1765-69. 9 v. 8°. L.R.
Decameron. G. Boccaccio; translated by W. K. Kelly. London, 1869. p. 8°. *L,328
Decatur, S., Life of. A. S. Mackenzie. Boston, 1846. 8°. . . . C,1106
The same. Boston, 1848. 12°. . . . . . . C,860,21
Decimal System for Libraries. N. B. Shurtleff. Boston, 1856. 8°. . . L.R.
Declaration of Independence, Lives of Signers. B. J. Lossing. Cinn. 1854. 12°. C,1046
Decoration, Inventions Décoratives. L. Solon. Paris, 1866. f°. . . L.R.
Decorations, Dresses of the Middle Ages. H. Shaw. Lond. 1858. 2 v. r. 8°. Q,188
Da Costa, I. Four Witnesses; Harmony of the Gospels. New York, 1855. 8°. P,496
De Costa, B. F. Pre-Columbian Discovery of America. Albany, 1868. 8°. B,625
De-Coo-Dah, Traditions of the. W. Pidgeon. New York, 1858. 8°. . B,601
De Cressy; a Tale. Leipzig, 1857. 16°. . . . . . . . . . J,110
Deep Down; a Tale of Cornish Mines. R. M. Ballantyne. Phila. 1869. 16°. J,1371
Deer, Antelopes, and Camels, Nat. Hist. of. Sir W. Jardine. Edin. n. d. 16°. N,470,21
Deerbrook; a Novel. H. Martineau. London, 1858. 12°. . . . . K,528

Deerslayer. J. F. Cooper. New York, 1864. 12°. . . . . . . . K,28
The same. New York, 1866. 12°. . . . . . . K,145
De Foe, D., and Churchill. J. Forster. London, 1856. p. 8°. . . I,661,3
Complete English Tradesman, etc., v. 2. London, 1845. 16°. . . I,590
History of the Devil. London, 1727. 8°. . . . . . . P,91
Journal of the Plague Year. London, 1839. 16°. . . . . I,612
Jure Divino; a Satyr. London, 1706. 12°. . . . . . . I,470
Life of. W. Chadwick. London, 1859. 8°. . . . . . . D,296
of, and newly-discov. Writings. W. Lee. Lond. 1869. 3 v. 8°. D,452
of Duncan Campbell. London, 1720. 8°. . . . . . U,249
Negotiations of M. Mesnager. London, 1717. 8°. . . . . U,250
New Voyage round the World. London, 1725. 8°. . . . V,1078
Robinson Crusoe. London, 1820. 2 v. 12°. . . . . . . K,531
The same. Boston, 1866. 12°. . . . . . . . . J,1522
The same. London, 1869. p. 8°. . . . . . . . L,146
The same. Leipzig, 1845. 16°. . . . . . . . J,111
Secret History of the White Staff. London, 1714. 12°. . . . U,248
The Storm; Disasters in the late Tempest. London, 1704. 8°. . N,83
Voyage to the World of Cartesius. London, 1692. 8°. . . . O,640
Works. London, 1854. 6 v. p. 8. . . . . . . . . . L,263

Vol. 1. Captain Singleton; Colonel Jack.
2. Memoirs of a Cavalier; Captain Carleton; Dickory Cronke.
3. Moll Flanders; History of the Devil.
4. Roxana; Mrs. Christian Davis.
5. History of the Plague of London, 1665; Great Fire in London, 1666; The Storm; True-Born Englishman.
6. Duncan Campbell; New Voyage round the World; Political Tracts.

De Forest, J. W. History of Indians of Connecticut. Hartford, 1853. 8°. B,627
Miss Ravenel's Conversion to Loyalty. New York, 1867. 12°. . J,628
Oriental Acquaintance. New York, 1856. 12°. . . . . . V,559
Degerando, J. M., *Baron*. Self-Education. Boston, 1860. 12°. . . O,978
De Hart, W. C. Observations on Military Law. New York, 1859. 8°. . U,527
Deistical Writers, View of the principal. London, 1837. 8°. . . . P,260
Deists, Short Method with. C. Leslie. New York, n. d. 18°. . . P,746,14
De Kay, J. Zoölogy of New York. Albany, 1842–44. 5 v. 4°. . *Q,101,1–5
Dekker, T. Knight's Conjuring. London, 1842. 12°. . . . L,606,5
and others. Patient Grissil; a Comedy. London, 1841. 8°. . I,885,6
De Kroyft, S. H. A Place in thy Memory. New York, 1858. 12°. . . H,115
De La Beche, H. T. Geological Manual. London, 1833. 8°. . . . N,800
Geological Observer. London, 1853. 8°. . . . . . . . N,843
Delaborde, H. La Peinture Religieuse en France. Paris, 1860. 8°. N,252,45
Delafield, R. Art of War in Europe, 1854–56. Washington, 1860. 4°. . P.D.
Delambre, J. B. J. Abrégé d'Astronomie. Paris, 1813. 8°. . . . N,283
Astronomie Théorique et Pratique. Paris, 1814. 3 v. 4°. . . N,381
Base du Système Métrique Décimal, v. 2–3. Paris, 1807–10. 4°. . M,817
Détermination d'un Arc du Méridien. Paris, 1799. 4°. . . M,1175
Histoire de l'Astronomie Ancienne. Paris, 1817. 2 v. 4°. . . N,383
du Moyen Age. Paris, 1819. . . . . . . . . N,382
Delamer, E. S. Flax and Hemp. London, 1854. 16°. . . . . M,438
Pigeons and Rabbits. London, 1866. 8°. . . . . . . . N,626
Delamotte, P. H. Practice of Photography. London, 1856. 12°. . . M,684
Delandine, F. A., and Chaudon. Diction. Historique. Caen, 1804. 13 v. 8°. C,597

Delepierre, O. Travaux de la Société des Philobiblon. Londres, 1862. 8°. L.R.
Historical Difficulties. London, 1868. 12°. . . . . . . A,31
De Liefede, J. Six Months among Charities of Europe. Lond. 1866. 2 v. 8°. O,356
Delille, J. Œuvres Choisies. Paris, 1856. 12°. . . . . . . . H,884
De Lolme, J. L. Progress of English Constitution. Lond. 1838. 2 v. 8°. B,51
The same. London, 1853. p. 8°. . . . . . . . L,178
Deloney, T. Garland of Good-Will. London, 1851. 12°. . . L,606,30
Strange Histories. London, 1841. 12°. . . . . . L,606,3
Delphine. Mad. de Stäel-Holstein. Paris, 1856. 12°. . . . . H,922
Delrieu, A. Le Rhin. Bruxelles, 1850. 12°. . . . . . . H,1024
Deluge, Mosaic, Physical Demonstrations of. G. Fairholme. Lond. 1837. 8°. N,803
Delusions, Extraordinary Popular. C. Mackay. Phil. 1850. 2 v. 12°. . O,332
Demeanor, Booke of. R. Weste. London, 1868. 8°. . . . . L,605,32
Demerara. H. Martineau. London, 1859. 16°. . . . . . K,551,2
Demerara Memorial, Observations on. London, 1827. . . . . O,396
De Mille, J. B. O. W. C. Series. Boston, 1871. 3 v. 16°. . . .
Vol. 1. The B. O. W. C. . . . . . . . . J,1505
2. Boys of Grand Pré School. . . . . . . J,1506
3. Lost in the Fog. . . . . . . . J,1507
Cryptogram. New York, 1871. 8°. . . . . . . . . K,357
Dodge Club. New York, 1869. 8°. . . . . . . . . K,102
Lady of the Ice. New York, 1870. 8°. . . . . . . . K,103
Demonology and Witchcraft, Letters on. Sir W. Scott. London, 1830. 16°. I,647
The same. New York, 1855. 16°. . . . . . . . L,344
De Morgan, A. Differential and Integral Calculus. London, 1842. 8°. M,1154
Essay on Probabilities. London, 1838. 12°. . . . . M,1028
The same. London, 1838. 12°. . . . . . . M,1163
Formal Logic. London, 1847. 8°. . . . . . . . . O,730
Democracy. G. S. Camp. New York, 1859. 18°. . . . . . L,430
in the United States. R. H. Gillet. New York, 1868. 12°. . . O,507
Democratic Review. Washington and New York, 1838–52. 31 v. 8°. T,56
Demosthenes. Oration on the Crown. Boston, 1856. 12°. . . . . U,404
Orations; translated by T. Leland. London, 1825. 8°. . . . A,114
The same; translated by T. Leland. N. Y. 1855. 2 v. 16°. U,360
The same; tr. by C. R. Kennedy. Lond. 1852–69. 5 v. p. 8°. L,52
Vol. 1. Olynthiac, and other Public Orations.
2. Oration on the Crown and on the Embassy.
3. Against the Law of Leptines, Midias, Androtion, and Aristocrates.
4. Private and other Orations.
5. Miscellaneous Orations, and Index.
Werke; übersetzt von H. A. Pabst. Stuttg. 1840–59. 19 v. in 3. 24°. E,318
Dempsey, G. D. Drainage and Sewerage. London, 1854. 12°. . . . M,904
Draining Districts and Lands. London, 1854. 12°. . . . . M,903
Locomotive Engines. London, 1857. 12°. . . . . . . M,905
Atlas to the same. London, 1859. 4°. . . . . . . Q,366
Denham, M. A. Proverbs and Popular Sayings. London, 1846. 12°. L,606,20
Denina, C. G. M. Ancient Republics of Italy. London, 1773. 8°. . . B,484
Dennis Duval. W. M. Thackeray. Boston, 1869. 12°. . . . K,1038,3
The same. Leipzig, 1867. 16°. . . . . . . . J,480
Denison, E. B. Clock and Watchmaking. London, 1850. 12°. . . M,907
Denison, M. A. Hannah's Triumph. Philadelphia, 1870. 16°. . . J,1705
Noble Sister. Philadelphia, 1870. 16°. . . . . . . . J,1704
Off the Track. Philadelphia, 1870. 16°. . . . . . . . J,1706

Denman, J. S. Fourth Reading Book. New York, 1853. 12°. . . . . O,786
Denmark, Ancient Shell-Mounds of. Mrs. Lubbock. London, 1864. 8°. V,1086,3
Geschichte von Dänemark. F. C. Dahlmann. Hamb. 1840–43. 3 v. 8°. E,11
Sweden and Norway, Tour in. H. D. Inglis. London, 1837. 12°. . V,549
History of. S. A. Dunham. Lond. 1839–40. 3 v. 12°. M,1002
in the Iron Age. C. Engelhardt. London, 1866. 4°. . . . . Q,110
Travels in. B. Taylor. New York, 1868. 12°. . . . . . V,543
Invasion of, 1824. A. Gallenga. London, 1864. 2 v. 12°. . . . B,575
Dennis, G. Cities and Cemeteries of Etruria. London, 1848. 2 v. 8°. . V,519
Dennis Donne. A. Cudlip. Leipzig, 1864. 2 v. in 1. 16°. . . . J,105
Denise. Leipzig, 1865. 16°. . . . . . . . . . . . . J,112
Dennistoun, J. Memoirs of the Dukes of Urbino. London, 1851. 3 v. 8°. D,735
Memoirs of Sir R. Strange and A. Lumisden. London, 1855. p. 8°. . D,228
Denon, V. Reise in Aegypten. Berlin, 1803. 8°. . . . . . . . E,226
Dental Surgery, Principles and Practice of. C. A. Harris. Phil. 1858. 8°. L,1008
Denton, D. Description of New York State. New York, 1845. 4°. . F,57
Depping, G. Wonders of Bodily Strength and Skill. New York, 1871. 12°. M,1062
De Profundis; a Tale of Social Deposits. W. Gilbert. Lond. 1864. 2 v. 12°. J,561
De Puy, H. W. Ethan Allen, and Green-Mountain Heroes. Bost. 1853. 12°. C,19
Kossuth and his Generals. Buffalo, 1852. 12°. . . . . . D,758
De Quincey, T. Beauties selected from his Writings. Boston, 1866. 12°. H,423
Cæsars. Boston, 1851. 16°. . . . . . . . . . . . H,422
Confessions of an English Opium-Eater. Boston, 1863. 16°. . . H,413
Essays on Philosophical Writers. Boston, 1854. 2 v. 16°. . . H,420
on Poets and other English Writers. Boston, 1855. 16°. . H,414
Historical and Critical Essays. Boston, 1853. 2 v. 16°. . . . H,415
Literary Reminiscences, v. 1. Boston, 1854. 16°. . . . . . H,416
Logic of Political Economy. Boston, 1859. 16°. . . . . . H,411
Memorials, and other Papers. Boston, 1856. 2 v. 16°. . . . H,417
Miscellaneous Essays. Boston, 1854. 16°. . . . . . . . H,418
Narrative and Miscellaneous Papers. Boston, 1853. 2 v. 16°. . H,419
Note-Book of an Opium-Eater. Boston, 1855. 16°. . . . . . H,413
Theological Essays. Boston, 1854. 2 v. 16°. . . . . . . H,421
Works. Edinburgh, 1862. 15 v. 12°. . . . . . . . . H,412

Vol. 1. Confessions of an English Opium-Eater.
2. Recollections of the Lakes, and of the Lake Poets—Coleridge, Wordsworth, and Southey.
3. Spanish Military Nun; Last Days of Immanuel Kant; Revelations of Lord Rosse's Telescopes; Joan of Arc; Casuistry of Roman Meals; Modern Superstition.
4. On Murder considered as one of the Fine Arts; Revolt of the Tartars; Dialogues of three Templars on Political Economy; On War; English Mail-Coach.
5. P. B. Shelley; Dr. Parr, or Whiggism in its relations to Literature; Oliver Goldsmith; Wordsworth's Poetry; John Keats; Homer, and the Homeridæ.
6. Judas Iscariot; Richard Bentley; Cicero; Secret Societies; Milton.
7. Walking Stewart; Marquess Wellesley; Schlosser's Literary History of the 18th Century; Protestantism; Pagan Oracles; Miracles as Subjects of Testimony; Casuistry; Greece under the Romans.
8. Alex. Pope; Theory of Greek Tragedy; Language; French and English Manners; Charles Lamb; Philosophy of Herodotus; Plato's Republic; Sortilege and Astrology; Notes on Walter S. Landor.
9. Cæsars; Theban Sphinx; Essenes; Aelius Lamia.
10. Incognito; or, Count Fitz-Hum; Rhetoric; Life of Milton; Revolution in Greece; Style; The Dice.
11. Ceylon; King of Hayti; Coleridge and Opium-Eating; Toilette of the Hebrew Lady; National Temperance Movements; Milton *versus* Southey and Landor; Fatal Marksman; Christianity as an organ of Political Movement; Notes on Godwin, Foster, and Hazlitt; Falsification of English History.

De Quincey, T. Works. *Continued.*

Vol. 12. Lord Carlisle on Pope; Glance at Works of Mackintosh; Anecdotage; Herder; Idea of a Universal History; Charlemagne; Goethe's Wilhelm Meister; Lessing.

13. Letter to a Young Man whose Education had been neglected; Orthographic Mutineers; J. Paul Richter; Art of Conversation; Presence of Mind; Knocking at the Gate of Macbeth; Antigone of Sophocles; Traditions of the Rabbins; Modern Greece.

14. Autobiographic Sketches, 1790-1803.

15. Biographies of Shakespeare, Pope, Goethe, and Schiller; A Tory's account of Toryism, Whiggism, and Radicalism; Political Parties of Modern England; Index.

Derby, *Earl* of. See *Stanley.*

Derby, G. H. Phœnixiana. New York, 1869. 12°. . . . . . . H,68

Squibob Papers. New York, 1865. 12°. . . . . . . . H,69

Derham, W. Astro-Theology. London, 1826. 8°. . . . . . . P,258

and others. Memorials of J. Ray. London, 1846. 8°. . . . O,297

Descartes, R. Œuvres Morale et Philosophique. Paris, 1855. 8°. . H,1004

Opera Philosophica. Amsterdam, 1656. 4°. . . . . . . O,636

Desert Home. M. Reid. Boston, 1866. 16°. . . . . . . J,1559

Deserted Family. J. T. Trowbridge. Philadelphia, n. d. 16°. . . . K,355

Deserted Mill. E. L. Llewellyn. Boston, 1870. 16°. . . . . J,1683

Deserted Wife. E. D. E. N. Southworth. Philadelphia, 1870. 12°. . . K,419

Design, Suggestions in. L. Limner. London, 1853. 4°. . . . . . Q,166

Designs, Original Geometrical Diaper. D. R. Hay. London, 1844. 4°. . Q,223

Desjardins, A. Vie de Jeanne d'Arc. Paris, 1854. 12°. . . . . . D,593

Desk and Debit. W. T. Adams. Boston, 1871. 16°. . . . . . J,1468,3

Dessables, M. Nouveau Manuel du Tourneur. Paris, 1839. 2 v. 18°. . M,596

De Staël, Mad. de. See *Staël-Holstein, Madame de.*

Desultoria; recovered MSS. of an Eccentric. New York, 1850. 12°. . H,232

Deutsche Abende. B. Auerbach. Stuttgart, 1864. 12°. . . . . E,311,19

Deutsche Arbeit. W. H. Riehl. Stuttgart, 1861. 8°. . . . . . . G,535

Deutsches Leben vor Fünfzig Jahren. E. Fritze. Hannover, 1863. 16°. G,277,1

Deutschlands Ehre, 1813; Hist. Roman. B. von Guseck. Leip. 1864. 16°. G,284

Deutschlands Laubhölzer im Winter. M. Willkomm. Dresden, 1864. 4°. Q,116

De Vere, A. English Misrule and Irish Misdeeds. London, 1848. 12°. . B,164

Sketches in Greece and Turkey. Philadelphia, 1850. 12°. . . V,564

De Vere S. The Great Empress; Agrippina. Philadelphia, 1870. 12°. . K,220

Devereux. Sir E. B. Lytton. Philadelphia, 1867. 12°. . . . . K,809

The same. Leipzig, 1842. 16°. . . . . . . . . J,307

Devey, J. Logic; or, Science of Inference. London, 1854. p. 8°. . . L,253

Devil, History of the. D. De Foe. London, 1727. 8°. . . . . . P,91

De Voe, T. F. Market Assistant. New York, 1867. 8°. . . . . . H,291

Devotions. J. Donne. London, 1840. 16°. . . . . . . . P,247

Dew, T. Digest of Laws, Customs, etc. New York, 1856. 8°. . . . A,28

Dew, Essay on. W. C. Wells. London, 1866. 8°. . . . . . . N,91

De Wahl, A. Hints on the Training of Girls. London, 1847. 16°. . O,1160

Dewar, D. Irish Character, Customs, and Superstitions. Lond. 1812. 8°. B,167

D'Ewes, Sir S. Autobiography and Correspondence. Lond. 1845. 2 v. 8°. D,40

Notes, Speeches, and Debates in Parliament. London, 1700. f°. . F,295

De Witte, Madame (*née Guizot*). French Country Family. N. Y. 1868. 12°. J,1367

Dexter, H. M. Congregationalism; what it is, etc. Boston, 1868. 8°. . P,218

Dialogues from Dickens. W. E. Fette. Boston, 1870. 16°. . . . . I,723

School-Day. A Clark. Philadelphia, n. d. 12°. . . . . O,1224

Dial of Love. M. Howitt. Philadelphia, 1854. 12°. . . . . J,1320
Diamond Rose. S. Tytler. London, 1867. 12°. . . . . . . . K,569
Diamonds and Precious Stones. H. Emanuel. London, 1867. 12°. . . N,854
Geognostische Vorkommen der. W. Haidinger. Wien, 1846. 8°. N,252,34
Diana of Meridor. A. Dumas. Philadelphia, n. d. 8°. . . . . . H,983
Diana's Crescent. A. Manning. London, 1868. 2 v. 16°. . . . J,582
Diary, A. F. Bremer. London, 1853. 12°. . . . . . . L,169,4
of a late Physician. S. Warren. New York, 1868. 3 v. 16°. K,1063
The same. Leipzig, 1844. 2 v. in 1. 16°. . . . . . J,513
of a Samaritan. New York, 1860. 12°. . . . . . . . H,264
of an Ennuyée. A. Jameson. Boston, 1857. 18°. . . . . V,1028
of an Officer of the Guards. S. C. Stepney. London, n. d. 12°. . H,168
of Mrs. Kitty Trevylyan. E. Charles. New York, 1864. 12°. . K,621
The same. Leipzig, 1869. 16°. . . . . . . . . J,64
Diaz, A. The William Henry Letters. Boston, 1870. 16°. . . J,1504
Dibdin, C. Songs; with Music. London, 1842. 8°. . . . . . . J,858
Dibdin, T. F. Bibliographical, Antiquarian, and Picturesque Tour in France and Germany. London, 1829. 3 v. 8°. . . . . . . . M,58
The same, illustrated. London, 1821. 3 v. r. 8°. . L.R.
The Director; a Literary Journal. London, 1807. 2 v. 8°. . . L.R.
Library Companion. London, 1824. 8°. . . . . . . . . L.R.
Rare Editions of Greek and Latin Classics. London, 1827. 2 v. 8°. L.R.
Reminiscences of a Literary Life. London, 1836. 2 v. 8°. . . L.R.
Diccionario de las Lenguas Española. M. Velasquez de la Cadena. N.Y. 1853. 8°. L.R.
Dichter und Kaufmann. B. Auerbach. Stuttgart, 1864. 2 v. 12°. . . E,311
Dicing, Dancing, etc., Treatise against. J. Northbrooke. London, 1843. 8°. I,885,14
Dick, T. Celestial Scenery. New York, 1855. 16°. . . . . . . L,398
Diffusion of Knowledge. New York, 1833. 18°. . . . . . L,381
Practical Astronomer. New York, 1846. 12°. . . . . . . N,262
Sidereal Heavens. New York, 1855. 18°. . . . . . . . L,405
Works. Philadelphia, 1869. 5 v. 12°. . . . . . . . . U,260
Vol. 1. Future State; Christian Philosopher.
2. Philosophy of Religion; Improvement of Society.
3. Moral Improvement; Covetousness.
4. Celestial Scenery; Sidereal Heavens.
5. Practical Astronomy; Solar System.
The same, v. 2. Cincinnati, 1854. 8°. . . . . . . U,195
Christian Philosopher; Celestial Scenery; Sidereal Heavens; Practical Astronomer; Solar System; Atmosphere.
Dick Rodney; Adventures of an Eton Boy. Boston, 1864. 16°. . . J,1625
Dickens, C. American Notes. Philadelphia, 1865. 8°. . . . . . V,123
The same. New York, 1865. 12°. . . . . . . . K,470
Barnaby Rudge. New York, 1868. 12°. . . . . . . . . K,467
The same. Philadelphia, 1868. 8°. . . . . . . . K,503
Bleak House. New York, 1868. 12°. . . . . . . . K,468
The same. Philadelphia, 1868. 8°. . . . . . . . K,504
Child's History of England. New York, 1851. 2 v. 16°. . J,1209
Christmas Stories. New York, 1868. 12°. . . . . . . . K,470
The same. Philadelphia, 1868. 8°. . . . . . . . K,505
David Copperfield. New York, 1868. 12°. . . . . . . K,473
The same. Philadelphia, 1868. 8°. . . . . . . K,506
Dialogues from; arranged by W. E. Fette. Boston, 1870. 16°. . I,723

Dickens, C. Dombey and Son. New York, 1868. 12°. K,471
The same. Philadelphia, 1868. 8°. K,508
Great Expectations. Philadelphia, 1868. 8°. K,509
Hard Times. New York, 1868. 12°. K,499
Hunted Down. New York, 1868. 12°. K,476
Lamplighter's Story. New York, 1868. 12°. K,477
Life of. R. S. Mackenzie. Philadelphia, 1870. 12°. D,191
Little Dorrit. New York, 1868. 12°. K,478
The same. Philadelphia, 1868. 8°. K,511
Little Paul. New York, n. d. 16°. J,1187
Martin Chuzzlewit. New York, 1868. 12°. K,480
The same. Philadelphia, 1868. 8°. K,512
Mystery of Edwin Drood. New York, 1871. K,521
New Stories. Philadelphia, 1860. 8°. K,502
Nicholas Nickleby. New York, 1868. 12°. K,482
The same. Philadelphia, 1868. 8°. K,513
Old Curiosity Shop. New York, 1868. 12°. K,485
The same. Philadelphia, 1868. 8°. K,520
Oliver Twist. New York, 1868. 12°. K,487
Our Mutual Friend. New York, 1868. 12°. K,489
The same. Philadelphia, 1868. 8°. K,514
Pickwick Papers. New York, 1868. 12°. K,493
The same. Philadelphia, 1868. 8°. K,516
Pictures from Italy. New York, 1868. 12°. K,470
Sketch of his Life. F. B. Perkins. New York, 1870. 12°. D,415
Sketches. New York, 1868. 12°. K,485
The same. Philadelphia, 1868. 8°. K,518
Tale of Two Cities. New York, 1868. 12°. K,499
The same. Philadelphia, 1868. 8°. K,519
Works; Riverside edition. New York, 1871. 28 v. 12°.

American Notes. K,1126
Barnaby Rudge, Sketches. 2 v. K,1127
Bleak House. 2 v. K,1128
Christmas Stories. K,1129
David Copperfield. 2 v. K,1131
Dombey and Son. 2 v. K,1130
Great Expectations. K,1139
Hard Times. K,1132
Little Dorrit. 2 v. K,1133
Martin Chuzzlewit. 2 v. K,1134
Master Humphrey's Clock. K,1135
Nicholas Nickleby. 2 v. K,1136
Old Curiosity Shop, Sketches. 2 v. K,1137
Oliver Twist. K,1138
Our Mutual Friend. 2 v. K,1140
Pickwick Papers. 2 v. K,1141
Tale of Two Cities. K,1142
Uncommercial Traveler, E. Drood. K,1143

The same; Tauchnitz edition. Leipzig, 1870. 92 v. 16°.

American Notes. J,113
Battle of Life; and Haunted Man. J,115
Bleak House. 4 v. J,114
Christmas Carol; Chimes; and Cricket on the Hearth. J,116
Christmas Stories. J,117
David Copperfield. 3 v. J,118
Dr. Marigold and Mugby Junction. J,119
Dombey and Son. 3 v. J,120
Great Expectations. 2 v. J,121
Hard Times. J,122
Household Words. 36 v. J,123
Hunted Down; and Uncommercial Traveler. J,124
Little Dorrit. 4 v. J,125
Martin Chuzzlewit. 2 v. J,126
Master Humphrey's Clock (Old Curiosity Shop; Barnaby Rudge) 3 v. J,127
Mystery of Edwin Drood. 2 v. J,128
Nicholas Nickleby. 2 v. J,129
No Thoroughfare. J,133
Novels and Tales from Household Words. 11 v. J,130
Oliver Twist. J,131
Our Mutual Friend. J,132
Pickwick Club. 2 v. J,134
Pictures from Italy. J,135
Sketches. J,136
Somebody's Luggage, etc. J,137
Tale of Two Cities. 2 v. J,138

Dickeson, M. W. American Numismatical Manual. Philadelphia, 1859. 4°. M,431
Dickinson, A. E. What Answer? Boston, 1869. 16°. . . . . . K,101
Dictionary, Biographical. J. L. Blake. Boston, 1854. 8°. . . . *C,622
Biographical. J. Gorton. London, 1851. 4 v. 8°. . . . . . *C,598
American. W. Allen. Boston, 1857. 8°. . . . *C,1018
T. J. Rogers. Boston, 1854. 8°. . . . . *C,1029
Brief. C. Hole and W. A. Wheeler. New York, 1866. 12°. L.R.
Imperial. J. Eadie and others. London, 1866. 6 v. 8°. . L.R.
Lippincott's. J. Thomas. Philadelphia, 1870–71. 2 v. 8°. L.R.
Botanical. J. Paxton and J. Lindley. London, 1845. 8°. . . N,943
Classical. C. Anthon. New York, 1869. 8°. . . . . . . L.R.
The same. New York, 1854. 8°. . . . . . . R.R.
J. Lempriere. New York, 1825. . . . . . . . L.R.
Commercial. J. R. M'Culloch. London, 1869. 8°. . . . . *O,611
Historical and Critical. P. Bayle. London, 1734–38. 5 v. f°. . *Q,139
Mathematical. C. Davis and W. G. Peck. New York, 1859. 8°. *M,1176
and Philosophical. C. Hutton. London, 1795. 2 v. 4°. . L.R.
Mercantile. I. de Veitelle. New York, 1864. 12°. . . . . . L.R.
of Archaic and Provincial Words. J. O. Halliwell. Lond. 1855. 2 v. 8°. L.R.
of Arts, Manufactures, and Mines. A. Ure. London, 1867. 3 v. 8°. *M,805
The same. New York, 1854–63. 3 v. 8°. . . . *M,804
The same. New York, 1856–57. 2 v. 8°. . . . . . S.C.
of Americanisms. J. R. Bartlett. Boston, 1859. 8°. . . . . L.R.
of Authors. S. A. Allibone. Philadelphia, 1858–71. 3 v. 8°. . L.R.
of Chronology. W. Tegg. London, 1854. 8°. . . . . . *A,306
of Dates. J. Haydn; edited by B. Vincent. London, 1866. 8°. *A,307
The same, with additions. New York, 1869. 8°. . . . *A,308
of Eminent Scotsmen. R. Chambers. Glasgow, 1855. 5 v. 8°. . S.C.
of Engineering, Spon's; ed. O. Byrne. Lon. 1869–70. v. 1 in 3 div. 8°. *M,731
of English and French Idioms. J. Roemer. New York, 1853. 12°. L,802
of the English Language. J. Ash. London, 1775. 8°. . . . . L.R.
A. Bailey. London, 1747. 2 v. 8°. . . . . . L.R.
J. Craig. London, 1854. 2 v. 8°. . . . . . L.R.
S. Johnson. London, 1854. r. 8°. . . . . . L.R.
S. Maunder. London, 1847. 12°. . . . . . L.R.
E. Phillips. London, 1720. f°. . . . . . . L.R.
C. Richardson. London, 1839. 2 v. 4°. . . . . L.R.
Supplement. London, 1856. 4°. . . . . L.R.
N. Webster. Springfield, 1867. 4°. . . . . R.R.
The same. Springfield, 1870. 4°. . . . . L.R.
J. E. Worcester. Boston, 1846. 4°. . . . . . L.R.
The same. Boston, 1869. 4°. . . . . . R.R.
Academic. N. Webster. New York, 1854. 8°. . . . . L.R.
Imperial. J. Ogilvie. Glasgow, 1859. 2 v. 8°. . . . . L.R.
New Royal. C. Marriott. London, 1780. 4°. . . . . L.R.
Pronouncing. J. Walker. Glasgow, 1850. 12°. . . . . L.R.
The same; edited by B. H. Smart. London, 1860. 8°. L.R.
Rhyming, 1570. P. Levins. London, 1867. 8°. . . L,605,27
J. Walker. Philadelphia, 1852. 8°. . . . . . L.R.
The same. New York, 1860. 12°. . . . . L.R.

Dictionary of Every-day Difficulties. E. Shelton. London, n. d. 12°. . L,556
of the Farm. W. L. Rham. London, 1858. 8°. . . . . M,495
of French Nouns. D. Boileau. London, 1827. 12°. . . . L,803
of French and English. A. Boyer. Paris, 1797. 2 v. 8°. . . L.R.
C. Fleming and Tibbins. Paris, 1854. 2 v. 4°. . . L.R.
A. Spiers and Surenne. New York, 1870. 8°. . . . L.R.
The same. New York, 1854. 8°. . . . . . R.R.
See also *Dictionnaire.*
of Geography. A. K. Johnston. London, 1852. 8°. . . . L.R.
of German and English. C. F. Grieb. Philadelphia, 1859. 2 v. 8°. L.R.
The same. Philadelphia, 1857. 2 v. 8°. . . . R.R.
J. G. Adler. New York, 1869. 8°. . . . . . L.R.
The same. New York, 1869. 8°. . . . . . . R.R.
of Greek and English. J. Groves. Philadelphia, 1858. 8°. . L.R.
H. G. Liddell and R. Scott. New York, 1870. 8°. . . R.R.
The same. New York, 1858. 8°. . . . . . L.R.
of Greek and Roman Antiquities. A. Rich, jr. Boston, 1854. 8°. . A,79
W. Smith. London, 1854. 8°. . . . . . S.C.
of Greek and Roman Biography, etc. W. Smith. Bost. 1849. 3 v. 8°. S.C.
of Greek and Roman Geography. W. Smith. Boston, 1854–57. 2 v. 8°. S.C.
of Latin Quotations. H. T. Riley. London, 1866. 12°. . . L,53
of Modern Slang. London, 1859. 16°. . . . . . . . L,562
of Music. W. Wilson. London, n. d. 12°. . . . . . . M,8
of Musicians. A. Choron. London, 1827. 2 v. 8°. . . . M,409
of Noted Names of Fiction. W. A. Wheeler. Boston, 1866. 12°. . L.R.
of Obsolete and Provincial English. T. Wright. Lon. 1857. 2 v. p. 8°. L,258
of Painters. M. Pilkington. London, 1840. 8°. . . . . *M,94
of Painters and Engravers. M. Bryan. London, 1853. 8°. . *M,138
of the Peerage. Sir J. B. Burke. London, 1856. 8°. . . *C,623
of Photography; edited by T. Sutton and G. Dawson. Lond. 1867. 12°. M,727
of Phrase and Fable. E. C. Brewer. Philadelphia, n. d. 12°. . L.R.
of Poetical Quotations. S. J. Hale. Philadelphia, 1866. 12°. . *I,163
of Quotations, Proverbs, etc. Philadelphia, 1856. 12°. . . . H,145
of Science, Literature, and Art. W. T. Brande. New York, 1870. 8°. L.R.
of the Scottish Language. J. Jamieson. Edinburgh, 1846. 8°. . L.R.
of Spanish Language. Neuman, Baretti, and Seoane. Lond. n. d. 2 v. 8°. L.R.
of Terms in Architecture, etc. London, 1858–59. 12°. . . . M,973
of Universal Biography. S. Maunder. London, 1845. 12°. . . C,488
of Universal Information. S. O. Beeton. London, n. d. 8°. . . L.R.
Pocket; Eng., French, Italian. F. Bottarelli. v. 2, 3. Venice, 1791. 8°. L.R.
Welsh and English. W. Evans. Carmarthon, 1812. 8°. . . L.R.
Dictionnaire de l'Académie Française. Bruxelles, 1835. 2 v. 8°. . . L.R.
The same; ed. par P. Lorain. Paris, 1858. 2 v. 8°. . . L.R.
de la Langue Française. F. J. Noel and C. P. Chapsal. Brux. 1839. 8°. L.R.
de Morale, Choix de Pensées. H. Logé. Bruxelles, 1844. 12°. H,1034
des Proverbes Français. Paris, 1821. 8°. . . . . . H,891
Encyclopédique de la France. P. Le Bas. Paris, 1840–45. 12 v. 8°. B,308
François-Anglois. A. Boyer. Paris, 1797. 2 v. 8°. . . . L.R.
Grec-François. J. Quénon. Paris, 1807. 8°. . . . . . . L.R.
Historique. L. M. Chaudon et F. A. Delandin. Caen, 1804. 13 v. 8°. C,597

Dictionnaire Historique et Critique. P. Bayle. Amsterdam, 1730. 4 v. f°. *Q,140
National, Langue Française. L. N. Rescherelle. Paris, 1866. 2 v. 4°. L.R.
des Sciences Naturelles. Strasbourg et Paris. 1816–30. 71 v. 8°. *Q,336
du Voyageur, François-Allemand-Latin. Basle, 1746. 8°. . . L.R.
Diderot, D. Œuvres choisies; précédées de sa Vie. Paris, 1856. 2 v. 12°. H,994
Didron, A. N. Christian Iconography, v. 1. London, 1851. p. 8°. . . L,102
Diefenbach, L. Wörterbuch der Gothischen Sprache. Frank.-a M.1851. 2 v. 8°. G,583
Dies Boreales; Christopher under Canvass. J. Wilson. Phila. 1850. 12°. H,607
Dietrich, D. Deutschland's Flora, v. 3, 6-9. Jena, 1844–48. 5 v. 8°. . G,862
Diez, F. C. Wörterbuch der Romanischen Sprache. Bonn, 1861–62. 2 v. 8°. G,585
Grammatik der Romanischen Sprachen. Bonn, 1836–44. 3 v. 8°. . G,584
Diffusion of Knowledge. T. Dick. New York, 1833. 16°. . . . . L,381
Digby, Sir K. Receipts in Physick and Chirurgery. London, 1675. 16°. . L,835
Digby Grand. G. J. W. Melville. Leipzig, 1862. 16°. . . . . . J,374
Dikes and Ditches. W. T. Adams. Boston, 1870. 16°. . . . J,1535,4
Dilke, C. W. Greater Britain, Travel in, 1866-67. New York, 1869. 12°. V,1076
Dillon, J. B. History of Indiana. Indianapolis, 1859. 8°. . . . . C,235
Dillwynn, L. W. British Confervæ. London, 1809. 4°. . . . . N,893
Dinájpúr in Bengal, Discription of. F. Buchanan. Calcutta, 1833. 8°. . V,698
Dinglestedt, F. The Amazon. New York, 1868. 12°. . . . . G,187
Dining, Classiques de la Table. J. Améro. Paris, 1855. 2 v. 12°. . . H,872
Hand-Book of. M. Brillat-Savarin. New York, 1865. 12°. . . H,305
Diodorus Siculus. Bibliotheca Historica. Parisiis, 1842–44. 2 v. 8°. . U,552
Diogenes Laërtius. Lives of Eminent Philosophers. London, 1853. p. 8°. L,55
Diplomat, Der. L. Storch. Frankfurt-a-Main, 1834. 24°. . . . G,480
Diplomatic Correspondence of American Revolution. Bost. 1829–30. 12 v. 8°. B,678
Diplomacy of the United States. W. H. Trescott. Boston, 1826. 8°. . B,858
Diptera of North America, Catalogue of. R. O. Sacken. Wash. 1858. 8°. O,53
Director, The; a Literary Journal. T. F. Dibdin. London, 1807. 2 v. 8°. L.R.
Discarded Daughter. E. D. E. N. Southworth. Philadelphia, 1870. 12°. . K,420
Disciplina Rediviva. J. S. Gilderdale. London, 1856. 16°. . . O,1021
Discipline appropriate to Schools. A. Hill. London, 1855. 8°. . O,1251,2
Early, illustrated. S. Wilderspin. London, 1840. 12°. . . O,1142
Rationale of. J. Pillans. Edinburgh, 1852. 8°. . . . . O,1234
Discoveries and Inventions. J. Beckmann. London, 1846. 2 v. p. 8°. . L,168
Discovery, Maritime and Inland. W. D. Cooley. Lond. 1830–31. 3 v. 12°. M,1006
Discovery of the Great West. F. Parkman. Boston, 1870. 8°. . . B,616
Diseases, Sources of Bodily and Mental. C. F. Lord. London, 1847. 8°. N,252,29
of Interior Valley of North America. D. Drake. Phil. 1854. 8°. . L,929
Disinfection, Principles and Practice of. R. Bartholow. Cin. 1867. 12°. . L,909
Disowned, The. Sir E. B. Lytton. Philadelphia, 1868. 12°. . . . K,808
The same. Philadelphia, 1823. 8°. . . . . . . K,881
The same. Leipzig, 1842. 16°. . . . . . . . J,308
Disraeli, B. Alroy. Leipzig, 1846. 16°. . . . . . . . . J,139
Coningsby. Leipzig, 1844. 16°. . . . . . . . . J,140
Contarini Fleming. Leipzig, 1846. 16°. . . . . . . . J,141
Henrietta Temple. Leipzig, 1859. 16°. . . . . . . . J,142
Lothair. New York, 1870. 12°. . . . . . . . . . K,674
The same. Leipzig, 1870. 2 v. in 1. 16°. . . . . . J,143

Disraeli, B. Novels and Tales. London, 1868. 5 v. 12°.
Coningsby; Henrietta Temple. K,671
Ixion; Vivian Grey. K,672
Sybil; Alroy. K,673
Venetia; Tancred. K,675
Young Duke; Contarini Fleming. K,676
Sybil; or, the Two Nations. Leipzig, 1845. 16°. J,144
Tancred; or, the New Crusade. Leipzig, 1847. 2 v. in 1. 16°. J,145
Venetia. Leipzig, 1858. 2 v. in 1. 16°. J,146
Vivian Grey. Leipzig, 1859. 2 v. in 1. 16°. J,147
Disraeli, I. Amenities of Literature. London, 1859. 2 v. 8°. H,647
Calamities and Quarrels of Authors. London, 1859. 8°. H,649
Curiosities of Literature. London, 1858. 3 v. 8°. H,650
Life and Reign of Charles I. London, 1851. 2 v. 8°. D,234
Literary Character; Men of Genius. London, 1859. 8°. H,651
Miscellanies of Literature. New York, 1841. 3 v. 12°. H,652
Distiller, Practical. M. L. F. Byrn. New York, 1870. 12°. M,650
Distinguished Men of Modern Times. H. Madden. London, 1838. 4 v. 16°. L,471
The same. New York, 1840. 2 v. 18°. L,419
District School; as it was. W. Burton. Boston, 1850. 18°. O,964
Ditson, G. L. Circassia; a Tour to the Caucasus. New York, 1850. 8°. V,679
Crescent and the French Crusaders. New York, 1859. 12°. V,774
Ditton, H. Institution of Fluxions. London, 1706. O,916
Dittrich, J. G. Deutsches Obstcabinet, Abbildungen. Jena, 1840. 8°. *F,90
Systematisches Handbuch der Obstkunde. Jena, 1837–41. 3 v. 8°. G,657
Divine Government, Method of the. J. M'Cosh. New York, 1858. 8°. P,159
Divine Love, Sixteen Revelations of. Mother Juliana. Boston, 1864. 16°. P,32
Divine Rule of Faith and Practice. W. Goode. Phil. 1842. 2 v. 8°. P,176
Dividing Line, History of the. W. Byrd. Richmond, 1866. 2 v. 4°. C,248
Divorce and Divorce Legislation. T. D. Woolsey. New York, 1869. 12°. O,372
Dixon, E. S. Dovecote and Aviary. London, 1851. 16°. O,85
Dixon, J. H. (Ed.). Ancient Poems of Eng. Peasantry. Lond. 1846. 12°. L,606,17
(Ed.) Scottish Versions of Ancient Ballads. London, 1865. 12°. L,606,17
Dixon, W. H. Free Russia. New York, 1870. 12°. V,533
Her Majesty's Tower. Leipzig, 1869–70. 2 v. in 1. 16°. J,149
Holy Land. London, 1865. 2 v. 8°. V,649
The same. Leipzig, 1865. 2 v. in 1. 16°. J,150
John Howard, and Prison-World of Europe. New York, 1869. 12°. O,351
New America. Philadelphia, 1867. 12°. V,105
The same. Leipzig, 1867. 2 v. in 1. 16°. J,151
Personal History of Lord Bacon. Leipzig, 1861. 16°. J,148
Spiritual Wives. Leipzig, 1868. 2 v. in 1. 16°. J,152
William Penn; a Biography. Philadelphia, 1851. 12°. D,153
Doane, G. W. Remains and Memoir of C. H. Wharton. Phil. 1834. 2 v. 12°. C,681
Dobie, D. Key to the Bible. New York, 1856. 12°. P,506
Dobson, E. Brickmaking, Tilemaking, etc. London, 1857. 12°. M,909
Building, Art of. London, 1854. 12°. M,908
Foundations and Concrete Works. London, 1850. 12°. M,910
Masonry and Stone-Cutting. London, 1856. 12°. M,911
Docteur Mathéus. E. Erckmann et A. Chatrian. Paris, 1861. 12°. H,1019
Doctor Antonio; a Tale of Italy. G. Ruffini. New York, 1867. 12°. K,912
The same. Leipzig, 1861. 16°. J,430

Doctor Austin's Guests. W. Gilbert. London, 1868. 12°. . . . . J,562
The same. London, 1866. 2 v. 12°. . . . . . . K,589
Doctor Jacob. M. B. Edwards. Boston, 1869. 16°. . . . . . . K,686
Doctor Johns. D. G. Mitchell. New York, 1866. 2 v. 16°. . . . K,215
Doctor Marigold's Prescriptions. C. Dickens. Leipzig, 1867. 16°. . . J,119
Doctor Thorne. A. Trollope. New York, 1867. 12°. . . . . K,1045
The same. Leipzig, 1858. 2 v. in 1. 16°. . . . . . J,497
Doctor's Wife, The. M. E. Braddon. Leipzig, 1864. 2 v. in 1. 16°. . J,36
Doctors, Book about. J. C. Jeaffreson. Leipzig, 1870. 2 v. in 1. 16°. . J,217
Doctrines, History of. K. R. Hagenbach. Edinburgh, 1850-52. 2 v. 8°. P,590
Dodd, G. Curiosities of Industry, and Applied Sciences. Leip. 1854. 8°. M,628
Dodd, W., Famous Forgery, Story of. P. Fitzgerald. Lond. 1865. 12°. . D,181
Dodd Family Abroad. C. Lever. New York, n. d. 8°. . . . . . K,774
The same. Leipzig, 1854. 3 v. 16°. . . . . . . I,275
Doddridge, J. Logan; a Dramatic Piece. Cincinnati, 1868. 4°. . . . I,730
Dodge, J. R. West Virginia and its Resources. Philadelphia, 1865. 12°. C,177
Dodge, M. A. *Gail Hamilton.* Battle of the Books. New York, 1870. 12°. H,59
Country Living and Country Thinking. Boston, 1866. 16°. . . H,52
Gala-Days. Boston, 1865. 16°. . . . . . . . . . H,67
New Atmosphere. Boston, 1865. 16°. . . . . . . . . H,53
Red-Letter Days in Applethorpe. Boston, 1866. 12°. . . . J,1287
Skirmishes and Sketches. Boston, 1865. 16°. . . . . . . H,54
Stumbling-Blocks. Boston, 1864. 16°. . . . . . . . H,55
Summer Rest. Boston, 1866. 16°. . . . . . . . . H,56
Woman's Wrongs. Boston, 1868. 16°. . . . . . . . H,57
Wool-Gathering. Boston, 1867. 16°. . . . . . . . H,58
Dodge, M. E. Few Friends; and how they were amused. Phil. 1868. 12°. H,43
Hans Brinker; or, the Silver Skates. New York, 1869. 12°. . J,1341
Dodge Club. J. De Mille. New York, 1869. 8°. . . . . . . K,102
Dodington, G. B. *Baron of Melcombe.* Diary. London, 1809. 8°. . . D,56
Dods, J. B. Spirit Manifestations examined and explained. N. Y. 1854. 12°. P,913
Dodsley, J. Select Collection of Old Plays. London, 1780. 12 v. 8°. . I,737
Dodsley, R. Economy of Human Life. London, 1809. 16°. . . . O,467
Döbereiner, J. W. Chemie des Platins. Stuttgart, 1836. 8°. . . N,252,5
Elemente der Pharmaceutischen Chemie. Jena, 1816. 8°. . . G,751
Essigbereitung. Jena, 1832. 16°. . . . . . . . . N,252,38
Dog, The. W. Youatt. London, 1861. 8°. . . . . . . . N,689
History of the. W. C. L. Martin. London, 1845. 18°. . . . M,441
in Health and Disease. J. H. Walsh. London, 1859. 8°. . . N,683
Dog Crusoe. R. M. Ballantyne. Philadelphia, n. d. 16°. . . . . J,1272
Dogs, Anecdotes of. E. Jesse. London, 1870. p. 8°. . . . . . . L,112
and Cats. H. Miller. London, 1868. 8°. . . . . . J,1186
and their Ways. C. Williams. London, 1865. 16°. . . . N,679
Management of. E. Mayhew. New York, 1856. 12°. . . . M,312
Natural History. C. H. Smith. Edinburgh, 1839-54. 2 v. 16°. N,470,18,19
Dolcino, F., and his Times. A. Gallenga. London, 1853. 12°. . . . D,732
Dollars and Cents. A. Warner. Philadelphia, 1863. 12°. . . . . . K,370
Domat, J. Civil Law in its Natural Order. Boston, 1850. 2 v. 8°. . U,517
Dombey and Son. C. Dickens. New York, 1868. 12°. . . . . . K,471
The same. Philadelphia, 1868. 8°. . . . . . . K,508

Dombey and Son. C. Dickens. New York, 1871. 2 v. 12°. . . . K,1130
The same. Leipzig, 1848. 3 v. 16°. . . . . . . J,120
Domenech, E. Adventures in Texas and Mexico. London, 1858. 8°. . . V,21
Seven Years in the Deserts of N. America. London, 1860. 2 v. 8°. V,77
Domestic Economy. M. Donovan. London, 1830. 12°. . . . . M,1041
Encyclopædia of. T. Webster and Mrs. Parkes. N. Y. 1849. 8°. L.R.
Lady Bountiful's Legacy. J. Timbs. London, 1868. 12°. . . . I,543
Treatise on. C. E. Beecher. New York, 1854. 12°. . . . . H,277
Domestic Science, Principles of. C. E. Beecher and H. B. Stowe. N.Y. 1869. 8°. O,366
Domestic Stories. D. M. Craik. Leipzig, 1862. 16°. . . . . . . J,86
Domherr, Der. J. D. H. Temme. Leipzig, 1867. 4 v. 16°. . . . G,514
Don, G. History of the Dichlamydeous Plants. Lond. 1831–38. 4 v. 4°. Q,12
Don Sebastian; or, House of Braganza. A. M. Porter. Lond. 1809. 4 v. 13°. J,576
Don Quichotte de la Manche. M. de Cervantes Saavedra. Paris, 1854. 12°. G,239
Don Quixote. M de Cervantes Saavedra. Boston, 1865. 4 v. 12°. . . G,234
The same. London, 1866. 8°. . . . . . . . G,233
The same; illustrated by G. Doré. London, n. d. 4°. . *Q,239
Donald Deane and his Cross. J. W. Bradley. Boston, 1868. 16°. . J,1653
Donaldson, J. Clay Lands and Loamy Soils. London, 1852. 12°. . . M,912
Donaldson, J. W. Classical Scholarship and Learning. Camb. 1856. 12°. O,833
New Cratylus. London, 1859. 8°. . . . . . . . . L,741
Varronianus; Ethnography of Ancient Italy. London, 1852. 8°. . N,436
Donati, V. Histoire Naturelle de la Mer Adriatique. A la Haye, 1758. 4°. N,749
Doniphan, A. W., Expedition of. J. S. Hughes. Cincinnati, 1850. 12°. B,883
Donnavan, C. Adventures in Mexico. Cincinnati, 1848. 8°. . . . T,19,3
Donne, J. Devotions. London, 1840. 16°. . . . . . . . P,247
Life of. I. Walton. New York, 1854. 8°. . . . . . . D,404
Poetical Works. Boston, 1855. 16°. . . . . . . . I,207
Donne, W. B. (Ed.) Corres. of George III. with Lord North. Lon. 1867. 2 v. 8°. D,427
Donovan, E. Insects of China. London, 1842. 4°. . . . . . . *Q,41
Insects of India. London, 1842. 4°. . . . . . . . *Q,42
Preserving Specimens of Natural History. London, 1794. 8°. . . N,541
Treatise on the Management of Insects. London, 1794. 8°. . . N,541
Donovan, M. Chemistry. London, 1832. 12°. . . . . . . M,1026
Domestic Economy. London, 1830. 12°. . . . . . M,1041
Doolittle, J. Social Life of the Chinese. New York, 1865. 2 v. 12°. V,595
Dora. J. Kavanagh. New York, 1868. 8°. . . . . . . . K,741
The same. Leipzig, 1868. 16°. . . . . . . . J,229
Dora Deane. M. J. Holmes. New York, 1867. 12°. . . . . . K,183
Dora d'Istria *pseud.* See *Koltoff-Massalski, H. G.*
Doran, J. Annals of the English Stage. New York, 1865. 2 v. 12°. . I,718
History of Court Fools. London, 1858. 12°. . . . . . . H,310
Knights and their Days. London, 1856. 8°. . . . . . . H,311
Monarchs retired from Business. London, 1857. 2 v. 8°. . . . C,531
New Pictures and Old Panels. London, 1859. 8°. . . . . . H,312
Queens of England of the House of Hanover. N. Y. 1855. 2 v. 12°. C,1206
(Ed.) Bentley Ballads. London, 1866. p. 8°. . . . . . . I,170
Dorchester, Mass., Early History of. S. G. Drake. Boston, 1851. 8°. . C,58
Oration at, July, 1855. E. Everett. Boston, 1855. 8°. . . . C,63
Doric Race, History of. C. O. Müller. London, 1839. 2 v. 8°. . . A,94

Dorn, J. F. Ausführung der Flachen Dachdeckung. Berlin, 1838. 8°. N,252,19
Dorotheus, *Bishop of Tyrus*. Lives and Martyrd. of Prophets. Lond. 1607. 4°. P,647
Dorothy; a Tale. Leipzig, 1857. 16°. . . . . . . . . . J,153
Dorothy Fox. Philadelphia, 1871. 8°. . . . . . . . . . K,410
Dorr, B. Egypt, Holy Land, Turkey, and Greece. Philadelphia, 1856. 12°. V,1042
Dorr, J. C. R. Sibyl Huntington. New York, 1870. 12°. . . . K,223
Dorr Rebellion, R. I., Might and Right. Providence, 1844. 12°. . . C,75
Dotty Dimple Stories. R. S. Clarke. Boston, 1870. 6 v. 16°. . . J,1650

Vol. 1. Dotty Dimple at her Grandmother's. Vol. 4. Dotty Dimple at Play.
2. Dotty Dimple at Home. 5. Dotty Dimple at School.
3. Dotty Dimple Out West. 6. Dotty Dimple's Flyaway.

Double-Counting on the Lathe, Art of. J. Ash. London, 1857. 8°. . . M,655
Double Play. W. Everett. Boston, 1871. 16°. . . . . . . . J,1337
Doubly False. A. S. Stephens. Philadelphia, n. d. 12°. . . . . K,320
Douce, F. Holbein's Dance of Death. London, 1858. p. 8°. . . . L,106
Douglas, A. M. Sydnie Adriance; or, Trying the World. Boston, 1869. 12°. K,120
Douglas, J. Antiquity of the Earth. London, 1785. 4°. . . . . N,747
Douglas, J. W., and Scott, J. British Hemiptera, v. 1. London, 1865. 8°. O,309
Douglas, S. A., Life of. J. W. Sheahan. New York, 1860. 12°. . . C,919
Life of. R. B. Warden. Columbus, 1860. 8°. . . . . C,807
Political Debates with A. Lincoln. Columbus, 1860. 8°. . . O,574
Douglass Farm. M. E. Bradley. New York, 1863. 16°. . . . . . J,1356
Dove, H. W. Entwickelung der Pflanzen. Berlin, 1846. 4°. . . N.252,43
Inductions Elektricität. Berlin, 1842. 4°. . . . . . N,252,43
Optische Studien. Berlin, 1853–59. 8°. . . . . . . . G,720
and Moser, L. (Eds.); Repertorium der Physik. Ber. 1837–49. 8 v. 8°. G,674
Dove, P. E. Elements of Political Science. Edinburgh, 1854. 8°. . . O,542
Dove in the Eagle's Nest. C. M. Yonge. New York, 1867. 12°. . K,1072
The same. Leipzig, 1866. 2 v. in 1. 16°. . . . . . J,548
Dovecote and Aviary. E. S. Dixon. London, 1851. 16°. . . . O,85
Dover, Lord. See *Ellis, G. J. W. A.*
Dow, L., Writings of. Cincinnati, 1855. 8°. . . . . . . . . U,130
Dowe, W. Junius Identified as Lord Chatham. London, 1857. 12°. . H,602
Down the Rhine. W. T. Adams. Boston, 1870. 16°. . . . . J,1535,6
Down the River. W. T. Adams. Boston, 1869. 16°. . . . . J,1534,6
Downing, A. J. Architecture of Country Houses. New York, 1851. 8°. M,185
The same. New York, 1866. 8°. . . . . . . . . M,190
Fruits and Fruit Trees of America. New York, 1856. 12°. . . M,536
The same. New York, 1859. 12°. . . . . . . . . M,537
The same. New York, 1869. 8°. . . . . . . . . M,542
Rural Essays; Memoir by G. W. Curtis. New York, 1853. 8°. . M,576
Theory and Practice of Landscape Gardening. New York, 1859. 8°. M,356
The same. New York, 1855. 8°. . . . . . . . . . S.C.
Downing, Maj. Jack. See *Smith, S.*
Dowse, T. Catalogue of his Library. Boston, 1870. 8°. . . . . L.R.
Doyle, J. A. American Colonies before Independence. London, 1869. 8°. B,626
Dragon-Fly, Libelludidées d'Europe. E. de Selys-Longchamps. Paris, 1840. 8°. O,38
Drainage. J. Parkes. London, 1846. 8°. . . . . . . . . . N,252,6
Desséchement des Terres. C. T. Chackeray. Paris, 1846. 8°. N,252,31
Letters to Lord John Russell on. London, 1847. 8°. . . . N,252,31
of Land, Essays on. J. Parkes. London, 1848. 8°. . . . N,252,31

Drainage of Districts and Lands. G. D. Dempsey. London, 1854. 12°. . M,903
of the Metropolis. A. Huxtable. London, 1847. 8°. . . N,252,25
of Strong Clays. P. Laws. Newcastle-upon-Tyne, 1850. 8°. . N,252,31
of Towns and Buildings. G. D. Dempsey. London, 1854. 12°. . M,904
Thorough and Deep Ploughing. J. Smith. Stirling, 1838. 8°. N,252,6
Drake, B. Life of Tecumseh. Cincinnati, 1858. 12°. . . . . . C,915
Sketches of Wm. H. Harrison. Cincinnati, 1847. 18°. . . . C,831
and Mansfield, E. D. Cincinnati in 1826. Cincinnati, 1827. 12°. . C,208
Drake, D. Diseases of Interior Valley of North America. Phil. 1854. 8°. L,929
Discourse on Intemperance. Cincinnati, 1828. 12°. . . . L,831
on the West. Cincinnati, 1834. 8°. . . . . . . T,19,2
Discourses. Cincinnati, 1852. 12°. . . . . . . . . . *L,830
Early Physicians, Scenery, and Society of Cincinnati.
Origin and Influence of Medical Periodical Literature, and the Benefits of Public Medical Libraries.
Medical Education and Profession in the U. S. Cincinnati, 1832. 12°. L,832
Pioneer Life in Kentucky. Cincinnati, 1870. 8°. . . . . C,222
Oration on Intemperance. Columbus, 1831. 8°. . . . . T,19,2
View of Cincinnati. Cincinnati, 1815. 12°. . . . . . *C,207
Life and Services of. E. D. Mansfield. Cincinnati, 1855. 12°. . C,789
Drake, Sir F. The World Encompassed; a Voyage. London, 1854. 8°. V,987
His Voyage, 1595. T. Maynarde. London, 1849. 8°. . . . V,992
Cavendish and Dampier. Lives and Voyages of. N. Y. 1854. 18°. L,363
Drake, J. R. The Culprit Fay. New York, 1864. 12°. . . . . I,31
Extracts from his Writings. New York, 1869. 12°. . . . I,41
Drake, N. Literary Hours; Sketches. Sudbury, 1800. 2 v. 8°. . . H,28
Siege of Pontefract Castle. Durham, 1860. 8°. . . . F,126,37
Drake, S. G. Biog. and Hist. of Indians of N. America. Boston, 1837. 8°. B,589
Early History of Dorchester. Boston, 1851. r. 8°. . . . . C,58
History and Antiquities of Boston. Boston, 1856. 8°. . . . C,62
Indian Captivities. Auburn, 1854. 12°. . . . . . . . B,591
Indians of North America. Boston, 1851. 8°. . . . . B,599
Founders of New England. Boston, 1865. 4°. . . . . F,56
Memoir of. J. H. Sheppard. Albany, 1863. 4°. . . . . C,1056
Drama. Account of the English Stage, 1660–1830. Bath, 1832. 10 v. 8°. I,716
Amateur Dramas. G. M. Baker. Boston, 1870. 12°. . . . I,722
Biographia Dramatica. D. E. Baker and I. Reed. London, 1812. 4 v. 8°. L.R.
British Theater. J. Bell. London, 1726–28. 20 v. . . . . . I,682

Vol. 1. Zara; Venice Preserved; Jane Shore; Siege of Damascus; Distressed Mother.
2. Provoked Wife; Every Man in his Humor; Beau's Stratagem; Old Bachelor; The Committee.
3. Earl of Essex; Tamerlane; Mourning Bride; Fair Penitent; Cato.
4. The Wonder; Rule a Wife and Have a Wife; Suspicious Husband; Conscious Lovers; Recruiting Officer.
5. All for Love; The Orphan; Tancred and Sigismunda; George Barnwell; Isabella.
6. Bold Stroke for a Wife; The Miser; Provoked Husband; Love makes a Man; She would and she would not.
7. Royal Convert; Alexander the Great; Mahomet; Theodosius; Lady Jane Grey.
8. Missing.
9. The Beggars' Opera; Polly; Achilles; Gentle Shepherd; Comus.
10. Merope; Barbarossa; Alzira; Phædra and Hippolitus; Oroonoko.
11. The Refusal; Way of the World; Amphitryon; The Drummer; The Relapse.
12 King Charles I.; The Gamester; Don Sebastian; Œphidus; The Revenge.
13. The Inconstant; The Double Dealer; The Foundling; The Spanish Friar; The Double Gallant.
14. The Albion Queens; Anna Bullen; Marianne; Ximena; The Brothers.
15. Constant Couple; Sir Harry Wildair; The Confederacy; The Rehearsal; The Chances.

Drama, British Theater. J. Bell. *Continued.* . . . . . . . . 1,682

16. Electra; Ambitious Step-Mother; Edward the Black Prince; Busiris Eurydice.
17. Twin Rivals; Country Wife; Fair Quaker of Deal; The Alchymist; Love's Last Shift.
18. Sophonisba; Philaster; Virginia; Ulysses; Gustavus Vasa.
19. Volpone; Country Lasses; Mistake; Gamesters; Lady's Last Stake.
20. Elvira; Boadicea; Creusa; Douglas; Roman Father.

British Theater. E. Inchbald. London, 1808. 25 v. 16°. . . . 1,685

Vol. 1. Comedy of Errors; Romeo and Juliet; Hamlet; King John; King Richard III.
2. King Henry IV.; Merchant of Venice; King Henry V.; Much Ado About Nothing.
3. As You Like It; Merry Wives of Windsor; King Henry VIII.; Measure for Measure; Winter's Tale.
4. King Lear; Cymbeline; Macbeth; Julius Cæsar; Antony and Cleopatra.
5. Coriolanus; Othello; Tempest; Twelfth Night; Every Man in His Humor.
6. Rule a Wife and Have a Wife; The Chances; New Way to Pay Old Debts; Rival Queens; All for Love.
7. Isabella, or, the Fatal Marriage; Oroonoko; Distressed Mother; Zara; Gustavus Vasa.
8. Constant Couple; The Inconstant; Recruiting Officer; Beau's Stratagem; Cato.
9. Provoked Wife; Provoked Husband; Love Makes a Man; She Would and She Would Not; The Careless Husband.
10. Tamerlane; Fair Penitent; Jane Shore; Lady Jane Grey; Siege of Damascus.
11. Busy-Body; The Wonder; Bold Stroke for a Wife; George Barnwell; Fatal Curiosity.
12. The Orphan; Venice Preserved; Conscious Lovers; The Revenge; Beggars' Opera.
13. Love for Love; Mourning Bride; Mahomet; Tancred and Sigismunda; Suspicious Husband.
14. Man of the World; The Foundling; Gamester; Roman Father; Edward the Black Prince.
15. Barbarossa; The Way to Keep Him; All in the Wrong; Grecian Daughter; Know Your Own Mind.
16. Country Girl; Jealous Wife; Clandestine Marriage; Countess of Salisbury; Douglas
17. Good-Natured Man; She Stoops to Conquer; Love in a Village; Maid of the Mill; Lionel and Clarissa.
18. The Brothers; West Indian; The Jew; First Love; Wheel of Fortune.
19. Earl of Warwick; The Rivals; The Duenna; Belle's Stratagem; Bold Stroke for a Husband.
20. The Dramatist; Count of Narbonne; Inkle and Yarico; Battle of Hexham; Surrender of Calais.
21. Mountaineers; Iron Chest; Heir-at-Law; John Bull; Poor Gentleman.
22. Castle of Andalusia; Fontainbleau; Wild Oats; The Heiress; Earl of Essex.
23. Such Things Are; Every One has His Fault; Wives as they Were and Maids as they Are; Lover's Vows; To Marry, or Not to Marry.
24. Road to Ruin; Deserted Daughter; The Strangers; De Montfort; Point of Honor.
25. Way to Get Married; Cure for the Heart-Ache; Speed the Plow; School of Reform; Honeymoon.

Collection of Farces. E. Inchbald. London, 1809. 7 v. 16°. . . 1,686

Vol. 1. Child of Nature; Wedding Day; Midnight Hour; Raising the Wind; Matrimony; Ella Rosenberg; Blind Boy; Who's the Dupe?; Love a la Mode.
2. Birthday; Jew and the Doctor; Irishman in London; Prisoner at Large; Poor Soldier; The Farmer; Highland Reel; Two Strings to Your Bow; The Deserter.
3. Hartford Bridge; Netley Abbey; Turnpike Gate; Lock and Key; Register Office; The Apprentice; The Critic; The Sultan; Rosina.
4. All the World's a Stage; Lying Valet; The Citizen; Three Weeks After Marriage; Catherine and Petruchio; Padlock; Miss in her Teens; The Quaker; Guardian.
5. High Life below Stairs; Bon Ton; Mock Doctor; Devil to Pay; Irish Widow; The Minor; Mayor of Garratt; The Lyar; Flora.
6. The Deuce is in Him; Edgar and Emmeline; Richard Cœur de Lion; Maid of the Oaks; Tom Thumb; Doctor and the Apothecary; The First Floor; The Appointed Child; The Farm-House.
7. Lodoiska; Ways and Means; School for Authors; Midas; The Waterman; The Author; The Old Maid; Miller of Mansfield; Comus, altered from Milton.

Dramatic Works. R. B. Sheridan. Leipzig, 1869. 16°. . . . J,460

Sir E. B. Lytton. Leipzig, 1860. 2 v. in 1. 16°. . . . J,309

Drawing-Room Plays. S. S. Steele. Philadelphia, 1865. 12°. . 1,731

London Playgoer. H. Morley. London, 1866. 12°. . . . . 1,709

Mimic Stage. G. M. Baker. Boston, 1870. 12°. . . . . . 1,721

Minor. New York, n. d. 39 v. in 23. 12°. . . . . . . 1,639

Vol. 1. Irish Attorney; Boots at the Swan; How to Pay the Rent; Loan of a Lover; Dead Shot; Last Legs; Invisible Prince; Golden Farmer.
2. Pride of the Market; Used Up; Irish Tutor; Barrack Room; Luke the Laborer; Beauty and the Beast; St. Patrick's Eve; Captain of the Watch. With Portrait and Memoir of Miss C. Wemyss.

Drama, Minor. *Continued.* . . . . . . . . . . . . . . 1,639

3. Secret; White Horse of the Peppers; Jacobite; Bottle; Box and Cox; Bamboozling; Widow's Victim; Robert Macaire. With Portrait and Memoir of Francis S. Chanfrau.
4. Secret Service; Omnibus; Irish Lion; Maid of Croissey; Old Guard; Raising the Wind; Slasher and Crasher; Naval Engagements. With Portrait and Memoir of Miss Rose Telbin.
5. Cockneys in California; Bombastes Furioso; Irish Ambassador; Weathercock; Who Speaks First? Macbeth Travestie; Delicate Ground; All that Glitters is not Gold. With Portrait and Memoir of William A. Goodall.
6. Grimshaw, Bagshaw, and Bradshaw; Bloomer Costume; Born to Good Luck; 'Twould Puzzle a Conjurer; Rough Diamond; Two Bonnycastles; Kiss in the Dark; Kill or Cure. With Portrait and Memoir of Frederick M. Kent.
7. Box and Cox Married and Settled; St. Cupid; Go-to-bed Tom; The Lawyers; Jack Sheppard; The Toodles; The Mobcap; Ladies Beware. With a Portrait and Memoir of Sol. Smith.
8. Morning Call; Popping the Question; Deaf as a Post; New Footman; Pleasant Neighbor; Paddy the Piper; Brian O'Linn; Irish Assurance.
9. Temptation; Paddy Carey; Two Gregories; King Charming; Po-ca-hon-tas; Clockmaker's Hat; Married Rake; Love and Murder.
10. Ireland and America; Pretty Piece of Business; Irish Broommaker; To Paris and Back for Five Pounds; That Blessed Baby; Our Gal; Swiss Cottage; Young Widow.
11. O'Flannigan and the Fairies; Irish Post; My Neighbor's Wife; Irish Tiger; P. P., or Man and Tiger; To Oblige Benson; State Secrets; Irish Yankee.
12. A Good Fellow; Cherry and Fair Star; Gale Breezely; Our Jemimy; Miller's Maid; Awkward Arrival; Crossing the Line; Conjugal Lesson.
13. My Wife's Mirror; Life in New York; Middy Ashore; Crown Prince; Two Queens; Thumping Legacy; Unfinished Gentleman; House Dog.
14. The Demon Lover; Matrimony; In and out of Place; I Dine with My Mother; Hi-a-wa-tha; Andy Blake; Love in '76; Romance under Difficulties.
15. One Coat for Two Suits; A Decided Case; Daughter; No! Glorious Minority; Coroner's Inquisition; Love in Humble Life; Family Jars; Personation.
16. Children in the Wood; Winning a Husband; Day after the Fair; Make Your Wills; Rendezvous; My Wife's Husband; Monsieur Tonson; Illustrious Stranger.
17. Mischief-Making; A Live Woman in the Mines; The Corsair; Shylock; Spoiled Child; Evil Eye; Nothing to Nurse; Wanted, a Widow.
18. Lottery Ticket; Fortune's Frolic; Is he Jealous?; Married Bachelor; Husband at Sight; Irishman in London; Animal Magnetism; Highways and By-ways.
19. Columbus; Harlequin Bluebeard; Ladies at Home; Phenomenon in a Smock Frock; Comedy and Tragedy; Opposite Neighbors; Dutchman's Ghost; Persecuted Dutchman.
20. Musard Ball; Great Tragic Revival; High, Low, Jack, and Game; A Gentleman from Ireland; Tom and Jerry; Village Lawyer; Captain's not A-miss; Amateurs and Actors.
21. Promotion; A Fascinating Individual; Mrs. Caudle; Shakespeare's Dream; Neptune's Defeat; Lady of the Bedchamber; Take Care of Little Charley; Irish Widow.
22. Yankee Peddler; Hiram Hireout; Double-Bedded Room; The Drama Defended; Vermont Wool Dealer; Ebenezer Venture; Principles form Character; Lady of the Lake (Travesty.)
23. Mad Dogs; Barney the Baron; Swiss Swains; Bachelor's Bedroom; A Roland for an Oliver; More Blunders than One; Dumb Belle; Limerick Boy.
24. Nature and Philosophy; Teddy the Tiler; Spectre Bridegroom; Matteo Falcone; Jenny Lind; Two Buzzards; Happy Man; Betsy Baker.
25. No. 1, round the Corner; Teddy Roe; Object of Interest; My Fellow Clerk; Bengal Tiger; Laughing Hyena; The Victor Vanquished; Our Wife.
26. My Husband's Mirror; Yankee Land; Norah Creina; Good for Nothing; The First Night; The Eaton Boy; Wandering Minstrel; Wanted, 1000 Milliners.
27. Poor Pillicoddy; The Mummy; Dont't Forget your Opera Glasses; Love in Livery; Anthony and Cleopatra; Trying it on; Stage-Struck Yankee; Young Wife and Old Umbrella.
28. Crinoline; A Family Failing; Adopted Child; The Turned Head; A Match in the Dark; Advice to Husbands; Siamese Twins; Sent to the Tower.
29. Somebody Else; Ladies' Battle; Art of Acting; The Lady of the Lions; The Rights of Man; My Husband's Ghost; Two can Play at that Game; Fighting by Proxy.
30. Unprotected Female; Pet of the Petticoats; Forty and Fifty; Who Stole the Pocket-Book?; My Son Diana; Unwarrantable Intrusion; Mr. and Mrs. White; A Quiet Family.
31. Cool as a Cucumber; Sudden Thoughts; Jumbo Jum; A Blighted Being; Little Toddlekins; A Lover by Proxy; Maid with the Milking Pail; Perplexing Predicament.
32. Dr. Dilworth; Out to Nurse; A Lucky Hit; The Dowager; Metamora (Burlesque); Dreams of Delusion; The Shaker Lovers; Ticklish Times.
33. Twenty Minutes with a Tiger; Miralda, or, the Justice of Tacon; A Soldier's Courtship; Servants by Legacy; Dying for Love; Alarming Sacrifice; Valet de Sham; Nicholas Nickleby.

Drama, Minor. *Continued.* . . . . . . . . . . . . . . 1,639

34. The Last of the Pigtails; King Renè's Daughter; The Grotto Nymph; A Devilish Good Joke; A Twice-Told Tale; Pas de Fascination; Revolutionary Soldier; A Man Without a Head.
35. The Olio, Part 1; The Olio, Part 2; The Olio, Part 3; The Trumpeter's Daughter; Seeing Warren; Green Mountain Boy; That Nose; Tom Noddy's Secret.
36. Shocking Events; A Regular Fix; Dick Turpin; Young Scamp; Young Actress; Call at No. 1-7; One Touch of Nature; Two B'hoys.
37. All the World's a Stage; Quash, or Nigger Practice; Turn Him Out; Pretty Girls of Stillberg; Angel of the Attic; Circumstances alter Cases; Katty O'Sheal; A Supper in Dixie
38. "Ici on Parle Français;" Who killed Cock Robin?; Declaration of Independence; Heads or Tails; Obstinate Family; My Aunt; That Rascal Pat; Don Paddy de Bazan.
39. Too much for Good Nature; Cure for the Fidgets; Jack's the Lad; Much Ado about a Merchant of Venice; The Artful Dodger; A Winning Hazard; A Day's Fishing; An Irishman's Maneuver.

Modern British. London, 1811. 5 v. 8°. . . . . . . 1,717

Vol. 1. Tragedies—Two Noble Kinsmen; King and No King; Maid's Tragedy; Thierry and Theodoret; Philaster; Bonduca; False One; Bondman; Fatal Dowry; Broken Heart; Rival Queens; Theodosius; All for Love; Don Sebastian; Orphan; Venice Preserved; Isabella; Oroonoko; Mourning Bride; Tamerlane; Fair Penitent; Jane Shore; Lady Jane Grey; Cato; Distressed Mother; Siege of Damascus.

2. Revenge; Brothers; Marianne; George Barnwell; Fatal Curiosity; Arden of Feversham; Zara; King Charles I.; Gustavus Vasa; Mahomet; Tancred and Sigismund; Irene; Roman Father; Elfrida; Caractacus; Gamester; Boadicea; Earl of Essex; Barbarossa; Douglas; Cleone; Orphan of China; Zenobia.
3. Comedies—Every Man in His Humour; Volpone; Alchemist; Rule a Wife and Have a Wife; Chances; New Way to Pay Old Debts; Committee; Rehearsal; Key to the Rehearsal; Country Girl; Plain Dealer; Old Bachelor; Double Dealer; Love for Love; Way of the World; Provoked Wife; Confederacy; Mistake; Provoked Husband; Spanish Friar; Love Makes a Man; She Would and She Would Not; Careless Husband.
4. The Hypocrite; Constant Couple; Sir Harry Wildair; Inconstant; Recruiting Officer; Beau's Stratagem; The Funeral; Tender Husband; Conscious Lovers; Busy-Body; The Wonder; Bold Stroke For a Wife; Drummer; Miser; Suspicious Husband; Way to Keep Him; Falstaff's Wedding; Jealous Wife; Clandestine Marriage; Good-Natured Man; She Stoops to Conquer; The Brothers; West Indian; Rivals.
5. Operas and Farces—Comus; Cheats of Scapin; Beggars' Opera; Contrivances; Chrononhotonthologus; Tom Thumb; Mock Doctor; Intriguing Chambermaid; Devil to Pay; King and Miller of Mansfield; Sir John Cockle at Court; Lying Valet; Miss in Her Teens; Lethé; Male Coquette; Guardian; Neck or Nothing; A Peep Behind the Curtain; Irish Widow; Bon Ton; High Life Below Stairs; Taste; Englishman in Paris.

Modern Standard. New York, n. d. 43 v. in 29. 12°. . . . . 1,690

Vol. 1. Ion; Fazio, or, the Italian Wife; Lady of Lyons; Richelieu, or, the Conspiracy; The Wife, a Tale of Mantua; Honeymoon; School for Scandal; Money. With Memoir of Anna Cora Mowatt.

2. Stranger; Grandfather Whitehead; Richard III.; Love's Sacrifice; Gamester; Cure for the Heartache; Hunchback; Don Cæsar de Bazan. With Portrait and Memoir of Charles Kean.
3. The Poor Gentleman; Hamlet; Charles II., or the Merry Monarch; Venice Preserved; Pizarro; Love-Chase; Othello; Lend Me Five Shillings. With Portrait and Memoir of Wm. E. Burton.
4. Virginius; King of the Commons; London Assurance; Rent-Day; Two Gentlemen of Verona; Jealous Wife; Rivals; Perfection. With Portrait and Memoir of J. H. Hackett.
5. A New Way to Pay Old Debts; Look Before You Leap; King John; Nervous Man; Damon and Pythias; Clandestine Marriage; William Tell; The Day After the Wedding. With Portrait and Memoir of George Coleman the elder.
6. Speed the Plough; Romeo and Juliet; Feudal Times; Charles the Twelfth; Bridal; Follies of a Night; Iron Chest; Faint Heart Never Won Fair Lady. With Portrait and Memoir of Sir E. Bulwer Lytton.
7. Road to Ruin; Macbeth; Temper; Evadne; Bertram; Duenna; Much Ado About Nothing; Critic. With Portrait and Memoir of Richard B. Sheridan.
8. Apostate; Twelfth Night; Brutus; Simpson & Co; Merchant of Venice; Old Heads and Young Hearts; Mountaineers; Three Weeks After Marriage. With Portrait and Memoir of George H. Barrett.
9. Love; As You Like It; Elder Brother; Werner; Gisippus; Town and Country; King Lear; Blue Devils. With Portrait and Memoir of Mrs. Shaw.
10. Henry the Eighth; Married and Single; Henry the Fourth, Part 1; Paul Pry; Guy Mannering; Sweethearts and Wives; The Serious Family; She Stoops to Conquer. With Portrait and Memoir of Charlotte Cushman.
11. Julius Cæsar; Vicar of Wakefield; Leap Year; The Catspaw; Passing Cloud; Drunkard; Rob Roy; George Barnwell. With Portrait and Memoir of Mrs. John Sefton.

Drama, Modern Standard. *Continued.*

12. Ingomar; Sketches in India; Two Friends; Jane Shore; Corsican Brothers; Mind your Own Business; Writing on the Wall; Heir-at-Law. With Portrait and Memoir of Thomas S. Hamblin.
13. Soldier's Daughter; Marco Spada; Sardanapalus; The Robbers; Douglas; Nature's Nobleman; Civilization; Katharine and Petruchio. With Portrait and Memoir of Edwin Forrest.
14. Game of Love; Midsummer Night's Dream; Ernestine; Rag-Picker of Paris; Flying Dutchman; Hypocrite; Therese; La Tour de Nesle. With Portrait and Memoir of John Brougham.
15. Ireland as it is; Sea of Ice; Seven Clerks; Game of Life; Forty Thieves; Bryan Boroihme; Romance and Reality; Ugolino. With Portrait andMemoir of Barney Williams.
16. The Tempest; The Pilot; Carpenter of Rouen; King's Rival; Little Treasure; Dombey and Son; Parents and Guardians; Jewess.
17. Camille; Married Life; Wenlock of Wenlock; Rose of Ettrickvale; David Copperfield; Aline, or the Rose of Killarney; Pauline; Jane Eyre.
18. Night and Morning; Æthiop; Three Guardsmen; Tom Cringle; Henriette, the Forsaken; Eustache Baudin; Ernest Maltravers; Bold Dragoons.
19. Dred, or the Dismal Swamp; Last Days of Pompeii; Esmeralda; Peter Wilkins; Ben the Boatswain; Jonathan Bradford; Retribution; Minerali.
20. French Spy; Wept of Wish-ton-Wish; Evil Genius; Ben Bolt; Sailor of France; Red Mask; Life of an Actress; Wedding Day.
21. All's Fair in Love; Hofer; Self; Cinderella; Phantom; Franklin; The Gunmaker of Moscow; The Love of a Prince.
22. Son of the Night; Rory O'More; Golden Eagle; Rienzi; Broken Sword; Rip Van Winkle; Isabelle; Heart of Mid-Lothian.
23. Actress of Padua; Floating Beacon; Bride of Lammermoor; Cataract of the Ganges; Robber of the Rhine; School of Reform; Wandering Boys; Mazeppa.
24. Young New York; The Victims; Romance after Marriage; Brigand; Poor of New York; Ambrose Gwinett; Raymond and Agnes; Gambler's Fate.
25. Father and Son; Massaniello; Sixteen-String Jack; Youthful Queen; Skeleton Witness; Innkeeper of Abbeville; Miller and his Men; Aladdin.
26. Adrienne the Actress; Undine; Jessie Brown; Asmodeus; Mormons; Blanche of Brandywine; Viola; Deseret Deserted.
27. Americans in Paris; Victorine; Wizard of the Wave; Castle Specter; Horse-Shoe Robinson; Armand; Fashion; Glance at New York.
28. Inconstant; Uncle Tom's Cabin; Guide to the Stage; Veteran; Miller of New Jersey; Dark Hour before Dawn; Midsummer Night's Dream, Laura Keene's edition; Art and Artifice.
29. Poor Young Man; Ossawattomie Brown; Pope of Rome; Oliver Twist; Pauvrette; Man with the Iron Mask; Knight of Arva; Moll Pitcher.
30. Black-Eyed Susan; Satan in Paris; Rosina Meadows; West End, or, Irish Heiress; Six Degrees of Crime; The Lady and the Devil; Avenger, or, Moor of Sicily; Masks and Faces.
31. Merry Wives of Windsor; Mary's Birthday; Shandy Maguire; Wild Oats; Michael Erle; Idiot Witness; Ticket-of-Leave Man; People's Lawyer.
32. Boy Martyrs; Lucretia Borgia; Surgeon of Paris; Patrician's Daughter; Shoemaker of Toulouse; Momentous Question; Love and Loyalty; Robber's Wife.
33. Dumb Girl of Genoa; Wreck Ashore; Clari; Rural Felicity; Wallace; Madelaine; The Fireman; Grist to the Mill.
34. Two Loves and a Life; Annie Blake; Steward; Captain Kyd; Nick of the Woods; Marble Heart; Second Love; Dream at Sea.
35. Breach of Promise; Review; Lady of the Lake; Still Water Runs Deep; The Scholar; Helping Hands; Faust and Marguerite; Last Man.
36. Belle's Stratagem; Old and Young; Raffaelle; Ruth Oakley; British Slave; A Life's Ransom; Giralda; Time Tries All.
37. Beatrice; Warlock of the Glen; Zelina; Ella Rosenberg; Neighbor Jackwood; Wonder; Robert Emmet; Green Bushes.
38. Flowers of the Forest; A Bachelor of Arts; The Midnight Banquet; Husband of an Hour; Love's Labor's Lost; Naiad Queen; Caprice; Cradle of Liberty.
39. The Lost Ship; Country Squire; Fraud and its Victims; Putnam; King and Deserter; La Fiammina; A Hard Struggle; Gwynneth Vaughan.
40. The Love Knot; Lavater, or, Not a Bad Judge; The Noble Heart; Coriolanus; The Winter's Tale; Eveleen Wilson; Ivanhoe; Jonathan in England.
41. The Pirate's Legacy; The Charcoal Burner; Adelgitha; Senor Valiente; Forest Rose; Duke's Daughter; Camilla's Husband; Pure Gold.
42. Ticket-of Leave Man; Fool's Revenge; O'Neil the Great; Handy Andy; Pirate of the Isles; Fanchon; Little Barefoot; Wild Irish Girl.
43. Pearl of Savoy; Dead Heart; Ten Nights in a Bar-Room; Dumb Boy of Manchester; Belphegor, the Mountebank; Cricket on the Hearth; Printer's Devil; Meg's Diversion.

Modern Theater. E. Inchbald. London, 1811. 10 v. 16°. . . 1,684

Vol. 1. The Will; The Rage; Life; How to Grow Rich; Notoriety.
2. Speculation; The Delinquent; Laugh When You Can; Fortune's Fool; Folly as it Flies.
3. Votary of Wealth; Zorinski; Secrets Worth Knowing; Who Wants a Guinea?; Werter.
4. Duplicity; School for Arrogance; He is Much to Blame; Seduction; School for Prejudice.

Drama, Modern Theater. E. Inchbald. *Continued.* . . . . . . I,684
5. False Impressions; Mysterious Husband; Box-Lobby Challenge; Natural Son; Carmelite.
6. Impostors; Wife of Two Husbands; Ramah Droog; Law of Lombardy; Braganza.
7. I'll Tell You What; Next-Door Neighbors; Wise Man of the East; Percy; Trip to Scarborough.
8. Matilda; Mary, Queen of Scots; Fugitive; He would be a Soldier; England Preserved.
9. Bank Note; Chapter of Accidents; English Merchant; School for Wives; Henry the Second, or, Fall of Rosamond.
10. Fashionable Levities; Time's a Tell-Tale; Which is the Man?; What is She?; Life of a Day.

New English; edited by W. Oxberry. London, 1818-22. 16 v. 12°. I,683
Vol. 1. New Way to Pay Old Debts; Rivals; West Indian; Hypocrite; Jealous Wife.
2. Beggars' Opera; Duenna; Lionel and Clarissa; Maid of the Mill; Love in a Village.
3. Richard the Third; Hamlet; Is He Jealous?; Alexander the Great; Way to Keep Him.
4. She Stoops to Conquer; Venice Preserved; The Wonder; Castle Specter; Woodman's Hut.
5. Clandestine Marriage; Soldier's Daughter; Othello; Distressed Mother; Provoked Husband.
6. Deaf and Dumb; Busy-Body; Romeo and Juliet; Belle's Stratagem; Recruiting Officer.
7. Bold Stroke for a Wife; Road to Ruin; Beau's Stratagem; As You Like It; King John.
8. Country Girl; Jane Shore; Coriolanus; Suspicious Husband; Merry Wives of Windsor.
9. Critic; Rosina; Honest Thieves; Mayor of Garratt; Three Weeks after Marriage; Shipwreck; Rugantine.
10. King Lear; Inconstant; Merchant of Venice; Rule a Wife and Have a Wife; Rob Roy.
11. Magpie; Quaker; Citizen; Deserter; Miser; Lying Valet; Who's the Dupe?
12. Guy Mannering; Cymbeline; Twelfth Night; Confederacy; Douglas.
13. Tobacconist; Midnight Hour; Fortune's Frolic; Love Laughs at Locksmiths; Review; Follies of a Day.
14. Know Your Own Mind; Macbeth; Grecian Daughter; Henry the Fourth; Evadne.
15. Wild Oats; Wheel of Fortune; Much Ado About Nothing; Blue Devils.
16. Every Man in His Humor; Measure for Measure; Julius Cæsar; Man of the World; Every One has his Fault.

Personal Recollections of the Stage. W. W. Wood. Phil. 1855. 12°. I,724
Record of the Boston Stage. W. W. Clapp. Boston, 1853. 12°. . I,714
Dramatic Art and Literature. A. W. von Schlegel. London, 1846. p. 8°. L,232
Dramatic Literature of Age of Elizabeth. W. Hazlitt. New York, 1845. 12°. H,701
Dramatic Poets, English. C. Lamb. New York, 1859. 12°. . . U,279,2
Dramatis Personæ. R. Browning. Boston, 1864. 12°. . . . . . I,294
Draper, H. Text-Book on Chemistry. New York, 1866. 12°. . . . N,220
Draper, J. W. Future Civil Policy of America. New York, 1865. 8°. . B,857
The same. New York, 1866. 8°. . . . . . . . . S.C.
History of the American Civil War. New York, 1867-70. 3 v. 8°. B,919
Human Physiology. New York, 1856. 8°. . . . . . . L,965
Intellectual Development of Europe. New York, 1864. 8°. . . O,707
The same. New York, 1865. 8°. . . . . . . . . S.C.
Text-Book on Natural Philosophy. New York, 1849. 12°. . . N,82
Draper, L. C. Reports on Schools of Wisconsin. Madison, 1858-59. 2 v. 8°. O,1212
Draughtsman, Practical. J. E. Armengaud and others. New York, 1854. 4°. Q,169
Drawing, Observations on. R. and J. Cochrane. Baltimore, 1857. 8°. M,1123
Cyclopædia of; edited by W. E. Worthen. New York, 1866. 8°. *M,230
Elements of. J. Ruskin. London, 1857. 8°. . . . . . . M,65
for Schools. T. Tate. London, 1854. 4°. . . . . . . . M,182
from Memory. M. E. Cavé. New York, 1869. 12°. . . . . M,24
from Nature. G. Barnard. London, 1865. 8°. . . . . . . M,135
Industrial. D. H. Mahan. New York, 1855. 8°. . . . . . M,224
of Ornaments, Principles of. R. Brown. London, 1822. 4°. . . Q,172
Text-Book of Geometrical. W. Minifie. Baltimore, 1849. 12°. . M,148

Drawing-Book, American. J. G. Chapman. New York, 1864. 4°. . . M,290
London. R. S. Burn. London, 1853. 8°. . . . . . . . M,43
Drawing-Room Plays and Evening Amusements. S. S. Steele. Phila. 1865. 12°. I,731
Drayson, A. W. The Earth we inhabit. London, 1859. 8°. . . . N,761
Drayton, M. Harmony of the Church. London, 1843. 12°. . . L,606,7
Draytons and Davenants. E. Charles. New York, 1868. 12°. . . . K,622
The same. Leipzig, 1868. 2 v. in 1. 16°. . . . . . J,63
Dream Life. D. G. Mitchell. New York, 1866. 12°. . . . . . . H,60
Dreams, Literature and Curiosities of. F. Seafield. London, 1868. 2 v. 8°. O,336
Dreamthorp. A. Smith. London, 1863. 12°. . . . . . . . H,483
Dred; or, Nina Gordon. H. B. Stowe. Boston, 1856. 2 v. 12°. . . K,285
Dred-Scott Case, Examination of the. T. H. Benton. New York, 1858. 8°. O,424
Drei Freunde. P. I. Wilcken. Hannover, 1861. 2 v. 16°. . . . G,515
Drei Jahre von Dreissigen; ein Roman. L. Rellstab. Leip. 1858. 5 v. 12°. G,426
Dresden, Warsaw, and Vienna, Courts of. Sir N. W. Wraxall. Lond. 1799. 8°. V,430
Dresses and Decorations of the Middle Ages. H. Shaw. Lond. 1858. 2 v. r. 8°. *Q,188
Drew, J. H. Life of S. Drew. New York, 1835. 12°. . . . . D,159
Drew, S. Life of T. Coke. New York, 1847. 12°. . . . . C,1000
Drifting Goodward. M. J. Lamb. Boston, 1870. 24°. . . . J,1395
Driftwood. H. W. Longfellow. Boston, 1866. 16°. . . . . . . U,1,1
Driven to Sea; Adventures of Norrie Seton. G. Cupples. Boston, 1870. 16°. J,1324
Droysen, J. G. Geschichte Alexanders des Groszen. Berlin, 1833. 8°. . E,13
Geschichte der Nachfolger Alexanders. Hamburg, 1836. 8°. . . E,14
Druids, Mythology and Rites of the British. E. Davies. London, 1809. 8°. P,831
Drummond, W., Poëtical Works. London, 1856. 16°. . . . . . I,346
Drummond, Sir W. Origines; the Origin of Empires. Lond. 1824-9. 4 v. 8°. A,110
Drury, D. Illustrations of Exotic Entomology. London, 1837. 3 v. 4°. *Q,5
Druyée's Brigade, History of. F. B. Hough. Albany, 1864. 8°. . . B,813
Druzes and Maronites, 1840-60. C. H. Churchill. London, 1862. 12°. . B,556
of the Lebanon. G. W. Chasseaud. London, 1855. 8°. . . . V,681
C. H. Churchill. London, 1853. 3 v. 8°. . . . . . V,641
Dryden, J., Critical and Prose Works of. London, 1800. 3 v. in 4. 8°. . U,254
Poetical Works; with Memoir. Boston, 1854. 5 v. 16°. . . I,208
The same; edited by R. Bell. London, 1854. 3 v. 16°. . I,248
Poetical Works. London, 1857. 16°. . . . . . . . . . I,340
The same. New York, 1868. 16°. . . . . . . . . I,342
Works; with Life by J. Mitford, v. 2, 3. New York, 1852. 2 v. 8°. U,253
Duane, W. Visit to Columbia in 1822-23. Philadelphia, 1826. 8°. . . V,260
Duane, W. J., Narrative and Correspondence. Philadelphia, 1838. 8°. . O,570
Dubief, L. F. Manuel du Fabricant de Cidre et de Poiré. Paris, 1834. 24°. . M,591
Dublin, Afternoon Lectures on Literature and Art, 1863-8. Lon. 1863-9. 5 v. 16°. H,566
Model Schools in. W. C. Taylor. Dublin, 1847. 8°. . . . O,1251,2
Dublin University Magazine. Dublin, 1833-62. 60 v. 8°. . . . . T,46
Du Bois, W. E. Gold and Silver Coins of all Nations. Phila. 1842. 4°. . M,391
Du Chaillu, P. B. Ashango-Land and Equatorial Africa. Lond. 1867. 8°. V,847
Explorations in Equatorial Africa. New York, 1861. 8°. . . V,869
Lost in the Jungle. New York, 1870. 12°. . . . . . J,1291
My Apingi Kingdom. New York, 1871. 12°. . . . . . J,1294
Stories of the Gorilla Country. New York, 1869. 12°. . . J,1491
Wild Life under the Equator. New York, 1870. 12°. . . J,1502

Duchess of Trajetto. A. Manning. London, 1863. 12°. . . . . . J,589
Ducis, J. F. and others. Chefs-d'Œuvre Tragiques. Paris, 1845. 12°. . H,883
Dudevant, Mad. *George Sand.* Antonia. Boston, 1870. 12°. . . K,1117
Autour de la Table. Paris, n. d. 12°. . . . . . . H,1025
Consuelo. Philadelphia, 1861. 8°. . . . . . . . . H,919
Fanchon; the Cricket. Philadelphia, n. d. 12°. . . . . H,954
Indiana; a Love Story. Philadelphia, 1850. 12°. . . . K,1120
Jealousy. Philadelphia, n. d. 12°. . . . . . . . K,1121
Les Dames Vertes. Paris, n. d. 12°. . . . . . . . H,1026
Mauprat. Boston, 1870. 12°. . . . . . . . . K,1118
M'lle Merquem. New York, 1868. 12°. . . . . . . H,959
Miller of Angibault. Boston, 1871. 12°. . . . . . . K,1123
Snow Man. Boston, 1871. 12°. . . . . . . . . K,1119
Teverino. New York, 1855. 12°. . . . . . . . . K,1122
Dudley, R. *Earl of Leicester*, Correspondence, 1585–86. London, 1844. 4°. . A,472
Dudley, T., Letter to Countess of Lincoln, 1631. See *Force's Tracts*, v. 2.
Dueling, History of. J. G. Millingen. London, 1841. 2 v. 8°. . . H,617
Duels and Dueling, Notes on. L. Sabine. Boston, 1859. 12°. . . . H,623
Duer, J. Law and Practice of Marine Insurance. N. Y. 1845–46. 2 v. 8°. U,529
Duer, W. A. Constitutional Jurisprudence of the U. S. N. Y. 1833. 12°. . O,469
The same. Boston, 1856. 12°. . . . . . . . . . U,490
The same; abridged. New York, 1855. 16°. . . . . L,446
Dürer, A., Life of. C. Heaton. London, 1870. 8°. . . . . . . M,122
Married Life of. L. Schefer. New York, 1867. 16°. . . . D,524
Duff, P. Book Keeping. New York, 1868. 8°. . . . . . . M,1171
Dufferin, Lord. See *Blackwood, F. T.*
Dufief, N. G. Nature displayed in teaching French. Lond. 1831. 2 v. 8°. L,800
Duflos, A. Die Wichtigsten Lebens-Bedürfnisse. Breslau, 1846. 8°. . G,752
Dufour, J. J. American Vine-Dresser's Guide. Cincinnati, 1826. 12°. . M,440
Dufton, J. National Education. London, 1847. 8°. . . . . . O,1251,2
Dugan, J. Hurlbut's Fighting Fourth Division. Cincinnati, 1863. 8°. . B,956
Dugdale, Sir W. History of Monasteries in England. Lond. 1846. 6 v. in 8. f°. Q,387
Vestitation of the County of Yorke, 1665. Durham, 1859. 8°. F,126,36
Du Hausset, Madame, Mémoires de. Paris, 1846. 12°. . . . . D,602
Dulcken, H. W. Picture History of England. London, 1866. 4°. . . A,403
Duller, E. Malerische und Romantische Donauländer. Leipzig, n. d. 8°. E,186,9
und Hagen. Vaterländische Gesch. Frank.-a-Main, 1853–58. 5 v. 8°. E,54
Dumas, A. Adventures of a Marquis. Philadelphia, n. d. 8°. . . H,979
Andrée de Taverney. Philadelphia, n. d. 8°. . . . . . H,980
Bragelonne. Philadelphia, n. d. 8°. . . . . . . . H,981
Chevalier. Philadelphia, n. d. 8°. . . . . . . . . H,975
Conscript. New York, 1855. 12°. . . . . . . . . H,972
Count of Monte-Cristo. Philadelphia, n. d. 8°. . . . . . H,982
Countess de Charny. Philadelphia, n. d. 8°. . . . . . H,976
Diana of Meridor. Philadelphia, n. d. 8°. . . . . . . H,983
Forty-Five Guardsmen. Philadelphia, n. d. 8°. . . . . . H,984
Iron Hand. Philadelphia, n. d. 8°. . . . . . . . H,985
Iron Mask. Philadelphia, n. d. 8°. . . . . . . . . H,986
Love and Liberty. Philadelphia, 1870. 12°. . . . . . . H,977
Louise la Valliere. Philadelphia, n. d. 8°. . . . . . . H,987

Dumas, A. Memoirs of a Maître d'Armes. London, 1865. p. 8°. . I,664,2
Memoirs of a Physician. Philadelphia, n. d. 8°. . . . . . H,988
Pictures of Travel in the South of France. London, n. d. 12°. . V,451
Queen's Necklace. Philadelphia, n. d. 2 v. in 1. 8°. . . H,1013
Six Years Later. Philadelphia, n. d. 8°. . . . . . . H,978
Tales of Algeria. Philadelphia, 1868. 12°. . . . . . H,973
Three Guardsmen. Philadelphia, n. d. 8°. . . . . . H,989
Twenty Years After. Philadelphia, n. d. 8°. . . . . . H,990
Dumas, A. *fils*. Camille; or, the Coquette. Philadelphia, n. d. 12°. . H,974
Dumas, J. B. Action du Calorique sur les Corps Organiques. Paris, 1838. 4°. N,252,57
Statique Chimique des Etres Organisés. Paris, 1841. 8°. . N,252,7
Dumouriez, C. F. D., Mémoires de. Paris, 1848. 2 v. 12°. . . . D,609
Duncan, A. Practical Surveyor's Guide. Philadelphia, 1860. 12°. . M,635
Duncan, H. Sacred Philosophy of the Seasons. New York, 1847. 4 v. 12°. M,761
Duncan, J. Beetles. Edinburgh, 1852. 16°. . . . . . . N,470,33
British Butterflies. Edinburgh, n. d. 16°. . . . . . N,470,29
British Moths. Edinburgh, n. d. 16°. . . . . . . N,470,30
Exotic Moths. Edinburgh, 1852. 16°. . . . . . . N,470,32
Foreign Butterflies. Edinburgh, 1852. 16°. . . . . . N,470,31
Introduction to Entomology. Edinburgh, 1853. 16°. . . N,470,28
Duncan, J. and Rabbe, A. History of Russia. London, 1854. 2 v. 12°. B,535
Duncker, M. Geschichte des Alterthums. Berlin, 1855-60. 4. v. 8°. . E,452
Dundee, Lord. See *Graham, J.*
Dunglison, R. Human Physiology. Philadelphia, 1856. 2 v. 8°. . . L,963
Dunham, S. A. Europe during Middle Ages. London, 1833-34. 4 v. 12°. M,998
History of Denmark, Sweden, and Norway. Lon. 1839-40. 3 v. 12°. M,1002
of the German Empire. London, 1834-35. 3 v. 12°. . . M,992
of Poland. London, 1831. 12°. . . . . . . M,1001
of Spain and Portugal. London, 1832. 5 v. 12°. . . M,991
The same. New York, 1854. 5 v. 16°. . . . B,452
Literary and Scientific Men of Great Britain. London, 1836. 3 v. 12°. M,1016
Dunlap, S. F. Vestiges of the Spirit-History of Man. New York, 1858. 8°. P,259
Dunlap, W. History of the American Theater. New York, 1832. 12°. . I,712
History of New Netherlands. New York, 1839-40. 2 v. 8°. . C,93
Dunlavy, J. Manifesto; or, Doctrine and Practice. New York, 1847. 8°. P,240
Dunlop, J. History of Fiction. Philadelphia, 1842. 2 v. 12°. . . H,642
Dunn Browne's Experiences in the Army. S. Fiske. Boston, 1866. 12°. B,915
Dunn, H. Principles of Teaching. London, 1837. 12°. . . . . O,960
Dunn, M. Steam-Jet applied to Ventilation of Mines. Newcastle, 1854. 8°. N,252,56
Explosions in Coal Mines. London, 1845. 8°. . . . N,252,35
Dunton, J. Letters from New England, 1686. Boston, 1867. 4°. . . C,66
Life and Errors. London, 1818. 2 v. in 1. 8°. . . . . D,518
Duparcq, E. de la B. Military Art. New York, 1863. 8°. . . . M,711
Dupin, C. Force Commerciale de la Grand-Bretagne. Paris, 1826. 2 v. 4°. M,818
Duplessis, G. Wonders of Engraving. New York, 1871. 12°. . M,1065
Duppa, R. Life of Michael Angelo Buonarroti. London, 1870. p. 8°. . L,126
Dupuy, A. E. Planter's Daughter. Philadelphia, 1870. 12°. . . . K,459
Durbin, J. P. Observations in the East. New York, 1854. 2 v. 12°. V,1058
Observations in Europe. New York, 1848. 2 v. 12°. . . . V,387
Dureau de La Malle, A. J. C. A. L'Algérie. Paris, 1852. 12°. . . V,807

Durch Nacht zum Licht. F. Spielhagen. Berlin, 1867. 3 v. 16°. . . G,453
Durfee, C. History of Williams College. Boston, 1860. 8°. . . . O,807
Durham, Ancient Monuments at. London, 1842. 8°. . . . F,126,15
Catalogues of the Cathedral Library. London, 1838. 8°. . F,126,7
Depositions from the Courts. London, 1845. 8°. . . . F,126,4
Historiæ Dunelmensis; Scriptores Tres; ed. J. Raine. Lon. 1839. 8°. F,126,9
Household Book. London, 1844. 8°. . . . . . . F,126,18
See of, Liber Vitæ Ecclesiæ. London, 1841. 8°. . . . F,126,13
Obituary Roll. London, 1856. 8°. . . . . F,126,31
Durrant, W. Kru Coast, Cape Palmas, and the Niger. London, 1862. 8°. V,1086,2
Durrieu, X. Present State of Morocco. London, 1854. p. 8°. . . I,658,2
Dussauce, H. Practical Guide for the Perfumer. Philadelphia, 1868. 12°. N,232
Tanning, Currying, and Leather-Dressing. Philadelphia, 1867. 8°. M,679
Treatise on the Manufacture of Soap. Philadelphia, 1869. 8°. . M,629
Dutch Republic, Rise of. J. L. Motley. New York, 1868. 3 v. 8°. . B,408
Dutchman's Fireside. J. K. Paulding. New York, 1868. 8°. . . . K,307
Du Terrail, P. *Chevalier Bayard*, Life of. W. G. Simms. N. Y. 1860. 12°. D,659
The Story of. E. Walford. New York, 1869. 16°. . . . . . I,563
Dutrochet, R. J. H. Recherches sur la Force Epipolique. Paris, 1842. 8°. N,252,17
Duval, J. La Question du Maroc. Paris, 1860. 8°. . . . . . N,252,45
Duverger, W. French and English Idioms compared. London, 1854. 12°. L,801
Duxbury Mass., History of. J. Winsor. Boston, 1849. 8°. . . . C,82
Duyckinck, E. A. Wit and Wisdom of Sydney Smith. N. Y. 1870. 8°. . H,461
and G. L. Cyclopædia of American Literature. N. Y. 1856. 2 v. 8°. S.C.
The same, and Supplement. New York, 1855-66. 3 v. 8°. H,669
Dwellings, Unhealthy Condition of. C. Girdlestone. London, 1845. 8°. N,252,29
Dwight, B. W. Modern Philology. New York, 1859. 8°. . . . L,532
Dwight, E. A. Life and Letters of Wilder Dwight. Boston, 1868. 8°. . C,712
Dwight, M. A. Grecian and Roman Mythology. New York, 1849. 8°. . P,922
Study of Art. New York, 1856. 12°. . . . . . . . M,10
Dwight, N. Lives of Signers of Declaration of Independ. N. Y. 1852. 12°. C,545
Dwight, Theo. History of the Hartford Convention. N. Y. 1833. 8°. . C,76
Dwight, Theo., jr. History of Connecticut. New York, 1859. 16°. . . L,427
Dwight, Timo., Life of. W. B. Sprague. Boston, 1860. 12°. . . C,860,14
Theology explained and defended. New York, 1867. 4 v. 8°. . P,716
Dyce, A. Strictures on Collier's edition of Shakespeare. London, 1859. 8°. I,887
(Ed.) Sir Thomas Moore; a Play. London, 1844. 8°. . . I,885,22
Timon; a Play. London, 1842. 8°. . . . . . I,885,11
Dyeing and Calico Printing. F. Calvert. Philadelphia, n. d. 12°. . M,653
Aniline and its Derivatives. M. Reimann. New York, 1868. 8°. . N,191
Blaufarben und Ultramarin. R. Meyer. Quedlinburg, 1845. 12°. N,252,23
Chemistry of. F. F. Runge. London, 1837. . . . . N,252,28
Dyer, G. Academic Unity. London, 1827. 8°. . . . . . O,1251,3
History of University of Cambridge. London, 1814. 2 v. 8°. . O,814
Privileges of University of Cambridge. London, 1824. 2 v. 8°. . O,1056
Dyer, J. Poetical Works. London, 1855. 16°. . . . . . . . I,274
Dyer, S. Olio of Love and Song. Indianapolis, 1855. 16°. . . . H,302,1
Dyer, T. H. Ancient Rome. London, 1864. 8°. . . . . . . A,178
History of Modern Europe. London, 1861-64. 4 v. 8°. . . A,337
of the Kings of Rome. London, 1868. 8°. . . . . A,162

Dyer, T. H. Life of John Calvin. New York, 1855. 12°. . . . D,645
Pompeii; its History and Antiquities. London, 1867. 8°. . . B,498
Dylks, J. C., Leatherwood God, Account of. R. R. Taneyhill. Cin. 1871. 8°. C,223
Dymond, J. Accordance of War with Christianity. Philad. n. d. 8°. . O,722
Essays on the Principles of Morality. New York, 1844. 8°. . . O,724
Dynamics; a Treatise on Motion. S. Earnshaw. Cambridge, 1844. 8°. . N,92
Dynevor Terrace. C. M. Yonge. New York, 1866. 2 v. 12°. . K,1079

Eadie, J. and others. Imperial Dictionary of Biography. Lond. 1866. 6 v. 8°. L.R.
Early Oriental History. London, 1852. 8°. . . . . . . A,22
Eagle Pass; or, Life on the Border. C. Montgomery. New York, 1852. 12°. K,218
Earl, G. W. Native Races of the Indian Archipelago. London, 1853. 12°. N,413
Earl's Daughter. E. M. Sewell. New York, 1869. 12°. . . . . K,995
Earl Whiting; or, the Nameless Boy. M. A. Atkins. Boston, 1870. 16°. J,1555
Early Dawn. E. Charles. New York, 1864. 12°. . . . . . . K,623
Early English Metrical Romances. G. Ellis. London, 1848. p. 8°. . L,8
The same. London, 1805. 3 v. 8°. . . . . . . H,699
Early English Text Society's Publications. London, 1867–71. 22 v. 8°. . L,605

1867. Vol. 24. Hymns to the Virgin and Christ; Parliament of Devils; and other Religious Poems; edited by F. J. Furnivall.
25. Stacions of Rome, verse 1370, prose 1460–70; Pilgrims' Sea Voyage, 1422; Clene Maydenhod, 1370; edited by F. J. Furnivall.
26. Religious Pieces in prose and verse, 1440; edited by G. G. Perry.
27. Levins, P. Manipulus Vocabulorum, 1570; edited by H. B. Wheatley.
28. Langland, W. Vision of Piers Plowman, with Vita de Dowel, Dobet et Dobest, 1362–1380, Part I. Vernon Text; edited by W. W. Skeat.
29. Old English Homelies, and Homeletic Treatises (Sawles Warde, and Wohunge of Ure Lauerd; Ureisuns of Ure Louerd and of your Lefdi, etc.) of the 12th 13th Centuries, Part I.; edited by Richard Morris.
30. Pierce the Ploughmans Crede, 1394; God spede the Plough, 1500.
1868. 31. Myrc, J. Instructions for Parish Priests, 1400; edited by E. Peacock.
32. Babees Book; The Bokes of Nurture of John Rhodes and John Russell; Wynkyn de Worde's Boke of Keruynge; The Booke of Demeanor; The Boke of Curtasye; Seager's School of Vertue, etc.; edited by F. J. Furnivall.
33. Book of the Knight of La Tour-Landry, for the Instruction of his Daughters.
34. Old English Homelies, Part II.
35. Lyndesay, Sir D. Works, Part III.: Hystorie of Squyer Meldrum; Testament of the said Williame Meldrum, Squyer; edited by F. Hall.
1869. 36. Merlin; or, Early History of King Arthur, a Prose Romance, 1450–60, Part III.; edited by H. B. Wheatley, with an Essay on Arthurian Localities by J. S. S. Glennie.
37. Lyndesay, Sir D. Works, Part IV.: Ane Satyre of the Thrie Estaits in Commendation of Vertew and Vitvperation of Vice; edited by C. F. Hall.
38. Langland, W. Vision of Piers Plowman, Part II.; Crowley Text.
39. Colonna, G. de. "Gest Hystoriale" of the Destruction of Troy, Part I.; edited by G. A. Panton and D. Donaldson.
1870. 40. English Gilds, their Statutes and Customs; edited by T. and L. T. Smith.
41. Lauder, W. Minor Poems; edited by J. Furnivall.
42. Bernardus de Cura Rei Famuliaris, with some Early Scotch Prophecies.
43. Ratis Raving, and other Moral and Religious Pieces in prose and verse.
1871. 44. Joseph of Arimathie; or, Holy Grail; edited by W. W. Skeat.
45. Gregory's Pastoral Care; King Alfred's West-Saxon Version, Part I.

The same; extra series. London, 1867–71. 13 v. 8°. . L,604

1867. Vol. 1. William of Parlerne; or, William and the Werwolf; Alliterative Romance of Alisaunder; edited by W. W. Skeat.
2. Ellis, A. J. Early English Pronunciation, with especial Reference to Shakespeare and Chaucer, Part I.; 14th, 16th, 17th and 18th Centuries.
1868. 3. Caxton's Book of Curtesye, 1477-78; edited by F. J. Furnivall.
4. Lay of Havelok the Dane, 1280; edited by W. W. Skeat.
5. Boethius, A. M. S. De Consolatione Philosophiæ, Chaucer's translation.
6. Romance of the Chevelere Assigne; re-edited by H. H. Gibbs.
1869. 7. Ellis, A. J. Early English Pronunciation, Part II.; Pronunciation of the 13th and Previous Centuries.
8. Gilbert, Sir H. Queen Elizabeth's Achademy; A Booke of Precedence, etc.; ed. by J. F. Furnivall; Rossetti, W. M. Italian Courtesy Books; Oswald, E. Early German Courtesy Books.

Early English Text Society's Publications; extra series. *Continued.* . . L,604

9. Awdeley, J. Fraternity of Vocabondes, 1565; Harman, T. Caueat or Warening for Commen Cursetors commonly called Vagabones, 1567; Sermon in Praise of Thieves and Thievery, by Parson Haben or Hyberdyne; edited by E. Viles and J. Furnivall.

1870. 10. Boorde, A. Introduction of Knowledge, 1547; Dyetary of Helth, 1542; Barnes, in the Defense of the Berde, 1542-43.

11. Barbour, J. The Bruce, 1375, Part I.; edited by W. W. Skeat.

1871. 12. Starkey, T. England in Henry VIII.'s Time, Part II.: Dialogue between Cardinal Pole and Thomas Lupset; edited by J. M. Cowper.

13. Fish, S. Supplicacyon for the Beggars, 1528–9; edited by F. J. Furnivall; Supplycacyon to Henry the Eyght, 1544; Supplicacyon of the Poore Commons, 1546; Decaye of England by the Great Multitude of Shepe, 1550-53; edited by J. M. Cowper.

Early Friendships. E. Copley. New York, 1852. 18°. . . . . . J,1243
Earnshaw, S. Dynamics; or, a Treatise on Motion. Cambridge, 1844. 8°. N,92
Earth, The. A. W. Drayson. London, 1859. 8°. . . . . . . N,761
R. Mudie. London, 1835. 16°. . . . . . . V,1131
and Animated Nature. O. Goldsmith. London. 1853. 8°. . . N,526
and Man. A. Guizot. Boston, 1855. 12°. . . . . . V,1138
Antiquity of. J. Douglas. London, 1785. 4°. . . . . . . N,747
Blicke in das Universum. L. Guison. Magdeburg, 1854. 8°. . . G,673
Cabinet of, unlocked. E. S. Jackson. London, 1867. 8°. . . N,609
Condition and Phenomena of. W. M. Higgins. New York, 1866. 16°. L,394
Macht des Kleinen. P. Harting. Leipzig, 1851. 8°. . . . . G,833
Phenomena of the Life of. E. Reclus. New York, 1871. 2 v. 8°. V,1110
Physical Condition of. W. M. Higgins. London, 1855. 16°. . . V,1132
Physik der Erde. H. Buff. Braunschweig, 1850. 12°. . . . G,672
Pflanze und Mensch. J. F. Schouw. Leipzig, 1851. 8°. . . . G,712
The same; translated. London, 1852. p. 8°. . . . . L,312
Sea and Sky. J. M. Wilson. London, 1859. 16°. . . . . N,257
Theory of the. Baron de Cuvier. Edinburgh, 1827. 8°. . . . N,792
Earthquakes and Volcanoes. M. Ponton. London, 1868. 12°. . . . V,1111
Erdbeben u. seine Erscheinungen. J. Bœgner. Frank. 1847. 8°. N,252,35
Earthly Paradise; a Poem. W. Morris. Boston, 1871. 3 v. 12°. . . I,334
Earthward Pilgrimage. M. D. Conway. London, 1870. 8°. . . . P,44
Eastman, E. C. White Mountain Guide. Concord, 1863. 16°. . . . V,26
East, The, Letters from. H. H. Leech. New York, 1869. 12°. . . V,669
Letters of a Sentimental Traveler in. W. C. Bryant. N.Y. 1869. 12°. V,1059
Ruined Cities of. W. K. Tweedie. London, 1859. 16°. . . J,1309
Travels in. A. W. Kinglake. New York, 1850. 12°. . . V,1037
Views in; Nelson's. London, 1857–58. 3 v. 16°. . . . V,1029
Yusef; a Crusade in. J. R. Browne. New York, 1865. 12°. . V,1041
East Boston, History of. W. H. Sumner. Boston, 1858. 8°. . . . C,81
East Hampton, Mass., Public Library Catalogue. East Hampton, 1871. 8°. L.R.
East Indian Archipelago, Travels in. A. S. Bickmore. London, 1868. 8°. V,896
East India Company, Annals of, 1600–1708. J. Bruce. Lond. 1810. 3 v. 4°. F,218
East Indies, Reise in Ostinden. L. von Orlich. Leipzig, 1845. 4°. . . Q,436
Six Voyages into, 1670. J. B. Tavernier. London, 1678. f°. . . Q,437
East Jersey under the Proprietary Governments. Newark, 1846. 8°. . C,107
East Lynne. Mrs. H. Wood. New York, n. d. 8°. . . . . . K,1066
The same. Leipzig, 1861. 3 v. 16°. . . . . . . J,519
Eastern Nations, Languages, Literature, etc. J. Richardson. Oxford, 1768. 8°. L,779
Eastlake, C. L. Household Taste in Furniture, etc. London, 1868. 4°. . M,158
Materials for a History of Oil Painting, v. 2. London, 1869. 8°. . M,60

Easton, A. Treatise on Street Railways. Philadelphia, 1859. 8°. . . . M,702
Eastwick, E. B. Venezuela. London, 1868. 8°. . . . . . . . V,261
Eating, Philosophy of. A. J. Bellows. New York, 1869. 12°. . . . L,899
Eaton, C. A. Rome in the Nineteenth Century. London, 1852. 2 v. p. 8°. L,155
Eaton, J. H. Life of Andrew Jackson. Cincinnati, 1827. 12°. . . . C,941
Eaton, W., Life of. Brookfield, Mass. 1813. 8°. . . . . . . . C,793
Life of. C. C. Felton. New York, 1860. 16°. . . . . . C,860,9
Ebchester, W. and Burnby, J. Obituary Roll from 1233. London, 1856. 8°. F,126,31
Eben Erskine. J. Galt. London, 1833. 3 v. 12°. . . . . . . J,565
Ebers, G. Daughter of an Egyptian King. Philadelphia, 1871. 12°. . G,226
Ebert, F. A. General Bibliographical Dictionary. Oxford, 1837. 4 v. 8°. L.R.
Ebrington, Viscount. See *Fortescue.*
Ecce Deus; Life and Doctrine of Jesus. J. Parker. Boston, 1867. 12°. . P,370
Ecce Homo. J. R. Seely. Boston, 1866. 12°. . . . . . . . P,371
Review of. W. E. Gladstone. London, 1868. 16°. . . . . P,372
Eccentrics, English. J. Timbs. London, 1866. 2 v. 8°. . . . . H,706
Ecclesiastical Antiquities of France. G. D. Whittington. London, 1811. 8°. M,174
Ecclesiastical Constitutions and Canons. Dublin, n. d. 32°. . . . P,337
Ecclesiastial History. Eusebius Pamphilus; tr. by C. F. Crusé. Lond. 1851. p. 8°. L,29
Philostratus; epitomized by Photius. London, 1855. p. 8°. . L,32
A. D. 305-445. Socrates Scholasticus. London, 1853. p. 8°. . . L,31
A. D. 322-594. Theodorit and Evagrius. London, 1854. p. 8°. . . L,33
A. D. 324-440. H. Sozomenus. London, 1855. p. 8°. . . . . L,32
Ancient. Eusebius, Socrates, and Evagrius. London, 1667. 4°. . . P,647
and Modern. J. L. Mosheim. New York, 1854. 2 v. 8°. . . P,611
Chronology of the Church. New York, 1859. f°. . . . . . Q,450
Manual of. H. E. F. Guericke. Andover, 1869. 8°. . . . . P,606
of 1st and 2d Centuries, Lectures on. F. D. Maurice. Camb. 1854. 8°. P,650
of England. Venerable Bede. London, 1849. p. 8°. . . . . L,1
and Normandy. O. Vitalis. London, 1853-56. 4 v. p. 8°. L,22
Remarks on. J. Jortin. London, 1751-73. 5 v. 8°. . . . . P,602
Ecclesiastical Laws, Reformation of. E. Cardwell. Oxford, 1850. 8°. . P,902
Ecclesiastical Memorials. J. Strype. Oxford, 1822. 6 v. 8°. . . . . P,688
Ecclesiastical Ornament, etc., Glossary of. A. W. Pugin. London, 1868. 4°. *Q,216
Eccleston, J. Introduction to English Antiquities. London, 1847. 8°. . A,443
Echinodermata, British Fossil of. T. Wright. . . . . . . . Q,30
of the British Tertiaries. E. Forbes. London, 1852. 4°. . . . Q,28
Echoes of the Universe. H. Christmas. Philadelphia, 1850. 12°. . . O,334
Eckermann, J. P. Conversations with Goethe. Boston, 1852. 12°. . . G,31
Eckfeldt, J. R. and Du Bois, W. E. Gold and Silver Coins. Phila. 1842. 4°. M,391
Eclectic Magazine, v. 1-30, 40-63. New York, 1844-64. 54 v. 8°. . . S,14
Eclectic Medical Journal, v. 15-17. Cincinnati, 1856-58. 3 v. in 2. 8°. . L,948
Eclectic Medical Society of New York, Transactions, 1870. Albany, 1870. 8°. L,953
Eclectic Museum. New York, 1843. 3 v. 8°. . . . . . . . . S,13
Eclipse of the Sun, Aug. 7, 1869, Reports on. B. F. Sands, etc. Wash. 1870. 4°. N,387
Eclipse of Faith. H. Rogers. London, 1867. 16°. . . . . . . P,26
Defence of the same. H. Rogers. Boston, 1854. 12°. . . . . P,97
Reply to the same. F. W. Newman. Boston, 1854. 12°. . . P,97
Eclipses. W. S. B. Woolhouse. London, 1836. 8°. . . . . . . N,342
Table for prediction of. C. F. A. Shadwell. London, 1847. 8°. . N,343

Economy of Human Life. R. Dodsley. London, 1809. 16°. . . . O,467
Economy, Practical, Elements of. A. L. Perry. New York, 1866. 8°. . O,515
Eddy, D. C. Scenes in Europa. Boston, 1858. 12°. . . . . . V,388
Walter in the East. New York, 1868. 6 v. 16°. . . . . . J,1707

Vol. 1. Walter in Egypt. 2. Walter in Jerusalem. 3. Walter in Samaria. Vol. 4. Walter in Damascus. 5. Walter in Constantinople. 6. Walter in Athens.

Young Man's Friend. Boston, 1866–68. 2 v. 12°. . . . H,223
Eddystone Lighthouse, Description of. J. Smeaton. London, 1791. f°. . Q,447
Ede, G. Management of Steel. New York, 1867. 12°. . . . . M,751
Edelmann und Bauer. F. G. Kühne. Leipzig, 1850. 12°. . . . G,339
Edelweiss. B. Auerbach. Stuttgart, 1864. 12°. . . . . . E,311,22
The same; translated by E. Frothingham. Boston, 1869. 16°. G,183
Eden, E. Portraits of Princes and People of India. London, 1844. f°. . *Q,444
Eden, Sir F. M. State of the Poor in England. London, 1797. 3 v. 4°. . O,610
Edersheim, A. History of the Jewish Nation. Edinburgh, 1856. 12°. . A,205
Edgar, J. G. Boyhood of Great Men. London, 1864. 8°. . . J,1515
Crusades and the Crusaders. Boston, 1860. 16°. . . . J,1513
Footprints of Famous Men. New York, 1854. 16°. . . . . C,487
The same. London, 1864. 16°. . . . . . . J,1514
History for Boys. London, 1855. 8°. . . . . . . J,1516
War of the Roses. London, 1867. 12°. . . . . . . J,1512
Edgar, J. E. Sea Kings and Naval Heroes. New York, 1863. 16°. . J,1521
Edgar, S. Variations of Popery. New York, 1850. 8°. . . . . P,816
Edgar Clifton; or, Right and Wrong. C. Adams. New York, 1870. 12°. J,1645
Edgar Huntley; Memoirs of a Sleep-Walker. C. B. Brown. Phil. 1858. 12°. K,464
Edged Tools. S. S. Robbins. New York, 1869. 16°. . . . . J,1663
Edgeworth, M. Belinda; Modern Griselda. London, 1820. 2 v. 12°. . K,550
Frank. New York, 1854. 2 v. 16°. . . . . . . . J,1486
Harry and Lucy. London, 1858. 16°. . . . . . . J,1485
Moral Tales. New York, 1867. 2 v. 16°. . . . . . K,677
Tales and Novels. New York, n. d. 20 v. in 10. 12°. . . . K,678

Vol. 1. Castle Rackrent; Essay on Irish Bulls; Self-Justification; Moral Tales.
2. Forrester; Prussian Vase; Good Aunt.
3. Angelina; Good French Governess; Mademoiselle Panache; Knapsack.
4. Lame Jervas; The Will; Limerick Gloves; Out of Debt, Out of Danger; Lottery; Rosanna.
5. Murad, the Unlucky; The Manufacturers; Contrast; Grateful Negro; To-morrow.
6. Ennui; The Dun.
7 Maneuvering; Almeria.
8. Vivian.
9. The Absentee.
10. The Absentee; Madame de Fleury; Emilie de Coulanges; Modern Griselda.
11, 12. Belinda.
13. Leonora.
14, 15. Patronage.
16. Patronage; Comic Dramas.
17. Harrington; Thoughts on Bores.
18. Ormond.
19, 20. Helen.

and R. L. Practical Education. New York, 1849. 12°. . . . O,946
Edgeworth, R. L. Essays on Professional Education. London, 1812. 8°. O,1205
Memoirs of; by himself and his daughters. London, 1844. 8°. . D,95
Edinburgh Annual Register, 1808–18. Edinburgh, 1810–23. 12 v. in 17. 8°. T,37
Edinburgh Encyclopædia; ed. by J. Brewster. Philadelphia, 1832. 18 v. 8°. S.C.
Edinburgh High School, History of. W. Steven. Edinburgh, 1849. 8°. O,1027
Edinburgh, History of. J. Anderson. Edinburgh, 1856. 8°. . . . B,130

Edinburgh, Royal Society of, Transactions. Edinb. 1788–1853. 20 v. 4°. *F,153
Traditions of. R. Chambers. Edinburgh, 1856. 12°. . . . . B,112
Edinburgh Philosophical Journal. Edinburgh, 1819–64. 89 v. 8°. . . R,16
Edinburgh Review. Edinburgh, 1804–67. 126 v. 8°. . . . . . R,6
Indexes to the same. Edinburgh, 1813–62. 4 v. 8°. . . R,6
Selections from; edited by M. Cross. Paris, 1835. 6 v. 8°. . . H,507
Edinburgh Sessional School, Account of. J. Wood. Edinburgh, 1840. 8°. O,1034
Edison, J. S. Legitimate System of National Education. Lond. 1855. 8°. O,1055
Edith; the Backwoods Girl. L. C. Tuthill. New York, n. d. 16°. . . J,1348
Edmonds, C. R. Life and Times of Washington. Lond. 1835–6. 2 v. 16°. I,633
Edmonds, J. W. and Dexter. Spiritualism, v. 1. New York, 1853. 8°. . P,873
Edmunds, F. Traces of History in the Names of Places. Lond. 1869. 12°. L,518
Edom, Egypt, and the Holy Land. Lord A. W. C. Lindsay. Lond. 1866. p. 8°. L,115
Education, Adult, History of. J. W. Hudson. London, 1851. 8°. . O,1040
Alliance of, with Civil Government. T. W. Lancaster. Lond. 1828. 4°. Q,327
American. E. D. Mansfield. New York, 1851. 8°. . . . O,954
American Journal of. Boston, 1826–29. 4 v. 8°. . . . . . S,23
American Journal of; ed. by H. Barnard. Hartford, 1855–62. 12 v. 8°. S,26
and Educational Institutions. J. Booth. London, 1846. 8°. . O,1251,2
and Self-Formation. J. C. Heinroth. London, 1838. 12°. . O,1008
as it is, and as it ought to be. J. Bentley. Cincinnati, 1849. 12°. O,1143
as it is, and as it ought to be. B. Parsons. London, 1850. 8°. O,1251,3
Book for his Daughters on. G. de La Tour-Landry. Lond. 1868. 8°. L,605,33
Boston Schoolmasters and Mr. Mann. Boston, 1844–46. 8°. . . O,927
British. T. Sheridan. London, 1756. 8°. . . . . . O,1230
British System of. J. Lancaster. Georgetown, 1812. 12°. . O,1128
Central Society of, Papers. London, 1837–39. 3 v. 12°. . O,1191
Christian. E. Biber. London, 1830. 8°. . . . . . . O,1202
Collegiate System of the United States. F. Wayland. Bost. 1842. 16°. O,961
Contributions to the Cause of. J. Pillans. London, 1856. 8°. O,1013
Crime and. W. J. E. Bennett. London, 1846. 8°. . . . O,1251,1
Crosby-Hall Lectures on. London, 1848. 8°. . . . . . O,1240
des Filles. F. de S. de L. M. Fénélon. Paris, 1854. 12°. . H,1000
Dialogues concerning. D. Fordyce. London, 1745–48. 2 v. 8°. O,1231
Discussions on. Sir W. Hamilton. New York, 1853. 8°. . . O,705
Doctrine of. J. P. F. Richter. Boston, 1864. 12°. . . . . O,995
Early. E. Appleton. London, 1821. 12°. . . . O,1171
W. Bainbrigge. London, 1854. 16°. . . . . . O,1124
Elementary Principles of. J. G. Spurzheim. London, 1828. 8°. O,1242
The same. New York, 1854. 12°. . . . . . . . O,972
English, German Letters on. L. Wiese. London, 1854. 16°. . O,1169
English Journal of. London, 1847–54. 8 v. 8°. . . . . . S,56
English University. W. Whewell. London, 1838. 8°. . . . O,924
Essay on. C. Atwater. Cincinnati, 1841. 8°. . . . . . O,1199
W. Barrow. London, 1802. 2 v. 12°. . . . . . . O,917
J. W. Parsons. London, 1794. 16°. . . . . . O,1152
Experimental. Cheltenham, 1843. 12°. . . . . . . O,1030
Female, Plan for. E. Darwin. Derby, 1797. 4°. . . . O,1269
Remarks on. A. E. Pendered. London, 1826. 12°. . O,1139
Strictures on. H. More. London, 1799. 2 v. 8°. . O,1196

Education, Fibel; erster Unter. im Denken., etc. K.A.Zoller. Reut.'43. 2v. 12°. o,888
for the People. H. Tuckfield. London, 1839. 16°. . . . . o,990
Hints on Forming Character. H. More. London, 1809. 2 v. 12°. o,1233
History and Plan of. H. Schmidt. New York, 1855. 18°. . . L,442
of Adult. J. W. Hudson. London, 1851. 8°. . . o,1040
Home. I. Taylor. New York, 1838. 12°. . . . . . . o,920
Household. H. Martineau. Philadelphia, 1849. 12°. . . o,1006
Improvements in. J. Lancaster. London, 1806. 8°. . . . o,925
in England. W. H. Teale. Oxford, 1850. 8°. . . . . . o,1251
and Europe. J. Kay. London, 1850. 2 v. 12°. . . . o,536
in Great Britain in 1851. H. Mann. London, 1854. 8°. . o,1239
Infant, Remarks on. C. and E. Mayo. London, 1849. 16°. . o,1161
Infant-School. J. Currie. Edinburgh, n. d. p. 8°. . . . o,1001
Infant-School Teachers, Model Lessons for. London, 1853. 12°. o,1119
Intellectual, Moral, and Physical. H. Spencer. New York, 1866. 12°. o,953
Practical Essay on. W. Jacques. London, 1817. 8°. . o,1183
its Nature, Import, and Necessity. J. Jenkins. London, 1848. 16°. o,1167
Journal of, for Upper Canada, v. 1, 2, 6. Tor. 1848. 3 v. 8° and 4°. T,60
Lectures on. Boston, 1831. 12°. . . . . . . . . o,1213
London, 1854. 8°. . . . . . . . . o,1177
G. Brewster. Columbus, 1833. 8°. . . . . . . o,926
H. Mann. Boston, 1848. 12°. . . . . . . . o,942
and Reports on. H. Mann. Cambridge, 1867. 2 v. 8°. . o,977
Lessons for Elementary Schools. G. Sydenham. Lond. 1857. 12°. o,1155
Letters on. Madame de Genlis. London, 1788. 3 v. 16°. . o,1162
C. M. Graham. London, 1790. 8°. . . . . . o,1038
E. Hamilton. Boston, 1825. 2 v. 12°. . . . . o,1195
Liberal. V. Knox. London, 1781. 12°. . . . . . . o,911
W. Whewell. London, 1850. 8°. . . . . . . . o,910
Observations upon. G. Turnbull. London, 1742. . . o,1184
Practical Essay on. J. W. Donaldson. Cambridge, 1856. 12°. o,833
Loose Hints upon. H. Home, *Lord Kames*. Edinburgh, 1782. 8°. o,1185
Minutes of Council on. London, 1840–57. 34 v. 8°. . . o,1058
Miscellaneous Papers on. London, 1841. 8°. . . . . .
Modern Theme, The. London, 1847. 12°. . . . . . . P,349
Moral. J. P. Potter. London, 1821. 12°. . . . . . o,1133
Moral and Intellectual. Mad. Bureaud Riofrey. London, 1843. 8°. o,1238
Moral and Religious. G. C. Crum. Cincinnati, 1851. 8°. . H,302,4
National. J. Dufton. London, 1847. 8°. . . . . . . o,1251,2
F. Hill. London, 1836. 2 v. 12°. . . . o,1031
O. De B. Priaulx. London, 1842. 8°. . . . o,1201
Chapters on. R. M. Macbrair. London, 1845. 8°. . o,1251,1
in Europe. H. Barnard. Hartford, 1854. 8°. . . o,1237
Lectures on. F. D. Maurice. London, 1839. 12°. . . o,1029
Legitimate System of. J. S. Edison. London, 1855. 8°. o,1055
Letter on. T. Page. London, 1843. 16°. . . . o,1163
Papers on. London, 1850. 16°. . . . . . . o,989
Outline of a System of. London, 1834. 12°. . . . . o,909
Observations relating to. J. Priestley. Bath, 1778. 8°. . . . o,955
of Children. J. Witherspoon. Andover, 1817. 12°. . . o,1157

Education of Girls, and Employment of Women. W.B.Hodgson. Lon.1869. 12°. o,458
of Mothers of Families. L. A. Martin. London, 1851. 8°. . . o,923
of the People. J. Willm. Glasgow, 1847. 8°. . . . . . o,919
in England. J. Kay. New York, 1863. 12°. . . . o,376
of India. C. E. Trevelyan. London, 1838. 12°. . . . o,921
of the Poor in England and Europe. J. Kay. London, 1846. 8°. o,1015
of the Young. S. Wilderspin. London, 1840. 16°. . . . . o,991
Ohio Journal of. Columbus, 1852-59. 8 v. 8°. . . . . . s,25
Philosophical Outlines of. G. Jardine. Glasgow, 1818. 8°. . o,1052
Philosophy of. J. Antrobus. London, 1850. 8°. . . . . . o,928
J. Simpson. Edinburgh, 1836. 8°. . . . . . . o,1175
T. Tate. London, 1854. 8°. . . . . . . . o,1218
Popular. I. Mayhew. New York, 1850. 12°. . . . . . . o,951
an Antidote for Crime. T. and F. Bullock. Lond. 1849. 12°. o,1126
First Principles of. S. S. Randall. New York, 1868. 12°. . o,975
Institutions of. R. W. Hamilton. Leeds, 1846. 8°. . o,1035
Lectures and Letters on. R. Sullivan. Dublin, 1842. 12°. o,1024
Lectures on. G. Combe. Edinburgh, 1848. 8°. . . o,1251,1
Observations on. H. Brougham. Boston, 1826. 8°. . o,1251,2
Practical. M. and R. L. Edgeworth. New York, 1849. 12°. . . o,946
Essays on. T. Markby. London, 1868. 12°. . . . . o,936
Importance of. E. Everett. New York, 1854. 12°. . . o,937
Principles of. London, 1854. 12°. . . . . . . . o,1145
L. Carpenter. London, 1820. 8°. . . . . . o,1051
W. Newnham. London, 1827. 2 v. 8°. . . . o,1241
E. M. Sewell. London, 1865. 2 v. 12°. . . . o,935
M. A. Stodart. London, 1844. 16°. . . . o,1026
and Practice of Common-School. J. Currie. Edinb. 1869. 12°. o,971
Private. E. Appleton. London, 1816. 12°. . . . . . o,1025
Professional, Essays on. R. L. Edgeworth. London, 1812. 8°. o,1205
promoted by Freedom. E. Baines. London, 1854. 8°. . . o,1251,1
Public. Sir J. K. Shuttleworth. London, 1853. 8°. . . o,1050
Discourses on. C. Wordsworth. London, 1844. 12°. . o,1037
Quarterly Journal of, v. 5-10. London, 1832-35. 6 v. 8°. . . s,44
Question, History of the. London, 1850. 8°. . . . . . o,1198
Reform in. T. Wyse. v. 1. London, 1836. 8°. . . . . o,929
Religious, Colloquies on. London, 1837. 8°. . . . . . P,215
Remarks on. R. Rantoul, jr. Boston, 1838. 8°. . . . . . o,927
School. J. Pycroft. Oxford, 1843. 12°. . . . . . . . o,996
Science of; Art of Teaching. J. Ogden. Cincinnati, 1859. 12°. . o,948
Self. J. M. Degerando. Boston, 1860. 12°. . . . . . o,978
W. Robinson. London, 1845. 16°. . . . . . . o,1120
Sketch of a Plan of. J. Neef. Philadelphia, 1808. 12°. . . . o,913
Spirit and Scope of. J. A. Stapf. Edinburgh, 1851. 8°. . . o,1172
State. B. Powell. London, 1840. 8°. . . . . . . o,1251,2
Rationalism in. H. Formby. Dublin, 1854. 8°. . . o,1251,2
Systematic. L. Carpenter and others. London, 1815. 2 v. 8°. o,1207
Systematic Technical. J. S. Russell. London, 1869. 8°. . . o,1018
Teachers' and Parents' Manual of. W. P. Lyon. N. Y. 1848. 18°. o,1113
Theologically considered. D. P. M. Hulbert. London, 1850. . o,1174

Education, Theory and Practice of, Notes of Lessons. J. Jones. Lon. 1856. 12°. O,1131
Thoughts on. G. Burnet. London, 1761. 16°. . . . . . O,1136
J. Locke. London, 1693. 8°. . . . . . . . . O,916
The same. London, 1836. 16°. . . . . . . O,992
A. S. Semple. London, 1812. 12°. . . . . . . O,1179
Wayside Thoughts on. D'A. W. Thompson. Edinburgh, 1868. 8°. O,976
Educational and Literary Journal, Scottish, v. 1. Edinburgh, 1853. 8°. . T,42
Educational Course. W. and R. Chambers. Edinburgh, 1852. 16°. . O,1153
Educational Essays. S. Skinner. London, 1844. 8°. . . . . . O,1217
E. Thomson. Cincinnati, 1856. 12°. . . . . . O,1178
Educational Expositor, v. 2. London, 1854. 8°. . . . . . . O,1255
Educational Institutions of the U. S. P. A. Siljeström. London, 1853. 12°. O,811
of Germany. G. P. R. James. London, 1835. 8°. . . . . O,1036
Educational Lectures at St. Martin's Hall. London, 1855. 16°. . . O,1020
Educational Reminiscences. London, 1838. 8°. . . . . . . O,1130
Educator, The. London, 1854. 2 v. 8°. . . . . . . . O,1189
Popular. London, 1853. 2 v. 4°. . . . . . . . . O,851
Edward the Confessor, Lives of. London, 1858. 8°. . . . . . W,153
Edward I., Year-Books of the Reign of. London, 1863–66. 3 v. 8°. . W,181
La Estoire de Seint Aedward le Rei.
Vita Beati Edvardi Regis et Confessoris.
Vita Æduuardi Regis qui apud Westmonasterium requiescit.
Edward VI., Mary, and Elizabeth, Reigns of. S. Turner. Lond. 1829. 2 v. 8°. A,434,11,12
Edward, D. B. History of Texas. Cincinnati, 1836. 12°. . . . . C,163
Edwards, A. B. Archie Lovell. Leipzig, 1867. 2 v. in 1. 16°. . . J,154
Barbara's History. New York, 1868. 8°. . . . . . . . K,679
The same. Leipzig, 1864. 2 v. in 1. 16°. . . . . J,155
Debenham's Vow. Leipzig, 1870. 2 v. in 1. 16°. . . . . J,156
Half a Million of Money. New York, 1866. 8°. . . . . K,680
The same. Leipzig, 1865. 2 v. in 1. 16°. . . . . J,157
Hand and Glove. New York, 1866. 8°. . . . . . . . K,685
The same. Leipzig, 1865. 16°. . . . . . . . J,158
Ladder of Life. New York, 1865. 8°. . . . . . . . K,681
Miss Carew. New York, n. d. 8°. . . . . . . . . K,682
The same. Leipzig, 1865. 2 v. in 1. 16°. . . . . J,159
My Brother's Wife. New York, n. d. 8°. . . . . . . K,684
Ordeal for Wives. London, 1865. 3 v. 12°. . . . . . J,564
Steven Lawrence, Yeoman. Leipzig, 1869. 2 v. in 1. 16°. . . J,160
Story of Cervantes. London, 1863. 16°. . . . . . . J,1202
Susan Fielding. New York, n. d. 8°. . . . . . . . K,687
Edwards, B. B. Biography of Self-taught Men. Boston, n. d. 12°. . . C,515
Memoir of Elias Cornelius. Boston, 1834. 12°. . . . . . C,750
Writings; Memoir by E. A. Park. Boston, 1853. 2 v. 12°. . . C,808
and others, Classical Studies. Boston, 1843. 12°. . . . . . L,549
Edwards, C. History and Poetry of Finger-Rings. New York, 1855. 12°. H,193
Pleasantries about Courts and Lawyers. New York, 1867. 8°. . H,509
Edwards, E. Free Town Libraries. London, 1869. 8°. . . . . . L.R.
Life of Sir Walter Raleigh. London, 1868. 2 v. 8°. . . . . D,453
Memoirs of Libraries. London, 1859. 2 v. 8°. . . . . . L.R.
Edwards, F. E. Eocene Mollusca, pts. 1, 2, 3. London, 1849–52. 3 pts. 4°. Q,15
The same, pt. 3, no. 2. London, 1856. 4°. . . . . . Q,30

Edwards, H. B. Punjab Frontier, 1848–49. London, 1851. 2 v. 8°. . V,697
Edwards, H. M., and Haime, J. British Fossil Corals. Lond. 1850–54. 4°. Q,34,1
Edwards, H. S. Life of Rossini. London, 1869. 8°. . . . . . . D,708
Edwards, J. History of the Work of Redemption. Worcester, 1808. 8°. . P,257
The same. New York, n. d. 18°. . . . . . . P,746,4
Life of. S. Miller. New York, 1860. 16°. . . . . . C,860,8
Life of David Brainerd. New York, n. d. 18°. . . . P,746,7
Treatise on Religious Affections. New York, n. d. 18°. . . P,746,3
Works. New York, 1856. 4 v. 8°. . . . . . . . . . P,727
Edwards, M. B. Doctor Jacob. Boston, 1869. 16°. . . . . . . K,686
Edwards, S. History of the Opera. London, 1862. 2 v. 12°. . . . M,408
Edwards, T. Canons of Criticism. London, 1752. 12°. . . . . . I,866
Edwin Brothertoft. T. Winthrop. Boston, 1865. 12°. . . . . . K,401
Edwin Drood, Mystery of. C. Dickens. New York, 1871. 16°. . . . K,521
Edwin the Fair. H. Taylor. London, 1864. 16°. . . . . . I,445,2
Edwin of Deira; a Poem. A. Smith. Boston, 1861. 16°. . . . . I,426
Egeria. W. G. Simms. Philadelphia, 1853. 12°. . . . . . . H,265
Eginhard, or Einhard. Œuvres. Paris, 1856. 12°. . . . . . . H,995
Egloffstein, F.W. v. Geology and Physical Geography of Mexico. N.Y.1864. 8°. N,751
Egypt, Ancient and Modern. M. Russell. New York, 1854. 18°. . . L,356
The same. London, 1857. 12°. . . . . . . . . V,792
Ancient Egypt under the Pharaohs. J. Kenrick. N. Y. 1852. 2 v. 12°. V,791
and the Books of Moses. E. W. Hengstenberg. Edinb. 1845. 8°. . P,242
and Constantinople, Harem Life in. E. Lott. Lond. 1866. 2 v. 12°. V,788
and India, Route through, to England. G. Fitzclarence. Lond. 1819. 4°. V,721
and Nubia. J. A. St. John. London, 1845. 8°. . . . . . V,845
Operations and Discoveries in. G. B. Belzoni. Lond. 1821. 4°. V,873
Assyria, and Persia, Histories of. J. Eadie. London, 1852. 8°. . A,22
Constantinople, the Crimea, etc., Visit to. T. Grey. N. Y. 1870. 12°. V,777
Daleth; Homestead of the Nations. E. L. Clark. Boston, 1864. 8°. V,868
Edom, and the Holy Land, Letters on. Lord Lindsay. Lond. 1858. p. 8°. L,115
Ethiopia, and Sinai, Letters from. R. Lepsius. London, 1853. p. 8°. L,16
Englishwoman in. S. Poole. London, 1851–53. 3 v. in 1. 24°. . V,768
Glimpses of the Land of. W. H. Bartlett. London, n. d. 4°. . . V,846
History of. S. Sharpe. London, 1842. 8°. . . . . . . V,756
The same. London, 1846. 8°. . . . . . . . . . V,848
Holy Land, and Italy, Visit to. I. Pfeiffer. London, 1853. 12°. V,1044
Letters from. N. C. Burt. Cincinnati, 1868. 12°. . . . . . V,638
Mehemed Ali's Reich. H. L. H. v. Pückler-Muskau. Stutt. 1844. 3 v. 16°. E,225
Monumental History of. W. Osburn. London, 1854. 2 v. 8°. . V,818
Monuments of. C. Forster. London, 1851–54. 3 v. 8°. . . L,530,2
Mountains of. F. L. Hawks. New York, 1850. 2 v. 8°. . . V,797
Observations in. J. P. Durbin. New York, 1854. 2 v. 12°. . V,1058
Pilgrimage to. I. F. Romer. London, 1846. 2 v. 8°. . . . V,675
J. V. C. Smith. Boston, 1859. 12°. . . . . . . . V,782
Place of, in Universal History. C. C. J. Bunsen. Lond. 1859–66. 5 v. 8°. V,849
Reise in Aegypten. V. Denon. Berlin, 1803. 8°. . . . . E,226
3300 Years ago. F. de Lanoye. New York, 1870. 12°. . . M,1056
Travels in. R. F. A. de Chateaubriand. London, 1812. 2 v. 8°. V,1083
B. Dorr. Philadelphia, 1856. 12°. . . . . . . V,1042

Egypt, Travels in. C. N. S. Sonnini de Manoncourt. London, 1800. 4°. . Q,431
F. L. Norden. London, 1757. 8°. . . . . . . . V,844
S. Olin. New York, 1851. 2 v. 12°. . . . . . V,1057
E. Warburton. Philadelphia, 1859. 8°. . . . . . V,830
under Mehemet Ali. H. L. H. v. Pückler-Muskau. Lond. 1845. 2 v. 12°. V,780
Village Life in. B. St. John. Boston, 1853. 2 v. 16°. . . . V,773
Egyptian Antiquities, British Museum. G. Long. Lond. 1832–36. 2 v. 16°. L,474
Egyptians, Ancient, Popular Account of. Sir J. G. Wilkinson. N.Y. 1854. 2 v. 12°. V,775
Modern, Manners and Customs of. E. W. Lane. Lond. 1836–37. 2 v. 16°. L,480
The same. London, 1842. 2 v. 8°. . . . . . . V,871
The same, abridged. London, 1846. 3 v. in 1. 16°. . . V,769
Ehrenberg, C. G. Das Leuchten des Meeres. Berlin, 1835. 4°. . N,252,43
Ehoron, F. Théorie des Atomes. Paris, 1837. 8°. . . . . N,252,4
Eichendorff, J. F. von. Sämmtliche Werke. Leipzig, 1864. 6 v. 16°. . E,319

Bd. 1. Leben; Gedichte.
2. Ahnung und Gegenwart; Dichter und ihre Gesellen.
3. Aus dem Leben eines Taugenichts; Das Marmorbild; Viel Lärmen um Nichts; Eine Meerfahrt, 1835; Das Schloss Dürande; Die Entführung; Die Glücksritter; Libertas und ihr Freier; Julian, Robert und Guiscard; Lucius.
4. Krieg den Philistern!; Meierbeth's Glück und Ende; Ezelin von Romano; Der letzte Held von Marienburg; Die Freier.
5. Das grosze Welttheater; Gift und Gegengift; König Ferdinand der Heilige; Das Schiff des Kaufmanns; Balthasars Nachtmahl; Der Göttliche Orpheus; Der Maler seiner Schande.
6. Die eherne Schlange; Amor und Psyche; Der Waldesdemuth Krone; Der Sünde Zauberei; Der Graf Lucanor von Don Juan Manuel

Eichwald, E. Caspische Meer und Caucasus, 1825–26. Stutt. 1834–37. 2 v. 8°. E,217
Eighteen Christian Centuries. J. White. Edinburgh, 1859. 8°. . . A,320
Eighty Years' Progress of the United States. New York, 1864. 8°. . . B,667
Eisenlohr, W. Lehrbuch der Physik. Stuttgart, 1852. 8°. . . . G,721
Eisenmann, G. Friedrichshaller Bitterwasser. Erlangen, 1847. 16°. N,252,37
Ekkoes from Kentucky. D. R. Locke. Boston, 1868. 12°. . . . H,70
Elaine. A. Tennyson; illustrated by G. Doré. London, 1867. f°. . *Q,241
Elam, C. Physician's Problems. Boston, 1869. 12°. . . . . . L,870
Elder, W. Biography of E. K. Kane. Philadelphia, 1858. 8°. . . . S.C.
Eldon, J. *Lord*, Life of. H. Twiss. Philadelphia, 1844. 2 v. 8°. . . D,298
Eldorado, California, and Mexico. B. Taylor. New York, 1865. 12°. . V,35
Eleanor's Victory. M. E. Braddon. Leipzig, 1863. 2 v. in 1. 16°. . . J,37
Electric Telegraph. See *Telegraph, Electric.*
Electrical Action, New View of. R. Laming. London, 1858. 8°. . N,252,46
Electricity. R. M. Ferguson. London, 1867. 16°. . . . . . . N,47
and the Electric Telegraph. G. Wilson. London, 1862. p. 8°. . I,666
Archives de l'Electricité. A. de La Rive. Paris, 1844. 8°. . N,252,55
Elektrische Polarisation. C. F. Schönbein. Basil, 1838. 8°. . N,252,1
der Galvanischen Kette. F. C. Henrici. Göttingen, 1840. 8°. N,252,8
Elements of. A. Bain. New York, 1849. 12°. . . . . N,168
W. J. Rolfe and J. A. Gillet. Boston, 1868. 12°. . . . N,228
Frictional, Treatise on. Sir W. S. Harris. London, 1867. 8°. . N,54
Inductions Elektricität. H. W. Dove. Berlin, 1842. 4°. . . N,252,43
Magnetism and Meteorology. D. Lardner. London, 1841. 2 v. 12°. M,1027
Magnetismus und Chemismus. G. F. Pohl. Berlin, 1829. 12°. N,252,23
Elektricität, etc. C. H. Schmidt. Leipzig, n. d. 12°. . N,252,23
Manual of. H. M. Noad. London, 1859. 8°. . . . . . . N,52
Phénomènes Electriques des Animaux. C. Matteucci. Paris, 1840. 8°. N,252,8

Electricity, Rudimentary. Sir W. S. Harris. London, 1848. 16°. . N,252,36
The same, 4th edition. London, 1854. 12°. . . . . . M,932
Student's Text-Book of. H. M. Noad. London, 1867. 8°. . . N,49
Treatise on. A. de La Rive. London, 1853-58. 3 v. 8°. . . N,51
Telegraphy and Magnetism, Questions on. W. McGregor. Lon. 1868. 12°. M,850
und Magnetismus. F. Eydam. Weimar, 1843. 8°. . . . N,252,8
Electro-Chemistry, Manipulations en. A. Brandely. Paris, 1848. 8°. N,252,34
Electro-Metallurgy. A. Watt. London, 1869. 12°. . . . . . M,861
Manual of. J. Napier. London, 1852. 12°. . . . . . M,752
Electro-Physiology. G. Huff. New York, 1852. 12°. . . . . L,888
Electron; a Telegraphic Epic. W. C. Richards. New York, 1858. 12°. . I,115
Electrotype Manipulation. C. V. Walker. London, 1841. 16°. . N,252,36
Elephant Club. M. Thomson. Philadelphia, n. d. 12°. . . . . K,348
Elephant, Natural History of. New York, 1855. 18°. . . . . . L,448
The Wild, in Ceylon. Sir J. E. Tennent. London, 1867. 16°. . . N,681
Elephants, Natural History of. Sir W. Jardine. Edinburgh, 1837. 16°. N,470,23
El Fureidis. M. S. Cummins. Boston, 1861. 12°. . . . . . . K,90
Elgin Marbles; with Account of Athens. E. I. Burrow. London, 1837. 8°. M,79
Elgin and Phigaleian Marbles, British Museum. Sir H. Ellis. Lond. 1833. 2 v. 16°. L,475
El Gringo; or, New Mexico. W. W. H. Davis. New York, 1857. 12°. . V,33
Elia, Essays of. C. Lamb. New York, 1859. 12°. . . . . . H,476
and Eliana. C. Lamb. Leipzig, 1869. 16°. . . . . . . J,252
Elijah the Tishbite. F. W. Krummacher. New York, n. d. 18°. . P,746,17
Eliot, C. W. and Storer, F. H. Manual of Inorganic Chemistry. N.Y. 1868. 8°. N,221
Eliot, George, *pseud.* See *Lewes, M. J.*
Eliot, J., Life of. N. Adams. Boston, 1870. 12°. . . . . . D,8,3
Life of. C. Francis. New York. 16°. . . . . . C,860,5
Progress of the Gospel among the Indians. Boston, 1868. 4°. . . B,583
Eliot, S. History of Liberty, Ancient Romans. Boston, 1853. 2 v. 12°. . A,155
History of Liberty, Early Christians. Boston, 1853. 2 v. 8°. . . P,400
Liberty of Rome. New York, 1849. 2 v. 8°. . . . . . . A,180
Eliot, W. G., jr. Lectures to Young Men. Boston, 1856. 12°. . . . H,263
Eliza Wharton; or, the Coquette. H. Foster. Philadelphia, 1866. 12°. . K,154
Elizabeth, Charlotte, *pseud.* See *Tonna, C. E.*
Elizabeth; or, Exiles of Siberia. Mad. Cottin. Philadelphia, 1868. 12°. . H,951
Elizabeth, Queen of England, and her Times. T. Wright. Lond. 1838. 2 v. 8°. D,356
Memoirs of the Court of. L. Aikin. London, 1819. 2 v. 8°. . A,501
History of. J. Abbott. New York, 1849. 16°. . . . . J,1389
Memoirs of. A. Strickland. Philadelphia, 1853. 8°. . . . D,203
Debates in Reign of. Sir S. D'Ewes. London, 1708. f°. . . F,295
Two Plays on the Life of. T. Heywood. London, 1851. 8°. . I,885,48
Elizabeth, Story of. A. I. Thackeray. Philadelphia, n. d. 12°. . K,1034
Elm Island Stories. E. Kellogg. Boston, 1869-71. 6 v. 16°. . . J,1473

Vol. 1. Lion Ben.
2. Charlie Bell.
3. Ark of Elm Island.
Vol. 4. Boy Farmers of Elm Island.
5. Young Ship-Builders.
6. Hard-Scrabble.

Ella of Garveloch. H. Martineau. London, 1859. 16°. . . . K,551,2
Ella; or, Turning over a New Leaf. W. Simonds. Boston, 1858. 16°. J,1431,3
Ellen Middleton. G. Fullerton. Leipzig, 1846. 16°. . . . . J,167

Ellen Montgomery's Book-Shelf. S. and A. B. Warner. N. Y. 1868. 16°. J,1423
Vol. 1. Mr. Rutherford's Children. Vol. 3. Hard Maple.
2. Sybil and Chryssa. 4. Karl Krinken.
Vol. 5. Casper and his Friends.

Ellenberger, J. L. Course of Arithmetic. London, 1854. 8°. . . M,1089
Ellery, W., Life of. E. T. Channing. New York, 1860. 12°. . . C,860,6
Ellet, C., jr. Mississippi and Ohio Rivers. Philadelphia, 1853. 8°. . . C,278
Ellet, E. F. Characters of Schiller. Boston, 1842. 12°. . . . . H,745
Domestic History of the American Revolution. New York, 1851. 12°. B,744
Family Pictures from the Bible. New York, 1849. 12°. . . . . P,136
Nouvellettes of the Musicians. New York, 1851. 12°. . . . K,697
Pioneer Women of the West. New York, 1852. 12°. . . . C,651
Queens of American Society. New York, 1868. 12°. . . . C,768
Rambles about the Country. New York, 1854. 16°. . . . H,184
Women Artists in all Ages. New York, 1859. 12°. . . . M,12
Women of the American Revolution. New York, 1852–54. 3 v. 12°. C,653
Elliot, J. Debates on Adoption of Federal Constitution. Phila. 1859. 5 v. 8°. O,427
Elliott, A. Forest, Jungle, and Prairie. London, 1868. 8°. . . . J,1151
Playground and the Parlor. London, 1868. 8°. . . . . M,341
Elliott, C. Delineations of Roman Catholicism. New York, n. d. 2 v. 8°. P,818
Elliott, C. B. Travels in Austria, Russia, etc. Philadelphia, 1839. 2 v. 12°. V,339
Elliott, C. W. New-England History. New York, 1857. 2 v. 8°. . . C,7
Elliott, E. N. Cotton is King; Pro-Slavery Arguments. Augusta, 1860. 8°. O,609
Elliott, F. R. Fruit Book. New York, 1859. 12°. . . . . . M,556
Elliptic Integrals, Theory of. J. Booth. London, 1851. 8°. . . M,1152
Ellis, A. J. Carliz Hous. Lundun, 1848. 18°. . . . . . . . L,672
Early English Pronunciation. London, 1867–69. 2 v. 8°. . L,604,2,7
Ferst Ideaz ov Relijun. Lundun, 1849. 18°. . . . . . . L,673
Fonetic Almanac, 1849, 51, 52. Lundun, 1849–52. 32°. . . . L,661
Fonetic Frend; a Munthli Jurnal. Lundun, 1850. 12°. . . . L,715
Romanic Ecsersizez. Lundun, 1849. 18°. . . . . . . L,672
Romanic Redin ecspland. Lundun, 1849. 18°. . . . . . L,672
Techerz Gid to the Fonetic Primer. Lundun, 1848. 18°. . . . L,673
Ellis, G. Early English Metrical Romances. London, 1805. 3 v. 12°. . H,699
The same. London, 1848. p. 8°. . . . . . . . L,8
Specimens of the Early English Poets. London, 1803. 3 v. 8°. . I,347
Ellis, G. A. Inquiries respecting Earl Clarendon. London, 1827. 12°. B,115
Ellis, G. E. Half-Century of the Unitarian Controversy. Boston, 1857. 8°. P,872
Life of J. Mason. Boston, 1860. 16°. . . . . . . C,860,13
of Anne Hutchinson. Boston, 1860. 12°. . . . C,860,16
of William Penn. Boston, 1860. 12° . . . . . C,860,22
Ellis, Sir H. Elgin and Phigaleian Marbles. London, 1833. 2 v. 16°. . L,475
Townley Gallery, British Museum. London, 1836. 2 v. 16°. . . L,490
Original Letters in English History. London, 1824–46. 11 v. 8°. B,2
Ellis, G. J. W. A. *Lord Dover*. Life of Frederick II. London, 1832. 2 v. 8°. D,529
The same. New York, 1855. 2 v. 18°. . . . . . . L,370
Ellis, S. S. Family Secrets. London, n. d. 3 v. 8°. . . . . . K,1037
First Impressions. New York, 1854. 16°. . . . . . . J,1180
Guide to Social Happiness. New York, n. d. 8°. . . . . . H,510
Minister's Family. New York, 1852. 18°. . . . . . . J,1194
Mothers of England. New York, 1844. 12°. . . . . . . H,471

Ellis, S. S. Prevention better than Cure. London, n. d. 12°. . . . O,389
Pictures of Private Life. London, 1868. 3 v. 16°. . . . K,918
Temper and Temperament. New York, 1846. 12°. . . . . K,698
Ellis, W. Madagascar revisited. London, 1867. 8°. . . . . V,863
Polynesian Researches. London, 1859. 4 v. 16°. . . . . V,874
Three Visits to Madagascar. New York, 1859. 8°. . . . . V,855
Tour through Hawaii. London, 1827. 8°. . . . . . . V,885
Ellis Bell *pseud.* See *Brontë, E.*
Elliston, R. W., Life and Enterprises of. G. Raymond. Lond. 1857. 12°. D,226
Ellsworth, H. W. Book-Keeping and Business Manual. N. Y. 1868. 16°. M,1164
Ellsworth, O., Life of. H. Flanders. Philadelphia, 1855. 8°. . . C,816,2
Life of. G. Van Santvoord. New York, 1854. 8°. . . . . C,817
Elocution, Art of. G. Vandenhoff. London, 1862. 12°. . . . . L,603
The same. New York, 1851. 12°. . . . . . . . L,600
and Reading. A. T. Randall. New York, 1870. 12°. . . . O,1244
and Rhetorical Gesture. J. Weaver. Philadelphia, 1846. 12°. . L,591
and Vocal Culture. R. Kidd. Cincinnati, n. d. 12°. . . . O,1249
Discourse on. D. Mac Leod. Cincinnati, 1855. 8°. . . . . T,19,2
Essay on. S. Kirkham. New York, 1865. 12°. . . . O,1226
Orthophony; or, Cultivation of the Voice. W. Russell. Bost. 1857. 12°. L,599
Elocutionist, Practical. J. W. S. Hows. Philadelphia, n. d. 12°. . O,1225
Eloquence, American; edited by F. Moore. New York, 1857. 2 v. 8°. . H,824
Clay Code; Text-Book of. H. Clay. New York, 1844. 12°. . . O,825
Essai sur l'Eloquence de la Chaire. J. S. Maury. Paris, 1850. 12°. H,870
Principles of. J. S. Maury. New York, 1857. 18°. . . . L,465
Elphinstone, M. History of India. London, 1866. 8°. . . . . . C,415
Kingdom of Caubul. London, 1839. 2 v. 8°. . . . . . . C,407
Elsie Venner. O. W. Holmes. Boston, 1867. 2 v. 16°. . . . . K,195
Elster's Folly. Mrs. H. Wood. Leipzig, 1866. 2 v. in 1. 16°. . . . J,520
Elton, C. A. History of the Roman Emperors. London, 1825. 12°. . . A,134
Elton, J. F. With the French in Mexico. London, 1867. 8°. . . . C,373
Elwin, F. H. Mens Corporis; the Mind in Sleep. London, 1843. 12°. . O,650
Ely, A. Journal of a Prisoner at Richmond. New York, 1862. 12°. . B,926
Elwyn, A. L. Glossary of supposed Americanisms. Philadelphia, 1859. 12°. L.R.
Emancipation, Results of. A. Cochin. Boston, 1863. 12°. . . . . O,391
Emancipation; a Tale. M. M. Sherwood. New York, 1860. 12°. . K,1008,5
Emanuel, H. Diamonds and Precious Stones. London, 1867. 12°. . . N,854
Embanking Lands from the Sea. J. Wiggins. London, 1852. 12°. . . M,974
Emblems, Divine and Moral. F. Quarles. London, 1859. 12°. . . . P,201
Embury, E. C. Pictures of Early Life. New York, 1854. 16°. . . . J,1200
Emerson, B. D. First-Class Reader. Philadelphia, 1839. 12°. . . . O,890
Emerson, G. B. School and Schoolmaster. New York, 1854. 12°. . . O,823
Trees and Shrubs of Massachusetts. Boston, 1846. 8°. . . N,1017
Emerson, R. W. Complete Works. London, 1868–70. 2 v. p. 8°. . . L,179
Vol. 1. Essays; New-England Reformers; Representative Men; Poems.
2. English Traits; Nature; Miscellanies; Conduct of Life.
Conduct of Life. Boston, 1861. 16°. . . . . . . . H,99
English Traits. Boston, 1865. 16°. . . . . . . . . H,103
Essays. Boston, 1866. 2 v. 12°. . . . . . . . . H,101
May Day, and other Pieces. Boston, 1867. 16°. . . . . . I,32

Emerson, R. W. Miscellanies. Boston, 1865. 16°. . . . . . . H,104
Representative Men. Boston, 1864. 12°. . . . . . . . H,105
Society and Solitude. Boston, 1870. 12°. . . . . . . . H,106
and others. Memoirs of M. F. Ossoli. New York, 1869. 2 v. 12°. U,96
Emerson, W. D. Occasional Thoughts in Verse. Springfield, 1851. 8°. . I,45
Emigrant. Sir F. B. Head. London, 1846. 8°. . . . . . . . H,314
Emigrants, Hints to. London, 1866. 12°. . . . . . . . . M,836
Emigrate, Where and why to. F. B. Goddard. Philadelphia, 1869. 8°. V,132
Emile; or, de l' Education. J. J. Rousseau. Paris, 1851. 18°. . . O,967
Emilia Galotti; a Tragedy. G. E. Lessing. Leipzig, 1868. 12°. . . G,39
Emilia Wyndham. A. Marsh-Caldwell. Leipzig, 1852. 2 v. in 1. 16°. . J,366
Emilius and Sophia. J. J. Rousseau. London, 1783. 4 v. 12°. . . O,912
Emily Chester. A. M. C. Seemuller. Boston, 1867. 12°. . . . . K,87
Eminent Americans. B. J. Lossing. New York, 1857. 8°. . . . . C,981
Eminent Men and Popular Books. London, 1859. 16°. . . . . . H,589
Emma; a Novel. J. Austen. Boston, 1864. 12°. . . . . . . K,593
Emmens, S. H. Treatise on Logic. London, 1865. 12°. . . . . . M,837
Emmons, E. Agriculture of New York. Albany, 1846–54. 5 v. 4°. *Q,101,15–19
Geology of New York. Albany, 1842. 4°. . . . . . *Q,101,10
Manual of Geology. Philadelphia, 1860. 12°. . . . . . . N,784
Emmons, N. Works, with Memoir by E. A. Park. Boston, 1860–63. 6 v. 8°. P,728
Emory, J., Life of. R. Emory. New York, 1841. 8°. . . . . . C,795
Emory, W. H. Military Reconnoissance to San Diego. Wash. 1848. 8°. . V,67
United States and Mexican Boundary Survey. Wash. 1857–58. 3 v. 4°. *Q,144
Emotions and the Will. A. Bain. London, 1859. 8°. . . . . . O,687
Empress Josephine. C. Mundt. New York, 1867. 8°. . . . . . G,198
Empires, Origin of. Sir W. Drummond. London, 1824–29. 4 v. 8°. . A,110
Enchiridion. F. Quarles. London, 1856. 16°. . . . . . . . P,29
Encke, J. F. Berechnung der Planetenstörungen. Berlin, 1851. 8°. . G,779
Encyclopædia. W. and R. Chambers. Philadelphia, 1865. 10 v. 8°. . L.R.
Allgemeine Weltkunde. J. G. A. Galletti. Leipzig, 1854. 4°. . E,207
Americana. Boston, 1853. 14 v. 8°. . . . . . . . . S.C.
The same. Boston, 1854. 14 v. 8°. . . . . . . . L.R.
Bibliographica. J. Darling. London, 1854–59. 3 v. 8°. . . . L.R.
Britannica; seventh edition. Edinburgh, 1842. 21 v. 4°. . . . S.C.
The same; eighth edition. London, 1853–60. 22 v. 4°. . L.R.
The same; eighth edition. London, 1853–60. 22 v. 4°. . R.R.
Conversations-Lexicon. See *Conversations-Lexicon.*
Edinensis. Edinburgh, 1827. 6 v. 4°. . . . . . . . . L.R.
English; conducted by C. Knight. Lond. 1854–70. 24 v. in 11. 4°. R.R.

Arts and Sciences. 8 v. in 4.
Biography. 6 v. in 3.
Geography. 4 v. in 2.
Supplement to Geography. 1 v.
Natural History. 4 v. in 2.
Supplement to Natural History. 1 v.

The same. London, 1854–70. 24 v. 4°. . . . . . L.R.
Iconographic. New York, 1864. 6 v. 8°. and 4°. . . . . . L.R.

Text, vol. 1. Mathematics and Astronomy; Physics and Meteorology; Chemistry; Mineralogy; Geognosy and Geology.
2. Botany; Zoology; Anthropology; Surgery.
3. Geography and Planography; History and Ethnology; Military Sciences; Naval Sciences.
4. Architecture; Mythology; Fine Arts; Technology.

Plates, vol. 1. Mathematics and Astronomy; Natural Sciences; Geography; History and Ethnology.
2. Military Sciences; Naval Sciences; Architecture; Mythology; Fine Arts; Technology.

Encyclopædia Metropolitana. London, 1845. 29 v. 4°. . . . . . L.R.

Vol. 1. Grammar, by Sir J. Stoddard; Logic, by R. Whately; Rhetoric, by R. Whately; Geometry, by P. Barlow; Arithmetic, by G. Peacock; Algebra, by D. Lardner; Geometrical Analysis, by D. Lardner; Theory of Numbers, by P. Barlow; Trigonometry, by G. B. Airy; Analytical Geometry, by H. P. Hamilton; Conic Sections, by A. P. Hamilton; Differential and Integral Calculus, by A. Levy.

2. Integral Calculus, by A. Levy; Calculus of Variations, by T. G. Hall; Calculus of Finite Differences, by T. G. Hall; Calculus of Functions, by A. De Morgan; Theory of Probabilities, by A. De Morgan; Definite Integrals, by H. Moseley; Moral and Metaphysical Philosophy, by F. D. Maurice; Law, General Principles, by R. Jebb; Law of Nations, by A. Polson; Roman and Canon Law, by J. T. Graves; Eng. Law, by A. Polson; Theology, by G. E. Corrie and J. Rose.

3. Mechanics, Hydrodynamics, Pneumatics, Optics, and Astronomy, by P. Barlow; Nautical Astronomy, by Capt. H. Kater; Physical Astronomy, by Sir J. F. W. Herschel; Magnetism, by P. Barlow.

4. Electro-Magnetism, by P. Barlow; Electricity, by F. Lunn; Galvinism, by P. M. Roget; Heat, by F. Lunn; Light, by Sir J. F. W. Herschel; Chemistry, by F. Lunn; Sound, by Sir J. F. W. Herschel.

5. Meteorology, by G. Harvey; Figure of the Earth, by G. B. Airy; Tides and Waves, by G. B. Airy; Architecture, by J. Narrien; Sculpture, by J. Westmacott, jr.; Painting, by J. T. James and J. Lindsay; Heraldry, by H. Thompson; Numismatics, by B. R. Green; Poetry, by J. Hughes; Music, by J. Gwilt; Engraving, by J. Lindsay.

6. Agriculture, by B. Russell; Horticulture, by G. Don; Commerce, by J. Lowe; Political Economy, by N. W. Senior; Carpentry, by P. Nicholson; Fortifications, by C. C. Mitchell; Naval Architecture, by G. Harvey; Crystallography, by J. H. Brooke; Mineralogy, by J. H. Brooke; Geology, by J. Phillips.

7. Botany, by T. Edwards; Zoology, by J. F. South; Anatomy, by J. F. South and F. Le Gros Cla5k; Materia Medica, by G. Johnson; Medicine, by R. Williams; Surgery, by W. Bowmau; Veterinary Art, by W. C. Spooner.

8. Principles of Manufactures, by C. Babbage; Manufactures, by P. Barlow.

9–13. History and Biography.

14–25. Miscellaneous and Lexicographical. 14, A–Asc; 15, Asc–Bri; 16, Bri–Coh; 17, Coh–Dif; 18, Dif–Fal; 19, Fam–Gue; 20, Gue–Ins; 21, Ins–Mas; 22, Mas–Ozo; 23, P–Rel; 24; Rel–Squa; 25, Squa–Zyg.

Plates, vol. 1. Mathematics; Sciences; Arts.
2. Natural History; Medical Science; Veterinary Art.
3. History; Miscellanies; Maps.
Index.

National, of Useful Knowledge. Boston, 1853. 12 v. 8°. . . . L.R.
Supplement. London, 1859. 8°. . . . . . . . . L.R.
The same. Boston, 1853. 12 v. 8°. . . . . . S.C.
New Edinburgh; edited by D. Brewster. Phil. 1832. 18 v. 8°. . S.C.
of Arts, Manufactures and Machinery. P. Barlow. Lond. 1851. 4°. L.R.
of Civil Engineering. E. Cresy. London, 1865. 8°. . . *M,712
of Industry of all Nations. C. Knight. New York, 1851. 8°. . M,709
of Pure Mathematics. London, n. d. 4°. . . . . . . . . L.R.
of Religious Knowledge; ed. by R. B. Edwards. Philadelphia, 1859. 8°. P,325
of Missions. H. Newcomb. New York, 1858. 8°. . . . . P,610
Penny. London, 1833–43. 27 v. in 14°. r. 8°. . . . . . L.R.
Supplement. London, 1845–46. 2 v. r. 8°. . . . . . L.R.
Popular. Glasgow, 1855–70. 8°. . . . . . . . . . L.R.
or, Universal Dictionary. A. Rees. Philadelphia, n. d. 41 v. 8°. L.R.
See also *Cyclopædia*.

Endlicher, S. and Unger, F. Grundzüge der Botanik. Wien, 1843. 8°. G,866
Enfield, W. History of Philosophy. London, 1791. 2 v. 4°. . . . Q,284
Engelhardt, C. Denmark in the Early Iron Age. London, 1866. 4°. . Q,110
Engelhardt, W. Nahrung der Pflanzen. Leipzig, 1856. 12°. . . . G,867
Engelmann, W. Bibliotheca Historico-Naturalis, v. 1. Leipzig, 1846. 8°. L.R.
Engineer and Machinist's Drawing-Book. Glasgow, 1855. r. 4°. . . S.C.
and Mech. Assistant. D. Scott and Jamieson. Glasg. 1847. 2 v. r. 4°. S.C.
Engineer's Guide to the Navy. D. F. M'Carthy. London, 1869. 12°. . M,849
Engineering, Agricultural. G. H. Andrews. London, 1852. 3 v. in 1. 16°. M,888
and Architecture, Mech. Principles of. H. Moseley. N. Y. 1856. 8°. M,703

Engineering, Civil, Encyclopædia of. E. Cresy. London, 1865. 8°. . *M,712
See also *Civil Engineering.*
Spon's Dictionary of; ed. by O. Bryne. v. 1 in 3 div. Lond. 1869–70. 8°. M,731
and Mechanics' Encyclopædia. L. Hebert. London, 1849. 2 v. 8°. M,803
England. J. G. Kohl. London, 1844. 8°. . . . . . . . . . V,398
American Farmer in. F. L. Olmsted. Columbus, 1859. 8°. . . M,516
The same. New York, 1852. 2 v. 12°. . . . . . V,335
and Brittany, Livere de Reis de. London, 1865. 8°. . . . W,192
and France, History of. H. Brougham. London, 1861. 8°. . . A,529
Social Life in. M. Berry. London, 1844. 2 v. 12°. . . H,313
New Chronicles of. R. Fabyan. London, 1811. 4°. . . . F,155
and Ireland, Reformation in. W. Corbett. London, 1829. 2 v. 8°. P,664
and Italy, Notes on. S. Hawthorne. New York, 1869. 12°. . . V,358
and Normandy, Eccles. Hist. of. Ord. Vitalis. Lond. 1853–4. 3 v. p. 8°. L,22
History of. F. Palgrave. London, 1851–64. 4 v. 8°. . . A,440
and Scotland, Border History, to 1603. G. Ridpath. Berw. 1848. 4°. F,30
King of Saxony's Journey through. C. G. Carus. Lond. 1846. 8°. V,399
and Wales, Antiquities of. F. Grose. London, n. d. 8 v. 4°. . A,563
Beauties of. J. Britton and Brayley. Lond. 1801–15. 18 v. in 25. 8°. *V,271
Endowed Grammar Schools in. N. Carlisle. Lond. 1818. 2 v. 8°. O,813
Anglo-Saxon Period, History of. F. Palgrave. London, 1831. 16°. I,602
Biographical History of. J. Granger. London, 1779. 4 v. 8°. . D,418
Biographical Index to Hume. S. Y. McMasters. Alton, 1854. 8°. . A,392
Cabinet History of. C. Macfarlane. Lond. 1851. 26 v. in 13. 12°. A,385
Chancellors of, Lives of. J. Campbell. Phil. 1851. 7 v. 8°. . D,249
Chief-Justices of, Lives of. J. Campbell. Phil. 1844. 2 v. 8°. . D,248
The same; v. 8–10. London, 1857. p. 8°. . . . . . D,424
Child's History of. C. Dickens. New York, 1851. 2 v. 16°. . J,1209
Chronicle of the Kings of. Sir R. Baker. London, 1674. f°. . F,289
William of Malmesbury. New York, 1847. p. 8°. . . L,27
Chronicles of. J. Capgrave. London, 1858. 8°. . . . . . W,151
Sir J. Froissart. London, 1868. 2 v. 8°. . . . . . A,345
R. Holinshed. London, 1807–8. 6 v. 4°. . . . . . F,161
J. Rastall. London, 1811. 4°. . . . . . . . . F,163
Church of, Eccles. Memorials J. Strype. Oxford, 1822. 3 v. in 6. 8°. P,688
Reformation of. G. Burnet. London, 1850. 2 v. . . . P,649
Civil Wars of. Sir F. Biondi. London, 1641. f°. . . . . . F,270
Civilization in, History of. H. T. Buckle. New York, 1862. 2 v. 8°. B,33
Comic History of. G. A. á Beckett. London, n. d. 8°. . . . A,445
Commentaries on Laws of. W. Blackstone. New York, 1854. 4 v. 8°. U,505
The same; edited by G. Sharswood. Phil. 1869. 2 v. 8°. W,502
Commonwealth of, History of. A. Bisset. London, 1867. 2 v. 8°. A,509
W. Godwin. London, 1824–28. 4 v. 8°. . . . . . A,510
Conquest of. R. Wace. London, 1860. 4°. . . . . . . F,170
by the Normans. J. N. A. Thierry. London, 1861. 2 v. p. 8°. L,242
Constitution of, Essay on. J. Russell. London, 1866. 16°. . . B,1
Rise and Progress of. E. S. Creasy. New York, 1859. 12°. B,47
J. L. de Lolme. London, 1838. 2 v. 8°. . . . B,51
The same. London, 1853. p. 8°. . . . L,178
Constitutional History of. H. Hallam. New York, 1867. 8°. . . B,55

England, Constitutional History of. H. Hallam. Boston, 1854. 3 v. 8°. . . B,50
T. E. May. New York, 1865–66. 2 v. 8°. . . . . . B,48
Costume in. F. W. Fairholt. London, 1860. 8°. . . . . M,366
Cottage History of. A. Manning. London, 1861. 16°. . . . A,384
Country Rambles in. J. L. Knapp. Buffalo, 1853. 12°. . . N,503
Court of, 1811–20. R. P. Grenville. London, 1856. 2 v. 8°. . A,552
Decline of. L. Rollin. London, 1850. 12°. . . . . . . A,477
Described. S. Aiken. London, 1818. 8°. . . . . . . V,267
Description of. W. Camden. London, 1789. 3 v. f°. . . . *F,121
Dialogue on the Common Laws of. T. Hobbs. n. t. 8°. . . . D,412
during the Middle Ages. S. Turner. London, 1825. 5 v. 8°. A,434,4-8
Ecclesiastical History of. Beda Venerabilis. London, 1849. p. 8°. L,1
First Impressions of. H. Miller. Boston, 1856. 12°. . . . . V,368
Four Conquests of. J. A. St. John. London, 1862. 2 v. 8°. . . A,499
Four Georges of. S. M. Smucker. New York, 1860. 12°. . C,1266
Gazetteer of, v. 1, 2. S. Whately. London, 1751. 12°. . . . V,297
Germany and Scotland. J. H. Merle d'Aubigné. N. Y. 1849. 12°. V,343
Geschichte von England. J. M. Lappenberg. Hamb. 1834-58. 5 v. 8°. E,42
Glory and Shame of. C. E. Lester. New York, 1850. 2 v. 12°. . V,367
Great Schools of. H. Staunton. London, 1865. 12°. . . . O,831
Historic Lands of. Sir J. B. Burke. London, 1849. 8°. . . . A,466
Historical Collections, Parliaments of Elizabeth. London, 1680. f°. F,279
Historical Relations, 1678–1714. N. Luttrell. Oxford, 1857. 6 v. 8°. B,17
Historia Anglicana. Bartholemew de Cotton. London, 1859. 8°. . W,166
History of. R. Brady. London, 1685–1700. 2 v. f°. . . . F,286
W. F. Collier. London, 1868. 12°. . . . . . . A,402
Sir E. S. Creasy. v. 1. London, 1869. 8°. . . . . A,437
J. A. Froude. London, 1858–67. 10 v. 8°. . . . . . A,398
The same. New York. 12 v. 8°. . . . . . A,400
T. Gaspey. London, n. d. 8 v. 8°. . . . . . . A,371
R. Grafton. London, 1809. 2 v. 4°. . . . . . . F,158
E. Hall. London, 1809. 4°. . . . . . . . . . F,159
D. Hume. New York, 1850. 6 v. 12°. . . . . . . A,393
The same. London, 1803. 10 v. 8°. . . . . . A,394
The same, abridged. New York, 1868. 8°. . . . A,391
The same, with Boydell's Illustrat. Lond. 1807. 5 v. f°. L.R.
T. Keightley. London, 1859–65. 2 v. 12°. . . . . . A,422
The same. New York, 1860. 5 v. 16°. . . . . L,416
J. Lingard. Boston, 1853–44. 13 v. 12°. . . . . . A,404
The same. Paris, 1840. 8 v. 8°. . . . . . A,405
C. Macaulay. London, 1763–71. 5 v. 4°. . . . . . F,262
Sir J. Mackintosh. London, 1830–40. 10 v. 12°. . . . M,986
W. Massey. London, 1865. 4 v. 12°. . . . . . . A,423
F. Palgrave. London, 1831. 16°. . . . . . . . . A,386
C. H. Pearson. London, 1867. 2 v. 8°. . . . . . A,436
P. Rapin de Thoyras. London, 1728–47. 28 v. 8°. . . . A,421
The same. London, 1732–37. 3 v. f°. . . . . S.C.
A. B. Thompson. London, 1865. 12°. . . . . . . A,390
H. Walter. London, n. d. 7 v. 12°. . . . . . . A,428
1603–1688. R. Vaughan. London, 1840. 2 v. 8°. . . . A,531

England, History of, 1701–13. P. H. Stanhope, *Lord Mahon*. Lond. 1870. 8°. A,433
1713–83. P. H. Stanhope, *Lord Mahon*. Bost. 1853–54. 7 v. 8°. A,401
The same. New York, 1849. 2 v. 8°. . . . A,411
The same. Leipzig, 1853–54. 7 v. 16°. . . . J,465
1760–1837. T. S. Hughes. London, 1855. 7 v. 8°. . . A,432
1773–1804. J. Adolphus. London, 1840–45. 7 v. 8°. . A,413
during his own time. G. Burnet. London, 1857. 8°. . . A,469
during the Peace, 1816–46. H. Martineau. Bost. 1865–6. 4 v. 8°. A,407
The same. London, 1849–50. 2 v. 8°. . . A,418,10–11
in Lives of Englishmen. G. G. Cunningham. Lond. 1853. 8 v. 8°. C,1270
from Acces. of James II. T. B. Macaulay. N. Y. 1866. 8 v. 8°. A,399
The same. Leipzig, 1849–61. 10 v. 16°. . . . J,336
to 1862; edited by W. Smith. New York, 1868. 16°. . . A,388
Illus. History of. J. F. Smith and W. Howitt. Lond. n. d. 8 v. 8°. A,467
in 1841. F. L. G. von Raumer. London, 1842. 2 v. 12°. . . V,371
Ladies' History of. C. Cowley. London, 1780. f°. . . . Q,309
Lectures on the History of. W. Longman. v. 1. London, 1863. 8°. A,438
Memoirs of the Court, 1688–1760. J. H. Jesse. London, 1843. 3 v. 8°. A,528
of Charles I. L. Aikin. London, 1833. 2 v. 8°. . . A,503
of Elizabeth. L. Aikin. London, 1819. 2 v. 8°. . . A,501
of James I. L. Aikin. London, 1822. 2 v. 8°. . A,502
of the Stuarts. J. H. Jesse. London, 1857. 3 v. p. 8°. L,267
Military Law of. London, 1810. 8°. . . . . . . . U,497
Month in. H. T. Tuckerman. New York, 1853. 12°. . . . V,359
Notabilities in. P. Chasles. New York, 1853. 12°. . . . C,519
Notes in Parliament. Sir S. D'Ewes. London, 1708. f°. . . F,295
Old; its Scenery and People. J. M. Hoppin. New York, 1867. 16°. V,303
Parliamentary Hist. of, to 1803. T. C. Hansard. Lond. 1806–20. 36 v. 8°. B,76
Passages from English Note-Books. N. Hawthorne. Bost. 1870. 2 v. 12°. H,92
Pictorial History of. G. L. Craik and C. Macfarlane. Lond. 1849. 11 v. 8°. A,418
The same. New York, 1846–48. 4 v. 8°. . . . . . A,415
Picture History of. H. W. Dulcken. London, 1866. 4°. . . A,403
Political History of. G. Smith. London, 1867. 8°. . . . C,1224
Political Poems and Songs. London, 1859–61. 2 v. 8°. . . W,164
Poor in State of. Sir F. M. Eden. London, 1797. 3 v. 4°. . . O,610
Popular History of. C. Knight. London, 1856–59. 8 v. 8°. . . A,406
Princesses of, Lives of the. M. A. E. Green. Lond. 1850–55. 6 v. 8°. D,338
Queens of, before the Conquest. M. Hall. London, 1854. 2 v. 8°. C,1250
from the Conquest. A. Strickland. Phil. 1854. 12 v. 12°. D,368
The same. London, 1868–69. 6 v. p. 8°. . . . L,270
Rebellion in, 1641. E. Hyde, *Earl Clarendon*. Oxford, 1849. 7 v. 8°. A,516
The same. Oxford, 1732. 3 v. in 1. f°. . . . . . F,122
Reformation in, Sketch of. I. J. Blunt. London, 1832. 16°. . I,603
Reign of Queen Anne, History of. A. Boyer. London, 1722. f°. Q,310
P. H. Stanhope, *Lord Mahon*. Leipzig, 1870. 2 v. in 1. 16°. . J,466
The same. London, 1870. 8°. . . . . . . A,433
Revolution for Popery, Counter. J. B. N. A. Carrel. Lond. 1846. 12°. A,476
Romance of English History. H. Neele. London, 1831. 3 v. 12°. K,884
Royal Princess of. M. Hall. London, 1858. 12°. . . . . D,437

England, Rural Life of. W. Howitt. Philadelphia, 1854. 2 v. 12°. . v,370
Sea-Kings of. W. H. D. Adams. London, 1861. 16°. . . . . c,1242
Secret History of Kings and Queens of. London, 1725. 2 v. 12°. A,482
Select Tracts relating to the Civil Wars. London, 1815. 8°. . . A,561
Social Condition of. J. Kay. New York, 1863. 12°. . . . O,376
Sports of. J. Strutt. London, 1855. 8°. . . . . . . M,314
State Papers of Reign of Henry VIII. W. Cecil. London, 1740. f°. F,290,1
Statesmen of the Commonwealth. J. Forster. New York, 1846. 8°. C,584
under Anglo-Saxon Kings. J. M. Lappenberg. Lond. 1845. 2 v. 8°. A,496
under the Norman Kings. J. M. Lappenberg. Oxford, 1857. 8°. A,497
under the Norman Occupation. J. F. Morgan. London, 1858. 12°. A,474
under Seven Administrations. A. Fonblanque. London, 1837. 3 v. 12°. B,3
Visit to; Bertha's Journal. London, 1851. 12°. . . . . . v,320
Visits to Remarkable Places. W. Howitt. Philadelphia, 1854. 2 v. 12°. v,342
Walk from London to J. O'Groat's. E. Burritt. London, 1864. 12°. v,375
Walk from London to Land's End. E. Burritt. London, 1868. 12°. v,395
Wars of the Roses. J. G. Edgar. London, 1867. 12°. . . . J,1512
Worthies of. T. Fuller. London, 1811. 2 v. 4°. . . . . . F,156
The same. London, 1840. 3 v. 8°. . . . . . . . B,18

English, The, and their Origin. L. O. Pike. London, 1866. 8°. . . B,53
Rule and Misrule in America. T. C. Haliburton. N. Y. 1851. 12°. . B,163
Sketches of. D. Jerrold. London, 1853. 16°. . . . . . H,599

English Antiquities, Introduction to. J. Eccleston. London, 1847. 8°. . A,443

English Catalogue of Books, 1835–62. S. Low. London, 1862. 8°. . . L.R.
Supplements, 1863–70. London, 1864–71. 8°. . . . . L.R.

English Colonies, History of. J. Marshall. Philadelphia, 1824. 8°. . B,622

English Composition. R. Armstrong. London, 1855. 2 v. 16°. . . O,775
R. Hiley. New York, 1855. 2 v. 16°. . . . . O,1062
R. G. Parker. Boston, 1852. 12°. . . . . . . H,8
Progressive Exercises in. J. Cornwell. London, 1855. 12°. . O,1067

English Cyclopædia; conducted by C. Knight. London, 1854–60. 18 v. 4°. L.R.
The same. London, 1854–70. 24 v. in 11. . . . . . R.R.

Arts and Sciences. 8 v. in 4.
Biography. 6 v. in 3.
Geography. 4 v in 2.
Supplement to Geography. 1 v.
Natural History. 4 v. in 2.
Supplement to Natural History. 1 v.

English and Foreign Life, Stories of. W. and M. Howitt. Lond. 1853. p. 8°. L,108

English Dramatic Poets, Specimens of; ed. by C. Lamb. London, 1854. p. 8°. L,15
The same. New York, 1859. 12°. . . . . . . U,278,4

English Envoy at the Court of Nicholas I. J. Corner. New York, 1854. 12°. K,94

English Etymology, Dictionary of, v. 1. H. Wedgwood. London, 1859. 8°. L.R.

English Gilds, Statutes, and Customs of; ed. by T. Smith. Lond. 1870. 8°. L,605,40

English Government and Constitution. J. Russell. London, 1865. 8°. . B,49
The same. London, 1866. 16°. . . . . . . B,1

English Historical Society; Collection of Monastic Chronicles, illustrative of English History. London, 1833–56. 29 v. 8°. . . . . U,616–635

Adam of Murimuth. Chronica. . U,630
Bede, V. Historia Ecclesiastica. . U,628
Opera Historica Minora. . . U,633
Chron. de la Traison de Richart Deux. U,629
Florence of Worcester. Chronicon. 2 v. U,617
Gesta Stephani. . . . . . . U,631
Gildas, St. De Excidio Britanniæ. U,635
Henrici Quinti Angliæ, Gesta. . . U,632
Kemble, J. M. Codex Diplomat. 6 v. U,616
Nenius. Historia Britonum. . . U,627
Richard of Devizes. Gesta Ricardi I. U,634
Roger of Wendover. Chronica. 5 v. U,622
Trivet, N. Annales sex Regum Angliæ. U,626
Walter of Hemingburgh. Chron. 2 v. U,621
William of Malmesbury. G. Ang. 2 v. U,618
William of Newbury. Hist. Ang. 2 v. U,619

English History, 1235–1273. Matthew Paris. London, 1852–54. 3 v. p. 8°. L,20
P. Vergilio, v. 1. London, 1846. 4°. . . . . . . A,471
Beauties of. J. Frost. New York, 1846. 18°. . . . . . . A,387
Cameos from. C. M. Yonge. New York, 1869. 12°. . . . A,478
Chronicles of. J. Hardynge and R. Grafton. London, 1812. 4°. . F,160
Half-Hours of. C. Knight. London, 1868. 8°. . . . . . A,444
in Shakespeare, Lectures on. H. Reed. Philadelphia, 1869. 12°. . I,891
Original Letters illustrative of. H. Ellis. London, 1824–46. 11 v. 8°. B,2
Revolutions in. R. Vaughan. New York, 1860–67. 3 v. 8°. . A,526
Tales from. A. Strickland. New York, 1868. 16°. . . . J,1276
Tales of Heroes from. London, 1869. 8°. . . . . . . J,1295
English Humorists of 18th Century. W. M. Thackeray. Bost. 1869. 12°. K,1038,4
The same. Leipzig, 1853. 12°. . . . . . . . . J,481
English Journal of Education. London, 1847–54. 8°. . . . . . S,56
English Lakes, Picturesque Tour of. R. Ackerman. London, 1821. 4°. Q,207
English Language. R. G. Latham. London, 1855. 2 v. 8°. . . . . L,575
Analytical System of. E. L. Price. Cincinnati, 1848. . . . Y,19,2
Anecdotes of. S. Pegge. London, 1844. 8°. . . . . . . L,617
and Literature, Five Centuries of. Leipzig, 1860. 16°. . . . J,164
Dictionary of. J. Ash. London, 1775. 8°. . . . . . . L.R.
A. Bailey. London, 1747. 2 v. 8°. . . . . . L.R.
J. Craig. London, 1856. 2 v. 8°. . . . . . L.R.
E. Phillips. London, 1720. f°. . . . . . . L.R.
S. Johnson. London, 1854. r. 8°. . . . . . L.R.
S. Maunder. London, 1847. 12°. . . . . . L.R.
C. Richardson. London, 1839. 2 v. 4°. . . . . L.R.
Supplement. London, 1856. 4°. . . . . L.R.
T. Sheridan. London, 1797. 2 v. 8°. . . . . L.R.
N. Webster. Springfield, 1867. 4°. . . . . . R.R.
The same. Springfield, 1870. 4°. . . . . L.R.
J. E. Worcester. Boston, 1846. r. 8°. . . . . L.R.
The same. Boston, 1869. 4°. . . . . . R.R.
Academic. N. Webster. New York, 1854. 8°. . . . . L.R.
Imperial. J. Ogilvie. Glasgow, 1859. 2 v. 8°. . . . . L.R.
New Royal. C. Marriott. London, 1780. 4°. . . . . L.R.
of Every-day Difficulties. E. Shelton. London, n. d. 12°. . L,556
of Obsolete and Provincial. T. Wright. Lon. 1857. 2 v. p. 8°. L,258
Pronouncing. J. Walker. Glasgow, 1850. 16°. . . . . L.R.
The same; edited by B. H. Smart. London, 1860. 8°. L.R.
Rhyming, 1570. P. Levins. London, 1867. 8°. . . L,605,27
J. Walker. Philadelphia, 1852. 8°. . . . . . L.R.
The same. New York, 1860. 12°. . . . . L.R.
The same. London, 1857. 2 v. 12°. . . . . . L.R.
Glossary of English Words. R. Nares. London, 1859. 2 v. 8°. . L.R.
R. C. Trench. New York, 1859. 12°. . . . . . L,547
Good English. E. S. Gould. New York, 1867. 12°. . . . L,548
Grammar. Dublin, 1854. 2 v. 18°. . . . . . . O,1059
Key to the same. Dublin, 1849. 18°. . O,1060
G. Brown. New York, 1866. 12°. . . . . L,540
J. T. Champlin. New York, 1850. 16°. . . . . L,558

English Language, Grammar. J. Chandler. Philadelphia, 1847. 12°. o,1074
W. C. Fowler. New York, 1852. 8°. . . . . . L,619
S. Kerl. Philadelphia, 1859. . . . . . . L,569
S. Kirkham. Rochester, N. Y. 1840. 12°. . . o,1071
T. L. Lyons. Cincinnati, 1850. 12°. . . . o,1081
L. Murray. New York, 1852. 16°. . . . o,1065
T. S. Pinneo. Cincinnati, 1850. 16°. . . . o,1079
J. M. Teeters. Canton, Ohio, 1836. 12°. . . o,1083
Grammar, Common School. J. R. Chandler. Phil. 1847. 12°. o,1074
Composition, etc., Guide to. New York, 1856. 12°. . . L,564
Digest of. L. T. Covell. New York, 1852. 12°. . . . L,577
Elements of. S. S. Greene. Philadelphia, 1853. 12°. . o,1084
D. B. Tower and B. F. Tweed. N. Y. 1854. 12°. . o,1068
English Teacher. S. S. Pinneo. New York, 1852. 12°. . o,1078
Eng. Sprach. für Deutsche. H. E. Lloyd. Hamb. 1837. 8°. L,774
First Lessons in. S. S. Greene. Philadelphia, 1848. 12°. o,1077
Grammar of. G. Brown. New York, 1858. 8°. . . . L,539
Grammatik der Eng. Sprache. J. F. Arnold. Stuttg. 1834. 12°. L,771
Introduction to. R. Lowth. Dublin, 1785. 16°. . . o,1073
Primary. T. S. Pinneo. Cincinnati, 1854. 16°. . . o,1064
Grammatical Structure of. J. Mulligan. New York, 1852. 8°. . L,571
Hand-Book of. R. G. Latham. New York, 1852. 12°. . . . L,544
of Engrafted Words. New York, 1857. 12°. . . . . L,543
Meaning of Words. A. B. Johnson. New York, 1854. 12°. . . L,512
Ollendorff's neue Meth. u. Schlüssel. P. Gands. N.Y. 1854-70. 2 v. 12°. L,775
Origin and History of. G. P. Marsh. New York, 1862. 8°. . . L,620
Past and Present. R. C. Trench. New York, 1858. 12°. . . L,546
Plea for the Queen's English. H. Alford. New York, n. d. 16°. . L,563
Philological Study of the. T. A. March. New York, 1865. 12°. . L,565
Practisches Lehrbuch. A. Baskerville. New York, 1870. 12°. . L,770
Pronunciation, Early. A. J. Ellis. London, 1867-69. 2 v. 8°. L,604,2,7
Guide to. E. J. Stearns. Boston, 1857. 16°. . . . L,560
Rise, Progress, and Structure of. M. Harrison. Phil. 1850. 12°. L,568
Synonyms and Antonyms. J. C. Smith. London, 1870. p. 8°. . L,254
Treatise on the. S. Kerl. Philadelphia, 1859. 12°. . . . L,569
Vulgarisms and other Errors of Speech. Philadelphia, 1868. 16°. . L,566
Young Analyzer of the. J. N. Mc. Elligott. New York, 1852. 8°. o,1088
English Literature, Bibliog. of. W. T. Lowndes. Lond. 1857-65. 10 v. p. 8°. L.R.
Compendium of. C. D. Cleveland. Philadelphia, 1859. 12°. . . H,682
Cyclopædia of. R. Chambers. Boston, 1854. 2 v. 8°. . . . H,713
Introduction to. H. N. Day. Boston, 1869. 12°. . . . . H,693
History of. W. F. Collier. London, 1869. 12°. . . . . H,679
G. L. Craik. New York, 1863. 2 v. 8°. . . . . H,711
W. Spalding. New York, 1868. 12°. . . . . . H,68
Lectures on. H. Reed. Philadelphia, 1855. 12°. . . . . H,677
Manual of. T. Arnold. London, 1867. 12°. . . . . . H,698
T. B. Shaw. New York, 1869. 12°. . . . . . H,695
of 13th Century, Glossarial Index to. H. Coleridge. Lond. 1859. 8°. L,573
of 19th Century. C. D. Cleveland. Philadelphia, 1859. 12°. . . H,682
Outlines of. T. B. Shaw. Philadelphia, 1854. 12°. . . . H,694

English Literature, Tables of. H. Morley. London, 1870. f°. . . . *F,173
English Merchants. H. R. F. Bourne. London, 1866. 2 v. 8°. . D,383
English Metrical Romances, Early. G. Ellis. London, 1805. 3 v. 12°. U,699
The same. London, 1848. 12°. . . . . . . . . L,8
English Misrule and Irish Misdeeds. A. De Vere. London, 1848. 12°. . B,164
English Nation, Manners and Customs of. J. Brookes. London, n. d. 8°. A,480
English Note-Book, Passages from. N. Hawthorne. Bost. 1870. 2 v. 12°. U,40,17,18
English Orphans. M. J. Holmes. New York, 1868. 12°. . . . . K,184
English Orthography, 1569. J. Hart. London, 1850. 24°. . . . L,666
English Pedagogy. Philadelphia, 1862. 8°. . . . . . . O,1216,5
English People, Pedigree of the. T. Nicholas. London, 1868. . . . N,379
English Poetry, History of. T. Warton. London, 1774–81. 3 v. 4°. . H,742
Reliques of Ancient. T. Percy. London, 1844. 3 v. 16°. . . I,578
The same. Leipzig, 1866. 3 v. 16°. . . . . . . J,411
English Poets, The Late; edited by H. R. Stoddart. New York, 1867. 12°. I,433
Lives of. R. Bell. London, 1839. . . . . . . . M,1015
S. Johnson. New York, 1857. 2 v. 12°. . . . . C,1220
The same. Leipzig, 1858. 2 v. in 1. 16°. . . . J,225
Selections from. L. Hunt. New York, 1857. 12°. . . . U,279,2
English Preachers, Pen Pictures of. London, 1852. 16°. . . . . C,838
English Punctuation, Treatise on. J. Wilson. Boston, 1856. 16°. . . L,561
English Reading, Course of. J. Pycroft. New York, 1854. 12°. . . O,966
English Revolution of 1640, Geschichte der. F. C. Dahlmann. Leip. 1846. 8°. E,43
History of. F. Guizot. London, 1854. 2 v. 8° . . . . . A,508
The same. London, 1864. 12°. . . . . . . . L,191
The same. New York, 1846. 12°. . . . . . . . . A,479
of 1688. Sir J. Macintosh. Philadelphia, 1835. 8°. . . . . H,841
English Revolutionary Period, Characters of. E. O. Jones. Lond. 1853. 12°. C,1286
English Shrines, Pilgrimages to. A. M. Hall. London, 1853. 8°. . C,1233
English Stage, Some Account of, 1660 to 1830. Bath, 1832. 10 v. 8°. . I,716
English Style. G. F. Graham. London, 1869. 16°. . . . . . . L,580
English Sketches. N. Hawthorne. Boston, 1866. 16°. . . . . K,162
English Stories of the Olden Time. M. Hack. v. 1. London, 1839. 12°. J,1207
English Surnames. M. A. Lower. London, 1849. 2 v. 8°. . . . L,516
in the Teutonic Family. R. Ferguson. London, 1858. 8°. . . L,515
English Synonyms. G. Crabb. New York, 1854. 8°. . . . . L,572
G. F. Graham. New York, 1858. 12°. . . . . . L,545
English Teacher. T. S. Pinneo. Cincinnati, 1852. 12°. . . . O,1078
English Traits. R. W. Emerson. Boston, 1852. 16°. . . . . H,103
English Universities. V. A. Huber. London, 1843. 2 v. in 3. 8°. . . O,815
English University, Five Years in an. C. A. Bristed. N. Y. 1852. 2 v. 12°. O,812
English Wars in France in Reign of Henry VI. London, 1861–64. 3 v. 8°. W,172
English Women of Letters. J. Kavanagh. Leipzig, 1862. 16°. . . J,230
English Writers. H. Morley. London, 1866–70. 2 v. in 4. 8°. . . H,712
Engraving, History and Art of. London, 1770. 12°. . . . . . . M,5
Wonders of. G. Duplessis. New York, 1871. 12°. . . M,1065
Wood, Art of. T. Gilks. London, n. d. 12°. . . . . . . M,62
Treatise on. J. Jackson and W. A. Chatto. London, 1861. 8°. . M,139
Engravings, Le Peintre-Graveur Français. A. P. F. Robert-Dumesnil. Paris, 1835–50. 8 v. 8°. . . . . . . . . . . . L.R.

Engravings, Le Peintre-Graveur Français, continué. P. de Baudicour. Paris, 1859–61. 2 v. 8°. . . . . . . . . . . . L.R.
Ennemoser, J. History of Magic. London, 1854. 2 v. p. 8°. . . . L,290
Ennis, J. Origin of the Stars. New York, 1868. 12°. . . . . . N,327
Enoch, Book of; translated by R. Laurence. Oxford, 1838. 8°. . . . P,432
Enoch Arden. A. Tennyson. Boston, 1864. 12°. . . . . . . I,446
Ensor, G. Inquiry concerning Population of Nations. London, 1818. 8°. O,516
Entertaining Knowledge by Popular Authors. London, n. d. 8°. . . . H,470
Entertaining Naturalist. J. W. Loudon. London, 1867. p. 8°. . . . L,119
Enthusiasm, Natural History of. I. Taylor. New York, 1856. 12°. . P,76
Entomological Magazine, v. 1–5. London, 1833–38. 8°. . . . . . R,15
Entomologist's Text-Book. J. O. Westwood. London, 1838. 12°. . . O,15
Entomology, Bibliothèque Entomologique. Paris, 1852. 2 v. 8°. . . O,31

Vol. 1. Kirby, W. Centurie d'Insectes; Eschscholtz, J. F. Œuvres Entomologiques; Macleay, W. S. Insectes de Java.
2. Bulletin de la Société Impériale des Naturalistes de Moscou.

British. J. Curtis. London, 1824–28. 5 v. 8°. . . . . . O,50
Elements of. W. S. Dallas. London, 1857. 12°. . . . . . O,30
Grammar of. E. Newman. London, 1835. 8°. . . . . . O,9
Handbuch der Entomologie. H. Burmeister. Berlin, 1832–55. 4 v. 8°. G,944
Atlas to the same. 4°. . . . . . . . . . . . G,964
Illustrations of British. J. F. Stephens. London, 1828–46. 12 v. 8°. O,70

Vol. 1–7. Mandibulata. Vol. 8–11. Haustellata. Vol. 12. Supplement.

of Exotic. D. Drury. London, 1837. 3 v. 4°. . . . *Q,5
Insecten Deutsche. W. F. Erichson and others. Ber. 1848–63. 4 v. 8°. G,945
Introduction to. J. Duncan. Edinburgh, 1853. 16°. . . . N,470,28
W. Kirby and W. Spence. London, 1815–26. 4 v. 8°. . *O,32
The same. London, 1856. 8°. . . . . . . O,29
The same. Philadelphia, 1846. 8°. . . . . . O,49
Manual of. H. Burmeister. London, 1836. 8°. . . . . . O,37
Miscellaneous Papers on. n. t. p. 4°. . . . . . . *Q,114

Macleay, W. S. Annulosa Javanica.
Horsfield, T. Descriptive Catalogue of the Lepidoptera of Java.
Westwood, J. O. Heteromera of Western Africa.
Sacred Beetles.
On Nycteribia.
Yarrell, W. On Athalia Centifoliæ.
Bonnett, E. T. On the Pteropine Bat.

Natural History of Insects. New York, 1859. 2 v. 18°. . . . L,341
Popular British. M. E. Catlow. London, 1852. 16°. . . . . O,4
Entomostraca, Natural History of British. W. Baird. London, 1850. 8°. O,302
of Cretaceous Formation of England. T. R. Jones. London, 1849. 4°. Q,27
Eoline. C. L. Hentz. New York, 1870. 12°. . . . . . . . K,166
Eōthen; Travels in the East. A. W. Kinglake. London, 1865. p. 8°. . I,657
The same. New York, 1858. 8°. . . . . . . V,1037
The same. Leipzig, 1846. 16°. . . . . . . . J,239
Epaminondas and Gustavus Adolphus. C. D. Yonge. London, 1858. 12°. C,486
Epictetus. Works; translated by E. Carter. London, 1758. 4°. . . U,594
Epidemics, Notes on. F. E. Anstie. London, 1866. 16°. . . . L,840
Epiploic Force, Recherches Physiques sur. R.J.H.Dutrochet. Paris, 1842. 8°. N,252,17
Epitaphs, Collections of. T. J. Pettigrew. London, 1857. p. 8°. . . L,6
and Inscriptions, American. T. Alden. New York, 1814. 5 v. 18°. *C,830
Equations, Differential, Treatise on. G. Boole. Cambridge, 1865. 12°. M,1147
Elementary Treatise on. I. Todhunter. London, 1867. 12°. M,1102

Equilibrium, Principes Fondamentaux de. L.N.M.Carnot. Paris, 1803. 8°. N,127
Equinoctial Regions, Reise in. A. v. Humboldt. Stutt. 1859–60. 4 v. 8°. E,177
The same. Stuttgart, 1861–62. 6 v. 16°. . . . . . E,168
Travels in. A. v. Humboldt and Bonpland. Lon. 1818–29. 8 v. in 7. 8°. V,257
The same. London, 1870. 3 v. p. 8°. . . . . . . L,296
Erasmus, D. Familiar Colloquies. London, 1725. 8°. . . . . . P,891
Manual for a Christian Soldier. London, 1687. 24°. . . . P,4
Moriæ Encomium. London, 1668. 18°. . . . . . . . P,11
Erato. W. D. Gallagher. Cincinnati, 1835. 2 v. 16°. . . . . I,25
Erben, Die. M. Ring. Prag und Leipzig, 1858. 24°. . . . . G,429
Erckern, L. Fleta Minor; Laws of Art and Nature. London, 1686. f°. Q,294
Erckmann, E. et Chatrian, A. Blockade of Phalsburg. N. Y. 1871. 12°. H,1009
Confidences d'un Joueur de Clarinette. Paris, 1861. 12°. . H,1015
Contes des Bords du Rhin. Paris, 1861. 12°. . . H,1014
Forest House and Catherine's Lovers. Boston, 1871. 12°. . G,225
Madame Thérèse. New York, 1869. 12°. . . . H,1010
Histoire d'un Paysun, 1789, 1792, 1793. Paris, 1861. 3 v. 12°. H,1017
Illustre Docteur Mathéus. Paris, 1861. 12°. . . H,1019
Invasion; ou, Fou Yégof. Paris, 1861. 12°. . . . H,1016
La Guerre. Paris, 1861. 12°. . . . . . . H,1018
Maitre Daniel Rock. Paris, 1861. 12°. . . . . H,1020
Erdmann, O. L. Grundriss der Allgemeinen Waarenkunde. Leip. 1833. 8°. N,252,10
Eric; or, Little by Little. F. W. Farrar. New York, n. d. 12°. . J,1470
Erichson, W. F. and others. Insecten Deutschlands. Berlin, 1848–63. 4 v. 8°. G,945
Erickson, D. S. Carl Bartlett; or, what can I do? Boston, 1869. 16°. . J,1658
Good Measure. Boston, 1869. 16°. . . . . . . . . . J,1659
Ericsson, J., Story Life of. P. C. Headley. New York, 1870. 12°. . J,1635
Erman, A. Travels in Siberia. Philadelphia, 1850. 2 v. 12°. . . V,615
Ermina. M. M. Sherwood. New York, 1860. 12°. . . . . K,1008,5
Ernest Linwood. C. L. Hentz. Philadelphia, 1870. 12°. . . . . K,456
Ernest Maltravers. Sir E. B. Lytton. Philadelphia, 1869. 12°. . . K,811
The same. Leipzig, 1842. 16°. . . . . . . . J,310
Ernst J. Philosophy of Freemasonry. Cincinnati, 1870. 16°. . . O,379
Errors, Popular. J. Timbs. London, 1849. 16°. . . . . . . M,809
The same. London, 1849. 16°. . . . . . . I,542,1
Erskine, J. E. Islands of the Western Pacific. London, 1853. 8°. . . V,900
Erzählungen eines alten Herrn. G. von Struensee. Breslau, 1860. 2 v. 16°. G,497
Erzählungen, Gesammelte. O. W. v. Horn. Frank.-a-M. 1861–62. 12 v. 18°. G,327
Escapes, Wonderful. F. Bernard. New York, 1871. 12°. . . M,1061
Eschenburg, J. J. Manual of Classical Literature. Philadelphia, 1852. 8°. H,733
Eschricht, D. F. Das Physische Leben. Kopenhagen, 1852. 8°. . . E,418
Eschscholtz, J. F. Œuvres Entomologiques. Paris, 1835. 8°. . . O,31,1
Espion Anglais. Londres, 1783–85. 7 v. 16°. . . . . . . H,859
Esprit de Mad. D. G. Girardin. Paris, n. d. 12°. . . . . H,1028
Espy, J. P. Meteorological Report. Washington, 1857. 4°. . . . P.D.
Esquemeling, J. Buccaneers of America. Boston, 1856. 8°. . . . C,383
Esquimaux, Life among the. C. F. Hall. New York, 1866. 8°. . . V,183
Esquiros, A. L'Angleterre et la Vie Anglaise. Paris, 1860. 8°. . N,252,45

Essayists, British. Boston, 1866. 38 v. 8°. . . . . . . . . H,536

| | | | | | |
|---|---|---|---|---|---|
| 1-4. | Tatler. | 22-24. | World. | 30-31. | Lounger. |
| 5-12. | Spectator. | 15-26. | Connoisseur. | 32-34. | Observer. |
| 13-15. | Guardian. | 27. | Idler. | 35-37. | Looker-On. |
| 16-18. | Rambler. | 28-29. | Mirror. | 38. | Index. |
| 19-21. | Adventurer. | | | | |

Modern British. New York and Boston, 1854-70. 7 v. 8°.

| | | | |
|---|---|---|---|
| A. Alison. . . . | H,621 | S. Smith. . . . . . | H,372 |
| F. Jeffrey. . . . | H,624 | T. N. Talfourd and J. Stephen. | H,373 |
| T. B. Macauley. . . . | H,374 | J. Wilson. . . . . . | H,609 |
| Sir J. Mackintosh. . . | H,370 | | |

Essays. D. Greenwell. London, 1866. 12°. . . . . . . . . H,323
and Tales in Prose. B. W. Proctor. Boston, 1853. 2 v. 16°. . H,307
and Reviews. Leipzig, 1862. 16°. . . . . . . . . . J,161
Temple, F. Education of the World.
Williams, R. Bunsen's Biblical Researches.
Powell, B. Study of the Evidences of Christianity.
Wilson, H. B. The National Church.
Goodwin, C. W. On the Mosaic Cosmogony.
Pattison, M. Tendencies of Religious Thought in England.
Jowett, B. Interpretation of Scripture.
in Biography and Criticism. P. Bayne. Boston, 1867. 2 v. 12°. . H,196
of an Optimist. J. W. Kaye. Philadelphia, 1871. 16°. . . H,442
of Elia. C. Lamb. New York, 1859. 12°. . . . . . H,476
Tales and Sketches. R. Macnish. London, 1844. 2 v. 16°. . . H,229
on Various Subjects. N. Wiseman. London, 1853. 3 v. 8°. . H,491
Este, D. K. Discourse on Jacob Burnet. Cincinnati, 1853. 8°. . . T,19,9
Estell, J. T. American Veterinarian. Cincinnati, 1867. 8°. . . . L,942
Estelle Russell. Leipzig, 1870. 2 v. in 1. 16°. . . . . . . J,162
Ester Reid; or, Asleep and Awake. Cincinnati, 1870. 12°. . . . K,276
Esther, the Captive Orphan. S. H. Tyng. New York, 1860. 12°. . . P,234
Estvàn, B. War Pictures from the South. New York, 1863. 12°. . . B,909
Etching and Etchers. P. G. Hamerton. London, 1868. 8°. . . . M,121
Etching on Copper, Art of. A. Ashley. London, n. d. . . . . . Q,203
Art and Practice of. H. Alken. London, 1849. 8°. . . . M,36
Ethan Allen and Green-Mountain Heroes. H.W.DePuy. Boston, 1853. 12°. C,19
Ethelwerd, F. Chronicle. London, 1848. p. 8°. . . . . . . L,26
Ethelyn's Mistake. M. J. Holmes. New York, 1870. 12°. . . . K,185
Etherization, with Surgical Remarks. J. C. Warren. Boston, 1848. 12°. L,849
Ethical and Social Studies. F. P. Cobbe. London, 1865. p. 8°. . . O,557
Ethics and Politics. Aristotle. London, 1797. 2 v. 4°. . . . . O,735
Grundprobleme der Ethik. A. Schopenhauer. Leipzig, 1860. 8°. G,571
for our Country and the Times. B. P. Aydelott. Cincinnati, 1866. 12°. P,345
Introduction to. T.S.Jouffroy; tr. W.H.Channing. Bost. 1856. 2 v. 12°. O,712
Manual of Political. F. Lieber. Boston, 1839-47. 2 v. 8°. . . O,522
Ethics, Nicomachean. Aristotle. London, 1853. p. 8°. . . . . . L,38
Ethiopia, Highlands of. W. C. Harris. London, 1844. 3 v. 8°. . . V,838
Letters from. R. Lepsius. London, 1853. p. 8°. . . . . . L,16
Ethiopians, Researches concerning the. A. H. L. Heeren. London, 1850. 8°. A,39
Ethnography, Lectures on Ancient. B. G. Niebuhr. Lond. 1853. 2 v. 8°. N,435
and Philology of U. S. Exploring Exped. H. Hale. Phila. 1846. 4°. *Q,281
Ethnology, Analytical. R. T. Massy. London, 1855. 12°. . . . N,393
Descriptive. R. G. Latham. London, 1859. 2 v. 8°. . . . N,446
of the British Islands. R. G. Latham. London, 1852. 16°. . . N,391
Our British Ancestors. S. Lysons. Oxford, 1865. p. 8°. . . N,439

Ethnology, Races of Man. C. Pickering. London, 1863. p. 8°. . . L,137
Races of the Old World. C. L. Brace. New York, 1863. 8°. . N,416
See also *Man, Species, Races.*
Etiquette. Habits of Good Society. New York, 1868. 12°. . . . H,742
Ladies' Guide to Politeness. E. Leslie. Philadelphia, n. d. 12°. . H,281
Etonians, Eminent. E. S. Creasy. London, 1850. 8°. . . . . D,101
Etruria, Cities and Cemeteries of. G. Dennis. London, 1848. 2 v. 8°. . V,519
History of. H. Gray. London, 1843-68. 3 v. 8°. . . . . A,76
Sepulchres of. H. Gray. London, 1843. 8°. . . . . . V,520
Stones of, and Roman Marbles. G. L. Taylor. London, 1859. 4°. . Q,285
Etruscan Literature, and Iberno-Celtic. Sir W. Betham. Dublin, 1842. 2 v. 8°. H,732
Ettingshausen, C. R. von. Kenntniss der Calamiten. n. p. n. d. 8°. . G,831
Nervation der Blätter bei den Celastrineen. Wien, 1857. 4°. . F,98
Euclid. Elements of Geometry. London, 1855. 12°. . . . . M,945
The same. Cambridge, 1845. 8°. . . . . . . M,1159
The same; edited by T. Tate. London, 1856. 12°. . M,1140
Elements of; edited by I. Todhunter. London, 1869. 16°. . M,1133
Eugene Aram. Sir E. B. Lytton. Philadelphia, 1869. 12°. . . . K,812
The same. Leipzig, 1842. 16°. . . . . . . . J,311
Eugenic Acid. C. G. Williams. London, 1858. 8°. . . . . . N,252,44
Euler, L. Introductio in Analysin Infinitorum. Lausannæ, 1748. 2 v. 4°. M,1186
Letters on Natural Philosophy. New York, 1854-58. 2 v. 18°. L,378
Methodus inveniendi Lineas Curvas. Lausannæ, 1748. 2 v. 4°. M,1185
Euphrates Expedition, British. F. R. Chesney. London, 1868. 8°. . V,706
Euripides. Crowned Hippolytus; tr. by M. P. Fitz-Gerald. Lond. 1867. 12°. U,380
Medea; translated by A. Webster. London, 1868. 16°. . . . U,381
Tragedies; translated by T. A. Buckley. London, 1854. 2 v. p. 8°. L,56
The same; translated by R. Potter. N. Y. 1848-52. 3 v. 18°. U,361
Europe, American Merchant in. G. F. Train. New York, 1857. 12°. V,1034
American Woman in. S. R. Urbino. Boston, 1869. 12°. . . V,331
Ancient History of. W. Russell. Philadelphia, 1801. 2 v. 8°. . A,330
and Africa, Travels in. M. M. Noah. New York, 1819. 8°. . V,1087
and the East, Travels in. S. I. Prime. New York, 1855. 2 v. 12°. V,1067
Appleton's Short-Trip Guide to. H. Morford. New York, 1868. 16°. V,295
Atlantic and transatlantic Sketches. L. Mackinnon. N. Y. 1852. 12°. V,36
Art and Scenery in. H. B. Wallace. Philadelphia, 1857. 12°. . M,86
At Home and Abroad. M. F. d'Ossoli. New York, 1869. 12°. . U,93
By-ways of. B. Taylor. New York, 1869. 12°. . . . . V,327
Civilization in. F. Guizot. New York, 1846. 4 v. 12°. . . A,301
The same. London, 1870. 3 v. p. 8°. . . . . . . L,192
The same. New York, 1853. 3 v. 8°. . . . . . . S.C.
Cruise of the North Star. J. O. Choules. Boston, 1854. 12°. . . V,338
during the Middle Ages. S. A. Dunham. London, 1833-34. 4 v. 12°. M,998
H. Hallam. Boston, 1853. 3 v. 8°. . . . . . A,243
The same. New York, 1867. 3 v. 8°. . . . A,229
The same. New York, 1854. 8°. . . . . A,244
Eleven Weeks in. J. F. Clarke. Boston, 1852. 12°. . . . . V,336
Eight Years in. G. Catlin. London, 1848. 2 v. 8°. . . . . B,985
Foreign Reminiscences. H. R. Fox. New York, 1851. 12°. V,1039
From Copenhagen to Venice. H. M. Field. New York, 1860. 12°. V,384

Europe, From the Oak to the Olive. J. W. Howe. Boston, 1868. 16°. . v,308
Glances at. H. Greeley. New York, 1852. 12°. . . . . . v,309
Hand-Book for. W. P. Fetridge. New York, 1862. 12°. . . v,1053
R. Park. New York, 1854. 12°. . . . . . . . v,302
Haps and Mishaps of a Tour in. S. J. Lippincott. Boston, 1854. 12°. v,356
Heroes of. H. G. Hewlett. Boston, 1861. 12°. . . . . c,547
Histoire de la Civilisation en. H. Roux-Ferrand. Paris, 1833-41. 6 v. 8°. A,311
History of, 1789-1815. Sir A. Alison. Edinburgh, 1849-50. 14 v. 8°. A,341
The same. New York, 1854. 4 v. 8°. . . . A,339
1815-1852. Sir A. Alison. New York, 1852. 5 v. 8°. . A,342
Modern. T. H. Dyer. London, 1861-64. 4 v. 8°. . . A,337
W. Russell. New York, 1853. 3 v. 8°. . . . A,343
The same. London, 1857. 12°. . . . . A,300
of Principal States of. J. Russell. London, 1826. 2 v. 12°. A,305
Holidays Abroad. E. M. Kirkland. New York, 1849. 2 v. 12°. v,324
Impressions of, 1867-68. H. W. Bellows. New York, 1868. 2 v. 12°. v,369
Intellectual Development of. J. W. Draper. New York, 1864. 8°. o,707
Journal of a Summer Tour. E. M. Sewell. New York, 1852. 12°. v,305
Letters from. J. W. Forney. Philadelphia, 1867. 12°. . . . v,330
from Abroad. E. M. Sedgwick. New York, 1841. 2 v. 12°. v,365
Literature of, 15th—17th Centuries. H. Hallam. N. Y. 1851. 2 v. 8°. H,739
of the South of. J. C. L. S. de Sismondi. Lond. 1850. 2 v. p. 8°. L,236
Loiterings in. J. W. Corson. New York, 1848. 12°. . . . v,366
Maritime Law of. D. A. Azuni. New York, 1806. 2 v. 8°. . U,542
Men and things in. N. Murray. New York, 1853. 12°. . . v,340
Memoirs, including Travels in. E. Watson. New York, 1856. 8°. c,723
Memories over the Water. H. Maney. Nashville, 1854. 12°. . v,333
National Education in. H. Barnard. Hartford, 1854. 8°. . o,1237
Nationalities of. R. G. Latham. London, 1863. 2 v. 8°. . . N,447
Notes of a Traveler in. S. Laing. London, 1862. p. 8°. . I,656,3
Observations in. J. P. Durbin. New York, 1848. 2 v. 12°. . . v,387
Origin of Representative Government in. F. Guizot. Lond. 1852. p. 8°. L,190
Outre-Mer. H. W. Longfellow. Boston, 1852. 16°. . . . v,315
Over the Ocean. C. Guild. Boston, 1871. 12°. . . . . v,292
Past and Present. F. H. Ungewitter. New York, 1850. 12°. . A,319
Pencilings by the Way. N. P. Willis. New York, 1852. 12°. . v,323
Pictures of. C. A. Bartol. Boston, 1855. 12°. . . . . v,386
Political Systems of. A. H. L. Heeren. London, 1857. 8°. . . A,41
Pilgrimage in. J. C. Beltrami. London, 1828. 2 v. 8°. . v,1074
Reisen in Europa, 1835-41. J. Russeger. Stutt. 1841-48. 2 v. in 7. 8°. E,161
Revolutions in. A. Crichton. Edinburgh, 1828. 3 v. 16°. . . I,512
Scenes and Thoughts in. G. H. Calvert. Boston, 1863. 16°. . . v,306
Scenes in. D. C. Eddy. Boston, 1858. 12°. . . . . . v,388
Six Months among the Charities of. J. DeLiefde. Lond. 1866. 2 v. 8°. o,356
Social and Political State of. S. Laing. Cincinnati, 1841. 8°. . v,391
Summer in. W. Channing. Boston, 1856. 12°. . . . . v,346
Sunny Memories of. H. B. Stowe. Boston, 1854. 2 v. 12°. . . v,337
Tour of the Continent in 1852. J. Barrow. London, 1853. p. 8°. I,656,2
Travels in. E. D. Clarke. New York, 1813-14. 2 v. 12°. . v,1035
W. Fisk. New York, 1843. 8°. . . . . . . . v,273

Europe, Travels in. J. Griffith. London, 1805. 4°. . . . . . v,1144
C. L. Pöllnitz. London, 1737–40. 4 v. 12°. . . v,328
in Greece, Turkey, etc. J. L. Stephens. N. Y. 1855. 2 v. 12°. v,341
in the South of. H. W. Adalbert. London, 1849. 2 v. 8°. v,1071
Views a-foot. B. Taylor. New York, 1868. 12°. . . . . . v,317
Visit to, 1851. B. Silliman. New York, 1854. 2 v. 12°. . . v,319
Vorhalle Europäischer Völkergeschichten. C. Ritter. Berlin, 1820. 8°. E,12
Voyage to. A. Tripp. Boston, 1855. 12°. . . . . . . v,385
Wanderings in. S. S. Cox. New York, 1852. 12. . . . . v,321
European Agriculture and Economy. H. Colman. Boston, 1850. 2 v. 8°. M,578
European Capitals, Sketches of. W. Ware. Boston, 1851. 12°. . v,1043
European Celebrities, Visits to. W. B. Sprague. Boston, 1855. 12°. . . C,520
European History, Conspiracies in. J. P. Lawson. Edinb. 1829. 2 v. 16°. I,518
European Life and Manners. H. Colman. Boston, 1850. 2 v. 12°. . . v,344
European Morals, History of. W. E. H. Lecky. New York, 1869. 2 v. 8°. O,723
European Seas, Natural History of. E. Forbes. London, 1859. 16°. . N,493
European Travel, Reminiscences of. A. P. Peabody. New York, 1868. 16°. v,307
European Vineyards. W. J. Flagg. New York, 1869. 12°. . . . M,502
Eusebius Pamphilus. Ecclesiastical History. London, 1607. 4°. . . P,647
The same; translated by C. F. Crusé. London, 1851. p. 8°. . L,29
Eustace, J. C. Classical Tour through Italy. London, 1813. 2 v. 4°. . Q,416
The same. London, 1841. 3 v. 16°. . . . . . . I,622
Eutaw; Sequel to the Foragers. W. G. Simms. New York, 1864. 12°. . K,251
Eutropius. Abridgment of Roman History. London, 1853. p. 8°. . . L,64
Eva; the Ill-Omened Marriage. Sir E. B. Lytton. Leipzig, 1842. 16°. . J,312
Evagrius Scholasticus. Ecclesiastical Historie. London, 1607. 4°. . . P,647
and Theodoretus. Church History, 322–594. London, 1854. p. 8°. L,33
Evangeline. H. W. Longfellow. Boston, 1866. 12°. . . . . . . I,65,2
Evangelists, Lives of the. J. Fleetwood. Auburn, 1853. 8°. . . . F,23
their Testimony examined. S. Greenleaf. London, 1847. 8°. . . P,510
Evans, A. J. See *Wilson, A. J.*
Evans, F. W. Autobiography of a Shaker. New York, n. d. 8°. . . P,859
Evans, M. J. See *Lewes, M. J.*
Evans, G. W. D. Classic and Connoisseur in Italy, etc. Lond. 1835. 3 v. 8°. M,102
Evans, T. Old Ballads, Historical and Narrative. London, 1784. 4 v. 12°. I,369
Evans, W. English-Welsh Dictionary. Carmarthen, 1812. 8°. . . L.R.
Evans, W. Agriculture in Canada. Montreal, 1835–36. 2 v. 8°. . . M,434
Agricultural Improvement by Education. Montreal, 1837. 16°. . M,433
Evelina. F. D'Arblay. London, 1820. 2 v. 12°. . . . . . K,545
The same. New York, n. d. 12°. . . . . . . . K,668
The same. Leipzig, 1850. 16°. . . . . . . . J,50
Evelyn, C. Companion; After-dinner Table-talk. New York, 1850. 12°. H,211
Evelyn, J. Diary and Correspondence. London, 1859. 4 v. p. 8°. . . L,265
Life of Mrs. Godolphin. New York, 1847. 12°. . . . . C,1222
Silva; a Discourse of Forest Trees, etc. London, 1706. f°. . . Q,121
Evelyn Marston. A. Marsh-Caldwell. Liepzig, 1856. 2 v. in 1. 16°. . J,367
Evenings at Donaldson Manor. M. J. McIntosh. New York, 1853. 12°. K,211
at Home. J. Aiken and A. L. Barbauld. Edinburgh, n. d. 16°. . J,1439
of a Working-Man. J. Overs. London, 1844. 16°. . . . H,466
with the Doctrines. N. Adams. Boston, 1866. 12°. . . . . . P,112

Evergreens, Book of. J. Hoopes. New York, 1868. 12°. . . . . . N,945
Everest, C. W. Poets of Connecticut. New York, 1847. 8°. . . . . J,873
Everett, A. H. Critical and Miscellaneous Essays. Boston, 1846. 2 v. 12°. H,85
Life of Patrick Henry. Boston, 1844. 16°. . . . . . C,860,11
Life of Gen. Joseph Warren. New York. 16°. . . . C,860,10
Everett, E. Importance of Practical Education. New York, 1854. 12°. . O,937
Life of John Stark. New York, 1848. 16°. . . . . . C,860,1
Life of George Washington. New York, 1860. 12°. . . . C,902
Mount Vernon Papers. New York, 1860. 12°. . . . . . . H,113
Oration at Dorchester, July, 1855. Boston, 1855. 8°. . . . . C,63
Orations and Speeches. Boston, 1853–68. 4 v. 8°. . . . . . H,821
Everett, W. Changing Base. Boston, 1870. 16°. . . . . . . J,1369
Double Play. Boston, 1871. 16°. . . . . . . . . . J,1337
Every Day. S. J. M. Pike. Boston, 1871. 12°. . . . . . . K,216
Every-Day Book. W. Hone. London, 1826–27. 2 v. 8°. . . . H,490
Every-Day Philosopher. A. K. H. Boyd. Boston, 1869. 12°. . . . H,306
Eversburg; Roman. M. Raven. Hannover, 1855. 3 v. 16°. . . . G,424
Evesham, Chronicon Abbatiæ, A. D. 1418. London, 1863. 8°. . . . W,179
Evidences of Christianity. See *Christianity.*
Evil, Nature of. H. James. New York, 1855. 12°. . . . . . P,148
Evils of Popular Ignorance. J. Foster. New York, 1853. 12°. . . H,440
Ewald, C. Our Constitution. London, 1867. 12°. . . . . . . O,483
Ewart, J. Agriculturist's Assistant. Glasgow, 1857. 16°. . . . . M,439
Ewart, W. Diseases incident to Lead Miners. Carlisle, 1846. 8°. . N,252,35
Ewbank, T. Hydraulics and Mechanics. New York, 1870. 8°. . . N,134
The same. New York, 1850. 8°. . . . . . . . . S.C.
The World a Workshop. New York, 1855. 12°. . . . . . M,759
Examples of Machinery and Mill-Work. Glasgow, 1845. 4°. . . . S.C.
Excursions. H. D. Thoreau. Boston, 1866. 16°. . . . . . . H,12
Exhibition of 1851. See *London Exhibition.*
Exiles in Babylon; or, Children of Light. C. Tucker. London, 1869. 12°. K,591
Exiles of Florida. J. R. Giddings. Columbus, 1858. 12°. . . . C,181
Exley, T. Important Facts in Chemistry, London, 1837. 8°. . N,252,2
Experience of Life. E. M. Sewell. New York, 1866. 12°. . . . K,996
Experimental Education. Cheltenham, 1843. 12°. . . . . . . O,1030
Extempore Speaking, Art of. M. Bautain. New York, 1868. 12°. . . L,601
Extraordinary Men. W. Russell. London, 1853. 8°. . . . . . C,501
Extraordinary Women. W. Russell. London, 1864. 8°. . . . . C,493
Eydam, F. Electricität und Magnetismus. Weimar, 1843. 8°. . . N,252,8
Eye, Education of the. J. Burnet. London, 1837. 4°. . . . . Q,170
Eyes, and how to care for them. H. W. Williams. Boston, 1871. 12°. . L,958
Eyma, X. Légendes du Nouveau Monde. Paris, 1863. 2 v. 12°. . H,1027
Eyre, E. J., Life of. H. Hume. London, 1867. 8°. . . . . . D,192
Eyre, V. Military Operations at Cabul. Philadelphia, 1843. . . V,1072
Eytelwein, J. A. Practical Hydraulics; tr. by T. Young. Lond. 1826. 8°. N,143

Fabens, J. W. Camel Hunt; a Narrative of Adventure. N. Y. 1853. 12°. K,293
Faber, F. Leben der Hochnordischen Vögel. Leipzig, 1827. 8°. . . G,920

Fabiola; or, Church of the Catacombs. N. Wiseman. London, 1855. 12°. K,695
Fable and Phrase, Dictionary of. E. C. Brewer. Philadelphia, n. d. 12°. L.R.
Fable for Critics. J. R. Lowell. New York, 1848. 12°. . . . . . I,95
Fable Land, Gems from. W. O. Bourne. New York, 1853. 12°. . . J,1208
Fable of the Bees. B. de Mandeville. Edinburgh, 1755. 2 v. 12°. . . O,349
Fables. J. P. C. de Florian. Paris, 1856. 12°. . . . . . . . H,863
J. de La Fontaine. Paris, 1853. 8°. . . . . . . . . H,893
and Epigrams. G. E. Lessing. London, 1825. 12°. . . . G,23
Choisies. J. de La Fontaine. v. 3. Paris, 1778. 16°. . . . H,854
et Œuvres Diverses. J. de La Fontaine. Paris, 1856. 12°. . H,879
Illustrated. J. de La Fontaine. New York, 1865. 2 v. 12°. . H,956
of Æsop. New York, 1848. 12°. . . . . . . . . . G,1
of Krilof. W. R. S. Ralston. London, 1869. 12°. . . . . H,625
of Phædrus, construed into English. London, 1847. 12°. . . U,399
Original and Selected. New York, 1869. 8°. . . . . . H,622
Fabyan, R. New Chronicles of England and France. London, 1811. 4°. F,155
Fact and Fiction. L. M. Child. New York, 1854. 12°. . . . . J,1220
Faded Hope, The. H. Sigourney. New York, 1854. 16°. . . . . J,1185
Fagel, F., Description Philosophique de feu. F. Hemsterhuis. Par. 1773. 16°. L,841
Fair Harvard; a Story of American College Life. New York, 1869. 12°. K,1099
Fair Maid of Perth. Sir W. Scott. Boston, 1858. 2 v. 16°. . . . K,934
The same. Philadelphia, 1866. 8°. . . . . . . K,96
The same. Philadelphia, 1869. 8°. . . . . . . K,1115
Fair Maid of the Exchange. T. Heywood. London, 1845. 8°. . . I,885,27
Fair Maid of the West. T. Heywood. London, 1850. 8°. . . . I,885,43
Fair Play. E. D. E. N. Southworth. Philadelphia, 1870. 12°. . . . K,423
Fairbairn, P. Prophecy; its Function and Interpretation. Edinb. 1856. 8°. P,160
Typology of Scripture. Philadelphia, 1859. 2 v. 8°. . . . P,161
Fairbairn, Sir W. Application of Iron to Buildings. London, 1870. 8°. . M,665
Mechanism and Machinery of Transmission. Philadelphia, 1867. 12°. M,610
Fairbanks, C. B. Aguecheek. Boston, 1859. 12°. . . . . . . H,125
Fairbanks, G. R. History of Florida till 1842. Philadelphia, 1871. 12°. . C,180
Fairchild Family. M. M. Sherwood. New York, 1858. 12°. . . K,1008,2
Faire Gospeller, The. A. Manning. London, 1866. 12°. . . . . . J,538
Fairfax, T. *Lord.* Fairfax Corresp., Reign of Charles I. Lond. 1848. 2 v. 8°. A,511,1,2
Life of. H. Coleridge. London, 1852. 16°. . . . . . C,1166,1
Memorials of the Civil War. London, 1849. 2 v. 8°. . . A,511,3,4
Fairfax; or, Master of Greenway Court. J. E. Cooke. New York, 1868. 12°. J,632
Fairholme, G. Physical Demonstrations of Mosaic Deluge. Lond. 1837. 8°. N,803
Fairholt, F. W. Costume in England. London, 1860. 8°. . . . . M,366
Tobacco; its History and Associations. London, 1859. 12°. . . H,467
(Ed.) Civic Garland; Songs. London, 1845. 12°. . . . . L,606,19
Lord Mayors' Pageants. London, 1843. 12°. . . . . L,606,10
Poems on George, Duke of Buckingham. London, 1850. 12°. L,606,29
Songs and Poems on Costume. London, 1849. 12°. . . L,606,27
Fairy Book. D. M. Craik. New York, 1867. 16°. . . . . . J,1204
Home Fairy Tales. J. Macé. New York, 1870. 12°. . . . J,1339
Fairy Egg, and what it held. H. H. Weston and others. Boston, 1870. 12°. J,1648
Fairy Fingers. A. C. Ritchie. New York, 1865. 12°. . . . . . K,233
Fairy Know-a-Bit. C. Tucker. London, 1868. 12°. . . . . . . . J,659

Fairy Legends and Tales, Danish. H. C. Andersen. London, 1861. p. 8°. L,92
of the South of Ireland. London, 1834. 16°. . . . . . . I,650
Fairy Mythology. T. Keightley. London, 1860. p. 8°. . . . . . L,14
of a Midsummer Night's Dream. London, 1845. 8°. . . I,885,24
Fairy Queen. E. Spenser. London, 1856. 16°. . . . . . . . I,432
Fairy Tales. H. C. Andersen. New York, 1869. 16°. . . . J,1660
H. Parr. London, 1869. 12°. . . . . . . . J,1443
of all Nations. E. Laboulaye. New York, 1867. 12°. . . J,1260
Faith and Practice, Divine Rule of. W. Goode. Philadelphia, 1842. 2 v. 8°. P,176
Development and Fruits of. G. B. Cheever. New York, 1849. 12°. P,262
and Modern Atheism compared. J. Buchanan. Edinb. 1855. 2 v. 8°. P,108
Hope and Love, Die Lehren der. J. F. Fries. Heidelberg, 1823. 16°. G,552
Nature and Royalties of. S. Bolton. London, 1656. 8°. . . . P,181
Nemesis of. J. A. Froude. London, 1849. 12°. . . . . P,276
Faith Gartney's Girlhood. A. D. T. Whitney. Boston, 1863. 12°. . . K,396
Faith Unwin's Ordeal. G. M. Craik. Leipzig, 1866. 16°. . . . . J,96
Falcon Family. M. W. Savage. London, 1845. 12°. . . . . . K,559
Falconer, W. Poetical Works. Boston, 1854. 16°. . . . . . . I,209
The same; with Life by G. Gilfillan. New York, 1854. 8°. . J,851
Falkland. Sir E. B. Lytton. Philadelphia, n. d. 8°. . . . . . K,826
Falkner Lyle. M. Lemon. Leipzig, 1866. 2 v. in 1. 16°. . . . J,263
Fallacies, Book of. J. Bentham. London, 1824. 8°. . . . . . . O,496
Fallen Pride. E. D. E. N. Southworth. Philadelphia, 1870. 12°. . . K,421
Fallersleben, H. von. Gedichte. Hannover, n. d. 16°. . . . . . E,260
Fallmerayer, J. P. Gesch. des Kaiserthums v. Trapezunt. Munch. 1827. 4°. E,34
Falloux, Count de. Life and Letters of Mad. Swetchine. Boston, 1868. 16°. D,746
False Heir. G. P. R. James. Leipzig, 1843. 16°. . . . . . . J,206
Fame and Fortune. H. Alger. Boston, 1868. 16°. . . . . . J,1430,2
Familie, Die. W. H. Riehl. Stuttgart, 1861. 16°. . . . . . . E,377
Family and Church. C. Loyson, *Father Hyacinthe.* New York, 1870. 12°. H,908
Family Doom. E. D. E. N. Southworth. Philadelphia, 1870. 12°. . . K,422
Family Magazine, 1836-41. Cincinnati, 1836-41. 6 v. 4°. . . . . S,20
Family Secrets. S. S. Ellis. London, n. d. 3 v. 8°. . . . . . K,1037
Family Topographer. S. Tymms. London, 1832-43. 7 v. 16°. . . . V,304
Family Tour through South of Holland. London, 1831. 16°. . . . . I,615
Famous Americans of Recent Times. J. Parton. Boston, 1869. 8°. . . C,910
Famous Persons and Places. N. P. Willis. New York, 1854. 12°. . . H,84
Fanaticism. I. Taylor. London, 1866. p. 8°. . . . . . . . P,96
Fanchon; the Cricket. Mad. Dudevant. Philadelphia, n. d. 12°. . . H,954
Fancourt, C. St. J. History of Yucatan until 1700. London, 1854. 8°. . C,374
Fanning, D. Narrative of Adventures in North Carolina. N. Y. 1865. 4°. C,315
Fanny, and other Poems. F. G. Halleck. New York, 1846. 12°. . . I,47
Fantosme, J. Chronicle of the War, 1173-74. London, 1840. 8°. . F,126,11
Far above Rubies. J. H. Riddell. Leipzig, 1867. 2 v. in 1. 16°. . . J,423
Faraday, M., as a Discoverer. J. Tyndall. London, 1868. 8°. . . . . D,205
Chemical Manipulations. London, 1842. 8°. . . . . . . . N,210
Lectures on the Chemical History of a Candle. New York, 1861. 16°. N,200
on the Forces of Matter. New York, 1860. 16°. . . . . N,64
on the Non-Metallic Elements. London, 1853. 16°. . . . M,754
Life and Letters of. B. Jones. London, 1870. 2 v. 8°. . . . . D,455

Faraday, M. Researches in Chemistry and Physics. London, 1859. 8°. . M,792
Review of his Report on Explosions. M. Dunn. London, 1845. 8°. N,252,35
and J. Stodart. Alloys of Steel. London, 1822. 4°. . . N,252,42
Farben-Laboratorium. C. H. Schmidt. Weimar, 1847. 16°. . . . G,627
Farel, W., and Story of the Swiss Reform. W. M. Blackburn. Edinb. 1867. 12°. D,698
Farley, J. L. Turkey. London, 1866. 8°. . . . . . . . . B,558
Farm, Dictionary of the. W. L. Rham. London, 1858. 8° . . . M,495
How to get a. E. Morris. New York, 1864. 12°. . . . . M,499
Farm Drainage. H. F. French. New York, 1859. 12°. . . . . M,518
Farm Engineer. R. Ritchie. Glasgow, 1849. 8°. . . . . . M,586
Farm Implements. J. J. Thomas. New York, 1854. 12°. . . . . M,512
Farmer and Rural Economist. T. G. Fessenden. New York, 1855. 12°. . M,519
Progressive. J. A. Nash. New York, 1854. 12°. . . . . M,517
Farmer's Dictionary. D. P. Gardner. New York, 1855. 12°. . . . M,494
Farmer's Reporter. Cincinnati, 1831–33. 8°. . . . . . . . T,32
Farmer's Text-Book. J. L. Blake. New York, 1856. 12°. . . . M,541
Farmers of Suffolk, Letters to. J. S. Henslow. London, 1843. 8°. . N,252,24
Farming, High, under Liberal Covenants. J. Caird. Edinburgh, 1849. 8°. N,252,31
High, vindicated. J. Caird. Edinburgh, 1850. 8°. . . . N,252,31
Outlines of Modern. R. S. Burn. London, 1865–69. 5 v. 12°. . M,832
What I know about. H. Greeley. New York, 1871. 12°. . . M,565
Faroe Islands, Historical and Descriptive Account of. New York, 1854. 16°. L,425
Yacht Voyage to. J. W. Clark. London, 1861. 8°. . . V,1086,1
Farquhar, G. Dramatic Works. London, 1866. 8°. . . . . . . I,728
Farquharson, M. Holidays at Roseland's. New York, 1870. 16°. . J,1323
Old-Fashioned Boy. Philadelphia, 1871. 16°. . . . . . . K,273
Farr, E. Ancient History. Cincinnati, 1856. 4 v. 12°. . . . . . A,9
Farragut, D. G., Story Life of. P. C. Headley. New York, 1870. 16°. J,1636
Farrar, A. S. Critical History of Free Thought. New York, 1866. 8°. . O,660
Farrar, F. W. Chapters on Language. London, 1865. 8°. . . . L,503
Eric; or, Little by Little. New York, n. d. 12°. . . . . J,1470
Julian Home. New York, n. d. 12°. . . . . . . J,1471
St. Winifred's. New York, n. d. 12°. . . . . . . J,1472
Farrar, J. Recollections of Seventy Years. Boston, 1866. 12°. . . C,546
Young Lady's Friend. New York, 1860. 12°. . . . . . . H,299
Farrers of Budge Row. H. Martineau. . . . . . . . K,551,9
Farriel, C. C. History of Provençal Poetry. New York, 1860. 12°. . H,761
Farrier, and Stud-Book. R. Mason. Philadelphia, 1858. 12°. . . . M,448
Every Man his own. F. and J. Clater. London, 1854. 12°. . . M,469
Farriery, Modern System of. G. Skeavington. London, n. d. 4°. . . M,585
Fasquelle, L. New Method of Learning French. New York, 1866. 12°. L,808
Fashion and Famine. A. S. Stephens. Philadelphia, 1870. 12°. . . K,444
Fatal Marriage. E. D. E. N. Southworth. Philadelphia, 1870. 12°. . . K,424
Father Brighthopes. J. T. Trowbridge. New York, 1869. 16°. . J,1213
Fathers, Christian, Lives and Acts of. W. Cave. Lond. 1687. 2 v. f°. F,105
Lives of. A. Butler. Dublin, 1866. 12 v. 12°. . . . . P,794
Magna Bibliotheca Veterum Patrum. Parisiis, 1644. 17 v. f°. Q,79
Fau, J. Anatomy of External Forms of Man. London, 1849. 8°. . . L,975
Atlas to the same. London, 1849. 8°. . . . . . *Q,194
Fauna Peruana, Untersuch. über die. J. J. Tschudi. St. Gallen, 1846. f°. Q,64

Faust. J. W. von Goethe. Stuttgart und Tübingen, 1854. 8°. . . . E,343,2
The same. Paris, 1836. 8°. . . . . . . . . E,344,2
The same. Stuttgart, 1867. 16°. . . . . . . E,327,5
The same; translated by C. T. Brooks. Boston, 1866. 12°. . G,49
The same; translated by A. Hayward. Boston, 1866. 16°. . G,48
The same; translated by B. Taylor. Boston, 1871. 2 v. 8°. G,173
Fauvel-Gouraud, F. Phreno-Mnemotechnic Dictionary. N. Y. 1844. 8°. L.R.
Fay, T. S. Countess Ida; a Tale of Berlin. New York, 1840. 2 v. 12°. K,110
Norman Leslie. New York, 1869. 12°. . . . . . . . . K,99
Ulric; or, the Voices. New York, 1851. 12°. . . . . . . I,33
Fayette Co. and Lexington, Ky., Direc. of. J. P. B. Mac Cabe. Lex. 1838. 12°. C,178
Feasts and Fasts of the Catholic Church. A. Butler. New York, 1852. 12°. P,823
Feathers for Arrows. C. H. Spurgeon. New York, n. d. 16°. . . . P,70
Featherstonhaugh, G. W. Voyage up the Minnay Sotor. Lond. 1847. 2 v. 8°. V,133
Féaux, B. Rechenbuch. Paderborn, 1857. 8°. . . . . . . . E,426
Fechner, G. T. Elemente der Psychophysik. Leipzig, 1860. 2 v. 8°. . G,548
Galvanische Kette. Leipzig, 1831. 4°. . . . . . . N,252,43
Nanna; das Seelenleben der Pflanzen. Leipzig, 1848. 16°. . . G,868
Federal Government, History of. E. A. Freeman. v. 1. London, 1863. 8°. A,89
Federalist, The. A. Hamilton and others. Hallowell, 1828. 8°. . . O,508
The same; edited by H. B. Dawson. v. 1. New York, 1864. 8°. O,528
Felice, G. de. History of the Protestants of France. London, 1853. 8°. . P,567
Félix, E. R. Memoirs of Rachel. A. de Barrera. New York, 1858. 12°. D,641
Felix Holt, the Radical. M. J. Lewes. New York, 1866. 8°. . . . K,793
The same. Leipzig, 1867. 2 v. in 1. 16°. . . . . . J,296
Fellenberg, L. R. Fibrine du Cheval. Berne, 1841. 8°. . . . N,252,14
Fellowes, W. D. Hist. Sketches of Charles I., Cromwell, etc. Lond. 1828. 4°. F,265
Felton, C. C. Greece, Ancient and Modern. Boston, 1867. 2 v. 8°. . A,83
Life of William Eaton. New York, 1860. 12°. . . . C,860,9
Female Poets of America. R. W. Griswold. Philadelphia, 1854. 8°. . H,667
Female Quixote. C. Lennox. London, 1820. 2 v. 12°. . . . . K,536
Female Soldier; Life of Deborah Sampson; ed. J. A. Vinton. Bost. 1866. 4°. C,1016
Female Sovereigns, Celebrated, Memoirs of. A. Jameson. Lond. 1870. 12°. C,550
Feminine Soul. E. Strutt. Boston, 1870. 16°. . . . . . . . O,373
Fénélon, F. de S. de L. M. Aventures de Télémaque. Paris, 1853. 8°. . H,939
The same. Paris, 1854. 12°. . . . . . . . . . H,886
The same. New York, 1854. 2 v. 18°. . . . . H,933
The same; translated. New York, n. d. 8°. . . . . H,947
De l'Education des Filles. Paris, 1854. 12°. . . . . H,1000
The same; translated. Boston, 1820. 24°. . . . O,1110
De l'Existence et des Attributs de Dieu. Paris, 1853. 12°. . . P,131
Life of. C. Butler. London, 1819. 8°. . . . . . . . D,605
Lives of Ancient Philosophers; tr. by J. Cormack. N. Y. 1854. 18°. L,432
Selections from the Writings of. Boston, 1851. 12°. . . . . H,907
Fenian Brotherhood; Life of S. Stephens. New York, 1866. 12°. . . D,378
Fenn, Sir J. Original Letters. London, 1787–1823. 5 v. 4°. . . . H,170
Paston Letters. London, 1849. p. 8°. . . . . . . . H,482
Fenning, D. Universal Spelling-Book. London, n. d. 16°. . . . O,778
Fenwick, T. and Baker, T. Subterraneous Surveying. London, n. d. 12°. M,839
Ferdinand and Isabella, Reign of. W. H. Prescott. Boston, 1858. 3 v. 8°. B,477

Ferdinand I. and Maximilian II. of Austria. L. Raube. Lond. 1864. p. 8°. I,661,2
Fergus, H. History of the United States. London, 1832. 2 v. 12°. . M,993
Ferguson, A. History of the Roman Republic. New York, 1856. 8°. . A,161
The same. New York, 1854. 16°. . . . . . . . L,468
Ferguson, R. English Surnames in the Teutonic Family. Lond. 1858. 8°. L,515
Swiss Men and Swiss Mountains. London, 1864. p. 8°. . . I,656,1
Teutonic Name-System. London, 1864. 8°. . . . . . . L,520
Ferguson, R. M. Electricity. London, 1867. 16°. . . . . . . N,47
Fergusson, J. Ancient Topography of Jerusalem. London, 1847. 8°. . V,716
History of Architecture. London, 1865–67. 3 v. 8°. . . *M,173
Illustrated Hand-Book of Architecture. London, 1855. 2 v. 8°. *M,189
Palaces of Nineveh and Persepolis restored. London, 1854. 8°. . V,655
Fern, Fanny, *pseud.* See *Parton, S. P.*
Fern Leaves, from Fanny's Portfolio. S. P. Parton. Auburn, 1854. 2 v. 12°. H,44
Ferns, British, History of. T. Moore. London, 1851. 16°. . . . N,921
British, and their Allies. T. Moore. London, 1867. 16°. . . N,914
Century of. Sir W. J. Hooker. London, 1854. 8°. . . . . N,894
Farrnkräuter. G. Kunze. Leipzig, 1840–47. 2 v. 4°. . . . G,963
Hardy. N. Bellairs. London, 1865. 8°. . . . . . . . N,942
Ferrara, Duchess of, Memorials of. London, 1859. 16°. . . . . D,638
Ferrier, J. F. Institutes of Metaphysic. Edinburgh, 1856. 12°. . . O,641
Lectures on Greek Philosophy. Edinburgh, 1866. 2 v. 8°. . . O,642
Ferrier, J. P. Caravan Journey. London, 1856. 8°. . . . . V,758
Ferris, B. G. Utah and the Mormons. New York, 1854. 12°. . . . C,166
Ferry, G. Vagabond Life in Mexico. New York, 1856. 12°. . . . K,300
Fertilization, Urbarmachung. C. Sprengel. Leipzig, 1846. 8°. . . G,661
Fessenden, T. G. American Kitchen Gardener. New York, 1856. 12°. . M,533
Complete Farmer and Rural Economist. New York, 1855. 12°. . M,519
Festivals, Games, and Amusements. H. Smith. New York, 1855. 16°. . L,358
Festive Songs of the 16th and 17th Centuries. London, 1848. 12°. . L,606,23
Festus; a Poem. P. J. Bailey. Boston, 1850. 12°. . . . . . . . I,283
Fétis, F. J. Treatise on Choir and Chorus Singing. London, 1854. 8°. M,421,1
Fetridge, W. P. Hand-Book for Europe and the East. New York, 1862. 12°. V,1053
Fette, W. E. Dialogues from Dickens. Boston, 1870. 16°. . . . . I,723
Feuerbach, A. Nachgelassene Scriften. Braunschweig, 1853. 4 v. 12°. E,320

Bd. 1. Leben, Briefe, und Gedichte. Bd 2–3 Geschichte der Griechischen Plastik. Bd. 4. Kunstgeschichtliche Abhandlungen.

Feuchtwanger, L. Popular Treatise on Gems. New York, 1869. 12°. . N,757
Treatise on Soluble or Water-Glass. New York, 1870. 12°. . . M,683
Few Friends, and their Amusements. M. E. Dodge. Philadelphia, 1869. 12°. H,43
Fibel; oder, erster Unterricht. K. A. Zoller. Reutlingen, 1842. 2 v. in 1. 12°. O,888
Fichte, J. G., Memoir of. W. Smith. Boston, 1846. 12°. . . . . . D,501
Sämmtliche Werke. Berlin, 1845–46. 8 v. 8°. . . . . . G,549

Vol. 1. Recensionen des Aenesidemus; Ueber den Begriff der Wissenschaftslehre, oder der sogenannten Philosophie; Grundlage der gesammten Wissenschaftslehre; Grundriss des Eigenthümlichen der Wissenschaftslehre; Erste und zweite Einleitung in die Wissenschaftslehre; Versuch einer neuer Darstellung der Wissenschaftslehre.
2. Darstellung der Wissenschaftslehre; Die Bestimmung des Menschen; Populairer und Kritischer Anhang.
3. Grundlage des Naturrechts; Der Geschlossene Handelsstaat.
4. System der Sittenlehre nach den Principien der Wissenschaftslehre; Staatslehre.

Fichte, J. G. Sämmtliche Werke. *Continued.* . . . . . . . G,549

6. Aphorismen über Religion und Deismus; Versuch einer Kritik aller Offenbarung; Ueber den Grund unseres Glaubens an eine Göttliche Weltregierung; Appellation an das Publicum gegen die Anklage des Atheismms; Gerichtliche Verantwortung gegen die Anklage des Atheismus; Rückerrinnerungen, Antworten, Fragen; Aus einem Privatschreiben; Die Anweisung zum seligen Leben, oder auch die Religionslehre.
6. Zurückforderung der Denkfreiheit von den Fürsten Europas; Beiträge zur Berichtigung der Urtheile über die Französische Revolution; Ueber die Bestimmung des Gelehrten; Ueber das Wesen des Gelehrten; Ueber die einzig mögliche Störung der akademischen Freiheit.
7. Grundzüge des gegenwärtigen Zeitalters; Reden an die Deutsche Nation; Politische Fragmente.
8. Nicolai's Leben und Sonderbare Meinungen; Deducirter Plan einer zu Berlin zu errichtenden höheren Lehranstalt; Vermischte Aufsätze; Recensionen; Poesien und metrische Uebersetzungen.

Vocation of Man; translated by W. Smith. London, 1848. 12°. . N,398
Vocation of the Scholar. London, 1847. 12°. . . . . . . G,34
und Schelling über Gott und Welt. J. F. Fries. Heidel. 1807. 16°. G,551
Fiction, History of. J. Dunlop. Philadelphia, 1842. 2 v. 12°. . . H,642
Fictitous Names, Hand-Book for. R. Thomas. London, 1868. 8°. . . L.R.
Field, G. Chromatics. London, 1845. 8°. . . . . . . . . M,109
Chromatography; a Treatise on Colours. London, 1835. 4°. . *Q,204
Treatise on Painting. London, 1858. 12°. . . . . . . M,913
Field, H. M. History of the Atlantic Telegraph. New York, 1866. 12°. M,693
Summer Pictures from Copenhagen to Venice. New York, 1860. 12°. V,384
Field, M. City Architecture. New York, 1854. 8°. . . . . . . M,225
Field, T. W. Pear Culture. New York, 1859. 12°. . . . . . . M,489
Field, W. Memoirs of Samuel Parr. London, 1828. 2 v. 8°. . . D,396
Field and Forest, Studies in. W. Flagg. Boston, 1857. 8°. . . . N,971
Field Artillery, Treatise on. Capt. Taubert. London, 1856. 12°. . . M,966
Field Fortification, Treatise on. D. H. Mahan. New York, 1864. 18°. . M,747
Field, Garden, and Woodland. London, 1838. 18°. . . . . . . N,910
Field-Sports of the United States. H. W. Herbert. N. Y. 1849. 2 v. 8°. M,315
Oriental. T. Williamson. London, 1819. 2 v. 4°. . . . Q,329
Fielding, H. History of Amelia. New York, 1850. 12°. . . . . K,699
History of Tom Jones. London, 1820. 3 v. 12°. . . . . . K,533
The same. Leipzig, 1844. 2 v. in 1. 16°. . . . . . J,163
Joseph Andrews. London, 1820. 12°. . . . . . . . . K,532
Miscellaneous Works. New York, 1858. 4 v. 12°. . . . . U,172

Vol. 1, 2. Tom Jones. Vol. 3. Amelia.
Vol. 4. Joseph Andrews, and Jonathan Wild.

Fielding T. H. Painting in Oil and Water Colors. London, 1846. 8°. . M,113
Fiesco, J. L., Conspiracy of. J. F. P. de Gondi. Boston, 1858. 12°. . B,482
Fighting Joe. W. T. Adams. Boston, 1869. 16°. . . . . . J,1536,5
Figuier, L. Insect World. London, 1868. 8°. . . . . . . . . O,48
Mammalia. New York, 1871. 8°. . . . . . . . . . N,530
Ocean World. London, 1868. 8°. . . . . . . . . . N,535
Primitive Man. New York, 1871. 8°. . . . . . . . N,507
Reptiles and Birds. New York, 1870. 8°. . . . . . . N,529
Vegetable World. London, 1867. 8°. . . . . . . . . N,982
World before the Deluge. New York, 1867. 8°. . . . . . N,820
Fiji and the Fijians. T. Williams and J. Calvert. New York, 1859. 8°. . V,899
and its Inhabitants. B. Seemann. London, 1862. 8°. . . . V,1086,2
Islands, Account of, 1860–61. B. Seemann. Cambridge, 1862. 8°. . V,898

Fillmore, A. D. Christian Psalmist. Cincinnati, 1847. 16°. . . . . P,887
Fillmore, M., Life of. W. L. Barré. Buffalo, 1856. 12°. . . . . . C,926
Filson, J. Settlement of Kentucky. London, 1793. 8°. . . . . . V,44
Finden, E. Ports, Harbors, etc., of Great Britain. Lond. 1841–44. 2 v. 4°. *Q,417
and W. Illustrations of Byron; ed. W. Brockedon. Lond. 1834. 3 v. 8°. *J,855
Findlay, A. G. Classical Atlas of Ancient Geography. New York, n. d. 8°. V,1127
Fine Art. W. M. Rosetti. London, 1867. 16°. . . . . . . . . M,39
Fine Arts, General View of. D. Huntington. New York, 1851. 12°. . M,40
History of. B. J. Lossing. New York, 1854. 16°. . . . . . L,408
Illustrated with Plates, Appleton's. New York, 1856. 2 v. 8°. . *Q,252
in Great Britain. W. B. S. Taylor. London, 1841. 2 v. 12°. . M,56
Pictorial Gallery of, v. 2. London, 1847. 4°. . . . . . . Q,205
Finger-Rings, History and Poetry of. C. Edwards. New York, 1855. 12°. H,193
Fink, G. W. Wesen und Geschichte der Oper. Leipzig, 1838. 8°. . . G,640
Finlay, G. Byzantine and Greek Empires. Edinburgh, 1854–56. 2 v. 8°. A,86
Greece under the Romans. Edinburgh, 1857. 8°. . . . . . A,85
The same. Edinburgh, 1857. 8°. . . . . . . . . A,107
History of Greece. Edinburgh, 1851. 8°. . . . . . . . A,105
The same. Edinburgh, 1856. 8°. . . . . . . . . A,106
History of the Greek Revolution, 1821. Edinburgh, 1861. 2 v. 8°. A,108
Finley, J. B. Autobiography; or, Pioneer Life in West. Cinn. 1858. 12°. C,787
Sketches of Western Methodism. Cincinnati, 1857. 12°. . . . P,843
Fior d' Aliza. A. de Lamartine. New York, 1869. 12°. . . . . H,964
Fireside Fairies. S. Pindar. New York, 1865. 16°. . . . . . . J,1360
Fireside Friend; or, Female Student. A. H. L. Phelps. New York, 1847. 12°. O,1144
Fireside Piety. J. Abbott. New York, 1835. 16°. . . . . . . J,1313
Fireside Travels. J. R. Lowell. Boston, 1865. 12°. . . . . . . V,310
Fireman, The; Fire Departments of the U. S. D. D. Dana. Boston, 1858. 12°. O,348
First Impressions. S. S. Ellis. New York, 1854. 16°. . . . . J,1180
Fischer, E. G. Lehrbuch der Arithmetik. Leipzig, 1842. 8°. . . . E,429
Fischer, N. W. Galvanische Elektricität. Berlin, 1830. 8°. . . N,252,8
Fish, H. C. Pulpit Eloquence of the Nineteenth Century. N. Y. 1857. 8°. P,764
Fish, S. Supplicacyon for the Beggars. London, 1871. 8°. . . L,604,13
Fish and Fishing of North America. H. W. Herbert. New York, 1851. 8°. M,310
Fish, Apodal, Catalogue of. J. J. Kaup. London, 1856. 8°. . . . N,702
Artificial Propagation of. T. Garlick. Cleveland, 1857. 8°. . . N,701
Fish-Breeding, Treatise on Artificial. W. H. Fry. New York, 1854. 12°. M,308
Fish-Culture, American. T. Norris. Philadelphia, 1868. 12°. . . M,320
in France. J. G. Bertram. London, 1864. 8°. . . V,1086,3
Fishes, Amphibious, and Reptiles. W. Swainson. London, 1838. 2 v. 12°. M,1034
British. R. Hamilton. Edinburgh, 1852. 2 v. 16°. . . N,470,36,37
History of. W. Yarrell. London, 1859. 2 v. 8°. . . N,703
of British Guiana. R. H. Schomburgk. Edinburgh, 1852. 16°. N,470,39,40
of the British Islands. J. Couch. London, 1866–67. 4 v. 8°. . N,704
Natural History of. J. S. Bushnan. Edinburgh, 1853. 16°. . N,470,35
Perch. Sir W. Jardine. Edinburgh, 1852. 16°. . . . N,470,38
Rare and Curious, of Ceylon. J. W. Bennett. London, 1851. . . Q,38
Fisher, G. P. Life of Benjamin Silliman. New York, 1866. 2 v. 12°. . C,706
Supernatural Origin of Christianity. New York, 1866. 8°. . . P,239
Fisher, R. S. Statistical Gazetteer of United States. New York, 1853. 8°. L.R.

Fisher, S. W. Lecture on William Penn. Cincinnati, 1847. 8°. . . H,302,4
Three Great Temptations of Young Men. Cincinnati, 1859. 12°. . H,262
Fishing and Whaling. C. Nordhoff. Cincinnati, 1856. 16°. . . . K,140
Fishing, Fly, Salmonia; Days of. Sir H. Davy. London, 1851. 16°. . M,301
Fishing in American Waters. G. C. Scott. New York, 1869. 12°. . . M,311
Fishing, Superior. R. B. Roosevelt. New York, 1868. 12°. . . . M,321
Fishing, Trout. G. P. R. Pulman. London, 1851. 16°. . . . . M,326
Fisk, F. Recollections of Mary Lyon. Boston, 1866. 12°. . . . C,695
Fisk, W. Travels in Europe. New York, 1843. 8°. . . . . . . V,273
Fisk, W., Life of. J. Holdich. New York, 1856. 8°. . . . . C,813
Fiske, D. W. First American Chess Congress. New York, 1859. 12°. . M,329
Fiske, J. Tobacco and Alcohol. New York, 1869. 16°. . . . . H,222
Fiske, S. Dunn Browne's Experiences in the Army. Boston, 1866. 12°. . B,915
Fison, W. Hints for the Earnest Student. London, 1850. 12°. . . C,986
Fitch, G. W. Origin of Geographical Names. New York, 1852. 18°. . O,897
Outlines of Physical Geography. New York, 1856. 12°. . V,1120
Fitch, J. Original Steamboat supported. Philadelphia, 1788. 8°. . B,809,1
Life of. T. Westcott. Philadelphia, 1857. 12°. . . . . C,925
The same. C. Whittlesey. Boston, 1860. 12°. . . C,860,16
Fitch, S. S. Lectures on the Functions of the Lungs. New York, 1856. 12°. L,916
Fitz-Boodle Papers. W. M. Thackeray. Boston, 1869. 12°. . . K,1038,4
The same. Philadelphia, 1866. 12°. . . . . . K,1087,4
The same. Leipzig, 1857. 16°. . . . . . . J,484,7
Fitzclarence, G. Route through India and Egypt. London, 1819. 4°. . V,721
Fitzgerald, P. Famous Forgery; Story of Dr. Dodd. London, 1865. 12°. D,181
Life of David Garrick. London, 1868. 2 v. 8°. . . . . D,443
Fitzosborne, Sir T., Letters of. W. Melmoth. London, 1795. 8°. . U,256,1
Five Acres too much. R. B. Roosevelt. New York, 1869. 12°. . . M,497
Five Black Arts; Painting, Pottery, Glass, etc. Columbus, 1861. 8°. . M,622
Five Centuries of English Language and Literature. Leipzig, 1860. 16°. . J,164
Five Gateways of Knowledge. G. Wilson. Philadelphia, 1857. 16°. . H,206
Five Great Monarchies of Ancient World. G. Rawlinson. Lond. 1867. 4 v. 8°. A,27
Five Weeks in a Balloon. New York, 1869. 12°. . . . . . . K,362
Five Years in an English University. C. A. Bristed. N. Y. 1852. 2 v. 12°. O,812
Flag of the United States, History of the. S. Hamilton. Phila. 1852. 12°. B,849
Flagg, E. Venice, the City of the Sea. New York, 1853. 2 v. 12°. . V,494
Flagg, W. Studies in the Field and Forest. Boston, 1857. 8°. . . . N,971
Flagg, W. J. Three Seasons in European Vineyards. N. Y. 1869. 12°. M,502
Flammarion, C. Wonders of the Heavens. New York, 1871. 12°. . M,1050
Flanders, H. Exposition of Constitution of United States. Phila. 1860. 12°. B,847
Lives of the Chief Justices of United States. Phila. 1855. 2 v. 8°. C,816
Flatbootman, Der. F. Gerstäcker. Prag und Leipzig, 1858. 24°. . . G,279
Flavel, J. Fountain of Life. New York, n. d. 12°. . . . . P,746,31
Flax and Hemp, Treatise on. E. S. Delamer. London, 1854. 16°. . . M,438
Flaxman, J. Compositions from Æschylus. London, 1831. 4°. . *Q,235
Compositions from Hesiod. London, 1817. 4°. . . . . *Q,237
Iliad of Homer, illustrated. London, 1805. 4°. . . . . . *Q,238
Lectures on Sculpture. London, 1865. p. 8°. . . . . . L,103
Odyssey of Homer, illustrated. London, 1805. 4°. . . . *Q,236
Fleetwood, J. History of the Holy Bible. New York, 1855. 8°. . . P,449

Fleetwood, J. Life of Jesus Christ. London, 1855. 4°. . . . . . F,23
The same. Auburn, 1853. 8°. . . . . . . . . P,375
Fleetwood; or, the New Man of Feeling. W. Godwin. London, 1832. 16°. K,525
Fleming, C. and Tibbins. French Dictionary. Paris, 1854. 2 v. 4°. . L.R.
Fleming, R. The Rise and Fall of Papal Rome. London, 1863. 12°. . P,562
Fleming, W. Vocabulary of Philosophy. London, 1858. 16°. . . . O,616
The same. Philadelphia, 1860. 8°. . . . . . . O,617
Fletcher, G. Russe Commonwealth, 1591. London, 1856. 8°. . . . V,989
Fletcher, J. History of Poland. New York, 1854. 16°. . . . . . L,357
Studies on Slavery. Natchez, 1852. 8°. . . . . . . . O,400
Fletcher, J. C. and Kidder, D. P. Brazil and the Brazilians. Bost. 1867. 8°. V,254
Fletcher, M., Life of; edited by H. Moore. New York, 1856. 12°. . . C,1170
Fletcher, P. Purple Island; a Poem. London, 1816. 8°. . . . . . J,859
Flint, A. Principles and Practice of Medicine. Philadelphia, 1868. 8°. . L,964
Flint, C. L. Milch Cows and Dairy Farming. Boston, 1868. 12°. . . M,453
Treatise on Grasses and Forage Plants. New York, 1857. 8°. . N,976
Flint, H. M. Mexico under Maximilian. Philadelphia, 1867. 12°. . . C,375
Flint, J. Letters from America. Edinburgh, 1822. 8°. . . . . . V,107
Flint, S. Making Honey; or, Frances Stuart. Boston, 1869. 16°. . . J,1656
Flint, T. History of the Mississippi Valley. Cincinnati, 1832. 8°. . . C,271
Lectures upon Natural History, Geology, etc. Cincinnati, 1833. 12°. N,502
Ten Years in the Valley of the Mississippi. Boston, 1826. 8°. . V,109
Flirtations in Fashionable Society. C. Sinclair. Philadelphia, n. d. 12°. . K,574
Flitch of Bacon. W. H. Ainsworth. Leipzig, 1854. 16°. . . . . J,9
Floating Light of Goodwin Sands. R. M. Ballantyne. Phila. 1871. 16°. J,1637
Flora, American. A. B. Strong. New York, 1848–49. v. 1–3. 4°. . N,1027
Beiträge zur Flora der Vorwelt. A. J. Corda. Prag, 1845. 4°. . Q,128
Deutsche und Schweizer. D. J. W. Koch. Leipzig, 1860. 16°. . G,877
Deutschlands. D. Dietrich. Jena, 1844. v. 3. 8°. . . . G,862
English. Sir J. E. Smith. London, 1828–36. 6 v. 8°. . . . N,989
Hibernica. J. T. Mackay. Dublin, 1836. 8°. . . . . . N,1020
im Winterkleide. E. A. Rossmässler. Leipzig, 1854. 8°. . . G,890
Medica. J. Lindley. London, 1838. 8°. . . . . . . N,1004
of the Coliseum of Rome. R. Deakin. London, 1855. 16°. . . N,937
of North America. J. Torrey and A. Gray. N. Y. 1838–40. v. 1. 8°. N,1021
Scottish Cryptogamic. R. K. Greville. Edinburgh, 1823–28. 6 v. 8°. N,1032
Wayside Flora; towards Rome. N. Bellairs. London, 1866. 16°. . N,940
Florence, and Affairs of Italy, History of. N. Machiavelli. Lond. 1854. 12°. L,207
History of the Commonwealth of. T. A. Trollope. Lond. 1865. 4 v. 8°. B,494
Museum Florentinum; ed. A. F. Gori. Florence, 1730–33. 6 v. f°. L.R.
Florence Erwin's Three Homes. Boston, 1865. 16°. . . . . . J,1626
Florence of Worcester. Chronicon; ed. B. Thorpe. Lond. 1848–49. 2 v. 8°. U,617
The same; with two continuations. London, 1854. p. 8°. . L,9
Florence Stories. J. Abbott. New York, 1867. 6 v. 16°. . . . J,1382

| | |
|---|---|
| Vol. 1. Florence and John. | Vol. 4. English Channel. |
| 2. Grimkie. | 5. Isle of Wight. |
| 3. Orkney Islands. | 6. Florence's Return. |

Florentine History, H. E. Napier. London, 1846–47. 6 v. 12°. . . B,486
Florian, J. P. C. de. Fables de; Ruth et Tobie, etc. Paris, 1856. 12°. . H,863
History of the Moors of Spain. New York, 1854. 16°. . . . L,459
Florida, Conquest of. T. Irving. New York, 1851. 12°. . . . . . C,184

Florida, Discovery and Conquest of. H. de Soto. London, 1851. 8°. . V,988
History of, till 1842. G. R. Fairbanks. Philadelphia, 1871. 12°. . C,180
Relation of a Discovery, 1663. See *Force's Tracts*, v. 4.
Florida War, History of. J. T. Sprague. New York, 1848. 8°. . . B,872
Florus, L. A. Epitome Rerum Romanarum. Parisiis, 1827. 8°. . . U,323
Roman History; translated by J. S. Watson. London, 1870. p. 8°. L,77
The same. New York, 1855. 12°. . . . . . . . A,136
Flourens, M. J. P. Fontenelle, Philosophie Moderne. Paris, 1847. 16°. N,252,38
Flower, Fruit, and Thorn Pieces. J. P. F. Richter. Boston, 1863. 2 v. 12°. G,220
Flower of the Family. E. Prentiss. New York, 1869. 16°. . . J,1638
Flower, W. H. Memoirs on the Cetacea. London, 1866. 4°. . . . Q,73
Flower-de-Luce. H. W. Longfellow. Boston, 1867. 16°. . . . . I,66
Flower-Painting, Art of. J. Andrews. London, n. d. 8°. . . . . M,141
Flowering-Plants and Ferns of Great Britain. A. Pratt. Lond. n. d. 5 v. 8°. N,1018
Flowers, Garden. E. S. Rand, jr. Boston, 1866. 12°. . . . . N,955
for Children. L. M. Child. Boston, 1865. 16°. . . . J,1433
for the Parlor and Garden. E. S. Rand, jr. Boston, 1864. 12°. . N,951
Haunts of the Wild. A. Pratt. London, 1863. 8°. . . . . N,923
Language of; Flora's Interpreter. S. J. Hale. Boston, 1854. 12°. N,941
of the Forest. M. M. Sherwood. New York, 1860. 12°. . . K,1008,5
Flügel, J. G. English and German Dictionary. Leipzig, 1847. 2 v. 8°. . L.R.
Fluids, Experiments on the Motion of. G. B. Venturi. London, 1826. 8°. N,143
Mischung von Flüssigkeiten. J. Vogel. Gottingen, 1846. 8°. N,252,33
Flusspiraten. F. Gerstäcker. Leipzig, 1862. 3 v. 16°. . . . . G,280
Fluxions, An Institution of. H. Ditton. London, 1706. 8°. . . . O,916
Fly-Catchers, Natural History of. W. Swainson. Edinb. n. d. 16°. N,470,13
Foe in the Household. C. Cheseboro'. Boston, 1871. 8°. . . . . K,150
Förster, E. Geschichte der Deutschen Kunst. Leipzig, 1860. 5 v. in 2. 12°. G,624
Follen, C. Works; with a Memoir. Boston, 1841. 5 v. 12°. . . . U,110
Follenberg, P. E. Letters on his Educational Institutions. Lond. 1842. 12°. O,1007
Following the Flag. C. C. Coffin. Boston, 1865. 16°. . . . J,1500
Folsom, G. Catalogue of Original Documents on Maine. N. Y. 1858. 8°. L.R.
Fonblanque, A. Eng. under Seven Administrations. Lond. 1837. 3 v. 12°. B,3
Fonblanque, A. jr. Rights and Wrongs. London, 1860. 16°. . . . U,481
and Holdsworth. How we are Governed. London, 1869. 12°. . O,504
Fonetic Advocat. See *Phonography*.
Fonetic Nuz; No. 1–15. n. t. p. . . . . . . . . . . . Q,385
Fonografic Corespondent. Lundun, 1849–55. 7 v. 18°. . . . . L,710
Fonthill Recreations. M. G. Sleeper. Boston, 1866–67. 3 v. 16°. . J,1695
Vol. 1. The Mediterranean Islands. Vol. 2. The Two Sicilies. Vol. 3. Sweden and Norway.
Fonvielle, W. de. Thunder and Lightning. London, 1868. 16°. . M,1048
Food and Climate. P. Harvey. Zanesville, 1849. 12°. . . . . L,906
Food, Chemistry of. J. von Liebig. Lowell, 1848. 12°. . . . . N,173
Feeding Stock with Prepared. J. Marshall. London, 1847. 8°. N,252,24
Fruits and Farinacea for Man. J. Smith. New York, 1856. 12°. . L,903
History of. A. Soyer. London, 1853. 8°. . . . . . H,321
in Chemischer Beziehung. F. C. Knapp. Brauns. 1848. 8°. N,252,30
Vegetable Substances used for. New York, 1855. 18°. . . . L,452
Verfälschungen. F. H. Walchner. Carlsruhe, 1840. 16°. . . N,252,37
Fool of Quality. H. Brooke. New York, 1860. 2 v. 12°. . . . K,612

Foot, J. Life of Arthur Murphy. London, 1811. 4°. . . . . . F,26
Foote, A. H. Africa and the American Flag. New York, 1854. 12°. . V,828
Foote, H. S. War of the Rebellion. New York, 1866. 12°. . . . B,913
Foote, J. P. Memoirs of S. E. Foote. Cincinnati, 1860. 12°. . . . C,845
Schools of Cincinnati and vicinity. Cincinnati, 1855. 8°. . O,1012
Footfalls on Boundary of another World. R. D. Owen. Phil. 1867. 12°. P,868
Footprints of Famous Men. J. G. Edgar. London, 1864. 16°. . J,1514
Footprints of the Creator. H. Miller. Boston, 1859. 12°. . . . . N,611
Footprints of our Forefathers. J. G. Miall. Boston, 1852. 12°. . . C,14
For each and for all. H. Martineau. London, 1859. 16°. . . . K,551,4
For ever and ever. F. Church. Leipzig, 1866. 2 v. in 1. 16°. . . J,348
For her sake. F. W. Robinson. New York, 1869. 8°. . . . . K,657
For richer, for poorer. H. Parr. Leipzig, 1870. 2 v. in 1. 16°. . . J,409
Foraminifera, Study of. W. B. Carpenter and others. London, 1862. 4°. Q,68
Forayers, The. W. G. Simms. New York, 1864. 12°. . . . . K,252
Forbes, C. S. Iceland; its Volcanoes, Geysers, etc. London, 1860. 8°. . V,191
Forbes, D. Familie of Innes. See *Spalding Club Publications*, v. 35.
Forbes, D., Life of. J. H. Burton. London, 1847. 8°. . . . . D,202
Forbes, E. British Naked-eyed Medusæ. London, 1848. f°. . . . Q,70
Echinodermata of the British Tertiaries. London, 1852. 4°. . . Q,28
Natural History of the European Seas. London, 1859. 16°. . . N,493
and Hanley, S. British Mollusca and Shells. London, 1853. 4 v. 8°. N,716
Forbes, F. E. Eleven Years in Ceylon. London, 1841. 2 v. 8°. . . V,696
Five Years in China. London, 1848. 8°. . . . . . V,642
Forbes, J. The Symmetrical Structure of Scripture. Edinb. 1854. 8°. . P,509
Forbes, Sir J. Physician's Holiday in Switzerland. London, 1852. 12°. . V,423
Sight-Seeing in Germany. London, 1856. p. 8. . . . . V,407
Norway and its Glaciers. Edinburgh, 1853. 8°. . . . . V,548
Papers on the Theory of Glaciers. Edinburg, 1859. 8°. . . . N,840
Tour of Mount Blanc and Monte Rosa. Edinburgh, 1845. 12°. . V,353
Forbes, J. D. Mathematical and Physical Science. Boston, 1856. 4°. . L.R.
Force, P. Tracts on the Colonies in North America. Wash. 1836–46. 4 v. 8°. B,810

Andros, Sir E. Commission of King James II. to him, June 3, 1686. v. 4.
Bacon's Rebellion in Virginia, 1675–76. v. 1.
Bermudas, Plaine Description of Bermudas, or Summer Islands, 1609. v. 3.
Bolzius, Mr. Journals in Georgia, 1734. v. 4.
Byfield, N. Account of the late Rebellion in New England, 1689. v. 4.
Child, J. New-Englands Jonas cast up at London, 1647. v. 4.
Clayton, J. Account of several Observations in Virginia, 1688. v. 3.
Cotton A. Account of our late Troubles in Virginia, 1675. v. 1.
Cotton, J. Abstract of Laws in New England, 1641 [*never passed*]. v. 3.
Dudley, T. Letter to Countess of Lincoln on New-England Plantation, 1631. v. 2.
Florida, Relation of a Discovery on the Coast of, 1664. v. 4.
Georgia, Account showing the Progress of, 1741. v. 1.
Brief Account of the Colony under Oglethorpe, 1733. v. 1.
Description of, 1741. v. 2.
State of the Province, 1740. v. 1.
True and Historical Narrative, by Tailfer, Anderson, and others, 1741. v. 1.
Gorton, S. Letter to Nathaniel Morton, 1669. v. 4.
Simplicities Defence against Seven-Headed Policy in New England, 1646. v. 4.
Guiana, News from Sir Walter Raleigh; with Description of, 1618. v. 3.
Hammond, J. Leah and Rachel; Virginia and Maryland, 1656. v. 3.
Higginson, F. New-England's Plantation, 1630. v. 1.
Maryland, Relation of the Colony of Lord Baltimore. v. 4.
Morton, T. New English Canaan; an Abstract of New England, 1632. v. 2.
Mountgomry, Sir R. Discourse concerning a new Colony south of Carolina, 1717. v. 1.
Narrative of the Imprisonment of two Presbyterian Ministers in New York, 1707. v. 4.
New England, Brief Relation of the State of, to 1689. v. 4.
Revolution in Justified, 1691. v. 4.
Norwood, Col. Voyage to Virginia. v. 3.

Force, P. Tracts on the Colonies of North America. *Continued.* . . B,810
Reck, Von. Extract of Journals on a Voyage to Georgia, 1733. v. 4.
Reformed Virginia Silk-worm, 1655. v. 3.
Shrigley, N. True Relation of Virginia and Maryland, 1669. v. 3.
Smith, Capt. John. Description of New England, 1614. v. 2.
New-Englands Trials; with present State of that happy Plantation, 1622. v. 2.
South Carolina, Description of the Province in 1731. v. 2.
Narrative of the Proceedings of the People in 1719. 2 v.
Virginia and Maryland; or, Lord Baltimore's case uncased, 1655. v. 2.
Richly Valued; translated from the Portuguese by R. Hakluyt, 1609. v. 4.
Declaration of the State of the Colony and Affairs, 1620. v. 3.
Description of the Province of New Albion, in North Virginia, 1648. v. 2.
Laws, Divine, Moral, and Martial, for the Colony, by W. Strachey, 1612. v. 3.
Narrative of Indian and Civil Wars, 1675-76. v. 1.
Nova Britannia, offering most excellent Fruits, 1609. v. 1.
New Life in Virginia; 2d part of Nova Britannia, 1612. v. 1.
Orders and Constitutions, 1619. v. 3.
Perfect Description of Present State of the Plantation, 1649. v. 2.
True Declaration of the Estate of the Colony, 1610. v. 3.
Virginia's Cure; An Advisive Narrative of the Church's Unhappiness, 1661. v. 3.
Ward, N. Simple Cobler of Aggawam in America, 1647. v. 3.
White, J. Planter's Plea; or, Grounds of Plantation in New England, 1630. v. 2.
Williams, E. Virginia richly and truly valued, 1650. v. 3.

Force and Nature, Attraction and Repulsion. C. F. Winslow. Phil. 1869. 8°. N,87
Eccentric and Centric. H. F. A. Pratt. London, 1862. 8°. . . N,93
Forces, Correlation and Conservation of. E. L. Youmans. New York, 1865. 12°. N,77
and continuity of. W. R. Grove. London, 1867. 8°. . . N,86
Lecture on. London, 1847. 8°. . . . . . . . N,252
of Matter, Lectures on. M. Faraday. New York, 1860. 16°. . N,64
Ford, R. Hand-Book for Travelers in Spain. London, 1869. 2 v. 12°. . V,469
Ford, S. R. Grace Truman. New York, 1864. 12°. . . . . K,107
Ford, T. History of Illinois. Chicago, 1854. 12°. . . . . . . C,170
Forde, J. Honour Triumphant, and a Line of Life. London, 1843. 8°. I,885,18
Fordyce, D. Dialogues concerning Education. London, 1745-48. 2 v. 8°. O,1231
Fore and Aft; Life of an Old Sailor. W. D. Phelps. Boston, 1871. 16°. J,1338
Foreign Quarterly Review. London, 1827-46. 37 v. 8°. . . . . . T,38
Foreigners Eminent in Piety, Lives of. Dublin, 1796. 12°. . . . C,535
Forest Arcadia of Northern New York. Boston, 1864. 16°. . . . V,147
Forest Creatures. C. Boner. London, 1861. 12°. . . . . . . N,634
Forest Days. G. P. R. James. Leipzig, 1843. 16°. . . . . . . J,207
Forest Exiles. M. Reid. Boston, 1868. 16°. . . . . . . . J,1558
Forest House. E. Erckmann and A. Chatrian. Boston, 1871. 12°. . . G,225
Forest, Jungle, and Prairie. A. Elliott. London, 1868. 8°. . . . J,1151
Forest Life in Norway and Sweden. H. Newland. London, 1859. 8°. . J,1318
Forest Scenery and Woodland Views. W. Gilpin. Edinb. 1834. 2 v. 8°. *M,350
Forest Tragedy, and other Tales. S. J. Lippincott. Boston, 1856. 12°. K,205
Forest Trees, Portraits of. J. G. Strutt. London, 1826. f°. . . . *Q,350
Forester, Fanny, *pseud.* See *Judson, E. C.*
Forester, Frank, *pseud.* See *Herbert, H. W.*
Forester, T. Norway in 1848-49. London, 1850. 8°. . . . . . V,547
Paris and its Environs. London, 1859. 12°. . . . . . . L,133
Rambles in Norway. London, 1854. p. 8°. . . . . . I,656,4
Forgery of Dr. Wm. Dodd. P. Fitzgerald. London, 1865. 12°. . . D,181
Forgiveness of Sin. J. Owen. New York, n. d. 12°. . . . . . P,204
Forgiven at Last. J. R. Haderman, *pseud.* Philadelphia, 1870. 12°. . K,572
Forkel, J. N. Johann Sebastian Bach's Leben, und Kunst. Leip. 1855. 4°. G,736
Forlorn Hope. E. Yates. Leipzig, 1867. 2 v. in 1. 16°. . . . J,539
Formby, H. State Rationalism in Education. Dublin, 1854. 8°. . O,1251,2

Forney, J. W. Letters from Europe. Philadelphia, 1867. 12°. . . v,330
Forrest, W. S. Historical Sketches of Norfolk, Va. Philadelphia, 1853. 8°. c,117
Forster, C. One Primeval Language. London, 1851–54. 3 v. 8°. . . l,530
Forster, G. Sämmtliche Schriften. Leipzig, 1843. 9 v. 12°. . . . e,322

Bd. 1–2. Reise um die Welt, 1772–75.
3. Ansichten vom Niederrhein, von Brabant, Flandern, Holland, England, und Frankreich.
4–6. Beitrag zur Länder u. Völkerkunde, Naturgesch. u. Philosophie des Lebens.
7. Leben; Briefwechsel.
8. Briefwechsel.
9. Briefwechsel; Sakontala, indisches Schauspiel von Kalidas.

Forster J. Life of Oliver Goldsmith. London, 1848. 8°. . . . d,426
Daniel De Foe and Charles Churchill. London, 1865. p. 8°. . i,661,3
Statesmen of the English Commonwealth. New York, 1846. 8°. . c,584
Walter Savage Lander; a Biography. Boston, 1869. 8°. . . d,84
Forster, J. G. J. Moleschott. Frankfort-a-M. 1854. 12°. . . . e,238
Forster, T. (Ed.) Letters of Locke, Sidney, and Shaftesbury. Lond. 1830. 8°. h,612
Forsyth, R. Beauties of Scotland. Edingburgh, 1805–8. 5 v. 8°. . . v,397
Forsyth, W. Culture and Management of Fruit Trees. London, 1824. 8°. m,562
History of Trial by Jury. London, 1852. 8°. . . . . o,422
Life of Cicero. London, 1867. 8°. . . . . . . . . d,736
Napoleon at St. Helena. New York, 1853. 2 v. 12°. . . . d,649
Fortescue, H. *Earl.* Unhealthiness of Towns. London, 1846. 16°. n,252,37
Fortune, R. Dreijährige Wanderungen in China. Göttingen, 1853. 8°. e,219
Journey to the Capitals of Japan and China. London, 1863. 8°. v,623
to the Tea Countries of China. London, 1852. 8°. . . . v,739
Residence among the Chinese. London, 1857. 8°. . . . . v,604
Fortune Seeker. E. D. E. N. Southworth. Philadelphia, 1870. 12°. . k,425
Fortunes of Glencore. C. Lever. London, 1865. 8°. . . . . k,775
The same. Leipzig, 1857. 2 v. in 1. 16°. . . . . j,276
Fortunes of Nigel. Sir W. Scott. Boston, 1858. 2 v. 16°. . . . k,935
The same. Philadelphia, 1869. 8°. . . . . . . k,1111
The same. Leipzig, 1846. 16°. . . . . . . . j,441
Forty-Five Guardsmen. A. Dumas. Philadelphia, n. d. 8°. . . . h,984
Fosbroke, T. D. Arts of the Greeks and Romans. Lond. 1833–35. 2 v. 12°. m,996
Fossil Balanidæ and Verrucidæ of Great Britain. C. Darwin. Lond. 1854. 4°. q,29
Fossil Botany. S. R. Pattison. London, 1849. 12°. . . . . . n,604
Fossil Brachiopoda, British. T. Davidson. London, 1851–54. 4°. . . q,33
Fossil Chelonian Reptilia. R. Owen. London, 1853. 4°. . . . q,22
Fossil Corals, British. H. M. Edwards and J. Haime. London, 1850–54. 4°. q,34,1
Fossil Echinodermata, British, pts. 1,3. T. Wright. London, 1859. 4°. q,30; q,32
Fossil Flora of Great Brit. J. Lindley and W. Hutton. Lond. 1831–7. 3 v. 8°. n,826
Fossil Insects in the Rocks of England. P. B. Brodie. London, 1845. 8°. n,816
der Kohlenformation v. Saarbrücken. F. Goldenberg. Cassel, 1854. 4°. g,847
Fossil Lepadidæ of Great Britain. C. Darwin. London, 1851. 4°. . q,29
Fossil Organic Remains. J. Parkinson. London, 1822. 8°. . . . n,788
Fossil Polyzoa of the Crag. G. Busk. London, 1859. 4°. . . . q,32
Fossil Remains of Mollusca in England. D. Sharpe. Lond. 1853–4. 2 pts. 4°. q,16
Fossil Remains of the Animal Kingdom. E. Pidgeon. London, n. d. 8°. n,802
Fossil Reptilia, pts. 1,3. R. Owen. London, 1859. 4°. . . . . q,30
History of British. R. Owen. London, 1849. 4°. . . . . q,3
of the Cretaceous Formation. R. Owen. London, 1851. 4°. . . q,23

Fossil Reptilia of Wealden Formations, v. 2. R. Owen. Lond. 1854. 4°. . Q,20
of the London Clay. R. Owen and T. Bell. London, 1849. 2 v. 4°. Q,21
Fossil Spirit; Boy's Dream of Geology. J. Mill. New York, 1854. 12°. N,595
Fossils, Catalogue of British. J. Morris. London, 1854. 8°. . . . N,819
Echinodermes Fossiles de la Suisse. L. Agassiz. Paris, n. d. 4°. . N,750
Fossile Säugethiere Würtemberg's. G. F. Jäger. Stuttg. 1835. f°. F,177
of the Bottom-Rocks. S. J. Mackie. London, 1860. 8°. . . N,783
Palæological Fossils of Cornwall, Devon. J. Phillips. Lond. 1841. 8°. N,825
Permian, of England. W. King. London, 1850. 4°. . . . Q,31
Tabular View of British. London, n. d. 4°. . . . . . . N,839
Foster, A. Life and Voyages of Americus Vespucius. New York, 1846. 8°. D,740
Foster, B. (Illustrator.) The Rhine; text by H. Mayhew. Lond. 1856. 8°. *V,436
The Upper Rhine; text by H. Mayhew. London, 1860. 8°. *V,437
Foster, C. A Harmony of Primeval Alphabets. London, n. d. 8°. . L,533
Foster, H. Coquette; or, Eliza Wharton. Philadelphia, 1866. 12°. K,154
Foster, J. Critical Essays in Eclectic Review. London, 1860–68. 2 v. p. 8°. L,182
Essays in a Series of Letters. London, 1870. p. 8°. . . . L,183
The same. New York, 1853. 12°. . . . . . . . H,439
Evils of Popular Ignorance, etc. London, 1865. p. 8°. . . . L,184
The same. New York, 1853. 12°. . . . . . . . H,440
Fosteriana; Thoughts, Reflections, and Criticisms. Lond. 1858. p. 8°. L,185
Lectures at Broadmead Chapel, Bristol. London, 1869. 2 v. p. 8°. L,181
Life and Correspondence of. London, 1852. 2 v. p. 8°. . . L,180
Life of. Boston, 1855. 8°. . . . . . . . . . D,198
Foster, J. W. Mississippi Valley; its Physical Geography. Chicago, 1869. 8°. C,280
Fouché, J. *Duke of Otranto.* Authentic Memoirs. London, 1839. 12°. . D,679
Foucard, E. Book of Illustrious Mechanics. New York, 1847. 12°. . M,633
Foul Play. C. Reade and D. Boucicault. Boston, 1868. 8°. . . . K,900
Found Dead. Leipzig, 1869. 16°. . . . . . . . . . . J,165
Foundations, Treatise on. E. Dobson. London, 1850. 12°. . . . M,910
Fountain of Life. J. Flavel. New York, n. d. 12°. . . . P,746,31
Four Seasons; Undine, and other Tales. Baron La M. Fouqué. N.Y. 1870. 12°. H,931
Four Years in Secessia. J. H. Browne. Hartford, 1865. 8°. . . . B,908
Four Years in the Saddle. H. Gilmor. New York, 1866. 12°. . . B,893
Fourier, C. Œuvres Complètes. Paris, 1843–48. 6 v. 12°. . . H,1001

Tome 1. Théorie des Quatre Mouvements et des Destinées Générales.
2–5. Théorie de l'Unité Universelle.
6. Le Nouveau Monde Industriel et Sociétaire.

Passions of the Human Soul. London, 1851. 2 v. 8°. . . . . O,685
Social Destiny of Man. New York, 1857. 8°. . . . . O,545
Fourier, J. B. J. *Baron.* Life of F. Arago. Boston, 1859. 12°. . . C,498
Fowle, W. B. Common-School Speller. Boston, 1855. 16°. . . . O,764
The Scholiast Schooled. Cambridge, 1846. 8°. . . . . O,927
Fowler H. American Pulpit. New York, 1856. 8°. . . . . C,946
Fowler, W. C. English Grammar. New York, 1852. 8°. . . . . L,619
Fowler, O. S. Home for All; Octagon Mode of Building. N.Y. 1854. 12°. M,201
Self-Culture and Perfection of Character. New York, 1854. 12°. . L,895
and L. N. Self-Instructor in Phrenology and Phys. N.Y. 1856. 12°. L,894
Fownes, G. Manual of Elementary Chemistry. Philadelphia, 1870. 12°. N,223
Treatise on Chemistry. London, 1857. 12°. . . . . . M,914
Fox, C. J. History of the Reign of James II. London, 1808. 4°. . . F,269

Fox, C. J. History of the Reign of James II. London, 1846. 12°. . . A,476
Memorials and Correspondence. *Earl* J. Russell. Lond. 1853–57. 4v. 8°. D,219
The same. Philadelphia, 1853. 2 v. 12°. . . . . . D,178
Speeches. London, 1853. 8°. . . . . . . . . . . H,800
Fox, H. R. *Lord Holland.* Foreign Reminiscences. New York, 1851. 12°. V,1039
Lives of Lope de Vega and G. de Castro. London, 1817. 8°. . . D,701
Fox, J. Book of Martyrs. Philadelphia, 1866. 12°. . . . . . . P,810
Fox, S. S. *Lady Holland.* Memoir of Sydney Smith. N. Y. 1856. 2 v. 12°. C,1209
Foxton, E., *pseud.* See *Palfrey, S.*
Fragments of Science for Unscientific People. J. Tyndall. N. Y. 1871. 12°. M,775
Framley Parsonage. A. Trollope. Leipzig, 1861. 2 v. in 1. 16°. . . J,498
Francatelli, C. E. Royal Confectioner. London, 1866. 8°. . . . H,304
France, Administration des Finances de. J. Necker. Paris, 1785. 3 v. 12°. O,468
Age of Louis XIV. H. Martin. Boston, 1865. 2 v. 8°. . . . B,369
Ancient Gaul, History of, v. 1. P. Godwin. New York, 1860. 8°. B,349,1
and England, Social Life in. M. Berry. London, 1844. 2 v. 12°. . H,313
and Belgium, 1815, War in. W. Siborne. Philadelphia, 1845. 8°. B,85
and Germany, Bibliographical Tour in. T. F. Dibdin. Lond. 1829. 3 v. 8°. M,58
The same, illustrated. London, 1821. 3 v. r. 8°. . . . L.R.
and Italy, Life in the Olden Time in. J. C. Colquhoun. Lond. 1858. 8°. D,709
Notes on. W. Colton. New York, 1860. 12°. . . . V,300
Sentimental Journey through. L. Sterne. London, n. d. 24°. V,445
The same. Leipzig, 1861. 16°. . . . . . . J,467
Stories and Sights of. S. J. Lippincott. Boston, 1867. 16°. J,1322
and its Revolutions. G. Long. London, 1850. 4°. . . . . . F,223
and Switzerland, Pedestrian in. G. Barrell, jr. New York, 1853. 12°. V,456
Annales du Parlement Français. Paris, 1839–46. 7 v. 8°. . . B,439
Annuaire des Marées des Côtes de. Paris, 1850, 52, 54, 57–62. 9 v. 24°. S,7
du Bureau des Longitudes. Paris, 1836, 1851. 2 v. 24°. . S,6
before Europe. J. Michelet. Boston, 1871. 12°. . . . . B,213
Chroniques de. Sir J. Froissart. Paris, 1853. 12°. . . . B,220
Chronicles of. Sir J. Froissart. London, 1868. 2 v. 8°. . . A,345
The same. London, 1812. 2 v. 4°. . . . F,157
E. de Monstrelet. London, 1853. 2 v. 8°. . . . B,275
Civil Wars and Monarchy in. L. Ranke. New York, 1853. 12°. . B,240
Claret and Olives; Garonne to the Rhone. A. B. Reach. Lond. 1852. 8°. V,479
Code Correctionnel et de Simple Police. Paris, n. d. 8°. . . . U,540
Constitution of. B. Boelker. Boston, 1848. 12°. . . . . . S.C.
Consulate and the Empire. A. Thiers. Philadelphia, 1865. 5 v. 8°. B,256
Cruise upon Wheels in. C. A. Collins. London, 1862. 2 v. 8°. . V,453
Decline of the French Monarchy. H. Martin. Boston, 1866. 2 v. 8°. B,370
Ecclesiastical Antiquities of. G. D. Whittington. London, 1811. 8°. M,174
Educational Tour in. H. Mann. London, 1853. 12°. . . . O,907
Fair; Impressions of a Traveler. D. M. Craik. New York, 1871. 12°. V,449
French Revolution, 1789, Essays on. J. W. Croker. London, 1857. 8°. B,258
Annals of. A. F. Bertrand de Moleville. Lond. 1800. 9 v. 8°. B,332
The same. London, 1800. 4 v. 8°. . . . . . B,285
Geschichte der. F. C. Dahlmann. Leipzig, 1847. 8°. . . E,87
W. Wachsmuth. Hamburg, 1840–44. 4 v. 8°. . . E,85
Histoire de. A. de Lamartine. Bruxelles, 1853. . . . B,441

France, French Revolution, 1789, Hist. View of. J. Michelet. Lond. 1848. p. 8°. L,211
History of. J. S. C. Abbott. New York, 1859. 8°. . . . B,257
T. Carlyle. London, 1857. 2 v. 8°. . . . . . B,206
The same. Leipzig, 1851. 3 v. 16°. . . . . J,60
F. A. Mignet. London, 1846. p. 8°. . . . . . B,225
The same. London, 1868. p. 8°. . . . L,212
H. von Sybel. London, 1867-69. 8°. . . . . . B,341
A. Thiers. New York, 1868. 4 v. in 2. 8°. . . . B,255
History of the Wars of. E. Baines. Philadelphia, 1835. 2 v. 8°. B,288
Lectures on. W. Smyth. London, 1855-60. 2 v. p. 8°. . L,239
Women of. J. Michelet. Philadelphia, 1855. 12°. . . . D,627
1830, Memoirs of Lafayette, and of. B. Savrens. Lond. 1832. 8°. D,666
1848, History of. A. de Lamartine. London, 1852. 12°. . L,202
The same. Boston, 1849. 2 v. in 1. 12°. . . . . S.C.
Girondins, Histoire des. A. de Lamartine. Bruxelles, 1851. 8°. . B,440
Girondists, History of. A. de Lamartine. New York, 1854. 4 v. 12°. B,224
Galignani's Guide through. Paris, 1828. 24°. . . . . . . V,444
Geological Notes on Auvergne. A. Geikie. London, 1862. 8°. V,1086,2
Geological Maps of. I. A. Knipe. London, 1843. 2 v. 8°. . . N,791
Hand-Book for. J. Murray. London, 1853. 12°. . . . . . V,448
Histoire de, jusqu'en 1789. H. Martin. Paris, 1865. 17 v. 8°. . . B,267
L. P. Anquetil. Paris, 1832. 13 v. 8°. . . . . . . B,329
C. Lacretelle. Paris, 1844. 14 v. 8°. . . . . . . B,261
Tom. 1-4. Pendant les Guerres de Religion.
5-10. Pendant le Dix-Huitième Siecle.
11-14. Depuis la Restauration.
History of. J. Adolphus. London, 1803. 2 v. 8°. . . . . B,333
E. de Bonnechose. London, 1868. 2 v. 8°. . . . B,342
E. E. Crowe. London, 1858-68. 5 v. 8°. . . . . B,340
The same. London, 1830-31. 3 v. 12°. . . . M,989
The same. New York, 1854. 3 v. 16°. . . . B,200
H. Martin. Boston, 1865. 2 v. 8°. . . . . . . B,369
J. Michelet. New York, 1847. 2 v. 12°. . . . . B,273
E. C. Penrose. New York, 1855. 12°. . . . . . B,205
J. Russell. Cincinnati, 1838. 12°. . . . . . B,223
Analyse Raisonnée de. R. F. A. de Chateaubriand. Paris, 1853. 12°. B,291
from 843 to 1529. E. Smedley. London, n. d. 8°. . . . B,347
Geschichte von. E. A. Schmidt. Hamburg, 1835-48. 4 v. 8°. E,86
of the Kings of. T. Wyatt. Philadelphia, 1846. 12°. . . D,558
of, to 1848. J. White. New York, 1859. 8°. . . . . . B,339
of, to 1852. New York, 1862. 12°. . . . . . . . B,269
Italy and Venice. H. Taine. New York, 1869. 8°. . . . . V,514
Lectures on History of. Sir J. Stephen. New York, 1852. 8°. . B,274
Literary and Scientific Men of. M. W. Shelley. Lond. 1838. 2 v. 12°. M,1014
Lois d'Instruction Criminelles et Pénales, v. 2. Paris, 1826. 8°. . U,525
Louis XIV. and the Court of. J. Pardoe. New York, 1865. 2 v. 12°. D,643
Memorial du Dépôt Général de la Guerre. Paris, 1826-40. 7 v. 4°. U,589
Memoirs of the History of. Napoleon I. London, 1823. 7 v. 8°. . D,583
Monarchy of. W. Tooke. London, 1855. 8°. . . . . . . B,264
Notabilities in. P. Chasles. New York, 1853. 12°. . . . . . C,519
Notes in France and Italy. W. Colton. Cincinnati, 1851. 12°. . V,300

France, Notes of a Traveler in. S. Laing. Philadelphia, 1846. 8°. . . v,272
Old Regime, Lectures on. C. Kingsley. London, 1867. 8°. . . B,337
and the Revolution. A. de Tocqueville. New York, 1856. 12°. B,241
Pictorial History of. G. M. Bussey and T. Gaspey. London, 1843. 8°. B,276
S. G. Goodrich. Philadelphia, 1846. 12°. . . . . . B,203
Pictures of Travel in the South of. A. Dumas. London, n. d. 12°. v,451
Pioneers of, in the New World. F. Parkman. Boston, 1865. 8°. . B,618
Protestant Reformation in. A. Marsh-Caldwell. Phila. 1851. 2 v. 12°. P,573
Reise durch Frankreich. H. F. Link. Kiel, 1801–4. 3 v. in 2. 12°. E,199
Religion and the Reign of Terror. E. de Pressensé. N. Y. 1869. 12°. P,576
Répertoire Alphabétique des Lois, Decrets, etc. Paris, 1810. 8°. . U,494
Restoration of Monarchy in. A. de Lamartine. N.Y. 1851–3. 4 v. 12°. B,243
The same. London, 1847–54. 4 v. p. 8°. . . . . . L,201
Revolutions from 1789 to 1849. F.W. Redhead. Phil. 1854. 3 v. 12°. B,221
Sentimental Journey in. L. Sterne. New York, 1857. 12°. . . v,452
Social and Religious Customs in. E. de Courcillon. N. Y. 1855. 12°. D,667
Social, Literary, and Political. Sir H. L. Bulwer. N. Y. 1857. 12°. v,450
Südliche Frankreich. J. Venedey. Frankfurt-a-M. 1846. 2 v. 8°. E,200
Switzerland and the Pyrenees. H. D. Inglis. Edinb. 1831. 2 v. 16°. I,532
Ten Years, 1830–40, History of. L. Blanc. Phila. 1848. 2 v. 8°. B,246
The same. London, 1844–45. 2 v. 8°. . . . . . . B,371
Tiers Etat, History of. A. Thierry. London, 1855. 2 v. 8°. . . B,242
The same. London, 1859. p. 8°. . . . . . . . L,243
Travels in, 1787–89. A. Young. Dublin, 1793. 2 v. 8°. . . v,458
under the Bourbons. C. D. Yonge. London, 1866–67. 4 v. 8°. . B,348
under Richelieu and Colbert. J. H. Bridges. Edinburgh, 1866. 8°. B,338
Wars with England, in Reign of Henry VI. Lond. 1861–64. 3 v. 8°. W,172
France, A. de. Prisoners of Abd-el-Kader. New York, 1845. 12°. . . H,925
Franchise and the Workman. F. D. Maurice. London, 1866. 8°. . . B,102
Francis I., Court and Reign of. J. Pardoe. Philadelphia, 1849. 2 v. 12°. D,640
Franciscans, Monumenta Franciscana. London, 1858. 8°. . . . W,154
French Country Family. Mad. De Witte. New York, 1868. 12°. . J,1367
French, B. F. Iron Trade of the United States, 1621–1857. N. Y. 1858. 8°. M,719
Francis, C. Life of John Eliot. New York. 16°. . . . . C,860,5
Life of Sebastian Rale. Boston, 1860. 16°. . . . . C,860,17
Francis, G. Magazine of Science and School of Arts. Lond. 1841–45. 6 v. 8°. S.C.
Francis, G. H. Orators of the Age. New York, 1854. 16°. . . . C,514
Francis, J. Annals and Anecdotes of Life Assurance. London, 1853. 12°. O,506
Chronicles and Characters of the Stock Exchange. Boston, 1850. 8°. O,552
Francis, J. B. Lowell Hydraulic Experiments. Boston, 1855. 4°. . . S.C.
Francis, J. G. Beach-Rambles in Search of Pebbles. London, 1866. 16°. N,472
Francis, J. W. New York during the last Half Century. N. Y. 1857. 8°. C,101
Francis, Sir P., Memoirs of. J. Parkes and H. Merivale. Lond. 1867. 2 v. 8°. D,354
Francœur, L. B. Astronomie Pratique. Paris, 1830. 8°. . . . . N,288
Traité de Mécanique Elémentaire. Paris, 1825. 8°. . . . N,125
Uranographie; ou, Traité d'Astronomie. Paris, 1837. 8°. . . N,287
Franconia, Wanderungen durch. G. von Heeringen. Leipzig, n. d. 8°. E,186,3
Frank. M. Edgeworth. New York, 1854. 2 v. 16°. . . . J,1486
Frank before Vicksburg. H. Castlemon, *pseud.* Cincinnati, 1870. 16°. J,1520,5
in the Woods. H. Castlemon. Cincinnati, 1870. 16°. . . J,1520,3

Frank on a Gunboat. H. Castlemon. Cincinnati, 1870. 16°. . . J,1520,2
on the Lower Mississippi. H. Castlemon. Cincinnati, 1870. 16°. J,1520,6
on the Prairie. H. Castlemon. Cincinnati, 1870. 16°. . . J,1520,4
the Young Naturalist. H. Castlemon. Cincinnati, 1870. 16°. J,1520,1
Frank Fairlegh. F. E. Smedley. Leipzig, 1864. 2 v. in 1. 16°. . . J,461
Frank Mildmay. F. Marryat. New York, 1868. 12°. . . . . K,838
Frank Warrington. M. Cole. New York, 1864. 12°. . . . . K,16
Frank Wildman's Adventures. F. Gerstäcker. Boston, 1870. 16°. . J,1624
Frank's Campaign. H. Alger. Boston, 1871. 16°. . . . . J,1592
Frankenstein. M. W. Shelley. Boston, 1869. 12°. . . . . K,1004
Frankland, Sir C. H.; or, Boston in Colonial Times. E. Nason. Alb. 1865. 8°. C,53
Frankland, E. Lecture-Notes for Chemical Students. London, 1866. 12°. N,186
Franklin, B., Autobiography. New York, n. d. 2 v. 16°. . . . L,401
The same; edited by J. Bigelow. Philadelphia, 1868. 12°. . C,810
The same; edited by H. H. Weld. Cincinnati, 1854. 8°. . C,811
Historical Review of Pennsylvania. London, 1759. 8°. . . . C,109
Letters from his Family and Friends. New York, 1859. 8°. . . H,171
Life of. J. Sparks. Boston, 1844. 8°. . . . . . . . C,791
W. M. Thayer. Boston, 1863. 16°. . . . . J,1292
M. L. Weems. Philadelphia, 1845. 12°. . . . . C,840
Life and Times of. J. Parton. Boston, 1867. 2 v. 12°. . . C,790
Life and Works; edited by W. Duane. New York, 1859. 2 v. 8°. C,685
Works; collected by W. T. Franklin, v. 2–6. Phil. 1808–17. 5 v. 8°. U,157
Works; with Life by J. Sparks. Boston, 1840. 10 v. 8°. . . U,104
Franklin, Sir J., Expeditions in Search of. J. Leslie. London, 1855. 12°. V,913
Fate of. F. L. M'Clintock. Boston, 1860. 12°. . . . . V,943
Journey to the Polar Sea, 1819–22. London, 1824. 2 v. 8°. . . V,942
Reise zur Aufsuchung. B. Seemann. Hannover, 1858. 2 v. in 1. 8°. E,162
Search for. S. M. Schmucker. New York, 1857. 12°. . . . V,937
Second Expedition to Polar Sea. London, 1828. 4°. . . V,1014
Franklin County, Ohio, History of. W. T. Martin. Columbus, 1858. 8°. . C,214
Franklin Institute, Journal of. Philadelphia, 1826–60. 70 v. in 39. 8°. . S,27
Franziska von Hohenheim. A. Bölte. Hannover, 1863. 2 v. 16°. . . G,261
Franz Kakoczy. C. Mundt. Leipzig und Wien, n. d. 2 v. in 1. 24°. . G,361
Fraser, J. History of Nadir Shah, Emperor of Persia. London, 1742. 8°. D,773
Fraser, J. B. Historical Account of Persia. New York 1854. 8°. . . L,388
Mesopotamia and Assyria. New York, 1842. 18°. . . . . L,443
Fraser, R. W. Sea-Side Naturalist. London, 1868. 12°. . . . . N,481
Fraser's Magazine. London, 1830–66. 75 v. 8°. . . . . . . R,5
Fraserian Papers. W. Maginn. New York, 1857. 12°. . . . . H,485
Frau Meisterin. C. Mundt. Berlin, n. d. 2 v. in 1. 24°. . . . . G,358
Frau von Brabantane. F. G. Kühne. Leipzig, 1850. 12°. . . . . G,339
Frau von Gampenstein. E. Willkomm. Leipzig, 1865. 3 v. 16°. . . G,516
Frau von Staël. A. Bölte. Wien, 1861. 3 v. 24°. . . . . . . G,262
Freaks of Fortune. W. T. Adams. Boston, 1868. 12°. . . . . J,1534,2
Fred, Maria, and Me. E. Prentiss. New York, 1871. 16°. . . J,1697
Frederick II. and his Court. C. Mundt. New York, 1867. 12°. . . G,200
and his Family. C. Mundt. New York, 1867. 8°. . . . . . G,201
and Philip of Macedon compared. C. D. Yonge. London, 1858. 12°. C,486
History of. T. Campbell. London, 1845. 2 v. 8°. . . D,511

Frederick II., History of. T. Carlyle. New York, 1858–66. 6 v. 12°. . D,510
The same. Leipzig, 1858–65. 13 v. 16°. . . . . J,59
Life of. G. J. W. A. Ellis, *Lord Dover*. London, 1832. 2 v. 8°. . D,529
The same. New York, 1855. 2 v. 16°. . . . . L,370
T. B. Macaulay. New York, 1865. 16°. . . . . . . D,492
Posthumous Works; trans. by T. Holcroft. London, 1789. 13 v. 8°. H,962
Free Government, Difficulties of a. W. Greene. Providence, 1851. 8°. . T,19,2
Free Nations, Industrial History of. W. T. McCullagh. Lond. 1846. 2 v. 8°. O,499
Free Schools, American System of. H. H. Barney. Cincinnati, 1851. 8°. O,1009
J. Mudd. Cincinnati, 1853. 8°. . . . . . . O,1009
Free Thought, Critical History of. A. S. Farrar. New York, 1866. 8°. . O,660
Free Trade, What is? E. Walter. New York, 1867. 12°. . . . O,559
and Finance, Essays on. P. Webster. Philadelphia, 1780–85. . P.D.
Freemasonry, Ahiman Rezon; History and Polity of. Phil. 1825. 8°. O,382
Constitutions of. J. Anderson. London, 1767. 4°. . . . . . O,383
Philosophy of. J. Ernst. Cincinnati, 1870. 16°. . . . . O,379
Freemason's Monitor. Z. A. Davis. Philadelphia, 1843. 12°. . . . O,380
Freedley, E. T. Philadelphia and its Manufactures. Phil. 1858. 12°. . M,624
Opportunities for Industry and Investment. Philadelphia, 1859. 12°. H,271
Practical Treatise on Business. Philadelphia, 1853. 12°. . . H,260
United States Mercantile Guide. Philadelphia, 1856. 8°. . . C,595
Freedman's Book. L. M. Child. Boston, 1868. 12°. . . . . . . H,97
Freeman, E. A. History of Architecture. London, 1859. 8°. . . . M,207
History of Federal Government, v. 1. London, 1863. 8°. . . A,89
Norman Conquest of England. Oxford, 1867–69. 3 v. 8°. . . A,435
Freeman, N. L. Reports of Supreme Court of Illinois, v. 44. Chicago, 1869. 8°. U,519
Freer, M. W. Regency of Anne of Austria. London, 1866. 2 v. 8°. . B,528
Freiberg's Bergbau, Erinnerungen an. Freiberg, 1839. 12°. . . N,252,23
Freibeuter, Der. L. Storch. Leipzig, 1861–62. 3 v. 16°. . . . . G,481
Freiligrath, F. Gedichte. Stuttgart, 1868. 12°. . . . . . . E,261
Sämmtliche Werke. New York, 1858. 6 v. in 3. 12°. . . . E,323

Bd. 1. Tagebuchblätter; Balladen und Romanzen; Terzinen; Alexandriner; Vermischte Gedichte; Gelegentliches; Zwischen den Garben.
2. Miss Hemans' Waldheiligthum; Longfellow's Sang von Hiawatha.
3. Uebersetzungen aus dem Englischen.
4. Aus den neuern Englischen Dichtern; Aus dem Italienischen; Aus dem Französischen.
5. Lyrische Gedichte von Victor Hugo.
6. Ein Glaubensbekenntniss, Zeitgedichte; Ça Ira! Neuere politische und soziale Gedichte.

Frelinghuysen, T., Memoir of. T. W. Chambers. New York, 1868. 12°. . C,767
Fremantle, Col. Three Months in the Southern States, 1863. N. Y. 1864. 12°. C,159
Frémont, J. C. Exploring Exped. to Rocky Mountains. Buffalo, 1852. 12°. V,2
The same. Washington, 1845. 8°. . . . . . . . V,78
Life of. C. W. Upham. Boston, 1856. 12°. . . . . . C,1004
French, B. F. Historical Collections of Louisiana. N. Y. 1846–50. 2 v. 8°. C,191
French, H. F. Farm Drainage. New York, 1859. 12°. . . . . M,518
French Comic Authors, Chefs-d'Œuvre des. Paris, 1845–46. 8 v. 12°. . H,860

Vol. 1. Missing.
2. Dancourt; Dufresny.
3. Brueys; Palaprat; Le Sage; Allainval; Lachaussée.
4. Destouches; Fagan; Boissy.
5. Marivaux; Piron; Gresset; Voltaire; J. J. Rousseau.
6. Desmahis; Delanoue; Saurin; Favart; Barthe; Poinsinet de Sivry.
7. Sedaine; Marmontel; Collé; Monvel; Andrieux; Chéron.
8. Collin d'Harleville; Fabre d'Eglantine; Desforges; Lemercier.

French and Indian War, Memoir upon. M. Pouchot. Boston, 1866. 2 v. 4°. F,68
French Court, Secret History of. V. Cousin. New York, 1859. 12°. . B,239
French Gardens, Gleanings from. W. Robinson. London, 1869. 12°. . N,957
French Government, Letter on the. R. Walsh. Baltimore, 1810. 8°. . B,270
French History, Beauties of. J. Frost. New York, 1846. 16°. . . . B,199
French in Algiers. C. Lamping and A. de France. New York, 1845. 12°. H,925
French Language, Choix des Morceaux. M. Moysant. Londres, 1800. 4 v. 8°. H,1021
Dictionnaire. F. J. M. Noël et C. P. Chapsal. Bruxelles, 1839. 8°. L.R.
Anglais-Français. C. Fleming et J. Tibbins. Paris, 1854. 4°. L.R.
de l'Academie Française. Bruxelles, 1835. 2 v. r. 8°. . L.R.
The same; ed. par P. Lorain. Paris, 1838. 2 v. r. 8°. L.R.
François-Allemand-Latin. Basle, 1746. 8°. . . . L.R.
François-Anglois et Ang.-Fr. A. Boyer. Paris, 1797. 2 v. 8°. L.R.
François-Italien. F. de Alberti di Villanova. Bassano, 1811. 2 v. 4°. L.R.
Français-Latin. F. J. M. Noël. Paris, 1822. 8°. . . L.R.
Grec-François. J. Quénon. Paris, 1807. 8°. . . . L.R.
Latin-Français. F. J. M. Noël. Paris, 1821. . . . L.R.
National. L. N. Bescherelle. Paris, 1866. 2 v. r. 4°. . L.R.
Dictionary of. C. Fleming and J. Tibbins. Paris, 1854. 4°. . . L.R.
A. Spiers and G. Surenne. New York, 1870. 8°. . L.R.
The same. New York, 1854. 8°. . . . L.R.
of English and French Idioms. J. Roemer. N. Y. 1853. 12°. L,802
of French Nouns. D. Boileau. London, 1827. 12°. . . L,803
French and English Idioms. W. Duverger. London, 1854. 12°. L,801
French Teacher. N. Pinney. New York, 1849. 12°. . . . L,805
French Translation Self-taught. G. H. Talbot. Boston, 1855. 12°. L,797
Grammaire Moderne des Ecrivains Français. Bruxelles, 1861. 12°. H,1022
Grammar of. J. P. V. L. de Levizac; ed. by A. Bolmar. Phil. 1854. 12°. L,804
F. J. M. Noël and C. P. Chapsal; ed. S. E. Saymore. N.Y. 1855. 12°. L,799
Count de Laporte. Boston, 1844. 8°. . . . . . . L,810
Method of Learning. L. Fasquelle. New York, 1866. 8°. . . L,808
Nature displayed in Teaching. N. G. Dufief. London, 1831. 2 v. 8°. L,800
Paidophilean System. J. Black. London, 1826. 2 v. 12°. . . L,806
Progressive Lessons in Reading. J. P. Barthélemy. Dayton, 1858. 12°. L,807
Serial and Oral Method. L. Manesca. Philadelphia, 1851. 12°. L,809
Vocabulaire Symbolique Anglo-Français. L. C. Ragonot. Lond. n. d. 4°. L.R.
French Literature, Leçons Françaises de. F. J. M. Noël. Bruxelles, 1840. 8°. H,918
in the Eighteenth Century. A. R. Vinet. Edinburgh, 1854. 8°. H,760
Modern. L. R. de Véricour. Boston, 1848. 12°. . . . . . H,759
French Love Songs, translated by H. Curwen. New York, 1871. 16°. . H,858
French Poetry, Early Studies in. W. Besant. London, 1868. 12°. . . H,757
French Poets, Early. H. F. Cary. London, 1846. 16°. . . . . . H,756
French Protestant Refugees, History of the. C. Weiss. N. Y. 1854. 2 v. 12°. B,364
French Revolution. See *France.*
French Songs, Illustrated Book of. J. Oxenford. London, 1855. 8°. . H,924
French Wines and Politics. H. Martineau. London, 1859. 16°. . K,551,4
French Women of Letters. J. Kavanagh. Leipzig, 1862. 16°. . . J,231
Frère, T. Morphy's Games and Frère's Tournament. New York, 1859. 18°. M,324
Fresenius, C. R. Qualitative Chemische Analyse. Brschw. 1843. 8°. N,252,11
The same; translated. London, 1864. 8°. . . . . . N,207

Fresenius, C. R. Quantitative Chemische Analyse. Brschw. 1845. 8°. N,252,11
The same; translated. London, 1865. 8°. . . . . . N,208
Fresh Hearts that Failed. R. T. S. Lowell. Boston, 1860. 16°. . . I,86
Fresnel, A. J., Life of. F. Arago. Boston, 1859. 12°. . . . C,498,2
Fret-Cutting and Perforated Carving. W. Bemrose, jr. London, n. d. 4°. Q,165
Frey, H. Mikroskop and Mikroskopische Technik. Leipzig, 1863. 8°. G,722
Freyberger Schmelzhüttenprozesse. K. A. Winkler. Freyberg, 1837. 8°. N,252,18
Freytag, G. Debit and Credit. New York, 1868. 12°. . . . . . G,188
Fridolin Schwertberger. C. Spindler. Stuttgart, 1844–45. 4 v. 24°. . G,468
Friend, The. S. T. Coleridge. London, 1867. p. 8°. . . . . L,173,1
Friends in Council; a Series of Readings. A. Helps. London, 1869. 4 v. 12°. H,324
Friends of Christ in New Testament. N. Adams. Boston, 1864. 12°. . P,147
Friendships, Celebrated. A. T. Thomson. London, 1861. 2 v. 8°. . C,561
Friendships of Women. W. R. Alger. Boston, 1868. 12°. . . . H,282
Fries, J. F. Beiträge zur Geschichte der Philosophie. Heidelberg, 1819. 12°. G,550
Deutsche Philosophie, Art und Kunst. Heidelberg, 1812. 16°. . G,557
Fichte und Schelling über Gott und Welt. Heidelberg, 1807. 16°. . G,551
Gefährdung der Deutschen durch die Juden. Heidelberg, 1816. 12°. G,533
Grundriss der Logik. Heidelberg, 1827. 12°. . . . . . G,554
Grundriss der Metaphysik. Heidelberg, 1824. 12°. . . . . G,555
Julius und Evagoras, die Schönheit der Seele. Heidel. 1822. 2 v. 16°. G,276
Liebe, Glauben, und Hoffnung. Heidelberg, 1823. 16°. . . . G,552
Μετανοεῖτε. Bekehrt Euch. Heidelberg, 1814. 24°. . . . G,532
Neue Kritik der Vernunft. Heidelberg, 1828–31. 3 v. 8°. . . G,553
Platons Zahl; eine Vermuthung. Heidelberg, 1823. 4°. . . G,556
Populäre Vorlesungen über die Sternkunde. Heidelberg, 1833. 12°. G,780
Atlas to the same. obl. 8°. . . . . . . . . . F,88
Verfassung und Verwaltung Deutscher Staaten. Heidelberg, 1831. 12°. G,534
Frisi, P. Treatise on Rivers and Torrents. London, n. d. 12°. . . M,840
Fritze, Ernst. Novellen. Hannover, 1863. 4 v. 16°. . . . . . G,277
Vol. 1. Deutsches Leben vor fünfzig Jahren. Vol. 3. Maske des Reichthums.
2. Berg oder Burg. 4. Zug um Zug.
Froissart, Sir J. Chroniques de France. Paris, 1853. 12°. . . . B,220
Chronicles of England, France, etc. London, 1812. 2 v. 4°. . F,157
The same. London, 1868. 2 v. 8°. . . . . . . A,345
True Tales of the Olden Time. London, 1854. 16°. . . . J,1201
From Cape Cod to Dixie and the Tropics. J. M. Mackie. N. Y. 1864. 12°. V,9
From Fourteen to Four-Score. S. W. Jewett. New York, 1871. 12°. . K,310
Fromberg, E. O. Painting on Glass. London, 1857. 12°. . . . M,915
Frontier Series. Boston, 1870–71. 5 v. 16°. . . . . . . .
Vol. 1. Pearson, C. H. Cabin on the Prairie. . . . . . . J,1609
2. Bishop, N. P. Thousand Miles Walk across South America. . J,1610
3. Barrows, W. Twelve Nights in the Hunters' Camp. . . . J,1611
4. McCabe, J. D. Planting the Wilderness. . . . . . J,1612
5. Pearson, C. H. Young Pioneers of the North-West. . . J,1613
Frontiers, Letters from the. G. A. McCall. Philadelphia, 1868. 12°. . V,117
Frost, J. Beauties of English History. New York, 1846. 18°. . . A,387
Beauties of French History. New York, 1846. 16°. . . . B,199
Pictorial Ancient History. Philadelphia, 1846. 8°. . . . A,50
Pictorial History of the Middle Ages. Philadelphia, 1846. 8°. . S.C.
Pictorial Modern History. Philadelphia, 1846. 8°. . . . A,49
Remarkable Events in American History. Philad. 1848 2 v. 8°. B,703

Frost, S. Parlor Stage. New York, 1866. 16°. . . . . . . . I,711
Frost and Fire. J. F. Campbell. Edinburgh, 1865. 2 v. 8°. . . . V,1112
Frothingham, N. L. Metrical Pieces. Boston, 1855. 16°. . . . . I,35
Frothingham, R. Siege of Boston, Battle of Bunker Hill, etc. Bost. 1849. 8°. C,43
Tribute to Thomas Starr King. Boston, 1865. 12°. . . . . . C,697
Froude, J. A. Calvinism; an Address. New York, 1871. 12°. . . . P,863
History of England. London, 1858–70. 12 v. 8°. . . . . . A,398
The same. New York, 1866–70 12 v. 8°. . . . . . A,400
Nemesis of Faith. London, 1849. 12°. . . . . . . . . P,276
Short Studies on Great Subjects. London, 1867. 8°. . . . . H,489
Fruit, Deutsches Obstcabinet. J. G. Dittrich. Jena, 1840. 8°. . . . *F,90
Systematisches Handbuch der Obstkunde. J. G. Dittrich. Jena, 1837. G,657
Fruit-Book, American. S. W. Cole. New York, 1858. 18°. . . . . M,435
American Growers' Guide. F. R. Elliott. New York, 1859. 12°. . M,556
Western. E. J. Hooper. Cincinnati, 1857. 8°. . . . . . . M,538
Fruit Culture, Practical and Scientific. C. R. Baker. Boston, 1866. 12°. . M,559
Fruit Culturist, American. J. J. Thomas. Auburn, 1854. 12°. . . . M,552
Fruit Trees, and Making of Cider. J. Evelyn. London, 1706. f°. . . . Q,121
Culture and Management of. W. Forsyth. London, 1824. 8°. . M,562
Fruits and Fruit Trees of America. A. J. Downing. New York, 1847. 12°. M,536
The same. New York, 1859. 12°. . . . . . . . . M,537
The same. New York, 1869. 8°. . . . . . . . . M,542
Fruits, Cultivation of Small. A. S. Fuller. New York, 1867. 12°. . M,488
History and Description of. London, 1830. 16°. . . . . . L,491
Fry, Caroline, Autobiography and Letters. Philadelphia, 1849. 12°. . . D,176
Fry, Elizabeth, Memoirs of. T. Timpson. New York, 1847. 12°. . C,1171
Fry, J. R. Address to St. Peter's Benevolent Society. Cincinnati, 1836. 8°. H,302,4
Fry, W. H. Treatise on Artificial Fish-Breeding. New York, 1854. 12°. M,308
Fryxell, A. History of Sweden. London, 1844. 2 v. 8°. . . . . B,577
Fuel, Economy of. T. S. Prideaux. London, 1853. 12°. . . . . . M,953
Für Stille Abende. L. Storch. Leipzig, 1856–57. 2 v. 16°. . . . . G,487
Fuller, A. S. Grape Culturist. New York, 1867. 12°. . . . . . M,491
Small Fruit Culturist. New York, 1867. 12°. . . . . . M,488
Fuller, A., Principal Works and Remains of. London, 1864. p. 8°. . . L,187
Fuller, M. V. Arctic Queen; a Poem. Sandusky, 1856. 12°. . . . T,19,2
Fuller, T. Church History of Britain. London, 1842. 3 v. 8°. . . P,581
Good Thoughts in Bad Times, etc. Boston, 1863. 16°. . . . . P,245
History of the Worthies of England. London, 1840. 3 v. 8°. . B,18
The same. London, 1811. 2 v. 4°. . . . . . . . F,156
Holy and Profane States. Boston, 1864. 16°. . . . . . . P,39
Life and Genius of. H. Rogers. London, 1864. p. 8°. . . I,661,2
Fullerton, G. Constance Sherwood. Leipzig, 1865. 2 v. in 1. 16°. . J,166
Ellen Middleton. Leipzig, 1846. 16°. . . . . . . . J,167
Grantley Manor. Leipzig, 1847. 2 v. in 1. 16°. . . . . . J,169
Lady-Bird. Leipzig, 1853. 2 v. in 1. 16°. . . . . . . J,170
Mrs. Gerald's Niece. Leipzig, 1870. 2 v. in 1. 16°. . . . . J,168
Stormy Life. New York, 1868. 8°. . . . . . . . . . K,701
The same. Leipzig, 1867. 2 v. in 1. 16°. . . . . . J,171
Too Strange not to be True. New York, 1865. 3 v. in 1. 8°. . K,702
The same. Leipzig, 1864. 2 v. in 1. 16°. . . . . . J,172

Fullom, S. W. History of Woman. London, 1855. 16°. . . . . . o,367
Fulton, R., Life of. J. Renwick. New York, 1860. 12°. . . . c,860,10
Fun Better than Physic. W. W. Hall. Springfield, 1871. 12°. . . L,959
Fun-Jottings. N. P. Willis. Auburn, 1855. 12°. . . . . . . H,79
Funck, K. W. F. von. Zeitalter der Kreuzzüge. Leipzig, 1821–24. 4 v. 8°. E,28
Fungi, Account of British. M. C. Cooke. London, 1862. 12°. . . . N,925
Study of Microscopic. M. C. Cooke. London, 1865. 12°. . . N,924
See also *Botany, Cryptogamia.*
Furber, G. C. 12 Months Volunteer; Campaign in Mexico. Cincin. 1857. 8°. B,879
Furlong, L. Christian Meditation. London, 1854. 16°. . . . . . P,346
Furnace, Descrip. d'un Fourneau à Coupelle. L.N.Vauquelin. Par. 1813. 8°. N,252,15
Furness, W. H. Remarks on the Four Gospels. Philadelphia, 1836. 12°. P,507
Unconscious Truth of the Four Gospels. Philadelphia, 1868. 12°. P,230
Furniture, Upholstery, etc., Taste in. C. L. Eastlake. London, 1868. 8°. . M,158
Fusel-Oil, Natur, Entstehung und Beseitigung. R. A. Thiele. Leip. 1853. 8°. N,252,44
Fuseli, H. Lectures on Painting. London, 1848. p. 8°. . . . . . L,303
The same. London, 1830. 4°. . . . . . . . . Q,167
Life and Writings. J. Knowles. London, 1831. 3 v. 8°. . . M,104
Fuss, J. D. Roman Antiquities. Oxford, 1840. 8°. . . . . . . A,166
Future, The; Political Essay. M. H. Throop. New York, 1864. 12°. . H,35
Future Life, Critical History of Doctrine of. W. R. Alger. N. Y. 1866. 8°. P,106
Future State, Philosophy of. T. Dick. Philadelphia, 1869. 12°. . U,260,1
Scripture Revelations concerning. R. Whately. London, 1870. 12°. P,224

Gaddis, M. P. Foot-Prints of an Itinerant. Cincinnati, 1857. 8°. . . P,113
Gärtner, C. F. von. Bastarderzeugung im Pflanzenreiche. Stutt. 1849. 8°. G,869
Gage, W. L. Life of Carl Ritter. New York, 1867. 12°. . . . D,513
Modern Historical Atlas. New York, 1869. 8°. . . . . V,1141
Gain of a Loss. Leipzig, 1866. 2 v. in 1. 16°. . . . . . . . J,173
Gajani, G. Roman Exile. Boston, 1856. 12°. . . . . . . . D,743
Gala Days. M. A. Dodge. Boston, 1865. 12°. . . . . . . . H,67
Galaxy, The; an Illustrated Magazine. New York, 1866–70. 10 v. 8°. T,25
Galerie Universelle des Hommes et des Femmes Celebres. Paris, n. d. 2 v. 4°. C,619
Galignani, A. and W. New Paris Guide. Paris, 1847. 16°. . . . V,446
Traveler's Guide through France. Paris, 1828. 24°. . . . V,444
Galileo-Galilei, Geschichtlicher Roman. M. Raven. Leipzig, 1860. 2 v. 12°. G,425
Galileo, Life of. J. E. D. Bethune. London, n. d. 8°. . . . . C,581
Private Life of; edited by Sister Maria Celeste. Boston, 1870. 12°. D,719
Tycho Brahe and Kepler, Lives of. J. Brewster. Lond. 1870. p. 8°. C,551
Gall, L. von. Gegen den Strom; Roman. Bremen, 1851. 2 v. 16°. . G,278
Gallagher, W. D. Erato; nos. 1, 2. Cincinnati, 1835. 2 v. 16°. . . I,25
Poetical Literature of the West. Cincinnati, 1841. 12°. . . . H,661
Progress in the North-West. Cincinnati, 1850. 8°. . . H,302,1
Gallaher, J. Pilgrimage of Adam and David. Cincinnati, 1846. 12°. . P,268
Gallaudet, T. H. History of Josiah. New York, n. d. 18°. . . P,746,28
Natural Theology. New York, n. d. 16°. . . . . P,746,28
Tribute to. H. Barnard. Hartford, 1852. 8°. . . . . C,1070
Gallenga, A. Frà Dolcino and his Times. London, 1853. 12°. . . D,732
History of Piedmont. London, 1855. 3 v. 12°. . . . . B,488

Gallenga, A. Invasion of Denmark in 1864. London, 1864. 2 v. 12°. . B,575
Italy in 1848. London, 1851. 12°. . . . . . . . . . B,490
Past and Present. London, 1849. 2 v. 12°. . . . . . B,487
Gallery of Historic Portraits. London, 1808–11. 7 v. 4°. . . . S.C.
Galletti, J. G. A. Allgemeine Weltkunde. Pest, 1854. 4°. . . . E,207
Gallus; Roman Scenes at Time of Augustus. W. A. Becker. Lon. 1853. 8°. A,153
Galt, J. Annals of the Parish. Edinburgh, 1844. 16°. . . . . . K,703
The same. London, 1841. 16°. . . . . . . K,1154
Ayrshire Legatees. London, 1841. 16°. . . . . . . K,1154
Eben Erskine. London, 1833. 3 v. 12°. . . . . . . J,565
Life of Lord Byron. New York, 1830. 18°. . . . . . . L,342
The same. London, 1830. 16°. . . . . . . . D,310
Lawrie Todd; or, the Settlers in the Woods. London, 1849. 16°. . K,522
Literary Life and Miscellanies. Edinburgh, 1834. 3 v. 8°. . . D,318
Life of Benjamin West. London, 1820. 8°. . . . . . . D,86
Life of Cardinal Wolsey. London, 1812. 4°. . . . . . . F,27
Southennan. London, 1830. 3 v. 12°. . . . . . . . K,523
Galton, F. Art of Travel. London, 1855. 12°. . . . . . V,1095
Hereditary Genius; its Laws and Consequences. New York, 1870. 8°. O,736
(Ed.) Vacation Tourists, for 1860–63. Lond. 1861–64. 3 v. 8°. . V,1086

1. Clark, W. G. Naples and Garibaldi.
Spottiswoode, G. A. Tour in Croatia and Hungary.
Slavonic Races.
Gossip on a Sutherland Hill-Side.
Bowen, C. C. Visit to Peru.
Cowell, J. J. Graian Alps and Mt. Iseran.
Stephen, L. The Allelein-Horn.
Hawkins, F. V. Ascent of Mount Cervin (Matterhorn).
Tyndall, J. From Lauterbrunnen to the Æggishhorn.
Clark, J. W. Yacht Voyage to the Faroe Islands and Iceland.
Tozer, H. F. Norway.
Galton, F. Visit to Spain at the Time of the Eclipse.
Noel, R. Syrian Travel and Syrian Tribes.

2. Weir, A. St. Petersburg and Moscow.
Marshall, W. The Country of Schamyl.
Tozer, H. F. The Monks of Mt. Athos.
Young, C. The Amazon and Rio Madeira.
Collinson, R. Nine Weeks in Canada.
Sclater, P. L. Naturalist's Impressions of Spain.
Geikie, A. Geological Notes on Auvergne.
Seemann, B. Fiji and its Inhabitants.
Durrant, W. The Kru Coast, Cape Palmas, and the Niger.
Grove, G. Nabloos and the Samaritans.
Christmas in Montenegro.

3. Tristram, H. B. Winter in Palestine.
Bertram, J. G. Fish Culture in France.
Kennedy, C. M. Turks of Constantinople.
Gordon, Lady Duff. Letters from the Cape.
Clark, W. G. Poland.
Powell, D. The Republic of Paraguay.
Tyrwhitt, R. St. J. Sinai.
Lubbock, Mrs. Ancient Shell-Mounds of Denmark.
Mayo, C. Med. Service of Federal Army.
Greive, W.T. Church and People of Servia.
Gordon, A. Wilderness Journeys in New Brunswick.

Galvanism, Chemische Verwandtschaft und. N. W. Fischer. Ber. 1830. 8°. N,252,8
Electric and Chemical Theories of. W. Ritchie. London, 1829. 4°. N,252,43
Galvanische Kette. G. T. Fechner. Leipzig, 1831. 4°. . . N,252,43
Kurze Darstellung des. J. Müller. Darmstadt, 1836. 8°. . N,252,4
Medical. W. H. Halse. London, n. d. 16°. . . . N,252,36
Treatise on. W. S. Harris. London, 1856. 12°. . . . . M,931
Gambler, Reformed. J. H. Green. Philadelphia, n. d. 12°. . . . M,343
Game, American, in its Seasons. H. W. Herbert. New York, 1853. 12°. M,328
Game Birds of the Northern States. R. B. Roosevelt. New York, 1866. 12°. M,318
Natural History of. Sir W. Jardine. Edinburgh, n. d. 16°. . N,470,8
Games, Established Rules for. E. Hoyle. Philadelphia, 1845. 24°. . . M,323
for Playground and Parlor. A. Elliott. London, 1868. 8°. . . M,341
Hand-Book of; edited by H. G. Bohn. London, 1867. p. 8°. . . L,292
Hoyle's Games Modernized. G. F. Pardon. London, n. d. 18°. . M,338
Manly Exercises. D. Walker. London, 1865. p. 8°. . . . L,152
Gammell, W. Life of Samuel Ward. Boston, 1860. 12°. . . . C,860,19
Life of Roger Williams. Boston, 1854. 16°. . . . . . C,1187

Gammel, W. Life of Roger Williams. Boston, 1860. 12°. . . c,860,14
Gammer Grethel's Fairy Tales. J. L. and W. K. Grimm. Lond. 1869. p. 8°. L,105
Gan-Eden; or, Pictures of Cuba. W. H. Hurlbut. Boston, 1854. 12°. . V,189
Ganot, A. Natural Philosophy; ed. by W. G. Peck. New York, 1860. 12°. N,72
Gands, P. Methode Eng. zu lernen, u. Schlüssel. N. Y. 1854–70. 2 v. 12°. L,775
Garbett, E. L. Architecture; Principles of Design. London, 1850. 12°. M,916
Garden, A. Anecdotes of the American Revolution. Brooklyn, 1865. 3 v. 4°. F,59
Garden, Book of the. E. MacIntosh. Edinburgh, 1853–55. 2 v. r. 8°. M,359
How to lay out a. E. Kemp. New York, 1858. 12°. . . . M,348
Manuel de l'Architecte des Jardins. P. Boitard. Paris, 1834. 18°. M,593
My Summer in a. C. D. Warner. Boston, 1871. 12°. . . . H,50
Garden Flowers. E. S. Rand, jr. Boston, 1866. 12°. . . . . . . N,955
Garden Vegetables. F. Burr, jr. Boston, 1866. 8°. . . . . . . M,511
Garden Walks with the Poets. C. M. Kirkland. New York, 1852. 12°. . I,365
Gardens, Remarks on laying out. Sir J. G. Wilkinson. London, 1858. 8°. M,93
Gardener's Almanac. J. Evelyn. London, 1706. f°. . . . . . Q,121
Gardener's Assistant. T. Bridgeman. New York, 1865. 12°. . . . M,520
Gardener's Chronicle, 1841–54. London, 1841–66. 26 v. 4°. . . . Q,374
Gardener's Magazine; conducted by J. C. Loudon. Lond. 1826–43. 19 v. 8°. R,19
Gardiner, M., *Countess of Blessington.* Country Quarters. Leip. 1850. 2 v. 16°. J,192
Correspondence with Lord Byron. Cincinnati, 1851. 12°. . . D,76
Idler in France. Philadelphia, 1841. 2 v. 12°. . . . . V,455
Idler in Italy. London, 1839. 2 v. 8°. . . . . . . V,517
Life and Correspondence of. R. R. Madden. N. Y. 1855. 2 v. 12°. C,1202
Marmaduke Herbert. Leipzig, 1847. 2 v. in 1. 16°. . . . J,193
Meredith. Leipzig, 1843. 16°. . . . . . . . . . J,194
Strathern; a Novel. Leipzig, 1844. 2 v. in 1. 16°. . . . J,195
Gardiner, W. Music of Nature. Boston, 1856. 8°. . . . . . . M,412
Gardner, C. K. Dictionary of Officers of U.S.Army. New York, 1853. 12°. L.R.
Gardner, D. P. Farmers' Dictionary. New York, 1855. 12°. . . . M,494
Garibaldi, G., and Naples. W. G. Clark. London, 1861. 8°. . . V,1086,1
Life, written by himself. New York, 1859. 12°. . . . . D,718
Rule of the Monk. New York, 1870. 8°. . . . . . G,241
Garland, H. A. Lectures on Protestantism and Gov't. St.Louis, 1852. 8°. T,19,2
Life of John Randolph of Roanoke. New York, 1854. 2 v. in 1. 8°. C,881
Garlick, T. Artificial Propagation of Fish. Cleveland, 1857. 8°. . . N,701
Garnier, J. G. Elemens d'Algèbre. Paris, 1811. 8°. . . . M,1116
Garnier-Audiger. Manuel du Tapissier, Décorateur, etc. Paris, 1830. 18°. M,590
Garrard, L. H. Wah-To-Yah and the Taos Trail. Cincinnati, 1850. 12°. V,155
Garrett, E. and R. White as Snow. New York, n. d. 12°. . . . K,138
Garrick, D., Life of. P. Fitzgerald. London, 1868. 2 v. 8°. . . . D,443
Mémoires de. Paris, 1855. 12°. . . . . . . . D,612
Garstangs of Garstang Grange. T. A. Trollope. Leipzig, 1870. 16°. . J,508
Gartenkunst, Theorie der. C. C. L. Hirschfeld. Leip. 1779–85. 5 v. in 3. 4°. G,742
Garter, Order of the. G. F. Beltz. London, 1841. 8°. . . . . D,279
Garvey, M. A. Manual of Human Culture. London, 1866. 12°. . O,1002
Gas and Ventilation. E. E. Perkins. Philadelphia, 1856. 12°. . . M,602
Gas, Appeal to the Consumers of London. London, 1849. 8°. . N,252,39
Dialogue concerning. C. Pearson. London, 1849. 8°. . . N,252,39
Domestic Uses of. A. A. Croll. Cottenham, 1848. 16°. . . N,252,37

Gas, Metropolitan Gas Inquiry. E. Cardwell. London, 1850. 8°. . N,252,39
Patent granted to G. Lowe. London, 1847. 8°. . . . . N,252,39
Second Dialogue with a Gas-Consumer. London, 1849. 8°. . N,252,39
Gas Consumer's Guide. Boston, 1871. 16°. . . . . . . . . M,667
Gas Consumers, Hints to. London, 1840. 16°. . . . . . . N,252,36
Gas-Lighting; its Progress, etc. J. O. M. Rutter. London, 1849. 8°. N,252.39
Gas-Making, Use of Clay Retorts for. J. Church. London, 1858. 8°. N,252,50
Gases, Dry, Action on Colouring Matter. G. Wilson. Edinburgh, 1848. 4°. N,252,42
Gaskell, E. C. Cousin Phillis, and other Tales. Leipzig, 1867. 16°. . . J,174
Cranford. New York, n. d. 16°. . . . . . . . . . K,704
The same. Leipzig, 1867. 16°. . . . . . . . J,175
Dark Night's Work. New York, 1863. 8°. . . . . . . K,705
The same. Leipzig, 1863. 16°. . . . . . . . J,176
Life of Charlotte Brontë. New York, 1857. 2 v. 12°. . . . C,1204
The same. Leipzig, 1859. 2 v. in 1. 16°. . . . . . J,178
Lois the Witch. Leipzig, 1861. 16°. . . . . . . . J,177
Mary Barton. New York, 1848. 8°. . . . . . . . . K,706
The same. Leipzig, 1849. 16°. . . . . . . . J,179
North and South. New York, n. d. 8°. . . . . . . . K,707
Right at Last, and other Tales. New York, 1860. 12°. . . . K,708
Ruth. New York, 1866. 12°. . . . . . . . . . . K,709
The same. Leipzig, 1853. 2 v. in 1. 16°. . . . . J,180
Sylvia's Lovers. Leipzig, 1863. 2 v. in 1. 16°. . . . . J,181
Wives and Daughters. New York, 1866. 8°. . . . . . . K,710
The same. Leipzig, 1866. 3 v. 16°. . . . . . . J,182
Gasparin, A. E. de. Science *vs.* Modern Spiritualism. N. Y. 1857. 2 v. 12°. P,871
Uprising of a Great People. New York, 1862. 12°. . . . B,900
Gaspey, T. History of England. London, n. d. 8 v. 8°. . . . A,371
and Bussey, G. M. History of France. London, 1843. 8°. . . B,276
Gassendi, P. Opera Omnia. Florentiæ, 1727. 6 v. f°. . . . . . Q,331
Gastronomic Regenerator; System of Cookery. A. Soyer. Lond 1861. 8°. H,320
Gates Ajar. E. S. Phelps. Boston, 1869. 16°. . . . . . . . K,231
Gates Wide Open. G. Wood. Boston, 1870. 12°. . . . . . . K,404
Gaudy, F. F. Sämmtliche Werke. Berlin, 1844. 24 v. in 12. 16°. . . E,325

Bd. 1. Biographie; Lieder.
2. Terzinen; Aus dem Tagebuche eines wandernden Schneidergesellen.
3. Der Liebe Loos; Das fünfzigjährige Jubiläum; Der Pfarrer von Weinsperg; Der verlorne Sohn;
4. Paulina; Der Stumme; Rede am Grabe des Musketiers Gröbel; Jugend-Liebe.
5, 6. Portogalli, Reise-und Lebensbilder aus Italien.
7. Kaiserlieder.
8. Lyrische Gedichte; Der moderne Paris; Aus den Papieren des Kandidaten Ballhorn.
9. Kopien des Laien; Die Bayerische Kellnerin; Der Deutsche in Trastevere.
10. Desengaño.
11. Balladen und Romanzen.
12. Nachricht von der allerneusten Schicksalen des Hundes Berganza; Ludwiga; Der junge Autor.
13–15. Venetianische Novellen.
16. Erzählende Dichtungen; Die Lebensüberdrüssigen; Wasserrosen.
17. Wandrers Schreibtafel; Die Verrathenen; Aus dem Gedenkbuche des Ritter Rudolf von Ehingen; Der Schweizer-Soldat in Bologna.
18. Elegien u. Epigramme; Schüler-Liebe; Dramatisches.
19–22. Mein Römerzug.
23. Vermischte Gedichte; Der Katzen-Raphael; Der Jahrestag; Aus dem Tagebuche eines Hessischen Jägers.
24. Genrebilder und Humoresken; Nachbildungen.

Gaudy, F. F. Werke; Neue Ausgabe, Auswahl. Berlin, 1853–4. 8 v. in 4. 16°. E,324
Bd. 1. Lieder; Romanzen; Terzinen; Aus dem Tagebuche eines wandernden Schneidergesellen.
2, 3. Mein Römerzug.
4. Kaiserlieder; Erzählende Dichtungen; Vermischte Gedichte.
5. Novellen u. Erzählungen.
6. Novellen u. Erzählungen: Humoresken.
7. Der Liebe Loos; Portogalli, Bilder aus Italien.
8. Venetianische Novellen.

Gaudy, J. P. and Gell, Sir W. Topography of Pompeii. London, 1852. 8°. *B,501
Gauss, C. F. Disquisitiones Arithmeticæ. Lipsiæ, 1801. 8°. . . M,1115
Recherches Arithmétiques. Paris, 1807. 4°. . . . . . M,1205
Theoria Motus Corporum Celestium. Hamburgi, 1809. 4°. . . N,386
Theory of the Motion of Heavenly Bodies. Boston, 1857. 4°. . M,823
Gaut Gurley; Trappers of Umbagog. D. P. Thompson. Phila. 1860. 12°. K,349
Gavazzi, A. Lectures in New York. New York, 1853. 12°. . . . P,796
Recollections of the Last Four Popes. London, 1859. 12°. . . C,548
Gavin, H. Unhealthiness of London. London, 1847. 8°. . . N,252,29
Gay, J. Poetical Works. Boston, 1854. 2 v. 16°. . . . . . . I,210
Gay Science, The. E. S. Dallas. London, 1866. 2 v. 8°. . . . O,796
Gayarré, C. History of Louisiana. New York, 1866. 3 v. 8°. . . . C,194
Philip II. of Spain. New York, 1866. 8°. . . . . . . B,475
Gaylord, G., *pseud.* See *Bradley, J. W.*
Gaylord, W. and Tucker, L. American Husbandry. N. Y. 1854. 2 v. 18°. M,436
Gay-Lussac, N. F. Essai d'Argent par la Voie humide. Paris, 1832. 4°. N,252,57
Gayworthys, The. A. D. T. Whitney. Boston, 1865. 12°. . . . K,399
Gazetteer of the British Islands. J. A. Sharp. London, 1852. 2 v. 8°. . L.R.
of Missouri. A. Wetmore. St. Louis, 1837. 8°. . . . . . C,241
of Ohio. G. W. Hawes. Cincinnati, 1860. 8°. . . . . . L.R.
W. Jenkins. Columbus, 1841. 12°. . . . . . . L.R.
of the United States, Colton's. R. S. Fisher. New York, 1853. 8°. L.R.
Lippincott's. T. Baldwin and J. Thomas. Phila. 1854. 8°. . L.R.
of the World. Edinburgh, 1856. 7 v. 8°. . . . . . . L.R.
A. K. Johnston. London, 1852. 8°. . . . . . L.R.
Harper's. J. C. Smith. New York, 1855. 8°. . . . L.R.
Imperial. W. G. Blackie. Glasgow, 1855. 2 v. 8°. . . L.R.
Lippincott's. J. Thomas and T. Baldwin. Philad. 1870. 8°. R.R.
The same. Philadelphia, 1858. 8°. . . . . . L.R.
Universal. J. R. McCulloch. New York, 1855. 2 v. 8°. . L.R.
Western; or, Emigrant's Directory. S. R. Brown. Auburn, N. Y. 1817. 8°. C,199
Gazlay, A. W. Races of Mankind. Cincinnati, 1856. . . . . N,395
Gefahrvolle Wege. G. Hiltl. Berlin, n. d. 4 v. 12°. . . . . G,312
Gegen den Strom. L. von Gall. Bremen, 1851. 2 v. 16°. . . . G,278
Gegenwart, Die. Leipzig, 1848-56. 12 v. 8°. . . . . . . . E,32
Geheimniss der alten Mamsell. E. John. Leipzig, 1868. 2 v. 16°. . G,336
Geheimniss der Stadt. F. W. Hackländer. Stuttgart, 1868. 3 v. 16°. . G,306
Geibel, E. Gedichte. Stuttgart, 1865. 12°. . . . . . . . E,262
Neue Gedichte. Stuttgart, 1865. 12°. . . . . . . . E,263
und Heyse, P. Spanishes Liederbuch. Berlin, 1852. 24°. . . E,265
und von Schack, A. F. Romanzero der Spanier. Stuttgart, 1860. 12°. E,264
Geijer, E. G. History of the Swedes. London, n. d. 8°. . . . . B,581
and Carlson, F. F. Geschichte Schwedens. Gotha, 1832–55. 4 v. 8°. E,112

Geikie, A. Geological Notes on Auvergne. London, 1862. 8°. . v,1086,2
Geinitz, H. B. and others. Steinkholen Europa's. München, 1865. 3 v. 4°. F,95
Geld und Geist. O. Ruppius. Berlin, 1863. 16°. . . . . . . G,430
Gell, Sir W. Topography of Rome, with map. London, 1846. 2 v. 8°. . A,179
Topography of Troy. London, 1804. f°. . . . . . . L.R.
and Gaudy, J. P. Pompeiana. Topography. London, 1852. 8°. . *B,501
Gem, The, for 1840. H. F. Anners. Philadelphia, 1839. 18°. . . . H,29
Gems, Natural History of. C. W. King. London, 1867. 8°. . . . N,864
Popular Treatise on. L. Feuchtwanger. New York, 1859. 12°. . N,757
Gemma; a Novel. T. A. Trollope. Philadelphia, n. d. 8°. . . K,1053
Genealogical Dictionary of New England. J. Savage. Bost. 1860–62. 4 v. 8°. *C,729
Genealogy, Hand-Book of American. W. H. Whitmore. Albany, 1862. 4°. F,39
of the Huntington Family. E. B. Huntington. Stamford, 1863. 8°. C,934
General Information. J. Timbs. London, 1867. 16°. . . . . . I,544
General Register for 1827. Edinburgh, 1828. 16°. . . . . . . I,505
Generals, Recollections of Distinguished. W. F. G. Shanks. N. Y. 1866. 12°. C,529
Generations of Animals, Alternation of. J. J. S. Steenstrup. Lond. 1845. 8°. O,291
Génevieve. A. de Lamartine. New York, n. d. 8°. . . . . . . G,242
Genghis Khan, History of. J. Abbott. New York, 1860. 16°. . . J,1392
Genii, Tales of the. J. Ridley. London, 1861. p. 8°. . . . . L,150
Genin, S. Selections from his Works. New York, 1855. 8°. . . . U,117
Genin, T. H. Selections from Writings, and Biography. N. Y. 1869. 8°. . C,728
Genius and Faith. W. C. Scott. New York, 1853. 12°. . . . . P,189
Genius, Illustrations of. H. Giles. Boston, 1854. 16°. . . . . H,37
Genlis, Comtesse de. Adelaide and Theodore. London, 1788. 3 v. 16°. . O,1162
Memoirs. London, 1825–26. 8 v. 12°. . . . . . . . D,668
The same. New York, 1825. 2 v. 8°. . . . . . . D,669
Genius of the West; a Magazine, v. 3–5. Cincinnati, 1855–56. 8°. . . T,15
Genoude, A. E. Vie de Jésus Christ. Paris, 1851. 12°. . . . . P,369
Gentility, Ladies' Guide to. E. Thornwell. New York, 1857. 12°. . . H,288
Gentleman, The, Character of. F. Lieber. Philadelphia, 1864. 12°. . H,228
Gentleman's Magazine. London, 1731–1860. 209 v. 8°. . . . . T,1
Selections from. London, 1811. 4 v. 8°. . . . . . T,3
Gentoo Laws, Code of; translated by N. B. Halbed. London, 1776. 4°. . Q,341
Geodosy, Opérations Géodésiques. P. Daussy. Paris, 1829. 4°. . . M,821
Traite de Géodésie. L. Puissant. Paris, 1819. 2 v. 4°. . . . M,815
Supplement. Paris, 1827. 4°. . . . . . . . M,1175
Geoffry Hamlyn. H. Kingsley. Leipzig, 1864. 2 v. in 1. 16°. . . J,248
The same. Boston, 1866. 12°. . . . . . . . K,755
Geoffrey de Vinsauf. Chronicle of the Crusades. London, 1848. p. 8°. . A,226
Geoffrey of Monmouth. British History. London, 1848. p. 8°. . . L,26
Geoffroy Saint-Hilaire, E. Principes de Philos. Zoologique. Paris, 1830. 8°. N,252,17
Geographical Distrib. of Animals and Plants. C. Pickering. Bost. 1854. 4°. *Q,282
Geographical Names, Origin of. A. J. Perkins and G. W. Fitch. N. Y. 1852. 18°. O,897
Geographical Reading Book. T. Crampton and T. Turner. Lond. 1857. 16°. O,895
Geographical Studies. C. Ritter. Boston, 1863. 12°. . . . V,1133
Geographical Teaching. Key to Guyot's Wall Maps. A. Guyot. N. Y. 1866. 12°. O,903
Geography. R. C. Smith. New York, 1852. 12°. . . . . . . O,900
Allgem. Länder- u. Volkerkunde. H. Berghaus. Stutt. 1837–44. 6v. 8°. E,157
Allgemeine Weltkunde. J. G. A. Galletti. Pest, 1854. 4°. . . E,207

Geography, Ancient. S. A. Mitchell. Philadelphia, 1860. 12°. . v,1135
Lectures on. B. G. Niebuhr. London, 1853. 2 v. 8°. . . N,435
and Mediæval. C. Anthon. New York, 1850. 8°. . v,1116
and History, Outlines of Scripture. E. Hughes. Phil. 1853. 12°. . P,459
Summary of. A. Adams. Edinburgh, 1794. 8°. . . v,1109
Atlas Classique et Universal. G. G. A. Goujon. Paris, 1835. f°. *Q,446
Atlas, Family. A. J. Johnston. New York, 1863. 4°. . . . R.R.
General. A. and C. Black. Edinburgh, 1853. 4°. . . R.R.
The same. Edinburgh, 1870. 4°. . . . *Q,469
G. W. Colton. New York, 1870. f°. . . . *Q,461
S. A. Mitchell. Philadelphia, 1868. 4°. . . *Q,464
Society for Diffus. of Knowledge. Lond. 1844. 2 v. f°. *Q,453
Modern Historical. W. L. Gage. New York, 1869. 8°. *v,1141
National. A. K. Johnston. Edinburgh, 1851. f°. . *Q,465
New Reference. S. A. Mitchell. Philadelphia, 1865. 4°. *Q,370
of Ohio and United States. H. F. Walling. N. Y. 1868. f°. *Q,392
Cities and Principal Towns of the World. London, 1830. 12°. M,1007
Class-Book of Local. E. E. White. Cleveland, 1860. 16°. . . O,899
Classical. S. Butler. Philadelphia, 1847. 12°. . . . v,1121
Atlas of. London, 1861. 8°. . . . . . . . . . L,79
S. Butler. Philadelphia, 1851. 8°. . . . v,1123
A. G. Findlay. New York, n. d. . . . . v,1127
Common-School. A. Guyot. New York, 1867–70. 4°. . . . Q,130
Comparative. C. Ritter. Philadelphia, 1865. 8°. . . . . P,290
Conversations on. Baroness Le Despencer. London, 1854. 8°. . O,902
De Orbis Situ. Pomponius Mela. Basileæ, 1522. f°. . . . Q,414
Dictionary of. A. K. Johnston. London, 1852. 8°. . . . L.R.
Dictionary of Greek and Roman. W. Smith. Bost. 1854–57. 2 v. 8°. S.C.
Elementary. A. Guyot. New York, 1868–70. 4°. . . . O,1219,1
Encyclopædia of. H. Murray; ed. by T. G. Bradford. Bost. 1853. 3 v. 8°. v,1128
English Cyclopædia. London, 1854–55. 4 v. r. 8°. . . . L.R.
Erdbeschreib. u. Staatenkunde. K. F. R. Schneider. Glog. 1857. 5 v. 8°. E,154
First Book of. A. Reid. Edinburgh, 1855. 18°. . . . . O,896
Hand-Book of Modern. H. G. Bohn. London, 1865. p. 8°. . . L,137
Intermediate. S. S. Cornell. New York, 1855. 4°. . . . Q,129
A. Guyot. New York, 1870. 4°. . . . . . . Q,102
Introductory. G. W. Colton and G. W. Fitch. New York, 1856. 4°. O,904
Manual of Modern. W. Pütz. New York, 1859. 12°. . . . A,302
Mediæval, Hand-Book of. W. Pütz. New York, 1858. . . . A,228
Mittheilungen aus Justus Perthes' Geographischer Anstalt. A. H. Petermann. Gotha, 1855–67. 14 v. 4°. . . . . . . E,205
Modern. J. Pinkerton. London, 1807. 3 v. 4°. . . . v,1142
S. A. Mitchell. Philadelphia, 1852. 12°. . . . O,901
R. M. Smith. Philadelphia, 1848. 4°. . . . Q,125
of Great Britain. G. Long and G. R. Porter. London, n. d. 8°. v,1126
Outlines of. G. Hogarth. London, 1853. 24°. . . . . O,894
Physical. M. Somerville. Philadelphia, 1854. 12°. . . v,1134
D. T. Ansted. Philadelphia, 1867. 8°. . . v,1118
and Intermediate. J. Monteith. New York, 1867. 4°. . . Q,187
Class-Book of. W. Rhind. Edinburgh, 1854. 16°. . . O,898

Geography, Physical, Historical and Military. T. S. Lavallée. Lond. 1868. 8°. V,1119
Outlines of. G. W. Fitch. New York, 1856. 12°. . V,1120
Primary. S. S. Cornell. New York, 1854. 4°. . . . . O,905
A. Guyot. New York, 1867. 4°. . . . . . . O,1219
Res Geographicæ. Strabo. Leipzig, 1819. 3 v. 18°. . . . U,384
Universal; edited by T. C. Callicot. New York, 1853. 12°. . V,1139
C. Malte-Brun. Philadelphia, 1827–29. 4 v. 8°. . . . S.C.
Universum. J. Meyer. Hildburghausen, 1834–60. 21 v. 16°. . E,307
Zeitschrift für Allgemeine. T. E. Gumprecht. Berl. 1853–56. 7 v. 8°. E,158
Zeitschrift für Vergleichende. J. G. Lüdde. Magdeb. 1842–50. 10 v. 8°. E,159
Geological Excursions round Isle of Wight. G. A. Mantell. Lond. 1854. p. 8. L,304
Geological Gossip. D. T. Ansted. London, 1860. 16°. . . . . N,600
Geological Magazine. London, 1864–68. 5 v. 8°. . . . . . . R,27
Geological Manual. Sir H. T. De la Beche. London, 1833. 8°. . . N,800
Geological Map of the United States. J. Marcou. Boston, 1853. 2 v. 8°. N,827
Geological Notes on Auvergne. A. Gerkie. London, 1862. 8°. . . V,1086,2
Geological Observer. Sir H. T. De la Beche. London, 1853. 8°. . . N,843
The same. Philadelphia, 1851. 8°. . . . . . . N,838
Geological Reconnaissance in California. W. P. Blake. N. Y. 1858. 4°. Q,49
of Tennessee. J. M. Safford. Nashville, 1856. 8°. . . N,877
Geological Sketches. L. Agassiz. Boston, 1866. 12°. . . . . N,608
Geological Society of London. See *London*.
Geological Survey of Canada. W. E. Logan. Montreal, 1845–57. 3 v. 8°, 4°. N,870
of California. San Francisco, 1864–67. 4 v. 4°. viz.:
Geology, Reports from 1860–64. J. D. Whitney. v. 1. . . N,741
Ornithology, Land Birds. J. G. Cooper. v. 1. . . . N,739
Palaeontology. F. B. Meek and W. M. Gabb. 2 v. . . N,740
of Connecticut. C. U. Shepard. New Haven, 1837. 8°. . . . N,871
of Del Rio Ranche, in Sonora. C. Cherry. Cincinnati, 1866. 8°. . O,501
of Illinois. A. H. Worthen and others. Chicago, 1866-70. 4 v. 8°. *N,742
of New Jersey. W. Kitchell. Trenton, 1856. 8°. . . . . . N,873
of Ohio, 1st and 2d Rep. 1837–8. W. W. Mather. Columbus, 1838. 8°. N,874,1–2
Report, 1869. J. S. Newberry. Columbus, 1869. 8°. . N,874,3
of Pennsylvania, 2d and 3d Rep. H. D. Rogers. Harrisburg, 1838–9. 8°. N,875
Final Report. H. D. Rogers. Edinburgh, 1858. 3 v. 4°. . *Q,50
Geologist, The; a Popular Magazine. London, 1858–64. 7 v. 8°. . . R,28
Geologist's Text-Book. D. T. Ansted. London, 1845. 12°. . . . N,601
Geology, Advanced Text-Book of. D. Page. Edinburgh, 1867. 12°. . N,765
and Agricult. Chem., Lectures on. J. F. W. Johnston. Edinb. 1847. 8°. M,573
and associate Sciences, Introd. to. G. F. Richardson. Lond. 1851. p. 8. L,310
and History. B. von Cotta. London, 1865. 16°. . . . . . N,598
and Mineralogy, with plates. W. Buckland. Lond. 1869–70. 2 v. p. 8°. L,280
The same. London, 1857. 2 v. p. 8°. . . . . . . N,805
W. Hooker. New York, 1865. 12°. . . . . . N,780
Treatise on. P. Cleaveland. v. 1. Boston, 1822. . . . N,858
and Natural History, Researches in. C. Darwin. N. Y. 1852. 2 v. 12°. N,633
and Zoölogy, Biography of. L. Agassiz. London, 1848–54. 4 v. 8°. O,300
Chemische und Physikalische. G. Bischof. Bonn, 1847–51. 3 v. 8°. G,844
Descriptive and Practical. D. T. Ansted. London, 1844. 2 v. 8°. N,806
Economical, of Massachusetts. E. Hitchcock. Boston, 1838. 8°. N,252,35

Geology, Elementary. E. Hitchcock. New York, 1855. 12°. . . . N,789
Elementary Course of. D. T. Ansted. Edinburgh, 1859. 8°. . . N,610
Elements of. A. Gray and C. B. Adams. New York, 1854. 12°. . N,605
J. F. W. Johnston. New York, 1855. 12°. . . . M,514
C. A. Lee. New York, 1855. 18°. . . . . . L,460
Sir C. Lyell. New York, 1866. 8°. . . . . . N,837
S. St. John. New York, 1851. 12°. . . . . . N,781
Familiar Compend of. A. M. Hillside. Philadelphia, 1859. 12°. . N,606
First Lessons in. G. A. Mantell. London, 1844. 2 v. 16°. . . L,305
for General Readers. D. Page. Edinburgh, 1866. 8°. . . . N,607
for Teachers and Students. S. Tenney. Philadelphia, 1860. 8°. . N,766
Geologie. K. C. von Leonhard. Stuttgart, 1836–44. 5 v. 12°. . G,834
Sir H. T. De la Beche. Berlin, 1836. 8°. . . N,252,4
der Gegenwart. B. von Cotta. Leipzig, 1866. 8°. . . G,829
Geologische Bilder. B. von Cotta. Leipzig, 1852. 8°. . . G,830
von Australien. L. Leichhardt. Halle, 1855. 4°. . . . Q,46
Taschenbuch der. K. C. von Leonhard. Stuttgart, 1845. 12°. G,835
und Geognosie. K. C. von Leonhard. Stuttgart, 1835. 8°. G,812,2
und Petrefactenkunde. C. Vogt. Braunschweig, 1846–47. 2 v. 8°. G,838
Great Stone-Book of Nature. D. T. Ansted. Philadelphia, 1863. 12°. N,767
Hand-Book of Geological Terms. D. Page. Edinburgh, 1859. 8°. N,786
Illustrated, with Plates, Appleton's. New York, 1856. 2 v. 8°. *Q,250
Illustrations of Surface. E. Hitchcock. Amherst, 1860. 4°. . . Q,56
Incentives to the Study of. S. S. Randall. New York, 1846. 12°. . N,593
Introduction to. R. Bakewell. London, 1838. 8°. . . . . . N,822
G. F. Richardson. London, 1851. p. 8°. . . . . . L,310
Lectures on. T. Flint. Cincinnati, 1833. 12°. . . . . . N,502
Manual of. J. D. Dana. Philadelphia, 1864. 8°. . . . . . N,801
E. Emmons. Philadelphia. 1860. 12°. . . . . . N,784
J. Phillips. London, 1855. 8°. . . . . . . . N,758
Manual of Elementary. Sir C. Lyell. New York, 1854. 8°. . N,837
Supplement. London, 1857. 8°. . . . . . . N,252,44
of Australia. G. H. Wathen. London, 1855. 8°. . . . . . V,875
of Bass Rock. H. Miller and T. Mac Crie. New York, 1852. 12°. N,612
of Berwickshire. R. D. Thomson. Berwickshire, 1831. 8°. . N,252,44
of California. P. T. Tyson. Washington, 1851. 8°. . . . . N,876
of New York. Albany, 1842–52. 6 v. 4°. viz.:
1st District. W. W. Mather. Albany, 1843. . . . *Q,101,9
2d District. E. Emmons. Albany, 1842. . . . *Q,101,10
3d District. L. Vanuxem. Albany, 1842. . . . *Q,101,11
4th District. J. Hall. Albany, 1843. . . . . *Q,101,12
Palæontology. J. Hall. Albany, 1847–52. 2 v. . *Q,101,13,14
of Pennsylvania. H. D. Rogers. Edinburgh, 1858. 3 v. 4°. . *Q,50
of Russia and Ural Mountains. R. I. Murchison. London, 1845. 2 v. 4°. Q,439
of Turko-Persian Frontier. W. K. Loftus. London, 1855. 8°. N,252,44
Old Red Sandstone. H. Miller. Boston, 1859. 12°. . . . N,614
Outlines of. J. L. Comstock. New York, 1837. 12°. . . . N,603
Passages in the History of. A. C. Ramsay. London, 1848. 8°. N,252,35
The same, continued London, 1849. 8°. . . . N,252,35
Popular Physical. J. B. Jukes. London, 1853. 16°. . . . N,597

Geology, Principles of. Sir C. Lyell. New York, 1854. 8°. . . . N,842
Rambles of a Geologist. H. Miller. Boston, 1859. 12°. . . V,357
Religion of. E. Hitchcock. Boston, 1855. 12°. . . . . P,252
Rudimentary Treatise on. J. E. Portlock. London, 1859. 12°. . M,952
Sketch-Book of Popular. H. Miller. Boston, 1859. 12°. . . N,613
Student's Manual of. J. B. Jukes. Edinburgh, 1862. 8°. . . N,790
Testimony of the Rocks. H. Miller. Boston, 1859. 12°. . . N,616
Text-Book of. J. D. Dana. Philadelphia, 1864. 8°. . . . N,762
Thoughts on a Pebble. G. A. Mantell. London, 1849. 12°. . . N,599
Treatise on. J. Phillips. London, 1837. 12°. . . . M,1040
Wonders of. G. A. Mantell. London, 1840. 2 v. p. 8°. . . N,596
The same. London, 1866. 2 v. p. 8°. . . . . . . L,307
Geometrical Drawing, Manual of. S. E. Warren. New York, 1868. 12°. M,156
Text-Book of. W. Minifie. New York. 1868. 8°. . . . . M,231
Geometrical Problems. M. Bland. London, 1842. 8°. . . . M,1132
Geometry, Analytical. J. Hann. London, 1850. 12°. . . . . M,845
Essai de. J. B. Biot. Paris, 1813. 8°. . . . . M,1127
Examples in. I. Todhunter. London, 1864. 8°. . . M,1107
and Trigonometry. T. Tate. London, 1855. 12°. . . . M,1087
Elements of. A. M. Legendre. New York, 1867. 8°. . M,1129
Algebra and Trigonometry. T. P. Kirkman. London, 1852. 12°. M,942
Descriptive, applied to Drawing. J. F. Heather. London, 1851. 12°. M,934
Elements of. C. Davies. New York, 1866. 8°. . . M,1124
Traité de. G. Monge. Paris, 1820. 4°. . . . . M,1190
L. L. Vallie. Paris, 1819. 2 v. 4°. . . . M,1191
Elémens de Géométrie. S. F. La Croix. Paris, 1814. 8°. . M,1126
Elements of. Dublin, 1854. 16°. . . . . . . . M,1086
The same; edited by R. Potts. Cambridge, 1847. 8°. . M,1159
The same; edited by I. Todhunter. London, 1869. 16°. M,1133
The same; three books; edited by T. Tate. London, 1856. 12°. M,1140
Euclid's Elements; edited by H. Law. London, 1855. 12°. . M,945
Geometrie der Stellung. L. N. M. Carnot. Altona, 1808–10. 2 v. 8°. E,433
Geometrische Anschauungslehre. B. Féaux. Paderborn, 1857. 8°. E,426
Lehrbuch der Geometrie. H. A. Brettner. Breslau, 1853. 12°. E,430
Methodus inveniendi Lineas Curvas. L. Euler. Laus. 1748. 2 v. 4°. M,1185
Perspective Drawing and Painting. C. Hayter. London, 1845. 8°. M,171
Plane Co-ordinate. I. Todhunter. London, 1867. 12°. . . M,1143
Practical, and Architectural Drawing. R. S. Burn. London, 1853. 8°. M,1125
Practical, Perspective, and Projective. T. Bradley. Lond. n. d. 8°. M,1131
Practical System of. R. and J. Cochrane. Baltimore, 1857. 8°. M,1123
Treatise on. D. Lardner. London, 1840. 12°. . . . M,1020
The same. London, 1840. 12°. . . . . . . M,1138
Vorschule der Darstellenden Geometrie. A. L. Busch. Berlin, 1846. 8°. E,434
George II., Memoirs of the Reign of. J. L. Hervey. Phil. 1848. 2 v. 12°. A,538
H. Walpole. London, 1847. 3 v. 8°. . . . . . . A,539
George III., Annals of the Reign of. J. Aikin. London, 1816. 2 v. 8°. A,540
Correspondence with Lord North. London, 1867. 2 v. 8°. . . D,427
Court and Cabinets of. R. P. Grenville. London, 1853–55. 4 v. 8°. A,551
History of the Reign of. London, 1770. 12°. . . . . . A,483
R. Bissett. Philadelphia, 1828. 3 v. 8°. . . . . A,409

George III., History of the Reign of. J. R. Miller. London, 1828. 8°. . A,541
Memoirs of. J. H. Jesse. London, 1867. 3 v. 8°. . . . D,114
Memoirs of the Reign of. H. Walpole. London, 1845. 4 v. 8°. D,357
Public and Private Life of. R. Huish. London, 1821. 4°. . . D,133
George IV., Life and Times of. G. Croly. New York, 1855. 18°. . . L,348
Memoirs of the Court of. R. P. Grenville. London, 1859. 2 v. 8°. A,553
Georges, The Four. W. M. Thackeray. Leipzig, 1861. 16°. . . . J,483
History of. S. M. Smucker. New York, 1860. 12°. . . . C,1266
Caricature History of. T. Wright. London, 1867. 8°. . . . A,537
George, A. Annals of the Queens of Spain. New York, 1850. 2 v. 12°. D,700
George Barnwell, Histoire de. G. Lillo. Londres, 1767. 12°. . . . H,855
George Canterbury's Will. Mrs. H. Wood. Philadelphia, 1870. 8°. . K,1068
The same. Leipzig, 1870. 2 v. in 1. 16°. . . . J,521
George Geith of Fen Court. J. H. Riddell. Boston, 1865. 8°. . . . K,910
The same. Leipzig, 1865. 2 v. in 1. 16°. . . . . J,424
George Ready. R. O'Lincoln. New York, 1865. 16°. . . . J,1351
Georgia. Account of the Colony, 1741. See *Force's Tracts*, v. 1.
Description of, 1741. See *Force's Tracts*, v. 2.
Establishment of a Colony, 1733. See *Force's Tracts*, v. 1.
History of. T. S. Arthur and W. H. Carpenter. Phil. 1852. 12°. C,154
Journal of Commissary Von Reck, 1734. See *Force's Tracts*, v. 4.
State of the Province, 1740. London, 1742. See *Force's Tracts*, v. 1.
True Narrative of the Colony. P. Tailfer, etc., 1741. See *Force's Tracts*, v. 1.
Georgia Plantation, Journal of Residence. F. A. Kemble. N. Y. 1864. 12°. V,88
Georgia Scenes. A. B. Longstreet. New York, 1840. 12°. . . . V,38
Georgian Era; Memoirs of Eminent Persons, v. 2-4. London, 1833-34. 8°. C,1229
Georgy Sandon; or, a Lost Love. A. Owen. Boston, 1865. 12°. . . K,872
Gerald Estcourt. F. Church. Leipzig, 1867. 2 v. in 1. 16°. . . . J,347
Geraudly, C. J. de. Art de conserver les Dents. Paris, 1737. 16°. . . L,842
Gerbier, Letters au les Maladies Cancereuse. Geneve, 1777. 2 v. 12°. . L,867
Gerhardt, C. Traite de Chimie Organique. Paris, 1860-63. 4 v. 8°. . N,180
Germaine. E. About. Boston, 1860. 12°. . . . . . . . H,966
German Alps, Deutsche Alpen. E. A. Schaubach. Jena, 1845-47. 5 v. 8°. E,202
German Archæology, Handbuch. G. Klemm. Dresden, 1836. 8°. . . E,453
German Art, Geschichte der. E. Förster. Leipzig, 1860. 5 v. in 2. 12°. G,624
German Emigrants, The. J. W. von Goëthe. London, 1854. p. 8°. L,188,4
German Empire, History of. S. A. Dunham. London, 1834-35. 3 v. 12°. M,992
German Hymns. Horæ Germanicæ. H. Mills. Auburn, 1845. 18°. . G,37
German Industry, Deutsche Arbeit. W. H. Riehl. Stuttgart, 1861. 8°. . G,535
German Language, Deutsche Orthographie. K. G. Andresen. Mainz, 1855. 8°. G,592
Deutsche Sprache. A. Schleicher. Stuttgart, 1860. 8°. . . . G,594
Geschichte der. J. L. C. Grimm. Leipzig, 1853-54. 2 v. 8°. G,593
Deutsch-Russisches Wörterbuch. J. A. E. Schmidt. Mosk. 1839. 2 v. 8°. L.R.
Deutsches Wörterbuch. J. L. and W. K. Grimm. Leip. 1854-62. 5 v. 8°. L.R.
Althochdeutsches. E. G. Graff u. Massmann. Berlin, 1846. 7 v. 4°. L.R.
Dictionary, German and English. G. J. Adler. New York, 1869. r. 8°. L.R.
The same. New York, 1869. r. 8°. . . . . . R.R.
C. F. Grieb. Philadelphia, 1857. 2 v. r. 8°. . . . . R.R.
The same. Philadelphia, 1869. 2 v. r. 8°. . . L.R.
N. N. W. Meissner. Leipzig, 1847. 2 v. 8°. . . . . . L.R.

German Language, Method of Learning. F. Ahn. New York, 1870. 8°. . L,553
Grammar of. G. H. Noehden. Andover, 1842. 8°. . . . L,798
W. D. Whitney. New York, 1870. 12°. . . . . . L,576
German Literature. W. Menzel; trans. by C. C. Felton. Boston, 1840. 12°. H,747
W. Menzel; translated by T. Gordon. Oxford, 1840. 4 v. 8°. . . H,748
Altdeutsche Märchen,Sagen, u. Legenden. R.Bechstein. Leip. 1863. 16°. G,260
Deutsche Nationalliteratur. R. Gottschall. Breslau, 1855. 2 v. 8°. E,249
Deutsches Lied in Hist. Entwicklung. A. Reissmann. Cassel, 1861. 8°. G,644
Geschichte der. A. Koberstein. Leipzig, 1845-66. 3 v. 8°. . . E,250
H. Kurz. Leipzig, 1861. 3 v. 8°. . . . . . E,254
A. T. C. Vilmar. Marburg, 1856. 8°. . . . . . E,253
seit Lessing's Tod. J. Schmidt. Leipzig, 1858. 3 v. 8°. . E,252
German Lyrics; translated by C. T. Brooks. Boston, 1853. 16°. . . G,45
German Poetry, Muster Sammlung. G. Schwab. Leipzig, 1857. 12°. . E,280
Historic Survey of. W. Taylor. London, 1830. 3 v. 8°. . . H,749
German Popular Stories. J. L. and W. K. Grimm. London, 1869. p. 8°. L,105
The same. Boston, 1857. 12°. . . . . . . . G,180
German Prose Writers, Fragments from. S. Austin. New York, 1841. 12°. H,746
German Novelists. T. Roscoe. London, 1826. 4 v. 12°. . . . . G,177
Vol. 1. Reynard, the Fox; Howleglass, the Merry Jester; Doctor Faustus.
2. Popular Traditions; Gottschalck; Eberhardt Büsching; Grimm; Lothar; La Motte Fouqué.
3. Musæus; Schiller.
4. Tieck; Langbein; Engel.

German Romance, Specimens of. T. Carlyle. Edinburgh, 1827. 4 v. 12°. G,51
Vol. 1. Musæus; La Motte Fouqué. Vol. 3. Richter.
2. Tieck; Hoffmann. 4. Goethe.

German States, Verfassung u.Verwaltung. J. F. Fries. Heidelberg, 1831. 12°. G,534
German Tales. B. Auerbach. Boston, 1869. 12°. . . . . . . G,172
German Theater; trans. by B. Thompson, v. 1, 3, 4, 6. London, 1806. 2 v. 12°. G,38
German Universities. K. von Raumer. New York, 1859. 8°. . . . O,816
Germany, Allemagne. Mad. de Staël-Holstein. Paris, 1856. 12°. . . H,880
The same. Paris, 1813. 3 v. 8°. . . . . . . . V,422
The same; translated. New York, 1859. 2 v. 12°. . . V,419
American Family in. J. R. Browne. New York, 1867. 12°. . . V,418
as it is. Baroness Blaze de Bury. London, 1851. 2 v. 8°. . . V,432
Atlas der Deutschen Bundes Staaten. A. Stieler. Gotha, 1848. 8°. *Q,363
Berg und Thal. H. Helff't. Berlin, 1854. 12°. . . . . . E,182
Christian Singers of. C. Winkworth. Philadelphia, n. d. p. 8°. . H,648
Deutsche Nationaleinheit. J. G. A. Wirth. Frankfurt-a-M. 1859. 8°. E,72
Deutschlands Flora, v. 3, 6-9. D. Dietrich. Jena, 1844. 8°. . . G,862
Educational Institutions of. G. P. R. James. London, 1835. 8°. O,1036
England and Scotland. J. H. Merle d'Aubigné. N. Y. 1849. 12°. . V,343
German Experiences. W. Howitt. London, 1844. 16°. . . . V,410
Geschichte der Deutschen. J. G. A. Wirth. Stuttgart, 1853. 4 v. 8°. E,52
der Deutschen Kaiserzeit. W. Giesebrecht. Braunschweig, 1860-68. 2 v. in 4. 8°. . . . . . . . E,65
der Deutsch. Freiheitskriege,1813-14. H.Beitzke. Berl.'64. 3v. 8°. E,70
der Deutsch. Staaten. J. G. A. Wirth, v.3,4. Karlsr. 1853. 2 v. 8°. E,53
Deutchlands, 1806-30. F. Bülau. Hamburg, 1842. 8°. . . E,69
des Groszen Deutschen Krieges. F. W. Barthold. Stuttgart, 1843. 2 v. in 1. 8°. . . . . . . . E,66

Germany, Geschichte des Teutschen. J. C. v. Pfister. Hamb. 1829–35. 5 v. 8°. E,48
des Teutschen Volkes. H. Luden. Gotha, 1825–37. 12 v. 8°. E,49
unter Fränk. Kaisern. A. H. H. Stenzel. Ber. 1827–8. 2 v. 8°. E,55
History of. F. Kolrausch. London, 1844. 8°. . . . . . . B,210
W. Menzel. London, 1849–53. 3 v. 12°. . . . . . L,208
E. C. Penrose. London, 1862. 12°. . . . . . . . B,207
Home Life in. C. L. Brace. New York, 1853. 12°. . . . V,417
Life in. Sir F. B. Head. London, 1848. 16°. . . . . V,411
Malerische und Romantische. Leipzig, n. d. 10 v. in 11. 8°. . . E,186
Bd. 1. Witzleben, C. A. F von. Die Sächsische Schweiz.
2. Schwab, G. Schwaben.
3. Heeringen, G. von. Franken.
4. Bechstein, L. Thüringen.
5. Blumenhagen, W. Der Harz.
6. Herlosssohn, G. C. Das Riesengebirge.
7. Seidl, J. G. Tyrol und Steiermark. 1 v. in 2.
8. Duller, E. Die Donauländer.
9. Simrock, K. Das Rheinland.
10. Kobbe, T. von und Cornelius, W. Wanderungen an der Ost- und Nordsee.
Peasant Life in. A. C. Johnson. New York, 1859. 12°. . . V,377
Poetry of. A. Baskerville. Philadelphia, 1856. 8°. . . . G,44
Rural and Domestic Life in. W. Howitt. Philadelphia, 1843. 8°. V,1072
Sight-Seeing in. Sir J. Forbes. London, 1856. p. 8°. . . . V,407
Student-Life in. W. Howitt. London, 1841. 8°. . . . . V,378
Tour in. J. Russell. Edinburgh, 1828. 2 v. 16°. . . . . I,510
Travels through. C. L. Baron de Pollnitz. London, 1737–40. 4 v. 8°. V,328
Vaterländische Gesch. C. Duller u. E. Hagen. Frank-a-M. 1853–8. 5 v. 8°. E,54
Gerstäcker, F. Flatbootman. Prag, 1858. 24°. . . . . . . . G,279
Flusspiraten des Mississippi. Leipzig, 1862. 3 v. 16°. . . . G,280
Frank Wildman's Adventures. Boston, 1870. 16°. . . . . J,1624
How a Bride was won. New York, 1869. 8°. . . . . . . K,711
Regulatoren in Arkansas. Leipzig, 1868. 3 v. in 1. 16°. . . G,285
Wild Sports in the Far West. Boston, 1870. 16°. . . . . J,1623
Gertrude. E. M. Sewell. New York, 1866. 12°. . . . . . . K,997
Gervinus, G. G. Geschichte des 19ten Jahrhunderts. Leip. 1855–66. 8 v. 8°. E,60
Einleitung zu demselben. Leipzig, 1853. 8°. . . . E,59
Introduction to History of the Nineteenth Century. Lond. 1853. 8°. A,313
Geschiedene, Die. M. Ring. Prag und Leipzig, 1858. 24°. . . . G,429
Geschwornen und ihre Richter. L. Schücking. Hannover, 1861. 3 v. 16°. G,447
Gesenius, W. Hebrew Grammar; edited by E. Rödiger. New York, 1852. 8°. L,783
Hebrew and English Lexicon. Boston, 1854. 8°. . . . . . L.R.
Gessart, M. A. Treatise on Glass Staining. London, 1857. 12°. . . M,917
Geubel, H. K. Grundriss der Zoophysiologisch. Chemie. Frank.-a-M. 1845. 8°. N,252,17
Gewerbehalle, 1863–67. Stuttgart, 1863–67. 5 v. 4°. . . . . *Q,219
Gfrörer, A. F. Geschichte Gustav Adophs. Stuttgart, 1837. 8°. . . E,113
Ghent, Documents of Negotiations at. J. Q. Adams. Washington, 1822. 8°. B,702
Ghosts, Apparitions, etc., Treatises on. London, 1820. 12°. . . B,111,3
Giant Cities of Bashan. J. L. Porter. London, 1866. 12°. . . . V,657
Giants and Dwarfs. E. J. Wood. London, 1868. 8°. . . . . N,401
Gibbes, R. W. Documentary History of Amer. Revolution. N. Y. 1853–7. 3 v. 8°. B,746
Gibbon, E. Autobiography. New York, 1846. 12°. . . . . . D,199
Decline and Fall of the Roman Empire. London, 1836. 8°. . . A,190
The same. London, 1853–55. 6 v. p. 8°. . . . . L,264
The same. Boston, 1854. 6 v. 8°. . . . . . . . A,148

Gibbon, E. Decline and Fall of the Roman Empire. Bost. 1854-55. 8 v. 8°. A,160
The same. Boston, 1854-55. 8 v. 8°. . . . . . . . S.C.
Geschichte des Römischen Weltreiches. Leipzig, 1843. 1 v. in 2. 8°. E,35
Miscellaneous Works. London, 1796. 2 v. 4°. . . . . . F,25
The same; with life. London, 1814. 5 v. 8°. . . . U,264
Reply to, on Miracles. R. Watson. New York, n. d. 18°. . P,746,14
Gibbon, L. and Herndon. Valley of the Amazon. Wash. 1854. 4 v. 8°. . V,263
Gibbons, D. Treatise on Law of Contracts. London, 1857. 12°. . . M,947
Gibbons, J. S. Banks of New York, their Dealers, etc. New York, 1870. 12°. O,503
Gibbs, G. Administration of Washington and Adams. N. Y. 1846. 2 v. 8°. B,811
Gibraltar, History of. F. Sayer. London, 1862. 8°. . . . . . . B,456
Giddings, J. R. Exiles of Florida. Columbus, 1858. 12°. . . . C,181
History of the Rebellion. New York, 1864. 8°. . . . . . B,935
Giebel, C. G. A. Allgemeine Palæontologie. Leipzig, 1852. 8°. . . G,832
Drei Reiche der Natur. Leipzig, 1859-64. 5 v. 8°. . . . G,965
Tagesfragen aus der Naturgeschichte. Berlin, 1857. 8°. . . . G,814
Giesebrecht, W. Gesch. der Deutsch. Kaiserzeit. Brauns. 1860-8. 2 v. in 4. 8°. E,65
Giesler, J. C. L. Text-Book of Church History. New York, 1855-58. 3 v. 8°. P,589
Gifford, G. Dialogue concerning Witches and Witchcraft. Lond. 1842. 12°. L,606,8
Gifford, W. (Ed.) Warreniana. Boston, 1851. 16°. . . . . . H,14
Gift-Book for Young Men. W. A. Alcott. Auburn, 1853. 12°. . . H,254
Gihon, J. H. and others. Annals of San Francisco. New York, 1855. 8°. C,247
Gilbert, Sir H. Queen Elizabeth's Achademy. London, 1869. 8°. . L,604,8
Gilbert, J. T. Celtic Records and Literature of Ireland. Dublin, 1861. 8°. H,709
Gilbert, J. W. Practical Treatise on Banking. London, 1849. 2 v. 8°. . O,567
Gilbert, W. De Profundis; a Tale of Social Deposits. London, 1864. 2 v. 12°. J,561
Dr. Austin's Guests. London, 1866. 2 v. 12°. . . . . . . K,589
The same. London, 1868. 12°. . . . . . . . . J,562
Magic Mirror. London, 1866. 12°. . . . . . . . . H,493
Wizard of the Mountain. London, 1867. 2 v. 12°. . . . . K,590
Gilbert Gurney; a Novel. T. E. Hook. London, 1841. 16°. . . . K,719
Gilbert's Last Summer at Rainford. W. J. Bradley. Boston, 1870. 16°. J,1677
Gilbert Starr and his Lessons. W. J. Bradley. Boston, 1870. 16°. . J,1676
Gil-Blas de Santillane, Historie de. A. R. Le Sage. Paris, 1855. 12°. . H,930
The same; translated by T. Smollett. Boston, 1865. 3 v. 12°. H,926
The same. Philadelphia, n. d. 8°. . . . . . . H,927
The same; illustrated. London, 1861. p. 8°. . . . L,104
Gildas, St., *the Wise*. Chronicle. London, 1848. p. 8°. . . . . . L,26
De Excidio Britannia; edited by J. Stevenson. London, 1838. 8°. . U,635
Gilder, W. H. New Rhetorical Reader. New York, 1852. 12°. . O,879
Gilderdale, J. S. Disciplina Rediviva. London, 1856. 16°. . . . O,1021
Gilds and Trades-Unions, History of. L. Brentano. London, 1870. 8°. L,605,40
Giles, C. Pioneer; a Narrative of his Experience. New York, 1844. 12°. C,844
Giles, H. Christian Thought on Life. Boston, 1850. 16°. . . . P,77
Illustrations of Genius. Boston, 1854. 16°. . . . . . . H,37
Lectures and Essays. Boston, 1851. 2 v. 16°. . . . . . H,38
Giles, J. A. History of the Ancient Britons. Oxford, 1854. 2 v. 8°. . A,495
Life of Alfred the Great. Oxford, 1854. 8°. . . . . . . A,494
Gilfillan, G. Bards of the Bible. New York, 1855. 12°. . . . . P,508
Galleries of Literary Portraits. Edinburgh, 1856-57. 3 v. 12°. . C,505

Gilks, T. Art of Wood Engraving. London, n. d. 12°. . . . . . M,62
Gill, T. Text-Book to School Management. London, 1858. 16°. . . O,1115
Gillespie, W. M. Manual of Road-Making. New York, 1853. 8°. . M,695
Treatise on Land-Surveying. New York, 1870. 8°. . . . M,699
Gillet, J. A. and Rolfe, W. J. Chemistry and Electricity. Boston, 1868. 12°. N,228
Elements of Astronomy. Boston, 1868. 12°. . . . . . N,325
Hand-Book of Natural Philosophy. Boston, 1868. 12°. . . . N,73
Gillet, R. H. Democracy in the United States. New York, 1868. 12°. . O,507
Gillies, J. History of Ancient Greece. Philadelphia, 1831. 8°. . . A,95
History of the World. Philadelphia, 1809. 3 v. 8°. . . . A,26
Memoirs of George Whitefield. Philadelphia, 1859. 12°. . . D,229
Gillies, R. P. Memoirs of a Literary Veteran. London, 1851. 3 v. 12°. D,382
Gilliss, J. M. U. S. Naval Astro. Expedition, v. 1,3,6. Wash. 1855–6. 4 v. 4°. Q,271
Gilman, J. Life of Samuel Taylor Coleridge. London, 1838. 8°. . C,1255
Gilmanton, N. H., History of. D. Lancaster. Gilmanton, 1845. 8°. . C,86
Gilmor, H. Four Years in the Saddle. New York, 1866. 12°. . . B,893
Gilmore, J. R. Adrift in Dixie. New York, 1866. 12°. . . . . . K,301
Among the Pines. New York, 1862. 12°. . . . . . . K,302
Down in Tennessee. New York, 1864. 12°. . . . . . . K,291
My Southern Friends. New York, 1863. 12°. . . . . . K,292
On the Border. Boston, 1867. 12°. . . . . . . . . K,95
Patriot Boys and Prison Pictures. Boston, 1866. 12°. . . . J,1265
Gillmore, Q. A. Artillery Operations against Charleston, 1863. N.Y. 1865. 8°. B,952
Gillray, J. Works; Caricatures. London, n. d. 2 v. f°. . . . . . L.R.
Account of the same. T. Wright and R. H. Evans. Lond. 1851. 8°. L.R.
Gilly, W. O. S. Shipwrecks of the Royal Navy. London, 1851. 12°. V,1081
Gilpin, S. Songs and Ballads of Cumberland. London, 1866. 8°. . . I,331
Gilpin, W. Forest Scenery and Woodland Views. Edin. 1834. 2 v. 8°. *M,350
Gilpin, W. S. Hints upon Landscape Gardening. London, 1835. 8°. . M,360
Gilson, A. Czar and the Sultan. New York, 1853. 16°. . . . . . C,490
Ginger Snaps. S. P. Parton. New York, 1870. 12°. . . . . . H,117
Ginx's Baby; his Birth and other Misfortunes. E. Jenkins. Bost. 1871. 16°. K,1039
Gipsies, History of. W. Simson. New York, 1866. 12°. . . . . D,706
Gipsy. G. P. R. James. New York, 1864. 12°. . . . . . . K,732
The same. Leipzig, 1847. 16°. . . . . . . . J,208
Gipsy Language, Specimens of. W. Simson. New York, 1866. 12°. . D,706
Gipsy's Prophecy. E. D. E. N. Southworth. Philadelphia, 1870. 12°. . K,426
Giraffe Hunters. M. Reid. Boston, 1870. 12°. . . . . . J,1588
Giraldus Cambrensis, S. Historical Works; tr. by R. C. Hoare. Lond. 1863. p. 8°. L,10
Opera. London, 1861–68. 5 v. 8°. . . . . . . . . . W,171
Girard, C. Cottoids of North America, v. 3. Washington, 1850. 4°. . Q,10
Herpetology of the U. S. Exploring Expedition. Phil. 1858. 4°. . *Q,279
Atlas to the same. Philadelphia, 1858. f°. . . . . . *Q,353
Girard College Observatory, Mag. and Meteorological Obs. Wash. 1863. 4°. Q,324,13
Girardin, D. G., Esprit de. Paris, n. d. 12°. . . . . . . H,1028
Girardin, E. de. Stories of an Old Maid; tr. by A. Elwes. N. Y. 1856. 16°. J,1355
Girardin, J. Fumiers considérés comme Engrais. Paris, 1847. 16°. . N,252,26
Giraud, G. Comedies; translated. New York, 1849. 12°. . . . I,739
Giraud, J. P., jr. Birds of Long Island. New York, 1844. . . . O,121
Girding on the Armor. S. S. Robbins. New York, 1869. 16°. . J,1664

Girdlestone, C. Unhealthy Condition of Dwellings. London, 1845. 8°. N,252,29
Girlhood of Shakespeare's Heroines. M. C. Clarke. London, 1864. 3 v. 12°. I,848
Girls, Education of, and Employment of Women. W.B.Hodgson. Lond. '69. 12°. O,458
Hints on the Training of. A. De Wahl. London, 1847. 12°. O,1160
Our. D. Lewis. New York, 1871. 12°. . . . . . . . L,854
Physical Life of. G. H. Napheys. Philadelphia, 1871. 12°. . . L,955
Girondists, Histoire des Girondins. A. de Lamartine. Bruxelles, 1851. 8°. B,440
History of the. A. de Lamartine. London, 1847–50. 3 v. p. 8°. L,200
The same. New York, 1854. 3 v. 12°. . . . . . B,224
Girtin, T. Picturesque Views; edited by T. Miller. London, 1854. 8°. . M,136
Gisli, the Outlaw; translated by G. W. Dasent. Edinburgh, 1866. 4°. . G,6
Glaciers, Mechanism of. R. Mallet. Dublin, 1838. 8°. . . . N,252,35
of the Alps. J. Tyndall. Boston, 1861. 8°. . . . . . . N,785
Papers on the Theory of. J. D. Forbes. Edinburgh, 1859. 8°. . N,840
Gladden, W. Plain Thoughts on the Art of Living. Boston, 1868. 16°. H,285
Gladiators. G. J. W. Melville. Leipzig, 1864. 2 v. in 1. 16°. . . J,375
Gladstone Government, Cabinet Pictures. London, 1869. 8°. . . . A,530
Gladstone, W. E. Church Principles. London, 1840. 8°. . . . P,312
"Ecce Homo," Review of. London, 1868. 16°. . . . . . P,372
Juventus Mundi; the Heroic Age. London, 1869. 12°. . . . H,734
Studies on Homer. Oxford, 1858. 3 v. 8°. . . . . . . H,727
Glanvil, J. Sadducismus Triumphatus; or, full and plain Evidence concerning Witches and Apparitions. London, 1726. 8°. . . . O,335
Glass and Porcelain, Manufactures of. G. R. Porter. London, 1832. 12°. M,1044
Manufacture of. H. Chance. London, 1856. 4°. . . . N,251,51
G. R. Porter. London, 1852. 8°. . . . . . . . . M,604
Soluble; or, Water-Glass, Treatise on. L. Feuchtwanger. N.Y. 1870. 12°. M,683
Glass-Making, Wonders of. A. Sauzay. New York, 1870. 12°. . M,1053
Glass-Staining. M. A. Gessert. London, 1857. 12°. . . . . M,917
Glass Tubes for Eudiometrical Purposes. C. T. Coathupe. Bristol, 1840. 4°. N,252,42
Glastenbury, Conn. Centennial Discourse by A. B. Chapin. Hartford, 1853. 8°. C,57
Glaube, Liebe, Hoffnung, Lehren von. J. F. Fries. Heidelberg, 1823. 16°. G,552
Glaucus; Wonders of the Shore. C. Kingsley. Boston, 1855. 16°. . . N,491
Gleanings from Harvest-Fields of Literature. C. C. Bombaugh. Balt. 1870. 12°. H,27
from the Poets. A. C. Lowell. Boston, 1862. 3 v. 12°. . . I,96
Glee-Hive. V. Novello. London, 1851–52. 3 v. 8°. . . . . M,400
Gleeman, A. M. Rhyme of North Countrie. Cincinnati, 1847. 12°. . I,43
Gleig, G. R. British Empire in India. London, 1830–35. 4 v. 16°. . I,604
Gleig, G. H. Leipzig Campaign. London, 1856. p. 8°. . . . I,661,1
British Military Commanders. London, 1831–32. 3 v. 12°. . M,1008
Chelsea Hospital and its Traditions. London, 1838. 3 v. 12°. . J,570
History of the Bible. New York, 1854. 2 v. 16°. . . . . L,345
Memoirs of Warren Hastings. London, 1841. 3 v. 8°. . . . D,116
Story of the Battle of Waterloo. New York, 1847. 12°. . . B,86
Glen Morris Stories. D. Wise. New York, 1869. 5 v. 16°. . . . J,1345

Vol. 1. Guy Carlton. Vol. 3. Jessie Carlton.
2. Dick Duncan. 4. Walter Sherwood.
Vol. 5. Kate Carlton.

Glennie, J. S. S. Arthurian Localities. . . . . . . . L,605,36
Gliddon, G. R. See *Nott, J. C. and Gliddon, G. R.*
Glimpse of the World. E. M. Sewell. New York, 1866. 12°. . . . K,998

Glimpse of the World. E. M. Sewell. Leipzig, 1863. 2 v. in 1. 16°. . J,455
Globe, Congressional, and Appendix. Washington, 1833–70. 90 v. 4°. . P.D.
Glory of the House of Israel. D. F. Strauss. Philadelphia, 1859. 12°. K,1021
Glossary of English Words. R. Nares. London, 1859. 2 v. 8°. . . L.R.
R. C. Trench. New York, 1859. 12°. . . . . . . L,547
Glover, D. L. (Ed.) Heroines of Shakespeare. Boston, n. d. 8°. . . *I,872
Glover, R. M. Physiological Properties of Picrotoxin. Edin. 1851. 8°. N,252,44
Applications of Chemistry to Medicine. London, 1841. 8°. . N,252,14
Physiological Properties of Bromine. n. t. p. 8°. . . . N,252,14
Medical Evidence at Trial of J. C. Belaney. Gateshead, 1844. 16°. N,252,37
Glycerine, Process of Manufacturing. G. F. Wilson. London, 1855. 8°. N,252,50
Glynn, J. Treatise on Constructing Cranes. London, 1854. 12°. . . M,923
Treatise on the Power of Water. London, 1853. 12°. . . . M,922
Glyster, G. Æsculapian Labyrinth Explored. Dublin, 1789. 8°. . . H,630
Gneisenau, Count. Life and Campaigns of Blücher. London, 1815. 8°. . D,517
Goadby, H. Vegetable and Animal Physiology. New York, 1858. 8°. . N,719
Goats, Sheep, Oxen, Natural History of. Sir W. Jardine. Edinb. n. d. 16°. N,470,22
Goblet, H. F. Theory of Sight. London, 1869. 8°. . . . . . . L,966
God in History. C. C. J. Bunsen. London, 1868–70. 3 v. 8°. . . P,121
H. Read. London, 1851. 16°. . . . . . . . P,169
Existence et Attributs de. M. Fénélon. Paris, 1853. 12°. . . P,131
Power, Wisdom, and Goodness of. T. Chalmers. Glasg. 1830–39. 2 v. 8°. P,216
H. Read. Glasgow, 1864. 12°. . . . . . . . P,221
Wonderful Workings of. S. Bolton. London, 1656. 4°. . . . P,181
God Spede the Plough (1500, A. D.); ed. W. W. Skeat. London, 1867. 8°. L,605,30
God's Glory in the Heavens. W. Leitch. London, 1867. 12°. . . . N,263
Goddard, F. B. Where to Emigrate and why. Philadelphia, 1869. 8°. . V,132
Godkin, E. L. History of Hungary. London, 1853. 8°. . . . . . B,530
Godman, J. D. American Natural History. Philadelphia, 1826–28. 3 v. 8°. N,684
The same. Philadelphia, 1846. 8°. . . . . . . N,524
Western Quarterly Reporter of Medical Science, v. 1, 2. Cin. 1822–3. 8°. L,934
Godolphin. Sir E. B. Lytton. Philadelphia, 1868. 12°. . . . . K,813
The same. Leipzig, 1842. 16°. . . . . . J,313
Godolphin, M., Life of. J. Evelyn. New York, 1847. 12°. . . . C,1222
Godwin, P. History of France; Ancient Gaul, v. 1. New York 1860. 8°. B,349,1
Out of the Past. New York, 1870. 12°. . . . . . . . H,241
Political Essays. New York, 1856. 12°. . . . . . . O,472
Godwin, W. Caleb Williams. London, 1831. 16°. . . . . . . K,524
Cloudesley; a Tale. London, 1830. 3 v. 12°. . . . . . . K,526
Fleetwood; or, the New Man of Feeling. London, 1832. 16°. . K,525
History of the Commonwealth of England. London, 1824–28. 4 v. 8°. A,510
St. Leon; a Tale of the Sixteenth Century. London, 1832. 16°. . K,527
Goebel, F. Reise in den Steppen Russlands. Dorpat, 1837-38. 2 v. 4°. . Q,433
Goepp, C. New Rome. New York, 1853. 12°. . . . . . . . G,35
Goeppert, H. R. Entstehung der Steinkohlen. Leiden, 1848. 4°. . . Q,44
Goergei, A. My Life and Acts in Hungary. New York, 1852. 12°. . D,771
Goethe, J. W. von. Autobiography; tr. A. J. W. Morrison. Lond. 1849. p. 8°. L,188,2
The same; translated by J. Oxenford. London, 1848. p. 8°. L,188,1
Biography of. T. De Quincey. Edinburgh, 1862. 12°. . . H,412,15
Conversations with. J. P. Eckermann. Boston, 1852. 12°. . . G,31

Goethe, J. W. von. Correspondence with a Child. Boston, 1859. 12°. . G,29
Correspondence with Schiller, 1794–1805, v. 1. New York, 1845. 12°. G,28
Essays on Art. Boston, 1845. 16°. . . . . . . . . M,9
Faust; translated by C. T. Brooks. Boston, 1866. 16°. . . . G,49
The same; translated by A. Hayward. Boston, 1866. 16°. . G,48
The same; translated by B. Taylor. Boston, 1871. 2 v. 8°. . G,173
Life of. G. H. Lewes. London, 1864. 8°. . . . . . . D,506
Life and Works. G. H. Lewes. Boston, 1856. 2 v. 12°. . . D,494
Minor Poetry. Philadelphia, 1859. 8°. . . . . . . . G,50
Sämmtliche Werke. Stuttgart und Tübingen, 1854–55. 6 v. 8°. . E,343

Bd. 1. Lieder; Gedichte.
2. Die Laune des Verliebten; Die Mitschuldigen; Claudine von Bella Villa; Erwin und Elmire; Jery und Bätely; Lila; Die Fischerin; Scherz, List, und Rache; Zauberflöte, zweiter Theil; Götz von Berlichingen; Egmont; Clavigo; Stella; Faust; Iphiginie auf Tauris; Torquato Tasso; Die Natürliche Tochter; Elpenor; Mahomet; Tancred; Theater und dramatische Poesie, etc.
3. Leiden des jungen Werthers; Briefe aus der Schweiz; Die Wahlverwandtschaften; Wilhelm Meister; Unterhaltungen deutscher Ausgewanderten; Die guten Weiber; Novelle.
4. Aus meinem Leben; Italiänische Reise; Ueber Italien, Fragmente; Campagne in Frankreich, 1792; Belagerung von Mainz, 1795; Aus einer Reise in der Schweiz, 1767; Reise am Rhein, Neckar, etc., 1811–15; Annalen; oder, Tag- und Jahreshefte; Biographische Einzelheiten.
5. Benvenuto Cellini; Rameaus' Neffe; Diderot's Versuch über die Malerei; Winckelmann; Philipp Hackert; Propyläen; Philostrat's Gemälde; Ferneres über Kunst; Deutsche Literatur; Auswärtige Literatur und Volks-Poesie.
6. Metamorphose der Pflanzen; Osteologie; Beiträge zur Optik; Zur Farbenlehre; Naturwissenschaftliche Einzelheiten; Mineralogie und Geologie; Meterologie Zur Naturwissenschaft im Allgemeinen; Chronologie der Entstehung Goethe'scher Schriften.

The same. Paris, 1836. 5 v. 8°. . . . . . . . E,344

Bd. 1. Leben; Lieder; Gedichte; West-öslicher Divan; Reineke Fuchs; Hermann und Dorothea; Achilleis; Pandora; Die Laune des Verliebten; Die Mitschuldigen; Die Geschwister; Mahomet; Tancred; Götz von Berlichingen; Egmont; Iphiginie auf Tauris; Torquato Tasso; Die Natürliche Tochter, etc.
2. Elpenor; Clavigo; Stella; Claudine von Bella Villa; Erwin u. Elmire; Jery und Bätely; Lila; Die Fischerin; Sherz, List und Rache; Zauberflöte, zweiter Theil; Faust; Dramen; Leiden des jungen Werthers; Briefe aus der Schweiz; etc.
3. Wilhelm Meister; Aus meinem Leben, Dichtung und Wahrheit; Italienische Reise.
4. Zweitzer Römischer Aufenthalt; Campagne in Frankreich, 1792; Aus einer Reise in der Schweiz, 1797; Aus einer Reise am Rhein, Main und Neckar, 1814–15; Benvenuto Cellini; Rameau's Neffe; Diderot's Versuch über die Malerei; Winckelmann; Philipp Hackert; Propyläen; Münzen, Medaillen, geschnittene Steine; Ferneres über Kunst.
5. Literatur; Zur Naturwissenschaft; Meteorologie; Zur Farbenlehre; Zur Pflanzenlehre; Osteologie.

Specimens of; translated by T. Carlyle. Edinburgh, 1827. 12°. . G,51,4
Theory of Colors. London, 1840. 8°. . . . . . . . M,48
Truth and Poetry. Autobiography, v. 2. New York, 1850. 12°. . D,509
Wilhelm Meister's Apprenticeship. Boston, 1867. 2 v. 12°. . . G,189
The same. London, 1868. p. 8°. . . . . . . L,188,5
Werke, Auswahl. Stuttgart, 1867–68. 36 v. in 18°. 16°. . . E,327

Bd. 1. Leben; Lieder; Balladen; Elegien; Episteln; Epigramme; Weissagungen des Bakis; Vier Jahreszeiten.
2. Sonnette; Vermischte Gedichte; Kunst; Parabolisch; Epigrammatisch; Politica; Gott und Welt; Chinesisch-Deutsche Jahres und Tages- Zeiten; Aus fremden Sprachen; Noten.
3. Hermann und Dorothea; Achilleïs; Reineke Fuchs.
4. Götz von Berlichingen; Egmont; Clavigo.
5. Faust.
6. Iphiginie auf Tauris; Torquato Tasso; Die natürliche Tochter; Elpenor.
7. Leiden des jungen Werthers; Briefe aus der Schweiz; Briefe eines Landgeistlichen; Zwo biblische Fragen; Die Wahlverwandschaften.
8, 9. Wilhelm Meister's Lehrjahre.
10. Wilhelm Meister's Wanderjahre.
11, 12. Aus meinem Leben, Wahrheit und Dichtung.
13. Sprüche in Reimen; Sprüche in Prosa; Ethisches.
14. West-östlicher Divan.

Goethe, J. W. von. Werke, Auswahl. *Continued.* . . . . . . . E,327

15. Alles an Personen und zu Festen Gedichtete.
16. Lustspiele und Farcen.
17. Singspiele.
18. Schauspiele; Zeitstücke.
19. Italienische Reise, 1786–88.
20. Italien; Ueber Italien, Fragmente.
21. Campagne in Frankreich; Belagerung von Mainz; Unterhaltungen Deutscher Ausgewanderten.
22. Schweizerreise, 1797; Reise am Rhein, Main und Neckar, 1814–15.
23. Annalen; oder, Tag- und Jahreshefte, 1749–1822; Biographische Einzelheiten.
24. Benvenuto Cellini.
25. Benvenuto Cellini; Diderot; Rameau's Neffe; Diderot's Versuch über die Malerei.
26. Winckelmann; Hackert; Propyläen.
27. Ferneres über Kunst.
28. Deutsche Literatur.
29. Auswärtige Literatur und Volks-Poesie.
30. Jugenddramen und Entwürfe; Gottfried von Berlichingen; Iphiginie in Prosa; Erwin und Elmire; Claudine von Bella Villa, etc.
31. Götz von Berlichingen, für die Bühne; Die Wette, ein Lustspiel; Mahomet; Tancred; Theater und dramatische Poesie.
32. Morphologie.
33, 34. Zur Farbenlehre.
35. Materiellen zur Geschichte der Farbenlehre.
36. Naturwissenschaftliche Einzelheiten; Mineralogie und Geologie; Meteorologie; Zur Naturwissenschaft im Allgemeinen.

Works. London, 1848–51. 5 v. p. 8°. . . . . . . . L,188

Vol. 1. Autobiography; translated by J. Oxenford
2. Same, trans. by A. J. W. Morrison; Letters from Switzerland; Travels in Italy.
3. Wilhelm Meister's Apprenticeship.
4. Novels and Tales; Elective Affinities; Sorrows of Werther; German Emigrants; Good Women; Nouvelette.
5. Dramatic Works; Faust; Iphigenia; Torquato Tasso; Egment; Götz von Berlichingen.

Goethe and Schiller; a Novel. C. Mundt. New York, 1868. 8°. . . G,202
Goquet, A. I. de. Origin of Laws, Arts, and Sciences. Edinb. 1775. 3 v. 8°. U,495
Gold, Probable Fall in the value of. M. Chevalier. New York, 1859. 8°. O,524
Production de l'Or et l'Argent. A. von Humboldt. Paris, 1848. 8°. N,252,30
Gold and Name. M. S. Schwartz. Boston, 1871. 8°. . . . . . G,223
Gold Brick. A. S. Stephens. Philadelphia, 1870. 12°. . . . . K,445
Gold Elsie; translated by A. L. Wister. E. John. Philadelphia, 1868. 12°. G,191
Goldelse, *in German.* E. John. Leipzig, 1868. 16°. . . . . . . G,337
Gold Foil. J. G. Holland New York, 1867. 12°. . . . . . . H,107
Gold-Hunter's Adventures, Life in Australia. W. H. Thomes. Bost. 1870. 12°. K,115
Gold Mines of the Gila. C. W. Webber. New York, 1849. 2 v. 12°. . K,308
Gold Thread. N. Macleod. London, 1867. 12°. . . . . . . J,1548
Golden Fetters. M. Lemon. Leipzig, 1868. 2 v. in 1. 16°. . . . J,264
Golden Legend. H. W. Longfellow. Boston, 1859. 16°. . . . I,67
Golden and Silver Ages. T. Heywood. London, 1851. 8°. . . I,885,47
Goldenberg, F. Fossile Insecten der Kohlenformation. Cassel, 1854. 4°. G,847
Goldoni, C. Life and Adventures of. E. Copping. London, 1857. 8°. . D,720
Mémoires de. Paris, 1855. 12°. . . . . . . . . . D,612
Giraud and Nota. Select Comedies, translated. N. Y. 1849. 12°. . I,739
Goldsmith, C. Earth and Animated Nature. London, 1853. 8°. . . N,526
The same. Philadelphia, 1863. 4 v. in 2. 8°. . . . . N,528
History of Greece. New York, 1855. 16°. . . . . . . A,58
The same; Pinnock's edition. Philadelphia, 1866. 12°. . A,67
History of Rome. New York, 1855. 16°. . . . . . . A,130
The same; Pinnock's edition. Philadelphia, 1868. 12°. . A,142
Life of. J. Forster. London, 1848. 8°. . . . . . . . D,426
W. Irving. New York, 1868. 12°. . . . . . . . U,9
The same. New York, 1867. 12°. . . . . . U,27

Goldsmith, O., Life of. W. Irving. New York, 1858. 2 v. 16°. . . . L,418
J. Prior. Philadelphia, 1837. 8°. . . . . . . . . D,99
Miscellaneous Works; edited by J. Prior. New York, 1859. 4 v. 12°. U,206
Select Works; Vicar of Wakefield; Poems. Leipzig, 1842. 16°. . J,183
Vicar of Wakefield. London, 1820. 12°. . . . . . . K,535
The same. New York, 1868. 12°. . . . . . . . . K,712
Goltz, B. Die Bildung und die Gebildeten. Berlin, 1867. 2 v. in 1. 16°. G,378
Typen der Gesellschaft. Berlin, 1867. 2 v. in 1. 16°. . . . E,379
Gondi, J. F. P. de, *Cardinal de Retz.* Conspiracy of Fiesco. Bost. 1828. 12°. B,482
Gongora; or, Philip III. and IV. of Spain. E. Churton. Lond. 1862. 2 v. p. 8°. B,455
Good, J. M. Book of Nature. Hartford, 1855. 8°. . . . . . . M,787
Life of. O. Gregory. London, 1828. 8°. . . . . . . D,371
Good Measure. D. S. Erickson. Boston, 1869. 16°. . . . . . J,1659
Good Fight, and other Tales. C. Reade. New York, 1859. 12°. . . K,917
Good for Nothing. G. J. W. Melville. Leipzig, 1862. 2 v. in 1. 16°. . J,376
Good French Governess. M. Edgeworth. New York, 1860. 12°. . K,678,2
Good Genius. H. and A. Mayhew. London, 1867. 16°. . . . . K,689
Good Old Times. A. Manning. London, 1857. 12°. . . . . . J,592
Good Time Coming. T. S. Arthur. Philadelphia, n. d. 16°. . . . J,610
Good Thoughts in Bad Times, etc. T. Fuller. Boston, 1863. 16°. . . P,245
Good Words; edited by N. Macleod. London, 1865–67. 8 v. 8°. . . S,19
Goode, W. Divine Rule of Faith and Practice. Phil. 1842. 2 v. 8°. . P,176
Gooding, R. Manual of Domestic Medicine. London, 1867. 12°. . . M,841
Goodrich, C. A. Child's History of the United States. Phil. 1855. 16°. J,1152
Select British Eloquence. New York, 1853. 8°. . . . . H,799
Goodrich, F. B. Man upon the Sea; Remarkable Voyages. Phil. 1858. 8°. V,1085
Goodrich, S. G. Cabinet Library. Boston, 1864. 20 v. 12°. . . J,1493

Vol. 1. Famous Men of Modern Times.
2. Famous Men of Ancient Times.
3. Curiosities of Human Nature.
4. Lives of Benefactors.
5. Lives of Celebrated Indians.
6. Lives of Celebrated Women.
7. Lights and Shadows of American History.
8. Lights and Shadows of European History.
9. Lights and Shadows of Asiatic History.
10. Lights and Shadows of African History.
Vol. 11. History of the American Indians.
12. Manners and Customs of the Indians.
13. Glance at the Physical Sciences.
14. Wonders of Zoölogy.
15. Anecdotes of the Animal Kingdom.
16. Glance at Philosophy
17. Ancient and Modern Literature.
18. Enterprise, Industry, and Art of Man.
19. Manners and Customs of Nations.
20. World and its Inhabitants.

Common-School History. Philadelphia, 1840. 12°. . . . . . A,18
Fifth School Reader. Louisville, 1846. 12°. . . . . . . O,889
History of all Nations. New York, 1856. 2 v. 4°. . . . . A,51
Lives of Celebrated Women. Boston, 1855. 12°. . . . . C,499
Parley's Panorama; or, Curiosities. Cincinnati, 1857. 8°. . . H,149
Pictorial History of France. Philadelphia, 1846. 12°. . . . B,203
of the United States. New York, 1852. 12°. . . . B,688
Goodsir, J. Anatomical Memoirs. Edinburgh, 1868. 2 v. 8°. . L,1005
Goodwin, H. Hulsean Lectures, 1856. London, 1856. 8°. . . . P,304
Problems and Examples in Mathematics. Cambridge, 1862. 8°. M,1174,1
Solution of the same. W. W. Hutt. Cambridge, 1863. 8°. M,1174,2
Goodwin, H. B. Sherbrooke. New York, 1866. 12°. . . . . K,127
Goodwin, J. (Ed.) Six Ballads, with Burdens. London, 1844. 12°. . L,606,13
Goodwin, T. G. Art of Mural Decoration. London, 1866. 8°. . . . M,27
Manual of Illumination. London, 1867. 12°. . . . . . M,26
Natural History of Secession. New York, 1864. 12°. . . . B,906

Gooseberry; its Culture, Uses, and History. G.W. Johnson. Lond. 1847. 16°. N,252,37
Gorboduc, Tragedie of. T. Norton and T. Sackville. London, 1847. 8°. I,885,32
Gordon, A. Wilderness Journeys in New Brunswick. London, 1864. 8°. V,1086,3
Gordon, G. H., *Earl of Aberdeen.* Grecian Architecture. London, 1860. 12°. M,843
Gordon, H. Lovers and Thinkers. New York, 1865. 12°. . . . . K,128
Gordon, Lady D. Letters from the Cape. London, 1864. 8°. . . V,1086,3
Gordon, P. Britaine's Distemper, 1639–49. See *Spalding Club Publications,* v. 16.
  Diary, 1635–99. See *Spalding Club Publications,* v. 33.
Gordon, J. History of Town of Aberdeen. See *Spalding Club Publications,* v. 9.
  Scots Affairs, 1637–41. See *Spalding Club Publications,* v. 1–3.
Gordon, M. Memoir of John Wilson. New York, 1863. 8°. . . . D,250
Gordon, T. History of the Greek Revolution. Edinburgh, 1844. 2 v. 8°. A,104
Gore, C. G. F. Castles in the Air. Leipzig, 1856. 16°. . . . . . J,184
  Dean's Daughter. Leipzig, 1853. 2 v. in 1. 16°. . . . . J,185
  Heckington. Leipzig, 1858. 2 v. in 1. 16°. . . . . . J,186
  Life's Lessons. Leipzig, 1857. 2 v. in 1. 16°. . . . . J,187
  Mammon; or, Hardships of an Heiress. Leipzig, 1855. 2 v. in 1. 16°. J,188
  Polish Tales. London, 1833. 3 v. 12°. . . . . . K,1036
  Progress and Prejudice. Leipzig, 1854. 2 v in 1. 16°. . . . J,189
  Two Aristrocracies. Leipzig, 1857. 2 v. in 1. 16°. . . . J,190
Gore, G. Liquid Metals in the Voltaic Circuit. London, 1860. 8°. . N,252,44
Gori, A. T. (Ed.) Museum Florentinum. Florence, 1730–33. 6 v. f°. . L.R.
  Antiqua Numismata, 3 v. Gemmæ Antiquæ, 2 v. Statuæ Antiquæ, 1 v.
Gorilla Country, Stories of. P. B. Du Chaillu. New York, 1869. 12°. J,1491
Gorilla Hunters. R. M. Ballantyne. Philadelphia, n. d. 16°. . . J,1614
Gorton, J. General Biographical Dictionary. London, 1854. 4 v. 8°. *C,598
Gorton, S. Letter to Nath. Morton, 1669. See *Force's Tracts,* v. 4.
  Life of. J. M. Mackie. Boston, 1860. 12°. . . . . . C,860,15
  Simplicities Defence. London, 1646. See *Force's Tracts,* v. 4.
Gospels. See *Bible, Gospels.*
Gosse, P. H. Canadian Naturalist. London, 1840. 12°. . . . . N,500
  Evenings at the Microscope. New York, 1860. 12°. . . . N,5
  Letters from Alabama on Natural History. London, 1859. 16°. . N,496
  Ocean. Philadelphia, 1856. 12°. . . . . . . . V,1136
  Text-Book of Zoölogy. London, 1851. 12°. . . . . . N,479
Gosson, S. School of Abuse. London, 1841. 8°. . . . . . I,885,2
Gossip on a Sutherland Hill-Side. London, 1861. 8°. . . . V,1086,1
Gothic Architecture. D. H. Arnot. New York, 1850. 4°. . . . M,295
  Essays on. T. Wharton and others. London, 1808. . 8°. . . M,208
  Examples of. A. and A. W. Pugin. London, 1850. 3 v. 4°. . *Q,345
  Specimens of. W. Caveler. London, 1839. 4°. . . . *Q,175
  Study of. J. H. Parker. Oxford, 1867. 8°. . . . . . M,146
Gothic Language, Affin. with Greek and Latin. J. Jamieson. Edinb. 1814. 8°. L,736
  Vergleich. Wörterbuch der. L. Diefenbach. Frank.-a-M. 1851. 2 v. 8°. G,583
Gotthelf, J. Wealth and Welfare. London, 1866. 2 v. 12°. . . . G,240
Gottlieb, D. J. Polizeilich-Chemische Skizzen. Leipzig, 1853. 8°. . . G,753
Gottschall, R. Deutsche National-literatur. Breslau, 1855. 2 v. 8°. . E,249
Gouge, W. M. Fiscal History of Texas. Philadelphia, 1852. 8°. . . C,193
Gough, J. B. Autobiography. Springfield, 1870. 8°. . . . . D,83

Gould, A. A. Principles of Zoölogy. Boston, 1854. 12°. . . . . . N,650
Report on Invertebrata of Massachusetts. Boston, 1870. 8°. . . N,721
and Kidder, F. History of New Ipswich, N. H. Boston, 1852. 8°. C,26
Gould, B. A. Reduction of Observations of Fixed Stars. Wash. 1866. 4°. Q,105
Gould, E. S. Good English. New York, 1867. 12°. . . . . . L,548
Gould, L. D. House-Carpenters' and Joiners' Assistant. N. Y. 1855. 4°. M,280
Gould, W. M. Zephyrs from Italy and Sicily. New York, 1852. 12°. . V,490
Goulding, F. R. Marooners Island. Philadelphia, 1869. 16°. . . J,1605
Young Marooners on the Florida Coast. Philadelphia, 1870. 16°. J,1604
Gove, M. S. Lectures to Women on Anatomy and Physiology. N. Y. 1846. 12°. L,869
Governesses; or, Modern Education. B. Riofrey. London, 1841. 8°. . O,1014
Government, Civil Liberty and Self. F. Lieber. Phil. 1853. 2 v. 12°. . O,477
Discoures on. A. Sidney. New York, 1805. 3 v. 8°. . . . O,569
Introduction to Science of. A. N. Young. Buffalo, 1851. 12°. . O,473
Principles of. N. Chipman. Burlington, 1833. 8°. . . . O,571
Science of. J. Alden. New York, 1867. 12°. . . . . . O,478
Governor's Pardon; Bridge of Sighs. H. N. Baker. Boston, 1870. 16°. J,1691
Gower, J. Confessio Amantis. London, 1857. 3 v. 8°. . . . . J,876
Illustrations of. H. J. Todd. London, 1810. 8°. . . . . H,705
Grabowski, S. G. Im Wald und Schloss. Leipzig, 1858. 2 v. in 1. 4°. . G,282
Grace Lee. J. Kavanagh. New York, 1866. 12°. . . . . . K,742
The same. Leipzig, 1855. 2 v. in 1. 16°. . . . . J,232
Grace Truman. S. R. Ford. New York, 1857. 12°. . . . . . K,107
Gräfe, H. Deutsche Volkschule. Leipzig, 1850. 3 v. 8°. . . . G,537
Gräfin und Marquise. G. von Struensee. Wien, 1865. 4 v. 16°. . . G,498
Graf Mirabeau. T. Mundt. Berlin, 1860. 4 v. 24°. . . . . . G,374
Graff, E. G. und Massmann. Althochdeutsche Sprache. Berl. 1834-46. 7 v. 4°. L.R.
Graffiti d'Italia. W. W. Story. Edinburgh, 1868. 16°. . . . . I,434
Grafton, R. Chronicle; or, History of England. London, 1809. 2 v. 4°. F,158
Continuation of Hardyng's Chronicle. London, 1812. 4°. . . F,160
Graham, A. J. Hand-Book of American Phonography. N. Y. 1858. 12°. L,692
Graham, C. M. Letters on Education. London, 1790. 8°. . . O,1038
Graham, G. F. English Style. London, 1869. 16°. . . . . . L,580
English Synonyms. New York, 1858. 12°. . . . . . L,545
Songs of Scotland. London, 1853. 3 v. 8°. . . . . . . M,414
Graham, J., *Marquis of Montrose*, Life of. J. Grant. London, 1858. 12°. D,311
Graham, J., *Earl of Deuchrie*. Exp. in Highlands, 1653-54. Lond. 1820. 12°. B,111,4
Graham, J., *Viscount Dundee*, Life of. M. Napier. Edinburgh, 1859. v. 1. 8°. D,430
Memoirs of. London, 1820. 12°. . . . . . . B,111,3
Graham, T. Arseniates, Phosphates, and Phosphoric Acid. Lond. 1833. 4°. N,252,57
Constitution of Salts, Oxalates, Nitrates, etc. London, 1837. 4°. . N,252,57
Elements of Chemistry. London, 1850-58. 2 v. 8°. . . . N,212
Essay on Agricultural Chemistry. Newcastle-on-Tyne, 1842. 12°. N,252,23
Graham, T. J. Preaching and Popular Education. London, 1850. 12°. O,1032
Graham, W. Brassfounder's Manual. London, 1870. 12°. . . . M,842
Grahame, J. History of the United States. Philadelphia, 1852. 2 v. 8°. B,624
Grandfather's Chair, History of. N. Hawthorne. Boston, 1866. 12°. U,40,12
Grammar, Principles of. S. Barrett, jr. Boston, 1858. 8°. . . . L,552
Comparative. F. Bopp London, 1862. 3 v. 8°. . . . . L,531
Grammaire Comparée. F. Bopp. Paris, 1866-69. 3 v. 8°. . . L,538

Grammar, Inquiry concerning. J. Harris. London, 1806. 8°. . . . L,524
Universal. J. Stoddart. London, 1849. 12°. . . . . . . L,508
Vergleichende. F. Bopp. Berlin, 1859–68. 3 v. 8°. . . . G,582
Grammont, P., *Chevalier de*, Mémoires de. A. Hamilton. Paris, 1851. 12°. D,608
Granada, Conquest of. W. Irving. Philadelphia, 1870. 16°. . . . U,16
The same. New York, 1867. 12°. . . . . . . . U,29
Grandpa's House. H. C. Weeks. New York, 1869. 16°. . . . J,1370
Granger, J. Biographical History of England. Lond. 1779. 4 v. 8°. . D,418
Grant, A., and the Mountain Nestorians. T. Laurie. Boston, 1853. 12°. . P,608
Nestorians; or, the Lost Tribes. London, 1844. 16°. . . V,1031
Grant, Mrs. A. Letters from the Mountains. Boston, 1809. 2 v. 12°. . V,351
Memoirs of an American Lady. New York, 1846. 12°. . . C,1002
Grant, E. Holiday Rambles. London, 1862. 16°. . . . . . J,1170
Grant, J. Cavaliers of Fortune. London, 1865. 16°. . . . . D,436
Dick Rodney; Adventures of an Eton Boy. Boston, 1864. 16°. J,1625
Memoirs of James, Marquis of Montrose. London, 1858. 12°. . D,311
Grant, R. History of Physical Astronomy. London, 1852. 8°. . . N,348
Grant, U. S., and his Campaigns. H. Coppée. New York, 1866. 8°. . B,930
Life of. C. A. Dana and J. H. Wilson. Springfield, Mass. 1868. 8°. C,772
E. D. Mansfield. Cincinnati, 1868. 12°. . . . . . C,957
C. A. Phelps. Boston, 1868. 12°. . . . . . . C,1001
Military History of. A. Badeau. v. 1. New York, 1868. 8°. . B,958
Grantham, J. Iron Ship-Building. London, 1857. 12°. . . . . M,924
Grantley Manor. G. Fullerton. Leipzig, 1848. 2 v. in 1. 16°. . . J,169
Granville, D. Works. Durham, 1860. 8°. . . . . . . F,126,37
Granville de Vigne. L. de la Rame. Philadelphia, 1870. 12°. . . K,877
Grape, Culture, and Wine-Making. R. Buchanan. Cincinnati, 1855. 12°. . M,490
P. B. Mead. New York, 1867. 8°. . . . . . . . . M,501
Grape Culturist. A. S. Fuller. New York, 1867. 12°. . . . . . M,491
Grapevine, Culture and Treatment of. J. F. Allen. New York, 1857. 12°. M,534
Grasses and Forage Plants. C. L. Flint. New York, 1859. 12°. . . N,976
Grasses, Die Süssgräser. C. E. Langethal. Jena, 1847. 8°. . . . G,880,1
Grattan, H. Defence of the Protestant Clergy against. Dublin, 1788. 8°. H,630
Memoirs of. H. Grattan, jr. London, 1849. 5 v. 8°. . . . D,361
Speeches; edited by D. O. Grattan. Dublin, 1867. 12°. . . . H,775
Grattan, T. C. Civilized America. London, 1859. 2 v. 8°. . . . V,129
History of the Netherlands. London, 1830. 12°. . . . . M,999
The same. New York, 1843. 12°. . . . . . . . . B,406
Gravenhorst, J. L. C. Wirtelschl. u. Krüppelfüssler. Breslau, 1851. 4°. . F,97
Graver Thoughts of a Country Parson. A. K. H. Boyd. Bost. 1865–69. 2 v. 12°. H,570
Graves, A. C. Seclusaval; or, the Arts of Romanism. Memphis, 1870. 12°. K,224
Graves, A. J. Woman in America. New York, 1855. 18°. . . . . L,450
Graves, G. Naturalist's Pocket-Book. London, 1818. 8°. . . . N,525
Graves, R. Spiritual Quixote. London, 1820. 2 v. 12.° . . . . . K,542
Gray, Alonzo. Elements of Natural Philosophy. New York, 1850. 12°. N,74
and Adams, C. B. Elements of Geology. New York, 1854. 12°. . N,605
Gray, Asa. Botanical Text-Book. New York, 1850. 8°. . . . . . N,972
Botany for Young People. New York, 1859. 4°. . . . . . N,948
of the Northern United States. Boston, 1848. 12°. . . N,974
The same. New York, 1856. 8°. . . . . . . . N,973

Gray, Asa. Botany of U. S. Exploring Exped., Atlas. New York. 1857. f°. *Q,354
Genera Floræ Americæ Boreali-Orientalis. New York, 1849. 2 v. 8°. N,1031
Introduction to Botany. New York, 1865. 12°. . . . . . N,991
Gray, Barry, *pseud.* See *Coffin, R. B.*
Gray, H. Anatomy, Descriptive and Surgical. Philadelphia, 1867. 8°. L,1035
Gray, Mrs. H. History of Etruria. London, 1843–68. 3 v. 8°. . . . A,76
Tour to the Sepulchres of Etruria. London, 1843. 8°. . . . V,520
Gray, J. C. Essays, Agricultural and Literary. Boston, 1856. 12°. . H,266
Gray, G. Z. Children's Crusade; Episode of 13th Century. N. Y. 1870. 12°. J,1545
Gray, Lady Jane, Life of. A. Strickland. London, 1868. 8°. . . . D,384
Gray, J. E., and Richardson, J. Zoology of Beechey's Voyage. Lond. 1839. 4°. *Q,6
Gray, T. Poetical Works. Boston, 1857. 16°. . . . . . . . I,212
Grazier, Practical. A. Henderson. London, 1856. 8°. . . . . . M,475
Great Architect and Material Universe. M. Ponton. London, 1866. 12°. N,269
Great Britain, Annals of the Coinage of. R. Ruding. Lond. 1840. 3 v. 4°. *Q,269
Annales sex Regum Angliæ. London, 1845. 8°. . . . . . U,626
Biographical Dictionary of Authors of. London, 1816. 8°. . . D,276
Calendar of Victory. N. Johns. London, 1860. p. 8°. . . . L,130
Chronica. Roger of Wendover. London, 1841–44. 5 v. 8°. . U,622
Chron. and Memor. during Middle Ages. Lond. 1858–69. 100 v. 8°.

1. Capgrave, J. Chronicle of England. . . . . . . W,151
2. Chronicon Monasterii de Abingdon. 2 v. . . . . . W,152
3. Lives of Edward the Confessor. . . . . . . . W,153
4. Monumenta Franciscana. . . . . . . . W,154
5. Netter, T. Fasciculi Zizaniorum J. Wyclif. . . . . W,155
6. Stewart, Wm. Metrical Version of Boece's Chronicles. 3 v. . W,156
7. Capgrave, J. Liber de Illustribus Henricis. . . . . . W,157
8. Thomas of Elmham. Historia Monasterii S. Augustini Cantuariensis. W,158
9. Eulogium (Historiarum sive Temporis); Chronicon ad 1366. . . W,159
10. Historia Regis Henrici Septimi. . . . . . . . W,160
11. Memorials of Henry the Fifth. . . . . . . . W,161
12. Munimenta Gildhallæ Londoniensis. 3 v. in 4. . . . W,162
13. John de Oxendes. Chronica. . . . . . . W,163
14. Political Songs and Poems, from 1326 to 1485. 2 v. . . . W,164
15. Bacon, Roger. Opera Inedita. . . . . . . . W,165
16. Bartholomew de Cotton. Historia Anglicana, 449–1298. . . W,166
17. Brut y Tywysogion; Chronicle of the Princes of Wales. . . W,167
18. Henry IV., Royal and Historical Letters during the Reign of. v. 1. W,168
19. Pecock, R. The Repressor of over-much Blaming of the Clergy. 2 v. W,169
20. Blegewryd. Annales Cambriæ. . . . . . . . W,170
21. Giraldus Cambrensis. Opera. v. 1–3, 5, 6. . . . . W,171
22. Wars of the English in France in the Reign of Henry VI. 2 v. in 3. W,172
23. Anglo-Saxon Chronicle. 2 v. . . . . . . . W,173
24. Letters during Reigns of Richard III. and Henry VII. 2 v. . W,174
25. Grosseteste, R., *Bishop.* Epistolæ. . . . . . . W,175
26. Hardy, T. D. Catalogue of Manuscripts relating to the History of Great Britain and Ireland. 2 v. in 3. . . . . . . W,176
27. Henry III., Royal Letters during the Reign of, 1216–72. 2 v. . W,177
28. Chronica Monasterii S. Albani. 7 v. . . . . . . W,178
29. Evesham, Abbatia de. Chronicon. . . . . . . W,179
30. Richard of Cirencester. Speculum Historiale de Gestis Regum. 2 v. W,180
31. Edward I. Year Books, 20–21; 30–31; 32–33. 3 v. . . . . W,181
32. Expulsion of the English from Normandy, 1449–50. . . . W,182
33. Historia et Cartularium Monasterii S. Petria Gloucestriæ. 3 v. . W,183
34. Neckam, A. De Naturis Rerum, etc. . . . . . . W,184
35. Leechdoms, Wortcunning, and Starcraft in Early England. 3 v. . W,185
36. Annales Monastici. 5 v. . . . . . . . . . W,186

Great Britain, Chron. and Mem. during Middle Ages. *Continued.*

37. Magna Vita S. Hugonis Episcopi Lincolniensis. . . . w,187
38. Richard I., Chronicles, etc., during the Reign of. 2 v. . . w,188
39. Waurin, J. de. Croniques de la Grant Bretaigne. 2 v. . . w,189
40. Wavrin, J. de. Chronicles of Great Britain. . . . . w,190
41. Higden, R. Polychronicon. 2 v. . . . . . . w,191
42. Le Livere de Reis de Brittanie e le Livere de Reis de Engleterre. . w,192
43. Chronica Monasterii de Melsa, 1150–1406. 3 v. . . . w,193
44. Matthæus Parisiensis. Historia Anglorum, 1067–1245. 3 v. . w,194
45. Liber Monasterii de Hyda. . . . . . . . w,195
46. Chronicon Scotorum; Chronicle of Irish Affairs till 1150. . . w,196
47. Pierre de Langtoft. Chronicle in French Verse. 2 v. . . w,197
48. War of the Gaedhill with the Gaill. . . . . . . w,198
49. Benedict of Peterborough. Gesta Regis Henrici Secundi. 2 v . w,199
50. Munimenta Academica. Academical Life and Studies at Oxford. 2 v. w,200
51. Roger de Houedene. Chronica. 2 v. . . . . . . w,201

Chronicon. Walter of Hemingburgh. London, 1848-49. 8°. . . U,621
Chronicon ex Chronicis. Florence of Worcester. Lond. 1848–9. 2 v. 8°. U,617
Chronicque de la Traïson et Mort de Richart II. London, 1846. 8°. U,629
Commoners of, History of. J. Burke. London, 1836–38. 4 v. 8°. B,75
Constitution of. C. Ewald. London, 1867. 12°. . . . . . O,483
A. Fonblanque and Holdsworth. London, 1869. 12°. O,504
Rise and Progress of. J. L. de Lolme. London, 1838. 2 v. 8°. B,51
Continental Interests of. A. H. L. Heeren. London, 1847. 8°. . A,42
De Excidio Britanniæ. St. Gildas. London, 1838. 8°. . . . U,635
Ecclesiastical History of. J. Collier. London, 1852. 8°. . . P,580
Education in. H. Mann. London, 1854. 8°. . . . . . O,1239
Educational Tour in. H. Mann. London, 1853. 12°. . . . O,907
Force Commerciale de la. C. Dupin. Paris, 1826. 2 v. 4°. . . M,818
Four Years in. C. Colton. New York, 1836. 12°. . . . . V,380
Galleries of Art in. G. F. Waagen. London, 1857. 8°. . . . M,59,4
Geography of. G. Long and G. R. Porter. London, n. d. 8°. . V,1126
Gesta Regum Anglorum. William of Malmesbury. Lond. 1840. 2 v. 8°. U,618
Historia Britonum Nennius. London, 1838. 8°. . . . . . U,627
Historia Ecclesiastica. V. Bede. London, 1841. 8°. . . . U,628
Historia Rerum Anglicarum. William of Newbury. Lond. 1856. 2 v. 8°. U,619
Gladstone Government; Cabinet Pictures. London, 1869. 8°. . . A,530
Historical Collections, 1618–40. J. Rushworth. Lond. 1659–80. 5 v. f°. F,40
History of. R. Henry. London, 1788–95. 12 v. 8°. . . . . A,463
1547–1603. J. P. Andrews. London, 1796. 2 v. 8°. . . A,464
1688–1802. W. Belsham. London, 1806–12. 12 v. 8°. . A,429
1760–1820. J. R. Miller. London, 1828. 8°. . . . . A,541
House of Commons, History of. London, 1742–44. 14 v. 12°. . B,101
Reports of Inspectors of Schools. London, 1852. 12°. . . O,1003
Literary and Scientific Men of. S. A. Dunham. Lond. 1856. 3 v. 12°. M,1016
Literature and Literary Men of. A. Mills. New York, 1851. 2 v. 8°. H,710
Monumenta Historica Britannica, v. 1. London, 1848. f°. . . F,120
National Sports of. H. Alken. London, 1825. f°. . . . . . M,342
Naval History of. J. Campbell. London, 1818. 8 v. 8°. . . B,93
Parliament, Notes of Debates in. Sir S. D'Ewes. London, 1708. f°. F,295
Peerage and Baronetage of. E. Lodge. London, 1870. 8°. . . C,624
Popular Antiquities of. J. Brand. London, 1849. 3 v. p. 8°. . L,3
Ports, Harbors, etc. W.H.Bartlett and W.Beattie. Lon. 1841–4. 2 v. 4°. *Q,417

Great Britain, Progress in, History of. R. K. Philp. London, 1859. 8°. . B,32
Public Accounts, Reports on. London, 1783–87. 3 v. 4°. . . P.D.
Public Expenditure. D. Wakefield. London, 1834. 8°. . . O,519
Public Libraries of, Rep. of Committee on. London, 1849–50. 2 v. f°. P.D.
Representative History of. T. H. B. Oldfield. Lond. 1816. 6 v. 8°. A,460
Royal Authors of. H. Walpole. London, 1806–23. 5 v. 8°. *C,1307
Secret History of. J. Macpherson. London, 1775. 2 v. 4°. . A,468
Specimens of Ancient Sculpture in. London, 1809–35. 2 v. f°. . S.C.
State Papers; collected by Earl Clarendon. Oxford, 1766–67. 3 v. f°. F,124
Tracts relating to History of. J. Somers. London, 1809–15. 13 v. 4°. F,130
Treasures of Art in. G. F. Waagen. London, 1854. 3 v. 8°. . M,59
Views in. T. Nelson. London, 1857–58. 3 v. 16°. . . *V,1029
and Ireland, Memoirs of. Sir J. Dalrymple. Lond. 1771–3. 2 v. 4°. A,470
Political Index to Histories of. R. Beatson. Lon. 1806–7. 3 v. 8°. A,461
Great Consummation. J. Cumming. New York, 1864. 2 v. 12°. . . P,249
Great Desert of Sahara. J. Richardson. London, 1848. 2 v. 8°. . . V,815
Great Deserts of N. America, Seven Years in. E.Domenech. Lon. 1860. 2 v. 8°. V,77
Great Events, by Distinguished Historians. F. Lieber. New York, 1847. 12°. A,24
Great Expectations. C. Dickens. Philadelphia, 1860. 8°. . . . K,509
The same. New York, 1871. 12°. . . . . . . K,1139
The same. Leipzig, 1861. 2 v. in 1. 16°. . . . . J,121
Great Harmonia. A. J. Davis. New York, 1860. 5 v. 12°. . . . P,866
Great Hoggarty Diamond. W. M. Thackeray. Boston, 1869. 12°. . K,1038,1
The same. Philadelphia, 1866. 12°. . . . . . K,1087,4
The same. Leipzig, 1849. 16°. . . . . . . J,484,1
Great Law of Consideration; or, Religious Life. A.Horneck. Lon. 1729. 8°. P,196
Great March to the Sea. G. W. Nichols. New York, 1865. 12°. . . B,907
Great Metropolis; New York City. J. H. Browne. Hartford, 1869. . C,106
Great Mysteries and Little Plagues. J. Neal. Boston, 1870. 16°. . . J,1325
Great Salt Lake, Exp. to Valley of. H. Stansbury. Phil. 1855. 2 v. 8°. V,112
Great Tribulation, The. J. Cumming. New York, 1860. 12°. . . P,253
Great Western Canal, Considerations on. Brooklyn, 1818. 8°. . B,809,2
Greater Britain; a Record of Travel. C. W. Dilke. New York, 1869. 12°. V,1076
Greatest Plague of Life. H. and A. Mayhew. London, n. d. 16°. . . J,654
Grecian Architecture. G. H. Gordon, *Earl of Aberdeen*. London, 1860. 12°. M,843
Greece and the Greeks. E. About. New York, 1857. 12°. . . . V,538
Ancient. A. H. L. Heeren. London, 1847. 8°. . . . . . A,42
Customs of. J. A. St. John. London, 1842. 3 v. 8°. . . A,102
Description of. J. A. Cramer. Oxford, 1828. 3 v. 8°. . A,97
History of. J. Gillies. Philadelphia, 1831. 8°. . . . A,95
Language and Literature of. W. Mure. Lond. 1854–9. 5 v. 8°. H,741
Literature of. C. O. Müller. London, 1858. 3 v. 8°. . A,109
and Ionian Islands, Reise durch. C. Müller. Leipzig, 1822. 16°. E,192
and the Levant. J. Hartley. London, 1833. 12°. . . . . V,568
and Turkey, Travels in. A. Slade. London, 1854. 8°. . . . V,580
Antenor's Reisen durch. Hamburg, 1805–6. 5 v. 16°. . . . E,191
Antiquities of. J. Potter. v. 2. Edinburgh, 1832. 8°. . . . A,113
Griechische Alterthümer. G.F.Schoemann. Ber. 1861–3. 2 v. 8°. E,456
of Athens. J. Stuart and N. Revett. London, 1858. p. 8°. . L,149
Manual of. C. Anthon. New York, 1852. 12°. . . . A,74

Greece, Antiquities of, Manual of. E. F. C. Bojesen. New York, 1854. 12°. A,72
Child's History of. J. Bonner. New York, n. d. 2 v. 16°. . J,1442
Description of. Pausanias; translated. London, 1794. 3 v. 8°. . A,93
Descriptive and Historical. C. Wordsworth. London, 1868. 8°. . A,100
Drama of. J. R. Darley. Dublin, 1840. 8°. . . . . . . H,731
Metrik der Griechischen Dramatiker und Lyriker. A. Rossbach und R. Westphal. Leipzig, 1854–61. 4 v. 8°. . . . . . G,598
Excursion in the Peloponnesus. T. Wyse. London, 1865. 2 v. 8°. V,576
First History of. E. M. Sewell. New York, 1853. 12°. . . A,60
Fragmenta Historicorum Græcorum. Paris, 1841–49. 4 v. 8°. . U,553
Geschichte des Hellenismus. J. G. Droysen. Hamburg, 1836. 8°. E,14
Hellenische Stämme u. Städte. C. O. Müller. Bres. 1820–4. 3 v. 8°. E,15
Hellenische Alterthumskunde. W. Wachsmuth. Halle, 1826. 2 v. 8°. E,457
History of. E. Curtius. London, 1868–70. 3 v. 8°. . . . . A,88
G. Finlay. Edinburgh, 1851. 8°. . . . . . . . . A,105
The same. Edinburgh, 1856. 8°. . . . . . A,106
O. Goldsmith. New York, 1855. 16°. . . . . . . . A,58
The same; ed. by W. Pinnock. Philadelphia, 1866. 12°. A,67
G. Grote. New York, 1854. 12 v. 12°. . . . . . A,80
The same. Boston, 1851–53. 11 v. 12°. . . . . S.C.
T. Keightley. London, 1858. 12°. . . . . . . A,71
The same. New York, 1853. 8°. . . . . A,87
W. Mitford. London, 1814–20. 10 v. 8°. . . . . . A,82
The same. Boston, 1823. 8. v. 8°. . . . . . A,115
E. Pococke and others. London, 1851. p. 8°. . . . . A,68
W. Smith. New York, 1859. 12°. . . . . . . . . A,66
C. Thirlwall. New York, 1851. 2 v. 8°. . . . . . A,98
The same. London, 1835–44. 8 v. 12°. . . . . M,994
Lectures on Ancient and Modern. C. C. Felton. Boston, 1867. 2 v. 8°. A,83
Macedonia and Syria, History of. W. R. Lyall and others. Lon. 1852. p. 8°. A,69
Modern. H. M. Baird. New York, 1856. 12°. . . . . . V,562
History of. Sir J. E. Tennent. London, 1845. 2 v. 8°. . A,116
Monks of Mount Athos. H. F. Tozer. London, 1862. 8°. . V,1086,2
Mythology of. T. Keightley. New York, 1866. 18°. . . . . P,909
Griech. Götterlehre. F. G. Welcker. Göttin. 1857–63. 3 v. 8°. E,463
Griechische Mythologie. L. Preller. Berlin, 1860–61. 2 v. 8°. E,462
Peloponnesian War. Thucydides; tr. by H. Dale. Lond. 1868. p. 8°. L,88
Ruines de la Grece. M. le Roy. Paris, 1757. f°. . . . . . L.R.
Russia and Crete, Travels in. B. Taylor. New York, 1868. 12°. . V,382
Sitten des Griechischen Heldenalters. C. G. Helbig. Leip. 1839. 16°. E,451
Sketches in. A. De Vere. Philadelphia, 1850. 12°. . . . . V,564
Theater of. Cambridge, 1827. 8°. . . . . . . . . . H,728
Travels in. R. F. A. de Chateaubriand. London, 1812. 2 v. 8°. V,1083
B. Dorr. Philadelphia, 1856. 12°. . . . . . V1042
T. S. Hughes. London, 1830. 2 v. 8°. . . . . . V,569
Travels of Anacharsis in. J. J. Barthélemy. Lond. 1806. 8 v. 8°, 4°. V,572
The same. London, 1817. 6 v. 8°. . . . . . V,573
Turkey and Asia Minor, Hand-Book for. J. Murray. Lon. 1845. 16°. V,1033
and Russia, Travels in. J. L. Stephens. N.Y. 1851–53. 2 v. 12°. V,341
under the Romans. G. Finlay. Edinburgh, 1857. 8°. . . . . A,85

Greece under the Romans. G. Finlay. Edinburgh, 1857. 8°. . . . . A,107
Voyage de Anacharsis en. J.J.Barthélemy. Paris, 1817. 7 v. 8°. V,571
Atlas to the same. Paris, 1817. f°. . . . . . *Q,388
Greek Anthology; translated by G. Burges. London, 1854. p. 8°. . . L,57
Greek and Roman Antiquities, Dictionary of. A. Rich, jr. Lond. 1860. 8°. A,79
W. Smith. Boston, 1854. 8°. . . . . . . . S.C.
Greek and Roman Biography and Mythology. W. Smith. Bost. 1849. 3 v. 8°. S.C.
Greek and Roman Philosophy, etc. C. J. Blomfield and others. Lon. 1853. 12°. O,633
Greek and the Turk. E. E. Crowe. London, 1853. 12°. . . . . V,531
Greek Bibliography, Νευελληνικὴ Φιλολογία. Α. Π. Βρετος. 'Αθήναις. 1854. 2v. 8°. L.R.
Greek Classic Poets, Study of. H. N. Coleridge. London, 1846. 16°. . I,320
Greek Classical Literature, History of. R. W. Brown. Philad. 1852. 8°. H,725
Greek Classics, Didot's Bibliothèque Grecque, avec la Traduction Latine et les Index. Paris, 1838-57. 16 v. 8°. . . . . . . . U,550

| | | | |
|---|---|---|---|
| Appianus. | U,550 | Arrianus. | U,551 |
| Diodorus Siculus. 2 v. | U,552 | Fragmenta Historicorum. 4 v. | U,553 |
| Herodotus. | U,554 | Josephus. 2 v. | U,555 |
| Plutarchus. 2 v. | U,556 | Polybius. | U,557 |
| Thucydides. | U,558 | Xenophon. | U,559 |

Greek Language, Analytical Lexicon of N. Test. Bagster's. Lond. 1852. 4°. L.R.
Dictionnaire Grec-Français. J. Planche. Paris, 1824. 8°. . . L.R.
J. Quénon. Paris, 1807. 8°. . . . . . . . . L.R.
Doctrine of the Greek Article. T. F. Middleton. London, 1808. 8°. P,544
Grammar of. C. Anthon. New York, 1849. 12°. . . . . L,733
The same. New York, 1856. 12°. . . .
P. Buttmann. Boston, 1822. 8°. . . . . . L,737
R. Kühner. New York, 1860. 8°. . . . . L,735
A. Matthiæ. London, 1837. 2 v. 8°. . . . L,740
R. Valpy. New York, 1852. 12°. . . . . L,731
of New Testament. G.B.Winer. Philadelphia, 1849. 2 v. 8°. P,484
of Idiom of New Test. G. B. Winer. Andover, 1870. 8°. . P,439
to the New Testament. W. Trollope. London, 1842. 8°. . L,739
Griechische Etymologie. G. Curtius. Leipzig, 1858-62. 2 v. in 1. 8°. G,596
Lessons in. C. Anthon. New York, 1852. 12°. . . . . L,732
Part second. New York, 1846. 12°. . . . . . . L,734
Lexicon of. J. Groves. Philadelphia, 1858. 8°. . . . . L.R.
H. G. Liddell and Scott. New York, 1858. r. 8°. . . R.R.
The same. New York, 1870. r. 8°. . . . . L.R.
J. Pickering. Boston, 1859. r. 8°. . . . . . L.R.
Græco-Latinum et Lat.-Græc. C. Schrevelius. N. Y. 1818. 8°. L.R.
of New Testament. E. Robinson. New York, 1858. 8°. . *P,451
of Roman and Byzantine Period. E.A.Sophocles. Bost. 1870. 8°. L.R.
Particles. H. Hoogeven; trans. by J. Seager. London, n. d. 8°. . L,738
Thesaurus Græcæ Linguæ. H.Stephanus. London, 1816-26. 8 v. f°. U,478
Prepositions. G. Harrison. Philadelphia, 1858. 8°. . . . L,743
Greek Literature, Geschichte der. C. O. Müller. Breslau, 1841. 2 v. 8°. E,251
History of. Sir T. N. Talfourd and others. London, 1850. 12°. . H,721
Manual of. C. Anthon. New York, 1853. 12°. . . . . H,724
Greek Philosophy, Lectures on. J. F. Ferrier. Edinburgh, 1866. 2 v. 8°. O,642
and Christianity. B. F. Cocker. New York, 1870. 8°. . . . P,144

Greek Poets and Poetry, Specimens of. W. Peter. Philadelphia, 1848. 8°. U,445
Study of. H. N. Coleridge. Boston, 1842. 12°. . . . . . I,320
Greek Mythology, Stories from. J. Wood. London, 1867. 16°. . . P,342
Greek Revolution, 1821. T. Keightley. Edinburgh, 1830. 2 v. 16°. . I,528
Historical Sketch of. S. G. Howe. New York, 1828. 12°. . . A,73
History of. G. Finlay. Edinburgh, 1861. 2 v. 8°. . . . . A,108
T. Gordon. Edinburgh, 1844. 2 v. 8°. . . . . . A,104
Greeks, Ancient Poets and Poetry of. A. Mills. Boston, 1854. 8°. . . U,446
and Romans, Arts, etc. of. T. D. Fosbroke. Lond. 1833-35. 2 v. 12°. M,996
Private Life of. W. A. Becker. London, 1854. 12°. . . . . A,152
Greeley, H. American Conflict, 1861-65. Hartford, 1864-66. 2 v. 8°. . B,920
Essays on Political Economy. Boston, 1870. 16°. . . . . . O,509
Exhibition at the Crystal Palace, N. Y. New York, 1853. 12°. . M,608
Glances at Europe. New York, 1851. 12°. . . . . . . V,309
Hints toward Reforms. New York, 1850. 12°. . . . . . O,457
Life of Henry Clay. Auburn, 1853. 12°. . . . . . . C,703
Life of. J. Parton. New York, 1855. 12°. . . . . . . C,678
Overland Journey to San Francisco. New York, 1860. 12°. . . V,118
Recollections of a Busy Life. New York, 1868. 8°. . . . . C,711
What I know of Farming. New York, 1871. 12°. . . . . . M,565
and Cleveland, J. F. Political Text-Book for 1860. N. Y. 1860. 8°. O,527
Green, A., Life of, written by himself. New York, 1849. 8°. . . . C,726
Green, F. H. and Congdon. Analytical Class-Book of Botany. N. Y. 1856. 4°. N,1033
Green, J. H. Mental Dynamics. London, 1847. 8°. . . . . . O,1039
Green, J. H. Reformed Gambler. Philadelphia, n. d. 12°. . . . M,343
Green, L. W., Memoir of. L. J. Halsey. New York, 1871. 12°. . . C,874
Green, M. A. E. Lives of Princesses of England, v. 2-6. Lond. 1850-55. 8°. D,338
Green, S. Life of Mahomet. London, 1840. 16°. . . . . . . I,630
Green Mountain Boys. D. P. Thompson. Boston, 1870. 12°. . . . K,391
Greene, G. Normandy during the Revolution. Lond. 1802. 8°. . . B,262
Greene, G. W. Biographical Studies. New York, 1860. 12°. . . . H,267
Historical Studies. New York, 1850. 12°. . . . . . . A,316
Historical View of the American Revolution. Boston, 1865. 12°. . B,742
History and Geography of Middle Ages. New York, 1851. 12°. . A,234
Life of Gen. Nathaniel Greene. Boston, 1860. 12°. . . C,860,20
Life of Gen. Nathaniel Greene, v. 1. New York, 1867. 8°. . . C,727
Greene, J. H. Irish Geography and Topography. Cincinnati, 1859. 8°. V,1124
Greene, J. R. Manual of the Animal Kingdom. London, 1861-63. 2 pts. 16°. O,2
Greene, Mrs. Grey House on the Hill. London, 1870. 12°. . . . J,1722
Greene, N., Life of. G. W. Greene. Boston, 860. 12°. . . . . C,860,20
The same, v. 1. New York, 1867. 8°. . . . . . C,727
W. G. Simms. Philadelphia, 1849. 12°. . . . . . C,762
Memoirs of. C. Caldwell. Philadelphia, 1819. 8°. . . . . C,771
Greene, R. and Marlowe. Poems; with Lives; ed. by R. Bell. Lond. 1856. I,249
and Peele. Dramatic and Poetical Works. London, 1861. 8°. . I,725
Greene, S. S. Elements of English Grammar. Philadelphia, 1853. 12°. O,1084
First Lessons in Grammar. Philadelphia, 1848. 12°. . . . O,1077
Greene, W. Difficulties of a Free Government. Providence, 1851. 8°. T,19,2
Greenhouse Botany. A. Catlow. London, 1857. 16°. . . . . . N,917
Greenhow, R. History of Oregon and California. New York, 1845. 8°. C,250

Greenland, Historical and Descriptive Account of. New York, 1854. 16°. L,425
History of. I. de La Peyrère. London, 1855. 8°. . . . . V,984
Observations in. F. Marten. London, 1711. 8°. . . . . V,961
The same. London, 1855. 8°. . . . . . . . V,984
Greenleaf, S. Testimony of the Four Evangelists. London, 1847. 8°. . P,510
Greenough, H., Memorial of. H. T. Tuckerman. New York, 1853. 12°. C,1003
Greenwell, D. Essays. London, 1866. 12°. . . . . . . . H,323
Poems. London, 1867. 12°. . . . . . . . . . I,171
Greenwood, F. W. P. Sermons of Consolation. Boston, 1842. 12°. . P,672
Greenwood, Grace, *pseud.* See *Lippincott, S. J.*
Greenwood, J. Treatise on Navigation. London, 1850. 12°. . . . M,925
Seven Curses of London. Boston, 1869. 12°. . . . . . H,118
True History of a Little Ragamuffin. London, n. d. 8°. . . K,694
Wild Sports of the World. London, 1864. 8°. . . . . N,636
Greg, T. Management of Heavy and Wet Lands. London, 1841. 8°. N,252,24
Gregg, J. Commerce of the Prairies. Philadelphia, 1850. 2 v. 12°. . V,158
Gregorovius, F. Corsica; Picturesque, Social, etc. London, 1855. p. 8°. I,656,2
Siciliana; Wanderungen in Neapel und Sicilien. Leipzig, 1861. 12°. E,197
Gregory, G. Life of Thomas Chatterton. London, 1789. 8°. . . . D,386
Gregory, St. Pastoral Care; Alfred's Anglo-Saxon Version. Lond. 1871. 8°. L,605,45
Gregory, O. Evidences, Doctrines of Christian Religion. Lond. 1851. p. 8°. L,189
Life of John Mason Good. London, 1828. 8°. . . . . D,371
Mathematics for Practical Men. London, 1862. 8°. . . M,1178
Plane and Spherical Trigonometry. London, 1816. 16°. . M,1139
Gregory, W. Letters on Animal Magnetism. Philadelphia, 1851. 12°. . L,877
Outlines of Chemistry. Cincinnati, 1851. 8°. . . . . . N,187
The same. New York, 1852. 8°. . . . . . . N,224
Schools of Chemistry in Great Britain. London, 1842. 8°. . N,252,21
Greive, W. T. Church and People of Servia. London, 1864. 8°. . V,1086,3
Grenville, G. N. T. Memorials of John Hampden. London, 1860. p. 8°. L,269
Grenville, R. and G. Grenville Papers; Corresp. Lond. 1852–53. 4 v. 8°. A,520
Grenville, R. P., *Duke of Buckingham and Chandos.* Court and Cabinets of
George III. London, 1853–55. 4 v. 8°. . . . . . A,551
Court of England during the Regency, 1811–20. Lond. 1856. 2 v. 8°. A,552
Memoirs of the Court of George IV., 1820–30. Lond. 1859. 2 v. 8°. A,553
Greswell, W. P. Annals of Parisian Typography. London, 1818. 8°. . L.R.
Gretton, A. L. V. Vicissitudes of Italy. London, 1859. 12°. . . . B,485
Greville, R. K. Scottish Cryptogamic Flora. Edinburgh, 1823–28. 6 v. 8°. *N,1032
Grey, C. Early Years of the Prince Consort. New York, 1867. 12°. . D,315
Grey, Sir G. Polynesian Mythology. London, 1855. 8°. . . . . P,920
Grey, H. G., *Earl.* Lord Russell's Colonial Policy. London, 1853. 2 v. 8°. B,52
Grey, J. Guano and other Manures. Hexham, 1843. 8°. . . N,252,25
Grey, R. Memoria Technica. Oxford, 1851. 16°. . . . . . O,999
Grey, T. Visit to Egypt, Constantinople, the Crimea, etc. N. Y. 1870. 12°. V,777
Grey House on the Hill. Mrs. Greene. London, 1870. 12°. . . . J,1722
Greyson Letters. H. Rogers. Boston, 1859. 12°. . . . . . H,270
Grieb, C. F. English and German Dictionary. Phila. 1857. 2 v. r. 8°. . R.R.
The same. Philadelphia, 1870. 2 v. r. 8°. . . . . . L.R.
Grier, W. Mechanic's Calculator. Glasgow, 1866. 16°. . . . . M,600
Griffin, G. Poetical Works. London, 1843. 16°. . . . . . . I,344

Griffin, G. W. Studies in Literature. Baltimore, 1870. 12°. . . . . H,645
Griffith, J. Travels in Europe, Asia Minor, and Arabia. London, 1805. 4°. V,1144
Griffin, J. J. Centigrade Testing in Pharmacy. London, 1851. 8°. . N,252,50
Chemistry of Non-Metallic Elements. London, 1860. 12°. . . N,177
Griffith, J. W. Text-Book of the Microscope. London, 1864. 12°. . . N,7
and Henfrey, A. Micrographic Dictionary. London, 1860. 2 v. in 3. 8°. N,9
Griffith, W. Notulæ ad Plantas Asiaticas, pts. 2–4. Calcutta, 1849–54. 3 v. 8°. N,981
Plates to the same. Calcutta, 1849–54. 3 v. 4°. . . . Q,126
Griffith Gaunt. C. Reade. Boston, 1867. 8°. . . . . . . . K,901
Griffiths, J. W. Marine and Naval Architecture. New York, 1851. 4°. . Q,220
Grimm, H. Life of Michael Angelo Buonarroti. Boston, 1866. 2 v. 12°. D,728
Grimm, J. L. Deutsche Mythologie. Göttingen, 1854. 8°. . . . E,460
Geschichte der Deutschen Sprache. Leipzig, 1853–54. 2 v. 8°. . G,593
and W. K. Deutsches Wörterbuch. Leipzig, 1854–62. 5 v. 8°. . L.R.
Gammer Grethel's Fairy Tales. London, 1869. p. 8°. . . L,105
German Popular Tales and Household Stories. Bost. 1867. 12°. G,180
Gallaudet, T. H. Scripture Biography for the Young. N.Y. n. d. 3 v. 16°. P,746,25–27
Natural Theology. New York, n. d. 16°. . . . . . P,746,28
Grindal, E., Life of. J. Strype. Oxford, 1821. 8°. . . . . . . P,687
Griscom, J. H. Animal Mechanism and Physiology. New York, 1855. 16°. L,399
Uses and Abuses of Air. New York, 1850. 12°. . . . . . L,883
Grisebach, A. H. R. Leistungen der Pflanzengeographie. Ber. 1845–56. 11 v. 8°. G,870
Griswold, R. W. Female Poets of America. Philadelphia, 1854. 8°. . H,667
Poets and Poetry of America. Philadelphia, 1855. 8°. . . . I,164
Prose Writers of America. Philadelphia, 1854. 8°. . . . H,665
Republican Court. New York, 1856. 8°. . . . . . . M,284
Sacred Poets of England and America. New York, 1850. 8°. . . I,162
Gros, Baron. Embassy to China and Japan. London, 1860. 12°. . . V,602
Grose, F. Antiquities of England and Wales. London, n. d. 8 v. 4°. *A,563
Grosseteste, R. Epistolæ. London, 1861. 8°. . . . . . . . W,175
Grote, G. History of Greece. New York, 1854. 12 v. 12°. . . . A,80
The same. Boston, 1851–53. 11 v. 12°. . . . . . S.C.
Plato and other Companions of Socrates. London, 1865. 3 v. 8°. . D,777
Grotius, H. De Jure Belli et Pacis. Cambridge, 1853. 3 v. 8°. . . U,543
Droit de la Guerre et de Paix. Basle, 1746. 4°. . . . . U,591
Memorials of. C. Barksdale. London, 1654. 8°. . . . . U,483
Selections from Law of War and Peace. London, 1655. 8°. . . U,483
Grove, G. Nabloos and the Samaritans. London, 1862. 8°. . . V,1086,2
Grove, W. R. Correlation of Physical Forces. London, 1867. 8°. . . N,86
Lectures on, 1843. London, 1846. 8°. . . . . . N,252,33
Groves, J. Greek and English Dictionary. Philadelphia, 1858. 8°. . L.R.
Grow, J. N. Hidden Life of the Soul. Philadelphia, 1871. 16°. . . P,200
Grün, A., *pseud.* See *Auersperg, A. A.*
Gruson, L. Universum, Blicke in das. Magdenburg, 1854. 8°. . . G,673
Guano and other Manures. J. Grey. Hexham, 1843. 8°. . . . N,252,25
as a Fertilizer. C. W. Johnson. London, 1843. 8°. . . N,252,25
Varieties, Analysis, and Application. A. Bourne. Lond. 1845. 8°. N,252,6
Guardian, The. J. Addison and others. Boston, 1866. 3 v. 8°. H,536,13–15
The same. Boston, 1856. 16°. . . . . . . . H,521
Guardian Angel. O. W. Holmes. Boston, 1867. 16°. . . . . . K,196

Günther, A. C. L. G. Reptiles of British India. London, 1864. f°. . Q,69
Günther, F.A. Homöopathischer Thierarzt. Sondershausen, 1855. 3 v. in 1. 8°. E,417
Guericke, H. E. F. Manual of Church History. Andover, 1869. 8°. . P,606
Guérin, E. de. Journal; edited by G. S. Trebutien. London, 1865. 8°. . D,636
Letters; edited by G. S. Trebutien. London, 1866. 8°. . . . D,637
Guernsey, A. H. and Alden. History of the Rebellion. N. Y. 1868. 2 v. f°. *Q,228
Guernsey, C. F. The New Boy. Philadelphia, 1871. 16°. . . . J,1723
Guerrazzi, F. D. Beatrice Cenci. New York, 1869. 12°. . . . . G,231
Guerre, La. E. Erckmann et A. Chatrian. Paris, 1861. 12°. . . H,1018
Guesclin, B. du, Life and Times of. D. F. Jamison. Lond. 1864. 2 v. 8°. D,681
Guesses at Truth. J. C. and A. W. Hare. Boston, 1865. 12°. . . . H,124
Guettée, Abbé; The Papacy; its origin and relations. New York, 1867. 12°. P,821
Guevara, A. de. Spanish Letters. London, 1657. 12°. . . . . H,905
Guiana, British, Discovery of. Sir W. Raleigh. London, 1848. 8°. . . V,981
History of. H. G. Dalton. London, 1855. 2 v. 8°. . . . V,248
News of. Sir W. Raleigh. See *Force's Tracts*, v. 3.
Guibourt, N.J.B.G. Pharmaceutische Waarenkunde. Nürnb. 1825. 2 v. in 1. 12°. G,754
Guicciardini, F. Aphorismes Civill and Militarie. London, 1629. f°. . F,71
History of Italy, 1490–1532. London, 1753–1756. 10 v. 8°. . . B,508
Maxims; translated by E. Martin. London, 1845. 18°. . . . H,899
Guiccioli, *Countess*. See *Boissy, T. G., Marquise de.*
Guide-Book, Short Trip to Europe. H. Morford. New York, 1868. 16°. . V,295
Guide for Young Disciples. J. G. Pike. New York, n. d. 18°. . P,746,11
Guide to Wealth. W. Smead. Cincinnati, 1856. 18°. . . . . O,466
Guild Court. G. Mac Donald. London, 1868. 3 v. 12°. . . . K,1101
Guild, C. Over the Ocean; Sights in Foreign Lands. Boston, 1871. 12°. V,292
Guild, R. A. Librarian's Manual. New York, 1858. 4°. . . . . . L.R.
Life of Roger Williams. See *Narragansett Club Publications*, v. 1.
Guildford, N. de. Owl and Nightingale; a Poem. London, 1843. 12°. L,606,11
Guileville, G. de. Pèlerinage de l'Homme, compared with Bunyan's Pilgrim's Progress. London, 1858. 4°. . . . . . . . . . Q,418
Pilgrimage of the Sowle. London, 1859. 4°. . . . . . . Q,419
Guillemin, A. The Heavens; Popular Astronomy, 2d ed. Lond. 1867. 8°. *N,346
The same; 4th edition. New York, 1871. 8°. . . . N,350
The Sun. New York, 1870. 12°. . . . . . . . M,1057
Guilt and Innocence. M. S. Schwartz. Boston, 1871. 8°. . . . . G,228
Guinevre. A. Tennyson. Illustrated by G. Doré. London, 1867. f°. . *Q,242
Guitar, Complete Method for. F. Carulli. Boston, n. d. 4°. . . . Q,189
Guizot, F. Corneille and his Times. New York, 1852. 12°. . . . D,658
Essay on the Character of Washington. New York, 1863. 16°. . C,901
History of Charles I. and English Revolution. London, 1854. 2 v. 8°. A,508
of Civilization in Europe. New York, 1846. 4 v. 12°. . . A,301
The same. London, 1868–70. 3 v. p. 8°. . . . L,192
The same. New York, 1850–52. 4 v. 12°. . . S.C.
of the English Revolution of 1640. New York, 1846. 12°. . A,479
The same. London, 1864. p. 8°. . . . . . . L,191
of Oliver Cromwell. Philadelphia, 1854. 2 v. 12°. . . D,402
The same. Philadelphia, 1854. 2 v. 12°. . . . S.C.
of Richard Cromwell and the Restoration. Lond. 1856. 2 v. 8°. A,525
of my Time. London, 1858–61. 4 v. 8°. . . . . . D,680

Guizot, F. Letter to Primary Teachers of France. Dublin, 1842. 12°. O,1024
Meditations on Christianity. New York, 1865. 8°. . . . . . P,84
Origin of Representative Government in Europe. Lond. 1852. p. 8°. L,190
Saint Louis and Calvin. Philadelphia, 1869. 12°. . . . . . D,655
Shakespeare and his Times. New York, 1852. 12°. . . . C,1200
The same. New York, 1855. 12°. . . . . . . . . I,844
Guizot, Madame. Moral Tales. London, 1853. 16°. . . . . J,1189
Popular Tales. Boston, 1859. 12°. . . . . . . . . J,1188
Gulistan; or, the Rose Garden; trans. by F. Gladwin. Boston, 1865. 16°. G,4
Gullick, T. J. and Timbs, J. Painting popularly explained. Lond. 1859. 16°. M,3
Gulliver's Travels. J. Swift. Philadelphia, 1867. 12°. . . . . J,1278
The same. London, 1867. 24°. . . . . . . . K,1025
The same. Leipzig, 1844. 16°. . . . . . . . . J,470
Gumprecht, T. E. Zeitschrift für Allgemeine Erdkunde. Berl. 1853–6. 7 v. 8°. E,158
Gunboat Series. H. Castlemon, *pseud.* Cincinnati, 1870. 6 v. 16°. . J,1520

1. Frank, the Young Naturalist.
2. Frank on a Gunboat.
3. Frank in the Woods.
4. Frank on the Prairie.
5. Frank before Vicksburg.
6. Frank on the Lower Mississippi.

Gunn, W. M. Religion and National Instruction. Edinburgh, 1840. 12°. O,1180
Gunning, H. Reminiscences of Cambridge, Eng. London, 1855. 2 v. 8°. B,59
Gunnison, J. W. Memoirs of the Great Salt Lake. Philadelphia, 1852. 12°. C,167
Gunpowder, Memoir on. J. Braddock. Madras, 1829. 8°. . . . N,252,50
Gunpowder Plot. D. Jardine. London, 1835. 16°. . . . . . L,473,2
Gurley, L. B. Memoir of William Gurley. Cincinnati, 1858. 12°. . . C,683
Gurley, R. R. Life of J. Ashmun. New York, 1839. 8°. . . . C,932
Gurlt, A. Fabrication de Fonte au moyen des Gaz. Paris, 1857. 8°. N,252,49
Gurney Married. T. Hook. London, n. d. 16°. . . . . . K,1152
Gurney, J. J. Journey in North America. Norwich, 1841. 8°. . . . V,159
Gurowski, A. G. de. America and Europe. New York, 1857. 12°. . O,489
Diary, 1861–65. Boston and Washington, 1862–66. 2 v. 12°. . B,902
Russia as it is. New York, 1854. 12°. . . . . . . . V,525
Guseck, B. von. Aus Eig'ner Kraft; Hist. Roman. Leip. 1858. 2 v. in 1. 24°. G,283
Deutschlands Ehre, 1813; Historischer Roman. Leipzig, 1864. 16°. G,284
Im Strom der Zeit. Prag, 1860. 4 v. in 2. 24°. . . . . . G,294
Mad. de Brandebourg; Historicher Roman. Wien, 1863. 2 v. in 1. 24°. G,295
Gustavus Adolphus and the Thirty Years' War. B. Chapman. Lond. 1856. 8°. D,760
compared with Epaminondas. C. D. Yonge. London, 1858. 12°. . C,486
Geschichte von. A. F. Gfrörer. Stuttgart, 1837. 8°. . . . . E,113
Life of. J. F. Hollings. London, 1838. 16°. . . . . . . I,624
Gutenberg, J., and the Art of Printing. E. C. Pearson. Boston, 1871. 12°. D,532
Guthrie, F. Elements of Heat. London, 1868. 12°. . . . . . N,39
Guthrie, T. Man and the Gospel. London, 1865. 12°. . . . . . P,263
Gutta Percha; ou, Caoutchouc. A. Adrianni. Utrecht, 1850. 8°. . N,252,50
in seiner Technischen Bedeuting. W. Bohne. Iserlohn, n. d. 16°. N,252,38
Gutzkow, C. Dramatische Werke. Leipzig, 1862–66. 20 v. in 5. 16°. . E,301
Hohenschwangau, Roman und Geschichte. Leipzig, 1867. 5 v. 16°. G,296
Ritter vom Geiste. Leipzig, 1865. 9 v. 16°. . . . . . . G,297
Guy, W. A. Defective Cleansing and Drainage of Towns. Lond. 1846. 8°. N,252,29
Guy Deverell. J. S. Le Fanu. Leipzig, 1865. 2 v. in 1. 16°. . . . J,261
Guy Livingstone. G. A. Lawrence. New York, 1868. 12°. . . . K,762
The same. Leipzig, 1860. 16°. . . . . . . . . J,257

Guy Mannering. Sir. W. Scott. Boston, 1852. 2 v. 16°. . . . . K,937
The same. Philadelphia, n. d. 12°. . . . . . . K,962
The same. Philadelphia, 1869. 8°. . . . . . K,1105
The same. Leipzig, 1846. 16°. . . . . . . . J,442
Guy Rivers. W. G. Simms. New York, 1859. 12°. . . . . . K,253
Guyer, J. D. History of Chicago. Chicago, 1869. 4°. . . . . C,314
Guyon, Mad. de la Mothe, Life of. T. C. Upham. New York, 1855. 12°. D,622
Guyot, A. Common-School Geography. New York, 1867. 4°. . . Q,130
The same. New York, 1870. 4°. . . . . . . . Q,130
Elementary Geography. New York, 1868. 4°. . . . O,1219,1
The same. New York, 1870. 4°. . . . . . . O,1219,1
Earth and Man. Boston, 1855. 12°. . . . . . . V,1138
Intermediate Geography. New York, 1870. 4°. . . . . Q,102
Key to Wall Maps. New York, 1866. . . . . . . . O,903
Primary; or, Introduction to Study of Geography. N. Y. 1867. 4°. O,1219,2
Gwendoline's Harvest. Leipzig, 1870. 16°. . . . . . . . J,191
Gwilt, J. Elements of Architectural Criticism. London, 1837. 8°. . . M,144
Encyclopædia of Architecture. London, 1867. 8°. . . . *M,172
Rudiments of Architecture. London, 1839. 8°. . . . . M,220
Gwynne, T. Nanette and her Lovers. London, 1854. 12°. . . . J,568
School for Dreamers. London, 1853. 12°. . . . . . . . K,716
Silas Barnstarke. London, 1853. 12°. . . . . . . . J,567
Young Singleton. London, 1856. 2 v. 16°. . . . . . . J,569
Gyll, G. W. J. Tractate on Language. London, 1859. 8°. . . . L,528
Gymnastic Exercises, Manual of. S. W. Mason. Boston, 1864. 16°. . O,1151
Gymnastics, Athletic and Gymnastic Exercises. J. A. Howard. Lon. 1860. 16°. M,305
New. D. Lewis. Boston, 1863. 12°. . . . . . . . M,345
Gypsies, Historical Survey of. J. Hoyland. York, 1816. 8°. . . . D,707
Zigeuner in Europa und Asien. A. F. Pott. Halle, 1844–45. 2 v. 8°. G,587
Zincali; the Gypsies of Spain. G. Borrow. London, 1861. 12°. D,705
Gypsies of the Dane's Dyke. G. S. Phillips. Boston, 1864. 12°. . . K,891
Gypsum as a Fertilizer. C. W. Johnson. London, 1842. 8°. . . N,252,25
Gypsy's Breynton Series. E. S. Phelps. Boston, 1869. 4 v. 16°. . J,1235
1. Gypsy Breynton.
2. Gypsy's Cousin Joy.
3. Gypsy's Sowing and Reaping.
4. Gypsy's Year at the Golden Crescent.

H—— Familie. F. Bremer. Leipzig, 1863. 12°. . . . . . . E,313,8
The same; translated. London, 1853. 12°. . . . L,169,4
Habitations of Animals. J. G. Wood. New York, 1866. 8°. . . . N,555
Habits of Good Society. New York, 1868. 12°. . . . . . . . H,472
Hack, M. English Stories of the Olden Time. London, 1839. v. 1. 12°. J,1207
Hackett, H. B. Commentary on Acts. Boston, 1870. 8°. . . . . P,534
Hackländer, F. W. Geheimniss der Stadt. Stuttgart, 1868. 3 v. 16°. . G,306
Künstlerroman. Stuttgart, 1866. 5 v. 12°. . . . . . . G,305
Zwölf Zettel. Stuttgart, 1868. 2 v. 12°. . . . . . . . G,307
Haddon, J. Arithmetic and Key. London, 1862. 2 v. 12°. . . . M,844
Algebra and Key. London, 1855. 2 v. 12°. . . . . . . M,926
Differential Calculus, Examples. London, 1851. 12°. . . . M,927
Haddon Hall, Evenings at. G. Cattermole. London, 1860. p. 8°. . . L,97

Hadermann, J. R., *pseud.* Forgiven at Last. Philadelphia, 1870. 12°. . K,572
Hadley, A. M. Teacher's Miscellany. Cincinnati, 1856. 12°. . . . . O,949
Hävernich, H. A. C. Introduction to the Old Testament. Edinb. 1852. 8°. P,512
Introduction to the Pentateuch. Edinburgh, 1850. 8°. . . . . P,511
Hagen, F. H. von der. Minnesinger. Leipzig, 1838. 4 pts. in 3 v. 8°. . E,308
Hagenbach, K. R. History of Doctrines. Edinburgh, 1850–52. 2 v. 8°. P,590
Hager, J. Elementary Characters of the Chinese. London, 1801. f°. . Q,247
Haidinger, W. Geognostisches Vorkommen der Diamanten. Wien, 1846. 8°. N,253,34
Haig, J. Symbolism; or, Mind—Matter—Language. Edinburgh, 1869. 12°. O,795
Hakewill, J. Elizabethan Architecture. London, 1835. 8°. . . . . M,221
Hakluyt, R. Divers Journeys in Discovery of America. Lond. 1850. 8°. V,994
Hakluyt Society, Publications of. v. 1–22. London, 1847–57. 8°. viz.:
Benzoni, G. History of the New World. . . . . . . V,979
Coats, W. Geography of Hudson's Bay, 1727–51. . . . . V,993
Columbus, C. Select Letters; translated by R. H. Major. . . . V,991
Drake, Sir F. The World Encompassed. . . . . . V,987
Hakluyt, R. Divers Voyages touching the Discovery of America. . V,994
Hawkins, Sir R. Observations in his Voyage into the South Sea, 1593. . V,995
Heberstein, Baron S. von. Notes upon Russia. . . . . V,978
India in the Fifteenth Century. . . . . . . . V,986
Japan, Memorials of the Empire of. . . . . . . V,982
Maynarde, T. Sir Francis Drake his voyage. . . . . V,992
Mendoza, J. G. de. Historie the Kingdome of China. 2 v. . . V,980
Middleton, Sir H. Voyage to Bantam and the Maluco Islands. . . V,996
Orleans, P. J. 'd. History of the two Tarter Conquerors of China. . V,997
Raleigh, Sir W. Discovery of the Empire of Guiana. . . . V,981
Rundall, T. Voyages in Search of a Passage to India, 1496–1631. . . V,983
Russia at the Close of the Sixteenth Century. . . . . . V,989
Soto, H. de. Discovery and Conquest of Terra Florida. . . . V,988
Spitzenbergen and Greenland, Documents on. . . . . . V,984
Strachey, W. Travaile into Virginia Britannica. . . . . V,985
Veer, G. de. Three Voyages by the North-East toward Cathay and China. V,990
Haldane, A. Lives of R. and J. A. Haldane. New York, 1853. 8°. C,1308
Hale, D., Memoir of. J. P. Thompson. New York, 1850. 12°. . . C,709
Hale, E. E. If, Yes, and Perhaps. Boston, 1868. 16°. . . . . H,32
Ingham Papers. Boston, 1869. 16°. . . . . . . . . H,33
Sybaris, and other Homes. Boston, 1869. 12°. . . . . . H,122
Ten times One is Ten. Boston, 1871. 16°. . . . . . . J,627
Hale, H. Ethnography and Philology of U. S. Explor. Exped. Phil. 1846. 4°. *Q,281
Hale, S. History of the United States. New York, 1840. 2 v. 18°. . L,417
Hale, S. J. Dictionary of Poetical Quotations. Philadelphia, 1866. 8°. *I,163
Flora's Interpreter. Boston, 1854. 12°. . . . . . . . N,941
Liberia; or, Mr. Peyton's Experiments. New York, 1853. 12°. . K,129
Manners. Boston, 1868. 8°. . . . . . . . . . . H,295
Woman's Record. Sketches of Distinguished Women. N. Y. 1855. 8°. *C,583
Hale, W. H. History of the Jews. London, 1854. 8°. . . . . . A,202
Half a Million of Money. A. B. Edwards. New York, 1866. 8°. . . K,680
The same. Leipzig, 1865. 2 v. in 1. 16°. . . . . . J,157
Half Century; Changes from 1800 to 1850. E. Davis. Boston, 1851. 12°. B,695
Half-Hours with the Best Authors. C. Knight. New York, 1867. 6 v. 12°. H,455
The same. London, n. d. 2 v. in 1. 8°. . . . . . H,456
The same. Philadelphia, 1869. 3 v. . . . . . . H,457
Half-Hours with the Best Letter-Writers. C. Knight. London, 1867. 8°. H,454
Half-hours with the Stars. R. A. Proctor. London, 1870. 4°. . . . N,388

Haliburton, T. C. Attaché, The. London, 1843. 2 v. 12°. . . . . K,713
Bubbles of Canada. London, 1839. 8°. . . . . . . . C,335
Historical Account of Nova Scotia. Halifax, 1829. 2 v. 8°. . . C,336
Nature and Human Nature. London, 1859. 12°. . . . . . J,572
Rule and Misrule of the English in America. New York, 1851. 12°. B,163
Sam Slick, the Clockmaker. Philadelphia, n. d. 12°. . . . K,714
Sam Slick's Wise Saws. London, 1859. 12°. . . . . . . K,130
Hall, A., against Universalism, Review of. J. H. Jordan. Indianap. 1848. 16°. P,867
Hall, A. M. Pilgrimages to English Shrines. London, 1853. 8°. . C,1233
Outlaw; an Historical Romance. London, 1847. 16°. . . . K,717
Sketches of Irish Character. London, 1842. r. 8°. . . . . . K,586
Hall, A. O. Manhattaner in New Orleans. New York, 1851. 12°. . . V,29
Hall, B. Patchwork. London, 1841. 3 v. 12°. . . . . . . V,376
Travels in North America. Edinburgh, 1829. 3 v. 8°. . . . V,160
Schloss Hainfeld; or, a Winter in Styria. London, 1836. 12°. . V,406
Voyage to Chili, Peru, and Mexico. Edinburgh, 1826–27. 2 v. 16°. I,492,2,3
Voyage to Loo-Choo and the Eastern Seas. Edinb. 1826–27. 16°. I,492,1
Hall, B. H. History of Eastern Vermont. New York, 1858. 8°. . . C,29
Hall, C. F. Arctic Researches. New York, 1866. 8°. . . . . . V,183
Hall, E. History of England. London, 1809. 4°. . . . . . . F,159
Hall, E. Puritans and their Principles. New York, 1846. 8°. . . C,9
Hall, E. B. Memoir of Mary L. Ware. Boston, 1853. 12°. . . . C,976
Hall, E. H. Hand-Book of American Travel. New York, 1869. 8°. . V,119
Hall, F. Travels in Canada and United States. London, 1818. 8°. . V,179
Hall, F. Life of Maximilian, Emperor of Mexico. N. Y. 1868. 12°. . D,507
Hall, G. J. Sought and Saved; Ragged Schools. London, 1855. 8°. O,1141
Hall, Judge James. Legends of the West. New York, 1854. 12°. . . C,142
Letters from the West. London, 1828. 8°. . . . . . . V,85
Life of Thomas Posey. Boston. 16°. . . . . . . C,860,19
Romance of Western History. Cincinnati, 1857. 12°. . . . C,143
Sketches of the West. Philadelphia, 1835. 2 v. 12°. . . . V,5
Statistics of the West. Cincinnati, 1837. 12°. . . . . . V,6
The West; its Soil, Surface, and Products. Cincinnati, 1848. 12°. . V,10
Western Reader. Cincinnati, 1833. 12°. . . . . . . . O,877
Hall, Prof. James. Geology of New York. Albany, 1843. 4°. . . . *Q,101,12
Palæontology of New York. Albany, 1847–52. 2 v. 4°. . *Q,101,13,14
and Whitney. Geologogical Survey of Iowa. n. p. 1858. 2 v. 8°. N,896
Hall, John. Hist. of Presbyterian Church in Trenton, N. J. N. Y. 1859. 12°. C,88
Hall, John. Papers for Home Reading. New York, 1871. 12°. . . H,224
Hall, Joseph. Satires, and other Poems. London, 1838. 8°. . . . J,861
Hall, J. B. The Little Book Open. Cincinnati, 1869. 16°. . . . I,28
Hall, J. C. Facts of the Animal Kingdom. London, 1841. 8°. . . N,445
Hall, M. Queens of England before the Conquest. Philadelphia, 1854. 12°. C,1249
The same. London, 1854. 2 v. 8°. . . . . . C,1250
The same. Boston, n. d. 8°. . . . . . . . . D,368,7
Royal Princesses of England. London, 1858. 12°. . . . . . D,437
Hall, N. From Liverpool to St. Louis. London, 1870. 12°. . . . V,23
Sermons. New York, 1868. 12°. . . . . . . . . P,670
Hall, R. Miscellaneous Works; with Memoir. London, 1849. p. 8°. . L.193
Works. New York, 1854. 4 v. 8°. . . . . . . . . . P,734

Hall, S. C. Book of British Ballads. London, 1853. 4°. . . . . . J,884
and Mrs. S. C. Ireland; its Scenery, etc. Lond. 1841–43. 3 v. 8°. V,274
Hall, Mrs. S. C. Lights and Shadows of Irish Life. Lond. 1838. 3 v. 12°. J,574
Can Wrong be Right? Leipzig, 1868. 16°. . . . . . . J,196
Hall, S. R. Instructor's Manual. Boston, 1852. 18°. . . . O,1111
Hall, W. W. Consumption. New York, 1857. 12°. . . . . . L,910
Fun better than Physic. Springfield, 1871. 12°. . . . . L,959
Health by good Living. New York, 1870. 12°. . . . . L,902
Sleep; or, the Hygiene of Night. New York, 1870. 12°. . . L,891
Hallam, A. H. Remains in Verse and Prose. London, 1863. 12°. . . H,553
Hallam, H. Constitutional History of England. New York, 1847. 8°. . B,55
The same. Boston, 1854. 3 v. 8°. . . . . . . B,50
Literature of Europe, 15th to 17th Centuries. N. Y. 1851. 2 v. 8°. H,739
The same. Boston, 1854. 3 v. 8°. . . . . . . H,738
State of Europe during the Middle Ages. New York, 1867. 3 v. 12°. A,229
The same. Boston, 1853. 3 v. 8°. . . . . . . . A,243
The same. New York, 1854. 8°. . . . . . . . A,244
Halle, J. Abusers of Chyrurgerie and Physyke. London, 1844. 12°. L,606,11
Halleck, F. G. Fanny, and other Poems. New York, 1846. 12°. . . I,47
Life and Letters of. J. G. Wilson. New York, 1869. 12°. . . C,924
Poetical Works. New York, 1859. 12°. . . . . . . . I,40
Poetical Writings, and Extracts from J. R. Drake. N. Y. 1869. 12°. I,41
Selections from the British Poets. New York, 1854. 2 v. 18°. . L,415
Halleck, H. W. Elements of Military Art and Science. N. Y. 1863. 12°. M,763
International Law and Laws of War. Philadelphia, 1866. 12°. . U,538
Haller, A. von. Primæ Lineæ Physiologiæ. Gottingæ, 1751. 16°. . . L,839
Halleur, G. C. H. and Schubert. Art of Photography. London, 1854. 12°. M,928
Hallier, E. Nordseestudien. Hamburg, 1863. 12°. . . . . . . G,681
Halliwell, J. O. Descriptive Notices of English Histories. Lond. 1848. 12°. L,606,23
Dictionary of Archaic and Provincial Words. London, 1855. 2 v. 8°. L.R.
Life of Shakespeare. London, 1848. 8°. . . . . . . C,1254
Notes of Family Excursions in North Wales. London, 1860. 4°. . V,329
Notices of Fugitive Tracts and Chap-Books. London, 1849. 12°. L,606,29
Hallock, J., Life of. C. Yale. New York, n. d. 12°. . . . . C,733
Hallock, W. A. Memoir of Harlan Page. New York, n. d. 18°. . P,746,23
Hallucinations. A. B. De Boismont. Philadelphia, 1853. 8°. . . . O,693
Halpin, N. J. Oberon's Vision. London, 1843. 8°. . . . . . I,885,16
Halpine, C. G. Adventures of Private Miles O'Reilly. New York, 1866. 12°. H,72
Baked Meats of the Funeral. New York, 1866. 12°. . . . H,75
Poetical Works. New York, 1869. 12°. . . . . . . . I,46
Halse, W. H. Medical Galvanism. London, n. d. 16°. . . . N,252,36
Halsey, L. Memoirs of J. F. Oberlin. London, 1857. 16°. . . . D,589
Halsey. L. J. Memoirs of Lewis W. Green. New York, 1871. 12°. . C,874
Halstead, M. Political Caucuses of 1860. Columbus, 1860. 8°. . . O,526
Halsted, C. A. Life of Margaret Beaufort. London, 1845. 8°. . . D,278
Richard III. as Duke and King. Philadelphia, 1844. 8°. . .
Haltaus, C. Geshichte Roms, im Punischen Kriege. Leipzig, 1846. 8°. E,17
Hamburg, Zoölogischer Garten. Brehm und Zimmermann. Hamb. 1865. 8°. G,932
Hamel, E. Histoire de A. L. L. Saint-Just. Bruxelles, n. d. 2 v. 12°. H,1029
Hamersly, L. R. Living Officers of the U. S. Navy. Philadelphia, 1870. 8°. C,753

Hamerton, P. G. Thoughts about Art. Boston, 1871. 12°. . . . . M,32
Etching and Etchers. London, 1868. 8°. . . . . . . M,121
Hamilton, A. Hamilton Club Series. New York, 1865-66. 3 v. 8°. . B,812
1. Williams, J. Life of Alexander Hamilton.
2. Hamilton, A. Observations on Certain Documents.
4. Callender, T. Letters to Alexander Hamilton.
Life and Times of. S. M. Schmucker. Philadelphia, 1856. 12°. . C,694
Works. New York, 1851. 7 v. 8°. . . . . . . . U,105
and Jay. Lives of. J. Renwick. New York, 1854. 18°. . . L,423
and others. The Federalist. Hallowell, 1828. 8°. . . . . O,505
The same, v. 1; edited by H. B. Dawson. N. Y. 1864. 18°. . O,528
Hamilton, A., *Comte.* Mémoires du Chevalier de Grammont. Paris, 1851. 12°. D,608
Hamilton, E. Cottagers of Glenburnie. Edinburgh, 1808. 8°. . . K,718
Letters of a Hindoo Rajah. London, 1811. 2 v. 12°. . . . H,830
Letters on Education. Boston, 1825. 2 v. 12°. . . . O,1195
The same. Alexandria, 1803. 2 v. 12°. . . . O,1019
Life of Agrippina, wife of Germanicus. London, 1811. 2 v. 8°. D,762
Hamilton, Gail, *pseud.* See *Dodge, M. A.*
Hamilton, J. Wanderings in North Africa. London, 1856. 12°. . . V,813
Hamilton, J. A. Reminiscences. New York, 1869. 8°. . . . . C,778
Hamilton, J. C. History of the Republic of the U. S. N. Y. 1858-65. 7 v. 8°. B,651
Hamilton, L. Memoirs and Speeches of R. Rantoul, jr. Boston, 1854. 8°. C,1102
Hamilton, N. E. S. A. Inquiry into Collier's Shakespeare, 1632. Lond. 1860. 4°. I,869
Hamilton, R. Amphibious Carnivora. Edinburgh, 1839. 16°. . N,470,25
Whales. Edinburgh, 1853. 16°. . . . . . . . N,470,26
Hamilton, R. W. Institutions of Popular Education. Leeds, 1846. 8°. O,1035
Hamilton, S. History of the United States Flag. Philadelphia, 1852. 12°. B,849
Hamilton, T. Men and Manners in America. Philadelphia, 1833. 8°. . V,79
Hamilton, W. Description of Hindostan. London, 1820. 2 v. 4°. . . V,720
Hamilton, Sir W. Engravings from Ancient Vases. Naples, 1791-95. 3 v. f°. L.R.
Observations on Vesuvius and other Volcanoes. London, 1773. 12°. V,1108
Hamilton, Sir W. An Analysis. J. H. Stirling. London, 1865. 8°. . O,684
Discussions in Philosophy and Literature. New York, 1853. 8°. . O,705
Lectures on Metaphysics and Logic. Boston, 1859-67. 2 v. 8°. . O,704
Philosophy of; edited by O. W. Wight. New York, 1854. 8°. . O,663
Hamilton, Sir W. R. Elements of Quaternions. London, 1866. 8°. M,1155
Lectures on Quaternions. Dublin, 1853. 8°. . . . . . M,1161
Hamiltons, The. C. Berkley. New York, 1856. 18°. . . . . J,1193
Hamlet; Roman. A. E. Brachvogel. Breslau, 1867. 3 v. 16°. . . G,264
Hamlin, A. C. Martyria; or, Andersonville Prison. Boston, 1866. 12°. B,895
Hamlin, H. A. L., Memorials of. M. W. Lawrence. Boston, 1854. 12°. . C,788
Hamm, W. Illustriter Katalog der Londoner Industrie Ausstellung. Leipzig, 1863-64. 2 v. 4°. . . . . . . . . . . *F,175
Hammer and Anvil. F. Spielhagen. New York, 1870. 12°. . . . G,217
Hammer and Rapier. J. E. Cooke. New York, 1870. 12°. . . . J,633
Hammer-Purgstall, J. von. Geschichte des Osmanischen Reiches. Pest, 1827-35. 10 v. 8°. . . . . . . . . . . . . E,119
Hammerschmied, J. Rundschau in der Naturwissenschaft. Wein, 1863. 8°. G,682
Hammond, J. Love Elegies. n. t. p. 12°. . . . . . . . I,325
Hammond, J. B. Political Parties in New York. Cooperstown, 1846. 2 v. 8°. C,92
Hammond, M. Life of John Cardinal de Cheverus. Philadelphia, 1839. 12°. D,642

Hammond, S. H. and Mansfield. Country Margins. New York, 1855. 12°. H,34
Wild Northern Scenes. Philadelphia, 1869. 12°. . . . . . J,1503
Hammond, W. A. Physics and Physiology of Spiritualism. N. Y. 1871. 12°. O,340
Hampden, J., Memorials of. G. N. T. Grenvill. London, 1860. p. 8°. . L,269
Hampden, R. D. Lectures on Moral Philosophy. London, 1856. 8°. . O,721
Hamst, O., *pseud.* See *Thomas, R.*
Hanaford, P. A. Life of George Peabody. Boston, 1870. 12°. . . . C,923
Hance, W. Address before the Botanic Society. Columbus, 1830. 4°. H,302,4
Hancock, A. British Nudibranchiate Mollusca. Lond. 1845–55. pts. 1–7. 8°. Q,67
Hand and Glove. A. B. Edwards. New York, 1866. 8°. . . . . K,685
The same. Leipzig, 1865. 16°. . . . . . . . . J,158
Hand, The; its Mechanism, etc. Sir C. Bell. London, 1870. p. 8°. . L,311
Hand und Fuss. J. C. G. Lucae. Frankfurt-a-Main, 1865. 4°. . . . E,481
Hand-Book of American Literature. Philadelphia, n. d. 18°. . . H,659
of Anglo-Saxon derivatives. New York, 1855. 12°. . . . . L,542
of Anglo-Saxon root-words. New York, 1857. 12°. . . . . L,541
of Domestic Medicine. London, 1855. 12°. . . . . . . L,291
of engrafted English Words. New York, 1854. 12°. . . . . L,543
Handel, G. F., Leben von. F. Chrysander. Leipzig, 1858–60. 2 v. 8°. . E,240
Life of. V. Schœler. New York, 1857. 12°. . . . . . . D,508
Oratorios; edited by V. Novello. London, n. d. 4 v. 8°. . . M,420
1. Israel in Egypt; The Messiah; Judas Maccabæus.
2. Joshua; Jeptha; Samson.
3. Saul; Solomon; Deborah.
4. Alexander's Feast; Te Deum; Coronation Anthem.

Handelman, H. Geschichte der Insel Hayti. Kiel, 1856. 8°. . . E,123
Geschichte der Amerikanischen Kolonisation. Kiel, 1856. 8°. . E,123
Handrailing, Treatise on. L. Reynolds. New Orleans, 1849. 8°. . . M,193
Handy Andy; Tale of Irish Life. S. Lover. London, n. d. 12°. . . K,799
Hanley, S. British Mollusca and their Shells. London, 1853. 4 v. 8°. N,716
Hanmar, N. Chronicle of Ireland till 1284. Dublin, 1809. 4°. . B,182,2
The same. Dublin, 1809. 4°. . . . . . . . A,565,2
Chronographie. London, 1607. 4°. . . . . . . . . . P,647
Hanmer, Sir T. Corresp. and Memoir; ed. by H. Bunbury. Lond. 1838. 8°. D,387
Hann, J. Elements of Plane and Spherical Trigonometry. Lond. 1854. 12°. M,930
Examples on the Integral Calculus. London, 1850. 12°. . . . M,929
Theoretical and Practical Mechanics. London, 1848. 8°. . . N,130
Treatise on Analytical Geometry. London, 1850. 12°. . . . M,845
Hanna, W. Life and Writings of Thomas Chalmers. N. Y. 1851–2. 4 v. 12°. D,230
Life of Christ. New York, n. d. 8°. . . . . . . . . . P,381
Hannaford, E. Story of the Sixth Ohio Regiment. Cincinnati, 1868. 8°. . B,960
Hannah Thurston. B. Taylor. New York, 1866. 12°. . . . . . K,304
Hannah's Triumph. M. A. Denison. Philadelphia, 1870. 16°. . . J,1705
Hannay, J. Satire and Satirists. New York, 1855. 12°. . . . . H,641
Hannibal, History of. J. Abbott. New York, 1868. 16°. . . . . J,1402
Life of. T. Arnold. New York, 1865. 16°. . . . . . . D,747
Passage of the Alps. H. L. Wickham and Cramer. London, 1828. 8°. A,159
Hannover, Notizblatt des Gewerbe-Vereins für. Hannover, 1847. 4°. N,252,53
Hanover, Mass., History of. J. S. Barry. Boston, 1853. 8°. . . . C,72
Hansard, T. C. History and Process of Printing. Columbus, 1861. 8°. . M,622
Parliamentary History of England to 1803. Lond. 1806–20. 36 v. 8°. B,76

Hans Breitman's Ballads. C. G. Leland. Philadelphia, 1869. 8°. . . . I,98
Hans Brinker; or, The Silver Skates. M. E. Dodge. New York, 1869. 12°. J,1341
Hanslick, E. Vom Musikalischen Schönen. Leipzig, 1865. 16°. . . . G,641
Hanson, J. H. The Lost Prince. New York, 1854. 12°. . . . . . D,575
Hanson, J. W. History of Massachusetts Sixth Regiment. Boston, 1866. 12°. B,912
Hanstein, J. Bau und Entwickelung der Baumrinde. Berlin, 1853. 8°. . G,872
Haps and Mishaps in the Brown Family. W. A. Boardman. Phil. 1870. 16°. J,1708
Harbaugh, H. Poems. Philadelphia, 1860. 12°. . . . . . . . I,29
Hard Cash. C. Reade. Boston, 1869. 16°. . . . . . . . K,904
The same. Leipzig, 1864. 3 v. 16°. . . . . . . J,418
Hard Times. C. Dickens. New York, 1868. 12°. . . . . . . V,499
The same. New York, 1871. 12°. . . . . K,1132
The same. Leipzig, 1854. 16°. . . . . . . . J,122
Harding, J. D. Elementary Art. London, n. d. 4°. . . . . . *Q,213
Lessons on Trees. London, n. d. 4°. . . . . . . *Q,212
Principles and Practice of Art. London, 1845. 4°. . . . . *Q,211
Hardware District of Birmingham; edited by S. Timmins. Lond. 1866. 8°. O,580
Hardwicke, Earl of. See *Yorke, P.*
Hardy, T. D. Materials for British History. London, 1862–65. 3 v. 8°. W,176
Memoirs of Henry, *Lord* Langdale. London, 1852. 2 v. 8°. . . D,130
Hardyng, J. and Grafton, R. Chronicles of English History. Lond. 1812. 4°. F,160
Hare, J. C. and A. W. Guesses at Truth. Boston, 1865. 12°. . . . H,124
Harem Life in Egypt and Constantinople. E. Lott. Lond. 1866. 2 v. 12°. V,788
Harford, J. S. Life of Michael Angelo Buonarroti. London, 1858. 2 v. 8°. D,761
Harland, Marion, *pseud.* See *Terhune, M. V.*
Harleian Miscellany; collection of Scarce Tracts. Lond. 1808–11. 12 v. 8°. F,254
Harley, A. J. Young Crusoe. Boston, n. d. 16°. . . . . . . J,1477
Harman, T. Caveat; Warening for Common Cursetors, 1567. Lond. 1869. 8°. L,604,9
Harmonies of Nature. G. Hartwig. London, 1866. 8°. . . . . . N,536
Harmony and Contrast of Colours. M. E. Chevreul. London, 1859. 12°. L,287
Rudiments of. J. F. Burrowes. Philadelphia, n. d. 12°. . . . M,403
Treatise on. C. S. Catel. London, 1854. 8°. . . . . . M,421,1
Harmony of Birds; a Poem. London, 1843. 12°. . . . . . L,606,7
Harold, the last of the Saxon Kings. Sir E. B. Lytton. Phila. 1868. 12°. K,814
The same. Leipzig, 1848. 2 v. in 1. 16°. . . . . . J,314
Harper's Gazetteer of the World. J. C. Smith. New York, 1855. r. 8°. . L.R.
Harper's Hand-Book for Europe and the East. New York, 1862. 12°. V,1053
Harper's New Monthly Magazine. New York, 1850–70. 41 v. 8°. . . S,3
Harper's Pictorial History of the Rebellion. New York, 1866–68. 2 v. f°. *Q,228
Harper's Story Books. J. Abbott. New York, 1870. 12 v. 12°. . . J,1629

Vol. 1. Bruno; Willie and the Mortgage; Strait Gate.
2. Little Louvre; Frank; Emma.
3. Virginia; Timboo and Joliba; Timboo and Fanny.
4. Harper Establishment; Franklin; The Studio.
5. Story of Ancient History; English History; American History.
6. John True; Elfred; Museum.
7. Engineer; Rambles Among the Alps; Three Gold Dollars.
8. Gibraltar Gallery; Alcove; Dialogues.
9. The Great Elm; Aunt Margaret; Vernon.
10. Carl and Jocko; Lapstone; Orkney.
11. Judge Justin; Minigo; Jasper.
12. Congo; Viola; Little Paul.

Harper, R. D. Memorials of United Presby. Church. Columbus, 1858. 8°. P,277
Harper, R. G. Select Works. Baltimore, 1841. 8°. . . . . . . H,797

Harrington. M. Edgeworth. New York, 1859. 12°. . . . . . K,678,9
Harrington, J. Oceana, and other Works. London, 1771. 4°. . . . . Q,302
Harris, C. A. Principles and Practice of Dental Surgery. Phila. 1858. 8°. L,1008
Harriet and Ellen. Cincinnati, 1856. 18°. . . . . . . . . . J,1460
Harris, J. Hermes; an Inquiry concerning Grammar. London, 1806. 8°. L,524
Works. London, 1801. 2 v. 4°. . . . . . . . . Q249,1,2
Harris, J. Mammon. New York, n. d. 18°. . . . . . . P,746,20
Man Primeval. Boston, 1854. 12°. . . . . . . . . . P,274
The Pre-Adamite Earth. Boston, 1856. 12°. . . . . . . P,275
Harris, J. J. H. The Schoolroom. London, 1842–48. 8°. . . . O,1251,3
Harris, T. M. Memorials of James Oglethorpe. Boston, 1841. 8°. . . D,301
Tour into the North-West Territory. Boston, 1805. 8°. . . . . V,65
Harris, T. W. Insects of New England injurious to Vegetation. Bost. 1852. 8°. O,36
The same; edited by C. L. Flint. Boston, 1863. 8°. . . . O,35
Harris, W. Life and Writings of James I. London, 1753. 8°. . . . D,32
Life and Writings of Charles I. London, 1772. 8°. . . . . . D,31
Lives of James I., Charles I., Cromwell, and Charles II. Lon. 1814. 5 v. 8°. D,393
Harris, W. C. Highlands of Æthiopia. London, 1844. 3 v. 8°. . . V,838
Harris, W. S. Electricity. London, 1854. 12°. . . . . . . . M,932
Galvanism, Animal and Voltaic Electricity. London, 1856. 12°. . M,931
Magnetism. London, 1850. 12°. . . . . . . . . M,933
Rudimentary Electricity. London, 1848. 16°. . . . . . N,252,36
Treatise on Frictional Electricity. London, 1867. 8°. . . . . N,54
Harrison, G. Treatise on the Greek Prepositions. Philadelphia, 1858. 8°. L,743
Harrison, J. P. Address on Professional Earnestness. Cincinnati, 1849. 8°. H,302,4
Harrison, M. Progress and Structure of English Language. Phila. 1850. 12°. L,568
Harrison, W. H., Civil and Military Services of. M. Dawson. Cin. 1824. 8°. C,797
Letter on the Battle of Tippecanoe. Cincinnati, 1840. 8°. . . . C,797
Eulogy on. E. D. Mansfield. Cincinnati, 1841. 8°. . . . H,302,4
Life of. H. Montgomery. Cleveland, 1852. 12°. . . . . . C,801
Sketches of. C. S. Todd and B. Drake. Cincinnati, 1847. 18°. . C,831
Harry and Lucy. M. Edgeworth. London, 1858. 16°. . . . . . J,1485
Harry Coverdale's Courtship and Marriage. F. E. Smedley. Phil. n. d. 12°. K,1014
Harry Lorrequer. C. Lever. London, n. d. 8°. . . . . . . K,776
The same. Leipzig, 1847. 2 v in 1. 16°. . . . . . J,277
Harry's Vacation. W. C. Richards. New York, 1864. 16°. . . . J,1557
Harsha, D. A. Life of James Hervey. Albany, 1865. 8°. . . . . D,100
Life of Charles Sumner. New York, 1856. 12°. . . . . . C,975
Hart, A. M. History of the Mississippi Valley. Cincinnati, 1853. 12°. . C,230
Hart, J. Orthography, 1569. London, 1850. 18°. . . . . . . L,666
Hart, J. C. Designs for Parish Churches. New York, 1857. 8°. . . M,229
Hart, J. S. Epitome of Greek and Roman Mythology. Phila. 1853. 12°. . P,914
Essay on Life and Writings of E. Spenser. New York, 1847. 8°. . H,708
In the School-Room. Philadelphia, 1868. 12°. . . . . . O,973
Harte, F. B. Condensed Novels. New York, 1867. 12°. . . . . . K,131
Luck of Roaring Camp, etc. Boston, 1870. 16°. . . . . . H,64
Poems. Boston, 1871. 12°. . . . . . . . . . . I,174
Hartford Convention, History of. T. Dwight. New York, 1833. 8°. . C,76
Hartig, G. L. von. Late Austrian Revolution. London, 1853. p. 8°. . L,177,4
Harting, P. Die Macht des Kleinen. Leipzig, 1851. 8°. . . . . . G,833

Hartley, C. B. Hunting Sports in the West. Philadelphia, n. d. 16°. . J,1608
Lives of H. Lee and T. Sumter. Philadelphia, 1859. 12°. . . C,552
Life of Daniel Boone. Philadelphia, 1865. 12°. . . . . J,1234
Hartley, D. Observations on Man. London, 1791. 3 v. 8°. . . . N,418
The same. London, 1801. 3 v. 8°. . . . . . . O,732
Hartley, J. Greece and the Levant. London, 1833. 12°. . . . . V,568
Hartwig, G. Harmonies of Nature. London, 1866. 8°. . . . . N,536
Leben des Meeres. Frankfurt-a-Main, 1857. 8°. . . . . G,815
Polar World; a Popular Description. New York, 1869. 8°. . . V,958
Sea and its Living Wonders. London, 1866. 8°. . . . . N,537
Tropical World. London, 1863. 8°. . . . . . . . . N,538
Harvard College, Annals of Astronomical Observatory, v. 5. G. P. Bond. Cambridge, 1867. 4°. . . . . . . . . . Q,106
History of. J. Quincy. Boston, 1860. 2 v. 8°. . . . . O,809
Memorial Biographies. Cambridge, 1867. 2 v. 8°. . . . C,1015
Necrology of Alumni, 1851–63. J. Palmer. Boston, 1864. 8°. . O,806
Harvey, P. Food and Climate. Zanesville, 1849. 12°. . . . . L,906
Harvey, W. Rheumatism, Gout, and Neuralgia. London, 1852. 8°. . L,923
Harvey, W. H. Algæ of the Southern Ocean. London, 1847–49. 8°. N,1041
British Marine Algæ. London, 1849. 8°. . . . . . . N,1005
History of British Sea-Weeds. London, 1846–51. 3 v. 8°. . N,1030
Sea-Side Book. London, 1857. 16°. . . . . . . N,474
Harz Mountains, Wanderung durch. W. Blumenhagen. Leip. n. d. 12°. E,183
Hase, C. History of the Christian Church. New York, 1855. 8°. . . P,591
Hassall, A. H. Adulterations detected. London, 1857. 8°. . . . L,905
Microscopic Anatomy of the Human Body. N. Y. 1851. 2 v. 8°. L,973
Hassard, J. R. Life of Archbishop John Hughes. New York, 1866. 8°. . C,963
Hassaurek, F. Four Years among Spanish-Americans. N. Y. 1867. 8°. . V,287
Hassler, F. R. Elements of Analytic Trigonometry. New York, 1826. 8°. M,1157
Haste and Waste. W. T. Adams. Boston, 1868. 16°. . . . J,1467,6
Hastings, T. Dissertation on Musical Taste. New York, 1853. 12°. . M,405
Hastings, W., Memoirs of. G. R. Gleig. London, 1841. 3 v. 8°. . . D,116
Hatfield, R. G. American House-Carpenter. New York, 1857. 8°. . . M,206
Hatfield, T. de. Possessions of the See of Durham. London, 1857. 8°. F,126,32
Hatherell, J. W. Repentance of David. London, 1847. 12°. . . . P,254
Hatsell, J. Precedents in the House of Commons. Lond. 1818. 4 v. 4°. Q,343
Hatton, Sir Christopher, Memoirs of. Sir H. Nicolas. London, 1847. 8°. D,62
Hauff, W. Arabian Days' Entertainments. Boston, 1868. 12°. . . J,1343
Sämmtliche Werke. Stuttgart, 1865–66. 5 v. 24°. . . . . E,329

Bd. 1. Hauff's Leben; Gedichte; Novellen: Vertrauliches Schreiben an Spöttlich; Jud Süss; Die Bettlerin von Pont des Arts; Die Sängerin; Die letzten Ritter von Marienburg.
2. Mittheilungen aus den Memoiren des Satan; Das Bild des Kaisers.
3. Othello; Der Mann im Monde; Controverspredigt über H. Clauren und den Mann in Mond; Phantasien im Bremer Rathskeller.
3. Mährchen für Söhne und Töchter gebildeter Stände; Skizzen: Die Bücher und die Lesewelt; Freie Stunden am Fenster; Der ästhetische Club; Ein Paar Reisestunden.
5. Lichtenstein, romantische Sage.

Haunted, and the Haunters. Sir E. B. Lytton. Phil. 1865. 2 v. 12°. K,829,2
Haunted Hearts. M. S. Cummins. Boston, 1864. 12°. . . . . K,89
Haunted Homestead. E. D. E. N. Southworth. Philadelphia, 1870. 12°. K,427
Haunted Man, and Battle of Life. C. Dickens. Leipzig, 1856. 16°. . J,115

Haupt, H. General Theory of Bridge Construction. New York, 1853. 8°. M,701
Haus, Das. F. Bremer. Leipzig, 1864. 2 v. 12°. . . . . . E,313,2,3
Havelock, Sir H., Biographical Sketch of. W. Brock. Leipzig, 1858. 16°. J,47
Memoirs of. J. C. Marshman. London, 1860. 8°. . . . . . D,468
Persian Campaign. G. H. Hunt. London, 1858. 12°. . . . V,629
Havelok the Dane, Lay of. London, 1868. 8°. . . . . . . L,604,4
Haven, A. B. Cousin Alice's Stories. New York, 1867. 8 v. 16°. viz.:
All's not Gold that Glitters. . . . . . . . . . J,1330
Contentment better than Wealth. . . . . . . . J,1328
No such Word as Fail. . . . . . . . . . . J,1327
Nothing Venture, Nothing Have. . . . . . . . J,1331
Out of Debt, Out of Danger. . . . . . . . . J,1332
Patient Waiting no Loss. . . . . . . . . . J,1329
Place for Everything. . . . . . . . . . . J,1333
Where There's a Will, There's a Way. . . . . . . J,1334
Memoir of. New York, 1868. 12°. . . . . . . . . C,734
The Coopers; or, Getting under Way. New York, 1866. 12°. . K,119
Haven, G. Pilgrim's Wallet; Travels in Europe. New York, 1866. 16°. V,316
Haven, J. Mental Philosophy. Boston, 1863. 12°. . . . . . . O,659
Studies in Philosophy and Theology. Andover, 1869. 12°. . . O,678
Hawaii; Past, Present, and Future. M. Hopkins. New York, 1869. 8°. . V,884
Tour Through. W. Ellis. London, 1827. 8°. . . . . . . V,885
Hawaiian Islands. R. Anderson. Boston, 1865. 8°. . . . . . . V,883
H. W. Baxley. New York, 1865. 8°. . . . . . . V,127
Haweis, T. History of the Church of Christ. London, 1847. 4 v. 12°. . P,574
Hawes, G. W. Ohio State Gazetteer. Cincinnati, 1859–60. 8°. . . . L.R.
Hawes, J. Life of Normand Smith. New York, n. d. 16°. . . P,746,23
Tribute to the Memory of the Pilgrims. Hartford, 1830. 12°. . P,839
Vindication of Congreg. Churches of New England. Hartf. 1830. 12°. P,839
Hawes, S. New-Testament Manual. Boston, 1871. 16°. . . . . P,184
Hawes, S. Pastime of Pleasure. London, 1845. 12°. . . . . L,606,18
Hawkesworth, J. Almoran and Hamet. London, 1820. 12°. . . . K,537
Hawkins, B. W. Artistic Anatomy of the Horse. London, 1866. 8°. . M,347
Hawkins, F. V. Partial Ascent of the Matterhorn. London, 1861. 8°. V,1086,1
Hawkins, J. General History of Music. London, 1853. 3 v. 8°. . . M,415
Hawkins, J. H. W., Life of. G. W. Hawkins. Boston, 1863. 12°. . . C,696
Hawkins, Sir R. Observations in the South Sea, 1593. Lond. 1847. 8°. . V,995
Hawkins, W. G. Life of John H. W. Hawkins. Boston, 1863. 12°. . . . C,696
Hawks, F. L. Narrative of the United States Japan Expedition, commanded by Com. Perry, 1852–54. Washington, 1856. 4°. . Q,413,1
Mountains of Egypt. New York, 1850. 8°. . . . . . . . V,797
Haworth, T. J. Leaves from a Teacher's Note-Book. Lond. 1857–58. 2 v. 16°. O,915
Hawthorne, N. The Blithedale Romance. Boston, 1852. 16°. . . . K,158
House of the Seven Gables. Boston, 1869. 12°. . . . . . K,159
Life of Franklin Pierce. Boston, 1852. 16°. . . . . . C,1010
Marble Faun. Boston, 1864. 2 v. 16°. . . . . . . . K,160
Mosses from an Old Manse. Boston, 1857. 12°. . . . . . K,157
Our Old Home. Boston, 1864. 12°. . . . . . . . . . K,162
Passages from his American Note-Books. Boston, 1868. 2 v. 12°. . H,235
Passages from the English Note-Books. Boston, 1870. 2 v. 12°. . H,92

Hawthorne, N. Snow-Image, and other Tales. Boston, 1865. 12°. . . K,164
Tanglewood Tales. Boston, 1870. 12°. . . . . . . J,1440
Twice-told Tales. Boston, 1853. 2 v. 12°. . . . . . . K,155
Wonder-Book for Girls and Boys. Boston, 1869. 12°. . . J,1335
Works. Boston, 1866–70. 18 v. 12°. . . . . . . . U,40

Vol. 1, 2. Twice-Told Tales.
3. Snow-Image, and other Tales.
4, 5. Mosses from an old Manse.
6. Scarlet Letter.
7. House of the Seven Gables.
8. Blithedale Romance.
9, 10. Marble Faun.
Vol. 11. Our Old Home.
12. True Stories from Hist. and Biography.
13. Wonder Book.
14. Tanglewood Tales.
15, 16. Passages from American Note-Books.
17, 18. Passages from the English Note-Books.

Scarlet Letter. Boston, 1865. 12°. . . . . . . . . . K,163
Hawthorne, S. Notes on England and Italy. New York, 1869. 12°. . V,358
Haxthausen, A. von, *Baron.* Transcaucasia. London, 1854. 8°. . . V,703
Transkaukasia. Leipzig, 1856. 2 v. 8°. . . . . . . . E,216
Hay, D. R. Laws of Harmonious Colouring. Edinburgh, 1847. 16°. . M,11
Nomenclature of Colours. Edinburgh, 1846. 8°. . . . . . M,54
Original Geometrical Draper Designs. London, 1844. 4°. . . Q,223
Science of Beauty. Edinburgh, 1856. 8°. . . . . . . . M,111
Hay, J. Pike County Ballads, and other Pieces. Boston, 1871. 8°. . . I,74
Haydn, F. J. Oratorios; edited by V. Novello. London, n. d. 8°. . . M,419

The Creation; The Seasons; Third Mass.

Sämmtliche Compositionen für das Pianoforte, v. 2. Wolfenb. n. d. 4°. Q,193
Life of. H. Beyle. London, 1817. 8°. . . . . . . . D,523
The same. Boston, 1839. 12°. . . . . . . . . . D,495
Haydn, J. Dictionary of Dates; ed. by B. Vincent. London, 1866. 8°. . *A,307
The same; with additions. New York, 1869. 8°. . . . *A,308
Universal Index of Biography; ed. by J. B. Payne. London, 1870. 8°. *C,582
Haydon, B. R. Lectures on Painting and Design. Lond. 1844–46. 2 v. 8°. M,44
Autobiography and Journals; ed. by T. Taylor. N. Y. 1853. 2 v. 12°. D,502
Hayes, E. Ballads of Ireland. London, 1855. 2 v. 12°. . . . . I,345
Hayes, I. I. Arctic Boat Journey. Boston, 1867. 12°. . . . . V,938
Cast away in the Cold. Boston, 1870. 12°. . . . . . J,1269
Open Polar Sea. New York, 1867. 8°. . . . . . . . V,954
Hayne, P. H. Poems. Boston, 1855. 16°. . . . . . . . . I,26
Haynes, G. Sketch of Massachusetts State Prison. Boston, 1870. 12°. . O,365
Hayter, C. Perspective Geometry, Drawing and Painting. Lond. 1845. 8°. M,171
Hayti, Geschichte von. H. Handelmann. Kiel, 1856. 8°. . . . . E,123
Hayward, A. Lord Chesterfield and George Selwyn. London, 1856. p. 8°. I,661,4
Hayward, C., jr. Life of Sebastian Cabot. New York, 1860. 12°. . C,860,9
Hazard, S. Annals of Pennsylvania, 1609–1682. Philadelphia, 1850. 8°. C,175
Hazen, E. Popular Technology. New York, 1855. 2 v. 16°. . . . L,439
Hazlitt, W. Dramatic Literature of the Age of Elizabeth. N. Y. 1845. 12°. H,701
Life of Napoleon I. London, 1852. 4 v. 8°. . . . . . . D,656
Miscellaneous Works. Philadelphia, 1866. 5 v. 12°. . . . U,216

Vol. 1, 2. Table Talk.
3. Dramatic Literature; Age of Elizabeth.
Vol. 4. English Poets and Comic Writers.
5. Spirit of the Age.

Principles of Human Action. London, n. d. 12°. . . . . . H,425
Round Table. London, 1869. 16°. . . . . . . . . . I,558
Spirit of the Age. Philadelphia, 1854. 8°. . . . . . . H,426
Hazlitt, W. C. History of the Venetian Republic. London, 1860. 4 v. 8°. B,496

He knew he was right. A. Trollope. Leipzig, 1869. 3 v. 16°. . . . . J,499
The same. New York, 1869. 8°. . . . . . . . K,1046
Head, Sir E. (Ed.) Hand-Book of Painting. London, 1854. 2 v. 12°. M,6
Head, Sir F. B. Bubbles from the Brunnen of Nassau. London, 1866. 12°. V,392
Journeys across the Pampas. London, 1846. 12°. . . . . . V,250
Emigrant. London, 1846. 8°. . . . . . . . . . . H,314
Fortnight in Ireland. London, 1852. 8°. . . . . . . . V,270
Life and Adventures of James Bruce. London, 1830. 16°. . . I,634
The same. New York, 1855. 18°. . . . . . . . L,422
Life in Germany. New York, 1848. 16°. . . . . . . . V,411
Head, J. H. Home Pastimes; or, Tableaux Vivants. Boston, 1860. 12°. H,245
Head of the Family. D. M. Craik. New York, n. d. 8°. . . . . K,643
The same. Leipzig, 1858. 2 v. in 1. 16°. . . . . . J,87
Headless Horseman. M. Reid. New York, 1870. 12°. . . . . J,1565
Headley, J. T. Adirondack; or, Life in the Woods. New York, 1869. 12°. V,25
History of the Great Rebellion. Hartford, 1865. 2 v. 8°. . . B,923
Imperial Guard of Napoleon I. New York, 1859. 12°. . . . B,87
Letters from Italy. New York, 1854. 12°. . . . . . . V,496
Luther and Cromwell. New York, 1850. 12°. . . . . . . C,491
Miscellaneous Works. New York, 1849. 2 v. 12°. . . . . H,213
Napoleon I. and his Marshals. New York, 1846. 2 v. 12°. . . D,619
The same. New York, 1865. 8°. . . . . . . . D,562
Second War with England. New York, 1853. 2 v. 12°. . . . B,850
Washington and his Generals. New York, 1854. 2 v. 12°. . . C,650
Headley, P. C. Life of General Lafayette. Auburn, 1851. 12°. . . D,620
Life of the Empress Josephine. New York, 1856. 12°. . . . D,557
Life of General Phil. H. Sheridan. New York, 1865. 16°. . . C,843
Massachusetts in the Rebellion. Boston, 1866. 8°. . . . . B,914
Story Life of Captain John Ericsson. New York, 1870. 12°. . J,1635
Story Life of General O. M. Mitchell. New York, 1870. 12°. . J,1634
Headlong Hall and Nightmare Abbey. T. L. Peacock. N. Y. 1845. 12°. K,890
Heads and Hands in the World of Labour. W. G. Blakie. Lond. 1865. 16°. H,468
Headsman, The. J. F. Cooper. New York, 1866. 12°. . . . . K,29
The same. New York, 1859. 8°. . . . . . . . . K,61
Heads of the People. K. Meadows. London, 1864. 2 v. 8°. . . . . H,616
Health and Happiness, Letters on. C. E. Beecher. New York, 1856. 16°. L,866
and Longevity, Code of. Sir J. Sinclair. London, 1844. 8°. . . L,927
by Good Living. W. W. Hall. New York, 1870. 12°. . . . L,902
Fun better than Physic. W. W. Hall. Springfield, 1871. 12°. . L,959
Hints on. W. E. Coale. Boston, 1852. 18°. . . . . . . L,837
The same; third edition. Boston, 1857. 12°. . . . . . L,846
Management of. J. Baird. London, 1868. 12°. . . . . . M,828
Interrupted, and Sick-Room Duties. H. Morley. Lond. 1847. 16°. N,252,37
its Friends and Foes. R. D. Mussey. Boston, 1866. 12°. . . L,863
Laws of. W. A. Alcott. Boston, 1860. 12°. . . . . . . L,864
Lectures on Life and. W. A. Alcott. Boston, 1853. 12°. . . L,847
Metropolitan Sewage Manure. London, 1847. 8°. . . . . N,252,29
of Towns' Association. R. A. Slaney. London, 1846. 16°. . N,252,37
Report of. H. Austin. London, 1847. 8°. . . . . N,252,29
Report on Sewerage. London, 1847. 8°. . . . . N,252,29

Health, Preservation of. B. N. Comings. New York, 1854. 12°. . . L,851
Tract upon, for Cottage Circulation. H. Morley. London, 1847. 16°. N,252,37
Heap, G. H. Central Route to the Pacific. Philadelphia, 1854. 8°. . . V,80
Heard, F. F. Curiosities of the Law Reporters. Boston, 1871. 12°. . . H,134
Hearne, S. Journey to the Northern Ocean, 1760-72. London, 1795. 4°. Q,424
Hearne, T. Works. Oxford, 1724. 4 v. 8°. . . . . . . . U,127
Vol. 1, 2. Robert of Gloucester's Chronicle.
3, 4. Peter Langtoft's Chronicle.
Heart and Hand. New York, 1858. 18°. . . . . . . . J,1173
Heart-Histories and Life-Pictures. T. S. Arthur. Philadelphia, n. d. 16°. J,611
Heart of the Continent. F. H. Ludlow. New York, 1870. 8°. . . . V,114
Heart of Mid-Lothian. Sir W. Scott. Boston, 1852. 2 v. 16°. . . K,938
The same. Philadelphia, n. d. 8°. . . . . . . . K,963
The same. Philadelphia, 1869. 8°. . . . . . . K,1107
The same. Leipzig, 1858. 2 v. in 1. 16°. . . . . . J,443
Hearts and Faces. J. T. Trowbridge. New York, 1859. 16°. . . J,1214
Hearth-Stone; Home-Life in Cities. S. Osgood. New York, 1860. 12°. . H,293
Heartsease. C. M. Yonge. New York, 1866. 2 v. 12°. . . . K,1081
The same. Leipzig, 1855. 2 v. in 1. 16°. . . . . J,549
Heat. J. Abbott. New York, 1871. 12°. . . . . . . . J,1729
as a Mode of Motion. J. Tyndall. New York, 1869. 12°. . . N,41
developed in Acids and Bases. T. Andrews. Dublin, 1841. 4°. N,252,42
Elements of. F. Guthrie. London, 1868. 12°. . . . . N,39
in its Relations to Water and Steam. C.W.Williams. Phil. 1867. 8°. N,43
Measurement of. A. Ure. London, n. d. 8°. . . . N,252,28
Metals and Alloys as conductors of. F. Calvert. Lond. 1858. 4°. N,252,52
Phenomena and Laws of. A. Cazin. London, 1868. 12°. . M,1058
Treatise on. D. Lardner. London, 1833. 12°. . . . M,1025
P. Stewart. Oxford, 1866. 16°. . . . . . . . N,37
Heath, J. Chronicle of the War. London, 1676. f°. . . . . . F,275
Heathen Philosophy comp. with Revelation. J. Priestley. North. 1804. 8°. U,294,13
Heather, J. F. Descriptive Geometry. London, 1851. 12°. . . . M,934
Use of Instruments. London, 1854. 12°. . . . . . . . M,935
Heaton, C. Life of Albrecht Dürer. London, 1870. 8°. . . . . M,122
Heaven and its Wonders. E. Swedenborg. New York, 1863. 8°. . . P,853
Heavenly Arcana. E. Swedenborg. New York, 1862-63. 10 v. 8°. . P,851
Heavenly Father. E. Naville. Boston, 1867. 12°. . . . . . . P,34
Heavens, The. A. Guillemin. London, 1867. 8°. . . . . . *N,346
The same; fourth edition. New York, 1871. 8°. . N,350
R. Mudie. London, 1854. 18°. . . . . . . N,261
Beauty of. C. F. Blunt. London, 1849. 4°. . . . . . . N,329
Wonders of. C. Flammarion. New York, 1871. 12°. . . M,1050
Wunder des Himmels. J. J. von Littrow. Stuttgart, 1854. 8°. . G,784
Heavenward Led; or, the Two Bequests. J.R.Sommers. Philad. 1871. 12°. K,225
Heber, A. Life of Reginald Heber. New York, 1830. 2 v. 8°. . . D,38
Memoir of Reginald Heber. Boston, 1856. 12°. . . . . . D,231
Heber, R. Journey from Calcutta to Bombay. London, 1828. 3 v. 8°. . V,737
Poetical Works. Philadelphia, 1841. 16°. . . . . . . I,343
Life of. A. Heber. New York, 1830. 2 v. 8°. . . . . . D,38
Memoir of. A. Heber. Boston, 1856. 12°. . . . . . . D,231

Heber, R. Catalogue of his Library. London, 1834–37. 4 v. 8°. . . . L.R.
Heberstein, S. von, *Baron.* Notes upon Russia. London, 1851–52. 2 v. 8°. V,978
Hebert, L. Engineer's and Mechanic's Encyclopædia. Lon. 1849. 2 v. 8°. M,803
Hebrew and English Lexicon. W. Gesenius. Boston, 1854. 8°. . . . L.R.
without Points. J. Parkhurst. London, 1813. 8°. . . . L.R.
Hebrew and Chaldee Lexicon. B. Davidson. London, n. d. 4°. . . . L.R.
Hebrew Antiquities, Hand-Book of. H. Browne. London, 1852. 12°. . A,200
Hebrew Chrestomathy. M. Stuart. Andover, 1838. 8°. . . . . . L,534
Hebrew Grammar. W. Gesenius. New York, 1852. 8°. . . . . . L.783
Hebrew Heroes; Tale of Jewish History. C. Tucker. London, 1869. 12°. K,576
Hebrew Lyrical History. T. Bulfinch. Boston, 1853. 16°. . . . . I,300
Hebrew Monarchy, History of. F. W. Newman. London, 1865. 8°. . A,207
Hebrew Nation, History of. S. Sharpe. London, 1869. 12°. . . . . A,206
Hebrew Poetry, Spirit of. I. Taylor. New York, 1862. 12°. . . . . P,80
Hebrew Politics in the Time of Sargon. E. Strachey. London, 1853. 8°. P,531
Hebrews, Ancient. A Mills. New York, 1856. 12°. . . . . . A,201
Laws of. E. C. Wines. New York, 1853. 8°. . . . A,220
Hebrides, Description of. D. Monro. Glasgow, 1820. 12°. . . B,111,2
Ramble in. H. Miller. Boston, 1859. 12°. . . . . . . V,357
Tour to, with Sam. Johnson. J. Boswell. London, 1852. 8°. . V,363
Hecht, E. Synopsis of the History of the Israelites. Cincinnati, 1857. 8°. A,238
Heck, J. G. Iconographic Encyclopædia. N. Y. 1864. 4 v. 8° and 2 v. 4°. L.R.
Hecker, I. T. Questions of the Soul. New York, 1856. 12°. . . . P,248
Heckington. C. G. F. Gore. Leipzig, 1858. 2 v. in 1. 16°. . . . J,186
Hedge, F. H. Primeval World of Hebrew Tradition. Boston, 1870. 12°. A,15
Recent Inquiries in Theology. Boston, 1861. 12°. . . . . . P,270
Hedge of Thorns. M. M. Sherwood. New York, 1860. 12°. . . K,1008,3
Hedged in. E. S. Phelps. Boston, 1870. 12°. . . . . . . . K,232
Hedges and Evergreens. J. A. Warden. New York, 1858. 12°. . . M,351
Heer, O. Pflanzen der Pfahlbauten. Zürich, 1865. 4°. . . . . . G,871
Heeren, A. H. L. Ancient Greece, and Historical Treatises. Lond. 1847. 8°. A,42
Carthaginians, Ethiopians, and Egyptians. London, 1857. 8°. . A,39
Manual of Ancient History. London, 1854. 8°. . . . . . A,43
Political System of Europe and Colonies. London, 1857. 8°. . . A,41
Principal Nations of Antiquity. London, 1854. 2 v. 8°. . . . A,40
Vol. 1. Persians, Phœnicians, Babylonians. Vol. 2. Scythians, Indians, Appendixes.
und Ukert, F. A. (Eds.) Geschichte der Europäischen Staaten. Hamburg u. Gotha, 1829–63. 68 v. 8°. viz.:
Böttiger, C. W. Kurstaat u. Königreich Sachsen, bis 1831. 2 v. E,84
Bülau, F. Geschichte Deutschlands, 1806–30. . . . . E,69
Dahlman, F. C. Dänemark, bis 1522. 3 v. . . . . . E,111
Geijer, E. G., und Carlson, F. F. Schweden, bis 1680. 4 v. . E,112
Kampen, N. G. von. Niederlande, bis 1815. 2 v. . . . E,83
Lappenberg, J. M. und Pauli, R. England, bis 1509. 5 v. . E,42
Lembke, F. W., und Schäfer, H. Spanien, bis 1276. 3 v. . E,92
Leo, H. Italienische Staaten, bis 1830. 5 v. . . . . E,101
Mailáth, J. von. Oestreich, bis 1849. 5 v. . . . . . E,77
Pfister, J. C. von. Geschichte der Teutschen, bis 1807. 5 v. . E,48
Roepell, R., und Caro, J. Polen, bis 1400. 2 v. . . . . E,107
Schäfer, H. Portugal, bis 1820. 5 v. . . . . . . . E,97

Heeren, A. H. L. and Ukert, F. A. (Eds.) Schmidt, E. A. Frankreich. . E,86
Stenzel, G.A.H. Der Preussische Staat, bis 1763. 5 v. . . E,74
Strahl, P. Der Russische Staat, bis 1792. 6 v. . . . E,108
Wachsmuth, E.W.G. Frankreich im Revolutionszeitalter. 4 v. E,85
Zinkeisen, J. W. Das Osmanische Reich, bis 1812. 7 v. . E,118
Heeringen, G. von. Wanderungen durch Franken. Leipzig. 8°. . E,186,3
Hegel, G. W. F. Philosophy of History. London, 1861. p. 8°. . . L,249
Secret of. J. H. Stirling. London, 1865. 2 v. 8°. . . . O,683
Werke; herausgegeben durch P. Marheineke u. A. M. Berlin, 1832–45. 19 v. in 22. 8°. . . . . . . . . . . G,562

Bd. 1. Philosophische Abhandlungen; Glauben und Wissen; Differenz des Fichteschen und Schellingschen Systems; Ueber das Verhältness der Naturphilosophie zur Philosophie überhaupt; Ueber die Wissenschaftliche Behandlungsarten des Naturrechts.
2. Phänomenologie des Geistes.
3–5. Wissenschaft der Logik.
6. Encyclopädie der Philosophischen Wissenchaften; 1ter Theil; Die Logik.
7. 2ter Theil; Vorlesungen über die Naturphilosophie.
3ter Thiel; Die Philosophie des Geistes. 2 v.
8. Grundlinien der Philosophie des Rechts.
9. Vorlesungen über die Philosophie der Geschichte.
10. Vorlesungen über die Aesthetik. 3 v.
11,12. Vorlesungen über die Philosophie der Religion.
13–15. Vorlesungen über die Geschichte der Philosophie.
16. Vermischte Schriften: Dissertatio Philosophica de Orbis Planetarum; Fünf Gymnasial-Reden zu Nürnberg; Kritiken.
17. Vermischte Schriften: Kritiken; Vorrede zu Hinrich's Religionsphilosophie; Drei Lateinische Reden an der Friedrich Wilhelm's Universität, Berlin; Schreiben in amtliche Angelegenheiten; Aufsätze vermischten Inhalts; Briefe.
18. Philosophische Propädeutik.
19. Hegel's Leben von K. Rosenkranz.

Heidelberg. G. P. R. James. Leipzig, 1846. 16°. . . . . . . J,209
Heidelberg Catechism, Lectures on. G. W. Bethune. N. Y. 1864. 2 v. 12°. P,904
Heidenmauer, The. J. F. Cooper. New York, 1865. 12°. . . . K,30
The same. New York, 1869. 12°. . . . . . . K,146
Heights of Eidelberg. M. H. Tatem. Philadelphia, 1871. 12°. . K,1158
Heideschenke, Die. L. Storch. Leipzig, 1855–56. 3 v. 16°. . . . G,482
Heine, H. Pictures of Travel; tr. by C. G. Leland. Philadelphia, 1853. 12°. G,32
Book of Songs; translated by C. G. Leland. Philadelphia, 1864. 12°. G,36
Poems; with Life by E. A. Bowring. London, 1866. p. 8°. . . L,194
Romanzero. Hamburg, 1854. 16°. . . . . . . . . . E,266
Sämmtliche Werke. Hamburg, 1867. 18 v. in 9. 16°. . . . E,330
Heine, W. Expedition in die Seen von China, etc. Leip. 1858. 3 v. in 2. 8°. E,232
Reise um die Erde nach Japan, 1853–55. Leipzig, 1856. 2 v. in 1. 8°. E,164
Heinroth, J. C. A. Education and Self-Formation. London, 1838. 12°. O,1008
Heir of Redclyffe. C. M. Yonge. New York, 1868. 2 v. 12°. . K,1080
The same. Leipzig, 1855. 2 v. in 1. 16°. . . . . . J,550
Heiress; an Autobiography. A. S. Stephens. Philadelphia, 1870. 12°. . K,446
Heiress of Haughton. A. Marsh-Caldwell. Leipzig, 1855. 2 v. in 1. . J,368
Helbig, C. G. Sitten des Griechischen Heldenalters. Leipzig, 1839. 16°. E,451
Helen. M. Edgeworth. New York, 1859. 12°. . . . . . . K,678,10
Helen and Arthur. C. L. Hentz. Philadelphia, 1870. 12°. . . . K,457
Helen and Olga; a Russian Tale. A. Manning. London, 1857. 12°. . J,590
Helen Gardner's Wedding Day. M. V. Terhune. New York, 1870. 12°. K,318
Helen Leeson; a Peep at New York Society. Philadelphia, 1855. 12°. . K,174
Helene, ein Frauenleben. R. Prutz. Prag, 1856. 3 v. 16°. . . . G,390
Helfft, H. Berg und Thal; Süd-Deutschland. Berlin, 1854. 12°. . . E,182

Helidorus, Longus, and Achilles Tatius; tr. by R. Smith. Lond. 1855. p. 8°. L,58
Heller, R. Reichspostreiter in Ludigwigsburg. Frankfurt-a-M. 1857. 12°. G,308
Helmes, J. Wetter und Wetterprophezeiung. Hannover, 1858. 8°. . G,723
Helmholtz, H. Lehre von den Tonempfindungen. Braunschweig, 1865. 8°. G,642
Helper, H. R. Impending Crisis of the South. New York, 1857. 12°. . B,878
Compendium of the same. New York, 1860. 12°. . . . . B,901
Helping-Hand Series. H. P. H. Nowell. Boston, 1869. 5 v. 16°. . J,1649
Vol. 1. Climbing the Rope. Vol. 3. Cruise of the Dashaway.
2. Billy Grimses's Favorite. 4. Little Spaniard.
Vol. 5. Salt-Water Dick.
Helps, A. Casimir Maremma. Boston, 1870. 12°. . . . . . . K,725
Companions of my Solitude. Boston, 1852. 16°. . . . . . H,438
Conversations on War and Culture. Boston, 1871. 12°. . . . H,325
Fruits of Leisure; Essays. New York, 1852. 12°. . . . . H,437
Friends in Council; First and Second Series. London, 1869. 4 v. 12°. H,324
Life of Columbus. Philadelphia, 1869. 12°. . . . . . . D,726
Life of Pizarro and Conquest of Peru. London, 1869. 12°. . . D,703
Realmah. Boston, 1869. 12°. . . . . . . . . . . . K,724
Spanish Conquest in America. New York, 1856–68. 4 v. 12°. . C,369
Helvetic Union, Destruction of the. J. Mallet-Dupan. London, n. d. 12°. B,222
Helvicus, C. Historical and Chronological Theater. London, 1687. 4°. F,233
Hemans, F. D. Poetical Works. Boston, 1857. 8°. . . . . . . J,860
The same. Boston, 1854. 12°. . . . . . . . . I,348
Select Poetical Works. Leipzig, 1865. 16°. . . . . . . J,197
Hemiptera, British. J. W. Douglas and J. Scott. London, 1865. 8°. . O,309
Hemsterhuys, F. Caractere de F. Fagel. Paris, 1773. 16°. . . . L,841
Henderson, A. History of Ancient and Modern Wines. London, 1824. 4°. Q,290
Practical Grazier. London, 1856. 8°. . . . . . . . . M,475
Henderson, E. Iceland in 1814 and 1815. Edinburgh, 1818. 2 v. 4°. . V,180
Henderson, J. Excursions in New South Wales. London, 1851. 2 v. 12°. V,886
Henfrey, A. Rudiments of Botany. London, 1858. 8°. . . . . . N,938
(Ed.) Botanical and Physiological Memoirs. London, 1853. 4°. . O,306
(Ed.) Reports and Papers on Botany. London, 1849. 8°. . . . O,295
and Smith. Micrographic Dictionary. London, 1860. 3 v. in 2. 8°. *N,9
Hengstenberg, E. W. Christology of the Old Testament. Edin. 1858. 4 v. 8°. P,528
Commentary on the Psalms. Edinburgh, 1851–57. 3 v. 8°. . . P,514
Egypt and the Books of Moses. Edinburgh, 1845. 8°. . . . P,242
Genuineness of Daniel and Zechariah. Edinburgh, 1848. 8°. . P,515
Genuineness of the Pentateuch. Edinburgh, 1847. 2 v. 8°. . . P,513
Revelation of St. John expounded. Edinburgh, 1851–52. 2 v. 8°. P,529
Henke, A. Handbuch der Speziellen Pathologie, v. 2. Berlin, 1808. 8°. E,413
Hennepin, L. Voyage dans l'Amerique. Amsterdam, 1704. 12°. . . V,149
Extracts from. J. G. Shea. New York, 1852. 8°. . . C,272
Henriade, La. F. M. A. de Voltaire. Paris, 1854. 12°. . . . . H,942
Henrici, F. C. Elektricität der Galvanischen Kette. Göttingen, 1840. 8°. N,252,8
Henrietta Temple; a Novel. B. Disraeli. London, 1868. 12°. . . K,671
The same. Leipzig, 1859. 16°. . . . . . . . . J,142
Henry Dunbar. M. E. Braddon. Leipzig, 1864. 2 v. in 1. 16°. . . J,38
Henry of Huntingdon. Chronicle. London, 1853. p. 8°. . . . . L,12
Henry II. and Richard I., Chronicle of the Reigns of. Benedict of Peterborough. London, 1867. 2 v. 8°. . . . . . . . . . . W,199

Henry III., Historical Letters on the Reign of. London, 1862–66. 2 v. 8°. w,177
Henry IV. of England, Royal and Hist. Letters in Reign of. Lond. 1860. 8°. w,168
Henry V., King of England. G. M. Towle. New York, 1866. 8°. . . D,373
Gesta, cum Chronica Neustriæ; ed. by B. Williams. Lond. 1850. 8°. U,632
Memorials of. London, 1858. 8°. . . . . . . . . . w,161
1. Redman, R. Vita Henrici V. 2. Versus Rhythmici de Henrico V.
3. Thomas, of Elmham. Liber Metricus de Henrico V.
Henry VII. Historia Regis. B. André. London, 1858. 8°. . . . . w,160
and Richard III., Letters in Reign of. London, 1861–63. 2 v. 8°. w,174
Henry VIII. of England, Life of. J. M. V. Audin. London, 1852. 8°. D,394
Life of. P. F. Tytler. London, 1854. 16°. . . . . . C,1183
Memoirs of. H. W. Herbert. New York, 1855. 12°. . . C,1190
Reign of. S. Turner. London, 1828. 2 v. 8°. . . . . A,434,9,10
Henry VIII. and his Court. C. Mundt. New York, 1868. 8°. . . G,203
Henry IV. of. France, History of. J. S. C. Abbott. Boston, 1856. 16°. J,1416
Life of. G. P. R. James. New York, 1847. 2 v. 12°. . . . D,647
Henry, C. S. History of Philosophy. New York, 1841. 2 v. 16°. . L,434
Henry, O. Analyse Chimique des Fontaines de Paris. Paris, 1848. 8°. N,252,39
Henry, P., Life of. A. H. Everett. Boston, 1860. 16°. . . . C,860,11
Life of. W. Wirt. Hartford, 1852. 8°. . . . . . . C,796
Henry, R. History of Great Britain. London, 1788–95. 12 v. 8°. . A,463
Henry, W. Action of Platinum on Gaseous Mixtures. Lond. 1824. 4°. N,252,42
Henry Esmond. W. M. Thackeray. Philadelphia, 1866. 12°. . K,1027
The same. Leipzig, 1865. 2 v. in 1. 16°. . . . . . J,482
Henry of Guise. G. P. R. James. New York, 1855. 2 v. in 1. 12°. . K,734
Henrys, Liber de Illustribus Henricis. J. Capgrave. London, 1858. 8°. w,157
Henslow, G. Lessons in Elementary Botany. London, 1864. 16°. . . N,911
Henslow, J. S. Letters to the Farmers of Suffolk. London, 1843. 8°. N,252,24
Descriptive and Physiological Botany. London, 1836. 12°. . M,1039
Henslowe, P. Diary from 1591 to 1609. London, 1845. 8°. . . I,885,26
Hentz, C. L. Banished Son. New York, 1870. 12°. . . . . . . K,165
Courtship and Marriage. Philadelphia, 1870. 12°. . . . . . K,455
Eoline. New York, 1870. 12°. . . . . . . . . . K,166
Ernest Linwood. Philadelphia, 1870. 12°. . . . . . . K,456
Helen and Arthur. Philadelphia, 1870. 12°. . . . . . . K,457
Linda; or, the Young Pilot. Philadelphia, 1869. 12°. . . . K,176
Lost Daughter. Philadelphia, 1870. 12°. . . . . . . K,458
Love after Marriage. Philadelphia, 1870. 12°. . . . . . K,460
Marcus Warland. New York, 1870. 12°. . . . . . . . K,167
Planter's Northern Bride. New York, 1870. 12°. . . . . K,168
Rena; or, the Snow Bird. New York, 1870. 12°. . . . . . K,169
Robert Graham; a sequel to Linda. Philadelphia, 1855. 12°. . K,175
Hepworth, G. H. Whip, Hoe, and Sword; Gulf Dep. in '63. Bost. 1864. 12°. H,39
Hequembourg, C. L. Plan of the Creation. Boston, 1859. 12°. . . P,250
Herald of Truth; edited by L. A. Hine. v. 1–3. Cincinnati, 1847–8. 8°. T,14
Heraldry, Elements of. W. H. Whitmore. Boston, 1866. 8°. . . . M,370
Introduction to. H. Clark. London, 1866. p. 8°. . . . . . L,288
Herbert, G., Life of. I. Walton. New York, 1854. 8°. . . . . . D,404
Poetical Works. Boston, 1855. 16°. . . . . . . . . I,213
The same; with Life by G. Gilfillan. New York, 1854. 8°. . J,853

Herbert, H. W. American Game in its Seasons. New York, 1853. 12°. . M,328
Captains of the Roman Republic. New York, 1854. 12°. . . C,500
Chevaliers of England. New York, 1852. 12°. . . . . . . K,190
Chevaliers of France. New York, 1853. 12°. . . . . . K,189
Field Sports of the United States. New York, 1849. 2 v. 8°. . M,315
Fish and Fishing of North America. New York, 1851. 8°. . . M,310
Hints to Horse-Keepers. New York, 1859. 12°. . . . . . M,461
Horse and Horsemanship of the United States. N. Y. 1857. 2 v. 8°. *M,733
Memoirs of Henry VIII., and of his Wives. New York, 1855. 12°. C,1190
Oliver Cromwell. New York, 1856. 12°. . . . . . . . . K,177
Sportsman's Vade Mecum. See *Mayhew, E.* New York, 1856. 12°. M,312
Herbert, W. Works; excepting Botany and Nat. Hist. Lond. 1842. 3 v. 8°. U,114
Herbert Lovell. F. W. B. Bouverie. London, n. d. 16°. . . . . J,1647
Herculaneum, Antiquities of; tr. by T. Martyn and J. Lettice. Lond. 1773. 4°. *Q,371
et Pompéi. L. Barré et H. R. Ainé. Paris, 1839–40. 8 v. 8°. *M,133
Pitture e Bronzi Antiche di Ercolano. Napoli, 1757–1771. 7 v. f°. L.R.
Herder, S. A. W. von. Erwärmung der Gebläseluft. Freiberg, 1840. 8°. N,252,18
Herder, J. G. von. Philosophy of the History of Man. London, 1800. 4°. N,465
Here and There in London. J. E. Ritchie. London, 1859. 16°. . . V,312
Hereditary Genius; its Laws and Consequences. F. Galton. N. Y. 1870. 8. O,736
Hereward, the Wake. C. Kingsley. Boston, 1866. 12°. . . . . . K,749
The same. Leipzig, 1866. 2 v in 1. 16°. . . . . . J,242
Herkimer Co. and Mohawk Valley, History of. N. S. Benton. Alb. 1856. 8°. C,89
Her Majesty's Tower. W. H. Dixon. Lepzig, 1869–70. 2 v. in 1. 16°. . J,149
Heringshändler; oder, Edelmann. C. Mundt. Berlin, 1864. 12°. . G,362,1
Herman; or, Young Knighthood. S. Palfrey. Boston, 1866. 2 v. 12°. . K,888
Hermann, E. Geschichte des Russischen Staates. Hamb. 1832–60. 6 v. 8°. E,108
Hermeneutics, Legal and Political. F. Lieber. Boston, 1839. 12°. . . O,481
Hermes, K. H. Geschichte der Neuesten Zeit. New York, 1848. 3 v. 12°. E,36
Hermits, The. C. Kingsley. Philadelphia, 1868. 12°. . . . . . P,795
Herndon, W. L. and Gibbon. Valley of Amazon, Maps. Wash. 1854. 4 v. 8°. V,263
Herodotus. Historiæ, Græce et Latine. Paris, 1845. 8°. . . . . . U,554
The same; translated by W. Beloe. New York, 1855. 3 v. 16°. U,363
The same; translated by H. Carey. London, 1870. p. 8°. . L,59
The same. New York, 1855. 12°. . . . . . A,64
The same; tr. and ed. by G. Rawlinson. Lond. 1858–61. 4 v. 8°. A,96
Analysis and Summary of. J. T. Wheeler. London, 1852. 12°. . L,251
Life and Travels of. J. T. Wheeler. New York, 1856. 2 v. 12°. . D,770
Notes on. D. W. Turner. London, 1853. 12°. . . . . . L,250
Heroes, The. C. Kingsley. Boston, 1864. 16°. . . . . . . J,1317
and Hero-Worship. T. Carlyle. New York, 1859. 12°. . . . H,429
in English History, Tales of. London, 1869. 8°. . . . . J,1295
Lectures on. T. Carlyle. London, 1858. 8°. . . . . . . H,428
of Europe. H. G. Hewlett. Boston, 1861. 12°. . . . . . C,547
of the Indian Rebellion. D. W. Bartlett. Columbus, 1859. 8°. C,1210
of the Laboratory and Workshop. C. L. Brightwell. Lond. 1859. 8°. J,1250
Heroine of a Week. London, 1845. 18°. . . . . . . . . . H,249
Heroines of Shakespeare; edited by D. L. Glover. Boston, n. d. 8°. . *I,872
Girlhood of. M. C. Clarke. London, 1864. 3 v. 12°. . . I,848

Herpetology of U. S. Exploring Expedition. C. Girard. Phil. 1858. 4°. *Q,279
Atlas to the same. Philadelphia, 1858. f°. . . . . . *Q,353
Herrera, A. de. General History of America. London, 1725-26. 6 v. 8°. B,582
Herrick, R. Hesperides. Boston, 1856. 2 v. 16°. . . . . . . I,214
Herring, J. Portrait Gal. of Distinguished Americans. Phil. 1836-39. 4 v. 4°. S.C.
Herschel, Sir J. F. W. Astronomy. London, 1833. 12°. . . . M,1023
Discourse on Natural Philosophy. London, 1851. 16°. . . . N,68
Familiar Lectures on Scientific Subjects. London, 1867. 8°. . . M,769
Life of. F. Arago. Boston, 1859. 12°. . . . . . . C,498,1
Meteorology. Edinburgh, 1861. 16°. . . . . . . . N,103
Outlines of Astronomy. London, 1869. 8°. . . . . . . N,349
The same. Philadelphia, 1853. 8°. . . . . . . . N,330
Study of Natural Philosophy. London, 1831. 12°. . . . M,1017
The Telescope. Edinburgh, 1861. 16°. . . . . . . . N,258
Hertha. F. Bremer. New York, 1856. 12°. . . . . . . K,605
Hervey, G. W. Principles of Courtesy. New York, 1852. 12°. . . H,283
Rhetoric of Conversation. New York, 1853. 12°. . . . . L,586
Hervey, J., Life of. D. A. Harsha. Albany, 1865. 8°. . . . . D,100
Theron and Aspasio. Berwick, 1802. 2 v. 12°. . . . . H,587
Hervey, J., *Lord.* Memoirs of Reign of George II. Phil. 1848. 2 v. 12°. A,538
Hervey, T. K. Illustrations of Modern Sculpture. London, 1834. 4°. *Q,215
Herzog von Bielitz. C. Mundt. Berlin, 1864. 12°. . . . . G,362,1
Hesekiel, J. G. L. Life of Bismark. New York, 1870. 8°. . . . D,528
Hesiod. Works; translated by J. Banks. London, 1856. p. 8°. . . L,60
Compositions from. J. Flaxman. London, 1817. 4°. . . *Q,237
Hesperian; or, Western Monthly Magazine. Columbus, 1838-39. 3 v. 8°. T,12
Hetherington, W. M. History of the Church of Scotland. N. Y. 1848. 8°. P,592
Westminster Assembly of Divines. New York, 1856. 12°. . . P,601
Hewitt, M. E. Memorial of Mrs. Frances S. Osgood. N. Y. 1851. 8°. . H,173
Hewlett, H. G. Heroes of Europe. Boston, 1861. 12°. . . . . C,547
Heyse, P. Neue Novellen. Stuttgart, 1858 24°. . . . . . . G,309
Novellen. Berlin, 1860. 24°. . . . . . . . . . G,310
Spanisches Liederbuch. Berlin, 1852. 24°. . . . . . . E,265
Vier Neue Novellen. Berlin, 1859. 16°. . . . . . . . G,311
Heywood, J. Dialogue on Wit and Folly. London, 1846. 12°. . L,606,20
Heywood, T. Fair Maid of the Exchange. London, 1845. 8°. . I,885,27
Fair Maid of the West. London, 1850. 8°. . . . . . I,885,43
Golden and Silver Ages; two Plays. London, 1851. 8°. . . I,885,47
King Edward IV.; parts 1 and 2. London, 1842. 8°. . . I,885,13
Life and Reign of Queen Elizabeth; two Plays. Lond. 1851. 8°. I,885,43
Marriage Triumph. London, 1842. 12°. . . . . . . L,606,3
Royal King and Loyal Subject. London, 1850. 8°. . . I,885,45
Woman killed with Kindness. London, 1850. 8°. . . . I,885,45
and Rowley, W. Fortune by Land and Sea. London, 1845. 8°. I,885,28
Hiatt, J. M. Political Manual. Indianapolis, 1864. 12°. . . . . O,474
Hiawatha, Song of. H. W. Longfellow. Boston, 1868. 16°. . . . I,70
Sang von; übersetzt von F. Freiligrath. New York, 1858. 12°. E,323,2
Hibberd, S. Rustic Adorments for Homes of Taste. London, 1870. 4°. . M,160
Hickey, W. (Ed.) Constitution of United States of America. Phila. 1853. 12°. B,718
Hickok, L. P. Empirical Psychology. Schenectady, 1855. 12°. . . O,647

Hickok, L. P. Rational Cosmology. New York, 1859. 8°. . . . . M,789
Rational Psychology. Schenectady, 1854. 8°. . . . . . . O,703
Hickox, J. H. Historical Account of American Coinage. Albany, 1858. 8°. M,390
Hicks, J.B. Humble Creatures; Earth-worm and House-fly. Lond. 1860. 8°. O,26
Hickson, W. E. Dutch and German Schools. London, 1840. 8°. . . O,1011
Hidden Life of the Soul. J. N. Grou. Philadelphia, 1871. 16°. . . P,200
Hidden Path. W. V. Terhune. New York, 1866. 12°. . . . . K,316
Hide and Seek. W. Collins. Leipzig, 1856. 2 v. in 1. 16°. . . . J,76
Hieroglyphica of Merkbeelden der oude Volkeren: Egyptenaren, Chaldeeuwen, Feniciers, enz. A. H. Westerhovius. Amsteldam, 1735. 4°. *Q,340
Higden, R. Polychronicon. London, 1869. 2 v. 8°. . . . . W,191
Higher-Water, Song of. J. W. Ward. New York, 1868. 8°. . . . I,72
Higgins, W. M. The Earth; its Physical Condition. London, 1855. 16°. V,1132
The same. New York, 1858. 16°. . . . . . . . . L,394
Entertaining Philosopher. London, 1844. 16°. . . . . . N,66
Higginson, F. New-Englands Plantation. Lond. 1630. See *Force's Tracts*, v. 1.
Higginson, T. W. Army Life in a Black Regiment. Boston, 1870. 12°. . B,892
Out-Door Papers. Boston, 1863. 12°. . . . . . . H,187
Highlanders, Sketches of. D. Stewart. Edinburgh, 1825. 2 v. 8°. . . V,361
Highlands and Highland Clans. J. Browne. Edinburgh, 1852–56. 4 v. 8°. B,128
Highmore, A. Pietas Londinensis; Public Charities, etc. London, 1810. 8°. O,418
Hilary St. Ives. W. H. Ainsworth. Leipzig, 1869. 2 v. in 1. 16°. . . J,10
Hildreth, R. Atrocious Judges. New York, 1856. 12°. . . . . D,180
History of the United States. New York, 1855. 6 v. 8°. . . B,638
Japan as it was and is. Boston, 1855. 12°. . . . . . V,620
Hildreth, S. P. Pioneer History; Account of Ohio Valley. Cin. 1848. 8°. C,270
Pioneer Settlers of Ohio. Cincinnati, 1852. 8°. . . . . C,710
Hiley, R. Practical English Composition. London, 1855. 2 v. 18°. O,1062,1
Key to the same. London, 1855. 18°. . . . O,1062,2
Hill, A. Discipline appropriate to Schools. London, 1855. 8°. . O,1251,2
Hill, F. National Education. London, 1836. 2 v. 12°. . . . . O,1031
Hill, G. C. Benedict Arnold. Philadelphia, 1868. 18°. . . . . C,835
Daniel Boone; a Biography. Philadelphia, 1865. 12°. . . . J,1198
Benjamin Franklin; a Biography. Philadelphia, 1860. 16°. . . J,1215
Gen. Israel Putnam; a Biography. Philadelphia, 1868. 16°. . . J,1228
Capt. John Smith; a Biography. Philadelphia, 1868. 16°. . . J,1229
Our Parish; or, Village Life. Philadelphia, n. d. 12°. . . . K,360
Hill, J. History of Animals. London, 1752. f°. . . . . . . Q,111
Hill, M. Juvenile Delinquency. London, 1853. 8°. . . . . . . O,354
Hill and Valley. H. Martineau. Cincinnati, 1853. 16°. . . . . J,1458
Hill Difficulty and other Papers. G. B. Cheever. New York, 1849. 12°. . H,462
Hill Side, The. A. Manning. London, n. d. 16°. . . . . . . J,580
Hillard, G. S. Life and Campaigns of G. B. McClellan. Phila. 1864. 12°. C,698
Life of Capt. John Smith. New York, 1860. 12°. . . . . C,860,2
Mercantile Profession; its Dangers and Duties. Boston, 1854. 8°. . H,301
Six Months in Italy. Boston, 1854. 2 v. 12°. . . . . . . V,506
Hilliard, H. W. Speeches and Addresses. New York, 1855. 8°. . . H,822
Hillern, W. von. Only a Girl. Philadelphia, 1871. 12°. . . . . G,176
Hillhouse, J. A. Dramas, Discourses, etc., v. 1. Boston, 1839. 12°. . . I,687
Hillside, A. M. Familiar Compendium of Geology. Philad. 1859. 12°. . N,606

Hillside and Border Sketches. W. H. Maxwell. London, 1847. 2 v. 8°. . V,349
Hillyars and Burtons. H. Kingsley. Boston, 1865. 12°. . . . . K,756
The same. Leipzig, 1865. 2 v. in 1. 16°. . . . . . J,249
Hilt to Hilt; or, the Shenandoah in 1864. J. E. Cooke. N. Y. 1869. 12°. J,630
Hiltl, G. Gefahrvolle Wege. Historischer Roman. Berlin, n. d. 4 v. 12°. G,312
Himalaya Mountains, Journey to. Sir W. Lloyd. London, 1840. 2 v. 8°. V,751
Himalayan Journals. J. D. Hooker. London, 1855. 2 v. 12°. . . V,673
Himself His Worst Enemy. A. P. Brotherhead. Philadelphia, 1871. 12°. K,311
Hind, J. R. Introduction to Astronomy. London, 1863. p. 8°. . . L,294
Solar System. New York, 1852. 12°. . . . . . . . N,268
Hindee-Roman Orthoepigraphical Ultimatum. J. B. Gilchrist. Lond. 1820. 8°. L,788
Hindoo Institutions compared with Moses'. J. Priestley. Northumb. 1799. 8°. U,294,14
Hindoos, The. London, 1834–35. 2 v. 16°. . . . . . . . L,488
Hindostan, Description of. W. Hamilton. London, 1820. 2 v. 4°. . . V,720
History of. T. Maurice. London, 1820. 2 v. 4°. . . . C,462
Modern History of. T. Maurice. London, 1802–3. 2 v. 4°. . . C,463
Views in. T. and W. Daniell. London, 1795–1804. 6 v. in 3. f°. . L.R.
Text. 1 v. London, 1795. 8°. . . . . . . . L.R.
Hinds, S. The Rise and Early Progress of Christianity. Lond. 1854. 12°. P,569
Hindu Philosophy, Christianity contrasted with. J. R. Ballantyne. Lon. '59. 8°. P,828
Hindustani and English Dialogues. J. B. Gilchrist. London, 1820. 8°. . L,787
Multum in Parvo. J. B. Gilchrist. London, 1820. 8°. . . . L,789
Hindustani Language, Grammar of, 2d ed. J. Shakespear. Lond. 1818. 4°. L,786
The same; 6th edition. London, 1855. 8°. . . . . L,784
Selections in. J. Shakespear. London, 1844–46. 4°. . . . L,785
Hine, L. A. Political and Social Economy. Cincinnati, 1855. 8°. . . O,514
Priz Esa on Muni-Getin. Sinsinati, 1854. 32°. . . . . . L,664
Hines, G. History of the Oregon Mission. Buffalo, 1850. 12°. . . . V,57
Hinman, R. R. The Blue Laws of several States. Hartford, 1838. 12°. . C,2
Hinton, J. H. Case of the Manchester Educationists. Lond. 1852–54. 8°. O,1251,3
History of the United States. London, n. d. 2 v. 4°. . . . S.C.
Hints for the Earnest Student. W. Fison. London, 1850. 12°. . . O,986
on Female Parochial Schools. London, 1848. 18°. . . . . O,1108
on Household Taste. C. L. Eastlake. London, 1868. 8°. . . M,158
to Emigrants. London, 1866. 12°. . . . . . . . . M,836
to Gas-Consumers. London, 1840. 16°. . . . . . . N,252,36
toward Reforms. H. Greeley. New York, 1850. 12°. . . . O,457
Hippolytus and his Age. C. C. J. Bunsen. London, 1854. 2 v. 8°. . . P,402
Hipsley, W. Equational Arithmetic, 2 pts. London, 1854. 12°. . . M,937
Hirschfeld, C. C. L. Theorie der Gartenkunst. Leipzig, 1779–85. 5 v. in 3. 4°. G,742
Histoire de la Coiffure. Paris, 1858. 8°. . . . . . . . . M,743
Hist. d'un Paysan, 1789, 92, 93. E. Erckmann et Chatrian. Paris, 1861. 3 v. 12°. H,1017
Histology, Human. A. Kölliker. London, 1853–54. 2 v. 8°. . . . L,970
Lectures on. J. Quekett. London, 1852–54. 2 v. 8°. . . . L,969
Historic Doubts relative to Battle of Bunker Hill. C. Hudson. Bost. 1857. 12°. B,741
relative to Napoleon I. R. Whately. London, 1859. 8°. . . D,585
relative to Richard III. H. Walpole. London, 1768. 4°. . . A,498
Historic Gallery of Portraits and Painting. London, 1807–9. 4 v. 8°. . C,593
Historical Atlas, Modern. W. L. Gage. New York, 1869. 8°. . . *V,1141
Historical and Chronological Theater. C. Helvicus. London, 1687. 4°. . F,233

Historical Characters. Sir H. L. Bulwer. London, 1868. 2 v. 8°. . . C,578
Vol. 1. Prince Talleyrand, the Politic man.
2. William Cobbett, the Contentious man; Sir James Mackintosh, the man of Promise; George Canning, the Brilliant man.
The same. Leipzig, 1868. 2 v. in 1. 16°. . . . . . J,332
Historical Collections of Gt. Britain, 1618–40. J. Rushworth. Lon. 1659. 5 v. f°. F,40
Historical Difficulties. O. Delepierre. London, 1868. 12°. . . . . A,31
Historical Essays. A. Thierry. Philadelphia, 1845. 8°. . . . . . A,344
Historical Life of Joanna of Sicily. London, 1824. 2 v. 8°. . . . D,738
Historical Magazine. Boston and New York, 1857–69. 16 v. 8°. . . F,149
Historical Memoirs. Sir N. W. Wraxall. Philadelphia, 1837. 8°. . . D,63
Historical Parallels. J. H. Malkin. London, 1831–35. 2 v. 16°. . . L,478
Historical Pictures of the Middle Ages. London, 1846. 2 v. 12°. . . A,236
Historical Revelations, 1848. L. Blanc. London, 1858. 8°. . . . B,245
Historical Studies. G. W. Greene. New York, 1850. 12°. . . . A,316
H. Merivale. London, 1865. 8°. . . . . . . . A,329
Historische Lebensbilder. C. Mundt. Berlin, 1864. 2 v. 12°. . . . G,362
Historisches Bilderbuch. C. Mundt. Berlin, 1862. 3 v. 24°. . . . G,359
History, Ancient. E. Farr. Cincinnati, 1856. 4 v. 12°. . . . . . A,9
J. Lord. New York, 1870. 8°. . . . . . . A,13
C. Rollin. New York, 1851. 2 v. 8°. . . . . . A,36
Geschichte des Alterthums. M. Duncker, Ber. 1855–60. 4 v. 8°. E,452
Histoire Ancienne. C. Rollin. Paris, 1846–49. 10 v. 12°. . A,55
Lectures on. B. G. Niebuhr. London, 1852. 3 v. 8°. . . A,25
Manual of. A. H. L. Heeren. London, 1854. 8°. . . . A,43
L. Schmitz. Philadelphia, 1855. 12°. . . . . A,19
W. C. Taylor. New York, 1854. 8°. . . . . . A,34
New Researches on. C. F. C. de Volney. New York, 1856. 12°. A,11
True Stories from. A. Strickland. New York, 1868. 16°. J,1377
and Biography, True Stories from. N. Hawthorne. Boston, 1866. 12°. U,40,12
and Ethnology, Illustrations to. Appleton's. New York, 1856. 8°. Q,258,2
and Geography, Summary of. A. Adam. Edinburgh, 1794. 8°. V,1109
and Harmony of the Evangelists. Dublin, 1759. 24°. . . . P,366
Chronology of. Sir H. Nicolas. London, 1833. 12°. . . . M,985
Common School. S. G. Goodrich. Philadelphia, 1840. 12°. . . A,18
Compendium of Ancient and Modern. M. J. Kerney. Balt. 1851. 12°. A,20
Curiosities of. J. Timbs. London, 1849. 16°. . . . . . . I,546
Flowers of. Matthew of Westminster. London, 1853. 2 v. p. 8°. . L,21
Roger de Wendover. London, 1849. 2 v. p. 8°. . . . L,19
for Boys. J. G. Edgar. London, 1855. 8°. . . . . . J,1516
Geschichte des 18ten Jahrhunderts. F. C. Schlosser. Heid. 1864–8. 8 v. 8°. E,37
God in. C. C. J. Bunsen. 1868–70. 3 v. 8°. . . . . . . P,121
Hand of God in. H. Read. London, 1851. 16°. . . . . . P,169
Landmarks of. C. M. Yonge. New York, 1867–69. 3 v. 12°. . A,230
Mediæval, Hand-Book of. W. Pütz. New York, 1858. . . . A,228
Student's Hand-Book of. I. MacBurney. London, 1857. 8°. A,235
Modern. J. Lord. Philadelphia, 1849. 12°. . . . . . . . A,317
J. Michelet. New York, 1865. 16°. . . . . . L,453
Geschichte der Neuesten Zeit. K. H. Hermes. N.Y. 1848. 3 v. 12°. E,36
Lectures on. T. Arnold. New York, 1847. 12°. . . . A,318
C. W. F. von Schlegel. London, 1849. p. 8°. . . L,233

History, Modern, Lectures on. W. Smyth. London, 1854. 2 v. p. 8°. . L,238
The same. Boston, 1855. 8°. . . . . . . A,321
Manual of. W. C. Taylor. New York, 1851. 8°. . . . A,327
Pictorial. J. Frost. Philadelphia, 1846. 8°. . . . A,49
True Stories from. A. Strickland. New York, 1868. 16°. J,1274
of all Nations. S. G. Goodrich. New York, 1856. 2 v. 4°. . . A,51
of his own Time. G. Burnet. London, 1857. 8°. . . . . . A,469
of my Time. F. Guizot. London, 1858–61. 4 v. 8°. . . . D,680
of the 18th Century. F. C. Schlosser. London, 1843–52. 8 v. 8°. . A,331
of the 16th and 17th Centuries. F. L. G. v. Raumer. Lond. 1835. 2v. 12°. A,315
Outlines of. T. Keightley. London, 1830. 12°. . . . . . M,984
of the World. J. Gillies. Philadelphia, 1809. 3 v. 8°. . . . A,26
J. von Müller. New York, 1855. 4 v. 12°. . . . . A,8
Sir W. Raleigh. London, 1614. f°. . . . . . . F,293
P. Smith. New York, 1865. 3 v. 8°. . . . . . . A,37
Outlines of. M. Willson. New York, 1869. 8°. . . . . . A,35
Petits Chefs-d'-Œuvre Historique. A. de Latour. Paris, 1854. 2 v. 12°. A,312
Philosophically Illustrated. G. Miller. London, 1848–53. 4 v. p. 8°. A,56
Philosophy of. E. Bloomfield. London, 1819. 4°. . . . . . F,225
C. W. F. von Schlegel. London, 1852. 12°. . . . . . L,231
Political, 15th–17th Centuries. J. Van Praet. London, 1868. 8°. . A,338
Sacred. H. White. Edinburgh, 1855. 16°. . . . . . . P,561
Study of. G. Smith. New York, 1866. 12°. . . . . . . A,23
Summary of Ancient and Modern. A. F. Tytler. Lond. 1849. 18°. A,16
Traces of, in Names of Places. F. Edmunds. London, 1869. 12°. . L,518
Universal. A. F. Tytler. Boston, 1843. 2 v. 8°. . . . . . A,38
The same. London, 1834. 6 v. 16°. . . . . . I,600
The same. New York, 1854. 6 v. 16°. . . . . L,400
Ancient Part. London, 1747–48. 20 v. 8°. . . . . . A,1
Modern Part. London, 1759–66. 44 v. 8°. . . . . . A,2
Elements of. H. White. Edinburgh, 1853–54. 3 v. 12°. . A,6
Discours sur. J. B. Bossuet. Paris, 1855. 12°. . . . P,59
Grand Dictionnaire de. L. Moréri. Basle, 1731–32. 6 v. f°. Q,246
Histoire Universelle. C. Cantu. Paris, 1853–56. 19 v. 8°. . A,14
Introduction to Study of. Sir J. Stoddart. London, 1850. 8°. A,21
on Scriptural Principles. M. Bowley. London, n. d. 6 v. 16°. A,5
Outlines of. G. Weber. Boston, 1853. 8°. . . . . . A,33
H. White. Edinburgh, 1855. 16°. . . . . . A,17
Weltgeschichte. G. Weber. Leipzig, 1857–66. 6 v. 8°. . . . E,10
für Deutsche. F. C. Schlosser. Frank.-a-M. 1855–56. 18v. in 9. 8°. E,6
The same. Frankfurt-a-Main, 1844–57. 19 v. 8°. . E,8
Zehn Jahre, 1840–50, Geschichte. R. Prutz. Leip. 1850–56. 2 v. 8°. E,38
Hitchcock, E. Economical Geology of Massachusetts. Boston, 1838. 8°. N,252,35
Elementary Geology. New York, 1855. 12°. . . . . . . N,789
Geology, Botany, and Zoölogy of Massachusets. Amherst, 1833. 8°. N,746
Illustrations of Surface Geology. Amherst, 1860. 4°. . . . Q,56
Religion of Geology. Boston, 1855. 12°. . . . . . . . P,252
Religious Truth illustrated from Science. Boston, 1857. 12°. . . P,251
Reminiscences of Amherst College. Northampton, 1863. 12°. . O,808
Zoölogical Temperance Convention. Northampton, 1854. 12°. . N,624

Hitchcock, E. and E., jr. Elementary Anat. and Physiology. N. Y. 1863. 12°. L,885
Hitherto; a Story of Yesterdays. A. D. T. Whitney. Boston, 1869. 12°. K,389
Hittell, J. S. Resources of California. San Francisco, 1868. 12°. . . V,94
Hive and Honey Bee, Treatise on. L. L. Langstroth. New York, 1859. 12°. M,464
Hoare, C. Treatise on the Slide-Rule, and its Use. London, 1869. 12°. . M,846
Hoaryhead. J. Abbott. New York, n. d. 12°. . . . . . . P,281,4
Hobart, N. Life of Emanuel Swedenborg. Boston, 1845. 16°. . . . D,754
Hobbes, T. English Works; ed. by Sir W. Molesworth. Lond. 1839–45. 11 v. 8°. O,794

Vol. 1. Elements of Philosophy, concerning Body.
2. Philosophical Rudiments, concerning Government and Society.
3. Leviathan; or, the Matter, Form, and Power of a Commonwealth, Civil and Ecclesiastical.
4. Human Nature; Elements of Law, Moral and Politic; Liberty and Necessity; Answer to Bishop Bramhall; Heresy and the Punishment thereof; Reputation, Loyalty, Manners, and Religion; Answer to Sir W. Davenant's Preface before Gondibert.
5. Questions concerning Liberty, Necessity, and Chance, Stated and Debated between Bishop Bramhall and T. Hobbes.
6. Dialogue between a Philosopher and a Student of the Common Laws of England; Behemoth, History of the Causes of the Civil Wars of England; Whole Art of Rhetoric; Art of Sophistry.
7. Seven Philosophical Problems and two Propositions of Geometry; Decameron Physiologicum: Proportion of a Straight Line to Half the Arc of a Quadrant; Six Lessons to the Savilian Professor of the Mathematics; Absurd Geometry of Dr. Wallis; Considerations on the Answer of Dr. Wallis.
8, 9. History of the Grecian War, translated from Thucydides.
10. Iliads and Odysses of Homer.
11. Index.

Miscellaneous Tracts. . . . . . . . . . . . H,504

Considerations upon Reputation, Loyalty, Manners, and Religion. London, 1680. 8°. 63 pp.
The Art of Rhetoric. London, 1681. 8°. 168 pp.
Dialogue of the Common Laws of England. London, 1681. 8°. 208 pp.
Decameron Physiologicum; or, Ten Dialogues of Natural Philosophy. London, 1678. 8°. 136 pp.

Opera Philosophica; ed. by Sir W. Molesworth. Londini, 1839–45. 5 v. 8°. O,793
Vita. Carolopoli, 1681. 8°. . . . . . . . . . D,412
Hochelaga; or, England in the New World. E. Warburton. N.Y. 1846. 12°. V,173
Hochstetter, F. von. Neu-Seeland. Stuttgart, 1863. 8°. . . . . . Q,430
Hodge, P. R. The Steam Engine; plates. New York, n. d. f°. . *Q,390
Hodgson, J. S. Considerations on Phrenology. London, 1839. 12°. . O,1033
Hodgson, W. B. Education of Girls, and Employment of Women. Lon. 1869. 12°. O,458
Hodson, W. S. R. Soldier's Life in India. Boston, 1860. 12°. . . . V,611
Höck, C. F. C. Römische Geschichte. Braunschweig, 1841–50. 8°. . . E,16
Höcker, G. Der Beseelte Schatten. Prag, 1859. 2 v. in 1. 24°. . . G,313
Hoefer, E. Auf Deutscher Erde. Stuttgart, 1860. 2 v. 16°. . . . G,323
Lorelei. Stuttgart, 1862. 24°. . . . . . . . . . G,324
Tolleneck. Wien, 1864. 3 v. 24°. . . . . . . . . G,325
Vergangene Tage. Prag, 1859. 24°. . . . . . . . . G,326
Hoefer, J. C. F. Nouvelle Biographie Générale. Paris, 1862–66. 46 v. 8°. L.R.
Höfflmayr, M. and Pruckner. Fabrikation des Blausalzes. Hof, 1837. 8°. N,252,10
Hölderlin. H. Rau. Leipzig, 1862. 2 v. 12°. . . . . . . G,410
Hoeven, J. van der. Handbuch der Zoologie. Leipzig, 1850–56. 2 v. 8°. G,919
Hoffman, C. F. Life of Jacob Leisler. Boston, 1860. 12°. . . . C,860,13
Hoffman, D. Chronicles of Cartaphilus. London, 1853. 2 v. 8°. . . H,627
Hoffman, M. Practice of the Court of Chancery. N. Y. 1839–43. 3 v. 8°. U,516
Hoffmann, G. F. Lichenes. Lipsiæ, 1784. 2 v. in 1. f°. . . . . Q,76
Pflanzenklimatologie. Leipzig, 1857. 8°. . . . . . . G,874
Hoffmann, H. Protein und seine Verbindungen. Giessen, 1842. 8°. . N,252,14

Hoffmann, R. Jahresbericht über Agriculturchemie. Berl. 1860–65. 6 v. 8°. G,755
Hoffnung, Liebe, Glauben, Lehren von. J. F. Fries. Heidelb. 1823. 16°. G,552
Hofland, B. Young Cadet. Philadelphia, n. d. 18°. . . . . J,1296
Hofmann, A. W. Introduction to Modern Chemistry. London, 1866. 8°. N,225
Hofmann, F. W. Cultur der Handelsgewächse. Prag, 1845. 8°. . . G,873
Hofmann, J. P. Laboratorium der Ludwig's Universität. Heid. 1842. 8°. N,252,7
Hoffmeister, W. Botanik der Reise des Prinzen Waldemar nach Ceylon. Berlin, 1862. 4°. . . . . . . . . . . . Q,127
Higher Cryptogamia. London, 1862. 8°. . . . . . . . O,307
Hofwyl, Sketches of. M. C. Woodbridge. London, 1862. 12°. . . O,1007
Hog, Breeds, and Management of. W. Youatt and Martin. N. Y. 1856. 12°. M,450
Hogarth, G. Memoirs of the Musical Drama. London, 1838. 2 v. 8°. . M,410
Memoirs of the Opera. London, 1851. 2 v. 8°. . . . . . M,406
Musical History, Biography, and Criticism. Lond. 1838. 2 v. 16°. M,399
Hogarth, G. Outlines of Geography. London, 1853. 24°. . . . O,894
Hogarth, W., as Painter, Engraver, Philosopher. G. A. Sala. Lond. 1866. 8°. C,1191
Erklärung der Hogarthischen Kupferstiche. Gött. 1794–1835. 2 v. 16°. G,622
Hogg, J. Elements of Natural Philosophy. London, 1853. 8°. . . N,80
The same. London, 1861. p. 8. . . . . . . . . L,293
The Microscope. London, 1856. 8°. . . . . . . . . . N,11
Hogg, J. Familiar Anecdotes of Sir Walter Scott. N. Y. 1834. 12°. . C,1165
Lecture on Writing and Spelling Reform. London, 1849. 32°. . L,661
Poetical Works of the Ettrick Shepherd. Glasgow, 1855. 5 v. 16°. I,357
Hogg, T. Culture of the Carnation. London, 1839. 12°. . . . . N,947
Hohenschwangau, Roman und Gesch. C. Gutzkow. Leipzig, 1867. 5 v. 16°. G,296
Hohenstaufen, Geschichte der. F. L. G. von Raumer. Leip. 1857–58. 6 v. 8°. E,68
Hohenstein, Die von. F. Spielhagen. Berlin, 1867. 3 v. 16°. . . . G,467
Hohensteins, The; a Novel. F. Spielhagen. New York, 1870. 12°. . G,222
Holbein, H. Dance of Death. F. Douce. London, 1858. 12°. . . L,106
Life and Works. R. N. Wornum. London, 1867. 8°. . . . M,292
Holcombe, J. P. Literature in Letters. New York, 1866. 8°. . . . H,219
Holcroft, T. Memoirs; by himself. London, 1856. p. 8°. . . I,661,4
Holdich, J. Life of Wilbur Fisk. New York, 1856. 8°. . . . . . C,813
Hole, C. Brief Biog. Dictionary; ed. by W. A. Wheeler. N. Y. 1866. 12°. L.R.
Hole, J. Prize Essay on Literary and other Institutions. Lond. 1853. 8°. O,1016
Hole, M. Discourses on the Liturgy. London, 1837–38. 4 v. 8°. . . P,899
Holiday Rambles. E. Grant. London, 1862. 16°. . . . . J,1170
Holidays at Roselands. M. Farquharson. New York, 1870. 16°. . . J,1323
Holinshed, R. Chronicles of England, Scotland, etc. Lond. 1807–8. 6 v. 4°. F,161
Holland, Belgium, Germany, Education in. W. E. Hickson. Lond. 1840. 8°. O,1011
Education in. V. Cousin. London, 1838. 8°. . . . . . O,1197
Educational Tour in. H. Mann. London, 1853. 12°. . . . O,907
Family Tour through the South of. London, 1831. 16°. . . . I,615
Histoire Métallique de Hollande. P. Bizot. Amst. 1688–90. 3 v. 8°. M,386
History of. C. M. Davies. London, 1851. 3 v. 8°. . . . . B,410
History of the United Netherlands. J. L. Motley. N. Y. 1861. 2 v. 8°. B,409
its Institutions, etc. E. Meeter. London, 1857. 12°. . . . . V,462
Rise of the Dutch Republic. J. L. Motley. N. Y. 1868. 3 v. 8°. B,408,2
Travels in. B. Silliman. New Haven, 1820. 16°. . . . . V,1030
Holland, E. H. Reviews and Essays. Boston, 1849. 12°. . . . . H,112

Holland, J. Manufactures in Metal. London, 1831. 3 v. 12°. . M,1043
Holland, J. G. Bay-Path; Tale of N. E. Colonial Life. N. Y. 1866. 12°. K,178
Bitter-Sweet; a Poem. New York, 1864. 12°. . . . . . . I,58
Gold-Foil; from Popular Proverbs. New York, 1867. 12°. . . H,107
History of Western Massachusetts. Springfield, 1855. 2 v. 12°. . C,40
Kathrina. New York, 1868. 12°. . . . . . . . . . I,59
Lessons in Life. New York, 1867. 12°. . . . . . . . H,108
Letters to the Joneses. New York, 1865. 12°. . . . . . . H,109
Letters to Young People. New York, 1867. 12°. . . . . . H,111
Life of Abraham Lincoln. Springfield, Mass. 1866. 8°. . . . C,878
Miss Gilbert's Career. New York, 1867. 12°. . . . . . . K,179
Plain Talks on Familiar Subjects. New York, 1866. 12°. . . H,110
Titcomb's Letters to Young People. New York, 1870. 12°. . . H,111
Holland, *Lady*. See *Fox, S. S.*
Hollands, The. V. F. Townsend. Boston, 1871. 12°. . . . . . K,277
Holley, M. A. Texas. Lexington, Ky. 1836. 12°. . . . . . . C,197
Holley, O. L. Description of the City of New York. New York, 1847. 16°. C,152
Hollick, F. Marriage Guide. New York, 1860. 16°. . . . . . L,836
Outlines of Anatomy. Philadelphia, 1846. 4°. . . . . . . Q,289
Hollings, J. F. Life of Cicero. London, 1839. 16°. . . . . . . I,628
Life of Gustavus Adolphus. London, 1838. 16°. . . . . . I,624
Holly, H. H. Country Seats. New York, 1866. 4°. . . . . . . M,195
Holmboe, C. A. Norske Sprogs sammenlignet med Sankrit. Wien, 1852. 4°. G,608
Holme Lee *pseud.* See *Parr, H.*
Holmes, E. Life of Mozart. New York, 1853. 12°. . . . . . . D,493
Holmes, J. Art of Rhetoric. Philadelphia, 1849. 12°. . . . . L,598
Holmes, M. J. Cameron Pride. Philadelphia, 1870. 12°. . . . . K,180
Darkness and Daylight. New York, 1869. 12°. . . . . . K,182
Dora Deane and Maggie Miller. New York, 1869. 12°. . . . K,183
English Orphans. New York, 1868. 12°. . . . . . . K,184
Ethelyn's Mistake. New York, 1870. 12°. . . . . . . K,185
Homestead on the Hillside. New York, 1869. 12°. . . . . K,186
Hugh Worthington. New York, 1869. 12°. . . . . . . K,187
Lena Rivers. New York, 1870. 12°. . . . . . . . K,188
Marian Gray. New York, 1869. 12°. . . . . . . . K,191
Meadow Brook. New York, 1868. 12°. . . . . . . . K,194
Millbank; or, Roger Irving's Ward. New York, 1871. 12°. . . K,173
Rose Mather. New York, 1869. 12°. . . . . . . . K,192
Tempest and Sunshine. New York, 1868. 12°. . . . . . K,193
Holmes, O. W. Autocrat of the Breakfast-Table. Boston, 1866. 12°. . H,61
Currents and Counter-Currents in Medical Science. Bost. 1861. 12°. L,862
Elsie Venner. Boston, 1867. 2 v. 16°. . . . . . . . K,195
Mechanism in Thought and Morals. Boston, 1871. 12°. . . . O,626
Guardian Angel. Boston, 1867. 16°. . . . . . . . . K,196
Poems. Boston, 1864. 16°. . . . . . . . . . . I,56
Professor at the Breakfast-Table. Boston, 1866. 12°. . . . . H,62
Songs in Many Keys. Boston, 1862. 12°. . . . . . . . I,53
Soundings from the Atlantic. Boston, 1866. 12°. . . . . . H,49
Holt, J., Memoirs of. T. C. Croker. London, 1838. 2 v. 8°. . . . . D,469
Holtzapffel, C. Turning and Mechanical Manipulation. Lond. 1866. 3 v 8°. M,666

Holy and Profane States. T. Fuller. Boston, 1864. 16°. . . . . . P,39
Holy Coat of Treves and German Cath. Church. J. Ronge. N.Y. 1845. 16°. P,792
Holy Grail, and other Poems. A. Tennyson. Boston, 1870. 16°. . . . I,451
or, Joseph of Arimathie; a Poem of 1350. London, 1871. 8°. L,605,44
Holy Land. See *Palestine.*
Holy Living. J. Taylor. Boston, 1864. 16°. . . . . . . . . P,31
and Dying. J. Taylor. London, 1870. p. 8°. . . . . . . L,241
Holy War. J. Bunyan. Philadelphia, 1841. 12°. . . . . . . P,17
Holyoake, G. J. Rudiments of Public Speaking. New York, 1853. 12°. . L,589
Homans, J. S. and J. S., jr. Cyclopædia of Commerce. New York, 1858. 8°. S.C.
Home, D. D. Incidents of my Life. New York, 1863. 12°. . . . D,29
Home, H., *Lord Kames.* Elements of Criticism. New York, 1855. 12°. . L,595
Loose Hints upon Education. Edinburgh, 1782. 8°. . . . O,1185
Sketches of the History of Man. Edinburgh, 1774. 2 v. 4°. . . N,466
The same. Edinburgh, 1813. 3 v. 8°. . . . . . . N,420
Home, The. F. Bremer. New York, 1843. 8°. . . . . . . . K,606
The same. London, 1853. p. 8°. . . . . . . L,169,3
Home and Social Philosophy; from Household Words. N. Y. 1852. 2 v. 12°. H,577
Home as Found. J. F. Cooper. New York, 1867. 12°. . . . . K,31
The same. New York, 1860. 12°. . . . . . . . K,60
Home-Book of Pleasure and Instruction. R. Valentine. London, 1868. 12°. M,331
or, Pocket Miscellany. W. and R. Chambers. Boston, 1868. 6 v. 12°. H,554
Home Cyclopædia of Literature and Arts. G. P. Putnam. N. Y. 1852. 12°. L.R.
Home for All; Octagon Mode of Building. O. S. Fowler. N. Y. 1854. 12°. M,201
Home-Heroes, Saints, and Martyrs. T. S. Arthur. Philadelphia, 1865. 12°. J,645
Home Influence. G. Aguilar. New York, 1866. 12°. . . . . . K,579
The same. Leipzig, 1859. 2 v. in 1. 16°. . . . . . J,2
Home-Life in Germany. C. L. Brace. New York, 1853. 12°. . . . V,417
its Divine Idea. J. B. Brown. New York, 1867. 12°. . . . P,20
Journal of a. E. M. Sewell. New York, 1867. 12°. . . . K,1148
The same. Leipzig, 1867. 2 v. in 1. 16°. . . . . J,456
Home-Lights and Shadows. T. S. Arthur. Philadelphia, n. d. 16°. . J,612
Home Pastimes; or, Tableau Vivants. J. H. Head. Boston, 1860. 12°. . H,245
Home Reading, Papers for. J. Hall. New York, 1871. 12°. . . . H,224
Home Scenes and Heart Studies. G. Aguilar. New York, 1864. 12°. . K,580
Home Stories. T. S. Arthur. New York, 1869. 6 v. 16°. . . . J,1478

Vol. 1. Hidden Wings. Vol. 4. The Peace-Maker.
2. Sowing the Wind. 5. Not anything for Peace.
3. Sunshine at Home. 6. After a Shadow.

Homespun; or, Five and Twenty Years Ago. New York, 1870. 12°. . H,73
Homer and Homeric Age, Studies on. W. E. Gladstone. Oxf. 1858. 3 v. 8°. H,727
and the Iliad. J. S. Blackie. Edinburgh, 1866. 4 v. 8°. . . . U,426

Vol. 1. Homeric Dissertations. Vol. 2, 3. Illiad in English verse.
Vol. 4. Notes Philological and Archæological.

Batrachomyomachia, Hymns, etc.; tr. G. Chapman. London, 1858. 16°. U,436
The same. London, 1859. p. 8°. . . . . . . . . L,140
Essay on the Genius of. R. Wood. London, 1824. 8°. . . . H,729
Iliad, *in Greek.* Halæ Saxon. 1785. 2 v. in 1. 8°. . . . . U,396
The same; first six books; ed. C. Anthon. N. Y. 1856. 12°. U,431
The same; illustrated by J. Flaxman. London, 1805. 4°. . *Q,238
The same; trans. by W. C. Bryant. Boston, 1870. 2 v. 8°. U,439

Homer. Iliad; translated by T. A. Buckley. London, 1856. p. 8°. . . U,428
The same. London, 1870. p. 8°. . . . . . . L,61
The same; tr. G. Chapman; ed. R. Hooper. Lond. 1857. 2 v. 12°. U,424
The same; tr. W. Cowper; ed. R. Southey. London, 1855. p. 8°. L,175,7
The same. New York, 1855. 8°. . . . . . . U,429
The same; translated by the Earl of Derby. N.Y. 1866. 2 v. 8°. U,432
The same; translated by Sir J. F. W. Herschel. Lond. 1866. 8°. U,437
The same; translated by C. Merivale. London, 1869. 2v. . U,435
The same; translated by W. Munford. Boston, 1846. 2 v. 8°. U,438
The same; translated by A. Pope. London, 1867. p. 8°. . L,139
The same. New York, 1855. 3 v. 16°. . . . U,365
The same; tr. P. S. Worsley, A. Conington. Edin. 1865–8. 2 v. 12°. U,433
Odyssey, *in Greek*. Halæ Saxon. 1784. 8°. . . . . . . U,397
The same; illustrated by J. Flaxman. London, 1805. 4°. *Q,236
The same; translated by T. A. Buckley. London, 1869. p. 8°. L,62
The same; translated by G. Chapman. Lond. 1857. 2 v. 16°. U,423
The same; tr. W. Cowper; ed. R. Southey. Lond. 1855. p. 8°. L,175,8
The same; translated by A. Pope. Hartford, 1854. 12°. . U,430
The same. New York, 1855. 2 v. 16°. . . . U,365,2,3
The same; tr. A. Pope; illus. J. Flaxman. Lond. 1859. p. 8°. L,140
The same; translated by P. S. Worsley. Edinb. 1868. 2 v. 8°. U,434
Werke; übersetzt von J. H. Voss. Stuttgart, 1866. 2 v. 16°. . E,290
Homes abroad. H. Martineau. London, 1859. 16°. . . . . . K,551,4
and Fortunes in West and South. F. R. Goddard. Phila. 1869. 8°. . V,132
and Haunts of British Poets. W. Howitt. New York, 1847. 2 v. 12°. D,19
of American Authors. New York, 1857. 4°. . . . . . . . H,664
of the New World. F. Bremer. New York, 1853. 2 v. 12°. . . V,53
without Hands. J. G. Wood. New York, 1866. 8°. . . . N,555
Homestead Architecture. S. Sloan. Philadelphia, 1867. 8°. . . . M,191
Homestead on the Hillside. M. J. Holmes. New York, 1864. 12°. . . K,186
Homeward Bound. J. F. Cooper. New York, 1865. 12°. . . . . K,32
The same. New York, 1860. 8°. . . . . . . . . K,62
Homilies, Old English, of 12th and 13th Centuries. London, 1868. . L,605,29,34
Homilist, The. D. Thomas. London, n. d. 8 v. 12°. . . . . . P,693
Hommaire de Hell, X. Steppes of the Caspian Sea. London, 1847. 8°. . V,704
Homœopathic Med. Soc. of New York. Trans. 1868, v. 6. Albany, 1868. 8°. L,945
Homöopathischer Thierarzt. F. A. Günther. Sonders. 1855. 3 v. in 1. 8°. E,417
Honan, M. B. Personal adventures in Italy. New York, 1852. 12°. . V,511
Hone, W. Every-Day Book. London, 1827. 3 v. 8°. . . . . . H,490
Honor May. M. Bartol. Boston, 1866. 12°. . . . . . . . K,21
Honor Triumphant, and Line of Life. J. Forde. London, 1843. 8°. I.885,18
Hood, C. Warming and Ventilation. London, 1869. 8°. . . . . . N,46
Hood, E. P. Lamps, Pitchers, and Trumpets. New York, 1869. 2 v. 12°. P,236
World of Anecdotes. London, 1870. 12°. . . . . . . H,574
Hood, T. Hood's Own. London, 1846. 8° . . . . . . . . H,169
Memorials; edited by his daughter and son. Boston, 1861. 2 v. 12°. D,6
Poetical Works. Boston, 4 v. 1856–59. 16°. . . . . . . I,215
Prose Works. New York, 1865. 3 v. 8°. . . . . . . U,276
Tylney Hall. Hartford, 1846. 12°. . . . . . . . . . K,726

Hood, T. Works; edited by E. Sargent. New York, 1860. 3 v. 12°. . I,349
Hoogeveen, H. Greek Particles. London, 1829. 8°. . . . . . L,738
Hooghe, R. de. Hieroglyphica of Merkbeelden. Amsterdam, 1735. 4°. . *Q,340
Hook, W. F. Church Dictionary. Philadelphia, 1854. 8°. . . . P,164
Hook, T. E. Gilbert Gurney; a Novel. London, 1841. 16°. . . . K,719
Gurney Married. London, n. d. 16°. . . . . . . K,1152
Jack Brag. London, n. d. 12°. . . . . . . . K,1151
Maxwell. London, 1840. 16°. . . . . . . . K,1150
Parson's Daughter. London, n. d. 16°. . . . . . . . K,720
Precepts and Practice. London, 1840. 12°. . . . . . K,721
Sayings and Doings. London, n. d. 3 v. 16°. . . . . K,722
Widow and the Marquess. London, n. d. 12°. . . . . K,723
Hook, W. F. Lives of Archbishops of Canterbury. Lond. 1861–68. 7 v. 8°. D,215
Hooke, Col. Negotiations in Scotland, 1707. Dublin, 1760. 16°. . . A,475
Hooke, N. Roman History, with Maps. London, 1806. 12 v. 8°. . A,157
Hooker, E. W. Life of Thomas Hooker. Boston, 1870. 12°. . . . D,8,6
Hooker, H. Child's Book on the Sabbath. New York, n. d. 18°. . P,746,29
Hooker, J. D. Himalayan Journals. London, 1855. 2 v. 12°. . . V,673
Hooker, R. Works. Oxford, 1807. 3 v. 8°. . . . . . . . P,725
The same. New York, 1851. 8°. . . . . . . . P,735
Life of. I. Walton. New York, 1854. 8°. . . . . . . D,404
Hooker, T., Life of. E. W. Hooker. Boston, 1870. 12°. . . . . D,8,6
Hooker, W. Child's Book of Nature. New York, 1869. 12°. . . . N,642
First Book in Chemistry. New York, 1862. 16°. . . . . N,166
Mineralogy and Geology. New York, 1865. 12°. . . . . N,780
Natural History. New York, 1860. 12°. . . . . . N,643
Science for the School and Family. New York, 1863–64. 2 v. 12°. . N,226
Vol. 1. Natural Philosophy. Vol. 2. Chemistry.
Hooker, Sir W. J. Century of Ferns. London, 1854. 8°. . . . N,894
Journal of Botany. London, 1842. . . . . . . . . N,1008
and Arnott, G. A. W. Botany of Beechey's Voyage. London, 1841. 4°. *Q,113
Hooper, E. J. Western Fruit Book. Cincinnati, 1857. 8°. . . . M,538
Hooper, J. J. Dog and Gun; Chapters on Shooting. . . . M,533,4
Hooper, W. Rational Recreations. London, 1794. 4 v. 8°. . . . H,505
Hooper, W. H. Ten Months among the Tuski. London, 1853. 8°. . V,953
Hoopes, J. Book of Evergreens. New York, 1868. 12°. . . . N,945
Hoover, D., Memoir of. I. H. Julian. Richmond, Ind. 1857. 8°. . . H,302,1
Hop, Analysis of the. J. C. Nesbit. London, 1846. 8°. . . . N,252,32
Hope and Have. W. T. Adams. Boston, 1868. 16°. . . . J,1467,5
Hope, I. Britanny and the Chase. London, 1853. p. 8°. . . I,656,7
Hope, T. Costume of the Ancients. London, 1812. 2 v. 8°. . . . M,369
Hope Leslie. C. M. Sedgwick. New York, 1862. 2 v. 12°. . . . K,237
Hope on, Hope Ever. M. Howitt. New York, 1867. 24°. . . . J,1159
Hopes. F. Bremer. London, 1857. 12°. . . . . . . . L,169,1
Hopes and Fears. C. M. Yonge. Leipzig, 1861. 2 v. in 1. 16°. . . J,551
Hopkins, J. H. American Citizen; his Rights and Duties. N. Y. 1857. 12°. O,415
Refutation of Milner's End of Controversy. N. Y. 1856. 2 v. 12°. P,197
Scriptural and Historical View of Slavery. New York, 1864. 12°. O,416
Hopkins, M. Hawaii; Past, Present, and Future. New York, 1869. 8°. V,884
Hopkins, M. Evidences of Christianity. Boston, 1870. 12°. . . . P,165

Hopkins, M. Lectures on Moral Science. Boston, 1870. 12°. . . . o,669
Law of Love and Love as a Law. New York, 1869. 12°. . . o,714
Miscellaneous Essays and Discourses. Boston, 1847. 8°. . . P,168
Hopkins, S. Youth of the Old Dominion. Boston, 1856. 12°. . . K,98
Puritans and Queen Elizabeth. Boston, 1859–65. 3 v. 8°. . . A,513
Hopley, T. Lecture on Respiration. London, 1855. 8°. . . . N,252,44
Hopper, I. T., Life of. L. M. Child. Boston, 1853. 12°. . . . . C,1011
Hoppin, J. M. Old England; its Scenery and People. New York, 1867. 16°. V,303
Horæ Lyricæ and Divine Songs. I. Watts. Boston, 1854. 16°. . . I,234
Horæ Paulinæ. W. Paley. London, 1845. 8°. . . . . . . P,709,3
Horæ Subsecivæ; Locke and Sydenham. J. Brown. Edinburgh, 1858. 8°. H,449
Horace Templeton's Diary. C. Lever. Leipzig, 1848. 16°. . . . J,289
Horatius Flaccus, Q., Deutscher Horatius. C. W. Binder. Bern, 1832. 16°. E,291
Dichtkunst. Wirzburg, 1780. 16°. . . . . . . . . . E,292
Odes; translated by T. Martin. Boston, 1861. 24°. . . . U,376
Odes and Epodes; tr. by Sir E. B. Lytton. New York, 1870. 12°. . U,457
The same. Leipzig. 1869. 2 v. in 1. 16°. . . . . . J,315
Opera ommia; curante N. E. Lemaire. Parisiis, 1829–31. 3 v. 8°. U,324
Satyren; übersetzt von C. M. Wieland. Leipzig, 1786. 2 v. 12°. E,293
Works; translated by P. Francis. London, 1831. 2 v. 16°. . . U,379
The same. New York, 1855. 2 v. 16°. . . . U,364
The same; translated by C. Smart. New York, 1855. 12°. . U,453
Hordynski, J. History of Late Polish Revolution. Boston, 1832. 8°. B,542
Horizontal Force. A. D. Bache. London, 1863. 4°. . . . Q,324,13
Horlock, *Scrutator*. Horses and Hounds. London, 1855. 12°. . . . M,447
Horn, W. O. v. Gesammelte Erzählungen. Frank.-a-M. 1861–62. 12 v. 16°. G,327
Schmiedjakobs Geschichten. Frankfurt-a-Main, 1853–62. 3 v. 12°. G,328
Hornby, E. Constantinople during the Crimean War. London, 1863. l. 8°. V,575
Horne, G. Discourses. Oxford, 1795. 4 v. 8°. . . . . . . P,708
Sixteen Sermons. Oxford, 1795. 8°. . . . . . . P,708,5
Horne, J. Controversial Letters. London, 1771. . . . . . . H,856
Horne, T.H. Introduction to Study of Bibliography. London, 1814. 2 v. 8°. L.R.
Horneck, A. Great Law of Consideration. London, 1729. 12°. . . P,196
Horner, F. Memoirs and Correspondence; ed. L. Horner. Bost. 1853. 2 v. 8°. D,97
Horner, W. E. Special Anatomy and Histology. Phil. 1851. 2 v. 8°. . L,1007
Horology and Astronomy. W. B. Carpenter. London, 1857. p. 8°. . L,283
Horry, P. and Weems. Life of Gen. Francis Marion. Philadel. 1863. 12°. C,1009
Horse, The. J. H. Walsh and I. J. Lupton. London, 1861. 8°. . . M,476
and Horsemanship of U. S. H. W. Herbert. N. Y. 1857. 2 v. 8°. *M,733
Artistic Anatomy of. B. W. Hawkins. London, 1866. 8°. . . M,347
Diseases of. W. Youatt. London, 1853. 18°. . . . . . . M,441
Foot of. W. Miles. New York, 1856. 12°. . . . . . . M,472
History of. W. C. L. Martin. London, 1853. 18°. . . . M,441
Trotting Horse of America. H. Woodruff. New York, 1868. 12°. M,460
Structure and Diseases of. W. Youatt. Auburn, 1854. 12°. . . . M,471
Horse-Doctor, Modern. G. H. Dadd. New York, 1854. 12°. . . . M,452
Horse-Keepers, Hints to. H. W. Herbert. New York, 1859. 12°. . . M,461
Horse Management; illustrated. E. Mayhew. Philadelphia, n. d. 8°. . M,478
Horsemanship, Method of. F. Baucher. Philadelphia, 1856. 12°. . . M,470
Horses and Hounds. Mr. Horlock, *Scrutator*. London, 1855. 12°. . . . M,447

Horses, Asses, etc., Natural History of. C. H. Smith. Edinb. n. d. 16°. N,470,20
Morgan. D. C. Linsley. New York, 1859. 12°. . . . . . M,462
Horsfield, T. Lepidoptera of Java. n. t. p. 4°. . . . . . . Q,114
Horse-Shoe Robinson. J. P. Kennedy. Philadelphia, 1865. 12°. . . K,230
Horsey, Sir J. Travels in Russia. London, 1856. 8°. . . . . . V,989
Horsford, M. G. Indian Legends and other Poems. New York, 1855. 12°. I,62
Hortense, History of. J. S. C. Abbott. New York, 1870. 16°. . J,1403
Hortense, Königin. C. Mundt. Berlin, 1861. 2 v. 12°. . . . . . G,360
The same; translated. New York, 1870. . . . . . G,213
Horticulture, Gleanings from French Gardens. W. Robinson. Lond. 1869. 12°. N,957
Theory of. J. Lindley. London, 1840. 8°. . . . . . . . M,564
Verhandlungen des Gartenbau Vereins in Preussen. Berlin, 1842–49. 19 v. in 18. 4°. . . . . . . . . . . . . . E,480
Horticulturist, The. J. C. Loudon. London, 1860. 8°. . . . . . M,543
Horton, R. G. Life of James Buchanan. New York, 1859. 12°. . . C,701
Hosking, W. Regulation of Buildings in Towns. London, 1848. 12°. . M,180
and others. Architecture, Building, Masonry, etc. N. Y. 1852. 4°. M,286
Hoskins, S. E. Charles II. in the Channel Islands. London, 1854. 2 v. 8°. A,519
Hosmer, J. K. The Color-Guard. Boston, 1864. 12°. . . . . . B,951
Hosmer, W. H. C. Poetical Works. New York, 1854. 2 v. 12°. . . *I,60
Hosmer, Z., Catalogue of the Library of. Boston, 1861. 8°. . . . L.R.
Hospital Life in Army of the Potomac. W. H. Reed. Boston, 1868. 12°. B,941
Hospital Sketches. L. M. Alcott. Boston, 1869. 16°. . . . . . K,2
Hotchkin, J. H. Settlement of Western New York. New York, 1848. 8°. C,95
Hot-Houses, Treatise on. R. B. Leuchars. New York, 1857. 12°. . . M,535
Hottentots, Journeys among, 1777–79. W. Paterson. London, 1789. 4°. . Q,422
Houdin, R. Sharper detected and exposed. London, 1863. 12°. . . D,663
Hough, F. B. History of Druryée's Brigade. Albany, 1864. 8°. . . B,813
Hist. of St. Lawrence and Franklin Counties, N.Y. Albany, 1853. 8°. C,120
Washingtonia; on Death of G. Washington. Roxbury, 1865. 2 v. 4°. F,60
Houghton, D. Geol. of Michigan; 2d and 3d Rep. Detroit, 1839–40. 2 v. 8°. N,881
Hours of Work and Play. F. P. Cobbe. London, 1867. 12°. . . . H,322
House and Home Papers. H. B. Stowe. Boston, 1865. 12°. . . . H,278
House by the Church-Yard. J. S. Le Fanu. New York, 1866. 12°. . K,763
House-Carpenter, American. R. G. Hatfield. New York, 1857. 8°. . M,206
House of Commons, History of. London, 1742–44. 14 v. 12°. . . B,101
Precedents in. J. Hatsell. London, 1818. 4 v. 4°. . . Q,343
House of Representatives, Rules of. J. M. Barclay. Washington, 1861. 8°. B,720
House of the Seven Gables. N. Hawthorne. Boston, 1869. 12°. . . K,159
The same. Boston, 1868. 12°. . . . . . . . U,40,7
House on the Moor. M. Oliphant. New York, 1861. 12°. . . . K,864
House on Wheels. Mad. de Stolz. Boston, 1871. 16°. . . . . J,1540
House-Painting, Treatise on. J. W. Masury. New York, 1868. 12°. . M,646
Household, Common Sense in the. M. V. Terhune. New York, 1871. 12°. H,328
Household Book of Poetry. C. A. Dana. New York, 1867. 8°. . . I,167
Household Library. T. S. Arthur. Philadelphia, 1859. 12 v. in 6. 12°.
Married Life; Home Scenes. . . . . . . . . J,600
Seed-Time and Harvest; Off-Hand Sketches. . . . . J,601
Stories for Young Housekeepers; Stories for Parents. . . J,602
The Two Wives; Lessons in Life. . . . . . . . J,603
Woman's Trials; Ways of Providence. . . . . . . J,604
Words for the Wise; The Tried and the Tempted. . . . J,605

Household of Bouverie; the Elixir of Gold. New York, 1860. 2 v. 12°. K,354
Household of Sir Thomas More. A. Manning. London. n. d. 12°. . . K,834
Household Science, Hand-Book of. E. L. Youmans. New York, 1868. 12°. M,762
Household Songs. H. E. G. Arey. New York, 1855. 12°. . . . I,7
Household Stories. J. L. and W. K. Grimm. Boston, 1867. 12°. . . G,180
Household Taste, Hints on. C. L. Eastlake. London, 1868. 8°. . . M,158
Household Verses. B. Barton. Philadelphia, 1849. 16°. . . . . I,2
Household Words; conducted by C. Dickens. Leipzig, 1851–56. 36 v. 16°. J,123
The same; v. 13–16. New York, 1857–58. 4 v. 8°. . . T,36
Novels and Tales from. Leipzig, 1856–59. 11 v. 16°. . . . J,130
Houssaye, A. Comédie à la Fenêtre. Paris, 1852. 12°. . . . . . I,743
Men and Women of the 18th Century. New York, 1852. 2 v. 12°. C,574
Philosophers and Actresses. New York, 1852. 2 v. 12°. . . C,575
Houston, S., Life of. New York, 1855. 12°. . . . . . . . C,677
How, D., Diary of a Private in the Revolution. Morrisania, 1865. 8°. . B,815
How a Bride was won. F. Gerstäcker. New York, 1869. 8°. . . . K,711
How could he escape? a Temperance Story. J. McN. Wright. N.Y. 1870. 16°. K,405
How could he help it? A. S. Roe. New York, 1869. 12°. . . . K,270
How he won her. E. D. E. N. Southworth. Philadelphia, 1870. 12°. . K,428
How to Conquer; or, Allen Ware. C. M. Trowbridge. Phil. 1870. 16°. J,1690
How to Talk; Manual of Conversation. New York, 1856. . . . . L,585
How we are Governed. A. Fonblanque and Holdsworth. Lond. 1869. 12°. O,504
Howadji in Syria. G. W. Curtis. New York, 1852. 12°. . . . . V,625
Howard, F. Color as a Means of Art. London, 1849. 8°. . . . M,47
Imitative Art. London, n. d. 12°. . . . . . . . . . M,28
Howard, G. W. F., *Earl of Carlisle.* Lectures and Addresses. Lond. 1862. p. 8°. I,667
Diary in Turkish and Greek Waters. London, 1855. 8°. . . V,566
Speech on Sanitary Reform. London, 1847. 8°. . . . N,252,29
Travels in America; Poetry of Pope. New York, 1851. 12°. . . V,17
Howard, H., *Earl of Surrey.* Poetical Works. Boston, 1854. 16°. . . I,230
The same; with Life. London, 1854. 16°. . . . . . I,254
Howard, J., and Prison World of Europe. W. H. Dixon. N. Y. 1869. 12°. O,351
Howard, J. H. Athletic and Gymnastic Exercises. London, 1860. 16°. . M,305
Howe, H. Historical Collections of Great West. Cincin. 1853. 2 v. in 1. 8°. C,277
Historical Collections of Ohio. Cincinnati, 1848. 8°. . . . C,225
The same. Cincinnati, 1854. 8°. . . . . C,213
Life and Death on the Ocean. New York, 1860. 8°. . . . V,951
Memoirs of Eminent American Mechanics. New York, 1858. 12°. C,652
and Barber, J.W. Hist. Collections of New York State. N.Y. 1842. 8°. C,94
Howe, J. W. From the Oak to the Olive. Boston, 1868. 16°. . . . V,308
Passion Flowers; Poems. Boston, 1854. 16°. . . . . . . I,90
Words for the Hour; Poems. Boston, 1857. 16°. . . . . . I,61
Howe, R., *Earl,* Life of. Sir J. Barrow. London, 1838. 8°. . . . D,277
Howe, S. G. History of Greek Revolution, 1821. New York, 1828. 12°. A,73
Howell, R. B. C. Early Baptists of Virginia. Philadelphia, 1857. 8°. *B,809,2
Howell, T. B. and T. J. Collection of State Trials. Lond. 1816–28. 34 v. 8°. U,701
Howells, W. D. Italian Journeys. New York, 1867. 8°. . . . . . V,509
No Love Lost; a Poem. New York, 1869. 12°. . . . . . I,172
Suburban Sketches. New York, 1871. 8°. . . . . . . H,128
Venetian Life. New York, 1867. 8°. . . . . . . . V,508

Howie, J. The Scots Worthies. Edinburgh, 1854. 8°. . . . . C,1311
Howitt, A. M. Art Student in Munich. Boston, 1854. 16°. . . . V,413
School of Life. Boston, 1855. 16°. . . . . . . . . J,1247
Howitt, Marg. Twelve Months with Frederika Bremer. Lond. 1866. 2 v. 8°. V,542
Howitt, Mary. Alice Franklin; a Tale. New York, 1854. 18°. . J,1154
Author's Daughter; a Tale. New York, n. d. 8°. . . . . K,727
Bright Days. Boston, 1869. 12°. . . . . . . . J,1667
Dial of Love. Philadelphia, 1854. 12°. . . . . . . J,1320
Pictorial Calendar of the Seasons. London, 1854. p. 8°. . . L,107
Popular History of the United States. New York, 1860. 2 v. 12°. B,690
Popular Tales. New York, 1867. 14 v. 24°.

| | | | |
|---|---|---|---|
| Alice Franklin. . . . | J,1154 | Sowing and Reaping. . . | J,1157 |
| Hope on! Hope ever! . . | J,1159 | Story of a Genius. . . | J,1182 |
| Little Coin, much Care. . | J,1184 | Strive and Thrive. . . | J,1155 |
| Love and Money. . . | J,1163 | Two Apprentices. . . | J,1162 |
| My Own Story. . . . | J,1165 | Which is the Wiser. . . | J,1156 |
| My Uncle, the Clockmaker. . | J,1181 | Who Shall be Greatest. . | J,1157 |
| No Sense like Common Sense. | J,1164 | Work and Wages. . . | J,1161 |

Sketches of Natural History. London, 1834. 16°. . . . . N,492
Strive and Thrive. New York, 1853. 12°. . . . . . J,1168
Trust and Trial. London, 1858. 12°. . . . . . . . J,573
Vignettes of American History. London, n. d. 12°. . . . J,1547
Which is the Wiser? New York, 1852. 18°. . . . . . J,1172
Wood Leighton; or, a Year in the Country. London, 1847. 16°. J,1368
Work and Wages. New York, 1852. 18°. . . . . . J,1158
and others. Poetical Works. Philadelphia, 1846. 8°. . . . I,487
Howitt, W. Boy's Adventures in Australia. London, 1866. 16°. . J,1232
Country Year-Book. New York, 1855. 12°. . . . . . . H,573
German Experiences. London, 1844. 16°. . . . . . . V,410
History of the Supernatural. Philadelphia, 1863. 2 v. 12°. . . P,42
Homes and Haunts of Eminent British Poets. London, 1857. 8°. C,1184
The same. New York, 1847. 2 v. 12°. . . . . . . D,19
Jack of the Mill. London, 1844. 2 v. in 1. 16°. . . . J,1240
Land, Labour, and Gold. London, 1855. 2 v. 12°. . . . . V,879
Northern Heights of London. London, 1869. 8°. . . . . . B,66
Rural and Domestic Life of Germany. Philadelphia, 1843. 8°. V,1072
Rural Life of England. Philadelphia, 1854. 2 v. 12°. . . . V,370
Student Life in Germany. London, 1841. 8°. . . . . . .. V,378
Visits to Remarkable Places. Philadelphia, 1854. 2 v. 12°. . . V,342
Woodburn Grange. Philadelphia, n. d. 12°. . . . . . K,1144
and M. Stories of English and Foreign Life. London, 1853. p. 8°. L,108
and Smith, J. W. Illustrated Hist. of England. Lond. n. d. 8 v. 8°. A,467
Howse, J. Grammar of the Cree Language. London, 1844. 8°. . . L,781
Hows, J. W. S. Practical Elocutionist. Philadelphia, n. d. 12°. . O,1225
Hoyland, J. Historical Survey of the Gypsies. York, 1816. 8°. . . D,707
Hoyle, E. Games, Established Rules. Philadelphia, 1845. 24°. . . M,323
Games Modernized. G. F. Pardon. London, n. d. 18°. . . M,338
Hozier, H. M. Seven Weeks' War; Prussia and Austria. Lon. 1867. 2 v. 8°. B,211
Hubback, J. May and December; a Tale of Wedded Life. Phil. 1866. 12°. K,1145
Hubbard, F. M. Life of W. R. Davie. Boston, 1860. 12°. . . . C,860,25
Huber, V. A. English Universities. London, 1843. 2 v. in 3. 8°. . . O,815

Huber, F. Natural History of Bees. Edinburgh, 1808. 12°. . . . . M,444
Huc, E. R. Christianity in China, Tartary, and Thibet. Lon. 1857–58. 3 v. 8°. V,622
Journey through the Chinese Empire. London, 1855. 2 v. 8°. . V,643
The same. New York, 1855. 2 v. 12°. . . . . . V,596
Journey through Tartary, Thibet, and China. N. Y. 1852. 2 v. 12°. V,588
The same. London, 1865. p. 8°. . . . . . . . . I,657
Hudibras. S. Butler. London, 1867. 12°. . . . . . . . I,301
The same. London, 1859. 2 v. p. 8°. . . . . . . L,96
The same; 3d part. London, 1678. 8°. . . . . . I,302
Hudson, C. Doubts concerning Battle of Bunker's Hill. Boston, 1857. 12°. B,741
Hudson, H., Historical Inquiry concerning. J. M. Read. Albany, 1866. 8°. C,105
Life of. H. R. Cleveland. New York, 1860. 12°. . . . C,860,10
Hudson, H. N. Lectures on Shakespeare. New York, 1848. 2 v. 12°. . I,890
Hudson, J. W. History of Adult Education. London, 1851. 8°. . O,1040
Hudson River, The. B. J. Lossing. New York, 1866. 8°. . . . V,70
Hudson's Bay, Geography of, 1727–1751. W. Coats. London, 1852. 8°. . V,993
Hudson's Bay Territory. J. McLean. London, 1849. 2 v. 12°. . . V,134
Hübener, J. W. P. Deutsche Lebermoose. Mannheim, 1834. 8°. . . G,875
Huen-Doubourg, J., *pseud.* See *Hamond, M.*
Hufeland, C. W. Art of Prolonging Life. Boston, 1854. 12°. . . . L,893
Huff, G. Electro-Physiology. New York, 1853. 12°. . . . . L,888
Huges, J. T. Doniphan's Expedition. Cincinnati, 1850. 12°. . . . B,883
Hugh Worthington. M. J. Holmes. New York, 1867. 12°. . . . K,187
Hughes, E. Outlines of Scripture Geography and History. Phil. 1853. 12°. P,459
Hughes, G. Natural History of Barbados. London, 1750. f°. . . F,72
Hughes, H. M. Clinical Introduction to Auscultation. London, 1845. 12°. L,855
Hughes, J., *Abp.*, *vs.* J. Breckenridge. Discus. on Romanism. Phil. 1836. 8°. P,819
Life of. J. R. Hazzard. New York, 1866. 8°. . . . . . C,963
Hughes, M. Aunt Mary's Stories, etc. New York, n. d. 16°. . . J,1216
Hughes, S. Treatise on Coal Gas. London. 12°. . . . . . . M,939
Water-Works for Cities and Towns. London, 1856. 12°. . . M,940
Hughes, T. Alfred the Great. London, n. d. 12°. . . . . . . A,491
School-Days at Rugby. Boston, 1866. 12°. . . . . . . K,729
Scouring of the White Horse. Cambridge, 1859. 12°. . . J,1445
Tom Brown at Oxford. Boston, 1864. 2 v. 12°. . . . . . K,728
Tom Brown's School-Days at Rugby. Leipzig, 1858. 16°. . . J,198
Hughes, T. S. History of England, 1760–1837. London, 1855. 7 v. 8°. A,432
Travels in Greece and Albania. London, 1830. 2 v. 8°. . . V,569
Hughes, W. Australian Colonies. London, 1862. p. 8°. . . . . . I,660
Class-Book of Physical Geography. London, 1868. 16°. . V,1129
Hughes, W. C. American Miller and Millwright. Philadelphia, 1869. 12°. M,637
Hugo, V. Brigand; or, Demon of the North. Philadelphia, n. d. 8°. . H,944
Hunchback of Notre Dame. Boston, 1866. 8°. . . . . H,949
Jargal; a Novel. New York, 1866. 12°. . . . . . . . H,955
Les Miserables; translated by C. E. Wilbour. New York, 1870. 8°. H,945
Life of, by his Wife. London, 1863. 2 v. 8°. . . . . D,607
Man who laughs. New York, 1869. 8°. . . . . . . . H,953
Toilers of the Sea. New York, 1866. 8°. . . . . . . H,946
Huguenots, The. S. Smiles. New York, 1868. 8°. . . . . . . B,365
History of. W. S. Browning. London, 1842. 8°. . . . . . B,367

Huish, R. Public and Private Life of George III. London, 1821. 4°. . D,133
Hulbert, D.P.M. Education; Theologically considered. London, 1850. O,1174
Emigration; Theologically considered. London, 1850. . . O,1174
Supremacy; Theologically considered. London, 1850. . . O,1174
Hull, W. Memoirs of the North-Western Army, 1812. Boston, 1824. 8°. B,873
Hullah, J. History of Modern Music. London, 1862. 12°. . . . M,407
Wilhelm's Method of Teaching Singing. London, 1841–42. 2 v. 8°. M,401
Hulsean Lectures, 1856. H. Goodwin. London, 1856. 8°. . . . P,304
Human Action, Principles of. W. Hazlitt. London, n. d. 12°. . . H,425
Human Body, The. J. J. G. Wilkinson. Philadelphia, 1851. 12°. . . L,886
Anatomical Atlas of. H. H. Smith. Philadelphia, 1851. 8°. . L,1036
Wonders of. A. Le Pileur. New York, 1870. 12°. . . M,1045
Human Character, Philosophy of. H. Strait. Nashville, 1846. 16°. . O,630
Human Culture, Manual of. M. A. Garvey. London, 1866. 12°. . O,1002
Human Intellect. N. Porter. New York, 1868. 8°. . . . . . . O,702
Human Life; its Condition and Duration. W. Sweetser. N. Y. 1867. 12°. L,937
Human Physiology. J. W. Draper. New York, 1856. 8°. . . . L,965
Treatise on. J. C. Dalton. Philadelphia, 1864. 8°. . . . L,962
Human Progression, Theory and Natural Probability of. Boston, 1851. 16°. O,535
Human Species, Natural History of the. C. H. Smith. London, 1852. 12°. N,392
Humanics. T. W. Collins. New York, 1860. 8°. . . . . . . O,673
Humanity in the City. E. H. Chapin. New York, 1854. . . . . P,46
Humble Creatures; Worm and Fly. J.Samuelson and J.B.Hicks. Lon.'60. 8°. O,26
Humboldt, C. W. von. Kawi-Sprache auf der Insel Java. Berl. 1839. 3 v. 4°. G,595
Letters to a Lady. Philadelphia, 1864. 12°. . . . . . . G,22
Life of. G. Schlesier. New York, 1853. 12°. . . . . . . D,521
Religious Thoughts and Opinions. Boston, 1851. 16°. . . . P,30
Humboldt, F. H. A. v. Ancient Inhabitants of America. Lond. 1814. 2 v. 8°. V,258
Ansichten der Natur. Stuttgart, 1849. 12°. . . . . . . G,684
The same. Stuttgart, 1860. 2 v. 16°. . . . . . . G,683
Aspects of Nature in Different Lands. Philadelphia, 1850. 12°. V,1137
Atlas de la Nouvelle-Espagne. Paris, 1811. f°. . . . . F,119
Biographischer Roman. H. Rau. Leipzig, 1861. 7 v. 12°. . G,411
Essay on the Superposition of Rocks. London, 1823. 8°. . . N,793
Institutions and Monuments of America. London, 1814. 2. v. 8°. V,256
Kleinere Schriften. Stuttgart, 1853. 8°. . . . . . . . G,685
Kosmos. Stuttgart und Tübingen, 1845–58. 4 v. 8°. . . . G,686
Atlas zum. Stuttgart, 1851. 8°. . . . . . . Q,283
The same; trans. by E. C. Otté. Lond. 1849–58. 5 v. p. 8°. L,295
The same. New York, 1853. 5 v. p. 8°. . . . . S.C.
Briefe über. B. Cotta and others. Leipzig, 1848–60. 6 v. 8°. G,700
Letters to Varnhagen von Ense. New York, 1860. 12°. . . . G,26
Life of. P. F. H. Klencke. New York, 1853. 12°. . . . . D,521
Life, Travels, and Books. New York, 1859. 12°. . . . . D,498
Political Essays on New Spain. London, 1811. 4 v. 8°. . . V,197
Productions de l'Or et de L'argent. Paris, 1848. 8°. . . N,252,30
Reise in die Aequinoctial-Gegenden. Stuttgart, 1859–60. 4 v. 8°. E,177
The same. Stuttgart, 1861–62. 6 v. 16°. . . . . . E,168
Travels and Researches of. W. MacGillivray. N. Y. 1869. 18°. L,377
Views of Nature. London, 1869. p. 8°. . . . . . . . L,297

Humboldt, A. von. Vulkanen von Quito und Mexico. Stuttgart, 1853. 4°. F,89
and Bonpland. Travels in Equinoctial America. Lond. 1870. 3 v. p. 8. L,296
The same. London, 1818–29. 8 v. in 7. 8°. . . . . V,257
Humbugs of the World. P. T. Barnum. New York, 1866. 12°. . . H,89
Hume, A. Learned Societies and Clubs of Great Britain. Lond. 1847. 12°. L.R.
The same, abridged. London, 1853. 12°. . . . . . L.R.
Hume, D. History of England. London, 1803. 10 v. 8°. . . . A,394
The same. New York, 1850. 6 v. 12°. . . . . A,393
The same, abridged. New York, 1868. 8°. . . . . . A,391
The same; with Boydell's illustrations. Lond. 1807. 5 v. f°. L.R.
Philosophical Works. Boston, 1854. 4 v. 8°. . . . . . . O,805
Letters of Eminent Persons to; ed. by J. H. Burton. Edinb. 1849. 8°. H,832
Life of E. J. Eyre. London, 1867. 8°. . . . . . . . D,192
Humming-Birds, Natural History of. Sir W. Jardine. Edinb. n.d. 2 v. 16°. N,470,6,7
W. C. L. Martin. London, 1852. 16°. . . . . . . . O,83
Humorists, English, of the 18th Century. W. M. Thackeray. N.Y. 1854. 12°. H,681
The same. New York, 1867. 12°. . . . . . . . . H,458
Humorous Poetry, from Chaucer to Saxe. J. Parton. Boston, 1867. 12°. I,94
Humorous Speaker. O. Oldham. New York, 1868. 12°. . . . . . O,827
Humphrey Clinker. T. Smollett. New York, 1867. 16°. . . . . K,1016
The same. London, 1820. 2 v. 12°. . . . . . . K,541
The same. Leipzig, 1846. 16°. . . . . . . . J,462
Humphrey, E. P. and Cleland, T. H. Memoirs of T. Cleland. Cin. 1859. 12°. C,802
Humphreys, H. N. Coin Collector's Manual. London, 1853. 2 v. p. 8°. L,298
History of the Art of Printing. London, 1867. 4°. . . . . *Q,296
Illuminated Books of the Middle Ages. London, 1849. f°. . *Q,467
Hunchback of Notre Dame. V. Hugo. Boston, 1866. . . . . . H,949
Hundertpfund, L. Painting restored to Simplest Principles. Lond. 1849. 12°. M,55
Hundeshagen, C. B. Einfluss des Calvinismus. Bern, 1842. 8°. . . N,252,33
Hungarian Brothers. A. M. Porter. London, 1850. 16°. . . . . . K,554
Hungarian Grammar. J. Csink. London, 1853. 8°. . . . . . . . L,778
Hungarian Lady, Memoirs of a. T. Pulszky. Philadelphia, 1850. 12°. . D,768
Hungarian Revolution. J. Pragay. New York, 1850. 12°. . . . B,537
Hungary. J. G. Kohl. London, 1843. 8°. . . . . . . . . . V,433
and Croatia, Tour in. G. A. Spottiswoode. London, 1861. 8°. V,1086,1
and her Institutions, 1839–40. J. Pardoe. London, 1840. 3 v. 12°. V,429
and its Revolutions. London, 1854. p. 8°. . . . . . . L,195
and Kossuth. B. F. Tefft. Philadelphia, 1852. 12°. . . . B,524
and Transylvania. J. Paget. Philadelphia, 1850. 2 v. 12°. . V,428
History of. E. L. Godkin. London, 1853. 8°. . . . . . B,530
in 1851. C. L. Brace. New York, 1853. 12°. . . . . . . V,427
My Life and Acts in. A. Görgei. New York, 1852. 12°. . . D,771
Scenes of the War, 1848–49. Philadelphia, 1850. 12°. . . . V,420
Hungerpastor, Der. W. Raabe. Berlin, 1867. 16°. . . . . . . G,391
Hunnewell, J. F. Lands of Scott. Boston, 1871. 12°. . . . . . V,350
Hunt, C. E. Shenandoah; the Last Confederate Cruiser. N.Y. 1867. 12°. B,916
Hunt, C. H. Life of Edward Livingston. New York, 1864. 8°. . . C,880
Hunt, F. Lives of American Merchants. New York, 1858. 2 v. 8°. C,1068
Worth and Wealth; a Collection of Maxims. New York, 1856. 12°. H,30
(Ed.) Merchant's Magazine. New York, 1839–64. 51 v. 8°. . . T,39

Hunt, G. H. Outram and Havelock's Persian Campaign. Lond. 1858. 12°. V,629
Hunt, L. Autobiography; with Reminiscences. New York, 1855. 2 v. 12°. D,273
Day by the Fire, and other papers. Boston, 1870. 16°. . . . H,583
Essays and Miscellanies. New York, 1857. 12°. . . . . H,584
Italian Poets translated into English Prose. New York, 1857. 12°. I,364
Lord Byron and his Contemporaries. Philadelphia, 1828. 8°. . D,78
Men, Women, and Books. New York, 1847. 2 v. 12°. . . . H,581
Poetical Works. Boston, 1864. 2 v. 24°. . . . . . . . I,354
Seer; or, Common-places refreshed. Boston, 1865. 2 v. 12°. . H,580
Selections from the English Poets. New York, 1857. 12°. . U,279,2
Selections in Prose and Verse, 1st ser. New York, 1852. 12°. . . H,582
Stories from the Italian Poets. New York, 1849. 8°. . . . I,364
Stories in Verse. London, 1855. 16°. . . . . . . . I,356
and Lee, S. A. Book of the Sonnet. Boston, 1867. 2 v. 16°. . I,361
Hunt, R. Poetry of Science. London, 1854. p. 8°. . . . . . L,299
Hunt, W. American Biographical Sketch-Book. New York, n. d. 8°. . C,776
Hunted Down. C. Dickens. Leipzig, 1860. 16°. . . . . . J,124
Hunter, H. History of London. London, 1811. 4°. . . . . . F,277
Sacred Biography; Lectures. New York. 1852. 8°. . . . . P,178
Hunter, J. Essays on Nat. Hist., Anatomy, Physiology, etc. Lond. 1861. 2v. 8°. N,720
Hunter, J. Founders of the Plymouth Colony. London, 1854. 8°. . . C,44
Hunter, W. W. Annals of Rural Bengal. London, 1868. 8°. . . . . C,403
Hunter's Feast. M. Reid. New York, n. d. 12°. . . . . . J,1567
Hunter's Life in South Africa. R. G. Cumming. New York, 1864. 2 v. 12°. V,802
Hunting Grounds of the World, Adventures on. V. Meunier. N.Y. 1870. 12°. M,1064
The same. London, 1868. 12°. . . . . . . J,1366
Hunting in South Africa. W. C. Baldwin. New York, 1863. 12°. . . V,803
Hunting Sports in the West. C. B. Hartley. Philadelphia, n. d. 16°. J,1608
Huntington, D. General View of the Fine Arts. New York, 1851. 12°. . M,40
Huntington, E. B. Genealogy of the Huntington Family. Stamford, 1863. 8°. C,934
Huntington, W. Autobiography. New York, 1843. 12°. . . . . P,28
Hurdis, J. L. Naturalist in Bermuda. London, 1859. 12°. . . . N,521
Hurlbut, W. H. Pictures of Cuba. London, 1856. p. 8°. . . . I,659,1
Hurry-Graphs; Sketches from Life. N. P. Willis. Boston, 1864. 12°. . H,83
Hurst, J. F. History of Rationalism. New York, 1865. 8°. . . . P,120
Hurtt, F. W. Cincinnati Diary and Guide. Cincinnati, 1856–57. 2 v. 24°. C,148
Husbandry, American. W. Gaylord and L. Tucker. N.Y. 1854. 2 v. 18°. M,436
Natural Laws of. J. von Liebig. New York, 1863. 8°. . . . M,560
Husbands and Homes. M. V. Terhune. New York, 1866. 12°. . . K,327
Huskisson, W. Select Speeches; with Life by R. Walsh. Phila. 1837. 8°. H,806
Husks. M. V. Terhune. New York, 1866. 12°. . . . . . K,328
Huss, J. Letters written during his Exile. Edinburgh, 1846. 12°. . . P,157
Hussey, T. J. Illustrations of Mycology. London, 1847–55. 2 v. 4°. . Q,122
Hutchings, J. M. Guide to the Yo-Semite Valley. New York, 1870. 8°. V,113
Hutchins, T. Account of Bouquet's Expedition, 1764. Cincinnati, 1868. 8°. C,217
Hutchinson, A., Life of. G. E. Ellis. Boston, 1860. 12°. . . . C,860,16
Hutchinson, F. Historical Essay on Witchcraft. London, 1718. 8°. . O,337
Hutchinson, L. Life of Col. John Hutchinson. London, 1848. p. 8°. . L,196
The same. London, 1838. 8°. . . . . . . . . C,596
Hutchinson, T. History of Massachusetts, 1628–1750. Salem, 1795. 2 v. 8°. C,41,1,2

Hutchinson, T. History of Massachusetts, 1749–74. London, 1828. 8°. . C,41,3
Papers relative to Massachusetts Bay. Boston, 1865. 2 v. 4°. . F,69
Witchcraft Delusion of 1692; ed. by W. F. Poole. Boston, 1870. 4°. O,324
Hutchinson, T. J. Niger, Tshadda, and Binuë Exped. Lond. 1865. p. 8°. I,658,1
Hutt, W. State and Prospects of British Agriculture. London, 1837. 8°. N,252,6
Hutt, W. W. Solutions of Goodwin's Problems. Cambridge, 1863. 8°. M,1174,2
Hutten, U. von, Leben. D. F. Strauss. Leipzig, 1858–60. 3 v. 8°. . . E,241
Hutton, C. Course of Mathematics. London, 1854. 8°. . . . M,1173
Mathematical and Philosophical Dictionary. Lond. 1795. 2 v. 4°. L.R.
Hutton, H. Follie's Anatomie; Satyres. London, 1842. 12°. . . L,606,6
Hutton, M. and others. Correspondence. London, 1843. 8°. . . F,126,17
Hutton, R. H. Studies in Parliament. London, 1866. 8°. . . . D,333
Huxley, T. H. Evidence as to Man's Place in Nature. N. Y. 1863. 12°. . N,400
Lay Sermons, Addresses, and Reviews. New York, 1871. 12°. . M,773
Lectures on Comparative Anatomy. London, 1864. 8°. . . . L,989
Origin of Species. New York, 1863. 12°. . . . . . . N,499
Oceanic Hydrozoa. London, 1859. 4°. . . . . . . . Q,74
and Youmans, W. J. Physiology and Hygiene. New York, 1868. 12°. L,872
Huxtable, A. Application and Economy of Manures. Southampt. 1846. 8°. N,252,25
Drainage of the Metropolis. London, 1847. 8°. . . . N,252,25
Present Prices. Blanford, 1850. 8°. . . . . . . . N,252,31
Science and Application of Manures. London, 1847. 8°. . . N,252,25
Hyacinthe, Father. See *Loyson, C.*
Hyde, H., *Earl of Clarendon.* Correspondence. London, 1828. 2 v. 4°. . F,29
Inquiries respecting. G. A. Ellis. London, 1827. 12°. . . . B,115
Life of, by himself. Oxford, 1759. f°. . . . . . . . F,123
Life of. J. Macdiarmid. London, 1807. 4°. . . . . . . F,24
Life and Administration of. T. H. Lister. London, 1837–38. 3 v. 8°. D,218
Rebellion and Civil Wars in England. Oxford, 1732. 3 v. in 1. f°. F,122
The same. Oxford, 1849. 7 v. 8°. . . . . . . A,516
State Papers, collected by. Oxford, 1766–67. 3 v. f°. . . . F,124
Hyde, J., jr. Mormonism; its Leaders and Designs. New York, 1857. 12°. P,836
Hydraulic Engineering. G. R. Burnell. London, 1858–59. 12°. . . M,896
Hydraulic Experiments. J. B. Francis. Boston, 1855. 4°. . . . S.C.
Hydraulics and Mechanics. T. Ewbank. New York, 1870. 8°. . . . N,134
The same. New York, 1850. 8°. . . . . . . . S.C.
Description des Travaux Hydraul. L. A. de Cessart. Par. 1806–8. 2 v. 4°. Q,295
Nouvelle Architecture Hydraul. M. de Prony. Paris, 1790–96. 2 v. 4°. M,820
Practical. J. A. Eytelwein. London, 1826. 8°. . . . . N,143
Treatise on. J. F. d'Aubuisson de Vorsins. Boston, 1852. 8°. . N,131
Hydropathy, Results of. E. Johnson. New York, 1854. 12°. . . . L,856
Hymers, J. Plane and Spherical Trigonometry. London, 1858. 8°. M,1156
Hymns and Songs of the Church. G. Wither. London, 1856. 16°. . . I,466
for the Christian Year; tr. by C. Winkworth. New York, 1856. 12°. G,43
Historical Sketches of. J. Belcher. Philadelphia, 1859. 12°. . . P,889
of the Ages; from Lyra Catholica, etc. Boston, 1865–66. 3 v. 12°. I,125
of Faith and Hope. H. Bonar. New York, 1868. 3 v. 16°. . . I,105
to the Virgin and Christ, etc. London, 1867. 8°. . . . L,605,24
Hypatia; or, New Foes. C. Kingsley. New York, 1866. 2 v. 16°. . . K,750
The same. Leipzig, 1857. 2 v. in 1. 16°. . . . . J,243

Hyperion. H. W. Longfellow. Boston, 1866. 16°. . . . . . . U,1,2
Hypocrisy, Treatise on. S. Bolton. London, 1656. f°. . . . . . P,181

I will be a Sailor. L. C. Tuthill. Boston, 1864. 16°. . . . . J,1266
I will be a Soldier. L. C. Tuthill. Philadelphia, 1867. 16°. . . . J,1684
Iceland and Faroe Islands, Yacht Voyage to. J. W. Clark. Lond. 1861. 8°. V,1086,1
Greenland and the Faroe Islands. New York, 1854. 18°. . . L,425
in 1814 and 1815. E. Henderson. Edinburgh, 1818. 2 v. 8°. . V,180
its Scenes and Sagas. S. Baring-Gould. London, 1863. 8°. . . V,170
its Volcanoes, Geysers, and Glaciers. C. S. Forbes. London, 1860. 8°. V,191
Journey to. I. Pfeiffer. New York, 1852. 12°. . . . . V,15
Summer in. C. W. Paijkull. London, 1868. 8°. . . . . V,182
Rambles in. P. Miles. New York, 1854. 12°. . . . . V,16
The same. London, 1854. p. 8°. . . . . . . I,656,4
Reise nach, in 1860. W. Preyer und F. Zirkel. Leipzig, 1862. 8°. E,174
und Spitzbergen, Reise nach. F. T. Blackwood. Braunschweig, 1860. 8°. E,172
Travels in, 1810. Sir G. S. Mackenzie. Edinburgh, 1811. 4°. . Q,440
Yacht Voyage to. F. T. Blackwood, *Lord Dufferin*. Bost. 1859. 12°. V,322
Ichnographs from Connecticut River. J. Deane. Boston, 1861. 4°. . Q,47
Iconographic Encyclopædia; ed. J. G. Heck. N. Y. 1851. 6 v. 8°. and 4°. L.R.
Text, vol. 1. Mathematics and Astronomy; Physics and Meteorology; Chemistry; Mineralogy; Geognosy and Geology.
2. Botany; Zoölogy; Anthropology; Surgery.
3. Geography and Planography; History and Ethnology; Military Sciences; Naval Sciences.
4. Architecture; Mythology; Fine Arts; Technology.
Plates, vol. 1. Mathematics and Astronomy; Natural Sciences; Geography; History and Ethnology.
2. Military Sciences; Naval Sciences; Architecture; Mythology; Fine Arts; Technology.
The same, *in German*. Leipzig. 20 v. in 5. 8°. and 4°. . L.R.
Idalia; a Romance. L. de la Rame. Philadelphia, 1869. 12°. . . K,886
The same. Leipzig, 1867. 2 v. in 1. 16°. . . . . J,414
Ide, G. B. Ministry demanded by the Present Crisis. Phila. 1844. 16°. . P,15
Ideal in Art. H. Taine. New York, 1869. 16°. . . . . . M,29
Idler, The. S. Johnson. Boston, 1866. 8°. . . . . . . H,536,27
The same. New York, n. d. 8°. . . . . . . U,227,1
in France. M. Gardiner. Philadelphia, 1841. 2 v. 12°. . . V,455
Idiotcy, Hand-Book of. J. Abbott. London, 1857. 12°. . . . . O,914
Idyls of the King. A. Tennyson. Boston, 1859. 12°. . . . . I,449
If, Yes, and Perhaps. E. E. Hale. Boston, 1868. 16°. . . . . H,32
Ignorance, Defence of. London, 1851. 16°. . . . . . . . O,963
Evils of Popular. J. Foster. New York, 1853. 12°. . . . H,440
Popular, Essay on. J. Foster. London, 1865. p. 8°. . . . L,184
Ik Marvel *pseud.* See *Mitchell, D. G.*
Iliad of Homer. See *Homer*.
Illinois, Campaign in, 1778–79. G. R. Clark. Cincinnati, 1869. 8°. . . C,219
Early Newspapers in. H. R. Boss. Chicago, 1870. 4°. . . . F,172
Geological Survey of. A. H. Worthen and others. Springfield and Chicago, 1866–70. 4 v. 4°. . . . . . . . . *N,742
History of, 1818–47. T. Ford. Chicago, 1854. 12°. . . . C,170
Reports of Supreme Court, v. 44. N. L. Freeman. Chicago, 1869. 8°. U,519

Illuminated and Missal Painting, Manual of. E. Jewett. London, n. d. 12°. M,84
Illuminated Books of the Middle Ages. H. N. Humphreys. London, 1849. f°. *Q,467
Illuminated Ornaments from 6th to 17th Century. H. Shaw. Lond. 1833. 4°. *Q,185
Illuminating, Hints on. H. M. Lucien. London, n. d. 12°. . . . M,61
History, Theory, and Practice of. M. D. Wyatt. London, n. d. 12°. M,83
Illumination, Manual of. J. W. Bradley and T. G. Goodwin. Lond. 1867. 12°. M,26,1
Companion to the above. J. J. Laing. London, 1866. 12°. . M,26,2
Illustrated London News. London, 1843–65. 47 v. f°. . . . . . *Q,335
Magazine of Art. New York, 1853. 2 v. 8°. . . . . . . T,54
Illustrative Gatherings for Preachers, Teachers. G. S. Bowes. Phil. 1864. 12°. P,90
Im Strom der Zeit. B. von Guseck. Prag, 1860. 4 v. in 2. 24°. . . G,294
Image of the Beast. S. B. Smith. New York, 1862. 18°. . . . . P,21
Image of his Father. H. and A. Mayhew. London, 1848. 12°. . . J,635
Imaginary Conversations of Greeks and Romans. W. S. Landor. Lon. 1853. 8°. H,446
Imatra, Les Pierres d'. G. F. Parrot. St. Petersburg, 1840. 4°. . N,252,42
Imhoff, L. Studium der Koleoptern. Basil, 1856. 8°. . . . . . G,947
Imitation of Christ. T. á Kempis. Dublin, 1817. 32°. . . . . . P,334
Imitative Art. F. Howard. London, n. d. 12°. . . . . . . . M,28
Imlay, G. Adventures of Daniel Boone. London, 1793. 8°. . . . V,44
Western Territory of North America. London, 1792. 8°. . . V,106
Immermann, C. Münchhausen. Berlin, 1864. 4 v. in 2. 16°. . . . G,334
Imperial Guard of Napoleon. J. T. Headley. New York, 1859. 12°. . B,87
Imposture, Deception, and Credulity, Sketches of. London, 1837. 16°. . I,646
Improvisatore. H. C. Andersen. New York, 1868. 8°. . . . . G,182
In Exile. From the German of W. von St. Philadelphia, 1871. 12°. . G,175
In Exitu Israel. S. Baring-Gould. New York, 1870. p. 8°. . . . K,585
In Memoriam. A. Tennyson. Boston, 1854. 16°. . . . . . . I,448
In Reih und Glied. F. Spielhagen. Berlin, 1868. 6 v. in 3. 16°. . . G,464
In School and Out. W. T. Adams. Boston, 1866. 16°. . . . J,1467,2
In the Tropics. R. B. Kimball. New York, 1863. 12°. . . . . K,133
In Wald und Schloss. S. Grabowski. Prag und Leipzig, 1858. 2 v. in 1. 24°. G,282
In War Time, and other Poems. J. G. Whittier. Boston, 1864. 16°. . I,151
In der zwölften Stunde. F. Spielhagen. Berlin, 1866. 16°. . . . G,454
Ina. K. Valerio. Boston, 1871. 8°. . . . . . . . . . . K,268
Inchbald, E. British Theatre. London, 1808. 25 v. 16°. . . . . I,685

Vol. 1. Comedy of Errors; Romeo and Juliet; Hamlet; King John; King Richard III.
2. King Henry IV.; Merchant of Venice; King Henry V.; Much Ado About Nothing.
3. As You Like It; Merry Wives of Windsor; King Henry VIII.; Measure for Measure; Winter's Tale.
4. King Lear; Cymbeline; Macbeth; Julius Cæsar; Antony and Cleopatra.
5. Coriolanus; Othello; Tempest; Twelfth Night; Every Man in His Humor.
6. Rule a Wife and Have a Wife; The Chances; New Way to Pay Old Debts; Rival Queens; All for Love.
7. Isabella, or, the Fatal Marriage; Oroonoko; Distressed Mother; Zara; Gustavus Vasa.
8. Constant Couple; The Inconstant; Recruiting Officer; Beau's Stratagem; Cato.
9. Provoked Wife; Provoked Husband; Love Makes a Man; She Would and She Would Not; The Careless Husband.
10. Tamerlane; Fair Penitent; Jane Shore; Lady Jane Grey; Siege of Damascus.
11. Busy-Body; The Wonder; Bold Stroke for a Wife; George Barnwell; Fatal Curiosity.
12. The Orphan; Venice Preserved; Conscious Lovers; The Revenge; Beggars' Opera.
13. Love for Love; Mourning Bride; Mahomet; Tancred and Sigismunda; Suspicious Husband.
14. Man of the World; The Foundling; Gamester; Roman Father; Edward the Black Prince.
15. Barbarossa; The Way to Keep Him; All in the Wrong; Grecian Daughter; Know Your Own Mind.

Inchbald, E. British Theater. *Continued.* . . . . . . . . . . I,685

16. Country Girl; Jealous Wife; Clandestine Marriage; Countess of Salisbury; Douglas.
17. Good-Natured Man; She Stoops to Conquer; Love in a Village; Maid of the Mill; Lionel and Clarissa.
18. The Brothers; West Indian; The Jew; First Love; Wheel of Fortune.
19. Earl of Warwick; The Rivals; The Duenna; Belle's Stratagem; Bold Stroke for a Husband.
20. The Dramatist; Count of Narbonne; Inkle and Yarico; Battle of Hexham; Surrender of Calais.
21. Mountaineers; Iron Chest; Heir-at-Law; John Bull; Poor Gentleman.
22. Castle of Andalusia; Fontainbleau; Wild Oats; The Heiress; Earl of Essex.
23. Such Things Are; Every One has His Fault; Wives as they Were and Maids as they Are; Lover's Vows; To Marry, or, Not to Marry.
24. Road to Ruin; Deserted Daughter; The Strangers; De Montfort; Point of Honor.
25. Way to Get Married; Cure for the Heart-Ache; Speed the Plow; School of Reform; Honeymoon.

Collection of Farces. London, 1809. 7 v. 16°. . . . . . I,686

Vol. 1. Child of Nature; Wedding Day; Midnight Hour; Raising the Wind; Matrimony; Ella Rosenberg; Blind Boy; Who's the Dupe?; Love a la Mode.
2. Birthday; Jew and the Doctor; Irishman in London; Prisoner at Large; Poor Soldier; The Farmer; Highland Reel; Two Strings to Your Bow; The Deserter.
3. Hartford Bridge; Netley Abbey; Turnpike Gate; Lock and Key; Register Office; The Apprentice; The Critic; The Sultan; Rosina.
4. All the World's a Stage; Lying Valet; The Citizen; Three Weeks After Marriage; Catherine and Petruchio; Padlock; Miss in her Teens; The Quaker; Guardian.
5. High Life below Stairs; Bon Ton; Mock Doctor; Devil to Pay; Irish Widow; The Minor; Mayor of Garratt; The Lyar; Flora.
6. The Deuce is in Him; Edgar and Emmeline; Richard Cœur de Lion; Maid of the Oaks; Tom Thumb; Doctor and the Apothecary; The First Floor; The Adopted Child; The Farm-House.
7. Lodoiska; Ways and Means; School for Authors; Midas; The Waterman; The Author; The Old Maid; Miller of Mansfield; Comus, altered from Milton.

Modern Theatre. London, 1811. 10 v. 16°. . . . . . . I,684

Vol. 1. The Will; The Rage; Life; How to Grow Rich; Notoriety.
2. Speculation; The Delinquent; Laugh When You Can; Fortune's Fool; Folly as it Flies.
3. Votary of Wealth; Zorinski; Secrets Worth Knowing; Who Wants a Guinea?; Werter.
4. Duplicity; School for Arrogance; He is Much to Blame; Seduction; School for Prejudice.
5. False Impressions; Mysterious Husband; Box-Lobby Challenge; Natural Son; Carmelite.
6. Imposter; Wife of Two Husbands; Ramah Droog; Law of Lombardy; Braganza.
7. I'll Tell You What; Next-Door Neighbors; Wise Man of the East; Percy; Trip to Scarborough.
8. Matilda; Mary, Queen of Scots; Fugitive; He would be a Soldier; England Preserved.
9. Bank Note; Chapter of Accidents; English Merchant; School for Wives; Henry the Second, or, Fall of Rosamond.
10. Fashionable Levities; Time's a Tell-Tale; Which is the Man?; What is She?; Lie of a Day.

Inchbald, E. S. Simple Story. London, 1820. 12°. . . . . . . K,539
Nature and Art. London, 1820. 12°. . . . . . . . K,538
Incidents and Sketches of Early History of the West. Cincinnati, n. d. 8°. C,149
Independence Hall, History of. D. W. Belisle. Philadelphia, 1859. 12°. B,848
Index Pseudonymorum, with Supplements. E. Weller. Leipzig, 1856–62. 8°. L.R.
Index to Periodical Literature. W. F. Poole. New York, 1853. 8°. . L.R.
India, Ancient and Modern. D. O. Allen. Boston, 1856. 8°. . . . V,757
and Egypt, Route through. G. Fitzclarence. London, 1819. 4°. . V,721
and the Hindoos. F. de W. Ward. New York, 1851. 12°. . . V,608
and its Inhabitants. C. Wright. Cincinnati, 1856. 8°. . . . . S.C.
and its People. H. Read. Columbus, 1859. 8°. . . . . . C,406
British, History of. J. Mill. London, 1817. 3 v. 4°. . . . . C,464
The same. London, 1848. 9 v. 8°. . . . . . C,414
H. Murray. London, 1858. 8°. . . . . . . . . C,401
The same. New York, 1855. 3 v. 16°. . . . . L,373
H. H. Wilson. London, 1848. 3 v. 8°. . . . . . C,402

India, British Empire in. E. H. Nolan. London, n. d. 2 v. 8°. . . C,429
History of. G. R. Gleig. London, 1830-35. 4 v. 16°. . I,604
British Rule in. H. Martineau. London, 1857. 12°. . . . C,424
Diary in, 1858-59. W. H. Russell. London, 1860. 2 v. 8°. . V,736
China and Japan, Visit to, 1853. B. Taylor. New York, 1862. 12°. V,606
Christianity in. J. W. Kaye. London, 1859. 8°. . . . . . P,593
Education in. C. E. Trevelyan. London, 1838. 12°. . . . O,921
General Description of. London, 1834-35. 2 v. 16°. . . . L,488
General Hypsometry of. R. Schlagtinweit. Leipzig, 1862. 2 v. 4°. . Q,380
History of. M. Elphinstone. London, 1866. 8°. . . . . . C,415
J. C. Marshman. London, 1867. 3 v. 12°. . . . . C,400
J. T. Wheeler. London, 1867. v. 1. 8°. . . . . . C,405
in the Fifteenth Century. London, 1857. 8°. . . . . . . V,986
History of the Indian Revolt. London, 1858. 8°. . . . . . C,461
Indian Mutiny in, History of. C. Ball. London, n. d. 2 v. r. 8°. F,263
Journal of a Tour in. Capt. Mundy. London, 1832. 2 v. 8°. . V,582
Journey through Oude. W. H. Sleeman. London, 1858. 2 v. 12°. V,735
Journeys in. R. Heber. London, 1828. 3 v. 8°. . . . . V,737
Knowledge of the Ancients of. W. Robertson. London, 1794. 8°. . V,694
Life in the Mission; Six Years in. C. Mackenzie. N. Y. '56. 2 v. 12°. V,607
Life of Indian Officers. J. W. Kaye. London, 1867. 2 v. 8°. . D,87
Pictorial, Descriptive, and Historical. J. Corner. Lond. 1857. p. 8°. L,110
Princes and People of; Sketches. E. Eden. London, 1844. f°. *Q,444
Picturesque Voyage to. T. and W. Daniell. London, 1810. f°. *Q,428
Rambles of an Indian Official. W. H. Sleeman. London, 1844. 2 v. 8°. V,686
Reise in Ostindien. L. von Orlich. Leipzig, 1845. 4°. . . Q,436
Reisen in Indien und nach Bukhara. A. Burnes. Stutt. 1835-36. 2 v. 8°. E,218
Scenery in Bengal. London, 1816. 8°. . . . . . . . V,695
Sepoy Revolt. H. Mead. London, 1857. 8°. . . . . . . C,428
Soldier's Life in. W. S. R. Hodson. Boston, 1860. 12°. . . V,611
Wanderings in. A. L. Adams. Edinburgh, 1867. 8°. . . . V,613
India; the Pearl of Pearl River. E. D. E. N. Southworth. Phil. 1870. 12°. K,429
Indian Archipelago, Native Races of. G. W. Earl. London, 1853. 12°. N,413
Indian Atrocities; Narratives of Dr. Knight and J. Slover. Cin. 1867. 12°. B,592
Indian Biography. B. B. Thatcher. New York, 1834. 2 v. 16°. . . L,372
Indian Captivities; or, Life in the Wigwam. S. G. Drake. Auburn, 1854. 12°. B,591
Indian Captivity; Capture of O. M. Spencer by Indians. N. Y. n. d. 16°. B,590
Indian Cottage. B. de St. Pierre. London, 1846. 12°. . . . U,123,1
Indian Language, Vocabulary of the Natick. J. Cotton. Camb. 1829. 8°. *L,618
Key to. R. Williams. See *Narragansett Club Publications*, v. 1.
Indian Languages, Literature of the. H. E. Ludewig. London, 1858. 8°. . H,666
Indian Legends, and other Poems. M. G. Horsford. New York, 1855. 12°. I,62
Indian Life and Indian History. G. Copway. Boston, 1860. 12°. . . B,628
Indian Mission, History of Dakotah or Sioux. Boston, 1841. 16°. . . J,1727
Indian Missions, History of the Baptist. J. McCoy. Washington, 1840. 8°. B,588
Indian Nations of Canada, History of the Five. C. Colden. London, 1747. 8°. B,584
Indian Pilgrim. M. M. Sherwood. New York, 1860. 12°. . . K,1008,4
Indian Races of America. C. De W. Brownell. Cincinnati, 1853. 8°. . S.C.
Indian Remains from Chile. T. Ewbank. Washington, 1855. 4°. . . P.D.
Indian Trader, Voyages and Travels of an. J. Long. London, 1791. 4°.

Indian Tribes of Guiana. W. H. Brett. London, 1868. 8°. . . . . v,246
of United States. H. R. Schoolcraft. Philadelphia, 1860. 6 v. 4°. *F,104
Indians, N. A., Captivity of Oatman Girls. R. B. Stratton. N. Y. 1858. 12°. B,596
Captivity with, 1755–59. Col. J. Smith. Cincinnati, 1870. 8°. . C,221
Eight Years in Europe. G. Catlin. London, 1848. 2 v. 8°. . . B,598
History of King Philip's War. I. and C. Mather. Albany, 1862. 4°. C,30
Journal of Two Visits to. D. Jones. New York, 1865. 8°. . . C,198
Manners and Customs of the. G. Catlin. London, 1851. 2 v. 8°. B,612,2
The same. London, 1866. 2 v. 8°. . . . . . . S.C.
Notes on the Iroquois. H. R. Schoolcraft. Albany, 1847. 8°. . B,615
of California; Chinigchinich. G. Boscana. New York, 1846. 12°. V,154
of Connecticut, History of. J. W. De Forest. Hartford, 1853. 8°. B,627
of New England, Progress of Gospel among. J. Eliot. Bost. 1868. 4°. B,583
Relation Exacte des Caraibes. M. de la Borde. Leide, 1704. 12°. V,149
Thirty Years with. H. R. Schoolcraft. Philadelphia, 1851. 8°. . B,611
Wars of the West. T. Flint. Cincinnati, 1833. 12°. . . . .
Indiana, Early Indiana Trials. O. H. Smith. Cincinnati, 1858. 8°. . C,236
History of. J. B. Dillon. Indianapolis, 1859. 8°. . . . . . C,235
Map of. J. H. Colton. New York, 1854. 24°. . . . . . C,151
Ohio and Kentucky, Tour in, in 1805. J. Espy. Cincinnati, 1871. 8°. C,223
Indiana; a Love Story. Mad. Dudevant. Philadelphia, 1850. 12°. . K,1120
Indies, Etablissements des Européens dans les deux. G. T. F. Raynal.
Amsterdam, 1773–74. 7 v. 16°. . . . . . . . . . C,425
The same; translated by J. O. Justamond. Lond. 1788. 8 v. 8°. C,426
Indigestion, Treatise on. A. P. W. Philip. Philadelphia, 1825. 8°. . L,890
Inductive Sciences, Philosophy of. W. Whewell. London, 1847. 2 v. 8°. O,698
Indus to the Euphrates. Nearchus Voyage, 325 B. C. London, 1797. 4°. V,722
Iudustrial Arts, Chefs-d'Œuvre of the. P. Burty. New York, 1869. 8°. M,120
Industrial Biography. S. Smiles. Boston, 1869. 12°. . . . . . C,549
Industrial Education, Lessons on. London, 1849. 12°. . . . . . O,1164
Industrial History of Free Nations. W. T. McCullagh. Lond. 1846. 2 v. 8°. O,499
Industry, Curiosities of. G. Dodd. London, 1854. 8°. . . . . . M,628
of all Nations, Encyclopædia of. C. Knight. New York, 1851. *M,709
Opportunities for. E. T. Freedley. Philadelphia, 1859. 12°. . H,271
Inez; a Tale of the Alamo. A. J. Wilson. New York, n. d. 12°. . . K,123
Infancy, Management of. A. Combe. New York, 1854. 12°. . . . L,852
Infant Education, Remarks on. C. and E. Mayo. London, 1849. 16°. . O,1161
Infant School Teachers, Model Lessons for. London, 1853. 12°. . . O,1119
Infant Schools, Manual for. W. Wilson. London, 1829. 12°. . . . O,1181
Infant System of Education. S. Wilderspin. London, 1840. 16°. . . O,1134
Infant's Progress. M. M. Sherwood. New York, 1860. 12°. . . K,1008,5
Infantry Tactics. H. B. Wilson. Philadelphia, 1862. 12°. . . . M,746
W. Scott. New York, 1854. 3 v. 18°. . . . . . . M,744
New System of. E. Upton. New York, 1869. 18°. . . . M,745
Infidelity, Cause and Cure of. D. Nelson. New York, n. d. 12°. . . P,860
Converts from. A. Crichton. Edinburgh, 1827. 2 v. 16°. . . I,495
Information for the People. W. and R. Chambers. Phil. 1866. 2 v. 8°. H,633
Infusoria, History of Living and Fossil. A. Pritchard. London, 1845. 8°. O,67
Ingeland, T. Disobedient Child. London, 1848. 12°. . . . . L,606,22
Ingelow, J. Monitions of the Unseen. Boston, 1871. 16°. . . . . I,385

Ingelow, J. Mopsa the Fairy. Boston, 1869. 16°. . . . . . J,1256
Poems. Boston, 1867. 16°. . . . . . . . . . . I,359
Sister's Bye-Hours. Boston, 1868. 16°. . . . . . . J,1427
Stories told to a Child. Boston, 1866. 12°. . . . . . J,1230
Story of Doom, and other Poems. Boston, 1867. 12°. . . . I,360
Studies for Stories. Boston, 1870. 16°. . . . . . . J,1257
Ingersoll, C. J. Second War of United States, 1812. Phil. 1845-53. 4 v. 8°. B,871
Ingham Papers. E. E. Hale. Boston, 1869. 16°. . . . . . . H,33
Ingleby, C. M. Shakespeare Fabrication. London, 1859. 16°. . . I,763
Inglis, H. D. Ireland in 1834. London, 1834. 2 v. 12°. . . . . . V,269
Journey through Norway and Sweden. London, 1837. 12°. . . V,549
The same. Edinburgh, 1829. 16°. . . . . . . . . I,514
Spain. London, 1837. 2 v. 12°. . . . . . . . . . V,465
Switzerland, France, and the Pyrenees. Edinburgh, 1831. 2 v. 16°. I,532
The same. London, 1837. 12°. . . . . . . . . V,409
Tyrol and Bavaria. London, 1837. 12°. . . . . . . . V,408
Ingoldsby Legends. R. H. Barham. London, 1866. 8°. . . . . . . K,597
Ingraham, J. H. Pillar of Fire; Israel in Bondage. Boston, 1865. 8°. . K,198
Prince of the House of David. New York, 1859. 12°. . . . K,199
Sunny South. Philadelphia, 1860. 12°. . . . . . . . K,299
Throne of David. Boston, 1864. 8°. . . . . . . . . K,197
Ingulphus and Peter of Blois. Chron. of Abbey of Croyland. Lond. 1854. p. 8°. L,13
Inhalation, Treatise on Medicated. S. S. Fitch. New York, 1856. 12°. . L,916
Initials, The. I. von Tautphoeus. Philadelphia, n. d. 12°. . . . G,236
The same. Leipzig, 1865. 2 v. in 1. 16°. . . . . . J,473
Innes, T. Civil and Ecclesiastical History of Scotland. Edinb. 1855. 4°. F,84,27
Innes, Family of. Edinburgh, 1867. 4°. . . . . . . . . F,84,35
Innocents Abroad. S. L. Clements. Hartford, 1870. 8°. . . . . . V,400
Inquire Within. New York, n. d. 12°. . . . . . . . . . H,290
Inquisition, Dealings with the. G. Achilli. London, 1851. 12°. . . P,822
Insanity, Medical Jurisprudence of. I. Ray. Boston, 1853. 8°. . . L,924
Reflex Insanity in Women. H. R. Storer. Boston, 1871. 12°. . L,938
Insect Architecture. J. Rennie; edited by J. G. Wood. Lond. 1869. p. 8°. L,111
J. Rennie and J. O. Westwood. London, 1845. 2 v. 18°. . . O,1
The same. London, n. d. 12°. . . . . . . . O,10
The same. London, 1857. 8°. . . . . . . . . . O,20
Insect Life, Episodes of. L. M. Budgen. New York, 1851-52. 3 v. 8°. . O,33
Wonders of. J. E. Willet. Philadelphia, 1871. 16°. . . . O,14
Insect Miscellanies. J. Rennie and J. O. Westwood. London, n. d. 12°. O,11
Insect Transformations. J. Rennie and J. O. Westwood. Lond. n. d. 12°. O,12
and Architecture. J. Rennie and Westwood. Lond. 1831-50. 3 v. 16°. L,479
Insect World. L. Figuier. London, 1868. 8°. . . . . . . . O,48
Insects, Arcana Entomologica. J. O. Westwood. London, 1845. 2 v. 8°. O,51
British Hemiptera. J. W. Douglas and J. Scott. Lond. 1865. 8°. O,309
Centurie d' Insectes. G. Kirby. Paris, 1834. 8°. . . . . O,31,1
Catalogue of Lepidoptera. W. Wood. London, 1854. 8°. . . O,52
Curious Facts about. F. Cowan. Philadelphia, 1865. 12°. . . O,23
Descriptions of Foreign. D. Drury. London, 1837. 3 v. 4°. . Q,5
Fossil, in the Rocks of England. P. B. Brobie. London, 1845. 8°. N,816
Genera Insectorum Linnæi et Fabricii. Vitodurum, 1789. 8°. . O,313

Insects, Genera et Species Insectorum. A. J. Retzius. Lipsiæ, 1873. 8°. . o,140
Historia Insectorum. J. Swammerdam. Leydae, 1737–38. 2 v. f°. *q,77
Histoire des Insectes. R. A. F. de Reaumur. 1734–42. 6 v. 8°. . *o,137
History and Arrangement of. W. Swainson. London, 1840. 12°. m,1036
Insecten Deutchlands. W. F. Erichson. Berlin, 1848–63. 4 v. 8°. g,945
Insectes de Java. M. W. S. Macleay. Paris, 1833. 8°. . . o,31,1
Introductory to History of. E. Newman. London, 1841. 8°. . . o,47
Modern Classification of. J. O. Westwood. Lond. 1839–40. 2 v. 8°. o,46
Natural History of. New York, 1859. 2 v. 18°. . . . . . l,341
J. Rennie and J. O. Westwood. London, 1829. 2 v. 16°. . i,644
North American. B. Jaeger and H. C. Preston. New York, 1859. o,22
of China. E. Donovan. London, 1842. 4°. . . . . . . q,41
of India. E. Donovan. London, 1842. 4°. . . . . . . q,42
of Massachusetts injurious to Vegetation. T. W. Harris. Bost. 1852. 8°. o,36
The same; edited by C. L. Flint. Boston, 1863. . . . o,35
on Fruit Trees. J. Major. London, 1829. 8°. . . . . . o,34
Pflanzenläuse, Aphiden. C. L. Koch. Nürnberg, 1857. 8°. . . g,946
Pilzkrankheit der Fliegen. H. Lebert. Stuttgart, n. d. 4°. . . g,956
Schädliche Forstins. Beckstein u. Scharfenberg. Leip. 1804–5. 3 v. 4°. g,957
Transactions of Entomological Society. London, 1836–62. 11 v. 8°. r,13
Treatise on Injurious. V. Köllar. London, 1840. 16°. . . . o,16
Treatise on the Management of. E. Donovan. London, 1794. 8°. . n,541
Inspiration, Human Element in. T. F. Curtis. New York, 1867. 12°. . p,501
Instinct, Indications of. T. L. Kemp. London, 1862. p. 8°. . . . i,666
Illustrations of. J. Couch. London, 1847. 12°. . . . . . n,652
W. Kirby. Philadelphia, 1836. 8°. . . . . . . n,686
W. Swainson. London, 1835. 12°. . . . . . m,1030
Instruction, Hints towards Improved. R. Dawes. London, 1853. 16°. . o,908
National, and Religion. W. M. Gunn. Edinburgh, 1840. 12°. o,1180
Prussian System of. C. E. Stowe. Cincinnati, 1836. 18°. . o,1112
Public, in Europe. C. E. Stowe. Columbus, 1837. 8°. . . o,125,1
Religious. E. Mayo. London, 1852. pt. 2. 16°. . . . o,1116
Instructor's Manual. S. R. Hall. Boston, 1852. 18°. . . . o,1111
Instrumenta Ecclesiastica. London, 1847. 4°. . . . . . . . m,293
Instrumentation and Orchestration. H. Berlioz. London, 1858. 8°. . m,421,2
Instruments, Treatise on Box of. T. Kentish. Philadelphia, 1852. 12°. . m,605
Treatise on Use of. J. F. Heather. London, 1854. 12°. . . m,935
Insurance Guide and Hand-Book. London, 1857. 8°. . . . . . o,497
Insurrection *vs.* Resurrection in America. M. D. Conway. Bost. 1862. 12°. h,88
Integral Calculus, Treatise on. I. Todhunter. London, 1868. 12°. . m,1146
Exercises de. A. M. L. Gendre. Paris, 1811–16. 3 v. 4°. . m,1204
See also *Calculus.*
Intellect, Emotions, and Moral Nature. W. Lyall. Edinburgh, 1855. 8°. o,691
Progress of. R. W. Mackay. London, 1850. 2 v. 8°. . . . o,681
Intellectual Development of Europe. J. W. Draper. New York, 1864. 8°. o,707
The same. New York, 1865. 8°. . . . . . . . . s.c.
Intellectual Observer. London, 1862–68. 12 v. 8°. . . . . . . r,34
Intellectual Philosophy. H. Winslow. Boston, 1850. 12°. . . . o,708
Elements of. F. Wayland. Boston, 1855. 12°. . . . . o,621
System of. A. Mahan. New York, 1847. 12°. . . . . . o,635

Intellectual Powers, Inquiries concerning. J. Abercrombie. N. Y. 1852. 18°. L,368
Intellectual System of the Universe. R. Cudworth. Andover, 1837–8. 2 v. 8°. P,142
The same. London, 1845. 3 v. . . . . . . . . P,141
Intemperance, Discourse on. D. Drake. Cincinnati, 1828. 12°. . . L,831
Oration on. D. Drake. Columbus, 1831. 8°. . . . . T,19,2
International Law and Laws of War. H. W. Halleck. Phil. 1866. 12°. . U,538
De Jure Belli et Pacis. H. Grotius. Cambridge, 1853. 3 v. 8°. . U,543
Elements of. H. Wheaton; edited by R. H. Dana, jr. Bost. 1866. 8°. U,507
Study of. T. D. Woolsey. Boston, 1860. 12°. . . . . . . U,492
Intermarriage. A. Walker. Philadelphia, 1856. 12°. . . . . . L,850
Interpreter. G. J. W. Melville. Leipzig, 1866. 2 v. in 1. 16°. . . J,377
Interrupted Wedding. A. Manning. London, 1864. 12°. . . . J,648
Intimate Friends. M. M. Sherwood. New York, 1860. 12°. . . K,1008,7
Intrigue, Die. L. Storch. Frankfurt-a-Main, 1833. 2 v. 24°. . . G,483
Introductory Lessons on Christian Evidences. London, 1868. 32°. . . P,3
on Morals. London, 1855. 24°. . . . . . . . . . . P,225
Invalide, Der. C. Spindler. Stuttgart, 1831. 5 v. 16°. . . . . . G,469
Invasion; ou, Fou Yégof. E. Erckmann et A. Chatrian. Paris, 1861. 12°. H,1016
Inventions and Discoveries, History of. J. Beckmann. Lond. 1846. 2 v. p. 8°. L,168
The same. London, 1814. 4 v. 8°. . . . . . . M,642
History of. F. C. Bakewell. New York, 1860. 12°. . . . . M,623
History of Wonderful. New York, 1855. 12°. . . . . . M,606
Wonderful. J. Timbs. London, 1868. 8°. . . . . . . . M,682
Inventors and Discoverers, Stories of. J. Timbs. New York, 1860. 12°. . C,521
Invertebrata, Comp. Anatomy and Physiology of. R. Owen. Lond. 1855. 8°. L,988
of Massachusetts. A. A. Gould; ed. by W. G. Binney. Bost. 1870. 8°. N,721
Investment of Money, Hints for. F. Playford. London, 1869. 12°. . . M,854
Ionian Islands. Reise durch die Ionischen Inseln. C. Müller. Leip. 1822. 16°. E,192
Iowa as it is in 1856. N. H. Parker. Chicago, 1856. 12°. . . . . . C,160
Geological Survey of. J. Hall and J. D. Whitney. n. p. 1858. 2 v. 8°. N,896
The same; and Plates. D. D. Owen. Philad. 1852. 2 v. 4°. Q,52
Irby, A. P. Travels in Turkey-in-Europe. London, 1866. 8°. . . V,570
Iredell, J. Life of G. J. Mac Ree. New York, 1857. 2 v. 8°. . C,1090
Ireland, Ancient Historians of. Dublin, 1809. 2 v. 4°. . . . . . B,182
Vol. 1. Spencer, E. View of the State of Ireland.
Campion, E. Historie of Ireland, 1571.
2. Hanmer, M. Chronicle of Ireland, 1571.
Marleburrough, H. Chronicle of Ireland, 1571.
and England, Connexion between. R. R. Madden. Dublin, 1845. 8°. B,169
Annals of the Famine in, 1847–49. A. Nicholson. N. Y. 1851. 12°. B,162
Ancient History of. J. Lynch. Dublin, 1848–52. 3 v. 8°. . . B,165
Ancient Laws of, v. 1. Dublin, 1865. 8°. . . . . . . B,171
Celtic Records and Literature of. J. T. Gilbert. Dublin, 1861. 8°. H,709
Chronicle of, to 1284. M. Hanmer. Dublin, 1809. 4°. . . A,565,2
The same, continued, 1285–1421. H. Marleburrough. Dub. 1809. A,565,2
Chronicles of. R. Holinshed. London, 1807–8. 6 v. 4°. . . F,161
Chronicon Scotorum. London, 1866. 8°. . . . . . . . W,196
Civil Wars in. W. C. Taylor. Edinburgh, 1831. 2 v. 16°. . . I,535
Constitutions and Canons Ecclesiastical. Dublin, 1715. 32°. . . P,337
Description of. W. Camden. London, 1789. 3 v. f°. . . . F,121
Fairy Legends of the South of. London, 1834. 16°. . . . . I,650

Ireland, Flowering Plants of. J. T. Mackay. Dublin, 1836. 8°. . . N,1020
Fortnight in. Sir F. B. Head. London, 1852. 8°. . . . . V,270
Historic Memories of. Sir J. Barrington. London, 1833. 2 v. 4°. F,287
Historical Songs of. London, 1841. 12°. . . . . . . L,606,1
History of. S. Barlow. London, 1814. 2 v. 8°. . . . . V,402
T. Leland. London, 1773. 3 v. 4°. . . . . . A,372
T. Moore. London, 1835–46. 3 v. 12°. . . . M,987
W. C. Taylor. New York, 1860–63. 2 v. 16°. . . L,375
T. Wright. London, n. d. 3 v. 8°. . . . . . F,267
till 1571. E. Campion. Dublin, 1809. 4°. . . . A,565,1
in 1834. H. D. Inglis. London, 1834. 2 v. 12°. . . . . V,269
Invasion of, by Danes and Norsemen. London, 1867. 8°. . . W,198
Irish Rebellion, 1798. W. H. Maxwell. London, 1868. 8°. . . B,160
its Scenery, etc. S. C. and Mrs. S. C. Hall. London, 1841–43. 3 v. 8°. . V,274
Legends of the Wars in. R. D. Joyce. Boston, 1868. 16°. . K,1013
Measurement of Lough Foyle Base. W. Yolland. Lond. 1847. 4°. Q,54
National Education in. J. C. Colquhoun. Cheltenham, 1838. 12°. O,1140
Natural History of. W. Thompson. London, 1849–51. 3 v. 8°. . O,109
'98 and '48; Revolutionary History of. J. Savage. N. Y. 1856. 12°. B,161
Protestant and Popish Families in. Dublin, 1736. 8°. . . . H,630
Orators of. Dublin, 1867. 7 v. 12°. . . . . . . . H,773–778
Repeal Prize Essays. Dublin, 1845. 8°. . . . . . . . B,168
State of in 1596. E. Spencer. Dublin, 1809. 4°. . . . A,565,1
Tour in. Prince Pückler Muskau. Philadelphia, 1833. 8°. . . V,291
Tour in, 1776–78. A Young. Dublin, 1780. 2 v. 8°. . . . V,390
Tour round, in 1835. J. Barrow. London, 1836. 12°. . . . V,268
vindicated. M. Carey. Philadelphia, 1837. 8°. . . . . . B,170
Ireland, W. H. Scribbleomania. London, 1815. p. 8°. . . . . I,471
Ireland, W. H. Confessions; Shakespeare Fabrication. London, 1805. 12°. I,889
Irish Bar, Sketches of. W. H. Curran. London, 1855. 2 v. 12°. . . D,432
Sketches of. R. L. Sheil. New York, 1854. v. 2. 12°. . . . D,413
Irish Character, Customs, and Superstitions. D. Dewar. London, 1812. 8°. B,167
Sketches of. A. M. Hall. London, 1842. r. 8°. . . . . K,586
Irish Chronicles of Eri, History of. A. O'Connor. Lond. 1822. 2 v. 8°. B,166
Irish Gentleman in search of a Religion. T. Moore. Baltimore, n. d. 12°. P,205
Irish Geography and Topography. J. H. Greene. Cincinnati, 1859. 8°. V,1124
Irish Language, Introduction to. W. Neilson. Dublin, 1808. 8°. . . L,780
Irish Life. W. S. Trench. Boston, 1869. 16°. . . . . . . K,1012
Lights and Shadows of. S. C. Hall. London, 1838. 3 v. 12°. . J,574
Irish Melodies. T. Moore. Dublin, 1859. 4°. . . . . . . . F,167
and Sacred Songs. T. Moore. New York, 1854. 12°. . . . I,378
with Accompaniments. T. Moore. Dublin, n. d. 2 v. 4°. . . M,413
Irish Misdeeds and English Misrule. A. De Vere. London, 1848. 12°. . B,164
Irish Names and Places, Origin and History of. P.W.Joyce. Dub. 1869. 16°. L,519
Irish Nation, Rise and Fall of. Sir J. Barrington. Dublin, 1868. 12°. . B,159
Irish Peasantry, Traits and Stories of. W. Carleton. London, 1868. 12°. K,619
Irish Sketch-Book. W. M. Thackeray. Boston, 1869. 12°. . . . K,1038,2
Irish, The, Abroad and at Home. New York, 1856. 12°. . . . V,1054
Irishmen, Lives of Distinguished. J. Wills. Dublin, 1847. v. 2–6. 8°. D,274
Iron and Brass-Founder's Guide. J. Larkin. Philadelphia, 1869. 12°. . M,636

Iron and Steel, Manufacture of. F. Kohn. London, 1869. f°. . . . Q,53
and Steel, Papers on. D. Mushet. London, 1840. 8°. . . . . M,725
Application of, to Buildings. W. Fairbairn. London, 1870. 8°. . M,665
Cast, Hot-Blast in manufacture of. T. Clark. Edinburgh, 1825. 4°. N,252,57
Chimie du Fer. Paris, 1826. 8°. . . . . . . . . N,252,18
Fabrication de, au Moyen des Gaz. A. Gurlt. Paris, 1857. 8°. N,252,49
Manufacture of. F. Overman. Philadelphia, 1851. 8°. . . . M,720
in Great Britain. W. Truran. New York, 1867. 4°. . . M,738
Metallurgy of. H. Bauerman. New York, 1868. 12°. . . . M,714
B. Kerl. London, 1869. 8°. . . . . . . . . M,717,2
Roofs of recent Construction. London, 1859. 4°. . . . . Q,174
Ship-Building. J. Grantham.. London, 1858. 12°. . . . M,924
Trade of United States, 1621–1857. B. F. French. N. Y. 1858. 8°. M,719
Verhalten des Eisens zum Sanerstoff. T.F.Schönbein. Basel, 1837. 8°. N,252,5
Iron Cousin. M. C. Clarke. New York, 1866. 12°. . . . . . . K,919
Iron Hand. A. Dumas. Philadelphia, n. d. 8°. . . . . . . H,985
Iron Mask. A. Dumas. Philadelphia, n. d. 8°. . . . . . . H,986
Ironthorpe, the Pioneer Preacher. J. T. Trowbridge. New York, 1869. 16°. J,1212
Iroquois, Notes on the. H. R. Schoolcraft. Albany, 1847. 8°. . . B,615
Irrawaddi, Up and down the. J. W. Palmer. New York, 1856. 12°. . V,593
Irving, D. Life and Writings of George Buchanan. Edinburgh, 1817. 8°. D,372
Irving, E. Last Days; a Discourse. London, 1850. 12°. . . . P,154
Life of. M. Oliphant. New York, 1862. 8°. . . . . . . D,299
Miscellanies. London, 1866. 8°. . . . . . . . . . H,243
Irving, P. M. Life of Washington Irving. Philadelphia, 1869. 3 v. 16°. U,10
Life and Letters of W. Irving. New York, 1867. 4 v. 12°. . . U,35
The same. New York, 1863-64. 4 v. 12°. . . . . C,1027
Irving, T. Conquest of Florida by Hernando de Soto. N. Y. 1851. 12°. C,184
Irving, W. Adventures of Capt. Bonneville. New York, 1868. 16°. . U,5
The same. New York, 1860. 12°. . . . . . . . . U,26
Alhambra. New York, 1868. 16°. . . . . . . . . . U,3
The same. New York, 1860. 12°. . . . . . . . . U,30
Astoria. New York, 1868. 16°. . . . . . . . . . U,4
The same. New York, 1860. 12°. . . . . . . . . U,24
Bracebridge Hall. New York, 1868. 16°. . . . . . . U,6
The same. New York, 1863. 12°. . . . . . . . .
Conquest of Granada. New York, 1870. 16°. . . . . . . U,16
The same. New York, 1860. 16°. . . . . . . . . U,29
Crayon Miscellany. New York, 1868. 16°. . . . . . . U,8
The same. New York, 1859. 12°. . . . . . . . . U,25
Discourse on. W. C. Bryant. New York, 1860. 12°. . . . C,847
Knickerbocker's History of New York. New York, 1869. 16°. . U,11
The same. New York, 1863. 12°. . . . . . . . U,36
The same. London, 1836. 16°. . . . . . . . . I,607
Life and Letters of. P. M. Irving. New York, 1869. 3 v. 16°. . U,10
The same. New York, 1860. 4 v. 12°. . . . . . U,35
The same. New York, 1863–64. 4 v. 12°. . . . . C,1027
Life and Voy. of Columbus and Companions. N. Y. 1868–9. 3 v. 16°. V,7
The same. New York, 1848–49. 3 v. 12°. . . . . . U,21
The same, abridged. London, 1830. 16°. . . . . . I,616

Irving, W. Life of Oliver Goldsmith. New York, 1868. 16°. . . . . U,9
The same. New York, 1860. 12°. . . . . . . U,27
The same. New York, 1858. 2 v. 16°. . . . . L,418
Life of George Washington. New York, 1869. 5 v. 16°. . . U,18
The same. New York, 1860. 5 v. 12°. . . . . U,34
The same. New York, 1856–60. 5 v. 12°. . . . . C,903
The same. New York, 1857–60. 5 v. 8°. . . . . C,885
Mahomet and his Successors. New York, 1868–69. 2 v. 16°. . U,13
The same. New York, 1860. 2 v. 12°. . . . . U,28
Sketch-Book. New York, 1870. 16°. . . . . . . . U,14
The same. New York, 1864. 12°. . . . . . . U,20
The same. London, 1834. 2 v. 16°. . . . . . I,648
Spanish Papers and Miscellanies. New York, 1868–69. 2 v. 16°. . U,15
The same. New York, 1866. 2 v. 12°. . . . . U,33
Tales of a Traveler. New York, 1869. 16°. . . . . . . U,17
The same. New York, 1864. 12°. . . . . . . . U,23
Voyages of the Companions of Columbus. London, 1831. 16°. . I,617
Wolfert's Roost. New York, 1868. 16°. . . . . . U,19
The same. New York, 1860. 12°. . . . . . . . U,31
and Paulding, J. K. Salmagundi. Philadelphia, 1869. 16°. . . U,12
The same. New York, 1857. 16°. . . . . . . . U,32
Irwin, R. B. Sherman and his Campaigns. New York, 1865. 8°. . . B,931
Is it I? a Book for every Man. H. B. Storer. Boston, 1868. 12°. . . L,834
Island Home; or, the Young Castaways. C. Romaunt. Boston, 1867. 16°. . J,1428
Island World of the Pacific. H. T. Cheever. New York, 1856. 12°. . V,882
Isle of Wight, Geological Excursions round the. G. A. Mantell. Lond. 1854. 12°. L,304
Isomorphism, Difficulty in. T. Clark. Aberdeen, 1836. 8°. . . N,252,2
Israel of the Alps. A. Muston. London, 1852. 12°. . . . . . B,363
The same. Glasgow, 1857. 2 v. 8°. . . . . . . B,368
Israelites, History of. E. Hecht. Cincinnati, 1857. 8°. . . . . A,238
Israelitish Nation, History of. A. Alexander. Philadelphia, 1853. 8°. . A,218
Isthmus of Panama. F. N. Otis. New York, 1867. 12°. . . . . V,242
Istria and Dalmatia, Voyage Pittoresque de. J. Lavallée. Paris, 1802. f°. Q,349
It is never too late to mend. C. Reade. Boston, 1856. 2 v. 12°. . . K,906
The same. Leipzig, 1856. 2 v. in 1. 16°. . . . . J,420
Italian Art, Wonders of. L. Viardot. New York, 1870. 12°. . . M,1051
Italian and English Dictionary. J. Millhouse. New York, 1861. 8°. . L.R.
Italian and French Dictionary. F. de A. di Villanova. Bassano, 1811. 2 v. 4°. L.R.
Italian Comedies; translated by C. Goldoni and others. New York, 1849. 12°. I,739
Italian Grammar, Grammaire Italienne. A. Vergani. Paris, 1842. 12°. L,772
Italian Novelists. T. Roscoe. v. 1, 3, 4. London, 1836. 3 v. 12°. . . G,232
Italian Painters, Memoirs of Early. A. Jameson. Boston, 1866. 16°. . M,19
Italian Poets, Stories from. L. Hunt. New York, 1849. 8°. . . . I,364
Italian Republics, History of. J. C. L. S. de Sismondi. N. Y. 1847. 16°. . B,481
The same. London, 1832. 12°. . . . . . . . M,997
Italian School of Design; Drawings. W. Y. Otley. London, 1823. f°. . L.R.
Italian Sights and Papal Principles. J. J. Jarves. New York, 1856. 12°. V,507
Italian Women, Decade of. T. A. Trollope. London, 1859. 2 v. 8°. . D,731
Italics; Brief Notes in Italy in 1864. F. P. Cobbe. London, 1864. 8°. . V,503
Italy, Autumn in. J. D. Sinclair. Edinburgh, 1829. 16°. . . . . I,520

Italy and England, Notes on. S. Hawthorne. New York, 1869. 12°. . v,358
and France, Life in the Olden Time. J. C. Colquhoun. Lon. 1868. 8°. D,709
Notes of. W. Colton. Cincinnati, 1851. 12°. . . . v,300
Sentimental Journey in. L. Sterne. New York, 1857. 12°. v,452
The same. Leipzig, 1861. 16°. . . . . . . J,467
and the Italian Islands. W. Spalding. New York, n. d. 3 v. 18°. L,440
and Sicily, Classic and Connoisseur in, G. D. Evans. Lond. 1835. 3 v. 8°. M,102
and Switzerland, Letters from. F. Mendelssohn. New York, 1865. 12°. v,504
Ancient Mythology of. T. Keightley. New York, 1866. 18°. . P,909
Ancient Republics of. C. G. M. Denina. London, 1773. 8°. . . B,484
Arms, Arts, and Literature of. J. Dennistoun. London, 1851. 3 v. 8°. D,735
Classical Tour through. J. C. Eustace. London, 1813. 2 v. 4°. *Q,416
The same. London, 1841. 3 v. 16°. . . . . . . I,622
Compendio della Storia d', 1534–1815. Parigi, 1834. 2 v. 12°. . B,483
Ethnography of Ancient. J. W. Donaldson. London, 1852. 8°. . N,436
Florence and Venice. H. Taine. New York, 1869. 8°. . . . v,514
Genius of. R. Turnbull. New York, 1852. 12°. . . . . . v,501
Geschichte der Italienischen Staaten. H. Leo. Hamb. 1829–48. 5 v. 8°. E,101
History of. I. Butt. London, 1860. 2 v. 8°. . . . . . . B,489
N. Green. New York, 1847. 16°. . . . . . L,395
G. Proctor. London, 1844. 8°. . . . . . . B,497
from 1490 to 1532. F. Guicciardini. Lon. 1753–1856. 10 v. 8°. B,508
Holy Land and Egypt, Visit to. I. Pfeiffer. London, 1853. 12°. v,1044
Idler in. Countess of Blessington. London, 1839. 2 v. 8°. . . v,517
Italian Journeys. W. D. Howell. New York, 1867. 8°. . . v,509
Journal of Residence in. S. O. Morgan. London, 1824. 3 v. 8°. . v,513
in 1848. A. Gallenga. London, 1851. 12°. . . . . . . B,490
in Transition. W. Arthur. New York, 1860. 12°. . . . . v,510
the Italian Sketch-Book. H. T. Tuckerman. New York, 1848. 12°. v.493
Landwirthschaft in Ober-Italien. J. Burger. Wien, 1851. 2 v. 12°. G,655
Letters from. J. T. Headley. New York, 1854. 12°. . . . v,496
F. Mendelssohn-Bartholdy. London, 1862. 2 v. 12°. . . G,25
Life in. H. C. Andersen. New York, 1867. 8°. . . . . G,182
Northern, Hand-Book for. J. Murray. London, 1853. 16°. . *v,489
Notes of a Traveler in. S. Laing. Philadelphia, 1846. 8°. . . v,272
Ost-Gothisches Reich in. J. C. F. Manso. Breslau, 1824. 8°. . E,100
Painting in. J. A. Crowe and G. B. Cavalcaselle. Lond. 1864–6. 3 v. 8° M,105
L. Lanzi. London, 1847. 3 v. p. 8°. . . . . . . L,204
Past and Present. A. Gallenga. London, 1849. 2 v. 12°. . . B,487
Personal Adventures in. M. B. Honan. New York, 1852. 12°. . v,511
Pictures from. C. Dickens. Leipzig, 1846. 16°. . . . . J,135
The same. New York, 1868. 12°. . . . . . . . K,470
Reformation in; Life of Savonarola. London, 1843. 12°. . . D,715
Rome and Naples. H. Taine. New York, 1868. 8°. . . . v,515
Six Months in. G. S. Hillard. Boston, 1854. 2 v. 12°. . . v,506
Southern, Hand-Book of. J. Murray. London, 1853. 16°. . *v,488
Spain and Portugal. W. Beckford. London, 1834. 2 v. 12°. . v,516
Travel and Study in. C. E. Norton. Boston, 1860. 16°. . . . v,47
Travels in. J. W. von Goethe. London, 1848–51. p. 8°. . L,188,2
Travels through, 1804–5. A. F. F. von Kotzebue. Lond. 1806. 4 v. 16°. v,486

Italy, Two Years in. F. Bremer. Philadelphia, 1860. 2 v. 8°. . . . V,416
Vicissitudes of. A. L. V. Gretton. London, 1859. 12°. . . . B,485
Zephyrs from. W. M. Gould. New York, 1852. 12°. . . . V,490
Itinéraire de Paris à Jérusalem. R.F.A.deChateaubriand. Par. 1854. 2 v. 12°. V,624
Ivanhoe. Sir W. Scott. Boston, 1852. 2 v. 16°. . . . . . . K,939
The same. Philadelphia, n. d. 8°. . . . . . . . K,964
The same. Philadelphia, 1869. 8°. . . . . . K,1108
The same. Leipzig, 1845. 16°. . . . . . . . J,444
I've been Thinking. A. S. Roe. New York, 1869. 12°. . . . . K,271
Ives, J. C. Explorations of the Colorado River. Washington, 1861. 4°. *Q,184
Ivors. E. M. Sewell. New York, 1857. 2 v. 12°. . . . . . . K,999
Ixion; a Novel. B. Disraeli. London, 1868. 12°. . . . . . . K,672

Jack Arcombe; Story of a Waif. W. J. Bradley. Boston, 1870. 16°. . J,1679
Jack Brag. T. E. Hook. London, n. d. 12°. . . . . . . K,1151
Jack Hinton, the Guardsman. C. Lever. Philadelphia, n. d. 8°. . . K,777
The same. Leipzig, 1849. 2 v. in 1. 16°. . . . . J,278
Jack Sheppard. W. H. Ainsworth. Leipzig, 1846. 16°. . . . . J,12
Jack Tier; or, the Florida Reef. J. F. Cooper. New York, 1866. 12°. . K,33
The same. New York, 1860. 8°. . . . . . . K,63
Jack of Dover. London, 1842. 12°. . . . . . . . . L,606,7
Jack of the Mill. W. Howitt. London, 1844. 2 v. in 1. 16°. . J,1240
Jackson, A., Achievements at N. O., 1814–15. A. Walker. N. Y. 1856. 12°. B,846
Life of. J. H. Eaton. Cincinnati, 1827. 12°. . . . . . C,941
J. Parton. New York, 1861. 3 v. 8°. . . . . . . C,943
Messages to Congress, and Life. Cincinnati, 1837. 12°. . . . O,482
Jackson, E. S. Cabinet of the Earth Unlocked. London, 1867. 8°. . . N,609
Jackson, J. and Chatto, W. A. Treatise on Wood Engraving. Lond. 1861. M,139
Jackson, J. C. How to treat the Sick without Medicine. N. Y. 1869. 12°. L,914
Jackson, J. G. Account of the Empire of Morocco. London, 1809. 4°. . V,862
Jackson, T. Life of Charles Wesley. New York, 1842. 8°. . . . D,293
Life of Richard Watson. New York, 1836. 8°. . . . . . D,33
Jacob, J. J. Biographical Sketches of Michael Cresap. Cincinnati, 1866. 4°. C,1054
Jacob, S. and others. History of the Ottoman Empire. London, 1854. 12°. B,555
Jacob, W. Production and Consumption of Metals. Lond. 1831. 2 v. 8°. M,722
Jacob Faithful. F. Marryat. New York, 1868. 12°. . . . . K,841
Jacobinism, History of. A. de Barruel. London, 1798. 4 v. 8°. . . B,271
Jacobites of 1715 and 1745. K. B. Thomson. London, 1845–46. 3 v. 8°. D,688
Jacobs, S. S. History of Nonantum and Natick, Mass. Boston, 1853. 12°. K,143
Jacobus, M. W. Notes on Acts. New York, 1863. 12°. . . . . P,526
Jaeger, B. Class-Book of Zoology. New York, 1860. 16°. . . . N,622
and Preston, C. H. Life of North-American Insects. N. Y. 1859. 12°. O,22
Jäger, G. F. Fossile Säugethiere Würtemberg's. Stuttgart, 1835. f°. . F,177
Jäger, H. Gedichte. Leipzig, 1851. 12°. . . . . . . . . E,267
Reichenau. Leipzig, 1851. 16°. . . . . . . . . . G,335
Jahn, J. Biblical Archæology. New York, 1856. 8°. . . . . . A,219
Jahr aus dem Leben August des Starken. F. Lubojatzky. Wien, 1863. 2 v. in 1. G,340

Jamaica, History of. E. Long. London, 1774. 3 v. 4°. . . . . . B,831
in 1850. J. Bigelow. New York, 1851. 12°. . . . . . . V,187
James I. of England, Court of. T. Birch. London, 1829. 2 v. 8°. . A,542
Life of. R. Chambers. Edinburgh, 1830. 2 v. 16°. . . . I,526
Life and Writings of. W. Harris. London, 1753. 8°. . . . D,32
The same. London, 1814. 5 v. 8°. . . . . . . D,393
Memoirs of the Court of. L. Aikin. London, 1822. 2 v. 8°. . A,502
James I. of Scotland, Murder of. Glasgow, 1820. 12°. . . . B,111,2
James II., History of Reign of. C. J. Fox. London, 1808. 4°. . . F,269
The same. London, 1846. 12°. . . . . . . . . A,476
James V. of Scotland, Life and Death of. Glasgow, 1819. 12°. . B,111,4
Navigation round Scotland. Glasgow, 1819. 12°. . . . B,111,3
James, C. Military Dictionary. London, 1802. 8°. . . . . . . M,765
James, C. P. Address at Camp McRea, July 4, 1842. Cincinnati, 1842. 8°. H,302,4
James, G. P. R. Agincourt. Leipzig, 1844. 16°. . . . . . . J,199
Arabella Stuart. Leipzig, 1844. 16°. . . . . . . . J,200
Arrah Neil; or, Times of Old. Leipzig, 1844. 16°. . . . J,201
Beauchamp; or, the Error. Leipzig, 1846. 16°. . . . . . J,202
Castle of Ehrenstein. Leipzig, 1847. 16°. . . . . . . J,203
Cavalier; Historical Novel. Philadelphia, 1859. 12°. . . . K,730
Convict. Leipzig, 1847. 2 v. in 1. 16°. . . . . . . . J,204
Corse De Leon; a Romance. New York, 1855. 2 v. in 1. 12°. . K,731
Darnley. Leipzig, 1847. 16°. . . . . . . . . . . J,205
Educational Institutions of Germany. London, 1835. 8°. . . O,1036
False Heir. Leipzig, 1843. 16°. . . . . . . . . J,206
Forest Days. Leipzig, 1843. 16°. . . . . . . . . J,207
Gipsy. New York, 1855. 2 v. in 1. 12°. . . . . . . K,732
The same. Leipzig, 1847. 16°. . . . . . . J,208
Heidelberg. Leipzig, 1846. 16°. . . . . . . . . J,209
Henry of Guise. New York, 1855. 2 v in 1. 12°. . . . K,734
History of Charlemagne. New York, 1854. 16°. . . . . B,198
The same. New York, n. d. 16°. . . . . . . . L,382
History of Chivalry. New York, 1855. 16°. . . . . . . L,353
Life of Henry IV. of France. New York, 1847. 2 v. 12°. . . D,647
Life of Richard Cœur de Lion. London, 1854. 2 v. p. 8°. . . L,197
Life and and Times of Louis XIV. London, 1851. 2 v. p. 8°. . L,198
Lord Montagu's Page. Philadelphia, 1858. 12°. . . . . K,736
Morley Ernstein. Leipzig, 1842. 16°. . . . . . . . J,210
One in a Thousand. New York, 1855. 2 v. in 1. 12°. . . . K,735
Philip Augustus. New York, 1855. 12°. . . . . . . K,733
Rose d'Albret. Leipzig, 1844. 16°. . . . . . . . J,211
Russell. Leipzig, 1847. 2 v. in 1. 16°. . . . . . . . J,212
Sir Theodore Broughton. Leipzig, 1848. 2 v. in 1. 16°. . . J,213
Smuggler. Leipzig, 1845. 16°. . . . . . . . . . J,214
Step Mother. Leipzig, 1845. 2 v in 1. 16°. . . . . . . J,215
Whim and its Consequences. Leipzig, 1847. 16°. . . . . J,216
James, H. Christianity the Logic of Creation. New York, 1857. 12°. . P,350
Lectures and Miscellanies. New York, 1852. 12°. . . . . . P,264
Nature of Evil. New York, 1855. 12°. . . . . . . . P,148
Secret of Swedenborg. Boston, 1869. 8°. . . . . . . P,847

James, H. Substance and Shadow. Boston, 1863. 8°. . . . . . P,167
James, J. A. Anxious Inquirer after Salvation. New York, n. d. 18°. P,746,21
Jameson, A. Beauties of the Court of Charles II. London, 1851. 4°. *D,300
Celebrated Female Sovereigns. New York, 1862. 2 v. 16°. . . L,366
Characteristics of Women. London, 1858. 2 v. 8°. . . . O,388
The same. Boston, 1866. 16°. . . . . . . . M,18
Common-Place Book of Thoughts and Memories. N. Y. 1855. 12°. H,508
Diary of an Ennuyée. Boston, 1857. 18°. . . . . . V,1028
History of our Lord. London, 1865. 2 v. 8°. . . . *M,117
Legends of the Madonna. London, 1867. 8°. . . . . . *M,118
The same. Boston, 1866. 16°. . . . . . . . M,21
Legends of the Monastic Orders. London, 1867. 8°. . . *M,119
The same. Boston, 1865. 24°. . . . . . . . M,1
Loves of the Poets. Boston, 1857. 18°. . . . . . . . H,561
Memoirs and Essays in Art, Literature, etc. London, 1846. 12°. . M,22
Memoirs of Celebrated Female Sovereigns. London, 1870. 12°. . C,550
Memoirs of Early Italian Painters. Boston, 1866. 16°. . . M,19
Sacred and Legendary Art. London, 1866. 2 v. 8°. . . *M,116
The same. Boston, 1866. 2 v. 16°. . . . . . . M,20
Sisters of Charity, and Communion of Labor. Boston, 1857. 12°. . H,562
Sketches in Canada. London, 1863. p. 8°. . . . . . I,659,2
Sketches of Art, Literature, and Character. Boston, 1866. 16°. . M,16
Studies, Stories, and Memories. Boston, 1866. 16°. . . . M,17
Jameson, R. The Polar Seas and Regions. London, 1855. 8°. . . V,913
and others. Discovery and Adventure in Africa. N. Y. 1855. 16°. L,349
Jamieson, A. Engineer and Mechanic's Assistant. Glasgow, 1847. 2 v. r. 4°. S.C.
Jamieson, J. Affinities of Greek and Latin to the Gothic. Edin. 1814. 8°. L,736
Dictionary of the Scottish Language. Edinburgh, 1846. 8°. . L.R.
Jamison, D. F. Life of Bertrand du Guesclin. London, 1864. 2 v. 8°. D,681
Jane Eyre. C. B. Nicholls. New York, 1870. 12°. . . . . . . K,856
The same. Leipzig, 1850. 2 v. in 1. 16°. . . . . . J,387
Jane Talbot. C. B. Brown. Philadelphia, 1857. 12°. . . . . . K,465
Jane Lomax. H. Smith. London, 1838. 3 v. 12°. . . . . . . K,565
Janet's Love and Service. M. M. Robertson. New York, 1869. 12°. . K,112
Janin, J. Portraits et Caractères Contemporains. Bruxelles, n. d. 12°. H,1030
January and June. B. F. Taylor. New York, 1865. 12°. . . . . . H,238
Japan and China, Journey to Capitals of. R. Fortune. London, 1863. 8°. V,623
Visit to. B. Taylor. New York, 1869. 12°. . . . . V,606
Baron Gros's Embassy. Marquis de Moges. Lond. 1862. 12°. V,602
and the Japanese. London, 1852. 12°. . . . . . . . V,610
and around the World. J. W. Spalding. New York, 1855. 12°. V,1065
as it was and is. R. Hildreth. Boston, 1855. 12°. . . . . . V,620
Geographical and Historical. C. Mac Farlane. N. Y. 1854. 12°. . V,609
The same. Hartford, 1856. 8°. . . . . . . . V,740
History of. E. Kaempfer. London, 1738. 2 v. f°. . . . F,236
Memorials of the Empire of. London, 1850. 8°. . . . . . V,982
Mission to, Lord Elgin's. L. Oliphant. Edinburgh, 1859. 2 v. 8°. V,738
Three Years' Residence in. Sir R. Alcock. N. Y. 1868. 2 v. 12°. V,617
United States Expedition, Perry's. F. L. Hawkes. Wash. 1856. 3 v. 4°. *Q,413
Japanese Botany. Philadelphia, n. d. 4°. . . . . . . . . . N,979

Japanese Fragments; Fac-similes of Illustrations. S. Osborn. Lond. 1861. 8°. V,612
Japanese, Manners and Customs of the. New York, 1859. 18°. . . L,426
Japhet in search of a Father. F. Marryat. New York, 1866. 12°. . . K,842
The same. Leipzig, 1843. 16°. . . . . . . . J,354
Jaques, J. History of Junius and his Works. London, 1843. 8°. . . H,603
Jaques, W. Essay on Intellectual Education. London, 1817. 8°. . O,1183
Jardine, D. Criminal Trials. London, 1832–35. 2 v. 16°. . . . L,473
Jardine, G. Outlines of Philosophical Education. Glasgow, 1818. 8°. O,1052
Jardine, Sir W. Naturalist's Library. Edinburgh, 1837–52. 40 v. 16°. N,470

Vol. 1–4. Jardine, Sir W. British Birds.
5. Sun Birds.
6, 7. Humming-Birds. 2 v.
8. Game Birds.
9. Selby, P. J. Pigeons.
10. Parrots.
11, 12. Swainson, W. Birds of Western Africa. 2 v.
13. Fly-Catchers.
14. Jardine. Sir W. Gallinaceous Birds.
15. Smith, C. H. Introduction to Mammalia.
16. Jardine, Sir W. Felinæ; Lions, Tigers, etc.
17. Macgillivray, W. British Quadrupeds.
18, 19. Smith, C. H. Dogs. 2 v.
20. Horses, Asses, etc.
21. Jardine, Sir W. Deer, Antelopes, etc.
22. Goats, Sheep, Oxen, etc.
23. Elephants and Thick-Skinned Quadrupeds.
24. Waterhouse, G. R. Marsupiala; or, Pouched Animals.
25. Hamilton, R. Amphibious Carnivora.
26. Whales.
27. Jardine, Sir W. Monkeys.
28. Duncan, J. Introduction to Entomology.
29. British Butterflies.
30. British Moths, Spinxes, etc.
31. Foreign Butterflies.
32. Exotic Moths.
33. Beetles.
34. Dunbar, —. Bees.
35. Bushman, J. S. Fishes; Their Structure and Uses.
36, 37. Hamilton, R. British Fishes. 2 v.
38. Jardine, Sir W. Perch Family.
39, 40. Schomburgk, R. H. Fishes of British Guiana.

The same. Edinburgh, 1852–54. 40 v. 16°. . . . . . S.C.
Jargal; a Novel. V. Hugo. New York, 1866. 12°. . . . . . . H,955
Jarves, J. J. Art Hints. New York, 1855. 12°. . . . . . . M,153
Art Idea; Sculpture, Painting, and Architecture. N. Y. 1866. 16°. M,4
Art Thoughts. New York, 1870. 16°. . . . . . . . . M,41
Italian Sights and Papal Principles. New York, 1856. 12°. . . V,507
Parisian Sights and French Principles. New York, 1856. 12°. . V,454
Java, Annulosa Javanica. W. S. Macleay and T. Horsfield. n. t. p. 4°. Q,114
Gestalt, Pflanzendecke, etc. F. Junghuhn. Leip. 1857. 3 v. in 2. 8°. E,231
History of. T. S. Raffles. London, 1830. 2 v. 8°. . . . . . C,409
Atlas to the same. London, 1844. 4°. . . . . . . F,235
Insectes de. W. S. Macleay. Paris, 1833. 8°. . . . . . O,31,1
Kawi-Sprache auf. W. von Humboldt. Berlin, 1836–39. 3 v. 4°. G,595
Lepidoptera of. T. Horsfield. n. t. p. 4°. . . . . . . Q,114
Naturwissenschaft. Reise durch. F. Junghuhn. Magd. 1845. 2 v. 8°. E,227
Jay, J., Life of. G. Van Santvoord. New York, 1854. 8°. . . . C,817
Life of. H. Flanders. Philadelphia, 1855. 8°. . . . . . C,816
and A. Hamilton, Lives of. J. Renwick. New York, 1854. 16°. . L,423
Jay, W. Autobiography. New York, 1855. 2v. . . . . . . C,961
Miscellaneous Writings on Slavery. Boston, 1853. 12°. . . . O,393
Jay, W. M. L. Shiloh; or, Without and Within. New York, 1870. 12°. K,573

Jeaffreson, J. C. Book about Doctors. Leipzig, 1870. 2 v. in 1. 16°. . J,217
Life of Robert Stephenson. London, 1864. 2 v. 8°. . . . . D,454
Jealousy. Mad. Dudevant. Philadelphia, n. d. 12°. . . . . K,1121
Jeames's Diary. W. M. Thackeray. Boston, 1869. 12°. . . . K,1038,1
The same. Philadelphia, 1866. 12°. . . . . . K,1087,2
The same. Leipzig, 1857. 16°. . . . . . . J,484,4
Jean Paul. See *Richter, J. P. F.*
Jebb, J. Translation of the Psalms. London, 1846. 2 v. 8°. . . . . P,431
Jefferson College, History of. J. Smith. Pittsburgh, 1857. 12°. . . O,835
Jefferson, T., Life of. H. S. Randall. New York, 1858. 3 v. 8°. . C,1069
Life of. G. Tucker. London, 1837. 2 v. 8°. . . . . . . C,944
Life and Times. S. W. Smucker. Philadelphia, 1858. 12°. . . C,940
Manual of Parliamentary Practice. New York, 1856. 12°. . . O,475
Sketches of the Life of. B. L. Rayner. New York, 1832. 8°. C,1049
Writings, Official and Private. Washington, 1853–54. 9 v. 8°. . U,107
and Cabell, J. C. History of University of Virginia. Richm. 1856. 8°. O,817
Jeffrey, F. Contributions to the Edinburgh Review. Boston, 1870. 8°. . H,624
Jona. Swift and Sam. Richardson. London, 1856. p. 8°. . . I,661,3
Life of. H. Cockburn. Philadelphia, 1856. 2 v. in 1. 12°. . . D,55
Jeffrey, R. V. Poems. Boston, 1858. 16°. . . . . . . . I,57
Jeffreys, G., *Judge*, Life of. H. W. Woolrych. Philadelphia, 1852. 12°. . D,177
Jeffries, B. J. The Eye in Health and Disease. Boston, 1871. 8°. . . L,954
Jenkin, C. Once and Again. Leipzig, 1865. 2 v. in 1. 16°. . . . J,218
Skirmishing. Leipzig, 1863. 16°. . . . . . . . . J,219
Two French Marriages. Leipzig, 1868. 2 v. in 1. 16°. . . . J,220
Who Breaks—Pays. Leipzig, 1861. 16°. . . . . . . . J,221
Within an Ace. Leipzig, 1869. 16°. . . . . . . . J,222
Jenkins, E. Ginx's Baby; his Birth and other Misfortunes. Bost. 1871. 16°. K,1039
Jenkins, J. Education. London, 1848. 16°. . . . . . . O,1167
Jenkins, J. S. History of Political Parties in N. Y. State. Aub. 1849. 8°. C,172
Life of John C. Calhoun. Auburn, 1856. 12°. . . . . . C,1043
Life of Silas Wright. Auburn, 1850. 12°. . . . . . . C,978
United States Exploring Expeditions. Auburn, 1852. 8°. . . V,963
War between United States and Mexico. Auburn, 1851. 12°. . . B,882
Jenkins W. Ohio Gazetteer. Columbus, 1837. 12°. . . . . . V,30
Jenks, J. W. Rural Poetry of the English Language. Boston, 1856. 8°. I,169
Jenks, W. Explanatory Bible Atlas. Boston, 1847. 4°. . . . . . Q,369
Jenkyn, T. W. Extent of the Atonement. Boston, 1846. . . . . . P,153
Jenner, S. Truth's Conflicts and Truth's Triumphs. London, 1854. 8°. . P,301
Jennings, D. Jewish Antiquities. London, 1766. 2 v. 8°. . . . A,215
Jennings, H. The Rosicrucians. London, 1870. 12°. . . . . . P,870
Jenty, C. N. Anatomico-Physiological Lectures, v. 3. London, 1757. 8°. . L,857
Jenyns, L. Observations in Natural History. London, 1846. 12°. . . N,653
Jenyns, S. Internal Evidence of Christianity. New York, n. d. 18°. P,746,14
Jerdan, W. Autobiography. London, 1852–53. 2 v. 12°. . . . . D,314
Men I have Known. London, 1866. 8°. . . . . . . . C,1247
Jeremie, J. A. History of the Early Christian Church. Lond. 1852. 12°. P,570
Jerrmann, E. Pictures from St. Petersburg. New York, 1852. 12°. . V,524
The same. London, 1854. p. 8. . . . . . . I,656,6
Jerrold, D., Life of. W. B. Jerrold. Boston, 1859. 12°. . . . . D,312

Jerrold, D., Life of. W. B. Jerrold. Philadelphia, n. d. 8°. . . . . U,180
Men of Character. Leipzig, 1852. 2 v. in 1. 16°. . . . . J,223
St. Giles and St. James. Leipzig, 1852. 2 v. in 1. 16°. . . . J,224
Specimens of his Wit. W. B. Jerrold. Boston, 1859. 16°. . . H,600
Works. London, 1851–54. 8 v. 12°. . . . . . . . . U,178

Vol. 1. St. Giles and St. James.
2. Men of Character.
3. Mrs. Caudle's Lectures; Story of a Feather; Sick Giant and Doctor Dwarf.
4. Cakes and Ale.
5. Punch's Letters to his Son; Punch's Complete Letter-Writer; Sketches of the English.
6. Man made of Money; Chronicles of Clovernook.
7. Comedies: Bubbles of the Day; Time works Wonders; The Catspaw; Prisoner of War; Retired from Business; St. Cupid, or, Timothy's Fortune.
8. Comedies and Dramas: Rent Day; Nell Gwynne; Housekeeper; Wedding Gown; Schoolfellows; Doves in a Cage; Painter of Ghent; Black-ey'd Susan.

The same. Philadelphia, n. d. 4 v. 12°. . . . . . U,179

Vol. 1. Memoir by his Son; St. Giles and St. James; Punch's Letters to his Son.
2. Story of a Feather; Cakes and Ale.
3. Mrs. Caudle's Curtain Lectures; Men of Character; Punch's Complete Letter-Writer.
4. Man made of Money; Sketches of the English; Chronicles of Clovernook; Sick Giant and Doctor Dwarf.

Jerrold, W. B. Brage-Beaker with the Swedes. London, 1854. 12°. . . V,537
Life and Remains of Douglas Jerrold. Boston, 1859. 12°. . . D,312
Life of Douglas Jerrold. Philadelphia, n. d. 12°. . . . . U,180
Travels in Sweden and Norway. London, 1854. 12°. . . . V,545
Jerry; or, the Sailor Boy Ashore. W. Simonds. Boston, 1867. 16°. . J,1431,7
Jersey, Sea-Side Studies at. G. H. Lewes. Edinburgh, 1858. 8°. . . N,520
Jerusalem, Ancient Topography of. J. Fergusson. London, 1847. 8°. . V,716
City of the Great King. J. I. Barclay. Philadelphia, 1858. 8°. . V,662
Recovery of. Captains Wilson and Warren. New York, 1871. 8°. V,668
Hebrew's Pilgrimage to. D. F. Strauss. Philadelphia, 1859. 12°. K,1021
Journey from Aleppo to. H. Maundrell. Oxford, 1707. 12°. . . V,639
Delivered. T. Tasso; tr. by A. C. Robertson. Edinburgh, 1853. 8°. I,406
The same; translated by J. H. Wiffen. New York, 1868. 16°. I,444
The same. London, 1854. p. 8°. . . . . . . L,158
The same, *in German.* Leipzig, 1847. 2 v. 16°. . . E,289
Jesse, E. Anecdotes of Dogs. London, 1870. p. 8°. . . . . . . L,112
Jesse, J. H. George Selwyn and his Contemporaries. Lond. 1843–44. 4 v. 8°. D,339
Literary and Historical Memorials of London. Lond. 1847. 2 v. 8°. B,62
London and its Celebrities. London, 1850. 2 v. 8°. . . . . B,61
Memoirs of the Court of England, 1688–1760. Lond. 1843. 3 v. 8°. A,528
Memoirs of the Court of the Stuarts. London, 1857. 3 v. p. 8°. . L,267
Memoirs of King George III. London, 1867. 3 v. 8°. . . . . D,114
Memoirs of the Pretenders and Adherents. London, 1858. p. 8°. . L,268
The same. Philadelphia, 1846. 2 v. 12°. . . . . . D,435
Jesse, W. Life of George *Beau* Brummell. London, 1844. 2 v. 8°. . D,466
Jessie; or, Trying to be Somebody. W. Simonds. Boston, 1859. 16°. J,1431,6
Jests and News out of Purgatory. R. Tarleton. London, 1844. 8°. . I,885,19
Jesuit Juggling. R. Baxter. New York, 1835. 12°. . . . . . . P,812
Jesuit Missions in North America. W. I. Kip. New York, 1846. 12°. . B,593
Jesuits, The. J. Michelet and E. Quinet. New York, 1845. 12°. . . P,808
Constitutiones Societatis Jesv, 1558. Romæ, 1858. 8°. . . . . P,892
Exposure of. B. Pascal. London, 1816. 8°. . . . . . . . P,93

Jesuits, History of. G. B. Nicolini. London, 1854. p. 8°. . . . . L,131
History of. A. Steinmetz. London, 1848. 3 v. 8°. . . . . P,627
in North America. S. Parkman. Boston, 1867. 8°. . . . . B,617
Relations des Jésuites dans la Nouvelle France. Quebec, 1858. 3 v. 8°. B,653
Jesus Christ and his Salvation. H. Bushnell. New York, 1869. 12°. . P,110
Character of, portrayed. D. Schenkel. Boston, 1866. 2 v. 12°. . P,378
Divinity of our Lord. H. P. Liddon. London, 1867. 8°. . . . P,527
Ecce Homo. J. R. Seely. Boston, 1866. 12°. . . . . . . P,371
History of. J. Taylor. London, 1851. 8°. . . . . . . P,368
Glory of, in the Manhood of Christ. H. Goodwin. London, 1856. 8°. P,304
History of, in Works of Art. A. Jameson. London, 1865. 2 v. 8°. *M,117
Imitation of. T. à Kempis. New York, 1851. 12°. . . . . . P,8
in Hades; a Poem. W. W. Lord. New York, 1851. 12°. . . . I,85
Life of. W. Hanna. New York, n. d. 8°. . . . . . . P,381
J. Fleetwood. London, 1855. 4°. . . . . . . F,23
A. Neander. New York, 1855. 8°. . . . . . P,376
The same. London, 1869. p. 8°. . . . . L,216
E. Renan. New York, 1867. 12°. . . . . . . P,374
D. F. Strauss. New York, 1856. 2 v. 8°. . . . P,377
and Lives of the Evangelists. J. Fleetwood. Auburn, 1853. 8°. P,375
Life and Teachings of. L. Abbott. New York, 1869. 8°. . . . P,379
Love of. S. Bolton. London, 1656. f°. . . . . . . . . P,181
Modern Representations of his Life. G. Uhlhorn. Boston, 1868. 16°. P,373
Notes on the Parables of our Lord. R. C. Trench. N. Y. 1855. 8°. P,516
Opinions concerning. J. Priestley. Birmingham, 1786. 4 v. 8°. U,294,20-23
Physical Cause of his Death. W. Stroud. New York, 1871. 12°. . P,380
Suffering Saviour. F. W. Krummacher. Boston, 1870. 12°. . . P,124
Words of the Lord Jesus. R. Stier. Edinburgh, 1855-58. 8 v. 8°. P,557
Vie de Jésus-Christ. A. E. Genoude. Paris, 1851. 12°. . . . P,369
Jevons, W. S. Coal Question. London, 1866. 8°. . . . . . . N,846
Jewell, J. Works. London, 1611. f°. . . . . . . . . . Q,311
Jewett, C. C. Construction of Catalogues. Washington, 1853. 8°. . . L.R.
Jewett, E. Illuminated and Missal Painting. London, n. d. 12°. . . M,84
Jewett, S. W. From Fourteen to Fourscore. New York, 1871. 12°. . . K,310
Jewish Antiquities. D. Jennings. London, 1766. 2 v. 8°. . . . . A,215
Jewish Church, History of. A. Stanley. New York, 1867-68. 2 v. 8°. . P,625
Jewish Nation, History of, from A. D. 70. A. Edersheim. Edinb. 1856. 12°. A,205
Jewish Scriptures and Antiq., Lectures on. J.G.Palfrey. Bost. 1838-52. 4 v. 8°. A,221
Jews, Creed and Ethics of the Maimonides. Cambridge, 1832. 8°. . . P,903
Gefährdung der Deutschen durch die. J. F. Fries. Heid. 1816. 12°. G,533
History of. W. H. Hale. London, 1854. 8°. . . . . . . A,202
F. Josephus. Edinburgh, n. d. 8°. . . . . . . A,217
H. H. Milman. New York, 1855. 3 v. 16°. . . . . L,336
The same. New York, 1866. 3 v. 8°. . . . . A,204
The same. London, 1839. 3 v. 16°. . . . . . I,601
Post-Biblical History of. M. J. Raphall. New York, 1866. 2 v. 12°. A,203
Joan of Arc, Life of. D. W. Bartlett. Auburn, 1854. 12°. . . . . D,595
Life of. J. Michelet. New York, 1865. 12°. . . . . . . D,591
Life and Death of. H. Parr. London, 1866. 2 v. 8°. . . . . D,618
Vie de. A. Desjardins. Paris, 1854. 12°. . . . . . . . D,593

Joan of Arc, and other Poems. R. Southey. London, 1857. 16°. . . . I,429
Joanna of Sicily, Historical Life of. London, 1824. 2 v. 8°. . . . . D,738
Jobson, F. J. America and American Methodism. New York, 1857. 8°. V,63
Jocelyn, E. Mother's Legacy to her Unborn Child. London, 1724. 24°. . P,336
John a Kent and John a Cumber. A. Munday. London, 1851. 8°. . I,885,46
John de Oxenedes. Chronica. London, 1859. 8°. . . . . . . . W,163
John, E. (*E. Marlitt, pseud.*) Countess Gisela. Philadelphia, 1869. 12°. . G,190
Geheimniss der alten Mamsell. Leipzig, 1868. 2 v. 16°. . . G,336
Goldelse. Leipzig, 1868. 16°. . . . . . . . . . . G,337
Gold Else. London, 1868. 12°. . . . . . . . . . G,191
Old Mam'selle's Secret. Philadelphia, 1868. 12°. . . . . . G,192
John Brent. T. Winthrop. Boston, 1864. 16°. . . . . . . . . K,402
John Godfrey's Caprice. H. Parr. Leipzig, 1868. 2 v in 1. 16°. . . J,408
John Godfrey's Fortunes. B. Taylor. New York, 1865. 12°. . . . K,303
John Halifax, Gentleman. D. M. Craik. New York, 1867. 12°. . . K,659
The same. Leipzig, 1857. 2 v. in 1. 16°. . . . . . J,88
John Law, the Projector. W. H. Ainsworth. Leipzig, 1864. 2 v. in 1. 16°. J,13
John Marchmont's Legacy. M. E. Braddon. Lepzig, 1864. 2 v. in 1. 16°. J,39
John, St., Pupils of. C. M. Yonge. London, n. d. 12°. . . . . . P,266
Johnes, M. Boy's Book of Modern Travel. London, n. d. 16°. . . J,1237
Boy's Book of Travel and Adventure. New York, 1870. 12°. . . J,1639
Prince Charlie, the Young Chevalier. New York, 1860. 12°. . . J,1646
Johns, N. Naval and Military Heroes of Great Britain. London, 1860. p. 8°. L,130
Johnson, A. B. Meaning of Words. New York, 1854. 12°. . . . . L,512
Physiology of the Senses. New York, 1856. 12°. . . . L,853
Treatise on Language. New York, 1836. 8°. . . . . . . L,517
Johnson, A. C. Peasant Life in Germany. New York, 1859. 12°. . . V,377
Johnson, A. J. Family Atlas. New York, 1863. 4°. . . . . . . R.R.
Johnson, C. W. Life of Sir Edward Coke. London, 1837. 2 v. 8°. . D,92
Several Tracts on Manures. London, 1836–43. 8°. . . . . N,252,25
Crushed Bones as a Manure. Gypsum as a Fertilizer.
Guano as a Fertilizer. Saltpeter and Nitrate of Soda as a Fertilizer.
Uses of Salt for Agricultural Purposes.
Johnson, E. Results of Hydropathy. New York, 1854. 12°. . . . . L,856
Johnson, E. Wonder-Working Providence of Sions Saviour in New England. London, 1654; edited by W. F. Poole. Boston, 1867. 4°. . C,34
Johnson, G. W. Cucumber; its Culture, Uses, and History. Lond. 1847. 16°. N,252,37
Gooseberry; its Culture, Uses, and History. London, 1847. 16°. N,252,37
Memoirs of John Selden. London, 1835. 8°. . . . . . . . D,57
Johnson, J. (Ed.) Scots Musical Museum; 600 Songs. Edinb. 1853. 4 v. 8°. M,411
Johnson, J. Typographia, the Printers' Instructor. Lond. 1824. 2 v. 12°. . L.R.
Johnson, J. Living to Purpose. London, 1868. 12°. . . . . . . H,129
Johnson, L. Every Lady her own Flower Gardener. New York, 1856. 12°. M,533
Johnson, M. J. Observations at Radcliffe Observatory. Oxf. 1861–7. 6v. 8°. N,362
Radcliffe Catalogue of 6317 Stars. Oxford, 1860. 8°. . . . N,361
Johnson, R. Crowne-Garland of Golden Roses. London, 1842. 12°. L,606,6
Johnson, R. Seven Champions of Christendom. London, 1867. 24°. C,1241
Johnson, R. V. Poems. Boston, 1858. 12°. . . . . . . . . I,57
Johnson, S., Anecdotes of. H. L. Piozzi. London, 1856. p. 8°. . . I,661,3
Dictionary of the English Language. London, 1854. r. 8°. . . L.R.
History of Rasselas. New York, 1853. 12°. . . . . . . K,737

Johnson, S. History of Rasselas. London, 1820. 12°. . . . . . K,537
The same. New York, 1869. 16°. . . . . . . . . I,562
Life of. Sir J. Hawkins. London, 1787. 8°. . . . . . . C,1214
J. Boswell. New York, 1858. 4 v. 12°. . . . . D,152
The same. New York, 1854. 2 v. 8°. . . . D,358
The same. Boston, n. d. . . . . . . . . S.C.
Life of; with Selections from Works. New York, 1855. 2 v. 16°. . L,413
Lives of Eminent English Poets. New York, 1857. 2 v. 12°. . C,1220
The same. Leipzig, 1858. 2 v. in 1. 16°. . . . . . J,225
Religious Life and Death of. New York, 1850. 12°. . . . D,158
Works; with Life by A. Murphy. New York, 1851. 2 v. 8°. . U,227

Vol. 1. Life; The Rambler; The Adventurer; The Idler; Rasselas; Tales of the Imagination; Letters; Irene, a Tragedy; Miscellaneous Poems.
2. Lives of the Poets; Lives of Eminent Persons; Political Tracts; Philological Tracts, etc.; Miscellaneous Tracts; Dedications; Opinions on Questions of Law; Reviews and Criticisms; Journey to the Western Islands of Scotland; Prayers and Meditations.

Johnson, W. R. Report on American Coal. Washington, 1844. 8°. . . N,794
Johnston, A. K. Dictionary of Geography. London, 1852. 8°. . . . . L.R.
Royal Atlas of Modern Geography. Edinburgh, 1868. 4°. . *Q,368
National Atlas. Edinburgh, 1851. f°. . . . . . . *Q,465
Physical Atlas. Edinburgh, 1849. f°. . . . . . . *Q,466
Johnston, C. Travels in Southern Abyssinia. London, 1844. 2 v. 8°. . V,806
Johnston, G. British Zoophytes. London, 1847. 2 v. 8°. . . . O,66
History of British Sponges. Edinburgh, 1842. 8°. . . . . O,68
Introduction to Conchology. London, 1850. 8°. . . . . . N,717
Johnston, J. Manual of Chemistry, Philadelphia, 1856. 12°. . . . N,231
Johnston, J. F. W. Chemistry of Common Life. New York, 1855. 2 v. 12°. N,170
Chemistry and Geology applied to Agriculture. New York, n. d. 12°. M,515
Economy of a Coal Field. Durham, 1838. 8°. . . . N,252,2
Elements of Agricultural Chemistry and Geology. N. Y. 1855. 12°. M,514
Lectures on Agricultural Chemistry and Geology. Edinb. 1847. 8°. M,573
Relation of Science to Agriculture. New York, 1850. 12°. . . M,496
What can be done for Agriculture? London, 1842. 8°. . . N,252,6
Johnstone, J. Memoirs of Samuel Parr. London, 1828. 8°. . . . P,285
Joinville, J., *Sieur* de. Crusade of Saint Louis. London, 1870. p. 8°. . L,5
Chronicle of the Crusades. London, 1848. p. 8°. . . . . . A,226
Memoirs. London, 1807. 2 v. in 1. 4°. . . . . . . . . F,36
Saint Louis, King of France. London, 1868. 16°. . . . . . I,564
Jolly, S. Vocation of the Teacher. London, 1854. 16°. . . . . O,1159
Jomini, H., *Baron de*. Art of War. Philadelphia, 1862. 12°. . . . M,113
History of the Campaign of Waterloo. New York, 1853. 12°. . B,204
Jonas Books. J. Abbott. New York, n. d. 18°. . . . . . . J,1714

Vol. 1. Jonas Stories.
2. Jonas a Judge.
3. Jonas on a Farm—Winter.
Vol. 4. Jonas on a Farm—Summer.
5. Caleb in Town.
6. Caleb in the Country.

Jones, A. Sketch of the Electric Telegraph. New York, 1852. 8°. . . M,708
Jones, B. Life and Letters of M. Faraday. London, 1870. 2 v. 8°. . D,455
Jones, C. A. Outlaw, and other Poems. Cincinnati, 1835. 16°. . . . I,55
Jones, C. C. Chatham Artillery in Southern Rebellion. Albany, 1867. 8°. C,65
Jones, D. Journal of Visits to Indians, 1772-73. New York, 1865. 8°. . C,198
Jones, D. F. Turnip Husbandry. Dublin, 1847. 16°. . . . . N,252,26
Jones, E. O. Characters of English Revolutionary Period. Lond. 1853. 12°. C,1286

Jones, G. Observations on the Zodiacal Light. Washington, 1856. 4°. Q,413,3
Jones, H. Regular Swiss Round in Three Trips. London, 1866. 16°. . F,424
Jones, I., Life of. P. Cunningham; edited by J. P. Collier. Lond. 1848. 8°. I,885,36
Jones, J. Theory and Practice of Notes of Lessons. London, 1856. 16°. O,1131
Jones, J. B. Rebel War Clerk's Diary. Philadelphia, 1866. 2 v. 12°. . B,911
Jones, J. H. Man, Moral and Physical. Philadelphia, 1860. 12°. . . L,896
Jones, J. M. and others. Naturalist in Bermuda. London, 1859. 12°. . N,521
Jones, J. P., Life of. A. S. Mackenzie. New York, 1854. 2 v. 8°. . . C,699
Life of. J. H. Sherburne. New York, 1851, 8°. . . . . C,1290
Jones, M. Nineveh and its Story. London, 1866. 16°. . . . . V,584
Jones, O. Grammar of Ornament. London, 1856. f°. . . . *Q,458
Jones, T. P. Conversations on Chemistry. Philadelphia, 1834. 12°. . N,171
Jones, T. R. Entomostraca of the Cretaceous Formation. Lond. 1849. 4°. Q,27
Introduction to Study of Foraminifera. London, 1862. f°. . . Q,68
Organization of the Animal Kingdom. London, 1861. 8°. . . N,554
Tertiary Entomostraca of England. London, 1856. 4°. . . . Q,30
Jones, W. Treasures of the Earth. New York, 1870. 16°. . . . J,1621
Jones, Sir W. Works; Life by Lord Teignmouth. London, 1807. 13 v. 8°. U,255

Vol. 1, 2. Memoir by Sir J. Shore, Lord Teignmouth; Correspondence; Prefatory Discourse to an Essay on the History of the Turks.
3. Discourse at a meeting of the Asiatic Society, 1794, by Sir J. Shore; Discourses on the Antiquities of Asia; on the Hindus; on the Arabs; on the Tartars; on the Persians; on the Chinese; on the Borderers; on the Origin and Families of Nations; on Asiatic History, Civil and Moral; on the Philosophy of the Asiatics; Dissertation on the Orthography of Asiatic Words in Roman Letters; on the Gods of Greece, Italy, and India.
4. Chronology of the Hindus; Literature of the Hindus; Musical Modes of the Hindus; Mystical Poetry of the Persians and Hindus; Sources and Course of the Nile; Indian Game of Chess; Cure for the Elephantiasis; Tales and Fables by Nizami.
5. Plants of India; Spikenard of the Ancients; Catalogue of Indian Plants; Grammar of the Persian Language; History of the Persian Language.
6. Poeseos Asiaticæ Commentariorum Libri sex; Testamentum Morale; Limon, seu Miscellaneorum Liber.
7. Charges to the Grand Juries; Institutes of Hindu Law.
8. Mahomedan Law of Succession to the Property of Intestates; Law of Inheritance; Essay on the Law of Bailments; Legal Mode of Suppressing Riots; Principles of Government; Character of Lord Ashburton.
9. Speeches of Issues in Causes concerning the Law of Succession to Property at Athens; Fragments of Isæus; Notes and Commentary on Isæus; Sacontalá, or, the Fatal Ring.
10. The Moallakat, or, Seven Arabian Poems suspended in the Temple at Mecca; Poems, chiefly translations from the Asiatic Languages; Examen de la Traduction des Livres attribués a Zoroastre.
11. Histoire de Nader Chah.
12. Traité sur la Poésie Orientale; Introduction to the History of Nader Shah.
13. Hitópadésa of Vishnusarman; Enchanted Fruit, an antediluvian Tale; Hymn to Camdeo; Two Hymns to Pracriti; Extracts from the Bhúshandá Rámáyan and Vedas.

Jonson, B. Conversations with W. Drummond; ed. D. Laing. Lond. 1842. 8°. I,885,8
Poetical Works; with Life by R. Bell. London, 1856. 16°. . . I,250
Works; with Memoir by W. Gifford. Boston, 1853. 8°. . . I,729
Jopling, J. Isometrical Perspective. London, n. d. 8°. . . . . M,222
Jordan, J. H. Review of A. Hall against Universalism. Indianap. 1848. 16°. P,867
Jordan and the Dead Sea; U. S. Expedition to. W. F. Lynch. Phil. 1852. 12°. V,636
Nile and Red Sea, The Rob Roy on. J. Mac Gregor. N. Y. 1870. 8°. V,1080
Jortin, J. Remarks on Ecclesiastical History. Lond. 1751–73. 5 v. 8°. P,602
Josselyn, J. New England Rarities. London, 1672; Boston, 1865. 4°. . F,65
Two Voyages to New England. London, 1674; Boston, 1865. 4°. . F,66
Joseph and his Friend. B. Taylor. New York, 1870. 12°. . . . K,306
Joseph Andrews. H. Fielding. London, 1820. 12°. . . . . K,532
Joseph im Schnee. B. Auerbach. Stuttgart, 1864. 12°. . . . E,311,21

Joseph in the Snow. B. Auerbach. Boston, 1868. 12°. . . . . . G,171
Joseph of Arimathie; or, the Holy Grail. London, 1871. 8°. . . L,605,44
Joseph II. and his Court. C. Mundt. New York, 1867. 8°. . . . G,205
Josephine, Confidential Correspondence of. J. S. C. Abbott. N. Y. 1856. 12°. D,604
History of. J. S. C. Abbott. New York, 1867. 16°. . . . J,1411
Life of. P. C. Headley. New York, 1856. 12°. . . . . D,557
Memoirs of. J. S. Memes. Edinburgh, 1831. 16°. . . . I,534
The same. New York, 1864. 16°. . . . . . . L,361
Josephus, F. Opera. Parisiis, 1845-47. 2 v. 8°. . . . . . . U,555
Works; translated by W. Whiston. London, 1848. 4 v. 8°. . A,216
The same. Edinburgh, n. d. 8°. . . . . . . . . A,217
Josh Billings, hiz Sayings. H. W. Shaw. New York, 1870. 12°. . . H,94
on Ice. H. W. Shaw. New York, 1870. 12°. . . . . H,95
Josiah, History of. T. H. Gallaudet. New York, n. d. 18°. . P,746,28
Joueur, Le; Tragedie Bourgeoise. Londres, 1767. 12°. . . . H,855,1
Jouffroy, T. S. Intro. to Ethics; tr. by W. H. Channing. Bost. 1856. 2 v. 12°. O,712
Journal des Sçavans, tome 1-6,10,11,13,14. Amsterdam, 1677-87. 10 v. 18°. S,5
of Botany. London, 1834-42. 4 v. 8°. . . . . . . N,1008
of Education for Upper Canada, v. 1, 2, 6. Tor. 1848-53. 3 v. 8°, 4°. T,60
of the Fine Arts, May to October, 1851. New York, 1851. 4°. . Q,156
of the Franklin Institute. Philadelphia, 1826-60. 70 v. 8°. . . S,28
of Man. J. R. Buchanan. v. 5. Cincinnati, 1855. 8°. . . . L,985
of Natural Philosophy, etc. W. Nicholson. Lond. 1797-1802. 5 v. 4°. T,41
The same; continued. Lond. 1802-13. 36 v. 8°. . . T,40
of English Agricultural Society. London, 1839-68. 29 v. 8°. . R,18
of the Royal Asiatic Society. London, 1834-56. 16 v. 8°. . . S,93
of Science and the Arts. London, 1816-31. 31 v. 8°. . . . S,30
Journal of a Home Life. E. M. Sewell. Leipzig, 1867. 2 v. in 1. 16°. . J,456
Joyce, J. Introduction to the Arts and Sciences. London, 1852. 12°. . M,786
Scientific Dialogues. London, 1852. p. 8°. . . . . . . L,300
Systematic Education. London, 1815. 2 v. 8°. . . . . O,1207
Joyce, P. W. Origin of Irish Names and Places. Dublin, 1869. 16°. . L,519
Joyce, R. D. Legends of the Wars in Ireland. Boston, 1868. 16°. . K,1013
Juan y Santacilia, J. and Ulloa. Voyage to South America. Lond. 1806. 2 v. 8°. V,253
Judæa Capta. C. E. Tonna. New York, 1869. 16°. . . . . . . J,1195
Judah's Lion. C. E. Tonna. New York, n. d. 16°. . . . . . J,1106
Judaism, Christianity without. B. Powell. London, 1857. 12°. . . P,222
before the Advent of Christ. D. T. Strauss. Philadelphia, 1859. 12°. K,1021
Judd, S., Life and Character of. A. Hall. Boston, 1857. 12°. . . . C,674
Margaret; a Tale of the Real and Ideal. Boston, 1871. 12°. . K,206
Philo; an Evangeliad. Boston, 1850. 12°. . . . . . . I,63
Judges, Atrocious. R. Hildreth. New York, 1856. 12°. . . . . D,180
Judicial Chronicle. Cambridge, 1834. 8°. . . . . . . . . U,526
Judicial Evidence, Rationale of. J. Bentham. London, 1827. 5 v. 8°. U,544
Junkin, D. X. George Junkin; a Historical Biography. Phil. 1871. 12°. C,825
Judkins, J. P. Introductory Lecture on Anatomy. Cincinnati, 1846. 8°. H,302,4
Judson, A., Memoirs of Life and Labors of. F. Wayland. Bost. 1853. 2 v. 12°. C,927
Judson, A. H., Memoir of. J. D. Knowles. Boston, 1855. 12°. . . C,834
S. B. and E. C., Lives of. A. W. Stuart. Boston, 1869. 12°. . . C,533
Judson, E. C. Alderbook. Boston, 1847. 2 v. 12°. . . . . . H,272

Judson, E. C. Life and Letters of. A. C. Kendrick. New York, 1869. 12°. . C,738
Memoir of Sarah B. Judson. New York, 1855. 18°. . . . C,833
My two Sisters. Boston, 1854. 16°. . . . . . . . J,1258
Jugendsünden. F. G. Kühne. Leipzig, 1850. 12°. . . . . . G,339
Jukes, J. B. Popular Physical Geology. London, 1853. 16°. . . . N,597
Student's Manual of Geology. Edinburgh, 1862. 8°. . . . N,790
Julia; a Poem. W. Brooke. Boston, 1855. 16°. . . . . . . I,287
Julia de Roubigné. H. Mackenzie. London, 1820. 12°. . . . . K,540
Julia Howard. M. Bell. New York, 1864. 8°. . . . . . . K,599
Julia Mandeville. F. M. Brooke. London, 1820. 12°. . . . . K,538
Julian, The Emperor, and his Generation. A. Neander. New York, 1850. 12°. D,722
Julian; or, Scenes in Judea. W. Ware. New York, 1865. 2 v. 12°. . K,353
Julian, I. H. Memoir of D. Hoover. Richmond, Ind. 1857. 8°. . H,302,1
Julian Home; Tale of College Life. F. W. Farrar. New York, n. d. 12°. J,1471
Juliana, Mother. Sixteen Revelations of Divine Love. Boston, 1864. 16°. P,32
Juliana Oakley. M. M. Sherwood. New York, 1860. 12°. . . K,1008,5
Julius and Evagoras; Schönheit der Seele. J. F. Fries. Heid. 1822. 2 v. 16°. G,276
Jungfrau Alp, Pilgrim to the. G. B. Cheever. New York, 1846. 8°. . V,500
Junghuhn, F. Java, seine Gestalt, Pflanzendecke. Leip. 1857. 3 v. in 2. 8°. E,231
Naturwissenschaftliche Reise durch Java. Magdeburg, 1845. 2 v. 8°. E,227
Atlas dazu. Madgeburg, 1845. obl. 4°. . . . . . *F,93
Junius (*pseud*) and his Works. J. Jaques. London, 1843. 8°. . . . H,603
identified as Lord Chatham. W. Dowe. London, 1857. 12°. . . H,602
identity with Sir P. Francis. J. Taylor. New York, 1818. 8°. H,604
Letters. Boston, 1851. 2 v. in 1. 12°. . . . . . . . H,601
with Evidence of Authorship. London, 1850. 2 v. p. 8°. L,199
Junkin, D. X. The Oath a Divine Ordinance. New York, 1845. 12°. . P,133
Junot, L. P., *Duchess d'Abrantes.* Memoirs of Napoleon. N. Y. 1869. 2 v. 8°. D,559
Souvenirs en Espagne et Portugal, 1808–11. Bruxelles, 1838. 2 v. 16°. H,1031
Jura, Quiet Nook in the. J. Ruffini. Leipzig, 1867. 16°. . . . J,434
Jure Divino; a Satyr. D. DeFoe. London, 1706. 12°. . . . . . I,470
Jurisprudence, Constitutional, of the U. S. W. A. Duer. Boston, 1856. 12°. U,490
The same. New York, 1833. 12°. . . . . . . O,469
The same. New York, 1855. 16°. . . . . . . L,446
Jussieu, A. de. Elements of Botany; ed. by J. H. Wilson. Lond. 1855. p. 8°. L,301
Juste, T. Memoirs of Leopold I. London, 1868. 2 v. 8°. . . . D,526
Vie de Marie de Hongrie. Bruxelles, 1861. 12°. . . . H,1032
Justinus. History of the World; tr. by J. S. Watson. London, 1853. p. 8°. L,64
Historiæ Phillippicæ; curante N. E. Lemaire. Parisiis, 1823. 8°. U,325
Works; translated by J. S. Watson. London, 1853. p. 8°. . . L,64
Juvenalis, D. J. Satiræ; ed. N. E. Lemaire. Parisiis, 1823–25. 2 v. 8°. U,326
The same. Amsterdam, 1684. 8°. . . . . . . . U,416
The same; translated by C. Bradham. New York, 1831. 18°. U,366
The same; translated by L. Evans. London, 1852. p. 8°. . L,65
Juvenile Choir. G. Kingsley. New York, 1845. 18°. . . . . . M,402
Juvenile Crime. S. P. Day. London, 1858. 8°. . . . . . . O,352
Juvenile Delinquency. C. F. Cornwallis. London, 1853. 8°. . . . O,354
M. Hill. London, 1853. 8°. . . . . . . . . . O,354
Juvenile Delinquents. M. Carpenter. London, 1853. 12°. . . . O,358
Half Century with. B. K. Peirce. New York, 1869. 8°. . . O,384

Juvenile Depravity. H. Worseley. London, 1849. 12°. . . . . . O,353
Juventus Mundi; the Heroic Age. W. E. Gladstone. London, 1869. 12°. H,734

Kaempfer, E. History of Japan. London, 1728. 2 v. f°. . . . . F,236
Kaffraria, Military Operations in. Sir G. Cathcart. London, 1856. 8°. . B,84
Kaines, J. Last Words of Eminent Persons. London, 1866. 8°. . . H,484
Kaleidoscope, History and Construction of. Sir D. Brewster. Lond. 1858. 8°. N,25
Karsten, C. J. B. Philosophie der Chemie. Berlin, 1843. 8°. . . N,252,7
Karsten, S. De Pulmonum Structura. Trajecti ad Rhenum, 1847. 8°. N,252,44
Kastner, K. W. G. Chemie zur Erläut. der Experimtalphys. Erl. 1850. 8°. N,252,33
Kaloolah; or, Adventures of J. Romer. W. S. Mayo. N. Y. 1850. 12°. J,638
Kampen, N. G. von. Geschichte der Niederlande. Hamb. 1831–33. 2 v. 8°. E,83
Kane, E. K., Biography of. W. Elder. Philadelphia, 1858. 8°. . . C,758
    The same. Philadelphia, 1858. 8°. . . . . . . S.C.
  First U. S. Grinnell Arctic Expedition, 1850–51. New York, 1854. 8°. V,940
  Second Grinnell Arctic Expedition, 1853–55. Phil. 1858. 2 v. 8°. V,939
  Tidal Observations in the Arctic Seas. Washington, 1863. 4°. Q,324,13
Kane, R. Nature of the Compounds of Ammonia. Dublin, 1839. 4°. N,252,42
Kansas, Conquest of. W. Phillips. Boston, 1856. 12°. . . . . . C,313
  Journey through. C. B. Boynton and Mason. Cincinnati, 1852. 12°. V,100
  Its Life and History. S. P. L. Robinson. Boston, 1857. 12°. . . C,182
  Summer Tour through. J. F. Meline. New York, 1868. 16°. . V,185
Kant, I. Critick of Pure Reason. London, 1838. 8°. . . . . . O,672
    The same. London, 1855. 12°. . . . . . . . L,252
  Last Days of. T. De Quincey. Edinburgh, 1863. 12°. . . H,412,3
  Sämmtliche Werke. Leipzig, 1867–68. 8 v. 8°. . . . . . G,565

Bd. 1. Die Wahre Schätzung der lebendigen Kräfte; Verändert die Erde ihre Achsenumdrehung? Ob die Erde veralte? physikalish erwogen; Naturgeschichte und Theorie des Himmels; Meditationes de Igne; Principiorum Primorum Cognitionis Metaphysicæ Nova Delucidatio; Ursache der Erderschütterungen, 1755; Geschichte und Beschreibung des Erdbebens, 1755; Fortgesetze Betrachtung der Erderschütterungen; Monadalogia Physica; Zur Erläuterung der Theorie der Winde.

2. Entwurf eines Collegii der physischen Geographie; Lehrbegriff der Berwegung und Ruhe; An Fräulein von Knobloch über Swedenborg; Betrachtungen über den Optimismus; Gedanken bei dem Ableben des Herrn von Funk; Die falsche Spitzfindigkeit der vier syllegistischen Figuren; Versuch den Begriff der negativen Grössen in die Weltweisheit einzuführen; Beweisgrund für das Dasein Gottes; J. P. D. Komarnicki; Krankheiten des Kopfes; Ueber das Gefühl des Schönen und Erhabenen; Deutlichkeit der Grundsätze der natürlichen Theologie und der Moral; Einrichtung seiner Vorlesungen, 1765–66; Träume eines Geistersehers; Von dem ersten Grunde des Unterschiedes der Gegenden im Raume; De Mundi Forma atque Principiis; Recensionen der Schrift von Moscati; Die verschiedenen Racen der Menschen; Das Basedow'sche Philanthropin betreffende Recensionen.

3. Kritik der Reinen Vernunft.

4. Prolegomena zu jeder künftigen Metaphysik; Recensionen von Schulz's Sittenlehre; Idee zu einer allgemeinen Geschichte in weltbürgerlicher Hinsicht; Was is Aufklärung?; Recensionen von Herder's Ideen zur Philosophie der Geschichte der Menschheit; Die Vulcane im Monde; Unrechtmässigkeit des Büchernachdrucks; Bestimmung des Begriffs einer Menschenrace; Grundlegung der Metaphysik der Sitten; Muthmasslicher Anfang der Menschengeschichte; Recensionen von Hufeland's Grundsatz des Naturrechts; Was heisst: sich im Denken Orientiren?; Metaphysische Anfangsgründe der Naturwissenschaft; Bemerkungen zu Jakob's Prüfung der Mendelssohn'schen Morgenstunden; Gebrauch teleologischer Principien in der Philosophie; Sieben Kleine Aufsätze, 1788–91.

5. Kritik der Praktischen Vernunft; Kritik der Urtheilskraft.

6. Entdeckung, nach der alle Kritik der reinen Vernunft entbehrlich werden soll; Schwärmerei; Misslingen aller philosophischen Versuche in der Theodicee; Religion innerhalb der Grenzen der blosen Vernunft; Ueber den Gemeinspruch: Das Mag in der Theorie richtig sein, taugt aber nichts für die Praxis;

Kant, I. Sämmtliche Werke. *Continued.* . . . . . . . . . G,655

Einfluss des Mondes auf die Witterung; Das Ende aller Dinge; Philosophie überhaupt; Zum ewigen Frieden; Zu Sömmerring, über das Organ der Seele; Von dem neuerdings erhobenen Ton in der Philosophie; Ausgleichung eines mathematischen Streits; Abschluss eines Tractats zum ewigen Frieden in der Philosophie.

7. Metaphysik der Sitten; Aus Menschenliebe zu lügen; Ueber die Buchmacherei; Der Streit der Facultäten; Anthropologie in pragmatischer Hinsicht.

8. Logik; Physische Geographie; Pädagogik; Fortschritte der Metaphysik seit Leibnitz und Wolf; Oeffentliche Erklärungen; Ehrendenksprüche auf verstorbene Collegen; Fragmente; Briefe.

Kapp, F. Life of F. W. von Steuben. New York, 1859. 12°. . . . D,516

Karlsbad, Mineral-Wasser von. S. Berzelius. Leipzig, 1825. 8°. . N,252,27

Karr, A. Tour round my Garden. London, 1865. 16°. . . . . . H,474

Kars, Narrative of the Defense of. A. Lake. London, 1857. 8°. . . A,522

Kate Coventry. G. J. W. Melville. Leipzig, 1860. 16°. . . . . . J,378

Kater, H. and Lardner, D. Mechanics. London, 1830. 12°. . . M,1021

Katharine Ashton. E. M. Sewell. New York, 1866. 2 v. 12°. . K,1000

Katharine Walton. W. G. Simms. New York, 1864. 12°. . . . K,254

Kathrina; her Life and mine. J. G. Holland. New York, 1868. 12°. . I,59

Katmandu, Nepaul, Journey to. L. Oliphant. New York, 1852. 12°. . V,586

Kaup, J. J. Catalogue of Apodal Fish in British Museum. Lond. 1856. 8°. N,702

and Klipstein, A. von. Dinotherus Giganteus. Darmstadt, 1836. 4°. N,252,57

Kavanagh. H. W. Longfellow. Boston, 1866. 16°. . . . . . . . U,1,2

Kavanagh, J. Adèle. New York, 1870. 3 v. in 1. 12°. . . . . K,739

The same. Leipzig, 1858. 3 v. 16°. . . . . . . J,226

Beatrice. New York, 1868. 12°. . . . . . . . . . K,656

The same. Leipzig, 1864. 2 v. in 1. 16°. . . . . . J,227

Daisy Burns. New York, 1867. 12°. . . . . . . . . K,740

The same. Leipzig, 1853. 2 v. in 1. 16°. . . . . . J,228

Dora. New York, 1868. 3 v. in 1. 8°. . . . . . . . K,741

The same. Leipzig, 1868. 2 v. in 1. 16°. . . . . . J,229

English Women of Letters. Leipzig, 1862. 16°. . . . . J,230

French Women of Letters. Leipzig, 1862. 16°. . . . . J,231

Grace Lee. New York, 1866. 12°. . . . . . . . . K,742

The same. Leipzig, 1855. 2 v. in 1. 16°. . . . . J,232

Madeleine; a Tale of Auvergne. New York, 1866. 12°. . . . K,747

Nathalie; a Tale. New York, 1863. 12°. . . . . . . K,743

The same. Leipzig, 1851. 2 v. in 1. 16°. . . . . J,233

Queen Mab. New York, 1864. 3 v. in 1. 12°. . . . . K,744

Rachel Gray. New York, 1868. 12°. . . . . . . . K,745

The same. Leipzig, 1856. 16°. . . . . . . . J,234

Seven Years, and other Tales. New York, 1866. 12°. . . . K,746

The same. Leipzig, 1859. 2 v. in 1. 16°. . . . . J,235

Silvia. Leipzig, 1870. 2 v. in 1. 16°. . . . . . . . J,236

Summer and Winter in the Two Sicilies. Leipzig, 1858. 2 v. in 1. 16°. J,238

Sybil's Second Love. New York, 1869. 12°. . . . . . . K,696

The same. Leipzig, 1867. 2 v. in 1. 16°. . . . . J,237

Women of Christianity. New York, 1852. 12°. . . . . . P,232

Kawi-Sprache auf der Insel Java. W. von Humboldt. Berl. 1836-39. 3 v. 4°. G,595

Kay, J. Education of the Poor. London, 1846. 8°. . . . . . O,1015

Social Condition of the English People. London, 1850. 2 v. 12°. . O,536

The same. New York, 1863. 12°. . . . . . . . O,376

Kaye, J. W. Christianity in India. London, 1859. 8°. . . . . . P,593
Essays of an Optimist. Philadelphia, 1871. 16°. . . . . . H,442
Lives of Indian Officers. London, 1867. 2 v. 8°. . . . . . D,87
War in Afghanistan. London, 1857–58. 3 v. 8°. . . . . . B,78
Keats, J., Life of. R. M. Milnes. London, 1820. 8°. . . . . . . D,194
Life, Letters, and Literary Remains. London, 1848. 2 v. . . . D,4
Poetical Works. Boston, 1848. 16°. . . . . . . . . . I,216
The same. Philadelphia, 1846. 8°. . . . . . . . I,487
Keble, J. Christian Year. Philadelphia, 1854. 24°. . . . . . . I,353
Letters of Spiritual Counsel. Oxford, 1870. 12°. . . . . P,127
Memoir of. Sir J. T. Coleridge. Oxford, 1869. 8°. . . . D,425
Keen, S. F. Orient Boys. Boston, 1870. 16°. . . . . . . J,1542
Keep a Good Heart. Cousin Carrie. New York, 1865. 16°. . . J,1363
Keferstein, W. See *Bronn, H. G. and Keferstein.*
Keightley, T. Fairy Mythology. London, 1860. p. 8°. . . . . . L,14
History of England. London, 1859–65. 2 v. 12°. . . . . A,422
The same. New York, 1860. 5 v. 18°. . . . . . . L,416
History of Greece. London, 1858. 12°. . . . . . . . . A,71
The same. New York, 1853. 8°. . . . . . . . . A,87
History of Rome. London, 1858. 16°. . . . . . . . . A,135
Life of John Milton. London, 1855. 8°. . . . . . . . C,1268
Mythology of Ancient Greece and Italy. New York, 1866. 8°. . P,921
The same; abridged. New York, 1866. 16°. . . . . . P,909
Outlines of History. London, 1830. 12°. . . . . . . . M,984
War of Independence in Greece. Edinburgh, 1830. 2 v. 16°. . I,528
Keil, K. F. Commentary on the Book of Joshua. Edinburgh, 1857. 8°. . P,530
and Bertheau, E. Commentary on Books of Kings. Edinb. 1857. 2 v. 8°. P,541
Keim, De B. R. Sheridan's Troopers on the Borders. Phil. 1870. 12°. . B,889
Keith, A. The Land of Israel. New York, 1844. 12°. . . . . . V,645
Keith, J., Memoir of. See *Spalding Club Publications*, v. 11.
Keith, R. Affairs of Church and State in Scotland. Edinb. 1844–50. 3 v. 8°. P,594
Keller, F. Lake Dwellings of Switzerland. London, 1866. 8°. . . M,175
Kellogg, A. G. Shakespeare's Delineations of Insanity, etc. N. Y. 1866. 12°. I,849
Kellogg, E. Labor and other Capital. New York, 1849. 8°. . . . O,547
Kellogg, E. Elm Island Stories. Boston, 1869–71. 6 v. 16°. . . J,1473
Vol. 1. Lion Ben. Vol. 3. Ark of Elm Island. Vol. 5. Young Shipbuilders.
2. Charlie Bell. 4. Boy Farmers. 6. Hard Scrabble.
Norman Cline. Boston, 1871. 16°. . . . . . . . . J,1724
Pleasant Cove Series. Boston, 1871. 2 v. 16°. . . . . J,1475
Vol. 1. Arthur Brown, the Young Captain. Vol 2. Young Deliverers.
Kelly, P. Universal Commercial Instructor. London, 1831. 2 v. in 1. 4°. Q,328
Kelly, W. K. History of the House of Austria. London, 1853. p. 8°. L,177,4
History of Russia. London, 1854. 2 v. p. 8°. . . . . . L,227
Syria and the Holy Land. London, 1844. 8°. . . . . . . V,661
Kelso, I. Danger in the Dark. Cincinnati, 1857. 12°. . . . . .. K,200
Kemble, F. A. Poems. Boston, 1859. 12°. . . . . . . . . I,123
Residence on a Georgia Plantation. New York, 1864. 12°. . . V,88
Kemble, J. M. (Ed.) Codex Diplomat., Ævi Saxonici. Lond. 1839–48. 6 v. 8°. U,616
State Papers and Correspondence, 1688–1714. Lon. 1857. 8°. . . A,521
Kemp, E. How to lay out a Garden. New York, 1858. 12°. . . . M,348
Kemp, G. Letter to J. Liebig on Animal Chemistry. Lond. 1844. 8°. N,252,14

Kemp, T. L. Indications of Instinct. London, 1862. p. 8°. . . . . I,666
Natural History of Creation. London, 1862. p. 8°. . . . . . I,666
Kempis, T. à. Imitation of Christ. Dublin, 1817. 32°. . . . . . P,334
The same. New York, 1851. 12°. . . . . . . . . P,8
Ken, T., Life of; by a Layman. London, 1851. 8°. . . . . . C,1291
Kendall, G. W. Texan Santa Fé Expedition. New York, 1844. 2 v. 12°. V,89
Kendrick, A. C. Life and Letters of Emily C. Judson. N. Y. 1869. 12°. . C,738
Kenilworth. Sir W. Scott. Boston, 1858. 2 v. 16°. . . . . . K,940
The same. Philadelphia, 1860. 8°. . . . . . . K,965
The same. Philadelphia, 1869. 8°. . . . . . K,1110
The same. Leipzig, 1845. 16°. . . . . . . . . J,445
Kennan, G. Tent-Life in Siberia. New York, 1870. 12°. . . . . V,682
Kennedy, C. M. Turks of Constantinople. London, 1864. 8°. . . V,1086,3
Kennedy, G. Profession is not Principle. Philadelphia, 1827. 12°. . . P,16
Kennedy, J. P. Horseshoe Robinson. Philadelphia, 1865. 12°. . . K,203
Life of William Wirt. Philadelphia, 1854. 2 v. 12°. . . . C,766
Mr. Ambrose's Letters on the Rebellion. New York, 1865. 12°. . B,890
Quodlibet, containing some Annals thereof. New York, 1866. 12°. K,312
Rob of the Bowl. Philadelphia, 1860. 12°. . . . . . . K,202
Swallow Barn. Philadelphia, 1866. 12°. . . . . . . . . K,201
Kennedy, W. S. Plan of Union; or, History of Presbyterian and Congregational Churches of the Western Reserve. Hudson, O. 1856. 12°. C,200
Kenneth. C. M. Yonge. New York, 1866. 12°. . . . . . K,1082
Kennion, E. Essay on Trees in Landscape. London, 1844. f°. . . Q,208
Kenrick, F. P. Primacy of the Apostolic See vindicated. Balt. 1855. 8°. P,817
Vindication of the Catholic Church. Baltimore, 1855. 12°. . . P,809
Kenrick, J. Ancient Egypt under the Pharaohs. N. Y. 1852. 2 v. 12°. V,791
Kent, J. Commentaries on American Law. Boston, 1867. 4 v. 8°. . U,421
Morning and Evening Service. London, n. d. 2 v. 8°. . . . M,426
Kentish, T. Box of Instruments and the Slide-Rule. Phila. 1852. 12°. . M,605
Kenton, S., Sketches of. J. MacDonald. n. p. n. d. 12°. . . . . C,839
Kentucky, Description of. J. Filson. London, 1793. 8°. . . . . V,44
Geological Survey in, 1854–55. D. D. Owen. Frank. 1856–57. 3 v. 8°. *N,743
Maps and Plates of the same. . . . . . . . . *N,745
History of. M. Butler. Cincinnati, 1836. 12°. . . . . C,231
H. Marshall. Frankfort, 1824. 2 v. 8°. . . . . *C,179
Indiana and Ohio, Tour in, in 1805. J. Espy. Cincinnati, 1871. 8°. C,223
Ohio and Tennessee, Travels to. F. A. Michaux. London, 1805. 8°. . V,73
Pioneer Life in. D. Drake. Cincinnati, 1870. 8°. . . . . . C,222
Sketches of. L. Collins. Maysville, Ky. 1847. 8°. . . . . . C,234
Tour in. F. Cuming. Pittsburgh, 1810. 12°. . . . . . . V,96
Kepler, J., Life of. Regensburg, 1842. 4°. . . . . . . . . F,176
Life of. J. E. D. Bethune. London, n. d. 8°. . . . . . . C,581
Galileo and Tycho Brahe, Lives of. D. Brewster. Lond. 1870. p. 8°. C,551
Keppel, G. T. Memoirs of Marquis of Rockingham. Lond. 1852. 2 v. 8°. D,431
Keppel, H. Expedition to Borneo. New York, 1846. 12°. . . . . V,235
Kerhallet, C. P. de. Navigation à la Côte Occident. d' Afrique. Paris, 1852. 4°. Q,425,2
Navigation dans la Mer des Antilles. Paris, 1854. 4°. . . . Q,425,1

Kerl, B. Practical Treatise on Metallurgy; edited by W. Crookes and E. Röhrig. London, 1868–70. 3 v. 8°. . . . . . . . M,717

Vol. 1. Lead, Silver, Zinc, Cadmium, Tin, Mercury, Bismuth, Antimony, Nickle, Arsenic, Gold, Platinum, Sulphur.
2. Copper, Iron. Vol. 3. Steel, Fuel.

Kerl, S. Grammar of the English Language. Philadelphia, 1859. . . L,569
Kern, G. M. Landscape Gardening. Cincinnati, 1855. 12°. . . . M,353
Kerner, J. Dichtungen. Stuttgart u. Tübingen, 1834. 12°. . . . E,268
Kerney, M. J. Compendium of Ancient and Modern Hist. Balt. 1851. 12°. A,20
Kerr, Orpheus C., *pseud.* See *Newell, R. H.*
Kerr, R. Collection of Voyages and Travels. Edinburgh, 1811–24. 18 v. 8°. V,1097
Key, F. S. Poems. New York, 1857. 12°. . . . . . . . . . I,54
Key, T. H. Philological Essays. London, 1868. 8°. . . . . . . L,550
Keyser, R. Private Life of the Old Northmen. London, 1868. 12°. . B,576
Religion of the Northmen. New York, 1854. 12°. . . . . . P,235
Khanikoff. Bokhara; its Amir and its people. London, 1845. 8°. . . V,700
Kidd, J. Adaptation of External Nature to Man. London, 1852. p. 8°. . L,276
The same. London, 1836. 16°. . . . . . . . N,89
Kidd, R. Vocal Culture and Elocution. Cincinnati, n. d. 12°. . O,1249
Kidder, D. P. and Fletcher, J. C. Brazil and the Brazilians. Phil. 1857. 8°. V,254
Kidder, F. Boston Massacre, March 5, 1770. Albany, 1870. 8°. . . B,748
Expeditions of Capt. John Lovewell. Boston, 1865. 4°. . . . B,888
and Gould, A. A. History of New Ipswich, N. H. Boston, 1852. 8°. C,26
Kieser, D. G. Grundzüge der Anatomie der Pflanzen. Jena, 1815. 8°. . G,876
Kiesewetter, R. G. Die Musik der Araber. Leipzig, 1842. 4°. . . . G,739
Weltlicheer Gesang vom Mittelalter. Leipzig, 1841. 4°. . . G,738
Killen, W. D. The Ancient Church. New York, 1859. 8°. . . . P,401
Kilpatrick, H. J. and our Cavalry. J. Moore. New York, 1865. 12°. . C,732
Kimball, J. K. Emancipation in the West Indies. New York, 1838. 12°. V,186
Kimball, R. B. In the Tropics. New York, 1863. 12°. . . . . K,133
Prince of Kashna. New York, 1866. 12°. . . . . . . K,132
Romance of Student Life Abroad. New York, 1865. 12°. . . K,135
Saint Ledger; or, Threads of Life. New York, 1850. 12°. . . K,137
Under-Currents. New York, 1864. 12°. . . . . . . . K,136
Was he Successful? New York, 1866. 12°. . . . . . . K,134
Kinder von Heute. C. Mundt. Berlin, 1864. 12°. . . . . . G,362,2
Kindergarten Guide. M. Mann and E. P. Peabody. New York, 1869. 12°. O,998
King and Commons; Cavalier and Puritan Song; ed. H. Morley. Lon. 1868. 16°. I,560
King, C. W. Antique Gems. London, 1866. 8°. . . . . . . M,100
Natural History of Gems. London, 1867. 8°. . . . . . . N,864
King, E. My Paris; French Character Sketches. Boston, 1868. 12°. . V,447
King, E., *Lord Kingsborough.* Antiquities of Mexico. Lon. 1830–48. 9 v. f°. *F,125
King, E. F. Ten Thousand Wonderful Things. London, n. d. 12°. . H,317
King, J. A. Twenty-Four Years in the Argentine Republic. Lond. 1846. 8°. V,249
King, Sir P. Life of John Locke. London, 1864. p. 8°. . . . . L,206
King, R. Journey to the Arctic Ocean. London, 1836. 2 v. 12°. . . V,914
King, T. S., Tribute to. R. Frothingham. Boston, 1865. 12°. . . . C,697
King, W. Permian Fossils of England. London, 1850. 4°. . . . Q,31
King, W. H. Lessons and Practical Notes on Steam. New York, 1864. 8°. M,700
King, W. R., Obituary Addresses on the Death of. Washington, 1854. 8°. C,799
King Arthur. Sir E. B. Lytton. London, 1851. 8°. . . . . . . I,383

King Arthur. Sir E. B. Lytton. Leipzig, 1849. 2 v. in 1. 16°. . . J,316
King of the Mountains. E. About. Boston, 1861. 12°. . . . . . H,971
King Philip's War, History of. B. Church; ed. S. G. Drake. Bost. 1827. 12°. B,685
History of. I. and C. Mather; ed. S. G. Drake. Boston, 1862. 4°. . C,30
King's Own. F. Marryat. New York, 1868. 12°. . . . . . . K,843
The same. Leipzig, 1869. 16°. . . . . . . . J,355
Kinglake, A. W. Eōthen; or, Travel in the East. New York, 1850. 12°. V,1037
The same. London, 1865. p. 8°. . . . . . . . I,657
The same. Leipzig, 1846. 16°. . . . . . . . J,239
Invasion of the Crimea. New York and Edinburgh, 1868. 4 v. 8°. B,81
The same. Leipzig, 1863–68. 8 v. 16°. . . . . . J,240
Kings and Queens; Life in the Palaces. J. S. C. Abbott. N. Y. 1855. 12°. J,1397
Kingsford, J., *pseud.* See *Barnard, C.*
Kingsley, C. Alton Locke. New York, 1867. 16°. . . . . . . K,748
The same. Leipzig, 1857. 16°. . . . . . . . J,241
Andromeda, and other Poems. Boston, 1858, 16°. . . . . . I,362
Glaucus; Wonders of the Shore. Boston, 1855. 16°. . . . N,491
Hereward, the Last of the English. Boston, 1866. 12°. . . . K,749
The same. Leipzig, 1866. 2 v. in 1. 16°. . . . . . J,242
Hermits. Philadelphia, 1868. 12°. . . . . . . . . P,795
Heroes; Greek Fairy Tales. Boston, 1864. 16°. . . . . J,1317
Hypatia. New York, 1866. 2 v. 16°. . . . . . . . K,750
The same. Leipzig, 1857. 2 v. in 1. 16°. . . . . . . J,243
Poems. Boston, 1856. 16°. . . . . . . . . . I,363
Sir Walter Raleigh and his Time. Boston, 1859. 12°. . . . D,405
Three Lectures on the Ancient Régime. London, 1867. 8°. . . B,337
Two Years Ago. Boston, 1864. 12°. . . . . . . . K,751
The same. Leipzig, 1857. 2 v. in 1. 16°. . . . . . J,244
Water Babies; a Fairy Tale. London, 1869. 12°. . . . . J,1728
Westward Ho; or, Sir Amyas Leigh. New York, 1866. 2 v. 16°. K,753
The same. Leipzig, 1855. 2 v. in 1. 16°. . . . . . J,245
Yeast; a Problem. New York, 1864. 12°. . . . . . . K,752
The same. Leipzig, 1851. 16°. . . . . . . . J,246
Kingsley, G. Juvenile Choir. New York, 1845. 16°. . . . . M,402
Kingsley H. Austin Elliot. Boston, 1863. 12°. . . . . . . K,754
The same. Leipzig, 1863. 16°. . . . . . . . J,247
Hillyars and the Burtons. Boston, 1865. 12°. . . . . K,756
The same. Leipzig, 1865. 2 v. in 1. 16°. . . . . . J,249
Leighton Court. Leipzig. 1866. 16°. . . . . . . J,250
Ravenshoe. Boston, 1866. 12°. . . . . . . . . K,757
The same. Leipzig, 1862. 2 v. in 1. 16°. . . . . . J,251
Recollections of Geoffry Hamlyn. Boston, 1866. 12°. . . . K,755
The same. Leipzig, 1864. 2 v. in 1. 16°. . . . . . J,248
Kingsley, J. L. Life of Ezra Stiles. Boston, 1860. 16°. . . . C,860,16
Kingston, W. H. G. Anthony Waymouth. Boston, 1865. 12°. . . J,1501
Cruise of the Frolic. Boston, 1866. 12°. . . . . . . J,1495
Lusitanian Sketches. London, 1845. 2 v. 12°. . . . . . V,473
Marmaduke Merry, the Midshipman. London, n. d. 12°. . . J,1720
Old Jack. London, 1869. 12°. . . . . . . . . . J,1259
Rob Nixon, the Old White Trapper. New York, 1866. 12°. . . J,1268

Kingston, W. H. G. Round the World. Boston, 1870. 16°. . . . J,1607
Schoolboy Days; or, Ernest Bracebridge. Boston, 1869. 16°. . J,1549
Kinzie, J. H. Wau-Bun; "Early Days" in the North-West. N.Y. 1856. 12°. C,275
Kip, W. I. Catacombs of Rome. New York, 1854. 12°. . . . . V,499
Christmas Holidays in Rome. Philadelphia, 1846. 12°. . . V,495
Early Conflicts of Christianity. New York, 1850. 12°. . . . P,566
Early Jesuit Missions in North America. New York, 1846. 12°. . B,583
Kipping, R. Mast-Making and Rigging of Ships. London, 1859. 12°. . M,941
Sails and Sail-Making. London, 1866. 12°. . . . . . . M,847
Kirby, G. Centurie d'Insectes. Paris, 1834. 8°. . . . . . . O,31,1
Kirby, W. History, Habits, and Instincts of Animals. Lond. 1852. 2 v. p. 8°. L,275
The same. Philadelphia, 1836. 8°. . . . . . . N,686
and S. W. Introduction to Entomology. Lond. 1815-26. 4 v. 8°. O,32
The same. London, 1856. 8°. . . . . . . . O,29
The same. Philadelphia, 1846. 8°. . . . . . . O,49
Kirby, W. F. Manual of European Butterflies. London, 1862. 8°. . O,21
Kirchhoff, G. Researches on the Solar Spectrum, etc. Cambridge, 1863. 4°. N,146
Kirk, J. F. History of Charles the Bold. Philadelphia, 1868. 3 v. 8°. B,350
Kirke, E., *pseud.* See *Gilmore, J. R.*
Kirkham, S. English Grammar in Familiar Lectures. New York, 1829. 12°. O,1071
Essays on Elocution. New York, 1865. 12°. . . . . . O,1226
Kirkland, C. M. Garden Walks with the Poets. New York, 1852. 12°. . I,365
Holidays Abroad; Europe from the West. New York, 1849. 2 v. 12°. V,324
Memoirs of Washington. New York, 1859. 12°. . . . . C,891
Patriotic Eloquence. New York, 1866. 12°. . . . . . . O,826
Kirkland, S., Life of. S. K. Lothrop. Boston. 16°. . . . . . C,860,25
Kirkman, T. P. Algebra, Geometry, and Trigonometry. Lond. 1852. 12°. M,942
Kirkwood, D. Meteoric Astronomy. Philadelphia, 1867. 12°. . . N,271
Kirkwood, J. P. Reports on the use of Lead Pipe. New York, 1859. 8°. N,215
Kirwan, *pseud.* See *Murray, N.*
Kitchell, W. Geological Survey New Jersey. 2d Report. Trenton, 1856. 8°. N,873
Kittlitz, F. H. von. Reise nach Russich Amerika. Gotha, 1858. 2 v. 8°. E,173
Kitto, J. Bible History of the Holy Land. London, n. d. 8°. . . V,650
Cyclopædia Biblical Literature; ed. W. Alexander. Phil. 1866. 3 v. 8°. *P,452
History of Palestine. Boston, 1852. 12°. . . . . . . V,635
Scripture Lands. London, 1850. p. 8°. . . . . . . . L,113
and Taylor, J. Cyclopædia of Biblical Literature. Boston, 1854. 8°. *P,788
Klaproth, J. H. Travaux de J. F. Champollion. Paris, 1832. 8°. . . V,854
Kleiner, S. Delineatio Templorum in Vienna. Augustæ-Vindel, 1724. f°. *Q,306
Kleinere Erzählungen. F. Bremer. Leipzig, 1863. 12°. . . . E,313,9
Kleist, H. von. Gesammelte Schriften. Berlin, 1863. 3 v. 16°. . . E,333

Bd. 1. Die Familie Schroffenstein; Penthesilea; Amphitryon.
2. Der zerbrochene Krug; Kätchen von Heilbronn; Prinz Friedrich von Homburg; Die Hermannsschlacht.
3. Erzählungen; Robert Guiskard, Trauerspiel; Gedichte, Epigramme, etc.; Anmerkungen.

Klemm, G. Die Frauen. Dresden, 1859. 6 v. 16°. . . . . E,380
Germanische Alterthumskunde. Dresden, 1836. 8°. . . . E,453
Klencke, P. T. H. Schlechte Kuhmilch. Braunschweig, 1847. 16°. N,252,37
Life of Alexander von Humboldt. New York, 1853. 12°. . . D,521
Klippart, J. H. Wheat Plant. Cincinnati, 1860. 12°. . . . . M,558
Klipstein, A. Schädel des Dinotherii Gigantei. Darmstadt, 1836. 4°. N,252,57

Klipstein, L. F. Grammar of Anglo-Saxon Language. N. Y. 1857. 12°. L,579
Selections from Anglo-Saxon Literature. New York, 1849. 2 v. 12°. H,743
Study of Modern Languages. New York, 1856. 8°. . . . L,638
Klopstock, F. G. Messias. Heidelberg, 1848. 2 v. in 1. 16°. . . . E,269
Klotzsch, F. and Garcke, A. Botanik der Reise des Prinzen Waldemar nach Ceylon. Berlin, 1862. 4°. . . . . . . . . . . . Q,127
Knapen, D. M. Mechanic's Assistant. New York, 1850. 12°. . M,1165
Knapp, A. and Baldwin, W. Newgate Calendar. London, 1824. 4 v. 8°. C,562
Knapp, F. C. Chemical Technology. London, 1848–49. 2 v. 8°. . N,192,2,3
Chemie der Nahrungsmittel. Braunschweig, 1848. 8°. . . N,252,30
Entstehung der Cyanursäure aus Melam. n. t. p. 8°. . . N,252,1
Knapp, J., *Elder*. Autobiography. New York, 1868. 12°. . . . C,763
Knapp, J. L. Country Rambles in England. Buffalo, 1853. 12°. . . N,503
Knapp, M. L. Lectures on Life Insurance. Philadelphia, 1853. 8°. . O,494
Knapp, S. L. Life of Aaron Burr. New York, 1835. 12°. . . . C,803
Life of Daniel Webster. Boston, 1831. 12°. . . . . . . C,1024
Knickerbocker, The, New York Monthly Magazine. N.Y. 1833–64. 63 v. 8°. S,10
Knickerbocker's History of New York. W. Irving. New York, 1869. 16°. U,11
The same. New York, 1863. 12°. . . . . . . . . U,36
The same. London, 1836. 16°. . . . . . . . . I,607
Knight, C. Encyclopædia of Industry. New York, 1851. 8°. . . . M,709
Half-Hours of English History. London, 1868. 8°. . . . . A,444
Half-Hours with the Best Authors. New York, 1867. 6 v. 12°. . H,455
The same. London, n. d. 4 v. in 2. 8°. . . . . . H,456
The same. Philadelphia, 1869. 3 v. 8°. . . . . . H,457
Half-Hours with the Best Letter-Writers. London, 1867. 8°. . H,454
Knowledge is Power. London, 1866. p. 8°. . . . . . . L,302
London. London, 1851. 6 v. in 3. 8°. . . . . . . . A,564
Popular History of England. London, 1856–62. 8 v. 8°. . . A,406
Shadows of the Old Booksellers. London, 1865. 8°. . . . D,336
William Shakespeare; a Biography. London, 1843. 8°. . C,1295
The same. London, 1843. 8°. . . . . . . . . I,783
Knight, Dr. and Slover, Narratives of, with Indians. Cincinnati, 1867. 12°. B,592
Knight, E. C. Marcus Flaminius. London, 1792. 2 v. 8°. . . . K,759
Knight, E. H. Library of Poetry and Song. New York, 1871. 8°. . *I,177
Knight, H. C. Life of James Montgomery. Boston, 1857. 12°. . . D,370
Knight of Gwynne. C. Lever. London, 1858. 2 v. 8°. . . . . K,778
The same. Leipzig, 1847. 3 v. 16°. . . . . . . J,279
Knight of St. John. A. M. Porter. London, 1818. 3 v. in 1. 12°. . K,556
Knighthood of the Bath. J. Anstis. London, 1725. 4°. . . . . . A,498
Knighton, D. Memoirs of Sir William Knighton. Philadelphia, 1858. 8°. C,1272
Knighton, W. Training in Streets and Schools. London, 1855. 16°. . O,1121
Knights and their Days. J. Doran. London, 1856. 8°. . . . . H,311
Knights of Malta. A. Sutherland. Edinburgh, 1830. 2 v. 16°. . . I,530
Knipe, I. A. Geological Maps of the British Isles. London, 1843. 2 v. 8°. N,791
Knout and the Russians. G. de Lagny. London, 1854. 12. . . . V,553
Knowledge, Five Gateways of. G. Wilson. Philadelphia, 1857. 16°. . H,206
is Power. C. Knight. London, 1866. p. 8°. . . . . . . L,302
Pursuit of, under Difficulties. G. L. Craik. London, 1868. p. 8°. . L,99
The same. London, 1834. 2 v. 16°. . . . . . . L,485

Knowledge, Pursuit of, under Difficulties. G. L. Craik. N. Y. 1868. 2 v. 16°. L,402
Knowles, J. D. Memoir of Ann H. Judson. Boston, 1855. 12°. . . . C,834
Knowles, J. S. Dramatic Works. London, 1856. 2 v. 12°. . . . . I,751
Vol. 1. Caius Gracchus; Virginius; William Tell; Alfred the Great; Hunchback; The Wife; Beggar of Bethnal Green; The Daughter.
2. The Love Chase; Woman's Wit; Maid of Mariendorpt; Love; John of Procida; Old Maids; Rose of Arragon; The Secretary.
Knox County, Ohio, History of. A. B. Norton. Columbus, 1862. 8°. . C,216
Knox, J. Reformation of Religion in Scotland. Glasgow, 1844. 8°. . P,663
Knox, T. W. Camp-Fire and Cotton-Field. New York, 1865. 8°. . . B,910
Overland through Asia. Hartford, 1870. 8°. . . . . . . V,670
Knox, V. Liberal Education. London, 1781. 12°. . . . . . . O,911
Kobbe, T. von und Cornelius, W. Wanderungen an der Ost- und Nordsee. Leipzig, n. d. 8°. . . . . . . . . . . . E,186,10
Kobell, F. von. Sketches from the Mineral Kingdom. Lond. 1852. p. 8°. L,312
Koberstein, A. Geschichte der Deutchen Nat.-Litteratur. Leip. 1845-6. 3 v. 8°. E,250
Koch, C. Crimea and Odessa. London, 1855. 12°. . . . . . . V,550
Krim und Odessa. Leipzig, 1854. 12°. . . . . . . . . E,198
Koch, C. L. Pflanzenläuse, Aphiden. Nürnberg, 1857. 8°. . . . . G,946
Koch, K. Kaukasische Länder u. Armenien. Leipzig, 1855. 8°. . . E,215
Koch, W. D. J. Deutsche und Schweizer Flora. Leipzig, 1860. 16°. . G,877
Köllar, V. Insects injurious to Gardeners. London, 1840. 16°. . . O,16
Kölliker, A. Darwin'sche Schöpfungstheorie. Leipzig, 1864. 8°. . . G,816
Human Histology. London, 1853-54. 2 v. 8°. . . . . . L,970
Human Microscopic Anatomy. London, 1860. 8°. . . . . . L,972
Koenig, H. Seltsame Geschichten. Wiesbaden, 1862. 12°. . . . G,338
Königin, Die. L. Storch. Leipzig, 1858. 4 v. 16°. . . . . . . G,486
Königin Hortense. C. Mundt. Berlin, 1861. 2 v. 12°. . . . . . G,360
König von Zion. C. Spindler. Stuttgart, 1854. 3 v. 24°. . . . . G,470
Königsmark; Legend of the Hounds, etc. G. H. Boker. Phil. 1869. 12°. I,10
Kœppen, A. L. The World in the Middle Ages. New York, 1854. 2 v. 12°. A,233
Körner, T. Sämmtliche Werke. Berlin, 1855. 4 v. in 2. 16°. . . . E,334
Bd. 1. Charakteristik und Biographie des Dichters; Leyer und Schwert; Vermischte Gedichte; Nachtrag, Ungedrucktes.
2. Toni; Die Sühne; Zriny; Hedwig.
3. Rosamunde; Joseph Heyderich; Die Braut; Der grüne Domino; Der Nachtwächter; Der Vetter aus Bremen; Die Gouvernante.
4. Das Fischermädchen; Der vierjährige Posten; Die Bergknappen; Alfred der Grosse; Der Kampf mit dem Drachen; Erzählungen, schriftlich bearbeitet von Caroline Pichler; Briefe; Zugabe.
Vaterländischer Roman. H. Rau. Leipzig, 1863. 2 v. 12°. . . G,412
Kohl, J. G. Austria, Hungary, Moravia, etc. London, 1843. 8°. . . V,433
History of the Discovery of Maine. Portland, 1865. 8°. . . C,123,7
Ireland, Scotland, and England. London, 1844. 8°. . . . V,398
Russia. London, 1844. 8°. . . . . . . . . . . V,535
Kohn, F. Iron and Steel Manufacture. London, 1868. f°. . . . . Q,53
Kolrausch. F. History of Germany. London, 1844. 8°. . . . . . B,210
Koltzoff-Massalski. Switzerland Pioneer of Reformation. Lond. 1858. 2 v. 8°. P,241
Komödianten, Die. A. Schrader. Leipzig, 1862. 4 v. 16°. . . . . G,445
Kopp, H. Gewicht der Chemischen Verbindungen. Frankf.-a-M. 1844. 8°. N,252,21
Koppe, C. Ebene Trigonometrie. Essen, 1853. 8°. . . . . . . . E,435
Planimetrie und Stereometrie. Essen, 1851. 8°. . . . . . E,431
Koran; translated, with notes by G. Sale. Philadelphia, 1855. 8°. . . P,423
Kossuth, L. and his Generals. H. De Puy. Buffalo, 1852. 12°. . . . D,758

Kossuth, L. and Hungary. B. F. Tefft. Philadelphia, 1852. 12°. . . . B,524
Memoirs of. London, 1854. p. 8°. . . . . . . . . . L,195
Select Speeches. New York, 1854. 12°. . . . . . . . . H,808
Kotzebue, A. F. F. von. Account of his Exile into Siberia. Lond. 1806. 3 v. 16°. D,748
Travels through Italy, 1804 and 1805. London, 1806. 4 v. 16°. . V,486
Kraitsir, C. Glossology; Treatise on Language. New York, 1852. 12°. . L,504
Krapf, J. L. Missionary Labors in Eastern Africa. Boston, 1860. 8°. . V,801
Kraus, L. A. Kritisch-etymolog. Medicinisches Lexikon. Gött. 1826. 12°. E,414
Krauss, F. Südafrikanische Crustaceen. Stuttgart, 1843. 4°. . . . F,96
Krauth, C. P. Conservative Reformation and its Theology. Phil. 1871. 8°. P,803
Krüsi, H. Life and Character of Pestalozzi. New York, 1854. 12°. O,820,24
Krilof and his Fables. W. R. S. Ralston. London, 1869. 12°. . . H,625
Krummacher, F. W. David, King of Israel. New York, 1868. 12°. . P,280
Elijah, the Tishbite. New York, n. d. 18°. . . . . . P,746,17
Parables; from 7th German edition. London, 1858. p. 8°. . . L,114
Suffering Saviour. Boston, 1870. 12°. . . . . . . . P,124
Kugler, F. T. Hand-Book of Painting; German, Flemish, and Dutch Schools; enlarged by Dr. Waagen. London, 1860. 2 pts. 8.° *M,87
Hand-Book of Painting, Italian Schools. London, 1860. 2 v. 8°. *M,88
Kühne, F. G. Drei Novellen. Leipzig, 1850. 16°. . . . . . . G,339
1. Frau von Brabantene. 2. Jugendsünden. 3. Edelmann u. Bauer.
Kühn, O. B. Chemische Untersuchungen. Leipzig, 1842. 8°. . . N,252,12
Cholestearine. Lipsiæ, n. d. 4°. . . . . . . . . N,252,41
Kühner, R. Grammar of the Greek Language. New York, 1857. 8°. . L,735
Kuhn, A. Idee des Schönen. Berlin, n. d. 12°. . . . . . . G,566
Kuhlman, F. Expériences Chemiques et Agronomiques. Paris, 1847. 8°. N,252,31
Kullak, A. Æsthetik des Klavierspiels. Berlin, 1861. 8°. . . . . G,643
Musikalische-Schöne. Leipzig, 1858. 16°. . . . . . . G,647
Kunisch, R. Bukarest und Stambul. Berlin, 1861. 12°. . . . . E,210
Künstlerroman. F. W. Hackländer. Stuttgart, 1866. 5 v. 12°. . . G,305
Kunz von Kauffungen. L. Storch. Leipzig, 1855. 3 v. 16°. . . . G,484
Kunze, G. Die Farrnkräuter. Leipzig, 1840–47. 2 v. 4°. . . . G,963
Kurr, J. G. von. Mineralogy illustrated. Boston, 1869. f°. . . . Q,55
Kurtz, J. H. History of the Old Covenant. Edinburgh, 1859. 2 v. 8°. P,637
Manual of Sacred History. Philadelphia, 1855. 12°. . . . P,457
Text-Book of Church History. Philadelphia, 1870. 2 v. 8°. . P,607
Kurz, H. Geschichte der Deutschen Litteratur. Leipzig, 1861. 3 v. 8°. E,254
Kützing, F. T. Grundüge der philosoph. Botanik. Leip. 1851–52. 2 v. in 1. 8°. G,878
Kyan, J. H. Elements of Light. London, 1838. 8°. . . . . . N,31

Labarte, J. Hand-Book of Arts of the Middle Ages. London, 1855. 8°. M,96
Labaume, E. Campaign in Russia. Hartford, 1850. 8°. . . . . . B,287
La Beche. See *De La Beche, Sir H. T.*
La Bédoyère, H. Public and Private Life of Napoleon, v. 2. Lond. 1839. 8°. D,582
Labor and other Capital. E. Kellogg. New York, 1849. 8°. . . . . O,547
La Borde, M. de. Voyage; Relation exacte des Caraibes. Leide, 1704. 12°. V,149
Laborer; Remedy for his Wrongs. W. Dealtry. Cincinnati, 1869. 12°. . O,487
Laboulaye, E. Abdallah; trans. by M. L. Booth. London, 1868. 16°. . I,566

Laboulaye, E. Fairy Tales of all Nations. New York, 1867. 12°. . . J,1260
Paris in America. New York, 1863. 12°. . . . . . . H,910
Labrador and Newfoundland, Summer Voyage to. L. L. Noble. N.Y. 1861. 12°. V,171
La Bruyère, J. de. Caractères de Théophraste, etc. Paris, 1852. 2 v. 12°. H,862
The same. Paris, 1853. 8°. . . . . . . . . . H,892
Caractères; ou, Mœurs de ce Siècle, etc. Paris, 1856. 12°. . . H,869
Lacemakers; Sketches of Irish Character. Mrs. Meredith. Lond. 1865. 12°. K,802
Lachmann, C. (Ed.) Nibelungen Noth und Klage. Berlin, 1841. 8°. . E,272
Lacombe, M. P. Arms and Armour. New York, 1870. 12°. . . . M,760
Lacon; or, Many Things in Few Words. C. C. Colton. New York, 1866. 8°. H,123
Lacretelle, J. C. D. de. Histoire de France. Paris, 1844. 14 v. 8°. . B,261
Tom. 1–4. Pendant les Guerres de la Religion.
5–10. Pendant le Dix-Huitième Siècle.
11–14. Depuis la Restauration.
Lacroix, P. Les Arts au Moyen Age. Paris, 1869. 2 v. 4°. . . *Q,360
and others. Histoire de la Charpenterie. Paris, 1858. 8°. . . M,743
Histoire des Cordonniers. Paris, 1852. 8°. . . . . M,741
Histoire de l'Imprimerie. Paris, 1852. 8°. . . . . M,742
Histoire de l'Orfévrerie-Joaillerie. Paris, 1850. 8°. . . M,743
La Croix, S. F. Elémens d'Algèbre, et Complément. Paris, 1817–18. 8°. M,1117
Elémens de Géométrie. Paris, 1814. 8°. . . . . . M,1126
Essais sur l'Enseignement des Mathematiques. Paris, 1816. 8°. . O,918
Traité Elémentaire d'Arithmétique. Paris, 1823. 8°. . . M,1103
Traité Elémentaire de Calcul. Paris, 1806. 8°. . . . M,1150
Traité du Calcul des Probabilités. Paris, 1822. 8°. . . . M,1148
Traité de Trigonométrie. Paris, 1813. 8°. . . . . M,1128
Ladder of Life. A. B. Edwards. New York, 1865. 8°. . . . . K,681
Ladies of the Reformation. J. Anderson. London, 1857. 12°. . . C,516
Ladies' Botany. J. Lindley. London, n. d. 2 v. 8°. . . . N,1035
Ladies' Guide to Perfect Gentility. E. Thornwell. New York, 1857. 12°. H,288
to True Politeness. E. Leslie. Philadelphia, n. d. 12°. . . H,281
Ladies' Repository, v. 2, 16–28. Cincinnati, 1842–68. 8°. . . . . S,47
Lady Adelaide's Oath. Mrs. H. Wood. Leipzig, 1867. 2 v. in 1. 16°. . J,522
Lady Audley's Secret. M. E. Braddon. Leipzig, 1862. 2 v. in 1. 16°. . J,40
Lady Bird. G. Fullerton. Leipzig, 1853. 2 v. in 1. 16°. . . . J,170
Lady Bountiful's Legacy. J. Timbs. London, 1868. 12°. . . . I,543
Lady of the Ice. J. De Mille. New York, 1870. 8°. . . . . K,103
Lady of the Isle. E. D. E. N. Southworth. Philadelphia, 1870. 12°. . K,430
Lady of the Lake. Sir W. Scott. New York, 1858. 16°. . . . I,411
Lady's Mile, The. M. E. Braddon. Leipzig, 1866. 2 v. in 1. 16°. . J,41
Lafayette, M. de., Life of. W. Cutter. Cincinnati, 1854. 12°. . . . D,631
Life of. P. C. Headley. Auburn, 1851. 12°. . . . . . . D,620
E. Mack. Ithaca, 1848. 12°. . . . . . . . . D,630
Private Life of. J. Cloquet. London, 1835. 8°. . . . . D,623
and French Revolution of 1830. B. Sarrens. London, 1832. 8°. . D,666
Lafever, M. Beauties of Modern Architecture. New York, 1849. 8°. . M,227
La Flechere, J. W. de., Life of. J. Benson. New York, 1855. 12°. . D,520
La Fontaine, J. de. Fables. Paris, 1853. 8°. . . . . . . . H,893
The same; translated by E. Wright. New York, 1865. 2 v. 12°. H,956
Fables Choisies, v. 3. Paris, 1778. 16°. . . . . . . H,854
Fables et Œuvres Diverses. Paris, 1856. 12°. . . . . H,879

La Gironière, P. de. Twenty Years in the Philippines. Lond. 1865. p. 8°. I,657
Lagny, G. de. The Knout and the Russians. London, 1854. 12°. . . V,553
Lagrange, J. L. Mecanique Analytique. Paris, 1853-55. 2 v. in 1. 4°. M,1080
Théorie des Functions Analytiques. Paris, 1813. 4°. . . M,1187
La Harpe, J. F. de. Lycée; Cours de Litterature. Paris, 1838-9. 18 v. in 9. 8°. H,646
La Hodde, L. de. History of Secret Societies. Philadelphia, 1856. 8°. . O,385
Laing, J. J. Companion to Manual of Illumination. London, 1866. 12°. M,26,2
Laing, M. History of Scotland. London, 1819. 4 v. 8°. . . . . B,138
Laing, S. Notes of a Traveler in Europe. Philadelphia, 1846. 8°. . V,272
The same. London, 1862. p. 8°. . . . . . . . . I,656,3
Pre-Historic Remains of Caithness. Edinburgh, 1866. 8°. . . N,438
Residence in Norway, 1834-36. London, 1862. p. 8°. . . I,656,3
Social and Political State of Europe. London, 1850. 8°. . . V,391
Laird of Norlaw. M. Oliphant. New York, 1860. 12°. . . . . . K,865
Laishley, R. History of British Birds' Eggs. London, 1858. 16°. . . O,82
Lake, A. Narrative of the Defense of Kars. London, 1857. 8°. . . A,522
Lake, W. J. Book of Object Lessons. London, 1857. 24°. . . . O,1109
Lake Champlain, History of. P. S. Palmer. Albany, 1866. 8°. . . C,90
Lake Ngami. C. J. Anderson. New York, 1861. 4°. . . . . . V,800
Lake Shore Series. W. T. Adams. Boston, 1870-71. 6 v. 16°. . J,1537

| | |
|---|---|
| Vol. 1. Through by Daylight. | Vol. 4. Switch Off. |
| 2. Lightning Express. | 5. Brake-Up. |
| 3. On Time. | 6. Bear and Forbear. |

Lake Superior, Ancient Mining on Shores of. C. Whittlesey. Wash. 1863. 4°. Q,324,13
Description of. L. Agassiz; Narrative by J. E. Cabot. Boston, 1850. 8°. V,1115
Life on the Lakes; a Trip to. New York, 1836. 2 v. 12°. . . V,40
and Red River, Exploration of. S. J. Dawson. Toronto, 1859. 4°. . Q,59
Lakes, Summer on the. M. F. Ossoli. Boston, 1844. 12°. . . . V,14
Lambert, E. Hand-Book of Needlework. London, 1842. 12°. . . H,478
Lambeth Library, Early Printed Books in. S. R. Maitland. Lond. 1843. 8°. L.R.
Lamartine, A. de. Additional Memoirs of my Youth. N. Y. 1860. 8°. . G,244
Confidences, Les. New York, 1849. 8°. . . . . . . . . H,928
Confidential Disclosures. New York, 1857. 12°. . . . . . H,969
Fior d'Aliza. New York, 1869. 16°. . . . . . . . H,964
Génevieve. New York, n. d. 8°. . . . . . . . . . G,242
Histoire des Girondins. Bruxelles, 1851. 8°. . . . . . . B,440
Histoire de la Revolution Française. Bruxelles, 1853. 8°. . . B,441
History of the French Revolution of 1848. London, 1852. p. 8°. . L,202
The same. Boston, 1849. 2 v. in 1. 12°. . . . . . S.C.
History of the Girondists. London, 1847-50. 3 v. p. 8°. . . L,200
The same. New York, 1854. 3 v. 12°. . . . . . B,224
History of Turkey. New York, 1855-57. 3 v. 12°. . . . . B,557
Life of Columbus. New York, 1865. 16°. . . . . . . D,712
Méditations Poétiques. Paris, 1821. 8°. . . . . . . H,1005
Memoirs of Celebrated Characters. New York, 1854-56. 3 v. 12°. C,525
Memoirs of my Youth. New York, n. d. 8°. . . . . . . G,243
Past, Present, and Future of the Republic. New York, 1850. 12°. B,244
Pilgrimage to the Holy Land. London, 1837. 3 v. 12°. . . V,656
Raphael; Pages de la Vingtième Année. New York, 1849. 8°. . H,928
The same; translated. New York, 1865. 12°. . . . . H,903
Restoration of the Monarchy in France. London, 1854. 4 v. p. 8°. L,201

Lamartine, A. de. Restoration of Monarchy in France. N.Y. 1851-3. 4 v. 12°. B,243
Stone Mason of Saint Point. New York, 1859. 12°. . . . H,904
Lamb, C. Essays of Elia. New York, 1859. 12°. . . . . . . H,476
Essays of Elia and Eliana. Leipzig, 1869. 16°. . . . . J,252
Life and Letters of. T. N. Talfourd. New York, 1859. 12°. . . C,1185
Literary Sketches and Letters of. T. N. Talfourd. N. Y. 1849. 12°. D,317
Memoir of. B. W. Procter. Boston, 1866. 16°. . . . . . D,313
Specimens of English Dramatic Poets. London, 1854. p. 8°. . L,15
Works; with Letters and Life by T. N. Talfourd. N. Y. 1852. 5 v. 12°. U,278
Vol. 1. Life and Letters.
2. Essays of Elia.
3. Rosamund Gray; Essays; Letters; Poems.
4. Specimens of English Dramatic Poets.
5. Final Memorials by T. N. Talfourd.
and Mary. Tales from Shakespeare. New York, 1869. 16°. . K,760
Lamb, Mrs. J. Tom and Sarah Neal. Philadelphia, 1871. 16°. . . J,1688
Mended Life; or, Carpenter's Family. Philadelphia, 1870. 16°. . J,1689
Lamb, M. J. Drifting Goodward. Boston, 1870. 24°. . . . . . J,1395
Lamborn, R. H. Metallurgy of Copper, Silver, etc. Lond. 1868-69. 2 v. 12°. M,848
Lame Jervas. M. Edgeworth. New York, 1860. 12°. . . . K,678,4
Laming, R. New View of Electrical Action. London, 1858. 8°. . N,252,46
Lamothe-Langon, E. L. de. Evenings with Cambacérès. Lond. 1837. 2 v. 8°. B,272
Lamotte, A. L. Metric System of Weights and Measures. Phil. 1867. 16°. M,1094
La Motte-Fouqué, Baron. Four Seasons; Undine, etc. N. Y. 1870. 12°. H,931
Specimens of; translated by T. Carlyle. Edinburgh, 1827. 12°. . G,51,1
Thiodolph the Icelander. New York, n. d. 12°. . . . . G,221
Undine, der Wassergeister. Braunschweig, 1860. 16°. . . . G,275
The same; translated. New York, 1864. 12°. . . . H,923
Lampadius, W. A. Life of F. Mendelssohn Bartholdy. N. Y. 1866. 16°. D,505
Lampert, I. Charakterbilder aus der Natur. Mainz, 1865. 2 v. 8°. . G,701
Lamping, C. French in Algiers. New York, 1845. 12°. . . . H,925
Lamplighter. M. S. Cummins. Boston, 1868. 12°. . . . . . . K,88
Lamplighter's Story and Nouvlettes. C. Dickens. Philadelphia, 1861. 8°. K,477
Lamps, Pitchers, and Trumpets. E. P. Hood. New York, 1869. 2 v. 12°. P,236
Lancashire Public School Association. London, 1850. 16°. . . . O,989
Lancashire Witches. W. H. Ainsworth. Leipzig, 1849. 2 v. in 1. 16°. . J,14
Lancaster, D. History of Gilmanton, N. H. Gilmanton, 1845. 8°. . . C,86
Lancaster, J. British System of Education. Georgetown, 1812. 12°. O,1128
Improvements in Education. London, 1806. 8°. . . . . O,925
Lancaster, T. W. Alliance of Education and Civil Gov't. Lond. 1828. 4°. Q,327
Lances of Linwood. C. M. Yonge. New York, 1856. 16°. . . J,1354
Lancet, London. New York, 1823-49. 53 v. 8°. . . . . . . L,951
Land and the Book. W. M. Thomson. New York, 1869. 2 v. 12°. . V,634
Land at Last. E. Yates. Leipzig, 1866. 2 v. in 1. 16°. . . . . J,540
Land of Burns. J. Wilson and R. Chambers. Glasgow, 1846. 4°. . . M,283
Land-Drainer, Practical. B. Munn. New York, 1855. 12°. . . . M,555
Land of Scott. T. Nelson. London, 1859. 16°. . . . . . . V,301
Land of Thor. J. R. Browne. New York, 1867. 12°. . . . . V,528
Land Surveying, Principles of. T. Tate. London, 1855. 12°. . . M,1087
Treatise on. W. M. Gillespie. New York, 1855. 8°. . . . M,699
Land we Live in; Sketch-Book of British Empire. Lond. n. d. 4 v. in 2. 4°. Q,421
Lander, R. and J. Journal of the Niger Expedition. Lon. 1832. 3 v. 16°. I,611

Lander, R. and J. Journal of the Niger Expedition. N. Y. 1854. 2 v. 18°. L,367
Landon, M. D. Franco-Prussian War in a Nutshell. N. Y. 1871. 12°. . B,212
Landor, W. S., Biography of. J. Forster. Boston, 1869. 8°. . . . D,84
Gebir, Count Julian, and other Poems. London, 1831. 12°. . . I,370
Imaginary Conversations of Greeks and Romans. London, 1853. 8°. H,446
Pericles and Aspasia. Philadelphia, 1839. 2 v. 8°. . . . H,151
Selections from; edited by G. S. Hillard. Boston, 1866. 12°. . . H,309
Works of. London, 1853. 2 v. 8°. . . . . . . . U,220
Vol. 1. Imaginary Conversations.
2. The same, concluded; Citation and Examination of Shakespeare; The Pentameron; Pericles and Aspasia; Minor Prose Pieces; Poems; Gebir; Acts and Scenes; Miscellaneous.

Land's End, Walk from London to. E. Burritt. London, 1868. 12°. . V,395
Lands of Sir Walter Scott. J. F. Hunnewell. Boston, 1871. 12°. . . V,350
of the Saracen. J. B. Taylor. New York, 1860. 12°. . . V,1051
of the Slave and Free. H. A. Murray. London, 1855. 2 v. 12°. V,144
Landsborough, D. British Sea-Weeds. London, 1851. 16°. . . . N,919
British Zoophytes, or Corallines. London, 1852. 16°. . . . O,5
Landscape Drawing, Progressive Fragments in. S. Prout. Lond. 1818. 8°. Q,209
Landscape Gardening. G. M. Kern. Cincinnati, 1855. 12°. . . . M,353
and Landscape Architecture. H. Repton. London, 1840. 8°. . M,355
C. H. J. Smith. New York, 1853. 12°. . . . . M,349
Beautifying Suburban Home-Grounds. F. J. Scott. N. Y. 1870. 8°. *M,361
Hints upon. W. S. Gilpin. London, 1835. 8°. . . . . M,360
Theory and Practice of. A. J. Downing. New York, 1859. 8°. . M,356
The same. New York, 1859. 8°. . . . . . . . S.C.
Landscape Painting in Oil Colours. J. Burnet. London, 1849. 4°. . . *Q,168
in Water-Colours. G. Barnard. London, 1861. 8°. . . . M,137
T. and T. L. Rowbotham. London, 1867. . 8°. . . . M,25
Lane, E. W. Account of the Modern Egyptians. London, 1842. 2 v. 8°. V,871
The same. London, 1836–37. 2 v. 16°. . . . . L,480
The same. London, 1846. 3 v. in 1. 24°. . . . . V,769
Lane, J. Public Accounts of Great Britain. London, 1785–87. 3 v. 4°. P.D.
Laneton Parsonage. E. M. Sewell. New York, 1863. 3 v. 12°. . K,1001
Lanfrey, P. Histoire Politique des Papes. Bruxelles, 1860. 12°. . H,1033
Lang, J. D. Religion and Education in America. London, 1840. 12°. . O,822
Langdale, Lord. See *Bickersteth, H.*
Langdon, Mary, *pseud.* See *Pike, M. H.*
Lange, J. P. Commentary on the Holy Scriptures. N. Y. 1868–71. 12 v. 8°. P,387

OLD TESTAMENT.

Vol. 1. Introduction; Genesis. J. P. Lange; translated by T. Lewis and A. Gorman.
10. Proverbs; Ecclesiastes; Song of Solomon. O. Zöckler; trans. by C. Aiken, etc.
11. Jeremiah; Lamentations. C. W. E. Naegelsbach; trans. by S. R. Asbury, etc.

NEW TESTAMENT.

Vol. 2. Introduction; Matthew. J. P. Lange; translated by P. Schaff.
3. Mark. J. P. Lange; translated by G. W. T. Shedd.
Luke. J. J. van Oesterzee; translated by P. Schaff and C. C. Starbuck.
12. John. J. P. Lange; translated by P. Schaff.
4. Acts. G. V. Lechler and C. Gerok; translated by C. F. Schaeffer.
5. Romans. J. P. Lange and F. R. Fay; translated by J. F. Hurst.
6. I. Corinthians. C. F. Kling; translated by D. W. Poor.
II. Corinthians. C. F. Kling; translated by C. P. Wing.
7. Galatians. O. Schmoller; translated by C. C. Starbuck.
Ephesians. K. Braune; translated by M. B. Riddle.
Philippians. K. Braune; translated by H. B. Hackett.
Colossians. K. Braune; translated by M. B. Riddle.

Lange, J. P. Commentary on Holy Scriptures. Old Testament. *Continued.* P,387
8. Thessalonians. C. A. Auberlen and C. J. Riggenbach; trans. by J. Lillie.
Timothy. J. J. van Oosterzee; trans. by E. A. Washburn and E. Harwood.
Titus. J. J. van Oosterzee; translated by G. E. Day.
Philemon. J. J. van Oosterzee; translated by H. B. Hackett.
Hebrews. C. B. Moll; translated by A. C. Kendrick.
9. James. J. P. Lange and J. J. van Oosterzee; trans. by J. I. Mombert.
Peter. G. F. C. Fronmüller; translated by J. I. Mombert.
John. K. Braune; translated by J. I. Mombert.
Jude. G. F. C. Fronmüller; translated by J. I. Mombert.

Lange, L. Römische Alterthümer. Berlin, 1863-67. 2 v. 8°. . . . E,454
Langethal, C. E. Hackfrüchte, Handelsgewächse, etc. Jena, 1864. 8°. . G,879
The same. Jena, 1855. 8°. . . . . . . . . G,880,3
Die Süssgräser. Jena, 1847. 8°. . . . . . . . . G,880,1
Langland, W. Vision of Piers Plowman; Vernon Text. Lond. 1867. 8°. L,605,28
The same; Crowley Text. London, 1869. 8°. . . . L,605,38
Vision and Creed of Piers Plowman. London, 1856. 2 v. 16°. . I,380
Langstroth, L. L. Hive and Honey Bee. New York, 1859. 12°. . . M,464
Langtoft, P. Chronicle. Oxford, 1724. 2 v. 8°. . . . . . U,127,3,4
Language and Life, Philosophy of. F. von Schlegel. London, 1866. p. 8°. L,229
The same. New York, 1855. 12°. . . . . . . . O,696
and the Study of Language. W. D. Whitney. New York, 1867. 8°. L,514
Chapters on. F. W. Farrar. London, 1865. 8°. . . . . . L,503
Compendium der Indo-Germanischen Sprachen. A. Schleicher. Weimar, 1861-62. 2 v. 8°. . . . . . . . . . . G,589
Etymologische Forschungen in den Indo-Germanischen Sprachen. A. F. Pott. Lemgo und Detmold, 1859-67. 4 v. 8°. . . G,586
Glossology; Treatise on. C. Kraitsir. New York, 1852. 12°. . L,504
Historical Relations of. Sir J. Stoddart. London, 1858. 12°. . L,510
One Primeval. C. Forster. London, 1851-54. 3 v. 8°. . . L,530
Origin of. H. Wedgwood. London, 1866. 8°. . . . . L,501
Origin and Progress of. J. Burnet. London, 1736-1809. 6 v. 8°. L,523
Philosophy of. J. Stoddart. London, 1849. 12°. . . . . L,508
Science of, Lectures on. F. M. Müller. New York, 1865. 8°. . L,513
Study of. H. Winslow. Boston, 1848. 12°. . . . . . O,820,18
Tractate on. G. W. J. Gyll. London, 1859. 8°. . . . . L,528
Treatise on. A. B. Johnson. New York, 1836. 8°. . . . L,517
Languages, Study of Modern. L. F. Klipstein. New York, 1848. 4°. . L,638
Study of Modern. J. F. Meline. Cincinnati, 1838. 8°. . . H,302,4
Study of. C. Marcel. New York, 1869. 12°. . . . . . L,502
System of Teaching. J. Black. London, 1826. 2 v. 12°. . . L,806
Lankester, E. Half-Hours with the Microscope. New York, 1868. 16°. . N,1
Vegetable Substances used for Food. London, 1832. 16°. . L,491,1
Lanman, C. Adventures in Wilds of America. London, 1863. p. 8°. I,659.2
Dictionary of United States Congress. Philadelphia, 1859. 8°. *C,777
Letters from Alleghany Mountains. New York, 1849. 12°. . . V,59
Private Life of Daniel Webster. New York, 1853. 12°. . . C,1008
Lanman, J. H. History of Michigan. New York, 1855. 18°. . . . L,431
Lanoye, F. de. Sublime in Nature. New York, 1870. 12°. . . M,1046
Rameses the Great; or, Egypt 3,300 Years ago. N. Y. 1870. 12°. M,1056
Lantier, E. F. de. Antenor's Reisen durch Griechenland. Ham. 1805-6. 5 v. 16°. E,191
Lanzi, L. History of Painting in Italy. London, 1847. 3 v. p. 8°. . L,204
Laocoon; or, Limits of Poetry and Painting. G. E. Lessing. Lond. 1838. 8°. M,45

La Peyrère, I. de. History of Greenland. London, 1855. 8°. . . . . v,984
La Place, G. F. M. J. de. Leçons de Litérature et Morale. Braux. 1848. 8°. H,190
La Place, P. S. de. Exposition du Système du Monde. Braux. 1827. 8°. N,285
Mécanique Céleste; tr. by N. Bowditch. Boston, 1829–39. 4 v. 4°. Q,104
Œuvres. Paris, 1843–47. 7 v. 4°. . . . . . . . . . Q,108
Tom. 1–5. Traité de Mécanique Céleste. 6. Exposition du Système du Monde. 7. Théorie Analytique des Probabilités.
Life of. F. Arago. Boston, 1859. 12°. . . . . . . C,498,1
Lapland, Travels in. B. Taylor. New York, 1865. 12°. . . . . v,543
La Plata, Argentine Confederation, and Paraguay. T.J.Page. N.Y. 1859. 8°. v,262
and Brazil. C. S. Stewart. New York, 1856. 12°. . . . . v,238
Map of the Basin of. T. J. Page. New York, n. d. 4°. . . . P,298
La Porte, Count de. French Grammar. Boston, 1844. 8°. . . . L,810
Lappenberg, J. M. England under Anglo-Saxon Kings. Lond. 1845. 2 v. 8°. A,496
England under the Norman Kings. Oxford, 1857. 8°. . . . A,497
und Pauli, R. Geschichte von England. Hamburg, 1834–58. 5 v. 8°. E,42
L'Ardeche, L. de. History of Napoleon I. New York, 1864. 2 v. in 1. 8°. D,563
Lardner, D. Cabinet Cyclopædia. London, 1830–46. 133 v. 12°.

HISTORY.

Keightly, T. Outlines of History. . . . . . . M,984
Nicolas, Sir N. H. Chronology of History. . . . . . M,985
Mackintosh, Sir J. History of England. 10 v. . . . M,986
Moore, T. History of Ireland. 4 v. . . . . . . M,987
Scott, Sir W. History of Scotland. 2 v. . . . . . M,988
Crowe, E. E. History of France. 3 v. . . . . . . M,989
Wilson, J. History of Switzerland. . . . . . . M,990
Dunham, S. A. History of Spain and Portugal. 5 v. . . M,991
History of the Germanic Empire. 3 v. . . . . . M,992
Fergus, H. History of the United States. 2 v. . . . . M,993
Thirlwall, C. History of Greece. 8 v. . . . . . M,994
History of Rome. 2 v. . . . . . . . . M,995
Fosbroke, T. D. Arts, Manufactures, etc., of Greeks and Romans. 2 v. M,996
Sismondi, J. C. L. S. de. History of the Italian Republics. . . M,997
Dunham, S. A. Europe during the Middle Ages. 4 v. . . . M,998
Grattan, T. C. History of the Netherlands. . . . . . M,999
Bell, R. History of Russia. 3 v. . . . . . . . M,1000
Dunham, S. A. History of Poland. . . . . . . M,1001
History of Denmark, Sweden, and Norway. 3 v. . . M,1002
Stebbing, H. History of the Christian Church. 2 v. . . . M,1003
Sismondi, J. C. L. S. de. Fall of the Roman Empire. 2 v. . . M,1004
Stebbing, H. History of the Reformation. 2 v. . . . . M,1005
Cooley, W. D. Maritime and Inland Discoveries. 3 v. . . M,1006
Cities and Towns of the World. . . . . . . . M,1007

BIOGRAPHY.

Gleig, G. R. British Military Commanders. 3 v. . . . . M,1008
Southey, R. British Admirals. 5 v. . . . . . . M,1009
Roscoe, H. Eminent British Lawyers. . . . . . . M,1010
Mackintosh, J., Foster, J., and Courtenay, T. P. Brit. Statesmen. 7 v. M,1011
Crowe, E. E. and James, G. P. R. Foreign Statesmen. 5 v. . M,1012
Shelley, M. W. and others. Literary and Scientific Men of Italy, Spain, and Portugal. 3 v. . . . . . . M,1013
Literary and Scientific Men of France. 2 v. . . . . M,1014
Bell, R. English Poets. 2 v. . . . . . . . M,1015
Dunham, S. A. and others. Literary and Scientific Men of Great Britain and Ireland. 3 v. . . . . . . . . M,1016

NATURAL PHILOSOPHY, ETC.

Herschel, Sir J. F. W. Study of Natural Philosophy. . . . M,1017
Powell, B. History of Natural Philosophy. . . . . . M,1018

Lardner, D. Cabinet Cyclopædia. *Continued.*

Lardner, D. Treatise on Arithmetic. . . . . . . M,1019
Treatise on Geometry. . . . . . . . M,1020
Kater, H. and Lardner, D. Mechanics. . . . . . M,1021
Lardner, D. Hydrostatics and Pneumatics. . . . . M,1022
Herschel, J. F. W. Treatise on Astronomy. . . . . M,1023
Brewster, D. Treatise on Optics. . . . . . . M,1024
Lardner, D. Treatise on Heat. . . . . . . . M,1025
Donovan, M. Treatise on Chemistry. . . . . . M,1026
Lardner, D. and Walker, C. V. Electricity, Magnetism, etc. 2 v. M,1027
De Morgan, A. Essay on Probabilities. . . . . . . M,1028

NATURAL HISTORY.

Swainson, W. Study of Natural History. . . . . . M,1029
Geography and Classification of Animals. . . . . M,1030
Natural History of Quadrupeds. . . . . . . M,1031
Animals in Menageries. . . . . . . . . M,1032
Natural History of Birds, 2 v. . . . . . . M,1033
Fishes, Amphibians, and Reptiles. 2 v. . . . . . M,1034
Shells, and Shell-Fish. . . . . . . . M,1035
and Shuckard, W. E. Insects. . . . . . . M,1036
Habits and Instincts of Animals. . . . . . . M,1037
Taxidermy and Bibliography of Zoölogists. . . . . M,1038
Henslow, J. S. Principles of Botany. . . . . . M,1039
Phillips, J. Treatise on Geology. 2 v. . . . . . . M,1040

USEFUL ARTS.

Donovan, M. Domestic Economy. 2 v. . . . . . . M,1041
Porter, G. R. Manufacture of Silk. . . . . . . M,1042
Holland, J. Manufactures in Metals. 3 v. . . . . . M,1043
Porter, G. R. Manufacture of Porcelain and Glass. . . . M,1044

Common Things explained. London, 1856. 12°. . . . . . H,195
Electricity, Magnetism, and Meteorology. London, 1841. 2 v. 12°. M,1027
Hand-Books of Natural Philos. and Astron. Phil. 1854. 3 v. 12°. N,79

Vol. 1. Mechanics; Hydrostatics; Hydraulics; Pneumatics; Sound; Optics.
2. Heat; Magnetism; Common Electricity; Voltaic Electricity.
3. Meteorology; Astronomy.

Hydrostatics and Pneumatics. London, 1831. 12°. . . . M,1022
Meteorology and Astronomy. Philadelphia, 1854. 12°. . . . M,772
Microscope. London, 1856. 8°. . . . . . . . . . . N,4
Museum of Science and Art. London, 1854–56. 12 v. in 6. 12°. . M,770
Popular Lectures on Science and Art. New York, 1855. 2 v. 8°. M,791
Railway Economy. New York, 1850. 12°. . . . . . . M,694
Steam Engine explained. Glasgow, 1839. 12°. . . . N,252,23
The same. New York, 1854. 8°. . . . . . . . . S.C.
Treatise on Arithmetic. London, 1834. 12°. . . . . . M,1019
The same. London, n. d. 16°. . . . . . . M,1095
Treatise on Geometry. London, 1840. 12°. . . . . . M,1138
The same. London, 1840. 12°. . . . . . . M,1020
Treatise on Heat. London, 1833. 12°. . . . . . . M,1025

Lardner, N. Works; with Life by Dr. Kippis. London, 1838. 10 v. 8°. P,714

Vol. 1-5. Life by A. Kippis; Credibility of the Gospel History; History of the Apostles and Evangelists.
6–8. Jewish and Heathen Testimonies; State of Gentileism under Christian Emperors; History of Heretics.
9. Sermons; Two Schemes of a Trinity considered.
10. Tracts; Dissertation on two new Epistles ascribed to Clement of Rome; Remarks upon Dr. Ward's Dissertations; Indexes.

La Rive, A. de. Archives de l'Electricité. Paris, 1844. 8°. . . . N,252,55
Treatise on Electricity. London, 1853–58. 3 v. 8°. . . . . N,51

La Rive, W. de. Life of Count Cavour. London, 1862. 8°. . . . . D,745

Larkin, J. Iron and Brass Founder's Guide. Philadelphia, 1869. 12°. . M,636
La Rochefoucauld, F. de. Maximes. Paris, 1855. 12°. . . . . . H,865
Moral Reflections, Sentences, and Maxims. New York, 1853. 12°. H,890
Pensées, Maximes, et Reflexions Morales. Paris, 1855. 8°. . . H,895
Travels in United States and Canadas. London, 1799. 4°. . . V,152
La Rochejaquelein, M. L. V. de, Memoirs of. Edinburgh, 1827. 16°. . I,494
Larrabee, W. C. Wesley and his Coadjutors. Cincinnati, 1853. 2 v. 16°. C,1181
Larwood, J. and Hotten, J. C. History of Signboards. London, n. d. p. 8°. H,397
La Salle, R. C., Life of. J. Sparks. Boston, 1860. 12°. . . . . C,860,11
Las Cases, M. J. E. D. Exile of Napoleon at St. Helena. N.Y. 1855. 4 v. 8°. D,634
The same. London, 1823. 4 v. 8°. . . . . . . D,670
Last Athenian. V. Rydberg. Philadelphia, 1869. 12°. . . . . . K,915
Last Chronicle of Barset. A. Trollope. New York, 1867. 8°. . . K,1047
The same. Leipzig, 1867. 3 v. 16°. . . . . . . J,500
Last Days; a Discourse. E. Irving. London, 1850. 12°. . . . . P,154
Last Days of Pompeii. Sir E. B. Lytton. Philadelphia, 1869. 12°. . . K,816
The same. Leipzig, 1842. 16°. . . . . . . . J,317
Last of the Barons. Sir E. B. Lytton. Philadelphia, 1869. 12°. . . K,815
The same. Leipzig, 1843. 2 v. in 1. 16°. . . . . . J,318
Last of the Cavaliers. Leipzig, 1862. 2 v. in 1. 16°. . . . . J,253
Last of the Mohicans. J. F. Cooper. New York, 1867. 12°. . . . K,37
The same. New York, 1859. 8°. . . . . . . . . K,66
Last of the Mortimers. M. Oliphant. New York, 1862. 12°. . . . K,866
The same. Leipzig, 1862. 2 v. in 1. 16°. . . . . . J,403
Last Words of Eminent Persons. J. Kaines. London, 1866. 8°. . . H,484
Lasteyrie, L. P. de. History of Auricular Confession. London, 1848. 12°. P,804
Lateinische Czarin u. ihr Schicksal. F. Lubojatzky. Wein, 1862. 2 v. 24°. G,341
Latham, R. G. Descriptive Ethnology. London, 1859. 2 v. 8°. . . N,446
Elements of Comparative Philology. London, 1862. 8°. . . . L,574
English Language. London, 1855. 2 v. 8°. . . . . . . L,575
Ethnology of the British Islands. London, 1852. 16°. . . . N,391
Hand-Book of the English Language. New York, 1852. 12°. . L,544
Nationalities of Europe. London, 1863. 2 v. 8°. . . . . N,447
Native Races of the Russian Empire. London, 1854. 8°. . . N,414
Lathburg, T. History of Book of Common Prayer. Oxford and Lond. 1858. 8°. P,900
Latin Delectus. Edinburgh, 1846. 16°. . . . . . . . O,1118
Latin Hymns of the Anglo-Saxon Church. Durham, 1851. 8°. . . F,126,23
Latin Language, Dictionary of Synonyms. L. Ramshorn. Bost. 1839. 12°. L,754
English-Latin Lexicon. Georges, Riddle, and Arnold. N.Y. 1856. 8°. L.R.
First and Second Book. T. K. Arnold. New York, 1858. 12°. . L,751
Grammar of. E. A. Andrews and S. Stoddard. Boston, 1864. 12°. L,753
I. N. Madvig. Oxford, 1857. 8°. . . . . . . . L,755
L. Schmitz. Philadelphia, 1851. 16°. . . . . . . L,750
Introduction to Prose Composition. T. K. Arnold. N. Y. 1854. 12°. L,752
Latin-English Lexicon. E. A. Andrews. New York, 1856. 8°. . R.R.
The same. New York, 1870. 8°. . . . . . L.R.
J. E. Riddle. London, 1851. 4°. . . . . . . . L.R.
Lat.-Eng. and Eng.-Latin Dict. C. D. Yonge. Lond. 1867–8. 2 v. 8°. L.R.
Lexicon totius Latinitatis. I. J. G. Scheller; tr. J. E. Riddle. Oxf. 1835. f°. L.R.
Philological Study of. J. W. Donaldson. London, 1852. 8°. . . N,436

Latin Language. Thesaurus Linguæ Latinæ. R. Stephanus. Lon. 1735. 4 v. f°. Q,138
Latin Quotations, Dictionary of. H. T. Riley. London, 1866. 12°. . . L,53
Latour, A. de (Ed.). Petits Chefs-d'Œuvre Historiques. Paris, 1854. 2 v. 12°. A,312
La Tour-Landry, G. de. Book for his Daughters. London, 1868. 8°. L,605,33
Latreille, P. A. and Baron Cuvier. Animal Kingdom. Lond. 1837. 4 v. 8°. N,663
Latter-Day Pamphlets. T. Carlyle. Boston, 1855. 12°. . . . . . H,427
Latter Days. M. M. Sherwood. New York, 1858. 12°. . . . K,1008,2
Lauder, W. Minor Poems. London, 1870. 8°. . . . . . . L,605,41
Laugel, A. United States during the War. London, 1866. 8°. . . B,933
Laurent, A. Chemical Method. London, 1855. 8°. . . . . . . N,190
Lauterbrunnen to the Æggisch-horn. J. Tyndall. London, 1861. 8°. V,1086,1
Laurie, T. Dr. Grant and the Mountain Nestorians. Boston, 1853. 12°. . P,608
Lavallée, J. Voyage Pittoresque de l'Istrie et de la Dalmatie. Paris, 1802. f°. *Q,349
Lavallée, T. S. Physical, Historical, and Military Geography. Lond. 1868. V,1119
Lavater, J. C. Essays on Physiognomy. London, 1792–98. 3 v. in 5. 4°. *Q,293
Lavergne, L. de. Adam Smith. Paris, 1860. 8°. . . . . . N,252,45
Lavinia. J. Ruffini. Leipzig, 1861. 2 v. in 1. 16°. . . . . . . J,431
Law, American, Commentaries on. J. Kent. Boston, 1867. 4 v. 8°. . U,421
Introduction to; 5th edition. T. Walker. Boston, 1869. 8°. U,500
and British Publications. R. Clarke & Co. Cincin. 1870. 8°. L.R.
Ancient. H. S. Maine. New York, 1864. 8°. . . . . . . U,636
and Practice of Legislative Assemblies. L. S. Cushing. Bost. 1856. 8°. U,503
Canon, Corpus Juris Canonici; ed. by A. L. Richter. Lipsiæ, 1833. 4°. Q,146
Civil, Corpus Juris Civilis. Lipsiæ. 3 v. 8°. . . . . . Q,342
The same. Göttingæ, 1776. 2 v. 4°. . . . . . Q,147
in its Natural Order. J. Domat. Philadelphia, 1850. 2 v. 8°. U,517
Curiosities of Law Reporters. F. F. Heard. Boston, 1871. 12°. . H,134
Every Man his own Lawyer. J. G. Wells. New York, 1867. 12°. U,488
International. H. Wheaton; ed. by R. H. Dana, jr. Bost. 1866. 8°. U,507
Library, New York State Library, Catalogue of. Albany, 1856. 8°. L.R.
Maritime, of Europe. D. A. Azuni. New York, 1806. 2 v. 8°. . U,542
Military, Observations on. W. C. De Hart. New York, 1859. 8°. U,527
of England. London, 1810. 8°. . . . . . . . . U,497
of Industrial and Provident Societies. E.W. Brabrook. Lond. 1869. 12°. O,508
of Nature and Nations. S. von Pufendorf. London, 1717. f° . Q,307
of Patents. F. W. Campin. London, 1869. 12°. . . . . . M,834
Principles of Natural and Politic. J. J. Burlamaqui. Lon. 1784. 2 v. 8°. U,541
Reign of. G. J. D. Campbell, *Duke of Argyll*. London, 1867. 8°. . U,539
Law, H. Civil Engineering. London, 1858–59. 3 v. in 1. 12°. . . M,943
Constructing and Repairing Roads. London, 1855. 12°. . . . M,944
Treatise on Logarithms, with Tables. London, 1859. 12°. . . M,946
Law, J., the Projector. W. H. Ainsworth. Leipzig, 1864. 2 v. in 1. 16°. J,13
and the Mississippi Bubble. A. Thiers. New York, 1859. 12°. . D,154
Lawrence, A., the Merchant Prince. W. M. Thayer. Boston, 1866. 16°. . J,1499
Diary and Correspondence; edited by W. R. Lawrence. Bost. 1855. 8°. C,1055
Lawrence, E. Lives of the British Historians. New York, 1855. 2 v. 12°. D,406
Lawrence, G. A. Barren Honor. Leipzig, 1862. 16°. . . . . . J,254
Border and Bastile. Leipzig, 1863. 16°. . . . . . . . J,255
Breaking a Butterfly. Leipzig, 1869. 2 v. in 1. 16°. . . . . J,256

Lawrence, G. A. Guy Livingstone. New York, 1868. 12°. . . . . K,762
The same. Leipzig, 1860. 16°. . . . . . . . . J,257
Maurice Dering Leipzig, 1864. 16°. . . . . . . . . J,258
Sans Merci. New York, 1866. 8°. . . . . . . . . . K,761
The same. Leipzig, 1866. 2 v. in 1. 16°. . . . . . J,259
Sword and Gown. New York, 1868. 8°. . . . . . . . . K,764
The same. Leipzig, 1860. 16°. . . . . . . . . J,260
Lawrence, M. W. Light on the Dark River; or, Memorials of Mrs. H. A. L. Hamlin. Boston, 1854. 12°. . . . . . . . . . . C,788
Lawrence, P. Model Speaker. Philadelphia, 1871. 12°. . . . . O,1227
Lawrence, Sir T., Life of. D. E. Williams. London, 1831. 2 v. 8°. . D,428
Lawrence, W. Lectures on Comparative Anatomy, etc. Lond. 1848. p. 8°. L,897
Lawrie Todd; or, the Settlers in the Woods. J. Galt. London, 1849. 16°. K,522
Laws, P. Draining Strong Clays. Newcastle-upon-Tyne, 1850. . N,252,31
Laws, Arts and Sciences, Origin of. A. I. de Goguet. Edinb. 1775. 3 v. 8°. U,495
Code of Gentoo; translated by N. R. Halbed. London, 1776. 4°. . Q,341
Customs, etc., Digest of. T. Dew. London, 1856. 8°. . . . . A,28
Esprit des Lois. C. de S., Baron de Montesquieu. Paris, 1856. 12°. U,493
of Business. T. Parsons. Boston, 1857. 8°. . . . . . . . U,508
of England, Commentaries on. Sir W. Blackstone. N. Y. 1854. 4 v. 8°. U,505
The same; edited by G. Sharswood. Phila. 1869. 2 v. 8°. . U,502
Lawson, J. P. Bible Cyclopædia. Edinburgh, n. d. 3 v. 8°. . . . . P,460
Conspiracies in European History. Edinburgh, 1829. 2 v. 16°. . I,518
Lawson, W. J. History of Banking. Boston, 1852. 8°. . . . . . O,568
Lawyer, Every Man his own. J. G. Wells. New York, 1867. 12°. . . U,488
in the School-Room. M. McN. Walsh. New York, 1867. 12°. . U,489
Lawyers and Courts, Pleasantries about. C. Edwards. New York, 1867. 8°. H,509
Lives of Eminent British. H. Roscoe. London, 1830. 12°. . M,1010
Lay of Havelok the Dane. London, 1868. 8°. . . . . . . . L,604,4
Lay Sermons, Addresses and Reviews. T. H. Huxley. New York, 1871. 12°. M,773
Layard, A. H. Discoveries at Nineveh. New York, 1857. 12°. . . V,591
The same. London, 1853. 8°. . . . . . . . . V,677
The same. New York, 1854. 8°. . . . . . . . . V,600
Nineveh and its Remains. London, 1849. 2 v. 8°. . . . . V,678
Laycock, T. Mind and Brain. New York, 1869. 2 v. 12°. . . . O,618
Lays of Ancient Rome. T. B. Macaulay. Leipzig, 1851. 16°. . . . . J,337
Lea, H. C. Historical Sketch of Sacerdotal Celibacy. Phila. 1867. 8°. . P,830
Lea, J. and Carey, H. C. Geography and Statistics of America. Lon. 1823. 8°. B,621
Lea, T. G. Plants of Cincinnati. Philadelphia, 1849. 8°. . . . . N,1010
Leach, D. and Swan, R. Elementary Intellectual Arithmetic. Bost. 1854. 16°. O,1093
Lead, Bleiweiss-Bereitung im Grossen. J. B. Trommsdorf. Erf. 1827. 4°. N,252,41
Bleiweiss und Bleizuckerfabrication. H. Ludowig. Weimar, 1847. 16°. N,252,38
R. Meyer. Quedlinburg, 1845. 12°. . . . . . N,252,23
Carbonates of. J. A. Phillips. London, n. d. 8°. . . . . N,252,50
Chromate of. T. Richardson. London, n. d. 8°. . . . . N,252,2
Effects of, on Chirurgical Disorders. J. Goulard. Dublin, 1777. 12°. L,838
Metallurgy of. B. Kerl. London, 1868. 8°. . . . . . M,717,1
Miners, Diseases incident to. W. Ewart. Carlisle, 1846. 8°. N,252,35
Observations to. T. Sopwith. London, 1846. 8°. . . N,252,35
Pipe, Reports on the use of. J. P. Kirkwood. New York, 1859. 8°. N,215

Lead, Silver, and Copper, Metallurgy of. R.H.Lamborn. Lond. 1869. 2 v. 12°. M,848
Leaders in Literature. T. De Quincey. Edinburgh, 1862. 12°. . H,412,8
Learned Societies and Clubs of Great Britain. A. Hume. Lond. 1847. 12°. L.R.
The same. London, 1853. 12°. . . . . . . . . L.R.
Learning and Working. F. D. Maurice. Cambridge, 1855. 8°. . . P,806
Leisure Moments Improved. New York, 1865. 16°. . . . . J,1365
Leather-Stocking Tales. J. F. Cooper. New York, 1870. 5 v. 12°. . K,20
Vol. 1. Deerslayer. Vol. 3. Pathfinder.
2. Last of the Mohicans. 4. Pioneers.
Vol. 5. Prairie.
Leatherwood God, J. C. Dylks. R. H. Taneyhill. Cincinnati, 1871. 8°. . C,223
Leaves from a Family Journal. E. Souvestre. New York, 1855. 12°. . H,968
from our Journal in the Highlands. Victoria I. N. Y. 1868. 12°. V,381
from Note-Book of a Naturalist. W. J. Broderip. Lond. 1852. 12°. N,655
Lebanon, Mount. C. H. Churchill. London, 1853. 3 v. 8°. . . . V,641
Druzes of. C. W. Chasseaud. London, 1855. 8°. . . . . V,681
and Maronites of. C. H. Churchill. London, 1862. 12°. . B,556
Le Bas, C. W. Life of Thomas Cranmer. London, 1833. 2 v. 16°. . . D,331
Life of John de Wycliffe. London, 1832. 16°. . . . . . . D,332
Le Bas, P. Dictionnaire Enclyclopédique de la France. Par. 1840–45. 12 v. 8°. B,308
Lebensbilder aus der Westl. Hemisphäre. C.Sealsfield. Stutt.1846. 5 v. 24°. E,357,9–13
Lebermoose, Deutsche. J. W. P. Hübener. Mannheim, 1834. 8°. . . G,875
Lebert, H. Ueber die Pilzkrankheit der Fliegen. Stuttgart, n. d. 4°. . G,956
Le Canu, L. R. Etudes Chimiques sur le Sang Humain. Paris, 1837. 4°. N,252,57
Recherches sur l'Urine Humaine. 1839. 8°. . . . . . N,252,14
Lechford, T. Plain Dealing; edited by J. H. Trumbull. Boston, 1867. 4°. F,64
Lecky, W. E. H. History of European Morals. New York, 1869. 2 v. 8°. O,723
History of Rationalism in Europe. New York, 1866. 2 v. 8°. . P,213
Leclerc, C. Bibliotheca Americana. Paris, 1867. 12 v. 8°. . . . L.R.
Leçons de Liter. et de Morale. F. J. M. Noël and de La Place. Brux.1840. 8°. H,918
Lecture-Room Talks. H. W. Beecher. New York, 1870. 12°. . . . P,237
Lectures and Addresses. G. W. F. Howard, *Earl of Carlisle.* Lond. 1865. p. 8°. I,667
and Essays. H. Giles. Boston, 1851. 2 v. 16°. . . . . . H,38
and Miscellanies. H. James. New York, 1852. 12°. . . . P,264
Early History of Massachusetts. Boston, 1869. 8°. . . . . . C,52
on the Evidences of Christianity. New York, 1856. 8°. . . . P,162
Pitts-Street Chapel. Boston, 1858. 12°. . . . . . . . P,673
to Young Men. H. W. Beecher. Boston, 1869. 12°. . . . H,221
W. G. Eliot, jr. Boston, 1856. 12°. . . . . . H,263
LeDespencer, *Viscountess Falmouth.* Conversations on Geography. Lon. '54. 8°. O,902
Le Docte, H. Chimie et Physiologie Végétales. Bruxelles, 1849. 8°. N,252,34
Ledyard, J., Life of. J. Sparks. Boston, 1860. 12°. . . . . C,860,24
Lee, C., Life of. J. Sparks. Boston, 1860. 12°. . . . . . . C,860,18
Lee, C. A. Elements of Geology. New York, 1855. 18°. . . . . L,460
Lee, E. B. Life of Jean Paul F. Richter. Boston, 1864. 12°. . . . D,519
Memoir of Joseph Buckminster. Boston, 1851. 12°. . . . C,752
Parthenia. Boston, 1858. 12°. . . . . . . . . . . K,715
Lee, H., Life of. C. B. Hartley. Philadelphia, 1859. 12°. . . . C,552
Lee, H. F. Sketches of Sculpture and Sculptors. Boston, 1854. 2 v. 12°. . M,13
Memoir of Pierre Toussaint. Boston, 1854. 16°. . . . . C,700
Lee, Holme, *pseud.* See *Parr, H.*

Lee, Mrs. R. African Crusoes. Boston, 1871. 16°. . . . . . . J,1552
Anecdotes of Habits of Animals. Boston, 1871. 16°. . . . J,1553
Anecdotes of Habits of Birds, Reptiles, and Fishes. Boston, 1871. 16°. J,1554
Australian Wanderings. Boston, 1871. 16°. . . . . . . J,1551
Memoirs of Baron Cuvier. London, 1833. 8°. . . . . D,682
Lee, R. H., jr. Memoir of Richard Henry Lee. Phil. 1825. 2 v. . . C,879
Lee, W. Life and Writings of Daniel DeFoe. London, 1860. 3 v. 8°. D,452
Leech, H. H. Letters of a Sentimental Idler from Greece. N. Y. 1869. 12°. V,669
Leechdoms, Wortcunning, etc., of Early England. Lond. 1864–66. 3 v. 8°. W,185
Leeds, Report on the Sewerage of. Capt. Vetch. Leeds, 1843. 16°. N,252,26
Leeds, L. W. Lectures on Ventilation. New York, 1868. 8°. . . N,45
Leeds, W. H. Orders of Architecture. London, 1854. 12°. . . . M,947
Le Fanu, J. S. Guy Deverell. Leipzig, 1865. 2 v. in 1. 16°. . . J,261
House by the Church-Yard. New York, 1866. 12°. . . . K,763
Lost Name. New York, 1868. 8°. . . . . . . . . . K,765
Uncle Silas. New York, n. d. 8°. . . . . . . . . . K,766
The same. Leipzig, 1865. 2 v. in 1. 16°. . . . . . J,262
Wylder's Hand. New York, 1866. 12°. . . . . . . . K,767
Lefèvre, M. Wonders of Architecture. New York, 1870. 12°. . M,1052
Legal and Political Hermeneutics. F. Lieber. Boston, 1839. 12°. . . O,481
Legend of Montrose. Sir W. Scott. Philadelphia, 1869. 8°. . . K,1108
The same. Boston, 1868. 12°. . . . . . . . . K,928
of the Wandering Jew; illustrated by G. Doré. London, n. d. f°. *Q,455
Legendary and Mythological Art. C. E. Clement. New York, 1871. 12°. M,82
Legende of Goode Women. G. Chaucer; ed. by H. Corson. Phil. 1864. 12°. I,243
Legendre, A. M. Elements of Geometry and Trigonometry. N. Y. 1867. 8°. M,1129
Exercises de Calcul Intégral. Paris, 1811–16. 3 v. 4°. . M,1204
Legends and Lyrics. A. A. Proctor. New York, 1859. 12°. . . . I,110
and Records. C. B. Taylor. New York, 1855. 12°. . . . C,530
of the War of Independence. T. M. Smith. Louisville, 1855. 8°. B,756
of the Wars in Ireland. R. D. Joyce. Boston, 1868. 16°. . K,1013
of Charlemagne. T. Bulfinch. Boston, 1866. 12°. . . . . A,224
of the Flowers. S. Pindar. New York, 1865. 16°. . . . J,1362
of the Madonna. A. Jameson. London, 1867. 8°. . . . *M,118
of the Monastic Orders. A. Jameson. London, 1867. 8°. . *M,119
The same. Boston, 1865. 16°. . . . . . . . M,1
of Montauk. J. A. Ayres. New York, 1849. 8°. . . . . . I,15
Legge, J. Life and Teachings of Confucius. Philadelphia, 1867. 12°. . D,774
Legislation, Principles of. J. Bentham. Boston, 1830. 8°. . . . O,495
Legislative Assemblies, Law and Practice of. L. S. Cushing. Bost. 1866. 8°. U,503
Legislative Guide. J. B. Burleigh. Philadelphia, 1865. 8°. . . . . B,719
Legitime und die Republikaner. C. Sealsfield. Stutt. 1845. 3 v. 24°. E,357,1–3
Le Gray, G. Treatise on Photography. Philadelphia, 1853. 12°. . . M,613
Lehmann, C. G. Zoochemie. Heidelberg, 1858. 8°. . . . . . G,756
Leibnitz, G. W. von. System of Theology. London, 1850. 8°. . . P,173
Opera Philosophica. Berolini, 1840. 8°. . . . . . . . . G,567
Leicester, Earl of, *R. Dudley*, Correspondence, 1585–86. London, 1844. 4°. A,472
Leigh, C. Natural History of Lancashire. London, 1700. f°. . . Q,62
Leichhardt, L. Beiträge zur Geologie von Australien. Halle, 1855. 4°. . Q,46
Leighton Court. H. Kingsley. Leipzig, 1866. 16°. . . . . . . J,250

Leighton, R. Whole Works; with Life. London, 1828. 2 v. 8°. . P,768
Leighton, W. A. British Species of Angiocarpous Lichens. Lond. 1851. 8°. O,303
Leila; or, the Seige of Granada. Sir E. B. Lytton. Philadelphia, 1868. 12°. K,817
The same. Philadelphia, 1868. 12°. . . . . . . K,818
Leila Books. A. F. Tytler. Boston, 1870. 5 v. 16°. . . . . J,1675
Vol. 1. Leila; or, the Island. Vol. 3 Leila at Home.
2. Leila in England. 4. Mary and Florence.
Vol. 5. Mary and Florence at Sixteen.

Leipzig Campaign. G. R. Gleig. London, 1856. p. 8°. . . . I,661,1
Leisler, J., Life of. C. F. Hoffman. Boston, 1860. 12°. . . . C,860,13
Leisure Hours. J. R. Mac Conochie. Louisville, Ky. 1846. 12°. . . I,79
Leisure Hours in Town. A. K. H. Boyd. Boston, 1869. 12°. . . . H,555
Leisure Moments improved. New York, 1855. 12°. . . . . . J,1254
Leitch, W. God's Glory in the Heavens. London, 1867. 12°. . . N,263
Lekain, H. L. Mémoires. Paris, 1855. 12°. . . . . . . . D,612
Leland, C. G. Hans Breitman's Ballads. Philadelphia, 1869. 8°. . . I,98
Leland, J. Divine Authority of the Scriptures. London, 1837. 8°. . . P,174
View of the Principal Deistical Writers. London, 1837. 8°. . . P,260
Leland, T. History of Ireland. London, 1773. 3 v. 4°. . . . A,372
Lelievre et Angers, M. M. Lower Canada Reports. Quebec, 1856. 2 v. 8°. C,344
Vol. 1. Seigniorial Questions. Vol. 2. Questions Seigneuriales.

Lemaire, N. E. Bibliotheca Classica Latina. Parisiis, 1819–38. 142 v. 8°.
Caesar, C. J. Opera Omnia. 4 v. . . . . . . . U,311
Catullus, C. V. Opera Omnia. . . . . . . . . U,312
Cicero, M. T. Opera Rhetorica et Oratoria. 2 v. . . . U,317
Orationes Omnes. 6 v. . . . . . . . U,315
Opera Philosophica. 6 v. . . . . . . . U,316
Epistolæ. 3 v. . . . . . . . . . U,313
Fragmenta. . . . . . . . . . U,314
Quinque Indices. . . . . . . . . U,318
Claudianus, C. Opera Omnia. 2 v. . . . . . . U,319
Cornelius Nepos. Opera . . . . . . . . U,334
Curtius Rufus, Q. De Rebus Gestis Alexandri Magni. 3 v. . . U,320
Florus, L. A. Epitome Rerum Romanarum. . . . . U,323
Horatius Flaccus, Q. Opera Omnia. 3 v. . . . . U,324
Justinus. Historiæ Philippicæ. . . . . . . U,325
Juvenalis, D. J. Sexdecim Satiræ. 2 v. . . . . . U,326
Livius Patavinus, T. Opera Omnia. 12 v. . . . . U,327
Lucretius Carus, T. De Rerum Natura. 2 v. . . . . U,330
Lucanus, M. A. Pharsalia. 3 v. . . . . . . . U,329
Martialis, M. V. Epigrammata. 3 v. . . . . . U,332
Ovidius Naso, P. Opera Omnia. 9 v. . . . . . U,335
Persius Flaccus, A. Sex Satiræ. . . . . . . . U,326,3
Phaedrus. Fabulæ Æsopiæ. 2 v. . . . . . . . U,336
Plautus, M. A. Comœdiæ. 4 v. . . . . . . . U,337
Plinius Secundus, C. Epistolæ. 2 v. . . . . . . U,338
Historiæ Naturales. 11 v. . . . . . . . U,339
Poetæ Latini Minores. 7 v. . . . . . . . U,340
Propertius, S. A. Elegiæ. . . . . . . . . U,341
Quintilianus, M. F. De Institutione Oratoria. 4 v. . . U,342,1–4
et Flaccus, C. Declamationes. 2 v. . . . . U,342,5,6
et Flaccus, C. Selecta Recentiorum Judicia; Annales. . U,342,7
Sallustius, C. C. Opera Omnia. . . . . . . . U,343
Seneca, L. A. Opera Philosophica. 3 v. . . . . . . U,345
Opera Declamatoria. . . . . . . . . U,344
Opera Tragica. 5 v. . . . . . . . . U,346
Silius Italicus, C. Punicorum Libri Septemdecim. 2 v. . . U,347
Statius, P. P. Opera Omnia. 4 v. . . . . . . U,348

Lemaire, N. E. Bibliotheca Classica Latina. *Continued.*

Suetonius Tranquillus, C. Opera Omnia. 2 v. . . . . . U,349
Tacitus, C. Opera. 5 v. . . . . . . . . U,350
Terentius Afrus, P. Comœdiæ. 2 v. . . . . . U,351
Tibullus, A. Opera Omnia. . . . . . . . U,352
Valerius Flaccus, C. Argonautica. 2 v. . . . . U,321
Valerius Maximus. Opera. 3 v. . . . . . . U,353
Velleius Paterculus, C. Opera. . . . . . . . U,354
Virgilius Maro, P. Opera Omnia. 8 v. . . . . . U,355
Appendix. . . . . . . . . . . U,356

Lembke, F. W. and Schäfer, H. Gesch. v. Spanien. Ham. 1831–61. 3 v. 8°. E,92
Lemon, M. Falkner Lyle. Leipzig, 1866. 2 v. in 1. . . . . . J,263
Golden Fetters. Leipzig, 1868. 2 v. in 1. 16°. . . . . . J,264
Leyton Hall. Leipzig, 1867. 2 v. in 1. 16°. . . . . . . J,265
Loved at Last. Leipzig, 1865. 2 v. in 1. 16°. . . . . . J,266
Up and Down the London Streets. Philadelphia, 1867. 8°. . . V,396
Wait for the End. Leipzig, 1864. 2 v. in 1. 16°. . . . . . J,267
Lempriere, J. Classical Dictionary. New York, 1853. 8°. . . . . L.R.
The same. New York, 1825. 8°. . . . . . . . . L.R.
Lemurs, Natural History of. J. Jackson. London, 1838. 16°. . L,482,1
Lena Rivers. M. J. Holmes. New York, 1868. 12°. . . . . . K,188
Lenau, *pseud.* See *Niembsch von Strehlenau, N.*
Lennox, C. Female Quixote. London, 1820. 2 v. 12°. . . . . . K,536
Lennox, W. P. Drafts on my Memory. London, 1866. 2 v. 8°. . . H,463
Lenormand, S. Nouveau Manuel du Relieur. Paris, 1840. 18°. . . M,595
Lenz, H. O. Botanik der Alten Griechen und Römer. Gotha, 1859. 8°. G,882
Schlangenkunde. Gotha, 1832. 8°. . . . . . . . . . G,918
Leo, X., Life and Pontificate of. W. Roscoe. London, 1853. 2 v. p. 8°. L,225
Leo, H. Geschichte der Italienischen Staaten. Hamburg, 1829–48. 5 v. 8°. E,101
Leon, J. A. Sugar and Coffee Planting. London, 1848. 8°. . . N,252,34
Leon y Gama, A. de. Descripcion de las dos Piedras que se está formando en la Plaza de Mexico. Mexico, 1792. 4°. . . . . . . C,377
Leonard, S. W. and Fillmore. Christian Psalmist. Cincinnati, 1847. 16°. . P,887
Leonard and Gertrude. J. H. Pestalozzi. London, 1825. 2 v. 8°. . . G,214
Leonhard, K. C. von. Geognosie und Geologie. Stuttgart, 1835. 8°. G,812,2
Geologie. Stuttgart, 1836–44. 5 v. 12°. . . . . . . . G,834
Jahrbuch für Mineralogie, Geognosie, etc. Stutt. 1848–52. 5 v. 8°. G,845
Taschenbuch für Freunde der Geologie. Stuttgart, 1845. 12°. . G,835
Vulkanen-Atlas. n. p. n. d. 8°. . . . . . . . . . . G,846
Lerebours, N. P. Treatise on Photography. London, 1843. 12°. . . M,615
Leonora. M. Edgeworth. New York, 1859. 12°. . . . . . K,678,7
Leopold I., Memoirs of. T. Juste. London, 1868. 2 v. 8°. . . . D,526
Leopold II. und seine Zeit. C. Mundt. Wien, 1861. 3 v. in 1. 24°. . G,363
Le Play, P. G. F. Fabrication des Fers à Acier. Paris, 1846. 8°. . N,252,34
Richesse Minérale de l'Espagne. Paris, 1834. 8°. . . . N,252,35
Lepsius, C. R. Alphabet for Reducing Unwritten Languages to a Uniform Orthography. London and Berlin, 1863. 8°. . . . . . . L,525
Letters from Egypt, Ethiopia, and Sinai. London, 1853. p. 8°. . L,16
Leroy, C. F. A. Stereotomie. Stuttgart, 1847. 4°. . . . . . . G,741
Atlas dazu. . . . . . . . . . . . . . *Q,85
Le Roy, M. Les Ruines de la Grece. Paris, 1757. f°. . . . . . . L.R.

Le Sage, A. R. Bachelor of Salamanca. Philadelphia, 1868. 2 v. 16°. . H,961
Histoire de Gil-Blas de Santillane. Paris, 1855. 12°. . . . H,930
The same; translated by T. Smollet. Boston, 1865. 3 v. 12°. H,926
The same. Philadelphia, n. d. 8°. . . . . H,927
The same; illustrated. London, 1861. p. 8°. . . L,104
Lesebuch, Zweites. Cincinnati, 1853. 16°. . . . . . . . . G,544
Leser, Amerikanischer, Zweites Buch. Cincinnati, n. d. 16°. . . . G,545
Lesley, J. P. Man's Origin and Destiny. Philadelphia, 1868. 8°. . . N,399
Leslie, C. Short Method with Deists. New York, n. d. 18°. . . P,746,14
Leslie, C. R. Autobiographical Recollections. Boston, 1860. 12°. . . C,761
Hand-Book for Young Painters. London, 1855. 12°. . . . M,51
Leslie, E. Ladies' Guide to True Politeness. Philadelphia, n. d. 12°. . H,281
Leslie, E. New Cookery Book. Philadelphia, 1857. 12°. . . . H,292
Leslie, J. and others. Polar Seas and Regions. London, 1855. 12°. . V,913
The same. New York, 1855. 16°. . . . . . . . . L,347
Leslie, Madeline, *pseud.* See *Baker, H. N.*
Leslie Tyrrell. G. M. Craik. Leipzig, 1867. 16°. . . . . . . J,97
Lesqeureux, L. Torfmoore im Allgemeinen. Berlin, 1847. 8°. . N,252,40
Lessing, G. E. Fables and Epigrams. London, 1825. 12°. . . . G,23
Life and Works. A. Stahr. Boston, 1866. 2 v. 12°. . . . D,522
Laocoon; Limits of Poetry and Painting. London, 1838. 8°. . . M,45
Nathan the Wise; translated by E. Frothingham. N. Y. 1868. 16°. G,41
and Emilia Galotti. Leipzig, 1868. 4°. . . . . . . G,39
Werke. Stuttgart, 1867. 10 v. in 5. 16°. . . . . . . E,335

Bd. 1. Leben; Singgedichte; Lieder; Oden; Fabeln und Erzählungen; Miss Sara Sampson, Trauerspiel.
2. Minna von Barnhelm; oder, das Soldatenglück, Lustspiel; Emilia Galotti.
3. Nathan der Weise.
4. Vade Mecum für den Pastor Lange; Wie die Alten den Tod gebildet; Briefe, antiquarischen Inhalts.
5. Sophokles; Laokoon; oder, über die Gränzen der Malerei und Poesie; Die Erziehung des Menschengeschlechts.
6. Hamburgische Dramaturgie.
7. Fragmente; Die Juden, Lustspiel; Der Freigeist, Lustspiel; Doktor Faust; Philotas, Trauerspiel; Briefe aus dem zweiten Theile der Schriften; Werther, der Bessere.
8. Rettungen des Horaz; Abhandlungen über die Fabel; Vorreden zu seinen Schriften; Vorrede zu den vermischten Schriften von C. Mylius; Vorreden zu den preussischen Kriegsliedern in den Feldzügen, 1756–7; Vorrede zu F. von Logau's Sinngedichten; Vorreden zu Diderot's Theater; Aus den Briefen, die neueste Literatur betreffend.
9. Ueber das Epigramm; Ueber Meusels Apollodor; Vom Alter der Oelmalerei; Zur Geschichte der Literatur; Ernst und Falk, Gespräche für Freimaurer; Noch nähere Berichtigung des Mährchens von 1000 Ducaten, oder Judas Ischarioth dem Zweiten.
10. Theologische Streitschriften; Briefe.

Lesson, R. P. Manual d'Ornithologie Domestique. Paris, 1834. 18°. . O,79
Lessons in Life. J. G. Holland. New York, 1867. 12°. . . . . H,108
on Industrial Education. London, 1849. 12°. . . . . O,1164
Lester, C. E. Glory and Shame of England. New York, 1850. 2 v. 12°. V,367
and Foster. Life and Voyages of Americus Vespucius. N. Y. 1846. 8°. D,740
L'Estrange, A. G. K. (Ed.) Life of M. R. Mitford. N. Y. 1870. 2 v. 12°. D,7
Letter-Writer, Sensible. A. Martine. New York, 1866. 16°. . . . H,6
Letter-Writing, History of. W. Roberts. London, 1843. 8°. . . . H,740
Letterman, J. Medical Recollections of the Army. Boston, 1866. 8°. . L,943
Letters by Eminent Persons in Bodleian Library. J. Aubrey. Lon. 1813. 3 v. 8°. H,823
from Abroad. H. Alford. London, 1865. 8°. . . . . . . V,487
C. M. Sedgwick. New York, 1855. 2 v. 12°. . . . V,365

Letters from the East. W. C. Bryant. New York, 1869. 12°. . . . v,1059
from the Frontiers. G. A. McCall. Philadelphia, 1868. 12°. . . v,117
from the Mountains. Mrs. A. Grant. Boston, 1809. 2 v. 12°. . v,351
from New York. L. M. Child. New York, 1850. 2 v. 12°. . . v,52
from Rome, A. D. 138. New York, 1854. 12°. . . . . . . v,498
of a Hindoo Rajah. E. Hamilton. London, 1811. 2 v. 12°. . H,830
of a Sentimental Traveler. H. H. Leech. New York, 1869. 12°. . v,669
of a Traveler. W. C. Bryant. New York, 1851. 12°. . . v,1052
of Royal and Illustrious Ladies. M. A. E. Wood. Lond. 1846. 3 v. 12°. H,837
of Spiritual Counsel. J. Keble. Oxford, 1870. 12°. . . . . P,127
sur l'Homme et ses Rapports. Paris, 1772. 16°. . . . . . L,841
to a Lady. W. von Humboldt. Philadelphia, 1864. 12°. . . . G,22
to B. Franklin from his Family. New York, 1859. 8°. . . . . H,171
to 'Squire Pedant by L. Altisonant. Cincinnati, 1856. 12°. . . H,253
to the Jones. J. G. Holland. New York, 1865. 12°. . . . H,109
to Young People. J. G. Holland. New York, 1867. 12°. . . H,111
writ by a Turkish Spy. G. P. Marana. London, 1748. 8 v. 16°. H,390
Leuchars, R. B. Construction and Ventilation of Hot-Houses. N. Y. 1857. 12°. M,535
Leuchs, J. C. Vollständige Bleich-Kunde. Nürnberg, 1845. 8°. . N,252,13
Leuckart, F. S. Einleitung in die Naturgeschichte. Stuttgart, 1832. 8°. G,812,1
Leuckart, R. Nachträge zu J. van der Hoeven's Zoölogie. Leip. 1856 8°. G,919,1
Physiolgische Uebersicht des Thierreichs. Stuttgart, 1851. 8°. . E,422
Lever, C. Arthur O'Leary. Leipzig, 1847. 2 v. in 1. 16°. . . . J,268
Barrington. London, 1863. 8°. . . . . . . . . . K,882
The same. New York, 1862. 8°. . . . . . . . . K,768
The same. Leipzig, 1863. 2 v. in 1. 16°. . . . . . J,269
Bramleighs of Bishop's Folly. Leipzig, 1868. 2 v. in 1. 16°. . J,270
Charles O'Malley. Philadelphia, 1865. 8°. . . . . . . K,769
The same. Leipzig, 1848. 3 v. 16°. . . . . . . . J,271
Con Cregan, the Irish Gil Blas. Philadelphia, n. d. 8°. . . K,770
Confessions of Harry Lorrequer. London, n. d. 8°. . . . . K,776
The same. Leipzig, 1847. 2 v. in 1. 16°. . . . . J,277
Daltons; or, Three Roads in Life. London, 1865. 2 v. 8°. . . K,772
The same. Leipzig, 1852. 4 v. 16°. . . . . . . J,272
Davenport Dunn; or, Man of the Day. London, 1859. 2 v. 8°. . K,773
The same. Leipzig, 1859. 3 v. 16°. . . . . . . J,273
Day's Ride: a Life's Romance. London, n. d. 8°. . . . . . K,771
The same. Leipzig, 1864. 2 v. in 1. 16°. . . . . . J,274
Diary of Horace Templeton. Leipzig, 1848. 16°. . . . . . J,289
Dodd Family Abroad. New York, n. d. 8°. . . . . . . K,774
The same. Leipzig, 1854. 3 v. 16°. . . . . . . J,275
Fortunes of Glencore. London, 1865. 8°. . . . . . . K,775
The same. Leipzig, 1857. 2 v. in 1. 16°. . . . . J,276
Jack Hinton, the Guardsman. Philadelphia, n. d. 8°. . . . K,777
The same. Leipzig, 1849. 2 v. in 1. 16°. . . . . J,278
Knight of Gwynne. London, 1858. 2 v. 8°. . . . . . . K,778
The same. Leipzig, 1847. 3 v. 16°. . . . . . . J,279
Luttrell of Arran. New York, 1865. 8°. . . . . . . K,780
The same. London, 1868. 8°. . . . . . . . K,883
The same. Leipzig, 1865. 2 v. in 1. 16°. . . . . . J,280

Lever, C. Martins of Cro' Martin. London, 1864. 2 v. 8°. . . . . K,781
The same. Leipzig, 1856. 3 v. 16°. . . . . . . J,281
Maurice Tiernay. London, 1865. 8°. . . . . . . . K,782
The same. Leipzig, 1861. 2 v. in 1. 16°. . . . . . J,282
The O'Donoghue. London, 1865. 8°. . . . . . . . K,783
One of Them. London, 1860. 8°. . . . . . . . . K,784
The same. Leipzig, 1860. 2 v. in 1. 16°. . . . . . J,283
Rent in a Cloud. London, n. d. 8°. . . . . . . . K,785
The same. Leipzig, 1869. 16°. . . . . . . . J,284
Roland Cashel. New York, 1856. 8°. . . . . . . . K,786
The same. Leipzig, 1858. 3 v. 16°. . . . . . . J,285
St. Patrick's Eve; Paul Gosslett's Confessions. Leipzig, 1870. 16°. J,286
Sir Brooke Fossbrooke. New York, 1867. 8°. . . . . . . K,788
The same. Leipzig, 1867. 2 v. in 1. 16°. . . . . . J,287
Sir Jasper Carew, Kt. New York, 1868. 8°. . . . . . . K,789
The same. Leipzig, 1861. 2 v. in 1. 16°. . . . . . J,288
That Boy of Norcott's. New York, 1869. 8°. . . . . K,1159
The same. Leipzig, 1869. 16°. . . . . . . . J,290
Tom Burke of Ours. London, 1865. 2 v. 12°. . . . . . K,790
The same. Leipzig, 1848. 3 v. 16°. . . . . . . J,291
Tony Butler. New York, 1865. 8°. . . . . . . . K,791
The same. Leipzig, 1866. 2 v. in 1. 16°. . . . . . J,292
Levi, L. Annals of British Legislation. London, 1857-59. 4 v. 8°. . B,181
Commercial Law; its Principles, etc. London, 1850-51. 2 v. 4°. . Q,218
Levins, P. Manipulus Vocabulorum; Rhyming Dictionary. Lon. 1867. 8°. L,605,27
Levis, J., Sixty Years of the Life of. New York, 1831. 2 v. 12°. . . C,676
Lévizac, J. P. V. L. de. Grammar of the French Language. Phil. 1854. 12°. L,804
Lewes, G. H. Biographical History of Philosophy. N. Y. 1857. 2 v. 8°. O,670
Biographical History of Philosophy; 3d ed. London, 1867. 2 v. 8°. O,737
Life of Goethe. London, 1864. 8°. . . . . . . . . D,506
Life and Works of Goethe. Boston, 1856. 2 v. 12°. . . . . D,494
Physiology of Common Life. Edinburgh, 1859-60. 2 v. 12°. . L,880
The same. Leipzig, 1866. 2 v. in 1. 16°. . . . . . J,293
Ranthorpe. Leipzig, 1847. 16°. . . . . . . . . J,294
Sea-Side Studies at Ilfracombe, etc. Edinburgh, 1858. 8°. . . N,520
Studies of Animal Life. New York, 1860. 12°. . . . . . N,648
Lewes, M. J. Adam Bede. New York, 1868. 12°. . . . . . . K,792
The same. Leipzig, 1859. 2 v. in 1. 16°. . . . . . J,295
Felix Holt, the Radical. New York, 1866. 8°. . . . . . K,793
The same. Leipzig, 1867. 2 v. in 1. 16°. . . . . . J,296
Mill on the Floss. New York, 1860. 12°. . . . . . K,795
The same. Leipzig, 1860. 2 v. in 1. 16°. . . . . . J,297
Romola. New York, 1868. 8°. . . . . . . . . K,796
The same. Leipzig, 1863. 2 v. in 1. 16°. . . . . . J,298
Scenes of Clerical Life. New York, n. d. 8°. . . . . . K,798
The same. Leipzig, 1859. 2 v. in 1. 16°. . . . . . J,299
Silas Marner, the Weaver of Raveloe. New York, 1861. 12°. . . K,794
The same. Leipzig, 1861. 16°. . . . . . . . J,300
Spanish Gipsy; a Poem. Boston, 1868. 16°. . . . . . . I,358
Lewin, T. Invasion of Britain by Julius Cæsar. London, 1859. 8°. . A,493

Lewin, W. Birds of Great Britain. London, 1797–1800. 8 v. in 4. 4°. Q,11
Lewis, D. New Gymnastics. Boston, 1863. 12°. . . . . . . M,345
Our Girls. New York, 1871. 12°. . . . . . . . . L,854
Talks about People's Stomachs. Boston, 1870. 12°. . . . L,940
Weak Lungs, and how to make them strong. Boston, 1863. 12°. . L,904
Lewis, E. J. American Sportsman. Philadelphia, 1868. 8°. . . . M,317
Lewis, G. C. Credibility of Early Roman History. London, 1855. 2 v. 8°. A,181
Methods of Reasoning in Politics. London, 1852. 2 v. 8°. . . O,546
Lewis, M. and Clarke, W. Expedition to Sources of the Missouri, Rocky Mountains, etc., 1804–6. Philadelphia, 1814. 2 v. 8°. . . . V,83
The same; abridged. New York, 1855. 2 v. 18°. . . L,441
Lewis, M. G. Life and Correspondence. London, 1839. 2 v. 8°. . . D,81
Monk; a Romance. London, 1829. 8°. . . . . . . . K,804
Lewis, S., Biography of. W. G. W. Lewis. Cincinnati, 1859. 8°. . . C,707
Lewis, S. and others. Maps of the several States, etc. Philad. 1794–95. f°. Q,394
Lewis, S. A. Records of the Heart; Poems. New York, 1844. 12°. . I,64
Lewis, W. G. W. Biography of Samuel Lewis. Cincinnati, 1857. 8°. . C,707
Lewis, W. M. People's Practical Poultry Book. New York, 1871. 8°. . M,454
Lexington and Fayette Co., Ky., Directory of. J.P.B. MacCabe. Lex. '38. 12°. C,178
Leypoldt, F. Trade Circular Annual for 1871. New York, 1871. 8°. . L.R.
Leyton Hall. M. Lemon. Leipzig, 1867. 2 v. in 1. 16°. . . . J,265
Lezaud, P. L. Résumés Philosophiques. Paris, 1853. 12°. . . . O,615
Liberia; or, Mr. Peyton's Experiments. S. J. Hale. N. Y. 1853. 12°. . K,129
Liberty. J. S. Mill. Boston, 1868. 16°. . . . . . . . . O,484
Liberty, Civil, and Self-Government. F. Lieber. Philad. 1853. 2 v. 12°. O,477
History of; Ancient Romans. S. Eliot. Boston, 1853. 2 v. 12°. . A,155
History of; Ancient Christians. S. Eliot. Boston, 1853. 2 v. 8°. . P,400
Libraire, Manuel du. J. C. Brunet. Bruxelles, 1838–43. 5 v. 8°. . . L.R.
The same. Paris, 1860–65. 6 v. 8°. . . . . . . L.R.
Librarian, The. J. Savage. London, 1808–9. 3 v. 8°. . . . . . L.R.
Librarian's Manual. R. A. Guild. New York, 1858. 4°. . . . L.R.
Libraries, Decimal System for. N. B. Shurtliff. Boston, 1856. 8°. . . L.R.
Free Town. E. Edwards. London, 1869. 8°. . . . . . L.R.
Memoirs of. E. Edwards. London, 1859. 2 v. 8°. . . . L.R.
Library Companion. T. F. Dibdin. London, 1824. 8°. . . . . . L.R.
Manual. Appleton's. New York, 1852. 8°. . . . . . . L.R.
of American History. Cincinnati, 1846. 8°. . . . . . . B,829
of Entertaining Knowledge. London, 1830–50. 43 v. 16°.
Craik, G. L. Pursuit of Knowledge under Difficulties. 2 v. . . L,485
Davis, J. F. The Chinese. 2 v. . . . . . . . . L,487
Distinguished Men of Modern Times. 4 v. . . . . . L,471
Ellis, Sir H. Elgin and Phigaleian Marbles. 2 v. . . . . L,475
Townley Gallery, British Museum. 2 v. . . . . L,490
Hindoos, The. 2 v. . . . . . . . . . . L,488
Jackson, J. Monkeys, Opossums, etc. 2 v. . . . . . L,482
Jardine, D. Criminal Trials. 2 v. . . . . . . L,473
Lane, E. W. Modern Egyptians. 2 v. . . . . . . L,480
Lankester, E. Vegetable Substances; Food. . . . . L,491,1
Long, G. Egyptian Antiquities. 2 v. . . . . . . L,474
Malkin, J. H. Historical Parallels. 2 v. . . . . . L,478
Menageries; Quadrupeds. 3 v. . . . . . . . L,481
New Zealanders. . . . . . . . . . . L,489
Paris and its Historical Scenes. 2 v. . . . . . . L,483

Library of Entertaining Knowledge. *Continued.*

Planché, J. R. British Costume. . . . . . . . L,472
Pompeii; its Past and Present. 2 v. . . . . . . L,484
Rennie, J. Architecture of Birds. . . . . . . L,469
Domestic Habits of Birds. . . . . . . . L,477
Faculties of Birds. . . . . . . . . L,476
and Westwood, J. O. Insects. 3 v. . . . . L,479
Secret Societies of the Middle Ages. . . . . . L,486
Traill, C. P. Backwoods of Canada. . . . . . L,470
Vegetable Substances: Materials of Manufactures. . . L,491,3
Vegetable Substances used in the Arts. . . . . L,491,2

of Poetry and Song. E. H. Knight. New York, 1871. 8°. . . I,177
of Wonders, illustrated. London and New York, 1868–71. 22 v. 12°.

Adams, W. H. D. Lighthouses and Lightships. . . . M,1054
Bernard, F. Wonderful Escapes. . . . M,1061
Cazin, A. Phenomena and Laws of Heat. . . . . M,1058
Depping, G. Bodily Strength and Skill. . . . . M,1062
Duplessis, G. Wonders of Engraving. . . . . . . M,1065
Flammarion, C. Wonders of the Heavens. . . . . M,1050
Fonvielle, W. de. Thunder and Lightning. . . . . M,1048
Guillemin, A. The Sun. . . . . . . . . M,1057
Lanoye, F. de. Rameses the Great; or, Egypt 3,300 Years ago. . M,1056
Sublime in Nature. . . . . . . . . M,1046
Lefèvre, M. Wonders of Architecture. . . . . M,1052
Marion, F. Wonders of Optics. . . . . . . M,1059
Wonderful Balloon Ascents. . . . . . . M,1063
Menault, E. Intelligence of Animals. . . . . M,1047
Meunier, V. Adventures on the Great Hunting Grounds. . . M,1064
Monnier, M. Wonders of Pompeii. . . . . . M,1055
Pileur, A. le. Wonders of the Human Body. . . . M,1045
Radau, R. Wonders of Acoustics. . . . . . . M,1060
Sauzay, A. Wonders of Glassmaking. . . . . . M,1053
Sonrel, L. Bottom of the Sea. . . . . . . . M,1049
Viardot, L. Wonders of European Art. . . . . . M,1066
Wonders of Italian Art. . . . . . . . M,1051

Libyan Desert, Adventures in. B. St. John. New York, 1849. 12°. . V,795
Lichens, British Species of Angiocarpous. W. A. Leighton. Lon. 1851. 8°. O,303
Descriptio et Adumbratio. G. F. Hoffman. Leipzig, 1784. f°. . Q,76
History of British. W. L. Lindsay. London, 1856. 16°. . . N,920
Inorganic Food of. R. D. Thomson. Glasgow, 1843. 8°. . N,252,21
Lichens, Proximate Principles of. J. Stenhouse. London, 1848. 4°. N,252,42
Lichtenberg, G. C. Erklärung der Hogarth. Kupferst. Göt. 1794–1835. 2 v. 16°. G,622
Liddell, H. G. History of Rome. London, 1855. 2 v. 8°. . . . A,151
Life of Julius Cæsar. New York, 1865. 16°. . . . . . D,713
and Scott, R. Greek-English Lexicon. New York, 1870. r. 8°. . L.R.
The same. New York, 1858. 8°. . . . . . . . R.R.
Liddle, J. Evils from Neglect of Sanitary Measures. Lond. 1847. 16°. N,252,37
Liddon, H. P. Divinity of our Lord; Bampton Lectures. Lond. 1867. 8°. P,527
Lidgate, J. Stans Puer ad Mensam. London, 1868. 8°. . . . L,605,32
Liebe, Glauben, Hoffnung, Lehren von. J. F. Fries. Heidelberg, 1823. 16°. G,552
Lieber, F. Character of the Gentleman. Philadelphia, 1864. 12°. . . H,228
Civil Liberty and Self-Government. Philadelphia, 1853. 2 v. 12°. O,477
The same. Philadelphia, 1859. 8°. . . . . . . O,551
Essays on Property and Labor. New York, 1854. 16°. . . . L,436
Legal and Political Hermeneutics. Boston, 1839. 12°. . . . O,481
Manual of Political Ethics. Boston, 1839–47. 2 v. 8°. . . . O,522

Lieber, O. M. Assayer's Guide. Philadelphia, 1869. 12°. . . . . M,715
Lieberkuhn, S. History of Jesus Christ in the Delaware Indian Language; translated by D. Zeisberger. New York, 1821. 16°. . *P,382
Great Events, described by Distinguished Historians. N.Y. 1847. 12°. A,24
Liebig, J. von. Analyse Chimique des Eaux Minerales. Paris, 1825. 8°. N,252,15
Analyse des Substances Organiques. Paris, 1838. 8°. . . N,252,15
Analyse Organischer Körper. Braunschweig, 1837. 8°. . . N,252,27
Animal Chemistry. Cambridge, 1842. 12°. . . . . . . N,233
Chemistry and Physics, Physiology and Pathology. Lond. 1846. 8°. N,252,32
Chemistry applied to Agriculture and Physiology. N. Y. 1856. 12°. M,540
Chemistry of Food. Lowell, 1848. 12°. . . . . . . . . N,173
Familiar Letters on Chemistry. New York, 1857. 12°. . . M,533,4
Handbuch der Organischen Chemie. Heidelberg, 1843. 8°. . . G,757
Motion of the Animal Juices. London, 1848. 8°. . . . . . L,936
Natural Laws of Husbandry. New York, 1863. 8°. . . . M,560
Studium der Naturwissenschaften. München, 1852. 8°. . . N,252,44
Studium der Naturwissenschaften in Preussen. Brschwg. 1840. 8°. N,252,7
Thier-Chemie. Braunschweig, 1846. 8°. . . . . . . . G,758
Thier-Chemie und Thier-Physiologie. Heidelberg, 1844. 8°. . N,252,7
Prüfung seiner Ackerbautherorie. F. G. Schulze. Jena, 1846. 8°. N,252,24
and others. Reports of Progress of Chemistry. Lond. 1849–53. 4 v. 8°. N,188
Lied, Das deutsche. A. Reissmann. Cassel, 1861. 8°. . . . . . G,644
Life, Art of Prolonging. C. W. Hufeland. Boston, 1854. 12°. . . . L,893
Christian Thought on. H. Giles. Boston, 1850. 16°. . . . P,77
Conduct of. R. W. Emerson. Boston, 1866. 12°. . . . . H,99
Economy of Human. R. Dodsley. London, 1809. 16°. . . . O,467
Here and There. N. P. Willis. New York, 1853. 12°. . . . H,78
in Italy and France in Olden Time. J. C. Colquhoun. Lond. 1868. 8°. D,709
in the Old World. F. Bremer. Philadelphia, 1860. 2 v. 8°. . V,416
in the Open Air. T. Winthrop. Boston, 1869. 16°. . . . H,42
Making the Best of. J. Johnson. London, 1868. 12°. . . . H,129
of Trust. G. Müller; edited by H. L. Wayland. Boston, 1870. 12°. P,43
on the Lakes; a Trip to Lake Superior. New York, 1836. 2 v. 12°. V,40
Theory of. S. T. Coleridge. Philadelphia, 1848. 12°. . . . P,291
Life and Alone. Boston, 1870. 16°. . . . . . . . . . . K,108
Life and Books. J. F. Boyes. London, 1859. 16°. . . . . . H,475
Life and Language, Philosophy of. F. von Schlegel. London, 1866. p. 8°. L,229
The same. New York, 1848. 12°. . . . . . . . . O,696
Life and Liberty in America. C. Mackay. New York, 1859. 12°. . . V,12
Life Drama, and other Poems. A. Smith. Boston, 1866. 16°. . . . I,425
Life Insurance, Annals and Anecdotes of. J. Francis. London, 1853. 12°. O,506
Lectures on. M. L. Knapp. Philadelphia, 1853. 8°. . . . O,494
Life and Death; a Novel. New York, 1871. 12°. . . . . . . K,208
Life and Death on the Ocean. H. Howe. New York, 1860. 8°. . . V,951
Life for a Life. D. M. Craik. New York, n. d. 12°. . . . . . K,660
The same. Leipzig, 1859. 2 v. in 1. 16°. . . . . . J,89
Life Saving Signal Book. H. J. Rogers. Baltimore, 1856. 8°. . . M,705
Life Thoughts from Discourses. H. W. Beecher. New York, 1866. 12°. . P,317
Life without and Life within. M. F. Ossoli. New York, 1869. 12°. . . U,94
Life's Lesson. C. G. F. Gore. Leipzig, 1857. 2 v. in 1. 16°. . . . J,187

Life's Secret. Mrs. H. Wood. Leipzig, 1867. 16°. . . . . . . J,523
Lifting the Veil. New York, 1870. 12°. . . . . . . . . . K,398
Light. J. Abbott. New York, 1871. 12°. . . . . . . . J,1730
and Electricity. J. Tyndall. New York, 1871. 12°. . . . N,29
Elements of. J. H. Kyan. London, 1838. 8°. . . . . . . N,31
Lectures on Polarized. J. Pereira. London, 1854. 16°. . . . N,19
Optice; sive de Reflexionibus, etc., Lucis. Sir I. Newton. Lond. 1706. 4°. N,30
Optics; or, the Reflections, etc., of. Sir I. Newton. Lond. 1730. 8°. N,27
Light of Nature Pursued. A. Tucker. Lond. 1852. 2 v. 8°. . . . P,104
The same. London, 1768–77. 3 v. in 5. 8°. . . . . P,313
Light of Nature; with other Treatises. N. Culverwel. London, 1854. 4°. P,311
Light on Shadowed Paths. T. S. Arthur. New York, 1864. 12°. . . K,6
Lights and Shadows of Irish Life. Mrs. S. C. Hall. Lond. 1838. 3 v. 12°. J,574
Lights and Shadows of Real Life. T. S. Arthur. Philadelphia, n. d. 16°. J,613
Lightfoot, J. On a Fresh Revision of Eng. New Testament. Lond. 1871. 12°. P,186
Lighthouse, Eddystone, Description of. J. Smeaton. London, 1791. f°. . Q,447
Lighthouses and Lightships. W. H. D. Adams. New York, 1870. 12°. M,1054
Construction and Illumination of. A. Stevenson. Lond. 1850. 12°. M,962
Lignac, J. A. V. L. de. L'Homme et la Femme, v. 1, 3. Lille, 1773–74. 8°. L,843
Like and Unlike. A. S. Roe. New York, 1869. 12°. . . . . . K,242
Lillo, G. Le Marchand de Londres, tragédie. Londres, 1767. 12°. . . H,855
Lilly and the Bee. S. Warren. Leipzig, 1851. 16°. . . . . . . J,514
Lily, J. Dramatic Works. London, 1858. 2 v. 16°. . . . . . I,748
Limes, Cements, and Mortars, Treatise on. G. R. Burnell. Lond. 1857. 12°. M,898
Limited Liability and Partnership Act. London, 1858–59. 12°. . . M,919
Limits of Religious Thought. H. L. Mansel. Boston, 1860. 12°. . . P,191
Limner, L. Suggestions in Design. London, 1853. 4°. . . . . *Q,166
Lincoln, A., Administration of. H. J. Raymond. New York, 1864. 12°. B,904
Expressions of Condolence at Death of. Washington, 1867. 4°. . Q,229
Life of. J. G. Holland. Springfield, Mass. 1866. 8°. . . . C,878
Life and Public Services of. H. J. Raymond. New York, 1865. 8°. C,886
Lincoln Memorial. W. T. Coggeshall. Columbus, 1865. 12°. . C,959
Six Months with. F. B. Carpenter. New York, 1866. 16°. . . C.916
and Douglas, S. A. Political Debates. Columbus, 1860. 8°. . . O,574
Lincoln, B., Life of. F. Bowen. Boston, 1860. 12°. . . . . . C,860,23
Linda; or, the Young Pilot. C. L. Hentz. Philadelphia, 1869. 12°. . K,176
Lindisfarm Chase. T. A. Trollope. New York, 1865. 8°. . . K,1054
Lindley, J. Flora Medica. London, 1838. 8°. . . . . . . N,1004
Introduction to Botany. London, 1835. 8°. . . . . . . N,978
Ladies' Botany. London, n. d. 2 v. 8°. . . . . . . N,1035
Natural System of Botany. London, 1836. 8°. . . . . N,1019
Pocket Botanical Dictionary. London, 1849. 8°. . . . . . N,943
Theory of Horticulture. London, 1840. 8°. . . . . . . M,564
Vegetable Kingdom. London, 1853. 8°. . . . . . . N,1003
and Hutton, W. Fossil Flora of Great Britain. Lond. 1831–7. 3 v. 8°. N,826
Lindner, E. O. Erste stehende Deutsche Oper. Berl. 1855. 2 v. 8° and 4°. G,743
Lindsay, A. W. C., *Lord*. Egypt, Holy Land. London, 1866. p. 8°. . . L,115
Lindsay, W. L. History of British Lichens. London, 1856. 16°. . . N,920
Linear Perspective. T. Bradley. London, n. d. 8°. . . . . . M,1131
explained. W. N. Bartholomew. Boston, 1866. 8°. . . . . M,210

Lingard, J. Antiquities of the Anglo-Saxon Church. Phil. 1848. 8°. . P,609
History of England. Boston, 1853–54. 8 v. 12°. . . . . A,405
The same. Paris, 1840. 13 v. 8°. . . . . . . . A,404
Lingard, R. Letter to a Young Gentleman. Dublin, 1670. 24°. . . P,2
Link, H. F. Bildung der Festen Körper. Berlin, 1841. 8°. . . N,252,21
Formation des Corps Solides. Berlin, 1841. 8°. . . . N,252,21
Icones Anatomico-Botanicae. Berlin, 1837–38. 3 v. in 1. f°. . Q,86
Reise durch Frankreich, Spanien, und Portugal. Kiel, 1801–4. 3 v. 12°. E,199
Linke, G. Bau der flachen Dächer. Braunschweig, 1841. 8°. . . N,252,19
Linn, E. A. and Sargent, N. Life of Lewis F. Linn. New York, 1857. 8°. C,1052
Linnæus, C. von. Dissertationes variæ. Lugd. Batav. 1749–85. 9 v. 8°. N,966
Species Plantarum. Vindobonae, 1764. 2 v. 8°. . . . . . N,964
Life of. D. H. Stoever. London, 1794. 4°. . . . . . . F,35
Linnean Society of London, Transactions of. London, 1868. 26 v. 4°. . F,129
Linsley, D. C. Morgan Horses. New York, 1859. 12°. . . . . M,462
Linton, E. L. Ourselves; Essays on Women. London, 1869. 16°. . . O,412
Lionel Lincoln. J. F. Cooper. New York, 1864. 12°. . . . . . K,34
The same. New York, 1859. 8°. . . . . . . . . K,64
Lions, Tigers, etc. Sir W. Jardine. Edinburgh, 1854. 16°. . . N,470,16
Lippincott, S. J. Forest Tragedy, and other Tales. Boston, 1856. 12°. . K,205
Haps and Mishaps of a Tour in Europe. Boston, 1854. 12°. . . V,356
Merrie England. Boston, 1863. 16°. . . . . . . J,1233
Poems. Boston, 1854. 16°. . . . . . . . . . . I,36
Records of Five Years. Boston, 1867. 16°. . . . . . H,284
Recollections of my Childhood. Boston, 1866. 16°. . . J,1461
Stories and Sights of France and Italy. Boston, 1867. 16°. . J,1322
Stories from Famous Ballads. Boston, 1866. 16°. . . . J,1246
Lippincott's Dict. of Biog. and Mythology. J. Thomas. Phil. 1870-71. 2 v. 8°. L.R.
Lippincott's Gazetteer of U. S. F. Baldwin and J. Thomas. Phil. 1854. 8°. L.R.
of the World. J. Thomas and T. Baldwin. Phil. 1870. 8°. L.R.
The same. Philadelphia, 1868. 8°. . . . . . R.R.
Lippincott's Magazine. Philadelphia, 1868–70. 5 v. 8°. . . . . T,47
List, F. National System of Political Economy. Philadelphia, 1856. 8°. O,554
Lister, T. H. Life of Edward Hyde, Earl of Clarendon. Lond. 1837–8. 3 v. 8°. D,218
The same. London, 1837–38. 3 v. 8°. . . . . . D,218
Litchfield Co., Conn., Centennial Celebration. Hartford, 1851. 8°. . . C,79
Literary Almanac, 1852. C. B. Norton. New York, 1851. 12°. . . L.R.
Literary and Educational Register. C. B. Norton. New York, 1854. 12°. L.R.
Literary Character; Men of Genius. I. Disraeli. London, 1859. 8°. . H,651
Literary Characters and Celebrated Places. A.T. Thomson. Lond. 1854. 2 v. 12°. H,396
Literary Hours; Sketches. N. Drake. Sudbury, 1800. 2 v. 8°. . . H,28
Literary Men of America. J. Wynne. New York, 1850. 12°. . . C,1045
Literary Portraits. G. Gilfillan. Edinburgh, 1856–57. 2 v. 8°. . . C,505
Literary Recreations and Miscellanies. J. G. Whittier. Bost. 1855. 16°. H,209
Literary, Scientific, and Mechanics' Institutions. J. Hole. Lond. 1853. 8°. O,1016
Literature, Amenities of. I. Disraeli. London, 1859. 2 v. 8°. . . H,647
The same. New York, 1855. 2 v. 12°. . . . . . H,653
Ancient and Modern. Mad. de Staël Holstein. London, 1803. 2 v. 8°. H,643
and Art, Afternoon Lectures in Dublin. London, 1863–69. 5 v. 12°. H,566
Cyclopædia of Anecdotes of. K. Arvine. Boston, 1870. 8°. . H,670

Literature and Art, Papers on. M. F. Ossoli. New York, 1846. 12°. . H,644
and Life, Lectures on. E. P. Whipple. Boston, 1853. 16°. . . H,207
and Literary Men of Great Britain. A. Mills. N. Y. 1851. 2 v. 8°. H,710
and Politics, Register of, for 1827. Edinburgh, 1828. 16°. . . I,505
and Science, Objects and Uses of. A. Potter. New York, 1858. 16°. L,461
Characteristics of. H. T. Tuckerman. Philadelphia, 1851. 12°. . H,696
Cours de Littérature. J. F. de La Harpe. Paris, 1838–9. 18 v. in 9. 8°. H,646
Curiosities of. I. Disraeli. London, 1858. 3 v. 8°. . . . H,650
Eléments de Littérature. J. F. Marmontel. Paris, 1854. 3 v. 12°. H,640
Essays illustrative of. A. Jameson. London, 1846. 12°. . . M,22
in Letters. J. P. Holcombe. New York, 1866. 8°. . . . . H,219
Lectures on General. J. Montgomery. New York, 1855. 16°. . L,385
Lectures on the History of. F. von Schlegel. London, 1868. 12°. L,230
Miscellanies of. I. Disraeli. New York, 1841. 3 v. 12°. . . H,652
of Europe in 15th, 16th, and 17th Cent. H. Hallam. Bost. 1854. 3 v. 8°. H,738
The same. New York, 1851. 2 v. 8°. . . . . . . H,739
of the Age of Elizabeth. E. P. Whipple. Boston, 1869. 12°. . . H,702
of the South of Europe. J. C. L. S. de Sismondi. N. Y. 1848. 2 v. 12°. H,764
The same. London, 1850. 2 v. p. 8°. . . . . . . L,236
Philosophy of. G. W. F. Hegel. London, 1861. p. 8°. . . . L,249
Pleasures, Objects, and Advantages of. R. A. Willmott. Lond. 1857. 16°. H,638
Pursuits of; a Satirical Poem. T. J. Mathias. London, 1803. 8°. . J,872
Rise and Progress of. Sir D. K. Sandford. Glasgow, 1847. 16°. . H,639
Studies in. G. W. Griffin. Baltimore, 1870. 12°. . . . . H,645
Tables of English. H. Morley. London, 1870. f°. . . *F,173
See also *American Literature, English, French, German, etc.*

Littérature Française Contemporaine. J. M. Quérard. Paris, 1842–57. 6v. 8°. L.R.
Littell, E. Select Reviews. Philadelphia, n. d. 8°. . . . . . H,618
Littell's Living Age. Boston, 1844–69. 103 v. 8°. . . . . . S,8
Little Agnes Library. H. N. Baker. Boston, 1868. 4 v. 16°. . . . J,1699

Vol. 1. Little Agnes. Vol. 3. I'll Try.
2. Trying to be useful. 4. Art and Artlessness.

Little Book open. J. B. Hall. Cincinnati, 1869. 16°. . . . . . I,28
Little Coin much Care. M. Howitt. New York, 1867. 24°. . . . J,1184
Little Dorrit. C. Dickens. New York, 1868. 12°. . . . . . . K,479
The same. Philadelphia, 1857. 8°. . . . . . K,511
The same. New York, 1871. 2 v. 12°. . . . . K,1133
The same. Leipzig, 1856–57. 4 v. 16°. . . . . J,125
Little Ferns. S. P. Parton. New York, 1868. 16°. . . . . . J,1496
Little Foxes. H. B. Stowe. Boston, 1869. 16°. . . . . . . . H,280
Little Henry and his Bearer. M. M. Sherwood. New York, 1860. 12°. K,1008,3
Little Lou's Sayings and Doings. E. Prentiss. New York, 1868. 8°. J,1340
Little Lucy and her Dhaye. M. M. Sherwood. New York, 1860. 12°. K,1008,3
Little Men; Life at Plumfield with Jo's Boys. L. M. Alcott. Bost. 1871. 16°. K,267
Little Paul. C. Dickens. New York, n. d. 16°. . . . . . J,1187
Little Peanut Merchant. M. A. Atkins. Boston, 1869. 16°. . . . J,1657
Little Pedlington and the Pedlingtonians. J. Poole. New York, 1852. 2 v. 12°. K,1097
Little Women. L. M. Alcott. Boston, 1870. 2 v. 16°. . . . . K,3
Littrow, J. J. von. Theoretische u. Pract. Astronomie. Wien, 1821–27. 3 v. 8°. G,782
Wunder des Himmels. Stuttgart, 1837. 8°. . . . . . . G,783

Littrow, J. J. von. Wunder des Himmels. Stuttgart, 1854. 8°. . . . G,784
Liturgy of Church of England, Discourses on. M. Hole. Lond. 1837. 4 v. 8°. P,899
Faith of. F. D. Maurice. London, 1860. 12°. . . . P,886
Live and Learn, Guide to Grammar, etc. New York, 1856. 12°. . . L,564
Live and Learn. H. N. Baker. Boston, 1869. 16°. . . . . . . J,1694
Livermore, Kate. M. Lee. New York, 1865. 16°. . . . . . J,1359
Live and Let Live. C. M. Sedgwick. New York, 1861. 18°. . . . J,1179
Lives of Eminent Persons. London, n. d. 8°. . . . . . . . . C,581

Galileo, by J. E. D. Bethune.
J. Kepler, by J. E. D. Bethune.
I. Newton, by J. B. Biot.
Mahomet, by J. A. Roebuck.
T. Wolsey, by A. T. Thomson.
Sir E. Coke, by E. P. Burke.
Lord J. Somers, by T. Jardine.
W. Caxton, by Stephenson.
R. Blake, by J. Gorton.
Adam Smith, by W. Draper.
C. Niebuhr, by S. Austin.
Sir C. Wren, by H. B. Ker.
Michael Angelo, by T. Roscoe.

of Foreigners Eminent in Piety. Dublin, 1796. 12°. . . . C,535
of Individuals raised from Poverty. London, 1841. 16°. . . I,636
of Remarkable Characters. London, 1814. 3 v. 8°. . . . C,1252
Records of Noble. W. H. D. Adams. London, 1870. 12°. . . C,1243
Living for Appearances. H. and A. Mayhew. London, 1855. 16°. . . J,636
Living, Philosophy of. H. Mayo. Philadelphia, 1852. 12°. . . . L,884
C. Ticknor. New York, 1855. 16°. . . . . . . . L,393
Living to Purpose. J. Johnson. London, 1868. 12°. . . . . H,129
Livingston, E., Life of. C. H. Hunt. New York, 1864. 8°. . . . C,880
Livingstone, D. Expedition to the Zambesi, 1858–64. New York, 1866. 8°. V,867
Missionary Travels in South Africa. New York, 1858. 8°. . . V,864
The same. New York, 1858. 8°. . . . . . . . S.C.
Missionsreisen in Süd-Afrika. Leipzig, 1858. 2 v. in 1. 8°. . . E,229
Live and Adventures of. H. G. Adams. London, n. d. 12°. . . D,366
Livius, T. Opera Omnia; curante. N. E. Lemaire. Paris, 1822. 12 v. 8°. U,327
History of Rome; tr. by D. Spillan and others. Lond. 1854. 4 v. p. 8°. L,66
The same; translated by G. Baker. London, 1822. 6 v. 8°. A,156
The same. New York, 1844–55. 5 v. 18°. . . . . U,368
Llewellyn, E. L. Deserted Mill; or, Reward of Industry. Bost. 1870. 16°. J,1683
Lloyd, C. A. A. Agricultural Chemistry. Shrewsbury, 1840. 8°. . N,252,6
Lloyd, H. E. Englische Sprachlehre für Deutsche. Hamburg, 1837. 12°. L,774
Lloyd, H. H. Atlas of Ohio and United States. New York, 1868. f°. *Q,392
Lloyd, Sir W. Journey from Caunpoor to Himalaya Mts. Lond. 1840. 2 v. 8°. V,751
Locke Amsden, the Schoolmaster. D. P. Thompson. Boston, 1848. 12°. K,350
Locke, D. R. Ekkoes from Kentucky. Boston, 1868. 12°. . . . H,70
Nasby; Divers Views, etc. Cincinnati, 1867. 12°. . . . H,71
Locke, J. Conduct of the Understanding. New York, 1868. 16°. . . L,454
Essay on the Human Understanding. London, 1866. 12°. . . M,838
Letters; edited by T. Forster. London, 1830. 8°. . . . . . H,612
Life of. Sir P. King. London, 1864. p. 8°. . . . . . . L,206
Philosophical Works. London, 1854. 2 v. p. 8°. . . . . . L,205

Vol. 1. Essay concerning the Human Understanding.
2. The same, concluded; Appendix; Examination of Malebranche's Opinion of seeing all things in God; Elements of Natural Philosophy; Reading and Study for a Gentleman.

Thoughts concerning Education. London, 1693. 8°. . . . . O,916
The same; edited by J. A. St. John. London, 1836. 16°. . O,992

Locke, J. Works. London, 1722–27. 3 v. f°. . . . . . . Q,312

Vol. 1. Essay concerning Human Understanding; Defenses of the same.
2. Essays on Money and Coinage; On Toleration; Reasonableness of Christianity; Vindications of the same.
3. Some Thoughts Concerning Education; Paraphrase and Notes on the Epistles of St. Paul; Posthumous Works; Letters.

Locke, J. Address on Agricultural Chemistry. Lebanon, Ohio, 1854. 8°. T,19,2
Locke, R. A. Moon Hoax. New York, 1859. 8°. . . . . . . N,347
Lockhart, J. G. Ancient Spanish Ballads. New York, 1842. 8°. . . J,862
Court and Camp of Napoleon I. London, 1829. 16°. . . . I,609
History of Napoleon I. London, 1829. 2 v. 16°. . . . . . I,608
The same. New York, 1868. 2 v. 16°. . . . . L,337
Life of Adam Blair and Matthew Wald. Edinburgh, 1849. 16°. . K,805
Life of Robert Burns. Edinburgh, 1828. 16°. . . . . . I,506
Life of Sir Walter Scott. Edinburgh, 1837–38. 7 v. 12°. . . D,175
The same. New York, 1851. 8 v. in 4. 12°. . . . C,1168
Lockhart Papers; from MSS. in possession of A. Aufrere. Lond. 1817. 2 v. 4°. F,266
Locks, Construction of. C. Tomlinson. London, 1858–59. 12°. . . M,967
Fire and Thief-Proof. G. Price. London, 1856. 8°. . . . M,660
Lockyer, J. N. Elementary Lessons in Astronomy. London, 1868. 16°. N,255
Locomotive Engine. Z. Colburn. Philadelphia, 1854. 12°. . . . M,634
Locomotive Engines. G. S. Dempsey. London, 1857. 12°. . . . M,905
Atlas to the same. London, 1859. 4°. . . . . . . Q,366
Locomotive Engineers, Water for. W. West. London, 1846. 8°. . N,292,39
Lodge, E. Illustrations of British History. London, 1791. 3 v. 4°. . F,276
The same. London, 1838. 3 v. 8°. . . . . . . A,524
Peerage and Baronetage of British Empire. London, 1870. 8°. *C,624
Portraits of Personages of Great Britain. Lond. 1849–50. 8 v. 8°. *L,116
Lodge, T. Defense of Poetry, Music, and Stage-Plays. London, 1853. 8°. I,885,49
Löwenthal, J. Games of the Chess Congress. London, 1864. p. 8°. . L,286
Löwig, K. Organic and Physiological Chemistry. Philadelphia, 1853. 8°. N,194
Loftus, W. K. Geology of the Turko-Persian Frontier. Lond. 1855. 8°. N,252,44
Travels in Chaldæa and Susiana. New York, 1857. 8°. . . . V,684
Lofty and the Lowly. M. J. McIntosh. New York, 1852. 2 v. 12°. . K,213
Log of the Water Lily. R. B. Mansfield. Leipzig, 1854. 16°. . . J,346
Logan, and Murder of Logan's Family. J. Doddridge. Cincinnati, 1868. 4°. I,730
Logan, J. Scottish Gaël; or, Celtic Manners. Hartford, n. d. 8°. . . B,127
Logan, O. Before the Footlights and behind the Scenes. Phil. 1870. 18°. I,719
Women and Theaters. New York, 1870. 12°. . . . . . I,720
Logan, W. E. Geological Survey of Canada, 1845, 49, 53, 56. Montreal and Toronto, 1845–57. 3 v. 8° and 4°. . . . . . . . . *N,870
Logarithms, Treatise on, and Tables. H. Law. London, 1859. 12°. . M,946
Tables. n. t. p. 8°. . . . . . . . . . . . M,1130
Tables. London, 1839. 16°. . . . . . . . . . M,1110
Tafeln. G. F. von Vega; hrsg. von J. A. Hülsse. Leipzig, 1840. 8°. E,436
Logé, Henri. Dictionnaire de Morale, Choix de Pensées. Brux. 1844. 12°. H,1034
Logic, and Metaphysics, Lectures on. Sir W. Hamilton. Bost. 1859–67. 2 v. 8°. O,704
and Rhetoric. R. Whately. London, 1855. p. 8°. . . . . . O,726
Elements of. H. Coppée. Philadelphia, 1870. 12°. . . . O,733
H. A. Day. New York, 1867. 12°. . . . . . . O,728
R. Whately. Boston, 1860. 12°. . . . . . . . O,727
Formal Logic. A. De Morgan. London, 1847. 8°. . . . . O,730

Logic, Grundriss der Logik. J. F. Fries. Heidelberg, 1827. 12°. . . G,554
in Theology. I. Taylor. New York, 1860. 12°. . . . . . P,81
im Abendlande, Geschichte der. C. Prantl. Leipzig, 1855-67. 3 v. 8°. G,568
or, the Science of Inference. J. Devey. London, 1854. p. 8°. . L,253
System of. P. Mac Gregor. New York, 1862. 12°. . . . O,628
J. S. Mill. London, 1868. 2 v. 8°. . . . . . . O,738
The same. New York, 1855. 8°. . . . . . . O,729
Treatise on. S. H. Emmens. London, 1865. 12°. . . . . M,837
Lois, the Witch. E. C. Gaskell. Leipzig, 1861. 16°. . . . . . J,177
Loménie, L. L. de. Beaumarchais and his Times. London, 1856. 4 v. 8°. D,660
The same. New York, 1857. 12°. . . . . . . D,648
London. C. Knight. London, 1851. 6 v. in 3. 8°. . . . . . . A,564
and its Celebrities. J. H. Jesse. London, 1850. 2 v. 8°. . . B,61
Bridge, Chronicles of. London, 1839. 16°. . . . . . . I,619
Club Life of. J. Timbs. London, 1866. 2 v. 12°. . . . B,58
Curiosities of. J. Timbs. London, 1855. 16°. . . . . . V,298
Customs of. R. Arnold. London, 1811. 4°. . . . . . F,154
Entomological Society, Transactions, 1834-62. Lond. 1836-64. 11 v. 8°. *R,13
Exhibition of 1851. J. Timbs. London, 1851. 16°. . . . . M,811
Official and Illustrated Catalogue. London, 1852. 3 v. 4°. . *F,239
Description of Crystal Palace, Tallis's. Lond. n. d. 2 v. 4°. S.C.
Illustrated Catalogue. See *Art Journal*, 1851.
Reports by Juries. London, 1852. 3 v. 4°. . . . . *F,240
Exhibition of 1862. J. Timbs. London, 1863. 16°. . . . . M,812
Illustriter Katalog der. W. Hamm. Leipzig, 1863-64. 2 v. 4°. *F,175
Geological Society, Quarterly Journal. London, 1845-68. 24 v. 8°. *R,38
Index to Publications of. G. W. Ormerod. London, 1858. 8°. *R,26
Proceedings, 1826-45, v. 1-4. London, 1837-46. 8°. . . *R,39
Transactions. London, 1811-56. 12 v. 4°. . . . . . *R,25
Her Majesty's Tower. W. H. Dixon. Leipzig, 1869-70. 2 v. in 1. 16°. J,149
Here and There in. J. E. Ritchie. London, 1859. 16°. . . V,312
History of. H. Hunter. London, 1811. 4°. . . . . . . F,277
History of the Public Charities of. A. Highmore. Lond. 1810. 8°. O,418
Horticultural Society, Transactions. London, 1815-48. 10 v. 4°. . *F,83
in 1850-51. J. R. McCulloch. London, 1865. p. 8°. . . . . I,667
Labor and London Poor. H. Mayhew. London, 1851-62. 4 v. 8°. O,360
Linnean Society, Transactions of. London, 1791-1865. 26 v. 4°. *F,129
Literary and Historical Memorials of. J. H. Jesse. Lond. 1847. 2 v. 8°. B,62
Malaria of. A. Ure. London, 1850. 8°. . . . . . . . N,252.29
Memorials of, 1276-1419; edited by H. T. Riley. London, 1868. r. 8°. F,261
Microscopical Society, Transactions of. v. 2, 3. Lond. 1849-52. 8°. *R,35
Munimenta Gildhallæ. London, 1859-62. 4 v. 8°. . . . . W,162
Night Side of. J. E. Ritchie. London, 1869. 8°. . . . . . V,294
Northern Heights of. W. Howitt. London, 1869. 8°. . . . . B,66
Photographic Society, Journal of Transactions. Lond. 1864-57. 3 v. 8°. *R,33
Pictorial Hand-Book of. London, 1854. 12°. . . . . . . L,136
Public Buildings of. J. Britton. London, 1823-28. 2 v. 4°. *Q,344
Queen's College, Introductory Lectures. London, 1849. 16°. . . H,392
Residence at the Court of. R. Rush. London, 1833. 8°. . . V,389
The same. Philadelphia, 1833. 8°. . . . . . . . V,401

London, Royal College of Surgeons, Fossils in Museum. London, 1845. 4°. Q,9
Index to Library Catalogue. London, 1853–55. . . . L.R.
Royal Geographical Society Journal. London, 1833–66. 36 v. 8°. *R,43
Index to v. 1–30. J. R. Jackson. London, 1844. 8°. . . *R,44
Royal Institution of. Lectures on Education. London, 1854. 8°. O,1177
Royal Society, Catalogue of Scientific Papers. Lond. 1867–70. 4 v. 4°. L.R.
History of. T. Thomson. London, 1812. 4°. . . . F,165
C. R. Weld. London, 1848. 2 v. 8°. . . . . F,164
Philosophical Transactions. London, 1749–1860. 124 v. *F,81
Abstracts, 1800–50. London, 1832–51. 5 v. 8°. . . *F,151
Report of Committee of Physics. London, 1840. 8°. . N,252,33
Shades and Echoes of Old. J. Stoughton. London, n. d. 12°. J,1277
Seven Curses of. J. Greenwood. Boston, 1869. 12°. . . . H,118
Society of Arts, Lectures. New York, 1854. 12°. . . . . M,609
Transactions, 1783–1844. London, 1789–1845. 55 v. 8°. . *R,37
Unhealthiness of. H. Gavin. London, 1847. 8°. . . . N,252,29
Vestiges of Old, Etchings. J. W. Archer. London, 1851. f°. *Q,308
Walk from, to John O'Groat's. E. Burritt. London, 1864. 12°. . V,375
Walk from, to Land's End. E. Burritt. London, 1868. 12°. . . V,395
Water Supply of. Sir W. Clay. London, 1849. 8°. . . N,252,39
J. L. Tabberner. London, 1847. 8°. . . . . . N,252,39
Water-Works of. W. Matthews. London, 1835. 8°. . . . N,129
World of. J. F. Murray. Edinburgh, 1843. 2 v. 12°. . . V,293
London Magazine, v. 26. London, 1757. 8°. . . . . . . . T,30
London Playgoer, Journal of a. H. Morley. London, 1866. 12°. . . I,709
London Romance. C. H. Ross. Leipzig, 1869. 2 v. in 1. 16°. . . J,428
Londiniana. E. W. Brayley. London, 1829. 4 v. 16°. . . . . . V,296
Long, E. History of Jamaica. London, 1774. 3 v. 4°. . . . . . B,831
Long, G. Egyptian Antiquities in Brit. Museum. Lond. 1832–6. 2 v. 16°. L,474
France and its Revolutions. London, 1850. r. 8°. . . . . . F,223
and Porter, G. R. Geography of Great Britain. London, n. d. 8°. V,1126
Long Island, History of. B. F. Thompson. New York, 1839. 8°. . . C,99
Long Look Ahead. A. S. Roe. New York, 1869. 12°. . . . . . K,244
Longacre, J. B. and Herring, J. Nat. Portrait Gallery. Phil. 1836–9. 4 v. 4°. S.C.
Longchamps, E. De S. Monographie des Libellulidées. Paris, 1840. 8°. . O,38
Longfellow, H. W. Flower-de-Luce. Boston, 1867. 16°. . . . . . I,66
Golden Legend. Boston, 1859. 16°. . . . . . . . . . I,67
New-England Tragedies. Boston, 1868. 16°. . . . . . . I,69
Outre-mer. Boston, 1852. 16°. . . . . . . . . . . V,315
Poems. Philadelphia, 1848. 8°. . . . . . . . . . I,178
The same. Boston, 1869. 2 v. 16°. . . . . . . I,65
Vol. 1. Miscellaneous Poems.
2. Evangeline; The Golden Legend; Hiawatha; Miles Standish.
Poetical Works. London, 1864. p. 8°. . . . . . . . L,117
Poets and Poetry of Europe. Philadelphia, 1847. 8°. . . . H,668
Prose Works. London, 1863. p. 8°. . . . . . . . . L,118
The same. Boston, 1866. 2 v. 16°. . . . . . . U,1
Vol. 1. Outre-mer; Driftwood. Vol. 2. Hyperion; Kavanagh.
Sang von Hiawatha; übersetzt von F. Freiligrath. N.Y. 1852. 12°. E,323,2
Song of Hiawatha. Boston, 1868. 16°. . . . . . . . . I,70
Tales of a Wayside Inn. Boston, 1863. 12°. . . . . . . I,71

Longley, E. American Manual of Phonography. Cincinnati, 1853. 12°. . L,688
Longman, W. Lectures on the History of England, v. 1. Lond. 1863. 8°. A,438
Longridge, J. A. Steam Jet as Motor for Ventilation. Newcastle, 1852. 8°. N,252,56
Longstreet, A. B. Georgia Scenes. New York, 1840. 12°. . . . . V,38
Longueville, Mad., Youth of. V. Cousin. New York, 1854. 12°. . . D,625
Longus. Greek Romances; translated by R. Smith. London, 1855. p. 8. L,58
Loo Choo and Eastern Seas, Voyage to. B. Hall. Edinburgh, 1826–27. 16°. I,492,1
Looker-on, The. W. Roberts. Boston, 1866. 3 v. 8°. . . H,536,35–37
Looking Around. A. S. Roe. New York, 1869. 12°. . . . . K,245
Looking-Glass for the Mind, New York, n. d. 18°. . . . . J,1298
Looking toward Sunset. L. M. Child. Boston, 1867. 12°. . . . H,294
Loomis, A. W. Confucius and the Chinese Classics. San Fran. 1867. 12°. G,5
Loomis, E. Introduction to Practical Astronomy. New York, 1855. 8°. N,359
Progress of Astronomy. New York, 1851. 12°. . . . . N,272
Treatise on Meteorology. New York, 1868. 8°. . . . . N,109
Loomis, J. R. Anatomy, Physiology, and Hygiene. New York, 1860. 12°. L,874
Lorain, P. Abrége du Diction. de l'Académie Française. Paris, 1838. 2 v. 8°. L.R.
Lord, C. F. J. Sources of Bodily and Mental Disease. Lond. 1847. 8°. N,252,29
Lord, E. Epoch of Creation. New York, 1851. 12°. . . . . P,134
Lord, J. Ancient History. New York, 1870. 8°. . . . . . . A,13
Ancient States and Empires. New York, 1869. 8°. . . . . A,12
Modern History from Luther to Napoleon. Philadelphia, 1849. 12°. A,317
Old Roman World. New York, 1868. 8°. . . . . . . A,154
Lord, W. W. Christ in Hades; a Poem. New York, 1851. 12°. . . I,85
Poems. New York, 1845. 12°. . . . . . . . . . I,80
Lord Erlistoun, etc. D. M. Craik. Leipzig, 1864. 16°. . . . . J,557
Lord Mayor of London. W. H. Ainsworth. London, n. d. 12°. . . J,560
The same. Leipzig, 1862. 2 v. in 1. 16°. . . . . J,15
Lord Montagu's Page. G. P. R. James. Philadelphia, 1858. 12°. . . K,736
Lord Oakburn's Daughters. Mrs. H. Wood. Leipzig, 1864. 2 v. in 1. 16°. J,524
Lorelei. E. Hoefer. Stuttgart, 1862. 24°. . . . . . . . . G,324
Lorenzana, F. A. Historia de Méjico. New York, 1828. 8°. . . . C,370
Lorenzo Benoni. G. Ruffini. New York, 1860. 12°. . . . . . K,913
The same. Leipzig, 1861. 16°. . . . . . . . J,432
Lorgnette; or, Studies of the Town. D. G. Mitchell. N. Y. 1851. 2 v. 12°. H,21
Lorrimer Littlegood. F. E. Smedley. Philadelphia, n. d. 12°. . K,1015
Lossing, B. J. Eminent Americans. New York, 1857. 8°. . . . C,981
History of the Fine Arts. New York, 1854. 18°. . . . . L,408
History of the United States, Common-School. New York, 1866. 12°. B,594
Pictorial. Hartford, 1868. 8°. . . . . . B,708
Primary. New York, 1864. 16°. . . . . B,595
Home of Washington. New York, 1866. 8°. . . . . . C,912
Hudson River, from the Wilderness to the Sea. New York, 1869. 8°. V,70
Pictorial Description of Ohio. New York, 1848. 8°. . . . C,205
Pictorial Field-Book of the Revolution. New York, 1860. 2 v. 8°. B,751
of the War of 1812. New York, 1865. 8°. . . . B,874
Signers of the Declaration of Independence. Cincinnati, 1854. 12°. C,1046
Lost and Saved. C. E. S. Norton. Leipzig, 1863. 2 v. in 1. 16°. . . J,393
Lost and Won. G. M. Craik. Leipzig, 1862. 16°. . . . . . J,98
Lost Cause; Southern History of the War. E. A. Pollard. N. Y. 1867. 8°. B,922

Lost Daughter. C. L. Hentz. Philadelphia, 1870. 12°. . . . . . K,458
Lost Heiress. E. D. E. N. Southworth. Philadelphia, 1870. 12°. . . K,431
Lost in Ceylon. W. Dalton. London, 1861. 16°. . . . . . J,1508
Lost in the Fog. J. De Mille. Boston, 1871. 16°. . . . . . J,1507
Lost in the Jungle. P. Du Chaillu. New York, 1870. 12°. . . J,1291
Lost Lenore. M. Reid. New York, 1870. 12°. . . . . . J,1566
Lost Love. A. Owen. Boston, 1871. 12°. . . . . . . . . K,872
Lost Name. J. S. Le Fanu. New York, 1868. 8°. . . . . . . K,765
Lost Prince, Louis XVII., identified. J. H. Hanson. New York, 1854. 12°. D,575
Lost Tribes, The; Saxons, Buddhism, etc. G. Moore. London, 1861. 8°. N,432
Loth, M. Our Prospects; a Tale of Real Life. Cincinnati, 1870. 8°. . K,409
Lothair. B. Disraeli. New York, 1870. 12°. . . . . . . . K,674
The same. Leipzig, 1870. 2 v. in 1. 16°. . . . . . J,143
Lothrop, S. K. Life of Samuel Kirkland. Boston, 1860. 12°. . C,860,25
Lott, E. Harem Life in Egypt and Constantinople. Lond. 1866. 2 v. 12°. V,788
Lottery, The. M. Edgeworth. New York, 1860. 12°. . . . K,678,2
Lotus-Eating. G. W. Curtis. New York, 1852. 12°. . . . . . . V,103
Loudon, J. C. Arboretum et Fruticetum Britannicum. Lond. 1844. 8 v. in 6. 8°. N,990
Loudon, J. C. Encyclopædia of Agriculture. London, 1844. 8°. . *M,574
Encyclopædia of Cottage Architecture. London, 1860. 8°. . *M,166
Horticulturist. London, 1860. 8°. . . . . . . . . . M,543
Villa Gardener. London, 1850. 8°. . . . . . . . . . M,357
(Ed.) Architectural Magazine. London, 1834–38. 5 v. 8°. . . M,265
Loudon, J. W. Entertaining Naturalist. London, 1867. 8°. . . . N,646
The same. London, 1867. p. 8°. . . . . . . . . L,119
Light of Mental Science. London, 1845. 12°. . . . . . . O,994
Young Naturalist's Journey. London, 1851. 16°. . . . . . N,620
Louie's Last Term at St. Mary's. M. Cole. New York, 1866. 12°. . . K,15
Louis IX., Saint, and John Calvin. F. Guizot. Philadelphia, 1869. 12°. D,655
Crusade of. J. *Sieur* de Joinville. London, 1870. p. 8°. . . . L,5
History of. J. *Sieur* de Joinville. London, 1868. 16°. . . . I,564
Louis XIV., Age of. H. Martin. Boston, 1865. 2 v. 8°. . . . . . B,369
and Court of France in 17th Century. J. Pardoe. N.Y. 1865. 2 v. 12°. D,643
and William III. Letters; ed. by P. Grimblot. Lond. 1848. 2 v. 8°. A,555
and the Writers of his Age. J. F. Astié. Boston, 1855. 12°. . . H,758
Life and Times of. G. P. R. James. London, 1851. 2 v. 12°. . L,198
Memoirs of L. de R. St. Simon. London, 1857. 4 v. 12°. . . D,661
Siècle de. F. M. A. de Voltaire. Paris, 1856. 12°. . . . . B,335
Louis XV., Siècle de. F. M. A. de Voltaire Paris, 1854. 12°. . . . B,336
Louis XVI., Private Memoirs of. A. F. B. de Moleville. London, 1797. 8°. D,677
Louis XVII., Life and Captivity of. A. de Beauchesne. N.Y. 1853. 2 v. 12°. D,646
Louis XVIII. and Charles X., Hist. of Reigns. E. E. Crowe. Lond. 1854. 2v. 8°. B,263
Louis's School-Days. E. J. May. New York, 1870. 12°. . . . J,1643
Louisa of Prussia and her Times. C. Mundt. New York, 1867. 8°. . G,206
Louise la Valliere. A. Dumas. Philadelphia, n. d. 8°. . . . . . H,987
Louisiana, Histoire de la. Le Page du Pratz. Paris, 1758. 3 v. 12°. . C,190
Historical Collections of. B. F. French. New York, 1846–50. 2 v. 8°. C,191
History of. F. de Barbé-Marbois. Philadelphia, 1830. 8°. . . C,187
E. Bunner. New York, 1855. 18°. . . . . . . L,458
C. Gayarré. New York, 1866. 3 v. 8°. . . . . . C,194

Louisiana, Views of. H. M. Brackenridge. Pittsburgh, 1814. 8°. . . . v,165
Lounger, The. H. Mackenzie and others. Boston, 1866. 2 v. 8°. . H,536,30,31
L'Ouverture, T. See *Toussaint l'Ouverture.*
Louvet de Couvret, J. B., Mémoires. Paris, 1848. 12°. . . . . D,609,2
Louvre, The; Biography of a Museum. B. St. John. London, 1855. 8°. v,457
Lovat, S. Lord, Life of. J. H. Burton. London, 1847. 8°. . . . . D,202
Love. J. Michelet. New York, 1869. 12°. . . . . . . . . H,911
after Marriage. C. L. Hentz. Philadelphia, 1870. 12°. . . . K,460
and Law. M. Edgeworth. New York, 1859. 12°. . . . K,678,8
and Liberty. A. Dumas. Philadelphia, 1870. 12°. . . . . H,977
and Mesmerism. H. Smith. London, 1845. 3 v. 12°. . . K,1010
and Money. M. Howitt. New York, 1867. 24°. . . . . J,1163
the Avenger. Leipzig, 1869. 2 v. in 1. 16°. . . . . . . J,301
Law of, and Love as a Law. M. Hopkins. New York, 1869. 16°. O,714
Love me Little, Love me Long. C. Reade. Boston, 1869. 16°. . . K,902
The same. Leipzig, 1859. 16°. . . . . . . . . J,419
Love Elegies. J. Hammond. n. p. n. d. . . . . . . . . . I,325
Love Songs, French; translated by H. Curwen. New York, 1871. 16°. . H,858
Love Story, from "The Doctor." R. Southey. London, 1865. p. 8°. I,664,2
Love's Conflict. F. Church. Leipzig, 1865. 2 v. in 1. 16°. . . . J,349
Love's Labor Won. E. D. E. N. Southworth. Philadelphia, 1870. 12°. . K,432
Loved at Last. M. Lemon. Leipzig, 1865. 2 v. in 1. 16°. . . . J,266
Lovel, the Widower. W. M. Thackeray. Leipzig, 1861. 16°. . . . J,483
Lovejoy, E. P.; Riots at Alton, and his Death. E. Beecher. Alton, 1838. 8°. C,158
Lover, S. Handy Andy. London, n. d. 12°. . . . . . . . . K,799
Rory O'More. London, n. d. 16°. . . . . . . . . K,800
Lovers and Thinkers. H. Gordon. New York, 1865. 12°. . . . K,128
Lovers of Gudrun; a Poem. W. Morris. Boston, 1870. 12°. . . . I,339
Loves of the Poets. A. Jameson. Boston, 1857. 18°. . . . . H,561
Lovewell, J., Expeditions of. F. Kidder. Boston, 1865. 4°. . . . B,888
Low, S. English Catalogue of Books, 1835–62. London, 1864. 8°. . . L.R.
Supplements, 1863–70. London, 1864–71. 8°. . . . L.R.
Lowe, E. J. Beautiful Leaved Plants. London, 1865. 8°. . . *N,1037
Lowe, G. Patent for Improvements in Gas. London, 1847. 8°. . N,252,39
Lowe's Edinburgh Magazine, 7th series, v. 2. Edinburgh, 1847. 8°. . S,43
Lowell, Mass., as it was and is. H. A. Miles. Lowell, 1845. 18°. . . C,37
Lowell, A. C. Gleanings from the Poets. Boston, 1862. 12°. . . I,96
Seed-Grain for Thought and Discussion. Boston, 1856. 2 v. 16°. H,186
Lowell, J. R. Among my Books. Boston, 1870. 12°. . . . . . H,239
Biglow Papers. Cambridge, 1848–67. 2 v. 12°. . . . . . I,8
Cathedral. Boston, 1870. 12°. . . . . . . . . . . I,51
Conversations on some of the Old Poets. Cambridge, 1845. 16°. . H,676
Fable for Critics. New York, 1848. 12°. . . . . . . I,95
Fireside Travels. Boston, 1865. 12°. . . . . . . . . V,310
My Study Windows. Boston, 1871. 12°. . . . . . . . . H,227
Poems. Boston, 1853–54. 2 v. 16°. . . . . . . . I,84
Under the Willows. Boston, 1869. 16°. . . . . . . . I,83
Vision of Sir Launfal. Boston, 1858. 16°. . . . . . . I,82
Year's Life. Boston, 1841. 12°. . . . . . . . . . I,52
Lowell, R. T. S. Fresh Hearts that Failed. Boston, 1860. 16°. . . . I,86

Lowell, R. T. S. New Priest of Conception Bay. New York, 1869. 12°. . K,797
Lower, M. A. English Surnames. London, 1849. 2 v. 8°. . . . L,516
Lowman, M. Commentary on the Revelation. Philadelphia, 1848. 8°. P,556,4
Lowndes, W. T. Bibliographer's Manual. London, 1860–64. 5 v. 8°. . L.R.
Lowth, R. Introduction to English Grammar. Dublin, 1785. 16°. . O,1073
New Translation of Isaiah. London, 1848. 8°. . . . . P,542
Lowth, W. Commentary; Prophets. Philadelphia, 1846. 8°. . P,556,3
Loyola, I. and Jesuitism in its Rudiments. T. Taylor. London, 1849. 8°. P,797
Loyson, C., *Father Hyacinthe.* Discourses; tr. L. W. Bacon. N. Y. 1869. 12°. P,63
Family and Church; edited by L. W. Bacon. New York, 1870. 12°. H,908
Lubojatzky, F. Jahr aus Leben August des Starken. Wein, 1863. 2 v. 24°. G,340
Lateinische Czarin und ihr Schicksal. Wein, 1862. 2 v. 16°. . G,341
Vor Hundert Jahren. Leipzig, 1851. 3 v. 16°. . . . . . G,342
Lubbock, Sir J. Origin of Civilization. New York, 1871. 12°. . . . O,534
Lubbock, Mrs. Ancient Shell Mounds of Denmark. London, 1864. 8°. V,1086,3
Lucae, J. C. G. Die Hand und der Fuss. Frankfurt-a-Main, 1865. 4°. . E,481
Lucanus, M. A. Pharsalia; ed. P. A. Lemaire. Parisiis, 1830–32. 3 v. 8°. U,329
The same; trans. by H. T. Riley. London, 1853. p. 8°. . L,67
Luckey, J. Life in Sing-Sing Prison. New York, 1866. 12°. . . . . O,347
Lucian. Comedies; translated by W. Maginn. New York, 1856. 12°. . U,427
Dialogues; translated by J. Carr, v. 1–3. London, 1774–86. 3 v. 8°. U,459
Lucien, H. M. Hints on Illuminating. London, n. d. 12°. . . . M,61
Lucile. E. R. B. Lytton. London, 1868. 16°. . . . . . . . . I,372
Lucilius, C. Satires; translated by L. Evans. London, 1852. p. 8°. . L,65
Luck and Pluck. A. Alger. Boston, 1870. 16°. . . . . . J,1595
Luck of Roaring Camp, etc. F. B. Harte. Boston, 1870. 16°. . . . H,64
Luckombe, P. (Ed.) Origin and Progress of Printing. London, 1770. 8°. M,638
Lucretia; or, the Children of Night. Sir E. B. Lytton. Philad. 1867. 12°. K,819
The same. Leipzig, 1846. 2 v. in 1. 16°. . . . . . J,320
Lucretius Carus, T. De Rerum Natura; cur. P. A. Lemaire. Par. 1838. 2 v. 8°. U,330
Nature of Things; translated by J. S. Watson. London, 1851. p. 8°. L,68
Lucy Arlyn. J. T. Trowbridge. Boston, 1866. 12°. . . . . . . K,121
Lucy Clare. M. M. Sherwood. New York, 1860. 12°. . . K,1008,3
Lucy Crofton. M. Oliphant. New York, 1860. 12°. . . . . . K,1165
Luden, H. Geschichte des Teutschen Volkes. Gotha, 1825–37. 12 v. 8°. . E,49
Ludewig, H. E. Literature of American Aborig. Languages. Lond. 1858. 8°. H,666
Ludlow, E. Memoirs. Vivay, 1698–99. 3 v. 16°. . . . . . C,1226
Ludlow, Fitz H. Heart of the American Continent. New York, 1870. 8°. V,114
Ludlow, J. M. Popular Epics of the Middle Ages. London, 1865. 2 v. 12°. H,735
Ludowig, H. Bleiweiss und Bleizuckerfabrication. Weimar, 1847. 16°. N,252,38
Ludus Coventriae; edited by J. O. Halliwell. London, 1841. 8°. . I,885,4
Lübben, A. Wörterbuch zur Nibelungen Noth. Oldenburg, 1854. 8°. . E,273
(Ed.) Pädagogischer Jahresbericht. v. 21. Leipzig, 1870. 8°. . G,539
Lübke, W. History of Art. London, 1868. 2 v. 8°. . . . . *M,115
Lüdde, J. G. Zeitschrift für Vergleichende Erdkunde. Magd. 1845–50. 10 v. 8°. E,159
Luke Darrell, the Chicago News-Boy. Chicago, 1870. 16°. . . . J,1671
Lumisden, A., Memoirs of. J. Dennistoun. London, 1855. 12°. . . . D,228
Lungs, Lectures on the Functions of. S. S. Fitch. New York, 1856. 12°. L,916
Weak, and how to make them Strong. D. Lewis. Boston, 1863. 12°. L,904
Lunt, G. Three Eras of New England. Boston, 1857. 12°. . . . H,190

Lupton, I. J. Horse in the Stable and the Field. London, 1861. 8°. . M,476
Lusiad; or, Discovery of India. L. de Camoëns. Oxford, 1776. 4°. . I,389
Lusitanian Sketches of Pen and Pencil. H. G. Kingston. Lond. 1845. 2 v. 12°. V,473
Lutfullah, Autobiography of. Leipzig, 1857. 16°. . . . . . . J,302
Luther, M., Autobiography of; ed. by M. Michelet. London, 1862. p. 8°. . L,209
The same; translated by J. P. Lawson. Edinburgh, 1836. 16°. D,490
and Oliver Cromwell. J. T. Headley. New York, 1850. 12°. . C,491
Boyhood of. H. Mayhew. New York, 1864. 8°. . . . . J,1463
Estimate of his Character. T. Carlyle. New York, 1865. 16°. . D,491
Leben und Wirken. C. F. G. Stang. Stuttgart, 1839. 8°. . . E,243
Life of. C. C. J. Bunsen. New York, 1865. 16°. . . . . D,491
Table-Talk; translated by W. Hazlitt. London, 1848. p. 8°. . . G,33
Luttrell of Arran. C. Lever. London, 1865. 8°. . . . . . . K,883
The same. New York, 1865. 8°. . . . . . . . K,780
The same. Leipzig, 1865. 2 v. in 1. 16°. . . . J,280
Luttrell, N. Hist. Relation of State Affairs, 1678–1714. Oxford, 1857. 6 v. 8°. B,17
Lyall, A. and others. Christian Church from 13th Century. Lond. 1858. 12°. P,572
Lyall, W. Intellect, Emotions, and Moral Nature. Edinburgh, 1855. 8°. . O,691
Lycett, J. Mollusca from the Great Oolite. London, 1850–54. 3 v. 4°. . Q,18
Lydgate, D. J. Minor Poems. London, 1840. 12°. . . . . . L,606,2
Lyell, Sir C. Alter des Menschengeschlechts. Leipzig, 1864. 8°. . . E,401
Elements of Geology. New York, 1866. 8°. . . . . . . N,837
Supplement. London, 1857. 8°. . . . . . . N,252,44
Geological Evidences of Antiquity of Man. Philadelphia, 1863. 8°. N,437
Principles of Geology. New York, 1854. 8°. . . . . . . N,842
Second Visit to the United States. New York, 1849. 2 v. 12°. . V,32
Review of his Report on Explosions. M. Dunn. London, 1845. 8°. N,252,35
Travels in North America, 1841–42. New York, 1852. 2 v. in 1. 12°. V,60
Lyman, S. P. Life and Memorials of Daniel Webster. N. Y. 1853. 2 v. 12°. C,675
Lynch, J. Cambrensis Eversus. Dublin, 1848–52. 3 v. 8°. . . . B,165
Lynch, T. Printer's Manual. Cincinnati, 1859. 8°. . . . . . . M,688
The same. Cincinnati, 1864. 12°. . . . . . . . L.R.
Lynch, W. F. Expedition to the Jordan and Dead Sea. Phila. 1850. 8°. V,660
The same; abridged. Philadelphia, 1852. 12°. . . . V,636
Lyndesay, Sir D. Works; part 3. London, 1868. 8°. . . . . L,605,35
Historie of Sqvyer Meldrum. Testament of Sqvyer Meldrum.
The same; part 4. London, 1869. 8°. . . . . . L,605,37
Ane Satyre of the Thrie Estates.
Lyon, G. F. Narrative of Attempt to reach Repulse Bay. London, 1825. 8°. V,955
Lyon, Mary, Life of. W. M. Thayer. Boston, 1866. 16°. . . . . J,1498
Recollections of. F. Fisk. Boston, 1866. 12°. . . . . . C,695
Lyon, Gen. N. and Missouri in 1861. J. Peckham. New York, 1866. 2 v. 12°. B,903
Lyon, W. P. Teachers' and Parents' Manual. New York, 1848. 18°. . O,1113
Lyons, T. L. English Grammar. Cincinnati, 1850. 12°. . . . . O,1081
Lyra Anglicana; Hymns. R. H. Baynes. Leipzig, 1868. 16°. . . J,32
Lyra Germanica; translated by C. Winckworth. New York, 1856. 12°. . G,43
Lyrics of Loyalty; edited by F. Moore. New York, 1864. 16°. . . I,77
Lysons, S. Our British Ancestors. Oxford, 1865. p. 8°. . . . . N,439
Lyteria; a Dramatic Poem. J. P. Quincy. Boston, 1855. 16°. . . I,112
Lytille Childrenes Lytil Boke. London, 1868. 8°. . . . . . L,605,32

Lyttleton, G., *Lord.* Conversion of St. Paul. New York, n. d. 18°. P,746,14

Lytton, E. B., *Lord.* Alice; or, the Mysteries. Philadelphia, 1868. 12°. . K,806

The same. Leipzig, 1842. 16°. . . . . . . . J,303

Athens; its Rise and Fall. New York, 1869. 12°. . . . . . A,70

The same. Leipzig, 1843. 2 v. in 1. 16°. . . . . . J,304

Caxtoniana. New York, 1863. 12°. . . . . . . . . . H,444

The same. Leipzig, 1864. 2 v. in 1. 16°. . . . . . J,305

Caxtons; a Family Picture. Philadelphia, 1868. 12°. . . . K,807

The same. Leipzig, 1849. 2 v. in 1. 16°. . . . . . J,306

Critical and Miscellaneous Writings. Philadelphia, 1841. 2 v. 12°. H,443

Vol. 1. Sir Walter Scott; Death of Sir Walter Scott; Art in Fiction; Conversation with an Ambitious Student in Ill Health; Zicci, a Tale; Poems of Laman Blanchard; Poems of Robert Montgomery; Tour of a German Prince; Present state of Poetry; Notices of Lord Brougham's Speeches.

2. Sir Thomas Browne; People's Charter; Public Opinion; Political Coalitions; Spirit of True Criticism; Authors and their Works; Proposals for a Literary Union; Literature considered as a Profession; International Law of Copyright; Modern Platonist; Knowledge of the World in Men and Books; English Notions of Morality; Willful Mistatements of the Quarterly Review; Influence and Education of Women; New Year; Position and Prospects of the Government, 1838; The Politician.

Devereux. Philadelphia, 1867. 12°. . . . . . . . . K,809

The same. Leipzig, 1842. 16°. . . . . . . . J,307

Disowned. Philadelphia, 1823. 8°. . . . . . . . . . K,881

The same. Philadelphia, 1868. 12°. . . . . . . K,808

The same. Leipzig, 1842. 16°. . . . . . . . J,308

Dramatic Works. Leipzig, 1860. 2 v. in 1. 16°. . . . . . J,309

The same. London, 1863. 8°. . . . . . . . . . I,738

Duchess de la Vallière; Richelieu; Lady of Lyons; Money; Not so bad as we seem.

Ernest Maltravers. Philadelphia, 1869. 12°. . . . . . . K,811

The same. Leipzig, 1842. 16°. . . . . . . . J,310

Eugene Aram. Philadelphia, 1869. 12°. . . . . . . . K,812

The same. Leipzig, 1842. 16°. . . . . . . . J,311

Eva; the Ill-Omened Marriage. Leipzig, 1842. 16°. . . . J,312

Falkland. Philadelphia, n. d. 8°. . . . . . . . . . K,826

Godolphin. Philadelphia, 1868. 12°. . . . . . . . . K,813

The same and Falkland. Leipzig, 1842. 16°. . . . J,313

Harold, the Last of the Saxon Kings. London, 1860. 12°. . . K,814

The same. Leipzig, 1848. 2 v. in 1. 16°. . . . . J,314

King Arthur. London, 1851. 12°. . . . . . . . . . I,383

The same. Leipzig, 1849. 2 v. in 1. 16°. . . . . J,316

Last Days of Pompeii. Philadelphia, 1869. 12°. . . . . K,816

The same. Leipzig, 1842. 16°. . . . . . . . J,317

Last of the Barons. Philadelphia, 1869. 12°. . . . . . . K,815

The same. Leipzig, 1843. 2 v. in 1. 16°. . . . . J,318

Leila, Calderon, and Pilgrims of the Rhine. Philadelphia, 1868. 12°. K,817

Lost Tales of Miletus. New York, 1866. 12°. . . . . . I,382

The same. Leipzig, 1866. 16°. . . . . . . . J,319

Lucretia; or, the Children of Night. Philadelphia, 1868. 12°. . K,819

The same; Leipzig, 1846. 2 v in 1. 16°. . . . . . J,320

Miscellaneous Prose Works. New York, 1868. 2 v. 12°. . . . I,556

Vol. 1. Reign of Terror, its Causes and Results; Oliver Goldsmith; Charles Lamb and some of his Companions; Thomas Gray's Works; Sir Thomas Browne; Pitt and Fox; Pym *vs.* Falkland; Life of Schiller.

Lytton, E. B., *Lord.* Miscellaneous Prose Works. *Continued.* . . . . I,556

2. Essays Written in Youth; Conversations with an Ambitious Student in his last illness; Influence of Love upon Literature and Real Life.

The same. Leipzig, 1868. 4 v. 16°. . . . . . . . J,321

My Novel; Varieties in English Life. Philadelphia, 1867. 2 v. 12°. K,820

The same. Leipzig, 1851. 4 v. 16°. . . . . . . . J,322

New Timon; a Poetical Romance. London, 1846. 8°. . . . . I,384

The same and St. Stephen's. Leipzig, 1860. 16°. . . . . J,323

Night and Morning. Philadelphia, 1869. 12°. . . . . . . K,821

The same. Leipzig, 1843. 16°. . . . . . . . . J,324

Odes and Epodes of Horace translated. Leipzig, 1869. 2 v. in 1. 16°. J,315

The same. New York, 1870. 12°. . . . . . . . . U,457

Paul Clifford. Philadelphia, 1868. 12°. . . . . . . . . K,822

The same. Philadelphia, 1830. 8°. . . . . . . K,823

The same. Leipzig, 1842. 16°. . . . . . . . J,325

Pelham. Philadelphia, 1868. 12°. . . . . . . . . . K,824

The same. Philadelphia, 1828. 8°. . . . . . . K,825

The same. Leipzig, 1842. 16°. . . . . . . . J,326

Pilgrims of the Rhine. Philadelphia, n. d. 8°. . . . . . K,826

Poems of Schiller translated. Liepzig, 1844. 16°. . . . . . J,328

Rienzi; the Last of the Roman Tribunes. Philadelphia, 1869. 12°. K,828

The same. Philadelphia, 1835. 8°. . . . . . . K,827

The same. Leipzig, 1842. 16°. . . . . . . . J,327

Strange Story. Philadelphia, 1868. 12°. . . . . . . . K,829

The same. Liepzig, 1861–62. 2 v. in 1. 16°. . . . . J,329

Student. Philadelphia, n. d. 8°. . . . . . . . . K,810

What will he do with it? Philadelphia, 1869. 2 v. 12°. . . . K,830

The same. Leipzig, 1853–58. 4 v. 16°. . . . . . J,330

Zanoni. Philadelphia, 1869. 12°. . . . . . . . . . K,831

The same. Leipzig, 1842. 16°. . . . . . . . J,331

Lytton, E. R. B., *Owen Meredith.* Lucille. Boston, 1868. 16°. . . . . I,372

Poems. Boston, 1866. 2 v. 16°. . . . . . . . . . I,373

The same. Leipzig, 1869. 2 v. in 1. 16°. . . . . . J,333

New Poems. Boston, 1868. 2 v. 16°. . . . . . . . . I,374

Ring of Amasis. New York, 1863. 12°. . . . . . . . . K,832

M. or N. "Similia Similibus Curantur." G. J. W. Melville. Leip. 1869. 16°. J,379

Mabel Ross, the Sewing Girl. Chicago, 1870. 16°. . . . . . J,1673

Mabel's Mistake. A. S. Stephens. Philadelphia, 1870. 12°. . . . K,447

McArthur, D., Sketches of. J. Mac Donald. n. p. n. d. 12°. . . . C,839

McCabe, J. D. Planting the Wilderness. Boston, 1870. 16°. . . J,1612

Macaria. A. J. Wilson. New York, 1869. 12°. . . . . . . . K,104

Macaulay, C. History of England. London, 1763–71. 5 v. 4°. . . F,262

Macaulay, T. B. Biographical Essays. Leipzig, 1857. 16°. . . . . J,334

Frederick II.; Bunyan; Goldsmith; Johnson; Barère.

Critical and Historical Essays. Leipzig, 1850. 5 v. 16°. . . J,335

Vol. 1. Milton; Machiavelli; Hallam's Constitutional History; Southey's Colloquies on Society; Robt. Montgomery's Poems; Civil Disabilities of the Jews; Moore's Life of Lord Byron; Croker's Boswell's Life of Johnson.

Macaulay, T. B. Critical and Miscellaneous Essays. *Continued.* . . . J,335

2. Southey's edition of Pilgrim's Progress; Nugent's Memorials of Hampden; Burleigh and his Times; Lord Mahon's War of the Succession in Spain; Walpole's Letters to Sir Horace Mann; Wm. Pitt, Earl of Chatham; Sir James Mackintosh.
3. Lord Bacon; Sir Wm. Temple; Gladstone on Church and State.
4. Lord Clive; Ranke's History of the Popes; Comic Dramatists of the Restoration; Lord Holland; Warren Hastings.
5. Madame D'Arblay; Life and Writings of Addison; Wm. Pitt, Earl of Chatham, 2d paper; Index.

Critical, Historical, and Miscellaneous Essays. N.Y. 1865-66. 6 v. 8°. H,433

Vol. 1. Biographical Sketch; Fragments of a Roman Tale; Royal Society of Literature; Scenes from Athenian Revels; Criticisms on Italian Writers; Law-suit between Parishes of St. Dennis and St. George; Conversation between Cowley and Milton touching the Great Civil War; Athenian Orators; The "Wellingtoniad" to be published, A. D. 2824; Mitford's History of Greece; Milton; Machiavilli; Dryden; History; Hallam's Constitutional History.
2. Mill on Government; Westminster Reviewer's Defense of Mill; Utilitarian Theory of Government; Southey's Colloquies on Society; Robt. Montgomery's Poems; Sadler's Law of Population; Southey's edition of Pilgrim's Progress; Sadler's Refutation Refuted; Civil Disabilities of the Jews; Moore's Life of Lord Byron; Croker's Boswell's Life of Johnson; Nugent's Memorials of Hampden.
3. Burleigh and his Times; Mirabeau; War of the Succession in Spain; Horace Walpole; Wm. Pitt, Earl of Chatham; Sir James Mackintosh; Lord Bacon.
4. Sir Wm. Temple; Gladstone on Church and State; Lord Clive; Ranke's History of the Popes; Comic Dramatists of the Restoration; Lord Holland.
5. Warren Hastings; Frederick the Great; Madame D'Arblay; Life and Writings of Addison; Barère.
6. Wm. Pitt, Earl of Chatham, 2d paper; Francis Atterbury; John Bunyan; Oliver Goldsmith; Samuel Johnson; Wm. Pitt; West Indies; London University; Social and Industrial Capacities of Negroes; The Present Administration, 1827; Index.

Critical and Miscellaneous Essays. Boston, 1854. 8°. . . . . H,374

The same. Philadelphia, 1843. 8°. . . . . . . H,435

History of England. New York, 1866. 8 v. 8°. . . . . . A,399

The same. New York, 1850-56. 4 v. 8°. . . . . . S.C.

The same. Leipzig, 1859-61. 10 v. 16°. . . . . . J,336

Lays of Ancient Rome. Leipzig, 1851. 16°. . . . . . . J,337

Life of Frederick the Great. New York, 1865. 16°. . . . D,492

Life of William Pitt. New York, 1865. 16°. . . . . . C,1180

Selections from Essays and Speeches. London, 1865. 2 v. p. 8°. I,663

Vol. 1. Warren Hastings; Lord Clive; William Pitt; Ranke's Popes; Gladstone on Church and State; Addison; Horace Walpole; Croker's Boswell's Johnson.
2. Lord Bacon; Lord Byron; Comic Dramatists; Frederick the Great; Hallam's Constitutional History; Speeches on Parliamentary Reform.

Speeches, Parliamentary and Miscellaneous. Lond. 1853. 2 v. in 1. 8°. H,795

The same. New York, 1853. 2 v. 12°. . . . . . . H,779

The same. Leipzig, 1853. 2 v. in 1. 16°. . . . . J,339

Wm. Pitt and Francis Atterbury. Leipzig, 1860. 16°. . . . J,338

and others. New Biographies of Illustrious Men. Boston, 1857. 12°. C,496

Macaulay, W. H. Kathay; a Cruise in the China Seas. N. Y. 1852. 12°. V,598

Macauley, E. W. Tales of the Drama. Hartford, 1853. 12°. . . . K,833

Macbrair, R. M. Chapters on National Education. London, 1845. 8°. O,1251,1

MacBride, J. Early Settlers of Butler Co., O. Cincinnati, 1869-71. 2 v. 8°. C,220

Symmes's Theory of Concentric Spheres. Cincinnati, 1826. 16°. . N,594

M'Burney, I. Student's Hand-Book of Mediæval History. Lond. 1857. 8°. A,235

MacCabe, J. P. B. Directory of Lexington and Fayette Co., Ky. Lex. 1838. 12°. C,178

McCall, G. A. Letters from the Frontiers. Philadelphia, 1868. 12°. . V,117

M'Carthy, D. F. Engineer's Guide to the Navy. London, 1869. 12°. . M,849

M'Caul, G. Philosophy of Mind and Matter. London, 1828. 8°. . . O,665

M'Causland, D. Adam and the Adamite. London, 1864. 12°. . . . P,915

McClellan, G. B. Art of War in Europe, 1854-56. Washington, 1857. 4°. P.D.

McClellan, G. B., Life and Campaigns of. G. S. Hillard. Phil. 1864. 12°. C,698
Report on the Army of the Potomac. Washington, 1864. 8°. . . P.D.
M'Clintock, F. L. Discovery of Fate of Sir J. Franklin. Boston, 1860. 12°. V,943
Meteorological Observations. Washington, 1863. 4°. . . Q,324,13
M'Clure, A. W. Life of John Cotton. Boston, 1870. 12°. . . . . . D,8,1
Lives of J. Wilson, J. Norton, and J. Davenport. Boston, 1870. 12°. D,8,2
M'Clure, R. Discovery of the North-West Passage. London, 1859. 8°. . V,944
MacCombie, W. Education; Essays and Lectures. Aberdeen, 1850. 16°. O,970
MacConochie, J. R. Leisure Hours. Louisville, Ky. 1846. 12°. . . I,79
McCosh, J. Christianity and Positivism. New York, 1871. 12°. . . P,577
Examination of J. S. Mill's Philosophy. New York, 1866. 12°. . O,701
Intuitions of the Mind. New York, 1860. 8°. . . . . . . O,674
Method of the Divine Government. New York, 1858. 8°. . . P,159
and Dickie, G. Typical Forms in Creation. New York, 1856. 8°. P,324
Mac Coy, F. Classification of British Palæozoic Rocks. London, 1855. 4°. Q,51
McCoy, I. History of Baptist Indian Missions. Washington, 1840. 8°. . B,588
M'Crie, T. History of the Bass Rock. New York, 1852. 12°. . . N,612
Works. Edinburgh, 1855–57. 4 v. 8°. . . . . . . . . P,761
McCullagh, W. T. Industrial History of Free Nations. Lond. 1846. 2 v. 8°. O,499
Memoirs of Richard Lalor Sheil. London, 1855. 2 v. 12°. . . D,204
M'Culloch, J. R. Commercial Dictionary. London, 1869. 8°. . . *O,611
Dictionary, Geographical, Statistical, etc. N. Y. 1855–58. 2 v. 8°. L.R.
London in 1850–51. London, 1865. p. 8°. . . . . . . I,667
Rate of Wages. London, 1854. 16°. . . . . . . . . O,470
Russia and Turkey. London, 1854. p. 8°. . . . . . I,656,6
Supplement to Commercial Dictionary. London, 1849. 8°. . N,252,48
Universal Gazetteer. New York, 1855. 2 v. 8°. . . . . . L.R.
Macdiarmid, J. Lives of British Statesmen, London, 1807. 4°. . . F,24
Sir Thomas More; William Cecil, Lord Burleigh; Thomas Wentworth, Earl of Strafford; Edward Hyde, Earl of Clarendon.
Mac Donald, G. Adela Cathcart. Boston, n. d. 12°. . . . . . K,1160
The same. London, 1864. 3 v. 12°. . . . . . . J,571
Alec Forbes, of Howglen. Leipzig, 1865. 2 v. in 1. 16°. . . J,340
Annals of a Quiet Neighborhood. New York, 1867. 12°. . . K,837
The same. Leipzig, 1867. 2 v. in 1. 16°. . . . . J,341
David Elginbrod. London, 1863. 3 v. 12°. . . . . . . K,803
Guild Court. London, 1868. 3 v. 12°. . . . . . . K,1101
Phantastes; a Faerie Romance. London, 1858. 12°. . . K,1102
The Portent; a Story. Boston, n. d. 12°. . . . . . K,1166
Robert Falconer. Boston, n. d. 12°. . . . . . . . . K,921
The same. London, 1868. 3 v. 12°. . . . . . . K,922
Seaboard Parish. London, 1868. 3 v. 12°. . . . . . . J,566
McDonald, J. Sketches of Gen. McArthur, Wells, and Kenton. n. t. p. 12°. C,839
M'Donner. J. Abbott. New York, n. d. 12°. . . . . . . P,281,4
Mac Dougall, G. F. Voyage to the Arctic Regions. London, 1857. 8°. . V,952
Macduff, J. R. Story of Bethlehem. New York, 1859. 12°. . . . J,1321
Macé, J. Fairy Book; Home Fairy Tales. New York, 1870. 12°. . . J,1339
History of a Mouthful of Bread. New York, 1868. 12°. . . L,901
Servants of the Stomach. New York, 1868. 12°. . . . . L,900
Macedonia, History of. E. Pococke. London, 1852. p. 8°. . . . A,69

McElligott, J. N. American Debater. New York, 1870. 12°. . . . . O,558
Manual of Orthography and Definition. New York, 1854. 8°. . O,893
Young Analyzer of the English Language. New York, 1852. 8°. . O,1088
Macfarlane, C. Cabinet History of England. Lond. 1851. 26 v. in 13. 12°. A,385
Great Battles of the British Army. London, 1860. 12°. . . B,77
Japan, Geographical and Historical Account of. N. Y. 1854. 12°. V,609
Life of Duke of Marlborough. London, 1854. 16°. . . . J,1231
Lives and Exploits of Banditti and Robbers. London, 1837. 16°. I,649
Turkey and its Destiny. Philadelphia, 1850. 2 v. 12°. . . . V,563
and Craik, G. L. Pictorial History of England. Lond. 1849. 8 v. 8°. A,418
Macfarlane, R. History of Propellers and Steam Navigation. N. Y. 1851. 12°. M,691
McFingal; a Modern Epic Poem. J. Trumbull. Hartford, 1856. 8°. . I,166
Mac Gauley, J. W. Treatise on Algebra. Dublin, 1854. 16°. . . M,1097
McGee, T. D'A. Poems. New York, 1869. 12°. . . . . . . I,368
Mac Gilchrist, J. Richard Cobden; a Biography. New York, 1865. 16°. D,3
Macgillivray, W. Conchologist's Text-Book. London, 1853. 16°. . . O,19
Travels and Researches of A. von Humboldt. New York, 1869. 16°. L,377
Macgregor J. Commercial Statistics. London, 1850. 5 v. 8°. . . O,607
History of the British Empire. London, 1852. 2 v. 8°. . . A,412
Progress of America. London, 1847. 2 v. 8°. . . . . . B,828
Macgregor, J. Rob Roy on the Baltic. London, 1867. 16°. . . . V,521
Rob Roy on the Jordan. New York, 1870. 8°. . . . V,1080
on Rivers and Lakes of Europe. London, 1870. 16°. . . V,383
Voyage alone in the. London, 1867. 12°. . . . V,1049
Mac Gregor, P. System of Logic. New York, 1862. 12°. . . . O,628
McGregor, W. Questions on Magnetism, Electricity, etc. London, 1868. 12°. M,850
McGuffey, W. H. Eclectic Third Reader. Cincinnati, 1853. 12°. . . O,875
Eclectic Fourth Reader. Cincinnati, 1853. 12°. . . . . O,788
Eclectic Spelling Book. Cincinnati, 1846. 12°. . . . . O,765
New Eclectic Speaker. Cincinnati, n. d. 12°. . . . . O,1228
Rhetorical Guide; or, Fifth Reader. Cincinnati, 1845. 12°. . . O,887
Second German Reader. Cincinnati, 1854. 16°. . . . . G,545
Machiavelli, N. History of Florence and Affairs of Italy. Lond. 1854. p. 8°. L,207
Works. London, 1680. f°. . . . . . . . . . . F,171
Mackarness, M. A. Sunbeam Stories. Leipzig, 1863. 16°. . . . J,412
Mac Henry, G. Cotton Trade. London, 1863. 8°. . . . . . . O,523
Machinery and Engineering, Mechanics of. J. Weisbach. Lond. 1848. 2 v. 8°. M,675
and Manufactures, Economy of. C. Babbage. London, 1846. 12°. . M,599
and Millwork. W. J. M. Rankine. London, 1869. 12°. . . M,726
Examples of. Glasgow, 1845. r. 4°. . . . . . . S.C.
Principles of. C. D. Abel. London, 1868. 12°. . . . . M,825
Atlas to same. London, 1860. 4°. . . . . . . Q,359
Machines and Mechanism. T. Baker. London, 1858. 12°. . . . M,891
for raising Water. T. Ewbank. New York, 1870. 8°. . . . N,134
The same. New York, 1850. . . . . . . . . . S.C.
Mechanics, Engineering, etc., Appleton's. New York, 1852. 2 v. 8°. *M,802
Principles and Practice of building. F. Overman. Phil. 1851. 12°. M,621
M'Ilvaine, C. P. Evidences of Christianity. Philadelphia, 1867. 12°. . P,166
Select Sermons. Columbus, 1838–39. 2 v. 8°. . . . . . P,779

Macilwain, G. Memoirs of John Abernethy. New York, 1853. 12°. . D,161
Mac Intosh, C. Book of the Garden. Edinburgh, 1853–55. 2 v. 8°. . M,359
McIntosh, M. J. Charms and Counter Charms. New York, 1864. 12°. K,212
Conquest and Self-Conquest. New York, 1854. 18°. . . . J,1175
Evenings at Donaldson Manor. New York, 1853. 12°. . . . K,211
Lofty and the Lowly. New York, 1852. 2 v. 12°. . . . K,213
Meta Gray. New York, 1863. 16°. . . . . . . . . . J,1352
Praise and Principle. New York, 1861. 18°. . . . . . . J,1178
Two Pictures. New York, 1863. 12°. . . . . . . . K,210
Year with Maggie and Emma. New York, 1861. 16°. . . . J,1364
Mack, E. Life of Lafayette. Ithaca, 1848. 12°. . . . . . . D,630
Mackay, A. Western World; Travels in the U. S. Phil. 1849. 2 v. 12°. V,31
Mackay, C. Extraordinary Popular Delusions. Phil. 1850. 12°. . . O,332
Life and Liberty in America. New York, 1859. 12°. . . . V,12
Voices from the Mountains and the Crowd. Boston, 1853. 12°. . I,366
(Ed.) Songs of London Prentices and Trades. London, 1841. 12°. L,606,1
Mackay, J. T. Flora Hibernica. Dublin, 1836. 8°. . . . . . N,1020
Mackay, R. W. Progress of the Intellect. London, 1850. 2 v. 8°. . O,681
Rise and Progress of Christianity. London, 1854. 12°. . . . P,603
Mackenzie, A. Voyages to Frozen and Pacific Ocean. London, 1801. 4°. Q,438
Mackenzie, A. S. Life of Stephen Decatur. Boston, 1846. 8°. . . C,1106
The same. Boston, 1860. 12°. . . . . . . C,860,21
Life of John Paul Jones. New York, 1854. 2 v. 8°. . . . C,699
Life of Oliver H. Perry. New York, 1854. 2 v. 16°. . . . L,421
Mackenzie, C. Life in the Mission; Six Years in India. N. Y. 1856. 2 v. 12°. V,607
Ten Thousands Receipts. Philadelphia, 1868. 8°. . . . . . H,631
Mackenzie, H. Julia de Roubigné. London, 1820. 12°. . . . . . K,540
Man of Feeling. London, 1820. 12°. . . . . . . . . K,540
The same. London, 1815. . . . . . . . . . K,853
Miscellaneous Works. New York, 1853. 12°. . . . . . . H,593
Mackenzie, G. M. and Irby. Travels in Turkey-in-Europe. Lond. 1866. 8°. V,570
Mackenzie, Sir G. S. Travels in Iceland, 1810. Edinburgh, 1811. 4°. . Q,440
Mackenzie, J. History of Scotland. London, 1867. 8°. . . . . B,113
Mackenzie, R. S. Life of Charles Dickens. Philadelphia, 1870. 12°. . D,191
M'Keever, H. B. Westbrook Parsonage. Philadelphia, 1870. 12°. . K,113
Mackie, J. M. Cosas de España; or, Going to Madrid. N. Y. 1855. 12°. V,470
From Cape Cod to Dixie and the Tropics. New York, 1864. 12°. . V,9
Life of Samuel Gorton. Boston, 1860. 12°. . . . . . C,860,15
Life of Tai-Ping-Wang. New York, 1857. 12°. . . . . D,756
Mackie, S. J. First Traces of Life on the Earth. London, 1860. 8°. . N,783
Mackinnon, L. Atlantic and Trans-Atlantic Sketches. N. Y. 1852. 12°. V,36
Mackintosh, Sir J. History of England. London, 1830–40. 10 v. 12°. . M,986
Life of; edited by R. J. Mackintosh. Boston, 1853. 2 v. 8°. C,1292
Miscellaneous Works. London, 1851. 8°. . . . . . . U,266
The same. Boston, 1854. 8°. . . . . . . . . . H,370
Revolution in England, 1688. Philadelphia, 1835. 8°. . . . H,841
The Man of Promise; Sir H. L. Bulwer. London, 1868. 8°. C,578,2
The same. Leipzig, 1868. . . . . . . . . . J,332
and others. Eminent British Statesmen. London, 1831. 7 v. 12°. M,1011
McLain, M. W. Daisy Ward's Work. Boston, 1871. 12°. . . . K,385

Maclaren, J. History of Currency. London, 1858. 8°. . . . . . o,531
Maclean, G. M. Somatology. New York, 1859. 12°. . . . . . N,76
M'Lean, J. Hudson's Bay Territory. London, 1849. 2 v. 12°. . . v,134
Macleay, W. S. Annulosa Javanica; Insects de Java. Paris, 1833. 8°. . o,31,1
and Horsfield, T. Insects of Java. n. t. p. 4°. . . . . . *Q,114
McLeod, A., Trial of; reported by M. T. C. Gould. New York, 1841. 8°. U,533
Macleod, D. Discourse on Elocution. Cincinnati, 1855. 8°. . . . T,19,2
Life of Sir W. Scott. New York, 1852. 12°. . . . . . . c,1167
Macleod, H. D. Theory and Practice of Banking. London, 1866. 2 v. 8°. o,566
Macleod, N. Gold Thread. London, 1867. 12°. . . . . . . J,1548
Old Lieutenant and his Son. London, 1862. 2 v. 12°. . . K,1103
The same. Leipzig, 1863. 16°. . . . . . . . J,342
Starling; a Scotch Story. London, 1867. 2 v. 12°. . . . K,923
and Guthrie, T. Wind-Wafted Seed. New York, 1869. 12°. . H,132
McMasters, S. Y. Biographical Index to Hume's History. Alton, 1854. 8°. A,392
McMicken, C. Will, and Sketch of his Life. Cincinnati, 1858. 4°. . *Q,291
Macmillan's Magazine. Cambridge, 1860–67. 15 v. 8°. . . . . S,42
Macknight, T. Life and Times of Edmund Burke. London, 1858–60. 3 v. 8°. D,251
Macnish, R. Philosophy of Sleep. New York, 1834. 12°. . . . L,889
Tales, Essays, and Sketches. London, 1844. 2 v. 16°. . . . H,229
McPherson, E. Political History of U. S. in the Rebellion. Wash. 1865. 8°. B,936
Macpherson, J. Baths and Wells of Europe. London, 1869. 16°. . L,919
Macpherson, J. Original Papers in English History. London, 1775. 2 v. 4°. A,468
Poems of Ossian. Leipzig, 1847. 16°. . . . . . . . J,406
McQueen, H. Orator's Touchstone. New York, 1854. 12°. . . . L,588
Macray, W. D. Annals of the Bodleian Library, Oxford. Lond. 1868. 8°. L.R.
McRee, G. J. Life of James Iredell. New York, 1857. 2 v. 8°. . . c,1090
McSherry, J. History of Maryland. Baltimore, 1849. 8°. . . . c,114
Madagascar Revisited. W. Ellis. London, 1867. 8°. . . . . v,863
Three Visits to. W. Ellis. New York, 1859. 8°. . . . . v,855
Madame Fontenoy. Leipzig, 1866. 16°. . . . . . . . . J,343
Madame de Brandebourg; Roman. B. von Guseck. Wien, 1863. 2 v. in 1. 24°. G,295
Madame Thérèse. E. Erckmann and A. Chatrian. New York, 1869. 12°. H,1010
Madden, R. R. Connexion between Ireland and England. Dublin, 1845. 8°. B,169
Life of Countess of Blessington. New York, 1855. 2 v. 12°. . c,1202
Phantasmata; or, Illusions and Fanaticisms. London, 1857. 2 v. 8°. H,506
Madeline. J. Kavanagh. New York, 1866. 12°. . . . . . K,747
Mademoiselle Merquem. Mad. Dudevant. New York, 1868. 12°. . . H,959
Mademoiselle Mori; Tale of Modern Rome. Leipzig, 1862. 2 v. in 1. 16°. J,344
Mademoiselle Panache. M. Edgeworth. New York, 1860. 12°. . K,678,2
Madison, J. Letters and other Writings. Philadelphia, 1865. 4 v. 8°. . U,108
Life of. J. Q. Adams. Buffalo, 1850. 12°. . . . . . c,918
Life and Times of. W. C. Rives. Boston, 1859. 3 v. 8°. . . c,815
Madonna, Legends of. A. Jameson. London, 1867. 8°. . . . *M,118
The same. Boston, 1866. 16°. . . . . . . . M,21
Madonna Mary. M. Oliphant. Leipzig, 1867. 2 v. in 1. 16°. . . J,404
Madras, Journey from. F. Buchanan. London, 1807. 3 v. 4°. . . v,717
Going to. J. M. Mackie. New York, 1855. 12°. . . . . v,470
Madvig, I. N. Latin Grammar. Oxford, 1857. 8°. . . . . . L,755
Mädler, J. H. Der Fixsternhimmel. Leipzig, 1858. 12°. . . . G,795

Männer der That. E. Willkomm. Leipzig, 1861. 4 v. 12°. . . . . G,517
Märchen, Sagen, und Legenden, Altdeutsche. R. Bechstein. Leip. 1863. 16°. G,260
Magasin Encyclopédique. Paris, 1795-96. 6 v. 8°. . . . . . T,27
Magazine of Natural History; ed. by E. Charlesworth. Lond. 1837-40. 4 v. 8°. R,42
ed. by J. C. Loundon. London, 1829-36. 9 v. 8°. . . R,45
Magazine of Science, and School of Arts, v. 7-15. Lond. 1846-51. 9 v. 8°. S.C.
Magazine of Zoology and Botany. Edinburgh, 1837-38. 2 v. 8°. . . R,29
Magee, J., Trial of, for Libel. Dublin, 1790. 8°. . . . . . . H,630
Magic, Chemical, Natural, and Physical. S. Piesse. London, 1865. 16°. M,340
History of. J. Ennemoser. London, 1854. 2 v. p. 8°. . . L,290
Letters on Natural. Sir D. Brewster. New York, 1855. 18°. . L,374
The same. London, 1832. 16°. . . . . . . . I,645
Philosophy of. A. J. E. B. Salverte. New York, 1847. 2 v. 12°. . O.326
Magic Mirror, The; Tales for Old and Young. W. Gilbert. Lond. 1866. 12°. H,493
Magic of Kindness. H. and A. Mayhew. New York, 1849. 16°. . . J,1464
Maginn, W. Fraserian Papers. New York, 1857. 8°. . . . . . H,485
Homeric Ballads and Lucian's Comedies. New York, 1856. 12°. . U,427
Odoherty Papers. New York, 1855. 2 v. 12°. . . . . H,477
Magnalia Christi Americana. C. Mather. Hartford, 1853-55. 2 v. 8°. . C,55
Magne, J. H. How to choose a good Milch Cow. Glasgow, 1857. 16°. . M,443
Magnet Stories. L. Palmer. Troy, 1867. 3 v. 16°. . . . . J,1627
Vol. 1. Drifting and Steering Vol. 2. One Day's Weaving. Vol. 3. Archie's Shadow.

Magnetic and Meteorological Observations at Girard College Observatory, 1840-45. A. D. Bache. Washington, 1863. 4°. . . . Q,324,13
Magnetic Declination, Influence of the Moon on. Washington, 1863. 4°. Q,324,13
Magnetical Investigations. W. Scoresby. London, 1839-52. 2 v. in 3. 8°. N,53
Magnetism. W. S. Harris. London, 1850. 12°. . . . . . . . M,933
D. Lardner. Philadelphia, 1854. 12°. . . . . . . N,79,2
Animal, Letters to a Candid Inquirer. W. Gregory. Phila. 1851. 12°. L,877
Electricity and Telegraphy, Quest. on. W. McGregor. Lon. 1868. 12°. M,850
Electricity, etc., Researches on. K. Reichenbach, *Baron v.* Lon. 1850. 8°. N,50
Elektricität und Chemismus. G. F. Pohl. Berlin, 1829. 12°. . N,252,23
Elektricität und Magnetismus. F. Eydam. Weimar, 1848. 8°. N,252,8
Manual of. A. Teste. Philadelphia, 1844. 12°. . . . . . L,879
Unterricht über. C. H. Schmidt. Leipzig, n. d. 12°. . . N,252,23
Magnus, A. Flusswasser und Kloaken grösserer Städte. Berlin, 1841. 8°. N,252,22
Magoon, E. L. Discourse on the Death of J. Q. Adams. Cin. 1848. 12°. . T,19,2
Orators of the American Revolution. New York, 1848. 12°. . . C,1026
Proverbs for the People. Boston, 1849. 12°. . . . . . . H,246
Republican Christianity. Boston, 1849. 12°. . . . . . . P,194
Westward Empire. New York, 1856. 12°. . . . . . . A,30
Magna Bibliotheca Veterum Patrum. Parisiis, 1644. 7 v. f°. . . . Q,79
Magyars, History of. E. L. Godkin. London, 1853. 8°. . . . . . B,530
Poetry of the. J. Bowring. London, 1830. 12°. . . . . . I,176
Mahan, A. System of Intellectual Philosophy. New York, 1847. 12°. . O,635
Mahan, D. H. Elementary Course of Civil Engineering. New York, 1857. 8°. M,706
Industrial Drawing. New York, 1865. 8°. . . . . . . M,224
Treatise on Field Fortification. New York, 1864. 18°. . . . M,747
Mahávansi, Rájá-Ratnácari, and Rájá-Vali. London, 1833. 3 v. 8°. . P,827

Mahomet. See *Mohammed.*
Mahon, Lord. See *Stanhope, P. H.*
Mahony, F. and Murphy, F. Reliques of Father Prout. Lond. 1866. 8°. L,143
Maiden Sisters. Leipzig, 1859. 16°. . . . . . . . . . . J,345
Maiden Widow. E. D. E. N. Southworth. Philadelphia, 1870. 12°. . . K,433
Maidment, J. (Ed.) Spottiswoode Miscellany. Edinburgh, 1844–45. 2 v. 8°. B,137
Mailáth, J. G. Geschichte von Oestreich. Hamburg, 1834–50. 5 v. 8°. . E,77
Maimonides, Creed and Ethics of the Jews. Cambridge, 1832. 8°. . . P,903
Main, R. Rudimentary Astronomy. London, 1852. 12°. . . . . M,948
Main, T. J. and Brown, T. Marine Steam Engine. Philadelphia, 1865. 8°. M,664
Maine, H. S. Ancient Law. New York, 1864. 8°. . . . . . . U,636
Maine, Catalogue of Original Documents. G. Folsom. New York, 1858. 8°. L.R.
Historical Society Collections. Portland, 1859–69. 7 v. 8°. . . C,123
History of. W. D. Williamson. Hallowell, 1832. 2 v. 8°. . . C,33
in the War. W. E. S. Whitman and C. H. True. Lewistown, 1865. 8°. B,950
Water-Power of. W. Wells. Augusta, 1869. 8°. . . . . . C,24
Maine Woods. H. D. Thoreau. Boston, 1868. 12°. . . . . . . V,71
Mainstone's Housekeeper. E. Meteyard. Boston, 1864. 12°. . . K,1164
Maintenon, F. d'A., Letters of. London, 1759. 2 v. 12°. . . . D,639,1,2
Life of. London, 1753. 2 v. 12°. . . . . . . . . D,639,3,4
Memoirs of. London, 1757. 2 v. 12°. . . . . . . D,639,5,6
Maitland, S. R. Early Printed Books in Lambeth Library. Lond. 1843. 8°. L.R.
Major, J. Insects on Fruit Trees. London, 1829. 8°. . . . . . O,34
Major Gahagan, Adventures of. W. M. Thackeray. Boston, 1869. 12°. K,1038,1
The same. Philadelphia, 1866. 12°. . . . . . . K,1087,1
The same. Leipzig, 1856. 16°. . . . . . . J,484,3
Make or Break. W. T. Adams. Boston, 1869. 16°. . . . . . J,1534,5
Making Honey; or, Frances Stuart. S. Flint. Boston, 1869. 16°. . J,1656
Maladies Squirrheuses, etc., Lettres sur. M. Gerbier. Geneve, 1777. 12°. L,867
Malan, S. C. Who is God in China? London, 1855. 8°. . . . . L,529
Malaria of London. A. Ure. London, 1850. 8°. . . . . . N,252,29
Malay Archipelago. A. R. Wallace. London, 1869. 2 v. 12°. . . V,881
Malayan Language, Dictionary of. W. Marsden. London, 1812. 4°. . L.R.
Malayan Waters, Journal in. S. Osborn. London, 1857. 12°. . . . V,616
Malcolm, Sir J. History of Persia. London, 1815. 2 v. 4°. . . . F,238
Malden, H. Origin of Universities and Academical Degrees. Lon. 1835. 16°. O,1156
Malet, H. P. Circle of Light. London, 1869. p. 8°. . . . . . H,244
Malherbe, A. Monographie des Picidées. Metz, 1861–62. 4 v. f°. . . Q,457
Malherbe, F. de and others. Œuvres de Poésie et Prose. Paris, 1852. 12°. H,996
Malkin, J. H. Historical Parallels. London, 1831–35. 2 v. 16°. . . L,478
Mallet, J. W. Cultivation of Cotton. London, 1862. 12°. . . . . M,647
Mallet, P. H. Northern Antiquities. London, 1847. p. 8°. . . . L,17
Mallet, R. Mechanism of Glaciers. Dublin, 1838. 8°. . . . . N,252,35
Neapolitan Earthquake, 1857; Principles of Observational Seismology. London, 1862. 2 v. r. 8°. . . . . . . . V,1107
Trap-Rocks in County of Galway. Dublin, 1838. 4°. . . . N,252,57
Mallet Du Pan, J. Destruction of the Helvetic Union. n. t. p. 12°. . B,222
Malta, Knights of. A. Sutherland. Edinburgh, 1830. 2 v. 16°. . . I,530
History of. W. Porter. London, 1858. 3 v. 8°. . . . A,237
Malte-Brun, C. Universal Geography. Philadelphia, 1827–29. 4 v. 8°. . S.C.

Malthus, T. R. Principles of Political Economy. London, 1836. 8°. . o,541
Principles of Population. London, 1826. 2 v. 8°. . . . . . o,517
Malus, S. L., Life of. F. Arago. Boston, 1859. 12°. . . . . . c,498,2
Mammalia. L. Figuier. New York, 1871. 8°. . . . . . . . N,530
Classification and Geograph. Distribution of. R. Owen. Lond. 1859. 8°. N,685
Popular History of. A. White. London, 1850. 16°. . . . N,678
Mammalogy and Ornithology of Exploring Exped. J. Cassin. Phil. 1858. 4°. *Q,277
Atlas to the same. Philadelphia, 1858. f°. . . . . . *Q,351
Mammals of North America. S. F. Baird. Philadelphia, 1857. 4°. . . Q,37
Mammiferous Animals, Natural History of. W. C. L. Martin. Lon. 1841. 8°. N,687
Mammon; or, Hardships of an Heiress. C. G. F. Gore. Leip.'55. 2 v. in 1. 16°. J,188
Man, Alter der Menscheit. O. Schmidt und F. Unger. Wein, 1866. 8°. . E,404
Alter des Menschengeschlechts. Sir C. Lyell. Leipzig, 1864. 8°. . E,401
and the Gospel. T. Guthrie. London, 1865. 12°. . . . . P,263
and his Motives. G. Moore. New York, 1848. 16°. . . . P,33
and his Relations. S. B. Brittan. New York, 1864. 8°. . . N,431
and Law, Forensic View of. R. B. Warden. Columbus, 1860. 8°. N,450
and Nature. G. P. Marsh. New York, 1867. 8°. . . . . . N,417
Anthropologie der Naturvölker. T. Waitz. Leip. 1859–64. 4 v. 8°. E,405
Antiquity of Intellectual. C. P. Smyth. Edinburgh, 1868. 8°. . N,402
The same. Berlin, 1855. 4°. . . . . . . . . . N,397
as he is not. R. Bage. London, 1820. 12°. . . . . . . K,549
Atlas der Anatomie des Menschen. C. E. Böck. Berlin, 1860. f°. *Q,292
Constitution of. G. Coombe. New York, 1835. 16°. . . . L,892
Descent of. C. Darwin. New York, 1871. 2 v. 8°. . . . N,440
General History of. N. Wanley. London, 1791. 4°. . . . N,464
Geological Evidences of the Antiquity of. Sir C. Lyell. Phila. 1863. 8°. N,437
How to be a. H. Newcomb. Boston, 1857. 8°. . . . . . J,1183
L'Homme et la Femme. M. de Lignac. v. 1, 3. Lille, 1773–4. 12°. L,843
Lettres sur l'Homme et ses Rapports. Paris, 1772. 16°. . . . L,841
Mensch im Spiegel der Natur. E.A. Rossmässler. Leip. 1868. 5 v. in 1. 16°. G,708
Moral and Physical. J. H. Jones. Philadelphia, 1860. 12°. . . L,896
Natural History of. G. L. L. Buffon. New York, 1853. 2 v. 12°. N,498
J. C. Prichard. London, 1855. 2 v. 8°. . . . . . N,448
J. G. Wood. London, 1870. 8°. . . . . . . . N,580
Observations on. D. Hartley. London, 1791. 3 v. 8°. . . . N,418
The same. London, 1801. 3 v. 8°. . . . . . . o,732
Origin and Destiny of. J. P. Lesley. Philadelphia, 1868. 8°. . N,399
Philosophy of the History of. J. G. von Herder. London, 1800. 4°. N,465
Physical History of. W. C. L. Martin. London, 1841. 8°. . . N,687
Place in Nature. T. H. Huxley. New York, 1863. 12°. . . . N,400
Primitive. L. Figuier. New York, 1871. 8°. . . . . . . N,507
Primeval. G. J. D. Campbell, *Duke of Argyll.* New York, 1869. 16°. N,390
J. Harris. Boston, 1854. 12°. . . . . . . . . . P,274
Proportionslehre der Menschlichen Gestalt. C. G. Carus. Leip. 1854. f°. *Q,448
Rechte des Menschen. T. Paine. Leipzig, 1851. 16°. . . . G,531
Seelenleben des Menschen. J. Schaller. Weimar, 1860. 8°. . . G,569
Sketches of the History of. H. Home, *Lord Kames.* Edinb. 1774. 2 v. 4°. N,466
The same. Edinburgh, 1813. 3 v. 8°. . . . . . . N,420
Social Destiny of. C. Fourier. New York, 1857. 8°. . . . . o,545

Man, Symbolik der Menschlichen Gestalt. C. G. Carus. Leipzig, 1858. 8°. E,400
Vestiges of the Spirit History of. S. F. Dunlap. New York, 1858. 8°. P,259
Vocation of; trans. by W. Smith. J. G. Fichte. London, 1848. 12°. N,398
where, whence, and whither. D. Page. Edinburgh, 1867. 16°. . N,394
Man and Wife. W. Collins. New York, 1870. 8°. . . . . . . K,631
The same. Leipzig, 1870. 3 v. 16°. . . . . . . J,77
Man in the Moon; English Fortune Teller. ed. J. O. Halliwell. Lond. 1849. 12°. L,606,29
Man made of Money, and Chronicles of Clovernook. D. Jerrold. Lond. 1853. U,178,6
Man of Feeling, The. H. Mackenzie. London, 1815. 12°. . . . K,853
The same. London, 1820. 12°. . . . . . . . K,540
Man upon the Sea; Remarkable Voyages. F. B. Goodrich. Phila. 1858. 8°. V,1085
Man who Laughs. V. Hugo. New York, 1869. 8°. . . . . . . H,953
Manby, C. Telegraphic Cables. London, 1858. 8°. . . . . . N,252,46
Manchester Educationists. J. H. Hinton. London, 1852–54. 2 pts. 8°. O,1251,3
Mandeville, B. de. Fable of the Bees. Edinburgh, 1755. 2 v. 12°. . O,349
Mandeville, Sir J. Voiage and Travaile. London, 1839. 8°. . . . V,701
Manesca, L. French Reader. Philadelphia, 1851. 12°. . . . . . L,809
Maneuvering. M. Edgeworth. New York, 1859. 12°. . . . K,678,4
Maney, H. Memories over the Water. Nashville, 1854. 12°. . . . V,333
Manhattaner in New Orleans. A. O. Hall. New York, 1851. 12°. . . V,29
Manifesto of the Church of Christ. J. Dunlavy. New York, 1847. 8°. . P,240
Mankind, Grundzüge der Ethnographie. M. Perty. Leipzig, 1859. 12°. E,402
Naturgeschichte des. J. C. Prichard. Leipzig, 1840–48. 4 v. in 5. 8°. E,403
Physical History of. J. C. Prichard. London, 1841–51. 5 v. 8°. . N,429
Atlas to the same. n. t. p. f°. . . . . . . . *Q,456
Races of. A. W. Gazlay. Cincinnati, 1856. . . . . . . N,394
Types of. J. C. Nott and G. R. Gliddon. Philadelphia, 1854. 8°. . N,449
Manly Exercises. D. Walker. London, 1865. p. 8°. . . . . . . L,152
Mann, H. Address at Antioch College. Yellow Springs, 1854. 12°. . O,1117
Answer to Boston Schoolmasters. Boston, 1845. 8°. . . . . O,927
Common School Controversy. Boston, 1844. 8°. . . . . . O,927
Educational Tour in Europe. London, 1853. 12°. . . . . O,907
Education in Great Britain. Boston, 1854. 8°. . . . . . O,1239
Lectures on Education. Boston, 1848. 12°. . . . . . . O,942
Lectures and Reports on Education. Cambridge, 1867. 2 v. 8°. . O,977
Life of. M. Mann. Boston, 1865. 8°. . . . . . . . C,930
Letters to. H. Walpole. Philadelphia, 1844. 2 v. 8°. . . . H,833
Slavery; Letters and Speeches. Boston, 1851. 12°. . . . . O,405
Mann, M. Life of Horace Mann. Boston, 1865. 8°. . . . . . . C,930
and Peabody. Culture of Infancy, and Kindergarten. N.Y. 1869. 12°. O,998
Mann, R. J. Guide to Natal. London, 1868. 12°. . . . . . . M,851
Mannering, May, *pseud.* See *Nowell, H. P. H.*
Manners. S. J. Hale. Boston, 1868. 8°. . . . . . . . . H,295
and Customs of all Nations. J. Blake. New York, 1853. 12°. V,1050
and Customs of the Japanese. New York, 1859. 18°. . . . . L,426
and Meals in the Olden Time, Poems on. London, 1868. 8°. . L,605,32
Illustrated Book of. Cincinnati, 1866. 12°. . . . . . . H,495
Manners, E. Sedgemoor. New York, 1857. 16°. . . . . . J,1353
Manning, A. Belforest. London, 1865. 2 v. 12°. . . . . . . J,593
Bessy's Money; a Tale. London, 1863. 16°. . . . . . . J,579

Manning, A. Caliph Haroun Alraschid. London, 1855. 12°. . . . . J,647
Cherry and Violet. London, 1870. 12°. . . . . . . . J,623
Chronicle of Ethelfled. London, 1861. 12°. . . . . . . J,585
Claude, the Colporteur. London, 1854. 12°. . . . . . . J,584
Colloquies of Edward Osborne. London, n. d. 12°. . . . J,586
Cottage History of England. London, 1861. 16°. . . . . . A,384
Deborah's Diary. London, 1860. 16°. . . . . . . . J,581
Diana's Crescent. London, 1868. 2 v. 16°. . . . . . . J,582
Duchess of Trajetto. London, 1863. 12°. . . . . . . J,589
Faire Gospeller. London, 1866. 12°. . . . . . . . . J,588
Good Old Times. London, 1857. 12°. . . . . . . . . J,592
Helen and Olga; a Russian Tale. London, 1857. 12°. . . . J,590
Hill-Side. London, n. d. 16°. . . . . . . . . . . . J,580
Household of Sir Thomas More. London, 1867. 12°. . . . . K,834
Interrupted Wedding. London, 1864. 12°. . . . . . . J,648
Maiden and Married Life of Mary Powell. New York, 1852. 16°. K,836
Masque at Ludlow. London, 1866. 12°. . . . . . . . . J,591
Miss Biddy Frobisher. London, 1868. 12°. . . . . . . J,583
Mrs. Clarinda Singlehart. London, 1855. 12°. . . . . . J,587
Noble Purpose Nobly Won. London, 1862. 2 v. 16°. . . . J,594
Old Chelsea Bun-House. London, 1860. 16°. . . . . . . J,626
Poplar-House Academy. London, 1859. 2 v. 16°. . . . J,595
Provocations of Madame Palissy. London, 1863. 16°. . . . J,596
Queen Philippa's Golden Booke. London, n. d. 12°. . . . I,403
Selvaggio; a Tale of Italian Life. London, 1865. 16°. . . . J,598
Spanish Barber. London, 1869. 12°. . . . . . . . . J,597
Tasso and Leonora. London, 1856. 12°. . . . . . . . J,625
Town and Forest. London, 1860. 12°. . . . . . . . . J,599
Valentine Duval. London, 1860. 12°. . . . . . . . . J,644
Village Bells. London, 1859. 16°. . . . . . . . . . J,624
Year Nine; Tale of the Tyrol. London, 1858. 12°. . . . . J,646
Manning, J. A. Speakers of the House of Commons. London, 1851. 8°. C,1309
Mansel, H. L. Limits of Religious Thought. Boston, 1860. 12°. . . P,191
Mansfield, C. B. Patent for Oils for Artificial Light. Glasgow, 1810. N,252,30
Mansfield, E. D. American Education. New York, 1851. 8°. . . . O,954
and Drake, B. Cincinnati in 1826. Cincinnati, 1827. 12°. . . C,208
Eulogy on W. H. Harrison. Cincinnati, 1841. 8°. . . . . H,302,4
History of the Mexican War. New York, 1850. 8°. . . . . B,884
Life and Service of Daniel Drake. Cincinnati, 1855. 12°. . . C,789
Life of Winfield Scott. New York, 1847. 12°. . . . . . C,1085
Lives of Ulysses S. Grant and Schuyler Colfax. Cincinnati, 1868. 12°. C,957
Political Grammar of the United States. Cincinnati, 1849. 16°. . O,471
Utility of the Mathematics. Cincinnati, 1835. . . . . . H,302,4
(Ed.) Monthly Chronicle. Cincinnati, 1839. 8°. . . . . . T,8
Mansfield, R. B. Log of the Water Lily. Leipzig, 1854. 16°. . . . J,346
School-Life at Winchester College. London, 1870. 12°. . . . O,830
Mansfield Park. J. Austen. Boston, 1864. 12°. . . . . . . K,594
The same. Leipzig, 1867. 16°. . . . . . . . . J,29
Manso, J. C. F. Ost Gothisches Reich in Italien. Breslau, 1824. 8°. . E,100
Mantell, G. A. Geological Excursions to Isle of Wight. Lond. 1854. p. 8°. L,304

Mantell, G. A. Medals of Creation. London, 1844. 2 v. p. 8°. . . . L,305
Petrifactions and their Teachings. London, 1851. p. 8°. . . . . L,306
Thoughts on a Pebble. London, 1849. 12°. . . . . . . . N,599
Wonders of Geology. London, 1840. 2 v. 12°. . . . . . N,596
The same. London, 1866. 2 v. f°. . . . . . . L,307
Manual for a Christian Soldier. E. Erasmus. London, 1687. 4°. . . P,4
Manual Pereira; Rule of South Carolina. F. C. Adams. Wash. 1853. 12°. K,1
Manufactures, Arts, and Mines, Dictionary of. A. Ure. Lond. 1867. 3 v. 8°. *M,805
History of American. J. L. Bishop. Philadelphia, 1868. 3 v. 8°. M,676
Philosophy of. A. Ure. London, 1861. p. 8°. . . . . . . L,322
in Metal. J. Holland. London, 1831. 3 v. 12°. . . . M,1043
of the United States. E. T. Freedley. Philadelphia, 1856. 8°. . C,595
Report on. A. Hamilton. Dublin, 1792. 8°. . . . . . . H,630
Manures, Application and Economy of. A. Huxtable. Southamp. 1846. 8°. N,252,25
The same. Southampton, 1846. 8°. . . . . . . N,252,31
Deceptions in Artificial. J. Robinson. London, n. d. 8°. . . N,252,25
Fumier de Basse Cour. C. T. Chackeray. Paris, 1847. 8°. . N,252,25
Fumiers considérés comme Engrais. J. Girardin. Paris, 1847. 16°. N,252,26
Relation to Crop, Soil, Atmosphere. F.S.M. de Sussex. Lond. 1848. 8°. N,252,31
Science and Application of. A. Huxtable. London, 1847. 8°. . N,252,25
Several Tracts on. C. W. Johnson. London, 1836–43. 8°. . . N,252,25
Crushed Bones as a Manure. Gypsum as a Fertilizer.
Guano as a Fertilizer. Saltpeter and Nitrate of Soda as Fertilizers.
Uses of Salt for Agricultural Purposes.
Maps, Construc. des Cartes Hydrograph. Beautemps-Beaupré. Par. 1811. 4°. M,819
of the Society for the Diffusion of Knowledge. London, 1844. 2 v. f°. *Q,453
of the several United States. S. Lewis and others. Phil. 1794–95. f°. Q,394
of U. S. Coast Survey, Catalogue of. Washington, 1862. 8°. . . L.R.
Marana, G. P. Letters of a Turkish Spy. London, 1748. 8 v. 16°. . H,390
Marble Faun. N. Hawthorne. Boston, 1864. 2 v. 16°. . . . . K,160
The same. Boston, 1868. 2 v. 12°. . . . . . U,40,9,10
Marble-Worker's Manual. New York, 1856. 16°. . . . . . . . M,603
Marcel, C. Study of Languages. New York, 1869. 12°. . . . . L,502
Marcet, A. Saline Contents of Sea Water. London, 1822. 4°. . . N,252,42
March, F. A. Philological Study of the English Language. N.Y. 1865. 12°. L,565
March Winds and April Showers. L. M. Budgen. London, 1854. 16°. . N,497
Marchand, R. F. Gundriss der Organischen Chemie. Leipzig, 1839. 8°. N,252,28
Marchese, P. Painters, Sculptors, etc., of S. Dominic. Order. Dubl. 1852. 2 v. 12°. M,154
Marchmont Papers, 1685–1752. London, 1831. 3 v. 8°. . . . . . A,556
Marco Paul's Voyages and Travels. J. Abbott. N. Y. 1852–53. 6 v. 16°. J,1380
Vol. 1. In New York. Vol. 4. In Vermont.
2. On the Erie Canal. 5. In Boston.
3. In Maine. 6. At Springfield Armory.
Marcou, J. Geological Map of the United States. Boston, 1853. 2 v. 8°. N,827
Marcus Flaminius. E. C. Knight. London, 1792. 2 v. 8°. . . . K,759
Marcus Warland. C. L. Hentz. New York, 1870. 12°. . . . . . K,167
Marcy, R. B. and McClellan, G. B. Exploration of Red River. Wash. 1853. 8°. V,81
Thirty Years of Army Life on the Border. New York, 1866. 8°. . V,108
Mardi, and a Voyage thither. H. Melville. New York, 1849. 2 v. 12°. K,214
Marey, Col. Memoir on Swords, etc. London, 1860. 12°. . . . . M,852
Margaret; a Tale of the Real and Ideal. S. Judd. Boston, 1871. 12°. . K,206
Margaret and her Bridesmaids. J. Stretton. Boston, 1864. 12°. . . K,852

Margaret Maitland. M. Oliphant. Leipzig, 1862. 16°. . . . . . J,397
Margaret of Anjou, History of. J. Abbott. New York, 1861. 16°. . J,1417
Margaret Percival. E. M. Sewell. New York, 1868. 2 v. 12°. . K,1002
Margaret Smith's Journal. J. G. Whittier. Boston, 1849. 16°. . . H.286
Margarinsäure. F. Varrentrapp. n. t. p. 8°. . . . . . . N,252,21
Maria Theresia und ihr Ofenheizer. C. Mundt. Berlin, 1864. 12°. . G.362,2
Maria Antoinette. Mémoires sur la Vie de. Mad. Campan. Paris, 1855. 16°. D,599
Court of. Madame Campan. Philadelphia, 1850. 2 v. 12°. . . D,621
History of. J. S. C. Abbott. New York, 1849. 16°. . . J,1384
and her Son. C. Mundt. New York, 1867. 8°. . . . . . G.207
Marie de Hongrie, Vie de. T. Juste. Bruxelles, 1861. 12°. . . H,1032
Marie de Medicis, Life of. J. Pardoe. London, 1852. 3 v. 8°. . . D,729
Marietta. T. A. Trollope. Philadelphia, 1870. 12°. . . . . . K,1041
Marine Animals, Nature and Habits of. F. C. L. Wraxall. Lond. 1860. 8°. N,505
Marine Insurance, Law and Practice of. J. Duer. N. Y. 1845-46. 2 v. 8°. U,529
Mariner, W. Account of the Tonga Islands. Edinburgh, 1827. 2 v. 16°. I,500
The same. London, 1818. 2 v. 8°. . . . . . . V,894
Marion, F. Wonderful Balloon Ascents. New York, 1870. 12°. . M,1063
Wonders of Optics. London, 1868. 12°. . . . . . . M.1059
Marion, F., Life of. P. Horry and M. S. Weems. Philadelphia, 1863. 12°. C,1009
Life of. W. G. Simms. Cincinnati, 1854. 12°. . . . . . C,682
Mariotti, L., *pseud.* See *Gallenga, A.*
Mariquita and New Grenada Mining Company. London, 1859. 8°. . N,252,46
Maritime and Inland Discovery. W. D. Cooley. Lond. 1830-31. 3 v. 12°. M,1006
Maritime Law of Europe. D. A. Azuni. New York, 1806. 2 v. 8°. . U,542
Mark, the Match Boy. H. Alger. Boston, 1869. 16°. . . . J,1430,3
Mark Rowland; a Tale of the Sea. J. S. Sleeper. Boston, 1867. 12°. . K,117
Markby, T. Practical Essays on Education. London, 1868. 12°. . . O,936
Market Assistant. T. F. De Voe. New York, 1867. 8°. . . . . . H.291
Markham, C. R. Cuzco; Journey to Ancient Capital of Peru. Lond. 1856. 8°. V,239
Marks, J. J. Peninsular Campaign in Virginia. Philadelphia, 1864. 12°. B,927
Marksmen, Instructions to Young. J. R. Chapman. New York, 1848. 12°. M.307
Marlborough, Duchess of, Memoirs of. A. T. Thompson. Lond. 1839. 2 v. 8°. D,163
Marlborough, Duke of. See *Churchill, J.*
Marleburrough, H. Chronicle of Ireland, 1285-1421. Dublin, 1809. 4°. A,565,2
The same. Dublin, 1809. 4°. . . . . . . B,182,2
Marlitt, E., *pseud.* See *John, E.*
Marlowe, C., Works of. London, 1865. 8°. . . . . . . . I,726
Marmaduke Herbert; or, Fatal Error. M. Gardiner. Leip. 1847. 2 v. in 1. 16°. J,193
Marmaduke Merry, the Midshipman. W. H. Kingston. London, n. d. 12°. J,1720
Marmontel, J. F. Contes Moraux. Londres, 1793. 6 v. 24°. . . . H,853
Eléments de Littérature. Paris, 1854. 3 v. 12°. . . . . H,640
Mémoires de. Paris, 1855. 12°. . . . . . . . . D,598
Memoirs of himself. Edinburgh, 1808. 4 v. 12°. . . . . . D,662
Maroon; or, Planter Life in Jamaica. M. Reed. New York, n. d. 12°. J,1568
Marooner's Island. F. R. Goulding. Philadelphia, 1869. 16°. . . J,1605
Maroons, Crimes committed against. J. R. Giddings. Columbus, 1858. 12°. C,181
History of. R. C. Dallas. London, 1803. 2 v. 8°. . . . C,427
Marquesas Islands, Residence in. H. Melville. London, 1847. 12°. . V,891
Marquette, J. Narrative of the Mississippi Valley. New York, 1852. 8°. C,272

Marquette, J., Life of. J. Sparks. New York, 1860. 12°. . . . c,860,10
Marriage Guide. F. Hollick. New York, 1860. 16°. . . . . . L,836
Marriage, Letters on. J. Witherspoon. Andover, 1817. 12°. . . o,1157
Physiology of. W. A. Alcott. Boston, 1868. 12°. . . . . . L,918
Married at Last. A. Cudlip. Philadelphia, n. d. 12°. . . . K,1147
Married for both Worlds. A. E. Porter. Boston, 1871. 12°. . . . K,266
Married or Single? C. M. Sedgwick. New York, 1858. 2 v. 12°. . . K,238
Marriott, C. New Royal English Dictionary. London, 1780. 4°. . . L.R.
Marryat, Florence. See *Church, F.*
Marryat, Frederick. Children of the New Forest. Leipzig, 1848. 16°. . J,353
Frank Mildmay, the Naval Officer. New York, 1868. 12°. . . K,838
Jacob Faithful. New York, 1868. 12°. . . . . . . . . K,841
Japhet in Search of a Father. New York, 1866. 12°. . . . K,842
The same. Leipzig, 1843. 16°. . . . . . . . . J,354
King's Own. New York, 1868. 12°. . . . . . . . . . K,843
The same. Leipzig, 1869. 16°. . . . . . . . . J,355
Masterman Ready. London, 1869. p. 8°. . . . . . . . L,120
Mr. Midshipman Easy. New York, 1866. 12°. . . . . K,844
The same. Leipzig, 1869. 16°. . . . . . . . . J,356
Mission; or, Scenes in Africa. London, 1864. p. 8°. . . . L,121
The same. Leipzig, 1845. 16°. . . . . . . . . J,357
Newton Forster. New York, 1868. 12°. . . . . . . . K,845
Pacha of Many Tales. New York. 1868. 12°. . . . . . K,846
Percival Keene. New York, 1868. 12°. . . . . . . . K,847
The same. Leipzig, 1842. 16°. . . . . . . . . J,359
Peter Simple. New York 1869. 12°. . . . . . . . . K,848
The same. Leipzig, 1842. 16°. . . . . . . . . J,360
Phantom Ship. New York, 1868. 12°. . . . . . . . . K,849
Pirate and Three Cutters. London, 1867. p. 8°. . . . . . L,122
Poacher. New York, 1868. 12°. . . . . . . . . . K,850
Privateersman. Leipzig, 1846. 16°. . . . . . . . . . J,361
The same. London, 1867. p. 8°. . . . . . . . . L,123
Settlers in Canada. New York, 1845. 2 v. 16°. . . . . J,1171
The same. London, 1869. p. 8°. . . . . . . . . L,124
The same. Leipzig, 1844. 16°. . . . . . . . . J,362
Snarleyyow; or, the Dog Fiend. New York, 1868. 12°. . . . K,851
Travels of Mons. Violet. Leipzig, 1843. 16°. . . . . . . J,358
Valerie; an Autobiography. Leipzig, 1849. 16°. . . . . . J,363
Marryatt, J. History of Pottery and Porcelain. London, 1868. 8°. . M,645
Marsden, J. B. History of Christian Churches and Sects. Lon. 1856. 2 v. 8°. P,604
History of the Later Puritans. London, 1854. 8°. . . . . . P,613
Marsden, W. Dictionary of Malayan Language. London, 1812. 4°. . L.R.
Marsh, C. Administration of Sir H. Barlow at Madras. London, 1813. 8°. C,408
Marsh-Caldwell, A. Aubrey. Leipzig, 1854. 2 v. in 1. 16°. . . . . J,364
Castle Avon. Leipzig, 1852. 2 v. in 1. 16°. . . . . . . J,365
Emilia Wyndham. Leipzig, 1852. 2 v. in 1. 16°. . . . . . J,366
Evelyn Marston. Leipzig, 1856. 2 v. in 1. 16°. . . . . . J,367
Heiress of Haughton. Leipzig, 1855. 2 v. in 1. 16°. . . . . J,368
Protestant Reformation in France. Philadelphia, 1851. 2 v. 12°. . P,573
Ravenscliffe. Leipzig, 1851. 2 v. in 1. 16°. . . . . . . . J,369

Marsh-Caldwell, A. Rose of Ashurst. Leipzig, 1857. 2 v. in 1. 16°. . J,370
Marsh, G. P. The Camel; his Organization, Habits, etc. Bost. 1856. 12°. M,446
History of the English Language. New York, 1862. 8°. . . . L,620
Man and Nature. New York, 1867. 8°. . . . . . . . N,417
Marsh, Mrs. G. P. Wolfe of the Knoll, and other Poems. N. Y. 1860. 12°. I,89
Marshall, H. History of Kentucky. Frankfort, 1824. 2 v. 8°. . . *C,179
Marshall, J. History of the English Colonies. Philadelphia, 1824. 8°. . B,622
Life of. G. Van Santvoord. New York, 1854. 8°. . . . . . C,817
H. Flanders. Philadelphia, 1855. 8°. . . . . . C,816,2
Life of Washington. Philadelphia, 1836. 2 v. 8°. . . . . . C,906
Writings upon the Federal Constitution. Boston, 1839. 8°. . . U,111
Marshall, J. Feeding Stock with prepared Food. London, 1847. 8°. N,252,24
Vaccination in relation to Public Health. London, 1847. 8°. . N,252,29
Marshall, W. Country of Schamyl. London, 1862. 8°. . . . V,1086,2
Marshall, W. Planting and Rural Ornament. London, 1803. 2 v. 8°. . M,561
Marshman, J. C. History of India. London, 1867. 3 v. 12°. . . C,400
Memoirs of Sir Henry Havelock. London, 1860. 8°. . . . . D,468
Marsigli, L. F. Danubius Pannonico-Mysicus. Hagæ Com. 1726. 6 v. in 3. f°. *F,301
Marston, J. Works. London, 1856. 3 v. 16°. . . . . . . I,749
Marstons; a Novel. H. Aïdé. Leipzig, 1868. 2 v. in 1. 16°. . . . J,5
Marten, F. Observations in Greenland. London, 1711. 8°. . . . V,961
Voyage to Spitzbergen. London, 1855. 8°. . . . . . . V,984
Martha Brown. Leipzig, 1861. 16°. . . . . . . . . . . J,371
Martialis, M. V. Epigrammata. Parisiis, 1825. 3 v. 8°. . . . U,332
The same; translated. London, 1865. p. 8°. . . . L,69
Martin, F. Statesman's Year-Book. London, 1869. 12°. . . . O,486
Martin, H. Histoire de France jusqu'en, 1789. Paris, 1865. 17 v. 8°. . B,267
History of France; Age of Louis XIV. Boston, 1865. 2 v. 8°. . B,369
The same; Decline of the Monarchy. Boston, 1866. 2 v. 8°. B,370
Martin, L. A. Education of Mothers of Families. London, 1851. 8°. . O,923
Martin, M. Voyage to St. Kilda. Glasgow, 1820. 12°. . . . B,111,2
Martin, R. M. Australia. London, 1853. 8°. . . . . . . . F,219
British Colonies; History, Condition, etc. London, n. d. 4°. . N,252,53
China; Political, Commercial, and Social. London, 1847. 2 v. 8°. V,619
Martin, T. Memoir of William E. Aytoun. Edinburgh, 1867. 8°. . . D,449
Martin, T. New Biographies of Illustrious Men. Boston, 1857. 12°. . C,496
Martin, W. C. L. History of Cattle. New York, 1858. 12°. . . . M,466
History of the Dog. London, 1845. 18°. . . . . . . . M,441
History of the Horse. London, 1853. 18°. . . . . . . M,441
Humming-Birds. London, 1852. 16°. . . . . . . . O,83
Natural History of Mammiferous Animals. London, 1841. 8°. . N,687
Martin, W. T. History of Franklin County, Ohio. Columbus, 1858. 8°. C,214
Martin Chuzzlewit. C. Dickens. New York, 1868. 12°. . . . . . K,480
The same. Philadelphia, 1844. 8°. . . . . . . K,512
The same. New York, 1871. 2 v. 12°. . . . . K,1134
The same. Leipzig, 1844. 2 v. in 1. 16°. . . . . . J,126
Martin Merrivale; his X Mark. J. T. Trowbridge. Boston, 1854. 12°. K,118
Martin Rattler. R. M. Ballantyne. London, 1867. 16°. . . . . J,1518
Martine, A. Sensible Letter-Writer. New York, 1866. 16°. . . . . H,6
Martine, G. Reliquiae Divi Andreae, See of St. Andrews. St. And. 1797. 4°. P,648

Martineau, H. Biographical Sketches. New York, 1869. 12°. . . . c,554
British Rule in India. London, 1857. 12°. . . . . . . c,424
Charles and Antoine Lucyon. Cincinnati, 1853. 18°. . . J,1452
Charmed Sea. Cincinnati, 1853. 18°. . . . . . . J,1453
Deerbrook; a Novel. London, 1858. 12°. . . . . . . K,528
Hill and Valley. Cincinnati, 1853. 16°. . . . . . J,1458
Hist. of England during the Peace, 1816–54. Bost. 1865–6. 4 v. 8°. A,407
The same. London, 1849–50. 2 v. 8°. . . . A,418,10,11
Introduction to the same. London, 1851. 8°. . A,418,9
Household Education. Philadelphia, 1849. 12°. . . . O,1006
Illustrations of Political Economy. London, 1834. 9 v. 18°. . K,551
Vol. 1. Life in the Wilds; Hill and Valley; Brooke and Brooke Farm.
2. Demerara; Ella of Garveloch; Weal and Woe in Garveloch.
3. Manchester Strike; Cousin Marshall; Ireland.
4. Homes Abroad; For Each and for All; French Wines and Politics.
5. Charmed Sea; Berkley, the Banker.
6. Messrs. Vanderput and Snoek; Loom and the Lugger.
7. Sowers not Reapers; Cinnamon and Pearls; Tale of the Tyne.
8. Briery Creek; Three Ages.
9. Farrers of Budge Row; Moral of Many Fables.
Illustrations of Taxation. London, 1834. 5 v. in 1. 18°. . . K,552
Life in the Sick Room. Boston, 1845. 16°. . . . . . . H,576
Miscellanies. Boston, 1836. 2 v. 12°. . . . . . . . H,594
Poor Laws and Paupers Illustrated. London, 1833. 4 v. in 1. 18°. K,553
Society in America. London, 1837. 3 v. 12°. . . . . V,104
Sowers not Reapers. Cincinnati, 1853. 18°. . . . . J,1455
Retrospect of Western Travel. London, 1838. 3 v. 12°. . . V,143
Martineau, J. Essays, Philosophical and Theological. Bost. 1868. 2 v. 12°. H,611
Miscellanies. Boston, 1852. 12°. . . . . . . . . H,488
Martinet, J. F. Religion in Society. New York, 1850. 12°. . . . P,192
Martins of Cro' Martin. C. Lever. London, 1864. 2 v. 8°. . . . K,781
The same. Leipzig, 1856. 3 v. 16°. . . . . . . J,281
Martyn, H., Memoir of. J. Sargent. New York, 1844. 12°. . . C,1228
The same. New York, n. d. 18°. . . . . . P,746,8
Martyria; or, Andersonville Prison. A. C. Hamlin. Boston, 1866. 12°. B,895
Martyrs, Book of. J. Fox. Philadelphia, 1866. 12°. . . . . . P,810
Les. R. F. A. de Chateaubriand. Paris, 1855. 12°. . . . . . H,936
The same, translated. New York, 1863. 12°. . . . . . H,934
of Science; or, Lives of Galileo, Tycho Brahe, and Kepler. Sir D. Brewster. New York, 1854. 16°. . . . . . . . . L,424
The same. London, 1870. p. 8°. . . . . . . C,551
of Spain. E. Charles. New York, 1865. 12°. . . . . . . K,624
Marvel, Ik, *pseud.* See *Mitchell, D. G.*
Marvell, A., Life of. H. Coleridge. London, 1852. 16°. . . . . C,1166,1
Poetical Works. Boston, 1857. 16°. . . . . . . . . . I,217
Marvels of Pond-Life. H. J. Slack. London, 1861. 12°. . . . . O,74
Marx, A. B. General Musical Instruction. London, 1854. 8°. . . M,421,1
Beethoven, Leben und Schaffen. Berlin, 1859. 2 v. 8°. . . . . G,638
Mary Barton. E. C. Gaskell. New York, 1848. 8°. . . . . . . K,706
The same. Leipzig, 1849. 16°. . . . . . . . J,179
Mary Derwent. A. S. Stephens. Philadelphia, 1870. 16°. . . . K,448
Mary Lee. K. Livermore. New York, 1865. 16°. . . . . . J,1359
Mary Powell, Maiden and Married Life of. A. Manning. N. Y. n. d. 16°. K,836

Mary, Queen of Scots, History of. J. S. C. Abbott. New York, 1868. 16°. J,1407
History of. F. A. A. Mignet. London, 1851. 2 v. 8°. . . . . D,127
The same. London, 1863. 12°. . . . . . . D,245
Letters of. London, 1842–43. 3 v. 12°. . . . . . . . H,815
Life of. H. G. Bell. Edinburgh, 1828. 2 v. 16°. . . . . . I,507
The same. New York, 1869. 2 v. 8°. . . . L,354
E. O. Benger, v. 2. Philadelphia, 1851. 12°. . . . C,1223
G. Chalmers. London, 1822. 3 v. 8°. . . . . . . D,128
vindicated. J. Whitaker. London, 1790. 3 v. 8°. . . . . D,112
Maryland, Growth of Toleration in. G. L. L. Davis. New York, 1855. 12°. C,168
History of. James Mac Sherry. Baltimore, 1849. 8°. . . . C,114
History of, 1633-1660. J. L. Bozman. Baltimore, 1837. 2 v. 8°. . C,124
Line in the Confederate Army. W. W. Goldsborough. Balt. 1869. 12°. B,963
Relation of the Colony. A. White. 1677. See *Force's Tracts*, v. 4.
Sketch of the History of. J. L. Bozman. Baltimore, 1811. 8°. . C,113
Masius, H. Skizzen aus der Pflanzen- und Thierwelt. Leipzig, 1852. 8°. . G,702
Thierwelt. Essen, 1862. 8°. . . . . . . . . . . G,930
Maske des Reichthums. E. Fritze. Hannover, 1863. 16°. . . . G,277,3
Mason, E. P. Introduction to Practical Astronomy. New York, 1841. 8°. N,293
Life and Writings. D. Olmsted. New York, 1842. 12°. . . C,1013
Mason, F. H. Twelfth Ohio Cavalry in the Rebellion. Cleveland, 1871. 8°. B,962
Mason, G. H. Life with the Zulus of Natal. London, 1855. p. 8°. . I,658,1
Mason, F. Story of a Working Man's Life. New York, 1870. 12°. . . C,730
Mason, G. C. Newport Illustrated. New York, 1854. 12°. . . . V,101
Mason, J., Life of. G. E. Ellis. Boston, 1860. 12°. . . . . C,860,13
Mason, J. Self-Knowledge. New York, n. d. 16°. . . . . P,746,21
Mason, J. M., Memoirs. J. Van Vechten. New York, 1856. 8°. . . D,37
Mason, R. Farrier and Stud-Book. Philadelphia, 1858. 12°. . . . M,448
Mason, S. W. Manual of Gymnastic Exercises. Boston, 1864. 16°. . O,1151
Mason, T. B. Journey through Kansas and Nebraska. Cincinnati, 1855. 12°. V,100
Mason, W., Life of. H. Coleridge. London, 1852. 16°. . . . C,1166,2
Spiritual Treasury for the Children of God. New York, n. d. 12°. P,193
Masonic Institution, Letters and Opinions on. J. Q. Adams. Cincin. 1851. 8°. O,381
See also *Freemasonry*.
Masonry and Stone-Cutting. E. Dobson. London, 1856. 12°. . . . M,911
Guide to Railway Masonry. P. Nicholson. London, 1840. 8°. . M,698
Masque at Ludlow. A. Manning. London, 1866. 12°. . . . . J,591
Masquerade; and other Poems. J. G. Saxe. Boston, 1866. 16°. . . I,120
Massachusetts, Adjutant-General's Report, 1866–68. Boston, 1866-68. 3 v. 8°. P.D.
Board of Health Report, 1871. Boston, 1871. 8°. . . . . . P.D.
Board of State Charities Reports, 1869–71. Boston, 1869-71. 2 v. 8°. P.D.
Charters and General Laws of the Colony. Boston, 1814. 8°. . . C,85
Chronicles of the First Planters of. A. Young. Boston, 1846. 8°. . C,45
Colony Records, 1628–1686; ed. N. B. Shurtleff. Bost. 1853–54. 5 v. in 6. 8°. F,85
Economical Geology of. E. Hitchcock. Boston, 1838. 8°. . N,252,35
Early History of; Lowell Institute Lectures. Boston, 1869. 8°. . C,52
General Court Manual. Boston, 1871. 16°. . . . . . . C,35
Geology, Botany, and Zoology of. E. Hitchcock. Amherst, 1833. 8°. N,746
Historical Collections of. J. W. Barber. Worcester, 1840. 8°. . C,54
Historical Society, Bibliography of. S. A. Green. Boston, 1871. 8°. L.R.

Massachusetts, Historical Society, Dowse Library Catalogue. Boston, 1870. 8°. L.R.
History of. New York, 1840. 2 v. 18°. . . . . . . J,1221
J. S. Barry. Boston, 1855–57. 3 v. 8°. . . . . . . C,67
W. H. Carpenter. Philadelphia, 1853. 12°. . . . . . C,38
1620–1820. A. Bradford. Boston, 1835. 8°. . . . C,47
The same, 1764–1765. Boston, 1822. 8°. . . . C,50
1628-1750. T. Hutchinson. Salem, 1795. 2 v. 8°. . C,41,1,2
The same, continued, 1749–74. London, 1828. 8°. . C,41,3
of the First Regiment. W. H. Cudworth. Boston, 1866. 12°. B,925
of the Second Regiment. A. H. Quint. Boston, 1864. 12°. . B,894
of the Sixth Regiment. J. W. Hanson. Boston, 1866. 12°. . B,912
of Slavery in. G. H. Moore. New York, 1866. 8°. . . C,46
of Western. J. G. Holland. Springfield, 1855. 2 v. 12°. . C,40
in the Civil War. W. Schouler. Boston, 1868. 8°. . . . . . B,939
in the Rebellion. P. C. Headley. Boston, 1866. 8°. . . . B,914
Invertebrata of. A. A. Gould; ed. by W. G. Binney. Boston, 1870. 8°. N,721
Judicial History of, 1630–1775. E. Washburn. Boston, 1840. 8°. C,42
Plymouth and the Pilgrims. J. Banvard. Boston, 1866. 16°. . C,17
Plymouth Colony Records, 1633-98. Boston, 1855–61. 12 v. in 10. 4°. F,86
Quartermaster's Report, 1862. Boston, 1862. 8°. . . . . . P.D.
Registration Reports, 1864–65. Boston, 1864–65. 2 v. 8°. . . P.D.
State Constitutional Convention, 1820. Boston, 1853. 8°. . . . C,70
State Library, Catalogue. Boston, 1858. 8°. . . . . . . L.R.
State Prison, Sketch of. G. Haynes. Boston, 1870. 12°. . . . O,365
Statistical Industry in, 1837. J. P. Bigelow. Boston, 1838. 8°. . C,36
Trees and Shrubs of. G. B. Emerson. Boston, 1846. 8°. . . N,1017
United States Constitutional Convention. 1788. Boston, 1856. 8°. . C,69
Massachusetts Teacher. Boston, 1848–53. 8°. . . . . . . O,1252
Massacre of St. Bartholomew. H. White. New York, 1868. 8°. . . B,366
Massey, G. Tale of Eternity, and other Poems. Boston, 1870. 16°. . I,158
Massey, W. History of England. London, 1865. 4 v. 12°. . . . A,423
Massie, J. C. Eclectic Southern Practice of Medicine. Philadlephia, 1854. 8°. L,967
Massillon, J. B. Chefs-d'Œuvre. Paris, 1855. 8°. . . . . . . P,724
Sermons et Morceaux Choisis. Paris, 1856. 12°. . . . P,61
Massinger, Philip. Believe as you List; a Tragedy. London, 1849. 12°. L,606,27
and Ford, J. Dramatic Works. London, 1869. 8°. . . . . I,727
Massmann, H. F. Wörterbuch der Althochdeutschen Sprache. Berl. 1846. 7 v. 4°. L.R.
Masson, D. British Novelists and their Styles. Boston, 1859. 12°. . . H,700
Life of John Milton, v. 1, 2. London, 1859-71. 8°. . . . C,1264
Recent British Philosophy. New York, 1866. 12°. . . . O,695
Massy, R. T. Analytical Ethnology. London, 1855. 12°. . . . N,393
Mast-Making. R. Kipping. London, 1859. 12°. . . . . . . M,941
Master-Builder's Plan in Forms of Animals. G. Ogilvie. London, 1858. 12°. N,645
Master Humphrey's Clock. C. Dickens. Leipzig, 1846. 3 v. 16°. . J,127
Old Curiosity Shop. Barnaby Rudge.
Introductory Chapters of. New York, 1871. 12°. . . . K,1135
Masterman Ready. F. Marryat. London, 1869. p. 8°. . . . . L,120
Masury, J. W. Treatise on House-Painting. New York, 1868. 12°. . M,648
Materialism, Discussions on, etc. J. Priestly. London, 1778. 8°. . U,294,9
Materialismus als Köhlerglaube. F. Michelis. Münster, 1856. 8°. E,443

Maternal Counsels. Mrs. Pullan. London, 1858. 12°. . . . . . O,959
Mathematical Analysis, Vorlesungen über. J. M. C. Bartels. Dorp. 1837. 2 v. 4°. E,437
Mathematical and Philosophical Dictionary. C. Hutton. Lond. 1795. 2 v. 4°. L.R.
Mathematical Dictionary. C. Davis and W. G. Peck. New York, 1859. 8°. M,1176
Mathematical Instruments, Treatise on. F. W. Simms. Baltimore, 1836. 8°. M,662
Mathematical Monthly. Cambridge, 1859–60. 3 v. 4°. . . . M,1188
Mathematics. J. Snape. London, 1847. 8°. . . . . . . N,252,33
Course of. C. Hutton. London, 1854. 8°. . . . . . M,1173
Elements of Quaternions. Sir W. R. Hamilton. Lond. 1866. 8°. M,1155
Encyclopædia of Pure. London, 1845. 4°. . . . . . . L.R.
Entwickelung einiger Math. Theorien. J. Schulz. Königs. 1803. 4°. M,1175
Enseignement des. S. F. La Croix. Paris, 1816. 8°. . . . O,918
Examples and Problems in. A. Wrigley. London, 1865. 8°. M,1121
for Practical Men. O. Gregory. London, 1862. 8°. . . M,1178
Historie des Mathematiques. J. E. Montucla. Paris, 1758–1802. 4 v. 4°. M,1203
Illustrated, Appleton's. New York, 1856. 2 v. 8°. . . . Q,259
Lectures on Quaternions. Sir W. R. Hamilton. Dublin, 1853. 8°. M,1161
Logic and Utility of. C. Davies. New York, 1850. 8°. . M,1172
Philosophy of. A. Comte. New York, 1851. 8°. . . . M,1189
Problems and Examples in. H. Goodwin. Cambridge, 1862. 8°. M,1174,1
Sammlung Mathematischer Tafeln. G. von Vega. Leip. 1840. 8°. E,436
Tables Definite Proportionals. W. T. Brande. London, 1828. 8°. M,1160
Utility of. E. D. Mansfield. Cincinnati, 1835. 8°. . . H,302,4
Vorlesungen über die Mathematik. G. v. Vega. Wein, 1793–1800. 4 v. 8°. E,428
Mather, C., and Salem Witchcraft. W. F. Poole. Boston, 1869. 8°. . O,341
and Witchcraft, Mr. Upham his reply. W. F. Poole. Bost. 1870. 16°. O,323
History of King Philip's War. Albany, 1862. 4°. . . . C,30
Magnalia Christi Americana. Hartford, 1853–55. 2 v. 8°. . . C,55
Life of. W. B. O. Peabody. Boston, 1860. 12°. . . . C,860,6
Wonders of the Invisible World. London, 1862. 12°. . . . O,339
The same; ed. by S. G. Drake. Roxbury, 1866. r. 8°. O,432,1
Mather, I. Early History of New England; ed. by S. G. Drake. Bost. 1864. 4°. B,603
With Historical Discourse concerning Prayer.
History of King Philip's War; ed. by S. G. Drake. Boston, 1862. 4°. C,30
Life of. E. Pond. Boston, 1846. 12°. . . . . . . . D,8,5
Remarkable Providences. London, 1856. 12°. . . . . . O,344
Mather, W. W. Geology of New York. Albany, 1843. 4°. . . *Q,101,9
Reports on Geological Survey of Ohio. Columbus, 1838. 8°. *N,874,1,2
Mathews, C., Memoirs of. A. J. Mathews. London, 1839. 4 v. 8°. . D,408
Mathias, T. J. Pursuits of Literature; Satirical Poem. London, 1798. 8°. J,871
The same. London, 1803. 8°. . . . . . . . J,872
Matins and Vespers. J. Bowring. London, 1823. 12°. . . . . I,286
Matrimonial Infelicities. R. B. Coffin. New York, 1865. 8°. . . K,12
Matteucci, C. Phénomènes Electriques des Animaux. Paris, 1840. 8°. N,252,8
Physical Phenomena of Living Beings. London, 1847. 8°. . . L,876
Matterhorn (Mt. Cervin), Ascent of. F. V. Hawkins. Lond. 1861. 8°. V,1086,1
Matthew Wald. J. G. Lockhart. Edinburgh, 1849. 16°. . . . K,805
Matthew of Westminster. Flowers of History; tr. C. D. Yonge. Lon. '53. 2 v. p. 8°. L,21
Matthew Paris. Historia Anglorum. London, 1866–69. 3 v. 8°. . W,194
Matthews, L. Life of Ebenezer Porter. Boston, 1837. 12°. . . . C,1100

Matthews, W. Hydraulia; the Water-Works of London. London, 1835. 8°. N,129
Matthiæ, A. Greek Grammar. London, 1837. 2 v. 8°. . . . . L,740
Matthias, B. Rules of Order for Business Meetings. Phil. 1851. 16°. . O,463
Mattie; a Stray. F. W. Robinson. New York, 1865. 8°. . . . . K,658
Mattocks, B. Minnesota as a Home for Invalids. Philadelphia, 1871. 16°. V,84
Maudsley, H. Physiology and Pathology of the Mind. New York, 1867. 8°. O,700
Maule, H. History of the Picts. Glasgow, 1820. 12°. . . . B,111,1
Maunder, S. Biographical Treasury. London, 1845. 12°. . . . C,488
Scientific and Literary Treasury. London, 1845. 12°. . . . L.R.
The same. London, 1848. 12°. . . . . . . . L.R.
Treasury of Knowledge and Library of Reference. Lond. 1845. 12°. L.R.
Treasury of Natural History. London, 1849. 12°. . . . . N,629
Maundrell, H. Journey from Aleppo to Jerusalem. Oxford, 1707. 8°. V,639
Mauprat. Mad. Dudevant. Boston, 1870. 12°. . . . . . . K,1118
Maurice, F. D. Church and State. London, 1839. 12°. . . . O,1029
Claims of the Bible and of Science. London, 1863. 12°. . . P,303
Conscience; Lectures on Casuistry. London, 1868. 8°. . . . O,720
Doctrine of Sacrifice. Cambridge, 1854. 12°. . . . . . P,694
Faith of the Liturgy. London, 1860. 12°. . . . . . . P,886
Learning and Working. Cambridge, 1855. 8°. . . . . . P,806
Lectures on the Apocalypse. London, 1861. 12°. . . . . P,68
Lectures on Eccles. Hist. of 1st and 2d Centuries. Camb. 1854. 8°. P,650
Lectures on Epistle to the Hebrews. London, 1846. 8°. . . P,537
Mediæval Philosophy. London, 1857. 8°. . . . . . O,637,3
Moral and Metaphysical Philosophy. London, 1854. 3 v. 12°. . O,637
Prophets and Kings of the Old Testament. Boston, 1853. 12°. . P,116
Religions of the World. London, 1861. 12°. . . . . . P,560
Theological Essays. Cambridge, 1853. 12°. . . . . . . P,67
Unity of the New Testament. London, 1854. 8°. . . . . P,522
Workman and the Franchise. London, 1866. 8°. . . . . B,102
Maurice, T. History of Hindostan. London, 1820. 2 v. 4°. . . . C,462
Modern History of Hindostan. London, 1802-3. 2 v. 4°. . . C,463
Oriental Trinities. London, 1800. 8°. . . . . . . . P,118
Maurice Dering. G. A. Lawrence. Leipzig, 1864. 16°. . . . . J,258
Maurice Tiernay. C. Lever. London, 1865. 8°. . . . . . K,782
The same. Leipzig, 1861. 2 v. in 1. 16°. . . . . J,282
Maury, J. S. Essai sur l'Eloquence de la Chaire. Paris, 1850. 12°. . H,870
Principles of Eloquence. New York, 1857. 18°. . . . . L,465
Maury, M. F. Physical Geography of the Sea. New York, 1855. 8°. V,1117
Physische Geographie des Meeres. Leipzig, 1859. 8°. . . . G,703
Maximilian I., Last Days of. F. Salm-Salm. London, 1868. 2 v. 8°. . C,382
Life of. F. Hall. New York, 1868. 12°. . . . . . D,507
Mexico under. H. M. Flint. Philadelphia, 1867. 12°. . . C,375
Maximilian, A. P., *Prinz zu Wied-Neuwied.* Reise nach Brasilien, 1815-1817.
Frankfurt-am-Main, 1820-21. 2 v. 4°. . . . . . . . *Q,434
Atlas dazu. 2 portfolios. . . . . . . . . . . *Q,470
Maximes du Duc de La Rochefoucauld. Paris, 1855. 12°. . . . H,865
Maxims of Francesco Guicciardini; trans. by E. Martin. Lond. 1845. 18°. H,899
of Washington; edited by J. F. Schroeder. N. Y. 1859. 12°. . H,269
Worth and Wealth, a Collection of. F. Hunt. New York, 1856. 12°. H,30

Maxwell. T. E. Hook. London, 1840. 16°. . . . . . . K,1150
Maxwell Drewitt. J. H. Riddell. Leipzig, 1866. 2 v. in 1. 16°. . . J,425
Maxwell, J. S. The Czar, his Court and People. New York, 1854. 12°. V,527
Maxwell, S. D. Suburbs of Cincinnati. Cincinnati, 1870. 4°. . . . C,226
Maxwell, W. H. Bivouac; Stories of the Peninsular War. Lond. 1857. 16°. K,1155
Brian O'Linn; or, Luck is Everything. London, 1849. 3 v. in 1. 12°. K,688
Hill-Side and Border Sketches. London, 1847. 2 v. 8°. . . V,349
Life of Duke of Wellington. London, 1867. p. 8°. . . . L,154
Irish Rebellion, 1798. London, 1868. 8°. . . . . . . B,160
Stories of Waterloo. London, 1835. 16°. . . . . . . J,637
Victories of Wellington and the British Armies. London, 1852. 16°. L,125
Wanderings in the Highlands and Islands. London, 1844. 2 v. 8°. V,405
Wild Sports of the West. London, 1838. 12°. . . . . V,404
May, C. L. Sweet Clover Stories. Boston, 1869. 4 v. 16°. . . . J,1698
Vol. 1. Nelly Milton's Housekeeping. 2. Brownie Sandford. Vol. 3. Sylvia's Burden. 4. Ruth Lovell.
May, E. J. Bertram Noel. New York, 1870. 12°. . . . . . J,1644
Louis's School Days. New York, 1870. 12°. . . . . . . J,1643
Mortimer's College Life. New York, 1870. 12°. . . . . J,1641
Sunshine of Greystone. New York, 1867. 12°. . . . . J,1642
Recollections of our Anti-Slavery Conflict. Boston, 1869. 12°. . O,390
May, Sophia, *pseud.* See *Clarke, R. S.*
May, T. E. Constitutional History of England. New York, 1865–66. 2 v. 8°. B,48
May and December; a Tale of Wedded Life. J. Hubback. Phil. 1866. 12°. K,1145
May-Day and other Pieces. R. W. Emerson. Boston, 1867. 16°. . . I,32
May-Flower and Miscellaneous Works. H. B. Stowe. Boston, 1869. 12°. K,288
May-Flowers. L. M. Bugden. London, 1855. 8°. . . . . . . J,1262
May Martin, and other Tales. D. P. Thompson. Boston, 1869. 12°. . K,393
Mayer, B. Capt. Canot; 20 years of an African Slaver. New York, 1864. 12°. V,783
Mexico as it was and as it is. New York, 1844. 8°. . . . V,196
Mayhew, E. Illustrated Horse Management. Philadelphia, n. d. 8°. . M,478
Sportsman's Vade Mecum. New York, 1856. 12°. . . . . M,312
Mayhew, H. Boyhood of Martin Luther. New York, 1864. 16°. . . J,1463
London Labor and London Poor. London, 1851–62. 4 v. 8°. . O,360
Mormons. London, n. d. 12°. . . . . . . . . . P,837
Mr. and Mrs. Sandboys at the Great Exhibition. London, n. d. 8°. V,313
Peasant Boy Philosopher. London, 1860. 16°. . . . . J,1465
Rhine; illustrated by B. Foster. London, 1856. 8°. . . . V,436
Upper Rhine; illustrated by B. Foster. London, 1860. 8°. . . V,437
Wonders of Science. London, 1856. 12°. . . . . . . D,2
and A. Acting Charades. London, n. d. 12°. . . . . . I,710
Good Genius. London, 1867. 16°. . . . . . . K,689
Greatest Plague of Life. London, n. d. 16°. . . . . J,654
Image of his Father. London, 1848. 12°. . . . . . J,635
Living for Appearances. London, 1855. 16°. . . . . J,636
Magic of Kindness. New York, 1849. 16°. . . . . J,1464
Whom to Marry, and how. London, n. d. 12°. . . . J,650
Mayhew, S. Popular Education. New York, 1850. 12°. . . . . . O,951
Practical System of Book-Keeping. New York, 1854. 12°. . M,1088
Mayne, F. Voyages and Discoveries of Arctic Regions. Lond. 1853. p. 8°. I,656,7

Maynarde, T. Sir Francis Drake; his voyage, 1595. London, 1849. 8°. . v,992
Mayo, C. Medical Service of the Federal Army. London, 1864. 8°. v,1086,3
Mayo, C. and E. Remarks on Infant Education. London, 1849. 16°. o,1161
Mayo, E. Lessons on Objects. New York, 1866. 12°. . . . . o,944
Lessons on Shells. London, 1846. 16°. . . . . . . . o,18
Lessons on the Miracles of our Lord. London, 1845. 16°. . . P,525
Model Lessons for Teachers. London, 1849–53. 3 v. 16°. . o,1119
Religious Instruction, pt. 2. London, 1852. 16°. . . . o,1116
Mayo, H. Philosophy of Living. Philadelphia, 1852. 12°. . . . L,884
Popular Superstitions. Philadelphia, 1852. 12°. . . . . o,329
Mayo, W. S. Kaloolah; or, Adventures of J. Romer. New York, 1850. 12°. J,638
Mazatlan Shells, Catalogue of. P. B. Carpenter. London, 1857. 16°. . o,17
Mead, H. Sepoy Revolt; its Causes and Consequences. London, 1857. 8°. C,428
Mead, P. B. Grape Culture and Wine Making. New York, 1867. 8°. . M,501
Meadows, K. Heads of the People. London, 1864. 2 v. 8°. . . . H,616
Meadow Brook. M. J. Holmes. New York, 1868. 12°. . . . . K,194
Meals and Manners in the Olden Times, Poems on. London, 1868. 8°. L,605,32
Means and Ends. C. M. Sedgwick. New York, 1839. 16°. . . . J,1222
Mears, J. W. Bible in the Workshop. New York, 1857. 12°. . . P,302
Mécanique Céleste, Traite de. P. S. La Place. Paris, 1843. . . *Q,108,1-5
The same; translated by N. Bowditch. Boston, 1829–39. 4 v. 4°. *Q,104
Mecca, Pilgrimage to. R. F. Burton. New York, 1856. 12°. . . . V,630
Méchain, P. F. A. et Delambre, J. B. J. Base du Systéme Métrique Decimal, v. 2,3. Paris, 1807–10. 4°. . . . . . . . . . M,817
Mechanic, American. C. Quill. Philadelphia, 1838. 18°. . . . H,250
Operative. J. Nicholson. Philadelphia, 1826. 2 v. in 1. 8°. . M,678
and Machinist. J. Nicholson. London, 1853. 8°. . . S.C.
Mechanical Examples. S. Newth. London, 1859. 8°. . . . M,1166
Mechanical Inventions of James Watt. J. P. Muirhead. Lond. 1854. 3 v. 8°. M,643
Mechanical Manipulation and Turning. C. Holtzapffel. Lond. 1856–66. 3 v. M,666
Mechanical Philosophy, Horology, etc. W. B. Carpenter. Lond. 1857. p. 8. L,283
Mechanics, Book of Illustrious. E. Foucaud. New York, 1847. 12°. . M,633
Memoirs of eminent American. H. Howe. New York, 1858. 12°. C,652
Mechanics' Assistant. D. M. Knapen. New York, 1850. 12°. . M,1165
Mechanics' Calculator. W. Grier. Glasgow, 1866. 16°. . . . . M,600
Mechanics' Companion. P. Nicholson. Philadelphia, 1868. 8°. . . M,630
Mechanics' Magazine, v. 1,2. London, 1830. 2 v. 8°. . . . . . S.C.
Mechanics' Magazine, v. 5. New York, 1835. 8°. . . . . . . T,21
Mechanics. O. Byrne. New York, 1860. 12°. . . . . . . . M,674
H. Kater and D. Lardner. London, 1830. 12°. . . M,1021
D. Lardner. Philadelphia, 1854. 12°. . . . . . . N,79,1
C. Tomlinson. London, 1859. 12°. . . . . . . M,968
Amateur Mechanic's Workshop. London, 1870. 8°. . . . M,661
for Beginners. I. Todhunter. London, 1870. 16°. . . . M,1136
Grundzüge der Mechanik. M. Rühlmann. Leipzig, 1860. 8°. . E,438
Illustrations of. H. Moseley. New York, 1855. 18°. . . . . L,462
Mécanique Analytique. J. L. Lagrange. Paris, 1853–55. 2 v. in 1. 4°. M,1080
Physical and Celestial. B. Peirce. Boston, 1855. 4°. . . . M,1081
The same. Boston, 1855. 4°. . . . . . . . . . S.C.
Theoretical and Practical. J. Hann. London, 1848. 8°. . . . N,130

Mechanics, Traité de Mécanique. S. D. Poisson. Paris, 1811. 2 v. 8°. . N,126
Traité de Mécanique Elémentaire. L. B. Francœur. Paris, 1830. 8°. N,125
Treatise on. A. W. Smith. New York, 1849. 8°. . . . . . N,133
Mechanism in Thought and Morals. O. W. Holmes. Boston, 1871. 12°. . O,626
Medals, Ancient and Modern Coins. J. Pinkerton. London, 1808. 2 v. 8°. M,387
Histoire Métallique de Hollande. P. Bizot. Amst. 1688–90. 3 v. 8°. M,386
of Creation. G. A. Mantell. London, 1844. 2 v. 16°. . . . L,305
Medbery, J. K. Men and Mysteries of Wall street. Boston, 1870. 12°. . O,505
Medhurst, W. H. China; its State and Prospects. London, 1857. 8°. . V,667
Mediæval Alphabets, Hand-Book of. H. Shaw. London, 1853. r. 8°. . *Q,160
Medical Chemistry, Elements of. B. H. Rand. Philadelphia, 1871. 12°. N,217
Medical Education and Profession in U. S. D. Drake. Cincin. 1832. 12°. L,832
Medical Electricity. J. Althaus. London, 1859. 8°. . . . . . . L,921
Medical Evidence at Trial of J. C. Belaney. R. M. Glover. Gatesh. 1844. 16°. N,252,37
Medical Galvanism. W. H. Halse. London, n. d. 16°. . . . N,252,36
Medical Jurisprudence. A. S. Taylor. London, 1856. 12°. . . . L,939
Lectures on. T. S. Traill. Edinburgh, 1836. 12°. . . . N,252,23
Medical Periodical Literature and Libraries. D. Drake. Cincin. 1852. 12°. L,830
Medical Science, Currents and Counter-Currents in. O. W. Holmes. Bos.'61. 12°. L,862
Medical Service of the Federal Army. C. Mayo. London, 1868. 8°. V,1086,3
Medici, Catharine de, Girlhood of. T. A. Trollope. London, 1856. 12°. . D,723
Medici, Lorenzo de, Life of. W. Roscoe. London, 1797. 2 v. 4°. . . F,28
The same. London, 1851. p. 8°. . . . . . . . . L,226
Medicine, Æsculapian Labyrinth Explored. G. Glyster. Dublin, 1789. 8°. *H,630
Dissertationes Medicæ. C. von Linnæus. Lugd. Batav. 1749–85. 9 v. 8°. N,966
Domestic. F. V. Raspail. London, 1853. 12°. . . . . . M,955
Hand-Book of. H. Davies. London, 1855. p. 8°. . . . L,291
Manual of. R. Gooding. London, 1867. 12°. . . . M,841
Eclectic Southern Practice. J. C. Massie. Philadelphia, 1854. 8°. L,967
Familiar Treatise on. J. M. Scudder. Cincinnati, 1869. 2 v. in 1. 8°. L,932
History and Heroes of. J. R. Russell. London, 1861. 8°. . . C,560
How to treat the Sick without. J. C. Jackson. New York, 1869. 12°. L,914
Institutes of. M. Paine. New York, 1867. 8°. . . . . L,1020
Principles and Practice of. A. Flint. Philadelphia, 1868. 8°. . L,964
Science and Practice of. W. Aiken. London, 1858. 8°. . . . L,873
Medicinisches Lexikon. L. A. Kraus. Göttingen, 1826. 12°. . . . E,414
Méditations Poétiques. A. de Lamartine. Paris, 1821. 8°. . . H,1005
Meditations on Christianity. F. Guizot. New York, 1865. 8°. . . . P,84
on Death and Eternity. J. H. D. Zschokke. Boston, 1865. 12°. . P,126
on Life and its Duties. J. H. D. Zschokke. Boston, 1863. 12°. . P,125
Mediterranean, Excursions along the. E. Napier. London, 1842. 2 v. 12°. V,1061
Shores of the. F. Schroeder. New York, 1846. 2 v. 12°. . V,1056
Summer Cruise in. N. P. Willis. New York, 1854. 12°. . V,1040
Winter and Spring on. J. H. Bennet. New York, 1870. 8°. . . V,345
Medusæ, British Naked-Eyed, Monograph of. E. Forbes. Lond. 1848. 8°. Q,70
Meek, A. B. Romantic Passages in South-Western History. N. Y. 1857. 12°. C,147
Meek, F. B. and Gabb, W. M. Palæntology. San Fran. 1864–66. 2 v. 4°. N,740
Meerkönig, Der. B. Möllhausen. Jena, 1867. 6 v. 16°. . . . . G,344
Meerman, G. Origines Typographicae. Hagae Com. 1765. 2 v. in 1. 4°. L.R.
Meeter, E. Holland; its Institutions, etc. London, 1857. 12°. . . . V,462

Meigs, R. J. Journal of Detachment of Benedict Arnold. Cin. 1852. 8°. C,710
Melancholy, Anatomy of. R. Burton. Philadelphia, 1859. 8°. . . . H,629
Melbourne and the Chincha Islands. G. W. Peck. New York, 1854. 12°. V,1064
Melbourne House. S. Warner. New York, 1866. 12°. . . . . . K,371
Meline, J. F. Study of the Modern Languages. Cincinnati, 1838. 8°. H,302,4
Two Thousand Miles on Horseback. New York, 1868. 12°. . . V,185
Mellichampe; a Legend of the Santee. W. G. Simms. New York, 1864. 12°. K,255
Melvil, Sir James, Memoirs of. G. Scott. Edinburgh, 1735. 8°. . . D,367
Melvill, H. Bible Thoughts. New York, n. d. 18°. . . . . . P,746,19
Melville, H. Confidence-Man. London, 1857. 16°. . . . . . . J,639
Mardi, and a Voyage thither. New York, 1849. 2 v. 12°. . . K,214
Omoo; Adventures in the South Seas. London, 1861. 12°. . . V,890
Piazza Tales. New York, 1856. 12°. . . . . . . . J,640
Redburn; his First Voyage. London, 1853. 2 v. 12°. . . . J,641
Typee; or, Residence in the Marquesas Islands. Lond. 1847. 12°. V,891
Whale. London, 1851. 3 v. 12°. . . . . . . . . . J,642
Melville, G. J. W. Brookes of Bridlemere. Leipzig, 1864. 2 v. in 1. 16°. J,372
Cerise; Tale of the Last Century. Leipzig, 1866. 2 v. in 1. 16°. . J,373
Digby Grand. Leipzig, 1862. 16°. . . . . . . . . . J,374
Gladiators. Leipzig, 1864. 2 v. in 1. 16°. . . . . . . J,375
Good for Nothing. Leipzig, 1862. 2 v. in 1. 16°. . . . . J,376
Interpreter. Leipzig, 1866. 2 v. in 1. 16°. . . . . . . J,377
Kate Coventry. Leipzig, 1860. 16°. . . . . . . . . J,378
M. or N. "Similia Similibus Curantur." Leipzig, 1869. 16°. . . J,379
Queen's Maries. Leipzig, 1862. 2 v. in 1. 16°. . . . . . J,380
White Rose. Leipzig, 1868. 2 v. in 1. 16°. . . . . . . J,381
Melvin, J. Journal of Expedition to Quebec, 1775. Philadelphia, 1864. 4°. Q,463
Memes, J. S. Memoirs of Empress Josephine. Edinburgh, 1831. 16°. . I,534
The same. New York, 1864. 18°. . . . . . . . L,361
Sculpture, Painting, and Architecture. Edinburgh, 1829. 16°. . I,515
Memoirs of a Maître d'Armes. A. Dumas. London, 1865. p. 8°. . I,664,2
and Essays in Art, Literature, etc. A. Jameson. London, 1846. 12°. . M,22
of Celebrated Characters. A. de Lamartine. N. Y. 1854–56. 3 v. 12°. C,525
of a Physician. A. Dumas. Philadelphia, n. d. 8°. . . . H,988
of my Youth. A. de Lamartine. New York, n. d. 8°. . . . G,243
Memorable Women. N. Crosland. Boston, 1857. 12°. . . . . C,504
Memorials of the Late War, 1806–15. Edinburgh, 1828. 2 v. 16°. . . I,509
Memory, Method of Artificial. R. Grey. Oxford, 1851. 16°. . . . O,999
Men I have known. W. Jerdan. London, 1866. 8°. . . . . . C,1247
of Character. D. Jerrold. London, 1851. 12°. . . . . U,178,2
The same. Leipzig, 1852. 2 v. in 1. 16°. . . . . J,223
of Letters and Science. H. Brougham. London, 1855. 12°. . . C,541
The same. Philadelphia, 1845–46. 2 v. 12°. . . . C,522
of the Time. E. Walford. New York, 1852. 12°. . . . . C,539
of our Times. H. B. Stowe. Hartford, 1868. 8°. . . . . C,774
Men, Women, and Books. L. Hunt. New York, 1847. 2 v. 12°. . . H,581
Women and Ghosts. E. S. Phelps. Boston, 1869. 12°. . . . K,228
Men's Wives. W. M. Thackeray. Leipzig, 1857. 16°. . . . . J,484,8
The same. Boston, 1869. 12°. . . . . . . . K,1038,3
The same. Philadelphia. . . . . . . . . . K,1087,4

Menageries; Quadrupeds described. London, 1830–40. 3 v. 16°. . . L,481
Menaï Straits Suspension Bridge. T. G. Cumming. London, 1842. 8°. . M,737
Menault, E. Intelligence of Animals. New York, 1869. 12°. . . M,1047
Mended Life; or, Carpenter's Family. J. Lamb. Philadelphia, 1870. 16°. J,1689
Mendelssohn-Bartholdy, F. E. Polko. New York, 1869. 16°. . . . D,496
Eighty-one Part Songs and Choruses. London, 1857. 8°. . . *M,422
Four-Part Songs; Op. 48. London, 1857. 8°. . . . . *M,422
Letters. London, 1862–63. 2 v. 12°. . . . . . . . G,25
Letters from Italy and Switzerland. New York, 1865. 12°. . . V,504
Lettres Inédites de. Paris, n. d. 12°. . . . . . . H,1035
Life of. W. A. Lampadius; trans. by W. L. Gage. N. Y. 1866. 16°. D,505
Six Four-Part Songs; Op. 41. London, 1857. 8°. . . . *M,422
Works; edited by V. Novello. London, n. d. 8°. . . . *M,423
St. Paul; Hymn of Praise; As the Hart Pants; Come, let us Sing; When Israel out of Egypt came; Not unto us, O Lord.
Mendoza, J. G. de. History of China. London, 1853–54. 2 v. 8°. . . V,980
Mensuration for Beginners. I. Todhunter. London, 1869. 16°. . . M,1135
Treatise on. T. Baker. London, 1859. 12°. . . . . . . M,892
Mental Action, Imperfect and Disordered. T. C. Upham. N. Y. 1852. 18°. L,406
Mental and Moral Culture. S. S. Randall. New York, 1855. 12°. . O,1168
Mental and Moral Science. A. Bain. London, 1868. 12°. . . . . O,645
Mental and Moral Training. H. Smith. London, n. d. 16°. . . O,1154
Mental Cultivation, Influence of, upon Health. A. Brigham. Hart. 1832. 12°. L,860
Mental Culture, Value of. W. Robinson. London, 1845. 16°. . . O,1120
Mental Development, Symmetrical. E. A. H. Allen. Boston, 1854. 12°. O,820,24
Mental Dynamics. J. H. Green. London, 1847. 8°. . . . . . O,1039
Mental Hygiene. W. Sweetser. New York, 1850. 12°. . . . . O,639
Mental Philosophy. J. Haven. Boston, 1863. 12°. . . . . . O,659
Elements of. C. C. Upham. New York, 1855. 2 v. 12°. . . O,622
Mental Science. R. Whately. London, 1855. 12°. . . . . . O,726
applied to Scripture Truth. J. Reid. Edinburgh, 1859. 12°. . . P,24
Menzel, W. German Literature. Oxford, 1840. 4 v. 8°. . . . . H,748
The same; trans. by C. C. Felton. Boston, 1840. 3 v. 12°. . H,747
History of Germany; trans. by G. Horrocks. Lond. 1849–53. 3 v. p. 8°. L,208
Menzies, A. Report of the Dick Bequest for Schools. Edinb. 1854. 8°. O,1235
Mercantile Dictionary. I. de Veitelle. New York, 1864. 12°. . . . L.R.
Mercantile Law, Compendium of. J. W. Smith. New York, 1866. 8°. . U,530
Mercantile Morals. W. H. Van Doren. New York, 1852. 12°. . . . H,252
Mercantile Profession, Dangers and Duties of. G. S. Hillard. Bost. 1854. 8°. H,301
Mercedes of Castile. J. F. Cooper. New York, 1866. 12°. . . . K,35
The same. New York, 1869. 12°. . . . . . . . K,147
Merchant, The. L. C. Tuthill. Cincinnati, 1854. 12°. . . . K,1094
Merchant of Berlin. C. Mundt. New York, 1867. 12°. . . . . G,208
Merchant Ships and Seamen, Law of. C. Abbott. Boston, 1854. 8°. . . U,531
Merchants' Magazine, Hunt's. New York, 1839–64. 51 v. 8°. . . . T,39
Merchants, Leading Pursuits and Leading Men. E. F. Freedley. Phila. 1856. 8°. C,595
Lives of American. F. Hunt. New York, 1858. 2 v. 8°. . C,1068
London. H. R. F. Bourne. New York, 1869. 16°. . . . . J,1670
Old, of New York City. J. A. Scoville. New York, 1870. 5 v. 12°. C,1044
Mercury, Recherches Chimiques sur. E. Millon. Paris, 1846. 8°. . N,252,32

Meredith. M. Gardiner. Leipzig, 1843. 16°. . . . . . . . J,194
Meredith, Mrs. Lacemakers; Sketches of Irish Character. London, 1865. 12°. K,802
Meredith, Owen, *pseud.* See *Lytton, E. R. B.*
Meredith, W. G. Memorials of Charles John, King of Sweden. Lond. 1829. 8°. D,775
Mérimé, P. Colomba. Boston, 1856. 16°. . . . . . . . . . H,967
Merivale, C. Conversion of the Roman Empire. New York, 1865. 8°. . A,173
Fall of the Roman Republic. London, 1853. 12°. . . . . . A,143
History of the Romans under the Empire. London, 1852–58. 6 v. 8°. A,172
The same. London, 1852–58. 6 v. 8°. . . . . . . . S.C.
Merivale, H. Historical Studies. London, 1865. 8°. . . . . . . A,329
Merkel, C. L. Anatomie und Physiologie des Stimm-Organs. Leip. 1857. 8°. E,419
Merle d'Aubigné, J. H. Germany, England, and Scotland. N. Y. 1849. 12°. V,343
History of the Reformation. Glasgow, 1854–55. 3 v. in 1. 8°. . P,659
The same. Glasgow, n. d. 5 v. 8°. . . . . . . P,660
History of the Reformation in time of Calvin. N. Y. 1870. 5 v. 12°. P,665
Merrick, J. L. Life and Religion of Mohammed. Boston, 1850. 8°. . D,776
Merrie England. S. J. Lippincott. Boston, 1863. 16°. . . . J,1233
Merrimack and Concord Rivers, Week on. H. D. Thoreau. Boston, 1862. 12°. V,24
Merry-Mount; a Romance. J. L. Motley. Boston, 1849. 12°. . . . K,142
Mervyn Clitheroe. W. H. Ainsworth. Leipzig, 1858. 2 v. in 1. 16°. . J,16
Mesmer and Swedenborg. G. Bush. New York, 1847. 12°. . . . P,842
Mesmerism, Popular Superstitions. H. Mayo. Philadelphia, 1852. 12°. O,329
and Phrenology. N. L. Rice. New York, 1849. 12°. . . . L,960
Mesnager, N., Negotiations of. D. De Foe. London, 1717. 8°. . . U,250
Mesopotamia and Assyria. J. B. Fraser. New York, 1842. 18°. . . L,443
Tour through. H. Southgate. New York, 1840. 2 v. 12°. . . V,646
Message Bird, August, 1850–April, 1851. New York, 1850–51. 4°. . . Q,156
Meta Gray. M. J. McIntosh. New York, 1863. 16°. . . . J,1352
Metal, Manufactures in. J. Holland. London, 1831. 3 v. 12°. . M,1043
New, found in Crude Platina. W. H. Wollaston. London, 1804. 4°. N,252,42
Metallic Wealth of the United States. J. D. Whitney. Philad. 1854. 8°. M,723
Metallurgy. J. Percy. London, 1864. 8°. . . . . . . . M,716
Electro. A. Watt. London, 1869. 12°. . . . . . . . M,861
Lehrbuch der Chem. Metallurgie. C. F. Rammelsberg. Berl. 1850. 8°. G,763
of Copper, Silver, and Lead. R. H. Lamborn. Lond. 1868–69. 2 v. 12°. M,848
of Iron. H. Bauerman. New York, 1868. 12°. . . . . . M,714
Practical Treatise on. B. Kerl; edited by W. Crookes and E. Röhrig. London, 1868. 3 v. 8°. . . . . . . . . . M,717

Vol. 1. Lead, Silver, Zinc, Cadmium, Tin, Mercury, Bismuth, Antimony, Nickel, Arsenic, Gold, Platinum, Sulphur.
2. Copper, Iron.
3. Steel, Fuel, Supplement.

Treatise on. F. Overman. New York, 1852. 8°. . . . . . M,718
The same. New York, 1854. 8°. . . . . . . . M,718
Traité Complet de. J. Percy. Paris et Liege, 1864–67. 5 v. 8°. . M,728
Metals, Ancient Artificers in. J. Napier. London, 1856. 12°. . . . M,713
and Alloys known to the Ancients. J. A. Phillips. n. t. p. 8°. N,252,44
Essays on. Sir J. Pettus. London, 1686. f°. . . . . . Q,294
Playbook of. J. H. Pepper. London, 1866. 12°. . . . . M,753
Precious, Consumption of. W. Jacob. London, 1831. 2 v. 8°. . M,722
Μετανοεῖτε, Bekehrt Euch. J. F. Fries. Heidelberg, 1814. 24°. . . G,532

Metaphysical Philosophy. F. D. Maurice. London, 1854. 8°. . . . O,637
Metaphysics. Aristotle; trans. by J. H. McMahon. London, 1857. p. 8°. L,40
and Ethics applied to Religion. F. Bowen. Boston, 1849. 8°. . O,706
and Logic, Lectures on. Sir W. Hamilton. Boston, 1859–67. 2 v. 8°. O,704
Grundriss der Metaphysik. J. F. Fries. Heidelberg, 1824. 12°. . G,555
Institutes of. J. F. Ferrier. Edinburgh, 1856. 12°. . . . O,641
Metastasio, P., Observations on. H. Beyle. Boston, 1839. 12°. . . D,523
Metcalf, S. L. Caloric; its Agency in Nature. Philadelphia, 1859. 2 v. 8°. N,44
Meteoric Astronomy. D. Kirkwood. Philadelphia, 1867. 12°. . . N,271
Meteorological Essays. F. Arago. London, 1855. 8°. . . . . . N,108
Meteorological Observations. Sir F. L. M'Clintock. Wash. 1863. 4°. Q,324,13
Meteorological Register, 1843–54, Army. Washington, 1855. 4°. . . Q,301
Meteorology. Sir J. F. W. Herschel. Edinburgh, 1861. 16°. . . . N,103
D. Lardner. Philadelphia, 1854. 12°. . . . . . . N,79,3
Atmospheric System and Prognost. T.B.Butler. Norwalk, 1870. 12°. N,102
Elements of. J. Brocklesby. New York, 1855. 12°. . . . . N,106
Illustrated, Appleton's. New York, 1856. 2 v. 8°. . . . Q,259
Lehrbuch der. J. Müller. Braunschweig, 1852. 2 v. 8°. . . G,726
Treatise on. E. Loomis. New York, 1868. 8°. . . . . . N,109
Meteors, Aerolites, and Falling Stars. T. L. Phipson. London, 1867. 12°. N,267
Meteyard, E. Life of Josiah Wedgewood. London, 1865–66. 2 v. 8°. . M,644
Mainstone's Housekeeper. Boston, 1864. 12°. . . . . . K,1164
Metford, J. General Discourse of Simony. London, 1682. 12°. . . . P,27
Method. S. T. Coleridge. London, 1855. 8°. . . . . . . . . O,726
Methodism, American. F. J. Jobson. New York, 1857. 8°. . . . V,63
History of. A. Stevens. New York, 1861. 3 v. 12°. . . . P,832
Rise and Progress of. R. Southey. New York, 1847. 2 v. 12°. C,1251
Sketches of Western. J. B. Finley. Cincinnati, 1857. 12°. . . P,843
Methodist Episcopal Church, History of. N. Bangs. N. Y. 1857. 4 v. 12°. P,841
History of. A. Stevens. New York, 1864. 4 v. 12°. . . . P,833
Journals of the General Conference. New York, 1855–56. 3 v. 8°. P,848
Methodist Magazine and Quarterly Review. New York, 1818–57. 39 v. 8°. S,11
Vols. 1–11. Methodist Magazine, 1818–20.
12–22. Methodist Magazine and Quarterly Review, 1830–40.
23–39. Methodist Quarterly Review, 1841–57.
Methodist Pulpit South. W. T. Smithson. Washington, 1859. 8°. . . P,862
Methodist Quarterly Review. See *Methodist Magazine.*
Metric System. Philadelphia, 1867. 16°. . . . . . . . . M,1094
Metrical Pieces. N. L. Frothingham. Boston, 1855. 16°. . . . . I,35
Metrical Romances; 13th–15th Centuries. H. Weber. Edinb. 1810. 3 v. 8°. I,468
Métrique, Base du Système. T. F. A. Méchain et J. B. J. Delambre, v. 2, 3. Paris, 1807–10. 4°. . . . . . . . . . . M,817
Metropolis Local Management Act. London, 1858–59. 12°. . . . M,949
Metropolitan Building Act. London, 1859. 12°. . . . . . M,921
T. Chambers and G. G. Tattersall. London, 1865. 12°. . U,486
Metropolitan Sanitary Commission, Report. London, 1848. f°. . N,252,54
Meunier, V. Adventures on the Great Hunting Grounds. N. Y. 1870. 12°. M,1064
Meuse, Tour through the Valley of. D. Costello. London, 1846. 12°. . V,393
Mexican Languages, Colleccion Polidiomica Mexicana. México, 1860. 4°. L,636
Lenguas Indigenas de México. F. Pimentel. México, 1862–65. 2 v. 8°. *L,616
Mexican War, Campaign of Gen. Scott. R. Semmes. Cincin. 1852. 12°. B,880

Mexican War, History of. N. C. Brooks. Philadelphia, 1849. 8°. . . B,885
History of. E. D. Mansfield. New York, 1850. 8°. . . . B,884
The same. New York, 1852. 12°. . . . . . S.C.
J. S. Jenkins. Auburn, 1851. 12°. . . . . . . B,882
R. S. Ripley, v. 2. New York, 1849. 8°. . . . . . B,886
Mexico, Across, in 1864–65. W. H. Bullock. London, 1866. 8°. . . V,192
Adventures in. C. Donnavan. Cincinnati, 1848. 8°. . . . T,19,3
and Researches in. R. A. Wilson. New York, 1856. 12°. . V,194
and Central America, Journey in. G. F. von Tempsky. Lond. 1858. 8°. V,204
and Rocky Mountains, Adventures in. G. F. Ruxton. Lond. 1849. 12°. V,139
and Texas, Adventures in. E. Domenech. London, 1858. 8°. . V,21
and U. S. Boundary Survey. W. H. Emory. Wash. 1857–58. 3 v. 4°. *Q,144
Antiquities of. E. King, *Lord Kingsborough*. Lond. 1830–48. 9 v. f°. *F,125
as it was and as it is. B. Mayer. New York, 1844. 8°. . . . V,196
Atlas de Nouvelle-Espagne. A. von Humboldt. Paris, 1811. f°. . *F,119
Chili and Peru, Voyage to. B. Hall. Edinburgh, 1826–27. 2 v. 16°. I,492,2,3
Conquest of. A. de Solis. London, 1724. f°. . . . . . . F,294
History of. W. H. Prescott. Boston, 1857. 3 v. 8°. . . C,388
Descripcion de las dos Piedras que se está formanda en la Plaza de.
A. de Leon y Gama. Mexico, 1792. 4°. . . . . . . C,377
Geology and Physical Geography of. F.W. Egloffstein. N. Y. 1864. 8°. N,751
Gulf of, Manuel de la Navigation. C. P. de Kerhallet. Paris, 1854. 4°. Q,425,1
Historia de Mejico. F. H. Lorenzana. New York, 1828. 8°. . . C,370
History of. F. S. Clavigero. Philadelphia, 1804. 3 v. 8°. . . C,371
J. M. Niles. Hartford, 1844. 12°. . . . . . . . C,368
P. Young. Cincinnati, 1847. 8°. . . . . . . . C,384
in 1827. W. G. Ward. London, 1828. 2 v. 8°. . . . . C,376
Journal of Campaign in. G. C. Furber. Cincinnati, 1857. 8°. . B,879
Memorias de la Revolucion de. W. D. Robinson. London, 1824. 8°. C,372
Monarchia Indiana. J. de Torquemada. Madrid, 1723. 3 v. f°. F,106
My Diary in, 1867. F. Salm-Salm. London, 1868. 2 v. 8°. . . C,382
Notes on, 1822. J. R. Poinsett. London, 1825. 8°. . . . V,198
Sale Catalogue of Books on. London, 1869. 8°. . . . . . L.R.
Travels in. W. H. Carpenter. New York, 1851. 12°. . . . V,195
under Maximilian. H. M. Flint. Philadelphia, 1867. 12°. . . C,375
Vagabond Life in. G. Ferry. New York, 1856. 12°. . . . K,300
With the French in. J. F. Elton. London, 1867. 8°. . . . C,373
Meyen, F. J. F. Outlines of the Geography of Plants. London, 1846. 8°. O,298
Pflanzen-Pathologie. Berlin, 1841. 8°. . . . . . . . G,883
Meyer, E. H. F. Geschichte der Botanik. Königsberg, 1854–57. 4 v. 12°. G,884
Meyer, J. Universum. Hildburghausen, 1834–60. 21 v. 16°. . . . *E,307
Meyer, R. Blaufarben und Ultramarin- Fabrikation. Quedlinb. 1845. 12°. N,252,23
Bleiweiss und Bleizucker Fabrikation. Quedlinburg, 1845. 12°. N,252,23
Meynier, H. A. Mémoire sur la Fabrication du Pyroxyle. Paris, 1848. 4°. N,252,41
Meyrick, S. R. Antient Armour from Norman Conquest. Lond. 1842. 3 v. 4°. *Q,372
Illustrations of Arms and Armour. J. Shelton. Lond. 1844. 2 v. 4°. *Q,373
Miall, J. G. Footsteps of our Forefathers. Boston, 1852. 12°. . . . C,14
Miami Country, Celebration of the 45th Anniversary of the Settlement.
Cincinnati, 1834. 8°. . . . . . . . . . . . . C,244
Michaelis, D. Introduction to the New Testament. Lond. 1801–2. 4 v. 8°. P,543

Michaud, J. F. History of the Crusaders. New York, 1853. 3 v. 12°. . A,225
Michaux, F. A. North American Sylva. Philadelphia, 1859. 3 v. 8°. *N,1039
Travels to the West of the Alleghany Mountains. Lond. 1805. 8°. V,73
Michel, F. X. Histoire des Hotelleries, Restaurants, etc., v. 2. Paris, 1851. 8°. H,632
Michelet, J. France before Europe. Boston, 1871. 12°. . . . . . B,213
Historical View of the French Revolution. London, 1848. p. 8°. . L,211
History of France. New York, 1847. 2 v. 12°. . . . . . B,273
History of the Roman Republic. New York, 1847. 12°. . . . A,139
The same. London, 1863. p. 8°. . . . . . . . . L,210
Life of Joan of Arc. New York, 1865. 16°. . . . . . . D,591
Love. New York, 1869. 12°. . . . . . . . . . . H,911
Modern History. New York, 1865. 18°. . . . . . . . L,453
La Montagne. Paris, 1868. 12°. . . . . . . . H,1036
The Bird; illustrated by Giacomelli. London, 1869. 8°. . *O,123
The People. New York, 1846. 12°. . . . . . . . . H,909
Women of the French Revolution. Philadelphia, 1855. 12°. . . D,627
and Quinet, E. Jesuits. New York, 1845. 12°. . . . . P,808
(Ed.) Life of Martin Luther. London, 1862. p. 8°. . . . L,209
Michelis, F. Kirchlicher Standpunkt in Naturforschung. Münster, 1855. 8°. E,443
Materialismus als Köhlerglaube. Münster, 1856. 8°. . . . E,443
Michigan, Early History of. E. M. Sheldon. New York, 1856. 12°. . C,238
Geology of, Annual Reports. D. Houghton. Detr. 1839–40. 2 v. 8°. N,881
History of. J. H. Lanman. New York, 1855. 18°. . . . L,431
Public Instruction of. F. W. Shearman. Lansing, 1852. 8°. . O,1215
Micke, R. Geschichte des zweiten Punischen Kriegs. Breslau, 1851. 12°. E,20
Micrographic Dictionary. J. W. Griffith and A. Henfrey. Lond. 1860. 3 v. 8°. *N,9
Microscope, The. J. Hogg. London, 1856. 8°. . . . . . . . N,11
D. Lardner. London, 1856. 8°. . . . . . . . N,4
and its Revelations. W. B. Carpenter. Philadelphia, 1856. 8°. . N,12
Anwendung für Pflanzen- Anatomie. H. Shacht. Berlin, 1855. 8°. G,727
Applied to Practical Medicine. L. Beal. London, 1858. 8°. . . L,971
Common Objects of. J. G. Wood. London, 1866. 16°. . . . N,3
Evenings at. P. H. Gosse. New York, 1860. 12°. . . . . N,5
Half-Hours with. F. Lankester. New York, 1868. 16°. . . . N,1
How to work with. L. S. Beale. London, 1868. 8°. . . . N,13
Mikroskop und Mikrokopische Technik. H. Frey. Leipzig, 1863. 8°. G,722
Practical Treatise on the Use of. J. Quekett. London, 1855. 8°. . *N,10
Text-Book of. J. W. Griffith. London, 1864. 12°. . . . . N,7
Use of, in Analysis. A. Ure. London, n. d. 8°. . . . N,252,28
Wunder des Mikroskops. M. Willkomm. Leipzig, 1856. 12°. . G,729
The same. Leipzig, 1861. 8°. . . . . . . . . . G,728
Microscopic and Molecular Science. M. Somerville. Lond. 1869. 2 v. 12°. N,14
Microscopic Fungi. M. C. Cooke. London, 1865. 12°. . . . . N,924
Microscopic Objects, Preparation of. T. Davies. London, n. d. 16°. . N,2
Microscopic Recreations, Marvels of Pond-Life. H. J. Slack. Lond. 1861. 12°. O,74
Microscopic World, Views of the. J. Brocklesby. New York, 1851. 12°. N,8
Microscopical Science, Quarterly Journal of. London, 1853–68. 16 v. 8°. R,24
Microscopist, The. J. H. Wythes. Philadelphia, 1853. 12°. . . . N,6
Middle Ages, Les Arts au Moyen Age. P. Lacroix. Paris, 1869. 2 v. 4°. *Q,360
Dresses and Decorations of. H. Shaw. London, 1858. 2 v. r. 8°. *Q,188

Middle Ages, England during. S. Turner. London, 1825. 5 v. 8°. A,434,4-8
Europe during. S. A. Dunham. London, 1833-34. 4 v. 12°. . M,998
H. Hallam. New York, 1867. 3 v. 12°. . . . . . A,229
The same. Boston, 1853. 3 v. 8°. . . . . . A,243
The same. New York, 1854. 8°. . . . . . A,244
Geschichte des Mittelalters. F. Rehm. Marburg, 1821-39. 4 v. in 8. 8°. E,23
Historical Pictures of. London, 1846. 2 v. 12°. . . . . . A,236
History and Geography of the. G. W. Greene. New York, 1851. 12°. A,234
Illuminated Books of. H. N. Humphreys. London, 1849. f°. . *Q,467
Popular Epics of. J. M. Ludlow. London, 1865. 2 v. 12°. . H,735
Secret Societies of. London, 1837. 16°. . . . . . . . L,486
World in. A. L. Kœppen. New York, 1854. 2 v. 12°. . . A,233
Middle Kingdom, The; China. S. W. Williams. New York, 1857. 2 v. 12°. V,618
Middleton, C. Life of Cicero. London, 1854. 8°. . . . . . . D,737
Miscellaneous Works. London, 1755. 5 v. 8°. . . . . . U,257
Middleton, Sir H. Voyage to Bantam and Maluco Islands. London, 1855. 8°. V,996
Middleton, T. F. Doctrine of the Greek Article. London, 1808. 8°. . P,544
Middleton Pomfret. W. H. Ainsworth. Leipzig, 1868. 2 v. in 1. 16°. . J,17
Midnight Sun; a Pilgrimage. F. Bremer. New York, 1860. 8°. . . K,608
Midshipman Easy. F. Marryat. New York, 1866. 12°. . . . . . K,844
The same. Leipzig, 1869. 16°. . . . . . . . J,356
Midsummer Fays. S. Pindar. New York, 1865. 16°. . . . . J,1361
Midwifery and Diseases of Women. J. Shew. New York, 1857. 12°. . L,912
Might and Right; Dorr Rebellion. Providence, 1844. 12°. . . . C,75
Mignet, F. A. A. Antonio Perezy and Philip II. London, 1846. 12°. . D,704
Histoire de la Revolution Française. Paris, 1855. 2 v. 12°. . B,218
History of the French Revolution. London, 1868. p. 8°. . . L,212
The same. London, 1846. 12°. . . . . . . . B,225
History of Mary, Queen of Scots. London, 1851. 2 v. 8°. . . D,127
The same. London, 1863. 12°. . . . . . . . D,245
Milburn, W. Oriental Commerce. London, 1825. 8°. . . . . . O,608
Milburn, W. H. Pioneers, etc., of the Mississippi Valley. N. Y. 1860. 12°. C,538
Pioneer Preacher. New York, 1858. 12°. . . . . . . P,101
Rifle, Ax, and Saddle Bags. New York, 1857. 12°. . . . . H,40
Ten Years of Preacher-Life. New York, 1859. 12°. . . . C,1005
Milch Cows and Dairy Farming. C. L. Flint. Boston, 1868. 12°. . . M,453
Mildred; a Novel. G. M. Craik. New York, 1868. 8°. . . . . . K,644
The same. Leipzig, 1868. 16°. . . . . . . . J,99
Mildred Arkell. Mrs. H. Wood. Leipzig, 1865. 2 v. in 1. 16°. . . J,525
Mile Stones in our Life Journey. S. Osgood. New York, 1855. 12°. . H,192
Miles, G. H. Mohammed; a Tragedy. Boston, 1850. 12°. . . . I,88
Miles, H. A. Lowell as it was and as it is. Lowell, 1845. 18°. . . C,37
Miles, P. Nordurfari; or, Rambles in Iceland. New York, 1854. 12°. . V,16
The same. London, 1854. p. 8°. . . . . . . I,656,4
Miles, W. Horse's Foot, and how to keep it sound. New York, 1856. 12°. M,472
The same. New York, 1856. 12°. . . . . . . M,533,3
Miles Standish. H. W. Longfellow. Boston, 1866. 12°. . . . . . I,65,2
Miles Wallingford; sequel to Afloat and Ashore. J. F. Cooper. N.Y. 1860. 12°. K,36
The same. New York, 1861. 8°. . . . . . . . K,65
Miletus, Lost Tales of. Sir E. B. Lytton. New York, 1866. 12°. . . I,382

Miletus, Lost Tales of. Sir E. B. Lytton. Leipzig, 1866. 16°. . . J,319
Milford Haven, Eligibility of, for Ocean Steamships. London, 1859. 4°. N,252,52
Military Adventure, Twelve Years of. London, 1829. 2 v. 8°. . . V,666
Military Art, Elements of. E. de la B. Duparcq. New York, 1863. 8°. . M,711
and Science, Elements of. H. W. Halleck. New York, 1863. 12°. . M,763
Military Commanders, Lives of British. G. R. Gleig. Lond. 1831-32. 3 v. 12°. M,1008
Military Dictionary. C. James. London, 1802. 8°. . . . . . . M,765
Military Heroes of the Revolution. C. J. Peterson. Philadelphia, 1848. 8°. C,686
of the War of 1812. C. J. Peterson. Philadelphia, 1848. 8°. . C,687
Military Law of England. London, 1810. 8°. . . . . . . . . U,497
Military Science; Elements of War. W. Müller. London, 1811. 3 v. 8°. M,814
Illustrations to, Appleton's. New York, 1856. 2 v. 8°. . . Q,256
Military Tactics, New System of. E. Upton. New York, 1869. 18°. . M,745
Milizia, F. Lives of Celebrated Architects. London, 1826. 2 v. 8°. . M,204
Milk, Frauenmilch. J. F. Simon. Berlin, 1838. 8°. . . . N,252,14
London; its Unhealthy Character. H. H. Rugg. London, n. d. 16°. N,252,38
Schlechte Kuhmilch. P. T. H. Klencke. Braunschweig, 1847. 16°. N,252,37
Mill, J. History of British India. London, 1817. 3 v. 4°. . . . C,464
The same. London, 1848. 9 v. 8°. . . . . . . C,414
Mill, J. Fossil Spirit; Boy's Dream of Geology. New York, 1854. 12°. N,595
Mill, J. S. Dissertations and Discussions. Boston, 1865. 4 v. 8°. . . H,610

Vol. 1. Contest in America; Right and Wrong of State Interference with Corporation and Church Property; The Currency Juggle; French Revolution; Poetry and its Varieties; Prof. Sedgwick's Discourse on the Studies of Cambridge University; Civilization; Aphorisms; Armand Carrel, a Prophecy; Writings of Alfred de Vigny; Bentham.
2. Coleridge; De Tocqueville's Democracy in America; Bailey on Berkeley's Theory of Vision; Michelet's History of France; Claims of Labor; Guizot's Essays and Lectures on History; Early Grecian History and Legend.
3. Vindication of the French Revolution of 1848; Enfranchisement of Women; Dr. Whewell on Moral Philosophy; Grote's History of Greece; Non-Intervention; Slave Power; Utilitarianism.
4. Parliamentary Reform; Recent Writers on Reform; Bain's Psychology; Non-Intervention; Contest in America; Austin on Jurisprudence; Grote's Plato; Inaugural Address.

Examination of Sir W. Hamilton's Philosophy. Bost. 1865. 2 v. 8°. O,658
On Liberty. Boston, 1868. 16°. . . . . . . . . . . O,484
Philosophy examined. J. McCosh. New York, 1866. 12°. . . O,701
Positive Philosophy of A. Comte. Boston, 1866. 8°. . . . O,627
Principles of Political Economy. Boston, 1848. 2 v. 8°. . . O,543
Representative Government. New York, 1867. 12°. . . . O,491
Subjection of Women. New York, 1869. 12°. . . . . . . O,370
System of Logic, Ratiocinative and Inductive. Lond. 1868. 2 v. 8°. O,738
The same. New York, 1855. 8°. . . . . . . . O,729
Millbank; or, Roger Irving's Ward. M. J. Holmes. New York, 1871. 12°. K,173
Mill on the Floss. M. J. Lewes. New York, 1860. 12°. . . . . K,795
The same. Leipzig, 1860. 2 v. in 1. 16°. . . . . J,297
Millwork and Machinery. R. Buchanan. London, 1841-42. 3 v. 8°. . M,680
W. J. M. Rankine. London, 1869. 12°. . . . . . M,726
Milledulcia; 1,000 Pleasant Things from Notes and Queries. N.Y. 1857. 12°. H,114
Millennial Rest. J. Cumming. New York, 1863. 12°. . . . . P,249
Miller, C. C. Architecture. Troy, N. Y. 1865. 4°. . . . . . *Q,200
Miller, E. H. Royal Road to Fortune. Chicago, 1870. 16°. . . J,1336
Miller, G. History Philosophically Illustrated. Lond. 1848-53. 4 v. p. 8°. A,56
Miller, H. Cruise of the Betsey. Boston, 1859. 12°. . . . . . . V,357

Miller, H. First Impressions of England. Boston, 1855. 12°. . . . v,368
Footprints of the Creator. Boston, 1859. 12°. . . . . . . n,611
Life and Letters of. P. Bayne. Boston, 1871. 2 v. 12°. . . d,210
Life and Times. T. N. Brown. New York, 1858. 12°. . . c,1205
My Schools and Schoolmasters. Boston, 1859. 12°. . . . . d,206
Old Red Sandstone. Boston, 1854. 12°. . . . . . . . n,614
Scenes and Legends of North of Scotland. Cincinnati, 1852. 8°. . v,362
Sketch-Book of Popular Geology. Boston, 1859. 12°. . . . n,613
Tales and Sketches. Boston, 1870. 12°. . . . . . . . h,119
Testimony of the Rocks. Boston, 1857. 12°. . . . . . . n,616
M'Crie, T. and others. Geology of the Bass Rock. N. Y. 1852. 16°. n,612
Miller, Mrs. H. Cats and Dogs. London, 1868. 8°. . . . . . j,1186
Miller, J. End of Religious Controversy. New York, 1851. 12°. . . p,206
Miller, J. R. History of Great Britain, 1760–1820. London, 1828. 8°. . a,541
Miller, J. S. Natural History of Crinoidea. Bristol, 1821. 4°. . . . q,40
Miller, S. Life of Jonathan Edwards. New York, 1860. 12°. . . c,860,8
Miller, T. Country Year-Book. London, n. d. 12°. . . . . . . h,564
History of the Anglo-Saxons. London, 1856. p. 8°. . . . l,127
Miller, W. A. Elements of Chemistry. N. Y. and Lond. 1864–67. 3 v. 8°. n,238
Miller and Millwright's Assistant. W. C. Hughes. Philadelphia, 1869. 12°. m,637
Miller of Angibault. Mad. Dudevant. Boston, 1871. 12°. . . . k,1123
Millhouse, J. English and Italian Dictionary. New York, 1861. 2 v. 8°. l.r.
Milliken, T. Address at Miami University. Rosseville, 1841. 8°. . *h,302,4
Millingen, J. G. History of Dueling. London, 1841. 2 v. 8°. . . h,617
Millon, E. Etudes de Chimie Organique. Lille, 1849. 8°. . . . n,252,32
Recherches Chimiques sur le Mercure. Paris, 1846. 8°. . n,252,32
Mills, A. Ancient Hebrews. New York, 1856. 12°. . . . . . . a,201
Literature and Literary Men of Great Britain. N. Y. 1851. 2 v. 8°. h,710
Poets and Poetry of the Ancient Greeks. Boston, 1855. 8°. . . u,446
Mills, C. History of the Crusades. London, 1821. 2 v. 8°. . . . a,247
Mills, H. Horæ Germanicæ; German Hymns. Auburn, 1845. 18°. . . g,37
Mills, Z. Index to the Laws of Ohio, 1802–45. Columbus, 1846. 8°. . p.d.
Mills of Tuxbury. V. F. Townsend. Boston, 1871. 12°. . . . . k,226
Milman, H. H. Annals of St. Paul's Cathedral. London, 1868. 8°. . . p,314
History of Christianity. New York, 1855. 8°. . . . . . . p,595
History of the Jews. London, 1839. 3 v. 16°. . . . . . i,601
The same. New York, 1866. 3 v. 8°. . . . . . . a,204
The same. New York, 1855. 3 v. 16°. . . . . . l,336
History of Latin Christianity. London, 1854–55. 6 v. 8°. . . p,605
Poetical Works. Philadelphia, 1846. 8°. . . . . . . . i,487
Milne, W. C. Life in China. London, 1857. 12°. . . . . . . v,592
Milner, J. and Haweis, T. History of Church of Christ. Lond. 1847. 4 v. 12°. p,574
Milner, T. Gallery of Nature. London, 1846. 8°. . . . . . . n,144
Milnes, R. M., *Lord Houghton.* Life of John Keats. London, 1820. 8°. . d,194
Poems of Many Years. Boston, 1846. 16°. . . . . . . i,87
Milton J. and his Times. M. Ring. New York, 1868. 8°. . . . g,216
Life of. T. Keightly. London, 1855. 8°. . . . . . c,1268
D. Masson. v. 1, 2. London, 1859–71. 2 v. 8°. . . c,1264
C. Symmons. London, 1822. 8°. . . . . . . c,1267
Paradise Lost; edited by T. Newton. London, 1754. 2 v. 4°. f,168,1,2

Milton, J. Paradise Lost; illustrated by G. Doré. London, n. d. f°. . *Q,244
Paradise Regained, Samson, etc. London, 1752. 4°. . . . F,168,3
Poetical Works. London, 1859. 8 v. 8°. . . . . . . J,867
The same. London, 1752. 3 v. 4°. . . . . . . F,168
The same. London, 1857. 16°. . . . . . . . I,338
The same. New York, 1868. 16°. . . . . . I,375
The same. Leipzig, 1850. 16°. . . . . . . . J,382
The same; ed. with Life, by H. J. Todd. Lond. 1801. 6 v. 8°. J,868

Vol. 1. Life of Milton; Nuncupative Will of Milton; List of editions, translations, and alterations of the Poetical Works; List of detached pieces of Criticism relating to the Poetical Works; Appendix to the Life; Prolegomena, etc.; Commendatory Verses; Addison's Criticism on Paradise Lost; Johnson's Remarks on Milton's Versification; Inquiry into the Origin of Paradise Lost.
2, 3. Paradise Lost.
4. Paradise Regained; Milton's Defense of Tragedy; Samson Agonistes.
5. Lycidas; L'Allegro; Il Penseroso; Arcades; Comus; Sonnets.
6. Odes; Miscellanies; Translations; Elegiarum Liber; Epigrammatum Liber; Silvarum Liber; Appendix; Glossarial Index.

The same; with Life by J. Mitford. Boston, 1853. 3 v. 16°. I,218
The same; with Memoir and Index. London, 1861. 2 v. p. 8°. L,128

Vol. 1. Memoir and Critical Remarks by J. Montgomery; Paradise Lost; Notes.
2. Paradise Regained; Samson Agonistes; Comus; Arcades; Minor Poems; Sonnets; Odes; Verbal Index.

Prose Works. Philadelphia, 1853. 2 v. 8°. . . . . . . U,221
The same; edited by J. A. St. John. London, 1853. 5 v. p. 8°. L,213

Vol. 1. Defense of People of England; Second Defense; Eikonoklastes.
2. Tenure of Kings and Magistrates; Areopagitica; Tracts on the Commonwealth; Observations on Ormond's Peace; Letters of State; Brief Notes on Dr. Griffith's Sermon; Reformation in England; Prelatical Episcopacy; Reason of Church Government urged against Prelaty; True Religion, Heresy, Schism; Toleration; Civil Power in Ecclesiastical Causes.
3. Likeliest Means to Remove Hirelings out of the Church; Animadversions upon the Remonstrant's Defense against Smectymnuus; Apology for Smectymnuus; Doctrine and Discipline of Divorce; Judgment of Martin Bucer concerning Divorce; Tetrachordon; Colasterion; Tractate on Education; Declaration for the Election of John III., King of Poland; Familiar Letters.
4. Treatise on Christian Doctrine, compiled from the Holy Scriptures alone, translated by C. R. Sumner.
5. Second Book of the same; History of Britain; History of Moscovia; Accedence commenced Grammar.

Treasures from his Prose Writings. Boston, 1866. 12°. . . . H,598
Works; with Life by J. Mitford. v. 2–8. London, 1851. 7 v. 8°. J,867

Vol. 1. Missing.
2. Paradise Lost; Paradise Regained.
3. Of Reformation in England; Of Prelatical Episcopacy; Reason of Church Government; Animadversions upon the Remonstrant's Defense against Smectymnuus; Apology against the Confutation of the Animadversions upon the Remonstrant, etc; Εἰκονοκλάστης, in answer to a Book entitled Εἰκὼν Βασιλική.
4. Doctrine and Discipline of Divorce; Tetrachordon; Martin Bucer concerning Divorce; Colasterion; Of Education; Areopagitica, or Unlicensed Printing; Tenure of Kings and Magistrates; On the Peace between Charles I. and the Irish Rebels.
5. History of Britain to the Conquest; Civil Power in Ecclesiastical Causes; Likeliest Means to Remove Hirelings out of the Church; Notes upon a Sermon, titled, The Fear of God and the King, by M. Griffith; Letter concerning Ruptures of the Commonwealth; Religion, Heresie, and the best means against the Growth of Popery; Ready Way to Establish a Free Commonwealth; Present Means of Establishing a Free Commonwealth.
6. Pro Populo Anglicano Defensio; J. Philippi Angli Responsio, etc.; Defensio Secunda; Defensio pro se Contra Alex. Morum; Ad Alex. Mori Supplementum Responsio; Accedence Commenc't Grammar.
7. Artis Logicæ Institutio; Praxis Logicæ Analytica; Petri Rami Vita; Literæ Senatus Anglicani; Literæ Oliverii Protect. Nomine; Literæ Richardi Protect. Nomine; Scriptum Domini Protectoris; Epistolarum Familiarum Liber; Prolusiones Quædam Oratoriæ.
8. Defense of the People of England; Letters of State during the Commonwealth; Letters written in the Names of Oliver and Richard, Protectors; Manifesto of the Lord Protector against the Spaniards; Declaration, or, Letters Patent for the Election of John III., of Poland; Brief History of Moscovia, etc.

und seine Zeit. M. Ring. Frankfurt-a-Main, 1857. 12°. . . . G,427

Milton, Mass. Catalogue of the Milton Public Library. Boston, 1871. 8°. L.R.
Milwaukee Young Men's Library Asso., Catalogue. Milwaukee, 1855. 12°. L.R.
Mimic Life; or, Before and Behind the Curtain. A.C. Ritchie. Bost. 1856. 12°. I,713
Mimic Stage; Dramas, Farces, etc. G. M. Baker. Boston, 1870. 12°. . I,721
Mind, Anatomy and Physiology of. J. Carlile. London, 1851. 16°. . O,710
and Brain. T. Laycock. New York, 1869. 2 v. 12°. . . . O,618
Obscure Diseases of the. F. Winslow. Philadelphia, 1866. 8°. L,930
and Matter. Sir B. Brodie. New York, 1857. 12°. . . . O,646
Philosophy of. G. Mac Caul. London, 1827. 8°. . . . O,665
Elements of the Philosophy of. D. Stewart. Boston, 1855. 12°. . O,651
Essays on the Powers of. T. Reid. Edinburgh, 1808. 3 v. 8°. . O,664
History of the Philosophy of. R. Blakey. London, 1850. 4 v. 8°. O,677
Improvement of. I. Watts. Boston, 1870. 16°. . . . . . O,638
in Nature. H. J. Clark. New York, 1865. 8°. . . . . . N,556
Intuitions of the. J. McCosh. New York, 1860. 8°. . . . O,674
Operations of, in Sleep. F. H. Elwin. London, 1843. 12°. . . O,650
Philosophy of. T. Brown. Hallowell, 1850. 2 v. 8°. . . . O,699
D. Stewart. Boston, 1847. 12°. . . . . . . O,686
Physiology and Pathology of. H. Maudsley. New York, 1867. 8°. O,700
World of. I. Taylor. New York, 1858. 12°. . . . . . O,620
Mine, The; or, Darkness and Light. C. Tucker. London, 1870. 16°. . J,662
Miner, T. B. American Bee-Keeper's Manual. New York, 1855. 12°. . M,467
Mineral Kingdom, Pseudomorphosen des. J. Blum. Stuttgart, 1847. 8°. N,252,35
Sketches from. F. von Kobell. London, 1852. p. 8°. . . . L,312
Mineral Resources of U. S. J. R. Browne and Taylor. Wash. 1867. 8°. N,861,1867
West of Rocky Mount. R.W.Raymond. Wash. 1870. 2 v. 8°. N,861,1869–70
Mineral Water, Action Thérapeutique des. P. Pattissier. Paris, 1839. 8°. N,252,22
Analyse Chimique des. Paris, 1825. 8°. . . . . . . N,252,15
Eaux Minérales Naturelles. P. Pattissier. Paris, 1841–44. 8°. . N,252,22
Fabrication des Artificielles. E. Soubeiran. Paris, 1840. 8°. . N,252,28
Friedrichsaller Bitterwasser. G. Eisenmann. Erlangen, 1847. 16°. N,252,37
Untersuchung der, von Karlsbad. J. Berzelius. Leipzig, 1825. 8°. N,252,27
Mineralogy. D. Varley. London, 1856. 12°. . . . . . . . M,972
and Geology. W. Buckland. London, 1869–70. p. 8°. Plates, obl. 8°. L,280
W. Hooker. New York, 1865. 12°. . . . . . . N,780
Treatise on. P. Cleaveland. v. 1. Boston, 1822. 8°. . . . N,858
British. J. Sowerby. London, 1804–17. 5 v. 8°. . . . . N,860
Descriptive. J. D. Dana. New York, 1868. 8°. . . . . . N,863
Geology and Mineral Analysis. T. Thomson. London, 1836. 2 v. 8°. N,859
Handbuch der Mineralogie. F. Quenstedt. Tübingen, 1863. 8°. . G,836
Illustrated, Appleton's. New York, 1856. 2 v. 8°. . . . Q,250
J. G. von Kurr. Boston, 1869. f°. . . . . . . Q,55
Introduction to. W. Phillips. Boston, 1852. 8°. . . . . N,856
Jahrbuch für. K. C. von Leonhard. Stuttgart, 1848–52. 5 v. 8°. . G,845
Manual of. J. Nicol. Edinburgh, 1849. 8°. . . . . . N,855
of New York. L. C. Beck. Albany, 1842. 4°. . . . *Q,101,8
Popular. H. Sowerby. London, 1850. 16°. . . . . . . N,755
Practical. F. Overmann. Philadelphia, 1854. 12°. . . . N,756
Rudiments of. A. Ramsay. London, 1868. 12°. . . . . M,855
System of. J. D. Dana. New York, 1850. 8°. . . . . . N,862

Minerals, Catalogue of American. S. Robinson. Boston, 1825. 8°. . . S.C.
Lithurgik oder Mineralien u. Felsarten. J. R. Blum. Stutt. 1840. 8°. G,812,1
Recherches sur la Composition des. S. F. Beudant. n. t. p. 8°. N,252,42
Recherches sur les Combustibles. H. V. Regnault. n. t. p. 8°. N,252,1
Richesse Minérale de l'Espagne. P. G. F. Le Play. Paris, 1834. 8°. N,252,35
Mines and Miners; Underground Life of. L. Simonin. New York, 1869. 8°. *M,739
Arts and Manufactures, Dictionary of. A. Ure. Lond. 1867. 3 v. 8°. *M,805
Minerals and Metals. W. Jones. New York, 1870. 12°. . J,1621
Minifie, W. Text-Book of Geometrical Drawing. Baltimore, 1849. 12°. M,148
The same. New York, 1868. 8°. . . . . . . . M,231
Mining and Metallurgy of Gold and Silver. J. H. Phillips. Lond. 1867. 8°. M,724
Compendium of British. J. Y. Watson. London, 1843. 8°. . N,252,40
Cornwall; its Mines and Miners. London, 1865. p. 8°. . . I,665
Erinnerungen an Freiberg's Bergbau. Freiberg, 1839. 12°. . N,252,23
Records of; edited by J. Taylor. London, 1829. 4°. . . N,252,43
Mining Records, National Import. of Preserving. T.Sopwith. Lon.1844. 8°. N,252,35
Mining Statistics. See *Mineral Resources.*
Minister's Family. S. S. Ellis. New York, 1852. 18°. . . . J,1194
Minister's Wife. M. Oliphant. Leipzig, 1869. 2 v. in 1. 16°. . . J,398
Minister's Wooing. H. B. Stowe. Boston, 1866. 12°. . . . . . K,283
Ministry demanded by the Present Crisis. G. B. Ide. Philad. 1844. 16°. P,15
Minnay Sotor, Voyage up the. G.W. Featherstonhaugh. Lond. 1847. 2 v. 8°. V,133
Minnesota and its Resources. J. W. Bond. New York, 1854. 12°. . . C,186
as a Home for Invalids. B. Mattocks. Philadelphia, 1871. 16°. . V,84
First Years of. H. E. Bishop. New York, 1857. 12°. . . . V,76
Geological Survey of, and plates. D. D. Owen. Philad. 1852. 4°. *Q,52
Hand-Book, for 1856–57. N. H. Parker. Boston, 1857. 16°. . C,185
Historical Society, Annals of. J. H. Simpson. St. Paul, n. d. 8°. B,809,1
History of. E. D. Neill. Philadelphia, 1858. 8°. . . . . . C,239
The same. Philadelphia, 1858. 4°. . . . . . . F,70
Minor Drama. See *Drama, Minor.*
Minisink Region, Orange County, New York, History of. C. E. Stickney.
Middletown, N. Y. 1867. 12°. . . . . . . . . . . C,144
Minstrelsy of the English Border. F. Sheldon. London, 1847. 8°. . . I,413
Mirabeau, H. G. R., *Comte de.* A Life History. Philadelphia, 1848. 12°. D,657
Secret History of the Court of Berlin. Dublin, 1789. 8°. . . B,209
Miracles, Dissertation on. G. Campbell. London, 1839. 8°. . . . P,518
Eight Lectures on. J. B. Mozley. London, 1865. 8°. . . . P,519
Notes on. R. Trench. New York, 1855. 8°. . . . . . P,517
of our Lord, Lessons on. E. Mayo. London, 1845. 16°. . . P,525
Past and Present. W. Mountford. Boston, 1870. 12°. . . . P,352
Scriptural and Ecclesiastical. J. H. Newman. London, 1870. 8°. P,353
Miracles of Heavenly Love in Daily Life. C. Tucker. London, 1870. 16°. J,660
Miriam, and other Poems. J. G. Whittier. Boston, 1871. 16°. . . . I,101
Miriam. M. V. Terhune. New York, 1866. 12°. . . . . . K,329
Mirror, The. G. Home, H. Mackenzie, and others. Bost. 1866. 2 v. 8°. H,536,28,29
Mirthfulness and its Exciters. B. F. Clark. Boston, 1870. 12°. . . H,121
Miscellanea Scotica; Collection of Tracts in Scotland. Glasg. 1818–20. 4 v. 12°. B,111

Vol. 1. Maule's (of Melgum) History of the Picts.
Monipennie, J., Summary of the Scots Chronicle.
History of the Feuds and Conflicts of the Clans.
Narrative of the Massacre of Glencoe.

Miscellanea Scotica; Collection of Tracts on Scotland. *Continued.* . . B,111
2. Life of James Sharp, Archbishop of St. Andrews.
Monro, D., Description of the Western Islands.
Martin, M., Voyage to Saint Kilda.
Buchanan, G., Chamæleon.
Death of King James I. of Scotland.
Buchan, A., Description of Saint Kilda.
3. Memoirs of Lord Dundee, the Highland Clans, and Massacre of Glencoe.
Navigation of James V. round Scotland.
Treatises on Second Sight.
4. Moncrieff, T. Alliance between France and Scotland.
Graham, J., Expedition of Earl Glencairn in the Highlands, 1653-54.
Life and Death of James V. of Scotland.
Buchanan, W., Genealogy of Ancient Scottish Surnames.

Miserables, Les. V. Hugo; trans. by C. E. Wilbour. New York, 1870. 8°. H,945
Miss Biddy Frobisher. A. Manning. London, 1868. 12°. . . . . . J,583
Miss Carew. A. B. Edwards. New York, 1867. 8°. . . . . . . K,682
The same. Leipzig, 1865. 2 v. in 1. 16°. . . . . . J,159
Miss Gilbert's Career. J. G. Holland. New York, 1867. 12°. . . . K,179
Miss Mackenzie. A. Trollope. New York, n. d. 8°. . . . . K,1048
Miss Marjoribanks. M. Oliphant. New York, 1866. 8°. . . . . . K,867
The same. Leipzig, 1870. 2 v. in 1. 16°. . . . . J,402
Miss Oona McQuarrie. A. Smith. Boston, 1866. 12°. . . . K,1011
Miss Patience Hathaway. J. W. Bradley. Boston, 1868. 16°. . . J,1655
Miss Ravenel's Conversion to Loyalty. J. W. DeForest. N. Y. 1867. 12°. J,628
Miss Van Kortland. New York, 1870. 8°. . . . . . . . . . K,149
Missing Bride. E. D. E. N. Southworth. Philadelphia, 1870. 12°. . . K,434
Mission; or, Scenes in Africa. F. Marryat. London, 1864. p. 8°. . . L,121
The same. Leipzig, 1845. 16°. . . . . . . . J,357
Missions, Cyclopedia of. H. Newcomb. New York, 1858. 8°. . . . P,610
Origin and History of. T. Smith and J. O. Choules. Bost. 1832. 2 v. 4°. Q,265
Mississippi River, Expedition to, 1820. H. R. Schoolcraft. Phila. 1855. 8°. V,110
Mississippi and Ohio Rivers. C. Ellet, jr. Philadelphia, 1853. 8°. . . C,278
Charts of. S. Cummings. Cincinnati, 1836. 8°. . . . M,689
Cincinnati Memorial on Navigation of. Cincinnati, 1844. 12°. C,201
Mississippi, State of, Report on Agriculture and Geology. B. L. C. Wailes. Washington, Miss. 1854. 8°. . . . . . . . . . . N,879
Mississippi Valley. J. Marquette. New York, 1852. 8°. . . . . . C,272
Aboriginal Monuments of the. E. G. Squier. New York, 1847. 8°. B,604
Ancient Monuments of. E. G. Squier and E. H. Davis. Wash. 1847. 4°. *Q,324,2
Discovery of. J. G. Shea. New York, 1852. 8°. . . . . . C,272
History of. A. M. Hart. Cincinnati, 1853. 8°. . . . . . C,230
J. W. Monette. New York, 1848. 2 v. 8°. . . . . . S.C.
History and Geography of. T. Flint. Cincinnati, 1832. 2 v. in 1. 8°. C,271
its Physical Geography. J. W. Foster. Chicago, 1869. 8°. . . C,280
Pioneers of. W. H. Milburn. New York, 1860. 12°. . . . C,538
Ten Years in. T. Flint. Boston, 1826. 8°. . . . . . . V,109
Missouri, Gazetteer of. A. Wetmore. St. Louis, 1837. 8°. . . . . C,241
Missouri River, Exped. to Sources of. M. Lewis and Clark. Phila. 1814. 2 v. 8°. V,83
Journal of a Voyage to, 1811. H. M. Brackenridge. Pitts. 1814. 8°. V,165
Mr. Ledbury, Adventures of. A. Smith. London, n. d. 16°. . . . . J,653
Mr. Pendleton's Cup. J. W. Bradley. Boston, 1868. 16°. . . . J,1654
Mr. Rutherford's Children. S. Warner. New York, 1868. 16°. . J,1423,1
Mistress and Maid. D. M. Craik. New York, n. d. 8°. . . . . . K,645

Mistress and Maid. D. M. Craik. Leipzig, 1862. 16°. . . . . . J,556
Mrs. Caudle's Curtain Lectures. D. Jerrold. London, 1852. 12°. . U,178,3
The same. Philadelphia, n. d. . . . . . . U,179,3
Mrs. Clarinda Singlehart. A. Manning. London, 1855. 12°. . . . J,587
Mrs. Gerald's Niece. G. Fullerton. Leipzig, 1870. 2 v. in 1. 16°. . . J,168
Mrs. Haliburton's Troubles. Mrs. H. Wood. Leipzig, 1863. 2 v. in 1. 16°. J,526
Mrs. Kitty Trevelyan, Diary of. E. Charles. New York, 1864. 12°. . K,612
The same. Leipzig, 1869. 16°. . . . . . . . . J,64
Mitchell, D. G. Battle Summer; Observations in Paris. N. Y. 1850. 12°. H,20
Doctor Johns. New York, 1866. 2 v. 12°. . . . . . . K,215
Dream Life. New York, 1866. 12°. . . . . . . . . . H,60
Fresh Gleanings from the Old Fields of Europe. N. Y. 1851. 12°. H,19
Lorgnette; or, Studies of the Town. New York, 1852. 2 v. 12°. . H,21
My Farm of Edgewood. New York, 1866. 12°. . . . . . M,550
Reveries of a Bachelor. New York, 1866. 12°. . . . . H,51
Rural Studies. New York, 1867. 12°. . . . . . . . M,549
Seven Stories, with Basement and Attic. New York, 1864. 12°. . K,217
Wet Days at Edgewood. New York, 1865. 12°. . . . . M,551
Mitchell, J. Life of Wallenstein, *Duke of Friedland*. London, 1840. 12°. D,503
Mitchell, J. Practical Assaying. London, 1854. 8°. . . . . . . N,193
Mitchell, O. M. Astronomy of the Bible. New York, 1870. 12°. . . N,332
Planetary and Stellar Worlds. New York, 1859. 12°. . . . N,322
Popular Astronomy. New York, 1860. 12°. . . . . . . N,320
Story Life of. P. C. Headley. New York, 1870. 12°. . . J,1634
Mitchell, S. A. Ancient Geography. Philadelphia, 1860. 12°. . . V,1135
General Atlas. Philadelphia, 1868. 4°. . . . . . . . *Q,464
Index to Map of the World. Philadelphia, 1838. 8°. . . V,1125
Modern Geography. Philadelphia, 1852. 12°. . . . . . O,901
New Reference Atlas. Philadelphia, 1865. 4°. . . . . . . *Q,370
Mitford, M. R., Life of; ed. by A. G. K. L'Estrange. N. Y. 1870. 2 v. 12°. D,7
Our Village. London, 1870. 2 v. 12°. . . . . . . . L,214
Recollections of a Literary Life. New York, 1852. 12°. . C,1246
Works. Philadelphia, 1846. 8°. . . . . . . . K,1091
Mitford, W. History of Greece. Boston, 1823. 8 v. 8°. . . . . . A,115
The same. London, 1814. 10 v. 8°. . . . . . . A,82
Mitla; Journey in Mexico and Cen. America. G. F. v. Tempsky. Lond. 1858. 8°. V,204
Mivart, St. G. Genesis of Species. New York, 1871. 12°. . . . N,403
Model-Drawing, Manual for Teaching. B. Williams. London, 1852. 8°. M,170
Model Lessons for Teachers. E. Mayo. London, 1849–53. 3 v. 16°. O,1119
Model Speaker. P. Lawrence. Philadelphia, 1871. 12°. . . . O,1227
Modeling, Architectural, in Paper. London, 1859. 12°. . . . . M,936
Modern Accomplishments. C. Sinclair. London, 1836. 12°. . . . K,563
Modern British Drama; edited by Sir W. Scott. London, 1811. 5 v. 8°. I,717

Vol. 1. Tragedies—Two Noble Kinsmen; King and No King; Maid's Tragedy; Thierry and Theodoret; Philaster; Bonduca; False One; Bondman; Fatal Dowry; Broken Heart; Rival Queens; Theodosius; All for Love; Don Sebastian; Orphan; Venice Preserved; Isabella; Oroonoko; Mourning Bride; Tamerlane; Fair Penitent; Jane Shore; Lady Jane Grey; Cato; Distressed Mother; Siege of Damascus.

2. Revenge; Brothers; Mariamne; George Barnwell; Fatal Curiosity; Arden of Feversham; Zara; King Charles I.; Gustavus Vasa; Mahomet; Tancred and Sigismunda; Irene; Roman Father; Elfrida; Caractacus; Gamester; Boadicea; Earl of Essex; Barbarossa; Douglas; Cleone; Orphan of China; Zenobia; The Grecian Daughter; Earl of Warwick; Matilda; Countess of Salisbury; Mysterious Mother; Comus; Fair Apostate.

Modern British Drama; edited by Sir W. Scott. *Continued.* . . . . I,717

3. Comedies—Every Man in His Humour; Volpone; Alchemist; Rule a Wife and Have a Wife; Chances; New Way to Pay Old Debts; Committee; Rehearsal; Key to the Rehearsal; Country Girl; Plain Dealer; Old Bachelor; Double Dealer; Love for Love; Way of the World; Provoked Wife; Confederacy; Mistake; Provoked Husband; Spanish Friar; Love Makes a Man; She Would and She Would Not; Careless Husband.
4. The Hypocrite; Constant Couple; Sir Harry Wildair; Inconstant; Recruiting Officer; Beaux Stratagem; The Funeral; Tender Husband; Conscious Lovers; Busy-Body; The Wonder; Bold Stroke For a Wife; Drummer; Miser; Suspicious Husband; Way to Keep Him; Falstaff's Wedding; Jealous Wife; Clandestine Marriage; Good-Natured Man; She Stoops to Conquer; The Brothers; West Indian; Rivals.
5. Operas and Farces—Comus; Cheats of Scapin; Beggars' Opera; Contrivances; Crononhotonthologus; Tom Thumb; Mock Doctor; Intriguing Chambermaid; Devil to Pay; King and Miller of Mansfield; Sir John Cockle at Court; Lying Valet; Miss in Her Teens; Lethé; Male Coquette; Guardian; Neck or Nothing; A Peep Behind the Curtain; Irish Widow; Bon Ton; High Life Below Stairs; Taste; Englishman in Paris; The Knights; Englishman returned from Paris; The Author; The Minor; Liar; Orators; Mayor of Garratt; The Patron; Commissary; Devil upon Two Sticks; Lame Lover; Maids of Bath; Apprentice; Upholsterer; Old Maid; Citizen; Three Weeks after Marriage; Love à la Mode; Love in a Village; Maid of the Mill; Padlock; Dr. Last in his Chariot; Sultan; The Deuse is in Him; Midas; Maid of the Oaks; Two Misers; Critic; Rosina.

Modern Griselda and Belinda. M. Edgeworth. London, 1820. 2 v. 12°. K,550
Modern Housewife; or, Ménagère. A. Soyer. London, 1861. 12°. . . H,319
Modern Inquiries. J. Bigelow. Boston, 1867. 8°. . . . . . . H,242
Modern Painters. J. Ruskin. New York, 1866. 5 v. 8°. . . . . M,76
Modern Society. C. Sinclair. London, 1837. 12°. . . . . . . K,564
Modern Standard Drama. New York, n. d. 43 v. in 29. 16°. . . . I,690
 Contents. See *Drama, Modern Standard.*
Modern War. E. Szabad. New York, 1863. 8°. . . . . . . M,750
Möllhausen, B. Der Meerkönig; eine Erzählung. Jena, 1867. 6 v. 16°. G,344
 Reisen in die Felsengebirge Nord-Amerikas. Leip. 1861. 2 v. in 1. 8°. E,175
Mörike, E. Gedichte. Stuttgart, 1867. 12°. . . . . . . . E,270
Moffat, J. C. Introduction to Study of Æsthetics. Cincinnati, 1856. 12°. O,625
 Life of Thomas Chalmers. Cincinnati, 1853. 12°. . . . . . D,196
Moffett, E. L. Crown Jewels. New York, 1871. 12°. . . . . . J,657
Moges, M. de. Baron Gros's Embassy to China and Japan. London, 1860. 12°. V,602
Mohammed and his Successors. W. Irving. New York, 1868–69. 2 v. 16°. U,13
 The same. New York, 1867. 2 v. 12°. . . . . . . U,28
 Life of. G. Bush. New York, 1854. 16°. . . . . . . L,343
 S. Green. London, 1840. 16°. . . . . . . . I,630
 J. A. Roebuck. London, n. d. 8°. . . . . . . . C,581
 Life and Religion of. J. L. Merrick. Boston, 1850. 8°. . . . D,776
 sein Leben und seine Lehre. G. Weil. Stuttgart, 1843. 12°. . E,242
 the Arabian Prophet; a Tragedy. G. H. Miles. Boston, 1850. 12°. I,88
Mohammedan System of Theology. W. H. Neale. London, 1831. 8°. . P,826
Mohawk Valley and Herkimer Co. N.Y., Hist. of. N. S. Benton. Alb. 1856. 8°. C,89
Mohl, H. von. Anatomy and Physiology of Vegetable Cell. Lond. 1852. 8°. N,1006
Mohun; or, the Last Days of Lee. J. L. Cooke. New York, 1869. 12°. . J,634
Molé, M. Mémoires; Eloge de M'lle. Dangeville. Paris, 1855. 12°. . D,612
Molecular and Microscopic Science. M. Somerville. London, 1869. 2 v. 12°. N,14
Moleschott, J. Kreislauf des Lebens. Mainz, 1852. 16°. . . . . E,412
 Georg Forster, der Naturforscher des Volks. Frank.-a-M. 1854. 16°. E,238
 Stoffwechsel in Pflanzen und Thieren. Erlangen, 1851. 8°. . . G,759
Molière, J. B. P. Œuvres. Paris, 1856. 2 v. 12°. . . . . . . H,881
 Œuvres Completes. Paris, 1854. 4 v. 8°. . . . . . . H,898

Mollusca and their Shells, British. E. Forbes and Hanley. Lond. 1853. 4 v. 8°. N,716
British Nudibranchiate. J. Alder and Hancock. Lond. 1845–55. 4°. Q,67
Eocene, pts. 1, 2, 3. F. E. Edwards. London, 1849. 4°. . . . Q,15
The same; pt. 3, no. 2. London, 1856. 4°. . . . . . Q,30
Fossil Remains of. D. Sharpe. London, 1856. 4°. . . . . Q,30
from the Great Oolite. J. Morris and J. Lycett. Lond. 1850–54. 3 v. 4°. Q,18
in England, Fossil Remains of. D. Sharpe. Lond. 1853–54. 2 v. 4°. Q,16
Manual of. S. P. Woodward. London, 1868. 12°. . . . . M,865
Monograph of the Crag. S. V. Wood. London, 1848–53. 4 v. 4°. Q,24
Popular History of. M. Roberts. London, 1851. 16°. . . . O,8
Moluccas, Voyage to the. Sir H. Middleton. London, 1855. 8°. . . . V,996
Mommsen, T. History of Rome. London, 1862–67. 5 v. 12°. . . . A,149
Römische Geschichte. Berlin, 1865–68. 3 v. in 4. 8°. . . . . E,18
Monaldi; a Tale. W. Allston. Boston, 1856. 12°. . . . . . . K,289
Monarchs retired from Business. J. Doran. London, 1857. 2 v. 8°. . C,531
Monasteries in England, History of. Sir W. Dugdale. Lond. 1846. 6 v. in 8. f°. *Q,387
of the Levant, Visits to. R. Curzon. London, 1849. 12°. . . V,1060
Monasterii de Abingdon Chronicon. London, 1858. 2 v. 8°. . . . W,152
Monasterii de Hyda Liber. London, 1866. 8°. . . . . . . . W,195
Monasterii de Melsa Chronicon. T. de Burton. London, 1866–68. 3 v. 8°. W,193
Monasterii S. Albani Chronica. London, 1863–69. 7 v. 8°. . . . W,178
Monasterii S. Augustini Cantuariensis Historia. Thomas of Elmham. London, 1858. 8°. . . . . . . . . . . . . . W,158
Monasterii S. Petri Gloucestriæ Historia. London, 1863–67. 3 v. 8°. . W,183
Monastery, The. Sir W. Scott. Boston, 1852. 2 v. 16°. . . . . K,941
The same. Philadelphia, 1869. 8°. . . . . . K,1109
The same. Leipzig, 1859. 16°. . . . . . . . J,446
Monastic Orders, Legends of. A. Jameson. London, 1867. 8°. . *M,119
The same. Boston, 1865. 24°. . . . . . . . M,1
Monastici Annales. London, 1864–69. 5 v. 8°. . . . . . W,186
Monckhoven, D. von. Photographic Optics. London, 1867. 12°. . . N,26
Popular Treatise on Photography. London, 1867. 12°. . . . M,853
Moncrieff, T. Ancient Alliance of the French and Scots. Glasgow, 1820. 12°. B,111,4
Monette, J. W. Valley of the Mississippi. New York, 1848. 2 v. 8°. . S.C.
Money. C. Moran. New York, 1863. 12°. . . . . . . . O,518
Chances to make. E. T. Freedley. Philadelphia, 1859. 12°. . H,271
Hints for investing. F. Plaford. London, 1869. 12°. . . . M,854
How to make and keep. T. A. Davies. New York, 1870. 12°. . H,492
in the Garden; Vegetable Manual. P. T. Quinn. N. Y. 1871. 12°. M,485
Science of; a Great Truth. W. B. Partee. Philadelphia, 1871. 12°. O,561
Moneyed Man, The. H. Smith. London, 1841. 3 v. 8°. . . . K,692
Monge, G. Géométrie Descriptive. Paris, 1820. 4°. . . . . M,1190
Mongols and Romans, Wars and Sports of. J. Ranking. London, 1826. 4°. M,430
Monikins, The. J. F. Cooper. New York, 1865. 12°. . . . . K,38
The same. New York, 1860. 8°. . . . . . . . K,67
Monitions of the Unseen. J. Ingelow. Boston, 1871. 16°. . . . I,385
Monk, The; a Romance. M. G. Lewis. London, 1829. 8°. . . . K,804
Monk of Cimiés. M. M. Sherwood. New York, 1855. 12°. . K,1008,4
Monks of Mt. Athos. H. F. Tozer. London, 1862. 8°. . . . V,1086,2
of the West. F. R. Montalembert. Edinburgh, 1861–67. 5 v. 8°. P,825

Monkeys. Sir W. Jardine. Edinburgh, 1843. 16°. . . . . . N,470,27
Histoire Naturelles des. J. B. Audebert. Paris, 1800. f°. . . Q,445
Natural History of. J. Jackson. London, 1838. 16°. . . . L,482
Opossums and Lemurs. London, 1838. v. 1. 16°. . . . L,482,1
Monnier, M. Wonders of Pompeii. New York, 1870. 12°. . . M,1055
Monro, D. Description of the Western Islands. Glasgow, 1820. 12°. B,111,2
Monroe, J., Life of. J. Q. Adams. Buffalo, 1850. 12°. . . . . C,918
Monroe, J. Science and Art of Chess. New York, 1859. 12°. . . . M,332
Monroe, L. B. Public and Parlor Readings. Boston, 1871. 12°. . O,1248
Monsell, J. S. B. Our new Vicar. New York, 1870. 16°. . . . P,69
Monsieur Violet. F. Marryat. Leipzig, 1843. 16°. . . . . . . J,358
Monstrelet, E. de. Chronicles of France. London, 1853. 2 v. 8°. . B,275
The same; translated by T. Johns. London, 1809. 5 v. 4°. *F,162
Mont Blanc and Monte Rosa, Tour of. J. D. Forbes. Edinburgh, 1845. 12°. V,353
Ascent of. J. Auldjo. London, 1864. p. 8°. . . . . . I,656,1
Story of. A. Smith. London, 1853. 12°. . . . . . . V,348
See also *Alps.*
Montagne, La. J. Michelet. Paris, 1868. 12°. . . . . . . H,1036
Montagu, B. Opinions on the Punishment of Death. Lond. 1812–13. 3 v. 8°. O,359
Selections from Taylor, Latimer, Hall, Milton, etc. N. Y. 1848. 8°. H,590
Montagu, E. Writings and Genius of Shakespeare; with three Dialogues of the Dead. London, 1810. 8°. . . . . . . . . . . I,888
Montagu, W. D. English Court from Elizabeth to Anne. Lond. 1864. 2 v. 8°. A,500
Montague, M. W. Letters; edited by S. J. Hale. Boston, 1869. 12°. . H,588
Letters and Works; ed. by Lord Wharncliffe. Lond. 1837. 3 v. 8°. U.129
Montaigne, M. de. Essais. Paris, 1838. 8°. . . . . . . . . H,958
Life of. B. St. John. London, 1858. 2 v. 12°. . . . . D,617
Works; edited by W. Hazlitt. Philadelphia, 1853. 8°. . . . H,916
The same; ed. W. Hazlitt and O. Wight. N. Y. 1859. 4 v. 12°. H,960
Montalembert, F. R. Monks of the West. Edinburgh, 1861–67. 5 v. 8°. P,825
Montalte, L. de, *pseud.* See *Pascal, B.*
Monte-Cristo, Count of. A. Dumas. London, 1858. 8°. . . . . H,982
Countess of. Philadelphia, 1871. 8°. . . . . . . H,1040
Monteith, J. Physical and Intermediate Geography. New York, 1867. 4°. Q,187
Montenegro, Christmas in. London, 1862. 8°. . . . . . . . V,1086,2
Montesquieu, C. de S., *Baron de.* Esprit des Lois. Paris, 1856. 12°. . U,493
Grandeur et Décadence des Romains. Paris, 1856. 12°. . . H,871
Pensées Diverses. Paris, 1855. 12°. . . . . . . . H,865
Reflections on the Roman Empire. Oxford, 1825. 16°. . . . A,131
Montfaucon, B. de. Antiquity explained in Sculpture. Lond. 1721–2. 7 v. f°. *Q,314
Montgomery, C. Eagle Pass; Life on the Border. New York, 1852. 12°. K,218
Montgomery, H. Life of William Henry Harrison. Cleveland, 1852. 12°. C,801
Montgomery, H. R. Memoirs of Sir Richard Steele. Edinburgh, 1865. 2 v. 8°. D,216
Montgomery, J., Life of. H. C. Knight. Boston, 1857. 12°. . . . D,370
Lectures on General Literature. New York, 1855. 16°. . . L,385
Poetical Works; with Memoir by R. Carruthers. Bost. 1858. 5 v. 16°. I,219
The same; with Memoir by R. W. Griswold. Boston, 1857. 8°. J,887
Sacred Poems and Hymns. New York, 1854. 12°. . . . . I,377
Montgomery, R., Life of. J. Armstrong. New York, 1860. 16°. . C,860,1
Montgomery, R. Poetical Works. London, n. d. 8°. . . . . . J,889

Montgomery, Sir R. Colony South of Carolina. See *Force's Tracts*, v. 1.
Monthly Chronicle,; edited by E. D. Mansfield. v. 1. Cincinnati, 1839. 8°. T,8
Montor, A. de. Lives and Times of the Roman Pontiffs. N. Y. 1867. 4 v. 8°. P,651
Montpelier, Vt., History of. D. P. Thompson. Montpelier, 1860. 8°. . C,27
Montpensier, A. P. d'O. Mémoires. Paris, 1855. 12°. . . . . . D,611
Montrose, Marquis of. See *Graham, J.*
Montrose and the Covenanters. M. Napier. London, 1838. 2 v. 8°. . B,118
Montucla, J. E. Histoire des Mathematiques. Paris, 1758–1802. 4 v. 4°. M,1203
Monumenta Franciscana. London, 1858. 8°. . . . . . . . W,154

1. Thomas de Eccleston de Adventu Fratrum Minorum in Angliam.
2. Adæ de Marisco Epistolæ.
3. Registrum Fratrum Minorum Londiniæ.

Monumental History of Egypt. W. Osburn. London, 1854. 2 v. 8°. . V,818
Monuments, Sepulchral. C. Tottie. London, 1843. f°. . . . . *Q,224
Moods. L. M. Alcott. Boston, 1865. 12°. . . . . . . . K,4
Moon, G. W. The Dean's English. London, 1865. 16°. . . . . . L,559
Moon Hoax. R. A. Locke. New York, 1859. 8°. . . . . . . N,347
Moonstone. W. Collins. Leipzig, 1863. 2 v. in 1. 16°. . . . . . J,78
Moor, E. Oriental Fragments. London, 1834. 12°. . . . . . V,565
Moore, A. Y. Life of Schuyler Colfax. Philadelphia, 1868. 12°. . . C,680
Moore, C. C. George Castriot, surnamed Scanderbeg. New York, 1850. 12°. D,759
Moore, C. H. What to Read and how to Read. New York, 1871. 12°. . O,984
Moore, F. (Ed.) American Eloquence. New York, 1857. 2 v. 8°. . H,824
Diary of the American Revolution. New York, 1863. 2 v. 8°. . B,750
Lyrics of Loyalty. New York, 1864. 16°. . . . . . . I,77
Rebellion Record. New York, 1861–69. 12 v. 8°. . . . . . B,982
Songs and Ballads of the Revolution. New York, 1856. 12°. . I,78
Women of the War. Hartford, 1866. 8°. . . . . . . B,949
Moore, G. Lost Tribes, and Saxons of the East and West. London, 1861. 8°. N,432
Man and his Motives. New York, 1848. 16°. . . . . . . P,33
Power of the Soul over the Body. New York, 1852. 16°. . . O,679
Use of the Body in relation to the Mind. New York, 1854. 16°. . O,652
Moore, G. H. History of Slavery in Massachusetts. New York, 1866. 8°. C,46
Moore, J. Kilpatrick and our Cavalry. New York, 1865. 12°. . . C,732
Moore, J. Zeluco. London, 1820. 2 v. 12°. . . . . . . . K,543
Moore, J. B. Governors of New Plymouth and Mass. Bay. N. Y. 1848. 8°. C,775
Moore, T. History of Ireland. London, 1835–46. 4 v. 12°. . . . M,987
Irish Gentleman in Search of a Religion. Baltimore, n. d. 12°. . P,205
Irish Melodies and Sacred Songs. New York, 1854. 12°. . . I,378
with Accompaniments. Dublin, n. d. 2 v. 4°. . . *M,413
with Symphonies. Dublin, 1859. 4°. . . . . . . *F,167
Life of Lord Byron, with Letters and Journals. Boston, n. d. 6 v. 16°. D,150
The same. Philadelphia, 1869. 2 v. 8°. . . . . . D,82
Life of Richard Brinsley Sheridan. New York, 1853. 2 v. 12°. . D,179
Memoirs, Journal, etc.; ed. by *Lord* J. Russell. Lond. 1853-6. 8 v. 8°. D,232
The same. New York, 1857. 2 v. 8°. . . . . . . D,397
Poetical Works. Boston, 1868. 8°. . . . . . . . . J,886
The same. Leipzig, 1842. 5 v. 16°. . . . . . . J,384
Moore, T. British Ferns and their Allies. London, 1867. 16°. . . N,914
British Ferns, History of. London, 1851. 16°. . . . . . N,921
Elements of Botany. London, 1865. 16°. . . . . . . . N,928

Moors of Spain, History of. J. P. C. Florian. New York, 1854. 16°. . L,459
Moos, H. M. Mortara; the Pope and his Inquisition. Cincin. 1860. 12°. I,81
Mopsa, the Fairy. J. Ingelow. Boston, 1869. 16°. . . . . . J,1286
Moral and Political Philosophy. W. Paley. New York, 1849. 12°. . . . P,233
The same. London, 1845. 8°. . . . . . . P,709,2
Moral Class-Book. W. and R. Chambers. London, 1856. 16°. . . . O,774
Moral Culture of Infancy. M. Mann and E. P. Peabody. New York, 1869. 12°. O,998
Moral Improvement of Mankind. T. Dick. Philadelphia, 1869. 12°. U,260,3
Moral Lessons, Elementary. M. F. Cowdery. Philadelphia, 1856. 12°. . O,785
Moral of many Fables. H. Martineau. London, 1859. 16°. . . K,551,9
Moral Philosophy. G. Combe. New York, 1840. 18°. . . . . . O,709
Lectures on. R. D. Hampden. London, 1856. 8°. . . . . O,721
of Courtship and Marriage. W. A. Alcott. Boston, 1857. 12°. . L,911
Moral Play of Wit and Science. J. O. Halliwell. London, 1848. 8°. I,885,35
Moral Reflections, Sentences, and Maxims. F. de Rochefoucauld. N.Y.'53. 12°. H,890
Moral Science. A. Bain. New York, 1869. 12°. . . . . . . O,716
Elements of. F. Wayland. Boston, 1855. 12°. . . . . O,717
Lectures on. M. Hopkins. Boston, 1870. 12°. . . . . O,669
Outlines of. A. Alexander. New York, 1855. 12°. . . . O,713
Moral Sentiment, Theory of. A. Smith. London, 1853. p. 8°. . . . L,237
Moral Tales. M. Edgeworth. New York, 1867. 2 v. 16°. . . . K,677
The same. Philadelphia, 1853. 16°. . . . . . . K,677
Madame Guizot. London, 1853. 12°. . . . . . . J,1189
Moral Training, Essay on. J. W. Loudon. London, 1845. 12°. . . O,994
Moral Uses of Dark Things. H. Bushnell. New York, 1868. 12°. . . P,51
Morality, Elements of. W. Whewell. New York, 1845. 2 v. 12°. . . O,711
Morals and Religion, True and Beautiful in. J. Ruskin. N. Y. 1868. 8°. M,75
History of European. W. E. H. Lecky. New York, 1869. 2 v. 8°. O,723
Introductory Lessons in. London, 1855. 24°. . . . . . . P,225
Moran, C. Money. New York, 1863. 12°. . . . . . . . . O,518
Mordecai, A. Military Commission to Europe, 1855–56. Wash. 1860. 4°. Q,346
More, H. Hints on the Character of a Young Princess. Lond. 1809. 2 v. 8°. O,1233
Memoirs of. W. Roberts. New York, 1855. 2 v. 12°. . . . D,337
Practical Piety. New York, n. d. 18°. . . . . . . P,746,30
Rural Tales. New York, 1854. 16°. . . . . . . . . J,1177
Shepherd of Salisbury Plain. New York, 1859. 12°. . . . K,854
Strictures on Female Education. London, 1799. 2 v. 8°. . O,1196
Works. New York, 1855. 7 v. 12°. . . . . . . . U,196

Vol. 1. Repository Tales.
2. Cœlebs in Search of a Wife; Essays; Moriana.
3. Christian Morals; Moral Sketches; Reflections on Prayer.
4. Practical Piety; Life and Writings of St. Paul.
5. On the Manners of the Great; Religion of the Fashionable World; Tragedies; Poems.
6. Strictures on the System of Female Education; Sacred Dramas.
7. Character of a Princess; Spirit of Prayer; Bible Rhymes.

The same. New York, 1854. 2 v. 8°. . . . . . . U,196
More, Sir T., Household of. A. Manning. New York, 1867. 16°. . . K,834
Life of. J. Macdiarmid. London, 1807. 4°. . . . . . . F,24
Utopia; or, the Happy Republic. London, 1852. 16°. . . . K,690
More Worlds than One. Sir D. Brewster. New York, 1854. 12°. . . N,260
Moreau de St. Méry, M. L. E. Description of St. Domingo. Phil. 1796. 2 v. 8°. S.C.
Morelet, A. Travels in Central America. New York, 1871. 12°. . . V,205

Morell, J. D. Hist. and Crit. View of Speculative Philosophy. N.Y. 1851. 8°. O,692
Morell, J. R. Algeria; its Topography and History. London, 1854. 8°. V,812
Moréri, L. Grand Dictionnaire de l'Histoire. Basle, 1731–32. 6 v. f°. *Q,246
Morfit, C. Chemical and Pharmaceutical Manipulations. Phil. 1857. 8°. N,211
Morford, H. Appleton's Short-Trip Guide to Europe. New York, 1868. 16°. V,295
Morgan, H. Ned Nevins, the Newsboy. Boston, 1869. 16°. . . J,1617
Morgan, H. J. Sketches of Celebrated Canadians. Montreal, 1865. 8°. . C,1231
Morgan, J. F. England under the Norman Occupation. London, 1858. 12°. A,474
Morgan, L. H. American Beaver and his Works. Philadelphia, 1868. 8°. N,688
Morgan, S. O., *Lady*. Italy, Journal of a Residence in. Lond. 1824. 3 v. 8°. V,513
Life and Times of Salvator Rosa. London, 1824. 2 v. 8°. . . M,91
Memoirs, Autobiography, Diaries, etc. Leipzig, 1863. 3 v. 16°. . J,383
Morgan Horses. D. C. Linsley. New York, 1864. 12°. . . . . . M,462
Moriæ Encomium. D. Erasmus. London, 1668. 18°. . . . . P,11
Morley Ernstein. G. P. R. James. Leipzig, 1842. 16°. . . . . J,210
Morley, H. English Writers. London, 1866–70. 2 v. in 4. 8°. . . H,712
Interrupted Health and Sickroom Duties. London, 1847. 16°. N,252,37
Journal of a London Playgoer. London, 1866. 12°. . . . I,709
King and the Commons. London, 1868. 16°. . . . . . . I,560
Life of Palissy, the Potter. Boston, 1853. 2 v. 16°. . . . D,653
Memoirs of Bartholomew Fair. London, 1859. 8°. . . . . H,619
Sketches of Russian Life. London, 1867. 12°. . . . . . V,529
Tables of English Literature. London, 1870. f°. . . . . *F,173
Tract upon Health for Cottage Circulation. London, 1847. 16°. N,252,37
Morley, J. Edmund Burke; a Historical Study. London, 1867. 8°. . D,252
Mormon, Book of. J. Smith, jr. Liverpool, 1854. 16°. . . . . P,426
Mormon Principle, Examination of. F. H. Ludlow. New York, 1870. 8°. V,114
Mormonism; from Edinburgh Review. London, 1865. p. 8°. . . . I,667
its Leaders and Designs. J. Hyde, jr. New York, 1857. 12°. . P,836
Mormons, The. H. Mayhew. London, n. d. 12°. . . . . . . P,837
City of the Saints. R. F. Burton. New York, 1862. 8°. . . . V,115
Latter-Day Saints. J. W. Gunnison. Philadelphia, 1852. 12°. . C,167
Utah and the. B. G. Ferris. New York, 1854. 12°. . . . C,166
Morning and Evening Exercises. H. W. Beecher. New York, 1871. 8°. P,897
Morning Communings with God. C. C. Sturm. London, 1858. 12°. . . L,240
Morning Stars of the New World. H. F. Parker. New York, 1854. 12°. C,518
Morocco, Account of the Empire of. J. G. Jackson. London, 1809. 4°. . V,862
Present State of. X. Durrieu. London, 1854. p. 8°. . . I,658,2
Sketches in. A. de Capell Brooke. London, 1831. 2 v. 8°. . . V,475
Travels in Morocco, Tripoli, etc. Ali Bey. Phila. 1816. 2 v. 8°. V,1082
Morphy, P., Exploits and Triumphs in Europe. F. M. Edge. N. Y. 1859. 12°. M,333
Games of Chess; edited by J. Löwenthal. London, 1869. p. 8°. . L,308
The same. New York, 1860. p. 8°. . . . . . . M,330
and Frère's Tournament. New York, 1859. 18°. . . . M,324
Morrell, B., jr. Four Voyages to the South Sea. New York, 1841. 8°. V,1098
Morris, B. F. Life of Thomas Morris. Cincinnati, 1856. 8°. . . . C,942
Morris, E. How to get a Farm and where to find one. N. Y. 1864. 12°. M,499
Ten Acres Enough. New York, 1864. 12°. . . . . . . M,498
Morris, E. J. Corsica; with a Sketch of Napoleon. Philadelphia, 1855. 12°. V,492
Morris, F. O. History of British Birds. London, 1868. 6 v. 8°. . . *O,87

Morris, F. O. Nests and Eggs of British Birds. London, 1867. 3 v. 8°. *O,88
Morris, G., Life of. J. Sparks. Boston, 1832. 3 v. 8°. . . . . C,818
Morris, J. Catalogue of British Fossils. London, 1854. 8°. . . . N,819
and Lycett, J. Mollusca from the Great Oolite. Lond. 1850–54. 3 v. 4°. *Q,18
Morris, T., Life of. B. F. Morris. Cincinnati, 1856. 12°. . . . . C,942
Morris, W. Earthly Paradise; a Poem. Boston, 1871. 3 v. 12°. . . I,334
Life and Death of Jason; a Poem. Boston, 1867. 12°. . . . I,335
Lovers of Gudrun; a Poem. Boston, 1870. 12°. . . . . I,339
Morrison, J. Elements of Book-Keeping. London, n. d. 8°. . . M,1169
Mortara; a Drama. H. M. Moos. Cincinnati, 1860. 8°. . . . . . I,81
Mortimer, C. B. Morton Montagu. New York, 1850. 12°. . . . K,219
Mortimer's College Life. E. J. May. New York, 1870. 12°. . . J,1641
Morton Montagu. C. B. Mortimer. New York, 1850. 12°. . . . K,219
Morton, N. New England's Memorial. Boston, 1855. 8°. . . . . . C,73
Morton, T. New English Canaan. London, 1632. See *Force's Tracts*, v. 2.
Morton; oder, die grosse Tour. C. Sealsfield. Stuttgart, 1846. 2 v. 24°. E,357
Mosaics. F. Saunders. New York, 1859. 12°. . . . . . . . H,234
Moschus. Idylls; translated by J. Banks. London, 1853. p. 8°. . . . L,87
Selections; translated by R. Polwhele. Exeter, 1786. 4°. . . U,480
Moscow and St. Petersburg. A. Weir. London, 1862. 8°. . . . V,1086,2
Moseley, H. Illustrations of Mechanics. New York, 1855. 18°. . . L,462
Mechanical Principles of Engineering and Architecture. N.Y. 1856. 8°. M,703
Mosen, J. Sämmtliche Werke. Oldenburg, 1863. 8 v. 16°. . . . E,339

Bd. 1. Gedichte.
2. Ritter Wahn; Ahasver.
3. Ueber die Tragödie; Heinrich der Finkler, König der Deutschen; Kaiser Otto III.; Cola Rienzi, der letzen Volktribun der Römer.
4. Wendelin und Helene; Die Bräute von Florenz; Johann von Oesterreich; Herzog Bernhard; Der Sohn des Fürsten; Cromwell.
5, 6. Der Congress von Verona.
7. Bilder im Moose.
8. Studien zur Kunst und Malerei; Ueber Goethe's Faust; Das neuere Deutsche Drama; Erinnerungen; Georg Venlot, Novelle mit Arabesken.

Moses, Divine Legation of. W. Warburton. London, 1846. 3 v. 8°. . P,316
Egypt and the Books of. E. W. Hengstenberg. Edinburgh, 1845. 8°. P,242
Institutions of, compared with Hindu. J. Priestley. Northum. 1799. 8°. U,294
Moses, H. Collection of Antique Vases. London, 1814. 4°. . . . M,98
Mosheim, J. L. v. Ecclesiastical History. New York, 1854. 2 v. 8°. . P,611
Moslih-Eddin Sádi Ben Abdallah. Gulistan; or, Rose Garden. Bost. 1865. 16°. G,4
Moss, L. Annals of the U. S. Christian Commission. Philadelphia, 1865. 8°. B,945
Moss, J. W. Manual of Classical Bibliography. London, 1825. 2 v. 8°. L.R.
Mosses from an Old Manse. N. Hawthorne. Boston, 1865. 2 v. 12°. . K,157
The same. Boston, 1868. 2 v. 12°. . . . . . U,40,4,5
Deutschland's Moose. K. Müller. Halle, 1853. 8°. . . . G,885
Muscologia Recent. S. E. v. Bridel-Brideri. 3 pts. Gothæ, 1797–1801. 4°. N,895
of Eastern North America. W. S. Sullivant. Cambridge, Mass. 1864. 8°. N,897
Moss-Side. M. V. Terhune. New York, 1857. 12°. . . . . . . K,330
Moth and Rust. Boston, 1870. 16°. . . . . . . . . J,1543
Mother and Offspring. S. Tracy. New York, 1853. 12°. . . . . L,913
at Home. J. S. C. Abbott. New York, 1855. 16°. . . . J,1398
The same. New York, n. d. 18°. . . . . . . P,746,24
Mother-in-Law. W. A. Boardman. Philadelphia, 1870. 16°. . . J,1710
E. D. E. N. Southworth. Philadelphia, 1870. 12°. . . . . K,435

Mother's Legacy to her unborn Child. E. Jocelyn. London, 1724. 24°. . P,336
Mother's Recompense; sequel to Home Influence. G. Aguilar. N.Y. 1867. 12°. K,581
The same. Leipzig, 1859. 2 v. in 1. 16°. . . . . . J,3
Mothers, Letters to. L. H. Sigourney. New York, 1848. 12°. . . . H,287
of England. S. Ellis. New York, 1844. 12°. . . . . . H,471
of the Wise and Good. J. Burns. Boston, 1855. 12°. . . . C,489
Moths, British. J. Duncan. Edinburgh, n. d. 16°. . . . . . N,470,30
Exotic. J. Duncan. Edinburgh, 1852. 16°. . . . . . N,470,32
Motion, Treatise on. S. Earnshaw. London, 1844. 8°. . . . . . N,92
Motley, J. L. History of the United Netherlands. New York, 1861. 4 v. 8°. B.409
Rise of the Dutch Republic. New York, 1868. 3 v. 8°. . . . B,408
Moulder's and Founder's Guide. F. Overman. Philadelphia, 1856. 12°. . M,748
Mound-Builders in America, Traditions of. W. Pidgeon. N. Y. 1858. 8°. B,601
Mount Athos, Thessaly, and Epirus. G. F. Bowen. London, 1852. 12°. . V,567
Mount Auburn Index, v. 1, 2. Cincinnati, 1869–70. 4°. . . . . . Q,358
Mount Vernon. S. F. Cooper. New York, 1859. 16°. . . . . . H,4
and its Associations. B. J. Lossing. New York, 1866. 8°. . . C.912
Mount Vernon and other Poems. H. Rice. Columbus, 1860. 8°. . . I,114
Mount Vernon Papers. E. Everett. New York, 1860. 12°. . . . H,113
Mountford, W. Miracles, Past and Present. Boston, 1870. 12°. . . P,352
Thorpe, a quiet English Town. Boston, 1852. 12°. . . . . K,363
Mourt's Relation; or, Journal of the Plantation at Plymouth; edited by H. M. Dexter. Boston, 1865. 4°. . . . . . . . . . . F,67
Movements; or, Exercises. M. Roth. London, 1852. 8°. . . . O,1251,1
Mowatt, A. C. See *Ritchie, A. C.*
Moysant, M. Bibliothèque Portative. Londres, 1800. 4 v. 8°. . H,1021
Mozart, W. A. E. Holmes. New York, 1853. 12°. . . . . . D,493
Künstlerleben. H. Rau. Frankfurt-am-Main, 1860. 3 v. 24°. . G,413
Letters, 1769–91. New York, 1866. 2 v. 16°. . . . . . G,27
Life of. M. Schlictegroll. Boston, 1839. 12°. . . . . . D,495
The same. London, 1817. 8°. . . . . . . . . D,523
Requiem Mass; edited by V. Novello. London, n. d. 8°. . *M,424
Sämmtliche Compositionen für Pianoforte. Wolfenbüttel, n. d. 2 v. 4°. *Q,191
Succinct Thorough Bass School. London, 1854. 8°. . . *M,421,1
Twelfth Mass; edited by V. Novello. London, n. d. 8°. . *M,424
Mozley, J. B. Eight Lectures on Miracles. London, 1865. 8°. . . P,519
Mudd, J. American System of Free Schools. Cincinnati, 1853. 8°. . O,1009
Mudge, Z. A. Witch-Hill; History of Salem Wichcraft. N. Y. 1870. 12°. O,325
Mudie, R. Earth. London, 1835. 16°. . . . . . . . V,1131
Feathered Tribes of the British Islands. London, 1854. 2 v. p. 8°. L,129
The same. London, 1854. 2 v. p. 8°. . . . . . . S.C.
Guide to the Observation of Nature. Edinburgh, 1832. 16°. . . I,537
The same. New York, 1860. 18°. . . . . . . . L,379
Heavens. London, 1854. 16°. . . . . . . . . . N,261
Sea. London, 1835. 16°. . . . . . . . . . . V,1130
Mügge, T. Afraja; Roman. Frankfurt-a-Main, 1857. 12°. . . . G,354
Nordisches Bilderbuch. Breslau, 1862. 12°. . . . . . E,196
Prophet; Historischer Roman. Leipzig, 1862. 3 v. 12°. . . G,355
Verloren und Gefunden. Frankfurt-am-Main, 1859. 2 v. 12°. . G,356
Mühlbach, L., *pseud.* See *Mundt, C.*

Müller, C. Deutschlands Moose. Halle, 1853. 8°. . . . . . . G,885
Die Natur, v. 1, 2, 8–11. Halle, n. d. 6 v. 4°. . . . . . G,740
Der Schüler der Natur. Halle, 1851. 16°. . . . . . . G,357
Reise durch Griechenland und Ionischen Inseln. Leipzig, 1822. 16°. E,192
Müller, C. O. Ancient Art and its Remains. London, 1852. 8°. . . M,97
Geschichte der Griechischen Literatur. Breslau, 1841. 2 v. 8°. . E,251
Geschichte Hellenischer Stämme und Städte. Breslau, 1824. 3 v. 8°. E,15
Handbuch der Archäologie der Kunst. Breslau, 1848. 8°. . . E,455
History of the Doric Race. London, 1839. 2 v. 8°. . . . A,94
Literature of Ancient Greece. London, 1858. 3 v. 8°. . . . A,109
Müller, F. Facts and Arguments for Darwin. London, 1869. 12°. . . N,519
Müller, F. M. Ancient Sanskrit Literature. London, 1859. 8°. . . H,730
Chips from a German Workshop. New York, 1869–71. 3 v. 8°. . G,20
The same. London, 1868. 2 v. 8°. . . . . . . G,21
Lectures on the Science of Language. New York, 1865–66. 2 v. 8°. L,513
Stratification of Language. London, 1868. 8°. . . . . L,526
Müller, G. Life of Trust; ed. by H. L. Wayland. Boston, 1870. 12°. . P,43
Müller, J. Grundriss der Physik und Meteorologie. Braunschweig, 1850. 8°. G,725
History of the World. New York, 1855. 4 v. 12°. . . . A,8
Kurze Darstellung des Galvanismus. Darmstadt, 1836. 8°. . N,252,4
Lehrbuch der Kosmischen Physik. Braunschweig, 1856. 8°. . . G,704
Atlas dazu. Braunschweig, 1856. 4°. . . . . . . G,705
Lehrbuch der Physik und Meteorologie. Braunschweig, 1852. 2 v. 8°. G,726
The same. Braunschweig, 1856–57. 3 v. 8°. . . . . G,724
Principles of Physics and Meteorology. London, 1847. 8°. . . N,88
The same. Philadelphia, 1848. 8°. . . . . . . N,90
Müller, J. Christian Doctrine of Sin. Edinburgh, 1852–53. 2 v. 8°. . P,122
Müller, L. Berzelius' Ansichten; Theoretische Chemie. Breslau, 1846. 8°. N,252,32
Fabrikation des Papiers. Berlin, 1849. 8°. . . . . . N,252,30
Müller, M. Dichtungen. Leipzig, 1868. 2 v. 12°. . . . . . . E,271
Müller, O. Charlotte Ackerman; a Theatrical Romance. Phil. 1871. 12°. G,169
Müller, W. Elements of the Science of War. London, 1811. 3 v. 8°. . M,814
Münchhausen. C. Immermann. Berlin, 1864. 4 v. in 2. 16°. . . G,334
Mugby Junction and Doctor Marigold. C. Dickens. Leipzig, 1867. 16°. J,119
Muhlenberg, H. Catalogus Plantarum Americæ. Lancaster, 1813. 8°. N,1022
Muhlenberg, H. A. Life of Peter Muhlenberg. Philadelphia, 1849. 12°. C,742
Muirhead, J. P. Life of James Watt. New York, 1859. 12°. . . D,30
Mechanical Inventions of J. Watt. London, 1854. 3 v. 8°. . M,643
The same; large paper. London, 1854. 3 v. 4°. . . . M,732
Mulder, G. J. Liebig's Question Tested. London, 1846. 8°. . . N,252,32
Mulford, E. The Nation. New York, 1870. 8°. . . . . . . O,498
Mullaly, J. Laying of the Cable. New York, 1858. 8°. . . . . . M,697
Mulligan, J. Grammatical Structure of the English Language. N. Y. 1852. 8°. L,571
Muloch, D. M. See *Craik, D. M.*
Munday, A. John a Kent and John a Cumber. London, 1851. 8°. I,885,46
Mundt, C., *Louise Mühlbach.* Andreas Hofer. New York, 1868. 12°. . G,194
Berlin and Sans-Souci. New York, 1868. 8°. . . . . . . G,195
Daughter of an Empress. New York, 1868. 8°. . . . . . G,197
Empress Josephine. New York, 1867. 8°. . . . . . G,198
Frederick the Great and his Court. New York, 1867. 12°. . . G,200

Mundt, C. Frederick the Great and his Family. New York, 1867. 8°. . G,201
Goethe and Schiller. New York, 1868. 8°. . . . . . . G,202
Henry the Eighth and his Court. New York, 1868. 8°. . . . G,203
Historisches Bilderbuch. Berlin, 1862. 3 v. 24°. . . . . G,359
Historische Lebensbilder. Berlin, 1864. 2 v. 12°. . . . G,362
Vol. 1. Herzog von Bielitz; Heringshändler oder Edelmann.
2. Maria Theresia und ihr Ofenheizer; Verschwörung durch ein Bild; Kinder von Heute.
Joseph II. and his Court. New York, 1867. 12°. . . . . . G,205
Kaiser Leopold II. und Seine Zeit. Wein, 1861. 3 v. in 1. 24°. . G,363
Königin Hortense. Berlin, 1861. 2 v. 12°. . . . . . . G,360
Louisa of Prussia. New York, 1867. 8°. . . . . . . G,206
Marie Antoinette and her Son. New York, 1867. 8°. . . . G,207
Merchant of Berlin. New York, 1867. 12°. . . . . . . G,208
Napoleon and Blucher. New York, 1867. 8°. . . . . . G,209
Napoleon and the Queen of Prussia. New York, 1868. 8°. . . G,210
Old Fritz and the New Era. New York, 1868. 8°. . . . . G,211
Prince Eugene and his Times. New York, 1869. 8°. . . . G,212
Prinz Eugen und Seine Zeit. Berlin, 1864. 3 v. 12°. . . . G,364
Queen Hortense. New York, 1870. 8°. . . . . . . . G,213
Mundt, T. Count Mirabeau. New York, 1868. 8°. . . . . . G,193
Graf Mirabeau. Berlin, 1860. 4 v. 24°. . . . . . . G,374
Robespierre. Berlin, 1859. 3 v. 16°. . . . . . . . G,375
Mundy, Capt. Tour in India. London, 1832. 2 v. 8°. . . . . V,582
Munich, Art Student in. A. M. Howitt. Boston, 1854. 16°. . . . V,413
Munimenta Academica; Academical Life at Oxford. Lond. 1868. 2 v. 8°. W,200
Munimenta Gildhallæ Londoniensis. London, 1859–62. 4 v. 8°. . . W,162
Vol. 1. Carpenter, J., Liber Albus. A. D. 1419.
2. Liber Custumarum.
3. Translations of the Anglo-Norman in the Liber Albus, etc.
Munn, B. Practical Land Drainer. New York, 1855. 12°. . . . M,555
Munsell, J., Catalogue of the Library of. New York, 1865. 8°. . . . L.R.
Chronology of Paper-Making. Albany, 1857. 8°. . . . . . M,659
Munson, J. E. Complete Phonographer. New York, 1868. 12°. . . L,693
Munster, Earl of. See *Fitzclarence, G.*
Mural Decoration, Art of. T. G. Goodwin. London, 1866. 8°. . . . M,27
Murchison, R. I. Geology of Cheltenham. London, 1845. 8°. . . . N,821
Geology of Russia and Ural Mountains. London, 1845. 2 v. 4°. . Q,439
Siluria; the Oldest Rocks. London, 1854. 8°. . . . . . . N,807
Murdoch, J. E. Patriotism in Poetry and Prose. Philadelphia, 1866. 12°. H,308
Mure, W. Language and Literature of Ancient Greece. Lond. 1859. 5 v. 8°. H,741
Murillo, B. E., Life of. C. Blanc. London, 1855. 4°. . . . . . . Q,179
Murphy, A., Life of. J. Foot. London, 1811. 4°. . . . . . . F,26
Murphy, J. Treatise on the Art of Weaving. Glasgow, 1857. 12°. . . M,656
Murphy, J. G. Review of Chemistry. Philadelphia, 1851. 12°. . . N,175
Murray, A. M. Letters from the U. S., Cuba, and Canada. N.Y. 1856. 12°. V,13
Murray, C. A. Travels in North America. London, 1854. 2 v. 12°. . V,11
Murray, H. History of British India. London, 1858. 8°. . . . . . C,401
Historical Account of British America. New York, 1848. 2 v. 16°. L,407
Polar Seas and Regions. London, 1855. 12°. . . . . . . V,913
Travels of Marco Polo. New York, 1864. 16°. . . . . . . L,456
and others. Encyclopædia of Geography. Phila. 1853. 3 v. 8°. V,1128

Murray, H. and others. Hist. Account of British India. N.Y.1855. 3 v. 16°. L,373
Murray, H. A. Lands of the Slave and Free. London, 1855. 2 v. 12°. . v,144
Murray, J. Fluid Magnesia. London, 1829. 8°. . . . . N,252,28
Murray, J. Family Library. London, 1829-61. 80 v. 16°. . . .

Vol. 1-6. Tytler, A. F. Universal History. 6 v. . . . . I,600
7-9. Milman, H. H. History of the Jews. 3 v. . . . I,601
10. Palgrave, F. Anglo-Saxon Period of England. . . . I,602
11. Blunt, I. J. Sketch of the Reformation in England. . . I,603
12-15. Gleig, G. R. History of the British Empire in India. 4 v. . I,604
16, 17. Sketches of Venetian History. 2 v. . . . . I,605
18. Trials of Charles I. and some of the Regicides. . . . I,606
19. Irving, W. Knickerbocker's History of New York. . . I,607
20, 21. Lockhart, J. G. History of Napoleon I. 2 v. . . . I,608
22. Court and Camp of Napoleon I. . . . . I,609
23, 24. Segur, P. de. Napoleon's Expedition to Russia. 2 v. . . I,610
25-27. Lander, R. and J. Journal of the Niger Expedition. 3 v. . I,611
28. DeFoe, D. Journal of the Plague Year, 1665. . . . I,612
29. Barrow, Sir J. Mutiny of the Bounty. . . . . I,613
30. Coleridge, H. N. Six Months in the West Indies, 1825. . . I,614
31. Family Tour through the South of Holland. . . . I,615
32. Irving, W. Life and Voyages of Columbus. . . . I,616
33. Voyages of the Companions of Columbus. . . . I,617
34. Davenport, R. A. History of the Bastile. . . . . I,618
35. Chronicles of London Bridge. . . . . . . I,619
36. Mutiny at Spithead and the Nore. . . . . . I,620
37, 38. Bucke, C. Ruins of Ancient Cities. 2 v. . . . . I,621
39-41. Eustace, J. C. Classical Tour through Italy. 3 v. . . I,622
42. Williams, J. Life of Alexander the Great. . . . . I,623
43. Hollings, J. F. Life of Gustavus Adolphus. . . . I,624
44. Aytoun, W. E. Life and Times of Richard I. . . . I,625
45. Barrow, Sir J. Life of Peter the Great. . . . . I,626
46. Davenport, R. A. Life of Ali Pasha. . . . . I,627
47. Hollings, J. F. Life of Cicero. . . . . . I,628
48. Roscoe, T. Life and Writings of M. de Cervantes. . . I,629
49. Green, S. Life of Mahomet. . . . . . . I,630
50. Bucke, C. Life of the Duke of Marlborough. . . . I,631
51. Southey, R. Life of Nelson. . . . . . . I,632
52, 53. Edmonds, C. R. Life of G. Washington. 2 v. . . . I,633
54. Head, Sir F. B. Life of J. Bruce, the African Traveler. . . I,634
55. Brewster, D. Life of Sir Isaac Newton. . . . . I,635
56. Lives of Individuals who have raised themselves from Poverty. . I,636
57, 58. Davenport, R. A. Narratives of Peril and Suffering. 2 v. . I,637
59-62. Cunningham, A. Lives of British Painters. 4 v. . . I,638
63. Lives of British Sculptors. . . . . . I,639
64. Lives of British Architects. . . . . . I,640
65. Lives of British Physicians. . . . . . . I,641
66-68. Tytler, P. F. Lives of Scottish Worthies. 3 v. . . . I,642
69-71. Wesley, J. Compendium of Natural Philosophy. 3 v. . . I,643
72, 73. Rennie, J., and Westwood, J. O. Natural History of Insects. 2 v. I,644
74. Brewster, D. Letters on Natural Magic. . . . . I,645
75. Sketches of Imposture, Deception, and Credulity. . . . I,646
76. Scott, Sir W. Letters on Demonology and Witchcraft. . . I,647
77, 78. Irving, W. Sketch-Book. 2 v. . . . . . . I,648
79. MacFarlane, C. Lives and Exploits of Banditti and Robbers. . I,649
80. Fairy Legends of the South of Ireland. . . . . . I,650

Hand-Book for Belgium. London, 1852. 16°. . . . . . v,412
for France. London, 1853. 16°. . . . . . . . v,448
for Greece, Turkey, and Asia Minor. London, 1845. 16°. v,1033
for Northern Italy. London, 1853. 16°. . . . . . v,489
for Spain. R. Ford. London, 1869. 2 v. 12°. . . . v,469

Murray, J. Hand-Book for Syria and Palestine. London, 1858. 2 v. 16°. V,626
Hand-Book of Southern Italy. London, 1853. 16°. . . . V,488
Murray, J. F. World of London. Edinburgh, 1843. 2 v. 12°. . . V,293
Murray, L. English Grammar. Philadelphia, 1827. 16°. . . . O,1065
Murray, N., *Kirwan.* Letter to Bishop John Hughes. N. Y. 1855. 12°. . P,800
Men and Things in Europe. New York, 1853. 12°. . . . . V,340
Preachers and Preaching. New York, 1860. 12°. . . . . P,100
Murray, W. H. H. Adventures in the Adirondacks. Boston, 1869. 12°. . V,98
Musæus, J. A., Specimens of; trans. by T. Carlyle. Edinburgh, 1827. 12°. G,51,1
Musci and Hepaticæ of the United States. W. S. Sullivant. N. Y. 1854. 8°. N,1029
Museum Criticum. Cambridge, 1814–26. 2 v. 8°. . . . . . U,386
Florentinum. A. F. Gori. Florence, 1730–33. 6 v. f°. . . . L.R.
of Science and Art. D. Lardner. London, 1854–56. 12 v. in 6. 12°. M,770
Musgrave, T. Cast away on the Auckland Isles. London, 1866. 8°. . . V,540
Music, Collections, The Church. Cincinnati, 1855. 8°. . . . . M,417
Singing-School Companion. J. and H. Bird. Bost. 1852. 8°. M,418
Das Deutsche Lied. A. Reissmann. Cassel, 1861. . . . . . G,644
Enharmonic Key-Board. H. W. Poole. New Haven, 1867. 8°. . M,398
Für Freunde der Tonkunst. F. Rochlitz. Leip. 1830–32. 4 v. 16°. G,645
General History of. J. Hawkins. London, 1853. 3 v. 8°. . . M,415
Geschichte der Griechischen Musik. C. F. Weitzmann. Berl. 1855. 4°. G,737
Geschichte der Musik. A. W. Ambros. Breslau, 1862–68. 3 v. 8°. G,636
Grenzen der Musik und Poesie. A. W. Ambros. Leipzig, 1855. 12°. G,637
History of. F. L. Ritter. Boston, 1870. 16°. . . . . . . M,397
W. C. Stafford. Edinburgh, 1830. 16°. . . . . . . I,524
History of Modern. J. Hullah. London, 1862. 12°. . . . M,407
Instrumentation and Orchestration. H. Berlioz. London, 1858. 8°. M,421,2
Jahrbücher fur Musikal.Wissenschaft. F.Chrysander. Leip.'67. 2 v. 8°. G,639
Musik der Araber. R. G. Kiesewetter. Leipzig, 1842. 4°. . . G,739
Musikalische-Schöne. E. Hanslick. Leipzig, 1865. 16°. . . G,641
A. Kullak. Leipzig, 1858. 16°. . . . . . . . G,647
New Dictionary of. W. Wilson. London, n. d. 12°. . . . M,8
of Nature. W. Gardiner. Boston, 1856. 8°. . . . . . . M,412
of Scotland. J. Johnson. Edinburgh, 1853. 4 v. 8°. . . . M,411
of the Olden Time, Popular. W. Chappell. London, n. d. 2 v. 8°. M,429
Perfect Harmony in. H. W. Poole. New Haven, 1867. 8°. . . M,398
Physiolog. Grundlage für Theorie der. H.Helmholtz. Brschwg.'65. 8°. G,642
Reinheit der Tonkunst. A. F. J. Thibaut. Heidelberg, 1826. 16°. G,646
Treatise on. C. C. Spencer. London, 1858. 2 v. in 1. 12°. . . M,960
Thorough-Base. J. F. Burrowes. Philadelphia, n. d. 12°. . . M,403
Voice of Singing. E. Seiler. Philadelphia, 1868. 12°. . . . M,404
Vom Musikalische-Schönen. E. Hanslick. Leipzig, 1865. 16°. . G,641
Wesen der Oper. G. W. Fink. Leipzig, 1838. 8°. . . . . G,640
Wilhelm's Method of Teaching Singing. J. Hullah. Lond. 1842. 2v. 8°. M,401
Musical Drama, Memoirs of. G. Hogarth. London, 1838. 2 v. 8°. . M,410
Musical History, Biography, and Criticism. G. Hogarth Lond. 1838. 2 v. 16°. M,399
Musical Instruction, General. A. B. Marx. London, 1854. 8°. . M,421,1
Musical Manual. B. Wilhem. Philadelphia, 1854. 8°. . . . . M,428
Musical Ratios. H. W. Poole. New Haven, 1868. 8°. . . . . M,398
Musical Taste, Dissertation on. T. Hastings. New York, 1853. 12°. . M,405

Musical Times and Singing-Class Circular. London, 1848-54. 6 v. in 3. 8°. M,427
Musical World. New York, 1852-53. 2 v. 4°. . . . . . . . . Q,157
Musicians, Dictionary of. London, 1827. 2 v. 8°. . . . . . . M,409
Mushet, D. Papers on Iron and Steel. London, 1840. 8°. . . . M,725
Muspratt, S. Chemistry applied to the Arts. Glasgow, n. d. 2 v. 8°. *N,253
Mussey, O. Review of E. Fisher's Lecture on North and South. Cincin. 1849. H,302,1
Mussey, R. D. Health; its Friends and Foes. Boston, 1866. 12°. . . L,863
Muston, A. Israel of the Alps. Glasgow, 1852. 2 v. 8°. . . . . . B,368
The same. London, 1852. 12°. . . . . . . . . B,363
Mute Singer. A. C. Ritchie. New York, 1866. 12°. . . . . . K,234
Mutiny at Spithead and the Nore. London, 1842. 16°. . . . . . I,620
of the Bounty. Sir J. Barrow. London, 1831. 16°. . . . I,613
My Apingi Kingdom. P. B. Du Chaillu. New York, 1871. 12°. . J,1294
My Aunt Kate. M. M. Sherwood. New York, 1860. 12°. . . K,1008,7
My Brother's Keepers. A. B. Warner. New York, 1866. 12°. . . . K,372
My Brother's Wife. A. B. Edwards. New York, n. d. 8°. . . . K,684
My Cave-Life in Vicksburg. New York, 1864. 12°. . . . . . . B,896
My Daughter Elinor. New York, 1871. 8°. . . . . . . . K,209
My Farm of Edgewood. D. G. Mitchell. New York, 1866. 12°. . . M,550
My Married Life at Hillside. R. B. Coffin. New York, 1865. 12°. . . K,13
My Novel; Varieties in English Life. Sir E. B. Lytton. Phil. 1867. 2 v. 12°. K,820
The same. Leipzig, 1851. 4 v. 16°. . . . . . . J,322
My own Story. M. Howitt. New York, 1867. 24°. . . . . . J,1165
My own Times. J. Reynolds. Illinois, 1855. 12°. . . . . . . C,740
My Recollections of Lord Byron. T. G. *Marq.* de Boissy. N. Y. 1869. 8°. D,75
My Schools and Schoolmasters. H. Miller. Boston, 1859. 12°. . . . D,206
My Southern Friends. J. R. Gilmore. New York, 1863. 12°. . . . K,292
My Summer in a Garden. C. D. Warner. Boston, 1871. 12°. . . . H,50
My Study Windows. J. R. Lowell. Boston, 1871. 12°. . . . . . H,227
My Three Neighbors in the Queen City. Cincinnati, 1858. 12°. . . K,274
My Two Sisters. E. C. Judson. Boston, 1854. 16°. . . . . . J,1258
My Uncle, the Clockmaker. M. Howitt. New York, n. d. 24°. . J,1181
My Uncle, the Curate. M. W. Savage. London, 1849. 3 v. 12°. . . K,558
Mycology, Illustrations of British. T. J. Hussey. London, 1855. 2 v. 4°. Q,122
Myrc, J. Instructions for Parish Priests. London, 1868. 8°. . . L,605,31
Mysteries of the Kingdom. J. Baylee. London, 1852. 16°. . . . P,287
of Paris. E. Sue. London, n. d. 12°. . . . . . . . . H,902
of Udolpho. A. Radcliffe. New York, 1857. 12°. . . . . K,893
The same. London, 1820. 3 v. 12°. . . . . . . K,548
Mystery of Edwin Drood. C. Dickens. New York, 1871. 16°. . . . K,521
The same. New York, 1871. 12°. . . . . . . . K,1143
The same. Leipzig, 1870. 2 v. in 1. 16°. . . . . . J,128
Mythology, Age of Fable. T. Bulfinch. Boston, 1871. 12°. . . . P,907
and Biography, Dictionary of. J. Thomas. Phil. 1870-71. 2 v. 8°. L.R.
and Fables of the Ancients. A. Banier. London, 1739-40. 4 v. 8°. P,918
and Rites of the British Druids. E. Davies. London, 1809. 8°. . P,831
Deutsche Mythologie. J. L. Grimm. Göttingen, 1854. 8°. . . E,460
C. Simrock. Bonn, 1864. 8°. . . . . . . . . . E,464
Epitome of Greek and Roman. J. S. Hart. Philadelphia, 1853. 12°. P,914
Grecian and Roman. M. A. Dwight. New York, 1849. 8°. . . P,922

Mythology, Grieschische Mythologie. L. Preller. Berlin, 1860–61. 2 v. 8°. E,462
Grieschische Götterlehre. F.G.Welcker. Göttingen, 1857–63. 3 v. 8°. E,463
Illustrated, Appleton's. New York, 1856. 2 v. 8°. . . . Q,253
Manual of. G. W. Cox. New York, 1868. 16°. . . . . P,910
Northern. B. Thorpe. London, 1851–52. 3 v. 12°. . . . P,917
of Greece and Italy. T. Keightley. New York, 1866. 8°. . . P,921
Pantheon of the Heathen Gods. A. Tooke. Baltimore, 1832. 12°. P,911
Polynesian. Sir G. Grey. London, 1855. 8°. . . . . . . P,920
Römische Mythologie. L. Preller. Berlin, 1865. 8°. . . . E,461
Stories from Greek. J. Wood. London, 1867. 16°. . . . P,342
Myths of the Middle Ages. S. Baring-Gould. Baltimore, 1867. 16°. . A,227
of the New World. D. G. Brinton. New York, 1868. 8°. . . P,916

Nabloos and the Samaritans. G. Grove, London, 1862. 8°. . . V,1086,2
Nachbarn, Die. F. Bremer. Leipzig, 1859. 2 v. 12°. . . . E,313,4,5
Nadir Shah, *Emperor of Persia*, History of. J. Fraser. London, 1742. 8°. D,773
Naked-Eyed Medusæ, British. E. Forbes. London, 1848. 4°. . . . Q,70
Names of Fiction, Dictionary of. W. A. Wheeler. Boston, 1866. 16°. . L.R.
of Places, Traces of History in. F. Edmunds. London, 1869. 12°. L,518
Personal, in the Bible. W. F. Wilkinson. London, 1865. 12°. . L,557
Name-System, Teutonic. R. Ferguson. London, 1864. 8°. . . . L,520
Nanette and her Lovers. T. Gwynne. London, 1854. 12°. . . . J,568
Napheys, G. H. Physical Life of Woman. Philadelphia, 1871. 12°. . L,955
Napier, Sir C. William the Conquerer; a Historical Romance. Lon. 1858. 8°. J,643
Napier, E. Excursions along the Mediterranean. London, 1842. 2 v. 12°. V,1061
Napier, H. E. Florentine History. London, 1846–47. 6 v. 12°. . . B,486
Napier, J. Chemistry applied to Dyeing. Philadelphia, 1853. 12°. . M,652
Manual of Electro-Metallurgy. London, 1852. 12°. . . . M,752
Napier, J. Ancient Artificers in Metal. London, 1856. 12°. . . . M,713
Napier, M. Life of John Graham, *Viscount Dundee*. v 1. Edinburgh, 1859. 8°. D,430
Montrose and the Covenanters. London, 1838. 2 v. 8°. . . B,118
Napier, Sir W. F. P. History of Peninsular War. N. Y. n. d. 5 v. 8°. . B,96
The same. New York, 1853. 8°. . . . . . . . . A,562
Naples and Garibaldi. W. G. Clark. London, 1861. 8°. . . . V,1086,1
History of the Kingdom of. P. Colletta. Edinburgh, 1858. 2 v. 8°. B,495
Neapolitan Earthquake, 1857. R. Mallet. London, 1862. 2 v. r. 8°. V,1107
Travels through the Kingdom of. C. U. v. Salis. London, 1795. 8°. V,483
Under Spanish Dominion. A. de Reumont. London, 1854. p. 8°. L,171
Napoleon I. and Blücher. C. Mundt. New York, 1867. 8°. . . . G,209
and the Queen of Prussia. C. Mundt. New York, 1867. 8°. . G,210
and his Marshals. J. T. Headley. New York, 1846. 2 v. 12°. . D,619
The same. New York, 1865. 8°. . . . . . . . . D,562
at Fontainebleau and Elba. Sir N. Campbell. London, 1869. 8°. . D,581
at St. Helena. J. S. C. Abbott. New York, 1855. 8°. . . . D,565
W. Forsyth. New York, 1853. 2 v. 12°. . . . . . D,649
Correspondence with Josephine; ed. J. S. C. Abbott. N. Y. 1856. 12°. D,604
Correspondence with his Brother Joseph. New York, 1856. 2 v. 12°. D,671
Court and Camp of. J. G. Lockhart. London, 1829. 16°. . . I,609

Napoleon I., Court and Camp of. J. G. Lockhart. New York, 1870. 16°. L,326

Early Life of. F. Gregorovius. Philadelphia, 1855. 12°. . . V,492

Expedition to Russia, 1812. P. de Ségur. London, 1827. 2 v. 8°. B,284

The same. London, 1836. 2 v. 16°. . . . . . . I,610

The same. New York, 1854. 2 v. 16°. . . . . . L,433

History of. J. S. C. Abbott. New York, 1864. 2 v. 8°. . . D,564

L. de L'Ardeche. New York, 1864. 2 v. in 1. 8°. . . D,563

J. G. Lockhart. London, 1829. 2 v. 16°. . . . . . I,608

The same. New York, 1858. 2 v. 18°. . . . L,337

Imperial Guard of. J. T. Headley. New York, 1859. 12°. . . B,87

in Exile. B. E. O'Meara. New York, 1853. 2 v. 12°. . . . D,555

Last Days of. F. Antommarchi. London, 1826. 2 v. in 1. 8°. . D,580

Life of. W. Hazlitt. London, 1852. 4 v. 8°. . . . . . D,656

Sir W. Scott. Edinburgh, 1851. 8°. . . . . . . D,566

The same. Exeter, 1828. 2 v. 8°. . . . . . S.C.

Life at St. Helena. M. J. E. D. Las Cases. London, 1823. 4 v. 8°. D,670

The same. New York, 1855. v. 2–4. 12°. . . . . . D,634

Memoirs of. F. de Bourrienne. Edinburgh, 1830–31. 4 v. 16°. . I,527

The same. Hartford, 1854. 8°. . . . . . . D,560

L. P. Junot, *Duchess d'Abrantes.* New York, 1869. 2 v. 8°. D,559

Memoirs of the History of France. London, 1823. 7 v. 8°. . . D,583

Public and Private Life. v. 2. H. La Bédoyere. London, 1839. 8°. D,582

Recueil de Lettres, Proclamat. etc. v. 1. M. Kermoysan. Par. '53. 12°. D,603

Sohn Napoleon's. M. Ring. Berlin, 1860. 2 v. 16°. . . . G,428

Table-Talk and Opinions. London, 1868. 16°. . . . . . I,567

Napoleon III., Coup d'Etat; or, Paris in Dec., 1851. E. Ténot. N.Y. 1870. 12°. B,346

Histoire de Jules César. New York, 1866. 2 v. 8°. . . . D,733

History of. J. S. C. Abbott. Boston, 1869. 8°. . . . . . D,584

S. M. Schmucker. Philadelphia, 1860. 12°. . . . . . D,556

History of Julius Cæsar. New York, 1866. 2 v. 8°. . . . D,742

Atlas to the same. New York, 1865–66. 2 v. 4°. . . . Q,462

Political and Historical Works. London, 1852. 2 v. 8°. . . D,561

Napoleon Museum. J. Sainsbury. London, 1845. f°. . . . . F,296

Naquet, A. Principles of Chemistry. London, 1868. 8°. . . . . N,214

Narbrough, Sir J. Voyage to the South Sea. London, 1711. 8°. . . V,961

Nares, E. Memoirs of William Cecil, *Lord Burghley.* Lon. 1828–31. 3 v. 4°. F,22

Thinks-I-to-Myself. Philadelphia, 1864. 16°. . . . . . K,860

Nares, R. Glossary of Words in English Authors. London, 1859. 2 v. 8°. L.R.

Narragansett Club, Publications of. v. 1–4. Providence, 1866–70. 4°. . C,84

Vol. 1. Guild, R. A. Life of Roger Williams.
Williams, R. Key into the Indian Language of America.
Cotton, J. Letter to Roger Williams.
Williams, R. John Cotton's Letter examined and answered.
2. Cotton, J. Reply to Roger Williams.
Queries of the highest Consideration.
3. Williams, R. The Bloody Tenent of Persecution, for Cause of Conscience.
4. The Bloody Tenent yet more Bloody.

Narratives of Peril and Suffering. R. A. Davenport. London, 1840. 16°. I,637

Nasby, P. V., *pseud.* See *Locke, D. R.*

Nash, F. Paris and its Environs. London, 1823. 2 v. in 1. imp. 4°. *Q,234

Nash, J. A. Progressive Farmer. New York, 1854. 12°. . . . M,517

Nash, S. Pleading and Practice under Civil Code. Cincinnati, 1856. 8°. U,515

Nash, T. Pierce Penniless's Supplication. London, 1842. 8°. . . . I,885,12
Nason, E. C.H. Frankland; Boston in Colonial Times. Albany, 1865. 8°. C,53
Nassau, Bubbles from the Brunnen of. Sir F. B. Head. London, 1866. 12°. V,392
Natal, Guide to. R. J. Mann. London, 1858. 12°. . . . . . . M,851
Natchez, Les. R. F. A. de Chateaubriand. Paris, 1853. 12°. . . . H,938
Nathalie; a Tale. J. Kavanagh. New York, 1863. 12°. . . . . K,743
The same. Leipzig, 1851. 2 v. in 1. 16°. . . . . . J,233
Nathan, the Wise. G. E. Lessing; tr. by E. Frothingham. N. Y. 1868. 16°. G,41
The same; and Emilia Galotti. Leipzig, 1868. 4°. . . G,39
Natick, Mass., History of. O. N. Bacon. Boston, 1856. 8°. . . . C,59
Nation, The. E. Mulford. New York, 1870. 8°. . . . . . . O,498
National Academy of Sciences, Memoirs. v. 1. Washington, 1866. 4°. . Q,107
National Almanac, 1863-64. Philadelphia, 1863-64. 2 v. 12°. . . *T,52
National Asso. for Social Science, Transactions. Lond. 1858-65. 8 v. 8°. O,413
National Cyclopædia of Useful Knowledge. Boston, 1853. 12 v. 8°. . S.C.
The same. Boston, 1853. 12 v. 8°. . . . . . . . L.R.
Supplement. London, 1859. 8°. . . . . . . L.R.
National Flag, History of. S. Hamilton. Philadelphia, 1852. 12°. . . B,849
National Orator. C. Northend. New York, 1859. 12°. . . . O,1229
National Portrait Gallery. J.B.Longacre and J.Herring. Phil. 1836-9. 4 v. 4°. S.C.
Nations of Antiq., Researches concerning. A.H.L.Heeren. Lon. 1854. 2 v. 8°. A,40
Native Georgian. See *Longstreet, A. B.*
Natural History. London, n. d. 8°. . . . . . . . . . . . Q,61
W. Hooker. New York, 1860. 12°. . . . . . . N,643
J. G. Wood. New York, 1854. 12°. . . . . . . N,632
Allgemeine Naturgeschichte. L. Oken. Stuttg. 1833-41. 8 v. in 14. 8°. G,822
Abbildungen dazu. Stuttgart, 1843. 4°. . . . . . *Q,60
Allgem. Formenlehre der Natur. C. G. Nees v. Esenbeck. Bres. 1861. 8°. G,680
American. J. D. Godman. Philadelphia, 1826-28. 3 v. 8°. . N,684
The same. Philadelphia, 1846. 8°. . . . . . . N,524
Anatomy, Physiology, etc., Essays on. J. Hunter. Lond. 1861. 2 v. 8°. N,720
Beobachtungen Naturhistor. Reisen. A. F. Schweigger. Berl. 1819. 4°. N,749
Bible Animals. J. G. Wood. London, 1869. 8°. . . . . . N,690
Bilder aus dem Zoologischen Garten zu Hamburg. C. L. Brehm und
G. F. Zimmermann. Hamburg, 1865. 8°. . . . . . G,932
Boy's Own Book of. J. G. Wood. London, 1861. 8°. . . . N,625
Charakterbilder der Natur. I. Lampert. Mainz, 1865. 2 v. 8°. . G,701
Curiosities of. F. Buckland. London, 1866. 2 v. 12°. . . . N,517
The same. New York, 1859. 12°. . . . . . . . N,516
de la Mer Adriatique. V. Donati. La Hate, 1758. 4°. . . O,1251,2
Entertaining Naturalist. J. W. Loudon. London, 1867. p. 8°. . L,119
First Lesson in. E. C. Agassiz. Boston, 1859. 16°. . . . N,494
Fresh and Salt-Water Aquarium. J. G. Wood. London, 1868. 16°. N,473
Geography and Classification of. W. Swainson. London, 1835. 12°. M,1030
Geology, Chemistry, etc., Lectures upon. T. Flint. Cin. 1833. 12°. N,502
Habits and Instincts of Animals. W. Swainson. Lond. 1840. 12°. M,1037
Histoire Naturelle des Crinoides. A. D. d'Orbigny. Paris, 1858. 4°. Q,57
de l'Espagne. P. G. F. Le Play. Paris, 1834. 8°. . N,252,35
des Singes et des Makins. J. R. Audebert. Paris, 1800. f°. . Q,445
Illustrated. J. G. Wood. London, 1862-63. 3 v. 8°. . . . N,558

Natural History, Instructions for Collect. Subjects. E. Donovan. Lon. 1794. 8°. N,541
Letters from Alabama relating to. P. H. Gosse. Lond. 1859. 16°. N,496
Mammalia. J. G. Wood. London, 1867. 4°. . . . . . . N,682
Methods of Study in. L. Agassiz. Boston, 1866. 12°. . . . . N,644
Naturgesch. der drei Reiche. G.W. Bischoff. Stutt. 1832–43. 14 v. 8°. G,812
Naturhistorischer Schulatlas. C. Arendts. Leipzig, 1866. 8°. . F,91
New England's Rarities Discovered. J. Josselyn. Boston, 1865. 4°. F,65
Observations in. L. Jenyns. London, 1846. 12°. . . . . . N,653
of Animals. J. Bigland. Philadelphia, 1849. 12°. . . . N,630
S. and A. A. Tenney. New York, 1866. 12°. . . . N,654
of Barbados. G. Hughes. London, 1750. f°. . . . . . F,72
of Birds. W. Swainson. London, 1836. 2 v. 12°. . . M,1033
The same. New York, 1855. 16°. . . . . . L,404
J. G. Wood. London, 1865. 4°. . . . . . . . . O,105
of Creation. T. L. Kemp. London, 1862. p. 8°. . . . . . I,666
of Crinoidea. J. S. Miller. Bristol, 1821. 4°. . . . . . Q,40
of the Earth and Animated Nature. O. Goldsmith. Edinb. 1853. 8°. N,526
of the Elephant. New York, 1855. 16°. . . . . . . . . L,448
of Fishes and Reptiles. W. Swainson. London, 1838. 2 v. 12°. M,1034
of Insects. J. Rennie and J. O. Westwood. London, 1829. 2 v. 16°. I,644
The same. New York, 1859. 2 v. 16°. . . . . . L,341
of Ireland. W. Thompson. London, 1849–51. 3 v. 8°. . . O,109
of Lancashire, etc. C. Leigh. Oxford, 1700. f°. . . . . . Q,62
of Man. G. L. L. de Buffon. New York, 1853. 2 v. 8°. . . N,498
of New York State. Albany, 1842–54. 19 v. 4°. . . . . . Q,101
of Quadrupeds. W. Swainson. London, 1835. 12°. . . M,1031
The same. New York, 1855. 16°. . . . . . . . . L,409
of Selborne. G. White. London, 1851. 8°. . . . . . . N,471
The same. London, 1851. 12°. . . . . . . . L,164
The same. Edinburgh, 1829. 16°. . . . . . . . . I,519
The same. New York, 1860. 16°. . . . . . . . . L,437
of the United States. L. Agassiz. Boston, 1857. 2 v. 4°. . . Q,115
Preservation of Specimens. T. Brown. London, 1870. 16°. . . N,480
Plates illustrating. London, n. d. ob. 8°. . . . . . . . . *Q,61
Recreations in. J. Anderson. London, 1799–1802. 6 v. 8°. . . H,615
Reptiles, Fishes. J. G. Wood. London, 1867. 4°. . . . . N,700
Researches in. C. Darwin. New York, 1852. 2 v. 12°. . . . N,633
Scripture. W. Carpenter. London, 1828. 8°. . . . . . . N,523
Seaside Studies in. E. C. and A. Agassiz. Boston, 1865. 8°. . . O,63
Sketches in. J. C. Atkinson. London, 1861. 8°. . . . . . N,628
Sketches of. M. Howitt. London, 1834. 16°. . . . . . . N,492
Study of. W. Swainson. London, 1834. 12°. . . . . M,1029
Treasury of. S. Maunder. London, 1849. 12°. . . . . . N,629
Tagesfragen aus der Naturgeschichte. C. G. A. Giebel. Berlin, 1857. 8°. G,814
Vulkanen Atlas. K. C. von Leonhard. n. t. p. 8°. . . . . G,846
Natural History Review. Dublin and London, 1854–65. 12 v. 8°. . . R,30
Natural Magic, Letters on. Sir D. Brewster. New York, 1855. 16°. . L,374
Natural Philosophy. W. Hooker. New York, 1863. 12°. . . . N,226,1
G. P. Quackenbos. New York, 1865. 12°. . . . . . . N,71
B. Powell. London, n. d. 16°. . . . . . . . . . . . N,61

Natural Philosophy. C. Tomlinson. London, 1859. 12°. . . . . . M,969
Compendium of. D. Olmsted. New Haven, 1848. 12°. . . . N,65
J. Wesley. London, 1836. 3 v. 16°. . . . . . . I,643
Dialogues of. T. Hobbs. London, 1678. 8°. . . . . . . H,504
Discourses on. Sir J. F. W. Herschel. London, 1851. 16°. . . N,68
Elements of. W. H. C. Bartlett. New York, 1851. 8°. . . . N,132
C. Brooke. London, 1867. 8°. . . . . . . . . N,67
A. Gray. New York, 1850. 12°. . . . . . . . N,74
J. Hogg. London, 1861. p. 8°. . . . . . . . L,293
The same. London, 1853. 8°. . . . . . . . N,80
S. A. Norton. Cincinnati, 1870. 12°. . . . . . . N,81
First Principles of. J. Renwick. New York, 1842. 12°. . . N,63
Hand-Book of. W. J. Rolfe and J. A. Gillet. Boston, 1868. 12°. . N,73
D. Lardner. Philadelphia, 1854. 3 v. 12°. . . . . N,79
Contents, see *Lardner, D.*
Introductory Course of. A. Ganot. New York, 1860. 12°. . . N,72
Journal of. W. Nicholson. London, 1797–1802. 5 v. 4°. . . T,41
The same; continued. London, 1802–13. 36 v. 8°. . . T,40
Kirkliche Standpunkt in. M. J. Schleiden. Münster, 1855. 8°. . E,443
Letters on. L. Euler. New York, 1854–58. 2 v. 18°. . . . L,378
Mechanische Theil der Naturlehre. H. C. Oersted. Brschwg. 1851. 8°. G,706
Physik der Erde. H. Buff. Braunschweig, 1850. 8°. . . . . G,672
Principia Mathematica. Sir I. Newton. Glasguæ, 1822. 4 v. 4°. M,1177
Study of. Sir J. F. W. Herschel. London, 1831. 12°. . . M,1017
Text-Book of. J. W. Draper. New York, 1849. 12°. . . . N,82
Natural Science, Gebiet der Naturkunde. F. Arago. Stutt. 1838. 3 v. in 1. 8°. G,670
Natural Sciences, Rundschau in der Naturwissenschaft. J. Hammerschmied. Wein, 1863. 8°. . . . . . . . . . G,682
Studium der Naturwissenschaften. J. v. Liebig. München, 1852. 8°. N,252,44
in Preussen. J. Liebig. Braunschweig, 1840. 8°. . . N,252,7
Natural Theology. T. Chalmers. New York, 1845. 12°. . . . P,208
W. Paley. London, 1845. 8°. . . . . . . . P,709,4
and Chemistry. W. Prout. London, 1855. p. 8°. . . . . L,279
Astron. and Physics with reference to. W. Whewell. Lond. 1852. p. 8°. L,277
Discourse of. H. Brougham. London, 1836. 12°. . . . . . P,155
The same. London, 1856. p. 8°. . . . . . . . P,171
Outline of a System of. G. Crabbe. London, 1840. 8°. . . . P,219
Naturalist, Adventures of a Young. L. Biart. New York, 1871. 12°. . J,1311
Entertaining. J. W. Loudon, 1867. 8°. . . . . . . . N,646
Leaves from the Note-Book of a. W. J. Broderip. Lond. 1852. 12°. N,655
Note-Book of a. E. P. Thompson. London, 1845. 12°. . . N,658
on the River Amazon. H. W. Bates. London, 1863. 2 v. 8°. . V,243
Practischer Naturforscher. F. H. Walchner. Karlsruhe, 1842. 8°. G,715
Sea-Side. R. W. Frasser. London, 1868. 12°. . . . . . N,481
Naturalist, The; a Magazine. London, 1851–58. 8 v. in 4. 8°. . . N,546
Naturalist's Cabinet. T. Smith. London, 1806–7. 6 v. 8°. . . . N,665
Naturalist's Library; ed. by Sir W. Jardine. Edinburgh, 1837–52. 40 v. 16°. N,470
Contents. See *Jardine, Sir W.*
The same. Edinburgh, 1852–54. 40 v. 16°. . . . . S.C.
Naturalist's Pocket-Book. G. Graves. London, 1818. 8°. . . . . N,525

Nature, Adaptation to Moral Const. of Man. T. Chalmers. Lond. 1853. p. 8°. L,278
Adaptation to Physical Condition of Man. J. Kidd. Lond. 1852. p. 8°. L,276
The same. Philadelphia, 1836. 8°. . . . . . . N,89
and Art. E. S. Inchbald. London, 1820. 12°. . . . . . K,538
and Elements of the External World. London, 1847. 8°. . . O,689
and Human Nature. T. C. Haliburton. London, 1859. 12°. . J,572
and the Supernatural. H. Bushnell. New York, 1864. 12°. . . P,52
Ansichten der Natur. A. von Humboldt. Stuttgart, 1860. 2 v. 16°. G,683
The same. Stuttgart, 1849. 12°. . . . . . . . G,684
Art and Life, Beautiful in. A. J. Symington. London, 1857. 2 v. 8°. M,53
Aspects of, in Different Lands. A. von Humboldt. Phil. 1850. 12°. D,1137
Aus der Natur. A. Abel. Leipzig, 1852–61. 16 v. in 5. 8°. . G,671
Beauties, Harmonies, and Sublimities of. C. Bucke. N. Y. 1855. 18°. L,435
Benedicite. G. C. Child. London, 1868. 16°. . . . . . P,348
Book of. J. M. Good. Hartford, 1855. 8°. . . . . . . M,787
F. Schoedler. Philadelphia, 1853. 8°. . . . . . . M,788
Child's Book of. W. Hooker. New York, 1869. 12°. . . . N,642
Drei Reiche der Natur. C. G. A. Giebel. Leipzig, 1859–64. 5 v. 8°. G,965
Etudes de la. J. H. B. de Saint-Pierre. Paris, 1856. 12°. . . M,757
Gallery of. T. Milner. London, 1846. 8°. . . . . . . N,144
Geschichte der Natur. H. G. Bronn. Stuttgart, 1841–43. 12 v. 8°. G,812
Great Stone Book of. D. T. Ansted. Philadelphia, 1863. 12°. . N,767
Harmonies of. G. Hartwig. London, 1866. 8°. . . . . . N,536
History of Animated. W. Bingley. Cincinnati, 1868. 8°. . . N,557
in Disease. J. Bigelow. Boston, 1854. 12°. . . . . . . L,848
Laws of, Appleton's. New York, 1856. 2 v. 8°. . . . . . Q,259
Die Natur, v. 1, 2, 8–11. O. Ule und K. Müller. Halle, n. d. 4°. G,740
Night-Side of. C. Crowe. New York, 1850. 12°. . . . . . O,333
Order of, and Claims of Revelation. B. Powell. London, 1859. 12°. P,223
Popular Guide to the Observation of. R. Mudie. Edinburgh, 1832. 16°. I,537
The same. New York, 1860. 16°. . . . . . . L,379
Remarkable Phenomena of. H. G. Bell. Edinburgh, 1827. 16°. . I,499
Schüler der Natur. K. Müller. Halle, 1851. 16°. . . . . G,357
Studies of. J. H. B. de Saint-Pierre. London, 1809. 4 v. 8°. . H,913
The same. London, 1846. 2 v. 12°. . . . . . . U,123
Sublime in. F. de Lanoye. New York, 1870. 12°. . . M,1046
True and Beautiful in. J. Ruskin. New York, 1868. 8°. . . M,75
Views. A. von Humboldt. London, 1869. p. 8°. . . . . . L,297
Wille in der Natur. A. Schopenhauer. Frankfurt-am-Main, 1854. 8°. G,575
Worship of, in America. E. G. Squier. New York, 1851. 8°. . B,607
Nature's Aristocracy; Plea for the Oppressed. J. Collins. Boston, 1871. 16°. H,120
Nautical Almanac, 1810–68. London, 1805–68. 60 v. in 44. 8°. . . R,21
Nautical Surveying, Treatise on. A. H. Alston. London, 1860. 8°. . M,755
Naval and Military Heroes of Great Britain. N. Johns. London, 1860. p. 8°. L,130
Naval Architecture. J. Peake. London, 1859. 12°. . . . . . . M,951
Modern System of. J. S. Russell. London, 1865. 3 v. f°. . . F,299
Naval Sciences, Illustrations to, Appleton's. New York, 1856. 8°. . Q,255,2
Nave, J. Handy-Book to Algæ, Diatoms, etc. London, 1867. 16°. . N,936
Navies of the World. H. Busk. London, 1859. 8°. . . . . . I,555
Navigation. J. Greenwood. London, 1850. 12°. . . . . . . M,925

Navigation and Nautical Astronomy. J. B. Young. London, 1858. 12°. . M,977
of all Ages, Appleton's. New York, 1856. 2 v. 8°. . . . Q,255
Thermometrical. J. Williams. Philadelphia, 1799. 8°. . . M,774
Naville, E. The Heavenly Father. Boston, 1867. 12°. . . . . P,34
Navy, British, History of. C. D. Yonge. London, 1863. 2 v. 8°. . . B,94
U. S., History of. J. F. Cooper. New York, 1853. 3 v. in 1. 8°. . B,855
during the Rebellion. C. B. Boynton. N. Y. 1868. 2 v. 8°. B,959
Neal, A. B. See *Haven, A. B.*
Neal, D. History of New England. London, 1747. 2 v. 8°. . . . C,18
History of the Puritans. New York, 1855. 2 v. 8°. . . . C,8
Neal, J. Great Mysteries and Little Plagues. Boston, 1870. 16°. . . J,1325
Neale, F. A. Residence in Siam. London, 1852. 12°. . . . . V,581
Neale, W. H. Mohammedan System of Theology. London, 1831. 8°. . P,826
Neander, A. Emperor Julian and his Generation. New York, 1850. 12°. D,722
History of the Christian Religion. Boston, 1854-55. 5 v. 8°. . P,612
The same. London, 1852-70. 9 v. in 10. p. 8°. . . . L,215
History of the Christian Dogmas. London, 1866. 2 v. p. 8°. . L,219
Life of Jesus Christ. New York, 1855. 8°. . . . . . . P,376
The same. London, 1869. p. 8°. . . . . . . . L,216
Memorials of Christian Life. London, 1852. 12°. . . . . L,218
Planting of the Christian Church. London, 1851. 2 v. p. 8°. . L,217
Nearchus's Voyage from the Indus to the Euphrates. London, 1797. 4°. . V,722
Nearer and Dearer. E. Bradley. New York, 1864. 12°. . . . . K,603
Neckam, A. De Naturis Rerum, etc. London, 1863. 8°. . . . . W,184
Necker, J. Administration des Finances de la France. Paris, 1785. v. 12°. O,468
Ned Myers. J. F. Cooper. New York, 1860. 12°. . . . . . K,39
Ned Nevins, the Newsboy. H. Morgan. Boston, 1869. 16°. . . . J,1617
Needlework, Hand-Book of. E. Lambert. London, 1842. 12°. . . H,478
Treasures in. Mrs. Warren and Mrs. Pullan. London, n. d. 12°. . H,473
Neef, J. Sketch of a Plan of Education. Philadelphia, 1808. 12°. . O,913
Neele, H. Romance of History; England. London, 1831. 3 v. 12°. . K,884
Nees v. Esenbeck, C. G. Allgemeine Formenlehre der Natur. Bres. 1861. 8°. G,680
Negro Emancipation, Practicability of. Bristol, 1830. 8°. . . . O,396
Neighbors. F. Bremer. New York, 1842. 8°. . . . . . . . K,609
The same. London, 1852. 12°. . . . . . . L,169,1
Neighbor's Wives. J. T. Trowbridge. Boston, 1867. 12°. . . . K,22
Neill, E. D. History of Minnesota. Philadelphia, 1858. 8°. . . . C,239
The same, large paper. Philadelphia, 1858. 4°. . . . . F,70
Neil, S. Epoch Men and Results of their Lives. Edinburgh, n. d. 12°. C,485
Neilson, W. Introduction to the Irish Language. Dublin, 1808. 8°. . L,780
Nelkenbrecher, J. C. Münz-, Mass-, und Gewichtskunde. Reutl. 1834. 12°. E,427
Nell, W. C. Colored Patriots of the American Revolution. Boston, 1855. 12°. B,740
Nelly Brooke. F. Church. Leipzig, 1869. 2 v. in 1. 16°. . . . J,350
Nellie Gates. W. A. Boardman. Philadelphia, 1870. 16°. . . . J,1709
Nelson, D. Cause and Cure of Infidelity. New York, n. d. 12°. . . P,860
Nelson, H., *Lord*, Life of. R. Southey. London, 1813. 2 v. 16°. . . C,1164
The same. London, 1867. 24°. . . . . . . . C,1162
The same. London, 1830. 16°. . . . . . . . I,632
The same. London, 1868. p. 8°. . . . . . . . L,147
The same. New York, 1862. 16°. . . . . . . . L,338

Nelson, R. Mercantile Arithmetic. Cincinnati, 1859. 16°. . . . o,1101
Nelson, T. The Land of Scott. London, 1859. 16°. . . . . . . v,301
Nelson's Views. London, n. d. 4°. . . . . . . . . . *q,426
The same. London, 1857–58. 3 v. 16°. . . . . *v,1029
Nemesis. M. V. Terhune. New York, 1866. 12°. . . . . . . k,317
Nennius. Historia Britonum; recensuit J. Stevenson. London, 1838. 8°. u,627
History of the Britons. London, 1848. 8°. . . . . . . . l,26
Nepos. See *Cornelius Nepos.*
Neptune, the Planet; an Exposition and Hist. J. P. Nichol. Edinb. 1848. 8°. n,333
Neptune's Heroes; or, Sea-Kings of Eng. W. H. D. Adams. Lond. 1861. 16°. c,1242
Nero, History of. J. Abbott. New York, 1864. 16°. . . . . . j,1386
Nesbit, J. C. Application of Chemistry to Agriculture. Lond. 1847. 8°. n,252,31
Analysis of the Hop. London, 1846. 8°. . . . . . . . n,252,32
Nest Hunters. W. Dalton. London, 1863. 16°. . . . . . . j,1719
Nests and Eggs of British Birds. J. C. Atkinson. London, 1861. 16°. . o,84
F. O. Morris. London, 1867. 3 v. 8°. . . . . . . . *o,88
Nestorians; or, Lost Tribes. A. Grant. London, 1844. 16°. . . . v,1031
Mountain, and Dr. Grant. T. Laurie. Boston, 1853. 12°. . . . p,608
Netherlands, Gesch. der Niederlande. N. G. Kampen. Hamb. 1831–33. 2 v. 8°. e,83
History of. T. C. Grattan. London, 1830. 12°. . . . . . m,999
The same. New York, 1843. 12°. . . . . . . . . b,406
History of United. J. L. Motley. New York, 1868. 4 v. 8°. . b,409
Revolt of. F. von Schiller. New York, 1847. 16°. . . . . b,407
The same. London, 1853–57. 2 v. p. 8°. . . . l,228,1,2
Netter, T. Fasciculi Zizaniorum J. Wyclif. London, 1858. 8°. . . . w,155
Neue Bahnen. L. Otto. Wien, 1864. 2 v. in 1. 24°. . . . . . g,376
Neue Stadtgeschichten. M. Ring. Prag und Leipzig, 1858. 3 v. 24°. . g,429
Vol. 1. Die Geschiedene. Vol. 2. Der Waisenknabe. Vol. 3. Die Erben.
Neues Leben. B. Auerbach. Stuttgart, 1864. 3 v. 12°. . . . e,311,14–16
Neuman, H., Baretti, and Seoane. Spanish Dictionary. Lond. n. d. 2 v. 8°. l.r.
Neuralgia affecting the Head. W. Harvey. London, 1852. 8°. . . . l,923
Neuwied, Prinz zu. See *Maximilian.*
Never too Late to Mend. C. Reade. Boston, 1866. 2 v. 12°. . . . . k,906
Nevin, A. Churches of the Valley; Presbyterian Churches of Cumberland and Franklin Counties, Penn. Philadelphia, 1852. 12°. . . . . c,87
Nevins, W. Practical Thoughts. New York, 1836. 18°. . . . . . p,13
The same. New York, n. d. 18°. . . . . . . . p,746,13
Nevius, J. L. China and the Chinese. New York, 1869. 12°. . . . . v,601
New America. W. H. Dixon. Philadelphia, 1867. 12°. . . . . . v,105
The same. Leipzig, 1867. 2 v. in 1. 16°. . . . . . j,151
New American Cyclopædia. New York, 1863. 16 v. 8°. . . . . . s.c.
The same. New York, 1870. 16 v. 8°. . . . . . r.r.
New American Magazine, v. 1, 2. Cleveland, 1852–54. 2 v. in 1. 8°. . t,13
New and Old; California and India. J. W. Palmer. New York, 1859. 12°. k,295
New Atlantis. F. *Lord* Bacon. London, 1852. 16°. . . . . . . k,690
New Atmosphere. M. A. Dodge. Boston, 1865. 16°. . . . . . . . h,53
New Bedford, Mass., History of. D. Ricketson. New Bedford, 1858. 12°. c,39
New Boy, The. C. F. Guernsey. Philadelphia, 1871. 16°. . . . j,1723
New Brunswick, Wilderness Journeys in. A. Gordon. London, 1864. 8°. v,1036,3
New Eclectic Speaker. W. H. McGuffey. Cincinnati, n. d. 12°. . . o,1228

New England, Abstract of Laws of. J. Cotton. 1641. See *Force's Tracts*, v. 3.
Brief Relation of the State of. London, 1689. See *Force's Tracts*, v. 2.
Chronology of, to 1820. A. Bradford. Boston, 1843. 12°. . . . C,1
Description of. J. Smith. London, 1616. See *Force's Tracts*, v. 2.
Early History of. I. Mather. Boston, 1864. 4°. . . . . . B,603
Ecclesiastical History of. C. Mather. Hartford, 1853–55. 2 v. 8°. C,55
Fathers, Lives of. Boston, 1870. 6 v. 12°. . . . . . . D,8
Vol. 1. Life of John Cotton; by A. W. M'Clure.
2. Lives of John Wilson, John Norton, and John Davenport; by A. W. M'Clure.
3. Life of John Eliot; by N. Adams.
4. Life of Thomas Shepard; by J. A. Albro.
5. Lives of Increase Mather and Sir Wm. Phipps; by E. Pond.
6. Life of Thomas Hooker; by E. W. Hooker.
Founders of. W. H. Bartlett. London, 1853. 8°. . . . . . C,74
S. G. Drake. Boston, 1865. 4°. . . . . . . . F,56
Genealogical Dictionary of. J. Savage. Boston, 1860–62. 4 v. 8°. *C,729
History of. J. W. Barber. Hartford, 1856. 8°. . . . . . C,20
C. W. Elliott. New York, 1857. 2 v. 8°. . . . C,7
D. Neal. London, 1747. 2 v. 8°. . . . . . C,18
from 1630 to 1649. J. Winthrop. Boston, 1853. 2 v. 8°. . C,6
from 1630 to 1689. J. G. Palfrey. Lond. 1859–68. 3 v. 8°. C,22
Letter to Countess of Lincoln. T. Dudley. 1630. See *Force's Tracts*, v. 2.
Letters from, 1686. J. Dunton. Boston, 1867. 4°. . . . . . C,66
New English Canaan. T. Morton. 1632. See *Force's Tracts*, v. 2.
News from. London, 1676. Boston, 1850. 4°. . . . . . . F,222
Planter's Plea. J. White. London, 1630. See *Force's Tracts*, v. 2.
Plain Dealing. T. Lechford; ed. by J. H. Trumbull. Bost. 1867. 4°. F,64
Proceedings of a Convention of Delegates, 1780. Albany, 1867. 4°. C,11
Rarities Discovered in. J. Josselyn. Boston, 1865. 4°. . . . F,65
Relation of the Troubles in. I. Mather. Boston, 1677. 4°. . . B,603
Revolution in. N. Byfield. London, 1689. See *Force's Tracts*, v. 4.
The same justified. London, 1691. See *Force's Tracts*, v. 4.
Three Eras of. G. Lunt. Boston, 1857. 12°. . . . . . . H,190
Two Voyages to, 1638 and 1663. J. Josselyn. Boston, 1865. 4°. . F,66
Wars with the Eastern Indians. S. Penhallow. Cincin. 1859. 4°. . B,610
Wonder-Working Providence. E. Johnson; ed. W. F. Poole. Bos. 1867. 4°. C,34
New-England Coast, Summer Cruise on. R. Carter. Boston, 1870. 16°. . V,49
New-England Farm-House, Autobiog. of. N. C. Chamberlain. N. Y. 1865. 12°. K,153
New-England Magazine, 1832–34. Boston, n. d. 7 v. 8°. . . . . . S,4
New-England Theocracy. H. F. Uhden. Boston, 1858. 12°. . . . P,835
New-England Tragedies. H. W. Longfellow. Boston, 1868. 16°. . . I,69
New-England's Jonas cast up. J. Child. London, 1647. Boston, 1869. 8°. C,10
The same. See *Force's Tracts*, v. 4.
New-England's Memorial. N. Morton. Boston, 1855. 8°. . . . . . C,73
New-England's Plantation. F. Higginson. Lond. 1630. See *Force's Tracts*, v. 1.
New-England's Prospect, 1634. W. Wood. Boston, 1865. 4°. . . . . C,31
New-England's Trials. J. Smith. London, 1622. See *Force's Tracts*, v. 2.
New Flower for Children. L. M. Child. Boston, 1865. 16°. . . J,1432
New Gospel of Peace. R. G. White. New York, 1866. 12°. . . . B,891
New Hampshire, History of, by Uncle Philip. N. Y. 1840–44. 2 v. 16°. J,1219
History of. G. Barstow. Boston, 1853. 8°. . . . . . . C,25
J. Belknap. Dover, N. H. 1812. 3 v. 8°. . . . . . C,128

New Ipswich, N. H., History of. F. Kidder and A. A. Gould. Bost. 1852. 8°. C,26
New Jersey, Bills of Credit. H. Phillips. Philadelphia, 1863. 8°. . . P.D.
East Jersey under Propriet.Govern'ts. W.Whitehead. Newark,1846. 8°. C,107
Geological Survey of. W. Kitchell. Trenton, 1856. 8°. . . . N,873
History of. J. W. Barber. Hartford, 1856. 8°. . . . . . C,20
W. H. Carpenter and T. S. Arthur. Philadelphia, 1853. 16°. C,156
New-Jersey Monumental Association, Address of. Trenton, 1859. 8°. B,809,2
New Mexico, El-Gringo. W. W. H. Davis. New York, 1857. 12°. . . V,33
Explorations in. J. R. Bartlett. New York, 1854. 2 v. 8°. . . V,124
New Moral World, Book of the. R. Owen. London, 1836. 8°. . . . O,525
New Netherlands, History of. W. Dunlap. New York, 1839-40. 2 v. 8°. C,93
History of. E. B. O'Callaghan. New York, 1846. 8°. . . . C,97
Register of, 1626-1674. E. B. O'Callaghan. Albany, 1865. 8°. . C,104
New Orleans, Gen. Jackson and. A. Walker. New York, 1856. 12°. . B,846
New Orleans Price Current, v. 16, 17. New Orleans, 1845-46. 2 v. in 1. f°. P.D.
New Pantheon. G. Crabb. London, 1854. 18°. . . . . . . . P,908
New Pictures and Old Panels. J. Doran. London, 1859. 8°. . . . H,312
New Priest of Conception Bay. R. T. S. Lowell. New York, 1869. 12°. . K,797
New Purchase; or, the Far West. R. Carlton *pseud.* N. Y. 1843. 2 v. 12°. V,156
New South Wales, Excursions in. J. Henderson. London, 1851. 2 v. 12°. V,886
History of. G. Barrington. London, n. d. 8°. . . . . . C,436
Religion and Education in. W. W. Burton. London, 1840. 8°. . P,175
New Spain, Political Essays on. A. von Humboldt. Lond. 1811. 4 v. 8°. V,197
New Testament Manual. S. Hawes. Boston, 1871. 16°. . . . . . P,184
See also *Bible, New Testament.*
New Timon; a Poetical Romance. Sir E. B. Lytton. London, 1846. 8°. . I,384
The same, and St. Stephen's. Leipzig, 1860. 16°. . . . J,323
New Voyage round the World. D. DeFoe. London, 1725. 8°. . . V,1078
New West; or, California in 1867-68. C. L. Brace. New York, 1869. 12°. V,153
New York City, Board of Education Documents, 1853-55. N.Y.1853-55. 3v. 8°. O,839
Banks of; their Dealers, etc. New York, 1870. 12°. . . . . O,503
Comptroller's Annual Report, 1854. New York, 1855. 8°. . . C,102
Custom-House, Reports on. Washington, 1867. 8°. . . . . . O,588
Description of; edited by O. L. Holley. New York, 1847. 18°. . C,152
during the last half Century. J. W. Francis. New York, 1857. 8°. C,101
Exhibition of Industry. New York, 1852. 8°. . . . . . B,809,1
Great Metropolis. J. H. Browne. Hartford, 1869. 8°. . . . C,106
Historical Sketch of. New York, 1853. 12°. . . . . . . C,162
History of. D. T. Valentine. New York, 1853. 8°. . . . . . C,100
House of Refuge and its Times. B. K. Peirce. New York, 1869. 8°. O,384
Imprisonment of two Presby. Ministers, 1707. See *Force's Tracts*, v. 4.
Journal of Commerce, v. 1-4. New York, 1828-29. 3 v. in 2. f°. . P.D.
Mercantile Library Association, Catalogue. New York, 1866. 8°. . L.R.
Supplement to the same. New York, 1869. 8°. . . . . L.R.
Old Merchants of. J. A. Scoville. New York, 1870. 5 v. 12°. C,1044
Past, Present, and Future. E. P. Belden. New York, 1850. 12°. . C,171
New York State, Agriculture of. E. Emmons. Albany, 1843. 5 v. 4°. Q,101,15
Antiquities of. E. G. Squier. Buffalo, 1851. 8°. . . . . . C,91
Code of Public Instruction. Albany, 1856. 8°. . . . . . . O,819
Forest Arcadia of Northern. Boston, 1864. 16°. . . . . . V,147

New York State, Historical Society, Charter and By-Laws. N. Y. 1857. 8°. C,101
Collections of, v. 1, 3. New York, 1811–21. 2 v. 8°. . . C,146
Discourse before. J. W. Francis. New York, 1857. 8°. . C,101
Proceedings at Dedication of Library. New York, 1857. 8°. C,101
Description of. D. Denton. New York, 1845. 4°. . . . . F,57
Documentary History. E. B. O'Callaghan. Alb. 1850–51. 4 v. 4°. S.C.
The same, v. 1, 2. Albany, 1849. 8°. . . . . . . C,96
Documents relative to its Colonial History. Alb. 1853–58. 11 v. 4°. F,234
Flora of. J. Torrey. Albany, 1843. 2 v. 4°. . . . . . *Q,101,6,7
Geology of. E. Emmons. Albany, 1842. 4°. . . . . . *Q,101,10
J. Hall. Albany, 1843. 2 v. 4°. . . . . . *Q,101,12,13
W. W. Mather. Albany, 1843. 4°. . . . . . . *Q,101,9
Historical Collections of. J. W. Barber and J. Howe. N.Y. 1842. 8°. C,94
History of. J. W. Barber. Hartford, 1856. 8°. . . . . . C,20
W. H. Carpenter and T. S. Arthur. Philadelphia, 1853. 16°. C,155
History of, 1609–1664. J. R. Brodhead. New York, 1853. 8°. . C,98
History of the Western Settlement of. J. H. Hotchkin. N.Y. 1848. 8°. C,95
Knickerbocker's History of. See *Irving, W.*
Library, Catalogue of Books on Bibliography. Albany, 1858. 8°. . L.R.
Catalogue of the General Library. Albany, 1856. 8°. . . L.R.
Catalogue of the Law Library. Albany, 1856. 8°. . . . L.R.
Catalogue of Maps, MSS., Engraving, etc. Albany, 1857. 8°. L.R.
Mineralogy of. L. C. Beck. Albany, 1842. 4°. . . . . *Q,101,8
Palæontology of. J. Hall. Albany, 1847–52. 2 v. 4°. . *Q,101,13,14
Phelps and Gorham's Purchase. O. Turner. Rochester, 1851. 8°. . C,145
Political Parties in. J. B. Hammond. Cooperstown, 1846. 2 v. 8°. C,92
J. S. Jenkins. Auburn, 1849. 12°. . . . . . . . C,172
Register of New Netherland, 1626–74. E.B.O'Callaghan. Alb. 1865. 8°. C,104
Report on Canals for 1859. V. R. Richmond. Albany, 1860. 2 v. 8°. P.D.
Zoölogy of. J. De Kay. Albany, 1842–44. 5 v. 4°. . . . *Q,101,1-5
New-Yorker, The; ed. H.Greeley and P. Benjamin. v. 6,7,8. N.Y.1838–40. 4°. Q,339
New Zealand and its Colonization. W. Swainson. London, 1859. 8°. . V,897
F. von Hochstetter. Stuttgart, 1863. 8°. . . . . . . . Q,430
New-Zealanders, The. London, 1830. 16°. . . . . . . . . L,489
Newberry, J. S. and Worthen. Palæontology of Illinois. Springf. 1866. 8°. N,742,2
Newbury and Newburyport, Mass., History of. J. Coffin. Boston, 1845. 8°. C,71
Newby, C. J. Common Sense. Leipzig, 1866. 2 v. in 1. 16°. . . . J,385
Newcastle-upon-Tyne, Hist. and Antiquities of. J. Brand. Lond. 1789. 2 v. 8°. F,288
Newcomb, H. Cyclopædia of Missions. New York, 1858. 8°. . . . P,610
Development of Christian Character. Boston, 1843. 12°. . . H,289
How to be a Man. Boston, 1857. 18°. . . . . . . J,1183
Young Lady's Guide. New York, 1853. 12°. . . . . . . H,298
Newcome, W. Improved Metrical Version of Ezekiel. London, 1836. 8°. P,545
Newcomes. W. M. Thackeray. New York, 1867. 2 v. in 1. 8°. . K,1028
The same. Leipzig, 1854. 4 v. 16°. . . . . . . . J,485
Newell, R. H., *Orpheus C. Kerr.* Versatilities; Poems. Boston, 1871. 12°. I,102
Newfoundland in 1842. R. H. Bonnycastle. London, 1842. 2 v. 12°. . V,177
Newgate Calendar. A. Knapp and W. Baldwin. London, 1824. 4 v. 8°. *C,562
Newland, H. Forest Life in Norway and Sweden. London, 1859. 8°. J,1318
Newman, E. Grammar of Entomology. London, 1835. 16°. . . . . O,9

Newman, E. Introduction to the History of Insects. London, 1841. 8°. . O,47
Newman, F. W. History of the Hebrew Monarchy. London, 1865. 8°. . A,207
Regal Rome. New York, 1852. 12°. . . . . . . . A,140
The Soul; its Natural History. London, 1868. 12°. . . . P,212
Reply to the Eclipse of Faith. Boston, 1854. 12°. . . . . P,97
Newman, J. Instructions for using Newman's Barometer. Lond. 1841. 8°. N,252,33
Newman, J. H. Apologia pro Vita Sua. New York, 1866. 12°. . . P,137
Analysis of his Apologia, by J. N. D. London, 1866. 12°. . . P,135
Arians of the Fourth Century. London, 1833. 8°. . . . . P,614
Callista; Sketch of the Third Century. Leipzig, 1869. 16°. . . J,386
Development of Christian Doctrine. London, 1845. 8°. . . . P,615
History of my Religious Opinions. London, 1865. 8°. . . . P,798
Letter on Dr. Pusey's Eirenicon. London, 1866. 8°. . . . P,220
Office and Work of Universities. London, 1856. 12°. . . . O,832
Parochial and Plain Sermons. London, 1869. 8 v. 8°. . . . P,674
Prophetical Office of the Church. London, 1837. 8°. . . . P,799
Scripture and Ecclesiastical Miracles. London, 1870. 8°. . . P,353
Newman, J. P. From Dan to Beersheba. New York, 1864. 12°. . . V,644
Newnham, W. Principles of Education. London, 1827. 2 v. 8°. . O,1241
Reciprocal Influence of Body and Mind. London, 1842. 8°. . . O,675
Newport, R. I., illustrated. G. C. Mason. New York, 1854. 12°. . . V,101
Newport, Ky., Laws and Ordinances; ed. by W. Stanley. Newport, 1856. 8°. U,518
News from New England. London, 1676. Boston, 1850. 4°. . . . F,222
Newspaper Literature, Specimens of. J. T. Buckingham. Bost. 1852. 2 v. 12°. C,720
Newspaper Record. W. T. Coggeshall. Philadelphia, 1856. 2 v. 8°. . M,639
Newspapers in Illinois. H. R. Boss. Chicago, 1870. 4°. . . . . F,172
Newton Forster. F. Marryat. New York, 1865. 12°. . . . . K,845
Newton, Sir I. Arithmetica Universalis. London, 1722. 8°. . . M,1105
Chronology of Ancient Kingdoms amended. London, 1728. 4°. . A,48
Life of. J. B. Biot. London, n. d. 8°. . . . . . . . C,581
Sir D. Brewster. London, 1831. 16°. . . . . . . I,635
The same. New York, 1831. 24°. . . . . L,359
Memoirs of. Sir D. Brewster. Edinburgh, 1855. 2 v. 8°. . . D,295
Optice; sive de Reflexionibus, etc., Lucis. London, 1706. 4°. . N,30
Optics; or, a Treatise of Light. London, 1730. 8°. . . . N,27
Principia Mathematica. Glasguæ, 1822. 4 v. 4°. . . . . M,1177
Newton, J. Cardiphonia; or, Utterance of the Heart. London, 1857. 16°. P,19
Newton, O. E. Asiatic Cholera as it appeared in Cincinnati. N. Y. 1867. 8°. L,928
Newton, T. Dissertations on Prophecies. Edinburgh, 1793. 2 v. 12°. . P,172
Life; by himself. London, 1816. 8°. . . . . . . C,1289
Newth, S. Arithmetical Examples. London, 1859. 8°. . . . M,1101
Mechanical Examples. London, 1859. 8°. . . . . . M,1166
Trigonometrical Examples. London, 1859. 8°. . . . . M,1144
Ney, Marshal, Memoirs of. Philadelphia, 1834. 8°. . . . . . . D,675
Ngami, Lake. C. J. Andersson. New York, 1861. 12°. . . . . . V,800
Nibelungen Noth, Wörterbuch zur. A. Lübben. Oldenburg, 1854. 8°. . E,273
und Klage; hrsg. von C. Lachman. Berlin, 1841. 8°. . . . . E,272
Nicaragua, Description of. E. G. Squier. New York, 1852. 2 v. in 1. 8°. V,203
its People, Scenery, etc. E. G. Squier. New York, 1860. 8°. . . V,203
War in. W. Walker. Mobile, 1860. 12°. . . . . . . C,367

Nichol, J. P. Architecture of the Heavens. London, n. d. 8°. . . N,336
Contemplations of the Solar System. Edinburgh, 1844. 8°. . . N,335
Cyclopædia of Physical Sciences. London, 1868. 8°. . . . M,793
Planet Neptune; an Exposition and History. Edinburgh, 1848. 8°. N,333
Planetary System. London, 1851. 8°. . . . . . . . N,328
Thoughts on the System of the World. Edinburgh, 1848. 8°. . . N,334
Nicholas I., *Czar of Russia*, Life and Reign of. S. M. Smucker. Phil. 1858. 12°. D,750
English Envoy at Court of. J. Corner. New York, 1854. 12°. . K,94
Nicholas, T. Pedigree of the English People. London, 1868. 8°. . . N,433
Nicholas Nickleby. C. Dickens. New York, 1869. 12°. . . . . K,482
The same. Philadelphia, n. d. 8°. . . . . . . . K,513
The same. New York, 1871. 12°. . . . . . K,1136
The same. Leipzig, 1843. 2 v. in 1. 16°. . . . . J,129
Nicholls, C. B., *Brontë, C.* Jane Eyre. New York, 1870. 12°. . . . K,856
The same. Leipzig, 1850. 2 v. in 1. 16°. . . . . J,387
Life of. E. C. Gaskell. New York, 1868. 2 v. in 1. 12°. . C,1204
The same. Leipzig, 1859. 2 v. in 1. 16°. . . . . J,178
Professor. New York, n. d. 12°. . . . . . . . . K,857
The same. Leipzig, 1857. 12°. . . . . . . J,388
Shirley. New York, 1867. 12°. . . . . . . . . . K,858
The same. Leipzig, 1849. 2 v. in 1. 16°. . . . . J,389
Villette. New York, 1867. 12°. . . . . . . . . K,859
The same. Leipzig, 1853. 2 v. in 1. 16°. . . . . J,390
and Brontë, A. and E. Poems. London, 1846. 16°. . . . I,285
Nicholls, G. F. Grammar of the Samaritan Languages. London, 1858. 12°. L,773
Nichols, G. W. Story of the Great March to the Sea. New York, 1866. 12°. B,907
Nichols, J. F. Life of Sebastian Cabot. London, 1869. 8°. . . . D,182
Nicholson, A. Annals of the Famine in Ireland, 1847–49. N. Y. 1851. 12°. B,162
Nicholson, E. Mortality Sermon on James iv: 14. Dublin, 1721. 8°. . P,340
Sermon on Trinity Sunday. Dublin, 1721. 8°. . . . . P,340
Three Sermons; James 1: 27, and Phil. 4: 8. Dublin, 1721. 8°. P,340
Nicholson, J. Operative Mechanic and Brit. Machinist. Phil. 1826. 2 v. 8°. M,678
The same. London, 1853. 8°. . . . . . . . S.C.
Nicholson, J. B. Art of Bookbinding. Philadelphia, 1856. 12°. . . M,620
Nicholson, P. Encyclopædia of Architecture; ed. Lomax. Lond. '52. 2 v. 4°. M,264
Guide to Railway Masonry. London, 1840. 8°. . . . . M,698
Mechanics' Companion. Philadelphia, 1868. 8°. . . . . M,630
Nicholson, W. Journal of Nat. Philosophy, etc. Lond. 1797–1802. 5 v. 4°. T,41
The same. London, 1802–13. 36 v. 8°. . . . . T,40
Nick of the Woods. R. M. Bird. New York, 1868. 12°. . . . J,1342
Nicol, J. Manual of Mineralogy. Edinburgh, 1849. 8°. . . . . N,855
Nicolas, Sir N. H. Battle of Agincourt. London, 1833. 8°. . . . B,97
Chronology of History. London, 1833. 12°. . . . . . M,985
History of the Royal Navy. London, 1847. 2 v. 8°. . . . B,95
Life of William Davison. London, 1823. 8°. . . . . D,39
Memoirs of Sir C. Hatton. London, 1847. 8°. . . . . D,62
Nicolay, C. G. Oregon Territory; Geographical and Physical. Lon. 1846. 16°. V,145
Nicole, P. Pensées de Pascal, et de Nicole. Paris, 1856. 12°. . . H,864
Nicolini, G. B. History of the Jesuits. London, 1854. p. 8°. . . . L,131
Nidworth and his three Magic Wands. E. Prentiss. Boston, 1870. 16°. J,1426

Niebuhr, B. G. Ancient Ethnography and Geography. Lond. 1853. 2 v. 8°. N,435
History of Rome. London, 1851. 3 v. 8°. . . . . . . A,171
Lectures on Ancient History. London, 1852. 3 v. 8°. . . . A,25
The same. London, 1852. 3 v. 8°. . . . . . . S.C.
Lectures on the History of Rome. London, 1852. 3 v. 8°. . . S.C.
Life and Letters. New York, 1852. 12°. . . . . . . D,514
Niebuhr, C., Life of. S. Austin. London, n. d. 8°. . . . . . . C,581
Niembsch von Strehlenau, N. Gedichte. Stuttgart, 1856. 2 v. in 1. 12°. E,274
The same. Stuttgart, 1865. 12°. . . . . . . . E,275
Savonarola, ein Gedicht. Stuttgart, 1853. 16°. . . . . . E,276
Niger River, Exped. to. W. Allen and T. R. H. Thomson. Lon. 1848. 2 v. 8°. V,837
R. and J. Lander. London, 1832. 3 v. 16°. . . . . . I,611
The same. New York, 1854. 2 v. 16°. . . . L,367
Kru Coast and Cape Palmas. W. Durrant. London, 1862. 8°. V,1086,2
Tshadda and Binuë Expedition. T. H. Hutchinson. Lon. 1865. p. 8°. I,658,1
Night and Morning. Sir E. B. Lytton. Philadelphia, 1869. 12°. . . K,821
The same. Leipzig, 1843. 16°. . . . . . . . J,324
Night Lessons from Scripture. E. M. Sewell. New York, 1860. 16°. . P,202
Night-Side of London. J. E. Ritchie. London, 1869. 8°. . . . V,294
Night-Side of Nature. C. Crowe. New York, 1850. 12°. . . . O,333
Nightingale, F. Notes on Nursing. New York, 1860. 12°. . . . L,915
Nightmare Abbey and Headlong Hall. T. L. Peacock. N. Y. 1845. 12°. . K,890
Nile, Discovery of the Source of. J. H. Speke. New York, 1864. 8°. . V,851
and its Banks. A. C. Smith. London, 1868. 2 v. 12°. . . . V,794
Notes of a Howadji. G. W. Curtis. New York, 1862. 12°. . . V,799
Travels to the Source of. J. Bruce. v. 2–8. Edinb. 1804–5. 4° and 8°. V,831
White, Expedition to. F. Werne. London, 1849. 2 v. 12°. . V,770
Tributaries of Abyssinia. Sir S. W. Baker. Philadelphia, 1868. 12°. V,781
Niles, J. M. History of South America and Mexico. Hartford, 1844. 12°. C,368
Niles's Weekly Register. v. 1–57, 60, 64. Baltimore, 1811–43. 4° and 8°. T,53
Nina. F. Bremer. Leipzig, 1857. 2 v. 12°. . . . . . . E,313,6,7
Nina Balatka; a Maiden of Prague. Leipzig, 1867. 16°. . . . . J,391
Nina Gordon. H. B. Stowe. Boston, 1867. 12°. . . . . . K,285
Nine Years a Sailor. C. Nordhoff. Cincinnati, 1866. 12°. . . J,1712
Nineteen Beautiful Years; or, a Girl's Life. New York, 1864. 16°. . C,719
Nineteenth Century; Claims of E. Swedenborg. New York, 1852. 8°. . P,845
Geschichte des 19ten Jahrhunderts. G. G. Gervinus. Leip. 1855–66. 8 v. 8°. E,60
Einleitung dazu. Leipzig, 1853. 8°. . . . . . . . . E,59
Introduction to the History of. G. G. Gervinus. London, 1853. 8°. A,313
Nineveh and Babylon, Discoveries at. A. H. Layard. London, 1853. 8°. . V,677
The same. New York, 1854. 8°. . . . . . . . . V,600
and its Palaces. J. Bononi. London, n. d. 8°. . . . . V,676
The same. London, 1857. p. 8°. . . . . . . . L,95
and Persepolis. W. S. W. Vaux. London, 1851. 8°. . . . V,590
Palaces of, Restored. J. Fergusson. London, 1851. 8°. . V,655
and its Remains. A. H. Layard. London, 1849. 2 v. 8°. . . V,678
and its Story. M. Jones. London, 1866. 16°. . . . . V,584
Discoveries at. A. H. Layard. New York, 1857. 12°. . . . V,591
Fall of. J. W. Bosanquet. London, 1853. 8°. . . . . A,328
Nitzsch, C. I. System of Christian Doctrine. Edinburgh, 1849. 8°. . P,139

Nitzsch, C. L. Pterylography; edited by P. L. Sclater. London, 1867. 4°. Q,72
Noad, H. M. Chemical Analysis. Philadelphia, 1849. 8°. . . . . N,205
Manual of Electricity. London, 1859. 8°. . . . . . . N,52
Student's Text-Book of Electricity. London, 1867. 8°. . . . . N,49
Noah, M. M. Travels in Europe and Africa. New York, 1819. . V,1087
No Church. Leipzig, 1861. 2 v. 16°. . . . . . . . . . J,392
No Love Lost; a Poem. W. D. Howells. New York, 1869. 12°. . . I,172
No Name. W. Collins. New York, 1863. 8°. . . . . . . . . K,636
The same. Leipzig, 1863. 3 v. 16°. . . . . . . J,79
No Sense like Common Sense. M. Howitt. New York, 1859. 24°. . J,1164
No Thoroughfare. C. Dickens. Leipzig, 1868. 16°. . . . . . . J,133
Noble, L. L. After Icebergs with a Painter. New York, 1861. 12°. . V,171
Life of Thomas Cole. New York, 1860. 12°. . . . . . . D,156
Noble Deeds of American Women. J. Clement. New York, 1856. 12°. . C,739
Noble Life. D. M. Craik. New York, 1867. 12°. . . . . . . K,661
The same. Leipzig, 1866. 16°. . . . . . . . J,558
Noble Purpose Nobly Won. A. Manning. London, 1862. 2 v. 16°. . J,594
Noble Sister. M. A. Denison. Philadelphia, 1870. 16°. . . . J,1704
Noctes Ambrosianæ. J. Wilson. New York, 1855. 5 v. 12°. . . . H,605
Noehden, G. H. Grammar of the German Language. Andover, 1842. 8°. L,798
Noël, F. J. M. Dictionnaire Latin-Français. Paris, 1821–22. 2 v. 8°. . L.R.
et Chapsal, C.P. Dictionnaire de la Langue Française. Brux.1839. 8°. L.R.
Nouvelle Grammaire Française. Philadelphia, 1857. 12°. . L,799
et La Place. Leçons de Litterature et de Morale. Brux. 1840. 8°. H,918
Noel, B. W. Essays on the Union of Church and State. N. Y. 1849. 12°. P,114
Noel, R. Syrian Travel and Syrian Tribes. London, 1861. 8°. . V,1086,1
Nolan, E. H. British Empire in India and the East. London, n. d. 2 v. 18°. C,429
Nollekins, Joseph, and his Times. J. T. Smith. London, 1828. 2 v. 8°. D,34
Nolte, V. Fifty Years in both Hemispheres. New York, 1856. 12°. V,1036
Nonantum and Natick, Mass. S. S. Jacobs. Boston, 1853. 12°. . . K,143
Nonconformist's Memorial. E. Calamy. London, 1802–3. 3 v. 8°. . D,233
Non-Metallic Elements, Lectures on. M. Faraday. London, 1853. 16°. M,754
Nordhoff, C. Cape Cod and all along Shore. New York, 1868. 12°. . K,139
Nine Years a Sailor. Cincinnati, 1866. 12°. . . . . . J,1712
Man-of-War Life; The Merchant Vessel; Whaling and Fishing.
Whaling and Fishing. Cincinnati, 1856. 16°. . . . . . . K,140
Nordisches Bilderbuch. T. Mügge. Breslau, 1862. 12°. . . . . . E,196
Norfolk, Va., Historical and Descrip. Sketches of. W.S.Forrest. Phil. 1853. 8°. C,117
Normal School, The. A. Wells. London, 1849. 16°. . . . . . O,969
Norman Cline. E. Kellogg. Boston, 1871. 16°. . . . . . J,1724
Norman Conquest of England. E. H. Freeman. Oxford, 1867–69. 3 v. 8°. A,435
Norman Leslie; a New York Story. T. S. Fay. New York, 1869. 12°. . K,99
Normandy and England, History of. F. Palgrave. London, 1851–64. 4 v. 8°. A,440
during the Revolution. G. Greene. London, 1802. 8°. . . . B,262
Ecclesiastical History of. Ordericus Vitalis. Lond. 1853–4. 4 v. p. 8°. L,22
Expulsion of the English from. London, 1863. 8°. . . . . W,182
Residence in. J. A. St. John. Edinburgh, 1831. 16°. . . . . I,531
Norris, T. American Fish Culture. Philadelphia, 1868. 12°. . . . M,320
Norske Sprogs, Det. C. A. Holmboe. Wein, 1852. 4°. . . . . . G,608
North, Christopher, *pseud.* See *Wilson, J.*

North America. A. Trollope. New York, 1862. 12°. . . . . . v,55
The same. Leipzig, 1862. 3 v. 16°. . . . . . . J,501
Adventurers of the first Explorers of. J. Banvard. Boston, 1853. 12°. B,686
Concise Account of. Maj. R. Rogers. London, 1765. 8°. . . V,161
Discovery of the Great West. F. Parkman. Boston, 1870. 8°. . B,616
Discovery and Settlement of. W. Robertson. N. Y. 1850. 3 v. 8°. U,205,1
Early Jesuit Missions in. W. I. Kip. New York, 1846. 12°. . B,593
Impressions of, 1849. R. Baird. Philadelphia, 1850. 16°. . . V,18
Journal of a Voyage into. P .F. X. de Charlevoix. Lon. 1761. 2 v. 8°. V,164
Journey in. J. J. Gurney. Norwich, 1841. 8°. . . . . V,159
Jesuits in. F. Parkman. Boston, 1867. 8°. . . . . . . B,617
Middle Settlements in. A. Burnaby. London, 1798. 4°. . . Q,442
Reisen in Nordamerika, 1852–53. M. Wagner. Leip. 1857. 3 v. 16°. E,169
Relation Exacte des Caraibes. M. de la Borde. Leide, 1704. 12°. V,149
Three Years in. J. Stuart. Edinburgh, 1833. 2 v. 12°. . . V,142
Tour in. H. Tudor. London, 1834. 2 v. 12°. . . . . . V,19
Travels into. P. Kalm. London, 1772. 2 v. 8°. . . . . V,163
Travels in. F. J. de Chastelleux. New York, 1828. 8°. . . V,86
Travels in, 1827–28. Capt. B. Hall. Edinburgh, 1829. 3 v. 8°. V,160
Travels in, 1841–42. C. Lyell. New York, 1852. 2 v. in 1. 12°. V,60
Travels through, 1825–26. Duke of Saxe-Weimar Eisenach. Philadelphia, 1828. 2 v. in 1. 8°. . . . . . . . . . V,45
Voyage dans l'Amerique. L. Hennepin. Amsterdam, 1704. 12°. . V,149
Western Territory of. G. Imlay. London, 1792. 8°. . . . V,106
North American Review. v. 1–86. Boston, 1815–58. 8°. . . . . . T,2
North British Review. Edinburgh, 1844–55. 23 v. 8°. . . . . . R,9
North Carolina, Historical Sketches of. J. W. Wheeler. Philad. 1851. 8°. C,192
History of. F. L. Hawks. Fayetteville, N. C. 1857. 2 v. 8°. . C,141
Narrative of Adventures in. D. Fanning. New York, 1865. 4°. . C,315
S. Carolina, Georgia, etc., Travels through. W. Bartram. Lon. 1792. 8°. V,162
North and the South. H. Chase and C. W. Sanborn. Boston, 1856. 12°. . O,394
North and South. E. C. Gaskell. New York, n. d. 8°. . . . . K,707
North Countrie, Rhyme of the. A. M. Gleeman. Cincinnati, 1847. 12°. I,43
North Georgia Gazette and Winter Chronicle. W. E. Parry. Lon. 1821. 4°. V,1012,5
North Pole, Attempt to reach the, 1827. W. E. Parry. London, 1828. 4°. V,1012,5
North Sea, Nordseestudien. E. Hallier. Hamburg, 1863. 12°. . . G,681
North Star, Cruise of the. J. O. Choules. Boston, 1854. 12°. . . . V,338
Northanger Abbey. J. Austen. Boston, 1864. 12°. . . . . . . K,595
Northbrooke, J. Treatise against Dicing, Dancing, etc. London, 1843. 8°. I,885,14
Northend, C. National Orator. New York, 1859. 12°. . . . O,1229
Teacher's Assistant. Boston, 1859. 12°. . . . . . . . O,938
Northern Antiquities. P. H. Mallet. London, 1847. p. 8°. . . . L,17
Illustrations of. R. Jamieson. Edinburgh, 1814. 4°. . . . F,232
Northern Ocean, Journey to the, 1760–72. S. Hearne. London, 1795. 4°. Q,424
Northern Picture-Book, Nordisches Bilderbuch. T. Mügge. Bres. 1862. 12°. E,196
Northern Travel. B. Taylor. New York, 1865. 12°. . . . . . V,543
Northmen, Discovery of America by. J. T. Smith. London, 1839. 12°. . B,698
History of the. H. Wheaton. London, 1831. 8°. . . . . . B,580
in New England. J. T. Smith. Boston, 1839. 12°. . . . . B,689
Private Life of the. R. Keyser. London, 1868. 12°. . . . . B,576

Northmen, Religion of. R. Keyser. New York, 1854. 12°. . . . P,235
North-West, Notes on. W. J. A. Bradford. New York, 1846. 12°. . C,164
North-West Passage, Discovery of. R. McClure. London, 1859. 8°. . V,944
Second Voyage in search of a, 1829–33. Sir J. Ross. Lond. 1835. 4°. Q,423
Voyages for Discovery of. W. E. Parry. London, 1821–28. 5 v. 4°. V,1012
The same, abridged. New York, 1855. 2 v. 16°. . . L,412
North-West Territory, Tour into. T. M. Harris. Boston, 1805. 8°. . V,65
Notes on the Early Settlement of. J. Burnet. Cincinnati, 1847. 8°. C,274
Norton, A. Notes on the Gospels. Boston, 1855. 2 v. 8°. . . . P,546
Tracts concerning Christianity. Cambridge, 1852. 8°. . . . P,140
Norton, A. B. History of Knox Co., O., 1779–1862. Columbus, 1862. 8°. C,216
Norton, C. B. Book-Buyer's Almanac, 1853. New York, 1853. 12°. . L.R.
Literary Almanac for 1852. New York, 1851. 12°. . . . L.R.
Literary and Educational Register, 1854. New York, 1854. 12°. . L.R.
Norton, C. E. Considerations on Recent Social Theories. Boston, 1853. 16°. O,368
Notes of Travel and Study in Italy. Boston, 1860. 16°. . . . V,47
Norton, C. E. S. Lost and Saved. Leipzig, 1863. 2 v. in 1. 16°. . . J,393
Old Sir Douglas. Philadelphia, 1867. 12°. . . . . . . K,873
The same. Leipzig, 1867. 2 v. in 1. 16°. . . . . J,394
Stuart of Dunleath. Leipzig, 1851. 2 v. in 1. 16°. . . . . J,395
Norton, J., Life of. A. W. McClure. Boston, 1870. 12°. . . . . . D,8,2
Norton, J. P. Elements of Scientific Agriculture. New York, 1855. 12°. M,513
Norton, S. A. Elements of Natural Philosophy. Cincinnati, 1870. 12°. . N,81
Norton, T. and Sackville, T. Tragedy of Gorboduc. London, 1847. 8°. I,885,32
Norton, W. A. Treatise on Astronomy. New York, 1867. 8°. . . N,345
Norway. H. F. Tozer. London, 1861. 8°. . . . . . . V,1086,1
and its Glaciers. J. D. Forbes. Edinburgh, 1853. 8°. . . . V,548
and its Scenery. E. Price. London, 1853. p. 8°. . . . . L,132
and Sweden. C. L. Brace. New York, 1859. 12°. . . . . V,541
Journey through. H. D. Inglis. Edinburgh, 1829. 16°. . I,514
Forest Life in. H. Newland. London, 1859. 8°. . . J,1318
Chronicles of the Kings of. Snorro Sturleson. London, 1844. 3 v. 8°. B,579
its People and Institutions. J. Bowden. London, 1867. 8°. . . V,544
in 1848–49. T. Forester. London, 1850. 8°. . . . . . . V,547
Rambles in. T. Forester. London, 1854. p. 8°. . . . I,656,4
Residence in, 1834–36. S. Laing. London, 1862. p. 8°. . I,656,3
Tour in. J. S. Maxwell. New York, 1854. 12°. . . . . V,527
Travels in. W. B. Jerrold. London, 1854. 12°. . . . . V,545
Unprotected Females in. London, 1857. 12°. . . . . . . V,554
Sweden and Denmark, Hist. of. S. A. Dunham. Lond. 1839–40. 3 v. 12°. M,1002
Tour in. H. D. Inglis. London, 1837. 12°. . . V,549
Norwood. H. W. Beecher. New York, 1868. 12°. . . . . . . K,10
Norwood, Col. Voyage to Virginia, 1649. See *Force's Tracts*, v. 3.
No such Word as Fail. A. B. Haven. New York, 1867. 16°. . . . J,1327
Not Wisely, but too Well. R. Broughton. New York, 1868. 8°. . . K,614
The same. Leipzig, 1867. 2 v. in 1. 16°. . . . . . J,53
Notabilities in France and England. P. Chasles. New York, 1853. 12°. C,519
Note-Book of a Naturalist. E. P. Thompson. London, 1845. 12°. . . N,658
Leaves from. W. J. Broderip. London, 1852. 12°. . . N,655
Notes and Queries; 1st Series. London, 1850–56. 12 v. 4°. . . . *S,90

Notes and Queries; 1st series; Index. London, 1856. 4°. . . . . S,90,13
2d series. London, 1856–61. 8 v. 4°. . . . . . . *S,91
3d series. London, 1862–67. 12 v. 4°. . . . . . *S,92
Milledulcia, 1000 Pleasant Things from. N. Y. 1857. 12°. . H,114
Notes from Books. H. Taylor. London, 1849. 12°. . . . . . . H,692
from Life. H. Taylor. Boston, 1853. 16°. . . . . . H,469
of Lessons. G. Sydenham. London, 1857. 12°. . . . . . O,1155
of Lessons, Theory and Practice of. J. Jones. London, 1856. 16°. O,1131
Nothing but Money. T. S. Arthur. New York, 1866. 12°. . . . K,7
Nothing New; Tales. D. M. Craik. New York, n. d. 8°. . . . . K,650
Nothing Venture, Nothing Have. A. B. Haven. New York, 1867. 16°. J,1331
Nott, J. C. and Gliddon, G. R. Types of Mankind. Philadelphia, 1854. 8°. N,449
Indigenous Races of the Earth. Philadelphia, 1857. 4°. . N,468
Nouveau Théatre Anglois, v. 1. Londres, 1767. 12°. . . . . . H,855
Nouvelle Biographie Générale. J. C. F. Hoefer. Paris, 1862–66. 46 v. in 23. 8°. L.R.
Nouvelletes of the Musicians. E. F. Ellet. New York, 1851. 12°. . . K,697
Nova Scotia, Historical Account of. T. C. Haliburton. Halifax, 1829. 2 v. 8°. C,336
Novelists, British, and their Styles. D. Masson. Boston, 1859. 12°. . H,700
German. T. Roscoe. London, 1826. 4 v. 12°. . . . . . G,177
Novello, V. (Ed.) Musical Library. London, 1854–58. 2 v. 8°. . *M,421

Vol. 1. Cherubini, L. Treatise on Counterpoint and Fugue.
Marx, A. B. General Musical Instruction.
Crotch, W. Elements of Musical Composition; Comprehending Rules of Thorough-Bass and Theory of Tuning.
Catel, C. S. Treatise on Harmony.
Fétis, F. J. Treatise on Choir and Chorus Singing.
Silcher, F. Guidance of Singing Schools and Choral Societies.
Mozart, W. A. Succinct Thorough-Bass School.
Novello, S. Voice and Vocal Art.
2. Albrechtsberger, J. G. Thorough-Bass; Harmony; Guide to Composition.
Berlioz, H. Modern Instrumentation and Orchestration.

Novels and Novelists of the Eighteenth Century. W. Forsyth. N.Y. 1871. 12°. H,684
and Tales from Household Words. Leipzig, 1856–59. 11 v. 16°. J,130

1. An Ordeal; Nemesis; Two College Friends; Rogue's Life; My Country Town.
2. Ninth of June; Bond and Free; My Blind Sister; Eric Walderthorn; Diary of Anne Rodway; My Little Ward; On 'Change in Paris; Dick Dallington; Black and Blue; Salome and I.
3. Day of Reckoning; Kester's Evil Eye; Poor Clare; My Brother Robert; Frenchman of Two Wives; Forbidden Fruit; Left and Never Called for; Wreck of the Golden Mary.
4. Dead Secret, by W. Collins.
5. Dead Secret, concluded; Murderer of Archbishop of Paris; New Boy at Styles's; How the Old Love Fared; Helena Mathewson; Agnes Lee; Yellow Tiger; My Window; Queen's Revenge; Amphlett Love-Match.
6. Eleanor Clare's Journal; Romantic Breach of Promise; Brave Coucou Driver; Mrs. Badgery; Our Family Picture; Lazy Tour of two Idle Apprentices.
7. Perils of Certain English Prisoners; Lynden Hall; Marie Courtenay; My Lost Home; Number Five, Hanbury Terrace; Two in a Legion; Old St. Ann's Gateway; Max and his Companions; Legend of my Native Town; Little Huguenot; Famine Abroad; Patagonian Brothers.
8. Well Authenticated Rappings; "A Gude Conceit o' Oursels;" Apparition of Mons. Bodry; Mr. Pearson; Shadowless Men; Little Constancy's Birthday; Tale of an Old Man's Youth; Years and Years Ago; Lost Alice; Balcome St. Mystery; Six Giants of Lehon; The Devil's Mark; Boscobel; Blood of the Sundons; History of a Miracle; End of the Fordyce Brothers.
9. My Lady Ludlow; Rev. Alfred Hoblush's Statement; Truth in Irons; Princess Royal; What Mr. Burleigh could not see.
10. House to Let; Canon's Clock; Her Face; Poisoned Meal; Tried Friendship; Heir of Hardington; Lina Fernie; Sin of a Father.
11. Fleur de Lys; Saving Little, Wasting Much; Her First Appearance; Gringe Family; Home Again; Gipsy King; New Mind; Ground and Lofty Tumbling; Clergyman's Wife; Smallchange Family; Miss Cicely's Portrait; Douglas Jerrold; My two Partners; Dishonored; Chetwyndes; Lucky Leg; From First to Last.

Novels employed by English Dramatic Poets. London, 1846. . . I,885,31

Novels, Vier Neue Novellen. P. Heyse. Berlin, 1859. 16°. . . . . G,311
Novelties in Arts and Manufactures. London, 1853. 16°. . . . . M,598
Novum Organum, etc. F. *Lord* Bacon. London, 1868. p. 8°. . . L.257
Nowell, H. P. H. Helping-Hand Series. Boston, 1869. 5 v. 16°. . . J,1649

Vol. 1. Climbing the Rope. Vol. 3. Cruise of the Dashaway.
2. Billy Grimes's Favorite. 4. Little Spaniard.
Vol. 5. Salt-Water Dick.

Noyes, G. R. Translation of the Book of Psalms. New York, 1863. 12°. P,503
Translation of Proverbs, Ecclesiastes, and Canticles. Boston, 1846. 12°. P,502
Noyes, J. H. History of American Socialisms. Philadelphia, 1870. 8°. . O,378
Nubia and Abyssinia. M. Russell. New York, 1854. 16°. . . . L,383
and Egypt. J. A. St. John. London, 1845. 8°. . . . . . V,845
Pilgrimage to. I. F. Romer. London, 1846. 2 v. 8°. . . . V,675
Reisen in Nubien und Arabien. E. Rüppell. Frank.-a.-M. 1829. 8°. E,228
Travels in. F. L. Norden. London, 1757. 8°. . . . . . V,844
Nubian Desert, Ride through. W. Peel. London, 1852. 8°. . . . V,810
Nürnberg, Roman. L. Otto. Prag, 1850. 3 v. 24°. . . . . . G,377
Nugent, E. Treatise on Optics. New York, 1868. 12°. . . . . . N,22
Nuisances and Diseases, Act on. London, 1855. 12°. . . . . M,950
Numerical Equations, Solution of. C. Sturm. London, 1835. 4°. . N,252,42
Numismatical Manual. M. W. Dickeson. Philadelphia, 1859. 4°. . *M,431
Numismatics, Coinage of Great Britain. R. Ruding. Lond. 1840. 3 v. 4°. *Q,269
Nun, The. M. M. Sherwood. New York, 1860. 12°. . . . K,1008,7
Nuremberg, Pictures of. H. J. Whittling. London, 1850. 2 v. 12°. . V,421
Nursery Rhymes of England; ed. by J. O. Halliwell. London, 1842. 12°. L,606,4
Nursing, Notes on. F. Nightingale. New York, 1860. 12°. . . . L,915
Nurture, Boke of. H. Rhodes. London, 1868. 8°. . . . . . L,605,32
J. Russell. London, 1868. 8°. . . . . . . L,605,32
Nussir-u-Deen, *King of Oude*. Private Life of an Eastern King. N.Y.'55. 12°. D,755
Nuttall, T. North American Sylva. Philadelphia, 1859. 2 v. 8°. . . N,1040
Ornithology of U. States and Canada; Land Birds. Boston, 1840. 8°. *O,101
Water Birds. T. Nuttall. Boston, 1834. 8°. . . *O,104
Nystrom, J. W. Treatise on Screw Propellers. Philadelphia, 1852. 8°. . M,704

Oak Openings. J. F. Cooper. New York, 1864. 12°. . . . . . K,40
The same. New York, 1860. 8°. . . . . . . . K,68
Oath, The, a Divine Ordinance. D. X. Junkin. New York, 1845. 12°. . P,133
Oberlin, J. F., Memoirs of. L. Halsey. London, 1857. 16°. . . . D,589
Oberlin-Wellington Rescue, History of. J. R. Shipherd. Boston, 1859. 8°. O,398
Oberon, ein Romantisches Heldengedicht. C. M. Wieland. Leip.1839. 16°. E,364,20
The same. Leipzig, 1868. 12°. . . . . . . . E,285
The same; tr. by W. Sotheby. Newport, R. I. 1810. 2 v. 12°. G,47
Oberon's Vision in Midsummer Night's Dream. N. J. Halpin. Lond. '43. 8°. I,885,16
Object Lessons. E. Mayo. New York, 1866. 12°. . . . . . . O,944
Book of. W. J. Lake. London, 1857. 24°. . . . . . . O,1109
Manual of. E. M. Sheldon. New York, 1867. 12°. . . . O,943
M. Willson. New York, 1862. 12°. . . . . . . O,945
Obsequens, J. Prodigiorum Libellus. Parisiis, 1823. 8° . . . . U,353,3
Observer, The; a Collection of Essays. R. Cumberland. Lond. 1798. 6 v. 12°. H,524

Observer, The; Collection of Essays. R. Cumberland. Bos. 1866. 3 v. 8°. H,536,32-34
O'Callaghan, E. B. American Editions of the Scripture. Albany, 1861. 4°. L.R.
History of New Netherlands. New York, 1846. 8°. . . . C,97
(Ed.) Documentary History of N. Y. State. Albany, 1853-61. 11 v. 4°. F,234
The same. Albany, 1849. 2 v. 8°. . . . . . G,96
Register of New Netherland, 1626-74. Albany, 1865. 8°. . C,104
Occult Sciences. A. J. E. B. Salverte. New York, 1847. 2 v. 12°. . O,326
E. Smedley and others. London, 1855. 8°. . . . . . . O,331
Occupation, Influence of, on Health. J. Pinney. London, 1856. 8°. . L,926
Ocean, The. P. H. Gosse. Philadelphia, 1856. 12°. . . . . V,1136
und Mittelmeer. C. Vogt. Frankfurt-am-Main, 1848. 2 v. 12°. . E,180
Ocean Waifs. M. Reid. Boston, 1870. 12°. . . . . . . . J,1587
Ocean World, The. L. Figuier. London, 1868. 8°. . . . . . . N,535
Ocean Work, Ancient and Modern. J. H. Wright. New York, 1853. 8°. J,1303
Oceana and other Works. J. Harrington. London, 1771. 4°. . . . Q,302
Oceanic Hydrozoa. T. H. Huxley. London, 1859. 4°. . . . . Q,74
Oceanic Tides. H. F. A. Pratt. London, 1865. 8°. . . . . . N,292
Ochsenheimer, F. Schmetterlinge von Europa. Leip. 1807-35. 10 v. in 17. 8°. G,955
Ockley, S. History of the Saracens. London, 1848. 12°. . . . L,220
O'Connell, D. Select Speeches. Dublin, 1867. 2 v. 12°. . . . H,777
O'Connor, A. Chronicles of Eri; History of the Irish. Lond. 1822. 2 v. 8°. B,166
Odd People. M. Reid. Boston, 1864. 16°. . . . . . . . J,1560
Odling, W. Acids and Salts. London, 1860. 8°. . . . . . N,252,44
Lectures on Animal Chemistry. London, 1866. 8°. . . . N,176
O'Doherty Papers. W. Maginn. New York, 1855. 2 v. 12°. . . H,477
O'Donoghue, The. C. Lever. London, 1865. 8°. . . . . . K,783
O'Donovan, J. Book of Rights. Dublin, 1847. 8°. . . . . . L,812
Odyssey of Homer. See *Homer*.
Oersted, H. C. Mechanischer Theil der Naturlehre. Braunschweig, 1851. 8°. G,706
Soul in Nature; tr. by L. and J. B. Horner. London, 1852. p. 8°. L,309
Off-Hand Sketches. T. S. Arthur. Philadelphia, 1858. 18°. . . . J,1302
Off the Track. M. A. Denison. Philadelphia, 1870. 16°. . . . J,1706
Offor, G. Life and Writings of William Tyndale. London, 1836. 8°. . P,417
Ogden, J. Science of Education; Art of Teaching. Cincinnati, 1859. 12°. O,948
Ogilvie, G. Master-Builder's Plan in Forms of Animals. Lond. 1858. 12°. N,645
Ogilvie, J. Imperial English Dictionary. Glasgow, 1859. 2 v. 8°. . L.R.
Ogilvies, The. D. M. Craik. New York, n. d. 8°. . . . . . K,647
The same. Leipzig, 1863. 16°. . . . . . . . J,90
Ogle County, Ill., Sketches of. Polo, Ill., 1859. 8°. . . . . . B,809,2
Oglethorpe, J., Memoir of. R. Wright. London, 1867. 8°. . . . D,292
Life of. W. B. O. Peabody. Boston, 1860. 12°. . . . . C,860,12
Memorials of. T. M. Harris. Boston, 1841. 8°. . . . . . D,301
Ohio, Atlas of, and of United States. H. F. Walling. New York, 1868. 4°. *Q,392
Celebration of the 45th Anniversary of the Settlement of Cincinnati and the Miami Country. Cincinnati, 1834. 8°. . . . . C,244
Celebration of 47th Anniversary of First Settlement of. Cin. 1835. 8°. C,252
The same. Cincinnati, 1835. 8°. . . . . . . . T,19,9
Com. of Statistics, Annual Report, 1857-62. Colum. 1858-63. 6 v. 8°. O,589
Constitution, adopted June 17, 1831. Cincinnati, 1853. 24°. . . C,150
Educational Monthly, v. 1. Columbus, 1860. 8°. . . . . O,1263

Ohio, Expedition against the Indians, 1764. H. Bouquet. Cincin. 1868. 8°. C,217
Gazetteer. Columbus, 1833. 18°. . . . . . . . . V,27
W. Jenkins. Columbus, 1837. 12°. . . . . . . . V,30
General and Local Laws, 1869–70. Columbus, 1869. 2 v. 8°. . U,534
Geological Survey, 1837–38. W.W. Mather. Columb. 1838. 2 v. 8°. N,874,1,2
Report, 1869. J. S. Newberry. Columbus, 1869. 8°. . N,874,3
Historical and Philosophical Society, Transactions. pt. 2, v. 1. Cincinnati, 1839. 8°. . . . . . . . . . . . . C,229
Historical Collections of. H. Howe. Cincinnati, 1848. 8°. . . C,225
The same. Cincinnati, 1854. 8°. . . . . . . . . C,213
History of. J. W. Taylor. Cincinnati, 1854. 12°. . . . . . C,206
in the War. W. Reid. Cincinnati, 1868. 2 v. 8°. . . . . . B,946
Journal of Education. Columbus, 1852–59. 8 v. 8°. . . . . S,25
Kentucky and Indiana, Tour in, in 1805. J. Espy. Cincin. 1871. 8°. C,223
and Tennessee, Travels to. F. A. Michaux. London, 1805. 8°. V,73
Notices of the House of Representatives. Columbus, 1857. 8°. H,302,1
The same; with Autographs. Columbus, 1857. 8°. . . C,203
Pictorial Description of. B. J. Lossing. New York, 1848. 8°. . C,205
Pioneer Settlers of. S. P. Hildreth. Cincinnati, 1852. 8°. . . C,710
Railroad Guide. Cincinnati, 1852. 12°. . . . . . . . M,692
Revised Statutes; collated by L. R. Swan. Cincin. 1860. 2 v. 8°. . U,514
River, Visits to Indians on, 1772–73. D. Jones. N. Y. 1865. 8°. . C,198
and Mississippi Rivers, Charts of. S. Cummings. Cincin. 1836. 8°. M,689
Memorial on Navigation of. Cincinnati, 1844. 12°. . . C,201
School Journal, 1846–50. Cleveland, 1846–50. 4 v. in 1. 8°. . . T,22
School System, Manual of the. J. W. Taylor. Cincinnati, 1857. 8°. O,1214
Sketch of the History of. S. P. Chase. Cincinnati, 1833. 8°. . . C,227
State Gazetteer. G. W. Hawes. Cincinnati, 1859–60. 8°. . . L.R.
Story of the Sixth Regiment. E. Hannaford. Cincinnati, 1868. 8°. B,960
Tour in. F. Cuming. Pittsburgh, 1810. 12°. . . . . . . V,96
Twelfth Cavalry in the Rebellion. F. H. Mason. Cleveland, 1871. 8°. B,962
Valley. S. P. Hildreth. Cincinnati, 1848. 8°. . . . . . . C,270

Ohio State Documents, viz.: . . . . . . . . . . . . P.D.
Ackerbau Bericht für 1869. Columbus, 1870. 8°.
Acts of a General Nature, 1854, v. 52. Columbus, 1854. 8°.
and Local Laws, v. 53, 54, 57. Columbus, 1856–60. 8°.
Acts of a Local Nature, 1847–49, v. 46–48. Columbus, 1848–50. 8°.
Adjutant-General, Reports, 1861–65. Columbus, 1861–66. 8°.
and Miami Canal, Rates of Toll on. Columbus, 1835. 8°.
Asylum for Idiotic and Imbecile Youth, Reports, 1857–60. Col. 1858–61. 8°.
Attorney-General, Annual Reports, 1846–61. Columbus, 1846–61. 8°.
Auditor, Reports, 1836–60. Columbus, 1836–60. 2 v. 8°.
Special Report. Columbus, 1840. 8°.
Bank Commissioners, Reports, 1839–44. Columbus, 1839–44. 8°.
Special Report, July 25, 1842. Columbus, 1842. 8°.
Board of Agricul. Rep. 1846–51, 53, 55–69. Colum. and Chil. 1851–57. 16 v. 8°.
Board of Public Works, Rep. 1836–50, 51–53, 54–60. Colum. 1836–60. 4 v. 8°.
Report on Book Accounts, etc. Columbus, 1845. 8°.
Canal Commissioners, Reports, 1827–36. Colum. 1827–36. 12 pam. in 1 v. 8°.
Canal Documents, 1825–32; edited by J. Kilbourn. Columbus, 1833. 8°.

Ohio State Documents. *Continued.* . . . . . . . . . . . P.D.

Canal Fund Commissioners, 1836–51. Colum. 1836–51. 15 pam. in 1 v. 8°.

Report of Examination of the Books. Columbus, 1845. 8°.

Census, 1850. Columbus, 1851. 8°.

Central Lunatic Asylum, Reports, 1839–60. Columbus, 1839–60. 8°.

Code of Civil Procedure. Columbus, 1853. 8°.

Commissary-General, Report, 1861. Columbus, 1862. 8°.

Commissioner on Railroads and Telegraphs, Reports, 1869–70. G.B.Wright. Columbus, 1870–71. 2 v. 8°.

Commissioners of Public Works, Reports. Columbus, 1845. 2 v. 8°.

Report, Jan. 20, 1847. Columbus, 1847. 8°.

Report of. Columbus, 1857. 8°.

Commissioners of Sinking Fund, 1st, 2d, and 4th Rep. Colum. 1852–54. 8°.

Commissioners on a Site for a New Penitentiary, Report. Colum. 1831. 8°.

Common School Director, v. 1, no. 6. Columbus, 1838. 8°.

Common Schools, Reports, 1825–60. Columbus, 1825–60. 4 v. 8°.

Constitution of the State of, 1851. Columbus, 1852. 8°.

Constitutional Convention, 1850–51; ed. J. V. Smith. Col. 1851. 2 v. 8°.

Documents, including Messages, etc. Columbus, 1846–54. 9 v. 8°.

Education Convention, Proceedings. Columbus, 1836. 8°.

Executive Documents; Message and Ann. Rep. 1869. Colum. 1870. 2 v. 8°.

Addresses and Messages, 1835–40, 42–45, 49, 50, 52, 54, 57–60. Columbus, 1835–60. 21 pam. in 1 v. 8°.

Executive and Legislative Documents. Columbus, 1822–63. 44 v. 8°.

Finance Report of Joint Committee. Columbus, 1856. 8°.

General and Local Laws, v. 60, 66. Columbus, 1863–69. 8°.

The same. Columbus, 1863–69. 2 v. 8°.

House of Representatives, Journal, 1808, 1809–17, 19, 20, 23–26, 28, 29, 31, 1832, 33, 34–49, 52, 54, 56-60, 62-66, 70. Chillicothe and Columbus, 1808–29. 51 v. 8°.

Appendix to the Journal, 1854. Columbus, 1854. 8°.

Impeachment Trial of C. Pease, Record of Proceedings. n. p. 1809. 8°.

Index to the Laws, 1802–45. Z. Mills. Columbus, 1846. 8°.

1845–57. W. T. Coggeshall. Columbus, 1858. 8°.

Index to Documents in House and Senate Journals, 1802–36. W. T. Coggeshall. Columbus, 1858. 8°.

Institution for the Deaf and Dumb, Reports, 1827–60. Colum. 1827–61. 8°.

Legislative Documents. Columbus, 1839–48. 11 v. 8°.

Life Insurance and Trust Co., Charter and By-Laws. Washington, 1867. 8°.

Miscellaneous State Papers, 1822–38. Columbus, 1822–38. 7 v. 8°.

Penitentiary, Reports, 1836–60. Columbus, 1836–60. 8°.

Quartermaster-General, Reports, 1856–61. Columbus, 1857–62. 8°.

Reform School, Reports, 1856–60. Columbus, 1856–60. 8°.

Regulations for the Military Forces of. H. B. Carrington. Colum. 1859. 8°.

The same, 2d edition. Columbus, 1861. 8°.

Report of Investigating Com. on Defalcation of State Treas. Colum. 1859. 8°.

Report on Auditor's Communication on Proceedings of Bank of United States against Officers of State. Columbus, 1821. 8°.

Report on Elementary Instruction in Europe. C. E. Stowe. Colum. 1837. 8°.

School Laws, 2d edition. Columbus, 1858. 8°.

Ohio State Documents. *Continued.* . . . . . . . . . . P.D.
School Laws, 3d edition. Columbus, 1862. 8°.
Secretary of State, Reports, 1836–60, 70. Columbus, 1836-60, 71. 8°.
Senate, Journal, 1808-11, 13-19, 22, 24, 25, 34-48, 50-52, 54, 56-61, 62, 1863, 64, 70. Chillicothe, Zanesville, and Colum. 1808–70. 47 v. 8°.
Southern Lunatic Asylum, Reports, 1855–60. Columbus, 1855–60. 8°.
Special Commissioners' Report to Investigate Claims on the National Road. Columbus, 1846. 8°.
State Boards of Equalization, 1853–59, Proceedings. Colum. 1854-60. 2 v. 8°.
State Commissioners of Com. Schools, Reports, 1857–59. Col. 1858-60. 8°.
State-House Commissioners, Annual Reports, 1838–60. Colum. 1838–60. 8°.
State Library, Reports, 1845-60, 61, 64, 65. Columbus, 1845–65. 8°.
State Lunatic Asylums, Reports, 1855–60. Columbus, 1856–61. 8°.
Statistics, Reports on, 1857, 60, 61, 62. Columbus, 1858–62. 8°.
Statutes at Large; edited by M. E. Curwen. Cincinnati, 1853–61. 4 v. 8°.
Statutes. J. R. Swan. Columbus, 1841. 8°.
The same. Cincinnati, 1854. 8°.
edited by M. E. Curwen. Cincinnati, 1854. 8°.
edited by J. R. Swan and L. J. Critchfield. Cincinnati, 1860. 2 v. 8°.
and of the North-West. Ter'y; ed. S. P. Chase. Cincin. 1833–35. 3 v. 8°.
Treasurer, Reports, 1836–60. Columbus, 1836–60. 8°.
Treasury, Investigation Reports, 1857. Columbus, 1857. 8°.
Report of Commissioners, 1857. Columbus, 1857. 8°.
Ohio Valley Historical Series. Cincinnati, 1868–71. 8 v. 8°. viz.:
No. 1. Bouquet, H. Expedition against the Ohio Indians, 1764. . . C,217
2. Walker, C. M. History of Athens County, Ohio. . . . C,218
3. Clark, Col. G. R. Campaign in the Illinois, 1778–79. . . C,219
4. McBride, J. Pioneer Biog.; Early Settlers of Butler Co. O. 2 v. C,220
5. Smith, Col. J. Captivity with the Indians, 1755–59. . . . C,221
6. Drake, D. Pioneer Life in Kentucky. . . . . . . C,222
7. Miscellanies. . . . . . . . . . . . . . . C,223
Espy, J. Tour in Ohio, Kentucky, and Indiana, in 1805
Williams, S. Two Western Campaigns in the War of 1812.
Taneyhill, R. H. The Leatherwood God, J. C. Dylks.
Oil Painting, History of. Sir C. L. Eastlake. London, 1869. 2 v. 8°. . M,60
Oils for Artificial Light, Patent for. C. B. Mansfield. Glasgow, 1810. 8°. N,252,30
Manufacture of Hydro-Carbon Oils. T. Antisell. N. Y. 1859. 8°. . N,195
Okavango River, Africa. C. J. Andersson. New York, 1861. 8°. . . V,850
O'Keeffe, J. Recollections; written by himself. London, 1826. 2 v. 8°. D,96
Oken, L. Allgemeine Naturgeschichte. Stuttgart, 1833–41. 8 v. in 14. 8°. G,822
Abbildungen dazu. Stuttgart, 1843. 4°. . . . . . *Q,60
Elements of Philosophy. London, 1847. 8°. . . . . . . O,299
Olbers, H. W. M. Berechnung der Bahn eines Cometen. Weimar, 1847. 8°. G,796
Old Battle Ground. J. T. Trowbridge. New York, 1869. 16°. . . J,1211
Old Chelsea Bun-House. A. Manning. London, 1860. 16°. . . . J,626
Old Court; a Novel. W. H. Ainsworth. Leipzig, 1867. 2 v. in 1. 16°. . J,18
Old Covenant, History of the. J. H. Kurtz. Edinburgh, 1859. 2 v. 8°. . P,637
Old Curiosity Shop. C. Dickens. New York, 1865. 12°. . . . . K,485
The same. New York, 1871. 2 v. 12°. . . . . K,1137
The same. Leipzig, 1846. 2 v. 16°. . . . . J,127,1,2
Old Deccan Days; Hindoo Fairy Legends. M. Frere. Phila. 1869. 12°. J,1372

Old Doctor's Son. M. D. Chellis. Boston, 1870. 16°. . . . . J,1619
Old English Homilies of 12th and 13th Centuries. Lond. 1868. 2 v. 8°. L,605,29,34
Old England and New England. A. Bunn. Philadelphia, 1853. 12°. . V,75
Old English Baron. C. Reeve. London, 1820. 12°. . . . . . . K,534
Old England's Worthies. London, 1853. f°. . . . . . . . *F,55
Old-Fashioned Boy. M. Farquharson. Philadelphia, 1871. 16°. . . K,273
Old-Fashioned Girl. L. M. Alcott. Boston, 1870. 16°. . . . . . K,5
Old Friends and New Acquaintances. A. Strickland. London, 1861. 8°. K,1022
Old Fritz and the New Era. C. Mundt. New York, 1868. 8°. . . . G,211
Old Helmet. S. Warner. New York, 1867. 12°. . . . . . . K,373
Old Homestead. A. S. Stephens. Philadelphia, 1870. 12°. . . . K,449
Old House by the River. W. C. Prime. New York, 1853. 12°. . . K,290
Old Jack. W. H. G. Kingston. London, 1869. 12°. . . . . . J,1259
Old Lieutenant and his Son. N. Macleod. London, 1862. 2 v. 12°. K,1103
The same. Leipzig, 1863. 16°. . . . . . . . J,342
Old Mam'selle's Secret. E. John. Philadelphia, 1868. 12°. . . . G,192
Old Manor House. C. Smith. London, 1820. 2 v. 12°. . . . . K,544
Old Masters; Princes of Art. Boston, 1870. 12°. . . . . . . M,202
Old Merchants of New York City. J. A. Scoville. N. Y. 1870. 5 v. 12°. C,1044
Old Mortality. Sir W. Scott. Boston, 1852. 2 v. 16°. . . . . K,942
The same. Philadelphia, 1869. 8°. . . . . . K,1106
The same. Leipzig, 1846. 16°. . . . . . . . J,447
Old Portraits and Modern Sketches. J. G. Whittier. Boston, 1850. 16°. . H,31
Old Red Sandstone. H. Miller. Boston, 1854. 12°. . . . . . . N,614
Old Regime and the Revolution. A. de Tocqueville. N. Y. 1856. 12°. . B,241
Old Roman World. J. Lord. New York, 1868. 8°. . . . . . . A,154
Old Sir Douglas. C. E. S. Norton. Philadelphia, 1867. 12°. . . . K,873
The same. Leipzig, 1867. 2 v. in 1. 16°. . . . . J,394
Old Testament. See *Bible, Old Testament.*
Old World in its New Face. H. W. Bellows. New York, 1868–69. 2 v. 12°. V,369
Oldfield, T. H. B. Representative History of Gt. Britain. Lond. 1816. 6 v. 8°. A,460
Oldham, J. Poetical Works, with Memoir; edit. by R. Bell. Lond. 1854. 16°. I,251
Oldham, O. Humorous Speaker. New York, 1868. 12°. . . . . . O,827
Oldtown Folks. H. B. Stowe. Boston, 1869. 12°. . . . . . . K,284
O'Lincoln, R. George Ready. New York, 1865. 16°. . . . . J,1351
Olin, S. Egypt, Arabia Petræa, and Holy Land. N. Y. 1851. 2 v. 12°. V,1057
Life of. New York, 1853. 2 v. 12°. . . . . . . . . C,708
Olio of Love and Song. S. Dyer. Indianapolis, 1855. 16°. . . H,302.1
Oliphant, L. Journey to Katmandu. New York, 1852. 12°. . . . . V,586
Lord Elgin's Mission to China and Japan. Edinb. 1859. 2 v. 8°. . V,738
Russian Shores of the Black Sea. New York, 1854. 12°. . . . V,526
Oliphant, M. Agnes. New York, 1867. 8°. . . . . . . . K,861
The same. Leipzig, 1865. 2 v. in 1. 16°. . . . . J,396
Athelings. New York, 1857. 8°. . . . . . . . . . K,862
Chronicles of Carlingford. New York, 1863. 8°. . . . . . K,874
The same, viz.:
Rector and Doctor's Family. Leipzig, 1870. 16°. . . . . J,399
Salem Chapel. Leipzig, 1870. 2 v. in 1. 16°. . . . . . J,400
Perpetual Curate. Leipzig, 1870. 2 v. in 1. 16°. . . . . J,401
Miss Marjoribanks. Leipzig, 1870. 2 v. in 1. 16°. . . . . J,402
Days of my Life. New York, 1863. 12°. . . . . . . . . K,863

Oliphant, M. House on the Moor. New York, 1861. 12°. . . . . K,864
Laird of Norlaw. New York, 1860. 12°. . . . . . . . K,865
Last of the Mortimers. New York, 1862. 12°. . . . . . . K,866
The same. Leipzig, 1862. 2 v. in 1. 16°. . . . . . J,403
Life of Edward Irving. New York, 1862. 8°. . . . . . D,299
Lucy Crofton. New York, 1860. 12°. . . . . . . K,1165
Madonna Mary. Leipzig, 1867. 2 v. in 1. 16°. . . . . J,404
Margaret Maitland. Leipzig, 1862. 18°. . . . . . . J,397
Minister's Wife. Leipzig, 1869. 2 v. in 1. 16°. . . . . J,398
Miss Marjoribanks. New York, 1866. 8°. . . . . . . K,867
Perpetual Curate. New York, 1865. 8°. . . . . . . K,868
Self-Sacrifice. Philadelphia, n. d. 12°. . . . . . . K,869
Son of the Soil. New York, 1865. 8°. . . . . . . K,870
Olive. D. M. Craik. New York, 1867. 8°. . . . . . . . K,649
The same. Leipzig, 1866. 2 v. in 1. 16°. . . . . . J,91
Oliver, J. Present to be given to Teeming Women. London, 1669. 12°. . P,339
Oliver, P. Puritan Commonwealth. Boston, 1856. 8°. . . . . . C,21
Oliver, T. Stephenson Monument. Newcastle, 1858. 8°. . . . N,252,46
Oliver Optic, *pseud.* See *Adams, W. T.*
Oliver Optic's Magazine, v. 1–8. Boston, 1867–70. 8 v. in 4. 8°. . . T,4
Oliver Twist. C. Dickens. New York, 1868. 12°. . . . . . . K,486
The same. New York, 1871. 12°. . . . . . . K,1138
The same. Leipzig, 1843. 16°. . . . . . . . J,131
Olmsted, D. Compendium of Natural Philosophy. New Haven, 1848. 12°. N,65
Letters on Astronomy. New York, 1855. 12°. . . . . . . N,266
Life and Writings of E. Porter Mason. New York, 1842. 12°. C,1013
Olmsted, F. L. American Farmer in England. New York, 1852. 2 v. 12°. V,335
The same. Columbus, 1859. 8°. . . . . . . . . M,516
Cotton Kingdom. New York, 1862. 2 v. 12°. . . . . . V,87
Journey in the Back Country. New York, 1863. 12°. . . . V,93
Journey in Seaboard Slave States. New York, 1863. 12°. . . V,74
Journey through Texas. New York, 1860. 12°. . . . . . V,91
Olshausen, H. Commentary on the New Testament. N. Y. 1858. 6 v. 8°. P,553
O'Meara, B. E. Napoleon in Exile. New York, 1853. 2 v. 12°. . . D,555
Omoo; Adventures in the South Seas. H. Melville. London, 1861. 12°. V,890
O'Neil, H. Lectures on Painting. London, 1866. 8°. . . . . . M,46
On Both Sides of the Sea. E. Charles. New York, 1868. 12°. . . . K,625
The same. Leipzig, 1868. 16°. . . . . . . . . J,65
On Guard. A. Cudlip. New York, 1865. 8°. . . . . . . . K,665
The same. Leipzig, 1865. 2 v. in 1. 16°. . . . . . . J,106
On the Border. J. R. Gilmore. Boston, 1867. 12°. . . . . . . K,95
On the Edge of the Storm. Leipzig, 1869. 16°. . . . . . . . J,450
On the Heights. B. Auerbach. Boston, 1869. 16°. . . . . . . G,184
The same. Leipzig, 1867. 16°. . . . . . . . G,185
On the Wing; a Book for Sportsmen. J. Bumstead. Boston, 1869. 12°. . M,319
Once and Again. C. Jenkin. Leipzig, 1865. 2 v. in 1. 16°. . . . . J,218
One-Armed Hugh. W. J. Bradley. Boston, 1870. 16°. . . . . J,1680
One in a Thousand. G. P. R. James. New York, 1855. 2 v. in 1. 12°. . K,735
One of Them. C. Lever. London, 1860. 8°. . . . . . . . K,784
The same. Leipzig, 1860. 2 v. in 1. 16°. . . . . . J,283

One Poor Girl; the Story of Thousands. W. Sikes. Phil. 1869. 12°. . K,122
One Year; or, a Story of Three Homes. F. M. Peard. Boston, 1871. 12°. K,1161
The same. Leipzig, 1869. 2 v. in 1. 16°. . . . . . J,410
Only a Clod. M. E. Braddon. Leipzig, 1865. 2 v. in 1. 16°. . . . J,42
Only a Fiddler! and O. T. H. C. Andersen. New York, 1862. 8°. . . G,181
Only a Girl. W. von Hillern. Philadelphia, 1871. 12°. . . . . G,176
Only Herself. A. Cudlip. Leipzig, 1870. 2 v. in 1. 16°. . . . . J,107
Onyx Ring. J. Sterling. Boston, 1856. 12°. . . . . . . K,1020
Opdyke, G. Political Economy. New York, 1861. 12°. . . . . O,563
Open Polar Sea. I. I. Hayes. New York, 1867. 8°. . . . . . . V,954
Open Timber Roofs of Middle Ages. R. and J. A. Brandon. Lond. 1849. 4°. *Q,176
Opera, Erste Deutsche. E. O. Lindner. Berlin, 1855. 2 v. 8° and 4°. . G,743
History of the. S. Edwards. London, 1862. 2 v. 12°. . . . M,408
Memoirs of the. G. Hogarth. London, 1851. 2 v. 8°. . . . M,406
Wesen und Geschichte der Oper. G. W. Fink. Leipzig, 1838. 8°. . G,640
Operas, Tales from the. G. F. Pardon. New York, 1866. 12°. . . K,889
Ophthalmic Science, Recent Advances in. H. W. Williams. Bost. 1866. 12°. L,881
Ophiology, Schlangenkunde. H. O. Lenz. Gotha, 1832. 8°. . . . G,918
Opie, A. Works. Philadelphia, n. d. 3 v. 8°. . . . . . . K,875

Vol. 1. Madeline; Adeline Mowbray; Black Velvet Pelisse; Death-Bed; Fashionable Wife and Unfashionable Husband; Robber; Mother and Son; Love and Duty; Soldier's Return; Brother and Sister; Revenge; Uncle and Nephew; Murder will Out; Orphan; Father and Daughter; Happy Faces.
2. Lady Anne and Lady Jane; Austin and his Wife; Mysterious Stranger; Appearance is against her; Valentine's Eve; Mrs. Arlington, or, All is not Gold that Glitters; Proposals of Marriage; White Lies; Henry Woodville; Quaker and Young Man of the World; Tale of Trials; Ruffian Boy; Welcome Home, or, the Ball.
3. Temper; Woman's Love; Wife's Duty; Two Sons; Opposite Neighbor; Love, Mystery, and Superstition; After the Ball, or, the two Sir Williams's; False or True; Confessions of an Odd-Tempered Man; Illustrations of Lying in all its Branches.

Opie, J. and others. Lectures on Painting. London, 1848. p. 8°. . . L,303
Opium-Eater, Confessions of an. T. De Quincey. Boston, 1862. 12°. . H,413
The same. Edinburgh, 1863. 16°. . . . . . . H,412,1
Opium-Habit, and its Remedy. H. Day. New York, 1868. 12°. . . L,868
Opossums, Natural History of. London, 1838. 16°. . . . . L,482,1
Opportunity. A. M. C. Seemuller. Boston 1867. 12°. . . . . K,86
Optic, Oliver, *pseud.* See *Adams, W. T.*
Optics. Sir D. Brewster. London, 1831. 12°. . . . . . . M,1024
D. Lardner. Philadelphia, 1854. 12°. . . . . . N,79,1
Sir I. Newton. London, 1730. 8°. . . . . . . . N,27
Light and Electricity. J. Tyndall. New York, 1871. 12°. . . N,29
Optice; sive Reflexionibus, etc., Lucis. Sir I. Newton. Lond. 1706. 4°. N,30
Optische Studien. H. W. Dove. Berlin, 1859. 8°. . . . . . G,720
Photographic. D. van Monckhoven. London, 1867. 12°. . . N,26
Physical. R. Potter. London, 1856–59. 2 v. 8°. . . . . N,28
Treatise on. E. Nugent. New York, 1868. 12°. . . . . N,22
S. Parkinson. London, 1866. 8°. . . . . . . . N,21
Undulatory Theory of. G. B. Airy. London, 1866. 12°. . . N,23
Wonders of. F. Marion. London, 1868. 12°. . . . . . M,1059
Optimist. H. T. Tuckerman. New York, 1850. 12°. . . . . H,9
Essays of an. J. W. Kaye. Philadelphia, 1871. 16°. . . . H,442
Orator, National. C. Northend. New York, 1859. 12°. . . . . O,1229

Oratores Attici; opera et stud. G. S. Dobson. London, 1828–38. 16 v. 8°. U,479

Æschines, Greek, v. 12; Latin, v. 16.
Andocides, Greek, v. 1; Latin, v. 13.
Antiphon, Greek, v. 1; Latin, v. 13.
Demades, Greek, v. 4; Latin, v. 14.
Demosthenes, Greek, v. 5–8; Latin, v. 15, 16.
Annotations (Reiske, etc), v. 9.
Indices, v. 11.
Demosthenes, Scholia Reiske, etc., v. 10.
Dinarchus, Greek, v. 4; Latin, v. 14.
Isæus, Greek, v. 4; Latin, v. 14.
Isocrates, Greek, v. 3; Latin, v. 14;
Lycurgus, Greek, v. 4; Latin, v. 14;
Lysias, Greek, v. 2; Latin, v. 13.
Sophistæ, Greek, v. 4; Latin, v. 14.

Orators of the Age. G. H. Francis. New York, 1854. 16°. . . . . C,514
of Ireland. Dublin, 1867. 7 v. 12°. . . . . . . H,773–778
Orator's Touchstone. H. MacQueen. New York, 1854. 12°. . . . L,588
Oratory, American. Philadelphia, 1853. 12°. . . . . . . . H,819
Golden Age of. E. G. Parker. Boston, 1857. 12°. . . C,528
Orbigny, A. D. d'. Histoire Naturelle des Crinoides. Paris, 1858. 4°. . Q,57
Paléontologie et Géologie Stratigraphiques. Paris, 1852. 4°. . . Q,35
Orchids, Zur Kenntniss der. H. G. Reichenbach. v. 1. Leipzig, 1858. 4°. Q,112
Fertilization of by Insects. C. Darwin. London, 1862. 8°. . . M,557
Ordeal for Wives. A. B. Edwards. London, 1865. 3 v. 12°. . . . J,564
Ordericus Vitalis. Ecclesiastical History. London, 1853-54. 4 v. p. 8°. L,22
Order of the Garter. G. F. Beltz. London, 1841. 8°. . . . . . D,279
Order of Nature and Claims of Revelation. B. Powell. London, 1859. 12°. P,223
Ordinance of 1787, History of. E. Coles. Philadelphia, 1856. 8°. . . B,860
The same. Philadelphia, 1856. 8°. . . . . . B,809,2
Oregon and California, History of. B. Greenhow. New York, 1845. 8°. . C,250
in 1848. J. Q. Thornton. New York, 1849. 2 v. 12°. . V,41
and Eldorado. T. Bulfinch. Boston, 1866. 8°. . . . . . C,183
Geographical and Physical Account. C. G. Nicolay. Lond. 1846. 16°. V,145
Oregon Mission, History of. G. Hines. Buffalo, 1850. 12°. . . . V,57
Orfévrerie-Joaillerie, Histoire de. P. Lacroix. Paris, 1850. 8°. . . M,743
Orfila, M. J. B. Recherches sur l'Acide Arsénieux. Paris, 1842. 8°. N,252,12
Orford, Earl of. See *Walpole, H.*
Organic Bodies, Anal. des Substances Organiques. J. Liebig. Paris, '38. 8°. N,252,16
Analyse Organischer Körper. J. Liebig. Braunschweig, 1837. 8°. N,252,27
Morphologische Studien über. H. G. Bronn. Leipzig, 1858. 8°. . G,719
Orient Boys. S. F. Keen. Boston, 1870. 16°. . . . . . . . J,1542
Orient, Poems of the. B. Taylor. Boston, 1855. 16°. . . . . . I,139
Oriental Acquaintance; Letters from Syria. J. W. DeForest. N.Y. 1856. 12°. V,559
Oriental Commerce. W. Milburn. London, 1825. 8°. . . . . . O,608
Oriental Field-Sports. T. Williamson. London, 1819. 2 v. 4°. . . *Q,329
Oriental Fragments. E. Moor. London, 1834. 12°. . . . . . . V,565
Oriental History, Early. J. Eadie. . . . . . . . . . . A,21
The same. London, 1852. 12°. . . . . . . . A,22
Oriental Nations, History of. L. Ritchie. London, 1848. 2 v. 8°. . C,404
Oriental Scenery; Views in Hindostan. T. and. W. Daniell. London, 1795–1804. 6 v. in 3. eleph. f°. . . . . . . . . L.R.
Text to the same. London, 1795. 8°. . . . . . . . L.R.
Oriental Trinities. T. Maurice. London, 1800. 8°. . . . . . . P,118
Origin of the Globe, Lectures on. G. Brewster. Columbus, 1850. 12°. . N,602
Origin of Species. C. Darwin. New York, 1860. 12°. . . . . . N,495
T. H. Huxley. New York, 1863. 12°. . . . . . . . . N,499
Original Letters in English History. Sir H. Ellis. Lond. 1824–46. 11 v. 8°. B,2
Original Tales. G. Cumberland. London, 1810. 2 v. 8°. . . . . K,667

Origines Ecclesiasticæ; Church Antiquities. J. Bingham. Lon. 1840. 9 v. 8°. P,784
Origines Typographicæ. G. Meerman. Hagæ Com. 1765. 2 v. in 1. 4°. L.R.
Orion, Observations on the Nebula of. G. P. Bond. Cambridge, 1867. 4°. Q,106,5
Orlando Furioso. L. Ariosto. London, 1823-31. 8 v. 8°. . . . G,78
The same; tr. by W. S. Rose. London, 1864-65. 2 v. p. 8°. L,93
Orléans, H.L.E., *Duchesse d'*, Memoir of. G.H. von Schubert. N.Y. 1860. 12°. D,615
Orléans, P. J. d'. Tartar Conquerors of China. London, 1854. 8°. . . V,997
Orleans, House of, Memoirs of. W. C. Taylor. Philadelphia, 1850. 2 v. 12°. D,687
Orley Farm. A. Trollope. New York, n. d. 8°. . . . . . K,1049
The same. Leipzig, 1862. 3 v. 16°. . . . . . . J,502
Orlich, L. von. Reise in Ostindien. Leipzig, 1845. 4°. . . . . . Q,436
Ormerod, G. W. Index to London Geological Society's Pub. Lon. 1858. 8°. *R,26
Ormond. M. Edgworth. New York, 1859. 12°. . . . . . K,678,9
Ormond and Clara Howard. C. B. Brown. Philadelphia, 1857. 12°. . K,461
Ornament, Analysis of. R. N. Wornum. London, 1856. 8°. . . . M,112
and Costume, Ecclesiastical. A. W. Pugin. London, 1868. 4°. *Q,216
Examples of; edited by J. Cundall. London, 1855. 4°. . . *Q,177
Floriated. A. W. Pugin. London, 1849. 4°. . . . . . *Q,181
Grammar of. O. Jones. London, 1856. f°. . . . . . *Q,458
Ornithological Biography, Amer. J. J. Audubon. Edinb. 1831-39. 5 v. 8°. *O,139
Ornithology, American. J. J. Audubon. London, 1827-38. 4 v. eleph. f°. L.R.
The same, reduced. New York, 1856. 7 v. 8°. *O,138
A. Wilson. New York, 1828-29. 3 v. 4°. . . . . . *Q,2
Plates to the same. New York, 1829. 4°. . . *Q,78
The same. New York, 1854. 8°. . . . . . . O,106
A. Wilson and C. L. Bonaparte. Edinburgh, 1831. 4 v. 16°. I,533
The same. Edinburgh, 1831. 4°. 16°. . . . . O,80
and Mammalogy of U. S. Exploring Exped. J. Cassin. Phil. 1858. 4°. *Q,277
Atlas to the same. Philadelphia, 1858. f°. . . *Q,351
and Oölogy of New England. E. A. Samuels. Boston, 1867. 8°. . O,122
Manuel d'Ornithologie Domestique. R. P. Lesson. Paris, 1834. 18°. O,79
of California. J.G. Cooper; ed. by S.F. Baird. v. 1. San Fran. 1870. 4°. N,739
of United States and Canada; Land Birds. T. Nuttall. Bost. 1840. 8°. *O,101
Water Birds. T. Nuttall. Boston, 1834. 8°. . . *O,104
Wake-Robin. J. Burroughs. New York, 1871. 12°. . . . . O,99
See also *Birds*.
Orphan Girls; a Tale of Southern Life. J. S. Peacocke. Philad. 1865. 12°. K,361
Orphans of Normandy. M. M. Sherwood. New York, 1858. 12°. . K,1008,2
Orr, W. S. (Ed.) Circle of the Sciences. London, 1859. 4 v. 8°. . . M,785
Vol. 1-3. Organic Nature. Vol. 4. Inorganic Nature.
Orthodox Congregationalism. D. Clarke. Boston, 1871. 12°. . . . P,864
Orthographie, Deutsche. K. G. Andresen. Mainz, 1855. 8°. . . . G,592
Orthography. J. Hart, 1569. London, 1850. 16°. . . . . . . L,666
and Definition, Manual of. J. N. Elligott. New York, 1854. 8°. . O,893
Orton, J. Andes and the Amazon. New York, 1870. 8°. . . . V,244
Orville College. Mrs. H. Wood. Leipzig, 1867. 16°. . . . . . J,527
Osborn, S. Japanese Fragments; Fac-Similes. London, 1861. 8°. . . V,612
Quedah; Journal in Malayan Waters. London, 1857. 12°. . . V,616
Stray Leaves from an Arctic Journal. New York, 1853. 12°. . V,936
(Ed.) McClure's North-West Passage. London, 1859. 8°. . . V,944

Osburn, W. Monumental History of Egypt. London, 1854. 2 v. 8°. . V,818
Oscanyan, C. Sultan and his People. New York, 1857. 12°. . . . V,557
Osceola, the Seminole. M. Reid. New York, n. d. 12°. . . . J,1569
Osgood, F. S., Memorial of; ed. by M. E. Hewitt. New York, 1851. 8°. H,173
Osgood, S. Hearth-Stone; Home-Life in Cities. New York, 1860. 12°. H,293
Mile-Stones in our Life-Journey. New York, 1855. 12°. . . H,192
Ossian, Gedichte; übersetzt von M. Denis. Wien, 1768–69. 3 v. in 1. 4°. E,305
Poems; translated by J. Macpherson. Boston, 1854. 12°. . . I,367
The same. Leipzig, 1847. 16°. . . . . . . . . J,406
Ossoli, M. F. Art, Literature, and the Drama. New York, 1869. 12°. . U,95
At Home and Abroad. New York, 1869. 12°. . . . . . U,93
The same. Boston, 1856. 12°. . . . . . . V,1032
Life Without and Life Within. New York, 1869. 12°. . . . U,94
Memoirs of. R. W. Emerson and others. New York, 1869. 2 v. 12°. U,96
Papers on Literature and Art. New York, 1846. 12°. . . . H,644
Summer on the Lakes. Boston, 1844. 12°. . . . . . . V,14
Woman in the Nineteenth Century. New York, 1869. 12°. . . U,97
Ost und West. G. von Struensee. Breslau, 1865. 4 v. 24°. . . . G,499
Ost-Gothisches Reich in Italien. J. C. F. Manso. Breslau, 1824. 8°. . E,100
Oswald, E. German Courtesy Books. London, 1869. 8°. . . L,604,8
Oswald Cray. Mrs. H. Wood. Leipzig, 1865. 2 v. in 1. 16°. . . . J,528
Oswinus, *King of Northumberland*, Life of. London, 1838. 8°. . . F,126,8
Other Worlds than Ours. R. A. Proctor. New York, 1871. 12°. . . N,274
Otis, F. N. Isthmus of Panama. New York, 1867. 12°. . . . . V,242
Studies of Animals. New York, 1866. 8°. . . . . . . Q,198
Otis, J., Life of. F. Bowen. Boston, 1860. 12°. . . . . . . C,860,12
Ott, A. Art of Making Soap and Candles. Philadelphia, 1867. 12°. . M,626
Ottley, W. Y. Early Florentine School. London, 1826. f°. . . . L.R.
Italian School of Design; a Series of Drawings. London, 1823. f°. L.R.
Otto, F. J. Lehrbuch der Essigfabrikation. Braunschweig, 1840. 8°. N,252,10
Otto, L. Neue Bahnen. Wien, 1864. 2 v. in 1. 24°. . . . . . G,376
Nürnberg, Roman. Prag, 1859. 3 v. 24°. . . . . . . G,377
Schultheissentöchter von Nürnberg. Wien, 1861. 3 v. 24°. . . G,378
Ottoman Empire, Geschichte des. J. v. H. Purgstall. Pest, 1827–35. 10 v. 8°. E,119
Geschichte des. J. W. Zinkeisen. Hamburg and Gotha, 1840–59. 7 v. 8°. E,118
History of. S. Jacob and others. London, 1854. 12°. . . . B,555
E. Upham. Edinburgh, 1828. 2 v. 16°. . . . . . I,516
Oude, Journey through. W. H. Sleeman. London, 1858. 2 v. 12°. . V,735
Ouida, *pseud.* See *Rame, L. de la.*
Our Artist in Cuba. G. W. Carleton. New York, 1865. 16°. . . . V,169
Our Garden Friends and Foes. J. G. Wood. London, 1864. 8°. . . N,647
Our Girls. D. Lewis. New York, 1871. 12°. . . . . . . . L,854
Our Life in the Highlands. Victoria I. New York, 1868. 12°. . . V,381
Our Mutual Friend. C. Dickens. Philadelphia, 1865. 8°. . . . K,514
The same. New York, 1868. 12°. . . . . . . . K,489
The same. New York, 1871. 2 v. 12°. . . . . K,1140
The same. Leipzig, 1864–65. 4 v. 16°. . . . . . J,132
Our New Vicar. J. S. B. Monsell. New York, 1870. 16°. . . . . P,69
Our New Way round the World. C. C. Coffin. Boston, 1869. 8°. . V,1075
Our New West. S. Bowles. Hartford, 1869. 8°. . . . . . . V,111

Our Old Home; English Sketches. N. Hawthorne. Boston, 1866. 16°. . K,162
The same. Boston, 1868. 12°. . . . . . . U,40,11
Our Parish; Pen-Paintings of Village Life. G. C. Hill. Phil. n. d. 12°. . K,360
Our Prospects; a Tale of Real Life. M. Loth. Cincinnati, 1870. 8°. . K,409
Our Social Bees. A. Wynter. London, 1869. 2 v. 12°. . . . . H,315
Our Village. M. R. Mitford. London, 1870. 2 v. p. 8°. . . . . L,214
Our Young Folks. Boston, 1865-70. 6 v. 8°. . . . . . . . T,45
Ourselves; Essays on Women. E. L. Linton. London, 1869. 16°. . . O,412
Out-Door Papers. T. W. Higginson. Boston, 1863. 12°. . . . . H,187
Out of Debt, out of Danger. A. B. Haven. New York, 1867. 16°. . J,1332
M. Edgeworth. New York, 1860. 12°. . . . . . K,678,2
Out of the Depths. Philadelphia, 1869. 12°. . . . . . . . K,871
Out of the Foam. J. E. Cooke. New York, 1871. 12°. . . . . J,655
Out of the Past. P. Godwin. New York, 1870. 12°. . . . . . H,241
Out of Town. R. B. Coffin. New York, 1867. 12°. . . . . . K,109
Out of the Wilderness. J. D. Chaplin. Boston, 1870. 12°. . . . K,96
Outlaw, The; an Historical Romance. A. M. Hall. London, 1847. 16°. . K,717
and other Poems. C. A. Jones. Cincinnati, 1835. 16°. . . . I,55
Outlines and Sketches. W. Allston. Boston, 1850. f°. . . . *Q,454
Outram and Havelock's Persian Campaign. G. H. Hunt. Lond. 1858. 12°. V,629
Outre-mer. H. W. Longfellow. Boston, 1852. 16°. . . . . . V,315
The same. Boston, 1866. 16°. . . . . . . . U,1,1
Outward Bound. W. T. Adams. Boston, 1870. 16°. . . . . J,1535,1
Overberg, B., Memoirs of. G. H. Schubert. London, 1838. 12°. . . D,499
Overbury, Sir T. Miscellaneous Works. London, 1856. 16°. . . . U,247
Overland Journey to San Francisco. H. Greeley. New York, 1860. 12°. V,118
Overland through Asia. T. W. Knox. Hartford, 1870. 8°. . . . V,670
Overman, F. Manufacture of Iron. Philadelphia, 1851. 8°. . . . M,720
Manufacture of Steel. Philadelphia, 1851-52. 12°. . . . . M,749
Mechanics for the Millwright, etc. Philadelphia, 1851. 12°. . . M,621
Moulder's and Founder's Guide. Philadelphia, 1856. 12°. . . M,748
Practical Mineralogy. Philadelphia, 1854. 12°. . . . . N,756
Treatise on Metallurgy. New York, 1854. 8°. . . . . . M,718
Over the Ocean. C. Guild. Boston, 1871. 12°. . . . . . . . V,292
Overs, J. Evenings of a Working Man. London, 1844. 16°. . . . H,466
Ovidius Naso, P. Opera Omnia; ed. J.A.Amar et al. Parisiis, 1820-4. 10v. 8°. U,335
Works; translated by Dryden, Pope, and others. N. Y. 1836. 2 v. 16°. U,378
The same; trans. by H. T. Riley. London, 1851-69. 3 v. p. 8°. L,70
Vol. 1. Fasti, Tristia, Pontic Epistles, Ibis, and Halieuticon.
2. Metamorphoses.
3. Heroides, Amours, Art of Love, and Minor Works.
Ovingdean Grange. W. H. Ainsworth. Leipzig, 1860. 16°. . . . J,19
Owen; a Waif. Leipzig, 1862. 2 v. in 1. 16°. . . . . . . J,407
Owen, A. Georgy Sandon; or, a Lost Love. Boston, 1865. 12°. . . K,872
Owen, D. D. Geological Survey in Kentucky, 1854-5. Frankf. 1856-7. 3 v. 8°. *N,743
Geological Survey of Wisconsin, Iowa, etc. Phil. 1852. 2 v. 4°. . *Q,52
Owen, J. Eshcol; or, Walking of the Saints. London, 1778. 32°. . . P,335
Owen, J. Forgiveness of Sin. New York, n. d. 12°. . . . . P,204
Owen, R. Anatomy of Vertebrates. London, 1866. 3 v. 8°. . . . L,986
Classification and Distribution of Mammalia. London, 1859. 8°. . N,685
Comparative Anatomy of Invertebrate Animals. London, 1855. 8°. L,988

Owen, R. Fossil Chelonian Reptilia. London, 1853. 4°. . . . . . Q,22
Fossil Reptilia; Cretaceous Pterosauria, pts. 1, 3. London, 1859. 4°. Q,32
of the Cretaceous Formation. London, 1851. 4°. . . . Q,23
of the Wealden Formations, v. 2. London, 1854. 4°. . . Q,20
History of British Fossil Reptiles. London, 1849. 4°. . . . . Q,3
National Museum of Natural History. London, 1862. 8°. . . N,527
Palæontology. Edinburgh, 1861. 8°. . . . . . . . N,823
Skeleton of Extinct Gigantic Sloth. London, 1842. 4°. . . . Q,43
and Bell, T. Fossil Reptilia of London Clay. Lond. 1849–50. 2 v. 4°. Q,21
Owen, R. Book of the New Moral World. London, 1836. 8°. . . . O,525
and Campbell, A. Evidences of Christianity. Cincinnati, 1852. 8°. P,115
Owen, R. D. Beyond the Breakers; Western Village Life. Phil. 1870. 8°. K,229
Footfalls on Boundary of Another World. Philadelphia, 1867. 12°. P,868
Hints on Public Architecture. New York, 1849. 4°. . . . Q,180
Owen, W. F. W. Voyages to Africa, Arabia, Madagascar. N.Y. 1833. 2 v. 12°. V,1079
Oxberry, W. (Ed.) New English Drama. London, 1818–22. 16 v. 12°. I,683
Contents, see *Drama, New English*.
Oxenford, J. Illustrated Book of French Songs. London, 1855. 8°. . H,924
Oxford Drawing-Book. N. Whitlock. London, n. d. 8°. . . . . . M,142
Oxford Essays, 1856. London, 1856. 8°. . . . . . . . . . H,451
Oxford, Munimenta Academica; Life at Oxford. London, 1868. 2 v. 8°. W,200
Oxford Reform and Oxford Professors. H. H. Vaughan. Lond. 1854. 8°. O,1251,1
Oxford Reformers of 1498. F. Seebohm. London, 1867. 8°. . . . P,623
Oxford University, Bodleian Library, Annals of. W. D. Macray. Lond. 1868. L.R.
Report on the State of. Oxford, 1853. 8°. . . . . . . O,818
Ozanam, A. F. Civilization in the Fifth Century. London, 1868. 2 v. 12°. A,303
Ozanam, J. Recreations in Science and Natural Philosophy. Lond. 1851. 8°. M,790
Ozark Mountains, Adventures in. H. R. Schoolcraft. Phil. 1853. 8°. . V,66
Ozon, Erzeugung von, auf Chemisch. Wege. C.F.Schönbein. Basel, 1844. 8°. N,252,21

Pabst, H. W. v. Landwirthschaftliche Erfahrungen. Stuttgart, 1849. 8°. G,658
Pacha of Many Tales. F. Marryat. New York, 1868. 12°. . . . K,846
Pacific Ocean, Among the Islands of Western. J. E. Erskine. Lond. 1853. 8°. V,900
Voyage to, 1776–80. J. Cook and J. King. London, 1784. 3 v. 4°. V,1010
Pacific Railroad, History of. F. B. Goddard. Philadelphia, 1869. 8°. . V,132
Reports on Surveys for. Washington, 1855–64. 13 v. 4°. . . P.D.
Pacific Slope and California. J. Todd. Boston, 1870. 16°. . . . V,92
Resources of. J. R. Browne. New York, 1869. 8°. . . . V,125
Pädagogik, Geschichte der, v. 1, 2, 4. K. Schmidt. Cöthen, 1867–69. 8°. G,538
Pädagogischer Jahresbericht, v. 21; hrsg. von A. Lüben. Leipzig, 1870. 8°. G,539
Paez, R. Wild Scenes in South America. New York, 1868. 12°. . . V,233
Page, D. Advanced Text-Book of Geology. Edinburgh, 1867. 12°. . N,765
Geology for General Readers. Edinburgh, 1866. 12°. . . . N,607
Hand-Book of Geological Terms and Geology. Edinburgh, 1859. 12°. N,786
Man; where, whence, and whither. Edinburgh, 1867. 16°. . . N,394
Past and Present Life of the Globe. Edinburgh, 1861. 8°. . . N,763
Page, D. P. Mutual Duties of Parents and Teachers. Boston, 1838. 8°. O,927
Theory and Practice of Teaching. New York, 1857. 8°. . . O,950

Page, H., Memoir of. W. A. Hallock. New York, n. d. 18°. . . P,746,23
Page, T. Milford Haven for Naval Arsenal. London, 1859. 4°. . N,252,52
Page, Rev. T. Letter to Lord Ashley on Education. London, 1843. 16°. O,1163
Page, T. J. La Plata, Argentine Confederation, and Paraguay. N.Y. 1859. 8°. V,262
Map of the Basin of La Plata. New York, n. d. 4°. . . . P,298
Pagésis, M. H. L'Amour qui dort; Comédie. Paris, 1864. 12°. . . I,743
Paget, J. Hungary and Transylvania. Philadelphia, 1850. 2 v. 12°. . V,428
Paijkull, C. W. Summer in Iceland. London, 1868. 8°. . . . . V,182
Paine, M. Institutes of Medicine. New York, 1861. 8°. . . . L,1020
The same. New York, 1867. 8°. . . . . . . . L,1020
Paine, R. T. Works in Verse and Prose. Boston, 1812. 8°. . . . U,141
Paine, T. Age of Reason. Paris, 1794-95. 12°. . . . . . P,37
Common Sense. See *American Revolution Tracts*, 8.
Political Writings. v 2. Boston, 1856. 8°. . . . . . U,143
Rechte des Menschen. Leipzig, 1851. 16°. . . . . . G,531
Reply to. R. Watson. New York, n. d. 18°. . . . P,746,14
Painters and Engravers, Dictionary of. M. Bryan. London, 1853. 8°. .*M,138
and Sculptors, British, Lives of. A. Cunningham. N.Y. 1845-68. 5 v. 1. 8°. L,352
Engravers, Sculptors, and Architects, Anecdotes of. S. Spooner. New York, 1865. 3 v. 12°. . . . . . . . . . M,52
General Dictionary of. M. Pilkington. London, 1840. 8°. . . *M,94
The same. London, 1857. 8°. . . . . . . *M,108
Hand-Book for Young. C. R. Leslie. London, 1855. 12°. . . M,51
Lives of British. A. Cunningham. London, 1830-33. 4 v. 16°. . I,638
Memoirs of Early Italian. A. Jameson. Boston, 1866. 16°. . . M,19
of all Nations, History of. C. Blanc. London, 1855. 4°. . . Q,179
of the Dutch and Flemish Schools. G. Stanley. London, 1855. p. 8°. L,314
of the English School. R. and S. Redgrave. London, 1866. 2 v. 8°. M,103
Sculptors and Architects, Lives of. G. Vasari. Lond. 1850-52. 5 v. p. 8°. L,244
Sculptors and Architects of the Order of S. Dominic. V. Marchese. Dublin, 1852. 2 v. 12°. . . . . . . . . . M,154
Painting. G. Field. London, 1858. 12°. . . . . . . . . M,913
and Design, Lectures on. B. R. Haydon. London, 1844-46. 2 v. 8°. M,44
and Sculpture, Early Florentine School. W. Y. Ottley. Lond. 1826. f°. L.R.
Epochs of, Characterized. R. N. Wornum. London, 1859. 12°. . M,31
Hand-Book of; edited by Sir E. Head. London, 1854. 2 v. 12°. . M,6
of Italian Schools. F. T. Kugler. London, 1867. 2 v. 8°. . M,88
of German and Flemish Schools. F. T. Kugler. Lond. '60. 2 v. 8°. M,87
History of. J. S. Memes. Edinburgh, 1829. 16°. . . . . I,515
Appleton's. New York, 1856. 2 v. 8°. . . . . *Q,252
in Italy. J. A. Crowe and G. B. Cavalcaselle. Lon. 1864. 3 v. 8°. M,105
House, Plain and Decorative. J. W. Masury. New York, 1868. 12°. M,648
in England, Anecdotes of. H. Walpole. London, 1849. 3 v. 8°. M,107
in Italy, History of. L. Lanzi. London, 1847. 3 v. p. 8°. . . L,204
in Oil and Water-Colors. T. H. Fielding. London, 1846. 8°. . M,113
in Water-Colors. G. F. Phillips. London, 1838. 4°. . . . Q,197
its Rise and Progress. Boston, 1846. 12°. . . . . . . M,14
Laocoon; Limits of Poetry and Painting. G. E. Lessing. Lond. 1838. 8°. M,45
Lectures on. J. Barry, J. Opie, and H. Fuseli. London, 1848. p. 8°. L,303
H. Fuseli. London, 1830. 4°. . . . . . . . Q,167

Painting, Lectures on. H. O'Niel. London, 1866. 8°. . . . . . M,46
J. Ruskin. New York, 1856. 12°. . . . . . . M,151
National Gallery of. A. J. Valpy. London, n. d. 8°. . . . . M,57
on Glass. E. O. Fromberg. London, 1857. 12°. . . . . . M,915
Popularly Explained. T. J. Gulleck. London, 1859. 16°. . . M,3
Restored to Simplest Principles. L. Hundertpfund. Lond. 1849. 12°. M,55
Treatise on. J. Burnet. London, 1850. 4°. . . . . . . *Q,170
L. da Vinci; translated by J. F. Rigaua. London, 1835. 12°. M,33
Works of Eminent Masters in. London, 1854. 2 v. in 1. 8°. . *Q,164
Paintings, Peintures Antiques Inédites. D. Raoul-Rochette. Paris, 1836. 4°. Q,171
Palace and Cottage. W. T. Adams. Boston, 1869. 16°. . . . . J,1535,5
of the Great King. H. Read. Glasgow, 1864. 12°. . . . P,221
Palacky, F. Geschichte von Böhmen. Prag, 1844–65. 5 v. in 9. 8°. . E,78
Palæontographical Society, Publications. London, 1850–59. 5 v. 4°.
Wright, T. British Fossil Echinodermata, pt. 1. . . . . Q,30
Sharpe, D. Fossil Remains of Mollusca, pt. 3. . . . . Q,30
Jones, T. R. Tertiary Entomostraca of England. . . . . Q,30
Owen, R. Fossil Reptilia, pt. 3. . . . . . . . Q,30
Wood, S. V. Crag Mollusca, v. 2. . . . . . . Q,30
King, W. Permian Fossils of England. . . . . . . Q,31
Wright, T. British Fossil Echinodermata, pt. 3. . . . . Q,32
Davidson, T. British Carboniferous Brachiopoda, pt. 5. . . . Q,32
Owen, R. Fossil Reptilia, suppl. 1. . . . . . . Q,32
Busk, G. Fossil Polyzoa of the Crag. . . . . . . Q,32
Davidson, T. British Fossil Brachiopoda, v. 1. . . . . Q,33
Edwards, H. M. and Haime, J. British Fossil Corals. . . . Q,34
Palæontologie. C. G. A. Giebel. Leipzig, 1852. 8°. . . . . . . G,832
Palæontology. F. B. Meek and W. M. Gabb. San Franc. 1864–66. 2 v. 4°. N,740
R. Owen. Edinburgh, 1861. 8°. . . . . . . . N,823
et Géologie Stratigraphiques. A. D. d'Orbigny. Paris, 1852. 4°. . Q,35
Palestine. M. Russell. New York, 1854. 18°. . . . . . . . L,360
The same. London, 1856. 16°. . . . . . . . V,628
and the Sinaitic Peninsula. C. Ritter. New York, 1866. 4 v. 8°. V,652
Bible History of the Holy Land. J. Kitto. London, n. d. 8°. . V,650
Biblical Researches in. E. Smith and E. Robinson. Bost. 1856–7. 3 v. 8°. V,665
Dan to Beersheba. J. P. Newman. New York, 1864. 12°. . . V,644
Domestic Life in. M. E. Rogers. London, 1863. 8°. . . . . V,632
Early Travels in; edited by T. Wright. London, 1848. p. 8°. . L,7
Egypt and Edom. A. W. C. *Lord* Lindsay. London, 1866. p. 8°. . L,115
and Arabia Petræa. J. L. Stephens. N. Y. 1854. 2 v. in 1. 8°. V,1073
and Italy, Visit to. I. Pfeiffer. London, 1853. 12°. . V,1044
and Nubia, Pilgrimage to. I. F. Romer. Lond. 1846. 2 v. 8°. V,675
Eōthen, Travels in. A. W. Kinglake. London, 1865. p. 8°. . . I,657
The same. New York, 1858. 8°. . . . . . . V,1037
The same. Leipzig. . . . . . . . . . . . J,239
Geography and Historical Sketch of. J. Schwarz. Phila. 1850. 8°. V,663
Giant Cities of Bashan. J. L. Porter. London, 1866. 12°. . . V,657
History of. J. Kitto. Boston, 1856. 12°. . . . . . . . . V,635
Holy Land. W. H. Dixon. London, 1865. 2 v. 8°. . . . . V,649
The same. Leipzig, 1865. 2 v. in 1. 16°. . . . . J,150
A. de Lamartine. London, 1837. 3 v. 12°. . . . . . V,656
Journey to Ararat. F. Parrot. New York, 1846. 12°. . . . . V,631

Palestine, Journey to. R. W. Stewart. Edinburgh, 1857. 8°. . . . . v,648
The Land and its Story. N. C. Burt. New York, 1869. 8°. . . v,651
The Land and the Book. W. M. Thomson. N. Y. 1869. 2 v. 12°. v,634
The Land of Israel. A. Keith. New York, 1844. 12°. . . . v,645
Lands of the Saracen. B. Taylor. New York, 1866. 12°. . v,1051
Letters from. N. C. Burt. Cincinnati, 1866. 12°. . . . . v,638
Letters on the Holy Land. A. W. C. *Lord* Lindsay. Lond. 1858. 12°. L,115
Notes of the Holy Land. R. Buchanan. London, 1859. 8°. . . v,633
Observations in. J. P. Durbin. New York, 1851. 12°. . . v,1058
Pathways of our Lord. J. M. Wainwright. New York, 1851. 12°. v,654
Physical Geography of the Holy Land. E. Robinson. Bost. 1865. 8°. v,653
Sermons during Tour in. A. P. Stanley. New York, 1864. 12°. . P,64
Sinai and. A. P. Stanley. New York, 1857. 8°. . . . . . v,664
Syria and the Holy Land. W. K. Kelly. London, 1844. 8°. . . v,661
Tent Life in the Holy Land. W. C. Prime. New York, 1867. 12°. v,637
Travels in. R. F. A. de Chateaubriand. London, 1812. 2 v. 8°. v,1083
B. Dorr. Philadelphia, 1856. 12°. . . . . . . . v,1042
S. Olin. New York, 1851. 2 v. 12°. . . . . . v,1057
E. Warburton. Philadelphia, 1859. 8°. . . . . . . v,830
Winter Ride in. H. B. Tristram. London, 1864. 8°. . . v,1086,3
Paley, W. Evidences of Christianity. New York, 1843. 16°. . . . P,344
Natural Theology. New York, 1847. 2 v. 16°. . . . . L,403
Principles of Moral and Political Philosophy. New York, 1849. 12°. P,233
Works. London, 1845. 5 v. 8°. . . . . . . . . . . P,709
Vol. 1. Evidences of Christianity.
2. Moral and Political Philosophy.
3. Horæ Paulinæ; Clergyman's Companion in visiting the Sick, etc.
4. Natural Theology.
5. Sermons, etc.
Palfrey, J. G. History of New England. London, 1859–68. 3 v. 8°. . C,22
Lectures on Jewish Scriptures and Antiquities. Bost. 1838–52. 4 v. 8°. A,221
Life of William Palfrey. Boston, 1860. 12°. . . . . . C,860,17
Palfrey, S. H. Herman; or, Young Knighthood. Boston, 1866. 2 v. 12°. K,888
Prémices. Boston, 1855. 16°. . . . . . . . . . . I,34
Palfrey, W., Life of. J. G. Palfrey. Boston, 1860. 12°. . . . C,860,17
Palgrave, F. History of England. London, 1831. 16°. . . . . A,386
History of the Anglo-Saxons. London, 1867. 12°. . . . . A,441
History of England, Anglo-Saxon Period. London, 1831. 16°. . I,602
History of Normandy and England. London, 1851–64. 4 v. 8°. . A,440
Palgrave, F. T. Essays on Art. New York, 1867. 16°. . . . . M,15
Palgrave, W. G. Journey through Arabia. London, 1865. 2 v. 8°. . V,750
Palissy, B., the Potter. F. M. Caulkins. Boston, 1858. 16°. . . . D,664
Life of. H. Morley. Boston, 1853. 2 v. 16°. . . . . D,653
Palm Trees of the Amazon. A. R. Wallace. London, 1853. 8°. . . N,954
Palmer, J. Necrology of Alumni of Harvard, 1851–63. Boston, 1864. 8°. O,806
Palmer, J. Travels over the Rocky Mountains, 1845–46. Cincin. 1847. 12°. V,37
Palmer, J. W. New and Old; California and India. New York, 1859. 12°. K,295
Poetry of Compliment and Courtship. Boston, 1868. 12°. . . I,488
Up and Down the Irrawaddi. New York, 1856. 12°. . . . V,593
Palmer, L. Magnet Stories. Troy, 1867. 3 v. 16°. . . . . . J,1627
Vol. 1 Drifting and Steering. Vol. 2. One Day's Weaving. Vol. 3. Archie's Shadow.
Palmer, P. S. History of Lake Champlain, 1609–1814. Albany, 1866. 8°. C,90

Palms, History of the. B. Seemann. London, 1856. 16°. . . . . . N,927
Die Palmen. B. Seemann. Leipzig, 1857. 8°. . . . . . . G,899
Structur der Jubæa Spectabilis. P. Wossidlo. Jena, 1861. 4°. . Q,117
Pampas and the Andes. N. H. Bishop. Boston, 1870. 16°. . . J,1610
Journeys across. F. B. Head. London, 1846. 12°. . . . . V,250
Pamphleteer, The. London, 1813–26. 27 v. 8°. . . . . . . . R,7
Panama in 1855. R. Tomes. New York, 1855. 16°. . . . . . V,172
Panama Railroad, History of. F. N. Otis. New York, 1867. 12°. . . V,242
Panopticon Penitentiary House. J. Bentham. London, 1791. 16°. . . O,465
Pantology, Survey of Human Knowledge. R. Park. Philadel. 1847. 8°. H,148
Pantropheon; or, History of Food. A. Soyer. London, 1853. 8°. . . H,321
Panzer, G.W. Annalen der Deutschen Lit. bis 1536. Nürm. 1788-1803. 2 v. 4°. L.R.
Annales Typographici ad annum 1536. Norimb. 1793–1803. 11 v. 4°. L.R.
Papacy, The; its Origin and Relations. Abbé Guettée. N. Y. 1867. 12°. P,821
Römische Päpste im 16 u. 17 Jahrh. L. Ranke. Ber. 1844–45. 3 v. 8°. E,30
Papal Conspiracy Exposed. E. Beecher. New York, 1855. 12°. . . P,820
Paper against Gold. W. Cobbett. New York, 1854. 18°. . . . . O,462
and Paper-Making, Chronology of. W. T. Coggeshall. Alb. 1856. 8°. M,639
Fabrikation des Papiers. L. Müller. Berlin, 1849. 8°. . . N,252,30
Paper-Making, Chronology of. J. Munsell. Albany, 1857. 8°. . . . M,659
Papers for Home Reading. J. Hall. New York, 1871. 12°. . . . H,224
for the People. W. and R. Chambers. Edinb. 1850–56. 12 v. in 6. 12°. H,558
The same, v. 1, 2. New York, 1860. 12°. . . . . . H,560
for the Schoolmaster, v. 2, 3, 4. London, 1852–54. 3 v. 12°. . O,1190
for the Teacher, series 1, 3–6. N. Y. and Phila. 1860–62. 5 v. 8°. O,1216
for Thoughtful Girls. S. Tytler. Boston, 1864. 12°. . . . J,1290
Parables. F. A. Krummacher. London, 1858. p. 8°. . . . . . L,114
of Our Lord explained and applied. F. Bourdillon. N. Y. n. d. 12°. P,365
with 21 illustrations. London, n. d. 16°. . . . . . P,367
Paradise Lost. J. Milton. London, 1861. p. 8°. . . . . . . L,128
The same. London, 1754. 2 v. 4°. . . . . . F,168,1,2
The same; illustrated by G. Doré. London, n. d. f°. . *Q,244
See also *Milton, J., Poetical Works.*
Paradise Regained. J. Milton. London, 1861. p. 8°. . . . . . L,128
and Samson Agonistes. J. Milton. London, 1752. 4°. F,168,3
Paraguay, History of. C. A. Washburn. Boston, 1871. 2 v. 8°. . . C,391
La Plata and Argentine Confederation. T. J. Page. N. Y. 1859. 8°. V,262
Letters from the Battles of. R. F. Burton. London, 1870. 8°. . V,247
Republic of. D. Powell. London, 1864. 8°. . . . . . V,1086,3
Paragreens on a Visit to Paris. J. Ruffini. Leipzig, 1869. 16°. . . J,433
Parallel Lives. C. D. Yonge. London, 1858. 12°. . . . . . . C,486
Paralysis and other Affections of the Nerves. G. H. Taylor. N. Y. 1871. 12°. L,957
Paramorphismus, Der. T. Scheerer. Braunschweig, 1854. 8°. . . G,710
Pardee, R. G. Cultivation of the Strawberry. New York, 1854. 12°. . M,539
Pardoe, J. Adopted Heir. Philadelphia, n. d. 12°. . . . . . K,587
City of the Magyar. London, 1840. 3 v. 12°. . . . . . V,429
City of the Sultan. London, 1837. 2 v. 8°. . . . . . . V,556
Court and Reign of Francis I. Philadelphia, 1849. 12°. . . D,640
Life of Marie de Medicis. London, 1852. 3 v. 8°. . . . . D,729
Louis XIV. and the Court of France. New York, 1865. 2 v. 12°. D,643

Pardon, G. F. Hoyle's Games Modernized. London, n. d. 18°. . . . M,338
Tales from the Operas. New York, 1865. 12°. . . . . . K,889
Parental Instructions. New York, 1846. 18°. . . . . . . . . H,3
Parents and Teachers, Duties of. D. P. Page. Boston, 1838. 8°. . . O,927
Stories for. T. S. Arthur. Philadelphia, 1858. 18°. . . . J,1196
Parents de Province; Vaudeville. E. Abraham et J. Prével. Paris, 1865. 12°. I,743
Parerga und Paralipomena. A. Schopenhauer. Berlin, 1860. 2 v. 8°. . G,572
Parietin; a Yellow Coloring Matter. R. D. Thomson. Glasgow, 1843. 8°. N,252,21
Paris, J. A. Philosophy in Sport. London, 1857. 8°. . . . . . N,70
Paris, M. English History, 1235–1273. London, 1852–54. 3 v. p. 8°. . L,20
Paris and its Environs. T. Forester. London, 1859. p. 8°. . . . L,133
Picturesque Views of. F. Nash. London, 1823. 2 v. in 1. 4°. *Q,234
and its Historical Scenes. London, 1831. 2 v. 16°. . . . L,483
The same. London, 1846. 2 v. 16°. . . . . . . B,202
and the Parisians in 1835. F. Trollope. New York, 1836. 8°. . V,459
Battle Summer, 1848. D. G. Mitchell. New York, 1850. 12°. . H,20
Bureau des Longitudes. Connaissance des Tems. Paris, 1834–42. 7 v. 8°. R,20
Exposition, 1867. Illustrirter Katalog. W. Hamm. Leip. 1868. 2 v. 4°. *F,180
Report of the United States Commissioners to; edited by W. P. Blake. Washington, 1870. 6 v. 8°. . . . . . F,280

Vol. 1. Introduction; General Survey of the Exhibition; Report on the United States Section; Report on the Fine Arts, by F. Leslie; Fine Arts applied to the Useful Arts, by F. Leslie, S. F. B. Morse, and T. W. Evans; Report on Weights, Measures, and Coins; Bibliography of the Exposition, by W. P. Blake.
2. The Production of Iron and Steel in its Economic and Social Relations, by A. S. Hewitt; Report upon the Precious Metals, by W. P. Blake; Progress and Condition of Industrial Chemistry, by J. L. Smith.
3. Machinery and Processes of the Industrial Arts, and Apparatus of the exact Sciences, by F. A. P. Barnard.
4. Telegraphic Apparatus, by S. F. B. Morse; Steam Engineering, by W. S. Auchincloss; Engineering and Public Works, by W. P. Blake; Béton-Coignet, its Fabrication and Uses, by L. P. Beckwith; Asphalt and Bitumen as applied in Construction, by A. Beckwith; Buildings, Materials, and Methods of Building, by J. H. Bowen; Mining and Mechanical Preparations of Ores, by H. F. Q. d'Aligny and others.
5. Statistics of Cereals, by S. B. Ruggles; Quality and Characteristics of Cereals Exhibited, by G. S. Hazard; Preparation of Food, by W. E. Johnston; Beet Sugar and Alcohol, Pressed and Agglomerated Coal, Photographs and Apparatus, and Atlantic Cables, by H. F. Q. d'Aligny; Culture and Products of the Vine, by M. P. Wilder and others; School Houses and Popular Education, by J. R. Freese; Munitions of War, by C. B. Norton and W. J. Valentine; Instruments of Medicine, Surgery, Hygiene, etc., by T. W. Evans; Musical Instruments, by P. Stevens.
6. Wool and Manufactures of Wool, by E. R. Mudge and J. L. Hayes; Report upon Cotton, by E. R. Mudge and B. F. Nourse; Silk and Silk Manufactures, by E. C. Cowdin; Clothing and Woven Fabrics, by P. Stevens; Report on Education, by J. W. Hoyt; List of the Reports.

in America. E. Laboulaye. New York, 1863. 12°. . . . H,910
in December, 1851; Napoleon's Coup d'Etat. E. Ténot. N.Y. 1870. 12°. B,346
My Paris; French Character Sketches. E. King. Boston, 1868. 12°. V,447
New Paris Guide. A. and W. Galignani. Paris, 1847. 16°. . . V,446
Purple Tints of. B. St. John. New York, 1854. 12°. . . .
Paris Sketch-Book. W. M. Thackeray. Boston, 1869. 12°. . . K,1038,2
Parisian Sights and French Principles. J. J. Jarves. New York, 1856. 12°. V,454
Park, E. A. Memoir of B. B. Edwards. Boston, 1853. 2 v. 12°. . . C.808
Park, M. Journal in Interior of Africa, 1805. London, 1815. 4°. . . V,718
Life and Travels of. Edinburgh, n. d. 12°. . . . . . . V,772
The same. New York, 1860. 16°. . . . . . . . L,410
Travels in the Interior of Africa, 1795–97. London, 1799. 4°. . V,719

Park, R. Hand-Book for Travelers in Europe. New York, 1854. 12°. . V,302
Pantology; Survey of Human Knowledge. Philadelphia, 1847. 8°. H,148
Parker, E. G. Golden Age of American Oratory. Boston, 1857. 12°. . C,528
Reminiscences of Rufus Choate. New York, 1860. 12°. . . C,751
Parker, H. F. Discoverers and Pioneers of America. New York, 1856. 12°. C,1047
Morning Stars of the New World. New York, 1854. 12°. . . C,518
Parker, J. Ad Clerum; Advice to a Young Preacher. Boston, 1871. 12°. H,511
Ecce Deus; Life and Doctrine of Jesus Christ. Boston, 1867. 12°. P,370
Parker, J. H. Domestic Architecture in England. Oxford, 1853–9. 3 v. 8°. M,186
Glossary of Terms used in Architecture. Oxford, 1850. 3 v. 8°. . M,205
Study of Gothic Architecture. Oxford, 1867. 8°. . . . . . M,146
Parker, M., Life and Acts. J. Strype. Oxford, 1821. 3 v. 8°. . . P,689
Parker, N. H. Iowa as it is in 1856. Chicago, 1856. 12°. . . . C,160
Minnesota Hand-Book for 1856–57. Boston, 1857. 12°. . . . C,185
Parker, R. A. Rosa Abbott Stories. Boston, 1871. 6 v. 16°. . . . J,1628
Vol. 1. Jack of all Trades. 2. Alexis, the Runaway. 3. Tommy Hickup. Vol. 4. Upside Down. 5. Young Detective. 6. Pinks and Blues.
Parker, R. G. English Composition. Boston, 1852. 12°. . . . . . H,8
Fourth Reader. New York, 1852. 12°. . . . . . . . O,790
Rhetorical Reader. New York, 1853. 12°. . . . . . . O,881
Parker, T., Life of. J. Weiss. New York, 1864. 2 v. 8°. . . . C,945
Critical and Miscellaneous Writings. Boston, 1867. 12°. . . H,87
Experience as a Minister. Boston, 1859. 8°. . . . . . . C,770
Speeches, Addresses, Occasional Sermons. Boston, 1859. 2 v. 12°. H,780
Ten Sermons. Boston, 1855. 12°. . . . . . . . . P,156
Trial of, with Defense. Boston, 1855. 8°. . . . . . . C,883
Parker, W. K. Introduction to Study of the Foraminifera. Lond. 1862. f°. Q,68
Parkes, B. R. Essays on Woman's Work. London, 1865. 12°. . . O,411
Parkes, J. Memoirs of Sir Philip Francis. London, 1867. 2 v. 8°. . D,354
Parkes, J. Essays on Land-Drainage. London, 1848. 8°. . . N,252,31
Lecture on Draining. London, 1846. 8°. . . . . . N,252,6
Parkhurst, H. M. Plowshare and American Reporter. Wash. 1853. 18°. L,674
Parkhurst, J. Hebrew and English Lexicon without Points. Lond. 1813. 8°. L.R.
Parkinson, J. Fossil Organic Remains. London, 1822. 8°. . . . N,788
Organic Remains of a Former World. London, 1804–11. 3 v. 4°. N,748
Parkinson, S. Treatise on Optics. London, 1866. 8°. . . . . N,21
Parkman, F. Book of Roses. Boston, 1866. 12°. . . . . . M,500
Discovery of the Great West. Boston, 1870. 8°. . . . . B,616
History of the Conspiracy of Pontiac. Boston, 1851. 8°. . . B,600
The same; 6th edition. Boston, 1870. 2 v. 8°. . . . B,613
Jesuits in North America in 17th Century. Boston, 1867. 8°. . B,617
Pioneers of France in the New World. Boston, 1865. 8°. . . B,618
Vassal Morton; a Novel. Boston, 1856. 12°. . . . . . K,141
Parkyns, M. Life in Abyssinia. New York, 1854. 2 v. 12°. . . . V,790
Parley, Peter, *pseud.* See *Goodrich, S. G.*
Parliament, British, Studies in. R. H. Hutton. London, 1866. 8°. . D,333
of Devils, etc. London, 1867. 8°. . . . . . . . L,605,24
Parliamentary Hist. of Eng. to 1803. T. C. Hansard. Lond. 1806–20. 36 v. 8°. B,76
Parliamentary Law and Practice. L. S. Cushing. Boston, 1866. 8°. . *U,503
Digest of. O. M. Wilson. Philadelphia, 1869. 8°. . . . U,491

Parliamentary Practice, Manual of. L. S. Cushing. Boston, 1856. 12°. . o,459
T. Jefferson. New York, 1856. 12°. . . . . . . o,475
Parliamentary Rules of Order. B. Matthias. Philadelphia, 1851. 16°. . o,463
Parlor Stage. S. A. Frost. New York, 1866. 16°. . . . . . . i,711
Parnell, T. Poetical Works. Boston, 1854. 16°. . . . . . . i,221
Parochial and Plain Sermons. J. H. Newman. London, 1869. 8 v. 8°. p,674
Parochiala. J. Sandford. London, 1845. 8°. . . . . . . . o,930
Parr, H., *Holme Lee.* For Richer, for Poorer. Leip. 1870. 2 v. in 1. 16°. j,409
Holme Lee's Fairy Tales. London, 1869. 12°. . . . . j,1443
John Godfrey's Caprice. Leipzig, 1868. 2 v. in 1. 16°. . . j,408
Life and Death of Jeanne d'Arc. London, 1866. 2 v. 8°. . . d,618
Sylvan Holt's Daughter. New York, 1860. 12°. . . . . k,230
Parr, S., Memoirs of. W. Field. London, 1828. 2 v. 8°. . . . d,396
Works; with Memoir by J. Johnstone. London, 1828. 8 v. 8°. . p,785
Parrain, Le, de Cendrillon. L. Ulbach. Paris, n. d. 12°. . . h,1039
Parrot, F. Journey to Ararat. New York, 1846. 12°. . . . . v,631
Parrot, G. F. Recherches sur les Pierres d'Imatra. St. Petersburg, 1840. 4°. n,252,42
Parrots, Natural History of. P. J. Selby. Edinburgh, n. d. 16°. . n,470,10
Parry, W. E. Voyage for Discov. of North-West Passage. Lon. 1821. 4°. v,1012,1
Appendix and Supplement. London, 1824. 4°. . v,1012,1
The same; second Voyage, 1821–23. London, 1824. 4°. . v,1012,2
Appendix to the same. London, 1825. 4°. . . v,1012,3
The same; third Voyage, 1824–25. London, 1826. 4°. . v,1012,4
The same; fourth Voyage, 1827. London, 1828. 4°. . v,1012,5
Three Voyages, abridged. New York, 1855. 2 v. 16°. . . . l,412
Parsons, B. Education the Want of every Human Being. Lond. 1850. 8°. o,1251,3
Parsons, J. W. Essays on Education. London, 1794. 16°. . . o,1152
Parsons, S. B. The Rose; its History, Poetry, Culture, etc. N.Y. 1850. 12°. m,352
Parsons, T. Essays. Boston, 1847. 16°. . . . . . . . . h,5
Laws of Business for Business Men. Boston, 1857. 8°. . . . u,508
Parsons, T. W. Poems. Boston, 1854. 8°. . . . . . . . i,381
Parson's Daughter, The. T. E. Hook. London, n. d. 16°. . . . k,720
Partee, W. B. Science of Money; a great Truth. Philadelphia, 1871. 12°. o,561
Parthenia; or, the Last Days of Paganism. E. B. Lee. Boston, 1858. 12°. k,715
Parthenogenesis in Moths and Bees. C. T. E. von Siebold. Lond. 1857. 8°. o,39
Parthey, G. Wanderungen durch Sicilien. Berlin, 1834–40. 2 v. 12°. . e,211
Atlas zum zweiten Theil. Berlin, 1840. portfolio. . . *q,84
Partisan, The; a Romance. W. G. Simms. New York, 1864. 12°. . . k,256
Partnership. Limited Liability and Partnership Act. Lond. 1858–59. 12°. m,919
Parton, J. Famous Americans of Recent Times. Boston, 1860. 8°. . c,910
General Butler in New Orleans. New York, 1864. 12°. . . . b,928
Humorous Poetry from Chaucer to Saxe. Boston, 1867. 12°. . . i,94
Life and Times of Aaron Burr. Boston, 1867. 2 v. 12°. . . c,792
Life and Times of Benjamin Franklin. Boston, 1867. 2 v. 12°. . c,790
Life of Andrew Jackson. New York, 1861. 3 v. 12°. . . . c,943
Life of Horace Greeley. New York, 1855. 12°. . . . . c,678
Smoking and Drinking. Boston, 1868. 16°. . . . . . . h,251
Topics of the Time. Boston, 1871. 12°. . . . . . . . h,131
Parton, S. P., *Fanny Fern.* Fern Leaves. Auburn, N. Y. 1854. 2 v. 12°. h,44
Ginger-Snaps. New York, 1870. 12°. . . . . . . . . h,117

Parton, S. P., *Fanny Fern.* Little Ferns. New York, 1868. 16°. . J,1496
Ruth Hall; a Domestic Tale. New York, 1855. 12°. . . . . K,920
Party, History of. G. W. Cooke. London, 1836–37. 8°. . . . . . B,31
Party Leaders; Sketches of Jefferson, etc. J. G. Baldwin. N. Y. 1868. 12°. C,527
Pascal, B. Lettres écrites à un Provincial. Paris, 1854. 12°. . . . P,92
Pensées de, précédées de la Vie. Paris, 1853. 8°. . . . . . H,894
Provincial Letters. London, 1816. 8°. . . . . . . . . P,93
The same; edited by O. W. Wight. New York, 1859. 12°. P,93
and Nicole, P. Pensées de Pascal, et de Nicole. Paris, 1856. 12°. H,864
Pasquier, E. Œuvres Choisies. Paris, 1849. 2 v. 12°. . . . . . H,997
Passion Flowers; Poems. J. W. Howe. Boston, 1854. 16°. . . . I,90
Passions of the Human Soul. C. Fourier. London, 1851. 2 v. 8°. . O,685
Past and Present. T. Carlyle. New York, 1852. 12°. . . . . H,430
Past Meridian. L. H. Sigourney. New York, 1854. 12°. . . . H,7
Past, the Present, and the Future. H. C. Carey. Philadelphia, 1848. 8°. O,549
Paston Letters; edited by Sir J. Fenn. London, 1849. p. 8°. . . . H,482
The same. London, 1787–1823. 5 v. 4°. . . . . . H,170
Pastoral Theology, Theory of. A. Vinet. New York, 1853. 12°. . . P,293
Pastor's Fireside. J. Porter. London, 1817. 4 v. 12°. . . . . J,575
Patagonia, Captive in. B. F. Bourne. Boston, 1853. 12°. . . . V,193
Patchwork. B. Hall. London, 1841. 3 v. 12°. . . . . . . V,376
Patent Office Reports, U. S. 1842-67. *Not complete.* Wash. 1842–69. 8°. .
Patents, Law of. F. W. Campin. London, 1869. 12°. . . . . . M,834
Paterculus, C. V. Abridgment of History of Rome. London, 1814. 8°. . A,158
Opera Omnia; illustr. by D. Ruhnkenius. Parisiis, 1822. 8°. . . U,354
The same; translated by J. S. Watson. New York, 1855. 12°. A,136
Pater-Mundi; Testimony of Modern Science. E. F. Burr. Boston, 1870. 12°. P,129
Paterson, W. Journeys among the Hottentots. London, 1789. 4°. . . Q,422
Pathfinder, The. J. F. Cooper. New York, 1863. 12°. . . . . . K,41
The same. New York, 1860. 8°. . . . . . . . . K,69
Patience Strong's Outings. A. C. F. Whitney. Boston, 1869. 12°. . . K,388
Patient Grisel, History of. London, 1842. 12°. . . . . . L,606,3
a pleasant Comedy. T. Dekker and others. London, 1841. 8°. I,885,6
Patient Waiting no Loss. A. B. Haven. New York, 1867. 16°. . J,1329
Patissier, P. Action Thérapeutique des Eaux Minérales. Paris, 1839. 8°. N,252,22
Eaux Minérales Naturelles. Paris, 1841. 8°. . . . . . N,252,22
Patmore, C. Angel in the House; the Betrothal. Boston, 1856. 16°. . I,93
The same; the Espousals. London, 1856. 16°. . . . I,92
Victories of Love. Boston, 1862. 16°. . . . . . . . I,91
Paton, A. A. Islands of the Adriatic. London, 1849. 2 v. 8°. . . V,435
Patrick, S., Lowth, and others. Comment. on Scriptures. Phil. 1846. 4 v. 8°. P,556
Patriot Boys and Prison Pictures. J. R. Gilmore. Boston, 1866. 12°. . J,1265
Patriotic Eloquence. C. M. Kirkland. New York, 1866. 12°. . . O,826
Patriotism in Poetry and Prose. J. E. Murdoch. Philadelphia, 1866. 12°. H,308
Patronage. M. Edgeworth. New York, 1859. 12°. . . . . . K,678,7,8
Patterson, R. Reporter's Assistant. Philadelphia, 1849. 12°. . . L,671
Pattison, S. R. Fossil Botany. London, 1849. 12°. . . . . . . N,604
Patton, J. History of the United States. New York, 1868. 8°. . . B,706
Patty Gray's Journey to Cotton Islands. C. H. Dall. Boston, 1870. 3 v. 16°. J,1701
Vol. 1. From Boston to Baltimore. Vol. 2. From Baltimore to Washington.
3. On the Way; or, Patty at Mount Vernon.

Paul, Saint. E. Renan. New York, 1869. 12°. . . . . . . P,130
Conversion of. G. *Lord* Lyttleton. New York, n. d. 18°. . P,746,14
Essays on the Difficulties of. R. Whately. London 1861. 8°. . P,523
Life and Epistles of. Conybeare and Howson. N. Y. 1858. 2 v. 8°. P,406
Paul and Virginia. J. H. B. de St. Pierre. London, 1846. 12°. . U,123,1
The same. Philadelphia, 1868. 12°. . . . . . . H,951
Paul und Virginie. J. H. B. de St. Pierre. Pforzheim, 1840. 8°. . . G,443
Paul Barton; or, Drunkard's Son. H. N. Baker. Boston, 1870. 16°. J,1692
Paul Clifford. Sir E. B. Lytton. Philadelphia, 1868. 12°. . . . K,822
The same. Philadelphia, 1830. 8°. . . . . . K,823
The same. Leipzig, 1842. 16°. . . . . . . . J,325
Paul Fane. N. P. Willis. New York, 1857. 12°. . . . . . . K,390
Paul Ferroll. C. Clive. Leipzig, 1856. 16°. . . . . . . . . J,68
Why he killed his Wife. C. Clive. Leipzig, 1856. 16°. . . J,69
Paul Gosslett's Confessions; St. Patrick's Eve. C. Lever. Leipzig, 1870. 16°. J,286
Paul the Pope and Paul the Friar. T. A. Trollope. London, 1861. 8°. K,1055
Paulding, J. K. Bulls and the Jonathans. New York, 1868. 8°. . . H,216
Dutchman's Fireside. New York, 1868. 12°. . . . . . . K,307
Life of Washington. New York, 1854. 2 v. 16°. . . . . . L,392
Literary Life of. W. I. Paulding. New York, 1867. 8°. . . C,958
Tale of the Good Woman. New York, 1867. 8°. . . . . . H,217
Pauli, R. Life of Alfred the Great. London, 1853. 12°. . . . . L,23
Pausanias. Description of Greece. London, 1794. 3 v. 8°. . . . A,93
Pavements, Tile, Specimens of. H. Shaw. London, 1858. 4°. . . *Q,186
Paxton, G. Illustrations of Holy Scriptures. Philadelphia, 1822. 2 v. 8°. P,474
Paxton, J. and Lindley, J. Pocket Botanical Dictionary. London, 1849. 8°. N,943
Payen, A. Fabrication et Raffinage des Sucres. Paris, 1832. 8°. . N,252,20
Payson, E., Memoir of. Portland, 1830. 12°. . . . . . . . . C,956
Memoirs of. A. Cummings. New York, n. d. 18°. . . P,746,12
Peabody, A. P. Reminiscences of European Travel. N. Y. 1868. 16°. . V,307
Record of a School. Boston, 1835. 12°. . . . . . . O,1176
Peabody, G., Life of. P. A. Hanaford. Boston, 1870. 12°. . . . C,923
Reception at Danvers, Mass., Oct. 9, 1856. Boston, 1856. 8°. . C,64
Peabody, G. H. Elements of Astronomy. Cincinnati, 1869. 8°. . . N,331
Peabody Institute, South Danvers, Mass., Catalogue of Library. Bost. 1855. 8°. L.R.
Peabody, O. W. B. Life of Israel Putnam. New York, 1860. 16°. . C,860,7
Life of John Sullivan. Boston, 1860. 12°. . . . . . C,860,13
Peabody, W. B. O. Life of David Brainard. Boston, 1860. 12°. . . C,860,8
Life of Cotton Mather. Boston, 1860. 12°. . . . . . C,860,6
Life of James Oglethorpe. Boston, 1860. 12°. . . . . C,860,12
Life of Alexander Wilson. Boston, 1860. 12°. . . . . C,860,2
Literary Remains of. Boston, 1850. 12°. . . . . . . H,218
Peace and War; an Essay. London, 1823. 8°. . . . . . . . . O,396
Peace Manual, The. G. C. Beckwith. Boston, 1847. 18°. . . . . O,461
Peacock, E. English Church Furniture, etc., at the Ref. London, 1866. 8°. M,161
Peacock, G. Treatise on Algebra. Cambridge, 1842–45. 2 v. 8°. . M,1120
Peacock, T. L. Headlong Hall and Nightmare Abbey. N. Y. 1845. 12°. K,890
Peacocke, J. S. Orphan Girls; a Tale of Southern Life. Philad. 1865. 12°. K,361
Peake, J. Naval Architecture. London, 1859. 12°. . . . . . M,951
Pear Culture. T. W. Field. New York, 1859. 12°. . . . . . . . M,489

Pearce, R. R. Memoirs of Richard, *Marquess* Wellesley. Lon. 1846. 3 v. 8°. D,35
Pearce, Z., Life; by himself. London, 1816. 8°. . . . . . C,1289,1
Peard, F. M. One Year; or, a Story of Three Homes. Boston, 1871. 12°. K,1161
One Year. Leipzig, 1869. 2 v. in 1. 16°. . . . . . . . J,410
Pearl of Orr's Island. H. B. Stowe. Boston, 1866. 12°. . . . . . K,286
Pearson, E. C. Gutenberg and the Art of Printing. Boston, 1871. 12°. . D,532
Pearson, C. H. Cabin on the Prairie. Boston, 1870. 16°. . . J,1609
History of England. London, 1867. 2 v. 8°. . . . . . . A,436
Young Pioneers of the North-West. Boston, 1871. 16°. . J,1613
Pearson, H. Memoir of Claudius Buchanan. New York, n. d. 18°. . P,746,16
Pearson, J. Exposition of the Creed. London, 1869. p. 8°. . . . L,221
Peasant-Boy Philosopher. H. Mayhew. London, 1860. 12°. . . J,1465
Peasant-Life in Germany. A. C. Johnson. New York, 1859. 12°. . . V,377
Peat, Bildung und das Wesen des Torfes. A.F.Weigmann. Brschwg.1837. 8°. N,252,4
Torfbetrieb in Russland. A. Bode. Mitau, 1846. 16°. . . N,252,38
Peat-Bogs, Torfmoore im Allgemeinen. L. Lesquereux. Berlin, 1847. 8°. N,252,40
Peck, G. W. Melbourne and the Chincha Islands. New York, 1854. 12°. V,1064
Peck, J. L. Dress and Care of the Feet. New York, 1871. 12°. . . L,956
Peck, J. M. Father Clark, the Pioneer Preacher. New York, 1855. 16°. C,829
Life of Daniel Boone. Boston, 1860. 12°. . . . . . C,860,23
Peck, W. G. Mathematical Dictionary. New York, 1859. 8°. . . M,1176
Peckham, J. Gen. Nathaniel Lyon and Missouri in 1861. N.Y. 1866. 2 v. 12°. B,903
Pecock, R. Repressor of Over-much Blaming of the Clergy; written 1449; edited by C. Babington. London, 1860. 2 v. 8°. . . . . W,169
Pedlar, Der. O. Ruppius. Berlin, 1867. 16°. . . . . . . . G,431
Peel, Sir R., Memoirs of. London, 1856–57. 2 v. 12°. . . . . . D,243
Speeches. London, 1853. 4 v. 8°. . . . . . . . . . H,796
Peel, W. Ride through the Nubian Desert. London, 1852. 8°. . . V,810
Peele, G. Dramatic and Poetical Works. London, 1861. 8°. . . . I,725
Peeps from a Belfry. F. W. Shelton. New York, 1855. 12°. . . . H,531
Peerage and Baronetage of British Empire. E. Lodge. London, 1870. 8°. *C,624
Romance of the. G. L. Craik. London, 1848–50. 4 v. 12°. . C,1230
Peg Woffington. C. Reade. Boston, 1866. 16°. . . . . . . K,907
Pegge, S. jr. Anecdotes of the English Language. London, 1844. 8°. . L,617
Peirce, B. Elementary Treatise on Sound. Boston, 1836. 8°. . . N,15
Physical and Celestial Mechanics. Boston, 1855. 4°. . . M,1081
Peirce, B. K. Half-Century with Juvenile Delinquents. N. Y. 1869. 8°. O,384
Pelet de la Lozère, P. J. C. Histoire des Etats-Unis d'Amérique. Par.'45. 8°. B,619
Pelham. Sir E. B. Lytton. Philadelphia, 1868. 12°. . . . . K,824
The same. Philadelphia, 1828. 8°. . . . . . . K,825
The same. Leipzig, 1842. 16°. . . . . . . J,326
Peligot, E. Composition Chimique de la Canne-à-Sucre. Paris, 1840. 8°. N,252,20
Fabrication du Sucre. Paris, 1843. 8°. . . . . . . N,252,20
Pellew, G. Life of Henry Addington. New York, 1847. 8°. . . C,1253,1
Pellico, S. Mes Prisons et des Devoirs. Paris, 1852. 12°. . . . D,716
Peloponnesian War. Thucydides; translated by H. Dale. Lon. 1868. 2 v. p. 8°. L,88
The same. New York, 1855. 12°. . . . . A,65
The same; translated by W. Smith. New York, n. d. 2 v. 16°. U,374
Peloponnesus, Excursion in. T. Wyse. London, 1865. 2 v. 8°. . . V,576
Pelouze, J. Fabrication du Coke et du Charbon de tourbe. Paris, 1842. 8°. N,252,10

Pelouze, J. Tannin et les Acides Gallique. Paris, n. d. 4°. . . . N,252,57
Transformation de l'Acide Hydrocyanique, etc. Paris, n. d. 8°. N,252,1
and Richardson, T. Decomposition of Cyanogen in Water. Newcastle, 1838. 8°. . . . . . . . . . N,252,2
Pelton, C. Key to his Hemispheres. Philadelphia, 1854. 8°. . . . . O,906
Physical Geography. Philadelphia, 1854. 8°. . . . . O,906
Pen-Pictures of Popular English Preachers. London, 1852. 16°. . . . C,838
Pencilings by the Way. N. P. Willis. Auburn, 1856. 12°. . . . H,82
Pendennis, History of. W. M. Thackeray. London, 1870. 8°. . . K,1029
The same. Leipzig, 1849. 3 v. 16°. . . . . . . J,486
Pendered, A. E. Remarks on Female Education. London, 1827. 12°. O,1139
Penhallow, S. Wars of New England with the Indians. Cincin. 1859. 4°. B,610
Peninsular Campaign in Virginia. J. J. Marks. Philadelphia, 1864. 12°. B,927
Peninsular War, History of the. W. F. P. Napier. New York, 1853. 8°. A,562
The same. New York, n. d. 5 v. 8°. . . . . . . B,96
Penn, W., Biography of. W. H. Dixon. Philadelphia, 1851. 12°. . . D,153
Lecture on. S. W. Fisher. Cincinnati, 1847. 8°. . . . . H,302,4
Life of. G. E. Ellis. Boston, 1860. 12°. . . . . . . C,860,22
M. L. Weems. Philadelphia, 1852. 12°. . . . . . . D,151
Pennsylvania, Annals of, 1609–82. S. Hazard. Philadelphia, 1850. 8°. . C,175
Early History of Western. Pittsburgh, 1848. 8°. . . . . . C,110
Geological Survey of, 2d and 3d Rep. H. D. Rogers. Harris. 1838–9. 8°. N,875
Geology of, Final Report. H. D. Rogers. Edinb. 1858. 2 v. in 3. 8°. *Q,50
Historical Collections of. S. Day. Philadelphia, 1843. 8°. . . C,111
History of. J. W. Barber. Hartford, 1856. 8°. . . . . . C,20
History of the 104th Regiment. W. W. H. Davis. Phila. 1866. 8°. B,964
Minutes of the Council, 1683–1790. Philadelphia, 1852–53. 16 v. 8°. C,119
Reserve Corps, History of. J. R. Sypher. Lancaster, 1865. 8°. . B,932
Review of the Constitution of. B. Franklin. London, 1859. 8°. . C,109
Penny Cyclopædia. London, 1833–43. 27 v. in 14. r. 8°. . . . . . L.R.
Supplement. London, 1845–46. 2 v. r. 8°. . . . . . L.R.
Penny Magazine, The, v. 1, 3. London, 1832–34. 3 v. 8°. . . . . Q,338
Penrose, E. C. History of France. New York, 1855. 12°. . . . . B,205
History of Germany. London, 1862. 12°. . . . . . . . B,207
People, The. J. Michelet. New York, 1846. 12°. . . . . . . H,909
I have met. N. P. Willis. New York, 1853. 12°. . . . . . H,76
Völker der Erde. A. B. Reichenbach. Leipzig, 1864. 8°. . . . E,155
People's Art Union, Historic Gallery of Portraits. London, n. d. 4 v. 8°. *C,593
People's Journal, v. 1, 2. New York, 1853–54. 2 v. 4°. . . . . . S,21
Pepper, J. H. Boy's Play-Book of Science. London, 1862. 12°. . . M,768
Play-Book of Metals. London, 1866. 12°. . . . . . . M,753
Scientific Amusements for Young People. London, 1865. 16°. . M,767
Pepperell, Groton, and Shirley, Mass., History of. C. Butler. Bost. 1848. 8°. C,126
Pepys, S. Diary and Correspondence. Philadelphia, 1855. 4 v. 8°. . D,450
Percival, J. G. Geological Survey of Wisconsin. Madison, 1855. 12°. . N,869
Life and Letters. J. H. Ward. Boston, 1866. 8°. . . . . . C,960
Poetical Works. Boston, 1859. 2 v. 24°. . . . . . . I,106
Report on the Geology of Connecticut. New Haven, 1842. 8°. . N,872
Percival Keene. F. Marryat. New York, 1868. 12°. . . . . . K,847
The same. Leipzig, 1842. 16°. . . . . . . . . J,359

Percy, J. Metallurgy. London, 1864. 8°. . . . . . . . . M,716
Traité Complet de Métallurgie. Paris et Liége, 1864–67. 5 v. 8°. . M,728
Percy, S. Tales of Kings and Queens of England. London, 1868. 16°. J,1556
Percy, T. Reliques of Ancient English Poetry. London, 1844. 3 v. 16°. I,379
The same. Leipzig, 1866. 3 v. 16°. . . . . . . J,411
Percy Anecdotes. T. Byerley and J. C. Robertson. London, n. d. 20 v. 18°. I,540
The same. London, 1868. 2 v. 12°. . . . . . . I,541
Percy Effingham. H. Cockton. London, 1853. 2 v. 12°. . . . . J,563
Percy Society, Publications of. London, 1840–52. 30 v. 12°. . . . *L,606

Vol. 1. Collier, J. P. (Ed.), Old Ballads; Mackay, C. (Ed.), Songs of the London 'Prentices and Trades; Croker, T. C. (Ed.), Historical Songs of Ireland; Pain and Sorrow of Evil Marriage; Parker, M., The King and a Poor Northern Man.
2. Lydgate, D. J., Minor Poems, Selections; Halliwell, J. O. (Ed.), Early Naval Ballads of England; Rowley, W., Search for Money; Mad Pranks and Merry Jests of Robin Goodfellow.
3. Wright, T. (Ed.). Political Ballads during the Commonwealth; Deloney, T., etc., Strange Histories; Heywood, T., Marriage Triumph; History of Patient Grisel.
4. Wright, T. (Ed.), Specimens of Lyric Poetry, Temp. Edward I.; Halliwell, J. O. (Ed.), Boke of Curtasye; Specimens of Old Christmas Carols; Halliwell, J. O. (Ed.), Nursery Rhymes of England.
5. Chettle, H., Kind-Heart's Dream; Dekker, T., Knight's Conjuring; Halliwell, J. O. (Ed.), Meeting of Gallants at an Ordinarie; Porter, H., Two Angry Women of Abington.
6. Rimbault, E. F. (Ed.), Poetical Tracts of the 16th Century; Rimbault, E. F. (Ed.), Cock Lorell's Bote; Johnson, R., Crown Garland of Golden Roses; Hutton, H., Follie's Anatomie; Wotton, Sir H., Poems.
7. Harmony of Birds; Brampton, T., Paraphrase on the Seven Penitential Psalms; Drayton, M., Harmony of the Church; Jack of Dover; Croker, T. C. (Ed.), A Kerry Pastoral.
8. Wright, T. (Ed.), Latin Stories; Gifford, G., Dialogue concerning Witches and Witchcraft.
9. Rowlands, S., The Four Knaves; Thomson, J., Poem to the Memory of W. Congreve; Halliwell, J. O. (Ed.), Pleasant Conceits of Old Hobson; Rimbault, E. F. (Ed.), Maroccus Extaticus, or, Bankes' Bay Horse in a Trance; Rimbault, E. F. (Ed.), Ballads illustrating the Great Frost of 1683–84.
10. Fairholt, F. W., Lord Mayors' Pageants.
11. Guildford, N. de, The Owl and Nightingale, a Poem; Croke, J., Thirteen Psalms, etc., in English Verse; Halle, J., Expostulation against the Abusers of Chyrurgerie and Physyke; Rich, B., Honestie of this Age.
12. Thoms, W. J (Ed.), Reynard the Fox.
13. Croker, T. C. (Ed.), The Keen of the South of Ireland; Goodwin, J. (Ed.), Six Ballads, with Burdens; Collier, J. P. (Ed.), Lyrical Poems, 1589–1600.
14. Audelay, J., Poems; Wright, T. (Ed.), St. Brandan, a Mediæval Legend of the Sea; Halliwell, J. O. (Ed.), Romance of the Emperor Octavian.
15. Halliwell, J. O. (Ed.), Friar Bakon's Prophesie, a Satire; Halliwell, J. O. (Ed.), Poetical Miscellanies of the Time of James I.; Crown Garland of Golden Roses, pt. 2.
16. Wright, T. (Ed.), Seven Sages, in English Verse; Halliwell, J. O. (Ed.), Romance of Syr Tryamoure.
17. Dixon, J. H. (Ed.), Scottish Traditional Versions of Ancient Ballads; Dixon, J. H. (Ed.), Ancient Poems, Ballads, etc., of the Peasantry of England.
18. Hawes, S., Pastime of Pleasure, an Allegorical Poem.
19. Fairholt, F. W. (Ed.), The Civic Garland; Songs; Robert of Gloucester, Life and Martyrdom of T. Beket.
20. Barnfield, R., The Affectionate Shepherd; Heywood, J., Dialogue on Wit and Folly; Denham, M. A., Collection of Proverbs and Popular Sayings; Halliwell, J. O. (Ed.), Song of Lady Bessy.
21. Croker, T. C. (Ed.), Songs of the French Invasion of Ireland.
22. Barclay, A., Cytezen and Uplondyshman; Halliwell, J. O. (Ed.), The Interlude of the Four Elements; Ingelend, T., The Disobedient Child; Croker, T. C. (Ed.), Autobiography of Mary, Countess of Warwick; Halliwell, J. O. (Ed.) Westward for Smelts, Stories.
23. Wright, T. (Ed.), Songs and Carols of the 15th Century; Wright, T. (Ed.), Festive Songs of the 16th and 17th Centuries; Halliwell, J. O., Descriptive Notices of Popular English Histories.
24–26. Chaucer, G., Canterbury Tales; edited by T. Wright, 3 v.
27. Massinger, P., Believe as you list, a Tragedy; Fairholt, F. W. (Ed.), Songs and Poems on Costume.
28. Hardwick, C. (Ed.), Passion of St. George; Hardwick, C. (Ed.), Poem on the Times of Edward II.; Shoreham, W. de, Religious Poems; Halliwell, J. O. (Ed.), Trial of Treasure.
29. Halliwell, J. O., Notices of Fugitive Tracts and Chap-Books; Man in the Moone; Manifest Detection of the use of Dice Play; Loyal Garland, Songs

Percy Society, Publications of. *Continued.* . . . . . . . . . . *L,606

of the 17th Century; Fairholt, F. W. (Ed.), Poems, Songs, etc., on George, Duke of Buckingham.

30. Deloney, T., Garland of Good-Will; Croker, T. C. (Ed.), Britannia's Pastorals; Black, W. H. (Ed.), Enterlude of John Bon and Mast Person.

Peregrine Pickle. T. Smollett. Leipzig, 1870. 2 v. in 1. 16°. . . . J,463
Pereira, J. Lectures on Polarized Light. London, 1854. 16°. . . . N,19
Père la Chaise, Promenade Philosoph. au. J. P. G. Viennet. Paris, 1855. 12°. H,866
Perfumer, Practical Guide for the. H. Dussauce. Philadelphia, 1868. 12°. N,232
Perfumes, Book of. E. Rimmel. London, 1865. 8°. . . . . H,447
Pericles and Aspasia. W. S. Landor. Philadelphia, 1839. 2 v. 8°. . H,151
The same. London, 1853. 8°. . . . . . . U,220,2
Peril and Suffering, Narratives of. R. A. Davenport. London, 1840. 2 v. 16°. I,637
Perils and Captivity. Edinburgh, 1827. 16°. . . . . . . . I,498
Perils of the Sea. New York, 1855. 18°. . . . . . . . . J,1217
Perilous Adventures. R. A. Davenport. New York, 1865. 16°. . . L,445
Periodical Literature, Index to. W. F. Poole. New York, 1853. 8°. . L.R.
Perkins, A. J. and Fitch, G. W. Origin of Geographical Names. N.Y. 1852. 18°. O,897
Perkins, C. C. Italian Sculptors. London, 1868. 4°. . . . *M,289
Tuscan Sculptors. London, 1864. 2 v. 4°. . . . . . *M,291
Perkins, E. E. Treatise on Gas and Ventilation. Philadelphia, 1856. 12°. M,602
Perkins, F. B. Charles Dickens; a Biography. New York, 1870. 12°. . D,415
Perkins, J. H. Annals of the West. Cincinnati, 1847. 8°. . . . C,273
Memoir and Writings; ed. by W. H. Channing. Cin. 1851. 2 v. 12°. C,846
Permian Fossils of England. W. King. London, 1850. 4°. . . . Q,31
Perpetual Curate. M. Oliphant. New York, 1865. 8°. . . . . K,868
The same. Leipzig, 1870. 2 v. in 1. 16°. . . . . J,401
Perry, A. L. Elements of Political Economy. New York, 1866. 8°. . O,515
Perry, M. C. U. S. Japan Expedition, 1852–54. Washington, 1856. 3 v. 4°. Q,413

Vol. 1. Hawks, F. L. Narrative of the Expedition.
2. Agriculture; Reports; Natural History.
3. Jones, G. Observations on the Zodiacal Light.

The same. Washington, 1856. 3 v. 4°. . . . . . P.D.
Perry, O. H., Life of. A. S. Mackenzie. New York, 1854. 2 v. 16°. . L,421
Inauguration of his Statue. Cleveland, 1861. 8°. . . . . C,173
Perry, W. S. Church of England and American Discovery. Portland, 1863. 8°. B,809,1
Persecutions of Popery. F. Shoberl. London, 1844. 2 v. 8°. . . P,621
Persia, Historical Account of. New York, 1854. 18°. . . . . L,388
History of. Sir J. Malcolm. London, 1815. 2 v. 4°. . . . F,238
History of Nadir Shah, Emperor of. J. Fraser. London, 1742. 8°. D,773
Mission to the Court of. Sir H. J. Brydges. London, 1834. 2 v. 8°. V,753
Northern, Journal of a Residence in. C. Stuart. London, 1854. 8°. V,752
Reise nach, und dem Lande der Kurden. M. Wagner. Leip. '52. 2v. 16°. E,213
Six Voyages into, 1670. J. B. Tavernier. London, 1678. f°. . . Q,247
Tour through. H. Southgate. New York, 1840. 2 v. 12°. . . V,646
Persian Language, English and Persian Vocabulary. Calcutta, 1800. 4°. L.R.
Persian War, Tale of the Great. G. W. Cox. London, 1861. 16°. . . A,132
Persius Flaccus, A. Satiræ Sex. Parisiis, 1830. 8°. . . . . . U,326,3
The same. Amsterdam, 1684. 8°. . . . . . . . U,416
Satires; translated by L. Evans. London, 1852. p. 8°. . . . L,65
The same; translated by Sir W. Drummond. N. Y. 1831. 18°. U,366
Persoz, J. F. Culture de la Vigne. Paris, 1849. 8°. . . . N,252,31

Persoz, J. F. Culture of the Vine. New York, 1858. 12°. . . . M,533,4
Perspective. G. Pyne. London, 1857. 12°. . . . . . . . . M,954
Elements of. J. Ruskin. New York, 1860. 12°. . . . . . M,69
Isometrical. J. Jopling. London, n. d. 8°. . . . . . . M,222
Manual of Linear. R. S. Smith. New York, 1857. 8°. . . M,110
Manual of Problems in Linear. S. E. Warren. New York, 1868. 8°. M,155
Perth Amboy, N. J., Early History of. W. A. Whitehead. N. Y. 1856. 8°. C,108
Perthes, C. T. Memoirs of Friedrich C. Perthes. Edinburgh, 1857. 2 v. 8°. D,531
Perthes, F. M. Life of Chrysostom. Boston, 1854. 12°. . . . . . D,744
Persuasion. J. Austen. Boston, 1863. 12°. . . . . . . . . K,596
Persuasives to Early Piety. J. G. Pike. New York, n. d. 18°. . P,746,10
Perty, M. Grundzüge der Ethnographie. Leipzig, 1859. 12°. . . . E,402
Peru, Chili, and Mexico, Voyage to. B. Hall. Edinburgh, 1826–7. 2 v. 16°. I,492,2,3
Conquest of. T. de Trueba y Cosio. Edinburgh, 1830. 16°. . . I,529
Conquest of, and Life of Pizarro. A. Helps. London, 1869. 12°. . D,703
Cuzco; a Journey. C. R. Markham. London, 1856. 8°. . . V,239
History of the Conquest of. W. H. Prescott. Boston, 1858. 2 v. 8°. C,389
Travels in. J. J. von Tschudi. New York, 1849. 12°. . . . V,236
Visit to. C. C. Bowen. London, 1861. 8°. . . . . . V,1086,1
Wanderungen durch. G. Byam. Dresden, 1852. . . . . . E,170
Peruvian Antiquities. M. E. de Rivero and J. J. Tschudi. N. Y. 1853. 8°. C,390
The same. Cincinnati, 1854. 12°. . . . . . . V,240
Pestalozzi, J. H. and his Plan of Education. E. Biber. London, 1831. 8°. D,527
and Pestalozzianism. H. Barnard. New York, 1862. 8°. . O,1216,6
Leonard and Gertrude. London, 1825. 2 v. 8°. . . . . . G,214
Life and System of. K. von Raumer. London, 1855. 8°. . . O,1010
Life and Character of. H. Krüsi. Boston, 1854. 12°. . . O,820,24
Sämmtliche Schriften. Stuttgart, 1819–26. 15 v. 8°. . . . E,340

Bd. 1-4. Lienhard and Gertrud.
5. Wie Gertrud ihre Kinder lehrt.
6. An die Unschuld, den Ernst, und den Edelmuth meines Vaterlands.
7. Meine Nachforschungen über den Gang der Natur in der Entwicklung des Menschengeschlechts; Ueber Gesetzgebung und Kindermord.
8. Ueber Gesetzgebung und Kindermord.
9. Vermischte Schriften, pädagogischen Inhalts.
10. Figuren zu meinem A B C-Buch.
11. Ansichten und Erfahrungen, die Idee der Elementarbildung betreffend; Zustand meiner pädagogischen Bestrebungen und Organisation meiner Anstalt, 1820; Einige meiner Reden.
12. Christoph und Else, zweistes Volksbuch.
13. Pestalozzi's Schwanengesang.
14. Praktische Elementarübungen.
15. Praktische Elementarbüngen; Rede an die Helevetische. Gesellschaft, 26 Apr. 1826.

Peter the Great, History of. J. Abbott. New York, 1865. 16°. . J,1394
Life of. Sir J. Barrow. London, 1861. 16°. . . . . . . I,626
The same. London, 1854. 16°. . . . . . . . . L,386
History of. S. H. Bradford. New York, 1865. 12°. . . . J,1357
Peter of Blois and Ingulphus. Chron. of Abbey of Croyland. Lon. 1854. p. 8°. L,13
Peter, W. Poets and Poetry of Greece and Rome. Philadelphia, 1848. 8°. U,445
Peter Parley, *pseud.* See *Goodrich, S. G.*
Peter Schlemihl's Wundersame Geschichte. A. v. Chamisso. Berl. 1864. 16°. E,317,2
Peter Simple. F. Marryat. New York, 1869. 12°. . . . . . . K,848
The same. Leipzig, 1842. 16°. . . . . . . . . J,360
Petermann, A. H. Geographische Mittheilungen. Gotha, 1855–67. 14 v. 4°. E,205
Peters, A., *E. von Taura.* Ring der Kaiserin. Leipzig, n. d. 2 v. in 1. 16°. G,502
Die Witkowetze. Wein, 1863. 3 v. 24°. . . . . . . G,503

Peters, A. Záwis von Rosenberg, Historischer Roman. Prag, 1860. 3 v. 24°. G,504
Peterson, C. J. Military Heroes of the Revolution. Philadelphia, 1848. 8°. C,686
Military Heroes of the War of 1812. Philadelphia, 1848. 8°. . C,687
Peterson, E. History of Rhode Island. New York, 1853. 8°. . . C,78
Petheram, J. Historical Sketches of Anglo-Saxon Literature. Lond. 1840. 8°. H,744
Peto, Sir S. M. Resources and Prospects of America. New York 1866. 16°. V,102
Petöfi, A., Translations from. J. Bowring. London, 1866. 16°. . . G,40
Petrarca, F. Gedichte. Berlin, 1855. 16°. . . . . . . . . E,288
Life of. T. Campbell. Philadelphia, 1841. 8°. . . . . . D,741
S. Dobson. London, 1838. 8°. . . . . . . . . C,596
Sonnets, Triumphs, and other Poems. London, 1859. p. 8°. . . L,134
Petrarch. See *Petrarca, F.*
Petrefacten-Buch. F. A. Schmidt. Stuttgart, 1846. 4°. . . . . . G,848
Petrefactions and their Teachings. G. A. Mantell. London, 1851. p. 8°. L,306
Die Versteinerungen. E. A. Rossmässler. Leipzig, 1853. 8°. . G,890
Petronel. F. Church. Leipzig, 1870. 2 v. in 1. 16°. . . . . . J,351
Petronius Arbiter, T. Satyricon; tr. by R. B. Sheridan. Lond. 1854. p. 8°. L,75
Pettenkofer, D. M. Chemie, Physiologie, und Pathologie. München, 1848. 4°. N,252,41
Pettigrew, T. J. Chronicles of the Tombs; Epitaphs. London, 1857. p. 8°. L,6
Pettus, Sir J. Essays on Metallic Words. London, 1686. f°. . . Q,294
Peveril of the Peak. Sir W. Scott. Boston, 1858. 2 v. 16°. . . . K,943
The same. Philadelphia, 1852. 8°. . . . . . . K,968
The same. Philadelphia, 1869. 8°. . . . . . K,1111
Pfarrhaus zu Hallungen. L. Storch. Berlin, 1851. 16°. . . . . G,485
Pfeiffer, I. Journey to Iceland, Sweden, and Norway. New York, 1852. 12°. V,15
Lady's Voyage round the World. London, 1862. p. 8°. . . I,660
The same. London, n. d. 12°. . . . . . . V,1062
Lady's Second Journey round the World. New York, 1856. 12°. V,1068
Last Travels. New York, 1861. 12°. . . . . . . . . V,809
Visit to the Holy Land, Egypt, and Italy. London, 1853. 12°. V,1044
Pfister, J. C. von. Geschichte der Teutschen. Hamburg, 1829–35. 5 v. 8°. E,48
Pflanze und ihr Leben. M. J. Schleiden. Leipzig, 1854. 8°. . . . G,896
Phædrus. Fables; construed into English. London, 1847. 12°. . . U,399
The same; translated by C. Smart. London, 1853. p. 8°. . L,86
Fabulæ Æsopiæ. Parisiis, 1826. 2 v. 8°. . . . . . . U,336
Phœnixiana. G. H. Derby. New York, 1869. 12°. . . . . . . H,68
Phantasmata; or, Illusions and Fanaticisms. R. R. Madden. Lond.'57. 2 v. 8°. H,506
Phantastes; a Faerie Romance. G. MacDonald. London, 1858. 12°. K,1102
Phantom Ship. F. Marryat. New York, 1868. 12°. . . . . . . K,849
Pharmaceutische Waarenkunde. N. J. B. G. Guibourt. Nürnb. 1823–24. 12°. G,754
Pharmacy, Centigrade Testing in. J. J. Griffin. n. t. p. 8°. . . N,252,50
Phelan, M. Game of Billiards. New York, 1865. 12°. . . . . M,336
Phelps, A. H. L. Fireside Friend; or, Female Student. N. Y. 1847. 12°. O,1144
Phelps and Gorham's Purchase, History of. O. Turner. Rochester, 1851. 8°. C,145
Phelps, C. A. Life and Services of Ulysses S. Grant. Boston, 1868. 12°. C,1001
Phelps, E. S. Gates Ajar. Boston, 1869. 12°. . . . . . . . . K,231
Gypsy Breynton Series. Boston, 1869. 4 v. 16°. . . . . J,1235
Vol. 1. Gypsy Breynton. 2. Gypsy's Cousin Joy. 3. Gypsy's Sowing and Reaping. 4. Gypsy's Year at the Golden Crescent.
Hedged in. Boston, 1870. 12°. . . . . . . . . . . . K,232

Phelps, E. S. Men, Women, and Ghosts. Boston, 1869. 12°. . . . . K,228
Silent Partner. Boston, 1871. 12°. . . . . . . . . . K,227
Phelps, Mrs. E. S. Sunnyside Series. New York, 1869. 18°. . . J,1399
Vol. 1. Sunnyside. Vol. 2. Peep at Number Five. Vol. 3. Tell-Tale.
Phelps, E. W. Bee-Keeper's Chart. New York, 1856. 12°. . . M,533,3
Phelps, R. H. History of Newgate of Connecticut. Albany, 1860. 4°. . C,77
Phelps, W. D. Fore and Aft; Life of an Old Sailor. Boston, 1871. 16°. J,1338
Phemie's Temptation. M. G. Terhune. New York, 1870. 12°. . . . K,332
Phenomena of Nature. H. G. Bell. Edinburgh, 1827. 16°. . . . I,499
Philadelphia and its Manufactures. E. T. Freedley. Philadelphia, 1858. 12°. M,624
History of. Philadelphia, 1839. 8°. . . . . . . . . . C,112
Philadelphia Mercantile Library, Catalogue of, 1870. Phil. 1870. 8°. . L.R.
Additions from 1850 to 1856. Philadelphia, 1856. 8°. . . L.R.
Catalogue of, 1850. Philadelphia, 1850. 8°. . . . . . . L.R.
Philbrick, J. D. American Union Speaker. Boston, 1869. 12°. . O,1243
Philip, Adventures of. W. M. Thackeray. Philadelphia, 1866. 12°. K,1026
The same. Leipzig, 1862. 2 v. in 1. 16°. . . . . . J,478
Philip Augustus; or, The Brothers in Arms. G. P. R. James. N.Y. 1855. 12°. K,733
Philip, A. P. W. Treatise on Indigestion. Philadelphia, 1825. 8°. . . L,890
Philip, King, History of. J. S. C. Abbott. New York, 1857. 16°. . J,1406
Philip of Macedon and Frederick the Great. C. D. Yonge. Lond. 1858. 12°. C,486
Philip II. of Spain. C. Gayarré. New York, 1866. 8°. . . . . B,475
History of the Reign of. W. H. Prescott. Boston, 1858–9. 3 v. 8°. B,476
R. Watson. London, 1839. 8°. . . . . . . . B,474
The same. London, 1777. 2 v. 4°. . . . . . B,573
Philip III. of Spain, History of Reign of. R. Watson. London, 1783. 4°. F,224
Philip, R. K. History of Progress in Great Britain. London, 1859. 8°. . B,32
Philip van Artevelde. H. Taylor. London, 1864. 12°. . . . . . I,445
Philippi, R. A. Conchyliologie und Malacozoologie. Halle, 1853. 8°. . G,922
Philippines, Twenty Years in. P. de La Gironière. London, 1865. p. 8°. I,657
Philleo, C. W. Twice Married; a Story of Connecticut Life. Phil. 1855. 12°. K,1100
Phillips, C. Curran and his Contemporaries. New York, 1854. 12°. . D,440
Speeches. London, 1822. 8°. . . . . . . . . . H,798
Phillips, E. Dictionary of the English Language. London, 1720. f°. . L.R.
Phillips, G. F. Painting in Water-Colors. London, 1838. 4°. . . . Q,197
Phillips, G. S. Gypsies of the Dane's Dike. Boston, 1864. 12°. . . K,891
Memoirs of William Wordsworth. London, 1852. 12°. . . C,1225
Phillips, H., jr. Discussion of the Maine Temperance Law. 1852. 8°. B,809,1
Phillips, J. Manual of Geology. London, 1855. 8°. . . . . . N,758
Palæozoic Fossils of Cornwall, Devon. London, 1841. 8°. . . N,825
Treatise on Geology. London, 1837. 12°. . . . . . M,1040
Phillips, J. A. Properties of the Carbonates of Lead. London, n. d. 8°. N,252,50
Metals and Alloys known to the Ancients. London, n. d. 8°. . N,252,44
Mining and Metallurgy of Gold and Silver. London, 1867. 8°. . M,724
Phillips, W. Conquest of Kansas by Missouri. Boston, 1856. 12°. . . C,313
Phillips, W. Introduction to Mineralogy. London, 1852. 8°. . . . N,856
Phillips, W. Speeches, Lectures, and Letters. Boston, 1871. 8°. . . H,816
Philo; an Evangeliad. S. Judd. Boston, 1850. 12°. . . . . . . I,63
Philo Judæus. Works; translated by C. D. Yonge. Lond. 1854–5. 4 v. p. 8°. L,30
Philobiblion, The; Bibliographical Journal. New York, 1862–63. 2 v. 4°. L.R.

Philological Essays. T. H. Key. London, 1868. 8°. . . . . . . L,550
Philological Grammar. W. Barnes. London, 1854. 8°. . . . . . L,527
Philology and Ethnography of U. S. Expl. Exped. H. Hale. Phil. 1846. 4°. *Q,281
Comparative, Elements of. R. G. Latham. London, 1862. 8°. . L,574
Outlines of. M. Schele de Vere. New York, 1853. 12°. . L,505
Modern. B. W. Dwight. New York, 1859. 8°. . . . . . L,532
Philosopher, Entertaining. W. M. Higgins. London, 1844. 16°. . . N,66
Philosophers and Actresses. A. Houssaye. New York, 1852. 2 v. 12°. . C,575
Lives of Ancient. F. de S. de La M. Fénélon. N. Y. 1854. 18°. . L,432
of the Time of George III. H. Brougham. London, 1855. 12°. . C,542
Philosophical Unbeliever, Letters to. J. Priestley. Birmingham, 1787. 8°. U,294,15
Philosophical Writers, Essays on. T. De Quincey. Boston, 1854. 2 v. 16°. H,420
Philosophy. Sir W. Hamilton; edited by O. W. Wight. N. Y. 1854. 8°. O,663
and Literature, Discussions on. Sir W. Hamilton. N. Y. 1853. 8°. O,705
and Theology, Studies in. J. Haven. Andover, 1869. 12°. . . O,678
Beiträge zur Geschichte der Philosophie. J.F.Fries. Heidel. 1819. 12°. G,550
Biographical History of. G. H. Lewes. New York, 1857. 2 v. 8°. O,670
The same, 3d edition. London, 1867. 2 v. 8°. . . . O,737
Deutsche Philosophie, Art, und Kunst. J. F. Fries. Heidel. 1812. 16°. G,557
Elements of. L. Oken. London, 1847. 8°. . . . . . . O,299
Examination of Sir W. Hamilton's. J. S. Mill. Boston, 1865. 2 v. 8°. O,658
Examination of J. S. Mill's. J. M'Cosh. New York, 1866. 8°. . O,701
Fontenelle; ou, Philos. Moderne. M.J.P. Flourens. Par. 1847. 16°. N,252,38
Fundamental. J. Balmes. New York, 1856. 2 v. 12°. . . . S.C.
Heathen, compared with Revelation. J. Priestley. Northum. 1804. 8°. U,294,3
History of. W. Enfield. London, 1791. 2 v. 4°. . . . . . Q,284
translated from the French by C. S. Henry. N.Y. 1841. 2 v. 18°. L,434
A. Schwegler; translated by J. H. Seelye. N. Y. 1866. 12°. . O,653
W.G. Tennemann; translated by A. Johnson. Lond. 1852. p. 8°. L,255
History of Ancient. W. A. Butler. Philadelphia, 1857. 2 v. 8°. O,662
History of Modern. V. Cousin. New York, 1854. 2 v. 8°. . . O,671
Intellectual. H. Winslow. Boston, 1850. 12°. . . . . . . O,708
in Sport. J. A. Paris. London, 1857. 8°. . . . . . . N,70
Inductive, Spirit of. B. Powell. London, 1855. 8°. . . . O,676
Mediæval. F. D. Maurice. London, 1857. p. 8°. . . O,637,3
Moral and Metaphysical. F. D. Maurice. London, 1854–7. 3 v. p. 8°. O,637
Moral. G. Combe. New York, 1840. 18°. . . . . . . O,709
and Political. W. Paley. London, 1845. 8°. . . P,709,2
Elementary Sketches of. S. Smith. New York, 1850. 12°. . O,719
Elements of. H. Winslow. New York, 1856. 12°. . . O,718
New System of. H. Spencer. New York, 1865. 12°. . . . O,656
of the Human Mind. D. Stewart. Boston, 1855. 12°. . . . O,651
of Life and Language. F. von Schlegel. London, 1866. p. 8°. . L,229
The same. New York, 1855. 12°. . . . . . . . O,696
of History. G. W. F. Hegel. London, 1861. p. 8°. . . . L,249
of the Moral Feelings. J. Abercombie. New York, 1854. 16°. . L,380
of Necessity. C. Bray. London, 1841. 2 v. 8°. . . . . O,682
of the Plays of Shakespeare. D. Bacon. Boston, 1857. 8°. . . I,868
of Ragged Schools. London, 1851. 16°. . . . . . . O,1123
of the Sciences. A. Comte. London, 1853. p. 8°. . . . . . L,289

Philosophy of Teaching. N. Sands. New York, 1869. 8°. . . . . O,956
Positive. A. Comte; tr. by H. Martineau. New York, 1853. 2 v. 12°. O,661
Positive of A. Comte. J. S. Mill. Boston, 1866. 8°. . . . . O,627
Recent British. D. Masson. New York, 1866. 12°. . . . . O,695
Résumés Philosophiques. P. L. Lezaud. Paris, 1853. 12°. . . O,615
Skeptical, Examined. B. P. Aydelott. Cincinnati, 1868. 16°. . P,228
Science and Religion. J. Bascom. New York, 1871. 12°. . . P,214
Speculative, from Kant to Hegel. H. M. Chalybäus. Andover, 1854. 8°. O,619
View of Speculative Philosophy of Europe. J. D. Morell. N.Y. '51. 8°. O,692
Vocabulary of. W. Fleming. London, 1858. 16°. . . . O,616
The same. Philadelphia, 1860. 8°. . . . . . . . O,617
Philostorgius, Ecclesiastical History; epit. by Photius. Lond. 1855. p. 8°. L,32
Phineas Finn. A. Trollope. New York, 1868. 8°. . . . . . K,1050
The same. Leipzig, 1869. 3 v. 16°. . . . . . . J,503
Phips, Sir W., Life of. E. Pond. Boston, 1870. 12°. . . . . D,8,5
Life of. F. Bowen. New York, 1860. 16°. . . . . . C,860,7
Phipson, T. L. Meteors, Aerolites, and Falling Stars. London, 1867. 12°. N,267
Phonetic Society of Great Britain. London, 1850. 32°. . . . . L,661
Phonography; or, Writing by Sound. I. Pitman. London, 1840. 8°. . L,694
American Manual of. E. Longley. Cincinnati, 1853. 12°. . . L,688
American Phonetic Journal. Cincinnati, 1855–58. 5 v. in 2. 8°. . L,727
American Phonographic Journal, v. 1, 2. Philadelphia, 1848–49. 18°. L,717
Bath Fables. S. Wilson. Lundun, 1850. 24°. . . . . . L,663
Book of Psalms in Short-Hand. London, 1853. 16°. . . . L,670
in Phonetic Short-Hand. B. Pitman. Cincinnati, n. d. 16°. L,670
Buc ov Izaa. Lundun, 1849. 24°. . . . . . . . . L,659
Carliz Hous. A. J. Ellis. Lundun, 1848. 18°. . . . . L,672
Childhod Ourz. E. V. Burns. Sinsinati, 1850. 18°. . . . L,667
Child's Transition Book. Boston, 1851. 16°. . . . . . . L,665
Complete Phonographer. J. E. Munson. New York, 1868. 12°. . L,693
Discorsez ov our Lord. Lundun, 1850. 32°. . . . . . . L,661
Divin and Moral Sonz. I. Watts. Lundun, 1849. 18°. . . . L,673
Esa on Man. A. Pope. Sinsinati, 1851. 24°. . . . . . . L,662
Exercises in. I. Pitman. London, 1849. 8°. . . . . . . L,718
Ferst Ideaz ov Relijun. A. J. Ellis. Lundun, 1849. 18°. . . L,673
Ferst Buc in Fonetic Redin. Lundun, 1849. 18°. . . . . L,673
Fonetic Advocat, v. 2. Sinsinati, 1850. 8°. . . . . . L,728
Fonetic Almanac, 1849, 51, 52. Lundun, 1849–52. 32°. . . . L,661
Fonetic Frend; a Munthly Jurnal. A. J. Ellis. Lundun, 1850. 12°. L,715
Fonetic Nuz; no. 1–15. n. t. p. 1°. . . . . . . . . Q,385
Fonetic Primer. n. t. p. 12°. . . . . . . . . . L,675
Fonografic Techer; an Esa. Lundun, 1847. 18°. . . . . L,668
Fonografic Correspondent, v. 2–10. Lundun, 1845–55. 8° and 16°. . L,710
Fonografic Magazen, 1849, 50. Lundun, 1849–50. 6 v. 18°. . . L,707
Fonografic Reporter, v. 1–4. Lundun, 1849–52. 4 v. 18°. . . L,711
Fonografic Star. Lundun, 1845–50. 6 v. 18°. . . . . L,708
Furst Fonetic Redur. Sinsinati, 1851. 16°. . . . . . . L,675
Guide to Phonetic Reading. Cincinnati, 1850. 16°. . . . L,675
Hand-Book of American. A. J. Graham. New York, 1852. 12°. . L,692

Phonography, History of Short-Hand. B. Pitman. Cincinnati, 1856. 12°. L,678
Lessons in. Sinsinati, 1850. 18°. . . . . . . . . . L,671
Manual of. B. Pitman. Cincinnati, 1855. 12°. . . . . L,686
The same. Cincinnati, 1867. . . . . . . . . . L,689
Manual of. I. Pitman. London, 1848. . . . . . . . L,718
The same. London, 1852. 18°. . . . . . . . L,719
The same. London, 1858. 18°. . . . . . . . L,668
Mirakelz ov our Lord. Lundun, 1853. 32°. . . . . . . L,661
Muni-Getin and Muni-Spendin. L. A. Hine. Sinsinati, 1854. 32°. L,664
Olmanac ov Olmanacs. A. J. Ellis. Lundun, n. t. p. . . . L,661
Phonetic Journal, 1848. London, 1848. 8°. . . . . . . L,824
The same; 1852–61. London, 1852–61. 9 v. 8°. . . . L,825
Phonetic Script Alphabet. n. t. p. . . . . . . . . . L,658
Phonographic and Pronouncing Vocab. I. Pitman. Lond. 1850. 16°. L,676
Phonographic Class-Book. S. P. Andrews and A. F. Boyle. . . L,690
Phonographic Correspondent, v. 2, 3. Bath, 1845–46. 8°. . L,710,2,3
edited by I. Pitman. Lond. 1847–55. 9 v. 18°. . . L,710,4–12
Phonographic Instructor. J. C. Booth. Philadelphia, 1850. 18°. . L,671
I. Pitman. London, 1852. 18°. . . . . . . . L,719
Phonographic Journal, v. 3. Bath, 1843–44. 8°. . . . . . L,726
Phonographic Magazine, 1849–50. London, 1849–50. 16°. . . L,707
The same; 1854, 55, 56, 58, 59. Cincinnati, 1854–59. 5 v. 12°. L,723
Phonographic Phrase-Book. T. A. Reed. London, 1855. 16°. . L,668
Phonographic Reader. S. P. Andrews and A. F. Boyle. N.Y.1848. 12°. L,691
Phonographic Reporter, v. 1–3. Cincinnati, 1854–55. 3 v. 12°. . L,712
Phonographic Star. London, 1845–46. 2 v. 12°. . . . . . L,708
Phonographic Teacher. E. Webster. New York, 1852. 16°. . L,685
Phonotypic Journal, v. 2–6, 8–10. London and Bath, 1844–60. 8°. . L,716
Phrase-Book; in Phonetic Short-Hand. B. Pitman. Cin. 1859. 12°. L,684
Plowshare and American Reporter. H. M. Parkhurst. Wash. 1853. 18°. L,674
Reporter's Assistant. R. Patterson. Philadelphia, 1849. 12°. . L,671
Reporter's Companion. I. Pitman. London, 1849. . . . . L,718
The same. London, 1853. 18°. . . . . . . L,719
B. Pitman. Cincinnati, n. d. 12°. . . . . . . . L,687
Reporter's Manual and Vocab. B. Pitman and Prosser. Cin. 1854. 12°. L,677
Reporterz Magazen. Lundun, 1847–48. 18°. . . . . . . L,709
Romanic Ecsersizez. A. J. Ellis. Lundun, 1849. 18°. . . . L,672
Romanic Redin Ecpland. A. J. Ellis. Lundun, 1849. 18°. . . L,672
Secund Fonetic Redur. Sinsinati, 1852. 16°. . . . . . . L 675
Selekt Dialogz for Children. Sinsinati, 1855. 18°. . . . . . L,675
Stenographic Short-Hand. I. Pitman. London, 1837. 24°. . . L,668
Teacher of. B. Pitman. Cincinnati, 1856. 12°. . . . . . L,680
Tecerz Gid to the Fonetic Primer. Lundun, 1848. 18°. . . . L,673
Te Samz ov David in Meter. Lundun, 1850. 12°. . . . . . P,1
Thousend Jemz ov Thot. Lundun, 1850. 32°. . . . . . L,660
Wa to Welth. B. Franklin. Lundun, 1850. 18°. . . . . . L,673
Weekli Fonetic Advocat, Supplement to. Sinsinati, 1851. 8°. . . L,728
What is Phonography? W. T. Coggeshall. n. t. p. . . . . L,675
Writing and Spelling Reform. J. Hogg. London, 1849. 32°. . L,661
Phosphates and Phosphoric Acid. T. Graham. London, 1833. 4°. . N,252,57

Photogenic Drawing. L. J. M. Daguerre. London, 1839. 16°. . . N,252,38
Photographic Manipulation. L. Price. London, 1858. 8°. . . . M,616
Photographic Optics. D. von Monckhoven. London, 1867. 12°. . . N,26
Photographs, Directions for making. J. H. Croucher. Phila. 1853. 12°. . M,613
Photography. G. C. H. Halleur and F. Schubert. London, 1854. 12°. . M,928
Dictionary of; edit. by T. Sutton and G. Dawson. Lond. 1867. 16°. M,727
Popular Treatise on. D. von Monckhoven. London, 1867. 12°. . M,853
Practice of. P. H. Delamotte. London, 1856. 12°. . . . . M,684
Treatise on. G. Le Gray. Philadelphia, 1853. 12°. . . . . M,613
N. P. Lerebours. London, 1843. 12°. . . . . . . M,615
C. Waldack. Cincinnati, 1865. 12°. . . . . . . M,614
Phrase and Fable, Dictionary of. E. C. Brewer. Philadelphia, n. d. 12°. L.R.
Phrenology and Mesmerism. N. L. Rice. New York, 1849. 12°. . . L,960
Considerations on. J. S. Hodgson. London, 1839. 12°. . . O,1033
Self-Instructor in. O. S. and S. N. Fowler. New York, 1856. 12°. L,894
Phreno-Mnemotechnic Dictionary. F. Fauvel-Gouraud. N. Y. 1844. 8°. L.R.
Physic and Chirurgery. Sir K. Digby. London, 1675. 16°. . . . L,835
Physical and Celestial Mechanics. B. Pierce. Boston, 1855. 4°. . M,1081
Physical Education, Thoughts on. C. Caldwell. Boston, 1834. 12°. . O,1132
Physical Forces, Correlation of. W. R. Grove. London, 1846. 8°. . N,252,33
and Conservation of. E. L. Youmans. New York, 1865. 12°. N,77
and Continuity of. W. R. Grove. London, 1867. 8°. . . N,86
Physical Geography. D. T. Ansted. Philadelphia, 1867. 8°. . . V,1118
A. Barrington. New York, 1851. 12°. . . . . . V,1122
E. Reclus. New York, 1871. 2 v. 8°. . . . . . V,1110
M. Somerville. Philadelphia, 1854. 12°. . . . . V,1134
R. M. Zornlin. Boston, 1855. 16°. . . . . . . . P,288
and Intermediate. J. Monteith. New York, 1867. 4°. . . . Q,187
Class-Book of. W. Hughes. London, 1868. 16°. . . . . V,1129
W. Rhind. Edinburgh, 1854. 16°. . . . . . . . O,898
of the Sea. M. F. Maury. New York, 1855. 8°. . . . . V,1117
Outlines of. G. W. Fitch. New York, 1856. 12°. . . . . V,1120
Physical History of Mankind. J. C. Prichard. London, 1841–51. 5 v. 8°. N,429
Physical Life, Das Physische Leben. D. F. Eschricht. Kopenhagen, 1852. 8°. E,418
of Woman. G. H. Napheys. Philadelphia, 1871. 12°. . . . L,955
Physical Phenomena of Living Beings. C. Matteucci. London, 1847. 8°. L,876
Physical Sciences, the Basis of Technology. G. Wilson. Edinb. 1857. 8°. N,252,49
Connection of. M. Somerville. New York, 1853. 12°. . . . N,69
Cyclopædia of. J. P. Nichols. London, 1868. 8°. . . . . . M,793
Philosophie Moderne relative aux. M. J. P. Flourens. Par. 1847. 16°. N,252,38
Physikalische Studien. A. Tellkampf. Hannover, 1854. 8°. . . G,713
Physical Theory of Another Life. I. Taylor. New York, 1852. 12°. . P,82
Physician's Holiday; a Month in Switzerland. J. Forbes. Lond. 1852. 12°. V,423
Physician's Problems. E. Elam. Boston, 1869. 12°. . . . . . . L,870
Physicians, Lives of British. London, 1830. 16°. . . . . . . I,641
Physics and Chemistry in the Arts. B. H. Paul. London, 1856. 8°. N,252,44
and Meteorology, Principles of. J. Müller. London, 1847. 8°. . N,88
The same. Philadelphia, 1848. 8°. . . . . . . . N,90
Dissertationes Physicæ. C. von Linnæus. Lugd. Batav. 1749–85. 9 v. 8°. N,966
Chemie und Experimentalphysik. K. W. G. Kastner. Erl. 1850. 8°. N,252,33

Physics, Elements of. N. Arnott. London, 1864-65. 2 v. 8°. . . . . N,84
Force and Nature. C. F. Winslow. Philadelphia, 1869. 8°. . . N,87
Grundriss der Physik u. Meteorologie. J. Müller. Brschwg. 1850. 8°. G,725
illustrated, Appleton's. New York, 1856. 8°. . . . . . . Q,259
Lehrbuch der Cosmischen Physik. J. Müller. Braunschweig, 1856. 8°. G,704
Atlas dazu. Braunschweig, 1856. 4°. . . . . . . . G,705
Lehrbuch der Physik. W. Eisenlohr. Stuttgart, 1852. 8°. . . . G,721
und Meteorologie. J. Müller. Brschwg. 1852. 2 v. 8°. G,726
The same. Braunschweig, 1856-57. 3 v. 8°. . G,724
Philosophy of the Mechanics of Nature. Z. Allen. N. Y. 1852. 8°. N,85
Principles of. B. Silliman, jr. Philadelphia, 1867. 12°. . . . N,78
Reportorium der. H. W. Dove and L. Moser. Berlin, 1837-49. 8 v. 8°. G,674
Report of Committee of Royal Society. London, 1840. 8°. . N,252,33
Science for the School and Family. W. Hooker. N.Y. 1863-64. 2 v. 12°. N,226
Thèses de Chimie et de Physique. A. Cahours. Paris, 1845. 4°. N,252,41
See also *Natural Philosophy.*
Physiognomy, Comparative, Men and Animals. J.W. Redfield. N.Y. 1852. 8°. L,917
Essays on. J. C. Lavater. London, 1792-98. 3 v. in 5. 4°. . *Q,293
New; or, Signs of Character. S. R. Wells. New York, 1866. 8°. . N,421
Physiology, Analysis of. J. J. Reese. London, 1852. 8°. . . . . . L,941
and Calisthenics. C. E. Beecher. New York, 1856. 16°. . . L,861
and Hygiene, Elements of. T. H. Huxley and W. J. Youmans.
New York, 1868. 12°. . . . . . . . . . L,872
Animal and Vegetable. J. S. Bushnan. Philadelphia, 1854. 12°. . L,887
P. M. Roget. London, 1867. 2 v. 12°. . . . . L,281
applied to Health and Education. A. Combe. N. Y. 1851. 16°. . L,389
Chemie in ihrer Verhältnisse zur. D. M. Pettenkofer. Mün. 1848. 4°. N,252,41
Comparative. L. Agassiz and A. A. Gould. London, 1870. p. 8°. . L,271
des Stoffwechsels in Pflanzen u. Thieren. J. Moleschott. Erl. 1851. 8°. G,759
Essays on. J. Hunter. London, 1861. 2 v. 8°. . . . . . N,720
Geschichte des leiblichen Lebens. C. G. Carus. Stuttgart, 1851. 8°. E,415
Human. J. C. Dalton. Philadelphia, 1864. 8°. . . . . . L,962
R. Dunglison. Philadelphia, 1856. 2 v. 8°. . . . . . L,963
History of a Mouthful of Bread. J. Macé. New York, 1868. 12°. L,901
of Common Life. G. H. Lewes. Edinburgh, 1859-60. 2 v. 12°. . L,880
The same. Leipzig, 1866. 2 v. in 1. 16°. . . . . . J,293
of Marriage. W. A. Alcott. Boston, 1868. 12°. . . . . L,918
Physiologische Briefe für Gebildete. C. Vogt. Gieszen, 1854. 8°. . E,421
Primæ Lineæ Physiologiæ. A. v. Haller. Göttingæ, 1751. 16°. . L,839
Principles of Comparative. W. B. Carpenter. Philadelphia, 1854. 8°. L,961
Self-Instructor in. O. S. and L. N. Fowler. New York, 1856. 12°. L,894
Physiophilosophy, Elements of. L. Oken, M. D.; tr. G. A. Sulk. Lon. 1847. 8°. O,299
Phytologist; Botanical Miscellany. London, 1844-63. 13 v. 8°. . . R,36
Pianoforte, Æsthetik des Klavierspiels. A. Kullak. Berlin, 1861. 8°. . G,643
Compositionen für. J. Haydn. v. 2. n. t. p. 4°. . . . . *Q,193
Instruction Book. C. C. Spencer. London, 1851. 12°. . . . . M,961
Original Sonaten für. M. Clementi. Wolfenbüttel, n. d. 3 v. 4°. *Q,192
Sämmtliche Compositionen für. W. A. Mozart. Wolfen. n. d. 2 v. 4°. *Q,191
Sonaten für das. L. von Beethoven. Wolfenbüttel, n. d. 2 v. 4°. *Q,190
Piazza Tales. H. Melville. New York, 1856. 12°. . . . . . . J,640

Picciola. X. B. Saintine. Philadelphia, 1857. 12°. . . . . . . H,948
Pichegru, C., Campaigns of. M. David. London, 1796. 8°. . . . B,331
Pickell, J. Early Life of George Washington. New York, 1856. 8°. . C,907
Pickering, C. Geographical Distribu. of Animals and Plants. Bost. 1854. 4°. *Q,282
Races of Man. London, 1863. p. 8°. . . . . . . . . L,135
Pickering, J. Lexicon of the Greek Lexicon. Boston, 1857. 8°. . . L.R.
Vocabulary of Words peculiar to the U. S. Boston, 1816. 8°. . . L.R.
Pickering, J. Working Man's Political Economy. Cincinnati, 1847. 8°. . O,490
Pickering, T. Corresp. bet. J. Adams and W. Cunningham. Salem, 1824. 8°. H,836
Picket, A. Address at the Western Literary Institute. Cincin. 1836. 8°. H,302,4
Pickwick Papers. C. Dickens. New York, 1869. 12°. . . . . K,493
The same. Philadelphia, n. d. 8°. . . . . . . . K,516
The same. New York, 1871. 2 v. 12°. . . . . K,1141
The same. Leipzig, 1842. 2 v. in 1. 16°. . . . . J,134
Picrotoxin, Physiological Properties of. R. M. Glover. Edinb. 1851. 8°. N,252,44
Pictorial Field-Book of the Revolution. B. J. Lossing. N. Y. 1860. 2 v. 8°. B,751
of the War of 1812. B. J. Lossing. New York, 1865. 8°. . . B,874
Pictorial Gallery of Useful and Fine Arts. London, 1847. 2 v. f°. *Q,364
Picts, History of. H. Maule. Glasgow, 1820. 12°. . . . . B,111,1
Picture-Book, New. N. Bohny. Edinburgh, 1858. 8°. . . . *Q,199
Picture History of England. H. W. Dulcken. London, 1866. 4°. . . A,403
Pictures of Country Life. A. Cary. New York, 1866. 12°. . . . K,11
from Italy. C. Dickens. Leipzig, 1846. 16°. . . . . . . J,135
The same. New York, 1868. 12°. . . . . . . . K,470
of Early Life. E. C. Embury. New York, 1854. 16°. . . J,1200
of Heroes and Lessons from their Lives. Philadelphia, n. d. 12°. J,1376
of Private Life. S. S. Ellis. London, 1868. 3 v. 16°. . . . K,918
Picturesque, The. Sir U. Price. Edinburgh, 1842. 8°. . . . . M,354
compared with Sublime and Beautiful. Sir U. Price. Lon. 1810. 3 v. 8°. M,89
Picturesque Views. J. W. M. Turner and T. Girtin. London, 1854. 8°. *M,136
Pidgeon, E. Fossil Remains of the Animal Kingdom. London, n. d. 8°. N,802
Pidgeon, W. Traditions of the De-Coo-Dah. New York, 1858. 8°. . B,601
Piedmont, History of. A. Gallenga. London, 1855. 3 v. 12°. . . B,488
Pierce, F., Life of. N. Hawthorne. Boston, 1852. 16°. . . . C,1010
Pierce Penniless's Supplication to the Devil. T. Nash. London, 1842. 8°. I,885,12
Pierce, the Ploughman's Crede; 1384. London, 1867. 8°. . . L,605,30
Pierpont, J. American First Class-Book. New York, 1835. 12°. . . O,882
National Reader. Boston, 1832. 12°. . . . . . . O,1105
Pierre de Langtoft, Chronicle. London, 1866–68. 2 v. 8°. . . . W,197
Piers Plowman, Vision of. W. Langland. Vernon Text. Lond. 1867. 8°. L,605,28
The same; Crowley Text. London, 1869. 8°. . . L,605,38
The same, and Creed. London, 1856. 2 v. 16°. . . . I,380
Piesse, G. W. S. Laboratory of Chemical Wonders. London, 1860. 12°. N,184
Piesse, S. Chemical, Natural, and Physical Magic. London, 1865. 16°. . M,340
Is Selenium a true Element? London, 1842. 8°. . . . N,252,21
Pietas Londinensis; Public Charities of London. A. Highmore. Lon. 1810. 8°. O,418
Piety, Persuasives to Early. J. G. Pike. New York, n. d. 18°. . P,746,10
Pigeons. P. J. Selby. Edinburgh, n. d. 16°. . . . . . . N,470,9
and Rabbits. E. S. Delamer. London, 1866. 8°. . . . . N,626
Pike County Ballads and other Pieces. J. Hay. Boston, 1871. 8°. . . I,74

Pike, J. G. Guide for Young Disciples. New York, n. d. 18°. . P,476,11
Persuasives to Early Piety. New York, n. d. 18°. . . P,746,10
Pike, L. O. The English and their Origin. London, 1866. 8°. . . B,53
Pike, M. H. Ida May; a Story. Boston, 1854. 12°. . . . . K,364
Pike, S. J. M. Every Day. Boston, 1871. 12°. . . . . . K,216
Pike, Z. M., Life of. H. Whiting. Boston, 1860. 12°. . . . C,860,15
Pileur, A. le. Wonders of the Human Body. New York, 1870. 12°. M,1045
Pilgrim's Progress. J. Bunyan. Leipzig, 1855. 16°. . . . . J,55
The same; illustrated by C. Bennett. New York, 1866. 12°. K,615
and John Bunyan, Lectures on. G. B. Cheever. Glasgow, 1864. 12°. H,675
Pilgrim Fathers; Founders of New England. W.H. Bartlett. Lond. 1853. 8°. C,74
Pilgrimage of Adam and David. J. Gallaher. Cincinnati, 1846. 12°. . P,268
of the Sowle. G. de Guileville; ed. by K. I. Cust. London, 1859. 4°. Q,419
Pilgrims at Plymouth, Journal of the. G. B. Cheever. New York, 1848. 12°. C,3
Tribute to to the Memory of. J. Hawes. Hartford, 1830. 12°. . P,839
Pilgrims of the Rhine, and Falkland. Sir E. B. Lytton. Philad. n. d. 8°. K,826
Pilgrims' Sea Voyage, etc. London, 1867. 8°. . . . . . . L,605,25
Pilkington, M. General Dictionary of Painters. London, 1840. 8°. *M,94
The same. London, 1857. 8°. . . . . . . *M,108
Pillans, J. Contributions to the Cause of Education. London, 1856. 8°. O,1013
Principles of Elementary Teaching. Edinburgh, 1829. 12°. . O,1135
Rationale of Discipline. Edinburgh, 1852. 8°. . . . O,1234
Pillar of Fire; Israel in Bondage. J. H. Ingraham. Boston, 1865. 8°. . K,198
Pillars of Hercules. D. Urquhart. New York, 1850. 2 v. 12°. . . V,472
Pilot, The. J. F. Cooper. New York, 1866. 12°. . . . . . . K,42
The same. New York, 1859. 8°. . . . . . . . . K,70
Pilzkrankheit der Fliegen. H. Lebert. Stuttgart, n. d. 4°. . . . . G,956
Pimentel, F. Lenguas Indígenas de México. México, 1862–65. 2 v. 8°. *L,616
Pindar, Peter, *pseud.* See *Wolcott, J.*
Pindar, S. Fireside Fairies. New York, 1865. 16°. . . . J,1360
Legends of the Flowers. New York, 1865. 16°. . . . J,1362
Midsummer Fays. New York, 1865. 16°. . . . . J,1361
Pindarus. Odes; translated by F. A. Paley. London, 1868. 12°. . . U,455
The same; translated by D. W. Turner. London, 1852. 12°. L,71
The same; translated into English Prose. Oxford, 1824. 8°. U,458
and Anacreon; tr. A. Wheelwright and Bourne. N. Y. 1844. 16°. . U,370
Pink and White Tyranny; a Society Novel. H. B. Stowe. Bost. 1871. 16°. K,383
Pinkerton, J. Inquiry into the History of Scotland. Edinb. 1814. 2 v. 8°. B,116
Medals; Ancient and Modern Coins. London, 1808. 2 v. 8°. . M,387
Modern Geography. London, 1807. 3 v. 4°. . . . . . V,1142
Pinkerton, J. N. Sleep and its Phenomena. London, 1839. 16°. . . L,844
Pinkney, W., Life of. W. Pinkney. New York, 1853. 8°. . . C,1050
H. Wheaton. Boston, 1860. 12°. . . . . . . C,860,6
Pinneo, T. S. Analytical English Grammar. Cincinnati, 1850. 12°. O,1079
English Teacher. Cincinnati, 1852. 12°. . . . . . O,1078
Primary English Grammar. Cincinnati, 1849. 16°. . . . O,1064
Pinney, J. Influence of Occupation on Health. London, 1856. 8°. . . L,926
Pinney, N. Practical French Teacher. New York, 1849. 12°. . . L,805
Pinnock, W. Exercises in False Spelling. London, n. d. 24°. . . O,760
Pioneer; a Narrative of Experience. C. Giles. New York, 1844. 12°. . C,844

Pioneer, Autobiography of a. J. Young. Cincinnati, 1859. 8°. . . . . C,722
Pioneer Biography of Butler Co., O. J. Mac Bride. Cincinnati, 1869. 2 v. 8°. C,220
Pioneer History. S. P. Hildreth. Cincinnati, 1848. 8°. . . . . . C,270
Pioneer Life in Kentucky. D. Drake. Cincinnati, 1870. 8°. . . . . C,222
Pioneer Preacher. W. H. Milburn. New York, 1858. 12°. . . . P,101
Pioneer Settlers of Ohio. S. P. Hildreth. Cincinnati, 1852. 8°. . . C,710
Pioneer Women of the West. E. F. Ellet. New York, 1852. 12°. . . C,651
Pioneers, The. J. F. Cooper. New York, 1866. 12°. . . . . . K,43
The same. New York, 1870. 12°. . . . . . . K,20,4
The same. New York, 1859. 8°. . . . . . . . K,71
Pioneers and Founders in the Mission Field. C. M. Yonge. Lond. n. d. 12°. C,512
of France in the New World. F. Parkman. Boston, 1865. 8°. . B,618
Piozzi, H. L. Anecdotes of Samuel Johnson. London, 1856. p. 8°. I,661,3
Autobiography, Letters, and Literary Remains. Boston, 1861. 12°. D,207
Pique; a Novel. Boston, n. d. 12°. . . . . . . . . . . K,124
Pirate, The. Sir W. Scott. Boston, 1853. 2 v. 16°. . . . . . K,944
The same. Philadelphia, 1869. 8°. . . . . . K,1110
The same. Leipzig, 1846. 16°. . . . . . . . J,448
Pirate and Three Cutters. F. Marryat. London, 1867. p. 8°. . . . L,122
Pitcairn's Island and Mutiny of the Bounty. J. Barrow. N. Y. n. d. 18°. L,364
Pitman, B. Book of Psalms in Phonetic Short-Hand. Cincinnati, n. d. 12°. L,670
Fonografic Reporter, v. 1–4. Lundun, 1849–52. 4 v. 18°. . . L,711
History of Short-Hand. Cincinnati, 1856. 12°. . . . . . L,678
Illustrated Manners Book. Cincinnati, n. d. 12°. . . . . L,683
Manual of Phonography. Cincinnati, 1865. 12°. . . . . L,686
The same. Cincinnati, 1867. 12°. . . . . . . . L,689
Phonographic Magazine, 1854. 5 v. Cincinnati, 1859. 12°. . . L,723
Phonographic Reporter, v. 1–3. Cincinnati, 1854–56. 3 v. 12°. . L,712
Phrase-Book in Phonetic Short-Hand. Cincinnati, 1859. 12°. . L,684
Teacher of Phonography. Cincinnati, 1856. 12°. . . . . . L,680
and Prosser, R. P. Reporter's Manual and Vocabulary. Cin. 1854. 16°. L,677
Pitman, I. Exercises in Phonography. London, 1849. 8°. . . . . L,718
Manual of Phonography. London, 1848. . . . . . . . . L,718
The same. London, 1852. 18°. . . . . . . . L,719
The same. London, 1858. 18°. . . . . . . . L,668
Phonographic and Pronouncing Vocabulary. London, 1850. 16°. . L,676
Phonographic Instructor. London, 1852. 18°. . . . . . . L,719
Phonography; or, Writing by Sound. London, 1840. 8°. . . L,694
Reporter's Companion. London, 1849. . . . . . . . L,718
The same. London, 1853. 18°. . . . . . . . L,719
Stenographic Short-Hand. London, 1837. 24°. . . . . . L,668
(Ed.) Fonographic Correspondent. London, 1847–55. 9 v. 18°. L,710,4–12
Pitt, J. How to brew good Beer. London, 1864. 12°. . . . . . M,669
Pitt, W., *Earl of Chatham*, Anecdotes of. J. Almon. Lond. 1810. 3 v. 8°. D,385
Correspondence. London, 1838–40. 4 v. 8°. . . . . . . . D,79
Life of. T. B. Macaulay. New York, 1865. 16°. . . . . C,1180
Pitt, W., *Rt. Hon.*, and Francis Atterbury. T. B. Macaulay. Leip. 1860. 16°. J,338
Life of. G. Tomline. London, 1821. 2 v. 4°. . . . . . F,21
Speeches of. London, 1817. 3 v. 8°. . . . . . . . . H,791
Pittsburgh, Pa., History of. N. B. Craig. Pittsburgh, 1851. 12°. . . C,169

Pitts-Street Chapel Lectures. Boston, 1858. 12°. . . . . . . P,673
Pitture e Bronzi Antiche di Ercolano. Napoli, 1757–71. 7 v. f°. . . L.R.
Pius IX., Letters Apostolic of, considered. T. Twiss. London, 1851. 8°. P,824
Pizarro, Life of, and Conquest of Peru. A. Helps. London, 1869. 12°. . D,703
Place for Every Thing. A. B. Haven. New York, 1867. 16°. . . J,1333
Place in Thy Memory; Letters. S. H. De Kroyft. New York, 1858. 12°. H,115
Plague-Year in London, Journal of. D. De Foe. London, 1839. 16°. . I,612
The same. London, 1854. p. 8°. . . . . . . L,263,5
Plain-Dealing. T. Lechford; edited by J. H. Trumbull. Boston, 1867. 4°. F,64
Plain Talks on Familiar Subjects. J. G. Holland. New York, 1866. 12°. H,110
Plain Thoughts on the Art of Living. W. Gladden. Boston, 1868. 16°. . H,285
Plan of Union, etc. W. S. Kennedy. Hudson, O. 1856. 12°. . . . C,200
Planche, J. Dictonnaire Grec-Français Paris, 1824. 8°. . . . L.R.
Planché, J. R. Descent of the Danube. London, 1828. 8°. . . . V,431
History of British Costume. London, 1836. 16°. . . . . L,472
The same. London, n. d. 12°. . . . . . . . M,365
Planché, M. A. See *Mackarness, M. A.*
Planchette; or, The Despair of Science. E. Sargent. Boston, 1869. 12°. O,327
Planetary and Stellar Worlds. O. M. Mitchell. New York, 1859. 12°. . N,322
Planetary System. J. P. Nichol. London, 1854. 8°. . . . . . . N,328
Planets, Berechnung der Planetenstörungen. J. F. Encke. Berlin, 1851. 8°. G,779
Planimetrie und Stereometrie. C. Koppe. Essen, 1851. 8°. . . . E,431
Plant, The; a Biography. M. J. Schleiden. London, 1853. 8°. . N,1002
Phytochemie. F. Rochleder. Leipzig, 1854. 8°. . . . . G,764
Pflanze und ihr Leben. M. J. Schleiden. Leipzig, 1854. 8°. . . G,896
Plant-Hunters. M. Reid. Boston, 1866. 16°. . . . . . . J,1584
Planter's Daughter. A. E. Dupuy. Philadelphia, 1870. 12°. . . . K,459
Planter's Guide. Sir H. Stewart. Edinburgh, 1848. 8°. . . . . M,571
Planter's Northern Bride. C. L. Hentz. Philadelphia, n. d. 12°. . . K,168
Planting and Rural Ornament. W. Marshall. London, 1803. 2 v. 8°. . M,561
Planting the Wilderness. J. D. Mc Cabe. Boston, 1870. 16°. . . J,1612
Plants, Anatomie and Physiologie der Gewächse. H. Schacht. Berl. 1854. 8°. G,893
and Animals, Chem. Relations between. L. Playfair. Lond. n. d. 8°. N,252,14
Geographical Distribution of. C. Pickering. Bost. 1854. 4°. Q,282
Anorganische Bestandtheile der Pflanzen. A. F. Wiegmann und L. Polstorf. Braunschweig, 1842. 8°. . . . . . . N,252,6
Atlas der Pflanzengeographie. L. Rudolph. Berlin, 1864. 4°. . Q,131
Bastarderzeugung im Pflanzenreiche. C. F. v. Gärtner. Stutt. 1849. 8°. G,869
Bau und Leben der Gewächse. E. A. Rossmässler. Leipzig, 1854. 8°. G,890
Brandpilze und Krankheiten der. A. de Bary. Berlin, 1853. 8°. . G,851
Cultur der Handelsgewächse. F. W. Hofmann. Prag, 1845. 8°. . G,873
Entwickelung der Pflanzen. H. W. Dove. Berlin, 1846. 4°. . N,252,43
Erde, Pflanzen, und Mensch. J. F. Schouw. Leipzig, 1851. 8°. . G,712
Ernährung der Pflanze. W. Schumacher. Berlin, 1864. 8°. . . G,898
Flowering, and Ferns of Great Britain. A. Pratt. Lond. n. d. 5 v. 8°. N,1018
Distribution of, thro' Northumberland. N. J. Winch. Newc. 1825. 8°. N,252,44
Growth of, in Glazed Cases. N. B. Ward. London, 1852. 12°. . M,493
Grundzüge der Anatomie der Pflanzen. D. G. Kieser. Jena, 1815. 8°. G,876
Metamorphose der Pflanze. A. Wigand. Leipzig, 1846. 8°. . . G,901
Nahrung der Pflanzen. W. Engelhardt. Leipzig, 1856. 12°. . . G,867

Plants, Nanna; das Seelenleben der Pflanzen. G. T. Fechner. Leip. 1848. 16°. G,868
Natürliches Pflanzensystem. H. G. L. Reichenbach. Leip. 1850. 8°. G,967
of the Bible. G. H. Balfour. London, 1857. 8°. . . . . N,1026
of the United States, Genera of. A. Gray. New York, 1849. 2 v. 8°. N,1031
of the World and where they grow. C. Daubeny. Lond. 1865. 16°. N,912
Outlines of the Geography of. F. J. F. Meyen. London, 1846. 8°. O,298
Pflanze und ihr Leben. M. J. Schleiden. Leipzig, 1855. 8°. . . G,896
Pflanzen der Pfahlbauten. O. Heer. Zürich, 1865. 4°. . . . G,871
Pflanzendecke der Erde. L. Rudolph. Berlin, 1859. 8°. . . G,892
Atlas dazu. Berlin, 1864. obl. 4°. . . . . . . . . *Q,131
Pflanzenklimatologie. H. Hoffmann. Leipzig, 1857. 8°. . . G,874
Pflanzen Pathologie. F. J. F. Meyen. Berlin, 1841. 8°. . . G,883
Physiologie der Pflanzen u. Thiere. M. J. Schleiden. Brschwg, 1850. 8°. G,659
Popular Geography of. 1855. 16°. . . . . . . . . N,918
Posthumous Papers on. W. Griffith. Calcutta, 1851. 8°. . . N,981
Standortsgewächse Deutschlands. J. T. C. Ratzeburg. Berlin, 1859. 8°. G,887
Stoffwechsel in Pflanzen und Thieren. J. Moleschott. Erlan. 1851. 8°. G,759
under Domestication. C. Darwin. New York, 1868. 2 v. 12°. . N,504
Wardian Cases for. S. H. Ward. London, 1854. 12°. . . . M,493

Platen, A. von. Gesammelte Werke. Stuttgart, 1853–54. 5 v. in 3. 16°. E,347

Bd. 1. Biographie; Lieder und Romanzen; Balladen; Vermischte und Gelegenheitsgedichte.
2. Gaselen; Sonette; Oden; Eklogen und Idyllen; Festgesänge; Epigramme; Uebersetzungen.
3. Die neuen Propheten; Mathilde von Valois; Der gläserne Pantoffel; Berengar; Der Schatz des Rhampsinit; Der Thurm mit sieben Pforten; Treue um Treue.
4. Die verhängnissvolle Gabel; Der Romantische Oedipus; Die Liga von Cambrai; Parabase; Der grundlose Brunnen; Die grossen Kaiser; Die Abassiden; Rosensohn.
5. Das Theater als ein Nationalinstitut; Ueber verschiedene Gegenstände der Dichtkunst und Sprache; Geschichten des Königreichs Neapel; Ursprung der Carraresen und ihrer Herrschaft in Padua; Lebensregeln.

Platinum, Action on Gaseous Mixtures. W. Henry. London, 1824. 4°. N,252,42
Chemie des Platins. J. W. Döbereiner. Stuttgart, 1836. 8°. . N,252,5
New Metal found in Crude. W. H. Wollaston. London, 1804. 4°. N,252,42
Two Metals found after solution of. S. Tennant. Lond. 1804. 4°. N,252,42

Plato against the Atheists; edited by T. Lewis. New York, 1855. 12°. . U,407
and other Companions of Socrates. G. Grote. London, 1865. 3 v. 8°. D,777
Gorgias; edited by T. D. Woolsey. Boston, 1856. 12°. . . . U,408
Opera; edited by I. Bekker et al. London, 1826. 11 v. 8°. . . U,469
Works; tr. by H. Cary, H. Davis, and G. Barges. Lond. 1851–4. 6 v. p. 8°. L,72

Vol. 1. Apology of Socrates; Crito, or, the Duty of a Citizen; Phædo, or, the Immortality of the Soul; Gorgias, or, on Rhetoric; Protagoras, or, the Sophists; Phædrus, or, the Beautiful; Theætetus, or, on Science; Euthyphron, or, on Holiness; Lysis, or, on Friendship.
2. The Republic; Timæus, on Nature; Critias.
3. Meno, or, respecting Virtue; Euthydemus, or, the vain Trifling of the Sophists; The Sophist; The Statesman; Cratylus, on the Rectitude of Names; Parmenides, or, on Idealities; The Banquet, or, on Love.
4. Philebus, on the Greatest Good; Charmides, on Temperance; Laches, or, on Fortitude; Menexemus, on Praise of the Slain in Battle; Hippias Major and Minor; Ion, on Poetry; First and Second Alcibiades, on Praying; Theages, on Political Wisdom.
5. The Laws.
6. Doubtful Works, attributed to Plato—Epinomis, or, the Philosopher; Axiochus, on Death; Eryxias, on Wealth; On Virtue; On Justice; Sisyphus, or, upon taking Counsel; Demodocus; Definitions; Treatise of Timæus, the Locrian, on the Soul of the World and Nature.
Lives of Plato by Diogenes Laertius, by Hesychius of Miletus, and by Olympiodorus; Introductions of Alcinous and Albinus to the Doctrines and Dialogues of Plato; Apuleius on the Doctrines of Plato; Other accounts of Plato; Index.

Plautus, M. A. Comœdiæ; cur. J. Naudet. Parisiis, 1830–32. 4 v. 8°. . U,337
The same; translated by H. T. Riley. London, 1852. 2 v. p. 8. L,73
Play and Study Series. H. N. Baker. Boston, 1869. 4 v. 16°. . J,1702
Vol. 1. Play and Study. 2. Motherless Children. Vol. 3. Howard and his Teacher. 4. Jack, the Chimney-Sweeper.
Played Out. A. Cudlip. Leipzig, 1867. 2 v. in 1. 16°. . . . . . J,108
Playfair, L. Chemical Relations of Plants and Animals. London, n. d. 8°. N,252,14
Playgoer, Journal of a London. H. Morley. London, 1866. 12°. . . I,709
Playground and the Parlor. A. Elliott. London, 1868. 8°. . . . M,341
Play-Hours and Half-Holidays. J. C. Atkinson. London, 1868. 8°. J,1378
Plays, Old, Select Collection of. J. Dodsley. London, 1870. 12 v. 8°. . I,737
Vol. 1. Prefaces; God's Promises, by J. Bale; The Four P's, by Heywood; Ferrex and Porrex, by T. Sackville; Damon and Pythias, by R. Edwards; New Custom.
2. Gammer Gurton's Needle; Alexander and Campaspe, by J. Lyly; Tancred and Gismunda, by R. Wilmot; Cornelia, by T. Kyd; Edward the Confessor, by C. Marlow.
3. George a Greene, the Pinner of Wakefield; First Part of Jeronymo; The Spanish Tragedy, by T. Kyd; Honest Whore, by T. Dekker.
4. The Malcontent, by J. Marston; All Fools, by G. Chapman; Eastward Hoe, by G. Chapman and others; Revenger's Tragedy, by C. Tourner; Dumb Knight, L. Machin.
5. Miseries of Enforced Marriage, by G. Wilkins; Lingua, by A. Brewer; Merry Devil of Edmonton; A Mad World, my Masters, by T. Middleton; Ram Alley, or, Merry Tricks, by L. Barry.
6. Roaring Girl, by T. Middleton and T. Dekker; Widow's Tears, by G. Chapman; White Devil, or, Vittoria Corombona, by J. Webster; The Hog hath lost his Pearl, by R. Tailor; The Four 'Prentices of London, by T. Heywood.
7. Green's tu quoque, or, the City Gallant, by J. Cooke; Albumazur, by Mr. Tomkis; A Woman Killed with Kindness, by T. Heywood; Match at Midnight, by W. Rowley; Fuimus Troes, the true Trojans, by J. Fisher.
8. 'Tis Pity she's a Whore, by J. Ford; The Heir, by T. May; The Bird in a Cage, by J. Shirley; Jew of Malta, by C. Marlow; The Wits, by Sir W. Davenant.
9. The Gamester, by J. Shirley; Microcosmus, by T. Nabbes; The Muse's Looking-Glass; by T. Randolph; The City Match, by J. Maine; The Queen of Arragon, by W. Habington.
10. The Antiquary, by S. Marmion; The Goblins, by Sir J. Suckling; The Ordinary, by W. Cartwright; The Jovial Crew, or, Merry Beggars, by R. Broome; The Old Couple, by T. May.
11. Andromana, or the Merchant's Wife, by J. Shirley; The Mayor of Quinborough, by T. Middleton; Grim, the Collier of Croydon; The City Night-Cap, by R. Davenport; The Parson's Wedding, by T. Killegrew.
12. Adventures of Five Hours, by Sir S. Tuke; Elvira, by G. Digby; The Widow, by B. Johnson and others; Historical Account of the English Stage, by J. Wright; Index.
Plea for the West. L. Beecher. Cincinnati, 1835. 12°. . . . . . O,987
Pleasant Cove Series. E. Kellogg. Boston, 1871. 16°. . . . J,1475
Vol. 1. Arthur Brown, the Young Captain. Vol. 2. Young Deliverers of Pleasant Cove.
Pleasant Memories of Pleasant Lands. L. H. Sigourney. Bost. 1856. 16°. H,275
Pleasantries about Courts and Lawyers. C. Edwards. New York, 1867. 12°. H,509
Pleasures of Taste and other Stories. J. Taylor. New York, 1847. 18°. J,1252
of the Imagination. M. Aikenside. Boston, 1854. 16°. . . . I,195
Pleiad, The; Evidences of Christianity. F. Wrangham. Edinb. 1828. 16°. I,508
Plinius Secundus, C. Hist. Naturalis; cur. C. Alexandre et al. Par. 1832. 11 v. 8°. U,339
The same; tr. by J. Bostock and Riley. Lond. 1855–7. 6 v. 8°. L,74
Plinius Cæcilius Secundus, C. Epistolæ et Panegyricus. Parisiis, 1823. 2 v. 8°. U,338
Letters. London, 1796. 2 v. 8°. . . . . . . . . U,256,7,8
Plot in Private Life. W. Collins. Leipzig, 1859. 16°. . . . . . J,80
Plowshare and American Reporter. H. M. Parkhurst. Wash. 1853. 18°. L,674
Plumer, W. Life of W. Plumer, jr. Boston, 1857. 8°. . . . . C,1053
Plunket, W. C., *Lord*. Speeches; with Memoir by J. C. Hoey. Dubl. 1867. 12°. H,778
Plurality of Worlds. W. Whewell; ed. by E. Hitchcock. Boston, 1861. 12°. N,273
Plutarch, British. London, 1776. 6 v. 12°. . . . . . . C,1188
Plutarchus. Plutarch's Lives; edited by A. H. Clough. Bost. 1859. 5 v. 8°. C,558

Plutarchus. Plutarch's Lives; ed. A. H. Clough; abridged. Lond. 1868. 12°. A,62
Plutarchi Vitæ; Græce et Latine. Parisiis, 1847–57. 2 v. 8°. . U,556
Plymouth and Massachusetts Bay, Governors of. J. B. Moore. N. Y. 1848. 8°. C,775
and the Pilgrims. J. Banvard. Boston, 1866. 16°. . . . . . C,17
History of. J. Thacher. Boston, 1835. 12°. . . . . . . C,5
Plymouth Colony, Founders of. J. Hunter. London, 1854. 8°. . . C,44
History of. F. Baylies. Boston, 1866. 2 v. 8°. . . . . . C,48
Plymouth Colony Records. Boston, 1855–59. 12 v. in 10. 4°. . . . F,86
Plymouth Plantation, History of; ed. by C. Deane. W. Bradford. Bost. 1856. 8°. C,61
Journal of; Mourt's Relation; ed. by H. M. Dexter. Bost. 1865. 4°. F,67
Plymouth Pulpit, Notes from. H. W. Beecher. New York, 1859. . . P,56
Pneumatics. D. Lardner. Philadelphia, 1854. 12°. . . . . . . N,79,1
C. Tomlinson. London, 1858–59. 12°. . . . . . . M,970
and Hydrostatics. D. Lardner. London, 1831. 12°. . . M,1022
Poacher, The. F. Marryat. New York, 1868. 12°. . . . . . . K,850
Pocock, E., Life of. L. Twells. London, 1816. 8°. . . . . . C,1289
Pococke, E. and others. History of Greece. London, 1852. p. 8°. . . A,68
History of Greece, Macedonia, and Syria. Lond. 1852. p. 8°. A,69
(Ed.) History of Roman Republic. London, 1852–53. 3 v. p. 8°. . A,141
Poe, E. A. Poems; with Memoir. New York, 1866. 12°. . . . . I,111
and his Critics. S. H. Whitman. New York, 1860. 12°. . . H,662
Works. New York, 1864. 4 v. 12°. . . . . . . . . U,91

Vol. 1. Notices of his Life, by J. R. Lowell and N. P. Willis; Memoir, by R. W. Griswold; Tales.
2. Poems; Eureka; Tales.
3. The Literati; Margenalia; Fifty Suggestions.
4. Arthur Gordon Pym, Miscellanies.

Pöllnitz, C. L. Memoirs; Travels through Germany, etc. Lond. 1740. 4 v. 8°. V,328
Poems, Ancient, Ballads, and Songs; ed. by R. Bell. London, 1857. 16°. I,244
Poeppig, E. Reise in Chile, Peru, etc., 1827–32. Leipzig, 1835–36. 2 v. . *Q,287
Atlas dazu. Leipzig, 1836. f°. . . . . . . . . *Q,460
Pösche, H. Das Leben der Hausthiere. Glogau, 1864. 8°. . . . . G,933
Poesche, T. and Goepp, C. The New Rome. New York, 1853. 12°. . G,35
Poet's Bazaar; Pictures of Travel in Europe. H. C. Andersen. N. Y. 1871. 12°. V,463
Poetæ Latini Minores. Parisiis, 1824–26. 7 v. 8°. . . . . . . . U,340
Poetical Quotations, Dictionary of. S. J. Hale. Philadelphia, 1866. 8°. *I,163
Poetical Register; Fugitive Poetry, 1801, 2, 4–7. London, 1802–11. 5 v. 8°. I,486
Poetry and Painting, Laocoon; or, Limits of. G. E. Lessing. Lond. 1838. 8°. M,45
and Song, Library of; edited by E. H. Knight. New York, 1871. 8°. *I,177
Class-Book of. E. Robbins. New York, 1852. 12°. . . . . I,116
Classical Arrangement of. J. Bell. Lond. 1789–97. 18 v. in 9. 16°. I,194
Grenzen der Musik und Poesie. A. W. Ambros. Leipzig, 1855. 12°. G,637
History of Provençal Poetry. C. C. Fauriel. New York, 1860. 12°. H,761
Household Book of; edited by C. A. Dana. New York, 1867. 8°. . I,167
Music and Stage-Plays, Defence of. T. Lodge. London, 1853. 8°. I,885,49
of Christian Art. A. F. Rio. London, 1854. 12°. . . . . . M,37
of Compliment and Courtship. J. W. Palmer. Boston, 1868. 12°. I,488
of the Magyars. J. Bowring. London, 1830. 12°. . . . . I,176
of the Orient. W. R. Alger. Boston, 1866. 12°. . . . . . I,6
Popular Epics of the Middle Ages. J. M. Ludlow. Lond. 1865. 2 v. 12°. H,735
Reliques of Ancient English. T. Percy. London, 1844. 3 v. 16°. I,379
The same. Leipzig, 1866. 3 v. 16°. . . . . . . J,411

Poetry, Rural, of the English Language. J. W. Jenks. Boston, 1856. 8°. I,169
Poets and other English Writers, Essays on. T. De Quincey. Boston, 1855. 16°. H,414
and Poetry of America. R. W. Griswold. Philadelphia, 1855. 8°. I,164
of the Ancient Greeks. A. Mills. Boston, 1854. 8°. . . U,446
of Europe. H. W. Longfellow. Philadelphia, 1847. 8°. . H,668
of Greece and Rome. W. Peter. Philadelphia, 1848. 8°. . U,445
of the West. W. T. Coggeshall. New York, 1864. 8°. . I,168
British. Boston, 1854–68. 130 v. 16°.

| | | | |
|---|---|---|---|
| Akenside, M. | I,195 | Keats. | I,216 |
| Ballads. 8 v. | I,196 | Marvell, A. | I,217 |
| Beattie, J. | I,197 | Milton, J. 3 v. | I,218 |
| Burns, R. 3 v. | I,198 | Montgomery, A. 5 v. | I,219 |
| Butler, S. 2 v. | I,199 | Moore, T. 6 v. | I,220 |
| Byron, G. G. N., *Lord*. 10 v. | I,200 | Parnell, T. and Tickell, T. | I,221 |
| Campbell, T. | I,201 | Pope, A. 3 v. | I,222 |
| Chatterton, T. 2 v. | I,202 | Prior, M. 2 v. | I,223 |
| Churchill, C. 3 v. | I,203 | Scott, W. 9 v. | I,224 |
| Coleridge, S. T. 3 v. | I,204 | Shakespeare, W. | I,225 |
| Collins, W. | I,205 | Shelley, P. B. 4 v. | I,226 |
| Cowper, W. 3 v. | I,206 | Skelton, J. 3 v. | I,227 |
| Donne, J. | I,207 | Southey, R. 10 v. | I,228 |
| Dryden, J. 5 v. | I,208 | Spenser, E. 5 v. | I,229 |
| Falconer, W. | I,209 | Swift, J. 3 v. | I,231 |
| Gay, J. 2 v. | I,210 | Thomson, J. 2 v. | I,232 |
| Goldsmith, O. | I,211 | Vaughan, H. | I,233 |
| Gray, T. | I,212 | Watts, I. | I,234 |
| Herbert, W. | I,213 | White, H. K. | I,235 |
| Herrick, R. 2 v. | I,214 | Wordsworth, W. 7 v. | I,236 |
| Hood, T. 5 v. | I,215 | Wyatt, Sir T. | I,237 |
| Howard, H., *Earl of Surrey*. | I,230 | Young, E. 2 v. | I,238 |

British. Bohn's Cabinet Edition. London, 1851. 4 v. 12°. . I,242

Vol. 1. Milton; Cowper; Goldsmith; Thomson; Falconer; Akenside; Collins; Gray; Somerville.
2. Missing.
3. H. More; I. Watts; Hayley; Mason; Prior; Grahame; Logan.
4. Dryden; Lyttleton; Hammond; Charlotte Smith; Richardson; Bloomfield; Gifford; Canning.

British, Lectures on. H. Reed. Philadelphia, 1860. 2 v. 12°. . H,678
British, Selections from the. F. G. Halleck. New York, 1854. 2 v. 16°. L,415
British, Specimens of. T. Campbell. Philadelphia, 1853. 8°. . J,856
Conversations on some of the Old. J. R. Lowell. Camb. 1845. 16°. H,676
Early French. H. F. Cary. London, 1846. 16°. . . . . . H,756
Eminent English, Lives of. S. Johnson. New York, 1857. 2 v. 12°. C,1220
The same. New York, 1857. 8°. . . . . . . U,227,2
The same. Leipzig, 1858. 2 v. in 1. 16°. . . . . J,225
English, Lives of. R. Bell. London, 1839. 2 v. 12°. . . M,1015
English, Selections from. L. Hunt. New York, 1857. 12°. . U,279,2
English, Specimens of the Early. G. Ellis. London, 1803. 3 v. 8°. I,347
English Dramatic, Specimens of; ed. by C. Lamb. Lond. 1854. 12°. L,15
Gleanings from. A. C. Lowell. Boston, 1862. 12°. . . . I,96
Homes and Haunts of Eminent British. W. Howitt. London, 1857. 8°. C,1184
The same. New York, 1847. 2 v. 12°. . . . . D,19
Late English; ed. by H. R. Stoddard. New York, 1867. 12°. . I,433
Laureate, Lives of the. W. S. Austin, jr. and J. Ralph. Lond. 1853. 8°. D,441
of Connecticut. G. W. Everest. New York, 1847. 8°. . . . J,873
Sacred, of England and America. R. W. Griswold. N. Y. 1850. 8°. I,162

Pohl, G. F. Magnetismus, Elektricität, und Chemismus. Berlin, 1829. 12°. N,252,23
Poinsett, J. R. Notes on Mexico, 1822. London, 1825. 8°. . . . . V,198
Poisoning, Trial of the Earl of Somerset for. A. Amos. London, 1846. 8°. B,30
Poisons, Treatise on. R. Christison. Edinburgh, 1845. 8°. . . . . L,968
Poisson, S. D. Traité de Mécanique. Paris, 1811. 2 v. 8°. . . . N,126
Poland. W. G. Clark. London, 1864. 8°. . . . . . . V,1086,3
Autocracy in. J. Allen. New York, 1854. 12°. . . . . . V,532
Geschichte Polens. R. Roepell and J. Caro. Hamburgh, 1840–63. 2 v. 8°. E,107
History of. S. A. Dunham. London, 1831. 12°. . . . M,1001
J. Fletcher. New York, 1854. 16°. . . . . . . L,357
Polar Sea, Expedition to. F. Wrangell. New York, 1861. 16°. . . L,438
Journey to, 1819–22. Sir J. Franklin. London, 1824. 2 v. 8°. . V,942
Polar Seas and Regions. J. Leslie and others. New York, 1855. 16°. . L,347
The same. London, 1855. 12°. . . . . . . . . V,913
Polar World; a popular Description. G. Hartwig. New York, 1869. 8°. V,958
See also *Arctic.*
Polish-German Dictionary. G. S. Bandtke. Breslau, 1806. 8°. . . L.R.
Polish Revolution, History of the. J. Hordynski. Boston, 1832. 8°. . B,542
Polish Tales. C. G. F. Gore. London, 1833. 3 v. 12°. . . . K,1036
Political and Moral Philosophy. W. Paley. London, 1845. 8°. . P,709,2
Political Ballads. W. W. Wilkins. London, 1860. 2 v. 12°. . . . I,99
Political Caucuses of 1860. M. Halstead. Columbus, 1860. 8°. . . . O,526
Political Class-Book. W. Sullivan. Boston, 1835. 12°. . . . . O,488
Political Economy. G. Opdyke. New York, 1861. 12°. . . . . O,563
A. Potter. New York, 1855. 16°. . . . . . L,464
N. W. Senior. London, 1854. 8°. . . . . . . . O,511
American. F. Bowen. New York, 1870. 12°. . . . . . O,513
and Social Economy. L. A. Hine. Cincinnati, 1855. 8°. . . O,514
Distribution of Wealth. W. Thompson. London, 1869. 8°. . . O,560
Elements of. A. L. Perry. New York, 1866. 12°. . . . . O,515
F. Wayland. Boston, 1869. 12°. . . . . . . . O,512
Essays on. H. Greeley. Boston, 1870. 16°. . . . . . . O,509
J. Ruskin. New York, 1866. 12°. . . . . . . . M,67
for the United States. C. Colton. New York, 1849. 8°. . . . O,544
Illustrations of; Tales. H. Martineau. London, 1834. 9 v. 18°. . K,551
Logic of. T. De Quincey. Boston, 1859. 16°. . . . . . H,411
Manual of. E. P. Smith. New York, 1853. 12°. . . . . O,510
National System of. F. List. Philadelphia, 1856. 8°. . . . O,554
Principles of. T. R. Malthus. London, 1836. 8°. . . . . O,541
J. S. Mill. Boston, 1848. 2 v. 8°. . . . . . . . O,543
Science of Wealth. A. Walker. Boston, 1866. 12°. . . . O,550
Treatise on. J. B. Say. Philadelphia, 1867. 8°. . . . . O,540
Working Man's. J. Pickering. Cincinnati, 1847. 8°. . . . O,490
Political Essays. P. Godwin. New York, 1856. 12°. . . . . O,472
Political Grammar of the U. S. E. D. Mansfield. Cincinnati, 1849. 16°. . O,471
Political History of the 15th, 16th, and 17th Centuries. J. Van Praet. London, 1868. 8°. . . . . . . . . . . . . . A,338
Political Index to the Histories of Great Britain and Ireland. R. Beatson. London, 1806–07. 3 v. 8°. . . . . . . . . . . . A,461
Political Manual. J. M. Hiatt. Indianapolis, 1864. 12°. . . . . . O,474

Political Parties in N. Y. State, Hist. of. J. B. Hammond. Coop. 1846. 2 v. 8°. c,92
J. S. Jenkins. Auburn, 1849. 8°. . . . . . . . c,172
Political Philosophy, v. 2, 3. H. *Lord* Brougham. London, 1853. 8°. . o,539
Political Poems from Edward III. to Richard III. Lond. 1859-61. 2 v. 8°. w,164
Political Science, Elements of. P. E. Dove. Edinburgh, 1854. 8°. . . o,542
Political Text-Book for 1860. H. Greeley and J. F. Cleveland. N.Y. 1860. 8°. o,527
Politics and Literature, Register of, for 1827. Edinburgh, 1828. 16°. . I,505
Methods of Reasoning in. G. C. Lewis. London, 1852. 2 v. 8°. . o,546
Polko, E. Reminiscences of F. Mendelssohn-Bartholdy. N. Y. 1869. 16°. D,496
Pollard, E. A. Life of Jeff. Davis. Philadelphia, 1869. 8°. . . . c,756
Lost Cause; Southern History of the War. New York, 1867. 8°. . B,922
Southern History of the War. New York, 1863-65. 3 v. 8°. . . B,934
Polo, M., Travels of; edited by H. Murray. New York, 1864. 16°. . . L,456
The same; edited by T. Wright. London, 1854. p. 8°. . . L,18
Pollok, R. Course of Time. New York, 1868. 12°. . . . . . . I,376
Polybius. Historiæ; Græce et Latine. Parisiis, 1839. 8°. . . . . U,557
Polynesia, History of. M. Russell. London, 1853. 16°. . . . . v,878
The same. New York, 1842. 16°. . . . . . . . L,444
Wandering Sketches in. W. M. Wood. Philadelphia, 1849. 12°. . v,241
Polynesian Mythology. Sir G. Grey. London, 1855. 8°. . . . . P,920
Polynesian Researches. W. Ellis. London, 1859. 4 v. 16°. . . . v,874
Polyzoa, Fresh-Water. G. J. Allman. London, 1856. 4°. . . . . Q,66
Pomological Manual. W. R. and W. Prince. New York, 1831. 8°. . . M,572
Pompeii and Herculaneum. W. H. D. Adams. London, 1868. 12°. . . B,499
et Herculanum. L. Barré et H. R. Ainé. Paris, 1839-40. 8 v. 8°. *M,133
its History and Antiquities. T. H. Dyer. London, 1867. 8°. . . B,498
its Past and Present. London, 1836. 2 v. 16°. . . . . . L,484
Last Days of. Sir E. B. Lytton. Leipzig, 1842. 16°. . . . J,317
Topography of. Sir W. Gell and J. P. Gaudy. London, 1852. 8°. *B,501
Wonders of. M. Monnier. New York, 1870. 12°. . . . . M,1055
Pompey the Little. F. Coventry. London, 1820. 12°. . . . . . K,535
Pomponius Mela. De Orbis Situ. Basileæ, 1522. f°. . . . . . Q,414
Pond, E. Lives of Increase Mather and Sir Wm. Phips. Boston, 1870. 12°. D,8,5
Pond-Life, Marvels of. H. J. Slack. London, 1861. 12°. . . . . o,74
Pontécoulant, G. C. de. Système du Monde. Paris, 1829-34. 3 v. 8°. . N,286
Pontefract Castle, Siege of. N. Drake. Durham, 1860. 8°. . . . F,126,37
Pontiac, Conspiracy of. F. Parkman. Boston, 1851. 8°. . . . . B,600
The same, 6th edition. Boston, 1870. 2 v. 8°. . . . B,613
Ponton, M. Earthquakes and Volcanoes. London, 1868. 12°. . . V,1111
Great Architect and Material Universe. London, 1866. 12°. . . N,269
Poole, H. W. Papers on Musical Theory. New Haven, 1867-68. 8°. . M,398
1. Perfect Harmony in Music; Enharmonic Key Board.
2. On Musical Ratios.

Poole, J. Comic Sketch-Book. London, 1835. 2 v. 12°. . . . . H,91
Little Pedlington and the Pedlingtonians. N. Y. 1852. 2 v. 12°. K,1097
Poole, J. English Parnassus; or, a Help to English Poesie. Lond. 1677. 8°. L,581
Poole, S. Englishwoman in Egypt. London, 1851-53. 24°. . . . . v,768
Poole, W. F. Catalogue of the Boston Mercantile Library. Bost. 1853. 8°. L.R.
Cotton Mather and Salem Witchcraft. Boston, 1869. 8°. . . . . o,341
C. Mather and Witchcraft; Mr. Upham his Reply. Bost. 1870. 16°. o,323

Poole, W. F. Index to Subjects in Reviews. New York, 1848. 8°. . . L.R.
Index to Periodical Literature. New York, 1853. 8°. . . . . L.R.
(Ed.) Hutchinson's Witchcraft Delusion of 1692. Boston, 1870. 4°. O,324
(Ed.) Johnson's Wonder-Working Providence, 1654. Bost. 1867. 4°. C,34
Poor, The, History of. T. Ruggles. London, 1793–94. 2 v. 8°. . . O,362
Poor Boy and Merchant Prince. W. M. Thayer. Boston, 1866. 16°. J,1409
Poor Laws and Paupers Illustrated. H. Martineau. Lond. 1833. 4 v. in 1. 18°. K,553
Poor Rich Man and Rich Poor Man. C. M. Sedgwick. N. Y. 1868. 16°. J,1425
Pope, A., Genius and Writings of. J. Wharton. London, 1806. 2 v. 8°. H,704
Life and Letters. R. Carruthers. London, 1857. p. 8°. . . . L,141
Poetical Works; edit. by R. Carruthers. London, 1858. 2 v. p. 8°. L,138
The same; edited by H. F. Cary. London, 1857. 12°. . . I,371
The same; edited by J. Lupton. London, 1867. 16°. . . I,482
The same; with Life by A. Dyce. Boston, 1856. 3 v. 16°. . I,222
Poetry of. G. W. F. Howard, *Earl of Carlisle.* N. Y. 1851. 12°. . V,17
Select Poetical Works. Leipzig, 1848. 16°. . . . . . . J,413
Translation of Homer's Iliad. London, 1867. p. 8°. . . . L,139
The same. New York, 1855. 2 v. 16°. . . U,365,1,2
of Homer's Odyssey. London, 1867. p. 8°. . . . . L,140
The same. New York, 1855. 2 v. 16°. . . U,365,2,3
Pope, A. R. American Educational Year-Book, 1857. Boston, 1857. 12°. O,1250
Popery, Persecutions of. F. Shoberl. London, 1844. 2 v. 8°. . . . P,621
Variations of. S. Edgar. New York, 1850. 8°. . . . . . P,816
Popes, Councils, and the Church, Glance at. London, 1866. 12°. . . P,135
Histoire Politique des Papes. P. Lanfrey. Bruxelles, 1860. 12°. H,1033
History of. L. M. de la Haye Cormenin. Phila. 1857. 2 v. in 1. 8°. P,815
L. Ranke. London, 1847–51. 3 v. p. 8°. . . . . . L,222
Recollections of the Last Four. A. Gavazzi. London, 1859. 12°. . C,548
N. Wiseman. London, 1858. 8°. . . . . . . . . C,559
Römische Päpste im 16 u. 17ten Jahrh. C.Ranke. Berl.1845. 3 v. 8°. E,30
Poplar-House Academy. A. Manning. London, 1859. 2 v. 16°. . . J,595
Poppe, J. H. M. von. Ausführliche Volks-Gewerbslehre. Stuttg. 1842. 8°. G,707
Popular Encyclopædia. D. K. Sandford. Glasgow, 1855. 7 v. 8°. . . L.R.
Popular Errors. J. Timbs. London, 1849. 16°. . . . . . . . M,809
The same. London, 1849. 16°. . . . . . . . . I,546
Popular Readings in Prose and Verse. J. E. Carpenter. Lon. 1867. 5 v. 12°. H,393
Popular Tales. Madame Guizot. Boston, 1859. 12°. . . . . J,1188
Popular Tales, etc., of the North; edited by B. Thorpe. London, 1853. p. 8°. L,28
Population, Essay on the Principle of. T. R. Malthus. London, 1826. 2 v. 8°. O,517
of Nations, Inquiry concerning. G. Ensor. London, 1818. 8°. . O,516
Porcelain and Glass, Manufactures of. G. R. Porter. London, 1832. 12°. M,1044
The same. London, 1852. 16°. . . . . . . . . M,604
and Pottery, Guide to the Knowledge. H. G. Bohn. Lond. 1857. p. 8°. L,142
History of. J. Marryat. London, 1868. 8°. . . . . M,645
History of. C. Tomlinson. Columbus, 1861. 8°. . . . . M,622
Porcupine, Peter, *pseud.* See *Cobbett, W.*
Porsoniana Table-Talk. S. Rogers. New York, 1856. 12°. . . . . H,571
Portent, The; a Story of the Highlanders. G. Mac Donald. Bost. 1871. 12°. K,1166
Porter, A. E. Married for both Worlds. Boston, 1871. 12°. . . . K,266
Porter, A. M. Barony. London, 1830. 3 v. 12°. . . . . . . K,557

Porter, A. M. Don Sebastian. London, 1809. 4 v. 12°. . . . . . J,576
Hungarian Brothers. London, 1850. 16°. . . . . . . K,554
Knight of St. John. London, 1818. 3 v. in 1. 12°. . . . K,556
Porter, C. B. Silver Cup of Sparkling Drops. Buffalo, 1852. 12°. . J,1286
Porter, E., Life of. L. Matthews. Boston, 1837. 12°. . . . C,1100
Rhetorical Reader. Cincinnati, 1848. 12°. . . . . O,1106
Porter, G. R. Geography of Great Britain. London, n. d. 8°. . V,1126
Manufactures of Porcelain and Glass. London, 1832. 12°. . M,1044
The same. London, 1852. 16°. . . . . . . M,604
Treatise on Silk Manufacture. London, 1831. 12°. . . . M,1042
Porter, H. Two Angrie Women of Abington. London, 1841. 12°. . L,606,5
Porter, J. Pastor's Fireside. London, 1817. 4 v. 12°. . . . . . J,575
Scottish Chiefs. Philadelphia, 1868. 12°. . . . . . . K,892
Thaddeus of Warsaw. Philadelphia, 1867. 12°. . . . . . K,885
Porter, J. A. Principles of Chemistry. New York, 1865. 12°. . . N,227
Porter, J. L. Five Years in Damascus. London, 1855. 2 v. 8°. . . V,658
Giant Cities of Bashan. London, 1866. 12°. . . . . . . V,657
Porter, N. American Colleges and American Public. New Haven, 1870. 12°. O,810
Books and Reading. New York, 1871. 12°. . . . . . . O,985
Human Intellect. New York, 1868. 8°. . . . . . . . . O,702
Porter, W. History of the Knights of Malta. London, 1858. 2 v. 8°. . A,237
Porter, W. T., Life of. F. Brinley. New York, 1860. 12°. . . . . C,737
Portia, and Stories of Shakespeare's Heroines. M.C.Clarke. N.Y. 1868. 12°. K,1149
Portlock, J. E. Geology. London, 1859. 12°. . . . . . . . . M,952
Porto Rico and Cuba, Travels in. D. Turnbull. London, 1840. 8°. . V,141
Portrait Gallery of Distinguished Men. London, 1853. 3 v. 8°. . *C,621
National. A. Chappel and E. A. Duyckinck. N. Y. n. d. 2 v. 4°. *Q,272
J. B. Longacre and J. Herring. Philadel. 1836–39. 4 v. 4°. S.C.
Portrait Painting, Hints on. J. Burnet. London, 1850. 4°. . . . *Q,161
Portraits and Paintings, Historic Gallery, of v. 1–4, 6, 7. Lon. 1807–11. 6 v. 8°. S.C.
Galerie Universelle des Hommes Celebres. Paris, n. d. 2 v. 4°. . *C,619
of Celebrated Women. C. A. Sainte-Beuve. Boston, 1868. 16°. . C,494
of the English. K. Meadows. London, 1864. 2 v. 8°. . . H,616
of Illustrious Persons of G. Britain. E. Lodge. Lon. 1849–50. 8 v. p. 8°. *L,116
People's Art Union. London, n. d. 4 v. 8°. . . . . . . C,593
Portugal and Spain, Ambassade en, 1808–11. L.P.Junot. Brux. 1838. 2 v. 16°. H,1031
History of. S. A. Dunham. London, 1832. 5 v. 12°. . M,991
Visit to. H. C. Andersen. New York, 1870. 12°. . . V,464
Geschichte. J. Aschbach. Frankfurt-a.-M. 1833–37. 2 v. 8°. E,93
Geschichte von Portugal. H. Schäfer. Gotha, 1836–54. 5 v. 8°. . E,97
Reise durch Portugal. H. F. Link. Kiel, 1801–4. 3 v. in 2. 12°. E,199
Posey, T., Life of. J. Hall. Boston, 1860. 12°. . . . . . C,860,19
Positive Philosophy. A. Comte; tr. by H. Martineau. N.Y. 1853. 2 v. 12°. O,661
The same, reviewed. J. S. Mill. Boston, 1866. 8°. . . . O,627
Positivism and Christianity. J. McCosh. New York, 1871. 12°. . . P,577
General View of. A. Comte. London, 1865. 8°. . . . . . O,643
Potato, Diseases in. London, 1845. 8°. . . . . . . . . N,252,6
its Diseases, Varieties, etc. J. M. Wilson. Edinburgh, 1850. 16°. M,437
Potiphar Papers. G. W. Curtis. New York, 1860. 12°. . . . . . K,92
Potomac and the Rapidan; Army Notes. A. H. Quint. Boston, 1864. 12°. B,894

Potomac Army, Hospital Life in. W. H. Reed. Boston, 1868. 12°. . B,941
Medical Recollections of. J. Letterman. New York, 1866. 8°. . L,943
Pott, A. F. Etymologische Forschungen auf dem Gebiete der Indo-Germanischen Sprachen. Lemgo and Detmold, 1859-67. 4 v. 8°. . G,586
Zigeuner in Europa und Asien. Halle, 1844-45. 2 v. 8°. . . G,587
Potter, A. Hand-Book for Readers and Students. New York, 1855. 18°. L,449
Objects and Uses of Science and Literature. New York, 1858. 16°. L,461
Political Economy. New York, 1855. 16°. . . . . . . L,464
Principles of Science. New York, 1847. 12°. . . . . . . M,611
Science applied to Domestic and Mechanic Arts. N. Y. 1855. 12°. M,607
and Emerson, G. B. School and Schoolmaster. N. Y. 1854. 12°. . O,823
Potter, J. Antiquities of Greece, v. 2. Edinburgh, 1832. 8°. . . . A,113
Potter, J. P. Moralist. London, 1821. 12°. . . . . . . O,1133
Potter, R. Physical Optics. London, 1856-59. 2 v. 8°. . . . N,28
Pottery and Porcelain, Guide to Knowledge of. H.G.Bohn. Lon. 1857. p. 8°. L,142
History of. J. Marryat. London, 1868. 8°. . . . M,645
History of. C. Tomlinson. Columbus, 1861. 8°. . . . M,622
Pottleton Legacy; a Story. A. Smith. London, n. d. 16°. . . . J,652
Potts, R. Appendix to Euclid. Cambridge, 1847. 8°. . . . M,1159
Pouched Animals, Natural History of. G.R.Waterhouse. Edin. n. d. 16°. N,470,24
Pouchot, M. French and Indian War, 1755-60. Boston, 1866. 2 v. 4°. F,68
Poulterer's Companion. C. N. Bement. New York, 1852. 12°. . . M,451
The same. New York, 1856. 4°. . . . . . . . M,473
Poultry Book. J. C. Bennett. Boston, 1854. 12°. . . . . . . M,445
People's Practical. W. M. Lewis. New York, 1871. 8°. . . M,454
Poussin, G. T. United States; its Power and Progress. Philad. 1851. 8°. B,704
Powell, B. Christianity without Judaism. London, 1857. 12°. . . P,222
Essays on Inductive Philosophy, etc. London, 1855. 8°. . . O,676
History of Natural Philosophy. London, n. d. 16°. . . . N,61
History of Physical and Mathematical Sciences. London, 1834. 12°. M,1018
Order of Nature and Claims of Revelation. London, 1859. 12°. . P,223
State Education considered. London, 1840. 8°. . . . O,1251,2
Powell, D. Republic of Paraguay. London, 1864. 8°. . . . V,1086,3
Power, T. Impressions of America. London, 1836. 2 v. 8°. . . . V,146
Practical Mechanic and Engineer's Magazine. Glasgow, 1842-47. 6 v. 4°. F,127
The same. Glasgow, 1842-45. 4 v. 4°. . . . . . S.C.
Practical Mechanic's Journal. Glasgow, 1848-56. 8 v. in 4. 4°. . . F,131
The same. Glasgow, 1848-53. 5 v. 4°. . . . . . S.C.
Practical Metal-Worker's Assistant. O. Byrne. Philadelphia, 1867. 8°. M,721
Practical Piety. H. More. New York, n. d. 18°. . . . . . P,746,30
Practical Thoughts. W. Nevins. New York, 1836. 18°. . . . P,13
The same. New York, n. d. 18°. . . . . . . P,746,13
Praed, W. M. Poetical Works. New York, 1853. 12°. . . . . . I,483
The same. New York, 1859-60. 2 v. 12°. . . . . . I,485
Pragay, J. Hungarian Revolution. New York, 1850. 12°. . . . . B,537
Prairie, The. J. F. Cooper. New York, 1856. 12°. . . . . . . K,44
The same. New York, 1870. 12°. . . . . . . K,20,5
The same. New York, 1859. 8°. . . . . . . . K,72
Prairie Crusoe. Boston, 1866. 16°. . . . . . . . . J,1383
Prairie du Chien, Tour to. C. Atwater. Columbus, 1831. 12°. . . V,28

Prairie Farming in America. J. Caird. New York, 1859. 12°. . . M,492
Prairie Travel; Wah-To-Yah. L. H. Garrard. Cincinnati, 1850. 12°. . V,155
Prairie-Teufel, Der. O. Ruppius. Berlin, 1861. 16°. . . . . . G,432
Prairies, Commerce of the. J. Gregg. Philadelphia, 1850. 2 v. 12°. . V,158
Praise and Principle. M. J. McIntosh. New York, 1861. 24°. . J,1178
Prantl, C. Geschichte der Logik im Abendlande. Leip. 1855–67. 3 v. 8°. G,568
Pratt, A. Flowering Plants and Ferns of G. Britain. London, n. d. 5 v. 8°. N,1018
Haunts of the Wild Flowers. London, 1863. 8°. . . . . . N,923
Pratt, H. F. A. Astronomical Investigations. London, 1865. 8°. . . N,292
Eccentric and Centric Force. London, 1862. 8°. . . . . . N,93
Pratt, J. H. Treatise on Attractions, etc., of the Earth. Camb. 1868. 12°. N,270
Pratz, Le Page du. Histoire de la Louisiane. Paris, 1758. 3 v. 12°. . C,190
Prayer, Book of Common, History of. T. Lathburg. Oxford, 1858. 8°. . P,900
Illustration of. C. Wheatley. London, 1857. p. 8°. . . L,247
Two Early Books compared. E. Cardwell. Oxford, 1852. 8°. P,901
Book of Public, Presbyterian Church. New York, 1857. 8°. . . P,898
Discourse concerning. I. Mather. Boston, 1677. 4°. . . . B,603
Prayers from Plymouth Pulpit. H. W. Beecher. New York, 1868. 12°. P,905
Praying and Working. W. F. Stevenson. London, 1863. 12°. . . C,506
Preacher, Advices to a Young. J. Parker. Boston, 1871. 12°. . . . H,511
Lectures on the Vocation of. E. P. Hood. New York, 1869. 2 v. 12°. P,236
Preachers and Preaching. N. Murray. New York, 1860. 12°. . . P,100
of the Ancient Church. W. Wilson. London, n. d. 16°. . . C,517
Preaching and Popular Education. T. J. Graham. London, 1850. 12°. O,1032
Pre-Adamite Earth. J. Harris. Boston, 1856. 12°. . . . . . . P,275
Preble, E., Life of. L. Sabine. Boston, 1860. 12°. . . . . . C,860,22
Precaution. J. F. Cooper. New York, 1865. 12°. . . . . . . K,45
The same. New York, 1861. 8°. . . . . . . . K,73
Precepts and Practice. T. E. Hook. London, 1840. 3 v. 12°. . . K,721
Prechtl, J. J. Chemie in technischer Beziehung. Wien, 1817. 2 v. 8°. . G,760
Pre-Historic Nations. J. D. Baldwin. New York, 1869. 12°. . . . A,10
Preller, L. Griechische Mythologie. Berlin, 1860–61. 2 v. 8°. . . E,462
Römische Mythologie. Berlin, 1865. 8°. . . . . . . . E,461
Prémices. S. H. Palfrey. Boston, 1855. 16°. . . . . . . . I,34
Prentice, G. D. Prenticeana; or, Wit and Humor. Philadelphia, 1871. 12°. H,126
Prentiss, E. Flower of the Family. New York, 1869. 16°. . . J,1638
Fred, Maria, and Me. New York, 1871. 16°. . . . . J,1697
Little Lou's Sayings and Doings. New York, 1868. 8°. . . J,1340
Nidworth and his Three Magic Wands. Boston, 1870. 16°. . J,1426
Stepping Heavenward. New York, 1869. 12°. . . . . . . K,116
Prentiss, S. S., Memoirs; edited by his brother. New York, 1856. 2 v. 12°. C,920
Pre-Raphaelitism. J. Ruskin. New York, 1851. 12°. . . . . . M,70
Presbyterian Church, Book of Public Prayer of. New York, 1857. 8°. . P,898
Presbyterian Churches of Cumberland and Franklin Co., Penn. A. Nevin. Philadelphia, 1852. 12°. . . . . . . . . . . . C,87
Presbyterianism, Western, Old Redstone, Sketches of. J. Smith. Phil. 1854. 8°. P,622
Prescott, G. B. History and Theory of Electric Telegraph. Bost. 1864. 12°. M,690
Prescott, H. E. See *Spofford, H. E.*
Prescott, W. H. Biographical and Critical Miscellanies. N. Y. 1845. 8°. H,147
The same. Boston, 1857. 8°. . . . . . . . . . S.C.

Prescott, W. H. History of the Conquest of Mexico. N. Y. 1854. 3 v. 8°. C,388
The same. New York, 1847. 3 v. 8°. . . . . . . S.C.
History of the Conquest of Peru. Boston, 1858. 2 v. 8°. . . C,389
The same, v. 2. New York, 1847. 8°. . . . . . . S.C.
History of Ferdinand and Isabella. Boston, 1858. 3 v. 8°. . . B,477
The same, v. 2, 3. Boston, 1857. 8°. . . . . . . S.C.
History of the Reign of Philip II. Boston, 1858-59. 3 v. 8°. . B,476
The same, v. 1, 2. Boston, 1856. 8°. . . . . . . S.C.
Life of. G. Ticknor. Boston, 1866. 8°. . . . . . . . C,875
The same. Boston, 1864. 4°. . . . . . . . . . C,759
Life of Charles Brockden Brown. Boston, 1860. 12°. . . C,860,1
and Robertson, W. Reign of Charles V. Boston, 1857. 3 v. 8°. . B,531
Present Hour, The. London, 1782. 8°. . . . . . . . . O,565
Preservation, Art de Conserver toutes les Substances. C. Appert. Par. 1831. 8°. N,252,13
of Timber, Canvas, etc., Patent for. Sir W. Burnett. Lond. 1848. 8°. N,252,40
President's Daughter and Nina. F. Bremer. London, 1852-53. 12°. L,169,2
The same. New York, n. d. 8°. . . . . . . . K,584
President's Messages, 1789-1846. E. Williams. New York, 1846. 2 v. 8°. O,591
Pressensé, E. de. Early Years of Christianity. New York, 1870. 12°. . P,575
Religion and the Reign of Terror. New York, 1869. 12°. . . P,576
Preston, H. C. Life of North-American Insects. New York, 1859. 12°. . O,22
Preston, H. W. Aspendale. Boston, 1871. 12°. . . . . . . K,222
Preston, S. School Education for the 19th Century. London, 1846. 8°. . O,947
Prestwich, J., jr. Water-bearing Strata around London. Lond. 1851. 8°. N,818
Pretenders and their Adherents, Memoirs of. J. H. Jesse. Lond. 1858. p. 8°. L,268
The same. Philadelphia, 1846. 2 v. 12°. . . . . . D,435
Pretty Widow. C. H. Ross. Leipzig, 1868. 16°. . . . . . . J,429
Prevention better than Cure. S. S. Ellis. London, n. d. 12°. . . . O,389
Préville, P. L. D., Mémoires de. Paris, 1855. 12°. . . . . . . D,612
Preyer, W. und Zirkel, F. Reise nach Island im Sommer, 1860. Leip. 1862. 8°. E,174
Priaulx, O. de B. National Education. London, 1842. 8°. . . O,1201
Genesis compared with Ancient Religions. London, 1854. 8°. . . P,179
Price, B. Principles of Currency. Oxford, 1869. 8°. . . . . . O,529
Price, E. Norway and its Scenery. London, 1853. p. 8°. . . . . . L,132
Price, E. L. Analytical System of the English Language. Cincinnati, 1848. T,19,2
Price, G. Fire and Thief-Proof Locks and Keys. London, 1856. 8°. . M,660
Price, L. Manual of Photographic Manipulation. London, 1858. 8°. . M,616
Price, Sir U. The Picturesque. Edinburgh, 1842. 8°. . . . . . M,354
Picturesque comp. with the Sublime and Beautiful. Lond. 1810. 3 v. 8°. M,89
Prichard, J. C. Eastern Origin of Celtic Nations. London, 1857. 8°. . N,434
Natural History of Man. London, 1855. 2 v. 8°. . . . . . N,448
Maps to the same. London, n. d. f°. . . . . . . Q,451
Naturgeschichte des Menschengeschlechts. Leip. 1840-8. 4 v. in 5. 8°. E,403
Physical History of Mankind. London, 1841-51. 5 v. 8°. . . N,429
Pride and Prejudice. J. Austen. Boston, 1864. 12°. . . . . . . K,595
The same. Leipzig, 1870. 16°. . . . . . . . . J,30
Prideaux, T. S. Economy of Fuel. London, 1853. 12°. . . . . . M,953
Priest and the Huguenot. L. F. Bungener. v. 2. Boston, 1856. 12°. . H,952
and Nun. J. McN. Wright. Philadelphia, 1869. 12°. . . . K,406
Priestley, J. Observations relating to Education. Bath, 1778. 8°. . . O,955

Priestley, J. Works. London, 1778–1804. 29 v. 8°. . . . . . U,294
Vol. 1–6. General History of the Christian Church. 6 v.
7, 8. History of the Corruptions of Christianity. 2 v.
9. Free Discussion on Materialism and Philosophical Necessity.
10–12. Discourses on Evidence of Revealed Religion. 3 v.
13. Doctrines of Heathen Philosophy and those of Revelation.
14. Institutions of Moses and those of the Hindoos.
15. Letters to a Philosophical Unbeliever. 2 v. in 1.
16–19. Notes on all the Books of Scripture. 4 v.
20–23. History of Early Opinions on Jesus Christ. 4 v.
24–29. Theological Repository; Essays, etc. 6 v.

Priests, Instruction for Parish. J. Myrc. London, 1868. 8°. . . L,605,31
Primacy of the Apostolic See vindicated. F. P. Kenrick. Bȧlt. 1855. 8°. P,817
Primary School Reader. W. D. Swan. Philadelphia, 1844. 12°. . . O,762
Prime, S. I. Letters from Switzerland. New York, 1860. 12°. . . V,415
Travels in Europe and the East. New York, 1855. 2 v. 12°. V,1067
Prime, W. C. Boat-Life in Egypt and Nubia. New York, 1867. 12°. . V,829
Old House by the River. New York, 1853. 12°. . . . . . K,290
Tent-Life in the Holy Land. New York, 1867. 12°. . . . V,637
Primer, Pictorial. C. W. and J. C. Sanders. New York, 1846. 12°. . . O,784
Standard School. E. Sargent. Boston, 1857. 12°. . . . . . O,772
Primeval World of Hebrew Tradition. F. H. Hedge. Boston, 1870. 12°. A,15
Prince Charlie, the Young Chevalier. M. Johnes. New York, 1860. 12°. J,1646
Prince, T. Catalogue of his Library. Boston, 1870. 8°. . . . . . L.R.
The same; American Portion. W. H. Whitmore. Bost. 1868. 12°. L.R.
Prince, W. R. and W. Pomological Manual. New York, 1831. 8°. . . M,572
Prince Eugene and his Times. C. Mundt. New York, 1869. 8°. . . G,212
Prince of Darkness. E. D. E. N. Southworth. Philadelphia, 1870. 12°. . K,436
Prince of the House of David. J. H. Ingraham. New York, 1859. 12°. . K,199
Prince of Kashna. R. B. Kimball. New York, 1866. 12°. . . . K,132
Princess, Character of a Young. H. More. London, 1809. 2 v. 8°. O,1233
Princesses of England, Lives of. A. E. Green. v. 2–6. Lond. 1850–55. 5 v. 8°. D,338
Principia Mathematica. Sir I. Newton. Glasguæ, 1822. 4 v. 4°. . M,1177
Printer, The; a Monthly Newspaper. v. 1. New York, 1859. 4°. . . Q,201
Printer-Boy, The; Ben Franklin. W. M. Thayer. Boston, 1863. 16°. . J,1292
Printer's Manual. T. Lynch. Cincinnati, 1859. 12°. . . . . . L.R.
The same. Cincinnati, 1864. 12°. . . . . . . . . L.R.
Printing, Annales de l'Imprimerie des Alde. A. A. Renouard. Par. 1825. 8°. L.R.
Annales Typographici ab artis inventæ origine ad annum 1536. G. W. Panzer. Norimbergæ, 1793–1803. 11 v. 4°. . . . . L.R.
Dictionary of the Art of. W. Savage. London, 1841. 8°. . . M,640
Gutenberg and the Art of. E. C. Pearson. Boston, 1871. 12°. . . D,532
Histoire de l'Imprimerie. P. Lacroix. Paris, 1852. 8°. . . . M,742
History and Process of. T. C. Hansard. Columbus, 1861. 8°. . M,622
History of the Art of. H. N. Humphreys. London, 1867. 4°. *Q,296
its Antecedents, History, etc. A. Stark. London, 1865. p. 8°. . I,667
Origin and Progress of. P. Luckombe. London, 1770. 8°. . . M,638
Specimens of Type, Cincinnati Type Foundry. Cincinnati, 1844. 4°. *M,740
New York Type Foundry. G. Bruce. New York, 1853. 8°. *M,641
U. S. Type Foundry. J. Conner & Sons. New York, 1859. 4°. *Q,382
Prints, Views of European Cities. n. t. p. . . . . . . . . . *Q,443
Prinz Eugen und seine Zeit. C. Mundt. Berlin, 1864. 4 v. 12°. . . G,364
Prior, J. Life of Edmund Burke. London, 1854. p. 8°. . . . . L,262

Prior, J. Memoir of Edmund Burke. Boston, 1854. 2 v. 12°. . . . D,193
Life of Oliver Goldsmith. Philadelphia, 1837. 8°. . . . . D,99
Prior, M. Poetical Works. Boston, 1853. 2 v. 16°. . . . . . I,223
Priory of Coldingham. Correspondence, Inventories, etc. London, 1841. 8°. F,126,12
of Finchdale, Charters of. London, 1837. 8°. . . . . F,126,6
of Hexham. Chronicles, Endowments, and Annals. Durham, 1864. 8°. F,126,44
Prison, Andersonville. A. C. Hamlin. Boston, 1866. 12°. . . . B,895
History of Newgate, in Conn. R. H. Phelps. Albany, 1860. 4°. . C,77
Prison Life in Sing-Sing. J. Luckey. New York, 1866. 12°. . . . O,347
Pictures from Mass. State Prison. G. Haynes. Boston, 1870. 12°. O,365
Prison Reform Congress, Transactions, 1870. Albany, 1871. 8°. . . P.D.
Prison-World of Europe. H. Dixon. New York, 1869. 12°. . . . O,351
Prisons, Mes, et des Devoirs. S. Pellico. Paris, 1852. 12°. . . . D,716
Pritchard, A. General History of Animalcules. London, 1843. 8°. . O,64
History of Infusoria. London, 1845. 8°. . . . . . . O,67
Private Life of an Eastern King. Nussir-u-Deen. New York, 1855. 12°. D,755
Private Miles O'Reilly, Adventures of. C. G. Halpine. New York, 1866. 12°. H,72
Privateers, American, in 1812–14. G. Coggeshall. New York, 1861. 8°. B,856
Privateersman. F. Marryat. London, 1867. p. 8°. . . . . . . L,123
The same. Leipzig, 1846. 16°. . . . . . . . J,361
Probabilities, Essay on. A. De Morgan. London, 1838. 12°. . . M,1028
The same. London, 1838. 12°. . . . . . . M,1163
History of the Theory of. I. Todhunter. London, 1865. 8°. M,1162
Problematic Characters. F. Spielhagen. New York, 1869. 12°. . . G,218
Problematische Naturen. F. Spielhagen. Berlin, 1866. 3 v. 16°. . . G,465
Proceedings of a Convention at Boston, 1780. Albany, 1867. 4°. . . C,11
Proceedings in the Trial of B. Arnold. New York, 1865. 4°. . . . F,37
Procter, A. A. Legends and Lyrics. New York, 1859. 12°. . . . I,110
Poems. Boston, 1866. 16°. . . . . . . . . . . I,109
Procter, B. W., *Barry Cornwall.* Charles Lamb; a Memoir. Boston, 1866. 16°. D,313
English Songs and other Poems. Boston, 1851. 16°. . . . I,321
Essays and Tales in Prose. Boston, 1853. 2 v. 16°. . . . H,307
Proctor, G. History of Italy. London, 1844. 8°. . . . . . B,497
Proctor, H. History of the Crusades. Philadelphia, 1856. 8°. . . A,245
Proctor, R. A. Half-Hours with the Telescope. London, 1868. 16°. . N,256
Other Worlds than ours. New York, 1871. 12°. . . . . N,274
The Sun. London, 1871. 8°. . . . . . . . . . N,289
Profession is not Principle. G. Kennedy. Philadelphia, 1827. 12°. . P,16
Professional Earnestness, Address on. J. P. Harrison. Cincin. 1849. 8°. H,302,4
Professor, The. C. B. Nicholls. New York, n. d. 12°. . . . . K,857
The same. Leipzig, 1857. 12°. . . . . . . . J,388
Professor at the Breakfast-Table. O. W. Holmes. Boston, 1866. 12°. . H,62
Progress, Illustrations of Universal. H. Spencer. New York, 1864. 12°. O,533
in Great Britain, History of. R. K. Philp. London, 1859. 8°. . B,32
in the North-West. W. D. Gallagher. Cincinnati, 1850. 8°. H,302,1
of Nations, Essays on. E. C. Seaman. New York, 1853. 12°. . O,493
Progress and Prejudice. C. G. F. Gore. Leipzig, 1854. 2 v. in 1. 16°. J,189
Progressive Speaker and Com. School Reader. S. Towne. Boston, n. d. 12°. O,1247
Projectiles for Military Purposes. W. Benson. Glasgow, 1860. 8°. N,252,49
Pronunciation, Early English. A. J. Ellis. London, 1867–69. 2 v. 8°. L,604,2,7

Prony, G. R. de. Nouvelle Architecture Hydraulique. Paris, 1796. 2 v. 4°. M,820
Propellers and Steam Navigation, History of. R. Mac Farlane. N.Y. 1851. 12°. M,691
Propertius, S. A. Elegiarum Libri Quatuor. Parisiis, 1832. 8°. . . U,341
Elegies; translated by R. B. Sheridan. London, 1854. 12°. . . L,75
Property and Labor, Essays on. F. Lieber. New York, 1854. 16°. . L,436
Property Law, Handy Book on. Sir E. B. Sugden. New York, 1858. 12°. U,487
Prophecies, Dissertations on the. T. Newton. Edinburgh, 1793. 2 v. 12°. P,172
Prophecy, its Nature, etc. P. Fairbairn. Edinburgh, 1856. 8°. . . P,160
a Preparation for Christ. R. P. Smith. Boston, 1870. 12°. . . P,143
Prophet, Der; Historischer Roman. T. Mügge. Leipzig, 1862. 3 v. 12°. G,355
Prophets and Kings of the Old Testament. F. D. Maurice. Bost. 1853. 12°. P,116
Lives and Martyrdoms of. Dorotheus, *Bishop of Tyrus*. Lon. 1607. f°. P,647
Proportions of the Human Figure. W. W. Story. London, 1866. 8°. . Q,159
Propria quæ Maribus, and Box Tunnel. C. Reade. Boston, 1857. 16°. . K,908
Prose Writers of America. R. W. Griswold. Philadelphia, 1854. 8°. . H,665
Prosser, R. P. and Pitman, B. Reporter's Manual and Vocab. Cin. 1854. 16°. L,679
Prostitution, History of. W. W. Sanger. New York, 1859. 8°. . . *O,363
Protein und seine Verbindungen. H. Hoffmann. Giessen, 1842. 8°. N,252,14
Protestant Churches, Variations of. J. B. Bossuet. N. Y. 1836–42. 2 v. 12°. P,568
Protestant Clergy in Ireland, Defense of. Dublin, 1788. 8°. . . . . H,630
Protestant Epis. Church in America, Hist. of. S. Wilberforce. Lon. 1844. 12°. P,838
Canon Law and Constitution of. F. Vinton. New York, 1870. 8°. P,834
Protestant Reformation in England and Ireland. W. Cobbett. Lond. '29. 2 v. 8°. P,664
Protestant Refugees, History of the French. C. Weiss. N. Y. 1854. 2 v. 12°. B,364
Protestant Religion, a safe Way. W. Chillingworth. London, 1854. p. 8°. P,658
Protestant Separatists, Collections concerning. J. Hunter. Lond. 1854. 8°. C,44
Protestantism and other Essays. T. De Quincey. Edinburgh, 1862. 12°. H,412,7
Lectures on. H. A. Garland. St. Louis, 1852. 8°. . . . T,19,2
Protestants of France, History of. G. de Félice. London, 1853. 8°. . P,567
Prout, Father, Reliques of. F. Mahoney and F. Murphy. London, 1860. 8°. L,143
The same. London, 1866. 8°. . . . . . . . . H,487
Prout, S. Progressive Fragments in Landscape Drawing. Lond. 1861. 8°. *Q,209,1
Studies of Boats and Coast Scenery. London, 1816. 4°. . . . *Q,195
Views of Rural Cottages. London, 1819. 8°. . . . . . *Q,209,2
Prout, W. Chemistry and Natural Theology. London, 1855. p. 8°. . L,279
Composition of Simple Alimentary Substances. London, 1827. 4°. N,252,42
Provençal Poetry, History of. C. C. Fauriel. New York, 1860. 12°. . H,761
Proverbial Philosophy. M. F. Tupper. New York, 1849. 8°. . . J,877
Proverb Series. M. E. Bradley and K. J. Neely. Boston, 1871. 6 v. 16°. J,1700

Vol. 1. Birds of a Feather.
2. Fine Feathers do not make fine Birds.
3. Handsome is that handsome does.
Vol. 4. Wrong confessed is half redressed.
5. One good turn deserves another.
6. Actions speak louder than words.

Proverbs, Dictionary of Quotations, Proverbs, etc. Philadelphia, 1856. 12°. H,145
Dictionnaire des Proverbes Français. Paris, 1821. 8°. . . . H,891
for the People. E. L. Magoon. Boston, 1849. 12°. . . . . H,246
Gold-Foil from Popular. J. G. Holland. New York, 1867. 12°. . H,107
Hand-Book of. J. Ray; edit. by H. G. Bohn. London, 1867. p. 8°. L,11
Polyglot of Foreign. H. G. Bohn. London, 1857. p. 8°. . . L,24
Wisdom, Wit, Whims, etc. J. Banvard. New York, 1855. 12°. . H,13
Providences, Remarkable, 1684. I. Mather. London, 1856. 12°. . . O,344
Provincial, Lettres. B. Pascal. Paris, 1853. 8°. . . . . . . P,92

Provincial Letters. B. Pascal; edited by O. W. Wight. N. Y. 1859. 12°. P,93
Provocations of Madame Palissy. A. Manning. London, 1863. 16°. . J,596
Prückner, C. P. und Höfflmayr. Fabrikation des Blausalzes. Hof, 1837. 8°. N,252,10
Prue and I. G. W. Curtis. New York, 1868. 12°. . . . . . . K,91
Prussia, Gesch. des Preussisch. Staats. G. A. H. Stenzel. Ham. 1830-54. 5 v. 8°. E,74
Geschichte Preussen's. J. Voigt. Königsberg, 1827-39. 9 v. 8°. . E,75
Notes of a Traveller in. S. Laing. Philadelphia, 1846. 8°. . . V,272
Queens of, Memoirs of. E. W. Atkinson. London, 1858. 8°. . . D,530
Verein zur Beförderung des Gartenbaues, etc.; Verhandlungen. Berlin, 1824-49. 19 v. in 18. 4°. . . . . . . . . *E,480
Prussian and French War in a Nutshell. M. D. Landon. N. Y. 1871. 12°. B,212
Prussiate, Fabrikation. M. Höfflmayr und C. P. Prückner. Hof, 1837. 8°. N,252,10
Prutz, R. Helene; ein Frauenleben. Prag, 1856. 3 v. 16°. . . G,390
Zehn Jahre; Geschichte, 1840-50. Leipzig, 1850-56. 2 v. 8°. . E,38
Psalms of David, fitted to Tunes. N. Brady and N. Tate. Camb. 1831. 8°. P,429
in Phonetic Short Hand; edit. by B. Pitman. Cincinnati, n. d. 12°. L,670
See also *Bible, Psalms.*
Pseudonymes et Anonymes Ouvrages. A. A. Barbier. Paris, 1822-27. 4 v. 8°. L.R.
Pseudonyms, Handbook of. R. Thomas. London, 1868. 8°. . . . . L.R.
Index Pseudonymorum; with Supplem. E. Weller. Leip. 1856-62. 8°. L.R.
Psyche; zur Entwicklungsgeschichte der Seele. C. G. Carus. Stutt. 1851. 8°. G,547
Psychological Inquiries. Sir B. C. Brodie. Lond. 1854-62. 2 v. in 1. 16°. O,694
Psychology. F. A. Rauch. New York, 1841. 12°. . . . . . . O,634
S. S. Schmucker. New York, 1845. 12°. . . . . . O,631
Elemente der Psychophysik. G. T. Fechner. Leipzig, 1860. 2 v. 8°. G,548
Empirical. L. P. Hickock. Schenectady, 1855. 12°. . . . . O,647
Principles of. J. Bascom. New York, 1869. 12°. . . . . . O,668
Rational. L. P. Hickock. Schenectady, 1854. 8°. . . . . . O,703
Seelenleben des Menschen. J. Schaller. Weimar, 1860. 8°. . . G,569
Pterylography. C. L. Nitzsch; edit. by P. L. Sclater. London, 1867. 4°. Q,72
Public and Parlor Readings. L. B. Monroe. Boston, 1871. 12°. . O,1248
Public Buildings, Select Designs for. S. H. Brooks. London, 1842. 4°. *M,297
Public Expenditure. D. Wakefield, jr. London, 1834. 8°. . . . . O,519
Public Libraries, Report of Select Committee on. Lond. 1849-50. 2 v. f°. P.D.
Public Men of the Revolution. W. Sullivan. Philadelphia, 1847. 8°. . C,882
Public School Advocate, v. 1. Columbus, 1851. 8°. . . . . . . . O,843
Public Speaking, Rudiments of. G. J. Holyoake. New York, 1853. 12°. L,589
Puck; his Vicissitudes, etc. L. de la Rame. Philadelphia, 1870. 12°. . K,894
The same. Leipzig, 1870. 2 v. in 1. 16°. . . . . . J,415
Pückler-Muskau, H. L. H. Aus Mehemed Ali's Reich. Stutt. 1844. 3 v. 16°. E,225
Egypt under Mehemet Ali. London, 1845. 2 v. 12°. . . . . V,780
Tour in England, Ireland, and France. Philadelphia, 1833. 8°. . V,291
Pütz, W. Hand-Book of Mediæval Geography and History. N. Y. 1858. 12°. A,228
Manual of Modern Geography and History. New York, 1859. 12°. A,302
Puffendorf, S. von. Law of Nature and Nations. London, 1717. f°. . Q,307
Pugin, A. and A. W. Examples of Gothic Architecture. Lond. 1850. 3 v. 4°. *Q,345
Pugin, A. W. Floriated Ornament. London, 1849. 4°. . . . . *Q,181
Glossary of Ecclesiastical Ornament and Costume. Lond. 1868. 4°. *Q,216
Photographs from Architec. Sketches. S. Ayling. Lond. 1865. 2 v. 4°. *M,281
Puissant, L. Description Géomét. de la France. Paris, 1832-40. 2 v. 4°. U,589,6,7

Puissant, L. Description Géomét. de la France, v. 1. Paris, 1832. 4°. . M,816
Méthode pour obtenir le Résultat d'Observations Astro. Par. 1823. 4°. M,1175
Traité de Géodésie. Paris, 1819. 2 v. 4°. . . . . . . M,815
Supplement to the same. Paris, 1827. 4°. . . . M,1175
Pulaski, K., *Count*, Life of. J. Sparks. Boston, 1860. 12°. . . C,860,14
Pullan, Mrs. Maternal Counsels. London, 1858. 12°. . . . . O,959
Treasures in Needlework. London, n. d. 12°. . . . . . H,473
Pulman, G. P. R. Fly-Fishing for Trout. London, 1851. 16°. . . . M,326
Pulpit, American. H. Fowler. New York, 1856. 8°. . . . . C,946
Annals of the American. W. B. Sprague. N. Y. 1859-69. 9 v. 8°. C,1122

Vol. 1, 2. Trinitarian Congregational.
3, 4. Presbyterian.
5. Episcopalian.
6. Baptist.
Vol. 7. Methodist.
8. Unitarian.
9. Lutheran.

Pulpit Eloquence of the 19th Century. H. C. Fish. New York, 1857. 8°. P,764
Pulszky, F. and T. Sketches of American Society. N. Y. 1853. 2 v. 12°. V,50
Pulszky, T. Memoirs of a Hungarian Lady. Philadelphia, 1850. 12°. . D,768
Pummell, J. Russet Leaves. Philadelphia, 1870. 12°. . . . . H,116
Pumpelly, R. Across American and Asia. New York, 1870. 8°. . V,1084
Punch; or, the London Charivari. London, 1841-68. 55 v. in 28. 4°. *Q 323
Punch's Complete Letter Writer. D. Jerrold. London, 1851. 12°. . U,178,5
The same. Philadelphia, n. d. 12°. . . . . U,179,3
Punch's Letters to his Son, etc. D. Jerrold. London, 1853. 12°. . U,178,5
The same. Philadelphia, n. d. 12°. . . . . U,179,1
Punctuation, Treatise on. J. Wilson. Boston, 1856. 16°. . . . . L,561
Punischer Krieg, Geschichte des zweiten. R. Micke. Breslau, 1851. 16°. E,20
Punishment by Death. G. B. Cheever. New York, 1855. 12°. . . . O,355
of Death, Opinions upon. B. Montagu. London, 1812-13. 3 v. 8°. O,359
Rationale of. J. Bentham. London, 1830. 8°. . . . . . O,553
Punishments, Thoughts on Secondary. R. Whately. London, 1832. 8°. . P,117
Punjab Frontier, 1848-49. H. B. Edwards. London, 1851. 2 v. 8°. . V,697
Punshon, W. M. Lectures and Sermons. Cincinnati, 1860. 12°. . . P,152
Pupils of St. John, the Divine. C. M. Yonge. London, n. d. 12°. . . P,266
Puritan Commonwealth. P. Oliver. Boston, 1856. 8°. . . . . . C,21
Puritans and Pilgrim Fathers, History of. W. H. Stowell and D. Wilson.
Cincinnati, 1856. 12°. . . . . . . . . . . C,4
and their Principles. E. Hall. New York, 1846. 8°. . . . C.9
History of. D. Neal. New York, 1855. 2 v. 8°. . . . . . C,8
History of the later. J. B. Marsden. London, 1854. 8°. . . P,613
Lives of. B. Brook. London, 1813. 3 v. 8°. . . . . . . D,132
of England and Queen Elizabeth. S. Hopkins. Bost. 1859-65. 3 v. 8°. A,513
Purple Island; a Poem. P. Fletcher. London, 1816. 8°. . . . . J,859
Pursuit of Knowledge under Difficulties. G. L. Craik. London, 1868. p. 8°. L,99
The same. London, 1834. 2 v. 16°. . . . . . . L,485
The same. New York, 1868. 2 v. 16°. . . . . . . L,402
Pursuits of Literature; a Satirical Poem. T. J. Mathias. London, 1798. 8°. J,871
The same. London, 1803. 8°. . . . . . . . . . J,872
Pursuits of Women. F. P. Cobbe. London, n. d. 12°. . . . . . O,410
Pusey, E. B. Church of England; an Eirenicon. New York, 1866. 12°. . P,238
Reply to the same. J. H. Newman. London, 1866. 8°. . P,220
Collegiate and Professorial Teaching. Oxford, 1854. 8°. . O,1203

Putnam, Gen. I. G. C. Hill. Philadelphia, 1868. 12°. . . . . J,1228
Discussion concerning. "Selah" and H. B. Dawson. Morris. 1860. 8°. B,814
Life of. O. W. B. Peabody. New York, 1860. 12°. . . . . C,860,7
Putnam, G. P. Home Cyclopædia of Literature and the Arts. N.Y.1852. 12°. L.R.
Putnam, M. L. Record of an Obscure Man. Boston, 1861. 12°. . . H,258
Putnam's Monthly Magazine. New York, 1853-57. 10 v. 8°. . . . . S,1
The same, new series, v. 1, 2. New York, 1868. 2 v. 8°. . S,2
Put Yourself in his Place. C. Reade. New York, 1870. 8°. . . . K,916
Puvis, A. Des Différens Moyens d'amender le Sol. Paris, 1837. 8°. N,252,24
Pycroft, J. Course of English Reading. New York, 1854. 12°. . . O,966
School Education. Oxford, 1843. 12°. . . . . . . . O,996
Pyne, G. Treatise on Perspective. London, 1857. 12°. . . . . . M,954
Pyramid, The Great. J. Taylor. London, 1859. 12°. . . . . . V,784
Life and Work at. C. P. Smyth. Edinburgh, 1867. 3 v. 8°. . V,836
Our Inheritance in. C. P. Smyth. London, 1864. 12°. . . . V,779
Pyrenees, The, and Béarn, Tour to. L. S. Costello. London, 1844. 2 v. 8°. V,477
France and Switzerland. H. D. Inglis. Edinburgh, 1831. 2 v. 16°. I,532
Pyrker, J. L. Sämmtliche Werke. Stuttgart, 1855-57. 3 v. 16°. . . E,348

Bd. 1. Tunisias; ein Heldengedicht.
2. Rudolph von Habsburg; ein Heldengedicht.
3. Perlen der heiligen Vorzeit.

Pyroxyle, Fabrication du. H. A. Meynier. Paris, 1848. 4°. . . N,252,41
Pyrrhus, History of. J. Abbott. New York, 1854. 16°. . . . . J,1421

Quackenbos, G. P. First Lessons in Composition. New York, 1855. 12°. O,1076
Natural Philosophy. New York, 1865. 12°. . . . . . . N,71
School History of the United States. New York, 1868. 12°. . . B,692
Quadroon; or, Adventures in Louisiana. M. Reid. New York, n. d. 12°. J,1570
Quadrupeds described. London, 1831-40. 3 v. 16°. . . . . . . L,481
Natural History of. New York, 1835. p. 8°. . . . . . . L,409
W. Swainson. London, 1835. 12°. . . . . . . M,1031
of North America. J.J. Audubon and J. Bachman. N.Y. 1854. 3 v. 8°. *N,467
Quakerism, Portraiture of. T. Clarkson. Indianapolis, 1870. 8°. . . P,861
Quakers, History of. W. Sewel. New York, 1844. 2 v. 8°. . . . P,624
Sufferings of the. J. Besse. London, 1733-38. 3 v. 8°. . . P,633
Quaritch, B. Catalogue of Books for sale. London, 1868. 8°. . . . L.R.
Quarles, F. Emblems, Divine and Moral. London, 1859. 12°. . . P,201
Enchiridion. London, 1856. 16°. . . . . . . . . P,29
Quarrying and Blasting Rocks. Sir J. Burgoyne. London, 1856. 12°. . M,894
Quarterly Journal of Education, v. 2-10. London, 1831-35. 9 v. 8°. . S,44
of the Geological Society of London. London, 1845-68. 24 v. 8°. R,38
of Microscopic Science. London, 1853-68. 16 v. 8°. . . . R,24
Quarterly Review. London, 1809-53. 93 v. 8°. . . . . . . R,8
Quartz Pebbles. J. Brainard. Cleveland, 1854. 8°. . . . . . . T,19,2
Quaternions, Elements of. Sir W. R. Hamilton. London, 1866. . . M,1155
Lectures on. Sir W. R. Hamilton. Dublin, 1853. 8°. . . M,1161
Treatise on. P. G. Tait. Oxford, 1867. 8°. . . . . . M,1153
Quatremère de Quincy, A. C. Life of Raphael. London, 1870. p. 8°. . L,126
Quebec, Expedition to, 1775. J. Melvin. Philadelphia, 1864. 4°. . . Q,463

Quebec Literary and Histor. Society, Transactions. Quebec, 1829–31. 2 v. 8°. *T,55
Queda; Journal in Malayan Waters. S. Osborn. London, 1857. 12°. . V,616
Queechy. S. Warner. Philadelphia, 1867. 12°. . . . . . . K,374
Queen Hortense. C. Mundt. New York, 1870. 8°. . . . . . . G,213
Queen Mab. J. Kavanagh. New York, 1864. 3 v. in 1. 12°. . . K,744
Queen-Mother and Rosamond. A. C. Swinburne. Boston, 1866. 12°. . I,435
Queen of the Air. J. Ruskin. New York, 1869. 8°. . . . . M,63
Queen of the County. J. C. Stretton. Boston, 1867. 12°. . . . K,855
Queen of Hearts. W. Collins. New York, 1859. 12°. . . . . K,638
Queen Phillippa's Golden Booke. A. Manning. London, n. d. 12°. . I,403
Queen's Maries. G. J. W. Melville. Leipzig, 1862. 2 v. in 1. 16°. . J,380
Queen's Necklace. A. Dumas. Philadelphia, n. d. 2 v. in 1. 8°. . H,1013
Queens of American Society. E. F. Ellet. New York, 1868. 12°. . . C,768
of England before the Conquest. M. Hall. London, 1854. 2 v. 8°. C,1250
The same. Philadelphia, 1854. 12°. . . . C,1249
The same. Boston, n. d. 8°. . . . . . . D,368,13
from the Conquest. A. Strickland. Phil. 1854. 12 v. 12°. D,368
Contents. See *Strickland, A.*
The same. London, 1868–69. 6 v. p. 8. . . . L,270
of the House of Hanover. J. Doran. New York, 1855. 2 v. 12°. C,1206
of Prussia, Memoirs of. E. W. Atkinson. London, 1858. 8°. . . D,530
of Scotland and Eng. Princesses. A. Strickland. N.Y. 1859–68. 8 v. 12°. D,17
of Society. K. B. and J. C. Thomson. London, 1870. 12°. . . C,590
The same. New York, 1861. 12°. . . . . . . . C,592
of Spain, Annals of. A. George. New York, 1850. 2 v. 12°. . D,700
Queer Bonnets. L. C. Tuthill. New York, n. d. 16°. . . . J,1347
Queer Little People. H. B. Stowe. Boston, 1868. 16°. . . . J,1279
Quekett, J. Lectures on Histology. London, 1852–54. 2 v. 8°. . . L,969
Treatise on the Use of the Microscope. London, 1855. 8°. . . N,10
Quénon, J. Dictionnaire Grec-François. Paris, 1807. 8°. . . . . L.R.
Quenstedt, F. A. Cephalopoden. Tübingen, 1849. 8°. . . . . . G,837
Handbuch der Mineralogie. Tübingen, 1863. 8°. . . . . . G,836
Quentin Durward. Sir W. Scott. Boston, 1858. 2 v. 16°. . . . K,945
The same. Philadelphia, 1852. 8°. . . . . . . K,970
The same. Philadelphia, 1869. 8°. . . . . . K,1112
The same. Leipzig, 1845. 16°. . . . . . . . J,450
Quérard, J. M. La France Littéraire. Paris, 1827–65. 12 v. 8°. . . L.R.
Les Supercheries Littéraires Dévoilées, v. 1, 2. Paris, 1869–70. 2 v. 8°. L.R.
Littérature Française Contemporaine. Paris, 1842–57. 6 v. 8°. . L.R.
Quesnel, P. The Gospels; with Reflections. Philadelphia, 1855. 2 v. 8°. P,547
Questions of Modern Thought; Lect. on Bible and Infidelity. Phil. 1871. 8°. P,284
McCosh, J. Renan's Life of Jesus.
Thompson, J. P. Unity of the Bible.
Adams, W. Advantages of a Written Revelation.
Schaff, P. Christ's Testimony to Christianity.
Hague, W. Self-Witnessing Character of the New Testament Christianity.
Haven, E. O. Soul; a Positive Entity.
Quevedo y Villegas, F. de. Works. Edinburgh, 1798. 3 v. 12°. . . H,963
Quiet Miss Godolphin. R. Garrett. Philadelphia, 1871. 12°. . . . K,382
Quiet Nook in the Jura. J. Ruffini. Leipzig, 1867. 16°. . . . . J,434
Quill, C. American Mechanic. Philadelphia, 1838. 18°. . . . . H,250
Quinby, M. Mysteries of Bee-Keeping explained. New York, 1857. 12°. M,468

Quincy, E. Life of Josiah Quincy. Boston, 1867. 12°. . . . . . C,877
Quincy, J. History of the Boston Athenæum. Cambridge, 1851. 8°. . O,829
History of Harvard College. Boston, 1860. 2 v. 8°. . . . O,809
Life of. E. Quincy. Boston, 1867. 12°. . . . . . . . C,877
Life of John Quincy Adams. Boston, 1858. 8°. . . . C,1089
Municipal History of Boston. Boston, 1852. 8°. . . . . C,60
Quincy, J. P. Charicles; a Dramatic Poem. Boston, 1856. 16°. . . I,113
Lyteria; a Dramatic Poem. Boston, 1855. 16°. . . . . . I,112
Quincy, Q. de. See *Quatremère de Quincy, A. C.*
Quinn, P. T. Money in the Garden; Vegetable Manual. N. Y. 1871. 12°. M,485
Quint, A. H. The Potomac and Rapidan; Army Notes. Boston, 1864. 12°. B,894
Quintilianus, M. F. De Institutione Oratoria. Parisiis, 1821-25. 7 v. 8°. U,342
The same; translated. London, 1856. 2 v. p. 8°. . . . L,76
Quitman, J. A., Life of. J. F. H. Claiborne. New York, 1860. 2 v. 12°. C,929
Quits; a Novel. I. von Tautphoeus. Philadelphia, 1866. 12°. . . . G,238
The same. Leipzig, 1858. 2 v. in 1. 16°. . . . . . J,474
Quodlibet; some Annals thereof. J. P. Kennedy. New York, 1866. 12°. K,312
Quotations, Dictionary of Aphorisms, Proverbs, and. Phil. 1856. 12°. . H,145
Dictionary of Latin. H. T. Riley. London, 1866. p. 8°. . . L,53
Dictionary of Poetical. S. J. Hale. Philadelphia, 1866. 8°. . . I,163
Familiar; 5th edition. J. Bartlett. Boston, 1869. 12°. . . . I,484

Raabe, W. Der Hungerpastor; ein Roman. Berlin, 1867. 16°. . . G,391
Rab and his Friends, etc. J. Brown. Leipzig, 1858. 8°. . . . . J,54
The same. Edinburgh, 1862. 16°. . . . . . . H,449
The same. Boston, 1864. . . . . . . . . H,185,1
Rabbe, A. and Duncan, J. History of Russia. London, 1854. 2 v. 12°. B,535
Rabelais, F. Œuvres. Paris, 1837. 8°. . . . . . . . . H,957
Works; translated by T. Urquhart. London, 1854-55. 2 v. p. 8°. *L,329
Rabener, G. W. Satiren, v. 3-5. Reuttlingen, 1777. 3 v. 16°. . . E,349
Race for Wealth. J. H. Riddell. Leipzig, 1866. 2 v. in 1. 16°. . . J,426
Races of the Earth, Indigenous. J. C. Nott and G. R. Gliddon. Phil. 1857. 4°. N,468
Mengenschlecht. J. C. Prichard. Leipzig, 1840-48. 4 v. in 5. 8°. E,403
of Man. C. Pickering. London, 1863. p. 8°. . . . . . L,135
See also *Ethnology.*
Rachel, M'lle. See *Félix, E. R.*
Rachel Gray. J. Kavanagh. New York, 1868. 12°. . . . . . K,745
The same. Leipzig, 1856. 16°. . . . . . . . J,234
Rachel Ray. A. Trollope. New York, n. d. 8°. . . . . . K,1035
The same. Leipzig, 1863. 2 v. in 1. 16°. . . . . J,504
Racine, J. Œuvres Poetiques. Paris, 1853. 3 v. 8°. . . . . . H,896
Théatre Complet. Paris, 1856. 12°. . . . . . . . H,888
Racine, L. Poésies. Paris, 1853. 12°. . . . . . . . . H,943
Radau, R. Wonders of Acoustics. New York, 1870. 12°. . . . M,1060
Radcliffe, A. Mysteries of Udolpho. New York, 1857. 12°. . . . K,893
The same. London, 1820. 3 v. 12°. . . . . . . K,548
Romance of the Forest. Philadelphia, 1864. 12°. . . . . K,1146
The same. London, 1820. 2 v. 12°. . . . . . . K,547

Radcliffe, A. Memoirs in Familiar Letters. Edinburgh, 1810. 8°. . . D,247
Radcliffe Observatory, Observations at. H. Main. Oxford, 1861–7. 5 v. 8°. N,362
Catalogue of 6,317 Stars. M. J. Johnson. Oxford, 1860. 8°. . N,361
Radde, G. Reisen in Ost-Siberien; Botanik von E. Regel. Mosk. 1861. 2 v. 8°. G,888
Radiation. J. Tyndall. New York, 1868. 12°. . . . . . . N,40
Rae, G. First Lessons in Arithmetic. Edinburgh, n. d. 16°. . . . O,1090
Raffaello Sanzio d'Urbino. Raphael's Cartoons. R. Cattermole. Lond. 1845. 8°. M,92
Life of. A. C. Quatremère de Quincy. London, 1870. p. 8°. . . L,126
Raffald, E. Experienced Housekeeper. London, 1801. 24°. . . . H,183
Raffles, Sir T. S. History of Java. London, 1830. 2 v. 8°. . . . C,409
Atlas to the same. London, 1844. 4°. . . . . . . F,235
Rafinesque-Schmalz, C. S. American Nations. Phila. 1836. 2 v. in 1. 12°. B,693
Ragamuffin, True History of a Little. J. Greenwood. London, n. d. 8°. K,694
Rag-Bag, The. N. P. Willis. New York, 1855. 12°. . . . . H,77
Ragged Dick Series. H. Alger. Boston, n. d. 6 v. 16°. . . . J,1430

Vol. 1. Ragged Dick.
2. Fame and Fortune.
3. Mark, the Match Boy.
Vol. 4. Rough and Ready.
5. Ben, the Luggage Boy.
6. Rufus and Rose.

Ragged Schools, Philosophy of. London, 1851. 16°. . . . . O,1123
Ragonot, L. C. Vocabulaire Symbolique Anglo-Français. London, n. d. 4°. L.R.
Raikes, T. Visit to St. Petersburg, 1829–30. London, n. d. 8°. . . V,534
Railroad Accidents and Steamboat Disasters. Worcester, 1846. 12°. . H,494
Railway Details. R. M. Stepheson. London, 1850. 12°. . . . . M,964
Railway Economy. D. Lardner. New York, 1850. 12°. . . . . M,694
Railway Machinery. D. K. Clark. Glasgow, 1855. 2 v. r. 4°. . . S.C.
Railway Masonry, Guide to. P. Nicholson. London, 1840. 8°. . . M,698
Railway Morals and Policy. H. Spencer. London, 1865. p. 8°. . . I,667
Railway Practice. S. C. Brees. London, 1847–56. 3 v. in 1. 4°. . . *Q,286
Plates to the same. London, 1849. f°. . . . . . . *Q,315
Railway Working in Great Britain. E. D. Chattaway. London, 1855. 12°. M,900
Raimund, G. Novellen. Hannover, 1860. 4 v. 16°. . . . . . G,393
Schloss Elkrath. Hannover, 1866. 3 v. 16°. . . . . . . G,392
Rainbow and Lucky Stories. J. Abbott. New York, 1860. 5 v. 16°. . J,1381

Vol. 1. Handie.
2. Rainbow's Journey.
Vol. 3. Three Pines.
4. Selling Lucky.
Vol. 5. Up the River.

Raine, J. (Ed.) Historiæ Dunelmensis; Scriptores tres. London, 1839. 8°. F,126,9
Rale, S., Life of. C. Francis. Boston, 1860. 12°. . . . . C,860,17
Raleigh, Sir W. and his Time. C. Kingsley. Boston, 1859. 12°. . . D,405
Discovery of Guiana. London, 1848. 8°. . . . . . . . V,981
History of the World. London, 1614. f°. . . . . . . F,293
Life of. E. Edwards. London, 1868. 2 v. 8°. . . . . D,453
J. A. St. John. London, 1869. 8°. . . . . . . D,407
News of; Description of Guiana, 1618. See *Force's Tracts*, v. 3.
Works; Lives by Oldys and Birch. Oxford, 1829. 8 v. 8°. . . U,237
Ralph, J. Lives of the Poets-Laureate. London, 1853. 8°. . . . D,441
Ralph the Heir. A. Trollope. New York, 1871. 12°. . . . K,1060
Ralph Roister Doister; a Comedy. N. Udall. London, 1847. 8°. . I,885,32
Ralston, W. R. S. Krilof and his Fables. London, 1869. 12°. . . H,625
Rambler, The. S. Johnson. Boston, 1866. 3 v. 8°. . . H,536,16–18
The same. New York, 1851. 8°. . . . . . . U,227,1
Rambles about the Country. E. F. Ellet. New York, 1854. 16°. . . H,184

Rambles of a Journalist. S. H. Hammond and L.W.Mansfield. N.Y.1855. 12°. H,34
Rame, L. de la., *Ouida*. Beatrice Boville. Philadelphia, 1867. 12°. . K,879
Cecil Castlemaine's Gage, etc. Philadelphia, 1867. 12°. . . K,880
Chandos. Philadelphia, 1869. 12°. . . . . . . . . . K,887
Granville de Vigne. Philadelphia, 1870. 12°. . . . . . K,877
Idalia; a Novel. Philadelphia, 1869. 12°. . . . . . . K,886
The same. Leipzig, 1867. 2 v. in 1. 16°. . . . . . J,414
Puck; his Vicissitudes, etc. Philadelphia, 1870. 12°. . . . K,894
The same. Leipzig, 1870. 2 v. in 1. 16°. . . . . J,415
Randolph Gordon, etc. Philadelphia, 1867. 12°. . . . . K,878
Strathmore. Philadelphia, 1870. 12°. . . . . . . . K,895
Tricotrin. Philadelphia, 1870. 12°. . . . . . . . K,876
The same. Leipzig, 1870. 2 v. in 1. 16°. . . . . J,416
Under Two Flags. Philadelphia, 1867. 12°. . . . . . . K,896
Rameses; or, Egypt 3300 Years Ago. F. de Lanoye. New York, 1870. 12°. M,1056
Rammelsberg, C. F. Lehrbuch der Chem. Metallurgie. Berlin, 1850. 8°. G,763
Lehrbuch der Stöchiometrie. Berlin, 1842. 8°. . . . . N,252,16
Quantitative und Metallurgische Analyt. Chemie. Berlin, 1845. 8°. N,252,16
Ramsay, A. Rudiments of Mineralogy. London, 1868. 12°. . . . M,855
Works; with Life by G. Chalmers. London, 1853–55. 3 v. 16°. . U,125
Ramsay, A. C. Passages in the History of Geology. Lond. 1848–9. 8°. N,252,35
Ramsay, A. M., *Chevalier*. Travels of Cyrus. London, 1727. 2 v. 8°. V,1069
Ramsay, D. History of the American Revolution. London, 1791. 2 v. 8°. B,739
History of the United States, 1607–1808. Phil. 1818. 2 v. 8°. . B,650
Life of Washington. London, 1807. 8°. . . . . . . . C,905
Ramsay, J. G. M. Annals of Tennessee. Philadelphia, 1853. 8°. . . C,276
Ramsay, W. Manual of Roman Antiquities. London, 1855. 12°. . . A,137
Ramshorn, L. Dictionary of Latin Synonymes. Boston, 1839. 12°. . L,754
Ran away to Sea. M. Reid. Boston, 1866. 16°. . . . . . J,1585
Rand, B. H. Elements of Medical Chemistry. Philadelphia, 1871. 12°. N,217
Rand, E. S. jr. Bulbs; Hardy and Tender. Boston, 1866. 12°. . . N,956
Flowers for the Parlor and Garden. Boston, 1864. 12°. . . . N,951
Garden Flowers. Boston, 1866. 12°. . . . . . . . N,955
Randall, A. T. Reading and Elocution. New York, 1870. 12°. . O,1244
Randall, H. S. Life of Thomas Jefferson. New York, 1858. 3 v. 8°. C,1069
Fine-Wool Sheep Husbandry. New York, 1863. 12°. . . . M,463
The same. New York, 1854. 8°. . . . . . . . M,474
Randall, S. S. First Principles of Popular Education. N. Y. 1868. 12°. O,975
Incentives to the Study of Geology. New York, 1846. 12°. . . N,593
Mental and Moral Culture. New York, 1855. 12°. . . . . O,1168
Randolph, J., of Roanoke, Life of. H. A. Garland. N. Y. 1854. 2 v. in 1. 8°. C,881
Randolph Gordon. L. de la Rame. Philadelphia, 1867. 12°. . . . K,878
Rangers and Regulators of the Tanaha. M. Reid. New York, 1870. 12°. J,1571
Rangers; or, The Tory's Daughter. D. P. Thomson. Boston, 1869. 12°. K,392
Ranke, L. Civil Wars and Monarchy in France. New York, 1853. 12°. B,240
Ferdinand I. and Maximilian II. of Austria. London, 1856. p. 8°. I,661,2
History of the Popes. London, 1847–51. 3 v. p. 8°. . . . . L,222
Romische Päpste im 16ten und 17ten Jahrh. Berl. 1844–45. 3 v. 8°. E,30
Servia and the Servian Revolution. London, 1853. p. 8°. . . . L,223
Rankine, W. J. M. Manual of the Steam Engine. Lond. and Glasg. 1859. 8°. M,617

Rankine, W. J. M. Machinery and Millwork. London, 1869. 12°. . . M,726
Ranking, J. Wars and Sports of the Mongols and Romans. Lond. 1826. 4°. M,430
Ranthorpe. G. H. Lewes. Leipzig, 1847. 16°. . . . . . . J,294
Rantoul, R. jr. Memoirs and Speeches; ed. by L. Hamilton. Bost. 1854. 8°. C,1102
Remarks on Education. Boston, 1838. 8°. . . . . . . O,927
Raphael. See *Raffaello Sanzio d' Urbino.*
Raphael. A. de Lamartine. New York, 1849. 8°. . . . . . . H,928
The same; translated. New York, 1865. 12°. . . . H,903
Raphall, M. J. Post-Biblical History of the Jews. N. Y. 1866. 2 v. 12°. A,203
Rapin de Thoyras, P. History of England. London, 1732–37. 3 v. f°. S.C.
The same. London, 1728–47. 28 v. 8°. . . . . . . A,421
Rasch, G. Ein Ausflug nach Rügen. Leipzig, 1856. 16°. . . . E,193
Raspail, F. V. Domestic Medicine. London, 1853. 12°. . . . . M,955
Raspe, R. E. Travels of Baron Munchausen. New York, 1869. 12°. J,1494
Rasselas, History of. S. Johnson. London, 1820. 12°. . . . . K,537
The same. New York, 1851. 8°. . . . . . . U,227,1
The same. New York, 1869. 16°. . . . . . . . I,562
Rastell, J. Pastime of People, Chronicles of England, etc. Lond. 1811. 4°. *F,163
Rat, The. J. Rodwell. London, 1863. 16°. . . . . . . . N,680
Rathbone, H. M. Lady Willoughby. New York, 1850. 8°. . . . D,157
Rathke, H. Morphologie; Reisebemerkungen aus Taurien. Riga, 1837. 4°. G,966
Rational Cosmology. L. P. Hickok. New York, 1859. 8°. . . . M,789
Rationalism, History of. J. F. Hurst. New York, 1865. 8°. . . . P,120
in Europe. W. E. H. Lecky. New York, 1866. 8°. . . . P,213
Ratisbonne, A. Life and Times of St. Bernardus. New York, 1855. 12°. D,635
Ratis Raving, Moral and Religious Pieces. London, 1870. 8°. . . L,605,43
Ratzeburg, J. T. C. Standortsgewächse Deutschlands. Berlin, 1859. 8°. G,887
Rau, H. Alex. von Humboldt; Biographischer Roman. Leip. 1861. 7 v. 12°. G,411
Hölderlin. Leipzig, 1862. 2 v. 12°. . . . . . . . . G,410
Mozart; ein Künstlerleben. Frankfurt-am-Main, 1860. 3 v. 24°. . G,413
Theodor Körner; Vaterländischer Roman. Leipzig, 1863. 2 v. 12°. G,412
William Shakespeare; Biographischer Roman. Berl. 1864. 4 v. 12°. G,414
Rauch, F. A. Psychology. New York, 1841. 12°. . . . . . . O,634
Raumer, F. L. G. von. America and the American People. N. Y. 1846. 8°. V,126
England in 1841; Letters. London, 1842. 2 v. 12°. . . . V,371
Geschichte der Hohenstaufen. Leipzig, 1857–58. 6 v. 8°. . . E,68
History of the XVI. and XVII. Centuries. London, 1835. 2 v. 12°. A,315
Raumer, K. von. German Universities. New York, 1859. 8°. . . . O,816
Life and System of Pestalozzi. London, 1855. 8°. . . . O,1010
Ravaillac, F., Trial of. M. de Béthune. Edinburgh, 1770. 12°. . D,597,5
Raven, M. Eversburg; ein Roman. Hannover, 1855. 3 v. 16°. . . G,424
Galileo Galilei; Geschichtlicher Roman. Leipzig, 1760. 2 v. 12°. G,425
Ravenscliffe. A. Marsh-Caldwell. Leipzig, 1851. 2 v. in 1. 16°. . . J,369
Ravenshoe. H. Kingsley. Boston, 1866. 12°. . . . . . . . K,757
The same. Leipzig, 1862. 2 v. in 1. 16°. . . . . J,251
Rawlinson, G. Five Great Monarchies of Anc. World. Lond. 1862–7. 4 v. 8°. A,27
Historical Evidences of the Truth of Scripture. Boston, 1860. 12°. P,53
History of Herodotus. New York, 1858–61. 4 v. 8°. . . . . A,96
Ray, D. B. Baptist Succession; Hand-Book of Baptist Hist. Cin. 1871. 12°. P,617
Text-Book of Campbellism. Cincinnati, 1871. 12°. . . . . P,618

Ray, I. Medical Jurisprudence of Insanity. Boston, 1853. 8°. . . . L,924
Ray, John, Correspondence of; edited by E. Lankester. London, 1848. 8°. O,301
Hand-Book of Proverbs; edited by H. G. Bohn. Lond. 1867. p. 8°. L,11
Memorials of. W. Derham and others. London, 1846. 8°. . . O,297
Ray, Joseph. Algebra; second Book. Cincinnati, 1866. 12°. . . M,1099
Arithmetic; part Second. Cincinnati, 1849. 16°. . . . O,1094
third Book. Cincinnati, n. d. 16°. . . . . . . O,1096
Child's Arithmetic. Cincinnati, 1853. 16°. . . . . O,1094
Intellectual Arithmetic. Cincinnati, 1853. 16°. . . . O,1080
Ray Society Publications, viz.:
Agassiz, L. Bibliographia Zoölogiæ et Geologiæ. London, 1848–54. 4 v. 8°. O,300
Alder, J. and Hancock. British Nudibranchiate Mollusca. Lond. 1845–55. 7 v. f°. Q,67
Allman, G. J. Monograph of Fresh-Water Polyzoa. London, 1856. f°. . Q,66
Baird, W. Natural History of the British Entomostraca. London, 1850. 8°. . O,302
Blackwall, J. History of the Spiders of Great Britain and Ireland. London, 1861–64. 2 v. f°. . . . . . . . . . . . Q,75
Botanical and Physiological Memoirs; edited by A. Henfrey. London, 1853. 8°. O,306
1. Braun, A. Phenomenon of Rejuvenescence in Nature.
2. Meneghini, G. Animal Nature of the Diatomeæ.
3. Cohn, F. Natural History of Protococcus Pluvialis.
Bowerbank, J. S. Monograph of the British Spongiadæ. Lond. 1864–66. 2 v. 8°. O,308
Brown, R. Miscellaneous Botanical Works, v. 1. London, 1864. 8°. . . O,310
Burmeister, H. Organization of Trilobites. London, 1846. f°. . . . Q,63
Carpenter, W. B. and others. Study of the Foraminifera. London, 1862. f°. . Q,68
Darwin, C. Monograph of the Sub-class Cirripedia. London, 1851–54. 2 v. 8°. O,304
Vol. 1. Lepadidæ. Vol. 2. Balanidæ, Verrucidæ, etc.
Douglass, J. W. and Scott, J. British Hemiptera, v. 1. London, 1865. 8°. . O,309
Eschricht, D. F. and others. Recent Memoirs of the Cetacea. London, 1866. f°. Q,73
Forbes, E. Monograph of the British Naked-Eyed Medusæ. London, 1848. f°. Q,70
Günther, A. C. L. G. Reptiles of British India. London, 1864. f°. . . Q,69
Hofmeister, W. Germination, etc., of the Higher Cryptogamia, and on the Fructification of the Coniferæ. London, 1862. 8°. . . . . O,307
Huxley, T. H. Oceanic Hydrozoa. London, 1859. f°. . . . . . Q,74
Leighton, W. A. British Species of Angiocarpous Lichens. London, 1851. 8°. O,303
Meyen, F. J. F. Outlines of the Geography of Plants. London, 1846. 8°. . O,298
Nitzsch, C. L. Pterylography. London, 1867. f°. . . . . Q,72
Oken, L. Elements of Physiophilosophy. London, 1847. 8°. . . . O,299
Ray, J. Correspondence; edited by E. Lankester. London, 1848. 8°. . . O,301
Memorials of; W. Derham and others. London, 1846. 8°. . . . O,297
Reports and Papers on Botany; edited by A. Henfrey. London, 1846. 8°. . O,293
1. Zuccarini, J. G. Morphology of the Coniferæ.
2. Grisebach, A. H. R. Report on the Contributions of Botanical Geography, for 1842.
3. Nägeli, C. On Vegetable Cells.
4. Link, H. F. Report on the Progress of Physiological Botany, 1842–43.
Reports and Papers on Botany; edited by A. Henfrey. London, 1849. 8°. . O,295
1. Mohl, H. von. On the Structure of the Palm-Stem.
2. Nägeli, C. On Vegetable Cells, part 2.
3. On the Utricular Structures in the Contents of Cells.
4. Link, H. F. Report on Progress of Physiological Botany, 1844–45.
5, 6. Grisebach, A. H. R. Report on the Progress of Geographical and Systematic Botany, for 1844–45.
Reports on the Progress of Zoölogy and Botany, 1841–42. C. L. Bonaparte, A. Wagner, and others. Edinburgh, 1845. 8°. . . . . . O,292
Reports on Zoölogy, 1843–44. A. Wagner and others. London, 1847. 8°. . O,294
Steenstrup, J. J. S. On the Alternation of Generations. London, 1845. 8°. . O,291

Raymond, G. Life and Enterprises of R.W. Elliston. London, 1857. 12°. D,226
Raymond, H. J. Administration of President Lincoln. N. Y. 1864. 12°. B,904
Life and Services of Abraham Lincoln. New York, 1865. 8°. . C,886
Raymond, R. W. Mineral Resources West of the Rocky Mountains. Washington, 1870. 2 v. 8°. . . . . . . . . . N,861,1869–70

Raynal, G. T. F. Histoire de Etablissements des Européens dans les deux Indes. Amsterdam, 1773-74. 7 v. 16°. . . . . . c,425
European Settlements in East and West Indies. Lon. 1788. 8 v. 8°. c,426
Rayner, B. L. Life of Thomas Jefferson. New York, 1832. 8°. . c,1049
Reach, A. B. Claret and Olives. London, 1852. 8°. . . . . . v,479
Read, H. Hand of God in History. Leipzig, 1851. 16°. . . . . . P,169
India and its People. Columbus, 1859. 8°. . . . . . . c,406
Palace of the Great King. Glasgow, 1864. 12°. . . . . P,221
Read, J. M. Henry Hudson; an Historical Inquiry. Albany, 1866. 8°. c,105
Read, T. B. Poetical Works. Philadelphia, 1867. 3 v. 16°. . . . I,107
New Pastoral. Philadelphia, 1855. 16°. . . . . . . . . I,108
Reade, C. Christie Johnstone. Boston, 1866. 16°. . . . . . . K,897
Cloister and the Hearth. New York, 1865. 8°. . . . . . K,898
The same. Leipzig, 1864. 2 v. in 1. 16°. . . . . . J,417
Clouds and Sunshine. Boston, 1855. 16°. . . . . . . K,899
Good Fight and other Tales. New York, 1859. 12°. . . . K,917
Griffith Gaunt. Boston, 1867. 8°. . . . . . . . . . K,901
Hard Cash. Boston, 1869. 16°. . . . . . . . . . K,904
The same. Leipzig, 1864. 3 v. 16°. . . . . . . J,418
It is Never too Late to Mend. Boston, 1856. 2 v. 12°. . . K,907
The same. Leipzig, 1856. 2 v. in 1. 16°. . . . . J,420
Love me Little, Love me Long. New York, n. d. 12°. . . K,902
The same. Leipzig, 1859. 16°. . . . . . . . J,419
Peg Woffington. Boston, 1866. 16°. . . . . . . . K,907
Put Yourself in his Place. New York, 1870. 8°. . . . . K,916
The same. Boston, 1870. 16°. . . . . . . . K,903
Propria quæ Maribus, and the Box Tunnel. Boston, 1857. 16°. . K,908
White Lies. Boston, 1867. 16°. . . . . . . . . . K,909
and Boucicault, D. Foul Play. Boston, 1868. 8°. . . . . . K,900
Reade, W. W. Savage Africa. New York, 1864. 8°. . . . . . V,866
Reader, American First Class-Book. J. Pierpont. New York, 1835. 12°. O,882
District School. W. D. Swan. Philadelphia, 1848. 12°. . . . O,789
Eclectic Third. W. H. McGuffey. Cincinnati, n. d. 12°. . . O,875
Eclectic Fourth. W. H. McGuffey. Cincinnati, 1853. 12°. . . O,788
Fifth School. S. G. Goodrich. Louisville, Ky. 1846. 12°. . . O,889
First Class. B. D. Emerson. Philadelphia, 1839. 12°. . . . O,890
Fourth. R. G. Parker. New York, 1852. 12°. . . . . O,790
Grammar School. W. D. Swan. Philadelphia, 1849. 12°. . . O,884
Instructive. W. D. Swan. Philadelphia, 1849. 12°. . . . O,886
National. J. Pierpont. Boston, 1832. 12°. . . . . . O,1105
New Rhetorical. W. H. Gilder. New York, 1852. 12°. . . . O,879
New North American; Fifth Book. L. Cobb. New York, 1853. 12°. O,878
North American. L. Cobb. Cincinnati, 1850. 12°. . . . . O,878
Primary School. W. D. Swan. Philadelphia, 1844-47. 2 pts. 16°. O,762
The same. Philadelphia, 1848. 12°. . . . . . . O,792
Rhetorical. R. G. Parker. New York, 1853. 12°. . . . . . O,881
E. Porter. Cincinnati, 1848. 12°. . . . . . . . O,1106
Rhetorical Guide; or, Fifth. W. H. McGuffey. Cincinnati, 1845. 12°. O,887
School. C. W. Sanders. Andover, 1841. 12°. . . . . . O,1107
Fourth Book. C. W. Sanders. New York, 1843. 12°. . . O,780

Reader, School, Fifth Book. C. W. and J. C. Sanders. New York, 1855. 12°. o,787
Shakespearian. J. W. S. Hows. New York, 1849. 12°. . . . I,843
Standard Second. E. Sargent. Boston, 1856. 12°. . . . . o,779
Standard Third. E. Sargent. Boston, 1856. 12°. . . . . o,892
Standard Fourth. E. Sargent. Boston, 1856. 12°. . . . . o,891
Western. J. Hall. Cincinnati, 1833. 12°. . . . . . o,877
Young Ladies'. W. D. Swan. Philadelphia, 1851. 12°. . . . o,885
Readers and Students, Hand-Book for. A. Potter. New York, 1855. 18°. L,449
Reading and Elocution. A. T. Randall. New York, 1870. 12°. . o,1244
Books and. N. Porter. New York, 1871. 12°. . . . . o,985
Boy's First Help to. T. A. Buckley. London, 1854. 16°. . o,768,1
Boy's Second Help to. T. A. Buckley. London, n. d. 16°. . o,768,2
Fourth Book of Lessons for. S. Worcester. Boston, 1838. 12°. . o,874
Girl's First Help to. T. A. Buckley. London, 1854. 16°. . o,767,1
Girl's Second Help to. T. A. Buckley. London, 1854. 16°. . o,767,2
Graduated. C. Baker. London, n. d. 16°. . . . . . o,756
Papers for Home. J. Hall. New York, 1871. 12°. . . . H,224
Use of Rules in Teaching. F. R. Russell. Boston, 1854. 12°. o,820,24
What to Read and how to Read. C. H. Moore. New York, 1871. 12°. o,984
Reading-Book, Fourth. J. S. Denman. New York, 1853. 12°. . . . o,786
Geographical. T. Crampton and T. Turner. London, 1857. 16°. . o,895
Zweites Lesebuch für Deutsche Volksschulen. Cincinnati, 1853. 12°. G,544
Reading-Books, Commis. of National Education. Dub. 1854-55. 8 v. 16°. o,781
New Series. L. Cobb. New York, 1850. 12°. . . . . . o,878
Reading-Lessons, Graduated. C. Baker. London, n. d. 16°. . . . o,756
Readings for the Young; selected from Sir W. Scott. Phil. 1848. 2 v. 16°. J,1283
Public and Parlor. L. B. Monroe. Boston, 1871. 12°. . . o,1248
Ready-Reckoner. London, 1861. 12°. . . . . . . . . . M,856
for Measurement of Land. A. Arman. London, 1862. 12°. . . M,826
Realmah. A. Helps. Boston, 1869. 12°. . . . . . . . K,724
Reason and Faith; with other Essays. H. Rogers. London, 1866. 16°. . P,22
and Instinct, Essay on. J. C. Atkinson. London, 1861. 8°. . . N,628
Critic of Pure. I. Kant. London, 1838. 8°. . . . . . o,672
The same. London, 1855. 12°. . . . . . . . L,252
Kritik der Vernunft. J. F. Fries. Heidelberg, 1828-31. 3 v. 8°. G,553
the only Oracle of Man. E. Allen. New York, 1836. 12°. . . P,227
Reason's Tribunal; a Poem. Dublin, 1735. 12°. . . . . . P,72
Reasoning, Easy Lessons on. London, 1853. 16°. . . . . . o,623
Reaumur, R. A. F. de. Histoire des Insectes. Paris, 1734-42. 6 v. 4°. . *o,137
Reavis, L. U. Thoughts for the Young of America. New York, 1871. 12°. H,17
Rebel War-Clerk's Diary. J. B. Jones. Philadelphia, 1866. 2 v. 12°. . B,911
Rebellion Record. F. Moore. New York, 1861-69. 12 v. 8°. . . . B,982
Récamier, Mad. Memoirs and Corresp.; tr. by J. M. Luyster. Bost. 1867. 16°. D,616
Receipts, Ten Thousand. C. Mackenzie. Philadelphia, 1868. 8°. . . H,631
Reclus, E. Earth; Phenomena of the Life of the Globe. N.Y. 1871. 2 v. 8°. V,1110
Recollections of a Busy Life. H. Greeley. New York, 1868. 8°. . . C,711
of a Literary Life. M. R. Mitford. New York, 1852. 12°. . C,1246
of Geoffry Hamlyn. H. Kingsley. Boston, 1866. 12°. . . . K,755
of my Childhood. S. J. Lippincott. Boston, 1866. 16°. . . J,1461
of Seventy Years. J. Farrar. Boston, 1866. 12°. . . . . C,546

Recommended to Mercy. Leipzig, 1864. 16°. . . . . . . . . J,421
Record of an Obscure Man. M. L. Putnam. Boston, 1861. 12°. . . H,258
Records of Five Years. S. J. Lippincott. Boston, 1867. 16°. . . . H,284
of the Heart; Poems. S. A. Lewis. New York, 1844. 12°. . . I,64
of Noble Lives. W. H. D. Adams. London, 1870. 12°. . . C,1243
Recreations of a Country Parson. A. K. H. Boyd. Boston, 1869. 2 v. 12°. H,569
of a Southern Barrister. Philadelphia, 1859. 8°. . . . . . H,268
of Christopher North. J. Wilson. Edinburgh, 1857. 2 v. 12°. . H,608
The same. Boston, 1854. 8°. . . . . . . . . . H,609
Rational. W. Hooper. London, 1794. 4 v. 8°. . . . . . H,505
Rector and Doctor's Family. M. Oliphant. Leipzig, 1870. 16°. . . J,399
Rector of St. Bardolph's. F. W. Shelton. New York, 1853. 12°. . . K,296
Red as a Rose is she. R. Broughton. New York, 1870. 8°. . . . K,607
The same. Leipzig, 1870. 2 v. in 1. 16°. . . . . . J,52
Red Court Farm. Mrs. H. Wood. Leipzig, 1868. 2 v. in 1. 16°. . . J,529
Red Cross; a Story. W. T. Adams. Boston, 1870. 16°. . . . J,1535,3
Red Eric; or, The Whaler's last Cruise. R. M. Ballantyne. Lond.1861. 16°. J,1271
Redgauntlet. Sir W. Scott. Boston, 1858. 2 v. 16°. . . . . . K,947
The same. Philadelphia, 1857. 8°. . . . . . . K,971
The same. Philadelphia, 1869. 8°. . . . . . K,1113
Red-Letter Days in Applethorpe. M. A. Dodge. Boston, 1867. 12°. J,1287
Red Race of America, History of. A. W. Bradford. New York, 1841. 8°. B,606
Mythology of. D. G. Brinton. New York, 1868. 12°. . . . P,916
Red River (of Canada) Expedition. G. L. Huyshe. London, 1871. 12°. . C,345
Settlement. A. Ross. London, 1856. 12°. . . . . . . C,338
and Lake Superior, Explor. between. S. J. Dawson. Toronto, 1859. 4°. Q,59
Red River (of Louisiana) Exploration. Washington, 1853. 2 v. 8°. . V,81
Red Rover. J. F. Cooper. New York, 1867. 12°. . . . . . . K,46
The same. New York, 1859. 8°. . . . . . . . . K,74
Redburn; his First Voyage. H. Melville. London, 1853. 2 v. 12°. . J,641
Redding, C. History and Description of Modern Wines. Lond. 1851. p. 8°. L,145
Redeemer and the Redeemed. C. Beecher. Boston, 1864. 12°. . . . P,128
Redemption, History of the Work of. J. Edwards. Worcester, 1808. 8°. P,257
The same. New York, n. d. 18°. . . . . . . P,746,9
Redfield, A. M. Zoölogical Science. Hartford, 1867. 12°. . . . N,649
Redfield, J. W. Compar. Physiognomy; Men and Animals. N.Y. 1852. 8°. L,917
Redgrave, R. and S. Century of Painters of Eng. School. Lond. 1866. 2 v. 8°. M,103
Redhead, T. W. French Revolution from 1789 to 1849. Phil. 1854. 3 v. 8°. B,221
Redman, R. Vita Henrici Quinti. London, 1858. 8°. . . . . W,161
Redouté, P. J. et Thory. Les Roses, peintes et décrites. Paris, 1828-9. 3 v. 8°. *N,1028
Redpath, J. Echoes from Harper's Ferry. Boston, 1860. 12°. . . H,18
Life of Capt. John Brown. Boston, 1860. 12°. . . . . . . C,693
Redskins, The. J. F. Cooper. New York, 1866. 12°. . . . . . K,47
The same. New York, 1860. 8°. . . . . . . . . K,75
Redtenbacher, J. Talgsäure. n. t. p. 8°. . . . . . . . . N,252,28
Reed, H. Lectures on the British Poets. Philadelphia, 1860. 2 v. 12°. . H,678
Lectures on English History in Shakespeare. Phil. 1869. 12°. . I,891
Lectures on Eng. Literature; Chaucer to Tennyson. Phil. 1855. 12°. H,677
Reed, J., Life of. H. Reed. Bost. 1860. 12°. . . . . . . C,860,18
Life of. W. B. Reed. Phil. 1847. 2 v. 8°. . . . . . . C,814

Reed, T. A. Phonographic Phrase-Book. London, 1855. 16°. . . . L,668
Reed, W. B. Life and Correspondence of Joseph Reed. Phil. 1847. 2 v. 8°. C,814
Reed, W. H. Hospital Life in Army of the Potomac. Boston, 1868. 12°. B,941
Reel in a Bottle. H. T. Cheever. New York, 1852. 12°. . . . J,1497
Reele, W. C. Provincial Justice; Crim. Law of Canada. Toronto, 1843. 8°. U,498
Reemelin, C. Vine-Dresser's Manual. New York, 1856. 12°. . . M,533,3
Rees, A. Cyclopædia; or, Universal Dictionary. Phil. n. d. 41 v. 4°. . L.R.
Reese, J. J. Analysis of Physiology. Philadelphia, 1852. 8°. . . . L,941
Reeve, C. Old English Baron. London, 1820. 12°. . . . . . K,534
Reeve, L. Conchologist's Nomenclator. London, 1845. 8°. . . . N,718
Reeves, P. Student's Own Speaker. New York, 1871. 12°. . . O,1245
Reformation, Conservative, and its Theology. C. P. Krauth. Phil. 1871. 8°. P,803
Reformation of 16th Century, Annals of. J. Strype. Oxford, 1824. 7 v. 8°. P,683
History of. J. H. Merle d'Aubigné. Glasgow, 1854–55. 3 v. in 1. 8°. P,659
The same. Glasgow, n. d. 5 v. 8°. . . . . . P,660
H. Stebbing. London, 1836–37. 2 v. 12°. . . . M,1005
J. Sleidan. London, 1689. 2 v. in 1. f°. . . . . . Q,305
in England, Sketch of. I. J. Blunt. London, 1832. 16°. . . I,603
in England and Ireland. W. Cobbett. London, 1829. 2 v. 8°. . P,664
in France. A. Marsh-Caldwell. Philadelphia, 1851. 2 v. 12°. . P,573
in Scotland. J. Knox. Glasgow, 1844. 8°. . . . . . . P,663
in time of Calvin. J. H. Merle d'Aubigné. New York, 1870. 5 v. 12°. P,665
Ladies of. J. Anderson. London, 1855. 12°. . . . . . . C,516
Leaders of. J. Tulloch. Boston, 1860. 12°. . . . . . . C,524
of the Church of England. G. Burnet. New York, 1843. 3 v. 8°. P,661
on the Continent, History of. G. Waddington. London, 1841. 3 v. 8°. P,662
Philosophische Weltanschaung der. M. Carriere. Stuttgart, 1847. 8°. E,33
Political Consequences of. A. H. L. Heeren. London, 1847. 8°. . A,42
Reformers before. C. Ullmann. Edinburgh, 1855. 2 v. 8°. . P,644
Spirit and Influence of. C. F. D. de Villers. Phila. 1833. 12°. . P,62
Switzerland Pioneer of. Princesse Koltzoff-Massalski. Lon. '58. 2 v. 8°. P,241
Reformatory Schools for Children. M. Carpenter. London, 1851. 12°. . O,922
Reformed Gambler, The. J. H. Green. Philadelphia, n. d. 12°. . . M,343
Reformed Virginian Silk Worm. London, 1688. See *Force's Tracts*, v. 3.
Reforms, Hints toward. H. Greeley. New York, 1850. 12°. . . . O,457
and Reformers, Sketches of. B. B. Stanton. New York, 1849. 12°. C,1287
Regel, E. Botanik von Ost-Sibirien. Moskau, 1861–62. 2 v. 8°. . . G,888
Parthenogenesis im Pflanzenreiche. St. Petersburg, 1859. 4°. . Q,119
Regenerate Life, Dissertations on. J. Arbouin. Boston, 1841. 16°. . O,988
Reginald Archer. A. M. C. Seemuller. Boston, 1871. 12°. . . . K,148
Regnard, J. F., Théatre de. Paris, 1855. 16°. . . . . . . . . H,887
Regnault, H. V. Elements of Chemistry. Philadelphia, 1853. 2 v. 8°. N,216
Recherches sur les Combustibles Minéraux. Paris, n. d. 8°. . N,252,1
Treatise on Crystallography. London, 1848. 8°. . . . . N,252,33
Regular Swiss Round in Three Trips. H. Jones. London, 1866. 16°. . V,424
Regulatoren, Die. F. Gerstäcker. Leipzig, 1868. 3 v. in 1. 16°. . . G,285
Rehm, F. Geschichtes des Mittelalters. Marburg, 1821–39. 4 v. in 8. 8°. E,23
Reichenbach, A. B. Völker der Erde. Leipzig, 1864. 8°. . . . E,155
Reichenbach, H. G. L. Natürliches Pflanzensystem. Leipzig, 1850. 8°. . G,967
Xenia Orchidacea, v. 1. Leipzig, 1858. 4°. . . . . . . . *Q,112

Reichenbach, K., *Baron von.* Researches on Magnetism, etc. Lond. 1850. 8°. N,50
Reichspostreiter in Ludwigsburg. R. Heller. Frankfurt-a.-M. 1857. 12°. G,308
Reid, A. First Book of Geography. Edinburgh, 1855. 18°. . . . . O,896
Reid, C. Valerie Aylmer. New York, 1871. 8°. . . . . . . . K,356
Reid, D. B. Rudiments of Chemistry. Philadelphia, 1846. 12°. . . . N,169
and Bain, A. Elements of Chemistry and Electricty. N. Y. 1849. 12°. N,168
Reid, H. Principles of Education. London, 1854. 12°. . . . . . O,1145
Reid, J. Sheaf; Mental Science applied to Scripture Truth. Edin. 1859. 12°. P,24
Reid, M. Afloat in the Forest. Boston, 1868. 12°. . . . . . . . J,1589
Boy Hunters. Boston, 1866. 16°. . . . . . . . . . . J,1561
Boy Slaves. Boston, 1868. 12°. . . . . . . . . J,1586
Boy Tar. Boston, 1869. 16°. . . . . . . . . . . J,1581
Bruin; the Grand Bear Hunt. Boston, 1866. 16°. . . . . J,1582
Bush-Boys. Boston, 1866. 16°. . . . . . . . . . J,1583
Cliff Climbers. Boston, 1866. 16°. . . . . . . . . . J,1563
Desert Home. Boston, 1866. 16°. . . . . . . . . . J,1559
Forest Exiles. Boston, 1868. 16°. . . . . . . . . . J,1558
Giraffe Hunters. Boston, 1869. 12°. . . . . . . . J,1588
Headless Horseman. New York, 1870. 12°. . . . . . . J,1565
Hunter's Feast. New York, n. d. 12°. . . . . . . . . J,1567
Lost Lenore. New York, 1870. 12°. . . . . . . . J,1566
Maroon; or, Planter Life in Jamaica. New York, n. d. 12°. . J,1568
Ocean Waifs. Boston, 1870. 12°. . . . . . . . . J,1587
Odd People. Boston, 1865. 16°. . . . . . . . . J,1560
Osceola, the Seminole. New York, n. d. 12°. . . . . J,1569
Plant Hunters. Boston, 1866. 16°. . . . . . . . . . J,1584
Quadroon; or, Adventures in Louisiana. New York, n. d. 12°. . J,1570
Ran away to Sea. Boston, 1866. 16°. . . . . . . . J,1585
Rangers and Regulators of the Tanaha. New York, 1870. 12°. . J,1571
Rifle Rangers; Adventures in Southern Mexico. New York, n. d. 12°. J,1572
Scalp Hunters; or, the Trappers. New York, n. d. 12°. . . J,1573
Tiger-Hunter. New York, 1870. 12°. . . . . . . . . J,1574
War-Trail; or, the Hunt of the Wild Horse. New York, 1870. 12°. J,1575
White Chief; a Legend of North Mexico. New York, 1869. 12°. J,1576
White Gauntlet. New York, 1870. 12°. . . . . . . . . J,1577
Wild Huntress. New York, n. d. 12°. . . . . . . . . J,1578
Wild Life; Adventures on the Frontier. New York, n. d. 12°. . J,1579
Wood-Rangers; or, Trappers of Sonora. New York, n. d. 12°. . J,1580
Young Voyageurs. Boston, 1866. 16°. . . . . . . . J,1562
Young Yägers. Boston, 1866. 16°. . . . . . . . . . J,1564
Reid, T. Essays on the Powers of the Human Mind. Edinburgh, 1808. 3 v. 8°. O,664
Reid, W. After the War; a Southern Tour. Cincinnati, 1866. 12°. . V,148
Ohio in the War. Cincinnati, 1868. 2 v. 8°. . . . . . B,946
Reid, W. Law of Storms and Winds. London, 1849. 8°. . . . . N,110
Reimann, M. Aniline and its Derivatives. New York, 1868. 8°. . . N,191
Reindeer, Dogs, and Snow-Shoes; Siberian Travel. R. J. Bush. N.Y. 1871. 12°. V,671
Reisen von Rambus & Co. A. von Winterfeld. Leipzig, 1865. 3 v. 16°. G,519
Reissmann, A. Das Deutsche Lied. Cassel, 1861. 8°. . . . . . G,644
Rejected Addresses. H. and J. Smith. Boston, 1860. 12°. . . . . I,428
Rejected Wife. A. S. Stephens. Philadelphia, 1870. 12°. . . . . K,450

Relations des Jésuites dans la Nouvelle-France. Quebec, 1858. 3 v. 8°. B,653
Religion, American. J. Weiss. Boston, 1871. 12°. . . . . . . P,583
Analogy of. J. Butler. New York, 1856. 12°. . . . . P,83
and Sermons. J. Butler. London, 1868. p. 8°. . . . L,170
and Chemistry. J. P. Cooke, jr. New York, 1867. 12°. . . P,217
and Culture. J. P. Shairp. New York, 1871. 12°. . . . P,182
and the Reign of Terror. E. de Pressensé. New York, 1869. 12°. . P,576
Evidences of, Revealed. J. Priestley. Lond. 1794–99. 3 v. 8°. U,294,10–12
History of. J. Evelyn. London, 1850. 2 v. 8°. . . . . . P,269
in America. R. Baird. New York, 1856. 8°. . . . . . P,582
in Society. J. F. Martinet. New York, 1850. 12°. . . . P,192
Metaphysics and Ethics applied to. F. Bowen. Boston, 1855. 12°. . O,706
Natural and Revealed. W. Warburton. London, 1753–54. 2 v. 12°. P,272
of the Present and of the Future. T. D. Woolsey. N. Y. 1871. 12°. P,198
Passing Thoughts on. E. M. Sewell. New York, 1867. 12°. . P,203
Philosophy of. T. Dick. Philadelphia, 1869. 12°. . . . U,260,2
Science and Philosophy. J. Bascom. New York, 1871. 12°. . P,214
Religions, of Ancient and Modern Times, Appleton's. New York, 1856. 8°. Q,253
of the World. F. D. Maurice. London, 1861. 12°. . . . P,560
Ten Great; Comparative Theology. J. F. Clarke. Boston, 1871. 8°. P,584
Religious Affections, Treatise on J. Edwards. New York, n. d. 18°. P,746,3
Religious Belief, Origin and Development of. S. Baring-Gould. N.Y. 1870. 12°. P,273
Religious Controversy, End of. J. Miller. New York, 1851. 12°. . P,206
Religious Duty. F. P. Cobbe. London, 1864. 12°. . . . . . . P,102
Religious Education, Colloquies on. London, 1837. 8°. . . . . . P,215
Religious Faith, Inquiry on. F. P. Cobbe. London, 1864. 12°. . . P,261
Religious Instruction, Duty of. T. J. Young. Charleston, 1841. 8°. O,1251,1
in a Series of Lessons. E. Mayo. London, 1852. 16°. . . . O,1116
Religious Knowledge, Encyclopædia of; ed. by J. N. Brown. Phil. 1859. 8°. P,325
Religious Liberty; Signs of the Times. C. C. J. Bunsen. N. Y. 1856. 12°. P,88
Denk- und Glaubensfreiheit. W. A. Schmidt. Berlin, 1847. 8°. . E,444
Struggles of our Forefathers for. J. G. Miall. Bost. 1852. 12°. . C,14
Religious Life, Necessity of a. A. Horneck. London, 1729. 12°. . . P,196
Religious Pieces in Prose and Verse; edit. by G. G. Perry. Lond. 1867. 8°. L,605,26
Religious Poems. H. B. Stowe. Boston, 1867. 16°. . . . . . . . I,145
Religious Subjects, Views of. H. W. Beecher. New York, 1859. 12°. . P,86
Religious Thoughts and Opinions. C. W. von Humboldt. Bost. 1851. 16°. P,30
Religious Training of Children. C. E. Beecher. New York, 1864. 12°. . P,38
Religious Truth illustrated from Science. E. Hitchcock. Boston, 1857. 12°. P,251
Religious Worship, History of. R. Whately. London, 1867. 8°. . . P,14
Reliques of Ancient English Poetry. T. Percy. London, 1844. 3 v. 16°. I,379
The same. Leipzig, 1866. 3 v. 16°. . . . . . . . J,411
of Father Prout. F. Mahoney and F. Murphy. London, 1860. 12°. L,143
The same. London, 1866. 8°. . . . . . . . . . . H,487
Rellstab, L. Drei Jahre von Dreissigen; ein Roman. Leipzig, 1858. 5 v. 12°. G,426
Gesammelte Schriften. Leipzig, 1860. 6 v. 12°. . . . . . E,350
Bd. 1–4. 1812, Historischer Roman.
5. Sagen und Romantische Erzählungen.
6. Kunst-Novellen.
Reminiscences. R. H. Gronow. London, 1862–66. 4 v. in 2. 12°. . . H,498
Vol. 1. Reminiscences.
2. Recollections and Anecdotes.
Vol. 3. Celebrities of London and Paris.
4. Last Recollections.

Reminiscences of a Literary Life. T. F. Dibdin. London, 1836. 2 v. 8°. L.R.
of a Scottish Gentleman; by Philo Scotus. London, 1861. 8°. . D,379
of Fifty Years. M. Boyd. New York, 1871. 12°. . . . . H,497
of Sixty-Five Years. E. S. Thomas. Hartford, 1840. 2 v. 12°. . C,980
Rena; or, the Snow Bird. C. L. Hentz. New York, 1870. 12°. . . K,169
Renan, E. The Apostles. New York, 1867. 12°. . . . . . . P,145
Life of Jesus. New York, 1867. 12°. . . . . . . . P,374
The same reviewed. J. McCosh. Philadelphia, 1871. 8°. . P,284
Saint Paul. New York, 1869. 12°. . . . . . . . . P,130
Renée, *Duchess of Ferrara*, Memorials of. London, 1859. 16°. . . . D,638
Rennie, J. Architecture of Birds. London, 1831. 16°. . . . . L,469
Domestic Habits of Birds. London, 1833. 16°. . . . . L,477
Faculties of Birds. London, 1835. 16°. . . . . . . . L,476
Fähigkeiten und Kräfte der Vögel. Leipzig, 1839. 16°. . . . G,910
Insect Architecture; edited by J. G. Wood. London, 1869. p. 8°. . L,111
Lebensweise der Vögel. Leipzig, 1835. 16°. . . . . . . G,911
Natural History of Birds. New York, 1855. 18°. . . . . L,404
and Westwood, J. O. Insect Architecture. London, n. d. 12°. . O,10
The same. London, 1845. 2 v. 18°. . . . . . O,1
The same. London, 1857. 8°. . . . . . . O,20
Insect Miscellanies. London, n. d. 12°. . . . . . O,11
Insect Transformations. London, n. d. 12°. . . . . . O,12
Miscellanies and Architecture. Lond. 1831–50. 3 v. 16°. L,479
Natural History of Insects. London, 1829. 2 v. 16°. . . I,644
Renouard, A. A. Annales de l'Imprimerie des Alde. Paris, 1825. 8°. . L.R.
Renunciation, The; a Romance. F. B. D'Arblay. Phila. 1840. 2 v. 12°. K,670
Rent in a Cloud and St. Patrick's Eve. C. Lever. London, n. d. 8°. . K,785
The same. Leipzig, 1869. 16°. . . . . . . . . J,284
Renton, H. Principles of the United Presbyterian Church. Edinb. 1853. 8°. O,1251,3
Renwick, J. First Principles of Natural Philosophy. N. Y. 1842. 12°. . N,63
Life of Benj. Thompson, *Count Rumford*. Boston. 16°. . . C,860,15
Life of David Rittenhouse. New York, 1860. 16°. . . . C,860,7
Life of De Witt Clinton. New York, 1854. 18°. . . . . L,420
Life of Robert Fulton. Boston, 1860. 12°. . . . . . C,860,10
Lives of John Jay and Alexander Hamilton. N. Y. 1854. 16°. . L,423
Treatise on the Steam Engine. New York, 1839. 8°. . . . M,663
Repeal Prize Essays. Dublin, 1845. . . . . . . . . . B,168
Repentance of David. J. W. Hatherell. London, 1847. 12°. . . . P,254
Treatise on. London, n. d. 18°. . . . . . . . . P,6
Répertoire Alphabétique des Lois, Decrets, etc. Paris, 1810. 8°. . . U,494
Repertorium der Physik; hrsg. H. W. Dove u. L. Moser. Ber. 1837–49. 8 v. 8°. G,674
Reporter's Manual and Vocab. B. Pitman and R. P. Prosser. Cincin. 1854. 12°. L,677
Reporterz Magazen. Lundun, 1847–48. 18°. . . . . . . . L,709
Representative Government. J. S. Mill. New York, 1867. 12°. . .. O,491
Representative Men. R. W. Emerson. Boston, 1849. 12°. . . . H,105
Reptiles, Amphibians, and Fishes. W. Swainson. London, 1838. 2 v. 12°. M,1034
and Birds. M. Figuier. New York, 1870. p. 8°. . . . . N,529
Classification Naturelle des. A. Brongniart. Paris, 1805. 4°. . N,744
Fossil Chelonian. R. Owen. London, 1853. 4°. . . . . Q,22
of British India. A. C. L. G. Gunther. London, 1864. 4°. . . Q,69

Reptiles, Our. M. C. Cooke. London, 1865. 12°. . . . . . . . N,699
Wirtelscheichen und Krüppelfüssler. J. L. C. Gravenhorst. Breslau und Bonn, 1851. 4°. . . . . . . . . . . . F,97
Reptilia of the Cretaceous Formation. R. Owen. London, 1851. 4°. . Q,23
of the London Clay. R. Owen. London, 1850. 4°. . . . . Q,21
of the Wealden Formations. R. Owen. London, 1854. 4°. . . Q,20
Repton, H. Landscape Gardening and Architecture. London, 1840. 8°. . M,355
Republic of the United States; its Duties to itself, etc. N. Y. 1848. 12°. . B,881
Republican Court. R. W. Griswold. New York, 1856. 8°. . . . M,284
Repulse Bay, Unsuccessful Attempt to reach. G. F. Lyon. London, 1825. 8°. V,955
Rescued from Egypt. C. Tucker. London, 1868. 12°. . . . . K,570
Residences, Cottage. A. J. Downing. New York, 1844. 8°. . . . M,167
Resolute, Voyage of. G. F. MacDougall. London, 1857. 8°. . . . V,952
Respectability, Golden Steps to. J. M. Austin. Auburn, 1853. 12°. . J,1466
Respiration, Lecture on. T. Hopley. London, 1855. 8°. . . . N,252,44
Restauration, Anecdotes Histor. du temps de la. A. Baudouin. Par. 1853. 12°. B,201
Restitutu; Titles, etc., of Old Books. Sir E. Brydges. Lond. 1814–16. 4 v. 8°. L.R.
Retribution. E. D. E. N. Southworth. Philadelphia, 1870. 12°. . . K,437
Retrospect of Medicine and Surgery. W. and J. Braithwaite. Lon. 1842–65. 12°. L,952
Retrospective Review. London, 1827–28. 16 v. 8°. . . . . . . *S,80
Retzius, A. J. Genera et Species Insectorum. Lipsiæ, 1783. 8°. . . O,140
Retzsch, M. Gallery to Shakespeare's Dramatic Works. Leip. 1848. obl. 4°. L.R.
Reuben Medlicott. H. W. Savage. London, 1864. 12°. . . . . K,560
Reumont, A. de. Carafas of Maddaloni. London, 1854. p. 8°. . . L,171
Revelation, Advantages of a written. W. Adams. Philadelphia, 1871. 8°. P,284
Christian, and Modern Astronomy. T. Chalmers. New York, 1855. 12°. P,35
Heathen Philosophy compared with. J. Priestley. North. 1804. 8°. U,294,13
Revels at Court; Reigns of Elizabeth and James I. London, 1842. 8°. I,885,7
Reveries of a Bachelor. D. G. Mitchell. New York, 1866. 12°. . . H,51
Revett, N. Antiquities of Athens. London, 1837. 16°. . . . . A,61
Revolutions in Europe. A. Crichton. Edinburgh, 1828. 3 v. 16°. . . I,512
Reybaud, L. Personnel de la Marine Française. Paris, 1860. 8°. . N,252,45
Reynard, the Fox; edited by W. J. Thoms. London, 1844. 12°. . *L,606,12
Pleasant History of; edited by T. Roscoe. London, 1826. 12°. G,177,1
Reynolds, F., Life and Times of; written by himself. Lond. 1827. 2 v. 8°. C,1211
Reynolds, J. My own Times. Illinois, 1855. 12°. . . . . . C,740
Reynolds, Sir J., Life and Writings of. A. Cunningham. N. Y. 1860. 12°. D,244
Literary Works. London, 1851–52. 2 v. p. 8°. . . . . L,224
Reynolds, J. N. Voyage of U. S. Frigate Potomac. New York, 1835. 8°. V,1077
Reynolds, L. E. Treatise on Hand-Railing. New Orleans, 1849. 8°. . M,193
Rham, W. L. Dictionary of the Farm. London, 1858. 8°. . . . M,495
Rheder und Matrose. E. Willkomm. Frankfurt-am-Main, 1857. 3 v. 12°. G,518
Rheider Burg, Die. L. Schücking. Leipzig, 1864. 16°. . . . . G,449
Rhemes and Douay. H. Cotton. Oxford, 1855. 8°. . . . . . P,813
Rhetoric. E. O. Haven. New York, 1871. 12°. . . . . . . L,615
J. Holmes. Philadelphia, 1849. 12°. . . . . . . L,598
and Oratory, Lectures on. J. Q. Adams. Cambridge, 1810. 2 v. 8°. L,551
Art of. T. Hobbes. London, 1681. 8°. . . . . . . . H,504
Elements of. R. Whately. New York, 1853. 12°. . . . . L,592
Lectures on. H. Blair. Philadelphia, 1829. 8°. . . . . . L,597

Rhetoric, Philosophy of. G. Campbell. Boston, 1823. 8°. . . . . L,596
The same. New York, 1854. 12°. . . . . . . . L,593
Treatise on. Aristotle. London, 1853. p. 8°. . . . . . . L,43
Rhind, W. Class-Book of Physical Geography. Edinburgh, 1854. 16°. . O,898
History of the Vegetable Kingdom. Glasgow, 1855. 8°. . . N,1036
Rhine, The. H. Mayhew; illustrated by B. Foster. London, 1856. 8°. *V,436
Le Rhin. A. Delrieu. Bruxelles, 1850. 12°. . . . . H,1024
Upper. H. Mayhew; illustrated by B. Foster. London, 1860. 8°. *V,437
Rhode Island, Colony Records, 1636–1776. Providence, 1856–62. 7 v. 8°. C,80
Educational Magazine, v. 1, 2. Providence, 1852–54. 8°. . . S,22
History of. E. Peterson. New York, 1853. 8°. . . . . C,78
Institute of Instruction, Journal, 1845–48. Prov. 1846–49. 3 v. 8°. S,24
Might and Right; Dorr Rebellion. Providence, 1844. 12°. . . C,75
Narragansett Club Publications. Providence, 1866–70. 4 v. 8°. . C,84
Record of, during the Rebellion. Providence, 1866. 8°. . . . F,61
Rhodes, H. Boke of Nurture. London, 1868. 8°. . . . . L,605,32
Rhyme and Reason of Country Life. S. F. Cooper. New York, 1854. 8°. I,44
of the North Countrie. A. M. Gleeman. Cincinnati, 1847. 12°. . I,43
Rhyming Dictionary, 1570. P. Levins. London, 1867. 8°. . . L,605,27
J. Walker. Philadelphia, 1852. 8°. . . . . . . L.R.
The same. New York, 1860. 12°. . . . . . L.R.
The same. London, 1857. 2 v. 12°. . . . . . L.R.
English Parnassus. J. Poole. London, 1677. 8°. . . . . L,581
Ribault, J., Life of. J. Sparks. Boston, 1860. 12°. . . . . C,860,17
Ricauti, T. J. Sketches for Rustic Work. London, 1848. 8°. . . . Q,202
Riccoboni, L. Account of the Theaters in Europe. London, 1741. 8°. . I,740
Rice, H. Mount Vernon and other Poems. Columbus, 1860. 8°. . . I,114
Rice, J. H. and B. H. Memoir of James Brainerd Taylor. N. Y. n. d. 18°. P,746,15
Rice, L., Memoir of. J. B. Taylor. Baltimore, 1840. 12°. . . . C,922
Rice, N. L. Phrenology and Mesmerism. New York, 1849. 12°. . . L,960
Rich, A. jr. Dictionary of Greek and Roman Antiquities. Lond. 1860. 8°. A,79
Rich Barnaby. Honestie of this Age. London, 1844. 12°. . . L,606,11
Rich and Humble. W. T. Adams. Boston, 1869. 16°. . . . . J,1467,1
Richard Cœur-de-Lion, Life of. G. P. R. James. London, 1864. 2 v. p. 8°. L,197
Chronicles during the Reign of. London, 1864–65. 2 v. 8°. . . W,188
Crusade of. Richard of Devizes. London, 1870. p. 8°. . . . L,5
De Rebus Gestis Ricardi I. Richard of Devizes. London, 1838. 8°. U,634
History of. J. Abbott. New York, 1857. 16°. . . . J,1418
Life and Times of. W. E. Aytoun. London, 1840. 16°. . . . I,625
and Henry II., Chronicle of the Reigns of. Benedict of Peterborough. London, 1867. 2 v. 8°. . . . . . . . . . . W,199
Richard II., of England. Chronicque de la Traïson et Mort de. Lon. 1846. 8°. U,629
History of. J. Abbott. New York, 1858. 16°. . . . J,1387
Richard III., Historic Doubts concerning. H. Walpole. London, 1768. 4°. A,498
History of. J. Abbott. New York, 1858. 16°. . . . J,1379
and Henry VII., Letters, etc., on Reigns of. London, 1861–63. 2 v. 8°. W,174
Richard of Cirencester. Ancient State of Britain. London, 1848. p. 8°. . L,26
Speculum Hist. de Gestis Regum Angliæ. London, 1863–69. 2 v. 8°. W,180
Richard of Devizes. Chronicle of the Crusades. London, 1848. p. 8°. . A,226
Crusade of Richard Cœur-de-Lion. London, 1870. p. 8°. . . . L,5

Richard of Devizes. De Rebus Gestis Ricardi I. London, 1838. 8°. . U,634
Richard the Fearless; or, the Little Duke. C. M. Yonge. N. Y. 1856. 16°. J,1238
Richard Hurdis. W. G. Simms. New York, 1864. 12°. . . . . . K,257
Richards, W. C. Electron; a Telegraphic Epic. New York, 1858. 12°. . I,115
Harry's Vacation. New York, 1864. 16°. . . . . . . J,1557
Richardson, A. D. Beyond the Mississippi. Hartford, 1869. 8°. . . V,130
Secret Service; Field, Dungeon, and Escape. Hartford, 1866. 8°. . B,929
Richardson, C. New English Dictionary. London, 1839. 2 v. 4°. . . L.R.
Supplement to the same. London, 1856. 4°. . . . . . L.R.
Richardson, G. F. Introd. to Geology and Assoc. Sciences. Lond. 1851. p. 8°. L,310
Richardson, J. Travels in the Great Desert of Sahara. Lond. 1848. 2 v. 8°. V,815
Richardson, Sir J. Arctic Searching Expedition. New York, 1852. 12°. V,912
and Gray, J. E. Zoölogy of Capt. Beechey's Voyage. Lond. 1839. 4°. Q,6
Richardson, J. Languages, Literature, etc., of Eastern Nations. Oxf. 1768. 8°. L,779
Richardson, S. Clarissa Harlowe. London, 1820. 8 v. 12°. . . . K,529
The same. Leipzig, 1862. 4 v. 16°. . . . . . . J,422
Sir Charles Grandison. London, 1776. 4 v. 12°. . . . . J,578
The same. London, 1820. 7 v. 12°. . . . . . . K,530
Essay on. F. Jeffrey. London, 1856. p. 8°. . . . . . I,661,3
Richardson, T. Chemical Composition of Human Blood. Lond. n. d. 8°. N,252,1
Chromate of Lead in Analysis of Organic Bodies. Lond. n. d. 8°. N,252,2
Composition of Coal. London, n. d. 8°. . . . . . . N,252,2
Decomposition of Cyanogen in Water. Newcastle, 1838. 8°. . N,252,2
Donium, a Subtance in Davidsonite. London, n. d. 8°. . . N,252,2
Zusammensetzung der Steinkohle. n. t. p. 8°. . . . . . N,252,1
and Ronalds, E. Chemical Technology. Lond. 1855. 3 v. in 4. 8°. N,191
Richardson, T. A. Architectural Modeling in Paper. London, 1859. 12°. M,936
Richelieu, A. J. du P., *Cardinal*, Life of. W. Robson. London, 1854. 16°. D,590
Richmond, L. Dairyman's Daughter. Philadelphia. n. d. 24°. . J,1297
Richmond during the War. New York, 1867. 12°. . . . . . . B,877
Richter, J. P. F. Flower, Fruit, and Thorn Pieces. Boston, 1863. 2 v. 12°. G,220
Levana; or, the Doctrine of Education. Boston, 1864. 12°. . . O,995
Life of. E. B. Lee. Boston, 1864. 12°. . . . . . . . D,519
Specimens of; translated by T. Carlyle. Edinburgh, 1827. 12°. . G,51,3
Titan; a Romance. Boston, 1868. 2 v. 12°. . . . . . G,215
Sämmtliche Werke. Paris, 1836–37. 4 v. r. 8°. . . . . . E,345

Bd. 1. Grönländische Prozesse; Auswahl aus des Teufel's Papieren; Die unsichtbare Loge (Mumien); Hesperus; Quintus Fixlein.
2. Biographische Belustigungen; Blumen-, Frucht- und, Dornenstücke; oder, Ehestand, Tod und Hochzeit des Armenadvokaten Siebenkäs; Jubelsenior; Kampaner Thal; Palingenesien; Briefe und bevorstehender Lebenslauf; Titan; Komischer Anhang zum Titan; Clavis Fichtiana.
3. Flegeljahre; Das Heimliche Klaglied; Vorschule der Aesthetik; Freiheit-Büchlein; Levana; Ergänzblatt zur Levana; Des Feldpredigers Schmelzle Reise nach Flätz; Dr. Katzenbergers Badereise.
4. Friedenpredigt; Dämmerungen; Herbst-Blumine; Leben Fibels; Mars und Phöbus; Museum; Politische Fastenpredigten; Ueber die deutschen Doppelwörter; Komet; Kleine Bücherschau.

Ricketson, D. History of New Bedford, Mass. New Bedford, 1858. 12°. C,39
Riddell, J. Architectural Designs for Country Residences. Phil. 1861. f°. *Q,245
Riddell, J. H. Far above Rubies. Leipzig, 1867. 2 v. in 1. 16°. . . J,423
George Geith of Fen Court. Boston, 1865. 8°. . . . . . K,910
The same. Leipzig, 1865. 2 v. in 1. 16°. . . . . . J,424
Maxwell Drewitt. Leipzig, 1866. 2 v. in 1. 16°. . . . . . J,425

Riddell, J. H. Race for Wealth. Leipzig, 1866. 2 v. in 1. 16°. . . . J,426
Riddell, J. L. Monograph of the Silver Dollar. New Orleans, 1845. 8°. M,388
Riddle, J. E. Latin-English Lexicon. London, 1851. 4°. . . . . L.R.
and Arnold, T. K. English-Latin Lexicon. New York, 1856. 8°. L.R.
Ridgely, D. Annals of Annapolis. Baltimore, 1841. 12°. . . . . C,140
Ridley, J. Tales of the Genii. London, 1861. p. 8°. . . . . . L,150
Ridpath, G. Border History of England and Scotland. Berwick, 1848. 4°. F,30
Riedesel, G., Memoirs of Residence in America. W. L. Stone. Alb.'68. 2 v. 8°. B,887
Riehl, W. H. Deutsche Arbeit. Stuttgart, 1861. 8°. . . . . . G,535
Die Familie. Stuttgart, 1861. 16°. . . . . . . . . . E,377
Rienzi. Sir E. B. Lytton. Philadelphia, 1835. 8°. . . . . . . K,827
The same. Philadelphia, 1869. 12°. . . . . . . K,828
The same. Leipzig, 1842. 16°. . . . . . . . J,327
Rifle, Ax, and Saddle Bags. W. H. Milburn. New York, 1857. 12°. . H,40
Rifle Rangers; Adventures in Southern Mexico. M. Reid. New York, n. d. 12°. J,1572
Riflemen, Hints to. H. W. S. Cleveland. New York, 1864. 8°. . . . M,337
Right at Last, and other Tales. E. C. Gaskell. New York, 1860. 12°. . K,708
Rights and Wrongs. A. Fonblanque, jr. London, 1860. 16°. . . . U,481
Riley, H. T. Dictionary of Latin Quotations. London, 1866. 12°. . . *L,53
Riley, J. Shipwreck on West Coast of Africa. London, 1817. 4°. . . Q,415
Rimbault, E. F. (Ed.) Ballads on the Great Frost, 1683–84. Lond. 1844. 12°. L,606,9
Cock Lorell's Bote; a Poem. London, 1843. 8°. . . . . L,606,6
Maroccus Extaticus; or, Banke's Bay Horse in a Trance. Lond. '43. 12°. L,606,9
Poetical Tracts of the Sixteenth Century. London, 1842. 12°. . L,606,6
Rimmel, E. Book of Perfumes. London, 1865. . . . . . . H,447
Ring, D. Three Thousand Exercises in Arithmetic. Philadelphia, 1845. 24°. O,1091
Ring, M. John Milton und seine Zeit. Frankfurt-am-Main, 1857. 12°. . G,427
John Milton and his Times. New York, 1868. 8°. . . . . G,216
Neue Stadtgeschichten. Prag und Leipzig, 1858. 3 v. 24°. . . G,429
Sohn Napoleons. Berlin, 1860. 2 v. 16°. . . . . . . G,428
Ring, The, and the Book. R. Browning. Boston, 1869. 12°. . . . I,296
Ring of Amasis. E. R. B. Lytton. New York, 1863. 12°. . . . K,832
Ring der Kaiserin. A. Peters. Leipzig und Wien, n. d. 2 v. in 1. 24°. G,502
Rio, A. F. Poetry of Christian Art. London, 1854. 12°. . . . M,37
Riofrey, B. Governesses; or, Modern Education. London, 1841. 8°. . O,1014
Moral and Intellectual Education. London, 1843. 8°. . . . O,1238
Riouffe, H. Mémoires de la Tyrannie de Robespierre. Paris, 1855. 12°. D,611
Ripley, G. Specimens of Foreign Standard Literature. Boston, 1840. 3 v. 12°. H,747
and Dana, C. A. (Eds.) New American Cyclopædia. N.Y. 1870. 16 v. 8°. R.R.
The same. New York, 1863. 16 v. 8°. . . . . . S.C.
Ripley, R. S. War with Mexico, v. 2. New York, 1849. 8°. . . B,886,2
Rita; an Autobiography. H. Aïdé. Leipzig, 1859. 16°. . . . . J,6
Ritch, J. W. American Architect. New York, n. d. 4°. . . . . M,296
Ritchie, A. C. Autobiography of an Actress. Boston, 1854. 12°. . . D,651
Clergyman's Wife, and other Sketches. New York, 1867. 12°. . K,221
Fairy Fingers; a Novel. New York, 1865. 12°. . . . . K,233
Mimic Life. Boston, 1856. 12°. . . . . . . . . I,713
Mute Singer. New York, 1866. 12°. . . . . . . . K,234
Ritchie, J. E. Here and There in London. London, 1859. 16°. . . V,312
Night Side of London. London, 1869. 8°. . . . . . . V,294

Ritchie, J. S. Wisconsin and its Resources. Philadelphia, 1858. 12°. . C,242
Ritchie, L. History of the Oriental Nations. London, 1848. 2 v. 8°. . C,404
Ritchie, R. Farm Engineer. Glasgow, 1849. 8°. . . . . . . M,586
Ritchie, W. Electric and Chemical Theories of Galvanism. Lond. 1829. 4°. N,252,43
Ritson, J. Scottish Songs and Ballads. London, 1866. 24°. . . . I,408
Rittenhouse, D., Life of. J. Renwick. Boston, 1860. 16°. . . C,860,7
Ritter, C. Die Erdkunde; oder, allgemeine vergleichende Geographie. Berlin, 1822–59. 11 v. in 23. 8°. viz.:
Erster Theil: Afrika. 1 v. . . . . . . . . . . E,153,1
Zweiter Theil: Asien. 9 v. in 22. . . . . . . . E,153,2–23

Bd. 1. Der Norden und Nord-Osten von Hoch-Asien.
2. Der Nord-Osten und der Süden von Hoch-Asien.
3. Der Süd-Osten von Hoch-Asien.
4. Die Indische Welt. 2 v.
5. West-Asien.
6. West-Asien; Iranische Welt. 2 v.
7. Das Stufenland des Euphrat- und Tigrissystems. 2 v.
8. Erste Abth. Die Halbinsel Arabien. 2 v.
Zweite Abth. Die Sinai-Halbinsel, Palästina, und Syrien. 6 v.
9. Klein-Asien. 2 v.
10. Namen- und Sach- Verzeichniss.

Comparative Geography. Philadelphia, 1865. 8°. . . . . P,290
Geographical Studies; translated by W. L. Gage. Boston, 1863. 12°. V,1133
Life of. W. L. Gage. New York, 1867. 12°. . . . . . D,513
Palestine and Sinaitic Peninsula; tr. by W. L. Gage. N. Y. 1866. 4 v. 8°. V,652
Vorhalle Europäischer Völkergeschichten. Berlin, 1820. 8°. . E,12
Ritter, F. L. History of Music. Boston, 1870. 16°. . . . . M,397
Ritter vom Geiste, Die. C. Gutzkow. Leipzig, 1865. 9 v. 16°. . . G,297
Rivero, M. E. and Tschudi, J. J. von. Peruvian Antiquities. Cin. 1854. 12°. C,390
Rivers and Torrents. P. Frisi. London, n. d. 12°. . . . . . M,840
Rives, W. C. Life and Times of James Madison. Boston, 1859–69. 3 v. 8°. C,815
Road-Making, Manual of. W. M. Gillespie. New York, 1853. 8°. . . M,695
Roads, Constructing and Repairing. H. Law. London, 1855. 12°. . . M,944
Rob of the Bowl. J. P. Kennedy. New York, 1860. 12°. . . . K,202
Robbins, C. Memoir of William Appleton. Boston, 1863. 8°. . . C,757
Rob Nixon; the Old White Trapper. W. H. G. Kingston. N. Y. 1866. 12°. J,1268
Rob Roy. Sir W. Scott. Boston, 1857. 2 v. 16°. . . . . . . K,948
The same. Philadelphia, 1869. 8°. . . . . . K,1107
The same. Leipzig, 1846. 16°. . . . . . . . J,451
Rob Roy on the Baltic. J. Macgregor. London, 1867. 16°. . . . V,521
on the Jordan. J. Macgregor. New York, 1870. 8°. . . V,1080
on Rivers and Lakes of Europe. J. Macgregor. London, 1870. 16°. V,383
Voyage alone in the. J. Macgregor. London, 1867. 12°. . V,1049
Roba di Roma. W. W. Story. London, 1863. 2 v. 12°. . . . . V,484
Robbers, The. F. von Schiller. London, 1853–57. 16°. . . . L,228,4
Robbers and Banditti, Lives of. C. MacFarlane. London, 1837. 16°. . I,649
Robbins, E. (Ed.) Class-Book of Poetry. New York, 1852. 12°. . . I,116
Robbins, S. S. Binding the Sheaves. New York, 1868. 16°. . . J,1662
Edged Tools. New York, 1869. 16°. . . . . . . J,1663
Girding on the Armor. New York, 1869. 16°. . . . J,1664
Robert Linton. New York, 1868. 16°. . . . . . . J,1665
Weighed in the Balance. New York, 1868. 16°. . . . J,1666
Robert-Dumesnil, A.P.F. Le Peintre-Graveur Français. Paris, 1850. 8 v. 8°. L.R.

Robert Falconer. G. Mac Donald. Boston, n. d. 12°. . . . . . K,921
The same. London, 1868. 3 v. 12°. . . . . . . K,922
Robert Graham. C. L. Hentz. Philadelphia, 1856. 12°. . . . K,175
Robert-Houdin, J. E. Sharper detected and exposed. London, 1863. 12°. D,663
Robert of Gloucester. Chronicle; ed. by T. Hearne. Oxford, 1724. 2 v. 8°. U,127,1,2
Life of Thomas à Becket. London, 1845. 12°. . . . L,606,19
Robert Linton. S. S. Robbins. New York, 1868. 16°. . . . J,1665
Roberts, M. Popular History of the Mollusca. London, 1851. 16°. . O,8
Voices from the Woodlands. London, 1850. 8°. . . . . . N,913
Roberts, O. W. Voyages in Central America. Edinburgh, 1827. 16°. . I,502
Roberts, W. History of Letter-Writing. London, 1843. 8°. . . . H,740
Looker-on; a Periodical Paper. Boston, 1866. 3 v. 8°. H,536,35–37
Memoirs of Hannah More. New York, 1835. 2 v. 12°. . . D,337
Robertson, C. L. Sanitary Condition of Great Yarmouth. Yar. 1847. 16°. N,252,37
Robertson, D. Reports of the Trial of Aaron Burr. Phil. 1808. 2 v. 8°. U,509
Robertson, F. W. Lectures and Addresses. Boston, 1859. 12°. . . P,55
Life and Letters of. S. A. Brooke. Boston, 1870. 12°. . . C,1212
Sermons at Trinity Chapel, Brighton. Boston, 1857–68. 5 v. 12°. P,54
The same. Leipzig, 1861–66. 4 v. 16°. . . . . . J,427
Robertson, M. M. Janet's Love and Service. New York, 1869. 12°. . K,112
Robertson, W. History of America. New York, 1850. 8°. . . U,205,1
The same. London, 1818. 3 v. 16°. . . . . . . B,683
The same, abridged. New York, 1854. 16°. . . . L,466
History of the Reign of Charles V. New York, 1848. 8°. . . U,205,2
The same, abridged. New York, 1869. 16°. . . . L,467
The same, continued by W. H. Prescott. Boston, 1857. 3 v. 8°. B,531
History of Scotland; Reigns of Mary and James V. N. Y. 1848. 8°. U,205,3
Knowledge of the Ancients about India. London, 1794. 8°. . . V,694
Works. London, 1840. r. 8°. . . . . . . . . . . U,236
Robespierre; Historischer Roman. T. Mundt. Berlin, 1859. 3 v. 16°. . G,375
Robin Goodfellow; his Mad Pranks, etc. London, 1841. 12°. . . L,606,2
Robin Hood; Songs and Ballads. London, 1867. 24°. . . . . I,355
Robbins, C. History of the Second Church, Boston. Boston, 1852. 8°. . C,83
Robins, S. Church Schoolmaster. London, 1850. 8°. . . . O,1138
Robinson, E. Greek and English Lexicon of New Text. N. Y. 1858. 8°. *P,451
Physical Geography of the Holy Land. Boston, 1865. 8°. . . V,653
and Smith, E. Biblical Researches in Palestine. Bost. 1856–57. 3 v. 8°. V,665
Robinson, F. Organization of the Army of U. S. Philad. 1848. 2 v. 8°. B,853
Robinson, F. W. For her Sake. New York, 1870. 8°. . . . . K,657
Mattie; a Stray. New York, 1865. 8°. . . . . . . . K,658
Robinson, G. Unhealthiness of Towns. Newcastle-on-Tyne, 1847. 8°. N,252,29
Robinson, H. C. Diary; edited by T. Sadler. Boston, 1870. 2 v. 12°. C,1245
Robinson, H. N. Treatise on Algebra. New York, 1863. 8°. . . M,1118
Robinson, J. Deceptions in Artificial Manures. London, n. d. 8°. . N,252,25
Robinson, S. Catalogue of American Minerals. Boston, 1825. 8°. . . S.C.
Robinson, S. P. L. Kansas; its Life and History. Boston, 1857. 12°. . C,182
Robinson, T. Scripture Characters. London, 1849. 2 v. 8°. . . . P,105
Robinson, T.A.L. v. J. Lang. and Lit. of Slavic Nations. N. Y. 1850. 12°. H,762
Robinson, W. Gleanings from French Gardens. London, 1869. 12°. . N,957
Robinson, W. Self-Education. London, 1845. 16°. . . . . . O,1120

Robinson, W. D. Memorias de la Revolucion de Méjico. Lond. 1824. 8°. C,372
Robinson, P. F. and Britton, J. Vitruvius Brittanicus; History of Woodburn Abbey, etc. London, 1847. f°. . . . . . . . . L.R.
Robinson Crusoe. D. DeFoe. Boston, 1864. 12°. . . . . . J,1522
The same. London, 1820. 2 v. 12°. . . . . . . K,531
The same. London, 1869. p. 8°. . . . . . . . L,146
The same. Leipzig, 1845. 16°. . . . . . . . J,111
Robison, J. and Tredgold, T. Carpentery and Joinery. London, 1859. 12°. M,957
Atlas of Engravings. London, 1859. 4°. . . . . Q,162
and others. Carpentry of Roofs. London, 1859. 12°. . . . . M,956
Robson, W. Great Sieges of History. London, 1855. 8°. . . . A,314
Life of Cardinal Richelieu. London, 1854. 12°. . . . . D,590
Roche, R. M. Children of the Abbey. Philadelphia, 1868. 12°. . . K,911
Rochette, D. R. Peintures Antiques inédites. Paris, 1836. 4°. . *Q,171
Rochleder, F. Phytochemie. Leipzig, 1854. 8°. . . . . . G,764
Genussmittel und Gewürze in Chem. Beziehung. Wien, 1852. 8°. N,252,49
Rochlitz, F. Für Freunde der Tonkunst. Leipzig, 1830–32. 4 v. 16°. . G,645
Rock Ahead. E. Yates. Leipzig, 1868. 2 v. in 1. 16°. . . . . J,541
Rockingham, Marquis of. See *Wentworth, C. W.*
Rocks, British Palæozoic. A. Sedgwick and F. MacCoy. London, 1855. 4°. Q,51
Essay on the Superposition of. A. von Humboldt. Lond. 1823. 8°. N,793
Testimony of the. H. Miller. Boston, 1859. 12°. . . . . . N,616
Rocky Mountains and Mexico, Adventures in. G. F. Ruxton. Lond. 1849. 12°. V,139
Expedition to. J. C. Frémont. Washington, 1845. 8°. . . . V,78
The same. Buffalo, 1852. 12°. . . . . . . V,2
M. Lewis and W. Clark. Philadelphia, 1814. 2 v. 8°. . V,83
The same, abridged. New York, 1855. 2 v. 16°. . L,441
Reisen in die. B. Möllhausen. Leipzig, 1861. 2 v. in 1. 8°. . . E,175
Travels over. J. Palmer. Cincinnati, 1847. 12°. . . . . V,37
Roderick Random. T. Smollett. Leipzig, 1845. 16°. . . . . J,464
Rodman, T. P. Studies for Mental Development. Boston, 1848. 12°. O,820,18
Rodwell, J. The Rat; its History and Character. London, 1863. 16°. . N,680
Roe, A. S. Cloud on the Heart. New York, 1869. 12°. . . . . . K,269
How could he help it? New York, 1869. 12°. . . . . . K,270
I've been Thinking. New York, 1869. 12°. . . . . . . K,271
Like and Unlike. New York, 1869. 12°. . . . . . . . K,242
Long Look Ahead. New York, 1869. 12°. . . . . . . K,244
Looking Around. New York, 1869. 12°. . . . . . . . K,245
Star and the Cloud. New York, 1869. 12°. . . . . . . K,272
Time and Tide. New York, 1869. 12°. . . . . . . . K,241
To Love and to be Loved. New York, 1869. 12°. . . . . K,243
Woman our Angel; a Novel. New York, 1867. 12°. . . . K,235
Röhrig, E. and Crookes, W. (Eds.) See *Kerl, B.*
Roemer, J. Cavalry; its History, Management, etc. New York, 1863. 8°. M,710
Dictionary of English and French Idioms. New York, 1853. 12°. L,802
Rœmer, J. J. Genera Insectorum Linnæi et Fabricii. Vito. Helv. 1789. 4°. O,313
Roepell, R. und Caro, J. Geschichte Polens. Hamburg, 1840–63. 2 v. 8°. E,107
Röschen vom Hofe. F. Spielhagen. Berlin, 1867. 16°. . . . . G,466
Roger, C. Rise of Canada, v. 1. Quebec, 1856. 8°. . . . . . . C,337
Roger de Hoveden. Annals, 732–1201; tr. H. T. Riley. Lond. 1853. 2 v. p. 8°. L,25

Roger de Hoveden. Chronica; ed. by W. Stubbs. London, 1868-69. 2 v. 8°.. W,201
Roger de Wendover. Chronica; sive Histori., et App. Lond. 1841-4. 5 v. 8°. U,622
Flowers of History. London, 1849. 2 v. p. 8°. . . . . . L,19
Rogers, C. Traits and Stories of the Scottish People. London, 1867. 12°. B,110
Rogers, H. Eclipse of Faith. London, 1867. 16°. . . . . . . P,26
Defense of the Eclipse of Faith. Boston, 1854. 12°. . . . P,97
Greyson Letters. Boston, 1859. 12°. . . . . . . . H,270
Life and Genius of Thomas Fuller. London, 1864. p. 8°. . I,661,2
Reason and Faith; with other Essays. London, 1866. 16°. . . P,22
New Biographies of Illustrious Men. Boston, 1857. 12°. . . C,496
Rogers, H. D. Geology of Pennsylvania; Final Rep. Edinb. 1858. 2 v. in 3. 4°. *Q,50
2d and 3d Reports. Harrisburgh, 1838-39. 8°. . . . N,875
Rogers, H. J. Life-Saving Signal-Book. Baltimore, 1856. 8°. . . M,705
Rogers, J. Biography of Barton W. Stone. Cincinnati, 1847. 12°. . C,1006
Rogers, M. E. Domestic Life in Palestine. London, 1863. 8°. . . . V,632
Rogers, R. Concise Account of North America. London, 1765. 8°. . V,161
Rogers, S., Poetical Works of. Boston, 1860. 12°. . . . . . I,124
Recollections. Boston, 1859. 16°. . . . . . . . C,1182
Table-Talk and Porsoniana. New York, 1856. 12°. . . . H,571
Rogers, T. J. American Biographical Dictionary. Easton, 1824. 8°. *C,1029
Roget, P. M. Animal and Vegetable Physiology. Lond. 1867. 2 v. p. 8°. L,281
Thesaurus of English Words and Phrases. Boston, 1855. 12°. *L,567
Rokeby, T. Memoir of Justice Rokeby. Durham, 1860. 8°. . . F,126,37
Roland, Madame, History of. J. S. C. Abbott. New York, 1867. 16°. J,1404
Mémoires, Notices Historiques et Anecdotes. Paris, 1855. 12°. . D,600
and Mad. de Stäel-Holstein, Memoirs of. L. M. Child. N.Y. 1854. 16°. D,652
Roland Cashel. C. Lever. New York, 1856. 8°. . . . . . . K,786
The same. Leipzig, 1858. 3 v. 16°. . . . . . . J,285
Roland Yorke. Mrs. H. Wood. Leipzig, 1869. 2 v. in 1. 16°. . . J,530
Rolfe, W. J. and Gillet, J. A. Elements of Chem. and Elect. Bost. 1868. 12°. N,228
Elements of Astronomy. Boston, 1868. 12°. . . . . N,325
Hand-Book of Natural Philosophy. Boston, 1868. 12°. . N,73
Rollin, C. Ancient History. New York, 1851. 2 v. 8°. . . . . . A,36
The same. Philadelphia, 1855. 4 v. 8°. . . . . . S.C.
Histoire Ancienne. Paris, 1846-49. 10 v. 12°. . . . . . A,55
Method of Teaching the Belles-Lettres, v. 1, 2. London, 1769. 8°. H,912
Traité des Etudes. Paris, 1854. 3 v. 12°. . . . . . . H,867
Rollin, L. Decline of England. London, 1850. 12°. . . . . . A,477
Rolling-Stone Series. H. Castlemon, *pseud.* Cincinnati, 1871. 3 v. 16°. J,1474
Vol. 1. Tom Newcombe. Vol. 2. Go Ahead. Vol. 3. No Moss.
Rollo Series. J. Abbott. New York, 1869. 14 v. 18°. . . . . J,1390
Vol. 1. Rollo Learning to Talk.
2. Rollo Learning to Read.
3. Rollo at Work.
4. Rollo at Play.
5. Rollo at School.
6. Rollo's Vacation.
7. Rollo's Experiment.
Vol. 8. Rollo's Museum.
9. Rollo's Travels.
10. Rollo's Correspondence.
11. Rollo's Philosophy—Water.
12. Rollo's Philosophy—Air.
13. Rollo's Philosophy—Fire.
14. Rollo's Philosophy—Sky.

Rollo's Tour in Europe. J. Abbott. New York, 1869. 10 v. 16°. . J,1391
Vol. 1. Rollo on the Atlantic.
2. Rollo in Paris.
3. Rollo in Switzerland.
4. Rollo in London.
5. Rollo on the Rhine.
Vol. 6. Rollo in Scotland.
7. Rollo in Geneva.
8. Rollo in Holland.
9. Rollo in Naples.
10. Rollo in Rome.

Romaine, W. Works. London, 1801. 8 v. 8°. . . . . . . . P,766
Roman Antiquities. A. Adam. New York, 1842. 8°. . . . . . A,165
C. Anthon. New York, 1854. 12°. . . . . . . A,138
J. D. Fuss. Oxford, 1840. 8°. . . . . . . . A,166
Trésor des. C. E. du Boulay. Paris, 1650. f°. . . . . . F,237
Manual of. W. Ramsay. London, 1855. 12°. . . . . . A,137
Römische Alterthümer. L. Lange. Berlin, 1863-67. 2 v. 8°. . E,454
Roman Baths. M. M. Sherwood. New York, 1855. 12°. . . . K,1008,14
Roman Catholic Bible in English. H. Cotton. Oxford, 1855. 8°. . . P,813
Roman Catholic Church, Corpus Juris Canonici. Lipsiæ, 1833. 4°. . Q,146
Glance at Popes, Councils, and the Church. London, 1866. 12°. . P,135
Lives and Times of Roman Pontiffs. A. de Montor. N.Y. 1867. 4 v. 8°. P,651
Origin and Relations of. Abbé Guettée. New York, 1867. 12°. . P,821
Safeguards against its Errors. J. Brogden. London, 1851. 3 v. 8°. P,814
Vindication of the. F. P. Kenrick. Baltimore, 1855. 12°. . . P,809
Roman Catholicism, Delineations of. C. Elliott. New York, n. d. 2 v. 8°. P,818
Discussion on. J. Hughes and J. Breckenridge. Phila. 1836. 8°. . P,819
Letter on Dr. Pusey's Eirenicon. J. H. Newman. London, 1866. 8°. P,220
Letters to Bishop Hughes. N. Murray. New York, 1855. 12°. . P,800
Römische Päpste im 16. u. 17t. Jahrh. L. Ranke. Ber. 1845. 3 v. 8°. E,30
Roman Catholics in England, Present Position. J. H. Newman. Lond. 1851. 8°. P,619
Roman Classical Literature. R. W. Browne. Philadelphia, 1857. 8°. . H,726
Roman Emperors, History of. C. A. Elton. London, 1825. 12°. . . A,134
Roman Empire, Conversion of. C. Merivale. New York, 1865. 8°. . . A,173
Decline and Fall of. E. Gibbon. Boston, 1854. 6 v. 12°. . . A,148
The same. Boston, 1854-55. 8 v. 8°. . . . . . . A,160
The same. London, 1836. 8°. . . . . . . . . A,190
The same. London, 1853-55. 6 v. p. 8°. . . . . . L,264
The same. Boston, 1854-55. 8 v. 8°. . . . . . . S.C.
Decline and Fall of; edited by E. Pococke. London, 1853. 12°. A,141,3
Etudes sur la Chute de. R. F. A. de Chateaubriand. Paris, 1855. 12°. A,164
The same. Bruxelles, 1831. 4 v. 16°. . . . . . . A,75
Fall of. J. C. L. S. de Sismondi. London, n. d. 2 v. 16°. . . A,133
The same. London, 1834. 2 v. 12°. . . . . . M,1004
History of; edited by E. Pococke. London, 1853. 12°. . . A,141,2
The Holy. J. Bryce. London, 1871. 12°. . . . . . . A,222
Reflections on. C. de S. *Baron* de Montesquieu. Oxford, 1825. 16°. A,131
Verfall und Untergang des. E. Gibbon. Leipzig, 1843. 2 v. 8°. . E,35
Roman Imperialism. J. R. Seely. Boston, 1871. 12°. . . . . . H,512
Roman Exile. G. Gajani. Boston, 1856. 12°. . . . . . . . D,743
Roman History. A. Florus; trans. by J. S. Watson. Lond. 1870. p. 8°. L,77
A. Marcellinus; trans. by C. D. Yonge. London, 1862. p. 8°. L,35
Credibility of Early. G. C. Lewis. London, 1855. 2 v. 8°. . . A,181
im Zeitalter der Punischen Kriege. C. Haltaus. Leipzig, 1846. 8°. E,17
Römische Geschichte. C. F. C. Höck. Braunschweig, 1841-50. 8°. E,16
T. Mommsen. Berlin, 1865-68. 3 v. in 4. 8°. . . . E,18
A. Schwegler. Tübingen, 1853-67. 3 v. in 4. 8°. . . . E,19
C. V. Paterculus; trans. by J. S. Watson. London, 1870. p. 8°. L,77
Roman Literature, History of. H. Thompson and others. Lond. 1852. 12°. H,720

Roman Mythology, Römische Mythologie. L. Preller. Berlin, 1865. 8°. E,461
See also *Mythology*.
Roman Question, The. E. About. New York, 1859. 12°. . . . . . V,497
Roman Republic, Fall of. C. Merivale. London, 1853. 12°. . . . . A,143
History of. A. Ferguson. New York, 1856. 8°. . . . . . A,161
The same. New York, 1854. 16°. . . . . . L,468
J. Michelet. London, 1863. p. 8°. . . . . . . . . L,210
The same. New York, 1847. 12°. . . . . . A,139
edited by E. Pococke. London, 1852. p. 8°. . . . . A,141,1
Revolutions in. R. A. de Vertot d'Aubeuf. London, 1721. 2 v. 8°. A,144
Roman Scenes of the time of Augustus. W. A. Becker. London, 1853. 12°. A,153
Roman World, The Old. G. Lord. New York, 1868. 8°. . . . . . A,154
Romance of American History. J. Banvard. Boston, 1860. 16°. . . B,699
of Cheuelere Assigne. London, 1868. 8°. . . . . . L,604,6
of the Forest. A. Radcliffe. Philadelphia, 1864. 12°. . . K,1146
The same. London, 1820. 2 v. 12°. . . . . . . K,547
of History; England. H. Neele. London, 1831. 3 v. 12°. . . K,884
of the Republic. L. M. Child. Boston, 1868. 12°. . . . . K,23
of the Revolution. Philadelphia, 1870. 16°. . . . . . . K,236
of Spanish History. J. S. C. Abbott. New York, 1869. 12°. . . B,453
of Student Life Abroad. R. B. Kimball. New York, 1865. 12°. . K,135
of Western History. J. Hall. Cincinnati, 1857. 12°. . . . C,143
Romances, Early English Metrical. G. Ellis. London, 1848. p. 8°. . . L,8
The same. London, 1805. 3 v. 12°. . . . . . . H,699
Romanische Sprachen, Grammatik der. F. C. Diez. Bonn, 1836–44. 3 v. 8°. G,584
Wörterbuch der. F. C. Diez. Bonn, 1861–62. 2 v. 8°. . . . G,585
Romans, Ancient, History of Liberty. S. Eliot. Boston, 1853. 2 v. 12°. A,155
and Greeks, Arts, Manufactures, etc., of. T. D. Fosbroke. London, 1833–35. 2 v. 12°. . . . . . . . . . . . . M,996
Grandeur et Décadence des. C. de S. de Montesquieu. Paris, 1856. 12°. H,871
History of, under the Empire. C. Merivale. London, 1852–58. 6 v. 8°. A,172
The same. London, 1852–58. 6 v. 8°. . . . . . . . S.C.
Romantic Belinda. L. C. Tuthill. Philadelphia, 1867. 16°. . . J,1686
Romantic Tales. D. M. Craik. Leipzig, 1861. 16°. . . . . . . J,93
Romaunt, C. Island Home; or, the Young Cast-Aways. Boston, 1867. 16°. J,1428
Romberg, A. Schiller's Lay of the Bell; in Vocal Score. London, n. d. 8°. M,424
Rome, Ancient. T. H. Dyer. London, 1864. 8°. . . . . . . A,178
and its Surrounding Scenery; illustrations by W. B. Cooke; descriptions by H. N. Humphreys. London, 1840. 4°. . . . *V,574
Catacombs of Rome. W. I. Kip. New York, 1854. 12°. . . . V,499
Child's First History of. E. M. Sewell. New York, 1849. 18°. J,1300
Child's History of. J. Bonner. New York, 1856. 2 v. 16°. . J,1422
Comic History of. G. A. à Beckett. London, n. d. 8°. . . . A,150
Fall of. J. G. Sheppard. London, 1861. 8°. . . . . . . A,163
History of. T. Arnold. New York, 1866. 8°. . . . . . . A,170
H. G. Liddell. London, 1855. 2 v. 8°. . . . . . . A,151
O. Goldsmith. New York, 1855. 18°. . . . . . . . A,130
The same; Pinnock's edition. Philadelphia, 1868. 12°. A,142
T. Keightley. New York, 1849. 12°. . . . . . . A,135
T. Livius; trans. by D. Spillan and others. Lond. 1854. 4 v. 12°. L,66

Rome, History of. T. Livius; trans. by G. Baker. London, 1822. 6 v. 8°. A,156
T. Mommson. London, 1862-67. 5 v. 12°. . . . . A 149
B. G. Niebuhr. London, 1851. 3 v. 8°. . . . . A,171
C. Thirlwall. London, 1834-35. 2 v. 12°. . . . . M,995
C. V. Paterculus; translated by G. Baker. London, 1814. 8°. A,158
History of the Kings of. T. H. Dyer. London, 1868. 8°. . . A,162
in the 19th Century. C. A. Eaton. London, 1852. 2 v. 12°. . . L,155
Lectures on the History of. B. G. Niebuhr. London, 1853. 3 v. 8°. S.C.
Letters from. C. P. Thompson. New York, 1854. 12°. . . . V,498
Liberty of. S. Eliot. New York, 1849. 2 v. 8°. . . . . . A,180
Papal, Rise and Fall of. R. Fleming. London, 1863. 12°. . . P,562
Poets and Poetry of. W. Peter. Philadelphia, 1848. 8°. . . U,445
Regal. F. W. Newman. New York, 1852. 12°. . . . . . A,140
Roba di Roma. W. W. Story. London, 1863. 2 v. 12°. . . V,484
Stacions of, 1370; Pilgrim's Sea Voyage, etc. London, 1867. 8°. L,605,25
Stones of Etruria, and Marbles of Antient. G. L. Taylor. Lond. 1859. 4°. Q,285
Topography of, with map. Sir W. Gell. London, 1846. 2 v. 8°. A,179
Romer, I. F. Pilgrimage to Egypt, Nubia, and Palestine. Lon. 1846. 2 v. 8°. V,675
Romilly, Sir S., Life of; written by himself. London, 1842. 2 v. 16°. . D,596
Romola. M. J. Lewes. New York, n. d. 8°. . . . . . . . K,796
The same. Leipzig, 1863. 2 v. in 1. . . . . . . J,298
Romulus, History of. J. Abbott. New York, 1865. 16°. . . . . J,1419
Ronge, J. Holy Coat of Treves and German Cath. Church. Edinb. 1845. 12°. P,792
Ronalds, E. and Richardson, T. Chem. Technology. Lon. 1855. 3 v. in 4. 8°. N,192
Roofing, Bau der flachen Dächer. J. Linke. Braunschweig, 1841. 8°. N,252,19
Das Lehmdach und der Theerfirniss. F. F. Runge. Berlin, 1837. 8°. N,252,19
Dorn'sche u. Sach'sche Dachdeckung. C.F.Michaut. Berl. 1837. 16°. N,252,23
Feuerfeste und Wasserdichte. S. Sachs. Berlin, 1837. 8°. . N,252,19
Flache Dachdeckung. J. F. Dorn. Berlin, 1838. 8°. . . . N,252,19
Roofs of the Middle Ages, Open Timber. R. and J. A. Brandon. Lon. 1849. 4°. Q,176
of Public Buildings, Atlas. London, 1859. 4°. . . . . . Q,174
Roorbach, O. A. Bibliotheca Americana, 1820-52. New York, 1852. 8°. L.R.
The same; 2d Supplement, 1858-61. New York, 1861. 8°. L.R.
Roosevelt, R. B. Fives Acres too much. New York, 1869. 12°. . . M,497
Game Birds of the Northern States. New York, 1866. 12°. . . M,318
Superior Fishing. New York, 1868. 12°. . . . . . . M,321
Root, N. W. T. School Amusements. New York, 1857. 12°. . . . O,997
Rory O'More. S. Lover. London, n. d. 16°. . . . . . . . K,800
Rosa Abbott Stories. R. A. Parker. Boston, 1871. 6 v. 16°. . . J,1628

Vol. 1. Jack of all Trades. Vol. 4. Upside Down.
2. Alexis, the Runaway. 5. Young Detective.
3. Tommy's Hickup. 6. Pinks and Blues.

Rosamund Gray. C. Lamb. New York, 1859. 12°. . . . . . U,278,3
Rosary, The. M. M. Sherwood. New York, 1855. 12°. . . . K,1008,14
Roscoe, H. Eminent British Lawyers. London, 1830. 12°. . . M,1010
Life of William Roscoe. London, 1833. 2 v. 8°. . . . . . D,457
Roscoe, H. Vittoria Colonna; Life and Poems. London, 1868. 12°. . D,724
Roscoe, H. E. Lessons in Elementary Chemistry. London, 1868. 16°. . N,219
Spectrum Analysis; six Lectures. New York, 1869. 8°. . . N,209
Roscoe, T. German Novelists; Selected Tales. London, 1826. 4 v. 12°. G,177
Italian Novelists, v. 1, 3, 4. London, 1836. 12°. . . . . . G,232

Roscoe, T. Life and Writings of M. de Cervantes. London, 1839. 16°. I,629
Life of Michael Angelo Buonarotti. London, n. d. 8°. . . . C,581
Roscoe, W. H., Life of. H. Coleridge. London, 1852. 16°. . . C,1166,3
Roscoe, W., Life of. H. Roscoe. London, 1833. 2 v. 8°. . . . D,457
Life and Pontificate of Leo X. London, 1853. 2 v. p. 8°. . . L,225
Life of Lorenzo de Medici. London, 1851. 12°. . . . . L,226
The same. London, 1797. 2 v. 4°. . . . . . . F,28
Rose, H. Anfangsgründe der Analytischen Chemie. Berlin, 1845. 8°. N,252,16
Traité d'Analyse Chimique. Paris, 1852. 2 v. 8°. . . . N,179
Rose d'Albret. G. P. R. James. Leipzig, 1844. 16°. . . . . J,211
Rose Family of Kilravock, Genealogy of. Edinburgh, n. d. 4°. . F,84,23
Rose-Garden. S. B. A. Moslih-Eddin. Boston, 1865. 16°. . . . G,4
Rose Mather; a Tale. M. J. Holmes. New York, 1869. 12°. . . . K,192
Rose of Ashurst. A. Marsh-Caldwell. Leipzig, 1857. 2 v. in 1. 16°. . J,370
Rose, The; its History, Poetry, Culture, etc. S. B. Parsons. N. Y. 1850. 12°. M,352
Thistle and Shamrock. M. Edgeworth. New York, 1859. 12°. K,678,8
Rosecran's (W. S.) Campaign with 14th Army Corps; or, Army of the Cumberland. W. D. Bickham. Cincinnati, 1863. 12°. . . . B,898
Rosenkranz, K. Hegel's Leben. Berlin, 1844. 8°. . . . . G,562,22
Roses, Book of. F. Parkman. Boston, 1866. 12°. . . . . . M,500
Peintes par P. J. Redouté; décr. par C. A. Thory. Par. 1829. 3 v. 8°. *N,1028
Rosi Zurflüh. J. Scherr. Prag, 1860. 24°. . . . . . . G,444
Rosicrucians, The. H. Jennings. London, 1870. 12°. . . . . P,870
Ross, A. Red River Settlement. London, 1856. 12°. . . . . C,338
Ross, C. H. London Romance. Leipzig, 1869. 2 v. in 1. 16°. . . J,428
Pretty Widow. Leipzig, 1868. 16°. . . . . . . J,429
Ross, D. B. Southern Speaker. Philadelphia, 1869. 12°. . . O,1246
Ross, J. Voyage of Discovery to Baffin's Bay. London, 1819. 2 v. 8°. . V,941
Second Voyage, 1829–33. London, 1835. 4°. . . . . . Q,423
Appendix to Second Voyage. London, 1835. 4°. . . Q,441
Ross, W. Papers on Teaching. London, 1859. 16°. . . . O,1022
Rossbach, A. and Westphal, R. Metrik der Griechischen Dramatiker und Lyriker. Leipzig, 1854–62. 4 v. in 5. 8°. . . . . . . G,596
Bd. 1. Rossbach. Griechische Rythmik.
2. Westphal. Harmonik und Melopöie der Griechen; Allgemeine Griechische Metrik, 2 v.
3. Rossbach und Westphal. Griechische Metrik nach den einzelnen Strophengattungen und metrischen Stilarten.
Supplement. Westphal. Die Fragmente und Lehrsätze der Griechischen Rhythmiker.
Rosse, J. W. Index of Dates. London, 1858–59. 2 v. p. 8°. . . . L,273
Rossel, E. P. E. de. Astronomie Nautique. Paris, 1810. 8°. . . N,299,4
Rossetti, C. G. Poems. Boston, 1870. 16°. . . . . . . . I,404
Rossetti, D. G. Poems. Boston, 1866. 16°. . . . . . . I,407
Rossetti, W. M. Fine Art, chiefly contemporary. London, 1867. 16°. . M,39
Italian Courtesy Books. London, 1869. 8°. . . . . L,604,8
Rossini, G., Life of. H. S. Edwards. London, 1869. 8°. . . . . D,708
Rossmässler, E. A. Anleitung zum Studium der Thierwelt. Leip. 1856. 8°. G,931
Botanische Unterhaltungen. Leipzig, 1858. 8°. . . . . G,855
Flora im Winterkleide. Leipzig, 1854. 8°. . . . . . G,890
Mensch im Spiegel der Natur. Leipzig, 1868. 5 v. in 1. 16°. . G,708
Reise Erinnerungen aus Spanien. Leipzig, 1854. 2 v. in 1. 12°. . E,194
Thiere des Waldes. Leipzig, 1864-67. 2 v. 8°. . . . . G,936

Rossmässler, E. A. Vier Jahreszeiten. Gotha, 1856. 8°. . . . . . G,891
Der Wald. Leipzig, 1863. 8°. . . . . . . . . . G,889
Das Wasser. Leipzig, 1858. 8°. . . . . . . . . . G,709
Roth, M. Movements; or, Exercises for the Body. London, 1852. 8°. O,1251,1
Rotrou, J. de and others. Chefs-d'Œuvre Tragiques, v. 1. Paris, 1851. 12°. H,882
Rough and Ready. H. Alger. Boston, 1869. 16°. . . . . . J,1430,4
Round Table, The. W. Hazlitt. London, 1869. 16°. . . . . . I,558
Round the World. W. H. G. Kingston. Boston, 1870. 16°. . . J,1607
Roundabout Papers. W. M. Thackeray. Boston, 1869. 12°. . . K,1038,4
The same. Leipzig, 1869. 2 v. in 1. 16°. . . . . . J,487
The same. New York, 1864. 12°. . . . . . K,1089
Roundhearts and other Stories. M. Cole. New York, 1867. 12°. . J,1436
Rousseau, J. B. Œuvres de Poesie et de Prose. Paris, 1852. 12°. . . H,996
Rousseau, J. J. Collection complete des Œuvres. Geneve, 1781–89. 33 v. 12°. H,991
Les Confessions de. Paris, 1856. 12°. . . . . . . . D,628
Emile; ou, de l'Education. Paris, 1851. 12°. . . . . . O,967
Emilius and Sophia. London, 1783. 4 v. 12°. . . . . O,912
Petits-Chefs d'Œuvre de. Paris, 1852. 12°. . . . . . H,868
Routledge, E. Every Boys' Annual. London, 1865–70. 6 v. 8°. . J,1350
Roux-Ferrand, H. Histoire de la Civilization en Europe. Par. 1833–41. 6 v. 8°. A,311
Roving Adventures. G. Borrow. Cincinnati, 1852. 8°. . . . . . K,600
Rowbotham, T. and T. L. Landscape-Painting in Water-Colors. Lon.'67. 8°. M,25
Rowlands, S. The Four Knaves. London, 1843. 12°. . . . L,606,9
Rowlands, W. Holwyddoreg ar Bynciau y Grefydd Gristionogol. Rome, N. Y. 1859. 16°. . . . . . . . . . . . . . P,840
Rowley, W. Search for Money. London, 1840. 12°. . . . L,606,2
Fortune by Land and Sea; Tragic-Comedy. London, 1845. 8°. I,885,28
Royal Agricultural Society's Journal. London, 1839–68. 29 v. 8°. . R,18
Royal Asiatic Society, Journal. London, 1834–56. 16 v. 8°. . . . S,93
Babylonian Text at Behistun. n. t. p. 8°. . . . . . S,93,14
Transactions, v. 1–3. London, 1827–35. 4°. . . . . . . F,128
Royal Confectioner. C. E. Francatelli. London, 1866. 8°. . . . H,304
Royal King and Loyal Subject. T. Heywood. London, 1850. 8°. . I,885,45
Royal Navy, History of the. Sir H. Nicolas. London, 1847. 2 v. 8°. . B,95
Shipwrecks of. W. O. S. Gilly. London, 1851. 12°. . . V,1081
Royal Road to Fortune. E. H. Miller. Chicago, 1870. 16°. . . J,1336
Royal Society of London. See *London.*
Royal Truths. H. W. Beecher. Boston, 1866. 16°. . . . . . . P,289
Rubens, P. P., Life of. C. Blanc. London, 1855. 4°. . . . . . . Q,179
Ruby Gray's Strategy. A. S. Stephens. Philadelphia, 1870. 12°. . . K,451
Ruby's Husband. M. V. Terhune. New York, 1869. 12°. . . . K,333
Ruding, R. Annals of the Coinage of Great Britain. Lond. 1840. 3 v. 4°. *Q,269
Rudolph, L. Atlas der Pflanzengeographie. Berlin, 1864. 4°. . . . Q,131
Pflanzendecke der Erde. Berlin, 1859. 8°. . . . . . . G,892
Atlas dazu. Berlin, 1864. obl. 4°. . . . . . . . *Q,131
Rückert, F. Gedichte. Frankfurt, 1843. 12°. . . . . . . . . E,278
Gesammelte Poetische Werke, v. 1–7. Frankf.-a.-M. 1868. 7 v. 12°. E,277
Rühlmann, M. Grundzüge der Mechanik. Leipzig, 1860. 8°. . . . . E,438
Rüppell, E. Reisen in Nubien, Kordofan, u. Arabien. Frank.-a.-M. 1829. 8°. E,228
Ruggles, H. I. Shakespeare as an Artist. New York, 1870. 16°. . . I,847

Ruggles, T. History of the Poor. London, 1793-94. 2 v. 8°. . . . o,362
Ruffini, G. Doctor Antonio; a Tale of Italy. New York, 1867. 12°. . K,912
The same. Leipzig, 1861. 16°. . . . . . . . J,430
Lavinia. Leipzig, 1861. 2 v. in 1. 16°. . . . . . . . J,431
Lorenzo Benoni. New York, 1860. 12°. . . . . . . . K,913
The same. Leipzig, 1861. 16°. . . . . . . . J,432
Paragreens on a Visit to Paris. Leipzig, 1869. 16°. . . . . J,433
Quiet Nook in the Jura. Leipzig, 1867. 16°. . . . . . J,434
Vincenzo; or, Sunken Rocks. New York, 1864. 8°. . . . K,914
The same. Leipzig, 1863. 2 v. in 1. 16°. . . . . . J,435
Rugg, H. H. London Milk; its Unhealthy Character. London, n. d. 16°. N,252,38
Ruins of Ancient Cities. C. Bucke. London, 1840. 2 v. 16°. . . . I,621
Revolutions of Empires. C. F. C. de Volney. New York, n. d. 16°. A,59
Rule of the Monk. G. Garibaldi. New York, 1870. 8°. . . . . . G,241
Rumford, Count. See *Thompson, B.*
Rumor. E. S. Sheppard. Boston, 1864. 8°. . . . . . . K,1007
Run to Earth. M. E. Braddon. Leipzig, 1869. 2 v. in 1. 16°. . . J,43
Rundall, T. Voyages in Search of a Passage to India. London, 1849. 8°. V,983
Runge, F. F. Chemistry of Dyeing. London, 1837. 8°. . . . N,252,28
Grundriss der Chemie. München, 1846-47. 2 v. 8°. . . . G,765
Das Lehmdach und der Theerfirniss. Berlin, 1837. 8°. . . N,252,19
Rupert, Prince, Memoirs of. E. Warburton. London, 1849. 3 v. 8°. . D,467
Rupert Godwin. M. E. Braddon. Leipzig, 1867. 2 v. in 1. 16°. . . J,44
Ruppius, O. Geld und Geist. Berlin, 1863. 16°. . . . . . G,430
Der Pedlar. Berlin, 1867. 16°. . . . . . . . . . G,431
Prairie-Teufel. Berlin, 1861. 16°. . . . . . . . . G,432
Vermächtniss des Pedlars. Berlin, 1859. 16°. . . . . . G,433
Rural Cyclopedia. J. M. Wilson. Edinburgh, 1852. 4 v. 8°. . . . M,587
Rural Economy, in relation to Chemistry. J. B. Boussingault. N. Y. 1856. 12°. M,521
Traite complet de. Madame Celnart. Paris, 1834. 8°. . . . M,592
Rural Hand-Books, Saxton's, 2d, 3d, and 4th ser. N. Y. 1855-58. 3 v. 12°. M,533

Vol. 1. Missing.
2. Johnson, E. Every Lady her own Gardener.
Bentz, L. and Roville, A. J. C. de. Elements of Agriculture.
Browne, D. J. American Bird Fancier.
Dana, S. L. Essay on Manners.
Fessenden, T. G. American Kitchen Gardener.
American Rose Culturist.
3. Miles, W. Horse's Foot, how to keep it sound.
Bement, C. N. Rabbit Fancier.
Weeks, J. M. Method of Managing Bees.
Reemelin, C. Vine-Dressers' Manual.
Phelps, E. W. Bee-Keeper's Chart.
Topham, T. Chemistry made Easy.
4. Liebig, J. Familiar Letters on Chemistry.
Hooper, J. J. Dog and Gun.
Persoz, J. F. Culture of the Vine.
Abell, Mrs. L. G. Skillful Housewife's Book.
Memoir of Indian Corn.

Rural Essays. A. J. Downing. New York, 1853. 8°. . . . . . M,576
Rural Homes. G. Wheeler. New York, 1868. 12°. . . . . . . M,157
Rural Hours. S. F. Cooper. New York, 1868. 12°. . . . . . . H,274
Rural Letters. N. P. Willis. New York, 1849. 12°. . . . . . . H,80
Rural Poems. W. Barnes. Boston, 1869. 16°. . . . . . . . I,75
Rural Rambles; by a Lady. Philadelphia, 1854. 8°. . . . . . . N,518
Rural Sports, Encyclopædia of. D. P. Blaine. London, 1852. 8°. . *M,316

Rural Studies. D. G. Mitchell. New York, 1867. 12°. . . . . . M,549
Rural Tales. H. More. New York, 1854. 16°. . . . . . . J,1177
Rush, B. Yellow Fever in Philadelphia in 1797. Philadelphia, 1798. 8°. L,935
Rush, J. Philosophy of the Human Voice. Philadelphia, 1855. 8°. . M,416
Rush, R. Residence at the Court of London, 1817–25. Phila. 1833. 8°. . V,401
The same. London, 1833. 8°. . . . . . . . V,389,1
The same, 2d series. London, 1845. 2 v. 8°. . . V,389,2,3
Washington in Domestic Life. Edinburgh, 1855. 2 v. 8°. . . C,884
Rushworth, J. Historical Collections, 1618–40. London, 1659–80. 5 v. f°. F,40
Tryal of the Earl of Strafford. London, 1680. f°. . . . . . F,41
Ruskin, J. Crown of Wild Olive. New York, 1866. 12°. . . . . M,72
Elements of Drawing. London, 1857. 8°. . . . . . . . M,65
Elements of Perspective. New York, 1860. 12°. . . . . M,69
Ethics of the Dust. New York, 1866. 12°. . . . . . . M,66
Lectures on Architecture and Painting. New York, 1856. 12°. . M,151
Lectures on Art. New York, 1870. 12°. . . . . . . . M,64
Modern Painters. New York and London, 1866. 5 v. 8°. . . M,76
Notes on the Construction of Sheepfolds. New York, 1851. 12°. . M,70
Political Economy of Art. New York, 1858. 12°. . . . . M,67
Pre-Raphaelitism. New York, 1851. 12°. . . . . . . . M,70
Queen of the Air. New York, 1869. 8°. . . . . . . . M,63
Sesame and Lilies. New York, 1865. 12°. . . . . . . M,71
Seven Lamps of Architecture. New York, 1857. 12°. . . . M,74
Stones of Venice. New York, 1851. 8°. . . . . . . . M,78
The True and Beautiful in Nature. New York, 1868. 8°. . . M,75
Two Paths; Lectures on Art. New York, 1859. 12°. . . . M,68
Unto this Last; Essays on Political Economy. New York, 1866. 12°. M,73
Russegger, J. Reisen in Europa, Asien, etc. Stutt. 1841–48. 4 v. in 7. 8°. E,161
Atlas dazu. portfolio. . . . . . . . . . *Q,459
Russell. G. P. R. James. Leipzig, 1847. 2 v. in 1. 16°. . . . . J,212
Russell, C. True Robinson Crusoes. Boston, 1871. 12°. . . . J,1538
Russell, F. J. Use of Rules in Teaching Reading. Boston, 1854. 12°. O,820,24
Russell, J. *4th Duke of Bedford.* Correspondence. Lond. 1842–46. 3 v. 8°. H,835
Russell, J. *Earl.* English Government and Constitution. Lond. 1866. 12°. B,1
History of English Government and Constitution. London, 1865. 8°. B,49
History of the Principal States of Europe. London, 1826. 2 v. 12°. A,305
Memorials of Charles James Fox. Philadelphia, 1853. 2 v. 12°. . D,178
The same. London, 1853–57. 4 v. 8°. . . . . . . D,219
Russell, J. Boke of Nurture. London, 1868. 8°. . . . . . L,605,32
Russell, J. History of France. Cincinnati, 1838. 12°. . . . . B,223
Russell, J. Tour in Germany. Edinburgh, 1828. 2 v. 16°. . . . I,510
Russell, J. R. History and Heroes of Medicine. London, 1861. 8°. . . C,560
Russell, J. S. Modern System of Naval Architecture. Lond. 1865. 3 v. f°. *F,299
Systematical Technical Education. London, 1869. 8°. . . O,1018
Russell, M. Ancient and Modern Egypt. London, 1857. 12°. . . V,792
The same. New York, 1854. 16°. . . . . . . . L,356
History and Condition of the Barbary States. New York, 1854. 2 v. 16°. L,391
History of Polynesia, including New Zealand. London, 1853. 16°. V,878
The same. New York, 1842. 16°. . . . . . . L,444
Life of Oliver Cromwell. Edinburgh, 1829. 2 v. 16°. . . . . I,521

Russell, M. Life of Oliver Cromwell. New York, n. d. 2 v. 18°. . . L,384
Nubia and Abyssinia. New York, 1854. 16°. . . . . . L,383
Palestine. London, 1856. 16°. . . . . . . . . . V,628
The same. New York, 1854. 16°. . . . . . . . . L,360
Russell, Lady R. Letters. Philadelphia, 1854. 12°. . . . . . D,290
Russell, W. Extraordinary Men. London, 1853. 8°. . . . . . C,501
Extraordinary Women. London, 1864. 8°. . . . . . . C,493
History of Ancient Europe. Philadelphia, 1801. 2 v. 8°. . . A,330
History of Modern Europe. London, 1857. 12°. . . . . . A,300
The same. New York, 1853. 3 v. 8°. . . . . . A,343
Russell, W. Orthophony; Cultivation of Voice in Elocution. Bost. 1857. 12°. L,599
Russell, W. H. Atlantic Telegraph. London, n. d. 4°. . . . . . Q,268
British Expedition to the Crimea. London, 1858. 8°. . . . . B,82
Canada; its Defences, etc. London, 1865. 8°. . . . . . V,22
Crimean War. London, 1856. 12°. . . . . . . . . . B,80
My Diary in India, 1858–59. London, 1860. 2 v. 8°. . . . . V,736
My Diary North and South. London, 1863. 2 v. 8°. . . . . V,138
Todleben's History of Defense of Sebastopol, 1854–55. Lond. 1865. 8°. B,88
Russet Leaves. J. Pummill. Philadelphia, 1870. 12°. . . . . . H,116
Russia. Marquis A. Custine. London, 1863. p. 8°. . . . . . . I,656,5
The same. New York, 1854. 12°. . . . . . V,530
J. G. Kohl. London, 1854. 8°. . . . . . . . . V,535
and Tartary, Pedestrian Journey thro. J. D. Cochrane. Edin.'29. 2 v. 16°. I,513
and Turkey. J. R. McCulloch. London, 1854. p. 8°. . . . . I,656,6
and the Ural Mountains, Geology of. R. I. Murchison. Lon. 1845. 2 v. 4°. *Q,439
as it is. A. de Gurowski. New York, 1854. 12°. . . . . . V,525
at the close of the Sixteenth Century. London, 1856. 8°. . . . V,989
Atlas Russicus. Petropoli, 1745. f°. . . . . . . . . F,118
Autocracy in. J. Allen. New York, 1854. 12°. . . . . . V,532
Campaign in. E. Labaume. Hartford, 1850. 8°. . . . . . B,287
Crimea and Odessa. C. Koch. London, 1855. 12°. . . . . V,550
Empire of. J. S. C. Abbott. New York, 1850. 12°. . . . . B,539
Expedition to, by Napoleon, in 1812. L. P. Ségur. N.Y. 1854. 2 v. 16°. L,433
Free Russia. W. H. Dixon. New York, 1870. 12°. . . . . V,533
Geologie de la Russie; Paléont. R. I. Murchison. Lond. 1845. 4°. *Q,439,2
Geschichte des Russischen Krieges, 1812. H. Beitzke. Berlin, 1862. 8°. E,88
des Russ. Staates. P. Strahl u. Hermann. Hamb. 1832. 6 v. 8°. E,108
History of. R. Bell. London, 1836–38. 3 v. 12°. . . . M,1000
W. K. Kelly. London, 1854. 2 v. p. 8°. . . . . . L,227
A. Rabbe and J. Duncan. London, 1854. 2 v. 12°. . . . B,535
History of the War with. H. Tyrrell. London, n. d. 3 v. 8°. . B,180
Invasion of, by Napoleon. Sir R. Wilson. London, 1860. 8°. . B,286
Nachrichten der Russ. Akademie. A. Schischkow. St. Pet. 1837. 8°. G,588
Napoleon's Expedition to. P. de Ségur. London, 1836. 2 v. 16°. I,610
Notes of a Residence in. G. A. Sala. Boston, 1858. 12°. . . . V,523
Notes upon. S. *Baron* von Heberstein. London, 1851–52. 2 v. 8°. V,978
Productive Forces of. L. de Tegoborski. London, 1856–56. 2 v. 8°. B,541
Progress of. D. Urquhart. London, 1853. 12°. . . . . . V,522
Reise in Steppen des Südlichen Russlands. F. Goebel. Dorp. '38. 2 v. 4°. Q,433
The Russe Commonwealth. G. Fletcher. London, 1856. 8°. . V,989

Russia, Russie sous Pierre le Grand. F. M. A. de Voltaire. Paris, 1856. 12°. D,749
Russian-Turkish Campaigns, 1828-9. F. R. Chesney. N. Y. 1854. 12°. B,536
St. Petersburg and Moscow. A. Weir. London, 1862. 8°. . V,1086,2
Secret History of. J. H. Schnitzler. London, 1854. 2 v. 8°. . B,543
Travels in. C. B. Elliott. Philadelphia, 1839. 2 v. 12°. . . V,339
Sir J. Horsey. London, 1856. 8°. . . . . . . V,989
Travels in Greece and. B. Taylor. New York, 1868. 12°. . . V,360
Travels in Greece, Turkey and. J. L. Stephens. N.Y. 1855. 2 v. 12°. V,341
Russian America, Reise nach. F. H. von Kittlitz. Gotha, 1858. 2 v. 8°. E,173
Russian Empire, Native Races of. R. G. Latham. London, 1854. 8°. . N,414
View of the. W. Tooke. London, 1800. 3 v. 8°. . . . B,540
Russian Language, Russ.-Germ. Dict. J. A. E. Schmidt. Mosk. 1839. 2 v. 16°. L.R.
Untersuchungen über die Sprache. A. Schischkow. St. Petersb. '37. 8°. G,588
Russian Life, Sketches of; edited by H. Morley. London, 1867. 12°. . V,529
Russian Poetry, Specimens of. J. Bowring. London, 1821-23. 2 v. in 1. 12°. I,160
Russian Shores of the Black Sea. L. Oliphant. New York, 1854. 12°. . V,526
Russians and the Knout. G. de Lagny. London, 1854. 12°. . . . V,553
of the South. S. Brooks. London, 1854. p. 8°. . . . . I,656,6
Rustic Adornments for Homes of Taste. S. Hibberd. London, 1870. 4°. M,160
Rustic Work, Sketches for. T. J. Ricauti. London, 1848. 8°. . . Q,202
Ruth. E. C. Gaskell. New York, 1866. 12°. . . . . . . . K,709
The same. Leipzig, 1853. 2 v. in 1. 16°. . . . . J,180
Ruth Hall; a Domestic Tale. S. P. Parton. New York, 1855. 12°. . K,920
Ruthe, J. F. Handbuch der Zoölogie. Berlin, 1853. 8°. . . . G,916
Rutledge. W. Cole. New York, 1868. 12°. . . . . . . . K,14
Rutledge, J., Life of. H. Flanders. Philadelphia, 1855. 8°. . . . C,816
Life of. G. Van Santvoord. New York, 1854. 8°. . . . . C,817
Rutter, J. O. M. Gas-Lighting; its Progress, etc. London, 1849. 8°. N,252,39
Ruxton, G. F. Adventures in Mexico and Rocky Mountains. Lond. 1849. 12°. V,139
Life in the Far-West. Edinburgh, 1849. 12°. . . . . V,137
Ruysdael, J., Life of. C. Blanc. London, 1855. 4°. . . . . Q,179
Ryan, J. Algebra. New York, 1843. 12°. . . . . . . M,1100
Rydberg, V. The Last Athenian. Philadelphia, 1869. 12°. . . . K,915

Sabbath, Child's Book on the. H. Hooker. New York, n. d. 18°. . P,746,29
Sabbath-Evening Readings. J. Cumming. Boston, 1856. 12°. . . . P,456
Sabbath-School Teaching, End of. Edinburgh, 1827. 12°. . . . . P,351
Sabine, L. American Loyalists. Boston, 1847. 8°. . . . . . C,1091
Life of Edward Preble. Boston, 1860. 12°. . . . . . C,860,22
Notes on Duels and Dueling. Boston, 1859. 12°. . . . . H,623
Sabine, R. History and Progress of Electric Telegraph. Lond. 1869. 12°. M,857
Sable Cloud; a Southern Tale. N. Adams. Boston, 1866. 12°. . . K,294
Sacerdotal Celibacy, Historical Sketch of. H. C. Lea. Phil. 1867. 8°. . P,830
Sachs, S. Feuerfeste Dachdeckung. Berlin, 1837. 8°. . . . . N,252,19
Sacken, R. O. Catalogue of the Diptera of N. America. Wash. 1858. 8°. O,53
Sackville, T., *Lord Buckhurst*. Works. London, 1859. 16°. . . . I,409
Sacred Allegories. W. Adams. Leipzig, 1864. 16°. . . . . . J,1
Sacred and Legendary Art. A. Jameson. London, 1866. 2 v. 8°. . *M,116

Sacred and Legendary Art. A. Jameson. Boston, 1866. 2 v. 16°. . M,20
Sacred History and Biography. F. A. Cox. London, 1850. 12°. . . P,458
  Manual of. J. H. Kurtz. Philadelphia, 1855. 12°. . . . . P,457
  of the World. S. Turner. New York, 1854. 3 v. 16°. . . . L,365
Sacred Philosophy. J. B. Walker. Boston, 1856. 12°. . . . . . P,271
Sacred Poets of England and America. R. W. Griswold. N. Y. 1850. 8°. I,162
Sacrifice, Doctrine of. F. D. Maurice. Cambridge, 1854. 12°. . . . P,694
Säulenordnungen und Baustyle. L. Bergmann. Leipzig, 1854. 8°. . . G,626
Safety Lamp, Invention of. W. R. Clanny. Gateshead, 1844. 12°. . N,252,23
Saffell, W. T. R. Records of the Revolutionary War. New York, 1858. 12°. B,755
Safford, J. M. Geological Reconnoissance of Tennessee. Nashv. 1856. 8°. N,877
Safford, W. H. Life of Harman Blennerhassett. Cincinnati, 1859. 12°. . C,746
Sahara, Great Desert of. H. B. Tristam. London, 1860. 8°. . . . V,811
Sailor Boy. W. T. Adams. Boston, 1869. 16°. . . . . . . J,1536,2
Sails and Sail-Making. R. Kipping. London, 1866. 12°. . . . . M,847
Sainsbury, J. Napoleon Museum. London, 1845. f°. . . . *F,296
St. Albans, Chronica Monasterii. London, 1863–69. 7 v. 8°. . . . W,178
St. Albans, Duchess of. Memoirs. M. Wilson. London, 1839. 12°. . D,416
St. Andrews, Reliquæ Divi Andreæ, See of. G. Martine. St. And. 1797. 4°. P,648
St. Bartholomew, Massacre of. H. White. New York, 1868. 8°. . . B,366
St. Domingo, Description of. M. L. E. Moreau de St. Méry. Phil. 1796. 8°. S.C.
  Life in. R. B. Kimball. New York, 1863. 12°. . . . . . K,133
St. Evremond, C. M. de St. D. de, Œuvres choisies de. Paris, 1852. 12°. . H,998
St. Elmo. A. J. Wilson. New York, 1870. 12°. . . . . . . K,125
St. Giles and St. James. D. Jerrold. London, 1851. 12°. . . . U,178,1
    The same. Philadelphia, n. d. 12°. . . . . . U,179,1
    The same. Leipzig, 1852. 2 v. in 1. 16°. . . . . . J,224
St. Helena and Cape of Good Hope. J. McG. Bertram. N. Y. 1852. 12°. V,808
St. James's; or, Court of Queen Anne. W. H. Ainsworth. Leipzig, 1844. 16°. J,20
St. John, Picture of. B. Taylor. Boston, 1866. 16°. . . . . . . I,140
St. John, B. Adventures in the Libyan Desert. New York, 1849. 12°. . V,795
  The Louvre; or, Biography of a Museum. London, 1855. 8°. . V,457
  Montaigne, the Essayist. London, 1858. 2 v. 12°. . . . . . D,617
  Purple Tints of Paris. New York, 1854. 12°. . . . . . . V,443
  Village Life in Egypt. Boston, 1853. 2 v. 16°. . . . . . V,773
St. John, H., *Lord Bolinbroke*, Philosophy of. W. Warburton. Lond. 1756. 16°. P,18
  Works. Philadelphia, 1841. 4 v. 8°. . . . . . . . . U,204
St. John, J. A. Customs of Ancient Greece. London, 1842. 3 v. 8°. . A,102
  Egypt and Nubia. London, 1845. 8°. . . . . . . . . V,845
  History of Ancient Greece. London, 1842. 3 v. 8°. . . . A,102
  History of the Four Conquests of England. London, 1862. 2 v. 8°. A,499
  Life of Sir Walter Raleigh. London, 1869. 8°. . . . . . D,407
  Lives of Celebrated Travelers. New York, 1854. 3 v. 16°. . . L,369
  Residence in Normandy. Edinburgh, 1831. 16°. . . . . . I,531
St. John, P. B. Arctic Crusoe. Boston, 1866. 16°. . . . . . J,1476
St. John, S. Elements of Geology. New York, 1851. 12°. . . . . N,781
St. John of Jerusalem, History of the Order of. J. Taaffe. Lond. 1852. 2 v. 8°. A,239
St. Just, A. L. L., Histoire de. E. Hamel. Bruxelles, n. d. 2 v. 12°. H,1029
St. Kilda, Description of. A. Buchan. Glasgow, 1820. 12°. . . B,111,2
  Voyage to. M. Martin. Glasgow, 1820. 12°. . . . . . B,111,2

St. Lawrence and Franklin Co's, N.Y., Hist. of. F. B. Hough. Alb. 1853. 8°. c,120
St. Ledger; or, Threads of Life. R. B. Kimball. New York, 1850. 12°. K,137
St. Leon; a Tale of the 16th Century. W. Godwin. London, 1832. 16°. K,527
St. Leonards, Lord. See *Sugden*.
St. Louis, *King of France*. J. *Sieur* de Joinville. London, 1868. 16°. . I,564
and John Calvin. F. Guizot. Philadelphia, n. d. 12°. . . . D,655
St. Louis Public Schools; 16th Annual Report. St. Louis, 1871. 8°. . O,840
Public School Library, Catalogue of. St. Louis, 1870. 8°. . . L.R.
St. Martin's Eve. Mrs. H. Wood. Leipzig, 1866. 2 v. in 1. 16°. . . J,531
St. Olaves; a Novel. New York, 1867. 8°. . . . . . . K,1018
St. Patrick's Eve; Paul Gosslet's Confessions. C. Lever. Leipzig, 1870. 16°. J,286
St. Paul's Cathedral. H. H. Milman. London, 1868. 8°. . . . . . P,314
St. Petersburg and Moscow. A. Weir. London, 1862. 8°. . . . V,1086,2
Pictures from. E. Jerrmann. New York, 1852. 12°. . . . V,524
The same. London, 1854. p. 8°. . . . . . . I,656,6
Visit to, 1829–30. T. Raikes. London, n. d. 8°. . . . . V,534
St. Philips. M. Cole. New York, 1865. 12°. . . . . . . K,17
St. Pierre, J. H. B. de. Etudes de la Nature. Paris, 1856. 12°. . . M,757
Œuvres choisies. Paris, 1854. 12°. . . . . . . . . H,885
Paul and Virginia. Philadelphia, 1868. 12°. . . . . . . H,951
Paul und Virginie. Pforzheim, 1840. 8°. . . . . . . . G,443
Studies of Nature. London, 1809. 4 v. 8°. . . . . . . H,913
Works; with Memoir by E. Clarke. London, 1846. 2 v. 12°. . U,123
Vol. 1. Paul and Virginia; Indian Cottage; Studies of Nature.
2. Studies of Nature.
St. Réal, C. V. de. Conspiracy of the Spaniards against Venice. 12°. . B,482
St. Rémy, M. de. Sur la Grande Route, Proverbe. Paris, 1865. 12°. . I,743
St. Ronan's Well. Sir W. Scott. Boston, 1858. 2 v. 16°. . . . K,949
The same. Philadelphia, 1864. 8°. . . . . . . K,973
The same. Philadelphia, 1869. 8°. . . . . . K,1112
St. Simon, L. *Duc de*. Mémoires. Paris, 1853. 12°. . . . . . . D,610
Memoirs on Louis XIV. and the Regency. Lond. 1857. 4 v. 12°. D,661
St. Stephen's and New Timon. Sir E. B. Lytton. Leipzig, 1860. 16°. . J,323
St. Vincent, Island of. C. Shephard. London, 1831. 8°. . . . . . V,184
St. Winifred's; or, the World of School. F. W. Farrar. N. Y. n. d. 12°. J,1472
Sainte-Beuve, C. A. Portraits of Celebrated Women. Boston, 1868. 16°. C,494
Sainte-Croix, Marquis de. Fabrication du Sucre. Paris, 1845. 8°. . N,252,20
Saintine, X. B. Picciola; the Prisoner of Fenestrella. Phila. 1857. 12°. H,948
Saints, Abrégé des Vie des. Paris, 1854. 2 v. 12°. . . . . . . P,793
Lives of. A. Butler. Dublin, 1866–67. 12 v. 12°. . . . . . P,794
Rules for the walking of. J. Owen. London, 1778. 32°. . . P,335
Saints' Everlasting Rest. R. Baxter. New York, 1855. 8°. . . . P,163
The same. New York, n. d. 18°. . . . . . . P,746,5
Sala, G. A. Baddington Peerage. London, 1861. 3 v. 12°. . . . K,562
Breakfast in Bed. Boston, 1863. 12°. . . . . . . . H,591
From Waterloo to the Peninsula. London, 1867. 2 v. 8°. . . V,379
My Diary in America in the midst of the War. London, 1865. 2 v. 8°. V,136
Notes of a Residence in Russia. Boston, 1858. 12°. . . . . . V,523
Seven Sons of Mammon. London, 1862. 3 v. 12°. . . . . . K,561
The same. Leipzig, 1869. 2 v. in 1. 16°. . . . . . J,436

Sala, G. A. Trip to Barbary. London, 1866. 8°. . . . . . . v,754
Wm. Hogarth; Painter, Engraver, and Philosopher. Lond. 1866. 8°. c,1191
Salem Chapel. M. Oliphant. Leipzig, 1870. 2 v. in 1. 16°. . . . J,400
Salem Witchcraft. See *Witchcraft.*
Salis, C. U. von. Travels through Kingdom of Naples. London, 1795. 8°. v,483
Salis, J. G. Gedichte. Zürich, 1800. 12°. . . . . . . . . E,279
Sallustius, C. C. Opera Omnia; cur. J. L. Burnouf. Parisiis, 1821. 8°. . U,343
übers. von A. von Goeriz. Stuttgart, 1828–36. 2 v. in 1. 24°. E,3
Florus and C. V. Paterculus; tr. by J. S. Watson. Lond. 1870. p. 8°. L,77
The same. New York, 1855. 16°. . . . . . . . . A,136
Salmagundi. W. Irving, J. K. Paulding, and Wm. Irving. Phil. 1869. 16°. U,12
The same. New York, 1864. 12°. . . . . . . . U,32
The same. New York, 1857. 16°. . . . . . . . H,230
Salmonia; Days of Fly-Fishing. Sir H. Davy. London, 1851. 16°. . M,301
Salm-Reifferscheid-Dyck, J. von. Monographia Generum Aloes et Mesembryanthemi. Düsseldorpii, 1836–63. 7 v. 4°. . . . . . . *Q,124
Salm-Salm, F. My Diary in Mexico in 1867. London, 1868. 2 v. 8°. . C,382
Salt for Agricultural Purposes. C. W. Johnson, London, 1830. 8°. N,252,25
Les Moyens d'Extraire le. Paris, n. d. 4°. . . . . . N,252,41
Salts, Oxalates, Nitrates, etc., Constitution of. T. Graham. Lond. 1837. 4°. N,252,57
Saltpetre and Nitrate of Soda as Fertilizers. C. W. Johnson. Lond. 1840. 8°. N,252,25
Salvation, Way of. A. Barnes. Philadelphia, 1863. 12°. . . . . P,111
Salvator Rosa, Life and Times of. S. O. Morgan. London, 1824. 2 v. 8°. M,91
Salverte, A.J.E.B. Occult Sciences; Philosophy of Magic. N.Y. 1847. 2 v. 12°. O,326
Sam Slick; the Clockmaker. T. C. Haliburton. Philadelphia, n. d. 12°. K,714
Sam Slick's Wise Saws. T. C. Haliburton. London, 1859. 12°. . . K,130
Samaritan, Diary of a. New York, 1860. 12°. . . . . . . . H,264
Samaritan Languages, Grammar of. G. F. Nicholls. London, 1858. 12°. L,773
Samaritans, The, and Nabloos. G. Grove. London, 1862. 8°. . . V,1086,2
Sampson D., the Female Soldier, Life of. J. A. Vinton. Boston, 1866. 4°. C,1016
Sampson, E. Brief Remarker on the Ways of Man. New York, 1855. 12°. H,210
Samuels, E. A. Ornithology and Oölogy of New England. Bost. 1867. 8°. O,122
Samuelson, J. and Hicks, J. B. Honey-Bee. London, 1860. 12°. . . O,27
Humble Creatures. Earthworm and Housefly. Lond. 1860. 8°. O,26
Sanborn, C. W. North and the South. Boston, 1856. 12°. . . . . . O,394
Sanctum Sanctorum. T. Tilton. New York, 1870. 12°. . . . . . H,240
Sand, George, *pseud.* See *Dudevant, Madame.*
Sand Hills of Jutland. H. C. Andersen. Boston, 1860. 16°. . . . J,1489
Sandboys at the Great Exhibition. H. Mayhew. London, n. d. 8°. . . V,313
Sanders, C. W. School Reader. Andover, 1841. 12°. . . . O,1107
School Reader; Fourth Book. New York, 1843. 12°. . . . O,780
and J. C. Pictorial Primer. New York, 1846. 12°. . . . O,784
School Reader; Fifth Book. New York, 1855. 12°. . . O,787
Sanderson, J. Biography of the Signers of the Declaration of Independence. Philadelphia, 1820–27. 9 v. 8°. . . . . . . . . C,655
Sanderson, R., Life of. I. Walton. New York, 1854. 8°. . . . . . D,404
Sandford, Sir D. K. Rise and Progress of Literature. Glasgow, 1847. 16°. H,639
Sandford, J. Parochialia. London, 1845. 8°. . . . . . . . O,930
Sandford, P. P. Memoirs of Wesleyan Preachers. New York, 1843. 12°. D,438
Sandford and Merton. T. Day. New York, 1867. 12°. . . . . . J,1205

Sands, B. F. Total Eclipse of the Sun, August 7, 1869. Wash. 1870. 4°. N,387
Sands, D., Life and Gospel Labors of. New York, 1848. 12°. . . C,1007
Sands, N. Philosophy of Teaching. New York, 1869. 8°. . . . . O,956
Sandstones of Craigleith, Composition of. T. Bloxam. Edinb. 1858. 8°. N,252,44
Sandwich Islands, Life in the. H. T. Cheever. New York, 1856. 12°. . V,876
Notes by a Häolé. New York, 1854. 12°. . . . . . . V,880
See also *Hawaii*, and *Hawaiian Islands*.
San Francisco, Annals of. F. Soulé and others. New York, 1855. 8°. . C,247
Overland Journey to. H. Greeley. New York, 1860. 12°. . . V,118
Sanger, W. W. History of Prostitution. New York, 1859. 8°. . *O,363
Sanitary Commission of United States, Sketch of its Work. Bost. 1863. 12°. B,897
Sanitary Fair, History of the Great Western. Cincinnati, 1864. 8°. . . B,944
Sanitary Measures, Evils from Neglect of. London, 1847. 16°. . . N,252,37
Sanitary Reform. G. W. F. Howard. London, 1847. 8°. . . . N,252,29
San Juan del Rio Ranche, Geological Report of. C. Cherry. Cin. 1866. 8°. O,501
Sans Merci. G. A. Lawrence. New York, 1866. 8°. . . . . . . K,761
The same. Leipzig, 1866. 2 v. in 1. 16°. . . . . . J,259
Sanscrit Grammar. M. Williams. Oxford, 1857. 8°. . . . . . L,742
Sanscrit Language, Glossarium Comparativum. F. Bopp. Berolini, 1866. 4°. L.R.
Comparative Grammar of. F. Bopp. London, 1862. 3 v. 8°. . L,531
Grammaire Comparée des. F. Bopp. Paris, 1869. 3 v. 8°. . L,538
Vergleichende Grammatik des. F. Bopp. Berlin, 1859-68. 3 v. 8°. G,582
Sanskrit Literature. F. M. Müller. London, 1859. 8°. . . . . H,730
Santa Fé Expedition, Narrative of. G. W. Kendall. New York, 1844. 2 v. 12°. V,89
Santa Fé Trader, Journal of. J. Gregg. Philadelphia, 1850. 2 v. 12°. . V,158
Santarem, M. F. Researches respecting Americus Vespucius. Bost. 1850. 16°. D,717
Saracens, History of. S. Ockley. London, 1848. p. 8°. . . . . . L,220
Sargent, E. Life of Henry Clay. New York, 1856. 8°. . . . . . C,703
Planchette; or, the Despair of Science. Boston, 1869. 12°. . . O,327
Songs of the Sea. Boston, 1849. 16°. . . . . . . . . I,117
Standard first Reader. Boston, 1856. 12°. . . . . . O,773
Standard second Reader. Boston, 1856. 12°. . . . . . . O,779
Standard third Reader. Boston, 1856. 12°. . . . . . . O,892
Standard fourth Reader. Boston, 1856. 12°. . . . . . . O,891
Standard School Primer. Boston, 1857. 12°. . . . . . . O,772
Standard Speaker. Philadelphia, 1867. 8°. . . . . . . O,828
Woman who Dared. Boston, 1870. 16°. . . . . . . . . I,122
Sargent, J. Memoir of Henry Martyn. New York, 1844. 12°. . . C,1228
The same. New York, n. d. 8°. . . . . . . P,746,8
Sargent, N. Life of Lewis F. Linn. New York, 1857. 8°. . . . C,1052
Sargent, W. Life and Career of Major John André. Boston, 1861. 8°. . C,1265
(Ed.) Braddock's Expedition against Fort Du Quesne. Phil. 1855. 8°. B,707
Sargent, W. L. Social Innovators and their Schemes. London, 1858. 8°. O,375
Sarmiento, D. F. Life in the Argentine Republic. New York, 1868. 12°. V,234
Sarrans, B. Memoirs of Lafayette and French Revolution, 1830. Lon. 1832. 8°. D,666
Sarratt, J. H. Game of Chess, v. 2. London, 1808. 8°. . . . . . M,335
Sartor Resartus. T. Carlyle. London, 1858. 8°. . . . . . . H,428
The same. New York, 1852. 12°. . . . . . . . H,430
Satanstoe. J. F. Cooper. New York, 1867. 12°. . . . . . . K,48
The same. New York, 1860. 8°. . . . . . . . . K,76

Satire and Satirists. J. Hannay. New York, 1855. 12°. . . . . . H,641
Saturday Review. London, 1856–64. 18 v. f°. . . . . . . *Q,379
Saulcy, L. F. J. C. de. Journey round the Dead Sea. London, 1854. 2 v. 8°. V,647
The same. Philadelphia, 1854. 2 v. 12°. . . . . . V,647
Saunders, F. Mosaics; by an Epicure. New York, 1859. 12°. . . H,234
Sauzay, A. Wonders of Glassmaking. New York, 1870. 12°. . . M,1053
Savage, E. H. History of the Boston Watch and Police. Boston, 1865. 8°. O,364
Savage, J. The Librarian. London, 1808–9. 3 v. 8°. . . . . . L.R.
Savage, J. Genealogical Dictionary of New England. Bost. 1860–62. 4 v. 8°. *C,729
Savage, J. '98 and '48; Revolutionary History of Ireland. N. Y. 1856. 12°. B,161
Savage, M. W. Bachelor of the Albany. London, 1854. 12°. . . . K,555
Falcon Family. London, 1845. 12°. . . . . . . . K,559
My Uncle, the Curate. London, 1849. 3 v. 12°. . . . . K,558
Reuben Medlicott. London, 1864. 12°. . . . . . . . K,560
Savage, W. Dictionary of the Art of Printing. London, 1841. 8°. *M,640
Savannah, Georgia, Census. Savannah, 1848. 8°. . . . . . B,809,2
Savonarola, G., Life and Times of. London, 1843. 12°. . . . . D,715
Savonarola; ein Gedicht. N. Lenau. Stuttgart, 1853. 16°. . . . E,276
Saxe, J. G. Masquerade, and other Poems. Boston, 1866. 16°. . . I,120
Poems. Boston, 1866. 16°. . . . . . . . . . . I,118
The same, Highgate edition. Boston, 1870. 12°. . . . I,121
Saxe-Weimer Eisenach, B. Travels through North America. Phil. 1828. 8°. V,45
Saxons of the East and West. G. Moore. London, 1861. 8°. . . . N,432
Saxony, Geschichte Sachsen's. C. W. Böttiger. Hamburg, 1830–31. 2 v. 8°. E,81
Say, J. B. Treatise on Political Economy. Philadelphia, 1867. 8°. . O,540
Say and Seal. S. and A. Warner. Philadelphia, 1867. 2 v. 12°. . . K,386
Sayer, F. History of Gibraltar. London, 1862. 8°. . . . . . . B,456
Sayings and Doings. T. E. Hook. London, n. d. 3 v. 16°. . . . K,722
of Dr. Bushwhacker. F. C. Cozzens. New York, 1867. 12°. . H,96
Saymore, S. E. New System of French Grammar. New York, 1855. 12°. L,799
Scalp Hunters; or, the Trappers. M. Reid. New York, n. d. 12°. . J,1573
Scanderbeg, G. Castriot, surnamed, Life of. C. C. Moore. N. Y. 1850. 12°. D,759
Scanderbeg; or, Love and Liberty. T. Whincop. London, 1747. 8°. . I,742
Scandinavia, Ancient and Mod. A. Crichton and Wheaton. N.Y. 1856. 2 v. 16°. B,429
The same. New York, 1856. 2 v. 16°. . . . . . B,574
History of. S. A. Dunham. London, 1839–40. 3 v. 12°. . M,1002
P. C. Sinding. London, 1866. 8°. . . . . . . . B,578
Scanland, A. L. Heights and Depths. Chicago, 1871. 12°. . . . K,365
Scapegoat, The. Philadelphia, 1871. 12°. . . . . . . . K,1098
Scarlet Letter. N. Hawthorne. Boston, 1865. 16°. . . . . . . K,163
The same. Boston, 1868. 12°. . . . . . . . U,40,6
Scenes and Legends of North of Scotland. H. Miller. Cincinnati, 1852. 8°. V,362
in Foreign Lands; Engravings. Paris, n. d. 16°. . . . *M,597
in my Native Land. L. H. Sigourney. Boston, 1845. 16°. . . H,248
of Clerical Life. M. J. Lewes. New York, n. d. 8°. . . . K,798
The same. Leipzig, 1859. 2 v. in 1. 16°. . . . . . J,299
of the War in Hungary, 1848–49. Philadelphia, 1850. 12°. . . V,420
Sceptical Philosophy Examined. B. P. Aydelott. Cincinnati, 1868. 16°. P,228
Scepticism and Christianity; Boston Lectures, 1870. Boston, 1870. 12°. . P,151
Schacht, H. Anatomie und Physiologie der Gewächse. Berlin, 1854. 8°. G,893

Schacht, H. Der Baum. Berlin, 1853. 8°. . . . . . . . . G,894
Das Mikroskop. Berlin, 1855. 8°. . . . . . . . . . G,727
Die Pflanzenzelle. Berlin, 1852. 8°. . . . . . . . G,902
Prüfung der Gewebe. Berlin, 1853. 8°. . . . . . . . . G,766
Schack, A. F. von u. Geibel, E. Romanzero der Spanier. Stutt. 1860. 12°. E,264
Schäfer, H. Geschichte von Portugal. Gotha, 1836–54. 5 v. 8°. . . . E,97
und Lembke, F. W. Geschichte von Spanien. Hamb. 1831–61. 3 v. 8°. E,92
Schaff, P. Christ's Testimony to Christianity. Philadelphia, 1871. 8°. . P,284
History of the Apostolic Church. New York, 1856. 8°. . . P,405
Life and Labors of St. Augustine. New York, 1854. 12°. . . D,757
Schaller, J. Seelenleben des Menschen. Weimar, 1860. 8°. . . . G,569
Schalk, E. Summary of the Art of War. Philadelphia, 1862. 12°. . M,764
Schamyl, Caucasus, the Country of. W. Marshall. London, 1862. 8°. V,1086,2
Life of. F. Wagner and F. Bodenstedt. London, 1856. p. 8°. I,661,1
Scharling, E. A. De Calculis Vesicariis. Hauniæ, 1839. 4°. . . N,452,41
Schatzkästlein des Gevattersmanns. B. Auerbach. Stutt. 1864. 2 v. 12°. E,311,17,18
Schaubach, E. A. Die Deutschen Alpen. Jena, 1845–47. 5 v. in 3. 8°. . E,202
Scheerer, T. Der Paramorphismus. Braunschweig, 1854. 8°. . . G,710
Schefer, L. Artist's Married Life. New York, 1867. 16°. . . . D,524
Scheiger, J. Geschichte des Zeughauses in Wien. Wien, 1833. 8°. . . E,80
Schele de Vere, M. Outlines of Comparative Philology. N. Y. 1853. 12°. L,505
Studies in English. London, 1867. 8°. . . . . . . . L,570
Wonders of the Deep. New York, 1870. 12°. . . . . N,501
Scheller, I. J. G. Lexicon totius Latinitatis. Oxford, 1853. f°. . . L.R.
Schelling, F. W. J. von. Sämmtliche Werke. Stutt. 1856–58. 2 pts. in 14 v. 8°. G,570

ERSTE ABTHEILUNG.

Bd. 1. Magisterdissertation; Ueber Mythen, Sagen, u. s. w.; Ueber die Möglichkeit einer Form der Philosophie; Theologische Examensdissertation; Vom Ich als Princip der Philosophie; Neue Deduktion des Naturrechts; Philosophische Briefe über Dogmatismus und Kriticismus; Erläuterung des Idealismus der Wissenschaftslehre; Aus der "Allgemeinen Uebersicht der neuesten philosophischen Literatur"; Ueber Offenbarung und Volksunterricht; Recension.
2. Ideen zu einer Philosophie der Natur; Von der Weltseele.
3. Entwurf eines Systems der Naturphilosophie; Einleitung dazu; System des transcendentalen Idealismus; Ueber die Jenaische Allgemeine Literaturzeitung.
4. Allgemeine Deduktion des dynamischen Processes; Ueber den wahren Begriff der Naturphilosophie; Darstellung meines Systems der Philosophie; Bruno, ein Gespräch; Fernere Darstellungen aus dem System der Philosophie; Die vier edlen Metalle; Miscellen.
5. Abhandlungen, u. s. w., aus dem Kritischen Journal der Philosophie; Vorlesungen über die Methode des akademischen Studiums; Philosophie der Kunst.
6. Immanuel Kant; Philosophie und Religion; Propädeutik der Philosophie; System der gesammten Philosophie und der Naturphilosophie insbesondere.
7. Darlegung des wahren Verhältnisses der Naturphilosophie zu der verbesserten Fichteschen Lehre; Aus den Jahrbüchern der Medicin als Wissenschaft; Ueber das Verhältniss der bildenden Künste zu der Natur; Philosophische Untersuchungen über das Wesen der menschlichen Freiheit; Stuttgarter Privatvorlesungen; Aufsätze und Recensionen aus der Jenaer und Erlanger Literaturzeitung und dem Morgenblatt.
8. Ueber das Wesen deutscher Wissenschaft; Denkmal der Schrift des Herrn F. H. Jacobi; Aus der Allgemeinen Zeitschrift von Deutschen für Deutsche; Die Weltalter, erstes Buch; Ueber die Gottheiten von Samothrake; Kleinere Aufsätze.
9. Ueber den Zusammenhang der Natur mit der Geisterwelt, ein Gespräch; Kunstgeschichtliche Anmerkungen zu J. M. Wagner's Bericht über die äginetischen Bildwerke; Erlanger Vorträge; Spicilegium observationum in novissimam Arnobii editionem; Abhandlungen philologischen und mythologischen Inhalts; Erste Vorlesung in München; Rede an die Studirenden der Ludwig-Maximilians-Universität, 29ten December, 1830; Reden in den öffentlichen Sitzungen der Akademie der Wissenschaften in München.
10. Zur Geschichte der neueren Philosophie; Vorrede zu einer philosophischen Schrift des Herrn Victor Cousin; Darstellung des philosophischen Empirismus; Anthropologisches Schema; Worte zum Andenken des Freiherrn von

Schelling, F. W. J. von. Sämmtliche Werke. *Continued.* . . . . . G,570

Moll und Sylvestre de Sacys; Darstellung des Naturprocesses; Vorwort zu H. Steffens nachgelassenen Schriften; Vorbemerkungen zu der Frage über den Ursprung der Sprache; Epigrammata; Gedichte und metrische Uebersetzungen.

ZWEITE ABTHEILUNG.

Bd. 1. Einleitung in die Philosophie der Mythologie.
2. Philosophie der Mythologie.
3, 4. Philosophie der Offenbarung.

und Fichte's Lehren von Gott u. Welt. J. F. Fries. Heidelb. 1807. 16°. G,551

Schenkel, D. Character of Jesus portrayed. Boston, 1866. 2 v. 12°. . . P,378

Scherer, J. J. Chem. u. Mikrosk. Untersuch. zur Pathologie. Heid. 1843. 8°. N,252,9

Scherr, J. Deutsche Kultur- und Sittengeschichte. Leipzig, 1858. 12°. . E,71

Rosi Zurflüh; Geschichte aus den Alpen. Prag, 1860. 24°. . . G,444

Scherzer, C. Travels in Central America. London, 1857. 2 v. 12°. . V,231

Schiller, J. C. F. von. Æsthetic Letters, etc.; tr. by J. Weiss. Bost. 1845. 16°. O,614

and Goethe, J.W. von. Correspondence, 1794–1805, v. 1. N.Y. 1845. 12°. G,28

Biography of. T. De Quincey. Edinburgh, 1862. 12°. . . H,412,15

Characters of. E. F. Ellet. Boston, 1842. 12°. . . . . . H,745

Correspondence with Körner. London, 1849. 3 v. 12°. . . . G,30

History of the Thirty Years' War, etc. Edinburgh, 1828. 2 v. 16°. I,503

The same. New York, 1852. 12°. . . . . . . . B,208

Lay of the Bell; in Vocal Score. A. Romberg. London, n. d. 8°. *M,424

Life of. T. Carlyle. London, 1857. 8°. . . . . . . . C,523

The same. Leipzig, 1869. 16°. . . . . . . . J,62

Poems and Ballads; trans. by Sir E. B. Lytton. Edinb. 1852. 16°. G,42

The same. Leipzig, 1844. 16°. . . . . . . . J,328

Revolt of the Netherlands. New York, 1847. 16°. . . . . . B,407

Song of the Bell; trans. by W. H. Furness. Philadelphia, 1850. 8°. G,46

Sämmtliche Werke. Stuttgart und Tübingen, 1838. 12 v. 16°. . E,354

Bd. 1. Gedichte; Metrische Uebersetzungen aus Vergil's Æneid: Zerstörung von Troja; Dido.
2. Die Räuber; Die Verschwörung des Fiesco zu Genua; Cabale und Liebe; Der Menschenfeind.
3. Metrische Uebersetzungen aus Euripedes: Iphiginie in Aulis; Scenen aus den Phonicierinnen; Don Carlos, Infant von Spanien.
4. Wallenstein, ein dramatisches Gedicht.
5. Maria Stuart; Die Jungfrau von Orleans; Die Braut von Messina, oder die feindlichen Brüder.
6. Wilhelm Tell; Die Huldigung der Künste; Macbeth; Turandot, Prinzessin von China.
7. Phädra; Der Parasit, oder die Kunst sein Glück zu machen; Der Neffe als Onkel; Nachlass.
8. Geschichte des Abfalls der vereinigten Niederlande.
9. Geschichte des dreissigjährigen Kriegs.
10. Prosaische Schriften.
11. Kleine Schriften vermischten Inhalts.
12. Æsthetische Erziehung des Menschen; Gränzen beim Gebrauch schöner Formen; Ueber naive und sentimentalische Dichtung; Ueber den moralischen Nutzen ästhetischer Sitten; Ueber das Erhabene; Ueber den Gebrauch des Gemeinen und Niedrigen in der Kunst; An den Herausgeber der Propyläen; Ueber Bürger's Gedichte; Ueber den Gartenkalender, 1795; Ueber Egmont von Gœthe; Ueber Matthisson's Gedichte; Anhang; Leben; Charlotte von Schiller.

Works. London, 1853–57. 4 v. p. 8°. . . . . . . . . L,228

Vol. 1. Historical. Thirty Years' War; Revolt of the Netherlands.
2. Historical and Dramatic. Revolt of the Netherlands, *continued*; Trials of Counts Egmont and Horn; Wallenstein and Wilhelm Tell; Historical Dramas.
3. Historical Dramas, continued. Don Carlos; Mary Stuart; Maid of Orleans; The Bride of Messina.
4. Early Dramas and Romances. The Robbers; Fiesco; Love and Intrigue; metrius; The Ghost-Seer; The Sport of Destiny.

Werke. Stuttgart, 1867. 12 v. in 6. 16°. . . . . . . E,355

Bd. 1. Leben; Charlotte von Schiller; Gedichte; Semele.
2. Die Räuber; Die Verschwörung des Fiesco zu Genua; Kabale und Liebe.

Schiller, J. C. F. von. Werke. *Continued.* . . . . . . . . . E,255

3. Don Carlos, Infant von Spanien ; Der Menschenfeind.
4. Wallenstein, ein dramatisches Gedicht.
5. Maria Stuart ; Jungfrau von Orleans.
6. Wilhelm Tell ; Huldigung der Künste ; Braut von Messina, oder die feindlichen Brüder.
7, 8. Fehlen.
9. Geschichte des dreissigjährigen Kriegs.
10. Prosaische Schriften.
11. Kleine Schriften, vermischten Inhalts.
12. Recensionen ; Nachlass.

Schinz, H. Verzeichniss aller Säugethiere. Solothurm, 1844. 2 v. in 1. . G,923

Schischkow, A. Nachrichten der Russischen Akad. St. Petersb. 1837. 8°. G,588

Inhalt: Untersuchungen über die Sprache.

Schism, Vindication of Brief Enquiry. London, 1690. 18°. . . . P,5

Schkuhr, C. Kryptogamische Gewächse. Wittenberg, 1809. 4°. . . G,903

Schlagintweit, H. and A. Physicalische Geog. der Alpen. Leipzig, 1850. 8°. E,206

and R. de. General Hypsometry of India, etc., v. 2. Leip. 1862. 4°. *Q,380

Schlegel, A. W. von. Lect. on Dramatic Art and Liter. Lond. 1846. p. 8°. L,232

Schlegel, C. W. F. von. Æsthetic and Miscel. Works. London, 1849. p. 8°. L,234

Lectures on the History of Literature. London, 1868. p. 8°. . . L,230

Lectures on Modern History. London, 1849. p. 8°. . . . . . L,233

Philosophy of History. London, 1852. p. 8°. . . . . . . L,231

Philosophy of Life and Language. London, 1866. p. 8°. . . L,229

The same. New York, 1855. 12°. . . . . . . . O,696

Schleicher, A. Compend. der Indo-German. Sprachen. Weimar, 1862. 2 v. 8°. G,589

Die Deutsche Sprache. Stuttgart, 1860. 8°. . . . . . . G,594

Schleiden, M. J. Medicinisch- Pharmaceutische Botanik. Leipzig, 1852. 8°. G,895

Physiologie der Pflanzen und Thiere. Braunschweig, 1850. 8°. . G,659

Pflanze und ihr Leben. Leipzig, 1858. 8°. . . . . . . G,896

Plant, The; a Biography. London, 1853. 8°. . . . . . N,1002

Poetry of the Vegetable World. Cincinnati, 1853. 12°. . . N,946

Principles of Scientific Botany. London, 1849. 8°. . . . . N,1001

Studien, Populäre Vorträge. Leipzig, 1855. 8°. . . . . . G,711

Ueber Fremdenpolizei in der Natur ; Franklin und Nordpolexpeditionen ; Natur der Töne und Töne der Natur ; Beeseelung der Pflanzen ; Swedenborg und der Aberglaube ; Wallenstein und die Astrologie ; Mondscheinschwärmereien eines Naturforschers ; Ueber Zauberei und Geisterspuk.

Theorie des Erkennens durch den Gesichtssinn. Leipzig, 1861. 8°. E,420

Schlesier, G. Life of William von Humboldt. New York, 1853. 12°. . D,521

Schleswig-Holstein, Geschichte von. G. Waitz. Göttin. 1851–52. 2 v. 8°. E,82

Schlichtegroll, A. H. F. de. Life of Mozart. London, 1817. 8°. . . D,523

Schloss Elkrath; Roman. G. Raimund. Hannover, 1866. 3 v. 16°. . G,392

Schloss Hainfeld; or, a Winter in Styria. B. Hall. London, 1836. 12°. . V,406

Schlossberger, J. E. Organische Chemie. Leipzig, 1860. 8°. . . . . G,767

Schlosser, F. C. Gesch. des 18ten Jahrhunderts. Heid. 1864–68. 8 v. 8°. E,37

History of the Eighteenth Century. London, 1843–52. 8 v. 8°. . A,331

Weltgeschichte für das Deutsche Volk. Frankf.-a.-M. 1844–57. 19 v. 8°. E,8

The same. Frankfurt-a.M., 1844–56. 18 v. in 9. 8°. . . E,6

Schmarda, L. K. Geograph. Verbreit. der Thiere. Wien, 1853. 3 v. in 1. 8°. G,921

Reise um die Erde, 1853–57. Braunschweig, 1861. 3 v. 8°. . . E,163

Schmidt, C. H. Magnetismus, Elekricität, etc. Leipzig, n. d. 12°. . .N,252,23

Vollständiges Farben-Laboratorium. Weimar, 1847. 16°. . . G,627

Schmidt, E. A. Geschichte von Frankreich. Hamburg, 1835–48. 4 v. 8°. E,86

Schmidt, F. A. Petrefacten-Buch. Stuttgart, 1846. 4°. . . . . . G,848

Schmidt, H. Education. New York, 1855. 18°. . . . . . . L,442
Schmidt, H. J. Deutsche Literatur seit Lessing's Tod. Leip. 1858. 3 v. 8°. E,252
Schmidt, J.A.E. Russisch-Deutsches Wörterbuch. Moskwa, 1839. 2 v. 12°. L.R.
Schmidt, J. F. J. Das Zodiacallicht. Braunschweig, 1856. 8°. . . . G,797
Schmidt, K. Geschichte der Pädagogik, v. 1, 2, 4. Cöthen, 1867–69. 3 v. 8°. G,538
Schmidt, O. and Unger, F. Alter der Menschheit. Wien, 1866. 8°. . . E,404
Schmidt, W. A. Denk- u. Glaubensfreiheit im 1ten Jahrh. Berlin, 1847. 8°. E,444
Schmiedjakobs Geschichten. W. O. von Horn. Frank.-a-M. 1862. 3 v. 12°. G,328
Schmitz, L. Grammar of the Latin Language. Philadelphia, 1859. 16°. L,750
Manual of Ancient History. Philadelphia, 1855. 12°. . . . A,19
Schmucker, S. M. Arctic Explorations in 19th Century. N. Y. 1857. 12°. V,937
History of Civil War in United States. Philad. 1862–65. 3 v. 8°. B,917
History of the Four Georges of England. New York, 1860. 12°. C,1266
History of Napoleon III. Philadelphia, 1860. 12°. . . . D,556
Life and Reign of Nicholas 1. Philadelphia, 1858. 12°. . . . D,750
Life and Times of Alexander Hamilton. Philadelphia, 1856. 12°. . C,694
Life and Times of George Washington. Philadelphia, 1860. 12°. . C,913
Life and Times of Thomas Jefferson. Philadelphia, 1858. 12°. . C,940
Life of Daniel Webster. Philadelphia, 1859. 8°. . . . . C,979
Memoirs of Catherine II. of Russia. New York, 1855. 12°. . . D,753
Schmucker, S. S. Psychology. New York, 1842. 12°. . . . . O,631
The same. New York, 1845. 12°. . . . . . . . O,632
Schneider, K.F.R. Erdbeschreibung u. Staatenkunde. Glogau, 1857. 5 v. 8°. E,154
Schnitzler, J. H. Secret History of Russia. London, 1854. 2 v. 8°. . B,543
Schoedler, F. Book of Nature. Philadelphia, 1853. 8°. . . . . M,788
Schoeler, V. Life of Handel. New York, 1857. 12°. . . . . D,508
Schoemann, G. F. Griechische Alterthümer. Berlin, 1861–63. 2 v. 8°. E,456
Schönbein, C. F. Elektrische Polarisation. Basel, 1838. 8°. . . N,252,1
Erzeugung des Ozons auf Chemischem Wege. Basel, 1844. 8°. N,252,21
Verhalten des Eisens zum Sauerstoff. Basel, 1837. 8°. . . N,252,5
Schönberg-Cotta Family. E. Charles. New York, 1864. 12°. . . . K,627
The same. Leipzig, 1867. 2 v. in 1. 16°. . . . . J,66
Schöne, Das, Idee des Shönen. A. Kuhn. Berlin, n. d. 12°. . . . G,566
Scholar, Vocation of the. J. G. Fichte. London, 1847. 12°. . . . G,34
Schomburgk, R. Reisen in Britisch-Guiana. Leipzig, 1847–48. 3 v. 4°. *Q,429
School and Schoolmaster. A. Potter and G. B. Emerson. N.Y. 1854. 12°. O,823
Graded. W. H. Wells. New York, 1867. 12°. . . . . O,939
Model. W. J. Unwin. London, 1849. 16°. . . . . . O,969
of the Future. F. B. Zincke. London, 1852. 12°. . . . O,1146
Record of a. E. P. Peabody. Boston, 1835. 12°. . . . O,1176
School Amusements. N. W. T. Root. New York, 1857. 12°. . . . O,997
School Architecture. H. Barnard. New York, 1854. 8°. . . . M,188
School Controversy, Boston. H. Mann. Boston, 1844. 8°. . . . O,927
School Economy. J. Symons. London, 1852. 16°. . . . . . O,965
J. P. Wickersham. Philadelphia, 1864. 12°. . . . . . O,940
School Education. J. Pycroft. Oxford, 1843. 12°. . . . . . O,996
for the 19th Century. S. Preston. London, 1846. 8°. . . . O,947
School for Dreamers. T. Gwynne. London, 1853. 12°. . . . . K,716
School-Life at Winchester College. R. B. Mansfield. London, 1870. 12°. O,830
School Management, Text-Book to. J. Gill. London, 1858. 16°. . O,1115

School of Abuse. S. Gosson. London, 1841. 8°. . . . . . I,885,2
School of Life. A. M. Howitt. Boston, 1855. 16°. . . . . . J,1247
School-Room, The. J. J. H. Harris. London, 1842–48. 2 pts. 8°. . O,1251,3
In the. J. S. Hart. Philadelphia, 1868. 12°. . . . . . . O,973
Lawyer in the. M. McN. Walsh. New York, 1867. 12°. . . . U,489
Schoolboy Days; or, Ernest Bracebridge. W. H. G. Kingston. Bos. 1869. 16°. J,1549
Schoolcraft, H. R. Adventures in the Ozark Mountains. Phil. 1853. 8°. V,66
Archives of Aboriginal Knowledge. Philadelphia, 1860–68. 6 v. 4°. *F,104
Expedition to Sources of the Mississippi, 1820. Philad. 1855. 8°. . V,110
Notes on the Iroquois. Albany, 1847. 8°. . . . . . . B,615
Thirty Years with Indian Tribes. Philadelphia, 1851. 8°. . . B,611
Schoolday Dialogues. A. Clark. Philadelphia, n. d. 12°. . . O,1224
Schoolmaster, The. London, 1836. 2 v. 12°. . . . . . . O,1194
The Church. S. Robins. London, 1850. 8°. . . . . . O,1138
Day-Dreams of a. D. W. Thompson. Edinburgh, 1864. 16°. . O,934
Papers for the, v. 2–4. London, 1853–54. 12°. . . . O,1190
Schools, Common, and Teachers' Seminaries. C. E. Stowe. Boston, 1839. 12°. O,1127
Deutsche Volksschule. H. Gräfe. Leipzig, 1850. 3 v. 8°. . . G,537
Dutch and German. W. E. Hickson. London, 1840. 8°. . O,1011
Hints on Female Parochial. London, 1848. 18°. . . . . O,1108
Model, in Dublin. W. C. Taylor. Dublin, 1847. 8°. . . O,1251,2
of Cincinnati. J. P. Foote. Cincinnati, 1855. 8°. . . . . O,1012
of England, The Great. H. Staunton. London, 1865. 12°. . . O,831
Ragged, Essay on. G. J. Hall. London, 1855. 8°. . . . . O,1141
Reformatory. B. Alderson. London, 1855. 8°. . . . . O,1251,2
for Children. M. Carpenter. London, 1851. 8°. . . . . O,922
Report of the Dick Bequest for. A. Menzies. Edinburgh, 1854. 8°. O,1235
Schopenhauer, A. Die beiden Grundprobleme der Ethik. Leip. 1860. 8°. G,571
Parerga u. Paralipomena; kleine philos. Schriften. Berl. 1862. 2 v. 8°. G,572
Ueber den Willen in der Natur. Frankfurt-a.-Main, 1854. 8°. . G,575
Vierfache Wurzel des Satzes. Leipzig, 1864. 8°. . . . . . G,573
Welt als Wille und Vorstellung. Leipzig, 1859. 2 v. 8°. . . . G,574
Schouler, W. Massachusetts in the Civil War. Boston, 1868. 8°. . . B,939
Schouw, J. F. Earth, Plants, and Man; tr. by A. Henfrey. Lond. 1852. p. 8°. L,312
Erde, Pflanzen, und Mensch. Leipzig, 1854. 8°. . . . . . G,712
Schrader, A. Die Komödianten. Leipzig, 1862. 4 v. 16°. . . . . G,445
Schrevelius, C. Lexicon Manuale Græco-Latinum. Novi-Eboraci, 1818. 8°. L.R.
Schrift und Volk. B. Auerbach. Stuttgart, 1864. 12°. . . . . E,311,20
Schroeder, F. Shores of the Mediterranean. New York, 1846. 2 v. 12°. V,1056
Schroeder, J. F. (Ed.) Maxims of Washington. New York, 1859. 12°. . H,269
Schubart u. seine Zeitgenossen. A. E. Brachvogel. Jena u. Leip. 1864. 4 v. 16°. G,265
Schubarth, E. L. Handbuch der Technischen Chemie. Berl. 1851. 3 v. 8°. G,768
Atlas dazu. Berlin, 1851. 4°. . . . . . . . . . F,94
Schubert, F. T. Populäre Astronomie. St. Petersburg, 1804–10. 3 v. 8°. G,798
Schubert, G. H. von. Memoir of the Duchess of Orleans. N.Y. 1860. 12°. D,615
Memoir of Bernard Overberg. London, 1838. 12°. . . . . . D,499
Schücking, L. Aus alter und neuer Zeit. Leipzig, 1865. 24°. . . . . G,446
Aus den Tagen der grossen Kaiserin. Prag und Leipzig, 1858. 24°. G,448
Die Geschwornen und ihr Richter. Hannover, 1861. 3 v. 16°. . G,447
Die Rheider Burg. Leipzig, 1864. 16°. . . . . . . . G,449

Schücking, L. Die Sphinx. Leipzig, 1856. 12°. . . . . . . G,450
Schüler der Natur. K. Müller. Halle, 1851. 16°. . . . . . . G,357
Schultheissentöchter von Nürnberg. L. Otto. Wien, 1861. 3 v. 24°. . G,378
Schultz, H. Refractors-Beobachtungen der K. Universitäts. Upsala, 1864. 8°. G,801
Schulz, J. Die Wichtigsten Mathematische Theorien. Königsb. 1803. 4°. M,1175
Schulze, F. Lehrbuch der Chemie für Landwirthe. Leipzig, 1846. 8°. . G,769
Schulze, G. F., Prüfung der Ackerbautheorie von J. v. Liebig. Jena, 1846. 8°. N,252,24
Schumacher, H. C. Astronomische Nachrichten. Altona, 1854-55. 3 v. 4°. G,849
Jahrbuch für 1836-43. Stuttgart, 1836-43. 7 v. 12°. . . . G,799
Sammlung von Hülfstafeln. Altona, 1845. 8°. . . . . . . G,781
Schumacher, W. Ernährung der Pflanze. Berlin, 1864. 8°. . . . G,898
Schwab, G. Fünf Bücher deutscher Lieder und Gedichte. Leip. 1857. 12°. E,280
Wanderungen durch Schwaben. Leipzig, n. d. 8°. . . . . E,186,2
Schwartz, M. S. Birth and Education. Boston, 1871. 8°. . . . . G,224
Gold and Name. Boston, 1871. 8°. . . . . . . . . . G,223
Guilt and Innocence. Boston, 1871. 8°. . . . . . . . G,228
Wife of a Vain Man. Boston, 1871. 8°. . . . . . . . G,229
Schwarz, J. Geography and Historical Sketch of Palestine. Phil. 1850. 8°. V,663
Schwarzwälder Dorfgeschichten. B. Auerbach. Stutt. 1863-64. 8 v. 12°. E,311,1-8
Schwegler, A. History of Philosophy; tr. by J. H. Seelye. N.Y. 1866. 12°. O,653
Römische Geschichte. Tübingen, 1853-67. 3 v. in 4. 8°. . . E,19
Schweigger, A. F. Beobachtungen auf Naturhistor. Reisen. Ber. 1819. 4°. N,749
Science and Art, Museum of. D. Lardner. Lond. 1854-56. 12 v. in 6. 12°. M,770

Vol. 1. The Planets; Weather Prognostics; Popular Fallacies; Latitudes and Longitudes; Lunar Influences; Meteoric Stones and Shooting Stars; Railway Accidents; Light.
2. Air; Locomotion by River and Railway in the United States; Cometary Influences; Water; The Potter's Art; Fire.
3. Locomotion and Transport; The Moon; The Earth; Terrestrial Heat; The Sun; Electric Telegraph.
4. Electric Telegraph, concluded; Earthquakes and Volcanoes; Barometer; Safety Lamp; Whitworth's Micrometric Apparatus; Steam.
5. Steam Engine; The Eye; The Atmosphere; Time; Pumps; Spectacles; The Kaleidoscope.
6. Clocks and Watches; Microscopic Drawing and Engraving; The Locomotive; The Thermometer; New Planets; Le Verrier and Adams' Planet; Magnitude and Minuteness.
7. The Almanac; Color; Optical Images; The Looking-Glass; Tides; How to Observe the Heavens; Stellar Universe.
8. Stellar Universe, concluded; Man; Magnifying Glasses; Instinct and Intelligence; Solar Microscope; Camera Lucida; Magic Lantern; Camera Obscura.
9. Microscope; White Ants; Surface of the Earth; Science and Poetry.
10. The Bee; Steam Navigation; Thunder and Lightning and Aurora Borealis; Electro-motive Power.
11. The Printing-Press; Geology; Stereoscope; Comets.
12. Pre-Adamite Earth; Eclipses; Sound.

and the Bible, Claims of. F. D. Maurice. London, 1863. 12°. . P,303
and Literature, Objects and Uses of. A. Potter. N. Y. 1858. 18°. . L,461
and Natural Philosophy, Recreations in. J. Ozanam. Lond. 1851. 8°. M,790
and Revealed Religion, Connexion between. N. Wiseman. And.'37. 8°. P,315
applied to Domestic and Mechanic Arts. A. Potter. N. Y. 1855. 12°. M,607
before the Norman Conquest. O. Cockayne. London, 1864-66. 3 v. 8°. W,185
Curiosities of. J. Timbs. London, 1849. 2 v. in 1. 16°. . . . I,545
Emancipation of; an Address. J. D. Cox. Salem, O. 1853. 8°. . T,19,2
for the Young. J. Abbott. New York, 1871. 2 v. 12°. viz:
Vol. 1. Heat. . . J,1729 Vol. 2. Light. . . J,1730
Fragments of, for Unscientific People. J. Tyndall. N.Y. 1871. 12°. M,775
Household. E. L. Youmans. New York, 1868. 12°. . . . . M,762
Literature and Art, Dictionary of. W. T. Brande. N. Y. 1870. 8°. L.R.

Science, Martyrs of; Galileo and others. Sir D. Brewster. Lond. 1870. p. 8°. c,551
The same. New York, 1854. 18°. . . . . . . . L,424
Molecular and Microscopic. M. Somerville. London, 1869. 2 v. 12°. N,14
Neue Encyklopädie der Wissenschaften. Stuttgart, 1848-50. 3 v. 8°. G,817
Zoologie. A. G. Bronn. Botanik. G. W. Bischoff.
of Gems, Jewels, Coins, and Medals. A. Billing. London, 1867. 8°. M,99
of Money; a Great Truth. Philadelphia, 1871. 12°. . . . O,561
Philosophy and Religion. J. Bascom. New York, 1871. 12°. . P,214
Poetry of. R. Hunt. London, 1854. 12°. . . . . . . L,299
Popular Lectures on. D. Lardner. New York, 1855. 2 v. 8°. . M,791
Principles of. A. Potter. New York, 1847. 12°. . . . . M,611
Religious Truth illustrated from. E. Hitchcock. Boston, 1857. 12°. P,251
Sciences, Circle of the; edited by W. S. Orr. London, 1859. 4 v. 8°. . M,785
Vol. 1-3. Organic Nature. Vol. 4. Inorganic Nature.
Classification of. H. Spencer. n. t. p. . . . . . . . O,667
illustrated, and Plates, Appleton's. New York, 1856. 2 v. 8°. . *Q,250
Inductive, History of. W. Whewell. New York, 1859. 2 v. 8°. . O,697
Philosophy of. A. Comte; tr. by G. H. Lewes. Lond. 1853. p. 8°. L,289
Physical and Mathematical, History of. B. Powell. Lond. 1834. 12°. M,1018
Studium der, in Preussen. J. Liebig. Braunschweig, 1840. 8°. N,252,7
Scientific American; 1st ser., v. 4-14, 1848-59. N. Y. 1848-59. 11 v. f°. Q,133
2d series, v. 1, 12, 14-23. New York, 1859-71. 12 v. f°. . Q,134
Scientific Amusements for Young People. J. H. Pepper. London, 1865. 16°. M,767
Scientific and Literary Treasury. S. Maunder. London, 1845. 12°. . L.R.
The same. London, 1848. 12°. . . . . . . . L.R.
Scientific Dialogues. J. Joyce. London, 1852. 12°. . . . . . . L,300
Scientific Discovery, Annual of; ed. D. A. Wells *et als*. Bos. 1850-71. 21 v. 12°. M,766
Scientific Knowledge, Guide to. E. C. Brewer. London, 1869. 18°. . N,16
Scientific Papers, Royal Society's Catalogue of. London, 1867-70. 4 v. 4°. L.R.
Scientific Subjects, Familiar Lectures on. Sir J.F.W. Herschel. Lon. 1867. 8°. M,769
Scilly Isles, Sea-Side Studies at. G. H. Lewes. Edinburgh, 1858. 8°. . N,520
Sclater, P. L. Birds of the Tanagrine Genus Calliste. London, 1857. 8°. O,107
Naturalist's Impressions of Spain. London, 1863. 8°. . . . V,1086,2
Scoresby, W. Voyage to the Northern Whale-Fishery. Edinb. 1823. 8°. V,181
Magnetical Investigations. London, 1839-52. 2 v. in 3. 8°. . . N,53
Scot, G. Memoirs of Sir James Melvil. Edinburgh, 1735. 8°. . . D,367
Scotia's Bards; with Biographical Sketches. New York, 1856. 8°. . . J,870
Scotland. J. G. Kohl. London, 1844. 8°. . . . . . . . . V,398
Affairs of, 1637-41. J. Gordon. Aberdeen, 1841. 3 v. 4°. . F,84,1-3
and England, Border History of, to 1603. G. Reidpath. Berwick, '48. 4°. F,30
Ballads of. W. E. Aytoun. Edinburgh, 1859. 2 v. 12°. . . . I,280
Baronial and Ecclesiastical Antiquities of. R. W. Billings. Edinburgh, n. d. 4 v. 4°. . . . . . . . . . . *Q,143
Beauties of. R. Forsyth. Edinburgh, 1805-8. 5 v. 8°. . . . V,397
Chronicles of England and. R. Holinshed. London, 1807-8. 6 v. 4°. *F,161
Church and State in. R. Keith. Edinburgh, 1844-50. 3 v. 8°. . P,594
Church of, History of. W. M. Hetherington. New York, 1848. 8°. P,592
T. Stephen. London, 1848. 4 v. 8°. . . . . . P,635
Church of, Sufferings of. R. Wodron. Glasgow, n. d. 4 v. 8°. . P,646
Church of, Ten Years' Conflict. R. Buchanan. Glasgow, 1857. 2 v. 12°. P,565

Scotland, Civil and Ecclesiastical History of. T. Innes. Aberdeen, 1853. 4°. F,84,27
Criminal Trials in. J. H. Burton. London, 1852. 2 v. 12°. . U,496
Domestic Annals of. R. Chambers. London, 1858. 2 v. 8°. . B,126
England and Germany. J. H. Merle D'Aubigné. N. Y. 1849. 12°. V,343
Hand-Book of. T. Nelson. London, 1859. 16°. . . . . . V,301
Highlands and Highland Clans. J. Browne. Edinb. 1852–56. 4 v. 8°. B,128
Hill-Side and Border Sketches. W. H. Maxwell. Lond. 1847. 2 v. 8°. V,349
History of. J. Aikman. Edinburgh, 1856. 6 v. 8°. . . . . S.C.
G. Buchanan. Edinburgh, 1821. 3 v. 8°. . . . . . B,125
J. H. Burton. Edinburgh, 1867. 4 v. 8°. . . . . . B,117
J. Mackenzie. London, 1867. 8°. . . . . . . . . B,113
G. Stuart. Dublin, 1782. 2 v. 8°. . . . . . . B,124
Sir W. Scott. London, 1830. 2 v. 12°. . . . . . M,988
P. F. Tytler. Edinburgh, 1864–67. 4 v. in 2. 12°. . . B,114
T. Wright. London, n. d. 3 v. 8°. . . . . . . F,264
History of, from 1603 to the Union. M. Laing. Lond. 1819. 4 v. 8°. B,138
History of; Reigns of Mary and James V. W. Robertson. N.Y.1848. 8°.U,205,3
Spottiswoode Miscellany; ed. by J. Maidment. Edinb. 1845. 2 v. 8°. B,137
Inquiry into the History of. J. Pinkerton. Edinb. 1814. 2 v. 8°. B,116
Legends of the North of. H. Miller. Cincinnati, 1852. 8°. . . V,362
Letters from the Mountains. A. Grant. Boston, 1809. 2 v. 12°. . V,351
Lockhart Papers. London, 1817. 2 v. 4°. . . . . . . F,266
Metrical Version of H. Boece's Chronicles. W. Stewart. Lon.'58. 3 v. 8°. W,156
Miscellanea Scotica; a Collection of Tracts. Glasg. 1818–20. 4 v. 12°. B,111
Contents, see *Miscellanea Scotica.*
Queens of, Lives of. A. Strickland. New York, n. d. 8 v. 12°. . D,17
Rare Animals of. Sir J. G. Dalyell. London, 1847–48. 2 v. 4°. . Q,7
Rebellions in, 1638–60. R. Chambers. Edinburgh, 1828. 2 v. 16°. I,511
Rebellions in, 1689 and 1715. R. Chambers. Edinburgh, 1829. 16°. I,517
Rebellions in, 1745–46. R. Chambers. Edinburgh, 1827. 2 v. 16°. I,501
Reformation in, History of the. J. Knox. Glasgow, 1844. 8°. . P,663
Secret History of Negotiations, 1707. Col. Hooke. Dublin, 1760. 16°. A,475
Sketches of the Highlanders. D. Stewart. Edinburgh, 1825. 2 v. 8°. V,361
Songs of. A. Cunningham. London, 1825. 4 v. 8°. . . . . I,350
G. F. Graham. London, 1853. 3 v. 8°. . . . . . M,414
Summer in Skye. A. Smith. London, 1865. 2 v. 12°. . . V,347
Travels in. B. Silliman. New Haven, 1820. 16°. . . . V,1030,3
Wanderings in the Highlands, etc. W. H. Maxwell. Lon. 1844. 2 v. 8°. V,405
Scots Musical Museum; 600 Songs. J. Johnson. Edinburgh, 1853. 4 v. 8°. *M,411
Scots Worthies. J. Howrie. Edinburgh, 1854. 8°. . . . . . . C,1311
Scotsmen, Dictionary of Eminent. R. Chambers. Glasgow, 1855. 5 v. 8°. S.C.
Scott, D., Memoir of. W. B. Scott. Edinburgh, 1850. 8°. . . . C,1271
Scott, D. and Jamison. Eng. and Mechanic's Assistant. Glas. 1847. 2 v. r. 4°. S.C.
Scott, F. J. Art of Beautifying Suburban Grounds. New York, 1870. 8°. *M,361
Scott, G. Memoirs of Sir James Melvil. Edinburgh, 1735. 8°. . . D,367
Scott, G. C. Fishing in American Waters. New York, 1869. 12°. . . M,311
Scott, J. British Hemiptera, v. 1. London, 1865. 8°. . . . . . O,309
Scott, R. Practical Cotton Spinner and Manufacturer. Philadelphia, 1851. 8°. M,658
Scott, R. H. Hand-Book of Volumetrical Analysis. London, 1862. 8°. . N,203
Scott, Sir W., Familiar Anecdotes of. J. Hogg. New York, 1834. 12°. . C,1165

Scott, Sir W. History of Scotland. London, 1830. 2 v. 12°. . . . M,988
Lands of. J. F. Hunnewell. Boston, 1871. 12°. . . . . . V,350
Letters on Demonology and Witchcraft. London, 1830. 16°. . . I,647
The same. New York, 1855. 16°. . . . . . . L,344
Life of. J. G. Lockhart. Edinburgh, 1837–38. 7 v. 12°. . . D,175
The same. New York, 1851. 8 v. in 4. 12°. . . C,1168
D. MacLeod. New York, 1852. 12°. . . . . . . C,1167
Life of Napoleon I. Edinburgh, 1851. 8°. . . . . . . D,566
Poetical Works. New York, 1868. 12°. . . . . . . . I,410
The same. New York, 1853. 6 v. 12°. . . . . . I,412

Vol. 1. Lay of the Last Minstrel; Ballads; Songs.
2. Marmion; Occasional Pieces.
3. Lady of the Lake; Vision of Don Roderick.
4. Rokeby; Bridal of Triermain.
5. Lord of the Isles; Field of Waterloo; Songs and Miscellanies.
6. Harold, the Dauntless; Dramatic Pieces.

The same; with Memoir. Boston, 1857. 9 v. 16°. . . . I,224

Vol. 1. Memoir; Lay of the Last Minstrel.
2. Marmion.
3. Lady of the Lake.
4. Rokeby; Vision of Don Roderick.
5. Lord of the Isles.
6. Imitations of the Ancient Ballads; Ballads from the German; Songs.
7. Miscellaneous Poems; Poems printed in Lockhart's Life; Lyrical Pieces, Mottoes, etc., from Waverley Novels.
8. Bridal of Triermain; Harold, the Dauntless; Field of Waterloo; Halidon Hill; MacDuff Cross.
9. Doom of Devorgoil; Auchindrane; House of Aspen; Goetz of Berlichingen.

The same. Edinburgh, 1821. 10 v. 8°. . . . . . J,878

Vol. 1–3. Minstrelsy of the Scottish Border.
4. Sir Tristram.
5. Lay of the Last Minstrel; Ballads.
6. Marmion.
Vol. 7. Lady of the Lake.
8. Rokeby; Vision of Don Roderick.
9. Lord of the Isles.
10. Miscellanies.

Poetical Works. Leipzig, 1861. 2 v. in 1. 16°. . . . . J,449

Vol. 1. Lay of the Last Minstrel; Marmion; Lady of the Lake.
2. Vision of Don Roderick; Rokeby; Lord of the Isles; Songs.

Readings for the Young, from his Works. Philad. 1848. 2 v. 16°. J,1283

Vol. 1. Tales of Chivalry; Narratives.
2. Narratives; Scottish Scenes and Characters.

Tales of a Grandfather. Boston, 1865. 6 v. 16°. . . . . J,1282
Waverly Novels; Household edition. Boston, 1868. 50 v. 12°. viz.:

Abbot. 2 v. . . . . . K,924
Anne of Geierstein. 2. . . K,925
Antiquary. 2 v. . . . . K,926
Betrothed; Highland Widow. . K,927
Black Dwarf; Montrose. 2 v. . K,928
Bride of Lammermoor. 2 v. . K,930
Chronicles of Canongate. . . K,931
Count Robert of Paris. 2 v. . K,932
Same, concluded; Castle Dangerous. . . . . . K,933
Fair Maid of Perth. 2 v. . . K,934
Fortunes of Nigel. 2 v. . . K,935
Guy Mannering. 2 v. . . K,937
Heart of Mid-Lothian. 2 v. . . K,938
Ivanhoe. 2 v. . . . K,939
Kenilworth. 2 v. . . K,940
Monastery. 2 v. . . K,941
Old Mortality. 2 v. . . K,942
Peveril of the Peak, 2 v. . K,943
Pirate. 2 v. . . . K,944
Quentin Durward. 2 v. . K,945
Redgauntlet. 2 v. . . K,947
Rob Roy. 2 v. . . . K,948
St. Ronan's Well. 2 v. . K,949
Surgeon's Daughter. 2 v. . K,950
Talisman, etc. 2 v. . . K,951
Waverley. 2 v. . . . K,952
Woodstock. 2 v. . . . K,953

The same. Philadelphia, n. d. 22 v. 8°. viz.:

Abbot. . . . . . . K,954
Anne of Geierstein. . . . K,955
Antiquary. . . . . K,956
Betrothed; Talisman. . . K,957
Chronicles of Canongate . . K,958
Count Robert of Paris. . . K,959
Kenilworth. . . . K,965
Monastery. . . . K,966
Old Mortality. . . . K,967
Peveril of the Peak. . . K,968
Pirate. . . . . K,969
Quentin Durward. . . K,970

Scott, Sir W. Waverly Novels. *Continued.* viz.:

| | | | |
|---|---|---|---|
| Fair Maid of Perth. . . . | K,960 | Redgauntlet. . . . | K,971 |
| Fortunes of Nigel. . . . | K,961 | Rob Roy. . . . | K,972 |
| Guy Mannering. . . . | K,962 | St. Ronan's Well. . . | K,973 |
| Heart of Mid-Lothian. . . | K,963 | Waverley. . . . | K,974 |
| Ivanhoe. . . . . | K,964 | Woodstock. . . . | K,975 |

The same, Abbotsford edition. Philad. 1869. 12 v. 8°. viz.:

Vol. 1. Waverley; Guy Mannering. . . . . . . . K,1105
2. Antiquary; Black Dwarf; Old Mortality. . . . . K,1106
3. Rob Roy; Heart of Mid-Lothian. . . . . . K,1107
4. Bride of Lammermoor; Montrose; Ivanhoe. . . . . K,1108
5. Monastery; Abbot. . . . . . . . . K,1109
6. Kenilworth; Pirate. . . . . . . . . K,1110
7. Fortunes of Nigel; Peveril of the Peak. . . . . K,1111
8. Quentin Durward; St. Ronan's Well. . . . . . K,1112
9. Redgauntlet; Betrothed; Talisman. . . . . . K,1113
10. Woodstock; Chronicles of Canongate. . . . . . K,1114
11. Fair Maid of Perth; Anne of Geierstein. . . . . K,1115
12. Count Robert of Paris; Castle Dangerous. . . . . K,1116

The same, Tauchnitz edition. Leip. 1845–60. 16 v. in 15. 16°. viz.:

| | | | |
|---|---|---|---|
| Abbot. . . . . . | J,437 | Ivanhoe. . . . | J,444 |
| Antiquary. . . . . | J,438 | Kenilworth. . . | J,445 |
| Black Dwarf; Montrose. . . | J,439 | Monastery. . . . | J,446 |
| Bride of Lammermoor. . . | J,440 | Old Mortality. . . | J,447 |
| Fortunes of Nigel. . . . | J,441 | Pirate. . . . | J,448 |
| Guy Mannering. . . . | J,442 | Quentin Durward. . . | J,450 |
| Heart of Mid-Lothian. 2 v. in 1. . | J,443 | Rob Roy. . . . | J,451 |
| Waverley. . . . . | J,452 | | |

Scott, W. B. Memoir of David Scott. Edinburgh, 1850. 8°. . . C,1271
Lectures on the Fine Arts. London, 1867. 12°. . . . . . M,81
Scott, W. C. Genius and Faith; or, Poetry and Religion. N. Y. 1853. 12°. P,189
Scott, Gen. W., Campaign of, in Mexico. R. Semmes. Cincinnati, 1852. 12°. B,880
Infantry Tactics. 1854–55. 3 v. 18°. . . . . . . . M,744
Life of. E. D. Mansfield. New York, 1847. 12°. . . . . . C,1085
Memoirs; written by himself. New York, 1854. 2 v. 12°. . . C,721
Scottish Cavaliers, Lays of. W. E. Aytoun. New York, 1866. 12°. . I,278
Scottish Chiefs. J. Porter. Philadelphia, 1868. 12°. . . . . K,892
Scottish Clans, Feuds and Conflicts of. Glasgow, 1820. 2 v. 12°. . B,111,1,2
Scottish Cryptogamic Flora. R. K. Greville. Edinburgh, 1823–28. 6 v. 8°. *N,1032
Scottish Dictionary. J. Jamieson. Edinburgh, 1846. 8°. . . . L.R.
Scottish Educational and Literary Journal, v. 1. Edinburgh, 1853. 8°. . T,42
Scottish Gaël, The. J. Logan. Hartford, n. d. 8°. . . . . . . B,127
Scottish People, Traits and Stories of. C. Rogers. London, 1867. 12°. . B,110
Scottish Songs and Ballads; edited by J. Ritson. London, 1866. 16°. . I,408
Scottish Surnames, Ancient. W. Buchanan. Glasgow, 1820. 12°. . B,111,4
Scottish Verse, Early. London, 1870. 8°. . . . . . . . . L,605,42
Scottish Worthies, Lives of. P. F. Tytler. London, 1832–33. 3 v. 16°. I,642
Scouring of the White Horse. T. Hughes. Cambridge, 1859. 12°. . J,1445
Scout, The. W. G. Simms. New York, 1868. 12°. . . . . . . K,258
Scoville, J. A. Old Merchants of New York. New York, 1870. 5 v. 12°. C,1044
Screw-Propeller; Trial of Lowe *v.* Penn. London, 1848. 8°. . . N,252,40
Screw-Propellers, Treatise on. J. W. Nystrom. Philadelphia, 1852. 8°. M,704
Scribbleomania. W. H. Ireland. London, 1815. p. 8°. . . . . I,471
Scribe, E. Œuvres Choisies, v. 1–3, 5. Paris, 1845. 4 v. 12°. . . H,999
Scripture and Ethnology, Harmony of. D. M'Causland. London, 1864. 12°. P,915

Scripture, Night Lessons from. E. M. Sewell. New York, 1869. 16°. . P,202
Scripture Biography for the Young. T. H. Gallaudet. N.Y. n. d. 3v. 18°. P,746.25–27
Scripture Characters. T. Robinson. London, 1849. 2 v. 8°. . . . P,105
Scripture Geography and History, Outlines of. E. Hughes. Phil. 1853. 12°. P,459
Scripture History, Smaller. W. Smith. New York, 1871. 16°. . . P,579
Scripture Lands. J. Kitto. London, 1850. 12°. . . . . . . L,113
Scripture Readings for Schools and Families. C. M. Yonge. Lon. 1871. 12°. P,185
Scripture Sights and Scenes. W. H. Bartlett. London, n. d. 12°. . V,1038
Scripture Testimony. C. Campbell. New York, 1863. 12°. . . . P,79
Scriptures and Geological Science. J. P. Smith. London, 1852. 12°. . L,313
Critical Knowledge of. T. H. Horne. New York, 1856. 2 v. 8°. P,453
Jewish, and Antiquities. J. G. Palfrey. Boston, 1838–52. 4 v. 8°. A,221
Rhemes and Doway Versions. H. Cotton. Oxford, 1855. 8°. . P,813
See also, *Bible.*
Scrutator, *pseud.* See *Horlock.*
Scudder, H. E. Seven Little People. New York, 1863. 12°. . . J,1267
Stories from my Attic. New York, 1869. 16°. . . . . . H,434
Scudder, J. M. Familiar Treatise on Medicines. Cin. 1869. 2 v. in 1. 8°. L,932
Sculptors, British, Lives of. A. Cunningham. London, 1830. 16°. . . I,639
and Painters, British, Lives of. A. Cunningham. N. Y. 1868. 5 v. 18°. L,352
Architects and Painters, Lives of Eminent. G. Vasari. Lon.'52. 5v. p. 8°. L,244
Familiar Sketches of. H. F. Lee. Boston, 1854. 2 v. 12°. . . M,13
Italian. C. C. Perkins. London, 1868. 4°. . . . . . *M,289
Tuscan. C. C. Perkins. London, 1864. 2 v. 4°. . . . *M,291
Sculptura Historico-Technica, Engraving. London, 1770. 12°. . . . M,5
Sculpture and Modeling, Works in. A. Canova. London, 1824–28. 3 v. 4°. *Q,225
and Painting, Early Florentine Schools. W. Y. Ottley. Lon. 1826. f°. L.R.
National Gallery of. A. J. Valpy. London, n. d. 8°. . . M,57
Ancient, in Great Britain, Specimens of. London, 1809–35. 2 v. f°. S.C.
History of, with Plates, Appleton's. New York, 1856. 2 v. 8°. . *Q,252
Illustrations of Modern. T. K. Hervey. London, 1834. 4°. . . *Q,215
Lectures on. J. Flaxman. London, 1865. p. 8°. . . . . . L,103
Painting and Architecture, History of. J. S. Memes. Edin. 1829. 16°. I,515
Sculptured Stones of Scotland. Aberdeen, 1856–57. 2 v. f°. . *F,84,29,30
Sea, The. R. Mudie. London, 1835. 16°. . . . . . . V,1130
Sea, The, and its Living Wonders. G. Hartwig. London, 1866. 8°. . . N,537
and the Sailor. W. Colton. New York, 1851. 12°. . . . . V,300
Bottom of. L. Sourel. New York, 1870. 12°. . . . . M,1049
Leben des Meeres. G. Hartwig. Frankfurt-am-Main, 1857. 8°. . G,815
Life in. F. C. L. Wraxall. London, 1860. 8°. . . . . N,505
Perils of. New York, 1855. 16°. . . . . . . . J,1217
Physische Geographie des Meeres. M. F. Maury. Leipzig, 1859. 8°. G,703
Sea Kings and Naval Heroes. J. E. Edgar. New York, 1863. 16°. . J,1521
of England. W. H. D. Adams. London, 1861. 16°. . . C,1242
Sea Lions. J. F. Cooper. New York, 1867. 12°. . . . . . . K,49
The same. New York, 1860. 8°. . . . . . . . K,77
Sea Shore, Common Objects of the. J. G. Wood. London, 1866. 12°. . N,475
Sea-Side Book. W. H. Harvey. London, 1857. 16°. . . . . . N,474
Sea-Side Naturalist. R. W. Fraser. London, 1868. 12°. . . . . N,481
Sea-Side Studies at Ilfracombe, etc. G. H. Lewes. Edinburgh, 1858. 8°. . N,520

Sea Voyage, Pilgrims, etc. London, 1867. 8°. . . . . . . L,605,25
Sea Water, Experiments on Saline Contents of. A. Marcet. Lond. 1822. 4°. N,252,42
Sea Weeds, British. D. Landsborough. London, 1851. 16°. . . . N,919
History of. W. H. Harvey. London, 1846–51. 3 v. 8°. *N,1030
Seaboard Parish, The. G. MacDonald. London, 1868. 3 v. 12°. . . J,566
Seager, F. Schoole of Vertue. London, 1868. 8°. . . . . L,605,32
Seafield, F. Literature and Curiosities of Dreams. Lond. 1865. 2 v. p. 8°. O,336
Sealsfield, C. Gesammelte Werke. Stuttgart, 1845–47. 15 v. 16°. . . E,357

Bd. 1–3. Der Legitime und die Republikaner.
4–6. Der Virey und die Aristokraten.
7, 8. Morton; oder, die grosse Tour.
9–13. Lebensbilder aus der westlichen Hemisphäre.
9. Georg Howard's, Esq., Brautfahrt.
10. Ralph Doughby's, Esq., Brautfahrt.
11. Pflanzerleben.
12. Pflanzerleben; Die Farbigen.
13. Nathan, der Squatter Regulator.
14, 15. Das Cajütenbuch; oder, nationale Charakteristiken.

Seaman, E. C. Essays on the Progress of Nations. New York, 1853. 12°. O,493
Seamanship in the Royal Navy. A. H. Alston. London, 1860. 8°. . . M,755
Seamen, Adventures of British. Edinburgh, 1827. 16°. . . . . I,493
Search, Edward, *pseud.* See *Tucker, A.*
Search for Winter Sunbeams. S. S. Cox. New York, 1870. 8°. . V,1070
Searing, E. Virgil's Æneid, six books; with Notes, Lexicon, etc. N.Y. 1870. 8°. U,422
Searle, January, *pseud.* See *Phillips, G. S.*
Sears, B. and others. Classical Studies. Boston, 1843. 12°. . . . L,549
Seasons, Die Vier Jahreszeiten. E. A. Rossmässler. Gotha, 1856. 8°. . G,891
Pictorial Calendar of. M. Howitt. London, 1854. p. 8°. . . L,107
Sacred Philosophy of. H. Duncan. New York, 1847. 4 v. 12°. . M,761
Seat of Empire. C. C. Coffin. Boston, 1870. 12°. . . . . . . V,51
Seaton, W. W., Biography of. Boston, 1871. 12°. . . . . . . C,939
Seaward, Sir E. Narrative of Shipwreck. London, 1865. p. 8°. . I,664,1
Sebastopol, Todleben's Defense of. W. H. Russell. London, 1865. 8°. . B,88
Secessia, Four Years in. J. H. Browne. Hartford, 1865. 8°. . . . B,908
Secession, Natural History of. T. S. Goodwin. New York, 1864. 12°. . B,906
Sketches of. W. G. Brownlow. Philadelphia, 1862. 12°. . . B,899
Seclusaval; or, the Arts of Romanism. A. C. Graves. Memphis, 1870. 12°. K,224
Second Sight, Apparitions, etc., Treatises on. Glasgow, 1820. 12°. . B,111,3
Second War with England, 1812–15. J. T. Headley. N. Y. 1853. 2 v. 12°. B,850
C. J. Ingersoll. Philadelphia, 1845–53. 4 v. 8°. . . . B,871
Secret Service, United States, History of. L. C. Baker. Phila. 1869. 8°. . B,924
Secret Societies, History of. L. de La Hodde. Philadelphia, 1856. 8°. . O,385
of the Middle Ages. London, 1837. 16°. . . . . . . . L,486
Sects, History of Christian Churches and. J. B. Marsden. Lond. 1856. 2 v. 8°. P,604
Sedgemoor; or, Home Lessons. E. Manners. New York, 1857. 16°. J,1353
Sedgwick, A. and McCoy, F. British Palæozoic Rocks. London, 1855. 4°. Q,51
Sedgwick, C. M. Boy of Mount Rhigi. Philadelphia, 1867. 16°. . J,1687
Hope Leslie. New York, 1862. 2 v. 12°. . . . . . . K,237
Letters from Abroad. New York, 1855. 2 v. 12°. . . . . V,365
Life of Lucretia M. Davidson. New York, 1860. 16°. . . C,860,7
Live and Let Live. New York, 1861. 18°. . . . . . J,1179
Married or Single. New York, 1858. 2 v. 12°. . . . K,238
Means and Ends. New York, 1839. 16°. . . . . . . J,1222
Memoir of Joseph Curtis. New York, 1858. 16°. . . . . C,841

Sedgwick, C. M. Poor Rich Man and Rich Poor Man. N. Y. 1868. 16°. J,1425
Stories for Young Persons. New York, 1860. 16°. . . . J,1245
See, G. vom. See *Struensee, G. von.*
Seebohm, F. Oxford Reformers of 1498. London, 1867. 8°. . . . . P,623
Seed Grain for Thought and Discussion. A. C. Lowell. Bost. 1856. 2 v. 16°. H,186
Seeds and Sheaves; or, Words of Scripture. A. C. Thompson. Bost. 1869. 12°. P,45
Seek and Find. W. T. Adams. Boston, 1869. 16°. . . . . . J,1534,4
Seelenleben des Menschen. J. Schaller. Weimar, 1860. 8°. . . . . G,569
Seely, J. R. Ecce Homo. Boston, 1866. 12°. . . . . . . . P,371
Roman Imperialism; Lectures and Essays. Boston, 1871. 12°. . H,512
Seemann, B. Fiji and its Inhabitants. London, 1862. 8°. . . . V,1086,2
Die Palmen. Leipzig, 1857. 8°. . . . . . . . . . G,899
History of the Palms. London, 1856. 16°. . . . . . . N,927
Reise um die Welt. Hannover, 1858. 2 v. in 1. 8°. . . . E,162
Viti; Account of the Fijian Islands, 1860–61. Cambridge, 1862. 8°. V,898
Seemuller, A. M. C. Emily Chester. Boston, 1865. 12°. . . . . K,87
Opportunity. Boston, 1867. 12°. . . . . . . . . K,86
Reginald Archer. Boston, 1871. 12°. . . . . . . . K,148
Seer, The; or, Common-Places Refreshed. L. Hunt. Bost. 1865. 2 v. 12°. H,580
Ségur, P. P., Comte de. Napoleon's Exped. to Russia, 1812. Lond. 1827. 2 v. 8°. B,284
The same. New York, 1854. 2 v. 16°. . . . . . . L,433
The same. London, 1836. 2 v. 16°. . . . . . . I,610
Seiler, E. The Voice in Singing. Philadelphia, 1868. 12°. . . . M,404
Selbourne, Natural History of. G. White. London, 1851. 8°. . . . N,471
The same. London, 1851. p. 8°. . . . . . . . L,164
The same. Edinburgh, 1829. 16°. . . . . . . . I,519
The same. New York, 1860. 8°. . . . . . . . L,437
Selby, P. J. Parrots. Edinburgh, n. d. 16°. . . . . . . N,470,10
Pigeons. Edinburgh, n. d. 16°. . . . . . . . . N,470,9
Selden, J., Memoirs of. G. W. Johnson. London, 1835. 8°. . . . D,57
Table-Talk. London, 1856. 16°. . . . . . . . . H,572
Select Tracts on the Civil Wars in England. London, 1815. 8°. . . A,561
Selections from Taylor, Latimer, Hall, Milton, etc. B. Montagu. N.Y. 1848. 8°. H,590
Selenium; is it a true Element? S. Piesse. London, 1842. 8°. . . N,252,21
Self-Cultivation. I. Taylor. Ithaca, 1842. 12°. . . . . . . O,1114
Self-Culture. O. S. Fowler. New York, 1854. 12°. . . . . . L,895
Self-Education. J. M. *Baron* Degerando. Boston, 1860. 12°. . . . O,978
Self-Help. S. Smiles. Boston, 1866. 12°. . . . . . . . H,394
Self-Knowledge. J. Mason. New York, n. d. 16°. . . . . . P,746,21
Self-Made Men. C. C. B. Seymour. New York, 1868. 12°. . . . C,526
Self-Sacrifice. M. Oliphant. Philadelphia, n. d. 12°. . . . . K,869
Self-Witnessing Charac. of New Test. Christianity. W. Hague. Phila. 1871. 8°. P,284
Selkirk, J. Recollections of Ceylon. London, 1844. 8°. . . . . V,699
Seltsame Geschichten. H. Koenig. Wiesbaden, 1862. 12°. . . . G,338
Selvaggio; a Tale of Italian Life. A. Manning. London, 1865. 12°. . J,598
Selwyn, G. and his Contemporaries. J. H. Jesse. London, 1843–44. 4 v. 8°. D,339
Life and Times of. A. Hayward. London, 1856. p. 8°. . . I,661,4
Selys-Longchamps, E. de. Monog. des Libellulidées d'Europe. Paris, 1840. 8°. O,38
Semmes, R. Campaign of Gen. W. Scott in Mexico. Cincinnati, 1852. 12°. B,880
Cruise of the Alabama and Sumter. London, 1864. 2 v. 12°. . B,954

Semple, A. S. Thoughts on Education. London, 1812. 12°. . . o,1179
Seneca, L. A. Opera Declamatoria; illus. M. N. Bouillet. Parisiis, 1831. 8°. u,344
Opera Philosphica; illus. M. N. Bouillet. Parisiis, 1827-30. 3 v. 8°. u,345
Opera Tragica; illus. J. Pierrot. Parisiis, 1829-32. 5 v. 8°. . . u,346
Werke. Stuttgart, 1828-51. 17 v. in 6. 24°. . . . . . g,530
Senior, N. W. Biographical Sketches. London, 1863. 8°. . . . c,537

Berryer; T. du Coudray; Campbell's Chief Justices; Feuerbach; J. H. Ramcke; Charles V.; Bacon; Lord King; Col. King; Anecdotes of Monkeys.

Political Economy. London, 1854. 8°. . . . . . . . o,511
Sense and Sensibility. J. Austen. Boston, 1864. 12°. . . . . k,596
The same. Leipzig, 1864. 16°. . . . . . . . j,31
Senses and the Intellect. A. Bain. London, 1855. 8°. . . . . o,688
Physiology of. A. B. Johnson. New York, 1856. 12°. . . . l,853
Sentimental Journey through France and Italy. L. Sterne. Leip. 1861. 16°. j,467
The same. London, n. d. 24°. . . . . . . . v,445
Seoane, M., Neuman, and Baretti. Spanish Dictionary. Lond. n. d. 2 v. 8°. l.r.
Sepoy Revolt; its Causes and Consequences. H. Mead. London, 1857. 8°. c,428
Sergeant Dale, his Daughter, etc. M. M. Sherwood. N. Y. 1860. 12°. k,1008,3
Seroux d'Agincourt, J. B. L. G. History of Art. Lond. 1847. 3 v. in 1. 4°. *q,468
Serpent Symbol and Nature Worship in America. E. G. Squier. N.Y. 1851. 8°. b,607
Serpents, Schlangenkunde. H. O. Lenz. Gotha, 1832. 8°. . . . g,918
Servia and the Servian Revolution. L. Ranke. London, 1853. 12°. . l,223
Church and People of. W. T. Greive. London, 1864. 8°. . v,1086,3
Sesame and Lilies. J. Ruskin. New York, 1865. 12°. . . . . m,71
Settlers in Canada. F. Marryat. New York, 1845. 2 v. 16°. . . j,1171
The same. London, 1869. p. 8°. . . . . . . . l,124
The same. Leipzig, 1844. 16°. . . . . . . . j,362
Seubert, M. Pflanzenkunde in populärer Darstellung. Leipzig, 1861. 8°. g,900
Seume, J. G. Sämmtliche Werke. Leipzig, 1839. 8 v. in 4. 16°. . . e,358

Bd. 1. Leben; Spaziergang nach Syrakus, 1802, erster Theil.
2. Spaziergang nach Syrakus, zweiter Theil; Anmerkungen dazu.
3. Mein Sommer, 1805; Rede des Phliasiers Patrokles in Athen, aus Xenophon's griechischer Geschichte; Die Belagerung, Eroberung und Zerstörung von Platäa, aus Thucydides; Praefatio ad fasciculum et conjecturarum in locos Plutarchi difficiliores.
4. Obolen; Apokryphen.
5. Einige Nachrichten über Polen im Jahre 1794; Veränderungen in Russland seit der Thronbesteigung Pauls des Ersten; Leben und Charakter der Kaiserin von Russland, Katharina II.
6. Dem Grafen von Igelström zum sechszehnten Geburtstage; Ueber Bewaffnung; Vorrede zu Percival's Beschreibung des Vorgebirgs der guten Hoffnung, aus dem Englishen; Die Impertinenzen; Kurzes Pflichten- und Sittenbuch für Landleute; Bruchstück einer Predigt, gehalten zu Knauthayn.
7. Gedichte.
8. Das polnische Mädchen; Adelaide; Die Weinlese; Miltiades, Trauerspiel; Der Schatz.

Seven Champions of Christendom. R. Johnson. London, 1867. 24°. j,1241
Seven Curses of London. J. Greenwood. Boston, 1869. 12°. . . . h,118
Seven Sleepers. Von den Siben Slafaeren. Heidelberg, 1839. 12°. . . e,281
Seven Sons of Mammon. G. A. Sala. London, 1862. 3 v. 12°. . . k,561
The same. Leipzig, 1869. 2 v. in 1. 16°. . . . . . j,436
Seven Stories, with Basement and Attic. D. G. Mitchell. N. Y. 1864. 12°. k,217
Seven Weeks' War; Prussia and Austria. H. M. Hozier. Lond. 1867. 2 v. 8°. b,211
Seven Wonders of the World. London, 1856. 16°. . . . . j,1224
Seven Years, and other Tales. J. Kavanagh. New York, 1866. 12°. . k,746
The same. Leipzig, 1859. 2 v. in 1. 16°. . . . . . j,235

Seven Years in Great Deserts of N. America. E. Domenech. Lond. 1860. 2v. 8°. v,77
Sévigné, M. de R. C. *Marquise de.* Lettres. Paris, 1856. 12°. . . . . H,874
The same. Paris, 1856. 6 v. 12°. . . . . . . . . H,873
Letters. London, 1764–8. 10 v. 12°. . . . . . . . H,900
The same; edited by Mrs. Hale. Boston, 1869. . . . H,901
Memoires de. C. A. Walckenaer. Paris, 1856. 5 v. 12°. . . D,613
Seward, W. H., Life of. G. E. Baker. New York, 1855. 12°. . . . C,745
Life of John Quincy Adams. Auburn, 1849. 12°. . . . . C,977
Works. New York, 1853. 3 v. 8°. . . . . . . . . U,126
Sewel, W. History of the Quakers. New York, 1844. 2 v. 8°. . . P,624
Sewell, E. M. After Life; sequel to Home Life. Leip. 1868. 2 v. in 1. 16°. J,453
Amy Herbert. Leipzig, 1857. 2 v. in 1. 16°. . . . . . . J,454
Child's First History of Greece. New York, 1353. 12°. . . . A,60
Child's First History of Rome. New York, 1849. 18°. . . J,1300
Cleve Hall. New York, 1868. 12°. . . . . . . . . K,994
Earl's Daughter. New York, 1869. 12°. . . . . . . K,995
Experience of Life. New York, 1866. 12°. . . . . . . K,996
Gertrude. New York, 1866. 12°. . . . . . . . . K,997
Glimpse of the World. New York, 1866. 12°. . . . . K,998
The same. Leipzig, 1863. 2 v. in 1. 16°. . . . . J,455
History of the Early Church. New York, 1867. 16°. . . . P,600
Ivors. New York, 1857. 2 v. 12°. . . . . . . . . K,999
Journal of a Home Life. New York, 1867. 12°. . . . K,1148
The same. Leipzig, 1867. 2 v. in 1. 16°. . . . . J,456
Journal of a Summer Tour. New York, 1852. 12°. . . . V,305
Katharine Ashton. New York, 1866. 2 v. 12°. . . . K,1000
Laneton Parsonage. New York, 1863. 3 v. 12°. . . . K,1001
Margaret Percival. New York, 1868. 2 v. 12°. . . . K,1002
Night Lessons from Scripture. New York, 1860. 16°. . . . P,202
Passing Thoughts on Religion. New York, 1867. 12°. . . . P,203
Principles of Education. London, 1865. 2 v. 12°. . . . . O,935
Ursula; a Tale. New York, 1865. 2 v. 12°. . . . . K,1003
The same. Leipzig, 1858. 2 v. in 1. 16°. . . . . J,457
Sewell, J. Steam applied to General Purposes. Lond. 1852–53. 2 v. in 1. 12°. M,958
Sewell, S. History of Woburn, Mass. Boston, 1868. 8°. . . . . C,68
Sewerage. G. D. Dempsey. London, 1854. 12°. . . . . . M,904
Fluswasser und Kloaken. A. Magnus. Berlin, 1841. 8°. . N,252,22
of Leeds, Report on. Leeds, 1843. 16°. . . . . . N,252,26
of Town's Bill, Report on. London, 1847. 8°. . . . . N,252,29
Sewerage Manure, Metropolitan. London, 1847. 8°. . . . . N,252,29
Sexegenarian, The. W. Beloe. London, 1817. 2 v. 8°. . . . . L.R.
Seymour, C. C. B. Self-Made Men. New York, 1868. 12°. . . . C,526
Sforgosi, L. History of Italy. New York, 1847. 18°. . . . . L,395
Shades, Shadows, and Linear Perspective. C. Davies. New York, 1856. 8°. M,211
Shadow of Ashlydyat. Mrs. H. Wood. Leipzig, 1863. 3 v. 16°. . . J,532
of Moloch Mountain. J. G. Austin. New York, 1870. 8°. . . K,207
Shadows of the Old Booksellers. C. Knight. London, 1865. 8°. . . D,336
Shadwell, C. F. A. Table for Prediction of Eclipses. London, 1847. 8°. N,343
Shaffner, T. P. Telegraph Manual. New York, 1859. 8°. . . . M,696
Shaftesbury, *Lord.* See *Cooper, A. A.*

Shairp, J. C. Culture and Religion. New York, 1871. 12°. . . . . P,182
Shaker, Autobiography of a. F. W. Evans. New York, n. d. 8°. . . P,859
Shakespear, J. Grammar of the Hindustani Language. London, 1855. 8°. L,784
The same, second edition. London, 1818. 4°. . . . . L,786
Selections in Hindustani. London, 1844–46. 2 v. in 1. 4°. . . L,785
Shakespeare, W. and English History, Lectures on. H. Reed. Phil. 1859. 12°. I,891
and his Times. F. Guizot. New York, 1852. 12°. . . . . C,1200
The same. New York, 1855. 12°. . . . . . . . . I,844
Autobiographical Poems; ed. by C. A. Brown. London, 1838. 12°. I,864
Biographischer Roman. H. Rau. Berlin, 1864. 4 v. 12°. . . G,414
Biography of. C. Knight. London, 1843. 8°. . . . . C,1295
The same. London, 1843. . . . . . . . . . *I,783
Concordance to. M. C. Clarke. Boston, n. d. 8°. . . . . . *I,892
Critical Examination of Text of. W. S. Walker. Lond. 1860. 3 v. 16°. I,842
Delineations of Insanity, etc. A. O. Kellogg. New York, 1866. 12°. I,849
Doubtful Plays. Leipzig, 1869. 16°. . . . . . . . . J,459

King Edward III.; Thomas Lord Cromwell; Locrine; Yorkshire Tragedy; London Prodigal; Birth of Merlin.

English of Shakespeare. Boston, 1867. 12°. . . . . . . I,846
First Sketch of Merry Wives of Windsor. London, 1842. 8°. I,885,9
Galerie des Femmes de. Paris, n. d. 8°. . . . . . . I,873
his Heroines, Girlhood of. M. C. Clarke. London, 1864. 3 v. 12°. I,848
The same; edited by D. L. Glover. Boston, n. d. 8°. . . *I,872
Henry IV., from a Contemporary Manuscript. London, 1845. 8°. I,885,25
in Germany. A. Cohn. London, 1865. 4°. . . . . . . I,788
Lectures on. H. N. Hudson. New York, 1848. 2 v. 12°. . . I,890
Legal Acquirements of. J. *Lord* Campbell. New York, 1859. 12°. I,865
Life of. J. O. Halliwell. London, 1848. 8°. . . . . . . C,1254
R. G. White. Boston, 1865. 8°. . . . . . . . C,1227
Marriage of Wit and Wisdom. London, 1846. 8°. . . I,885,29
Medical Knowledge of. C. W. Stearns. New York, 1865. 12°. . I,841
Method of, as an Artist. H. I. Ruggles. New York, 1870. 16°. . I,847
Miscellaneous Papers. London, 1796. 8°. . . . . . . I,867
Notes and Emendations to Text of. J. P. Collier. New York, 1853. 12°. I,845
Inquiry into the same. N. E. S. A. Hamilton. Lond. 1860. 4°. I,869
Strictures on the same. A. Dyce. London, 1859. 8°. . . I,887
Text Vindicated. S. W. Singer. London, 1853. 8°. . . I,870
Philosophy of the Plays of. D. Bacon. Boston, 1857. 8°. . . I,868
Poems of. Boston, 1864. 16°. . . . . . . . . . . I,225
Poems; with Life; edited by R. Bell. London, 1855. 16°. . . I,252
Portia, and Stories of his Heroines. M. C. Clarke. N. Y. 1868. 12°. K,1149
Remarks on the Plots of his Plays. C. Simrock. Lond. 1850. 8°. I,885,44
Scholar; Studies of his Text, etc. R. G. White. New York, 1854. 8°. I,871
Shakespearean Reader. J. W. S. Hows. New York, 1849. 12°. . I,843
Sonnets never before interpreted. London, 1866. 8°. . . . I,886
Tales from. C. M. Lamb. New York, 1869. 16°. . . . . . K,760
Werke; übersetzt von F. Bodenstedt *et als.* Leip. 1867. 12 v. in 4. E,303

Bd. 1. Othello.
2. König Johann.
3. Antonius und Kleopatra.
4. Die lustigen Weiber von Windsor.
5. Viel Lärmen um Nichts.
6. König Richard der Zweite.
Bd. 7. Macbeth.
8, 9. König Heinrich der Vierte.
10. Romeo und Julia.
11. Coriolanus.
Bd. 12. Timon von Athen.

Shakespeare, W. Werke; übersetzt von A. W. von Schlegel und L. Tieck. Berlin, 1825–33. 9 v. in 5. 12°. . . . . . . . . . . E,302

Bd. 1. König Johann; König Richard der Zweite; König Heinrich der Vierte.
2. König Heinrich der Fünfte; König Heinrich der Sechste.
3. König Richard der Dritte; König Heinrich der Achte; Sommernachtstraum; Viel Lärmen um Nichts.
4. Heilige-Drei-Königs-Abend, oder Was ihr wollt; Der Kaufmann von Venedig; Der Sturm.
5. Coriolanus; Julius Cäsar; Antonius und Kleopatra; Maas für Maas.

Works. London, 1868. 12°. . . . . . . . . . . . I,756

The same. Philadelphia, n. d. 8°. . . . . . . I,767

The same. Boston, 1851. 7 v. 8°. . . . . . . I,781

Vol. 1. Life of Shakespeare; New Facts; Will; Preface of the Players; Tempest; Two Gentlemen of Verona; Merry Wives of Windsor; Twelfth Night; Measure for Measure; Much Ado about Nothing.
2. Midsummer Night's Dream; Love's Labor's Lost; Merchant of Venice; As you like it; All's well that ends well; Taming of the Shrew.
3. Winter's Tale; Comedy of Errors; Macbeth; King John; King Richard II.; King Henry IV., part 1.
4. King Henry IV., part 2; King Henry V.; King Henry VI., parts 1, 2, 3.
5. King Richard III.; King Henry VIII.; Troilus and Cressida; Timon of Athens; Corolanus.
6. Julius Cæsar; Antony and Cleopatra; Cymbeline; Titus Andronicus; Pericles.
7. King Lear; Romeo and Juliet; Hamlet; Othello.

The same; illustrated. Boston, 1850. 7 v. 8°. . . . . *I,782

Contents, *the same as the preceding.*

The same; edited by A. Dyce. Leipzig, 1868. 7 v. 16°. . J,458

Vol. 1. Measure for Measure; Comedy of Errors; Much Ado about Nothing; Love's Labor's Lost; Midsummer Night's Dream; Merchant of Venice; As you like it.
2. Taming of the Shrew; All's well that ends well; Twelfth Night; Winter's Tale; King John; King Richard II.
3. King Henry IV.; King Henry V.; King Henry VI., parts 1, 2.
4. King Henry VI., part 3; King Richard III.; King Henry VIII.; Troilus and Cressida; Titus Andronicus.
5. Coriolanus; Romeo and Juliet; Timon of Athens; Julius Cæsar; Macbeth.
6. Hamlet; King Lear; Othello; Antony and Cleopatra; Cymbeline.
7. Pericles; Tempest; Two Gentlemen of Verona; Merry Wives of Winsor; Poems; Life; Glossary.

The same; edited by W. Hazlitt. London, 1865. 4 v. 12°. I,761

Vol. 1. Merry Wives of Windsor; Twelfth Night; Tempest; Two Gentlemen of Verona; Measure for Measure; Much Ado about Nothing; Midsummer Night's Dream; Love's Labor's Lost; Merchant of Venice; As you like it.
2. All's well that ends well; Taming of the Shrew; Winter's Tale; Comedy of Errors; Macbeth; King John; King Richard II.; King Henry IV., pts. 1, 2.
3. King Henry V.; King Henry VI., parts 1, 2, 3.; King Richard III.; King Henry VIII.; Troilus and Cressida; Coriolanus.
4. Julius Cæsar; Antony and Cleopatra; Timon of Athens; Cymbeline; King Lear; Romeo and Juliet; Hamlet; Othello.

The same; edited by H. N. Hudson. Boston, 1851. 11 v. 12°. I,758

Vol. 1. Tempest; Two Gentlemen of Verona; Merry Wives of Windsor; Twelfth Night.
2. Measure for Measure; Much Ado about Nothing; Midsummer Night's Dream; Love's Labor's Lost.
3. Merchant of Venice; As you like it; All's well that ends well; Taming of the Shrew.
4. Winter's Tale; Comedy of Errors; Macbeth; King John.
5. Richard II.; Henry IV., parts 1, 2; Henry V.
6. Henry VI., parts 1–3.
7. Richard III.; Henry VIII.; Troilus and Cressida.
8. Timon of Athens; Coriolanus; Julius Cæsar; Antony and Cleopatra.
9. Cymbeline; Titus Andronicus; Pericles; King Lear.
10. Romeo and Juliet; Hamlet; Othello;
11. Life; History of the Drama; Poems and Sonnets.

The same; edited by S. W. Singer. London, 1856. 10 v. 12°. I,757

Vol. 1. Life of Shakespeare by W. W. Lloyd; Tempest; Two Gentlemen of Verona; Merry Wives of Windsor; Measure for Measure.
2. Comedy of Errors; Much Ado about Nothing; Love's Labor's Lost; Midsummer Night's Dream; Merchant of Venice.
3. As you like it; Taming of the Shrew; All's well that ends well; Twelfth Night.
4. Winter's Tale; Pericles; King John; King Richard II.
5. King Henry IV., parts 1, 2; King Henry V.
6. King Henry VI., parts 1–3; King Richard III.

Shakespeare, W. Works; edited by S. W. Singer. *Continued.* . . . 1,757

7. King Henry VIII.; Troilus and Cressida; Coriolanus; Pericles.
8. Titus Andronicus; Romeo and Juliet; Timon of Athens; Julius Cæsar.
9. Macbeth; Hamlet; King Lear.
10. Othello; Antony and Cleopatra; Cymbeline.

The same, Companion edition; ed. C. Knight. Lon. 1860. 6 v. 12°. 1,764

Vol. 1. Biography; *Histories:*—King John; King Richard II.; King Henry IV., pts. 1, 2.
2. King Henry V.; King Henry VI., parts 1-3; King Richard III.; King Henry VIII.
3. *Tragedies:*—Romeo and Juliet; Hamlet; Othello; Timon of Athens; King Lear; Macbeth.
4. Troilus and Cressida; Cymbeline; Coriolanus; Julius Cæsar; Antony and Cleopatra; Titus Andronicus; Pericles.
5. *Comedies:*—Two Gentlemen of Verona; Love's Labor's Lost; Merry Wives of Windsor; Comedy of Errors; Much Ado about Nothing; Tempest; Measure for Measure.
6. Midsummer Night's Dream; Merchant of Venice; As you like it; Taming of the Shrew; All's well that ends well; Twelfth Night; Winter's Tale.

The same, Handy-volume edition. New York, 1867. 13 v. 24°. 1,760

Vol. 1. Tempest; Two Gentlemen of Verona; Comedy of Errors.
2. Merry Wives of Windsor; Measure for Measure; Midsummer Night's Dream.
3. Much Ado about Nothing; Twelfth Night; Love's Labor's Lost.
4. As you like it; Merchant of Venice; Winter's Tale.
5. Taming of the Shrew; All's well that ends well; King John.
6. King Richard II.; King Henry IV., parts 1, 2.
7. King Henry V.; King Henry VI., parts 1, 2.
8. King Henry VI., part 3; King Richard III.; King Henry VIII.
9. Julius Cæsar; Antony and Cleopatra; Troilus and Cressida.
10. Othello; Coriolanus; Timon of Athens.
11. Hamlet; Romeo and Juliet; Pericles.
12. King Lear; Cymbeline; Titus Andronicus.
13. Macbeth; Poems and Sonnets; Glossary.

The same, Pictorial edition; ed. by C. Knight. Lon. 1853. 8 v. 8°. *1,784

Vol. 1. *Comedies:*—Two Gentlemen of Verona; Love's Labor's Lost; Merry Wives of Windsor; Comedy of Errors; Taming of the Shrew; Midsummer Night's Dream; Merchant of Venice.
2. All's well that ends well; Much Ado about Nothing; Twelfth Night; As you like it; Measure for Measure; Winter's Tale; Tempest;
3. *Tragedies:*—Romeo and Juliet; Hamlet; Cymbeline; Othello; Timon of Athens; King Lear.
4. Macbeth; Troilus and Cressada; Coriolanus; Julius Cæsar; Antony and Cleopatra; Poems.
5. *Histories:*—King John; King Richard II; King Henry IV., parts 1, 2; King Henry V.
6. Essay on King Henry VI. and Richard III.; King Henry VI., parts 1-3; Contentions of the Houses of York and Lancaster; King Richard III.; King Henry VIII.
7. Titus Andronicus; Pericles; Two Noble Kinsmen; Plays ascribed to Shakespeare; Dedication, Address, etc., prefixed to the editions of 1623 and 1632; History of Opinion on the Writings of Shakespeare; Shakespeare in Germany; Indexes.

The same, Stratford edition; ed. C. Knight. Lond. 1867. 6 v. 12°. 1,762

Vol. 1. Life of Shakespeare by C. Knight; *Histories:*—King John; King Richard II.; King Henry IV., parts 1, 2.
2. King Henry V.; King Henry VI., parts 1-3; King Richard III.; King Henry VIII.
3. *Tragedies:*—Macbeth; Coriolanus; Julius Cæsar; Antony and Cleopatra; Cymbeline; Troilus and Cressida.
4. *Comedies:*—Tempest; Two Gentlemen of Verona; Merry Wives of Windsor; Measure for Measure; Comedy of Errors; Much Ado about Nothing; Love's Labor's Lost.
5. Midsummer Night's Dream; Merchant of Venice; As you like it; Taming of the Shrew; All's well that ends well; Twelfth Night; Winter's Tale.
6. *Tragedies:*—Romeo and Juliet; Timon of Athens; Hamlet; King Lear; Othello; Pericles; Titus Andronicus.

Writings and Genius of. E. Montagu. London, 1810. 8°. . . 1,888

Shakespeare Fabrication. C. M. Ingleby. London, 1859. 16°. . . . 1,763

Shakespeare Forgeries, Confessions concerning. W. H. Ireland. Lon. 1805. 12°. 1,889

Shakespeare Society Publications. London, 1841–53. 49 v. 8°. . . 1,885

Vol. 1. Collier, J. P. Memoirs of Edward Alleyn, Founder of Dulwich College.
2. Gosson, S. School of Abuse, Pleasant Invective against Poets, etc.
3. Heywood, T. Apology for Actors, 1612.
4. Ludus Coventriæ, Collection of Mysteries; edited by J. O. Hallowell.
5. Thynn, F. Debate between Pride and Lowliness.

Shakespeare Society Publications. *Continued.* . . . . . . . . I,885

6. Dekker, T. and others. Patient Grissil; a Comedy, 1603.
7. Accounts of the Revels at Court in the Reigns of Elizabeth and James I.
8. Jonson, B. Notes of his Conversations with Drummond of Hawthornden, 1619.
9. First Sketch of Shakespeare's Merry Wives of Windsor.
10. Fools and Jesters; Armin, R. Nest of Ninnies, 1608.
11. Timon; a Play; edited by A. Dyce.
12. Nash, T. Pierce Penniless's Supplication to the Devil, 1592.
13. Heywood, T. King Edward IV.
14. Northbrooke, J. Treatise against Dicing, Dancing, Plays, and Interludes, 1577.
15. First Sketches of the Second and Third Parts of King Henry the Sixth.
16. Halpin, N. J. Oberon's Vision compared with Lylie's Endymion.
17. The Alleyn Papers; illustrative of the Early English Stage.
18. Forde, J. Honour Triumphant; A Line of Life.
19. Tarlton's Jests and News out of Purgatory.
20. Legge, T. True Tragedie of Richard the Third, and the Latin Play of Richardus Testius.
21. The Ghost of Richard the Third; a Poem, 1614; edited by J. P. Collier.
22. Sir Thomas More; a Play; edited by A. Dyce.
23. The Old Taming of a Shrew, upon which Shakespeare founded his Comedy; The Wife Lapped in Morels Skin.
24. Illustrations of the Fairy Mythology of a Midsummer Night's Dream; edited by J. O. Halliwell.
25. Shakespeare's Play of King Henry the Fourth, from a Contemporary Manuscript.
26. Diary of Philip Henslowe, 1591–1609; edited by J. P. Collier.
27. Heywood, T. Fair Maid of the Exchange; a Comedy.
28. Heywood, T. and Rowley, W. Fortune by Land and Sea; a Tragi-Comedy.
29. Marriage of Wit and Wisdom, an Interlude; Illustrations of Shakespeare and the Early English Drama.
30. Collier, J. P. Memoirs of the Principal Actors in Shakespeare's Plays.
31. Riche, B. Farewell to Militaire Profession.
32. Udall, N. Ralph Roister Doister; a Comedy. Norton, T. and Sackville, T. Tragedie of Gorboduc.
33, 34. The Chester Plays; a Collection of Mysteries founded on Scriptural Subjects. 2 v.
35. The Moral Play of Wit and Science and Early Poetical Miscellanies.
36. Cunningham, P. Inigo Jones; a Life of the Architect. Planché, J. R. Remarks on some of his Sketches for Masks and Dramas. Five Court Masks by Jonson, etc.
37–40. Shakespeare Society Papers. 4 v.
41. Extracts from the Registers of the Stationers' Company of Works entered for Publication from 1557–1570; edited by J. P. Collier. v. 1.
42. The same, v. 2, from 1570–1587.
43. Heywood, T. The Fair Maid of the West; or, a Girle worth Gold.
44. Simrock, K. Remarks on the Plots of Shakespeare's Plays.
45. Heywood, T. The Royal King and Loyal Subject; a Woman killed with Kindness.
46. Munday, A. John a Kent and John a Cumber; a Comedy, etc.
47. Heywood, T. Golden and Silver Ages; Two Plays.
48. Heywood, T. If you know not me; a Woman kilde with Kindnesse.
49. Lodge, T. Defence of Poetry, Music, and Stage-Plays; Alarum against Usurers; Forbonius and Prisceria.

Shamrock and Thistle. W. T. Adams. Boston, 1868. 16°. . . J,1535,2

Shanks, W. F. G. Recollections of Distinguished Generals. N. Y. 1866. 12°. C,529

Sharp, J., Life of. Glasgow, 1820. 12°. . . . . . . . . B,111,2

Sharp, J. A. Gazetteer of the British Islands. London, 1852. 2 v. 8°. . L.R.

Sharpe, D. Fossil Remains of Mollusca. London, 1856. 4°. . . . . Q,30

Fossil Remains of Mollusca in England. London, 1853–54. 2 v. 4°. Q,16

Sharpe, E. Supplying Town of Lancaster, Eng., with Water. Lan. 1850. 16°. N,252,37

Sharpe, S. Historic Notes on the Bible. London, 1858. 8°. . . . . P,540

History of Egypt. London, 1842. 8°. . . . . . . . . V,756

The same. London, 1846. 8°. . . . . . . . . . V,848

History of the Hebrew Nation. London, 1869. 12°. . . . . A,206

Sharper detected. J. E. Robert-Houdin. London, 1863. 12°. . . . D,663

Shaw, E. Civil Architecture. Boston, 1852. 4°. . . . . . . M,287

Rural Architecture. Boston, 1843. 4°. . . . . . . . . M,294

Shaw, H. Dresses and Decorations of the Middle Ages. Lond. 1858. 2 v. r. 8°. *Q,188

Hand-Book of Mediæval Alphabets. London, 1853. f°. . . *Q,160

Illuminated Ornaments from 6th to 17th Centuries. Lond. 1833. 4°. *Q,185

Shaw, H. Specimens of Tile Pavements. London, 1858. 4°. . . . *Q,186
Shaw, H. W. Josh Billings; hiz Sayings. New York, 1870. 12°. . . H,94
Josh Billings on Ice, etc. New York, 1870. 12°. . . . . H,95
Shaw, T. B. Manual of English Literature. New York, 1869. 12°. . H,695
Outlines of English Literature. Philadelphia, 1854. 12°. . . H,694
Shea, J. G. Discovery of the Mississippi Valley. New York, 1852. 8°. . C,272
Sheahan, J. W. Life of Stephen A. Douglas. New York, 1860. 12°. . C,919
Shearman, F. W. System of Public Schools of Michigan. Lansing, 1852. 8°. O,1215
Shedd, W. G. T. Sermons to the Natural Man. New York, 1871. 8°. . P,710
Shee, M. A. Life of Sir Martin Archer Shee. London, 1860. 2 v. 8°. . D,364
Sheep, History and Diseases of. W. C. Spooner. London, 1844. 12°. . M,449
Management and Diseases of. M. Youatt. New York, 1857. 8°. . M,477
Sheep Husbandry. H. S. Randall. New York, 1854. 8°. . . . . M,474
Fine Wool. H. S. Randall. New York, 1863. 12°. . . . M,463
Sheet-Iron, Copper Plate, etc., Workers. L. J. Blinn. Phila. 1869. 12°. . M,671
Sheffield, J., *Duke of Buckingham*, Works. London, 1729. 2 v. 8°. . . U,251
Sheil, R. L., Memoirs of. W. T. MacCullagh. London, 1855. 2 v. 12°. . D,204
Sketches; Legal and Political. London, 1855. 2 v. 8°. . . . D,417
Sketches of the Irish Bar, v. 2. New York, 1854. 12°. . . . D,413
Speeches. London, 1847. 8°. . . . . . . . . . . H,803
Speeches; with Memoir by T. Macnevin. Dublin, 1867. 12°. . . H,776
Sheldon, E. A. (Ed.) Lessons on Objects. . . . . . . . . O,944
Manual of Object Lessons. New York, 1867. 12°. . . . . O,943
Sheldon, E. M. Early History of Michigan. New York, 1856. 12°. . . C,238
Sheldon, F. Minstrelsy of the English Border. London, 1847. 8°. . . I,413
Shelley, M. W. Frankenstein. Boston, 1869. 12°. . . . . . K,1004
and others. Liter. and Scient. Men of So. Europe. Lond. 1835. 3v. 12°. M,1013
Literary and Scientific Men of France. Lond. 1838. 2 v. 12°. M,1014
Shelley, P. B. Essays, Letters from Abroad, etc. London, 1840. 2 v. 12°. H,445
Memorials; edited by M. W. Shelly. Boston, 1859. 12°. . C,1169
Poetical Works. Boston, 1854. 12°. . . . . . . . . . I,414
The same. Boston, 1857. 4 v. 16°. . . . . . . . I,226
and Lord Byron, Last Days of. E. J. Trelawny. Boston, 1859. 12°. C,1244
Shells and Shell-Fish. W. Swainson. London, 1840. 12°. . . . M,1035
British, Land and Fresh-Water. W. Turton. London, 1857. 12°. . O,62
Lessons on. E. Mayo. London, 1846. 16°. . . . . . . O,18
Shelton, E. Dictionary of Every-Day Difficulties. London, n. d. 12°. . L,556
Shelton, F. W. Crystalline; or, Heiress of Fall-Down Castle. N. Y. 1854. 12°. K,297
Peeps from a Belfry; or, Paris Sketch-Book. New York, 1855. 12°. H,531
Rector of St. Bardolph's. New York, 1853. 12°. . . . . K,296
Shenandoah; or, Last Confederate Cruiser. C. E. Hunt. N. Y. 1867. 12°. B,916
Shenstone, W. Poetical Works. New York, 1854. 8°. . . . . J,854
Shepard, C. Island of St. Vincent. London, 1831. 8°. . . . . V,184
Shepard, C. U. Report Geological Survey of Connecticut. N. Haven, 1837. 8°. N,871
Shepard, T., Life of. J. A. Albro. Boston, 1870. 12°. . . . . D,8,4
Shepherd, W. Life of Poggio Bracciolini. London, 1837. 8°. . . . D,739
and others. Systematic Education. London, 1815. 2 v. 8°. . O,1207
Shepherd of Bethlehem. C. Tucker. London, 1869. 12°. . . . . K,592
of Salisbury Plain. H. More. New York, 1859. 12°. . . . K,854
Sheppard, E. S. Charles Auchester. New York, n. d. 8°. . . . K,1005

Sheppard, E. S. Counterparts. Boston, 1869. 8°. . . . . . . K,1006
Rumor. Boston, 1864. 8°. . . . . . . . . . K,1007
Sheppard, J. G. Fall of Rome. London, 1861. 8°. . . . . . . A,163
Sheppard, J. H. Memoir of Samuel G. Drake. Albany, 1863. 4°. . C,1056
Sherbrooke. H. B. Goodwin. New York, 1866. 12°. . . . . . K,127
Sherburne, J. H. Life of John Paul Jones. New York, 1851. 8°. . C,1290
Sheridan, P. H., Life of. P. C. Headley. New York, 1865. 16°. . . C,843
Sheridan's, P. H., Troopers on the Borders. De B. R. Keim. Phila. 1870. 12°. B,889
Sheridan, R. B. Dramatic Works; with Life. London, 1854. p. 8°. . L,235

Rivals; St. Patrick's Day; Duenna; School for Scandal; Critic; Trip to Scarborough; Pizarro.

The same. Leipzig, 1869. 16°. . . . . . . . . J,460
Life of. T. Moore. New York, 1853. 2 v. 12°. . . . . . D,179
Speeches. London, 1842. 3 v. 8°. . . . . . . . . H,804
Sheridan, T. British Education. London, 1756. 8°. . . . O,1230
Dictionary of the English Language. London, 1797. 2 v. 8°. . L.R.
Life of Jonathan Swift. London, 1803. 2 v. 12°. . . . U,246,1,2
Sherman, W. T. and his Campaigns. S. M. Bowman and R. B. Irwin. New York, 1865. 8°. . . . . . . . . . B,931
Great March to the Sea. G. W. Nichols. New York, 1866. 12°. . B,907
Sherwood, J. D. Comic History of the United States. Boston, 1870. 12°. B,697
Sherwood, M. M., Life of; chiefly Autobiographical. London, 1857. 8°. D,297
Works. New York, 1866. 16°. . . . . . . . K,1008

Vol. 1. Henry Milner.
2. Fairchild Family; Orphans of Normandy; Latter Days.
3. Little Henry and his Bearer; Little Lucy and her Dhaye; Sergeant Dale, his Daughter, and the Orphan Mary; Susan Gray; Lucy Clare; Hedge of Thorns; Recaptured Negro; Susannah, or, the Three Guardians; Theophilus and Sophia; Abdallah.
4. Indian Pilgrim; Broken Hyacinth; Little Woodman; Babes in the Wood; Clara Stephens; Golden Clew; Katharine Seward; Mary Anne; Iron Cage; Little Beggars.
5. Infant's Progress; Flowers of the Forest; Juliana Oakley; Ermina; Emancipation.
6. The Governess; Little Momiere; Stranger at Home; Père la Chaise; Infant's Grave; English Mary; My Uncle Timothy.
7. The Nun; Intimate Friends; Aunt Kate; Emmeline; Obedience; Gipsy Babes; Basket-Maker; Butterfly; Alune; Procrastination; Mourning Queen.
8. Victoria; Arzoomund; Birthday Present; Errand Boy; Orphan Boy; Two Sisters; Julian Percival; Edward Mansfield; The Infirmary; Mrs. Catherine Crawley; Joan, or, Trustworthy; Young Forester; Bitter-Sweet; Common Errors.
9-12. The Lady of the Manor.
13. The Mailcoach; My three Uncles; Old Lady's Complaint; Shepherd's Fountain; Hours of Infancy; Economy; "Hoc Age;" Old Things and New Things; Swiss Cottage; Obstinacy Punished; Infant's Grave; Father's Eye; Red Book; Dudley Castle; The Happy Grandmother; Blessed Family; My Godmother; Useful Little Girl; Caroline Mordaunt; Le Fevre; The Penny Tract; Potters' Common; China Manufactory; Emily and her Brothers.
14. Monk of Cimiés; The Rosary; Roman Baths; Saint Hospice; Violet Leaf; Convent of St Clair.
15. Henry Milner; Sabbaths on the Continent; Idler.
16. John Marten.

Shetland and the Shetlanders. C. Sinclair. New York, 1840. 12°. . . V,364
Shew, J. Midwifery and Diseases of Women. New York, 1857. 12°. . *L,912
Shifting Winds. R. M. Ballantyne. Philadelphia, 1870. 16°. . J,1674
Shiloh; or, Without and Within. W. M. L. Jay. New York, 1870. 12°. K,573
Ship and Shore. W. Colton. New York, 1851. . . . . . . . V,311
Shipherd, J. R. History of the Oberlin-Wellington Rescue. Boston, 1859. 8°. O,398
Shipmaster's Assistant. J. Blunt. New York, 1851. 8°. . . . . . U,528

Ships and Boats. W. Bland. London, 1868. 12°. . . . . . . M,830
Construction of. H. A. Sommerfeldt. London, n. d. 12°. . . M,859
Rigging of. R. Kipping. London, 1859. 12°. . . . . . M,941
Ships' Anchors. G. Cotsell. London, 1856. 12°. . . . . . . M,901
Shipwreck, Narrative of. Sir E. Seaward. London, 1865. p. 8°. . I,664,1
Shipwrecks and Disasters at Sea. Edinburgh, 1833. 2 v. 16°. . . I,538
of the Royal Navy. W. O. S. Gilly. London, 1861. 12°. . V,1081
Shirley. C. B. Nicholls. New York, 1867. 12°. . . . . . . K,858
The same. Leipzig, 1849. 2 v. in 1. 16°. . . . . . J,389
Shirley, J. Dramatic Works and Poems. London, 1833. 6 v. 8°. . I,753
Shirley, Groton, and Pepperell, Mass., History of. C. Butler. Bost. 1848. 8°. C,126
Shoberl, F. Persecutions of Popery. London, 1844. 2 v. 8°. . . P,621
Shoemakers, Hist. des Cordonniers. P. Lacroix and others. Paris, 1852. 8°. M,741
Lives of Distinguished. Portland, 1829. 12°. . . . . . . D,335
Shooting; Manual of Practical Information. R. Blakey. London, n. d. 16°. M,339
Recreations in. J. W. Carleton. London, 1859. 12°. . . . L,144
Shore, Sir J., *Lord Teignmouth*, Life of; by his Son. London, 1843. 2 v. 8°. D,126
Life of Sir William Jones. London, 1807. 2 v. 8°. . . U,255,1,2
Shoreham, W. de. Religious Poems. London, 1849. 12°. . . L,606,28
Short Studies on Great Subjects. J. A. Froude. London, 1867. 8°. . . H,489
Shrines, English, Pilgrimages to. A. M. Hall. London, 1853. 8°. . . C,1233
Shurtleff, N. B. Decimal System for Libraries. Boston, 1856. 8°. . . L.R.
Shuttleworth, Sir J. K. Public Education. London, 1853. 8°. . O,1050
Siam, Residence in. F. A. Neale. London, 1852. 12°. . . . . . V,581
Siberia, Botanik zu Radde's Reisen in. E. Regel. Moskau, 1861. 2 v. 8°. G,888
Oriental and Western. T. W. Atkinson. New York, 1865. 12°. . V,685
Tent Life in. G. Kennan. New York, 1870. 12°. . . . . . V,682
Travels in. A. Erman. Philadelphia, 1852. 2 v. 12°. . . V,615
Siberian Travel; Reindeer, Dogs, and Snow-Shoes. R. J. Bush. N.Y. 1871. 12°. V,671
Siborne, W. War in France and Belgium, 1815. Philadelphia, 1845. 8°. B,85
Sibyl Huntington. J. C. R. Dorr. New York, 1870. 12°. . . . . K,223
Sibyls, Treatise of the. D. Blondel. London, 1861. f°. . . . . . Q,264
Sicilian Summer, and other Poems. H. Taylor. London, 1864. 16°. . I,445
Sicilian Vespers, History of Wars of. M. Amari. London, 1850. 3 v. 12°. B,509
Sicilies, Summer and Winter in. J. Kavanagh. Leipzig, 1858. 2 v. in 1. 16°. J,238
Sicily and Malta, Travels in. P. Brydone. Aberdeen, 1848. 12°. . . V,491
a Pilgrimage. H. T. Tuckerman. New York, 1852. 12°. . . V,467
and Levant, Wanderungen durch. G. Parthey. Berl. 1834–40. 2 v. 12°. E,211
Atlas zum zweiten Theil. Berlin, 1840. . . . . . . Q,84
Pictures from. W. H. Bartlett. London, 1853. 8°. . . *V,518
Wanderungen in Neapel und Sicilien. F. Gregorovius. Leip. '61. 12°. E,197
Zephyrs from Italy and. W. M. Gould. New York, 1852. 12°. . V,490
Sick Room, Life in the. H. Martineau. Boston, 1845. 16°. . . . H,576
Sick-Room Duties. H. Morley. London, 1847. 16°. . . . . N,252,37
Sickness and Health of Bleaburn. Boston, 1853. 16°. . . . . . K,239
Sidereal Heavens. T. Dick. New York, 1855. 16°. . . . . . . L,405
The same. Philadelphia, 1869. 12°. . . . . . U,260,4
Sidney, A. Discourses on Government. New York, 1805. 3 v. 8°. . O,569
Life of. G. Van Santvoord. New York, 1851. 12°. . . . D,270
Original Letters; edited by T. Forster. London, 1830. 8°. . . H,612

Sidney, H. Diary of the Times of Charles II. London, 1843. 2 v. 8°. . A,517
Sidney, Sir P. Countess of Pembroke's Arcadia. London, 1868. 16°. K,1009
Life and Times of. S. M. Davis. Boston, 1859. 12°. . . . D,271
Memoir of. H. R. F. Bourne. London, 1862. 8°. . . . C,1269
Miscellaneous Works, with Life by W. Gray. Boston, 1860. 8°. . U,128
Sidney, S. Three Colonies of Australia. London, 1853. 8°. . . . V,892
Sieber, F. W. Reise nach der Insel Kreta in 1817. Leipzig, 1823. 2 v. 8°. E,201
Siebold, C. T. E. von. True Parthenogenesis in Moths and Bees. Lon. 1857. 8°. O,39
Sieges of History. W. Robson. London, 1855. 8°. . . . . . . A,314
Sight and Hearing. J. H. Clark. New York, 1856. 8°. . . . . . L,878
Theorie des Erkennens. M. J. Schleiden. Leipzig, 1861. 8°. . E,420
Theory of. H. F. Goblet. London, 1869. 8°. . . . . . L,966
Sight-Seeing in Germany. Sir J. Forbes. London, 1856. p. 8°. . . V,407
Signboards, History of. J. Larwood and J. C. Hotten. London, n. d. p. 8°. H,397
Signers, Book of, Fac-Simile Letters; ed. by W. Brotherhead. Phil. 1861. 4°. *F,73
of the Declaration of Independence. B. J. Lossing. Cin. 1854. 12°. C,1046
The same. New York, 1859. 12°. . . . . C,1046
Biography of. J. Sanderson. Philadelphia, 1820–27. 9 v. 8°. C,655
Lives of. N. Dwight. New York, 1852. 12°. . . . C,545
Signs of the Times; Religious Liberty. C. C. J. Bunsen. N. Y. 1856. 12°. P,88
Sigourney, L. H. Daily Counsellor. Hartford, 1859. 8°. . . . . I,97
Faded Hope. New York, 1854. 16°. . . . . . . . J,1185
Letters to Mothers. New York, 1848. 12°. . . . . . H,289
Past Meridian. New York, 1854. 12°. . . . . . . . H,7
Pleasant Memories of Pleasant Lands. Boston, 1856. 16°. . . H,275
Scenes in my Native Land. Boston, 1845. 16°. . . . . H,248
Select Poems. Philadelphia, n. d. 12°. . . . . . . . I,175
Sikes, W. One Poor Girl; the Story of Thousands. Philadelphia, 1869. 12°. K,122
Silas Barnstarke. T. Gwynne. London, 1853. 12°. . . . . . J,567
Silas Marner. M. J. Lewes. New York, 1861. 12°. . . . . . K,798
The same. Leipzig, 1861. 16°. . . . . . . . J,300
Silcher, F. Instructions for Singing Schools. London, 1857. 8°. . M,421,1
Silent Partner. E. S. Phelps. Boston, 1871. 12°. . . . . . K,227
Silent Struggles. A. S. Stephens. Philadelphia, 1870. 12°. . . . K,452
Silius Italicus, C. Punicorum Libri 17; cur. N. E. Lemaire. Par. 1823. 2 v. 8°. U,347
Siljeström, P. A. Educational Institutions of the U. S. London, 1853. 12°. O,811
Silk, Cotton, Linen, and Wool, History of. New York, 1845. 8°. . . M,657
Manufacture of. G. R. Porter. London, 1831. 12°. . . M,1042
Silk-Worm, Reformed Virginia. London, 1655. See *Force's Tracts*, v. 3.
Sill, E. N. Discourse on the Settlement of Tallmadge. Akron, O. 1857. 8°. C,204
Silliman, B., Life of. G. P. Fisher. New York, 1866. 2 v. 8°. . . C,706
Travels in England, Holland, and Scotland. N. Haven, 1820. 3 v. 16°. V,1030
Visit to Europe in 1851. New York, 1854. 2 v. 12°. . . . V,319
and others, (Eds.). American Journal of Science, 1st ser. v. 1–7, 13–49; 2d ser. 1–9, 26. New Haven, 1819–58. 54 v. 8°. . S,32
Silliman, B., jr. First Principles of Chemistry. Philadelphia, 1867. 12°. N,229
Principles of Physics. Philadelphia, 1867. 12°. . . . . N,78
Silloway, T. W. Text-Book of Modern Carpentry. Boston, 1858. 12°. . M,631
Siluria; the Oldest Rocks. Sir R. I. Murchison. London, 1854. 8°. . N,807
Silver, Lead, and Copper, Metallurgy of. R. H. Lamborn. Lond. 1869. 2 v. 12°. M,848

Silver, Essai d'Argent par Voie Humide. N.F. Gay-Lussac. Paris, 1832. 4°. N,252,57
Metallurgy of. B. Kerl. London, 1868. 8°. . . . . . M,717,1
Silbererze. K. A. Winkler. Freiberg, 1848. 8°. . . . N,252,30
Silver Casket. C. Tucker. London, 1870. 16°. . . . . . . . . J,661
Silver Cord. S. Brooks. Leipzig, 1862. 3 v. 16°. . . . . . . J,48
Silver Cup of Sparkling Drops. C. B. Porter. Buffalo, 1852. 12°. . . J,1286
Silver Dollar, Monograph of. J. L. Riddell. New Orleans, 1845. 8°. . M,388
Silver-Pen. See *Meteyard, E.*
Silver Region of Arizona and Sonora. S. Mowry. New York, 1864. 12°. . C,246
Silver Store, The; Mediæval Poems. S. Baring-Gould. London, 1868. 12°. I,281
Silvia. J. Kavanagh. Leipzig, 1870. 2 v. in 1. 16°. . . . . . J,236
Simmonds, P. L. Commercial Products of Veget. Kingdom. Lond. 1854. 8°. N,1009
Simms, F. W. Practical Tunneling. London, 1859. 4°. . . . . . M,288
Treatise on Mathematical Instruments. Baltimore, 1836. 8°. . . M,662
Simms, W. G. Beauchampe. New York, 1864. 12°. . . . . . . K,247
Border Beagles. New York, 1864. 12°. . . . . . . . K,248
Charlemont. New York, 1866. 12°. . . . . . . . . K.249
Confession. New York, 1864. 12°. . . . . . . . . K,250
Egeria; Voices of Thought and Counsel. Philadelphia, 1853. 12°. H,265
Eutaw; a Sequel to The Forayers. New York, 1864. 12°. . . K,251
Forayers. New York, 1864. 12°. . . . . . . . . K,252
Guy Rivers. New York, 1859. 12°. . . . . . . . . K,253
History of South Carolina. New York, 1860. 12°. . . . . C,195
Katharine Walton. New York, 1864. 12°. . . . . . . K,254
Life of Capt. John Smith. Philadelphia, 1867. 12°. . . . C,553
Life of Chevalier Bayard. New York, 1860. 12°. . . . . D,659
Life of Francis Marion. Cincinnati, 1854. 12°. . . . . . C,682
Life of Nathaniel Green. Philadelphia, 1849. 12°. . . . . C,762
Mellichampe; a Legend of the Santee. New York, 1864. 12°. . K,255
Partisan; a Romance. New York, 1864. 12°. . . . . . . K,256
Poems. New York, 1853. 2 v. 12°. . . . . . . . . . I,141
Richard Hurdis. New York, 1864. 12°. . . . . . . . K,257
Scout. New York, 1868. 12°. . . . . . . . . . . K,258
Southward Ho! New York, 1865. 12°. . . . . . . . K,259
Vasconselos; a Romance. New York, 1859. 12°. . . . . . K,261
Views and Reviews in American Literature. New York, 1845. 8°. H,660
Wigwam and the Cabin. New York, 1864. 12°. . . . . . K,260
Woodcraft. New York, 1864. 12°. . . . . . . . . . K,262
Yemassee. New York, 1866. 12°. . . . . . . . . . K,264
Simon, B. A. The Ten Tribes of Israel. London, 1836. 8°. . . . C,387
Simon, J. F. Animal Chemistry. London, 1845–46. 2 v. 8°. . . . N,189
Frauenmilch nach ihrem chemischen Verhalten. Berlin, 1838. 8°. N,252,14
Simonds, W. Aimwell Stories. Boston, 1865–70. 7 v. 16°. . . . J,1431

| | | |
|---|---|---|
| Vol. 1. Oscar. | Vol. 3. Ella. | Vol. 6. Jessie. |
| 2. Clinton. | 4. Whistler. | 7. Jerry. |
| | 5. Marcus. | |

Simonin, L. Underground Life; or, Mines and Miners. N. Y. 1869. 8°. *M,739
Simony, General Discourse of. J. Metford. London, 1682. 12°. . . . P,27
Simple Cobler of Aggawam. N. Ward. London, 1647. See *Force's Tracts*, v. 3.
Simple Story. E. S. Inchbald. London, 1820. 12°. . . . . . . K,539
Simplicity and Fascination. A. Beale. Boston, 1866. 12°. . . . K,598

Simpson, J. Philosophy of Education. Edinburgh, 1836. 8°. . . o,1175
Simpson, J. H. Annals of Minnesota Historical Society. St. Paul, 1852. 8°. B,809,1
Simrock, K. Deutsche Mythologie. Bonn, 1864. 8°. . . . . . E,464
Plots of Shakespeare's Plays. London, 1850. 8°. . . . I,885,44
Das Rheinland. Leipzig, n. d. 8°. . . . . . . . E,186,9
Simson, W. History of the Gipsies. New York, 1866. 12°. . . . D,706
Sin, Christian Doctrine of. J. Müller. Edinburgh, 1852–53. 2 v. 8°. . P,122
Christian Doctrine of the Forgiveness of. J. F. Clarke. Bost. 1852. 16°. P,283
Forgiveness of. J. Owen. New York, n. d. 12°. . . . . . P,204
the Greatest Evil. S. Bolton. London, 1656. f°. . . . . . P,181
Sinai. R. St. J. Tyrwhitt. London, 1864. 8°. . . . . . . . V,1086,3
and Palestine. A. P. Stanley. New York, 1857. 8°. . . . . V,664
Tent and Khan; a Journey to. R. W. Stewart. Edinb. 1857. 8°. V,648
Letters from. R. Lepsius. London, 1853. p. 8°. . . . . . L,16
Sinclair, C. Flirtations in Fashionable Life. Philadelphia, n. d. 12°. . K,574
Modern Accomplishments. Edinburgh, 1836. 12°. . . . . . K,563
Modern Society. London, 1837. 12°. . . . . . . . K,564
Shetland and the Shetlanders. New York, 1840. 12°. . . . V,364
Sinclair, Sir J. Code of Health and Longevity. London, 1844. 8°. . . L,927
Correspondence. London, 1831. 2 v. 8°. . . . . . . . H,834
Sinclair, J. D. Autumn in Italy. Edinburgh, 1829. 16°. . . . . I,520
Sinding, P. C. History of Scandinavia. London, 1866. 8°. . . . B,578
Sing-Sing Prison, Life in. J. Luckey. New York, 1866. 12°. . . . O,347
Singer, S. W. Text of Shakespeare vindicated. London, 1853. 8°. . . I,870
Singing, Choir and Chorus, Treatise on. F. J. Fétis. London, 1854. 8°. M,421,1
Voice in. E. Seiler. Philadelphia, 1868. 12°. . . . . . M,404
Wilhelm's Method of Teaching. J. Hullah. London, 1841–42. 2 v. 8°. M,401
Singing-School Companion. J. and H. Bird. Boston, 1852. 16°. . . M,418
Singing-Schools, Instructions for. F. Silcher. London, 1857. 8°. . M,421,1
Sink or Swim. H. Alger. Boston, 1871. 16°. . . . . . . . J,1596
Sioux or, Dakotah; Indian Mission, History of. Boston, 1841. 16°. . . J,1727
Sir Amyas Leigh; Westward Ho! C. Kingsley. N. Y. 1866. 2 v. 16°. . K,753
The same. Leipzig, 1855. 2 v. in 1. 16°. . . . . . J,245
Sir Brooke Fossbrooke. C. Lever. New York, 1867. 8°. . . . K,788
The same. Leipzig, 1867. 2 v. in 1. 16°. . . . . . J,287
Sir Charles Grandison. S. Richardson. London, 1820. 7 v. 12°. . . K,530
The same. London, 1776. 4 v. 12°. . . . . . . J,578
Sir Jasper Carew, Knt. C. Lever. New York, 1868. 8°. . . . . K,789
The same. Leipzig, 1861. 2 v. in 1. 16°. . . . . J,288
Sir Jasper's Tenant. M. E. Braddon. Leipzig, 1866. 2 v. in 1. 16°. . J,45
Sir Roger de Coverley. J. Addison. London, 1865. p. 8°. . . . I,664,2
Sir Theodore Broughton. G. P. R. James. Leipzig, 1848. 2 v. in 1. 16°. J,213
Sir Thomas More; a Play; edited by A. Dyce. London, 1844. 8°. . I,885,22
Siris; Virtues of Tar-Water in Disease. G. Berkeley. n. t. p. . . O,648
Sismondi, J. C. L. S. de. Fall of the Roman Empire. London, n. d. 2 v. 16°. A,133
The same. London, 1834. 2 v. 12°. . . . . . M,1004
History of the Italian Republics. London, 1832. 12°. . . . M,997
The same. New York, 1858. 12°. . . . . . . B,481
Literature of the South of Europe. London, 1850. 2 v. p. 8°. . L,236
The same. New York, 1848. 2 v. 12°. . . . . . H,764

Sister's Bye-Hours. J. Ingelow. Boston, 1868. 16°. . . . . . J,1427
Sister's Triumph. W. A. Boardman. Philadelphia, 1870. 16°. . . J,1711
Sisters of Charity. A. Jameson. Boston, 1857. 12°. . . . . . H,562
Sisters of Orleans; a Tale. New York, 1871. 12°. . . . . K,1157
Six Boys; a Mother's Story. Boston, 1871. 16°. . . . . . J,1108
Six Old English Chronicles; edited by J. A. Giles. London, 1848. 8°. . L,26

Ethelwerd, F. Chronicle.
Asserius, J. Life of King Alfred.
Geoffrey of Monmouth. British History.
Gildas, the Wise. Chronicle.
Nennius, Abb. History of the Britons.
Richard of Cirencester. Ancient State of Britain.

Six Years Later. A. Dumas. Philadelphia, n. d. 8°. . . . . . H,978
Sixty Years of the Life of Jeremy Levis. New York, 1831. 2 v. 12°. . C,676
Skeavington, G. Modern System of Farriery. London, n. d. 4°. . . M,585
Skelton, J. Illustrations of Meyrick's Arms and Armor. Lond. 1844. 2 v. 4°. *Q,373
Poetical Works. Boston, 1856. 3 v. 16°. . . . . . . I,227
Skelton, P., Life of. S. Burdy. London, 1816. 8°. . . . . . C,1289,2
Sketch-Book. W. Irving. New York, 1870. 16°. . . . . . . U,14
The same. New York, 1866. 12°. . . . . . . U,20
The same. London, 1834. 2 v. 16°. . . . . . . I,648
Sketches by "Boz." C. Dickens. Philadelphia, 1839. 8°. . . . K,518
The same. New York, 1868. 12°. . . . . . . K,485
The same. New York, 1871. 12°. . . . . . K,1127
The same. Leipzig, 1843. 16°. . . . . . . . J,136
abroad with Pen and Pencil. F. O. C. Darley. Boston, 1869. 8°. . V,403
Legal and Political. R. L. Sheil. London, 1855. 2 v. 8°. . . D,417
of Imposture, Deception, and Credulity. London, 1837. 16°. . I,646
of Society and Adventure. N. P. Willis. Auburn, 1853. 12°. . H,78
Tales and Essays. R. Macnish. London, 1844. 2 v. 16°. . . H,229
Skin, Healthy. E. Wilson. Philadelphia, 1854. 12°. . . . . L,858
Skinner, S. Educational Essays. London, 1844. 8°. . . . . O,1217
Skirmishes and Sketches. M. A. Dodge. Boston, 1865. 16°. . . . H,54
Skirmishing. C. Jenkin. Leipzig, 1863. 16°. . . . . . . . J,219
Skye, Summer in. A. Smith. Boston, 1865. 12°. . . . . . . V,332
The same. London, 1865. 2 v. 12°. . . . . . . V,347
Slack, H. J. Marvels of Pond Life. London, 1861. 12°. . . . O,74
Slade, A. Travels in Turkey, Greece, etc. London, 1854. 8°. . . V,580
Slang, Dictionary of Modern. London, 1859. 16°. . . . . . *L,562
Slater, S., Memoir of. G. S. White. Philadelphia, 1836. 8°. . . . D,363
Slave Power, The. J. E. Cairnes. New York, 1863. 8°. . . . . . O,397
Slave States, Journey in the Back Country. F. L. Olmsted. N. Y. 1863. 12°. V,93
Journey in Seaboard. F. L. Olmsted. New York, 1863. 12°. . V,74
Slave Trade, Domestic and Foreign. H. C. Carey. Philadelphia, 1853. 12°. O,407
Slavery, Discussion concerning. W. G. Brownlow and A. Pryne. Phil.'58. 12°. O,408
in Massachusetts. G. H. Moore. New York, 1866. 8°. . . . C,46
Law of, in United States, v. 1. T. R. R. Cobb. Philadelphia, 1858. 8°. O,399
Letters and Speeches on. H. Mann. Boston, 1851. 12°. . . . O,405
Miscellaneous Tracts on. London, 1823–30. 8°. . . . . . *O,396

1. Case of the Vigilante, employed in the Slave Trade.
2. Debate in House of Commons, May 15, 1823.
3. Debate in House of Commons, June 23, 1825, on Mr. Buxton's motion.
4. Second Report of the Society for the Abolition of, 1825.

Slavery, Miscellaneous Tracts on. *Continued.* . . . . . . . . . *o,396
5. Apology for the Ladies' Anti-Slavery Associations, 1828.
6. Further Progress of Colonial Reform, 1827.
7. Observations on the Demerara Memorial, 1829.
8. A Word from the Bible on behalf of Enslaved British Subjects.
9. Practicability, Safety, and Advantages of Emancipation.
10. Address to Christian Proprietors and Freeholders.
11. Duty of prompt and complete Abolition, by S. C. Wilks.
12. Peace and War; an Essay.

Miscellaneous Writings on. W. Jay. Boston, 1853. 12°. . . . o,393
Pro-Slavery Arguments. E. N. Elliott. Augusta, Ga. 1860. 8°. . o,609
Results of. A. Cochin. Boston, 1863. 12°. . . . . . . . o,402
Scriptural and Historical View of. J. H. Hopkins. N.Y. 1864. 12°. o,416
South-Side View of. N. Adams. Boston, 1860. 12°. . . . . o,406
Studies on. J. Fletcher. Natchez, 1852. 8°. . . . . . . . o,400
Slavic Languages and Literature. T. A. L. v. J. Robinson. N. Y. 1850. 12°. H,762
Slavonic Races. London, 1861. 8°. . . . . . . . . . . . V,1086,1
Sleeman, W. H. Journey through Oude. London, 1858. 2 v. 12°. . V,735
Rambles and Recollections of an Indian Official. Lond. 1844. 2 v. 8°. V,686
Sleep and its Phenomena. J. N. Pinkerton. London, 1839. 16°. . . L,844
the Hygiene of Night. W. W. Hall. New York, 1870. 12°. . L,891
Operations of the Mind in. F. H. Elwin. London, 1843. 12°. . o,650
Philosophy of. R. Macnish. New York, 1834. 12°. . . . L,889
Sleeper, J. S. Mark Rowland; a Tale of the Sea. Boston, 1867. 12°. . K,117
Sleeper, M. G. Fonthill Recreations. Boston, 1866-67. 3 v. 16°. . J,1695
Vol. 1. The Mediterranean Islands. Vol. 2. The Two Sicilies. Vol. 3. Sweden and Norway.

Sleidan, J. History of the Reformation. London, 1689, 1789. 2 v. in 1. f°. Q,305
Slide-Rule, and its Use. C. Hoare. London, 1869. 12°. . . . . M,846
Treatise on the. T. Kentish. Philadelphia, 1852. 12°. . . . M,605
Sloan, S. City and Suburban Architecture. Philadelphia, n. d. 4°. . *Q,222
Constructive Architecture. Philadelphia, 1859. 4°. . . . *Q,173
Homestead Architecture. Philadelphia, 1867. 8°. . . . . M,191
Model Architect. Philadelphia, 1860. 2 v. 4°. . . . . *Q,221
Sloth, Description of a Gigantic Extinct. R. Owen. London, 1842. 4°. Q,43
Slover, J., Memoir of. Cincinnati, 1867. 12°. . . . . . . . B,592
Small House at Allington. A. Trollope. New York, 1864. 8°. . K,1051
The same. Leipzig, 1864. 3 v. 16°. . . . . . . J,505
Smart, C. Poems. London, 1752. 4°. . . . . . . . . . F,166
Smead, W. Guide to Wealth. Cincinnati, 1856. 18°. . . . . . o,466
Smeaton, A. C. Builder's Pocket Companion. Philadelphia, 1850. 12°. M,145
Smeaton, J. Description of Eddystone Lighthouse. London, 1791. f°. . Q,447
Power of Water and Wind to turn Mills. London, 1826. 8°. . N,143
Smedley, E. History of France from 843 to 1529. London, n. d. 8°. . B,347
Sketches of Venetian History. New York, 1860. 2 v. 18°. . . L,371
and others. Occult Sciences. London, 1855. 8°. . . . . . o,331
Smedley, F. E. Frank Fairlegh. Leipzig, 1864. 2 v. in 1. 16°. . . J,461
Harry Coverdale's Courtship and Marriage. Philadelphia, n. d. 12°. K,1014
Lorrimer Littlegood. Philadelphia, n. d. 12°. . . . . K,1015
Smelting, Freyberger Schmelzhüttenprozesse. K. A. Winkler. Frey. 1837. 8°. N,252,18
Smiles, S. Brief Biographies. Boston, 1864. 12°. . . . . . . C,495
The Huguenots. New York, 1868. 8°. . . . . . . . . B,365
Industrial Biography. Boston, 1869. 12°. . . . . . . . C,549

Smiles, S. Life of George Stephenson. Columbus, 1859. 12°. . . . . D,272
Lives of George and Robert Stephenson. New York, 1868. 8°. . C,1294
Lives of Matthew Boulton and James Watt. London, 1865. 8°. . D,59
Self-Help. Boston, 1866. 12°. . . . . . . . . . . H,394
Smith, Adam, Life of. W. Draper. London, n. d. 8°. . . . . C,581
Nature and Causes of the Wealth of Nations. Edinburgh, 1853. 8°. O,521
Theory of Moral Sentiments. London, 1853. p. 8°. . . . . L,237
Smith, Albert. Adventures of Mr. Ledbury. London, n. d. 16°. . . J,651
Month at Constantinople. London, 1851. 16°. . . . . . . V,551
Pottleton Legacy; a Story. London, n. d. 16°. . . . . . J,652
Story of Mont Blanc. London, 1853. 12°. . . . . . . V,348
Wild Oats and Dead Leaves. London, 1860. 12°. . . . . . J,653
Smith, Alex. City Poems. Boston, 1857. 16°. . . . . . . . I,424
Dreamthorp. London, 1863. 12°. . . . . . . . . . H,483
Edwin of Deira; a Poem. Boston, 1861. 16°. . . . . . . I,426
Life Drama and other Poems. Boston, 1866. 16°. . . . . . I,425
Miss Oona McQuarrie. Boston, 1866. 12°. . . . . . K,1011
Poems. Boston, 1853. 16°. . . . . . . . . . . I,427
Summer in Skye. London, 1865. 2 v. 12°. . . . . . . V,347
The same. Boston, 1865. 12°. . . . . . . . V,332
Smith, A. C. Nile and its Banks. London, 1868. 2 v. 12°. . . . . V,794
Smith, A. W. Treatise on Mechanics. New York, 1849. 8°. . . N,133
Smith, C. Old Manor House. London, 1820. 2 v. 12°. . . . . K,544
Smith, C. H. Dogs. Edinburgh, 1839–54. 2 v. 16°. . . . N,470,18,19
Horses, Asses, etc. Edinburgh, n. d. 16°. . . . . . N,470,20
Introduction to Mammalia. Edinburgh, n. d. 16°. . . . N,470,15
Natural History of the Human Species. London, 1852. 16°. . . N,392
Smith, C. H. J. Landscape Gardening. New York, 1853. 12°. . . M,349
Smith, C. J. Synonyms and Antonyms. London, 1870. p. 8°. . . L,254
Smith, E. P. Incidents of U. S. Christian Commission. Philad. 1869. 8°. B,961
Smith, E. P. Manual of Political Economy. New York, 1853. 12°. . O,510
Smith, E. R. Araucanians; Indians of Chili. New York, 1855. 12°. . V,251
Smith, G. Lectures on the Study of History. New York, 1866. 12°. . A,23
Three English Statesmen. London, 1867. 8°. . . . . . C,1224
John Pym, Oliver Cromwell, and Wm. Pitt.
Smith, Henry. Mental and Moral Training. London, n. d. 16°. . O,1154
Smith, Horace. Adam Brown, the Merchant. Lond. 1843. 3 v. in 1. 12°. K,691
Brambletye House. London, 1826. 3 v. 12°. . . . . . . J,649
Festivals, Games, and Amusements. New York, 1855. 18°. . . L,358
Jane Lomax. London, 1838. 3 v. 12°. . . . . . . . K,565
Love and Mesmerism. London, 1845. 3 v. 12°. . . . . K,1010
Moneyed Man; or, the Lesson of a Life. London, 1841. 3 v. 8°. . K,692
Tor Hill. London, 1826. 3 v. in 1. 12°. . . . . . . . K,567
Walter Colyton. London, 1830. 3 v. in 1. 12°. . . . . K,568
Zillah; a Tale. London, 1828. 4 v. in 2. 12°. . . . . K,566
and James. Rejected Addresses. Boston, 1860. 12°. . . . . I,428
Smith, H. B. Chronological Tables of the Church. New York, 1859. f°. *Q,450
Smith, H. H. Anatomical Atlas of the Human Body. Philadel. 1851. 8°. L,1036
Smith, Col. James. Captivity with the Indians, 1755–59. Cincin. 1870. 8°. C,221
Smith, James. Thorough Draining and Deep Plowing. Stirling, 1838. 8°. N,252,6

Smith, James. Voyage and Shipwreck of St. Paul. London, 1848. 8°. . P,278
Smith, Capt. John, Biography of. G. C. Hill. Philadelphia, 1868. 16°. J,1229
Description of New England. London, 1616. See *Force's Tracts*, v. 2.
Life of. G. S. Hillard. Boston, 1860. 12°. . . . . . C,860,2
W. G. Simms. Philadelphia, 1867. 12°. . . . . . C,553
New England's Trials. London, 1622. See *Force's Tracts*, v. 2.
True Travels, 1593. Richmond, 1819. 2 v. 8°. . . . . . C,115
Smith, John. Fruits and Farinacea proper Food of Man. N. Y. 1856. 12°. L,903
Smith, J. C. Correspondence and Miscellanies. New York, 1847. 12°. . H,214
Smith, J. C. Practical Book-Keeping. Cincinnati, 1853. 8°. . . M,1170
Smith, Sir J. E. English Flora. London, 1828–36. 6 v. 8°. . . . N,989
Smith, J. F. and Howitt, W. Illus. History of England. Lond. n. d. 8 v. 8°. A,467
Smith, J. J. Summer's Jaunt across the Water. Phil. 1846. 2 v. in 1. 12°. V,299
and Watson, J. F. American Historical and Literary Curiosities.
Philadelphia, 1861. 4°. . . . . . . . . . *Q,227
The same; large paper. New York, 1852. f°. . . S.C.
Smith, J. J. (Ed.) Cambridge Portfolio. London, 1840. 2 v. 4°. . . Q,214
Smith, John P. Holy Scriptures and Geological Science. Lond. 1852. 12°. L,313
Smith, Julia P. Chris and Otho. New York, 1870. 12°. . . . . J,656
Widow Goldsmith's Daughter. Hartford, 1870. 12°. . . . K,152
Smith, John T. Nollekens and his Times. London, 1828. 2 v. 8°. . D,34
Smith, John W. Compendium of Mercantile Law. New York, 1866. 8°. U,530
Smith, Joseph. History of Jefferson College. Pittsburgh, 1857. 12°. . O,835
Old Redstone; Sketches of Western Presbyterianism. Phil. 1854. 8°. P,622
Smith, Joseph, jr. Book of Mormon. Liverpool, 1854. 16°. . . . P,426
Smith, Joshua T. Discovery of America by Northmen. Lond. 1839. 12°. B,698
Northmen in New England. Boston, 1839. 12°. . . . B,689
Smith, Josiah D. Truth in Love; Sermons. Philadelphia, 1864. . . P,190
Smith, J. V. C. Pilgrimage to Egypt. Boston, 1859. 12°. . . . V,782
Smith, M. Geog. View of Brit. Possessions in N. America. Balt. 1814. 24°. V,1027
Smith, O. H. Early Indiana Trials. Cincinnati, 1858. 8°. . . . C,236
Smith, P. History of the World. New York, 1865–66. 3 v. 8°. . . A,37
Smith, R. C. Geography on the Productive System. New York, 1852. 12°. O,900
Smith, R. M. Modern Geography. Philadelphia, 1848. 4°. . . . Q,125
Smith, R. P. Prophecy; a Preparation for Christ. Boston, 1870. 12°. . P,143
Smith, R. S. Manual of Linear Perspective. New York, 1857. 8°. . . M,110
Manual of Topographical Drawing. New York, 1864. 8°. . . M,209
Smith, Seba, *Jack Downing*. Thirty Years out of the Senate. N. Y. 1859. 12°. H,74
Way Down East; or, Yankee Life. Philadelphia, 1866. 12°. . . H,93
Smith, Sydney. Elementary Sketches of Moral Philosophy. N. Y. 1850. 12°. O,719
Memoir of S. S. Fox, *Lady Holland*. New York, 1856. 2 v. 12°. C,1209
Selections from his Writings. London, 1863. 2 v. in 1. p. 8°. . I,662
Wit and Wisdom of. E. A. Duyckinck. New York, 1870. 8°. . H,461
Works. London, 1859. 2 v. 12°. . . . . . . . . U,124
The same. Boston, 1857. 8°. . . . . . . . . H,372
Smith, S. B. Image of the Beast. New York, 1862. 18°. . . . . P,21
Smith, T. Naturalist's Cabinet. London, 1806–7. 6 v. 8°. . . . N,665
Smith, Sir T., Life of. J. Strype. Oxford, 1820. 8°. . . . . P,690
Smith, T. and Choules, J. O. Origin and Hist. of Missions. Bost. 1832. 2 v. 4°. Q,265
Smith, T. M. Legends of the War of Independence. Louisville, 1855. 8°. B,756

Smith, T. R. Acoustics in Public Buildings. London, n. d. 12°. . . M,858
Smith, W. Dictionary of the Bible. Boston, 1863. 3 v. 8°. . . *P,450
Dictionary of Greek and Roman Antiquities. New York, 1854. 8°. S.C.
Dictionary of Greek and Roman Geography. Bost. 1854–57. 2 v. 8°. S.C.
Greek and Roman Biography and Mythology. Bost. 1849. 3 v. 8°. S.C.
History of England, to 1862. New York, 1868. 16°. . . . A,388
History of Greece. New York, 1854. 12°. . . . . . . A,66
Smaller Scripture History. New York, 1871. 16°. . . . . . P,579
Smith, W. Thorndale; or, the Conflict of Opinions. Boston, 1859. 12°. K,1168
Smith, W. Memoir of S. G. Fichte. Boston, 1846. 12°. . . . . D,501
Smith, W. H. Canada; Past, Present, and Future. Toronto, n. d. 2 v. 8°. C,341
Smith, W. L. G. Observations on China. New York, 1863. . . . V,597
Smith, W. R. History of Wisconsin, v. 1, 3. Madison, Wis. 1851. 2 v. 8°. C,233
Smith, Sir W. S., Life of. J. Barrow. London, 1848. 2 v. 8°. . . D,129
Smithson, W. T. Methodist Pulpit South. Washington, 1859. 8°. . . P,862
Smithsonian Institution, Contributions to Knowledge. Wash. 1848–71. 17 v. 4°. Q,324

Vol. 1. Squier, E. G., and Davis, E. H. Ancient Monuments of the Mississippi Valley.
2. Walker, S. C. Researches relative to the Planet Neptune.
Lieber, F. Vocal Sounds of Laura Bridgeman.
Bailey, J. W. Microscopical Examination of Soundings off the Atlantic Coast of the United States.
Ellet, C., jr. Physical Geography of the Mississippi Valley.
Gibbes, R. W. Memoir on Mosasaurus and Allied Genera.
Agassiz, L. Embryological Classification of Insects.
Hare, R. Explosiveness of Niter.
Bailey, J. W. Microscopical Observations in So. Carolina, Georgia, and Florida.
Squier, E. G. Aboriginal Monuments of the State of New York.
Downes, J. Occultations visible in the United States during 1851.
3. Locke, J. Observations on Terrestrial Magnetism.
Secchi, A. Researches on Electrical Rheometry.
Girard, C. Fresh-Water Fishes of North America. Cottoids.
Harvey, W. H. Marine Algæ of North America, part 1. Melanospermeæ.
Gray, A. Plantæ Wrightianæ Texano-Neo-Mexicanæ, part 1.
Davis, C. H. Law of Deposit of the Flood-Tide.
Whittlesey, C. Description of Ancient Works in Ohio.
Appendix; Ephemeris of Neptune, and Occultations in 1852.
4. Riggs, S. R. Grammar and Dictionary of the Dakotah Language.
5. Leidy, J. A Fauna and Flora within Living Animals.
Leidy, J. Memoir upon the Extinct Species of American Ox.
Wyman, J. Anatomy of the Nervous System of Rana Pipiens.
Harvey, W. H. Marine Algæ of North America, part 2. Rhodospermeæ.
Gray, A. Plantæ Wrightianæ Texano-Neo-Mexicanæ, part 2.
6. Torrey, J. Plants collected by J. C. Frémont in California.
Torrey, J. Observations on the Batis Maritima of Linnæus.
Torrey, J. On the Darlingtonia Californica; a new Pitcher Plant.
Stimpson, W. Marine Invertebrata of Gr. Manan, New Brunswick.
Coffin, J. H. Winds of the Northern Hemisphere.
Leidy, J. Ancient Fauna of Nebraska.
Appendix. Occultations in 1853.
7. Chappelsmith, J. Tornado in Indiana, April 30, 1852.
Bailey, J. W. New Species of Microscopical Organisms.
Lapham, I. A. Antiquities of Wisconsin.
Leidy, J. Extinct Sloth Tribe of North America.
Publications of Society and Periodicals in Smithsonian Library, part 1.
8. Haven, S. F. Archæology of the United States.
Olmsted, D. Recent Secular Period of the Aurora Borealis.
Alvord, B. Tangencies of Circles and of Spheres.
Jones, J. Researches concerning certain N. American Vertebrata.
Force, P. Auroral Phenomena in Higher Northern Latitudes.
Publications of Soc. and Periodicals in Smithsonian Library, part 2.
9. Meech, L. W. Heat and Light of the Sun in different Latitudes.
Hitchcock, E. Illustrations of Surface Geology.
Mayer, B. Mexican Archæology and Zapotec Remains.
Gibbs, W. A. and Genth, F. A. Ammonia-Cobalt Bases.
Runkle, J. D. New Tables of Planetary Motions.
Runkle, J. D. Asteroid Supplement to New Tables.
10. Harvey, W. H. Marine Algæ of North America, part 3. Chlorospermæ.
Kane, E. K. Magnetical Observations in Arctic Seas.
Bowen, T. J. Grammar and Dictionary of the Yoruba Language.
11. Brewer, T. M. North-American Oology. Raptores and Fissirostres.
Gillis, J. M. Total Eclipse of the Sun, September, 7, 1858, in Peru.

Smithsonian Institution, Contributions to Knowledge. *Continued.* . . Q,324

Bache, A. D. Magnetic and Meteorological Observations, part 1.
Kane, E. K. Meteorological Observations in the Arctic Seas.
LeConte, J. L. Coleoptera of Kansas and Eastern New Mexico.
Sonntag, A. Observations on Terrestrial Magnetism in Mexico.
Loomis, E. Certain Storms in Europe and America, December, 1836.
12. Kane, E. K. Astronomical Observations in the Arctic Seas.
Whittlesey, C. Fluctuations in Level in North American Lakes.
Caswell, A. Meteorological Observations at Providence, R. I., 28½ years.
Smith, N. D. Meteorological Observations near Washington, Ark., 20 years.
Mitchell, S. W. Researches upon the Venom of the Rattlesnake.
13. Kane, E. K. Tidal Observations in the Arctic Seas.
McClintock, L. Meteorological Observations in the Arctic Seas.
Whittlesey, C. Ancient Mining on the Shores of Lake Superior.
Bache, A. D. Astronomical Discussions. Girard College, parts 1–6.
Bache, A. D. Magnetic Survey of Pennsylvania.
Mitchell, S. W. and Morehouse, G. R. Anatomy of Chelonia.
14. Bache, A. D. Astronomical Discussions. Girard College, parts 7–12.
Draper, H. Construction and Use of a Silvered Glass Telescope.
Meek, F. B. and Hayden, F. V. Palæontology of the Missouri.
Leidy, J. Cretaceous Reptiles of the United States.
15. Newcomb, S. Orbit of Neptune.
Whittlesey, C. Fresh-Water Glacial Drift of the North-Western States.
Pumpelly, R. Geological Researches in China and Japan.
Hayes, I. I. Physical Observations in the Arctic Seas, 1860–61.
16. Dean, J. The Gray Substance of the Medulla, Oblongata, and Trapezium.
Cleaveland, P. Results of the Meteorological Observations made at Brunswick, Me., 1807–59, reduced and discussed by C. A. Schott.
Hildreth, S. P. and Wood, J. Results of Meteorological Observations at Marietta, O., 1817–59, reduced and discussed by C. A. Schott.
Pickering, C. On the Gliddon Mummy Case in the Museum of the Smithsonian Institute.
Coffin, J. H. Orbit and Phenomena of a Meteoric Fire-Ball seen July 20, 1860.
Gould, B. A. On the Transatlantic Longitude.
Swan, J. G. The Indians at Cape Flattery, Washington Territory.
17. Morgan, L. H. Systems of Consanguinity and Affinity of the Human Family.

Miscellaneous Collections. Washington, 1862–69. 9 v. 8°. . . F,152

Vol. 1. Directions for Meteorological Observations.
Coffin, J. H. Psychometrical Tables.
Guyot, A. Meteorological and Physical Tables.
2. Booth, J. C. and Morfit, C. Recent Improvements in Chemical Arts.
Proceedings in Relation to Electro-Magnetic Telegraph.
Stanley, J. M. Catalogue of Portraits of North-American Indians.
Baird, S. F. Catalogue of North-American Birds.
Baird, S. F. and Girard, C. Catalogue of North-American Serpents.
Check-List of North-American Shells.
Directions for Collecting Specimens.
Circular to Officers of Hudson's-Bay Company.
Instructions for Collecting Nests and Eggs.
North-American Grasshoppers.
North-American Shells.
Morgan, L. H. Circular on Relationship in Different Nations.
3. Osten Sacken, R. Catalogue of Diptera of North America.
Morris, J. G. Catalogue of Lepidoptera of North America.
LeConte, J. L. Classification of Coleoptera, part 1.
Catalogue of Publications of Societies in Smithsonian Library.
4. Hagen, H. Synopsis of North-American Neuroptera.
Morris, J. G. Synopsis of North-American Lepidoptera.
5. Binney, W. G. Bibliography of North-American Conchology.
Catalogue of Publications of Smithsonian Institution to June, 1862.
List of Foreign Correspondents of Smithsonian Institution.
6. Loew, Monograph of Diptera, parts 1 and 2.
LeConte, J. L. List of Coleoptera of North America.
Le Conte, J. L. New Species of Coleoptera of North America.
7. Allen, H. Monograph of the Bats of North America.
Binney, W. G. Land and Fresh-Water Shells of North America, parts 2 and 3.
Stimpson, W. Researches upon the Hydrobiinæ and allied Forms.
Prime, T. Monograph of American Corbiculadæ.
Conrad, T. A. Check-List of the Invertebrate Fossils of North America. Eocene and Oligocene.
Meek, F. B. Check-List of the Invertebrate Fossils of North America. Miocene, Cretaceous, and Jurassic.
Egleston, T. Catalogue of Minerals, with their Formulas.
Gibbs, G. Dictionary of the Chinook Jargon; or, Trade Language of Oregon.
Gibbs, G. Instructions for Research relative to the Ethnology and Philology of America.
List of Works published by the Smithsonian Institution, January, 1866.
8. Osten Sacken, R. Monographs of the Diptera of North America, part 4.
Scudder, S. H. Catalogue of the Orthoptera of North America.

Smithsonian Institution, Miscellaneous Collections. *Continued.* . . . F,152
Binney, W. G. and Bland, T. Land and Fresh-Water Shells of N. America, pt. 1.
Arrangement of Families of Birds.
Circular to Officers of the Hudson's-Bay Company.
Suggestions relative of Scientific Investigation in Russian America.
Circular relating to Collections in Archæology and Ethnology.
Circular to Entomologists.
Circular relative to Collection of Birds from Middle and South America.
Smithsonian Museum Miscellanea.
9. Binney, W. G. Bibliography of North-American Conchology, part 2.
Catalogue of Publications of Societies and of Periodical Works belonging to the Smithsonian Institution.
Reports of Regents, 1853-61, 63-67. Washington, 1854-68. 14 v. 8°. P.D.
Smoke, Methods of Consuming. W. West. London, 1842. 8°. . . N,252,13
Prevention of. C. W. Williams. London, 1858. 12°. . . . M,975
Steam without. R. Armstrong. London, n. d. 8°. . . . N,252,30
Smoking and Drinking. J. Parton. Boston, 1868. 16°. . . . . H,251
Smollett, T. Humphrey Clinker. New York, 1867. 16°. . . . K,1016
The same. London, 1820. 2 v. 12°. . . . . . . K,541
The same. Leipzig, 1846. 16°. . . . . . . . J,462
Peregrine Pickle. Leipzig, 1870. 2 v. in 1. 16°. . . . . J,463
Roderick Random. Leipzig, 1845. 16°. . . . . . . . J,464
Smooth Stones taken from Ancient Brooks. C. H. Spurgeon. N. Y. 1860. 12°. P,25
Smucker, S. S. See *Schmucker, S. S.*
Smuggler. G. P. R. James. Leipzig, 1845. 16°. . . . . . J,214
Smyth, C. P. Antiquity of Intellectual Man. Edinburgh, 1868. 8°. . N,402
The same. Berlin, 1855. 4°. . . . . . . . . N,397
Life and Work at the Great Pyramid. Edinburgh, 1867. 3 v. 8°. V,836
Our Inheritance in the Great Pyramid. London, 1864. 12°. . . V,779
Smyth, W. Lectures on the French Revolution. Lond. 1855-60. 2 v. p. 8°. L,239
Lectures on Modern History. London, 1854. 2 v. p. 8°. . . L,238
The same. Boston, 1855. 8°. . . . . . . . . A,321
Snape, J. Mathematics. London, 1847. 8°. . . . . . . N,252,33
Snarleyyow; or, the Dog Fiend. F. Marryat. New York, 1868. 12°. . K,851
Snorri Sturleson. The Heimskringla; or, Chronicle of the Kings of Norway, from the Icelandic. London, 1844. 3 v. 8°. . . . . . B,579
Snow-Bound; a Poem. J. G. Whittier. Boston, 1867. 12°. . . . I,154
Snow Image and other Tales. N. Hawthorne. Boston, 1865. 16°. . . K,164
The same. Boston, 1868. 12°. . . . . . . . U,40,3
Snow Man. Madame Dudevant. Boston, 1871. 12°. . . . K,1119
Snowball, J. C. Elements of Plane Trigonometry. Cambridge, 1837. 8°. M,1158
Snowden, J. R. Description of Ancient and Modern Coins. Phila. 1860. 8°. *M,389
Soap, Art of Manufacturing. A. Ott. Philadelphia, 1867. 12°. . . M,626
Rapport sur la Fabrication des Savons. Paris, n. d. 8°. . . N,252,41
Treatise on the Manufacture of. H. Dussauce. Phila. 1869. 8°. . M,629
Social and Ethical Studies. F. P. Cobbe. London, 1865. p. 8°. . . O,557
Social Condition of England and Europe. J. Kay. London, 1850. 2 v. 12°. O,536
Social Destiny of Man. C. Fourier. New York, 1857. 8°. . . . O,545
Social Happiness, Guide to. S. S. Ellis. New York, n. d. 8°. . . . H,510
Social Innovators and their Schemes. W. L. Sargent. London, 1858. 8°. O,375
Social Life in England and France. M. Berry. London, 1844. 2 v. 12°. H,313
Social Morals, Memoirs illustrative of. A. Jameson. London, 1846. 12°. M,22
Social Philosophy, Political Economy applied to. J. S. Mill. Bost. 1848. 2 v. 8°. O,543
Social Science, Introduction to. G. H. Calvert. New York, 1856. 12°. . O,369

Social Science, National Association for, Transactions. Lon. 1858–65. 8 v. 8°. O,413
Principles of. H. C. Carey. Philadelphia, 1858–59. 3 v. 8°. . O,548
Social Statics; Conditions essential to Happiness. H. Spencer. N.Y. 1865. 12°. O,532
Social Theories, Considerations on recent. C. E. Norton. Boston, 1853. 16°. O,368
Socialisms, History of American. J. H. Noyes. Philadelphia, 1870. 8°. O,378
Société Royale des Antiquaires du Nord, Mémoires. Copenhagen, n. d. 8°. R,32
Societies, Friendly, Loan, etc. N. White. London, 1867. 12°. . . . M,862
Society and Solitude. R. W. Emerson. Boston, 1870. 12°. . . . H,106
as it is and should be. J. R. Buchanan. Cincinnati, 1846. 8°. H,302,4
Improvement of. T. Dick. Philadelphia, 1869. 12°. . . U,260,2
in America. H. Martineau. London, 1837. 3 v. 12°. . . . V,104
of Jesus, Constitutiones Societatis Jesu, 1558. Romæ, 1858. 8°. . P,892
See also *Jesuits.*
Typen der Gesellschaft. B. Goltz. Berlin, 1867. 2 v. in 1. 16°. . E,379
Wits and Beaux of. K. B. and J. C. Thomson. New York, 1861. 12°. C,591
Socrates and the Socratic School. E. Zeller. London, 1868. 12°. . . D,772
Plato and the Companions of. G. Grote. London, 1865. 3 v. 8°. . D,777
Socrates Scholasticus. Ecclesiastical History, A. D. 305–445. Lon. 1853. p. 8°. L,31
The same. London, 1607. 4°. . . . . . . . . P,647
Sohn Napoleons. M. Ring. Berlin, 1860. 2 v. 16°. . . . . . G,428
Soil, Différens Moyens d'amender le Sol. A. Puvis. Paris, 1837. 8°. N,252,24
Die Bodenkunde. C. Sprengel. Leipzig, 1844. 8°. . . . . . G,660
Lehre von den Urbarmachungen. C. Sprengel. Leipzig, 1846. 8°. G,661
Solar System. J. R. Hind. New York, 1852. 12°. . . . . . . N,268
Contemplations of. J. P. Nichol. Edinburgh, 1844. 8°. . . . N,335
Destiny of. D. Vaughan. Cincinnati, n. d. 8°. . . . . . T,19,2
with Reflections. T. Dick. Philadelphia, 1869. 12°. . . U,260,5
Soldier Boy. W. T. Adams. Boston, 1869. 16°. . . . . . J,1536,1
Soldier's Orphans. A. S. Stephens. Philadelphia, n. d. 12°. . . . K,321
Solid Bodies, Bildung der Festen Körper. H. F. Link. Berlin, 1841. 8°. N,252,21
Formation des Corps Solides. H. F. Link. Berlin, 1841. 8°. N,252,21
Solio, A. de. Conquest of Mexico. London, 1724. f°. . . . . F,294
Solitary, The. F. Bremer. London, 1852. p. 8°. . . . . . L,169,1
Solitudes of Nature and Man. W. R. Alger. Boston, 1869. 16°. . . H,236
Solon, L. Inventions Décoratives. Paris, 1866. f°. . . . . . . L.R.
Solubilities of Chemical Substances. F. H. Storer. Cambridge, 1864. 8°. . N,246
Somatology. G. M. Maclean. New York, 1859. 12°. . . . . . N,76
Somebody's Luggage, etc. C. Dickens. Leipzig, 1867. 16°. . . . . J,137
Somers, J. *Lord.* Collection of Tracts relating to Great Britain; edited by W. Scott. London, 1809–15. 13 v. 4°. . . . . . . F,130

Vol. 1. Reign of Elizabeth and prior. Vol. 7, 8. Reign of Charles II.
2, 3. Reign of James I. 9. Reign of James II.
4, 5. Reign of Charles I. 9–12. Reign of William III.
6, 7. Commonwealth. 12, 3. Reign of Queen Anne.
13. Reign of Queen Anne; Reign of George I.

Life of. T. Jardine. London, n. d. 8°. . . . . . . . C,581
Somerset, Earl of, Trial of, for Poisoning. A. Amos. London, 1846. 8°. . B,30
Somerville, M. Connection of the Physical Sciences. New York, 1853. 12°. N,69
Molecular and Microscopic Science. London, 1869. 2 v. 12°. . N,14
Physical Geography. Philadelphia, 1854. 12°. . . . V,1134
Sommerfeldt, H. S. Construction of Ships. London, n. d. 12°. . . M,859
Sommers, J. R. Heavenward Led; or, the Two Bequests. Phila. 1871. 12°. K,225

Son of the Soil. M. Oliphant. New York, 1865. 8°. . . . . . K,870
Sonatas, Original, für das Pianoforte. M. Clementi. Wolfenb. n. d. 3 v. 4°. *Q,192
für das Pianoforte. L. von Beethoven. Wolfenbüttel, n. d. 2 v. 4°. *Q,190
Song and Poetry, Library of. E. H. Knight. New York, 1871. 8°. . *I,177
of the Bell; trans. by W. H. Furness. F. von Schiller. Phila. 1850. G,46
of Hiawatha. H. W. Longfellow. Boston, 1868. 16°. . . . I,70
of Higher-Water. J. W. Ward. New York, 1868. 8°. . . . I,72
Songs and Ballads of Cumberland; edited by S. Gilpin. London, 1866. 8°. I,331
of the Revolution; edited by F. Moore. New York, 1859. 12°. I,78
before Sunrise. A. C. Swinburne. Boston, 1871. 12°. . . . I,438
from the Dramatists; edited by R. Bell. London, 1855. 16°. . . I,253
of the Cavaliers. G. W. Thornbury. London, 1857. 12°. . . I,100
of Labor, and other Poems. J. G. Whittier. Boston, 1856. 16°. . I,159
of Scotland. A. Cunningham. London, 1825. 4 v. 8°. . . . I,350
G. F. Graham. London, 1853. 3 v. 8°. . . . . . M,414
of the Sea. E. Sargent. Boston, 1849. 16°. . . . . . . I,117
of Summer. R. H. Stoddard. Boston, 1857. 16°. . . . . . I,147
Song-Tide, and other Poems. P. B. Marston. Boston, 1871. 12°. . . I,126
Sonnet, Book of the. L. Hunt and S. A. Lee. Boston, 1867. 2 v. 16°. . I,361
Sonnini de Manoncour, C. N. S. Travels in Egypt. London, 1800. 4°. . Q,431
Sooner or Later. S. Brooks. Leipzig, 1868. 3 v. 16°. . . . . . J,49
Sonrel, L. Bottom of the Sea. New York, 1870. 12°. . . . . M,1049
Sophia Dorotha, Consort of George I., Memoirs of. R. F. Williams. London, 1846. 2 v. 8°. . . . . . . . . . . . . . . D,676
Sophocles. Antigone; with Notes by T. D. Woolsey. Boston, 1855. 12°. U,409
Electra; with Notes by T. D. Woolsey. Boston, 1854. 12°. . . U,410
Tragedies; Oxford translation. New York, 1855. 12°. . . . U,400
The same; translated by E. H. Plumptre. London, 1867. 8°. U,398
The same; translated by T. Franklin. New York, n. d. 16°. U,373
Sophocles, E. A. Greek Lexicon of Rom. and Byzan. Periods. Bost. 1870. 8°. L.R.
Soprano, The; a Musical Story. C. Barnard. Boston, 1869. 8°. . . K,204
Sopwith, T. Importance of Preserving Mining Records. Lond. 1844. 8°. N,252,35
Observations to Miners in Lead Mines. London, 1846. 8°. N,252,35
Sordella, Strafford, Christmas Eve, etc. R. Browning. Boston, 1864. 12°. I,295
Sorrows of Werther. J. W. von Goethe. London, 1848–51. 16°. . L,188,4
Soto, H. de. Conquest of Florida. T. Irving. New York, 1851. 12°. . C,184
Discovery of Terra Florida. London, 1851. 8°. . . . . . V,988
Soubeiran, E. Fabrication des Eaux minérales artificielles. Paris, 1840. 8°. N,252,28
Soul, The; a Positive Entity. E. O. Haven. Philadelphia, 1871. 8°. . P,284
Diet of. R. Dexter. London, 1597. 16°. . . . . . . . P,6
Feminine. E. Strutt. Boston, 1870. 18°. . . . . . . O,373
in Nature. H. C. Oersted. London, 1852. 12°. . . . . . L,309
its Natural History. F. W. Newman. London, 1868. 12°. . . P,212
Power of, over the Body. G. Moore. New York, 1852. 16°. . O,679
Questions of. I. T. Hecker. New York, 1856. 12°. . . . P,248
Seelenleben des Menschen. J. Schaller. Weimar, 1860. 8°. . . G,569
Soulé, F. and others. Annals of San Francisco. New York, 1855. 8°. . C,247
Sound. D. Lardner. Philadelphia, 1854. 12°. . . . . . . . N,79,1
and its Phenomena. E. C. Brewer. London, 1863. 18°. . . N,17
Eight Lectures on. J. Tyndall. London, 1867. 8°. . . . . N,18

Sound, Elementary Treatise on. B. Peirce. Boston, 1836. 8°. . . . N,15
Soundings from the Atlantic. O. W. Holmes. Boston, 1866. 12°. . . H,49
South, R. Sermons. New York, 1856. 4 v. 8°. . . . . . . P,715
South, The, and the North. J. S. C. Abbott. New York, 1860. 12°. . . V,90
Impending Crisis of. H. R. Helper. New York, 1857. 12°. . . B,878
Compendium of. H. R. Helper. New York, 1860. 12°. . B,901
Tour in, after the War. W. Reid. Cincinnati, 1866. 12°. . . V,148
South America, History of. J. M. Niles. Hartford, 1844. 12°. . . C,368
Journeys across the Pampas. F. B. Head. London, 1846. 12°. . V,250
Reisen durch Südamerika. J. J. von Tschudi. Leipzig, 1866–8. 4 v. 8°. E,178
Thousand Miles' Walk across. N. P. Bishop. Boston, 1870. 16°. J,1610
Twenty Years' Residence in. W. B. Stevenson. London, 1825. 3 v. 8°. V,206
Voyage to. J. Juan y Santacilia and A. de Ulloa. Lond. 1806. 2 v. 8°. V,253
Wandering Sketches in. W. M. Wood. Philadelphia, 1849. 12°. V,241
Wanderings in. C. Waterton. London, 1836. 16°. . . . . V,230
Wild Scenes in. R. Paez. New York, 1863. 12°. . . . . . V,233
South Carolina, Description of the Province, 1731. See *Force's Tracts*, v. 2.
Historical Collections of. B. R. Carroll. New York, 1836. 2 v. 8°. C,196
History of. W. G. Simms. New York, 1860. 12°. . . . . C,195
Proceedings of the People, 1719. Lond. 1726. See *Force's Tracts*, v. 2.
Sovereign Rule of. F. C. Adams. Washington, 1853. 12°. . . K,1
South Danvers, Mass., Catalogue of Peabody Inst. Library. Bost. 1855. 8°. L.R.
South Sea, Four Voyages to the. B. Morrell, jr. New York, 1841. 8°. . V,1098
Observations in, 1593. Sir R. Hawkins. London, 1847. 8°. . . V,995
Voyage to. Sir J. Narbrough. London, 1711. 8°. . . . . . V,961
South-Sea Bubble. W. H. Ainsworth. Leipzig, 1868. 2 v. in 1. 16°. . J,21
South-Sea Scheme; Mississippi Bubble. L. A. Thiers. New York, 1859. 12°. D,154
Southennan. J. Galt. London, 1830. 3 v. 12°. . . . . . . K,523
Southern Generals. New York, 1865. 8°. . . . . . . . . . C,1087
Southern History of the War. E. A. Pollard. New York, 1863–65. 3 v. 8°. B,934
Southern Speaker. D. B. Ross. Philadelphia, 1869. 12°. . . . . O,1246
Southern States, Three Months in. Col. Fremantle. New York, 1864. 12°. C,159
South-Western History, Romantic Passages in. A. B. Meek. N. Y. 1857. 12°. C,147
South-Western Industrial Fair, 1852. New Orleans, 1852. 8°. . . . B,809,1
Southey, C. B. Chapters on Churchyards. Edinburgh, 1829. 2 v. 16°. . H,585
Southey, R. Chronicle of the Cid. Lowell, 1846. 8°. . . . . . B,478
Common-Place Book. New York, 1855. 2 v. 8°. . . . . . H,628
Joan of Arc, and other Poems. London, 1857. 16°. . . . . I,429
Life and Correspondence; edited by his Son. New York, 1851. 8°. D,115
Life of Horatio *Lord* Nelson. London, 1813. 2 v. 16°. . . C,1164
The same. London, 1868. p. 8°. . . . . . . . . L,147
The same. New York, 1862. 16°. . . . . . . . . L,338
The same. London, 1830. 16°. . . . . . . . . I,632
Life of John Wesley. New York, 1847. 2 v. 12°. . . . . C,1251
The same. London, 1864. p. 8°. . . . . . . . . L,245
Lives of the British Admirals. London, 1833–40. 5 v. 12°. M,1009
Love Story; from "The Doctor." London, 1865. p. 8°. . . I,664,2
Poetical Works; with Life. Boston, 1860. 10 v. 16°. . . . . I,228

Vol. 1. Life, by H. T. Tuckerman; Joan of Arc; Vision of the Maid of Orleans.
2. The Triumph of Woman; Wat Tyler; Poems concerning the Slave-Trade; Botany Bay Eclogues; Sonnets; Monodramas; Amatory Poems of Abel

Southey, R. Poetical Works; with Life. *Continued.* . . . . . . I,228
Shufflebottom; Lyric Poems; Songs of the American Indians; Occasional Pieces; The Retrospect; Hymn to the Penates.
3. English Eclogues; Nondescripts; Devil's Walk; Inscriptions; Carmen Triumphale, for 1814; Odes; Epistles to Allan Cunningham; Op eene Verzameling van mijne Afbeeldingen.
4. Thalaba the Destroyer.
5. Madoc.
6. Ballads and Metrical Tales.
7. Tale of Paraguay; All for Love; Pilgrim to Compostella.
8. Curse of Kehama.
9. Roderick, the last of the Goths.
10. Poet's Pilgrimage to Waterloo; Lay of the Laureate; Funeral Song for the Princess Charlotte of Wales; Vision of Judgment; Oliver Newman; Miscellaneous Poems.

Reminiscences of. J. Cottle. New York, 1847. 12°. . . . . C,1248
Southgate, H. Tour thro' Armenia, Persia, Mesopotamia, etc. N.Y.'40. 2v. 12°. V,646
Southward Ho! W. G. Simms. New York, 1865. 12°. . . . . . K,259
Southwell, R. Poetical Works. London, 1856. 16°. . . . . . I,430
Southworth, E. D. E. N. Allworth Abbey. Philadelphia, 1870. 12°. . K,412
Bridal Eve. Philadelphia, 1870. 12°. . . . . . . . K,413
Bride of Llewellyn. Philadelphia, 1870. 12°. . . . . K,415
Bride's Fate. Philadelphia, 1870. 12°. . . . . . . . K,414
Changed Brides. Philadelphia, 1870. 12°. . . . . . . K,416
Christmas Guest. Philadelphia, 1870. 12°. . . . . . . K,417
Cruel as the Grave. Philadelphia, 1871. 12°. . . . . . K,411
Curse of Clifton. Philadelphia, 1870. 12°. . . . . . . K,418
Deserted Wife. Philadelphia 1870. 12°. . . . . . . K,419
Discarded Daughter. Philadelphia, 1870. 12°. . . . . . K,420
Fair Play. Philadelphia, 1870. 12°. . . . . . . . K,423
Fallen Pride. Philadelphia, 1870. 12°. . . . . . . . K,421
Family Doom. Philadelphia, 1870. 12°. . . . . . . K,422
Fatal Marriage. Philadelphia, 1870. 12°. . . . . . . K,424
Fortune Seeker. Philadelphia, 1870. 12°. . . . . . . K,425
Gipsy's Prophecy. Philadelphia, 1870. 12°. . . . . . . K,426
Haunted Homestead. Philadelphia, 1870. 12°. . . . . . K,427
How he won her. Philadelphia, 1870. 12°. . . . . . . K,428
India; the Pearl of Pearl River. Philadelphia, 1870. 12°. . . K,429
Lady of the Isle. Philadelphia, 1870. 12°. . . . . . . K,430
Lost Heiress. Philadelphia, 1870. 12°. . . . . . . . K,431
Love's Labor Won. Philadelphia, 1870. 12°. . . . . . . K,432
Maiden Widow. Philadelphia, 1870. 12°. . . . . . . K,433
Missing Bride. Philadelphia, 1870. 12°. . . . . . . K,434
Mother-in-Law. Philadelphia, 1870. 12°. . . . . . . K,435
Prince of Darkness. Philadelphia, 1870. 12°. . . . . . K,436
Retribution. Philadelphia, 1870. 12°. . . . . . . . K,437
Three Beauties. Philadelphia, 1870. 12°. . . . . . . K,439
Tried for her Life. Philadelphia, 1871. 12°. . . . . . K,397
Two Sisters. Philadelphia, 1870. 12°. . . . . . . . K,438
Vivia; or, the Secret of Power. Philadelphia, 1870. 12°. . . K,440
Widow's Son. Philadelphia, 1870. 12°. . . . . . . . K,441
Wife's Victory. Philadelphia, 1870. 12°. . . . . . . K,442
Souvestre, E. Attic Philosopher in Paris. New York, 1868. 12°. . . H,906
The same. London, 1865. p. 8°. . . . . . . . I,664,1
Brittany and La Vendée. New York, 1857. 12°. . . . . . H,950

Souvestre, E. Confessions d'un Ouvrier. Bruxelles, 1852. 16°. . H,1037
Confessions of a Workingman. London, 1865. p. 8°. . . I,664,1
Leaves from a Family Journal. New York, 1855. 12°. . . H,968
Sowerby, G. B., jr. Conchological Manual. London, 1852. 8°. . . O,65
Popular British Conchology. London, 1854. 16°. . . . . O,7
Popular History of the Aquarium. London, 1857. 16°. . . . N,477
Sowerby, H. Popular Mineralogy. London, 1850. 16°. . . . . N,755
Sowerby, J. British Mineralogy. London, 1804–17. 5 v. 8°. . . . N,860
Sowers not Reapers. H. Martineau. Cincinnati, 1853. 18°. . . J,1455
Sowing and Reaping. M. Howitt. New York, 1867. 24°. . . J,1160
Soyer, A. Culinary Campaign to the Crimea. London, 1857. 12°. . . B,89
Gastronomic Regenerator; System of Cookery. London, 1861. 8°. H,320
Memoirs of. F. Volant and J. R. Warren. London, 1859. 16°. . D,654
Modern Housewife; or, Ménagère. London, 1861. 12°. . . . H,319
Pantropheon; or, History of Food. London, 1853. 8°. . . . H,321
Sozomenus, H. Ecclesiastical History, A. D. 324 to 440. London, 1855. p. 8°. L,32
Spain. H. D. Inglis. London, 1837. 2 v. 12°. . . . . . . V,465
Ancient Poetry and Romances of. J. Bowring. Lond. 1824. 12°. I,161
and France, Travels in, 1787–89. A. Young. Dublin, 1793. 2 v. 8°. V,458
and Morocco, Travels in. D. Urquhart. New York, 1850. 2 v. 12°. V,472
and Portugal. W. Beckford. London, 1834. 12°. . . . . . V,516
Ambassade en, 1808–11. L. P. Junot. Brux. 1838. 2 v. 16°. H,1031
Geschichte von. J. Aschbach. Frank.-a.-M. 1833–37. 2 v. in 1. 8°. E,93
History of. S. A. Dunham. London, 1832. 5 v. 12°. . M,991
The same. New York, 1854. 5 v. 16°. . . . B,452
Visit to. H. C. Andersen. New York, 1870. 12°. . . V,464
Zwei Jahren in. M. Willkomm. Dresden, 1847. 3 v. 12°. E,195
Annals of the Queens of. A. George. New York, 1850. 2 v. 12°. D,700
Attaché in Madrid. Mad. Calderon de la Barca. N. Y. 1858. 12°. V,468
Bible in. G. Borrow. Philadelphia, 1843. 8°. . . . . . V,476
Dominion of the Arabs in. J. A. Condé. London, 1854. 3 v. p. 8°. L,174
Geschichte der Ommaijaden in. J. Aschbach. Frankfurt-am-Main, 1829–30. 2 v. in 1. 8°. . . . . . . . . . E,95
Geschichte von Spanien. F. W. Lembke and H. Schäfer. Hamburg, 1831–61. 3 v. 8°. . . . . . . . . . . E,92
Gypsies of. G. Borrow. London, 1861. 12°. . . . . . . D,705
Hand-Book for Travelers in. R. Ford. London, 1869. 2 v. 12°. V,469
Hist. Naturelle, et Richesse Minérale de. M.F.LePlay. Par.1834. 8°. N,252,35
History of Ferdinand and Isabella. W.H.Prescott. N.Y.1853. 3 v. 8°. B,477
Institutions and Public Men of. S. T. Wallis. Boston, 1853. 12°. V,466
Lands of the Saracen. B. Taylor. New York, 1866. 12°. . V,1051
Life in. W. Thornbury. New York, 1860. 12°. . . . . V,471
Naturalists' Impressions of. P. L. Sclater. London, 1862. 8°. V,1086,2
Reise durch Spanien. H. F. Link. Kiel, 1801–4. 3 v. in 2. 12°. E,199
Reise Erinnerungen aus. E. A. Rossmässler. Leip. 1854. 2 v. in 1. 12°. E,194
Sketches in. A. de Capell Brooke. London, 1831. 2 v. 8°. . V,475
Spanien und die Spanier. E. von Cuendias. Brüssel, 1851. 8°. . E,203
under Charles II. A. Stanhope. London, 1840. 8°. . . . B,479
Visit to, at the Time of the Eclipse. F. Galton. London, 1861. 8°. V,1086,1
War in the Peninsula. Sir W. F. P Napier. N. Y. 1853. 8°. . A,562

Spain, War in the Peninsula. Sir W. F. P. Napier. N. Y. n. d. 5 v. 8°. B,96
Spalding Club Publications. Aberdeen and Edinburgh, 1840-69. 37 v. 4°. F,8

1-3. Gordon, J. History of Scott's Affairs, 1637-41. 3 v.
4-8. Miscellany of the Club. 5 v.
9. Gordon, J. History of both Touns of Aberdeene.
10. Presbytery Book of Strathbogie, 1631-54.
11. Keith, J. Memoir of, 1714-34.
12-15. Shires of Aberdeen and Banff. 5 v.
16. Gordon, P. Britane's Distemper.
17. Blakhal, G. Breiffe Narration.
18, 19. Aberdeen Burgh Records. 2 v.
20, 21. Registrum Episcopatus Aberdonensis. 2 v.
22. Aberdeen, Records of Kirk Session, etc.
23. Genealogy of Family of Rose of Kilravock.
24, 25. Spalding, J. Trubles in Scotland and England, 1624-45. 2 v.
26. Letters to Earl of Aberdeen, 1681-84.
27. Innes, T. Civil and Ecclesiastical History of Scotland, 80-818.
28. Fasti Aberdonenses, 1494-1814.
29, 30. Sculptured Stones of Scotland. 2 v.
31. Brus, The; Collection of Cambridge and Edinburgh MSS.
32. Book of the Thanes of Cawdor, 1236-1742.
33. Gordon, P. Diary of 1635-99.
34. Brodie, A. Diary of 1680-85.
35. Forbes, D. Familie of Innes.
36. Stuart, J. The Book of Deer.

Spalding, J. W. Japan and around the World. New York, 1855. 12°. V,1065
Spalding, W. History of English Literature. New York, 1868. 12°. . H,683
Italy and the Italian Islands. New York, n. d. 3 v. 18°. . . L,440
Spanisches Liederbuch. E. Geibel und P. Heyse. Berlin, 1852. 24°. . E,265
Spanish-Americans, Four Years among. F. Hassaurek. N. Y. 1867. 8°. V,237
Spanish and English Dictionary. G. Baretti and H. Neuman. N. Y. 1852. 8°. R.R.
H. Neuman, Baretti, and Seoane. London, n. d. 2 v. 8°. . L.R.
M. Velasquez de la Cadena. New York, 1852. 8°. . . R.R.
and Portugese Literature. F. Bouterwek. London, 1823. 2 v. 8°. H,766
Spanish Barber, The. A. Manning. London, 1869. 12°. . . . . . J,597
Spanish Brothers; a Tale. London, 1871. 12°. . . . . . . K,618
Spanish Conquest in America. A. Helps. New York, 1856-68. 4 v. 12°. C,369
Spanish Gipsy; a Poem. M. J. Lewes. Boston, 1868. 16°. . . . I,358
Spanish History, Romance of. J. S. C. Abbott. New York, 1869. 12°. . B,453
Spanish Letters. A. de Guevara. London, 1657. 12°. . . . . H,905
Spanish Literature, History of. F. Bouterwek. London, 1847. 12°. . H,763
History of. G. Ticknor. New York, 1849. 3 v. 8°. . . . H,767
Spanish Match. W. H. Ainsworth. Leipzig, 1865. 2 v. in 1. 16°. . J,22
Spanish Papers. W. Irving. New York, 1868-69. 2 v. 16°. . . . U,15
The same. New York, 1866. 2 v. 12°. . . . . . U,33
Spanish State Papers; England and Spain. London, 1862-68. 3 v. 8°. . B,183
Spare Hours. J. Brown. Boston, 1866. 12°. . . . . . . . H,185
Sparing to Spend. T. S. Arthur. Philadelphia, n. d. 16°. . . . J,614
Sparks, J. Life of Ethan Allen. Boston, 1860. 12°. . . . C,860,1
Life of Benedict Arnold. Boston, 1860. 12°. . . . . . C,860,3
Life of Benjamin Franklin. Boston, 1844. 8°. . . . . C,791
Life of Robert *Sieur* de La Salle. Boston, 1860. 12°. . . . C,860,11
Life of John Ledyard. Boston, 1860. 12°. . . . . . C,860,24
Life of Charles Lee. Boston, 1864. 12°. . . . . . . C,860,18
Life of *Pere* Jacques Marquette. Boston, 1860. 12°. . . . C,860,10
Life of Governeur Morris. Boston, 1832. 3 v. 8°. . . . C,818
Life of *Count* K. Pulaski. Boston, 1860. 12°. . . . . C,860,14
Life of John Ribault. Boston, 1860. 12°. . . . . . C,860,17
Life of George Washington. New York, 1855. 12°. . . . C,904

Sparks, J. List of Books on American History. Boston, 1855. 8°. . . A,321
(Ed.) Correspondence of American Revolution. Bost. 1853. 4 v. 8°. B,749
The same. Boston, 1853. 4 v. 8°. . . . . . S.C.
(Ed.) Diplomatic Corresp. of Am. Revolution. Bost. 1829–30. 12 v. 8°. B,678
(Ed.) Library of American Biography. Boston, 1860. 25 v. 12°. . C,860

Vol. 1. Stark, J., by E. Everett.
Brown, C. B., by W. H. Prescott.
Montgomery, R., by J. Armstrong.
Allen, E., by J. Sparks.
2. Wilson, A., by W. B. O. Peabody.
Smith, Capt. J., by G. S. Hillard.
3. Arnold, B., by J. Sparks.
4. Wayne, A., by J. Armstrong.
Vane, Sir H., by C. W. Upham.
5. Eliot, J., by C. Francis.
6. Pinkney, W., by H. Wheaton.
Ellery, W., by E. T. Channing.
Mather, C., by W. B. O. Peabody.
7. Phips, Sir W., by F. Bowen.
Putnam, I., by O. W. B. Peabody.
Davidson, L. M., by C. M. Sedgwick.
Rittenhouse, D., by J. Renwick.
8. Edwards, J., by S. Miller.
Brainerd, D., by W. B. O. Peabody.
9. Steuben, Baron, by F. Bowen.
Cabot, S., by C. Hayward, jr.
Eaton, W., by C. C. Felton.
10. Fulton, R., by J. Renwick.
Hudson, H., by H. R. Cleveland.
Warren, J., by A. H. Everett.
Marquette, by J. Sparks.
11. Salle, R. de la, by J. Sparks.
Henry, P., by A. H. Everett.
12. Otis, J., by F. Bowen.
Oglethorpe, J., by W. B. O. Peabody.
Vol. 13. Sullivan, J., by O. W. B. Peabody.
Leisler, J., by C. F. Hoffman.
Bacon, N., by W. Ware.
Mason, J., by G. E. Ellis.
14. Williams, R., by W. Gammell.
Dwight, T., by W. B. Sprague.
Pulaski, Count, by J. Sparks.
15. Rumford, Count, by J. Renwick.
Pike, Z. M., by H. Whiting.
Gorton, S., by J. M. Mackie.
16. Stiles, E., by J. L. Kingsley.
Fitch, J., by C. Whittlesey.
Hutchinson, A., by G. E. Ellis.
17. Ribault, J., by J. Sparks.
Rale, S., by C. Francis.
Palfrey, W., by J. G. Palfrey.
18. Lee, C., by J. Sparks.
Reed, J., by H. Reed.
19. Calvert, L., by G. W. Burnap.
Ward, S., by W. Gammell.
Posey, T., by J. Hall.
20. Greene, N., by G. W. Greene.
21. Decatur, S., by A. S. Mackenzie.
22. Preble, E., by L. Sabine.
Penn, W., by G. E. Ellis.
23. Boone, D., by J. M. Peck.
Lincoln, B., by F. Bowen.
24. Ledyard, J., by J. Sparks.
25. Davie, W. R., by F. M. Hubbard.
Kirkland, S., by S. K. Lothrop.

The same. Boston, 1837. 12 v. 8° . . . . . . . . S.C.
(Ed.) Life and Writings of George Washington. Bost. 1847. 12 v. 8°. U,64

Vol. 1. Life, by J. Sparks.
2. Official Letters relating to the French War, and Private Letters before the American Revolution.
3–8. Correspondence and Miscellaneous Papers relating to American Revolution.
9. Correspondence from his Resignation as Commander-in-Chief to his Inauguration as President.
10, 11. Correspondence from the beginning of his Presidency to the end of his Life.
12. Speeches and Messages to Congress; Proclamations and Address.

(Ed.) Life and Works of Benj. Franklin. Boston, 1840. 10 v. 8°. U,104

Vol. 1. Autobiography; Life continued, by Sparks.
2. Essays on Religious and Moral Subjects, and the Economy of Life; Essays on Politics, Commerce, and Political Economy.
3. Essays and Tracts, Historical and Political, before the American Revolution; Constitution and Government of Pennsylvania.
4. Essays and Tracts, continued.
5. Political Papers during and after the American Revolution; Letters and Papers on Electricity.
6. Letters and Papers on Philosophical Subjects.
7. Correspondence: Part 1, Private Letters to the time of the Author's First Mission to England, 1725–57. Part 2, Letters, Private and Official, from the time of the Author's First Mission to England to the Revolution, 1757–75.
8. Correspondence: Part 2, continued, 1757–75. Part 3, Letters, Private and Official, from the beginning of the Revolution to end of the Author's Mission to France, 1775–85; Appendix; Fragment of Polybius on the Athenian Government; Memoir of Sir John Dalrymple.
9. Correspondence: Part 3, continued; Journal of the Negotiation of the Treaty of Peace.
10. Correspondence: Part, 3, continued. Part 4, Private Letters, from the termination of the Author's Mission to France to the end of his Life, 1785–90; Supplement; Indexes; Chronological List of the Author's Writings.

Sparks from the Anvil. E. Burritt. London, n. d. 12°. . . . . . H,133
Sparrowgrass Papers. F. S. Cozzens. New York, 1870. 12°. . . . H,66
Speaker, American Union. J. D. Philbrick. Boston, 1869. 12°. . O,1243
Model. P. Lawrence. Philadelphia, 1871. 12°. . . . O,1227
National Orator. C. Northend. New York, 1859. 12°. . . O,1229

Speaker, New Eclectic. W. H. McGuffey. Cincinnati, n. d. 12°. . o,1228
Practical Elocutionist. J. W. S. Hows. Philadelphia, n. d. 12°. o,1225
Progressive, and Common-School Reader. S. Towne. Bost. n. d. 12°. o,1247
Southern. D. B. Ross. Philadelphia, 1869. 12°. . . . o,1246
Student's Own. P. Reeves. New York, 1871. 12°. . . o,1245
Universal. N. A. Calkins and W. T. Adams. Boston, 1861. 12°. o,1223
Speakers of the House of Commons. J. A. Manning. London, 1850. 8°. c,1309
Species, Entstehung der Arten. C. Darwin. Stuttgart, 1863. 8°. . . G,813
Genesis of. St. G. Mivart. New York, 1871. 12°. . . . . N,403
Origin of. C. Darwin. New York, 1860. 12°. . . . . N,495
T. H. Huxley. New York, 1863. 12°. . . . . . . N,499
Variation of. T. V. Wollaston. London, 1856. 12°. . . . N,506
Spectator. J. Addison and Sir R. Steele. Cincinnati, 1851. 2 v. 8°. . H,459
The same. Boston, 1866. 8 v. 8°. . . . . . c,536,5–12
Selections from. New York, 1859. 2 v. 16°. . . . . . L,463
The same. London, 1849. 2 v. 12°. . . . . . H,530
Spectrum Analysis; Six Lectures. H. E. Roscoe. New York, 1869. 8°. N,209
Spectrum, Researches on the Solar. G. Kirchoff. Cambridge, 1863. 4°. . N,146
Speculum Naturale. Vicentius Bellovacensis. Argentinæ, 1469. 2 v. f°. *Q,355
Speight, T. Brought to Light. New York, 1867. 8°. . . . K,1017
Speke, J. H. Discovery of the Source of the Nile. New York, 1864. 8°. V,851
Speller, Common-School. W. B. Fowle. Boston, 1855. 16°. . . . o,764
Spelling, Exercises in False. W. Pinnock. London, n. d. 24°. . . o,760
Spelling-Book. A. H. McGuffey. Cincinnati, 1846. 12°. . . . . o,765
W. D. Swan. Philadelphia, 1849. 12°. . . . . . o,791
New. L. Cobb. Cincinnati, 1849. 12°. . . . . . . o,771
Universal. D. Fenning. London, n. d. 16°. . . . . . o,778
Spence, J. Anecdotes of Books and Men. London, 1858. 16°. . . H,575
Spence, W. and Kirby, W. Introd. to Entomology. Lond. 1815–26. 4 v. 8°. o,32
The same. London, 1856. 8°. . . . . . . . o,29
The same. Philadelphia, 1846. 8°. . . . . . . o,49
Spencer, C. C. Pianoforte Instruction-Book. London, 1851. 12°. . . M,961
Treatise on Music. London, 1858. 2 v. in 1. . . . . . M,960
Spencer, E. Fall of the Crimea. London, 1854. 12°. . . . . B,79
State of Ireland in the Year 1596. Dublin, 1809. 2 v. 4°. . . A,565
The same. Dublin, 1809. 4°. . . . . . . . B,182,1
Spencer, H. Classification of the Sciences. New York, 1865. 8°. . . o,667
Education, Intellectual, Moral, Physical. New York, 1866. 12°. . o,953
Essays, Moral, Political, and Æsthetic. New York, 1865. 12°. . o,655
First Principles of Philosophy. New York, 1865. 12°. . . . o,656
Illustrations of Universal Progress. New York, 1865. 12°. . . o,533
Principles of Biology. New York, 1866–67. 2 v. 12°. . . . o,657
Railway Morals and Policy. London, 1865. p. 8°. . . . . . I,667
Social Statics; conditions essential to Happiness. N. Y. 1865. 12°. o,532
Spencer, J. A. History of the United States. New York, 1866. 4 v. 8°. B,677
Spencer, O. M., Narrative of his Capture by the Indians. New York, n. d. 16°. B,590
Spendthrift, The; a Tale. W. H. Ainsworth. Leipzig, 1856. 16°. . . J,23
Spenser, E., Essay on the Life and Writings of. J. S. Hart. N. Y. 1847. 8°. H,708
Faerie Queene. London, 1856. 16°. . . . . . . . I,432

Spenser, E. Poetical Works; with Life. Boston, 1855. 5 v. 16°. . . . I,229
Vol. 1. Life; Faerie Queene.
2-4. Faerie Queene; Miscellaneous Poems.
5. Miscellaneous Poems.
The same; with Life and Notes. Philadelphia, 1857. 5 v. 12°. I,431
Contents, *same as preceding.*
Spermatorrhœa. R. Bartholow. New York, 1866. 12°. . . . . . L,908
Sphinx, Die. L. Schücking. Leipzig, 1856. 12°. . . . . . . G,450
Spiders, British. E. F. Stavely. . . . . . . . . . . . . O,24
of Great Britain and Ireland. J. Blackwall. Lond. 1861. 2 pts. 4°. Q,75
Spielhagen, F. Auf der Düne. Berlin, 1866. 16°. . . . . . . . G,451
Clara Vere. Berlin, 1866. 16°. . . . . . . . . . G,452
Hammer and Anvil. New York, 1870. 12°. . . . . . . G,217
Die von Hohenstein. Berlin, 1867. 3 v. 16°. . . . . . G,467
The same; translated. New York, 1870. 12°. . . . G,222
Durch Nacht zum Licht. Berlin, 1867. 2 v. 16°. . . . . . G,453
In der zwölften Stunde. Berlin, 1866. 16°. . . . . . . G,454
In Reich und Glied. Berlin, 1868. 6 v. 16°. . . . . . . G,464
Problematic Characters. New York, 1869. 12°. . . . . G,218
Problematische Naturen. Berlin, 1866. 3 v. 16°. . . . . . G,465
Röschen vom Hofe. Berlin, 1866. 16°. . . . . . . . G,466
Through Night to Light. New York, 1870. 12°. . . . . G,219
Spiers, A. Commercial Terms in English and French. Phila. 1847. 12°. L.R.
and Surenne, G. French and English Dictionary. N. Y. 1870. 8°. L.R.
The same. New York, 1854. 8°. . . . . . . . R.R.
Spindler, C. Fridolin Schwertberger. Stuttgart, 1844-45. 4 v. 24°. . G,468
Der Invalide. Stuttgart, 1831. 5 v. 16°. . . . . . . . G,469
Der König von Zion. Stuttgart, 1854. 3 v. 24°. . . . . G,470
Der Vogelhändler von Imst. Stuttgart, 1841-42. 4 v. 24°. . . G,471
Spinoza, B. Opera Omnia. Jenae, 1802-3. 2 v. 8°. . . . . . P,722
Spinoza; ein Denkerleben. B. Auerbach. Stuttgart, 1864. 2 v. 12°. E,311,10,11
Spirit of the Age. W. Hazlitt. Philadelphia, 1854. 8°. . . . . . H,426
Spirit History of Man. S. F. Dunlap. New York, 1858. 8°. . . . P,259
Spirit Manifestations examined and explained. J. B. Dods. N. Y. 1854. 12°. P,913
Spiritual Quixote. R. Graves. London, 1820. 2 v. 12°. . . . . . K,542
Spiritual Treasury for the Children of God. W. Mason. N. Y. n. d. 12°. P,193
Spiritual Wives. W. H. Dixon. Leipzig, 1868. 2 v. in 1. 16°. . . J,152
Spiritualism. J. W. Edmonds and G. T. Dexter. v. 1. New York, 1853. 8°. P,873
Incidents in my Life. D. D. Home. New York, 1863. 12°. . . D,29
Physics and Physiology of. W. A. Hammond. New York, 1871. 12°. O,340
Planchette; or, the Despair of Science. E. Sargent. Bost. 1869. 12°. O,327
Science *vs.* Modern. A. E. de Gasparin. New York, 1857. 2 v. 12°. P,871
Strange Visitors; Papers by eminent Spirits. New York, 1869. 12°. O,330
Spitzbergen and Greenland, Documents on. London, 1855. 8°. . . . V,984
Yacht Voyage to. F. P. Blackwood. Boston, 1859. 12°. . . V,322
Voyage to. F. Marten. London, 1855. 8°. . . . . . . V,984
Spix, J. B. von, and Martius, C. F. P. Reise in Brasilien, 1817-20. München, 1823-31. 3 v. 4°. . . . . . . . . . . . *Q,427
Atlas dazu. 3 portfolios. . . . . . . . . . *Q,471
Spofford, H. E. Amber Gods, and other Stories. Boston, 1869. 12°. . K,246
Azarian; an Episode. Boston, 1864. 12°. . . . . . . K,144

Spohr, L. God, Thou art Great; edited by V. Novello. London, n. d. 8°. M,425
The Last Judgment; edited by V. Novello. London, n. d. 8°. . M,425
Sponges, History of British. G. Johnston. Edinburgh, 1842. 8°. . . O,68
Monograph of the British. J. S. Bowerbank. Lond. 1864-66. 2 v. 8°. O,308
Spon's Dictionary of Engineering; ed. O. Byrne. Lond. 1869-70. 1 v. in 3. 8°. M,731
Spooner, S. Anecdotes of Painters, Engravers, etc. N. Y. 1865. 3 v. 12°. M,52
Spooner, W. C. History and Diseases of the Sheep. London, 1844. 12°. . M,449
Sporting, On the Wing. J. Bumstead. Boston, 1869. 12°. . . . M,319
Shot Gun and Sporting Rifle. J. H. Walsh. London, 1859. 12°. . M,306
Sports and Games, American Boy's Book of. New York, 1864. 12°. . J,1326
National, of Great Britain. H. Alken. London, 1825. f°. . . M,342
of England. J. Strutt. London, 1855. 8°. . . . . . . M,314
of the World, Wild. J. Greenwood. London, 1864. 8°. . . N,636
Oriental Field. T. Williamson. London, 1819. 2 v. 4°. . . *Q,329
Sportsman, American. E. J. Lewis. Philadelphia, 1868. 8°. . . . M,317
Spottiswoode, G. A. Tour in Croatia and Hungary. London, 1861. 8°. V,1086,1
Sprague, C. Poetical and Prose Writings. Boston, 1850. 16°. . . . U,92
Sprague, J. T. History of the Florida War. New York, 1848. 8°. . . B,872
Sprague, W. B. Annals of the American Pulpit. N. Y. 1859-69. 9 v. 8°. C,1122

Vol. 1, 2 Trinitarian Congregational.
3, 4. Presbyterian.
5. Episcopalian.
6. Baptist.
Vol. 7. Methodist.
8. Unitarian.
9. Lutheran.

Excellent Woman as described in Proverbs. Boston, 1852. 12°. J,1281
Life of Timothy Dwight. Boston, 1860. 12°. . . . . . C,860,14
Visits to European Celebrities. Boston, 1855. 12°. . . . . C,520
Spread-Eagleism. G. F. Train. New York, 1859. 12°. . . . . H,36
Sprengel, C. Bodenkunde. Leipzig, 1844. 8°. . . . . . . . G,660
Lehre von den Urbarmachungen. Leipzig, 1846. 8°. . . . G,661
Spring, G. Fragments from the Study of a Pastor, v. 1. N. Y. 1838. 12°. H,189
Personal Reminiscences of. New York, 1866. 2 v. 12°. . . . C,764
Spring Comedies. Lady Barker. London, 1871. 12°. . . . K,1163
Spring Grove Cemetery, Report for 1857. Cincinnati, 1857. 8°. . . C,228
its History, Improvements, etc. Cincinnati, 1869. 4°. . . . *F,42
Sproat, A. D. Endeavor towards a Universal Alphabet. Chill. 1857. 8°. H,302,1
Spurgeon, C. H. Feathers for Arrows. New York, n. d. 16°. . . . P,70
Sermons. New York, 1857-69. 8 v. 12°. . . . . . . P,195
(Ed.) Smooth Stones from Ancient Brooks. New York, 1860. 12°. P,25
Spurzheim, J. G. Education. New York, 1854. 12°. . . . . . O,972
Elementary Principles of Education. London, 1828. 8°. . O,1242
Spy, The. J. F. Cooper. New York, 1867. 12°. . . . . . . K,50
The same. New York, 1859. 8°. . . . . . . . . K,80
Squibob Papers. G. H. Derby. New York, 1865. 12°. . . . . . H,69
Squier, E. G. Aboriginal Monuments of Mississippi Valley. N. Y. 1847. 8°. B,604
Antiquities of the State of New York. Buffalo, 1851. 8°. . . C,91
Monograph of Authors on Central America. Albany, 1861. 4°. . F,63
Nicaragua; its People, Scenery, etc. New York, 1860. 8°. . . V,203
Rare Documents concerning America. Albany, 1860. 4°. . . F,62
Serpent Symbol and Worship of Nature. New York, 1851. 8°. . B,607
Staaten von Central-Amerika. Leipzig, 1865. 8°. . . . . E,171
States of Central America. New York, 1858. 8°. . . . . V,202

Squier, E. G. and Davis, E. H. Ancient Monuments of the Mississippi Valley. Washington, 1847. 4°. . . . . . . . . Q,324,1
Squire Trevlyn's Heir. Mrs. H. Wood. Philadelphia, 1863. 8°. . K,1067
Staal, M. J. C. de L. *Baroness* de. Mémoires. Paris, 1853. 12°. . . D,610
Stable Book; Management of Horses. J. Stewart. New York, 1864. 12°. M,459
Stadt Geheimniss, Das. F. W. Hackländer. Stuttgart, 1868. 3 v. 16°. . G,306
Staël-Holstein, Madame de. De l'Allemagne. Paris, 1813. 3 v. 8°. . V,422
The same. Paris, 1856. 12°. . . . . . . . . . H,880
Ancient and Modern Literature. London, 1803. 2 v. 8°. . . H,643
Considerations sur la Révolution Francaise. Paris, 1818. 3 v. 8°. B,226
Corinne; ou l'Italie. Paris, 1855. 12°. . . . . . . . H,932
Corinne; or, Italy. New York, n. d. 12°. . . . . . H,921
Delphine. Paris, 1856. 12°. . . . . . . . . . . H,922
Frau von Staël; Biographischer Roman. A. Bölte. Wien, 1861. 3 v. 24°. G,262
Germany. New York, 1859. 2 v. 12°. . . . . . . . V,419
Memoirs of. L. M. Child. New York, 1854. 16°. . . . . . D,652
Stafford, W. C. History of Music. Edinburgh, 1830. 16°. . . . I,524
Stage, English, Annals of. J. Doran. New York, 1865. 2 v. 12°. . I,718
English, Some Account of, 1660–1830. Bath, 1832. 10 v. 8°. . I,716
Personal Recollections of. W. W. Wood. Philadelphia, 1855. 12°. I,724
Record of the Boston. W. W. Clapp. Boston, 1853. 12°. . . I,714
Stage-Plays, Defence of. T. Lodge. London, 1853. 8°. . . . . I,885,49
Stahr, A. Life and Works of Gotthold Ephraim Lessing. Bost. 1866. 2 v. 12°. D,522
Standard First Reader. E. Sargent. Boston, 1856. 12°. . . . . O,773
Standard Library Cyclopædia. London, 1849–53. 4 v. p. 8°. . . . *L,248
Standard Speaker. E. Sargent. Philadelphia, 1867. 8°. . . . . O,828
Stang, C. F. G. Martin Luther; sein Leben und Wirken. Stutt. 1839. 8°. E,243
Stanhope, A. Spain under Charles II. London, 1840. 8°. . . . B,479
Stanhope, H. L., *Lady*. Travels. London, 1846. 3 v, 12°. . . V,1066
Stanhope, P. H., *Lord Mahon*. History of England. Boston, 1854. 7 v. 8°. A,401
The same. New York, 1849. 2 v. 8°. . . . . . . . A,411
The same. Leipzig, 1853–54. 7 v. 16°. . . . . . J,465
History of the Reign of Queen Anne. London, 1870. 8°. . . A,433
The same. Leipzig, 1870. 2 v. in 1. 16°. . . . . . J,466
Stanhope, P. D., *Lord Chesterfield*. Letters. London, 1845-53. 5 v. 8°. . H,831
Letters, Sentences, and Maxims. New York, 1870. 16°. . . I,559
and G. Selwyn. A. Hayward. London, 1856. p. 8°. . . . I,661,4
Stanley, A. P. History of the Jewish Church. New York, 1867–68. 2 v. 8°. P,625
Life and Correspondence of Thomas Arnold. London, 1868. 2 v. 8°. D,209
The same. Boston, 1860. 2 v. 12°. . . . . . . D,208
Memorials of Westminster Abbey. London, 1868. 8°. . . . B,60
Sermons during Tour in the East. New York, 1864. 12°. . . P,64
Sinai and Palestine. New York, 1857. 8°. . . . . . . V,664
Stanley, E. Diseases of the Bones. London, 1849. 8°. . . . . L,931
Stanley, E. Familiar History of Birds. London, 1865. 12°. . . . O,100
Stanley, G. Painters of the Dutch and Flemish Schools. London, 1855. p. 8°. L,314
(Ed.) Bryan's Dictionary of Painters and Engravers. Lond. 1853. 8°. M,138
Stansbury, H. Expedition to Great Salt Lake, with Maps. Phil. 1855. 2 v. 8°. V,112
Stanton, H. B. Sketches of Reforms and Reformers. New York, 1849. 12°. C,1287
Stapf, J. A. Spirit and Scope of Education. Edinburgh, 1851. 8°. . O,1172

Stapleton, A. G. George Canning and his Times. London, 1859. . . . D,61
Star and the Cloud. A. S. Roe. New York, 1869. 12°. . . . . . K,272
Star-Chamber, The. W. H. Ainsworth. Leipzig, 1854. 2 v. in 1. 16°. . J,24
Star Papers. H. W. Beecher. New York, 1855. 12°. . . . . . H,231
New. H. W. Beecher. New York, 1859. 12°. . . . . . P,86
Stark, A. Printing; its History, Antecedents, etc. London, 1865. p. 8°. I,667
Stark, J., Life of. E. Everett. Boston, 1860. 12°. . . . . C,860,1
Memoir and Correspondence. C. Stark. Concord, 1860. 8°. . . C,933
Starkey, T. England in reign of Henry VIII., p. 2. . . . . . L,604,12
Starling, E. Noble Deeds of Woman. London, 1864. p. 8°. . . . L,148
Starling, The; a Scotch Story. N. Macleod. London, 1867. 2 v. 12°. . K,923
Starry Flag. W. T. Adams. Boston, 1869. 16°. . . . . . J,1534,1
Stars, The, and the Angels. Philadelphia, 1860. 12°. . . . . N,265
Chemistry of. G. Wilson. London, 1862. p. 8°. . . . . . I,666
Fixsternhimmel. J. H. Mädler. Leipzig, 1858. 12°. . . . G,795
Half-Hours with the. R. A. Proctor. London, 1870. 4°. . . N,388
Origin of. J. Ennis. New York, 1868. 12°. . . . . . . N,327
Reduction of Observations of. B. A. Gould. Washington, 1866. 4°. Q,105
Wunder der Sternenwelt. O. Ule. Leipzig, 1860. 8°. . . . G,800
State of the Union in 1854. Washington, 1855. 8°. . . . . . . B,639
State Trials, Collection of. T. B. and T. J. Howell. Lond. 1816–28. 34 v. 8°. U,701
Statesmen, Eminent British. Sir J. Mackintosh and others. Lon. '31. 7 v. 12°. M,1011
Eminent Foreign. E. E. Crowe. London, 1833. 5 v. 12°. . M,1012
in the Time of George the III. H. Brougham. Phil. 1840. 2 v. 8°. C,556
The same. Philadelphia, 1854. 2 v. 12°. . . . . . C,543
The same. London, 1856. 3 v. 12°. . . . . . . C,540
of the English Commonwealth. J. Forster. New York, 1846. 8°. C,584
Statesman's Year-Book. F. Martin. London, 1869. 12°. . . . . O,486
Statics, Analytical. I. Todhunter. London, 1866. 8°. . . . M,1108
and Dynamics. T. Baker. London, 1851. 12°. . . . . . M,893
Stationers Company, Register of, v. 1, 1557–1570. London, 1848. 8°. . I,885,41
The same, vol. 2, 1570–1587. London, 1849. 8°. . . I,885,42
Statius, P. P. Opera Omnia; ed. N. E. Lemaire. Parisiis, 1825–30. 4 v. 8°. U,348
Thebiad; tr. into English Verse by W. L. Lewis. Lond. 1773. 2 v. 8°. U,456
Staunton, H. Chess-Player's Companion. London, 1849. p. 8°. . . M,327
Chess-Player's Hand-Book. London, 1870. p. 8°. . . . . . L,315
Chess Praxis; supplement to Hand-Book. London, 1860. p. 8°. . L,316
Chess Tournament. London, 1852. p. 8°. . . . . . . L,318
Great Schools of England. London, 1865. 12°. . . . . . O,831
Stavely, E. F. British Spiders. London, 1866. 8°. . . . . . . O,24
Steam, applied to general purposes. J. Sewell. Lond. 1852–53. 2 v. in 1. 12°. M,958
Lessons and Practical Notes on. W. H. King. New York, 1864. 8°. M,700
Spannkraft in Salzlösungen. L. von Babo. Freiburg, 1847. 8°. N,252,33
Steam Boilers. R. Armstrong. London, 1857. 12°. . . . . . M,889
Steam Engine, Catechism of. J. Bourne. New York, 1871. 12°. . . M,685
Chimneys and Furnaces of. R. Armstrong. London, n. d. 8°. N,252,30
Description of Patent Condensing. T. Craddock. Lond. 1847. 8°. N,252,40
Explained. D. Lardner. Glasgow, 1839. 12°. . . . N,252,23
The same. New York, 1854. 8°. . . . . . . . . S.C.
Hand-Book of the. J. Bourne. New York, 1865. 12°. . . . M,618

Steam Engine, Invention and Improvement of, v.1. T.Tredgold. Lon.1838. 4°. *Q,367
Marine. T. J. Main and T. Brown. Philadelphia, 1865. 8°. . M,664
Manual of. W. J. M. Rankine. London, 1859. 8°. . . . M,617
Origin and Improvement of. P. R. Hodge. New York, n. d. f°. . *Q,390
Treatise on. J. Bourne. London, 1868. 4°. . . . . . . *Q,267
J. Renwick. New York, 1839. 8°. . . . . . M,663
Steamboat Disasters and Railroad Accidents. Worcester, 1846. 12°. . H,494
Steamboats, Account of the Origin of. W. Thornton. Washington, 1814. 8°. B,809,1
Stearic Acid, Zusammensetzung der Talgsäure. R. Redtenbacher. n. t. p. N,252,28
Stearns, C. W. Shakespeare's Medical Knowledge. New York, 1865. 12°. . I,841
Stearns, E. J. Guide to English Pronunciation. Boston, 1857. 16°. . L,560
Stebbing, H.. History of Chivalry and the Crusades. Edinb. 1830. 2 v. 16°. I,523
History of the Christian Church. London, 1833-34. 2 v. 12°. M,1003
History of the Church of Christ. London, 1842. 3 v. 8°. . . P,626
History of the Reformation. London, 1836-37. 2 v. 12°. . M,1005
Stedman, C. History of the American War. London, 1794. 2 v. 4°. . B,830
Stedman, E. C. Blameless Prince. Boston, 1869. 16°. . . . . I,144
Poems, Lyrical and Idyllic. New York, 1860. 12°. . . . I,142
Steel, S. H. Sanitary Condition of Abergavenny. Abergavenny, 1847. 8°. N,252,29
Steel, Alloys of. J. Stodart and M. Faraday. London, 1822. 4°. . N,252,42
and Iron Manufacture. F. Kohn. London, 1869. f°. . . . Q,53
Fabrication des Fers à Acier. P. G. F. Le Play. Paris, 1846. 8°. N,252,34
Management of. G. Ede. New York, 1867. 12°. . . . . . M,751
Manufacture of. F. Overman. Philadelphia, 1851-52. 12°. . . M,749
Manufacture of Wrought. W. Clay. London, 1858. 4°. . N,252,51
Metalurgy of. B. Kerl. London, 1870. 8°. . . . . . M,717,3
Steele, A. Chief of the Pilgrims; Life of Wm. Brewster. Phil. 1857. 8°. C,812
Steele, Sir R., Memoirs of. H. R. Montgomery. Edinburgh, 1865. 2 v. 8°. D,216
Steele, S. S. Drawing-Room Plays and Evening Amusements. Phil. 1865. 12°. I,731
Steenstrup, J. J. S. Alternation of Generations of Animals. Lond. 1845. 8°. O,291
Steiermark zur Zeit der Braunkohlenbildung. F. Unger. Wien, 1866. 8°. E,404
Steinmetz, A. History of the Jesuits. London, 1848. 3 v. 8°. . . P,627
Sunshine and Showers. London, 1867. 12°. . . . . . . N,107
Stenhouse, J. Proximate Principles of some of the Lichens. Lond. 1848. 4°. N,252,42
Stenzel, G.A.H. Deutschland unter den Fränkisch. Kaisern. Ber.1828. 2v. 8°. E,55
Geschichte des Preussichen Staats. Hamburg, 1830-54. 5 v. 8°. . E,74
Step-Mother. G. P. R. James. Leipzig, 1845. 2 v. in 1. 16°. . . J,215
Stephanus, R. Thesaurus Linguæ Latinæ. Londini, 1734-35. 4 v. f°. *Q,138
Stephanus, H. Thesaurus Græcæ Linguæ. Londini, 1816-26. 8 v. f°. *U,478
Stephen, King of England. Gesta Stephani, Regis Anglorum. Lond. 1846. 8°. U,631
Stephen, Sir J. Essays in Ecclesiastical Biography. London, 1860. 8°. C,594
Lectures on the History of France. New York, 1852. 8°. . . B,274
Critical and Miscellaneous Essays. Boston, 1857. 8°. . . . H,373
Stephen, L. The Allelein-Horn. London, 1861. 8°. . . . . V,1086,1
Stephen, T. History of the Church of Scotland. London, 1848. 4 v. 8°. P,635
Stephens, A. Memoir of John Horne Tooke. London, 1813. 2 v. 8°. . D,77
Stephens, A. H. Constitutional View of Late War. Phil. 1868-70. 2 v. 8°. B,937
Stephens, A. S. Curse of Gold. Philadelphia, 1870. 12°. . . . K,443
Doubly False. Philadelphia, n. d. 12°. . . . . . . . K,320
Fashion and Famine. Philadelphia, 1870. 12°. . . . . . K,444

Stephens, A. S. Gold Brick. Philadelphia, 1870. 12°. . . . . . K,445
Heiress; an Autobiography. Philadelphia, 1870. 12°. . . . K,446
Mabel's Mistake. Philadelphia, 1870. 12°. . . . . . . K,447
Mary Derwent. Philadelphia, 1870. 12°. . . . . . . K,448
Old Homestead. Philadelphia, 1870. 12°. . . . . . . K,449
Rejected Wife. Philadelphia, 1870. 12°. . . . . . . . K,450
Ruby Gray's Strategy. Philadelphia, 1870. 12°. . . . . . K,451
Silent Struggles. Philadelphia, 1870. 12°. . , . . . K,452
Soldier's Orphans. Philadelphia, n. d. 12°. . . . . . . K,321
Wife's Secret. Philadelphia, 1870. 12°. . . . . . . . K,453
Wives and Widows. Philadelphia, 1870. 12°. . . . . K,454
Stephens, J., Organizer of the Irish Republic. New York, 1866. 12°. . D,378
Stephens, J. F. Illustrations of Brit. Entomology. Lond. 1828–46. 12 v. 8°. *O,70
Vol. 1-7. Mandibulata. Vol. 8-11. Haustellata. Vol. 12. Supplement.
Stephens, J. L. Incidents of Travel in Central America. N. Y. 1853. 2 v. 8°. V,199
Incidents of Travel in Yucatan. New York, 1860. 2 v. 8°. . . V,200
Travels in Egypt, Arabia, and Holy Land. N.Y. 1854. 2 v. in 1. 12°. V,1073
Travels in Greece, Turkey, Russia, and Poland. N. Y. 1855. 2 v. 12°. V,341
Stephenson, G., Life of. S. Smiles. Columbus, 1859. 12°. . . . D,272
Monument to. T. Oliver. Newcastle-upon-Tyne, 1858. 8°. . N,252,46
and R., Lives of. S. Smiles. New York, 1868. 8°. . . . C,1294
Stephenson, R., Life of. J. C. Jeaffreson. London, 1864. 2 v. 8°. . . D,454
Stephenson, R. M. Railway Details. London, 1850. 12°. . . . M,964
Stepney, S. C. Diary of an Officer of the Guards. London, n. d. 12°. . H,168
Steppes of the Caspian Sea, Travels in. X. Hommaine de Hell. Lon. 1847. 8°. V,704
Stepping Heavenward. E. Prentiss. New York, 1869. 12°. . . . K,116
Steps of Belief; or, Christianity *vs.* Atheism. J. F. Clarke. Bost. 1870. 12°. P,71
Stereoscope, History and Construction of. Sir D. Brewster. Lond. 1856. p. 8°. N,24
Sterling, J., Life of. T. Carlyle. Boston, 1852. 12°. . . . . . . D,246
The same. London, 1857. 8°. . . . . . . . C,523
Onyx Ring. Boston, 1856. 12°. . . . . . . . K,1020
Sterne, L. Sentimental Journey through France and Italy. Lond. n. d. 24°. V,445
The same. Leipzig, 1861. 16°. . . . . . . . J,467
Sentimental Journey, Letters, and Sermons. New York, 1857. 12°. V,452
Tristram Shandy. Philadelphia, 1867. 12°. . . . . . K,1019
The same. Leipzig, 1849. 16°. . . . . . . . J,468
Works; Life by himself; illustrated by Darley. Phila. 1864. 8°. K,1096
Stewart, Sir H. Planter's Guide. Edinburgh, 1848. 8°. . . . . . M,571
Steuben, F. W. B., *Baron*, Life of. F. Bowen. Boston, 1860. 12°. . C,860,9
Life of. F. Kapp. New York, 1859. 12°. . . . . . . D,516
Steven, W. History of the High School at Edinburgh. Edinb. 1849. 8°. O,1027
Steven Lawrence, Yeoman. A. B. Edwards. Leipzig, 1869. 2 v. in 1. 16°. J,160
Stevens, A. History of Methodism. New York, 1861. 3 v. 12°. . . P,832
The same. New York, 1864. 4 v. 12°. . . . . . . P,833
Stevens, G. E. The Queen City in 1869. Cincinnati, 1869. 16°. . . . C,209
Stevens, T., Memorial Addresses on. Washington, 1869. 8°. . . . C,800
Stevenson, A. Construction and Illumination of Lighthouses. Lon. 1850. 12°. M,962
Stevenson, D. Civil Engineering of North America. Lond. 185–. 12°. . M,963
Stevenson, W. B. Twenty Years' Residence in So. America. Lon. 1825. 3 v. 8°. V,206
Stevenson, W. F. Praying and Working. London, 1863. 12°. . . . C,506

Stewart, C. S. Brazil and La Plata. New York, 1856. 12°. . . . . v,238
Stewart, David. Sketches of Highlanders. Edinburgh, 1825. 2 v. 8°. . v,361
Stewart, Dugald. Collected Works; ed. Sir W. Hamilton. Lon. 1858. 10 v. 8°. o,799

Vol. 1. Dissertation; Progress of Philosophy.
2-4. Elements of the Philosophy of the Human Mind.
5. Philosophical Essays.
6, 7. Philosophy of the Active and Moral Powers of Man.
8, 9. Lectures on Political Economy.
10. Biographical Memoirs of Adam Smith, W. Robertson, and T. Reid; with Memoir of Stewart, by J. Veitch.

Philosophy of the Human Mind. Boston, 1847. 12°. . . . . o,686
The same; edited by F. Bowen. Boston, 1855. 12°. . . o,651
Stewart, J. Stable Book; Management of Horses. New York, 1864. 12°. M,459
Stewart, P. Treatise on Heat. Oxford, 1866. 16°. . . . . . . . N,37
Stewart, R., *Lord Castlereagh*, Memoirs and Correspond. Lond. 1848-9. 4 v. 8°. D,58
Stewart, R. W. Tent and the Khan; Sinai and Palestine. Edinb. 1857. 8°. v,648
Stewart, W. Metrical Version of H. Boece's Chronicles. Lond. 1858-63. 3 v. 8°. w,156
Stickney, C. E. Minisink Region, Orange Co., N.Y. Middletown, 1867. 12°. c,144
Stieler, A. Atlas der Deutschen Bundes-Staaten. Gotha, 1848. obl. 8°. . Q,363
Hand-Atlas und Bericht dazu. Gotha, 1850. 2 v. f°. . . *Q,393
Schul-Atlas, Supplement. H. Berghaus. Gotha, 1851. obl. 8°. . Q,362
Stier, R. Words of the Lord Jesus. Edinburgh, 1855-58. 8 v. 8°. . P,557
Stiff, E. Texan Emigrant. Cincinnati, 1840. 12°. . . . . . . v,20
Stiles, E., Life of. J. L. Kingsley. Boston, 1860. 12°. . . . c,860,16
Stiles, W. H. Austria in 1848-49. New York, 1852. 2 v. 8°. . . . B,529
Still Waters. Leipzig, 1857. 16°. . . . . . . . . . . . J,469
Stillingfleet, E. Origines Britannicæ. London, 1685. f°. . . . . Q,304
Stirling, J. H. Secret of Hegel. London, 1865. 2 v. 8°. . . . . o,683
Sir William Hamilton; an Analysis. London, 1865. 8°. . . . o,684
Stirling, W. Cloister Life of Charles V. Boston, 1853. 12°. . . . D,515
Velasquez and his Works. London, 1855. 16°. . . . . . D,699
Stith, W. History of the Discovery and Settlement of Virginia. N.Y. 1865. 8°. c,127
Stock Exchange, Chronicles and Characters of. J. Francis. Boston, 1850. 8°. o,552
Stockbridge, J. C. Memoir of Baron Stow, the Model Pastor. Bost. 1871. 12°. c,713
Stockton, R. F., Sketch of the Life of. New York, 1856. 8°. . . . c,962
Stodart, J. and Faraday, M. Alloys of Steel. London, 1822. 4°. . N,252,42
Stodart, M. A. Principles of Education. London, 1844. 16°. . . o,1026
Stoddard, D. T., Memoir of. J. P. Thompson. New York, 1859. 12°. . c,736
Stoddard, R. H. Late English Poets. New York, 1867. 12°. . . . I,433
Poems. Boston, 1852. 16°. . . . . . . . . . . . I,143
Songs of Summer. Boston, 1857. 16°. . . . . . . . . I,147
Town and Country, and Voices in the Shells. New York, 1858. 12°. J,1261
Stoddart, Sir J. Grammar; from Encyclopædia Metropolitana. Lon. 1849. 12°. L,508
Glossology; from Encyclopædia Metropolitana. London, 1858. 12°. L,510
History and Biography; from Encyc. Metropolitana. Lond. 1850. 12°. A,21
Stöckhardt, J. A. Chemical Field Lectures. London, 1855. p. 8°. . . L,320
The same. Cambridge, 1853. 12°. . . . . . . . . N,174
Chemische Feldpredigten. Leipzig, 1856. 8°. . . . . . . G,770
Principles of Chemistry. Philadelphia, 1868. 12°. . . . . N,230
Schule der Chemie. Braunschweig, 1855. 16°. . . . . . G,771
Stoever, D. H. Life of Charles von Linnæus. London, 1794. 4°. . . F,35
Stokes, J. Cabinet-Maker's and Upholster's Companion. Phila. 1850. 12°. M,147

Stolz, Madame de. House on Wheels. Boston, 1871. 16°. . . J,1540
Stomach, Servants of the. J. Macé. New York, 1868. 12°. . . . L,900
Stomachs, Talks about Peoples'. D. Lewis. Boston, 1870. 12°. . . L,940
Stone, B. W., Biography of. J. Rogers. Cincinnati, 1847. 12°. . C,1006
Stone, W. L. Border Wars of the American Revolution. N. Y. 1864. 2 v. 18°. L,451
Life of Joseph Brant. Buffalo, 1851. 2 v. 8°. . . . . . C,724
Poetry and History of Wyoming. Albany, 1864. 12°. . . . C,174
(Ed.) Memoirs of General Riedesel. Albany, 1868. 2 v. 8°. . B,887
Stone, Blasting and Quarrying of. Sir J. Burgoyne. London, 1862. 12°. M,894
Stone Cutting. E. Dobson. London, 1856. 12°. . . . . . . . M,911
Stone Mason of Saint Point. A. de Lamartine. New York, 1859. 12°. . H,904
Stone River, Battle of. W. D. Bickham. Cincinnati, 1863. 12°. . . B,898
Stonhenge, *pseud.* See *Walsh, J. H.*
Stones of Venice. J. Ruskin. New York, 1851. 8°. . . . . . . M,78
Recherches sur les Pierres d'Imatra. G. F. Parrot. St. Pet. 1840. 4°. N,252,42
Stony Point, Assault on. H. B. Dawson. Morrisania, 1863. 8°. . . F,58
Storch, L. Der Diplomat; Novelle. Frankfurt-am-Main, 1834. 24°. . G,480
Der Freibeuter. Leipzig, 1861–62. 3 v. 16°. . . . . . . G,481
Für Stille Abende. Leipzig, 1856–57. 2 v. 16°. . . . . . G,487
Die Heideschenke. Leipzig, 1855–56. 3 v. 16°. . . . . . G,482
Die Intrigue. Frankfurt-am-Main, 1833. 2 v. 24°. . . . G,483
Die Königin. Leipzig, 1858. 4 v. 16°. . . . . . . . . G,486
Kunz von Kauffungen. Leipzig, 1855. 3 v. 16°. . . . . . G,484
Das Pfarrhaus zu Hallungen. Berlin, 1851. 16°. . . . . G,485
Storer, F. H. Dictionary of Solubilities of Chemical Substances. Cam. 1864. 8°. N,246
Manual of Inorganic Chemistry. New York, 1868. 8°. . . . N,221
Storer, H. R. Is it I? a Book for every Man. Boston, 1868. 12°. . . L,834
Reflex Insanity in Women. Boston, 1871. 12°. . . . . . L,938
Why Not? a Book for every Woman. Boston, 1868. 16°. . . L,833
Stories and Sights of France and Italy. S. J. Lippincott. Boston, 1867. 16°. J,1322
and Tales. H. C. Andersen. New York, 1871. 12°. . . J,1519
for Freemason's Fireside. C. W. Towle. Cincinnati, 1868. 12°. . K,9
for Young Persons. C. M. Sedgwick. New York, 1860. 16°. . J,1245
from famous Ballads. S. J. Lippincott. Boston, 1866. 16°. . J,1246
from History. A. Strickland. New York, 1868. 16°. . . J,1275
from History and Biography. N. Hawthorne. Boston, 1866. 12°. U,40,12
from my Attic. H. E. Scudder. New York, 1869. 16°. . . . H,434
in Verse. L. Hunt. London, 1855. 16°. . . . . . . . I,356
of an Old Maid. E. de Girardin; trans. by A. Elwes. N. Y. 1856. 16°. J,1355
of English and Foreign Life. W. and M. Howitt. Lond. 1853. p. 8°. L,108
of the Gorilla Country. P. B. Du Chaillu. New York, 1868. 12°. J,1491
of the Prairie. J. F. Cooper. New York, 1868. 12°. . . J,1374
of the Sea. J. F. Cooper. New York, 1868. 12°. . . . J,1373
of the Woods. J. F. Cooper. New York, 1869. 12°. . . J,1375
told to a Child. J. Ingelow. Boston, 1866. 12°. . . . J,1230
Storm, The. D. De Foe. London, 1704. 8°. . . . . . . . N,83
Storms, Development of the Law of. W. Reid. London, 1849. 8°. . . N,110
Mechanical Theory of. T. Bassnett. New York, 1854. 12°. . . N,105
Stormy Life. G. Fullerton. New York, 1868. 8°. . . . . . K,701
The same. Leipzig, 1867. 2 v. in 1. 16°. . . . . J,171

Story, J. Exposition of Constitution of the U. S. New York, 1868. 12°. U,511
Life and Letters; edited by W. W. Story. Boston, 1851. 2 v. 8°. C,1092
Miscellaneous Writings; edited by W. W. Story. Boston, 1852. 8°. . U,142
Story, W. W. Graffiti d'Italia. Edinburgh, 1868. 16°. . . . . I,434
Poems. Boston, 1856. 12°. . . . . . . . . . . I,146
Proportions of the Human Figure. London, 1866. 8°. . . *Q,159
Roba di Roma. London, 1863. 2 v. 12°. . . . . . . V,484
(Ed.) Life and Letters of Joseph Story. Boston, 1851. 2 v. 8°. C,1092
(Ed.) Miscellaneous Writings of Joseph Story. Boston, 1852. 8°. U,142
Story Book. H. C. Andersen. New York, 1869. 16°. . . . . J,1437
Story of a Bad Boy. T. B. Aldrich. Boston, 1870. 16°. . . . J,1713
of Bethlehem. J. R. Macduff. New York, 1859. 12°. . . J,1321
of the Captives in Abyssinia. H. Blanc. London, 1868. 16°. . V,787
of Doom, and other Poems. J. Ingelow. Boston, 1867. 12°. . . I,360
of Elizabeth. A. I. Thackeray. Leipzig, 1863. 16°. . . . J,477
of a Genius. M. Howitt. New York, 1867. 24°. . . . . J,1182
of the Great March to the Sea. G. W. Nichols. N. Y. 1866. 12°. . B,907
of Kennett. B. Taylor. New York, 1866. 12°. . . . . . K,305
of my Life. H. C. Andersen. New York, 1871. 12°. . . . D,533
of the 6th Ohio Regiment. E. Hannaford. Cincinnati, 1868. 8°. . B,960
of a Working Man's Life. F. Mason. New York, 1870. 12°. . . C,730
Stoughton, J. Shades and Echoes of Old London. London, n. d. 12°. . J,1277
Stow, B., Memoir of. J. C. Stockbridge. Boston, 1871. 12°. . . . C,713
Stowe, C. E. Common Schools and Teachers' Seminaries. Bost. 1839. 12°. O,1127
Elementary Public Instruction in Europe. Columbus, 1837. 8°. O,1251,1
History of the Books of the Bible. Hartford, 1867. 8°. . . . P,448
Letter on the Millennial Arithmetic. Cincinnati, 1843. 8°. . H,302,4
Prussian System of Instruction. Cincinnati, 1836. 18°. . . O,1112
Stowe, H. B. Agnes of Sorrento. Boston, 1867. 12°. . . . . . K,281
Chimney Corner. Boston, 1868. 16°. . . . . . . . . H,276
Dred; or, Nina Gordon. Boston, 1856. 2 v. 12°. . . . . . K,285
House and Home Papers. Boston, 1865. 12°. . . . . . . H,278
Key to Uncle Tom's Cabin. Boston, 1853. 8°. . . . . . . O,404
Lady Byron vindicated. Boston, 1870. 12°. . . . . . . H,279
Little Foxes. Boston, 1869. 16°. . . . . . . . . . H,280
May Flower, and Miscellaneous Works. Boston, 1869. 12°. . . K,288
Men of our Times. Hartford, 1868. 8°. . . . . . . . C,774
Minister's Wooing. Boston, 1867. 12°. . . . . . . . K,283
Oldtown Folks. Boston, 1869. 12°. . . . . . . . . K,284
Pearl of Orr's Island. Boston, 1866. 12°. . . . . . . K,286
Pink and White Tyranny. Boston, 1871. 16°. . . . . . K,383
Queer Little People. Boston, 1868. 16°. . . . . . . J,1279
Religious Poems. Boston, 1867. 16°. . . . . . . . I,145
Sunny Memories of Foreign Lands. Boston, 1854. 2 v. 12°. . V,337
Uncle Tom's Cabin. Boston, 1868. 12°. . . . . . . . . K,287
Stowell, W. H. and Wilson, D. Puritans and Pilgrim Fathers. Cin. 1856. 12°. C,4
Strabo. Geographica; *in Greek.* Leipzig, 1819. 3 v. 18°. . . . . U,384
Geography; tr. H.C.Hamilton and W. Falconer. Lon. 1854-7. 3v. p.8°. L,80
Strachey, E. Hebrew Politics in the Time of Sargon. London, 1853. 8°. P,531
Strachey, W. Laws of Virginia, 1612. See *Force's Tracts*, v. 3.

Strachey, W. Travaile into Virginia Britannica. London, 1849. 8°. . v,985
Strafford, Earl of. See *Wentworth, T.*
Strahl, P., and Hermann. Gesch. des Russisch. Staates. Ham. 1832–60. 6 v. 8°. E,108
Strait, H. Philosophy of the Human Character. Nashville, 1846. 16°. . O,630
Strange, Sir R., Memoirs of. J. Dennistoun. London, 1855. 12°. . . D,228
Strange Story. Sir E. B. Lytton. Philadelphia, 1868. 12°. . . . K,829
The same. Leipzig, 1861–62. 2 v. in 1. 16°. . . . J,329
Strange Visitors; original papers by eminent spirits. New York, 1869. 12°. O,330
Strathbogie, Presbytery Book of, 1631–54. Aberdeen, 1843. 4°. . F,84,10
Strathern; a Novel. M. Gardiner. Leipzig, 1844. 2 v. in 1. 16°. . . J,195
Strathmore. L. de la Rame. Philadelphia, 1870. 12°. . . . . . K,895
Stratification of Language. F. M. Müller. London, 1868. 8°. . . . L,526
Stratton, R. B. Captivity of Oatman Girls among the Indians. N.Y. 1858. 12°. B,596
Strauss, D. F. Glory of the House of Israel. Philadelphia, 1859. 12°. K,1021
Life of Jesus. New York, 1856. 2 v. 8°. . . . . . . P,377
Ulrich von Hutten. Leipzig, 1858–60. 3 v. 8°. . . . . . E,241
and Renan, E. E. Zeller. London, 1866. 8°. . . . . . H,736
Strawberry, Cultivation of. R. G. Pardee. New York, 1854. 12°. . . M,539
Stray Leaves from an Arctic Journal. S. Osborn. New York, 1853. 12°. . V,936
Street, A. B. Poems. New York, 1845. 8°. . . . . . . . I,165
Woods and Waters. New York, 1860. 12°. . . . . . . K,97
Street, G. E. Brick and Marble in the Middle Ages. London, 1855. 8°. . M,203
Street Railways, Treatise on. A. Easton. Philadelphia, 1859. 8°. . . M,702
Streit and Friede. F. Bremer. Leipzig, 1857. 12°. . . . . . E,313,10
Stretton, J. C. Margaret and her Bridesmaids. Boston, 1864. 12°. . . K,852
Queen of the County. Boston, 1867. 12°. . . . . . . K,855
Strickland, A. Lives of the Bishops sent to the Tower, 1688. Lon. 1866. 12°. C,1288
Lives of the Queens of England. Boston, n. d. 12 v. in 6. 8°. . D,368

Vol. 1. Matilda of Flanders, 1066; Matilda of Scotland, 1100; Adelicia of Louvaine, 1120; Matilda of Boulogne, 1136; Eleanora of Aquitaine, 1154.
2. Berengaria of Navarre, 1191; Isabella of Angoulême, 1200; Eleanor of Provence, 1236; Eleanora of Castille, 1273; Marguerite of France, 1299; Isabella of France, 1308; Philippa of Hainault, 1327; Anne of Bohemia, 1380.
3. Isabella of Valois, 1397; Joanna of Navarre, 1402; Katherine of Valois, 1402; Margaret of Anjou, 1444; Elizabeth Woodville, 1464; Anne of Warwick, 1473.
4. Elizabeth of York, 1486; Katherine of Arragon, 1509; Anne Boleyn, 1533; Jane Seymour, 1536; Anne of Cleves, 1539; Katherine Howard, 1540.
5. Katherine Parr, 1543; Mary, 1553.
6. Elizabeth, 1558.
7. Elizabeth; Anne of Denmark, 1603.
8. Henrietta Maria, 1628; Catherine of Braganza, 1661.
9. Mary Beatrice of Modena, 1685.
10. Mary Beatrice of Modena; Mary II., 1688.
11, 12. Mary II.; Anne, 1702.

The same. London, 1868–69. 6 v. p. 8. . . . . . L,270

Vol. 1. Matilda of Flanders, 1066; Matilda of Scotland, 1100; Adelicia of Louvaine, 1120; Matilda of Boulogne, 1136; Eleanora of Aquitaine, 1154; Berengaria of Navarre, 1191; Isabella of Angoulême, 1200; Eleanor of Provence, 1236; Eleanora of Castille, 1273; Marguerite of France, 1299; Isabella of France, 1308; Philippa of Hainault, 1327; Anne of Bohemia, 1380; Isabella of Valois, 1397; Joanna of Navarre, 1402; Katherine of Valois, 1402; Margaret of Anjou, 1444.
2. Elizabeth Woodville, 1464; Anne of Warwick, 1473; Elizabeth of York, 1486; Katharine of Arragon, 1509; Anne Boleyn, 1533; Jane Seymour, 1536; Anne of Cleves, 1539; Katharine Howard, 1540; Katharine Parr, 1543; Mary, 1553.
3. Elizabeth, 1558.
4. Anne of Denmark, 1603; Henrietta Maria, 1628; Catharine of Braganza, 1661; Mary Beatrice of Modena, 1685.
5. Mary II., 1688.
6. Anne, 1702.

The same; abridged by C. G. Parker. New York, 1867. 12°. D,369

Strickland, A. Lives of the Queens of Scotland. N. Y. 1859–68. 8 v. 12°. D,17
Vol. 1. Margaret Tudor; Magdalene of France; Mary of Lorraine.
2. Mary of Lorraine; Lady Margaret Douglas.
3–7. Mary Stuart.
8. Elizabeth Stuart; Sophia, Electress of Hanover.
Lives of the Tudor Princesses. London, 1868. 8°. . . . . D,384
Memoirs of Elizabeth of England. Philadelphia, 1853. 8°. . . D,203
Old Friends and New Acquaintances. London, 1861. 8°. . K,1022
Stories from History. New York, 1868. 16°. . . . . J,1275
Tales from English History. New York, 1868. 16°. . . J,1276
True Stories from Ancient History. New York, 1868. 16°. . J,1377
True Stories from Modern History. New York, 1868. 16°. . J,1274
Strickland, W. Reports on Canals, Railways, etc. Philadelphia, 1826. 4°. *Q,90
Strickland, W. P. History of the American Bible Society. N. Y. 1856. 8°. P,645
Pioneer Bishop; Life of Francis Asbury. New York, 1858. 8°. C,1285
Strife and Peace. F. Bremer. London, 1833. p. 8°. . . . L,169,3
Strive and Thrive. M. Howitt. New York, 1853. 12°. . . . J,1168
Strong, A. B. American Flora. New York, 1848–49. 3 v. 4°. . N,1027
Stroud, W. Physical Cause of the Death of Christ. New York, 1871. 12°. P,380
Struensee, G. von. Erzählungen eines alten Herrn. Breslau, 1860. 2 v. 16°. G,497
Gräfin und Marquise. Wien, 1865. 4 v. 16°. . . . . . G,498
Ost und West. Breslau, 1865. 4 v. 24°. . . . . . . G,499
Vor fünfzig Jahren. Breslau, 1859. 3 v. 12°. . . . . G,500
Zwei gnädige Frauen. Breslau, 1860. 2 v. 16°. . . . . G,501
Strum, C. Solution of Numerical Equations. London, 1835. 4°. . N,252,42
Strumpf, F. L. Fortschritte der angewandten Chemie. Berlin, 1853. 8°. . G,772
Strutt, E. Feminine Soul. Boston, 1870. 16°. . . . . . . . O,373
Strutt, J. The Sports and Pastimes of England. London, 1855. 8°. . M,314
Strutt, J. G. Sylva Brittanica; or, Portraits of Forest Trees. Lon. 1826. f°. Q,350
Stryker, J. (Ed.) Amer. Quarterly Register, v. 1–3, 5. Phil. 1848–51. 4 v. 8°. T,58
Strype, J. Annals of the Reformation. Oxford, 1824. 4 v. in 7. 8°. *P,683
Ecclesiastical Memorials. Oxford, 1822. 3 v. in 6. 8°. . . *P,688
Life and Acts of Edmund Grindal. Oxford, 1821. 8°. . . *P,687
Life and Acts of John Aylmer. Oxford, 1821. 8°. . . . *P,684
Life and Acts of Matthew Parker. Oxford, 1821. 3 v. 8°. . *P,689
Life of Sir John Cheke. Oxford, 1821. 8°. . . . . . *P,686
Life of Sir Thomas Smith. Oxford, 1820. 8°. . . . . . *P,690
Life and Acts of John Whitgift. Oxford, 1822. 3 v. 8°. . *P,691
Memorials of Thomas Cranmer. Oxford, 1840. 2 v. 8°. . *P,685
The same. London, 1853. 2 v. 12°. . . . . . . D,316
General Index to his Works. Oxford, 1828. 2 v. 8°. . . *P,692
Stuart, C. Residence in Northern Persia, etc. London, 1854. 8°. . . V,752
Stuart, G. History of Scotland. Dublin, 1782. 2 v. 8°. . . . . . B,124
Stuart, J. (Ed.) Book of Deer. Edinburgh, 1869. 4°. . . . F,84,36
Stuart, J. Three Years in North America. Edinburgh, 1833. 2 v. 12°. V,142
and Revett, N. Antiquities of Athens. London, 1858. p. 8°. . L,149
The same. London, 1837. 16°. . . . . . . . . A,61
Stuart, M. Commentary on Book of Proverbs. New York, 1859. 12°. . P,504
Commentary on Ecclesiastes. Andover, 1864. 12°. . . . P,536
Commentary on Epistle to the Hebrews. London, 1856. 8°. . . P,532
Commentary on Epistle to Romans. London, 1857. 8°. . . . P,533

Stuart, M. Hebrew Chrestomathy. Andover, 1838. 8°. . . . . . L,534
Stuart, R. Cyclopædia of Architecture. New York, 1854. 2 v. in 1. 8°. *M,168
Stuart of Dunleath. C. E. S. Norton. Leipzig, 1851. 2 v. in 1. 16°. . J,395
Student, The. Sir E. B. Lytton. Philadelphia, n. d. 8°. . . . K,810
Student and Intellectual Observer, v. 1, 2. London, 1868. 2 v. 8°. R,34,11,12
Student-Life in Germany. W. Howitt. London, 1841. 8°. . . . V,378
Student's Manual. J. Todd. Northampton, 1854. 12°. . . . O,1028
Student's Own Speaker. P. Reeves. New York, 1871. 12°. . . O,1245
Studies appropriate to Mental Development. T.P.Rodman. Bost. 1848. 12°. O,820,18
for Stories. J. Ingelow. Boston, 1870. 16°. . . . . . J,1257
from Life. D. M. Craik. New York, 1861. 12°. . . . . K,662
The same. Leipzig, 1867. 16°. . . . . . . . . J,94
in English. M. Schele de Vere. London, 1867. 8°. . . . L,570
of Nature. J. B. de St. Pierre. London, 1846. 2 v. 12°. . . U,123
Stories and Memoirs. A. Jameson. Boston, 1866. 16°. . . . M,17
Stumbling-Blocks. M. A. Dodge. Boston, 1864. 16°. . . . . . H,55
Stunden der Andacht. H. Zschokke. Aurau, 1863. 10 v. . . E,367,20-29
Sturleson. See *Snorri Sturleson*.
Sturm, C. C. Morning Communings with God. London, 1858. p. 8°. . L,240
Style, English. G. F. Graham. London, 1869. 16°. . . . . . L,580
Styria, Lower, Winter in. B. Hall. London, 1836. 12°. . . . . V,406
Sublime in Nature. F. de Lanoye. New York, 1870. 12°. . . M,1046
Substance and Shadow. H. James. Boston, 1863. 8°. . . . . P,167
Subtle Brains and Lissom Fingers. A. Wynter. London, 1863. 8°. . H,318
Suburban Grounds, Art of Beautifying. F. J. Scott. New York, 1870. 8°. *M,361
Suburban Sketches. W. D. Howells. New York, 1871. 8°. . . . H,128
Success in Life; the Lawyer. L. C. Tuthill. Cincinnati, 1854. 12°. . K,1092
the Mechanic. L. C. Tuthill. Cincinnati, 1854. 12°. . K,1093
the Merchant. L. C. Tuthill. Cincinnati, 1854. 12°. . K,1094
Suchet, L. G., *Maréchal duc d'Albuféra*. Mémoires. Paris, 1834. 2 v. 8°. D,650
Atlas pour Mémoires. Paris, 1834. f°. . . . . . Q,449
Sue, E. Mysteries of Paris. London, n. d. 12°. . . . . . H,902
Wandering Jew. Philadelphia, n. d. 8°. . . . . . H,915
Suetonius Tranquillus, C. Duodecim Cæsares, etc. Parisiis, 1828. 2 v. 8°. U,349
Lives of the Twelve Cæsars. London, 1855. p. 8°. . . . . L,84
Sugar and Coffee Planting. J. A. Leon. London, 1848. 8°. . . N,252,34
Sugar Cane, Composition Chimique de. E. Peligot. Paris, 1840. 8°. N,252,20
Sugar Cultivation. J. A. Leon. London, 1848. 8°. . . . . N,252,34
Sugar, Fabrication du Sucre. E. Peligot. Paris, 1843. 8°. . . N,252,20
Fabrication du Sucre aux Colonies Françaises. C. L. F. F. *Marquis* Renouard de Sainte-Croix. Paris, 1843. 8°. . . . N,252,20
Fabrication et Raffinage des Sucres. A. Payen. Paris, 1832. 8°. N,252,20
Treatise on Boiling. H. Weatherby. Philadelphia, 1865. 12°. . M,646
Sugden, Sir E. B. Handy Book on Property Law. New York, 1858. 12°. U,487
Sullivan, E. Bungalow and the Tent; Visit to Ceylon. London, 1854. 12°. V,585
Sullivan, J., Life of. O. W. B. Peabody. Boston, 1860. 12°. . . C,860,13
Sullivan, R. Methods of Teaching in Male Model Schools. Dub. 1843. 16°. O,958
Popular Education. Dublin, 1842. 12°. . . . . . . O,1024
Sullivan, W. Political Class-Book. Boston, 1835. 12°. . . . . O,488
Public Men of the Revolution. Philadelphia, 1847. 8°. . . . C,882

Sullivant, W. S. Mosses of Eastern North America. Cambridge, 1864. 8°. N,897
Musci and Hepaticæ of the United States. New York, 1856. 8°. N,1029
Sully, Duc de, *M. de Béthune*, Memoirs of. London, 1856. 2 v. p. 8°. . L,327
with Trial of Francis Ravaillac. Edinburgh, 1770. 5 v. 12°. D,597
Sulpicia. Satires; translated by L. Evans. London, 1852. p. 8°. . . L,65
Sultan and his People. C. Oscanyan. New York, 1857. 12°. . . . V,557
Summer Cruise on New-England Coast. R. Carter. Boston, 1870. 16°. . V,49
Summer Evening Tales. H. Conscience. New York, n. d. 12°. . K,1023
Summer in Leslie Goldthwaite's Life. A. D. T. Whitney. Boston, 1871. 12°. K,395
Summer Pictures; from Copenhagen to Venice. H. M. Field. N. Y. 1860. 12°. V,384
Summer Rest. M. A. Dodge. Boston, 1866. 16°. . . . . . . H,56
Summer Tour, Journal of. E. M. Sewell. New York, 1852. 12°. . . V,305
Summer's Jaunt across the Water. J. J. Smith. Phila. 1846. 2 v. in 1. 12°. V,299
Summit County, Reminiscences of. L. V. Bierce. Akron, O. 1854. 16°. . C,153
Sumner, C. Duel between France and Germany. Boston, 1871. 12°. . B,214
Life of. D. A. Harsha. New York, 1856. 12°. . . . . C,975
Orations and Speeches. Boston, 1850. 2 v. 12°. . . . . H,817
Recent Speeches and Addresses. Boston, 1856. 12°. . . . H,818
Sumner, W. H. History of East Boston. Boston, 1858. 8°. . . . C,81
Sumter, T., Life of. C. B. Hartley. Philadelphia, 1859. 12°. . . . C,552
Sun, The. A. Guillemin. New York, 1870. 16°. . . . . M,1057
Ruler of the Planetary System. R. A. Proctor. London, 1871. 8°. N,289
Sunbeam Stories. M. A. Mackarness. Leipzig, 1863. 16°. . . . J,412
Sun Birds. Sir W. Jardine. Edinburgh, n. d. 16°. . . . . . N,470,5
Sunday Magazine, 1865–67. London, 1865–67. 3 v. 8°. . . . . . S,29
Sunday-School Speaker. O. A. Cheney. Boston, 1869. 12°. . . . O,824
Sunday-Schools, Forty Years' Experience in. S. H. Tyng. N. Y. 1860. 12°. P,23
Sunny Bank. M. V. Terhune. New York, 1867. 12°. . . . . K,334
Sunnyside Series. Mrs. E. S. Phelps. New York, 1869. 3 v. 18°. J,1399
Vol. 1. Sunnyside. Vol. 2. Peep at Number Five.
Vol. 3. Tell-Tale.

Sunny Skies. B. H. Channing. Boston, 1869. 12°. . . . . . J,1668
Sunny South. J. H. Ingraham. Philadelphia, 1860. 12°. . . . K,299
Sunset Land; the Great Pacific Slope. J. Todd. Boston, 1870. 16°. . V,92
Sunshine and Showers. A. Steinmetz. London, 1867. 12°. . . . N,107
of Greystone. E. J. May. New York, 1867. 12°. . . . J,1642
Supercheries, Les. J. M. Quérard. v. 1–3. Paris, 1869–71. 3 v. 8°. . L.R.
Superior Fishing. R. B. Roosevelt. New York, 1868. 12°. . . . M,321
Supernatural, History of. W. Howitt. Philadelphia, 1863. 2 v. 12°. . P,42
Nature and the. H. Bushnell. New York, 1864. 12°. . . . P,52
Superstition, Popular. H. Mayo. Philadelphia, 1852. 12°. . . . O,329
Surenne, G. French and English Dictionary. New York, 1854. 8°. . R.R.
Sur la Grande Route; Comedie. M. de Saint-Remy. Paris, 1865. 12°. . I,743
Surgeon's Daughter. Sir W. Scott. Boston, 1859. 2 v. 16°. . . . K,950
Surnames, English. M. A. Lower. London, 1849. 2 v. 8°. . . . L,516
English, Place of, in the Teutonic Family. R. Ferguson. Lond. 1858. 8°. L,515
Surrey, Earl of, *H. Howard*. Poetical Works. Boston, 1854. 16°. . . I,230
The same; with Life. London, 1854. 16°. . . . . I,254
Surry of Eagles' Nest. J. E. Cooke. New York, 1866. 12°. . . . J,631
Surtees, R., Memoir of. G. Taylor. Durham, 1852. 8°. . . . F,126,24

Surtees Society, Publications. London and Durham, 1835-65. 45 v. 8°. F,126

Vol. 1. Reginaldi Monachi Dunelmensis Libellus de Beati Cuthberti Virtutibus.
2. Wills and Inventories of the Northern Counties from the 11th Century.
3. The Towneley Mysteries.
4. Testamenta Eboracensia; or, Wills registered at York, part 1.
5. Sanctuarium Dunelmense et Sanctuarium Beverlacense.
6. Charters of Endowment, Inventories, etc., of the Priory of Finchale.
7. Catalogi Veteres Librorum Ecclesiæ Cathedralis Dunelm.
8. Miscellanea Biographica: Oswinus, Rex Northumbriæ; Cuthbertus, Episcopus Lindisfarnensis; Eata, Episcopus Haugustaldensis.
9. Historiæ Dunelmensis Scriptores tres, Gaufridus de Coldingham, Robertus de Graystanes, Willielmus de Chambre.
10. Rituale Ecclesiæ Dunelmensis.
11. Fantosme, J. Chronicle of the War between the English and the Scots, 1173-74.
12. Correspondence, Inventories, Account Rolls, etc., of the Priory of Coldingham.
13. Liber Vitæ Ecclesiæ Dunelmensis.
14. Correspondence of Robert Bowes, Ambassador of Elizabeth to Scotland.
15. Description of the Ancient Monuments, Rites, and Customs of the Monastical Church of Durham before the Suppression. Written in 1593.
16. Anglo-Saxon and English Psalter, v. 1.
17. Correspondence of Dr. Matthew Hutton, Archbishop of York.
18. Durham Household Book: Accounts of the Bursar, 1530-1534.
19. Libellus de Vita et Miraculis S. Godrici, Herimetæ de Finchale.
20. Anglo-Saxon and Early English Psalter, v. 2.
21. Depositions and other Ecclesiastical Proceedings from the Courts of Durham. 1311—Reign of Elizabeth.
22. Injunctions and other Ecclesiastical Proceedings of Richard Barnes, Bishop of Durham, 1575-1587.
23. Latin Hymns of the Anglo-Saxon Church.
24. Taylor, G. Memoir of Robert Surtees.
25. Boldon Buke, Survey of the Possessions of the See of Durham, 1183.
26. Wills and Inventories from the Registry of Richmond.
27. Pontifical of Egbert, Archbishop of York, A. D. 732-766.
28. Lindisfarne and Rushworth Gospels: Matthew.
29. Inventories and Account Rolls of the Benedictine Houses Jarrow and Monk-Wearmouth.
30. Testamenta Eboracensia, part 2.
31. Obituary Roll of William Ebchester and John Burnby, Priors of Durham.
32. Bishop Hatfield's Survey of the Possessions of the See of Durham.
33. Best, H., of Elmswell. Rural Economy in Yorkshire in 1641.
34. Acts of the High Commission Court within the Diocese of Durham.
35. Fabric Rolls of York Minster.
36. Dugdale, W. Visitation of the County of Yorke, 1665-66.
37. Miscellanea:
 1. Works and Letters of Dennis Granville, Dean of Durham.
 2. Nathan Drake's account of the Siege of Pontefract Castle.
 3. Brief Memoir of Justice Rokeby.
38. Wills and Inventories from the Registry at Durham, part 2.
39. Lindisfarne and Rushworth Gospels, part 2: Mark.
40. Depositions from the Castle of York on Offences in the Northern Counties.
41. Tonge, T. Heraldic Visitation of the Northern Counties in 1530.
42. Memorials of the Abbey of St. Mary of Fountains.
43. Lindisfarne and Rushworth Gospels, part 3: Luke.
44. Priory of Hexham, its Chroniclers, Endowments, and Annals, v. 1.
45. Testamenta Eboracensia, v. 3.

Surveying, Land and Engineering. T. Baker. London, 1859. 12°. . M,890
 Subterraneous. T. Fenwick and T. Baker. London, n. d. 12°. . M,839
 Treatise on Land-Surveying. W. M. Gillespie. New York, 1870. 8°. M,699
Surveyor's Guide. A. Duncan. Philadelphia, 1860. 12°. . . . M,635
Susan Fielding. A. Edwards. New York, n. d. 8°. . . . . . . K,687
Susan Gray. M. M. Sherwood. New York, 1860. 12°. . . . K,1008,3
Suspension Bridge over Menaï Straits. T. G. Cumming. London, 1824. 8°. M,737
Sussex, F. S. M. de. Manures. London, 1848. 8°. . . . . . N,252,31
Sutherland, A. Knights of Malta. Edinburgh, 1830. 2 v. 16°. . . I,530
Sutherland Hill-Side, Gossip on a. London, 1861. 8°. . . . V,1086,1
Sutherlands, The. M. Cole. New York, 1867. 12°. . . . . . . K,18
Sutton, T. and Dawson, G. Dictionary of Photography. London, 1867. 12°. M,727
Swainson, W. Animals in Menageries. London, 1838. 12°. . . M,1032
 Birds of Western Africa. Edinburgh, n. d. 2 v. 16°. . N,470,11,12
 Fishes, Amphibians, and Reptiles. London, 1839. 2 v. 12°. M,1034

Swainson, W. Fly Catchers. Edinburgh, n. d. 16°. . . . . . N,470,13
Geography and Classification of Animals. London, 1835. 12°. M,1030
Habits and Instincts of Animals. London, 1840. 12°. . . M,1037
History and Arrangements of Insects. London, 1840. 12°. . M,1036
Natural History and Classification of Birds. London, 1836. 2 v. 12°. M,1033
Natural History and Classification of Quadrupeds. Lond. 1835. 12°. M,1031
New Zealand and its Colonization. London, 1859. 8°. . . . V,897
Study of Natural History. London, 1834. 12°. . . . M,1029
Taxidermy and Bibliography of Zoölogy. London, 1840. 12°. M,1038
Treatise on Shells and Shell-Fish. London, 1840. 12°. . M,1035
Swallow Barn. J. P. Kennedy. Philadelphia, 1866. 12°. . . . K,201
Swammerdam, J. Biblia Naturæ; sive Historia Insectorum. Leyd. 1738. 2 v. f°. *Q,77
Swan, J. G. Three Years in Washington Territory. New York, 1857. 12°. V,128
Swan, R. and Leach, D. Intellectual Arithmetic. Boston, 1854. 16°. O,1093
Swan, W. D. District School Reader. Philadelphia, 1848. 12°. . . O,789
Grammar School Reader. Philadelphia, 1844. 12°. . . . O,884
Instructive Reader. Philadelphia, 1849. 12°. . . . . O,886
Primary School Reader. Philadelphia, 1847. 2 pts. 16°. . . O,762
Spelling Book. Philadelphia, 1849. 12°. . . . . . . O,791
Young Ladies' Reader. Philadelphia, 1851. 12°. . . . . . O,885
Sweden and Norway, Journey through. H. D. Inglis. Edinburgh, 1829. 16°. I,514
The same. London, 1837. 12°. . . . . . . V,549
Travels in. W. B. Jerrold. London, 1854. 12°. . . . V,545
I. Pfeiffer. New York, 1852. 12°. . . . . . V,15
Denmark and Lapland; Northern Travel. B. Taylor. N. Y. 1865. 12°. V,543
and Norway, History of. S. A. Dunham. Lon. 1840. 3 v. 12°. M,1002
History of. A. Fryxell. London, 1844. 8°. . . . . . . B,577
Geschichte Schwedens. E.G. Geijer and Carlson. Gotha, 1832–55. 4 v. 8°. E,112
Swedenborg, E. Angelic Wisdom concerning Divine Love. N. Y. 1863. 8°. P,855
Apocalypse Revealed. New York, 1862. 2 v. 8°. . . . . . P,850
Compendium of his Writings. Boston, 1853. 8°. . . . . . P,874
Conjugal Love. New York, 1860. 8°. . . . . . . . P,852
Dictionary of Correspondences. Boston, 1847. 12°. . . . . P,846
Examination of the claims of. New York, 1852. 8°. . . . . P,845
Four Leading Doctrines of the New Church. New York, 1862. 8°. P,857
Heaven and its Wonders. New York, 1863. 8°. . . . . . P,853
Heavenly Arcana contained in Holy Scriptures. N.Y. 1854–63. 10 v. 8°. P,851
Life of. N. Hobart. Boston, 1845. 16°. . . . . . . . D,754
Life and Writings of. W. White. London, 1867. 2 v. 8°. . . P,849
Mesmer and. G. Bush. New York, 1847. 12°. . . . . . P,842
Miscellaneous Theological Works. New York, 1863. 8°. . . P,854
Practical Nature of his Doctrines. A. Clissold. Boston, 1839. 12°. P,844
True Christian Religion. New York, 1858. 8°. . . . . . P,858
Secret of. H. James. Boston, 1869. 8°. . . . . . . . P,847
Swedes, Brage-Beaker with the. W. B. Jerrold. London, 1854. 12°. . V,537
History of. E. G. Geijer. London, n. d. 8°. . . . . . . B,581
Swedish and Eng. Pocket-Dictionary. C. Deleen. Orebro, 1829. 16°. L.R.
Sweet-Clover Stories. C. L. May. Boston, 1869. 16°. . . . J,1698

Vol. 1. Nelly Milton's Housekeeping. Vol. 3. Sylvia's Burden.
2. Brownie Sandford. 4. Ruth Lovell.

Sweetser, W. Human Life; its Condition and Duration. N. Y. 1867. 12°. L,937
Mental Hygiene. New York, 1850. 12°. . . . . . . . o,639
Swetchine, Mad., Life and Letters. Count de Falloux. Boston, 1868. 16°. D,746
Swift, J., *Dean*, Essay on. F. Jeffrey. London, 1856. p. 8°. . . . I,661,3
Gulliver's Travels. Philadelphia, 1867. 12°. . . . . . J,1278
The same. London, 1867. 24°. . . . . . . . K,1025
The same. Leipzig, 1844. 16°. . . . . . . . J,470
Poetical Works. Boston, 1854. 3 v. 16°. . . . . . . I,231
Tale of a Tub. London, 1867. 24°. . . . . . . . K,1024
Works, with Life. New York, 1859. 6 v. 12°. . . . . U,245

Vol. 1. Life of Dean Swift, by T. Roscoe; Poetical Works; Riddles; Poems composed at Market Hall.
2. Gulliver's Travels; Tale of a Tub; History of Martin; Battle of the Books; Mechanical Operation of the Spirit; Drapier's Letters; Memoirs of Capt. John Creichton.
3. Journal to Stella; Change in Queen Anne's Ministry; Contests and Dissensions at Athens and Rome; The Examiner; Character of Thomas, Earl of Wharton; Remarks on a Letter to the seven Lords; Mr. Prior's Journey to Paris.
4–6. Miscellaneous Prose Writings.

The same; *incomplete*. London, 1803. 23 v. 12°. . . . U,246
Swinburne, A. C. Atalanta in Calydon. Boston, 1866. 16°. . . . I,436
Chastelard; a Tragedy. New York, 1866. 16°. . . . . I,437
Queen-Mother and Rosamond. Boston, 1866. 12°. . . . . I,435
Songs before Sunrise. Boston, 1871. 12°. . . . . . . I,438
Swindell, J. G. Well Digging and Boring. London, 1854. 12°. . . M,965
Swinton, W. Rambles among Words. New York, 1864. 12°. . . . L,507
Twelve Decisive Battles of the War. New York, 1867. 8°. . . B,938
Swiss Family Robinson. J. R. V. Wyss. London, n. d. 16°. . . J,1444
Swiss Men and Swiss Mountains. R. Ferguson. London, 1864. p. 8°. I,656,1
Switzerland, Allelein-Horn. L. Stephen. London, 1861. 8°. . . V,1086,1
Ascent of the Matterhorn. F. V. Hawkins. London, 1861. 8°. V,1086,1
W. Farel and Reform in. W. M. Blackburn. Edinburgh, 1867. 12°. D,698
France and the Pyrenees. H. D. Inglis. Edinburgh, 1831. 2 v. 16°. I,532
From Lauterbrunnen to the Æggisch-horn. J. Tyndall. Lon. 1861. 8°. V,1086,1
Graian Alps and Mount Iseran. J. J. Cowell. London, 1861. 8°. V,1086,1
History of. J. Wilson. London, 1832. 12°. . . . . . . M,990
A. Vieusseux. London, 1846. 8°. . . . . . . . B,417
A. Zschokke. New York, 1858. 12°. . . . . . . B,416
Lake Dwellings of. F. Keller. London, 1866. 8°. . . . . M,175
Letters from. J. W. von Goethe. London, 1848–51. 16°. . L,188,2
F. Mendelssohn-Bartholdy. London, 1862. 2 v. 12°. . . G,25
S. I. Prime. New York, 1860. 12°. . . . . . . V,415
Month in; Physician's Holiday. J. Forbes. London, 1852. 12°. . V,423
Notes of a Traveler in. S. Laing. Philadelphia, 1846. 8°. . . V,272
Pioneer of Reformation. Princesse Koltzoff-Massalski. Lon.'58. 2v. 8°. P,241
Regular Swiss Round, in Three Trips. H. Jones. London, 1866. 16°. V,424
Schweizerland's Geschichte. H. Zschokke. Aarau, 1853. 16°. E,367,37
South of France and Pyrenees. H. D. Inglis. London, 1837. 12°. V,409
Story of Mont Blanc. A. Smith. London, 1853. 12°. . . . V,348
Two Years in. F. Bremer. Philadelphia, 1860. 2 v. 8°. . . V,416
Sword and Gown. G. A. Lawrence. New York, 1868. 8°. . . . K,764
The same. Leipzig, 1860. 16°. . . . . . . . . . J,260

Swords, Memoir on. Col. Marey. London, 1860. 12°. . . . . M,852
Sybaris, and other Homes. E. E. Hale. Boston, 1869. 12°. . . . H,122
Sybel, H. von. French Revolution. London, 1867–69. 4 v. 8°. . . B,341
Sybil; or, the Two Nations. B. Disraeli. London, 1868. 12°. . . K,673
The same. Leipzig, 1845. 16°. . . . . . . J,144
Sybil's Second Love. J. Kavanagh. New York, 1869. 12°. . . . K,696
The same. Leipzig, 1867. 2 v. in 1. 16°. . . . . J,237
Sydenham, G. Notes of Lessons. London, 1857. 12°. . . . O,1155
Sydnie Adriance; or, Trying the World. A. M. Douglas. Boston, 1869. 12°. K,120
Sylva Brittanica; Portraits of Forest Trees. J. G. Strutt. Lond. 1826. f°. Q,350
Sylvan Holt's Daughter. H. Parr. New York, 1860. 12°. . . . K,230
Sylvester Sound, the Somnambulist. H. Cockton. Londoo, 1867. p. 8°. . K,630
Sylvia's Lovers. E. C. Gaskell. Leipzig, 1863. 2 v. in 1. 16°. . . J,181
Symbolic Anglo-German Vocabulary. London, n. d. 8°. . . . . . L.R.
Symbolism; or, Mind-Matter-Language. J. Haig. Edinburgh, 1869. 12°. O,795
Symes, M. Embassy to Ava in 1795. Edinburgh, 1827. 2 v. 16°. . . I,496
Symington, A. J. Beautiful in Nature, Art, and Life. Lond. 1857. 2 v. 8°. M,53
Symmes's Theory of Concentric Spheres. J. McBride. Cincin. 1826. 16°. N,594
Symmons, C. Life of John Milton. London, 1822. 8°. . . . . C,1267
Symons, J. School Economy. London, 1852. 16°. . . . . . . O,965
Synonyms and Antonyms. C. J. Smith. London, 1870. p. 8°. . . . L,254
English. G. Crabb. New York, 1854. 8°. . . . . . . L,572
G. F. Graham. New York, 1858. 12°. . . . . . . L,545
Sypher, J. R. History of Pennsylvania Reserve Corps. Lancaster, 1865. 8°. B,932
Syracuse, N.Y., Board of Education Reports, 1870–71. Syracuse, 1870–71. 8°. O,595
Central Library, Catalogue of Books. Syracuse, 1869. 8°. . . L.R.
Syria and the Holy Land. W. K. Kelly. London, 1844. 8°. . . . . V,661
and Palestine, Hand-Book for. J. Murray. Lond. 1858. 2 v. 16°. V,626
History of. E. Pococke. London, 1852. 12°. . . . . . . A,69
Howadji in. G. W. Curtis. New York, 1852. 12°. . . . V,625
Letters from. J. W. De Forest. New York, 1856. 12°. . . . V,559
Syriac Grammar. M. Uhlemann. New York, 1855. 8°. . . . . . L,782
Syrian Travel and Syrian Tribes. R. Noel. London, 1861. 8°. . V,1086,1
Syrus, P. Moral Sayings; tr. by D. Lyman. Cleveland, 1856. 12°. . U,405
Szabad, E. Modern War. New York, 1863. 8°. . . . . . . M,750

Taaffe, J. History of Order of St. John of Jerusalem. Lond. 1852. 4 v. 8°. A,239
Tabberner, J. L. Supply of Water to London. London, 1847. 8°. . N,252,39
Table-Talk. W. Hazlitt. New York, 1845. 8°. . . . . . . . U,216,1,2
M. Luther. London, 1848. 12°. . . . . . . . G,33
S. Rogers. New York, 1856. 12°. . . . . . . . H,571
J. Selden. London, 1856. 16°. . . . . . . . H,572
and Opinions. Napoleon I. London, 1868. 16°. . . . . I,567
Selections from the Ana. Edinburgh, 1827. 16°. . . . . I,497
Tableaux Vivants; Home Pastimes. J. H. Head. Boston, 1860. 12°. . H,245
Tablets. A. B. Alcott. Boston, 1868. 16°. . . . . . . . . H,188
Tacitus, C. C. Opera; illust. by J. J. Oberlin. Parisiis, 1819–20. 5 v. 8°. U,350
Werke; übersetzt von H. Gutmann. Stutt. 1829–40. 10 v. in 2. 24°. E,4

Tacitus, C. C. Works; Oxford translation. London, 1870. 2 v. p. 8°. . L,85
Taeping Rebellion in China. L. Brine. London, 1862. 12°. . . . . V,603
Taine, H. A. Ideal in Art. New York, 1869. 16°. . . . . . . . M,29
Italy, France, and Venice. New York, 1869. 8°. . . . . . V,514
Rome and Naples. New York, 1868. 8°. . . . . . V,515
Philosophy of Art. London, 1865. 12°. . . . . . . . . M,30
Tai-Ping-Wang, Life of. J. M. Mackie. New York, 1857. 12°. . . D,756
Tait, P. G. Treatise on Quaternions. Oxford, 1867. 8°. . . . M,1153
Talbot, G. H. French Translation Self-taught. Boston, 1855. 12°. . . L,797
Philosophy of French Pronunciation. New York, 1868. 12°. . . L,796
Talbot Harland. W. H. Ainsworth. Leipzig, 1870. 16°. . . . . . J,26
Tale of the Good Woman. J. K. Paulding. New York, 1867. 8°. . . H,217
of a Tub. J. Swift. London, 1867. 24°. . . . . . . . K,1024
The same. London, 1803. 12°. . . . . . . U,246,3
The same. New York, 1859. 12°. . . . . . . U,245,2
of Two Cities. C. Dickens. Philadelphia, 1859. 8°. . . . . K,519
The same. New York, 1868. 12°. . . . . . . . . K,499
The same. New York, 1871. 12°. . . . . . . K,1142
The same. Leipzig, 1859. 2 v. in 1. 16°. . . . . . J,138
of the Tyne. H. Martineau. London, 1859. 16°. . . . K,551,7
Tales and Sketches. H. Miller. Boston, 1870. 12°. . . . . . . H,119
Essays and Sketches. R. Macnish. London, 1844. 2 v. 16°. . H,229
from American History. New York, 1830–52. 3 v. 16°. . . J,1218
from English History. A. Strickland. New York, 1868. 16°. . J,1276
from the Operas. G. F. Pardon. New York, 1865. 12°. . . . K,889
from Shakespeare. C. and M. Lamb. New York, 1869. 16°. . . K,760
of Algeria. A. Dumas. Philadelphia, 1868. 12°. . . . . . H,973
of the Borders. J. M. Wilson. Edinburgh, 1857. 10 v. 16°. K,1065
of the Crusaders. Sir W. Scott. Philadelphia, 1852. 8°. . . K,957
of the Drama. E. W. Macauley. Hartford, 1853. 12°. . . . K,833
of the Genii. J. Ridley. London, 1861. p. 8°. . . . . . L,150
of the Gods and Heroes. G. W. Cox. London, 1862. 16°. . . P,912
of a Grandfather. Sir W. Scott. Boston, 1865. 6 v. 16°. . J,1282
of Heroes from English History. London, 1869. 8°. . . J,1295
of the Irish Peasantry. W. Carleton. New York, n. d. 16°. . . K,588
of Kings and Queens of England. S. Percy. London, 1868. 16°. J,1556
of the American Revolution. New York, 1836. 16°. . . J,1223
of a Traveler. W. Irving. New York, 1869. 16°. . . . . . U,17
The same. New York, 1867. 12°. . . . . . . . U,23
of a Wayside Inn. H. W. Longfellow. Boston, 1863. 12°. . . . I,71
Talfourd, T. N. Critical and Miscellaneous Writings. Boston, 1854. 8°. . H,371
The same. Boston, 1857. 8°. . . . . . . . . . H,373
Final Memorials of Charles Lamb. New York, 1859. 12°. . U,278,5
Life and Letters of Charles Lamb. New York, 1859. 12°. . U,278,1
The same. New York, 1859. 12°. . . . . . . C,1185
Literary Sketches and Letters. New York, 1849. 12°. . . . . D,317
Vacation Rambles and Thoughts. Lond. 1845–54. 3 v. 12° and 16°. V,352
(Ed.) Works of C. Lamb; with Letters and Life. N.Y. 1852. 2 v. 12°. U,277
and others. History of Greek Literature. London, 1850. 12°. . . H,721
Talisman, The. Sir W. Scott. Boston, 1858. 2 v. 16°. . . . . . K,951

Talisman, The. Sir W. Scott. Philadelphia, 1864. 8°. . . . . . K,957
The same. Philadelphia, 1869. 8°. . . . . . K,1113
Talk about Fruits, Flowers, and Farming. H. W. Beecher. N. Y. 1859. 12°. H,90
Talleyrand, C. M. de, the Politic Man. Sir H. L. Bulwer. Lon. 1868. 8°. C,578,1
The same. Leipzig, 1868. . . . . . . . . . J,332
Tallis, J. Description of the Crystal Palace. London, n. d. 2 v. 4°. . S.C.
Tallmadge, Ohio, 50th Anniversary of Settlement. Akron, O. 1857. 8°. . C,204
Talmage, T. De W. Crumbs Swept Up. Philadelphia, 1870. 12°. . . H,130
Tamerlain, History of. Cherefeddin Ali. London, 1723. 2 v. 8°. . . D,769
Tancred; or, the New Crusade. B. Disraeli. London, 1868. 12°. . . K,675
The same. Leipzig, 1847. 2 v. in 1. 16°. . . . . J,145
Taney, R. B., Life of. G. Van Santvoord. New York, 1854. 8°. . . C,817
Taneyhill, R. H. The Leatherwood God, J. C. Dylks. Cincinnati, 1871. 8°. C,223
Tanglewood Tales. N. Hawthorne. Boston, 1870. 16°. . . . J,1440
The same. Boston, 1868. 12°. . . . . . . . . U,40,14
Tangled Talk. London, 1864. 8°. . . . . . . . . . . . H,532
Tanner, H. S. Description of Central United States. Phila. 1841. 16°. . V,1
Tannin, Acides Gallique, etc., Mémoire sur. J. Pelouze. Paris, n. d. 4°. N,252,57
Tanning, Currying, and Leather Dressing. H. Dussauce. Phila. 1867. 8°. M,679
Tappan, B. Discourse before the Historical Society of Ohio. Colum. 1833. 8°. T,19,9
The same. Columbus, 1833. 8°. . . . . . . H,302,1
Tappan, H. P. Step from the New World to the Old, v. 2. N. Y. 1852. 12°. V,325
Tar-Water, Virtues of, in Disease. G. Berkeley. London, 1747. 8°. . O,648
Tara; a Mahratta Tale. M. Taylor. Leipzig, 1864. 3 v. 16°. . . . J,475
Tariff Question. E. B. Bigelow. Boston, 1862. 4°. . . . . . . Q,217
Tarleton, R. Jests and News out of Purgatory. London, 1844. 8°. I,885,19
Tartary and Russia, Journey through. J. D. Cochrane. Edinb. 1829. 2 v. 16°. I,513
China and Thibet, Christianity in. E. R. Huc. Lond. 1857–58. 3 v. 8°. V,622
Thibet and China, Journey through. E. R. Huc. N. Y. 1852. 2 v. 12°. V,588
The same. London, 1865. p. 8°. . . . . . . . . I,657
Tasso, T. L. Hunt. New York, 1857. 12°. . . . . . . . . I,364
Conjectures concerning, v. 2. R. H. Wilde. New York, 1842. 12°. D,730
Das Befreite Jerusalem; übers. von K. Streckfuss. Leip. 1847. 2 v. 16°. E,289
Godfrey of Bulloigne. New York, 1848. 8°. . . . . . . G,77
Jerusalem Delivered; trans. by A. C. Robertson. Edinb. 1853. 8°. I,406
The same; translated by J. H. Wiffen. London, 1854. 12°. . L,151
The same. New York, 1868. 16°. . . . . I,444
Opere. Venezia, 1722–42. 12 v. 4°. . . . . . . . Q,320
Tasso and Leonora. A. Manning. London, 1856. 12°. . . . . . J,625
Taste, Essays on the Nature and Principles of. A. Alison. N. Y. 1854. 12°. O,624
Tate, T. Algebra made Easy. London, 1856. 16°. . . . . . M,1092
Drawing for Schools. London, 1854. 4°. . . . . . . M,182
First Principles of Arithmetic. London, 1857. 8°. . . . M,1090
Geometry, Mensuration, Trigonometry, etc. London, 1855. 12°. M,1087
Philosophy of Education. London, 1854. 8°. . . . . . O,1218
Tatem, M. H. Heights of Eidelberg. Philadelphia, 1871. 12°. . . K,1158
Tatler, The. J. Addison. Boston, 1866. 4 v. 8°. . . . . . H,536,1–4
Tattered Tom; or, the Story of a Street Arab. H. Alger. Boston, 1871. 16°. J,1598
Tattersall, G. and Chambers, T. Metropol. Buildings Act. Lon. 1865. 12°. U,486
Taubert, Capt. Field Artillery. London, 1856. 12°. . . . . . M,966

Tauler, J., Life of, with twenty-five Sermons. New York, 1858. 4°. . . D,500
Taura, E. von., *pseud.* See *Peters, A.*
Tautphoeus, I. von., *Baroness.* At Odds. Philadelphia, 1863. 12°. . . G,237
The same. Leipzig, 1863. 2 v. in 1. 16°. . . . . . J,471
Cyrilla. Leipzig, 1853. 2 v. in 1. 16°. . . . . . . . J,472
Initials. Philadelphia, n. d. 12°. . . . . . . . . . G,236
The same. Leipzig, 1865. 2 v. in 1. 16°. . . . . . J,473
Quits. Philadelphia, 1866. 12°. . . . . . . . . . G,238
The same. Leipzig, 1858. 2 v. in 1. 16°. . . . . . J,474
Tavernier, J. B. Grand Seignor's Seraglio. London, 1677. f°. . *Q,437
Voyages through Turkey, Persia, and Indies. London, 1678. f°. *Q,437
Taverns, Histoire des Hotelleries, etc. F. X. Michel. v. 2. Paris, 1851. 8°. H,632
Taxation, Illustrations of. H. Martineau. London, 1834. 5 v. in 1. 18°. K,552
of the United Kingdom. R. D. Baxter. London, 1869. 8°. . . O,555
Taxidermist's Manual. T. Brown. London, 1870. 16°. . . . . N,480
Taxidermy. W. Swainson. London, 1840. 12°. . . . . . M,1038
Taylor, A. S. Medical Jurisprudence. London, 1856. 12°. . . . L,939
Taylor, B. At Home and Abroad. New York, 1866. 2 v. 12°. . V,1055
By-Ways of Europe. New York, 1869. 12°. . . . . . . V,327
Colorado; a Summer Trip. New York, 1867. 8°. . . . . . V,34
Eldorado, California, and Mexico. New York, 1868. 12°. . . V,35
Hannah Thurston. New York, 1866. 12°. . . . . . . K,304
John Godfrey's Fortunes. New York, 1865. 12°. . . . . . K,303
Joseph and his Friend. New York, 1870. 12°. . . . . . K,306
Journey to Central Africa. Philadelphia, 1870. 12°. . . . V,776
Lands of the Saracen. New York, 1866. 12°. . . . . V,1051
Northern Travel; Sweden, Denmark, and Lapland. N. Y. 1868. 12°. V,543
Picture of St. John. Boston, 1866. 16°. . . . . . . . . I,140
Poems. Boston, 1866. 16°. . . . . . . . . . . . I,137
Poems of Home and Travel. Boston, 1855. 16°. . . . . . I,138
Poems of the Orient. Boston, 1855. 16°. . . . . . . I,139
Story of Kennett. New York, 1866. 12°. . . . . . . K,305
Travels in Greece and Russia. New York, 1859. 12°. . . . V,360
Views a-Foot in Europe. New York, 1867. 12°. . . . . V,317
Visit to China and Japan. New York, 1869. 12°. . . . . V,606
Taylor, B. F. January and June. New York, 1865. 12°. . . . H,238
Taylor, C. B. Legends and Records. New York, 1855. 12°. . . . C,530
Taylor, G. Memoir of Robert Surtees. Durham, 1852. 8°. . . F,126,24
Taylor, G. H. Paralysis and other Nerve Affections. N. Y. 1871. 12°. . L,957
Taylor, G. L. Stones of Etruria and Ancient Rome. London, 1859. 4°. . Q,285
Taylor, H. Edwin, the Fair. London, 1864. 16°. . . . . . I,445,2
Notes from Books. London, 1849. 12°. . . . . . . . H,692
Wordsworth's Poetical Works and Sonnets; De Vere's Poems; Ways of the Rich and Great.
Notes from Life. Boston, 1853. 16°. . . . . . . . . H,469
Money; Choice in Marriage; Humility and Independence; Children; Wisdom; The Life Poetic; Ways of the Rich and Great.
Philip van Artevelde. London, 1864. 16°. . . . . . . I,445,1
Sicilian Summer and other Poems. London, 1864. 16°. . . . I,445,3
Taylor, I. Elements of Thought. New York, 1851. 12°. . . . . O,654
Fanaticism. London, 1866. p. 8°. . . . . . . . . . P,96

Taylor, I. Home Education. New York, 1838. 12°. . . . . . . o,920
Logic in Theology, and other Essays. London, 1859. 16°. . . P,74
The same. New York, 1860. 12°. . . . . . . . . P,81
Loyola and Jesuitism in its Rudiments. London, 1849. 8°. . . P,797
Natural History of Enthusiasm. New York, 1856. 12°. . . P,76
Physical Theory of Another Life. New York, 1852. 12°. . . P,82
Restoration of Belief. Boston, 1867. 12°. . . . . . . P,75
Self-Cultivation. Ithaca, 1842. 12°. . . . . . . . . o,1114
Spirit of the Hebrew Poetry. New York, 1862. 12°. . . . P,80
Transmission of Ancient Books to Modern Times. London, 1859. 8°. H,722
Wesley and Methodism. London, 1851. 8°. . . . . . . P,829
Words and Places. London, 1865. 12°. . . . . . . . L,511
World of Mind. New York, 1858. 12°. . . . . . . . o,620
Taylor, James. Encyclopædia of Biblical Literature. Boston, 1854. 8°. . P,788
Taylor, Jane. The Pleasures of Taste. New York, 1847. 18°. . J,1252
Taylor, Jeremy. History of Jesus Christ. London, 1851. 8°. . . . P,368
Holy Living. Boston, 1864. 16°. . . . . . . . . P,31
Holy Living and Dying. London, 1870. p. 8°. . . . . . L,241
Whole Works. London, 1853. 3 v. 8°. . . . . . . . P,786
Taylor, John. Arator; Agricultural Essays. Georgetown, 1814. 12°. . M,486
Taylor, John. The Great Pyramid. London, 1859. 12°. . . . V,784
Taylor, John. Identity of Junius with Sir P. Francis. N. Y. 1818. 8°. . H,604
Taylor, John. Records of Mining. London, 1829. 4°. . . . . N,252,43
Taylor, J. B., Memoir of. J. H. and B. H. Rice. New York, n. d. 18°. P,746,15
Taylor, J. B. Memoir of Luther Rice. Baltimore, 1840. 12°. . . C,922
Taylor, J. W. Early History of the State of Ohio. Cincinnati, 1854. 12°. C,206
Manual of the Ohio School System. Cincinnati, 1857. 8°. . o,1214
Victim of Intrigue; a Tale. Cincinnati, 1847. 8°. . . . . *H,302,1
Taylor, J. W Mineral Resources of U. States. Washington, 1867. 8°. N,861,1867
Taylor, M. Tara; a Mahratta Tale. Leipzig, 1864. 3 v. 16°. . . J,475
Taylor, R. C. Statistics of Coal. Philadelphia, 1855. 8°. . . . N,847
Taylor, S. H. Method of Classical Study. Boston, 1861. 12°. . . o,974
Taylor, T. Thackeray, the Humorist and Man of Letters. N. Y. 1864. 12°. D,448
Taylor, W. Historic Survey of German Poetry. London, 1830. 3 v. 8°. H,749
Taylor, W. B. S. Fine Arts in G. Britain and Ireland. Lon. 1841. 2 v. 12°. M,56
Taylor, W. C. Civil Wars in Ireland. Edinburgh, 1831. 2 v. 16°. . I,535
History of Ireland. New York, 1860–63. 2 v. 16°. . . . L,375
Manual of Ancient History. New York, 1854. 8°. . . . A,34
Manual of Modern History. New York, 1851. 8°. . . . A,327
Memoirs of the House of Orleans. Philadelphia, 1850. 2 v. 12°. D,687
Model Schools in Dublin. Dublin, 1847. 8°. . . . . . o,1251,2
Modern British Plutarch. New York, 1846. 12°. . . . . D,439
National Portrait Gallery. London, n. d. 2 v. in 1. 8°. . C,1312
Tea, Cultivation and Manufacture of, in China. S. Ball. London, 1848. 8°. M,575
Tea Countries of China, Journey to. R. Fortune. London, 1852. 8°. . V,739
Teacher. J. Abbott. New York, 1856. 12°. . . . . . . . o,941
and the Taught, Conversations for. London, 1845. 18°. . . . H,249
Massachusetts. Boston, 1848–53. 6 v. 8°. . . . . . o,1252
Papers for, v. 1, 3–6. New York and Philadelphia, 1860–62. 5 v. 8°. o,1216
Taught. E. Davis. Boston, 1839. . . . . . . . . o,1173

Teachers, Vocation of. S. Jolly. London, 1854. 16°. . . . . o,1159
Teachers' Assistant. C. Northend. Boston, 1859. 12°. . . . . . o,938
Teachers' Miscellany. J. L. Campbell and A. M. Hadley. Cincin. 1856. 12°. o,949
Teachers' Note-Book, Leaves from. T. J. Haworth. Lond. 1857-58. 2 v. 16°. o,915
Teachers, Memoirs of. H. Barnard. New York, 1859. 8°. . . o,1057
Teaching, Art of. J. Ogden. Cincinnati, 1859. 12°. . . . . . . o,948
Collegiate and Professional. E. B. Pusey. Oxford, 1854. 8°. o,1203
Elementary, Principles of. J. Pillans. Edinburgh, 1829. 12°. o,1135
Geschichte der Pädagogik. C. Schmidt. v. 1, 2, 4. Cöthen, 1869. 3 v. 8°. G,538
in Male Model Schools. R. Sullivan. Dublin, 1843. 16°. . . o,958
Lecture on Thorough. W. H. Brooks. Boston, 1838. 8°. . o,1260,2
Papers on. W. Ross. London, 1859. 16°. . . . . . o,1022
Philosophy of. N. Sands. New York, 1869. 8°. . . . . . o,956
Principles of. H. Dunn. London, 1837. 12°. . . . . . . o,960
Theory and Practice of. D. P. Page. New York, 1857. 8°. . . o,950
Theory of. Boston, 1841. 12°. . . . . . . . . . o,1004
Teale, W. H. Education in England. Oxford, 1850. 8°. . . . o,1251
Technology and Industrial Museums, Objects of. G. Wilson. Edin. 1856. 4°. N,252,52
Ausführl. Volks-Gewerbslehre. J. H. M. v. Poppe. Stutt. 1842. 8°. G,707
Chemical. F. Knapp. Philadelphia, 1848-49. 2 v. 8°. . N,192,2,3
illustrated, Appleton's. New York, 1856. 2 v. 8°. . . . Q,251
Popular. E. Hazen. New York, 1845-55. 2 v. 18°. . . . L,439
Theorie u. Praxis der Gewerbe. J. R. Wagner. Leip. 1858-64. 5 v. 8°. G,773
What is Technology? G. Wilson. Edinburgh, 1855. 8°. . N,252,49
Tecumseh, Life of. B. Drake. Cincinnati, 1858. 12°. . . . . . C,915
Teeters, J. M. English Grammar. Canton, O. 1836. 12°. . . . o,1083
Teeth, Art de conserver les Dents. C. J. de Geraudly. Paris, 1737. 16°. L,842
Dissertation concernant les Dents. R. Bunon. Paris, 1741. 16°. . L,842
Essai sur les Maladies des Dents. R. Bunon. Paris, 1743. 16°. . L,842
Tefft, B. F. Hungary and Kossuth. Philadelphia, 1852. 12°. . . . B,524
Tegg, W. Dictionary of Chronology. London, 1854. 8°. . . . . A,306
Tegoborski, L. de. Productive Forces of Russia. Lond. 1855-56. 2 v. 8°. B,541
Tehauntepec, Isthmus of. J. J. Williams. New York, 1852. 2 v. 8°. . V,201
Teignmouth, Lord. See *Shore, Sir J.*
Telegraph, Electric, and Electricity. G. Wilson. London, 1862. p. 8°. . I,666
History and Progress of. R. Sabine. London, 1869. 12°. . M,857
History and Theory of. G. B. Prescott. Boston, 1864. 12°. M,690
Sketch of. A. Jones. New York, 1852. 8°. . . . . . M,708
Hand-Book of. R. Bond. London, 1870. 12°. . . . . . M,831
Oceanic, Laying of the Cable. J. Mullaly. New York, 1858. 8°. . M,697
Telegraph Manipulation. C. V. Walker. London, 1850. 16°. . . N,252,36
Telegraph Manual. T. P. Shaffner. New York, 1859. 8°. . . . M,696
Telegraphic Cables; edited by C. Manby. London, 1858. 8°. . . N,252,46
Telegraphy, Electricity, etc., Questions on. W. McGregor. Lond. 1868. 12°. M,850
Télémaque, Aventures de. F. de S. de L. M. Fénélon. Paris, 1854. 12°. . H,886
The same. New York, 1854. 2 v. 18°. . . . . . . . H,933
The same. Paris, 1853. 8°. . . . . . . . . . . H,939
The same; translated. New York, n. d. 8°. . . . . . H,947
Telescope, The. Sir J. F. W. Herschel. Edinburgh, 1861. 16°. . . N,258
Half-Hours with. R. A. Proctor. London, 1868. 16°. . . . N,256

Tellkampf, A. Physikalische Studien. Hannover, 1854. 8°. . . . . G,713
Temme, J. D. H. Der Domherr; Historischer Roman. Leip. 1867. 4 v. 16°. G,514
Temper and Temperament. S. S. Ellis. New York, 1846. 12°. . . K,698
Temperance Cause, Church's Duties in. B. P. Aydelott. Cin. 1865. 24°. P,10
Temperance Convention, World's. New York, 1851. 8°. . . . B,809,1
Zoological. E. Hitchcock. Northampton, 1854. 12°. . . . N,624
Temperance Law, Maine. H. Phillips, jr. n. p. 1852. 8°. . . *B,809,1
Tempest and Sunshine. M. J. Holmes. New York, 1868. 12°. . . K,193
Temple, H. J., *Lord Palmerston*, Life of. H. L. Bulwer. Phil. 1871. 2 v. 12°. C,1213
Temple, Sir W., Life of. T. P. Courtenay. London, 1836. 2 v. 8°. . . D,80
Works. London, 1720. 2 v. f°. . . . . . . . . . Q,303
Temple Bar. London, 1861–68. 22 v. 8°. . . . . . . . . . R,3
Tempsky, G. F. von. Mitla; Journey in Mexico and Cen. Am. Lon. 1858. 8°. V,204
Temptations, Three Great, of Young Men. S. W. Fisher. Cincin. 1859. 12°. H,262
Ten Acres Enough. E. Morris. New York, 1864. 12°. . . . . . M,498
Ten Great Religions; Comparative Theology. J. F. Clarke. Bost. 1871. 8°. P,584
Ten Nights in a Bar-Room. T. S. Arthur. Philadelphia, n. d. 16°. . J,615
Ten times One is Ten. E. E. Hale. Boston, 1871. 16°. . . . . . J,627
Ten Thousand a Year. S. Warren. Philadelphia, n. d. 8°. . . K,1064
The same. Leipzig, 1845. 3 v. 16°. . . . . . . J,515
Ten Thousand Wonderful Things. E. F. King. London, n. d. 12°. . H,317
Ten Tribes of Israel. B. A. Simon. London, 1836. 8°. . . . . . C,387
Ten Years of Preacher Life. W. H. Milburn. New York, 1859. 12°. C,1005
Tenant of Wildfell Hall. A. Brontë. New York, n. d. 12°. . . . K,611
Tennant, S. Metals found after Solution of Platina. London, 1804. 4°. N,252,42
Tennemann, W. G. History of Philosophy. London, 1852. 12°. . . L,255
Tennent, Sir J. E. Christianity in Ceylon. London, 1850. 8°. . . . P,636
History of Modern Greece. London, 1845. 2 v. 8°. . . . . A,116
Wild Elephant, Method of Capturing, etc. London, 1867. 16°. . N,681
Tennessee, Annals of. J. G. M. Ramsey. Philadelphia, 1853. 8°. . . C,276
Code enacted, 1857–58. R. J. Meigs and W. F. Cooper. Nash. 1858. 8°. P.D.
Down in. J. R. Gilmore. New York, 1864. 12°. . . . . . K,291
House Journal, 1859–60. Nashville, 1859. 8°. . . . . . . . P.D.
Public Acts, 1859–60. Nashville, 1860. 8°. . . . . . . . P.D.
Kentucky and Ohio, Travels to. F. A. Michaux. Lond. 1805. 8°. V,73
Senate Journal, 1859–60. Nashville, 1859. 8°. . . . . . P.D.
Report of Agricultural Bureau, 1855–57. Nashville, 1856–58. 2 v. 8°. P.D.
Reports, 1857–58. Nashville, 1858. 8°. . . . . . . . P.D.
Reports from Public Officers, 1859–60. Nashville, 1860. 8°. . . P.D.
Statute Laws, v 1. Knoxville, 1831. 8°. . . . . . . . . P.D.
Tenney, A. A. Natural History of Animals. New York, 1866. 12°. . N,654
Tenney, S. Geology. Philadelphia, 1860. 8°. . . . . . . . N,766
Manual of Zoölogy. New York, 1866. 8°. . . . . . . N,654
Tennyson, A. Elaine; illustrated by G. Doré. London, 1867. f°. . . *Q,241
Enoch Arden, etc. Boston, 1864. 12°. . . . . . . . . I,446
Guinevere; illustrated by G. Doré. London, 1867. f°. . . . *Q,242
Holy Grail, and other Poems. Boston, 1870. 16°. . . . . . I,451
Idyls of the King. Boston, 1859. 12°. . . . . . . . . I,449
In Memoriam. Boston, 1854. 16°. . . . . . . . . . I,448

Tennyson, A. Poetical Works. Boston, 1866. 2 v. 16°. . . . . . I,447

Vol. 1. Minor Poems; Princess; Enoch Arden.
2. In Memoriam; Maud; Charge of the Light Brigade; Idylls of the King.

The same. Leipzig, 1860. 6 v. 16°. . . . . . . J,476

Vol. 1. Idylls of the King; Maud. Vol. 3, 4. Miscellaneous.
2. In Memoriam; Princess. 5 Enoch Arden, etc.
Vol. 6. Holy Grail, etc.

Vivien; illustrated by G. Doré. London, 1867. f°. . . . *Q,243

Ténot, E. Paris in December, 1851. New York, 1870. 12°. . . . B,346

Tent on the Beach, and other Poems. J. G. Whittier. Boston, 1867. 16°. I,153

Tenterden, *Lord.* See *Abbott, C.*

Terentius, A. P. Comœdiæ; illustrav. N. E. Lemaire. Parisiis, 1828. 2 v. 8°. U,351

The same; translated by H. T. Riley. London, 1853. p. 8°. L,86

Terhune, M. V., *Marion Harland.* Alone. New York, 1869. 12°. . . K,315

At Last. New York, 1870. 12°. . . . . . . . . K,331

Common Sense in the Household; Housewifery. New York, 1871. 12°. H,326

Helen Gardner's Wedding Day. New York, 1870. 12°. . . . K,318

Hidden Path. New York, 1866. 12°. . . . . . . . K,316

Husbands and Homes. New York, 1866. 12°. . . . . K,327

Husks, and Col. Floyd's Wards. New York, 1866. 12°. . . . K,328

Miriam. New York, 1866. 12°. . . . . . . . . K,329

Moss-Side. New York, 1857. 12°. . . . . . . . . K,330

Nemesis. New York, 1866. 12°. . . . . . . . . K,317

Phemie's Temptation. New York, 1870. 12°. . . . . . K,332

Ruby's Husband. New York, 1869. 12°. . . . . . K,333

Sunny Bank. New York, 1867. 12°. . . . . . . . K,334

Ternaux, H. Bibliothèque Américaine, jusqu'a 1700. Paris, 1837. 4°. . L.R.

Teniers, D., Life of. C. Blanc. London, 1855. 4°. . . . . . . Q,179

Test, A. Manual of Animal Magnetism. Philadelphia, 1844. 12°. . . L,879

Testimony; its Posture in the Scientific World. n. t. p. 8°. . . . N,252,46

of the Rocks. H. Miller. Boston, 1857. 12°. . . . . . N,616

Teutonic Name-System. R. Ferguson. London, 1864. 8°. . . . . L,520

Teverino. Madame Dudevant. New York, 1855. 12°. . . . K,1122

Texan Emigrant. E. Stiff. Cincinnati, 1840. 12°. . . . . . . V,20

Texas. M. A. Holley. Lexington, 1836. 12°. . . . . . . . . C,197

and Mexico, Adventures in. E. Domenech. London, 1858. 8°. . V,21

and New Mexico, Explorations in. J. R. Bartlett. N. Y. 1854. 2 v. 8°. V,124

Fiscal History of. W. M. Gouge. Philadelphia, 1852. 8°. . . C,193

History of. D. B. Edward. Cincinnati, 1836. 12°. . . . C,163

H. Yoakum. New York, 1856. 2 v. 8°. . . . . . C,188

Journey through. F. L. Olmsted. New York, 1860. 12°. . . V,91

Textile Fabrics. Prüfung der Gewebe. H. Schacht. Berlin, 1853. 8°. . G,766

Thacher, J. History of Plymouth. Boston, 1835. 12°. . . . . . C,5

Thackeray, A. I. Story of Elizabeth. Philadelphia, n. d. 12°. . K,1034

The same. Leipzig, 1863. 16°. . . . . . . . J,477

Village on the Cliff. New York, 1868. 8°. . . . . . K,1169

Thackeray, W. M. Ballads. Boston, 1856. 16°. . . . . . . . I,452

Catherine. Leipzig, 1870. 16°. . . . . . . . . . J,479

Denis Duval. Leipzig, 1867. 16°. . . . . . . . . . J,480

Early and Late Papers. Boston, 1867. 12°. . . . . . K,1090

English Humorists of the Eighteenth Century. New York, 1854. 12°. H,681

Thackeray, W. M. English Humorists of the 18th Century. N. Y. 1867. 12°. H,458
The same. Leipzig, 1853. 12°. . . . . . . . . J,481
Four Georges; Lovel the Widower. Leipzig, 1861. 16°. . . J,483
History of Henry Esmond. Philadelphia, 1866. 12°. . . K,1027
The same. Leipzig, 1852. 2 v. in 1. 16°. . . . . . J,482
History of Pendennis. London, 1868. 12°. . . . . K,1029
The same. Leipzig, 1849. 3 v. 16°. . . . . . . J,486
Humorist and the Man of Letters. T. Taylor. New York, 1864. 12°. D,448
Miscellanies. Boston, 1869–70. 5 v. 12°. . . . . K,1038

Vol. 1. Memoirs of Barry Lyndon; Great Hoggarty Diamond; Novels by Eminent Hands; Jeames's Diary; Adventures of Maj. Gahagan; Legend of the Rhine; Rebecca and Rowena; Next French Revolution; Cox's Diary.
2. Paris Sketch-Book; Yellowplush Papers; Irish Sketch-Book; Journey from Cornhill to Grand Cairo.
3. Book of Snobs; Sketches and Travels in London; Character Sketches; Denis Duval; Men's Wives; Mr. and Mrs. Frank Berry; Dennis Haggarty's Wife; Bedford Row Conspiracy; Little Dinner at Timmins's; Fatal Boots.
4. Four Georges; English Humorists; Charity and Humor; Roundabout Papers; Second Funeral of Napoleon; Little Travels and Roadside Sketches; Fitz-Boodle Papers; Critical Reviews; Wolves and the Lambs.
5. Catherine; Titmarsh among Pictures and Books; Fraser Miscellanies; Christmas Books; Selections from Punch; Ballads, etc.

The same. Philadelphia, 1866. 4 v. 12°. . . . K,1087

Vol. 1. Ballads; Book of Snobs; Fatal Boots; Cox's Diary; Maj. Gahagan.
2. Yellowplush Papers; Jeames's Diary; Sketches in London; Prize Novels; Character Sketches.
3. Barry Lyndon; Legend of the Rhine; Rebecca and Rowena; Little Dinner at Timmins's; Bedford Row Conspiracy.
4. Fitz-Boodle Papers; Men's Wives; Shabby Genteel Story; Great Hoggarty Diamond.

The same. Leipzig, 1849–57. 8 v. 16°. . . . . . J,484

Vol 1. Great Hoggarty Diamond; Book of Snobs.
2. Kickleburys Abroad; Legend of the Rhine; Rebecca and Rowena; Second Funeral of Napoleon; Chronicle of the Drum.
3. Adventures of Maj. Gahagan; Fatal Boots; Ballads.
4. Yellowplush Papers; Jeames's Diary; Cox's Diary.
5. Sketches and Travels in London; Novels by Eminent Hands; Character Sketches.
6. Memoirs of Barry Lyndon.
7. Little Dinner at Timmins's; Bedford Row Conspiracy; Fitz-Boodle Papers; Shabby Genteel Story.
8. Men's Wives.

Newcomes. New York, 1867. 2 v. in 1. 8°. . . . . . K,1028
The same. Leipzig, 1854. 4 v. 16°. . . . . . . J,485
Philip on his Way through the World. Philadelphia, 1866. 12°. K,1026
The same. Leipzig, 1862. 2 v. in 1. 16°. . . . . J,478
Roundabout Papers. New York, 1864. 12°. . . . . K,1089
The same. Leipzig, 1869. 2 v. in 1. 16°. . . . . J,487
Vanity Fair. Philadelphia, 1866. 12°. . . . . . K,1031
The same. Leipzig, 1848. 3 v. 16°. . . . . . J,488
Virginians. New York, 1859. 8°. . . . . . . . K,1032
The same. Leipzig, 1858–59. 4 v. 16°. . . . . . J,489
Thaddeus of Warsaw. J. Porter. Philadelphia, 1867. 12°. . . . K,885
Thaër, A. D. Principles of Agriculture. New York, 1846. 8°. . . M,563
That Boy of Norcott's. C. Lever. New York, 1869. 8°. . . . K,1159
The same. Leipzig, 1869. 16°. . . . . . . . . J,290
Thatcher, B. B. Indian Biography. New York, 1834. 2 v. 16°. . . L,372
Thayer, W. M. Bobbin Boy; or, how Nat got his Learning. Bost. 1863. 16°. J,1293
Good Girl and True Woman. Boston, 1866. 16°. . . . . . J,1498

Thayer, W. M. Poor Boy and Merchant Prince. Boston, 1866. 16°. . J,1499
Printer Boy; Ben. Franklin. Boston, 1863. 16°. . . . . J,1292
Youth's History of the Rebellion. Boston, 1864–66. 4 v. 12°. . J,1280
Vol. 1. Sumter to Roanoke. Vol. 3. Murfreesboro' to Fort Pillow.
2. Roanoke to Murfreesboro'. 4. Fort Pillow to the End.
Theater, American, History of. W. Dunlap. New York, 1832. 12°. . I,712
British; edited by J. Bell. London, 1776–78. 20 v. 12°. . . I,682
Contents. See *Drama, British Theater.*
Modern; edited by E. Inchbald. London, 1811. 10 v. 16°. . . I,684
Contents. See *Drama, Modern Theater.*
of the Greeks. Cambridge, 1827. 8°. . . . . . . . H,728
de Famille. E. Boquet-Liancourt. Paris, 1870. 12°. . . . I,743
Les Gentillatres; Après le Duel; L'Indécis; Le Retour d'Ulysse; L'Envers d'un Beau Mariage; Les Trois Sœurs; Oscar.
Theaters in Europe, Account of. L. Riccoboni. London, 1741. 8°. . . I,740
Theism, Treatise on. F. Wharton. Philadelphia, 1859. 12°. . . . P,267
Thénard, L. J. Description d'un Fourneau à Coupelle. Paris, 1813. 8°. N,252,15
Theodore Leigh; a Novel. A. Cudlip. New York, 1865. 8°. . . . K,666
Theocritus. Idylliums; tr. with Notes by F. Fawkes. Lond. 1767. 8° . U,452
Bion, Moschus, and Tyrtæus. Idylls; trans. by J. Banks. Lond. 1853. L,87
Selections; tr. by R. Polwhele. Exeter, 1786. 4°. . . U,480
Theodoretus and Scholasticus, E. Church Hist., 322–594. Lond. 1854. p. 8°. L,33
Theognis. Works; translated by J. Banks. London, 1856. p. 8°. . . L,60
Theological Essays. F. D. Maurice. Cambridge, 1853. 12°. . . . P,67
Theological Repository. J. Priestley. London, 1784–95. 6 v. 8°. U,294,24–29
Theology, Comparative; Ten Great Religions. J. F. Clarke. Boston, 1871. 8°. P,584
explained and defended. T. Dwight. New York, 1867. 4 v. 8°. . P,716
Geology in its Bearings on. H. Miller. Boston, 1859. 12°. . . N,616
Institutes of. H. Venema. Andover, 1853. 8°. . . . . . P,119
Logic in, and Essays. I. Taylor. London, 1859. 16°. . . . P,74
Natural. T. Chalmers. New York, 1845. 2 v. 12°. . . . P,208
T. H. Gallaudet. New York, n. d. 16°. . . P,746,28
W. Paley. New York, 1847. 2 v. 18°. . . . L,403
Astronomy and Physics. W. Whewell. London, 1852. p. 8°. L,277
Discourse on. H. Brougham. London, 1836. 12°. . . P,155
The same. London, 1856. p. 8°. . . . . . . P,171
Lectures on. P. A. Chadbourne. New York, 1869. 12°. . P,66
Outline of a System of. G. Crabbe. London, 1840. 8°. . P,219
of Inventions. J. Blakely. New York, 1856. 12°. . . . . P,85
Recent Inquiries in; edited by F. H. Hedge. Boston, 1861. 12°. . P,270
System of. G. W. von Leibnitz. London, 1850. 8°. . . . P,173
Theophrastus, Caractères de Théophraste. J. de La Bruyère. Par. 1852. 2v. 12°. H,862
The same. Paris, 1853. 8°. . . . . . . . . H,892
Theoria Motus. C. F. Gauss; tr. by C. H. Davis. Boston, 1857. 4°. . M,823
Theory of Teaching, with Practical Illustrations. Boston, 1841. 12°. O,1004
Thermometrical Navigation. J. Williams. Philadelphia, 1799. 8°. . . M,774
Theron and Aspasio. J. Hervey. Bewick, 1802. 2 v. 12°. . . . H,587
Thibaut, A. F. J. Reinheit der Tonkunst. Heidelberg, 1826. 16°. . . G,646
Thibet, China, and Tartary, Christianity in. E. R. Huc. Lond. 1857–58. 3 v. 8°. V,622
China and Tartary, Journey thro'. E. R. Huc. N. Y. 1852. 2 v. 12°. V,588
The same. London, 1865. p. 8°. . . . . . . . I,657

Thiele, R. A. Fuselöl. Leipzig, 1853. 8°. . . . . . . . . N,252,44
Thieme, A. Gedichte. Naumburg, 1855. 24°. . . . . . . . E,282
Thierry, A. Conquest of England by the Normans. Lond. 1861. 2 v. p. 8°. L,242
Formation and Progress of the Tiers Etat. London, 1855. 2 v. 8°. B,242
The same. London, 1859. p. 8°. . . . . . . . L,243
Historical Essays. Philadelphia, 1845. 8°. . . . . . . A,344
Moeurs et Caractères au 19me Siècle et au 18me. Bruxelles, 1836. 16°. H,1038
Œuvres. Bruxelles, 1839. 8°. . . . . . . . . . . H,1006
Lettres sur l'Histoire de France; La Conquète d'Angleterre; Dix ans d'Etudes historiques.
Thiers, A. History of the Consulate and Empire. Phila. 1864-65. 5 v. 8°. B,256
The same. Philadelphia, 1861. 4 v. 8°. . . . . . S.C.
History of the French Revolution. New York, 1868. 4 v. in 2. 8°. B,254
Mississippi Bubble; Memoir of John Law. New York, 1859. 12°. . D,154
Things by their Right Names. A. L. Barbauld. New York, 1854. 16°. J,1462
not generally known. J. Timbs. London, 1846-49. 6 v. in 3. 16°. I,544
edited by D. A. Wells. New York, 1859. 12°. . . . H,233
to be remembered. J. Timbs. London, 1863. 16°. . . . . M,808
Thinks-I-to-myself. E. Nares. Philadelphia, 1864. 16°. . . . . K,860
Thiodolf, the Icelander. F. La Motte Fouqué. New York, n. d. 12°. . G,221
Thirlwall, C. History of Greece. New York, 1851. 2 v. 8°. . . . A,98
The same. London, 1835-44. 8 v. 12°. . . . . . . M,994
History of Rome. London, 1834-35. 2 v. 12°. . . . . M,995
Thirty-Ninth Congress, History of. W. H. Barnes. Indianapolis, 1867. 8°. B,722
Thirty Years in the Senate. T. H. Benton. New York, 1856-58. 2 v. 8°. B,665
out of the Senate. S. Smith. New York, 1859. 12°. . . . H,74
Thirty Years' War; Revolt of Netherlands. F. v. Schiller. Lon. 1857. 2v. p.8°. L,228,1,2
The same. New York, 1852. 12°. . . . . . . . B,208
The same. Edinburgh, 1828. 2 v. 16°. . . . . . I,503
Warriors of. E. Cust. London, 1865. 2 v. 12°. . . . . . D,512
Thomas de Burton. Chronicon Monasterii de Melsa. Lond. 1866-68. 3 v. 8°. W,193
Thomas, A. See *Cudlip, A.*
Thomas Aquinas. Commentary of the Four Gospels. Oxf. 1841-45. 4 v. in 8. 8°. P,473
Thomas, D. (Ed.) The Homilist. London, n. d. 8 v. 12°. . . . . P,693
Thomas, E. S. Reminiscences of Sixty-five Years. Hartford, 1840. 2 v. 12°. C,980
Thomas, F. W. Address on the Institution of Odd Fellows. Cin. 1834. 8°. H,302,4
Clinton Bradshaw. Cincinnati, 1847. 2 v. in 1. 8°. . . . *T,19,3
Thomas, J. and Baldwin, T. Gazetteer of the United States. Phila. 1854. 8°. L.R.
Pronouncing Gazetteer of the World. Philadelphia, 1870. 8°. L.R.
The same. Philadelphia, 1858. 8°. . . . . . . R.R.
Dictionary of Biography. Philadelphia, 1870-71. 2 v. 8°. . . L.R.
Thomas, J. J. American Fruit Culturist. Auburn, 1854. 12°. . . . . M,552
Farm Implements. New York, 1854. 12°. . . . . . . M,512
Thomas, R. Hand-Book of Fictitious Names. London, 1868. 8°. . . L.R.
Thomas of Elmham. Hist. Monasterii S. Augustini. London, 1858. 8°. . W,158
Liber Metricus de Henrico V. London, 1858. 8°. . . . . . W,161
Thome, J. A. and Kimball, J. H. Emancipat. in West Indies. N.Y. 1838. 12°. V,186
Thomes, W. H. Bushrangers; Yankee's Advent. in Australia. Bost. 1870. 12°. K,114
Gold Hunters' Adventures. Boston, 1870. 12°. . . . . . . K,115
Thompson, A. B. History of England. London, 1865. 12°. . . . . A,390

Thompson, A. C. Better Land. Boston, 1869. 12°. . . . . . . . P,50
Seeds and Sheaves; or, Words of Scripture. Boston, 1869. 12°. . P,45
Thompson, B., *Count of Rumford*, Life of. J. Renwick. Boston, 1860. 12°. C,860,15
Memoir of. G. E. Ellis. Philadelphia, 1871. 8°. . . . . . C,848
Thompson, B. F. History of Long Island. New York, 1859. 8°. . . C,99
Thompson, C. P. Letters from Rome. New York, 1854. 12°. . . . V,498
Thompson, D. P. Centeola and other Tales. New York, 1864. 12°. . K,298
Gaut Gurley; or, the Trappers of Umbagog. Philadelphia, 1860. 12°. K,349
Green Mountain Boys. Boston, 1870. 12°. . . . . . . K,391
History of Montpelier, 1781–1860. Montpelier, 1860. 8°. . . C,27
Locke Amsden, the Schoolmaster. Boston, 1848. 12°. . . . K,350
May Martin, and other Tales. Boston, 1869. 12°. . . . . K,393
Rangers; or, the Tory's Daughter. Boston, 1869. 12°. . . . K,392
Thompson, D. W. Day-Dreams of a Schoolmaster. Edinburgh, 1864. 16°. O,934
Wayside Thoughts on Education. Edinburgh, 1868. 8°. . . . O,976
Thompson, E. P. Note-Book of a Naturalist. London, 1845. 12°. . . N,658
Thompson, H. and others. History of Roman Literature. Lond. 1852. 12°. H,720
Thompson, J. P. Memoir of David Hale. New York, 1850. 12°. . . C,709
Memoir of David T. Stoddard. New York, 1859. 12°. . . C,736
Unity of the Bible. Philadelphia, 1871. 8°. . . . . . . P,284
Thompson, W. Distribution of Wealth. London, 1869. 8°. . . . O,560
Natural History of Ireland. London, 1849–51. 3 v. 8°. . . O,109
Thompson, Z. History of Vermont. Burlington, 1842. 8°. . . . C,28
Thoms, W. J. (Ed.) Reynard the Fox. London, 1844. 12°. . . L,606,12
Thomson, A. T. Celebrated Friendships. London, 1861. 2 v. 8°. . . C,561
Life of G. Villiers, *Duke of Buckingham*. London, 1860. 3 v. 12°. D,162
Literary Characters and Celebrated Places. London, 1854. 2 v. 12°. H,396
Memoirs of Sarah, *Duchess of Marlborough*. London, 1839. 2 v. 8°. D,163
Thomson, E. Educational Essays. Cincinnati, 1856. 12°. . . O,1178
Sketches, Biographical and Incidental. Cincinnati, 1857. 12°. . H,256
Thomson, J. Poem to the Memory of W. Congreve. London, 1843. 12°. L,606,9
Poetical Works; illustrated by B. Foster. London, 1855. 16°. . I,453
The same; with Memoir by N. H. Nicolas. Lond. 1847. 2 v. 16°. I,454
The same. Boston, 1857. 2 v. 16°. . . . . . I,232
The same. Edinburgh, n. d. 12°. . . . . . . . I,455
The same. Philadelphia, 1848. 8°. . . . . . . J,857
The same; with Life; edited by R. Bell. Lond. 1855. 2 v. 16°. I,255
The same. Leipzig, 1853. 16°. . . . . . . . J,490
Thomson, J. B. Practical Arithmetic. Cincinnati, 1848. 12°. . . O,1100
Thomson, K. B. Jacobites of 1715 and 1745. London, 1845–46. 3 v. 8°. D,688
and J. C. Queens of Society. London, 1870. 12°. . . . . C,590
The same. New York, 1861. 12°. . . . . C,592
Wits and Beaux of Society. London, 1867. 12°. . . . C,589
The same. New York, 1861. 12°. . . . . C,591
Thomson, M. Doesticks' Letters; and what he says. Philadel. n. d. 12°. K,347
Elephant Club. Philadelphia, n. d. 12°. . . . . . . . K,348
Witches of New York. Philadelphia, n. d. 12°. . . . . K,346
Thompson, R. Illustrations of British History. Edinburgh, 1828. 2 v. 16°. I,504
Thomson, R. D. Examination of the Cowdie Pine Resin. Glasg. 1843. 8°. N,252,21
Geology of Berwickshire. Berwickshire, 1831. 8°. . . . . N,252,44

Thomson, R. D, Parietin; a yellow Coloring Matter. Glasgow, 1843. 8°. N,252,21
Thomson, R. S. Calisthenic and Hygienic Exercises. London, 1854. 16°. M,304
Thomson, S. Wild Flowers. London, 1866. 16°. . . . . . N,922
Thompson, T. History of the Royal Society. London, 1812. 4°. . . F,165
Mineralogy, Geology, and Mineral Analysis. London, 1836. 2 v. 8°. N,859
Thomson, W. M. The Land and the Book. New York, 1869. 2 v. 12°. V,634
Thoreau, H. D. Cape Cod. Boston, 1866. 12°. . . . . . . . . V,72
Excursions. Boston, 1866. 16°. . . . . . . . . . H,12
Maine Woods. Boston, 1868. 12°. . . . . . . . . . V,71
Walden. Boston, 1869. 12°. . . . . . . . . . . H,11
Week on the Concord and Merrimack Rivers. Boston, 1862. 12°. . V,24
Yankee in Canada, etc. Boston, 1866. 12°. . . . . . . V,176
Thornbury, G. W. Life in Spain. New York, 1860. 12°. . . . V,471
Songs of the Cavaliers. London, 1857. 12°. . . . . . . I,100
Turkish Life and Character. London, 1860. 2 v. 12°. . . . V,552
Thorndale; or, the Conflicts of Opinions. W. Smith. Boston, 1859. 12°. K,1168
Thornton, J. Q. Oregon and California in 1848. New York, 1849. 2 v. 12°. V,41
Thornton, J. W. Landing at Cape Ann. Boston, 1854. 8°. . . . C,49
Thornton, R. Religious Pieces; edited by G. G. Perry. London, 1867. 8°. P,897
Thornton, W. Account of the Origin of Steamboats. Wash. 1814. 8°. *B,809,1
Thornwell, E. Ladies' Guide to Gentility. New York, 1857. 12°. . . H,288
Thorough-Bass and Theory of Tuning. W. Crotch. London, 1856. 8°. *M,421,1
Harmony and Composition. J. G. Albrechtsberger. Lon. 1855. 3v. 8°. *M,421,2
Thorough-Bass School. W. A. Mozart. London, 1854. 8°. . . *M,421,1
Thorpe, a Quiet English Town. W. Mountford. Boston, 1852. 12°. . K,363
Thorpe, B. Northern Mythology. London, 1851–52. 3 v. 12°. . . P,917
Thorpe, C. and others. British Marine Conchology. London, 1844. 12°. O,25
Thory, C. A. et Redouté. Les Roses peintes et décrites. Paris, 1829. 3 v. 8°. *N,1028
Thou, J. A. de. Historiæ sui Temporis. London, 1733. 7 v. f°. . . Q,316
Life of. J. Collinson. London, 1807. 8°. . . . . . . D,665
Thought and Morals, Mechanism in. O. W. Holmes. Boston, 1871. 12°. O,626
Elements of. I. Taylor. New York, 1851. 12°. . . . . O,654
Investigation of the Laws of. G. Boole. London, 1854. 8°. . . O,690
Limits of Religious. H. L. Mansel. Boston, 1860. 12°. . . . P,191
Thoughts and Things at Home and Abroad. E. Burritt. Bost. 1854. 12°. P,149
Thoughts for the Thoughtful. B. P. Aydelott. Cincinnati, 1866. 24°. . P,9
Thoughts on Bores. M. Edgeworth. New York, 1859. 12°. . . K,678,17
Thousand Miles' Walk across South America. N. P. Bishop. Bost. 1870. 16°. J,1610
Three Beauties. E. D. E. N. Southworth. Philadelphia, 1870. 12°. . K,439
Three Clerks. A. Trollope. New York, 1860. 12°. . . . . K,1052
Three Courses and a Dessert. G. Cruikshank. London, 1867. p. 8°. . L,100
Three English Statesmen. G. Smith. London, 1867. 8°. . . . C,1224
Three Eras of a Woman's Life. T. S. Arthur. Philadelphia, n. d. 16°. J,616
Three Gardens; Eden, Gethsemene, Paradise. W. Adams. N.Y. 1868. 12°. P,95
Three Guardsmen. A. Dumas. Philadelphia, n. d. 8°. . . . . H,989
Three Proverb Stories. L. M. Alcott. Boston, 1871. 16°. . . . . K,19
Three Scouts. J. T. Trowbridge. Boston, 1865. 12°. . . . J,1446
Three Successful Girls. J. Crouch. New York, 1871. 12°. . . . K,151
Three Tales of the Olden Time. Sir J. Froissart. London, 1854. 16°. J,1201
Throne of David. J. H. Ingraham. Boston, 1864. 8°. . . . . . K,197

Throop, M. H. The Future; a Political Essay. New York, 1864. 12°. . H,35
Through Night to Light. F. Spielhagen. New York, 1870. 12°. . . G,219
Thrower, W. Questions in Arithmetic. London, 1855. 12°. . . O,1099
Thuanus. See *Thou, J. A. de.*
Thucydides, Analysis and Summary of. J. T. Wheeler. Lond. 1855. p. 8°. L,256
Historia Belli Peloponnesiaci. Paris, 1840. 8°. . . . . . U,558
Peloponnesian War; trans. by S. T. Bloomfield. Lond. 1829. 3 v. 8°. A,84
The same; translated by H. Dale. London, 1868. 2 v. p. 8°. L,88
The same. New York, 1855. 12°. . . . . . A,65
The same; translated by W. Smith. New York, 1753. 2 v. 18°. U,374
Thunder and Lightning. W. de Fonvielle. London, 1868. 12°. . M,1048
Thuringia, Wandurung durch Thüringen. L. Bechstein. Leip. n. d. 12°. E,184
Thurston, D. History of Winthrop, Maine. Portland, 1855. 12°. . . C,16
Thynn, F. Debate between Pride and Lowliness. London, 1841. 8°. I,885,5
Tibullus, A. Opera; ed. P. A. de Goldbéry. Parisiis, 1826. 8°. . . U,352
and Catullus, C.V. Poems; trans. by W. K. Kelly. Lond. 1854. p. 8°. L,46
Ticknor, C. Philosophy of Living. New York, 1855. 16°. . . . L,393
Ticknor, G. History of Spanish Literature. New York, 1849. 3 v. 8°. H,767
Life of William H. Prescott. Boston, 1866. 12°. . . . . C,875
The same. Boston, 1864. 4°. . . . . . . . . *C,759
Tiers Etat, Formation and Progress of. A. Thierry. Lond. 1855. 2 v. 8°. B,242
The same. London, 1859. p. 8°. . . . . . . . L,243
Tiger-Hunter. M. Reid. New York, 1870. 12°. . . . . J,1574
Tilemaking. E. Dobson. London, 1857. 12°. . . . . . . M,909
Tile Pavements, Specimens of. H. Shaw. London, 1858. 4°. . . *Q,186
Tileston, E. G. Hand-Book of Admin. of United States. Bost. 1871. 16°. B,682
Tilton, T. Sanctum Sanctorum. New York, 1870. 12°. . . . . H,240
Timber, Canvas, etc., Preservation of. Sir W. Burnett. Lond. 1848. 8°. N,252,40
Timber Trees, British. J. Blenkarn. London, 1859. 8°. . . . . N,950
History and Description of. London, 1830. 16°. . . . L,491,2
Timbs, J. Book of Wonders, Events, and Discoveries. London, n. d. 12°. M,681
Club-Life of London. London, 1866. 2 v. 12°. . . . . B,58
Curiosities of London. London, 1855. 16°. . . . . . V,298
English Eccentrics and Eccentricities. London, 1866. 2 v. 8°. . H,706
Lady Bountiful's Legacy. London, 1868. 12°. . . . . . I,543
Painting explained. London, 1859. 16°. . . . . . . . M,3
Popular Errors. London, 1849. 16°. . . . . . . M,809
Stories of Inventors and Discoverers. New York, 1860. 12°. . . C,521
Things not generally known. Lond. 1866–69. 6 v. in 3. 16°. viz.:
Vol. 1. General Information. . . . . . . I,544
2. Curiosities of Science. . . . . . . I,545
3. Curiosities of History; Popular Errors. . . . I,546
Things to be remembered. London, 1863. 16°. . . . . M,808
Wonderful Inventions. London, 1868. 8°. . . . . . M,682
Year-Book of Facts, 1839–71. London, 1839–71. 33 v. 16°. . . M,810
Extra vol. Exhibition of 1851. London, 1851. 16°. . . M,811
International Exhibition of 1862. London, 1862. 16°. M,812
Time and Tide. A. S. Roe. New York, 1869. 12°. . . . . . K,241
Timmins, S. (Ed.) Birmingham and Midland Hardware Dist. Lond. 1866. 8°. O,580
Timpson, T. Memoirs of Elizabeth Fry. New York, 1847. 12°. . C,1171

Timur-Bec; or, Tamerlain, History of. Cherefeddin Ali. Lond. 1723. 2v. 8°. D,769
Tin, Sheet-Iron, and Copper-Plate Workers. L. J. Blinn. Phil. 1869. 12°. M,671
Tindal, N. History of England. London, 1744-47. 13 v. 8°. . A,421,16-28
Tinn, G. Treatise on Cholera. Newcastle, 1837. 8°. . . . . N,252,1
Tippecanoe, Letters on the Battle of. W. H. Harrison. Cincin. 1840. 8°. *C,797
Titan; a Romance. J. P. F. Richter. Boston, 1868. 2 v. 12°. . . G,215
Titcomb, Timothy, *pseud.* See *J. G. Holland.*
Titles to Real Property, Manual upon. M. E. Curwen. Cincin. 1865. 16°. U,484
Tobacco and Alcohol. J. Fiske. New York, 1869. 16°. . . . . H,222
its History and Associations. F. W. Fairholt. London, 1859. 12°. H,467
Tobique, New Brunswick, Two Months on the. London, 1866. 12°. . . V,175
Tochter des Präsidenten. F. Bremer. Leipzig, 1857. 12°. . . E,313,1
Tocqueville, A. de. Democracy in America. New York, 1854. 2 v. in 1. 8°. V,68
Memoirs, Letters, and Remains. Boston, 1862. 2 v. 8°. . . . D,629
Old Regime and the Revolution. New York, 1856. 12°. . . . B,241
Todd, C. S. and Drake, B. Sketches of Wm. H. Harrison. Cin. 1847. 18°. C,831
Todd, H. J. Illustrations of Gower and Chaucer. London, 1810. 8°. . H,705
Todd, J. Student's Manual. Northampton, 1854. 12°. . . . O,1028
Sunset Land; Great Pacific Slope. Boston, 1870. 16°. . . . V,92
Todd, R. B. (Ed.) Cyclop. of Anat. and Physiology. Lond. 1859. 5 v. in 6. 8°. *L,1034
Todhunter, I. Algebra. London, 1866. 12°. . . . . . . M,1098
Algebra for Beginners. London, 1869. 16°. . . . . . M,1109,1
Key to the same. London, 1869. 8°. . . . . . M,1109,2
Algebra for Schools. London, 1870. 8°. . . . . . . M,1098,1
Key to the same. London, 1870. 8°. . . . . . M,1098,2
Analytical Statics. London, 1866. 8°. . . . . . . M,1108
Differential Calculus. London, 1864. 8°. . . . . . . M,1106
Elementary Treatise on Equations. London, 1867. 12°. . . M,1102
Elements of Euclid. London, 1869. 16°. . . . . . M,1133
Examples of Analytical Geometry. London, 1864. 8°. . . M,1107
History of the Theory of Probability. London, 1865. 8°. . M,1162
Mechanics for Beginners. London, 1870. 16°. . . . . M,1136
Mensuration for Beginners. London, 1869. 16°. . . . M,1135
Plane Trigonometry. London, 1864. 12°. . . . . M,1142
Spherical Trigonometry. London, 1863. 8°. . . . . . M,1137
Treatise on the Integral Calculus. London, 1868. 12°. . . M,1146
Treatise on Plane Co-ordinate Geometry. London, 1867. 12°. M,1143
Trigonometry for Beginners. London, 1868. 16°. . . . M,1134
Todleben's Defense of Sebastopol. W. H. Russell. London, 1865. 8°. . B,88
To Love and to be Loved. A. S. Roe. New York, 1869. 12°. . . . K,243
Toilers of the Sea. V. Hugo. New York, 1866. 8°. . . . . . . H,946
Tolleneck. E. Hoefer. Wien, 1864. 3 v. 24°. . . . . . . . G,325
Tom and Sarah Neal. J. Lamb. Philadelphia, 1871. 16°. . . J,1688
Tom Bentley; Story of a Prodigal. Boston, 1870. 16°. . . . J,1541
Tom Brown at Oxford. T. Hughes. Boston, 1864. 2 v. 12°. . . . K,728
Tom Brown's School Days. T. Hughes. Leipzig, 1858. 16°. . . . J,198
Tom Burke of Ours. C. Lever. London, 1865. 2 v. 12°. . . . K,790
The same. Leipzig, 1848. 3 v. 16°. . . . . . . J,291
Tom Jones, History of. H. Fielding. London, 1820. 3 v. 12°. . . K,533
The same. New York, 1858. 2 v. 12°. . . . . U,172,1,2

Tom Jones, History of. H. Fielding. Leipzig, 1844. 2 v. in 1. 16°. . J,163
Tomes, R. The Champagne Country. New York, 1867. 12°. . . . V,460
Panama in 1855. New York, 1855. 16°. . . . . . . . V,172
Tomline, G. Life of William Pitt. London, 1821. 2 v. 4°. . . . F,21
Tomlinson, C. Construction of Locks. London, 1858-59. 12°. . . M,967
History of Pottery and Porcelain. Columbus, 1861. 8°. . . . M,622
Mechanics. London, 1859. 12°. . . . . . . . . . M,968
Natural Philosophy. London, 1859. 12°. . . . . . . . M,969
Pneumatics. London, 1858-59. 12°. . . . . . . . M,970
Warming and Ventilation. London, 1858. 12°. . . . . M,971
Tone-Masters. C. Barnard. Boston, 1871. 3 v. 16°. . . . J,1344
Vol. 1. Mozart and Mendelssohn. Vol. 2. Handel and Haydn. Vol. 3. Bach and Beethoven.
Tonempfindungen, Lehre von. H. Helmholtz. Braunschweig, 1865. 8°. G,642
Tonga Islands. W. Mariner. London, 1818. 2 v. 8°. . . . . . V,894
The same. Edinburgh, 1827. 2 v. 16°. . . . . . I,500
Tonge, T. Heraldic Visitation of Northern Counties, 1530. Durh. 1863. 8°. F,126,41
Tonna, C. E. Conformity; Falsehood and Truth. N. Y. 1866. 2 v. in 1. 16°. J,1105
Judæa Capta. New York, 1869. 16°. . . . . . . J,1195
Judah's Lion. New York, n. d. 16°. . . . . . . J,1106
Wrongs of Women. New York, n. d. 16°. . . . . . J,1107
Tony Butler; a Novel. C. Lever. New York, 1865. 8°. . . . . . K,791
The same. Leipzig, 1866. 2 v. in 1. 16°. . . . . . J,292
Too Strange not to be True. G. Fullerton. New York, 1865. 3 v. in 1. 8°. K,702
The same. Leipzig, 1864. 2 v. in 1. 16°. . . . . . J,172
Tooke, A. Pantheon of the Heathen Gods. Baltimore, 1832. 12°. . . P,911
Tooke, J. H. Letter to Lord Ashburton. London, 1782. 8°. . . . O,565
Memoir of. J. H. Stephens. London, 1813. 2 v. 8°. . . . D,77
Tooke, W. Monarchy of France. London, 1855. 8° . . . . . B,264
View of the Russian Empire. London, 1800. 3 v. 8°. . . . B,540
Topham, J. Chemistry made easy. New York, 1856. 12°. . . M,533,3
Topics of the Time. J. Parton. Boston, 1871. 12°. . . . . . . H,131
Topographical Drawing, Manual of. R. S. Smith. New York, 1864. 8°. M,209
Tor Hill. H. Smith. London, 1826. 3 v. in 1. 12°. . . . . . K,567
Torquemada, J. de. Monarchia Indiana con el Origen y Guerras de los Indios Ocidentales. Madrid, 1723. 3 v. f°. . . . . . . F,106
Torrey, J. Flora of the State of New York. Albany, 1843. 2 v. 4°. *Q,101,6,7
and Gray, A. Flora of North America, v 1. New York, 1838-40. 8°. N,1021
Tortoise Shell, Chemische Untersuchungen des. A. Völcker. Göttin. 1847. 8°. N,252,40
Tottie, C. Designs for Sepulchral Monuments. London, 1843. f°. . *Q,224
Tour of Doctor Syntax. W. Combe. London, 1866. 24°. . . . . . I,326
Tour round my Garden. A. Karr. London, 1865. 16°. . . . . . H,474
Toussaint, C. J. Manuel complet d'Architecture. Paris, 1837. 2 v. 24°. M,589
Toussaint l'Ouverture, Life of. J. R. Beard. London, 1853. 8°. . . C,876
Toussaint, P., Memoir of. H. F. Lee. Boston, 1854. 16°. . . . C,700
Tower, D. B. Key to Intellectual Algebra. New York, 1845. 16°. O,1098
and Tweed, B. F. Elements of English Grammar. N. Y. 1854. 16°. O,1068
Tower, F. B. Illustrations of the Croton Aqueduct. N. Y. 1845. 4°. . *Q,270
Towle, C. W. Stories for Freemason's Fireside. Cincinnati, 1868. 12°. . K,9
Towle, G. M. History of Henry V., King of England. N. Y. 1866. 8°. . D,373

Towle, N. C. Hist. and Analysis of Constitution of U. S. Bost. 1861. 12°. O,492
Town and Country, and Voices in Shells. R. H. Stoddard. N.Y. 1858. 12°. J,1261
and Forest. A. Manning. London, 1860. 12°. . . . . J,599
Towne, P. A. Primary Arithmetic. Louisville, Ky. 1867. 12°. . . M,1093
Towne, S. Progressive Speaker and Common School Reader. Bost. n. d. 12°. O,1247
Towneley Mysteries, The. London, 1836. 8°. . . . . . . F,126,3
Townley Gallery, British Museum. Sir H. Ellis. London, 1836. 2 v. 16°. L,490
Townley, J. Illustrations of Biblical Literature. New York, 1842. 2 v. 8°. P,472
Towns, Cleansing and Drainage of. W. A. Guy. London, 1846. 8°. N,252,29
Townsend, L. T. Credo. Boston, 1870. 16°. . . . . . . . . P,40
Townsend, V. F. Hollands. Boston, 1871. 12°. . . . . . . K,277
Mills of Tuxbury. Boston, 1871. 12°. . . . . . . . K,226
Townsend, W. C. Modern State Trials. London, 1850. 2 v. 8°. . . O,423
Townshend, H. Hist. Collect. of Parliaments of Elizabeth. Lond. 1680. f°. F,279
Tozer, H. F. Monks of Mount Athos. London, 1862. 8°. . . V,1086,2
Norway. London, 1861. 8°. . . . . . . . . . V,1086,1
Tracts relating to Great Britain. J. Somers; edited by Sir W. Scott. London, 1809–15. 13 v. 4°. . . . . . . . . . . F,130
Tracy, S. Mother and her Offspring. New York, 1853. 12°. . . . L,913
Trade Circular Annual for 1871. F. Leypoldt. New York, 1871. 8°. . L.R.
Trades, Book of. J. Wylde. London, 1866. 16°. . . . . . . M,668
Boy's Book of. London, 1866. sm. 4°. . . . . . . J,1284
of the United States. E. F. Freedley. Philadelphia, 1856. 8°. . C,595
Theorie und Praxis der Gewerbe. J.R.Wagner. Leip. 1858–64. 5v. 8°. G,773
Tradesman, Complete English. D. De Foe. v. 2. London, n. d. 16°. . I,590
Tradesman's Companion. M. L. Byrn. New York, 1867. 12°. . . M,673
Trades-Unions, Origin of, and History of Gilds. L.Brentano. Lon. 1870. 8°. L,605,40
Trälinnan. F. Bremer. London, 1852. 12°. . . . . . . L,169,1
Trafford, F. G. See *Riddell, J. H.*
Traill, C. P. Backwoods of Canada. London, 1839. 16°. . . . . . I,470
Canadian Crusoes. Boston, n. d. 16°. . . . . . . J,1616
Stories of the Canadian Forest. Boston, n. d. 16°. . . J,1615
Traill, T. S. Lectures on Medical Jurisprudence. Edinburgh, 1836. 12°. N,252,23
Train, G. F. American Merchant in Europe, Asia, etc. N. Y. 1857. 12°. V,1034
Spread-Eagleism. New York, 1859. 12°. . . . . . . H,36
Young America in Wall Street. New York, 1857. 12°. . . O,485
Training in Streets and Schools. W. Knighton. London, 1855. 16°. O,1121
Philosophy of. A. R. Craig. London, 1843. 16°. . . . O,1122
Trans-Kaukasia. A. F. von Haxthausen. Leipzig, 1856. 2 v. 8°. . E,216
The same; translated. London, 1854. 8°. . . . . V,703
Transmission, Mechanism and Machinery of. W. Fairbairn. Phil. 1867. 12°. M,610
of Ancient Books to Modern Times. I. Taylor. London, 1859. 8°. H,722
of Life; the Masculine Function. G. H. Napheys. Phil. 1871. 12°. L,978
Transportation, Colonization, Thoughts on. R. Whately. London, 1832. 8°. P,117
Transubstantiation, History of Popish. J. Cosin. Oxford, 1850. 12°. . P,807
Trap-Rocks in the County of Galway. R. Mallet. Dublin, 1838. 4°. N,252,57
Travel and Adventure, Boy's Book of. M. Johnes. London, n. d. 16°. J,1237
Art of. F. Galton. London, 1855. 12°. . . . . . . V,1095
Pictures of. H. Heine. Philadelphia, 1858. 12°. . . . . G,32

Traveler's Library. London, 1864. 25 v. p. 8°. viz.:

|  |  |  |
|---|---|---|
| Vol. 1. | Ferguson, R. Swiss Men and Swiss Mountains. | 1,656,1 |
| | Auldjo, J. Ascent of Mont Blanc. | 1,656,1 |
| | Tschudi, F. von. Sketches of Nature in the Alps. | 1,656,1 |
| 2. | Gregorovius, F. Corsica. | 1,656,2 |
| | Barrow, J. Tour on the Continent in 1852. | 1,656,2 |
| 3. | Laing, S. Residence in Norway. | 1,656,3 |
| | Laing, S. Notes of a Traveler in Europe. | 1,656,3 |
| 4. | Miles, P. Nordurfari; or, Rambles in Iceland. | 1,656,4 |
| | Forrester, T. Rambles in Norway. | 1,656,4 |
| 5. | Custine, A. Russia. | 1,656,5 |
| 6. | McCulloch, J. R. Russia and Turkey. | 1,656,6 |
| | Jerrmann, E. Pictures from St. Petersburgh. | 1,656,6 |
| | Brooks, S. Russians of the South. | 1,656,6 |
| 7. | Hope, I. Brittany and the Bible. | 1,656,7 |
| | Hope, I. Brittany and the Chase. | 1,656,7 |
| | Baines, E. Visit to the Vaudois of Piedmont. | 1,656,7 |
| | Mayne, F. Voyages and Discoveries in Arctic Regions. | 1,656,7 |
| 8. | Kinglake, A. W. Eothen; Travels in the East. | 1,657 |
| | Huc, E. R. Tartary, Thibet, and China. | 1,667 |
| | La Gironière, P. de. Twenty Years in the Philippines. | 1,657 |
| 9. | Mason, G. H. Life with the Zulus of Natal. | 1,658,1 |
| | Hutchinson, T. J. Niger, Tshadda, and Binu's Exped. | 1,658,1 |
| 10. | Durrieu, X. Present State of Morocco. | 1,658,2 |
| | Werne, F. African Wanderings. | 1,658,2 |
| 11. | Wilberforce, E. Brazil through a Naval Glass. | 1,659,1 |
| | Hurlbut, W. H. Pictures of Cuba. | 1,659,1 |
| 12. | Lanman, C. Adventures in the Wilds of North America. | 1,659,2 |
| | Jameson, A. Sketches of Canada. | 1,659,2 |
| 13. | Hughes, W. The Australian Colonies. | 1,660 |
| | Pfeiffer, I. Lady's Voyage round the World. | 1,660 |
| 14. | Memoir of the Duke of Wellington. | 1,661,1 |
| | Cockayne, T. O. Life of Marshal Turenne. | 1,661,1 |
| | Gleig, G. R. The Leipzig Campaign. | 1,661,1 |
| | Wagner, F. and Bodenstedt. F. Schamyl. | 1,661,1 |
| 15 | Rogers, H. Life and Genius of T. Fuller. | 1,661,2 |
| | Turkey and Christendom; from Edinburgh Review. | 1,661,2 |
| | Ranke, L. Ferdinand I. and Maximilian II. of Austria. | 1,661,2 |
| 16. | Forster, J. D. De Foe and C. Churchill. | 1,661,3 |
| | Piozzi, H. L. Anecdotes of S. Johnson. | 1,661,3 |
| | Jeffrey, F. J. Swift and S. Richardson. | 1,661,3 |
| 17. | Holcroft, T. Memoirs by himself. | 1,661,4 |
| | Arago, F. History of my Youth. | 1,661,4 |
| | Hayward, A. Lord Chesterfield and G. Selwyn. | 1,661,4 |
| 18. | Smith, S. Selections from his Writings. | 1,662 |
| 19, 20. | Macaulay, T. B. Selections from Essays and Speeches. 2 v. | 1,663 |
| 21. | Seaward, Sir E. Narrative of his Shipwreck. | 1,664,1 |
| | Souvestre, E. Confessions of a Workingman. | 1,664,1 |
| | Souvestre, E. Attic Philosopher in Paris. | 1,664,1 |
| 22. | Southey, R. A Love Story; from "The Doctor." | 1,664,2 |
| | Addison, J. Sir Roger de Coverley. | 1,664,2 |
| | Dumas, A. Memoir of a Maitre d'Armes. | 1,664,2 |
| 23. | Our Coal and our Coal Pits. | 1,665 |
| | Cornwall; its Mines and Miners. | 1,665 |
| 24. | Kemp, T. L. Natural History of Creation. | 1,666 |
| | Kemp, T. L. Indications of Instinct. | 1,666 |
| | Wilson, G. Electricity and Electric Telegraph. | 1,666 |
| | Wilson, G. Chemistry of the Stars. | 1,666 |
| 25. | Carlisle, Earl. Lectures and Addresses. | 1,667 |
| | Mormonism; from Edinburgh Review. | 1,667 |
| | McCulloch, J. R. London in 1850–51. | 1,667 |
| | Spencer, H. Railway Morals and Policy. | 1,667 |
| | Stark, A. Printing; its Antecedents, History, etc. | 1,667 |

Travels, Over the Ocean. C. Guild. Boston, 1871. 12°. . . . . . v,292
Treasures of the Earth. W. Jones. New York, 1870. 16°. . . . J,1621
Treatise on Repentance. London, n. d. 18°. . . . . . . . P,6
Trebizond, Geschichte des Kaiserthums von. J.P.Fallmerayer. Mün.1827. 4°. E,34
Tredgold, T. Carpentery and Joinery. London, 1859. 12°. . . . M,957
 Carpentry of Roofs. London, 1859. 12°. . . . . . . . M,956
 Steam Engine; its Invention and Improvement, v. 1. Lond. 1838. 4°. Q,367
  Atlas to the same. London, 1840. f°. . . . . . . Q,391
 (Ed.) Tracts on Hydraulics. London, 1826. 8°. . . . . . N,143
  Smeaton, J. Power of Wind and Water to turn Mills.
  Venturi, G. B. Experiments on the Motion of Fluids.
  Eytelwein, J. A. Practical Hydraulics; translated by T. Young.
Tree, What may be learned from a. New York, 1863. 12°. . . . N,1023
Trees and Shrubs of Massachusetts. G. B. Emerson. Boston, 1846. 8°. N,1017
 Arboretum et Fruticetum Britan. J. C. Loudon. Lond. 1844. 6 v. 8°. N,990
 Der Baum. H. Schacht. Berlin, 1853. 8°. . . . . . . G,894
 British Timber. J. Blenkarn. London, 1859. 8°. . . . . . N,950
 Entwickelung der Baumrinde. J. Hanstein. Berlin, 1853. 8°. . G,872
 from Nature. G. Barnard. London, 1868. f°. . . . . *Q,452
 in Landscape, Treatise on. E. Kennion. London, 1844. f°. . *Q,208
 Lesson on. J. D. Harding. London, n. d. 4°. . . . . *Q,212
 North-American Sylva. F. A. Michaux. Philadelphia, 1859. 3 v. 8°. N,1039
  The same continued by T. Nuttall. Philadel. 1859. 2 v. 8°. N,1040
 of America. D. J. Browne. New York, 1846. 8°. . . . . N,1024
 Portraits of Forest. J. G. Strutt. London, 1826. f°. . . . *Q,350
 Silva; a Discourse of Forest. J. Evelyn. London, 1706. f°. . Q,121
Trelawney, E. J. Adventures of a Younger Son. London, n. d. 16°. . K,693
 Last Days of Shelley and Byron. Boston, 1859. 12°. . . . C,1244
Tremenheere, H. S. Constitutions of U. S. and England comp. Lond. 1854. 8°. O,576
Trench, R. C. Authorized Version of the New Testament. N. Y. 1858. 12°. L,729
 Calderon; his Life and Genius. New York, 1856. 12°. . . . D,702
 English Language, Past and Present. New York, 1858. 12°. . . L,546
 Epistles to the Seven Churches in Asia. London, 1861. 8°. . . P,521
 Glossary of English Words. New York, 1859. 12°. . . . . L,547
 Holy Scriptures; Hulsean Lectures, 1845-46. Phila. 1854. 12°. . P,48
 Lessons in Proverbs. New York, 1853. 12°. . . . . . . L,506
 Notes on the Miracles of our Lord. New York, 1855. 8°. . . P,517
 Notes on the Parables of our Lord. New York, 1855. 8°. . . P,516
 Poems. New York, 1856. 12°. . . . . . . . . . . I,456
 Studies in the Gospels. London, 1867. 8°. . . . . . . P,279
 Study of Words. London, 1869. 16°. . . . . . . . L,509
 Synonyms of the New Testament. New York, 1858. 12°. . . L,730
Trench, W. S. Realities of Irish Life. Boston, 1869. 12°. . . . K,1012
Trent, W. Journal from Logstown to Pickawillany, 1752. Cincinnati, 1871. 8°. C,253
  The Miami Confederacy; Historical Sketch of the Post at Pickawillany; Biographical Sketch of William Trent; Gov. R. Dinwiddie's Letters to the Board of Trade, 1752; Journal of Capt. Wm. Trent, 1752.
Trent, Council of, Catechism of; trans. by T. A. Buckley. London, 1852. 8°. P,890
  Canons of. T. A. Buckley. London, 1851. 12°. . . . . P,888
Trenton, N. J., Presbyterian Church, History of. J. Hall. N. Y. 1859. 12°. C,88
Trescot, W. H. Diplomacy of the Revolution. New York, 1852. 12°. . B,743
Trevelyan, C. E. Education of the People of India. London, 1838. 12°. O,921

Trevelyn Hold. Mrs. H. Wood. Leipzig, 1864. 2 v. in 1. 16°. . . . . J,533
Trial, The; more Links of Daisy Chain. C. M. Yonge. N. Y. 1866. 12°. K,1083
The same. Leipzig, 1864. 2 v. in 1. 16°. . . . . . J,552
Trial by Jury, History of. W. Forsyth. London, 1852. 8°. . . . O,422
Trial of J. Magee for Libel. Dublin, 1790. 8°. . . . . . . . P.D.
Trials and Confessions of a Housekeeper. T. S. Arthur. Phila. n. d. 16°. J,617
Modern State. W. C. Townsend. London, 1850. 2 v. 8°. . . . O,423
State, Collection of. T. B. and T. J. Howell. Lond. 1816-28. 34 v. 8°. U,701
State, of the United States. F. Wharton. Philadelphia, 1849. 8°. . O,426
Tribune Almanac, 1838-68. New York, 1868. 2 v. 12°. . . . . . T,50
Tricotrin. L. de la Rame. Philadelphia, 1870. 12°. . . . . . . K,876
The same. Leipzig, 1870. 2 v. in 1. 16°. . . . . . J,416
Tried for her Life. E. D. E. N. Southworth. Philadelphia, 1871. 12°. . K,397
Trigonometrical Examples. S. Newth. London, 1859. 8°. . . M,1144
Trigonometry. J. Hann. London, 1849. 12°. . . . . . . . . M,930
T. P. Kirkman. London, 1852. 12°. . . . . . . . M,942
Ebene Trigonometrie. C. Koppe. Essen, 1853. 8°. . . . . E,435
Elements of. A. M. Legendre. New York, 1867. 8°. . . M,1129
Elements of Analytic. F. R. Hassler. New York, 1826. 8°. . M,1157
Elements of Plane. J. C. Snowball. Cambridge, 1837. 8°. . M,1158
for Beginners. I. Todhunter. London, 1868. 16°. . . . M,1134
Plane. I. Todhunter. London, 1869. 12°. . . . . . M,1142
Plane and Spherical. J. Hymers. London, 1858. 8°. . . M,1156
O. Gregory. London, 1816. 16°. . . . . . . M,1139
Plane, Solutions of Examples in. J. W. Colenso. Lond. 1856. 16°. M,1085
Spherical. I. Todhunter. London, 1863. 8°. . . . . . M,1137
Traité de, Rectiligne et Sphérique. Paris, 1813. 8°. . . M,1128
Treatise on. G. B. Airy. London, 1855. p. 8°. . . . . M,1141
Trilobites, Organisation der Trilobiten. H. Burmeister. Berlin, 1843. 8°. Q,4
Organization of. H. Burmeister. London, 1846. 4°. . . . . Q,63
Tripp, A. Crests from the Ocean World. Boston, 1855. 12°. . . . . V,385
Tristram, H. B. Great Sahara. London, 1860. 8°. . . . . . . V,811
Winter Ride in Palestine. London, 1864. 8°. . . . . V,1086,3
Tristram Shandy. L. Sterne. Philadelphia, 1867. 12°. . . . . K,1019
The same. Leipzig, 1849. 16°. . . . . . . . . J,468
Triumph over Midian. C. Tucker. London, 1869. 12°. . . . . . K,571
Trivet, N. Annales sex Regum Angliæ. London, 1845. 8°. . . . . U,626
Trollope, A. Barchester Towers. Leipzig, 1859. 2 v. in 1. 16°. . . J,491
Belton Estate. New York, 1866. 8°. . . . . . . . K,1059
The same. Leipzig, 1866. 2 v. in 1. 16°. . . . . J,492
Bertrams. Leipzig, 1859. 2 v. in 1. 16°. . . . . . . . J,493
Can you forgive her? New York, n. d. 8°. . . . . . K,1042
The same. Leipzig, 1865. 3 v. 16°. . . . . . . J,494
Castle Richmond. New York, 1860. 12°. . . . . . . . K,1043
The same. Leipzig, 1860. 2 v. in 1. 16°. . . . . J,495
Claverings. New York, 1866. 8°. . . . . . . . . K,1044
The same. Leipzig, 1867. 2 v. in 1. 16°. . . . . J,496
Doctor Thorne. New York, 1867. 12°. . . . . . . K,1045
The same. Leipzig, 1858. 2 v. in 1. 16°. . . . . J,497
Framley Parsonage. Leipzig, 1861. 2 v. in 1. 16°. . . . . J,498

Trollope, A. He knew he was Right. New York, 1869. 8°. . . K,1046
The same. Leipzig, 1869. 3 v. 16°. . . . . . . J,499
Last Chronicle of Barset. New York, 1867. 8°. . . . K,1047
The same. Leipzig, 1867. 3 v. 16°. . . . . . . J,500
Miss Mackenzie. New York, n. d. 8°. . . . . . . K,1048
North America. New York, 1862. 12°. . . . . . . . V,55
The same. Leipzig, 1862. 3 v. 16°. . . . . . . J,501
Orley Farm. New York, n. d. 8°. . . . . . . . K,1049
The same. Leipzig, 1862. 3 v. 16°. . . . . . . J,502
Phineas Finn. New York, 1868. 8°. . . . . . . . K,1050
The same. Leipzig, 1869. 3 v. 16°. . . . . . . J,503
Rachel Ray. Leipzig, 1863. 2 v. in 1. 16°. . . . . . J,504
Ralph the Heir. New York, 1871. 12°. . . . . . . K,1060
Small House at Allington. New York, 1864. 8°. . . . K,1051
The same. Leipzig, 1864. 3 v. 16°. . . . . . . J,505
Three Clerks. New York, 1860. 12°. . . . . . . K,1052
Vicar of Bullhampton. Leipzig, 1870. 2 v. in 1. 16°. . . . J,559
Warden. Leipzig, 1859. 16°. . . . . . . . . . J,506
West Indies and Spanish Main. Leipzig, 1860. 16°. . . . J,507
Trollope, F. Paris and the Parisians in 1835. New York, 1836. 8°. . V,459
Trollope, T. A. Beppo. Philadelphia, 1870. 12°. . . . . . K,1040
Decade of Italian Women. London, 1859. 2 v. 8°. . . . D,731
Garstangs of Garstang Grange. Leipzig, 1870. 2 v. in 1. 16°. . J,508
Gemma; a Novel. Philadelphia, n. d. 12°. . . . . . K,1053
Girlhood of Catharine de Medici. London, 1856. 12°. . . . D,723
History of the Commonwealth of Florence. London, 1865. 4 v. 8°. B,494
Lindisfarn Chase. New York, 1865. 8°. . . . . . . K,1054
Marietta. Philadelphia, 1870. 12°. . . . . . . . K,1041
Paul the Pope and Paul the Friar. London, 1861. 8°. . . K,1055
Trollope, W. Greek Grammar to the New Testament. London, 1842. 8°. L,739
Trommsdorff, J. B. Bereitung des Bleiweisses im grossen. Erfurt, 1827. 4°. N,252,41
Tropical World. G. Hartwig. London, 1863. 8°. . . . . . . N,538
Tropics, Health Trip to the. N. P. Willis. New York, 1853. 12°. . . V,135
Troschel, F. H. and Ruthe, J. F. Handbuch der Zoologie. Berlin, 1853. 8°. G,916
Trout, Fly-Fishing for. G. P. R. Pulman. London, 1851. 16°. . . M,326
Trowbridge, C. M. How to Conquer; or, Allen Ware. Phila. 1870. 16°. J,1690
Trowbridge, J. T. Burrcliff. New York, 1869. 16°. . . . . . J,1210
Cudjo's Cave. Boston, 1869. 12°. . . . . . . . . K,351
Deserted Family. Philadelphia, n. d. 16°. . . . . . . K,355
Father Brighthopes. New York, 1869. 16°. . . . . . J,1213
Hearts and Faces. New York, 1869. 16°. . . . . . J,1214
Ironthorpe, the Pioneer Preacher. New York, 1869. 16°. . J,1212
Lucy Arlyn. Boston, 1866. 12°. . . . . . . . . K,121
Martin Merivale; his × Mark. Boston, 1854. 12°. . . . . K,118
Neighbors' Wives. Boston, 1867. 12°. . . . . . . . K,22
Old Battle Ground. New York, 1869. 16°. . . . . . J,1211
Three Scouts. Boston, 1865. 12°. . . . . . . . J,1446
Vagabonds, and other Poems. Boston, 1869. 16°. . . . . I,148
Troy, Topography of. W. Gell. London, 1804. f°. . . . . . . L.R.
Troyes, J. de. Secret History of Louis XI. London, 1856. 2 v. 8°. . L,326

True, the Beautiful, and the Good. V. Cousin. New York, 1854. 8°. . O,629
and Beautiful and Nature. J. Ruskin. New York, 1868. 8°. . . M,75
True History of a Little Ragamuffin. J. Greenwood. London, n. d. 8°. . K,694
True Manliness. L. C. Tuthill. Philadelphia, 1867. 16°. . . . J,1685
True Riches, and other Tales. T. S. Arthur. Philadelphia, n. d. 16°. . J,618
True Robinson Crusoes. C. Russell. Boston, 1871. 12°. . . . J,1538
True Secret History of England. London, 1725. 2 v. 8°. . . . A,482
True Stories from Ancient History. A. Strickland. New York, 1868. 16°. J,1377
from History and Biography. N. Hawthorne. Boston, 1866. 12°. U,40,12
from Modern History. A. Strickland. New York, 1868. 16°. . J,1274
Trueba y Cosio, T. de. Conquest of Peru. Edinburgh, 1830. 16°. . . I,529
Life of Hernando Cortes. Edinburgh, 1829. 16°. . . . . . I,522
Trübner, N. Guide to American Literature. London, 1859. 8°. . . L.R.
Trumbull, B. History of the United States. Boston, 1840. 8°. . . B,620
Trumbull, J. M'Fingal; a Modern Epic Poem. Hartford, 1856. 8°. . I,166
Trumps; a Novel. G. W. Curtis. New York, 1870. 12°. . . . . K,126
Truran, W. Iron Manufacture of Great Britain. New York, 1867. 8°. . M,738
Trust and Trial. M. Howitt. London, 1858. 12°. . . . . . . J,573
Truth and Poetry; Autobiography. J. W. von Goethe. v. 2. N. Y. 1850. 12°. D,509
Guesses at. J. C. and A. W. Hare. Boston, 1865. 12°. . . . H,124
in Love; Sermons. J. D. Smith. Philadelphia, 1864. 12°. . . P,190
Truth's Advocate and Anti-Jackson Expositor. Cincinnati, 1828. 8°. . O,593
Truth's Conflicts and Truth's Triumphs. S. Jenner. London, 1854. 8°. . P,301
Tschudi, F. von. Thierleben der Alpenwelt. Leipzig, 1865. 8°. . . G,935
Sketches of Nature in the Alps. London, 1865. p. 8°. . . I,656,1
Tschudi, J. J. von and Rivero, M. E. Peruvian Antiquities. Cin. 1854. 12°. C,390
Reisen durch Südamerika. Leipzig, 1866–68. 4 v. 8°. . . . E,178
Travels in Peru. New York, 1849. 12°. . . . . . . . V,236
Untersuchungen über die Fauna Peruana. St. Gallen, 1844–46. f°. *Q,64
Tucker, A. Light of Nature. London, 1668–77. 3 v. in 5. 8°. . . P,313
The same; with Life by Sir H.P.St.J.Mildmay. Lon.'52. 2 v. 8°. P,104
Tucker, C., *A.L.O.E.* Crown of Success. London, 1870. 16°. . . . J,663
Claudia. New York, 1870. 16°. . . . . . . . . K,575
Exiles in Babylon; or, Children of Light. London, 1869. 12°. . K,591
Fairy Know-a-bit; or, a Nutshell of Knowledge. London, 1868. 12°. J,659
Hebrew Heroes; Tale of Jewish History. London, 1869. 12°. . K,576
The Mine; or, Darkness and Light. London, 1870. 16°. . . J,662
Miracles of Heavenly Love in Daily Life. London, 1870. 16°. . J,660
Rescued from Egypt. London, 1868. 12°. . . . . . . K,570
Shepherd of Bethlehem. London, 1869. 12°. . . . . . . K,592
Silver Casket. London, 1870. 16°. . . . . . . . . J,661
Triumph over Midian. London, 1869. 12°. . . . . . . K,571
Young Pilgrim. London, 1869. 12°. . . . . . . . . K,577
Tucker, G. History of the United States. Philadelphia, 1856–57. 4 v. 8°. B,652
Life of Thomas Jefferson. London, 1837. 2 v. 8°. . . . . C,944
Tucker, L. American Husbandry. New York, 1854. 2 v. 18°. . . M,436
Tuckerman, H. T. America and her Commentators. New York, 1864. 8°. V,69
Artist-Life; American Painters. New York, 1847. 12°. . . . M,38
Biographical Essays. Boston, 1857. 8°. . . . . . . C,555
Book of the Artists; American Artist-Life. New York, 1867. 8°. . M,282

Tuckerman, H. T. Character and Portraits of Washington. N. Y. 1858. 4°. *F,38
Criterion. New York, 1866. 12°. . . . . . . . . . H,41
Italian Sketch-Book. New York, 1848. 12°. . . . . . . V,493
Memorial of Horatio Greenough. New York, 1853. 12°. . . C,1003
Month in England. New York, 1853. 12°. . . . . . . V,359
Optimist. New York, 1850. 12°. . . . . . . . . . H,9
Poems. Boston, 1851. 16°. . . . . . . . . . . I,149
Sicily; a Pilgrimage. New York, 1852. 12°. . . . . . . V,467
Sketch of American Literature. Philadelphia, 1854. 12°. . . H,694
Tuckerman, J. Ministry at Large in Boston. Boston, 1838. 12°. . . P,49
Tuckey, J. K. Exploration of the River Congo. New York, 1818. 8°. . V,833
Tuckfield, H. Education for the People. London, 1839. 16°. . . . O,990
Tudor, H. Tour in North America. London, 1834. 2 v. 12°. . . V,19
Tudor Princesses, Lives of. A. Strickland. London, 1868. 8°. . . D,384
Tulloch, J. Beginning Life. London, 1864. 16°. . . . . . . H,565
Leaders of the Reformation. Boston, 1860. 12°. . . . . . C,524
Tunneling, Practical. F. W. Simms. London, 1859. 4°. . . . . . M,288
Tupper, M. F. Proverbial Philosophy. New York, 1849. 8°. . . . J,877
Turenne, Marshal, Life of. T. O. Cockayne. London, 1856. p. 8°. . I,661,1
Turk and the Greek. S. G. W. Benjamin. New York, 1867. 16°. . . V,539
E. E. Crowe. London, 1853. 12°. . . . . . . . V,531
Turkey. J. L. Farley. London, 1866. 8°. . . . . . . . . . B,558
and Christendom; from Edinburgh Review. London, 1856. p. 8°. I,661,2
and Greece, Travels in. A. Slade. London, 1854. 8°. . . . . V,580
and its Destiny. C. MacFarlane. Philadelphia, 1850. 2 v. 12°. . V,563
and Russia. J. R. McCulloch. London, 1854. p. 8°. . . I,656,6
City of the Sultan. J. Pardoe. London, 1837. 2 v. 8°. . . V,556
Greece, Russia, etc., Travels. J. L. Stephens. New York, 1855. 12°. V,341
History of. A. de Lamartine. New York, 1855–57. 3 v. 12°. . B,557
in Europe, Travels in. G. M. Mackenzie and A.P. Irby. Lond. 1866. 8°. V,570
Month at Constantinople. A. Smith. London, 1851. 16°. . . V,551
Russia, Austria, etc., Travels in. C. B. Elliott. Phil. 1839. 2 v. 12°. V,339
Russo-Turkish Campaigns, 1828–29. F. R. Chesney. N. Y. 1854. 12°. B,536
Six Voyages through, 1670. J. B. Tavernier. London, 1678. f°. . Q,437
Sketches in. A. De Vere. Philadelphia, 1850. 12°. . . . V,564
Turkish and Greek Waters, Diary in. G. W. F. Howard. Lond. 1855. 8°. V,566
Turkish Empire. A. de Bessé. Philadelphia, 1854. 12°. . . . . V,560
Turkish Language, Grammaire Turke. A. L. Davids. London, 1836. 4°. L,637
Turkish Life and Character. G. W. Thornbury. London, 1860. 2 v. 12°. V,552
Turkish Spy, Letters of. G. P. Marana. London, 1748. 8 v. 16°. . . H,390
Turko-Persian Frontier, Geology of. W. K. Loftus. London, 1855. 8°. N,252,44
Turks in Europe. F. Bouvet. New York, 1853. 16°. . . . . . C,490
of Constantinople. C. M. Kennedy. London, 1864. 8°. . . V,1086,3
Year with the. W. W. Smyth. New York, 1854. 12°. . . . V,561
Turnbull, D. Travels in Cuba and Porto Rico. London, 1840. 8°. . . V,141
Turnbull, G. Observations upon Liberal Education. London, 1742. O,1184
Turnbull, R. Genius of Italy. New York, 1852. 12°. . . . . . V,501
Turner, D. W. Notes on Herodotus. London, 1853. p. 8°. . . . . L,250
Turner, J. W. M. and Girtin. Picturesque Views; ed. T. Miller. Lon. 1854. 8°. *M,136
Turner, O. History of Phelps' and Gorham's Purchase. Rochester, 1851. 8°. C,145

Turner, S. History of the Anglo-Saxons. London, 1823. 3 v. 8°. A,434,1-3
The same. Paris, 1840. 3 v. 8°. . . . . . . . A,492
History of England during Middle Ages. London, 1825. 5 v. 8°. A,434,4-8
Reign of Edward VI., Mary, and Elizabeth. Lond. 1829. 2 v. 8°. A,434,11,12
Reign of Henry VIII. London, 1828. 2 v. 8°. . . . A,434,9,10
Sacred History of the World. New York, 1854. 3 v. 16°. . . L,365
Turner, T. Geographical Reading Book. London, 1857. 16°. . . O,895
Turner, T. H. Domestic Architecture in England, 13th Century. Oxf. 1851. 8°. M,159
Turner's Companion. Philadelphia, 1851. 12°. . . . . . . M,601
Turning and Mechanical Manipulation. C. Holtzapffel. Lon. 1866. 3 v. 8°. M,666
Hand, in Wood, Ivory, Shell, etc. F. Campin. London, 1868. 12°. M,687
Manuel du Tourneur. M. Dessables. Paris, 1839. 2 tom. 16°. . M,596
Turnip Husbandry. D. F. Jones. Dublin, 1847. 16°. . . . N,252,26
Turnips, Experiments on, with Guano, etc. J. Grey. Hexham, 1843. 8°. N,252,25
Turton, W. British Land and Fresh-Water Shells. London, 1857. 12°. O,62
Tuscany, Life in. M. S. Crawford. Columbus, 1859. 8°. . . . . V,512
Tuski, Ten Months among the. W. H. Hooper. London, 1853. 8°. . V,953
Tuthill, L. C. Beautiful Bertha. New York, 1870. 16°. . . . . J,1346
Edith. New York, 1870. 16°. . . . . . . . . . J,1348
I will be a Sailor. Boston, 1864. 16°. . . . . . . . J,1266
I will be a Soldier. Philadelphia, 1867. 16°. . . . . . J,1684
Queer Bonnets. New York, 1870. 16°. . . . . . . J,1347
Romantic Belinda. Philadelphia, 1867. 16°. . . . . . J,1686
Success in Life; the Lawyer. Cincinnati, 1854. 12°. . . K,1092
the Mechanic. Cincinnati, 1854. 12°. . . K,1093
the Merchant. Cincinnati, 1854. 12°. . . K,1094
True Manliness. Philadelphia, 1867. 16°. . . . . . J,1685
Tweed, B. F. Elements of English Grammar. New York, 1854. 16°. . O,1068
Tweedie, W. K. Ruined Cities of the East. London, 1859. 16°. . . J,1309
Twells, L. Life of Edward Pocock. London, 1816. 8°. . . . . C,1289,2
Twelve Months' Campaign in Mexico. G. C. Furber. Cincinnati, 1857. 8°. B,879
Twelve Nights in the Hunters' Camp. W. Barrows. Boston, 1870. 16°. J,1611
Twelve Years' Military Adventure. London, 1829. 2 v. 8°. . . . V,666
Twenty Years after. A. Dumas. Philadelphia, n. d. 8°. . . . . H,990
Twice Married; a Story of Connecticut Life. C. W. Philleo. N. Y. 1855. 12°. K,1100
Twice-Told Tales. N. Hawthorne. Boston, 1865. 2 v. 16°. . . . K,155
The same. Boston, 1868. 2 v. 12°. . . . . . U,40,1,2
Twins, The. F. Bremer. London, 1852. p. 8°. . . . . . L,169,1
Twiss, H. Life of John Scott, *Lord Eldon*. Philadelphia, 1844. 2 v. 8°. D,298
Twiss, T. Letters Apostolic of Pope Pius IX. considered. London, 1851. 8°. P,824
Two Admirals. J. F. Cooper. New York, 1867. 12°. . . . . K,51
The same. New York, 1867. 8°. . . . . . . . . K,78
Two Apprentices. M. Howitt. New York, 1867. 24°. . . . . J,1162
Two Aristocracies. C. G. F. Gore. Leipzig, 1857. 2 v. in 1. 16. . . J,190
Two Baronesses; a Romance. H. C. Andersen. New York, 1869. 12°. . G,227
Two Cosmos; Tale of Fifty Years Ago. Leipzig, 1861. 16°. . . . J,509
Two French Marriages. C. Jenkin. Lepzig, 1868. 2 v. in 1. 16°. . . J,220
Two Guardians. C. M. Yonge. New York, 1866. 12°. . . . K,1084
The same. Leipzig, 1869. 16°. . . . . . . . J,553
Two Marriages. D. M. Craik. New York, 1867. 12°. . . . . K,663

Two Marriages. D. M. Craik. Leipzig, 1867. 16°. . . . . . . J,95
Two Months on the Tobique, New Brunswick. London, 1866. 12°. . . V,175
Two Pictures. M. J. McIntosh. New York, 1863. 12°. . . . . . K,210
Two Sisters. E. D. E. N. Southworth. Philadelphia, 1870. 12°. . . K,438
Two Thousand Miles on Horseback. J. F. Meline. New York, 1868. 16°. V,185
Two Vocations. E. Charles. New York, 1855. 12°. . . . . . K,628
Two Years Ago. C. Kingsley. Boston, 1864. 12°. . . . . . . K,751
The same. Leipzig, 1857. 2 v. in 1. 16°. . . . . . J,244
Two Years before the Mast. R. H. Dana, jr. Boston, 1869. 12. . . V,157
Tyburn Chronicle; or, Villainy Displayed. London, 1768. 4 v. 8°. . *C,563
Tycho Brahe, Galileo, and Kepler, Lives of. D. Brewster. Lond. 1870. p. 8°. C,551
The same. New York, 1854. 16°. . . . . . . . . L,424
Tylney Hall. T. Hood. Hartford, 1846. 12°. . . . . . . . K,726
Tymms, S. Family Topographer. London, 1832–43. 7 v. 16°. . . V,304
Tyndale, W., Life of. G. Offor. London, 1836. 8°. . . . . . . P,417
Tyndall, J. Faraday as a Discoverer. London, 1868. 8°. . . . . D,205
Fragments of Science for Unscientific People. New York, 1871. 12°. M,775
From Lauterbrunnen to the Æggisch-horn. London, 1861. 8°. V,1086,1
Glaciers of the Alps. Boston, 1861. 8°. . . . . . . . . N,785
Heat as a Mode of Motion. New York, 1869. 12°. . . . . N,41
Light and Electricity. New York, 1871. 12°. . . . . . N,29
Radiation. New York, 1868. 12°. . . . . . . . . . N,40
Sound; Eight Lectures. London, 1867. 8°. . . . . . . . N,18
Tyng, S. H. Captive Orphan; Esther. New York, 1860. 12°. . . P,234
Forty Years' Experience in Sunday Schools. New York, 1860. 12°. P,23
Memoirs of Gregory T. Bedell. London, 1835. 12°. . . . . C,809
Type of the Times, v. 7, 8. Cincinnati, 1854–55. 2 v. f°. . . . . *Q,383
Type, Specimens of. See *Printing.*
Typee; or, Residence in the Marquesas Islands. H. Melville. Lond.'47. 12°. V,891
Typical Forms in Creation. J. Mc Cosh and G. Dickie. N. Y. 1856. 8°. P,324
Typographia; the Printer's Instructor. J. Johnson. Lond. 1824. 2 v. 12°. L.R.
Typographical Antiquities. J. Ames. London, 1785–1819. 4 v. 4°. . L.R.
Typography, Parisian, Annals of. W. P. Greswell. London, 1818. 8°. . L.R.
Tyrol, The, and Bavaria. H. D. Inglis. London, 1837. 12°. . . . . V,408
Tyrrell, H. History of the War with Russia. London, n. d. 3 v. 8°. . B,180
Tyrtæus. Selections; translated by R. Polwhele. Exeter, 1786. 4°. . U,480
War Songs; translated by J. Banks. London, 1853. p. 8°. . . L,87
Tyrwhitt, R. St. J. Hand-Book of Pictorial Art. Oxford, 1868. 8°. . M,95
Sinai. London, 1864. 8°. . . . . . . . . . . . V,1086,3
Tyson, P. T. Geology of California. Washington, 1851. 8°. . . . N,876
Tytler, A. F. Leila Books. Boston, 1870. 5 v. 16°. . . . . J,1675

Vol. 1. Leila; or, the Island. Vol. 3. Leila at Home.
2. Leila in England. 4. Mary and Florence.
Vol. 5. Mary and Florence at Sixteen.

Tytler, A. F., *Lord Woodhouselee.* Universal History. Boston, 1843. 2 v. 8°. A,38
The same. London, 1834. 6 v. 16°. . . . . . . I,600
and Nares, E. Universal History. New York, 1854. 6 v. 16°. . L,400
The same, abridged by J. D. Hincks. London, 1849. 18°. . A,16
Tytler, P. F. History of Scotland. Edinburgh, 1864–67. 4 v. in 2. 12°. B,114
Life of Henry VIII. London, 1854. 16°. . . . . . . C,1183

Tyler, P. F. Lives of Scottish Worthies. London, 1832–33. 3 v. 16°. . I,642
Discovery on Northern Coasts of America. New York, 1833. 16°. L,376
Tytler, S. Citoyenne Jacqueline. London, 1865–66. 3 v. 16°. . K,1056
Days of Yore. London, 1866. 2 v. 8°. . . . . . . K,1057
Diamond Rose. London, 1867. 12°. . . . . . . . . K,569
Papers for Thoughtful Girls. Boston, n. d. 12°. . . . J,1290

Udall, N. Ralph Roister Doister; a Comedy. London, 1847. 8°. . I,885,32
Uhden, H. F. New England Theocracy. Boston, 1858. 12°. . . . P,835
Uhland, L. Gedichte. Stuttgart, 1868. 12°. . . . . . . . E,283
Uhlemann, M. Syriac Grammar. New York, 1855. 8°. . . . . . L,782
Uhlhorn, G. Modern Representations of the Life of Jesus. Boston, 1868. 16°. P,373
Ulbach, L. Le Parrain de Cendrillon. Paris, n. d. 12°. . . . H,1039
Ulcers on the Leg, Treatment of. H. T. Chapman. Cincinnati, 1853. 8°. L,922
Ule, O. und Müller, C. Das Weltall. Halle, 1859. 8°. . . . . . G,714
Die Wunder der Sternenwelt. Leipzig, 1860. 8°. . . . . . G,800
(Eds.) Die Natur, v. 1, 2, 8–11. Halle, 1852–62. 6 v. 4°. . . G,740
Ullmann, C. Reformers before the Reformation. Edinburgh, 1855. 2 v. 8°. P,644
Ulric; or, the Voices. T. S. Fay. New York, 1851. 12°. . . . I,33
Unbeliever, Letters to a Philosophical. J. Priestley. Birming. 1787. 8°. U,294,15
Uncle Ralph. Leipzig, 1858. 16°. . . . . . . . . . . J,510
Uncle Silas. J. S. Le Fanu. New York, n. d. 8°. . . . . . . K,766
The same. Leipzig, 1865. 2 v. in 1. 16°. . . . . . J,262
Uncle Tom's Cabin. H. B. Stowe. Boston, 1868. 12°. . . . . . K,287
Key to. H. B. Stowe. Boston, 1853. 8°. . . . . . . O,404
Uncommercial Traveler. C. Dickens. New York, 1871. 12°. . . K,1143
The same. New York, 1869. 12°. . . . . . . K,501
and Hunted Down. C. Dickens. Leipzig, 1860. 16°. . . . J,124
Under Two Flags. L. de la Rame. Philadelphia, 1867. 12°. . . . K,896
Under the Willows. J. R. Lowell. Boston, 1869. 16°. . . . . . I,83
Undercurrents. R. B. Kimball. New York, 1864. 12°. . . . . K,136
Understanding, Conduct of. J. Locke. New York, 1868. 16°. . . L,454
Essay on. J. Locke. London, 1866. 12°. . . . . . . M,838
Undine, *in German*. F. La Motte-Fouqué. Braunschweig, 1860. 16°. . G,275
or, the Water-Spirit. F. La Motte-Fouqué. New York, 1864. 12°. H,923
and other Tales. F. La Motte-Fouqué. New York, 1870. 12°. . H,931
Ungava; a Tale of Esquimaux-Land. R. M. Ballantyne. Boston, 1859. 16°. J,1469
Unger, F. Alter der Menschheit und das Paradies. Wien, 1866. 8°. . E,404
Steiermark zur Zeit der Braunkohlenbildung. Wien, 1866. 8°. . E,404
Wachsthum des Stammes. Wien, 1858. 4°. . . . . . . Q,118
und Endlicher, S. Gründzüge der Botanik. Wien, 1843. 8°. . G,866
Ungewitter, F. H. Europe, Past and Present. New York, 1850. 12°. . A,319
Unhealthiness of Towns. H. Fortescue. London, 1846. 16°. . . N,252,37
G. Robinson. Newcastle, 1847. 8°. . . . . . . . N,252,29
Unitarian Controversy, Half-Century of. G. E. Ellis. Boston, 1857. 8°. P,872
United Presbyterian Church, Principles of. H. Renton. Edinburgh, 1853. 8°. O,1251,3
United States, Administration of Lincoln. H. J. Raymond. N. Y. 1864. 12°. B,904
of Washington and Adams. G. Gibbs. N. Y. 1846. 2 v. 8°. B,811

United States, Agriculture, Reports on, 1860–69. Wash. 1866–70. 8 v. 8°. P.D.
American Archives, 4th ser., v. 2–5. P. Force. Washington, n. d. f°. P.D.
American Citizen. J. H. Hopkins. New York, 1857. 12°. . . O,415
American History. M. Willson. New York, 1847. 8°. . . B,701
American Pocket Atlas. M. Carey. Philadelphia, 1814. 12°. . V,1146
American State Papers. Washington, 1832–61. 33 v. f°. . . P.D.

Claims.
Commerce and Navigation, v. 2.
Finance. v. 3–5.
Foreign Relation. 6 v.
Indian Affairs. v. 2.
Military Affairs. v. 2–7.
Miscellaneous. 2 v.
Naval Affairs. 4 v.
Post Office Department. v. 1.
Public Lands. 8 v.

and Canada, Tour in. C. R. Weld. London, 1855. 12°. . . V,140
Tour in. F. A. F. de La Rochfoucauld-Liancourt. Lond. 1799. 4°. V,152
Travels in. F. Hall. London, 1818. 8°. . . . . . V,179
Appeal respecting. R. J. Walsh. Philadelphia, 1819. 8°. . . B,623
Army, Dictionary of Officers, 1789–1853. C.K.Gardner. N.Y.1853. 12°. L.R.
Meteorological Register, 1843–54. T. Lawson. Wash. 1855. 4°. P.D.
Organization of. F. Robinson. Philadelphia, 1848. 2 v. 8°. B,853
Report on Mortality, 1839-55. R. H. Coolidge. Wash. 1856. 4°. P.D.
The same; 1855–60. Washington, 1855–60. 4°. . P.D.
Assassination of Abraham Lincoln. Washington, 1867. 4°. . . *Q,229
Census, 1840, Compendium of. Washington, 1841. 4°. . . . . Q,299
Census, 1850, and Appendix. Washington, 1853. 4°. . . . P.D.
Mortality Statistics. Washington, 1855. 8°. . . P.D.
Preliminary Report on. Washington, 1853. 8°. . . P.D.
Statistical View of. Washington, 1854. 8°. . . P.D.
Census, 1860. Washington, 1864–66. 4 v. 4°. . . . . . P.D.
Preliminary Report on. Washington, 1862. 8°. . P.D.
Child's History of the. J. Bonner. New York, 1866. 3 v. 12°. . J,1248
C. A. Goodrich. Philadelphia, 1855. 16°. . . . . . J,1152
Coast Survey; Catalogue of Maps. Washington, 1862. 8°. . . L.R.
Report for 1850. A. D. Bache. Washington, 1851. 8°. . P.D.
for 1851. Washington, 1852. 2 v. 8°. and 4°. . . P.D.
for 1854–67. Washington, 1854–69. 15 v. 4°. . . P.D.
Report on History and Progress of, to 1858. Camb. 1858. 8°. P.D.
Colonial and Lake Trade, Report on. I. D. Andrews. Wash. '54. 2 v. 8°. P.D.
Colorado and New Mex. Geolog. Survey. F.V.Hayden. Wash.1869. 8°. P.D.
Colorado River, Report on, 1857–58. J. C. Ives. Washington, 1861. 4°. P.D.
Comic History of. J. D. Sherwood. Boston, 1870. 12°. . . . B,697
Commerce and Navigation, 1853, 55, 63–69. Wash. 1854–70. 9 v. 8°. P.D.
Foreign and Domestic, Statistics of. Washington, 1864. 8°. P.D.
of the Prairies. J. Gregg. Philadelphia, 1850. 2 v. 12°. . V,158
Report of Committee on. Washington, 1830. 8°. . . . . P.D.
Commercial and Revenue System. R. Mayo. Wash. 1847. 2 v. 4°. P.D.
Commercial Relations, 1855–65. Wash. 1856–66. 12 v. 8°. and 4°. P.D.
Common-School History of. B. J. Lossing. New York, 1866. 12°. B,594
Congress, Annals of; Debates, 1789–1825. Wash. 1834–56. 42 v. 8°. P.D.
Debates in, Abridged. T. H. Benton. N. Y. 1857–59. 12 v. 8°. P.D.
Dictionary of. C. Lanman. Philadelphia, 1859. 8°. . . *C,777
Directory, 42d Cong., 1st Sess. B. P. Poore. Wash. 1871. 8°. B,969
Documents, 34th Congress. Washington, 1856–57. 50 v. 8°. P.D.

United States, Congress, Documents, 35th Congress. Wash. 1858–59. 92 v. 8°. P.D.
36th Congress. Washington, 1860–61. 72 v. 8°. . P.D.
37th Congress. Washington, 1862–63. 56 v. 8°. . P.D.
38th Congress. Washington, 1864–65. 50 v. 8°. . P.D.
39th Congress. Washington, 1866–67. 61 v. 8°. . P.D.
40th Congress. Washington, 1868–69. 65 v. 8°. . P.D.
Miscellaneous, 1827–59. Wash. 1827–59. 22 v. 8°. . P.D.
History of, from 1789 to 1793. Philadelphia, 1843. 8°. . B,666
Journal, Nov. 1782–Nov. 1783. Philadelphia, 1800. 8°. . P.D.
Secret Journals, 1775–88. Boston, 1820–21. 4 v. 8°. . . P.D.
Library Catalogue. Washington, 1864. 8°. . . . . . L.R.
Additions, Dec. 1865–Dec. 1866. Washington, 1866. 8°. L.R.
Dec. 1866–Dec. 1867. Washington, 1868. 8°. . L.R.
Dec. 1868–Dec. 1869. Washington, 1870. 8°. . L.R.
Congressional Globe, 1833–70. Washington, 1833–70. 90 v. 4°. . P.D.
Constitution of; edited by J. M. Barclay. Washington, 1860. 8°. . B,720
The same; ed. by W. Hickey. Philadelphia, 1853. 12°. B,718
and of the several States. New York, 1852. 8°. . . . B,664
compared with the British. H. S. Tremenheer. Lond. 1854. 8°. O,576
Debates on Adoption of. J. Elliot. Philadelphia, 1859. 5 v. 8°. O,427
Exposition of. J. Bayard. Philadelphia, 1833. 12°. . . O,480
H. Flanders. Philadelphia, 1860. 12°. . . . B,847
J. Story. New York, 1854. 12°. . . . . . . U,511
History and Analysis of. N. C. Towle. Boston, 1861. 12°. O,492
Massachusetts Convention, 1788. Boston, 1856. 8°. . . C,69
Origin and Adoption of. G. F. Curtis. N. Y. 1854–59. 2 v. 8°. B,663
Proceedings of the Convention. R. Yates. Cin. 1838. 12°. O,479
Questions on. W. B. Wedgewood. Philadelphia, 1844. 12°. O,1087
War Powers under. W. Whiting. Boston, 1871. 8°. . . . U,510
Writings upon. J. Marshall. Boston, 1839. 8°. . . . U,111
Constitutional Jurisprudence of. W. A. Duer. Boston, 1856. 12°. . U,490
The same. New York, 1833. 12°. . . . . . . . O,469
The same, abridged. New York, 1855. 16°. . . . . L,446
Covode Investigation, etc. Washington, 1860. 8°. . . . . P.D.
Cuba and Canada. A. M. Murray. New York, 1856. 12°. . . V,13
H. A. Murray. London, 1855. 2 v. 12°. . . . . V,144
Democracy in. R. H. Gillet. New York, 1868. 12°. . . . O,507
A. de Tocqueville. New York, 1854. 8°. . . . . V,68
Diplomacy of. T. Lyman. Boston, 1826. 8°. . . . . . B,858
Diplomatic Correspondence. Washington, 1863–65. 4 v. 8°. . . P.D.
District of Columbia, Documents on. Washington, 1827–56. 8°. . P.D.
Eastern and Western States. J. S. Buckingham. Lond. n. d. 3 v. 8°. V,122
Educational Institutions of. P. A. Siljeström. London, 1853. 12°. O,811
Eighty Years' Progress of. New York, 1864. 8°. . . . . B,667
Exploring Expedition and Reports, 1838–42, viz.:
Wilkes, C. Narrative of the Expedition. Phila. 1850. 5 v. 8°. V,962
Cassin, J. Mammalogy and Ornithology. Phila. 1858. 4°. . *Q,277
Atlas to the same. Philadelphia, 1858. f°. . . . *Q,351
Dana, J. D. Zoophytes. Philadelphia, 1848. 4°. . . . *Q,278
Atlas to the same. Philadelphia, 1849. f°. . . . *Q,352

United States, Exploring Expedition and Reports, 1838–42. *Continued.* viz.:
Girard, C. Herpetology. Philadelphia, 1858. 4°. . . *Q,279
Atlas to the same. Philadelphia, 1858. f°. . . . *Q,353
Gray, A. Botany, pt. 1; Phanerogamia; Atlas. N.Y. 1857. f°. *Q,354
Hale, H. Ethnography and Philology. Philadelphia, 1846. 4°. *Q,281
Pickering, C. Geographical Distribution of Animals and Plants. Boston, 1854. 4°. . . . . . . . . *Q,282
Exploring Expeditions. J. S. Jenkins. Auburn, 1852. 8°. . . V,963
Finances, Rep. 1849, 52, 55–57, 61–63, 65, 67–70. Wash. 1850–70. 8°. P.D.
From Liverpool to St. Louis. N. Hall. London, 1870. 12°. . . V,23
from 1800–1850; Half-Century. E. Davis. Boston, 1851. 12°. . B,695
Gold Panic Investigation. Washington, 1870. 8°. . . . . . P.D.
Geological Expl. of 40th Parallel, v. 3; Mining Industry and Atlas. J. D. Hague and C. King. Wash. and N.Y. 1870. 2 v. 4°, f°. *Q,356
History of the Federal Government. A. Bradford. Boston, 1840. 8°. B,721
Hand-Book of the Administration. E. G. Tileston. Bost. 1871. 16°. B,682
Histoire des. J. Pelet de la Lozère. Paris, 1845. 8°. . . . B,619
Historical Tracts on the Colonies. P. Force. Wash. 1836–46. 4 v. 8°. B,810
Contents. See *Force, P.*
History of. G. Bancroft. Boston, 1848–67. 9 v. 8°. . . . . B,637
H. Fergus. London, 1830–32. 2 v. 12°. . . . . . M,993
J. Grahame. Philadelphia, 1852. 2 v. 8°. . . . . . B,624
S. Hale. New York, 1840. 2 v. 16°. . . . . . . . L,417
J. C. Hamilton. New York, 1858–65. 7 v. 8°. . . . . B,651
R. Hildreth. New York, 1855. 6 v. 8°. . . . . . B,638
J. H. Hinton. London, n. d. 2 v. 4°. . . . . . . S.C.
J. Patton. New York, 1868. 8°. . . . . . . . . B,706
D. Ramsay. Philadelphia, 1818. 2 v. 8°. . . . . . B,650
J. A. Spencer. New York, 1866. 4 v. 8°. . . . . . B,677
G. Tucker. Philadelphia, 1856–57. 4 v. 8°. . . . . . B,652
B. Trumbull. Boston, 1840. 8°. . . . . . . . . B,620
N. Webster. Cincinnati, 1835. 12°. . . . . . . B,684
M. Willson. New York, 1855. 12°. . . . . . . B,691
History of the National Flag. S. Hamilton. Philadelphia, 1852. 12°. B,849
History of the War of 1812. H. M. Brackenridge. Phila. 1836. 12°. B,854
Immigration to. W. J. Bromwell. New York, 1856. 8°. . . B,862
in 1861. *Count* A. de Gasparin. New York, 1862. 12°. . . . B,900
Indian Affairs, 1854–66, Report on. Washington, 1855–66. 8°. . P.D.
Indian Tribes, Special Com. Report on. Washington, 1867. 8°. . P.D.
Industrial Resources of. J. D. B. De Bow. N. Y. 1854. 3 v. 8°. . B,705
Internal Revenue System, Report on. Washington, 1864. 8°. . . P.D.
its Power and Progress. G. T. Poussin. Philadelphia, 1851. 8°. . B,704
Japan Expedition, 1852–54. M. C. Perry. Washington, 1856. 3 v. 4°. Q,413
Contents. See *Perry, M. C.*
The same. Washington, 1856. 3 v. 4°. . . . . . . P.D.
Kansas Troubles, Report on. Washington, 1856. 8°. . . . . P.D.
Lakes, Survey of the. G. G. Meade. Detroit, 1861. 8°. . . . P.D.
Land Office, Report of, 1868. Washington, 1868. 8°. . . . . P.D.
Lands of the Slave and Free. H. A. Murray. Lond. 1855. 2 v. 12°. V,144
Last Winter in. F. B. Zincke. London, 1868. 12°. . . . . . V,62

United States, Letters from. A. M. Murray. New York, 1856. 12°. . . v,13
Library of American History. Cincinnati, n. d. 8°. . . . B,709
Maps of. S. Lewis and others. Philadelphia, 1794–95. f°. . . *Q,394
Meteorological Observations, 1854-59. Washington, 1861–64. 2 v. 4°. P.D.
Meteorological Report, Fourth. J. P. Espy. Washington, 1857. 4°. P.D.
Mexican Boundary Survey. W. H. Emory. Wash. 1857–58. 3 v. 4°. *Q,144
The same. Washington, 1856-59. 3 v. 4°. . . . . . P.D.
Middle States, Description of. H. S. Tanner. Phila. 1841. 16°. . v,1
Mining Statistics. J. R. Browne and Taylor. Wash. 1868. 8°. N,861,1867
R. W. Raymond. Washington, 1870. 2 v. 8°. . N,861,1869–70
Naval Astronomical Expedition, 1849–52, v. 1, 2, 3, 6. J. M. Gilliss. Washington, 1855–56. 4 v. 4°. . . . . . . . Q,271
Navy and Marine Corps, Living Officers. R. Hamersly. Phila. 1870. 8°. C,753
History of the. J. F. Cooper. New York, 1853. 8°. . . B,855
The New Rome. T. Poesche and C. Goepp. New York, 1853. 12°. G,35
Pacific Railroad, Reports on Surveys for. Wash. 1855–64. 13 v. 4°. P.D.
Patent Office Reports. *Not complete.* Washington, 1842–69. 8°. . P.D.
Paraguayan Investigation. Washington, 1870. 8°. . . . . . P.D.
Pictorial History of. S. G. Goodrich. New York, 1852. 12°. . . B,688
B. J. Lossing. Hartford, 1868. 8°. . . . . . . . B,708
Popular History of. M. Howitt. New York, 1860. 2 v. 12°. . B,690
President's Messages, Apr. 3, 1798, and Jan. 18, 1799. Phila. 1799. 8°. P.D.
Washington to Jackson; comp. E. Williams. N.Y. 1846. 2 v. 8°. O,591
and Documents. Washington, 1855–71. 36 v. 8°. . . P.D.
Primary History of. B. J. Lossing. New York, 1864. 16°. . . B,595
Public Economy for. C. Colton. New York, 1849. 8°. . . . O,544
Reduction of American Tonnage, Report on. Washington, 1870. 8°. P.D.
Reports on the Art of War in Europe, 1854–56. viz.:
Delafield, R. Art of War in Europe. Wash. 1860. 4°. . Q,333
McClellan, G. B. Report on Organization. Wash. 1857. 4°. Q,347
Mordecai, A. Report on Ordnance. Wash. 1860. 4°. . . Q,346
The same. Washington, 1857–61. 3 v. 4°. . . P.D.
Rocky-Mountains Exploring Exped. J. C. Frémont. N. Y. 1846. 8°. P.D.
The same. Washington, 1845. 8°. . . . . . . . V,78
The same. Buffalo, 1852. 12°. . . . . . . . V,2
Romance of American History. J. Banvard. Boston, 1860. 16°. . B,699
School History of. G. P. Quackenbos. New York, 1868. 12°. . B,692
Second Visit to. Sir C. Lyell. New York, 1849. 2 v. 12°. . . V,32
Second War with Great Britain. J. T. Headley. N. Y. 1853. 2 v. 12°. B,850
C. J. Ingersoll. Philadelphia, 1845–53. 4 v. 8°. . B,871
Society in. M. Chevalier. Boston, 1839. 8°. . . . . . . V,46
United States, Southern Rebellion, viz.:
Administration on the Eve of. J. Buchanan. New York, 1866. 8°. B,953
American Conflict, 1861–65. H. Greeley. Hartford, 1864–66. 2 v. 8°. B,920
Army Life in a Black Regiment. T. W. Higginson. Boston, 1870. 12°. B,892
Attack on Petersburg. Washington, 1865. 8°. . . . . . . P.D.
Battle of Murfreesboro'. W. S. Rosecrans. Washington, 1863. 8°. P.D.
Border and Bastile. G. A. Lawrence. Leipzig, 1863. 16°. . . J,255
Camp-Fire and Cotton-Field. T. W. Knox. New York, 1865. 8°. . B,910
Christian Commission, Annals of. L. Moss. Philadelphia, 1868. 8°. B,945

United States, Southern Rebellion. *Continued.* viz.:

Christian Commission, Incidents of. E. P. Smith. Phila. 1869. 8°. B,961
Report, 1864-65. Philadelphia, 1865. 2 v. in 1. 8°. . . B,942
Color-Guard. J. K. Hosmer. Boston, 1864. 12°. . . . . B,951
Constitutional View of. A. H. Stephens. Phila. 1868-70. 2 v. 8°. B,937
Cruise of the Alabama and Sumter. R. Semmes. Lond. 1864. 2 v. 12°. B,954
Days and Nights on Battle Field. C. C. Coffin. Boston, 1868. 16°. J,1236
Debates in Peace Conventions, 1861. L. E. Chittenden. N. Y. 1864. 8°. B,921
Diary, 1861-65. A. Gurowski. Bost. and Wash. 1862-66. 2 v. 12°. B,902
Dunn Brown in the Army. S. Fiske. Boston, 1866. 12°. . . B,915
Fort-Pillow Massacre. Washington, 1864. 8°. . . . . . . P.D.
Four Years in the Saddle. H. Gilmor. New York, 1866. 12°. . B,893
Four Years in Secessia. J. H. Browne. Hartford, 1865. 8°. . . B,908
Four Years of Fighting. C. C. Coffin. Boston, 1866. 8°. . . B,940
Gen. Butler in New Orleans. J. Parton. New York, 1864. 12°. . B,928
Gen. Grant and his Campaigns. H. Coppée. New York, 1866. 8°. B,930
See also *Grant, U. S.*, and Lives of other Generals.
Gen. Nath. Lyon, and Missouri in 1861. J. Peckham. N. Y. 1866. 12°. B,903
Gen. Sherman and Campaigns. S. M. Bowman and Irwin. N.Y. '65. 8°. B,931
Great Rebellion. J. M. Botts. New York, 1866. 12°. . . . B,905
Harper's Pictorial History of. New York, 1866-68. 2 v. 4°. . *Q,228
Historical Sketch of the Chatham Artillery. C. C. Jones. Alb. 1867. 8°. C,65
History of. J. W. Draper. New York, 1867-70. 3 v. 8°. . . B,919
J. S. C. Abbott. Springfield, 1866. 2 v. 8°. . . . B,918
S. M. Schmucker. Philadelphia, 1862-65. 3 v. 8°. . . B,917
History of the Great Rebellion. J. T. Headley. Hartf. 1865. 2 v. 8°. B,923
History of Hurlbut's Fighting Fourth. J. Dugan. Cincin. 1863. 8°. B,956
History of the Navy during. C. B. Boynton. N. Y. 1867-68. 2 v. 8°. B,959
History of the Rebellion. J. R. Giddings. New York, 1864. 8°. . B,935
History of the Secret Service. L. C. Baker. Philadelphia, 1869. 8°. B,924
Hospital Life in Potomac Army. W. H. Reed. Boston, 1868. 12°. B,941
Journal of Prisoner at Richmond. A. Ely. New York, 1862. 12°. B,926
Lost Cause. E. A. Pollard. New York, 1867. 8°. . . . . . B,922
Loyal West in Times of. J. W. Barber and H. Howe. Cincin. 1865. 8°. B,957
Maine in the War. W. E. S. Whitman and C. H. True. Lewis. 1865. 8°. B,950
Martyria; or, Andersonville Prison. A. C. Hamlin. Boston, 1866. 12°. B,895
Maryland Line in Confed. Army. W. W. Goldsborough. Balt. 1869. 12°. B,963
Massachusetts in the Civil War. W. Schouler. Boston, 1868. 8°. . B,939
Massachusetts in the Rebellion. P. C. Headley. Boston, 1866. 8°. B,914
Massachusetts' First Regiment. W. H. Cudworth. Boston, 1866. 12°. B,925
Massachusetts' Sixth Regiment. J. W. Hanson. Boston, 1866. 8°. B,912
Medical Service in the Federal Army. C. Mayo. London, 1864. 8°. V,1086,3
Military History of U. S. Grant, v. 1. A. Badeau. N. Y. 1868. 8°. B,958
Mr. Ambrose's Letters on. J. P. Kennedy. New York, 1865. 12°. B,890
My Cave Life in Vicksburg. New York, 1864. 12°. . . . . B,896
My Diary in America during the War. G. A. Sala. Lon. 1865. 2 v. 8°. V,136
My Diary North and South. W. H. Russell. London, 1863. 2 v. 8°. V,138
Natural History of Secession. T. S. Goodwin. N. Y. 1864. 12°. . B,906
New Gospel of Peace. R. G. White. New York, 1866. 12°. . . B,891
New Orleans Riots. Washington, 1867. 8°. . . . . . . P.D.

United States, Southern Rebellion. *Continued.* viz.:
Newspapers lettered "Southern Records of the Rebellion," viz.:
New York Herald, March, 1856–February, 1861. . . F,102,2
New York Herald, March–August, 1861. . . . . F,102,3
New York Times, February, 1854–March, 1861. . . . F,101,1
New York Times, March–July, 1861. . . . . F,101,2
Ohio Cavalry, 12th, History of. F. H. Mason. Cleveland, 1871. 8°. B,962
Ohio in the War. W. Reid. Cincinnati, 1868. 2 v. 8°. . . B,946
Ohio Regiment, 6th, Story of. E. Hannaford. Cincinnati, 1868. 8°. B,960
Operations against Charleston, 1863. Q. A. Gillmore. N.Y. 1865. 8°. B,952
Organization of Potomac Army. G. B. McClellan. Wash. 1864. 8°. P.D.
Peninsular Campaign in Virginia. J. J. Marks. Phila. 1864. 12°. B,927
Penn. Regiment, 104th, History of. W. W. H. Davis. Phila. 1866. 8°. B,964
Penn. Reserve Corps, History of. J. R. Sypher. Lancaster, 1865. 8°. B,932
Political History during the War. E. McPherson. Wash. 1865. 8°. B,936
Potomac and the Rapidan. A. H. Quint. Boston, 1864. 12°. . . B,894
Rebellion Record; edited by F. Moore. New York, 1861–69. 12 v. 8°. B,982
Rebel War-Clerk's Diary. J. B. Jones. Philadelphia, 1866. 2 v. 12°. B,911
Report of Committee on Conduct of the War. Wash. 1863–66. 8 v. 8°. B,943
Rhode Island during the Rebellion. Providence, 1866. 8°. . . F,61
Richmond during the War. New York, 1867. 12°. . . . . B,877
Rosecrans' Campaign. W. D. Bickham. Cincinnati, 1863. 12°. . B,898
Sanitary Commission; its Purposes and Work. Boston, 1863. 12°. . B,897
Scylla and Charybdis. H. S. Foote. New York, 1866. 12°. . . B,913
Secret History of Southern Confederacy. E. A. Pollard. Phil. 1869. 8°. C,756
Secret Service; Field, Dungeon, etc. A. D. Richardson. Hartf.'66. 8°. B,929
Shenandoah; the last Confederate Cruiser. C.E. Hunt. N.Y. 1867. 12°. B,916
Sheridan's Troopers on the Borders. B. R. Keim. Phila. 1870. 12°. B,889
Sherman's Great March to the Sea. G. W. Nichols. N.Y. 1866. 12°. B,907
Sketches of Secession, etc. W. G. Brownlow. Philadel. 1862. 12°. B,899
Southern History of the War. E. A. Pollard. N. Y. 1863–65. 3 v. 8°. B,934
Twelve Decisive Battles of the War. W. Swinton. N. Y. 1867. 8°. B,938
United States during the War. A. Laugel. London, 1866. 8°. . B,933
Uprising of a Great People. A. de Gasparin. New York, 1862. 12°. B,900
War of the Rebellion. H. S. Foote. New York, 1866. 12°. . . B,913
War Pictures from the South. B. Estvàn. New York, 1863. 12°. . B,909
Wearing the Gray. J. E. Cooke. New York, 1867. 8°. . . . B,955
Whip, Hoe, and Sword. G. H. Hepworth. Boston, 1864. 12°. . H,39
Women of the War. F. Moore. Hartford, 1866. 8°. . . . B,949
Youth's History of. W. M. Thayer. Boston, 1864–66. 4 v. 12°. J,1280
Contents. See *Thayer, W. M.*
United States, State of the Union in 1854. Washington, 1855. 8°. . . B,639
State Trials of. F. Wharton. Philadelphia, 1849. 8°. . . . O,426
Statistical Gazetteer of. R. S. Fisher. New York, 1853. 8°. . . L.R.
Statutes at Large, 1849–63; edit. by G. Minot. Bost. 1850–63. 15 v. 8°. P.D.
Travels in. A. Mackay. Philadelphia, 1849. 2 v. 12°. . . V,31
J. P. Brissot de Warville. Paris, 1791. 2 v. 8°. . . . V,43
The same. London, 1792. 8°. . . . . . . V,106
I. Weld, jr. London, 1799. 4°. . . . . . . . V,151
Western Travel. H. Martineau. London, 1838. 3 v. 12°. . . V,143

United States Almanac, 1844. Philadelphia, 1844. 12°. . . . . . T,49
United States Christian Commission, Annals of. L. Moss. Phila. 1865. 8°. B,945
Incidents of. E. P. Smith. Philadelphia, 1869. 8°. . . . B,961
Reports, 1864, 65. Philadelphia, 1865. 2 v. in 1. 8°. . . . B,942
United States Sanitary Commission, Sketch of its Work. Boston, 1863. 12°. B,897
Universal Alphabet, Endeavor towards. A. D. Sproat. Chillicothe, 1857. 8°. H,302,1
Universal History. See *History, Universal.*
Universal Progress, Illustrations of. H. Spencer. New York, 1865. 12°. . O,533
Universal Speaker. N. A. Calkins and W. T. Adams. Boston, 1861. 12°. O,1223
Universe, Blicke in das Universum. L. Gruson. Magdeburg, 1854. 8°. . G,673
Echoes of the. H. Christmas. Philadelphia, 1850. 12°. . . . O,334
Geschichte der Schöpfung des Weltalls. C. Vogt. Brschwg. 1858. 8°. G,839
Das Weltall. O. Ule. Halle, 1859. 8°. . . . . . . . G,714
Die Wunder des Himmels. J. J. von Littrow. Stuttgart, 1837. 8°. G,783
The same. Stuttgart, 1854. 8°. . . . . . . . G,784
Universities and Academical Degrees, Origin of. H. Malden. Lond. 1835. 16°. O,1156
English. V. A. Huber. London, 1843. 2 v. in 3. 8°. . . . O,815
Office and Work of. J. H. Newman. London, 1846. 12°. . . O,832
University of Virginia. T. Jefferson and J. C. Cabell. Richmond, 1856. 8°. O,817
University Reform, Discussions on. Sir W. Hamilton. New York, 1853. 8°. O,705
Unkind Word, and other Stories. D. M. Craik. New York, 1870. 12°. . K,664
The same. Leipzig, 1869. 2 v. in 1. 16°. . . . . . J,101
Unprotected Females in Norway. London, 1857. 12°. . . . . . V,554
Unsere Zeit; Deutsche Revue der Gegenwart. Leipzig, 1865–67. 6 v. 8°. L.R.
Untersuchungen über Thierstaaten. C. Vogt. Frankfurt-a.-M. 1851. 8°. . G,914
Unwin, W. J. Model School. London, 1849. 16°. . . . . . . O,969
Up and Down the London Streets. M. Lemon. Philadelphia, 1867. 8°. . V,396
Up the Baltic. W. T. Adams. Boston, 1871. 16°. . . . . . J,1544,1
Upham, C. W. History of Salem Witchcraft. Boston, 1867. 2 v. 8°. . O,328
The same reviewed. W. F. Poole. Boston, 1867. . . . . O,341
Lectures on Salem Witchcraft. Boston, 1831. 16°. . . . . . O,343
Life of John C. Frémont. Boston, 1850. 12°. . . . . . C,1004
Life of Sir Henry Vane. Boston, 1860. 12°. . . . . . C,860,4
Upham, E. History of the Ottoman Empire. Edinburgh, 1829. 2 v. 16°. I,516
Upham, T. C. Elements of Mental Philosophy. N. Y. 1841–55. 2 v. 12°. O,622
Imperfect and Disordered Mental Action. New York, 1852. 16°. . L,406
Life of Madame Guyon. New York, 1855. 2 v. 12°. . . . . D,622
Upholsterer's and Cabinet-Maker's Companion. J. Stokes. Phila. 1850. 12°. M,147
Upholstery, Manuel du Tapissier, Decorateur, etc. A. Garnier. Paris, 1830. 18°. M,590
Upsala, Refractors-Beobachtungen, 1862–64. Upsala, 1864. 8°. . . . G,801
Upton, E. New System of Infantry Tactics. New York, 1869. 18°. . M,745
Upward and Onward Series. W. T. Adams. Boston, 1871. 3 v. 16°. J,1468
Vol. 1. Field and Forest. Vol. 2. Plane and Plank.
Vol. 3. Desk and Debit.
Urbino, Dukes of, Memoirs of. J. Dennistoun. London, 1851. 3 v. 8°. . D,735
Urbino, S. R. American Woman in Europe. Boston, 1869. 12°. . . . V,331
and Day, H. Art Recreations. Boston, 1869. 12°. . . . . . M,35
Ure, A. Cotton Manufacture of Great Britain. London, 1861. 2 v. p. 8°. L,321
Dictionary of Arts, Manufactures, and Mines. N. Y. 1857. 2 v. 8°. S.C.
The same, and Supplement. New York, 1854–63. 3 v. 8°. . M,804
The same, 6th edition; ed. by R. Hunt. Lond. 1867. 3 v. 8°. M,805

Ure, A. Essays on Heat and the use of the Microscope. London, n. d. 8°. N,252,28
Malaria of London. London, 1850. 8°. . . . . . . N,252,29
Philosophy of Manufactures. London, 1861. p. 8°. . . . . . L,322
Revenue in Jeopardy from Spurious Chemistry. London, 1843. 8°. N,252,30
Ultimate Analysis of various Substances. London, 1822. 4°. . N,252,42
Urine, Humaine, Nouvelles recherches sur l'. L. R. Le Canu. Paris, n. d. 8°. N,252,14
Urquhart, D. Pillars of Hercules. New York, 1850. 2 v. 12°. . . V,472
Progress of Russia. London, 1853. 12°. . . . . . . . V,522
Ursula; a Tale of Country Life. E. M. Sewell. New York, 1865. 2 v. 12°. K,1003
The same. Leipzig, 1858. 2 v. in 1. 16°. . . . . . J,457
Useful Arts in Connection with Science. J. Bigelow. N. Y. 1853. 2 v. 12°. M,612
Utah and the Mormons. B. G. Ferris. New York, 1854. 12°. . . . C,166
Great Salt Lake Valley. H. Stansbury. Philadelphia, 1855. 2 v. 8°. V,112
Utopia; or, the Happy Republic. Sir T. More. London, 1852. 16°. . K,690

Vacation Rambles and Thoughts. T. N. Talfourd. Lon. 1845–54. 3 v. 12°. 16°. V,352
Vacation Story-Books. Boston, 1870. 6 v. 16°. . . . . . J,1703
Vol. 1. Worth, not Wealth. Vol. 4. The Charm.
2. Country Life. 5. Walter Seyton.
3. Karl Keigler. 6. Holidays at Chestnut Hill.
Vacation Tourists, for 1860–63; ed. by F. Galton. Lond. 1861–64. 3 v. 8°. V,1086
Contents. See *Galton, F.*
Vaccination in relation to Public Health. J. Marshall. London, 1847. 8°. N,252,29
Vagabond Life in Mexico. G. Ferry. New York, 1856. 12°. . . . K,300
Vagabonds, and other Poems. J. T. Trowbridge. Boston, 1869. 16°. . I,148
Valcourt, R. de. Illustrated Book of Manners. Cincinnati, 1866. 12°. . H,495
Vale of Cedars. G. Aguilar. New York, 1868. 12°. . . . . . . K,583
Valentine, D. T. History of the City of New York. New York, 1853. 8°. C,100
Valentine, R. Home Book of Pleasure and Instruction. Lond. 1868. 12°. M,331
Valentine Duval. A. Manning. London, 1860. 12°. . . . . . J,644
Valentine Vox, the Ventriloquist. H. Cockton. Philadelphia, n. d. 8°. . K,632
Valerie; an Autobiography. F. Marryat. Leipzig, 1849. 16°. . . . J,363
Valerie Aylmer. C. Reid. New York, 1871. 8°. . . . . . . K,356
Valerio, K. Ina. Boston, 1871. 8°. . . . . . . . . . . . K,268
Valerius Flaccus, C. Argonauticon; ed. N. E. Lemaire. Parisiis, 1825. 2 v. 8°. U,321
Valerius Maximus. De Dictis Factisque Memorabilibus; et J. Obsequens, De Prodigiis, etc.; ed. C. B. Hase. Parisiis, 1822–23. 2 v. in 3. 8°. U,353
Vallée, L. L. Traité de la Géométrie descriptive. Paris, 1819. 2 v. 4°. M,1191
Valpy, A. J. National Gallery of Painting and Sculpture. Lond. n. d. 8°. M,57
Valpy, R. Elements of Greek Grammar. New York, 1852. 12°. . . L,731
Vámbéry, A. Travels in Central Asia. New York, 1865. 8°. . . . V,680
Van Dieman's Land, Visit to. W. Howitt. London, 1855. 2 v. 12°. . V,879
Van Doren, W. H. Mercantile Morals. New York, 1852. 12°. . . H,252
Van Praet, J. Political History, 15th to 17th Centuries. London, 1868. 8°. A,338
Van Santvoord, G. Life of Algernon Sidney. New York, 1851. 12°. . D,270
Lives of the Chief Justices of the United States. N. Y. 1854. 8°. C,817
The same. New York, 1854. 8°. . . . . . . . . S.C.
Van Vechten, J. Memoirs of John M. Mason. New York, 1856. 8°. . D,37
Vanbrugh, J. Dramatic Works. London, 1866. 8°. . . . . . . I,728

Vandenhoff, G. Art of Elocution. London, 1862. 12°. . . . . L,603
The same. New York, 1851. 12°. . . . . . . . L,600
Vane, Sir H., Life of. C. W. Upham. Boston, 1860. 12°. . . . C,860,4
Vanity Fair. W. M. Thackeray. Philadelphia, 1866. 12°. . . K,1031
The same. Leipzig, 1848. 3 v. 16°. . . . . . . J,488
Vanity Fair; a Humorous Serial. New York, 1860–62. 6 v. 4°. . *Q,322
Vanuxem, L. Geology of New York. Albany, 1842. 4°. . . . *Q,101,11
Variation of Species. T. V. Wollaston. London, 1856. 12°. . . . N,506
Varley, D. Mineralogy; with additions by J. D. Dana. Lond. 1856. 12°. M,972
Varnhagen von Ense, K.A.L.P., Letters to. A. v. Humboldt. N.Y. 1860. 12°. G,26
Tagebücher. Leipzig, 1863. 4 v. 8°. . . . . . . . . E,239
Varnum, J. P. Washington Sketch-Book. New York, 1864. 12°. . . V,42
Varrentrapp, F. Ueber Margarinsäure. n. t. p. 8°. . . . . N,252,21
Vasari, G. Lives of Painters, Sculptors, etc. London, 1851–2. 5 v. p. 8°. L,244
Vasconselos; a Romance. W. G. Simms. New York, 1859. 12°. . . K,261
Vases, Engravings from Ancient. W. Hamilton. Naples, 1791–5. 3 v. f°. L.R.
Vashti. A. J. Wilson. New York, 1869. 12°. . . . . . . . K,106
Vassal Morton; a Novel. F. Parkman. Boston, 1856. 12°. . . . K,141
Vathek; an Arabian Tale. W. Beckford. New York, 1868. 16°. . . K,616
Vaudois of Piedmont, History of. A. Muston. Glasgow, 1857. 2 v. 8°. B,368
Visit to. E. Baires. London, 1853. p. 8°. . . . . I,656,7
Vaughan, D. Destiny of the Solar System. Cincinnati, n. d. 8°. . *T,19,2
Popular Physical Astronomy. Cincinnati, 1858. 8°. . . . N.290
Vaughan, H. Sacred Poems. Boston, 1856. 16°. . . . . . . I,233
Vaughan, H. H. Oxford Reform and Oxford Professors. Lond. 1854. 8°. O,1251,1
Vaughan, R. History of England from 1603 to 1688. Lond. 1840. 2 v. 8°. A,531
Revolutions in English History. New York, 1860–67. 3 v. 8°. . A,526
Vauquelin, L. N. et Thénard, L. J. Fourneau à Coupelle. Paris, 1813. 8°. N,252,15
Manuel de l'Essayeur. Paris, 1812. 8°. . . . . . . N,252,15
Vauvenargues, L. de C. de. Œuvres Choisies. Paris, 1852. 12°. . . H,865
Vaux, C. Villas and Cottages. New York, 1857. 8°. . . . . M,183
Vaux, W. S. W. Nineveh and Persepolis. London, 1851. 8°. . . V,590
Veer, G. de. Three Voyages towards Cathay and China. Lond. 1853. 8°. V,990
Vega, G. von. Sammlung Mathematischer Tafeln. Leipzig, 1840. 8°. . E,436
Vorlesungen über die Mathematik. Wien, 1793–1800. 4 v. 8°. . E,428
Vega Carpio, L. de, Life of. H. R. Fox, *Lord Holland*. London, 1817. 8°. D,701
Vegetable and Animal Physiology. H. Goadby. New York, 1859. 8°. . N,719
and Animal Substances, Analysis of. A. Ure. London, 1822. 4°. N,252,42
Vegetable Cell, Anatomy of. H. von Mohl. London, 1852. 8°. . N,1006
Vegetable Kingdom. J. Lindley. London, 1853. 8°. . . . . N,1003
Atlas des Pflanzenreichs. Breslau, n. d. 4°. . . . . . . G,854
Commercial Products of. P. L. Simmonds. London, 1854 8°. . N,1009
History of. W. Rhind. Glasgow, 1857. 8°. . . . . . . N,1036
Parthenogenesis im Pflanzenreiche. E. Regel. St. Petersburg, 1859. 4°. Q,119
Vegetable Manual; Money in the Garden. P. T. Quinn. . . . . M,485
Vegetable Physiology. P. M. Roget. London, 1867. 2 v. 12°. . . L,281
and Systematic Botany. W. B. Carpenter. London, 1858. 8°. . L,284
Vegetable Substances; Materials of Manufacture. London, 1833. 16°. L,491,3
used for Food. New York, 1855. 18°. . . . . . . . L,452
E. Lankester. London, 1832. 16°. . . . . . L,491,1

Vegetable Substances used in the Arts. London, 1830. 8°. . . . L,491,2
Vegetable World. L. Figuier. London, 1867. 8°. . . . . . N,982
Aesthetik der Pflanzenwelt. F. T. Bratranek, Leipzig, 1853. 8°. . G,859
Poetry of. M. J. Schleiden. Cincinnati, 1853. 12°. . . . N,946
Skizzen aus der Pflanzen- und Thierwelt. H. Masius. Leip. 1852. 8°. G,702
Vegetables, Hackfrüchte und Küchenkräuter. C.E.Langethal. Jena, 1864. 8°. G,879
Vehse, E. Memoirs of the Court of Austria. London, 1856. 2 v. 12°. . B,525
Veitelle, I. de. Mercantile Dictionary. New York, 1864. 12°. . . L.R.
Velasquez de la Cadena, M. Diccionario de las Lenguas Esp. N.Y. 1853. 8°. L.R.
Spanish and English Dictionary. New York, 1852. . . . . L.R.
Velasquez, J. R. de S., and his Works. W. Stirling. London, 1855. 16°. D,699
Velleius Paterculus. See *Paterculus*.
Venedey, J. Das Südliche Frankreich. Frankfurt-a.-M. 1846. 2 v. 8°. . E,200
Venegas, M. History of California. London, 1759. 2 v. 8°. . . . C,245
Venema, H. Institutes of Theology; tr. A.W.Brown. Andover, 1853. 8°. P,119
Venetia; a Novel. B. Disraeli. London, 1868. 12°. . . . . . K,675
The same. Leipzig, 1858. 2 v. in 1. 16°. . . . . J,146
Venetian History, Sketches of. London, 1831-32. 2 v. 16°. . . . I,605
The same. New York, 1860. 2 v. 16°. . . . . L,371
Venetian Life. W. D. Howells. New York, 1867. 8°. . . . . V,508
Venetian Republic, History of. W. C. Hazlitt. London, 1860. 4 v. 8°. . B,496
Venezuela. E. B. Eastwick. London, 1868. 8°. . . . . . . V,261
Venice from 1797 to 1849. E. Flagg. New York, 1853. 2 v. 12°. . V,494
Conspiracy of the Spaniards against. C. V. de St. Real. n. t. p. 12°. B,482
Italy and France. H. Taine. New York, 1869. 8°. . . . V,514
Past and Present. W. H. D. Adams. London, 1869. 12°. . . B,500
République de Venise. P. A. N. B. Daru. Paris, 1821. 8 v. 8°. . B,527
Stones of. J. Ruskin. New York, 1870. 3 v. 8°. . . . M,78
Venn, H. Complete Duty of Man. New York, n. d. 12°. . . P,746,33
Ventilation and Warming. C. Hood. London, 1869. 8°. . . . N,45
C. Tomlinson. London, 1858. 12°. . . . . M,971
History and Art of. W. Bernan. London, 1845. 2 v. in 1. 16°. L,865
by Furnace and Steam-Jet. W. Armstrong, jr. Durham, 1853. 8°. N,252,56
W. Barkus and others. Durham, 1853. 8°. . . . N,252,56
Lectures on. L. W. Leeds. New York, 1868. 8°. . . . . N,45
Treatise on. E. E. Perkins. Philadelphia, 1856. 12°. . . . M,602
M. Wyman. Boston, 1846. 12°. . . . . . . M,619
Venturi, G. B. Experiments on Motion of Fluids. London, 1826. 8°. . N,143
Vergangene Tage. E. Hoefer. Prag, 1859. 24°. . . . . . G,326
Vergani, A. Grammaire Italienne. Paris, 1842. 12°. . . . . L,772
Vergil, Polydore. English History, v. 1. London, 1846. 4°. . . . A,471
Véricour, L. R. de. Modern French Literature. Boston, 1848. 12°. . H,759
Verloren und Gefunden. T. Mügge. Frankfurt-a.-M. 1859. 2 v. 12°. . G,356
Vermächtniss des Pedlars. O. Ruppius. Berlin, 1859. 16°. . . . G,433
Vermont, Geology of. C. B. Adams. Burlington, 1846. 8°. . . . N,878
History of. W. H. Carpenter and T. S. Arthur. Philad. 1865. 16°. C,15
Z. Thompson. Burlington, 1842. 8°. . . . . . C,28
History of Eastern. B. H. Hall. New York, 1858. 8°. . . C,29
Natural and Civil History of. S. Williams. Burlington, 1809. 2 v. 8°. C,32
Verner's Pride. Mrs. H. Wood. Philadelphia, n. d. 8°. . . . K,1069

Verner's Pride. Mrs. H. Wood. Leipzig, 1863. 3 v. 16°. . . . . J,534
Vernon, J. Letters Illustrative of Reign of William III. Lon. 1841. 3 v. 8°. A,554
Véronique. F. Church. Leipzig, 1869. 2 v. in 1. 16°. . . . . J,352
Versatilities; Poems. R. H. Newell. Boston, 1871. 12°. . . . I,102
Verschwörung durch ein Bild. C. Mundt. Berlin, 1864. 12°. . . G,362,2
Vertebrates, Anatomy of. R. Owen. London, 1866. 2 v. 8°. . . . L,986
Vertot d'Aubeuf, R. A. de. Revolutions in Roman Repub. Lon. 1721. 2 v. 8°. A,144
Vespucci, A., Life and Voyages of. C.E.Lester and A. Foster. N. Y. 1846. 8°. D,740
Researches respecting. E. F. de B. y S. Santarem. Bost. 1850. 16°. D,717
Vestiges of the Natural History of Creation. New York, 1854. 18°. . N,441
Vesuvius, Ætna, and other Volcanoes. Sir W. Hamilton. London, 1773. 12°. V,1108
Veterinarian, American. J. T. Estell. Cincinnati, 1867. 8°. . . . L,942
Viardot, L. Wonders of European Art. New York, 1871. 12°. . M,1066
Wonders of Italian Art. New York, 1870. 12°. . . . M,1051
Vicar of Bullhampton. A. Trollope. Leipzig, 1870. 2 v. in 1. 16°. . J,559
Vicar of Wakefield. O. Goldsmith. London, 1820. 12°. . . . . . K,535
The same. New York, 1868. 12°. . . . . . . K,712
The same. Leipzig, 1842. 16°. . . . . . . . J,183
Vicarious Sacrifice. H. Bushnell. Boston, 1866. 8°. . . . . P,109
Vicars, H., Memorials of. New York, 1857. 16°. . . . . . D,28
Vicksburg, My Cave Life in. New York, 1864. 12°. . . . . . B,896
Victim of Intrigue; a Tale. J. W. Taylor. Cincinnati, 1847. 8°. . *H,302,1
Victoria I. Journal of our Life in the Highlands. New York, 1868. 12°. V,381
Victoria; a Tale. M. M. Sherwood. New York, 1856. 12°. . . K,1008,8
Victoria, Australia, in 1854. G. H. Wathen. London, 1855. 12°. . . V,875
Two Years in. W. Howitt. London, 1855. 2 v. 12°. . . . V,879
Victories of Love; a Poem. C. K. Patmore. Boston, 1862. 12°. . . I,91
of Wellington and the British Armies. W. H. Maxwell. Lon. '52. p. 8°. L,125
Vidocq, E. F., Memoirs of, by himself. Philadelphia, n. d. 12°. . . D,574
Vienna, Delineatio Templarum, etc., in. S. Kleiner. Aug. Vindel, 1724. f°. *Q,306
Geschichte des bürgerlichen Zeughauses in. J. Scheiger. Wien, 1833. 8°. E,80
Viennet, J. P. G. Mélanges de Poésie. Paris, 1853. 12°. . . . H,940
Promenade au Cimetière du Père la Chaise. Paris, 1855. 12°. . H,866
Vierenklee, J. E. Arithmetik und Geometrie. Leipzig, 1822. 8°. . . E,432
Vierfache Wurzel des Satzes. A. Schopenhauer. Leipzig, 1864. 8°. . G,573
Vieusseux, A. History of Switzerland. London, 1846. 8°. . . . B,417
Viga Glum's Saga; translated by Sir E. Head. London, 1866. 16°. . G,230
Vigilante, Slaver, Case of the. London, 1823. 8°. . . . . . . O,396
Vignettes of American History. M. Howitt. London, n. d. 12°. . . J,1547
Villa on the Rhine. B. Auerbach. New York, 1869. 2 v. 16°. . . G,186
Village Belles. A. Manning. London, 1859. 16°. . . . . . . J,624
Village Life in the West. R. D. Owen. Philadelphia, 1870. 8°. . . K,229
Village on the Cliff. A. I. Thackeray. New York, 1868. 8°. . . K,1169
Villas and Cottages. C. Vaux. New York, 1857. 8°. . . . . . M,183
Villers, C. F. D. de. Spirit of the Reformation. Philadelphia, 1833. 12°. P,62
Villette. C. B. Nicholls. New York, 1867. 12°. . . . . . . K,859
The same. Leipzig, 1853. 2 v. in 1. 16°. . . . . . J,390
Villiers, G., *Duke of Buckingham*, Life of. A.T. Thomson. Lond. 1860. 3 v. 12°. D,162
Poems on; edited by F. W. Fairholt. London, 1850. 12°. . L,606,29
Vilmar, A. F. C. Geschichte der Deutschen Nat. Literatur. Marburg, 1856. 8°. E,253

Vincentius Bellovacensis. Speculum Naturale. Argentinæ, 1469. 2 v. f°. *Q,355
Vincenzo; or, Sunken Rocks. G. Ruffini. New York, 1864. 8°. . . . K,914
The same. Leipzig, 1863. 16°. . . . . . . . . J,435
Vinci, L. da. Treatise on Painting; tr. by J. F. Rigaud. Lond. 1835. 12°. M,33
Vine, Culture de la Vigne. J. F. Persoz. Paris, 1849. 8°. . . . N,252,31
Culture of. J. F. Persoz. New York, 1858. 12°. . . . . M,533,4
Weinbau in Sud-Deutschland. J. P. Bronner. Heid. 1833–42. 2 v. 8°. G,860
Vine-Dresser's Guide, American. J. J. Dufour. Cincinnati, 1826. 12°. . M,440
Vinegar, Bereitung verschiedener Essige. D. W. Döbereiner. Jena, 1832. 8°. N,252,38
Lehrbuch der Essigfabrikation. F. J. Otto. Braunschweig, 1840. 8°. N,252,10
Manufacture of. C. M. Wetherill. Philadelphia, 1860. 12°. . M,686
Vinet, A. R. Pastoral Theology. New York, 1853. 12°. . . . . P,293
French Literature in the Eighteenth Century. Edinburgh, 1854. 8°. H,760
Vineyards, European. W. J. Flagg. New York, 1869. 12°. . . . . M,502
Vinton, F. Canon Law of Protestant Episcopal Church. New York, 1870. 8°. P,834
Virey, Der, und die Aristokraten. C. Sealsfield. Stuttgart, 1845. 3 v. 24°. E,257,4–6
Virgilius Maro, P. Æneid; trans. by J. Conington. New York, 1867. 8°. *U,419
Æneid, First Six Books; with Notes. E. Searing. N. Y. 1870. 8°. U,422
Bucolics and Georgics; ed. by T. Keightley. London, 1847. 12°. . U,417
Omnia Opera quæ extant; ed. N. E. Lemaire. Parisiis, 1819–22. 8 v. 8°. U,355
Werke; übers. von W. Binder. Stuttgart, 1856–57. 3 v. in 1. 16°. E,294
Works; translated by J. Davidson. London, 1869. p. 8°. . . . *L,89
with interlinear translation by L. Hart and V. R. Osborn. Baltimore, 1868. 12°. . . . . . . . . . *U,418
Virgin, The, and Christ, Early Hymns to. London, 1867. 8°. . . . L,605,24
Virginia and Maryland; Leah and Rachel. Lond. 1656. See *Force's Tracts*, v. 3.
Lord Baltimore's Case. London, 1655. See *Force's Tracts*, v. 2.
True Relation. N. Shrigley. 1669. See *Force's Tracts*, v. 3.
Bacon's Rebellion, 1675–76. See *Force's Tracts*, v. 1.
List of those executed. Sir W. Berkeley. See *Force's Tracts*, v. 1.
Britannica, Travaile into. W. Strachey. London, 1849. 8°. . . V,985
Debates of the Convention of, 1788. Richmond, 1805. 8°. . . . O,395
Declaration of the State of. London, 1620. See *Force's Tracts*, v. 3.
Description of New Albion. London, 1648. See *Force's Tracts*, v. 2.
Extracts from MSS., Annals of. See *Force's Tracts*, v. 1.
History of. C. Campbell. Philadelphia, 1860. 8°. . . . . C,116
W. H. Carpenter and T. S. Arthur. Philadelphia, 1865. 16°. C,176
History of the Discovery and Settlement of. W. Stith. N.Y. 1865. 8°. C,127
Laws Divine, Moral, and Martial, 1612. See *Force's Tracts*, v. 3.
Mineral Springs. W. Burke. Richmond, 1853. 12°. . . . . V,39
Narrative of Indian and Civil Wars, 1675–76. See *Force's Tracts*, v. 1.
New Life in. London, 1612. See *Force's Tracts*, v. 1.
Nova Brittania. London, 1609. See *Force's Tracts*, v. 1.
Observables in. J. Clayton. 1688. See *Force's Tracts*, v. 3.
Orders and Constitutions of, 1619–20. See *Force's Tracts*, v. 3.
Our Late Troubles in, 1676. A. Cotton. See *Force's Tracts*, v. 1.
Perfect Description of. London, 1649. See *Force's Tracts*, v. 2.
Richly Valued. London, 1609. See *Force's Tracts*, v. 4.
the South Part. E. Williams. London, 1650. See *Force's Tracts*, v. 3.
True Declaration of the Colony. London, 1610. See *Force's Tracts*, v. 3.

Virginia, True Travels of Capt. J. Smith, 1593-1629. Richm. 1819. 2 v. 8°. C,115
Virginia's Cure. London, 1662. See *Force's Tracts*, v. 3.
Voyage to. Col. Norwood. 1649. See *Force's Tracts*, v. 3.
Western, Early Settlement of. W. De Haas. Wheeling, 1851. 8°. C,281
Virginians, The. W. M. Thackeray. New York, 1859. 8°. . . K,1032
The same. Leipzig, 1858-59. 4 v. 16°. . . . . . J,489
Visigoths, Geschichte der Westgothen. J. Aschbach. Frankfurt-a.-M. 1827. 8°. E,24
Vision of Sir Launfal. J. R. Lowell. Boston, 1858. 16°. . . . I,82
Visit to my Discontented Cousin. Boston, 1871. 16°. . . . . J,1715
Visits to European Celebrities. W. B. Sprague. Boston, 1855. 12°. . C,520
Vital Principle, Discovery of; Physiology of Man. London, 1838. 8°. . L,976
Vitruvius Brittanicus; History of Woburn Abbey. P. F. Robinson and J. Britton. London, 1847. f°. . . . . . . . . . . . L.R.
Vitruvius Pollio, M. Architecture; trans. by J. Gwilt. Lond. 1860. 12°. M,860
Vittoria Colonna; Life and Poems. Mrs. Roscoe. London, 1868. 12°. . D,724
Vivia; or, the Secret of Power. E. D. E. N. Southworth. Phil. 1870. 12°. K,440
Vivian. M. Edgeworth. New York, 1859. 12°. . . . . . K,678,4
Vivian Grey. B. Disraeli. London, 1868. 12°. . . . . . . K,672
The same. Leipzig, 1859. 2 v. in 1. 16°. . . . . . J,147
Vivien; illustrated by G. Doré. A. Tennyson. London, 1867. f°. . *Q,243
Vocal Culture and Elocution. R. Kidd. Cincinnati, n. d. 12°. . O,1249
Vocal Organs, Anatomie und Physiologie der. C. L. Merkel. Leip. 1857. 8°. E,419
Völcker, A. Chemische Untersuchung des Schildpatts. Gött. 1847. 8°. N,252,40
Vogel, J. Mischung von Flüssigkeiten. Göttingen, 1846. 8°. . . N,252,33
Untersuchungen über Eiter. Erlangen, 1838. 8°. . . . . N,252,9
Vogelhändler von Imst. C. Spindler. Stuttgart, 1841-42. 4 v. 24°. . G,471
Vogt, C. Bilder aus dem Thierleben. Frankfurt-a.-M. 1852. 8°. . . G,915
Lehrbuch der Geologie und Petrefactenkunde. Brschwg. 1847. 2 v. 8°. G,838
Natürliche Geschichte der Schöpfung. Braunschweig, 1851. 8°. . G,839
Ocean und Mittelmeer. Frankfurt-a.-M. 1848. 2 v. 16°. . . E,180
Physiologische Briefe fur Gebildete aller Stände. Giessen, 1854. 8°. E,421
Untersuchungen über Thierstaaten. Frankfurt-a.-M. 1851. 8°. . G,914
Vorlesungen über Nützliche und Schädliche Thiere. Leip. 1864. 16°. G,912
Zoologische Briefe. Frankfurt-a.-M. 1851. 2 v. 8°. . . . G,929
Voice and Vocal Art. S. Novello. London, 1856. 8°. . . . . M,421,1
in Singing. E. Seiler. Philadelphia, 1868. 12°. . . . . M,404
Orthophony; Cultivation of. W. Russell. Boston, 1857. 12°. . L,599
Philosophy of the Human. S. Rush. Philadelphia, 1855. 8°. . M,416
Voices from the Mountains and the Crowd. C. Mackay. Bost. 1853. 12°. I,366
of Freedom; Poems. J. G. Whittier. Philadelphia, 1846. 12°. . I,150
Voigt, F. S. Lehrbuch der Zoologie. Stuttgart, 1835-40. 6 v. in 3. 8°. G,812,8-11
Voigt, J. Geschichte Preussens. Königsberg, 1827-39. 9 v. 8°. . . E,75
Volant, F. and Warren, J. R. Memoirs of Alexis Soyer. Lond. 1859. 16°. D,654
Volcanoes, Active and Extinct. C. G. B. Daubeny. London, 1848. 8°. V,1114
and Earthquakes. M. Ponton. London, 1868. 12°. . . V,1111
Zurcher and Margollé. London, 1868. 12°. . . . V,1140
Observations on, etc. Sir W. Hamilton. London, 1773. 12°. . V,1108
Umrisse von Vulkanen aus den Cordilleren von Quito und Mexico. A. von Humboldt. Stuttgart, 1853. obl. 8°. . . . . . F,89
Vulkanen-Atlas. K. C. von Leonhard. n. t. p. 8°. . . . . G,846

Volckhausen, A. von. Why did he not die? Philadelphia, 1871. 12°. . G,170
Volkmann, A. W. Zustandekommen der Muskelcontractionen. Berl. n. d. 8°. G,779
Volney, C. F. de. New Researches on Ancient History. N. Y. 1856. 12°. A,11
Ruins; Meditations on Revolutions of Empires. N. Y. n. d. 16°. . A,59
Voltaic Circles with Sulphuric Acid. T. Andrews. Dublin, 1838. 4°. N,252,57
Voltaic Electricity. D. Lardner. Philadelphia, 1854. 12°. . . . N,79,2
Voltaire, F. M. A. de. Commentaires sur Corneille. Paris, 1851. 12°. . H,876
Contes, Satires, Epitres, etc. Paris, 1850. 12°. . . . . . H,941
La Henriade. Paris, 1854. 12°. . . . . . . . . H,942
Histoire de Charles XII. New York, 1854. 16°. . . . . D,592
et Russie sous Pierre le Grand. Paris, 1856. 12°. . . . D,749
History of Charles the Twelfth. New York, 1858. 12°. . . . D,751
Œuvres complètes. Paris, 1784–89. 70 v. 8°. . . . H,1007

Vol. 1. *Tragédies:*—Œdipe; Artémire; Mariamne; Discours sur la Tragédie; Brutus; Eryphile.
2. Zaïre; Adélaïde Du Guesclin; Amélie, ou, le Duc de Foix; La Mort de César; Alzire, ou, les Américains.
3. Zulime; Le Fanatisme, ou, Mahomet; Lettre au Pape Benoit XIV.; Mérope; Sémiramis; Dissertation sur la Tragédie ancienne et moderne.
4. Oreste; Rome sauvée, ou, Catalina; L'Orphelin de la Chine; Tancrède.
5. Olimpie; Le Triumvirat; Les Scythes; Les Guebres, ou, la Tolérance; Sophonisbe.
6. Les Lois de Minos; Don Pèdre; Les Pélopides, ou, Atrée et Thieste; Irène; Agathocle.
7. L'Indiscret; L'Enfant Prodigue; La Prude; Nanine, ou, le Préjugé vaincu; La Femme qui a Raison.
8. L'Ecossaise; Le Droit du Seigneur; Charlot, ou, La Comtesse de Givry; Le Dépositaire; Socrate.
9. Samson; La Princesse de Navarre; Le Temple de la Gloire; Le Baron d'Otrante; Pandore; Les Deux Tonneaux; Tanis et Zélide; Jules César; L'Héraclius Espagnol.
10. La Henriade; Essai sur les Guerres Civiles de France; Sur la Mort de Henri IV.; Essai sur la Poësie Epique.
11. La Pucelle d'Orléans.
12. *Poëmes et Discours en Vers:* Discours en Vers sur L'Homme; Le pour et le contre; Poëme sur la Loi Naturelle; Poëme sur le Désastre de Lisbonne en 1755; Le Temple du Goût; Le Temple de l'Amitié; Sur les Evénements de l'Année, 1744; Poëme de Fontenoi; Voyage à Berlin; Précis de l'Ecclesiaste et du Cantique des Cantiques; La Guerre Civile de Genève, ou, les Amours de Robert Covelle; La Fête de Bellebat; La Bastille; La Mort de M'lle Lecouvreur; La Police sous Louis XIV.; Sur la Campagne d'Italie; Apologie de la Fable; Jean qui pleure et qui rit; L'Hôte et l'Hotesse; Lettres à M. de Cromot.
13. Epîtres en Vers; Stances; Odes.
14. Contes en Vers; Satires; Poésies mêlées.
15. Lettres en Vers et en Prose.
16–19. Essai sur les Mœurs et l'Esprit des Nations.
20, 21. Siècle de Louis XIV.
22. Précis du Siècle de Louis XV.
23. Histoire de Charles XII.
24. Histoire de l'Empire de Russie sous Pierre le Grand.
25. Annales de l'Empire de Charlemagne.
26. Histoire du Parlement de Paris; Fragmens Historiques sur l'Inde.
27. *Mélanges Historiques:*—Le Pyrrhonisme de l'Histoire; Réponse à la Beaumelle; Supplément au Siècle de Louis XIV.; La Défense de mon Oncle; Un Chrétien contre six Juifs; De quelques Niaiseries; Incursion sur Nonotte, ex-Jésuite.
28. Fragments sur l'Histoire; Examen de quelques Objections contre Plusieurs faits rapportés dans l'essai sur les mœurs et l'esprit des nations; Des Mensonges imprimés et du Testament Politique du Cardinal de Richelieu.
29. *Politique et Législation:*—La Voix du Sage et du Peuple; Idées de la Mothe Le Vayer; Pensées sur l'Administration publique; De la Paix perpétuelle; Les Droits des Hommes et les Usurpations des Papes; Le Tocsin des Rois; Fragment des Instructions pour le Prince royal de * * *; Le Cri des Nations; Observations sur Jean Law, Melon et Dutot, sur le Commerce, le Luxe, les Monnaies et les Impôts; Des Embellissemens de Paris; Requête à tous les Magistrats du Royaume; Idées républicaines; Commentaire sur le Livre des Délits et des Peines; Prix de la Justice et de l'Humanité; Commentaire sur l'Esprit des Lois; Diatribe a l'Auteur des

Voltaire, F. M. A. de. Œuvres complètes. *Continued.* . . . H,1007

Ephémérides; Ecrits pour les Habitans du Mont-Jura et du Pays de Gex; Rémonstrances du Pays de Gex au roi.

30. Fragment d'une Lettre sur un Usage très-utile établi en Hollande; Discours du Conseiller Anne Dubourg à ses Juges; Jusqu' à quel point on doit tromper le Peuple; Timon; Les Païnes et les Sous-Fermiers; Ce qu'on ne fait pas et ce qu'on pourrait faire; Sermon du Papa Nicolas Charisteski; Discours aux Confédérés Catholiques de Kaminiek en Pologne; Traité sur la Tolérance à l'Occasion de la Mort de Jean Calas; Essai sur les Probabilités en fait de Justice; Supplément aux Causes Célebres; Lettre d'un Ecclésiastique sur le prétendu Rétablissement des Jésuites dans Paris; Petit Ecrit sur l'Arrêt du conseil qui permet le libre Commerce des Blés dans le Royaume; Les Edits de Louis XVI. pendant l'Administration de Turgot.

31. Philosophie de Newton.

32. *Philosophie Générale, Métaphysique, Morale et Théologie:*—Traité de Métaphysique; Le Philosophe ignorant; Il faut prendre un Parti, ou, le Principe d'Action, Diatribe; Tout en Dieu, Comment. sur Mallebranche; De l'Ame; Lettres de Memmius à Cicéron; Remarques sur les Pensées de Pascal; Profession de Foi des Théistes; Sermons et Homélies; Discours de M. Belleguier, Ancien Avocat.

33. Examen important de Milord Bolinbroke; Dieu et les Hommes; Remonstrances du Corps des Pasteurs du Gévaudan à A. J. Rustan; Instructions à A. J. Rustan; Conseils raisonnables à Bergier pour la Défense du Christianisme, par une Société de Bacheliers en Théologie; Les Questions de Zapata, trad. par Tamponet; Epître aux Romains, trad. de l'Italien de M. le Comte de Corbera.

34. La Bible enfin expliquée par plusieurs Aumôniers de S. M. L. R. D. P.

35. Nouveau Testament.

36. Dialogues et Entretiens philosophiques.

37-43. Dictionnaire philosophique.

44. *Romans:*—Zadig; Le Monde comme il va, Vision de Babouc; Memnon; Les deux Consolés; Histoire des Voyages de Scarmentado; Micromégas; Histoire d'un bon Bramin; Le Blanc et le Noir; Jeannot et Colin; Candide, ou, l'Optimisme; l'Ingenu.

45. L'Homme aux quarante Ecus; La Princesse de Babylone; Les Lettres d'Amabed; Histoire de Jenni; Les Oreilles du Comte de Chesterfield et le Chapelain Goudman; Le Taureau blanc; Le Crocheteur borgne; Cosi-Sancta; Songe de Platon; Bababec et les Fakirs; Aventure de la Mémoire; Les aveugles Juges des Couleurs; Aventure Indienne; Voyage de la Raison.

46. *Facéties:*—Diatribe du Docteur Akakia; Réflexions pour les Sots; Femmes, soyez soumises à vos Maris; Conformez-vous aux Temps; De l'horrible Danger de la Lecture; Rescrit de l'Empereur de la Chine à l'occasion d'un Projet de Paix perpétuelle; Extrait de la Gazette de Londres, 20 Février, 1762; Relation du Jésuite Bertier; Lettres de Chabres Couju à ses Frères; Balance Egale; Petit Avis à un Jésuite; Les Quand, les Si, les Qui, les Quoi, les Ah, Ah! etc.; La Prière Universelle de M. Pope; Lettre d'un Quaker; Instruction Pastorale; Avis à tous les Orientaux; Lettre Pastorale; A Warburton; Canonisation de Saint Cucufin, en 1767; Disc. aux Velches, par A. Vadé; Questions sur les Miracles; Sur l'Encyclopédie.

47. *Mélanges Littéraires:*—Discours de Voltaire à sa Réception à l'Académie Française, avec des notes; Panégyrique de Louis XV.; Eloge Funébre des Officiers qui sont mort dans la Guerre de 1741; Eloge historique de la Marquise Du Chatelet; Eloge de Crébillon; Eloge funèbre de Louis XV.; Vie de Molière; Traduction du Poëme de J. Plokof, sur les Affaires présentes; Lettres Chinoises, Indiennes et Tartares; Des divers Changemens arrivés à l'Art Tragique; De la Tragédie Anglaise; Sur la Comédie Anglais; Du Théâtre Anglais, par Jérôme Carré; Parallèle d'Horace, de Boileau et de Pope; Lettres à S. A. Mgr. le Prince de *** sur Rabelais, et sur d'autres Auteurs accusés d'avoir mal parlé de la Religion Chrétienne: Vanini, Warburton, Toland, Locke, Tailord, Tindal, Collins, Wolston, Bolingbroke, T. Chubb, Swift, B. Desperiers, Théophile, Des Barreaux, La Mothe-le-Vayer, Saint-Evremont, Fontenelle, L'Abbé de Saint-Pierre, Bayle, M'lle Huber, Barbeirac Fréret, Boulanger, Montesquieu, La Métrie, Le curé Meslier, Orobio, Spinosa; Conseils à un Journaliste, sur la Philosophie, l'Histoire, le Théâtre, les Pièces de Poésie, les Mélanges de Littérature, les Anecdotes littéraires, les Langues et le Style; Conseils à Racine sur son Poëme de la Religion; Utile examen des trois dernières Epîtres du Sieur Rousseau; Sur l'anti-Machiavel; Mémoire sur la Satire à l'Occasion d'un Libelle de l'Abbé Desfontaines contre l'Auteur; Le Préservatif; Petit Commentaire sur l'Eloge du Dauphin de France, composé par Thomas; Quelques petites Hardiesses de Clair, à l'Occasion d'un Panégyrique de Saint-Louis.

Voltaire, F. M. A. de. Œuvres complètes. *Continued.* . . . . H,1007

48. Réfutation d'un Ecrit anonyme, contre la Mémoire de J. Saurin; Les Honnêtetés Littéraires; Commentaire historique sur les Œuvres de l'Auteur de la Henriade; Extrait d'un Ecrit periodique, intitulé Nouvelle Bibliothèque; Observation sur plusieurs Ouvrages de Marat, Stern, Guérin, du Rocher, de Noailles, etc.; Connaissance des Béautés et des Défauts de la Poésie, et de l'Eloquence dans la Langue Française; Panégyrique de Saint-Louis.
49. Sur la Considération qu'on doit aux Gens de Lettres; Lettres diverses.
50, 51. Commentaires sur Corneille.
52–63. *Recueil des Lettres de Voltaire:*
52. 1715–1737.
53. 1738–1743.
54. 1744–1752.
55. 1753–1757.
56. 1758–1760.
57. 1761–1762.
58. 1763–1764.
59. 1765–1766.
60. 1767–1768.
61. 1769–1771.
62. 1772–1774.
63. 1775–1778.
64–66. Lettres du Prince Royal de Prusse et de Voltaire, 1736–1777.
67. Lettres de l'Impératrice de Russie (Catherine II.) et de Voltaire, 1763–1777; Lettres de plusieurs Souverains à Voltaire.
68, 69. Lettres de Voltaire et d'Alembert, 1746–1778.
70. Vie de Voltaire par de Condorcet, suivie des Mémoires de Voltaire, Ecrits par lui-même; Tables, etc.

Romans. Paris, 1851. 12°. . . . . . . . . . H,877
Siècle de Louis XIV. Paris 1856. 12°. . . . . . . . B,335
Siècle de Louis XV. Paris, 1854. 12°. . . . . . . . B,336
Théatre de. Paris, 1856. 12°. . . . . . . . . . H,875
Volumetrical Analysis, Hand-Book of. R. H. Scott. London, 1862. 8°. . N,203
Vor Fünfzig Jahren. G. von Struensee. Breslau, 1859. 3 v. 12°. . . G,500
Vor Hundert Jahren. F. Lubojatzky. Grimma und Leipzig. 3 v. 16°. . G,342
Voyage alone in the Rob Roy. J. Macgregor. London, 1867. 12°. . V,1049
Expedition in die Seen von China. W. Heine. Leipzig, 3 v. in 2. 8°. E,232
of the U. S. Frigate Potomac. J. N. Reynolds. New York, 1835. 8°. V,1077
Reise um die Erde nach Japan, '53–5. W. Heine. Leip. 1856. 2 v. in 1. 8°. E,164
round the World. G. Hines. Buffalo, 1850. 12°. . . . . V,57
I. Pfeiffer. London, 1862. p. 8°. . . . . . . . I,660
The same. London, n. d. 12°. . . . V,1062
Second Voyage. I. Pfeiffer. New York, 1856. 12°. V,1068
round the World in 1740–44. G. Anson. London, 1748. 4°. . . Q,432
The same. London, 1853. 8°. . . . . . . . N,252,45
to the World of Cartesius. D. DeFoe. London, 1692. 8°. . . O,640
Voyages and Discoveries, Account of. London, 1711. 8°. . . . . V,961

Narbrough, Sir J. Voyage to the South Sea.
Tasman, A. J. Discoveries on the South Terra Incognita.
Wood, J. Attempt to Discover a North-East Passage to China.
Marten, F. Observations made in Greenland and other countries.

and Travels, Collection of. O. and J. Churchill. Lond. 1744–46. 6 v. f°. Q,435

Vol. 1. History of Navigation.
Navarette, D. F. Account of the Empire of China.
Baumgarten, M. Travels through Egypt, Arabia, Palestine, etc.
Brewer, H. and Herckeman, E. Voyage to the Kingdom of Chile.
Candidius, G. Account of the Island of Formosa.
Candidius, G. Curious Remarks on the Empire of Japan.
Monck, Capt. J. Voyage to Hudson's Straits, 1619–20.
Beauplan, G. le V. de. Description of Ukraine, of Poland.
Angelo, M. (of Gattina) and Carli, D. de. Voyage to Congo, 1666–67.
Merolla da Sorrento, J. Voyage to Congo, 1682.
Roe, Sir T. Journal as Embassador to India.
2. Nieuhoff, J. Voyages and Travels into Brasil and the East Indies.
Smith, Capt. J. Travels and Adventures, 1592–1629.

Voyages and Travels, Collections of. O. and J. Churchill. *Continued.* . Q,435

Two Journals kept by seven Sailors in Greenland, 1633–34.
Account of 42 who perished by Shipwreck near Spitzbergen, 1646.
Peyrere, J. de la. Account of Iceland.
Peyrere, J. de la. Account of Greenland.
James, Capt. T. Voyage for Discovery of North-West Passage, 1631–2.
Backhoff, F. I. Voyages into China.
Wagener, Z. Voyages thro' a great part of the World.
Columbus, D. F. History of Cristopher Columbus.
Greaves, J. Pyramidographia; or, Description of the Pyramids.
Greaves, J. Discourse of the Roman Foot and Denarius.
Borri, C. Account of Cochin-China.
3. Ovalle, A. de. Historical Relation of the Kingdom of Chile.
Monson's, Sir W. Naval Tracts.
Baldæus, P. Coasts of Malabar and Coromandel and of Ceylon.
4. Gemelli-Careri, J. F. Voyage round the World.
Gemelli-Careri, J. F. Travels through Europe.
Rolamb, N. Relation of a Journey to Constantinople.
Shipwreck of a Dutch Vessel, with a Description of Corea.
Pelham, E. Preservation of Eight Men in Greenland, 1630.
Merin, J. B. Journey to the Mines in Hungary, 1615.
Rhyne, W. T. Account of the Cape of Good Hope and the Hottentots.
Bolland, R. Draught of the Straights of Gibraltar.
5. Barbot, J. Description of the Coasts of North and South Guinea.
Barbot, J. Abstract of a Voyage to New Calabar River.
Barbot, J. Description of the Lower Æthiopia.
Barbot, J. Voyage to the Congo River, 1700.
Barbot, J. Description of the Islands of Cape Verde.
Herrera, A. de. First Discovery of America by Columbus.
Herrera, A. de. Brief Description of the Caribbee Islands.
Rise and Progress of our Trade to Africa preceding 1697.
Sepp, A. and Behme, A. Voyage from Spain to Paraquaria.
Discovery of the Islands of Salomon.
6. Techo, N. del. History of the Provinces of Paraguay, Tucuman, Rio de la Plata, Parana, Guaira, Urvaica, and Chili.
Baron, S. Description of the Kingdom of Tonqueen.
Norwood, R. Voyage to Virginia, 1649.
Phillips, T. Journal of a Voyage to Cape Monseradae in Africa to Barbadoes.
Gatonbe, J. Voyage into the North-West Passage, 1612.
Everard, R. Three Years' Suffering of, on the Coast of Assada, 1686.
The Mosqueto Indian and his Golden River.
Lord, H. Discovery of the Banian Religion.
Lord, H. Religion of the Persees.
May, C. Wonderful Preservation of the Ship Terra Nova, 1688.
Account of the King of Mocha.
Some Reasons for the Unhealthfulness of the Island of Bombay.
Skippon, P. Journey through Lower Countries, Germany, Italy, and France, 1663.

and Travels, Collection of. R. Kerr. Edinburgh, 1811–24. 18 v. 8°. V,1097
World Displayed. Philadelphia, 1795–96. 8 v. 8°. . V,1096
Contents. See *World, Displayed.*
Circumnavigation of the Globe. New York, 1859. 16°. . . . L,397
in Search of a Passage to India. T. Rundall. London, 1849. 8°. . V,983
Man upon the Sea. F. B. Goodrich. Philadelphia, 1858. 8°. . V,1085
round the World; from Death of Capt. Cook. New York, 1865. 16°. L,455
Weltumsegelung mit Kriegsfregatte Eugenie. N. T. Andersson. Leipzig, 1854. 12°. . . . . . . . . . . . E,160
Vriese, W. H. de and Harting, P. Monogr. des Marattiacées. Leide, 1853. 4°. Q,132
Vulgarisms and other Errors of Speech. Philadelphia, 1868. 16°. . . L,566

Waagen, G. F. Galleries of Art in Great Britain. London, 1857. 8°. M,59,4
Treasures of Art in Great Britain. London, 1854. 3 v. 8°. . M,59,1–3
Wace, R. Conquest of England, from the Roman de Rou. Lond. 1860. 4°. F,170
Wachsmuth, W. Hellenische Alterthumskunde. Halle, 1826–30. 2 v. in 4. 8°. E,457
Frankreich im Revolutionszeitalter. Hamburg, 1844. 4 v. 8°. . E,85

Waddington, G. History of the Church. London, 1835. 3 v. 8°. . . P,634
History of the Reformation on the Continent. London, 1841. 3 v. 8°. P,662
Wade, J. British History. London, 1847. 8°. . . . . . . . A,439
Wages, Rate of. J. R. M'Culloch. London, 1854. 16°. . . . . O,470
Wagner, F. and Bodenstedt, F. Schamyl. London, 1856. p. 8°. . I,661,1
Wagner, J. R. Theorie und Praxis der Gewerbe. Leipzig, 1858–64. 5 v. 8°. G,773
Wagner, M. Kaukasus und das Land der Kosaken. Dresden, 1848. 2 v. 16°. E,212
Reise nach Kolchis und jenseits des Kaukasus. Leipzig, 1850. 12°. E,214
Reise nach Persien und dem Lande der Kurden. Leip. 1852. 2 v. 16°. E,213
und Scherzer, C. Reisen in Nordamerika in 1853. Leip. 1857. 3 v. 16°. E,169
Wagner, R. Comparative Anatomy of Vertebrate Animals. Phil. 1845. 8°. L,990
Fortschritte der Chemie und Physik. Berlin, 1850. 8°. . . N,252,49
Wah-To-Yah; and the Taos Trail. L. H. Garrard. Cincinnati, 1850. 12°. V,155
Wailes, B. L. C. Agriculture and Geology of Mississippi. Wash. 1854. 8°. N,879
Wainwright, J. M. Pathways of our Lord. New York, 1851. 8°. . . V,654
Waisenknabe, Der. M. Ring. Prag und Leipzig, 1858. 24°. . . G,429,2
Wait for the End. M. Lemon. Leipzig, 1864. 2 v. in 1. 16°. . . J,267
Waiting for the Verdict. R. K. Davis. New York, 1868. 8°. . . . K,100
Waitz, G. Schleswig-Holsteins Geschichte. Göttingen, 1851–52. 2 v. 8°. E,82
Anthropologie der Naturvölker. Leipzig, 1859–64. 4 v. 8°. . E,405
Bk. 1. Einheit des Menschengeschlechtes und der Naturzustand des Menschen.
2. Die Negervölker und ihre Verwandten.
3, 4. Die Amerikaner.
Wake-Robin. J. Burroughs. New York, 1871. 12°. . . . . . O,99
Wakefield, D., jr. Public Expenditure apart from Taxation. Lon. 1834. 8°. O,519
Walchner, F. H. Der Practische Naturforscher. Karlsruhe, 1842. 8°. . G,715
Verfälschungen der Nahrungsmittel. Karlsruhe, 1840. 16°. . N,252,37
Walckenaer, C. A. Vie et Ecrits de Mme. de Sévigné. Paris, 1856. 5 v. 12°. D,613
Waldack, C. Treatise on Photography. Cincinnati, 1865. 12°. . . M,614
Walden. H. D. Thoreau. Boston, 1869. 12°. . . . . . . . H,11
Wales, Annales Cambriæ, 447–1288. Blegewryd. London, 1860. 8°. . W,170
Antiquities of. F. Grose. London, n. d. 8 v. 4°. . . . . A,563
Brut y Tywysogion. Caradoc of Llancarvan. London, 1860. 8°. W,167
Itinerary through. Giraldus Cambrensis. London, 1863. 12°. . L,10
Family Excursions in North. J. O. Halliwell. London, 1860. 4°. V,329
Walford, E. Story of Chevalier Bayard. New York, 1869. 16°. . . I,563
Walford, E. Men of the Time. New York, 1852. 12°. . . . . C,539
Walk from London to John O'Groat's. E. Burritt. London, 1864. 8°. . V,375
Walk from London to Land's End. E. Burritt. London, 1868. 12°. . V,395
Walks in the Black Country. E. Burritt. London, 1868. 8°. . . . V,394
Talks, etc., of Two Schoolboys. J. C. Atkinson. London, 1864. 16°. J,1517
Walker, A. Beauty; chiefly Beauty in Woman. London, 1836. 8°. *M,106
Intermarriage; or, Results from certain Unions. Philad. 1856. 12°. L,850
Walker, A. Jackson and New Orleans. New York, 1856. 12°. . . B,846
Walker, A. Science of Wealth. Boston, 1866. 8°. . . . . . . O,550
Walker, C. M. History of Athens Co., Ohio. Cincinnati, 1869. 8°. . C,218
Walker, D. Manly Exercises. London, 1865. p. 8°. . . . . . L,152
Walker, C. V. Electric Telegraph Manipulation. London, 1850. 16°. N,252,36
Electrotype Manipulation. London, 1841. 16°. . . . N,252,36
Walker, J. Critical Pronouncing Dictionary. Glasgow, 1850. 16°. . L.R.
Dictionary of the English Language. Philadelphia, 1852. 8°. . L.R.

Walker, J. Key to Classical Pronunciation, etc. Philadelphia, 1808. 8°. L.R.
Pronouncing Dictionary. London, 1860. 8°. . . . . . . L.R.
Rhyming Dictionary. Philadelphia, 1852. 8°. . . . . . . L.R.
The same. New York, 1860. 12°. . . . . . . . L.R.
The same. New York, 1857. 2 v. 12°. . . . . L.R.
Walker, J. B. Sacred Philosophy. Boston, 1856. 12°. . . . . . P,271
Walker, M. S. Both Sides of the Street. Boston, 1870. 16°. . . J,1539
Down in a Saloon. Boston, 1871. 16°. . . . . . . J,1109
Walker, T. Companion for the Afflicted. New York, 1851. 12°. . . P,292
Walker, T. Discourse before Ohio Historical Society. Cincinnati, 1838. 8°. *T,19,9
Introduction to American Law. Boston, 1869. 8°. . . . . . U,500
Oration on Daniel Webster. Cincinnati, 1852. 8°. . . . H,302,4
Walker, W. War in Nicaragua. Mobile, 1860. 12°. . . . . C,367
Walker, W. S. Critical Exam. of Text of Shakespeare. Lon. 1860. 3 v. 16°. I,842
Wall Street, Men and Mysteries of. J. K. Medbery. Boston, 1870. 12°. O,505
Wallace, A. R. Malay Archipelago. London, 1869. 2 v. 12°. . . V,881
Palm-Trees of the Amazon. London, 1853. 8°. . . . . . N,954
Wallace, H. B. Art and Scenery in Europe. Philadelphia, 1857. 12°. . M,86
Literary Criticisms and other Papers. Philadelphia, 1856. 12°. . H,655
Wallace, Sir W., Life of. J. D. Carrick. Edinburgh, 1830. 2 v. 16°. . I,525
Wallenstein, *Duke of Friedland*, Life of. J. Mitchell. London, 1840. 12°. D,503
Waller, E. Poetical Works with Life; edited by R. Bell. Lon. 1854. 16°. I,256
Walling, H. F. Atlas of Ohio and of the United States. N. Y. 1868. 4°. *Q,392
Wallis, S. P. Spain; her Institutions and Public Men. Boston, 1853. 16°. V,466
Walpole, H. Anecdotes of Painting in England. London, 1849. 3 v. 8°. M,107
Castle of Otranto. London, 1820. 12°. . . . . . . . . K,534
Catalogue of Royal and Noble Authors. London, 1806–23. 5 v. 8°. *C,1307
Historic Doubts on Richard III. London, 1768. 4°. . . . A,498
Letters to Horace Mann. Philadelphia, 1844. 2 v. 8°. . . H,833
Memoirs of. E. Warburton. London, 1852. 2 v. 8°. . . . D,36
Memoirs of the Reign of George III. London, 1845. 4 v. 8°. . D,357
Reign of King George II. London, 1846–47. 3 v. 8°. . . . A,539
Walsh, J. H. The Dog in Health and Disease. London, 1859. 8°. . N,683
Shot Gun and Sporting Rifle. London, 1859. 16°. . . . . . M,306
and Lupton, T. J. Horse in the Stable and Field. Lond. 1861. 8°. M,476
Walsh, M. McN. Lawyer in the School-Room. New York, 1867. 12°. . U,489
Walsh, R. Appeal respecting the United States. Philadelphia, 1819. 8°. B,623
Letter on the French Government. Philadelphia, 1810. 8°. . . B,270
(Ed.) American Review of Hist. and Politics. Phil. 1811–12. 4 v. 8°. T,43
Walter, E. What is Free Trade? New York, 1867. 12°. . . . . O,559
Walter, H. History of England. London, n. d. 7 v. 12°. . . . . A,428
Walter and Frank; or, Lathrop Farm. H. N. Baker. Boston, 1870. 16°. J,1693
Walter Colyton. H. Smith. London, 1830. 3 v. in 1. 12°. . . . K,568
Walter Goring. A. Cudlip. Leipzig, 1866. 2 v. in 1. 16°. . . . J,109
Walter of Hemingburgh. Chronicon. London, 1848–49. 2 v. 8°. . . U,621
Walter's Tour in the East. D. C. Eddy. New York, 1868. 6 v. 16°. . J,1707

Vol. 1. Walter in Egypt.
2. Walter in Jerusalem.
3. Walter in Samaria.
Vol. 4. Walter in Damascus.
5. Walter in Constantinople.
6. Walter in Athens.

Walton, I. Choice English Biography. New York, 1854. 8°. . . D,404

Dr. John Donne; Sir Henry Wotton; Richard Hooker; George Herbert; Dr. Robert Sanderson; with Account of the Author, by T. Zouch.

Walton, I. Lives of Donne, Wotton, Hooker, and others. Lond. 1838. 8°. . C,596
and Cotton, C. Complete Angler. London, 1853. 12°. . . . M,309
The same; edited by E. Jesse. London, 1870. p. 8°. . . L,153
Wandering Jew. E. Sue. Philadelphia, n. d. 8°. . . . . . . H,915
Chronicles of. D. Hoffman. London, 1853. 2 v. 8°. . . . H,627
Designs on. G. Doré. London, n. d. f°. . . . . . . *Q,455
Wanley, N. General History of Man. London, 1791. 4°. . . . N,464
War and Christianity. J. Dymond. Philadelphia, n. d. 8°. . . . O,722
and Culture, Conversations on. A. Helps. Boston, 1871. 12°. . H,325
Art of. H. *Baron* de Jomini. Philadelphia, 1862. 12°. . . M,813
Art of, in Europe, 1854-56. R. Delafield. Washington, 1860. 4°. Q,333
G. B. McClellan. Washington, 1857. 4°. . . . . Q,347
A. Mordecai. Washington, 1860. 4°. . . . . . Q,346
The same. Washington, 1857-60. 3 v. 4°. . P.D.
between the United States and Mexico. See *Mexican War*.
Droit de la Guerre, et de la Paix. H. Grotius. Basle, 1746. 4°. . U,591
Elements of the Science of. W. Müller. London, 1811. 3 v. 8°. M,814
in France and Belgium, 1815. W. Siborne. Philadelphia, 1845. 8°. B,85
Laws of, and International Law. H. W. Halleck. Phila. 1866. 12°. U,538
of 1812, Campaign of the N. W. Army. W. Hull. Boston, 1824. 8°. B,873
History of. H. M. Brackenridge. Philadelphia, 1836. 12°. B,854
Journal of Ky. Volunteers, etc. E. Darnell. Phil. 1854. 18°. C,269
Military Heroes of. C. J. Peterson. Philadelphia, 1848. 8°. C,687
Military Occurrences. W. James. London, 1818. 2 v. 8°. B,875
Pictorial Field-Book of. B. J. Lossing. New York, 1865. 8°. B,874
Second War with England. J. T. Headley. N. Y. 1853. 2 v. 12°. B,850
C. J. Ingersoll. Philadelphia, 1845-53. 4 v. 8°. . B,871
Two Western Campaigns in. S. Williams. Cincinnati, 1871. 8°. C,223

1. Brush, Capt. H. Expedition with supplies for Gen. Hull, 1812.
2. Meigs, Gov. R. J. Expedition for the relief of Fort Meigs, 1813.

of the Gaedhill with the Gaill. London, 1867. 8°. . . . . . W,198
of the Rebellion. See *United States, Southern Rebellion.*
Summary of the Art of. E. Schalk. Philadelphia, 1862. 12°. . M,764
War Pictures from the South. B. Estvàn. New York, 1863. 12°. . . B,909
War Powers under the U. S. Constitution. W. Whiting. Boston, 1871. 8°. U,510
War Tiger. W. Dalton. London, 1869. 16°. . . . . . . . . J,1264
War Trail; or, the Hunt of the Wild Horse. M. Reid. New York, 1870. 12°. J,1575
Warburton, E. Conquest of Canada. New York, 1850. 2 v. 12°. . . C,340
Crescent and the Cross. New York, 1850. 8°. . . . . . V,627
The same. Leipzig, 1852. 2 v. in 1. 16°. . . . . . J,511
Darien; or, the Merchant Prince. Leipzig, 1853. 2 v. in 1. 16°. J,512
Hochelaga; or, England in the New World. New York, 1846. 12°. V,173
Memoirs of Horace Walpole. London, 1852. 2 v. 8°. . . . D,36
Memoirs of Prince Rupert. London, 1849. 3 v. 8°. . . . D,467
Travels in Egypt and the Holy Land. Philadelphia, 1859. 8°. . V,830
Warburton, W. Divine Legation of Moses demonstrated. Lond. 1846. 3 v. 8°. P,316
Life of. J. S. Watson. London, 1863. 8°. . . . . . . D,456
Natural and Revealed Religion. London, 1753-54. 2 v. 12°. . P,272
View of Lord Bolingbroke's Philosophy. London, 1756. 16°. . P,18
Ward, F. de W. India and the Hindoos. New York, 1851. 12°. . . V,608

Ward, H. G. Mexico in 1827. London, 1828. 2 v. 8°. . . . . . C,376
Ward, J. Young Mathematician's Guide. Dublin, 1755. 8°. . . M,1119
Ward, J. H. Life and Letters of James G. Percival. Boston, 1866 8°. . C,960
Ward, J. W. Song of Higher-Water. New York, 1868. 8°. . . . I,72
Ward, M. F., Trial of, for Murder of W. H. G. Butler. Louisville, 1854. 12°. U,537
Ward, N., Memoir of. J. W. Dean. Albany, 1868. 8°. . . . . . C,909
Simple Cobler of Aggawam. London, 1647. See *Force's Tracts*, v. 3.
Ward, N. B. Growth of Plants in Glazed Cases. London, 1852. 12°. . M,493
Ward, S., Life of. W. Gammell. Boston, 1860. 12°. . . . C,860,19
Ward, T. Errata to the Protestant Bible. Dublin, 1807, 4°. . . . P,461
Warden. A. Trollope. Leipzig, 1859. 16°. . . . . . . . . J,506
Warden, R. Ardvoirlich; a Romantic Tragedy. Cincinnati, 1857. . H,302,1
Warden, R. B. Familiar Forensic View of Man and Law. Columbus, 1860. 8°. N,450
Life of Stephen A. Douglas. Columbus, 1860. 8°. . . . . . C,807
Warder, J. A. American Pomology; Apples. New York, 1867. 12°. . M,553
Hedges and Evergreens. New York, 1858. 12°. . . . . . M,351
Wardlaw, R. Lectures on the Book of Ecclesiastes. Philadelphia, 1822. 8°. P,471
Ware, M. L., Memoir of. E. B. Hall. Boston, 1853. 12°. . . . C,976
Ware, W. Aurelian. New York, 1866. 2 v. 12°. . . . . . . K,352
Julian; or, Scenes in Judea. New York, 1865. 2 v. 12°. . . K,353
Life of Nathaniel Bacon. Boston, 1860. 12°. . . . . . C,860,13
Sketches of European Capitals. Boston, 1851. 12°. . . V,1043
Works and Genius of Washington Allston. Boston, 1852. 12°. . M,50
Warfield, C. Household of Bouverie. New York, 1860. 2 v. 12°. . K,354
Waring, G. E. jr. Elements of Agriculture. New York, 1855. 12°. . M,484
Waring, J. B. The Arts connected with Architecture. London, 1858. f°. *Q,348

1. Stained Glass.
2. Fresco Ornament.
3. Marquetry; or, Inlay of Wood.
4. Marble and Enamel Inlay.

Warming and Ventilating, Hist. and Art of. W. Bernan. Lon. '45. 2 v. in 1. 16°. L,865
and Ventilation. C. Hood. London, 1869. 8°. . . . . . N,46
C. Tomlinson. London, 1858. 12°. . . . . . . M,971
Warner, A. B. Dollars and Cents. Philadelphia, 1863. 12°. . . . K,370
My Brother's Keeper. New York, 1866. 12°. . . . . . . K,372
Warner, C. D. My Summer in a Garden. Boston, 1871. 12°. . . . H,50
Warner, S. Daisy. Philadelphia, 1869. 2 v. 12°. . . . . . . K,369
Melbourne House. New York, 1866. 12°. . . . . . . K,371
Old Helmet. New York, 1867. 12°. . . . . . . . K,373
Queechy. Philadelphia, 1867. 12°. . . . . . . . . K,374
Say and Seal. Philadelphia, 1869. 2 v. 12°. . . . . . . K,386
Wide, Wide World. Philadelphia, 1868. 12°. . . . . . K,375
and A. B. Ellen Montgomery's Book-Shelf. New York, 1868. 16°. J,1423

Vol. 1. Mr. Rutherford's Children.
2. Sybil and Chryssa.
Vol. 3. Hard Maple.
4. Karl Krinken.
Vol. 5. Casper and his Friends.

Warren, E. Life of J. C. Warren. Boston, 1860. 2 v. 8°. . . . C,1088
Warren, E. Bloomfield. Boston, 1870. 16°. . . . . . . . J,1630
Warren, J., Inauguration of Statue of. Boston, 1858. 8°. . . . C,23
Life of. A. H. Everett. Boston, 1860. 12°. . . . . . C,860,10
Warren, J. C. Etherization; with Surgical Remarks. Boston, 1848. 12°. L,849
Life of. E. Warren. Boston, 1860. 2 v. 8°. . . . . . C,1088
Warren, Mrs. and Pullan, Mrs. Treasures in Needlework. London, n. d. 12°. H,473

Warren, S. Diary of a late Physician. New York, 1868. 3 v. 16°. K,1063
The same. Leipzig, 1844. 2 v. in 1. 16°. . . . . . J,513
Duties of Attorneys and Solicitors. New York, 1849. 16°. . . U,485
Extracts from Blackstone's Commentaries. London, 1837. . . U,501
Lily and the Bee. Leipzig, 1851. 16°. . . . . . . . J,514
Miscellanies. Edinburgh, 1855. 2 v. 8°. . . . . . . H,441

Vol. 1. The Bracelets, a Tale; My First Circuit; Sir William Follett; Memoir of John William Smith; Who is the Murderer? a Problem in the Law of Circumstantial Evidence; Duke of Marlborough; Paradise in the Pacific; Uncle Tom's Cabin; Calais; Pegsworth, a Press-Room Sketch.
2. The Mystery of Murder and its Defense; Modern State Trials; The Martyr Patriots; Speculations among the Stars; Personal Recollections of Christopher North.

Ten Thousand a Year. Philadelphia, n. d. 8°. . . . K,1064
The same. Leipzig, 1845. 3 v. 16°. . . . . . . J,515
Warren, S. E. Manual of Problems in Linear Perspective. N. Y. 1868. 8°. M,155
Manual of Geometrical Drawing. New York, 1868. 12°. . . M,156
Warreniana; with Notes by W. Gifford. Boston, 1851. 16°. . . . H,14
Warriors of the Thirty Years' War. Sir E. Cust. London, 1865. 2 v. 12°. D,512
Warton, J. Essay on Genius and Writings of Pope. Lond. 1806. 2 v. 8°. H,704
Warton, T. History of English Poetry. London, 1774–81. 3 v. 4°. . H,742
Warwick, Mary *Countess of*. Autobiography. London, 1848. 12°. . L,606,22
Was he Successful? R. B. Kimball. New York, 1866. 12°. . . . K,134
Washburn, C. A. History of Paraguay. Boston, 1871. 2 v. 8°. . . C,391
Washburn, E. Judicial History of Massachusetts, 1630–1775. Bost. 1840. 8°. C,42
Washington, G. and his Generals. J. T. Headley. N. Y. 1854. 2 v. 12°. C,650
Character and Portraits of. H. T. Tuckerman. N. Y. 1859. 4°. . *F,38
Early Life of. J. Pickell. New York, 1856. 8°. . . . . C,907
Essay on the Character of. F. Guizot. New York, 1863. 16°. . C,901
Home of, and its Associations. B. J. Lossing. N. Y. 1866. 8°. . C,912
in Domestic Life. R. Rush. Edinburgh, 1855. 2 v. 8°. . . C,884
Life of. E. Everett. New York, 1860. 12°. . . . . . C,902
W. Irving. New York, 1856–57. 4 v. 12°. . . . . C,903
The same, v. 1–3, 5. New York, 1857–59. 8°. . . C,885
The same. New York, 1867. 5 v. 12°. . . . U,34
The same. New York, 1869. 5 v. 16°. . . . U,18
J. Marshall. Philadelphia, 1836. 2 v. 8°. . . . . C,906
J. K. Paulding. New York, 1854. 2 v. 16°. . . . L,392
D. Ramsay. London, 1807. 8°. . . . . . . . C,905
J. Sparks. New York, 1855. 12°. . . . . . . . C,904
M. L. Weems. Philadelphia, 1869. 12°. . . . . C,873
Life and Times of. C. R. Edmonds. London, 1835–36. 2 v. 16°. I,633
S. M. Schmucker. Philadelphia, 1860. 12°. . . . . C,913
Maxims of; edited by J. F. Schroeder. New York, 1859. 12°. . H,269
Memoirs of. C. M. Kirkland. New York, 1859. 12°. . . . C,891
Memoirs of the Administration of. G. Gibbs. N. Y. 1846. 2 v. 8°. B,311
Recollections and Private Memoirs of. G. W. P. Custis. N. Y. 1860. 8°. C,1104
Revolutionary Orders. New York, 1844. 8°. . . . . . . B,747
Washingtonia; Memorials of Death of. F. B. Hough. Roxb. '65. 2v. 4°. F,60
Writings; with Life by J. Sparks. New York, 1847–48. 12 v. 8°. U,64

Vol. 1. Life by J. Sparks.
2. Official Letters relating to the French War, and Private Letters before the American Revolution.

Washington, G. Writings; with Life by J. Sparks. *Continued.* . . . u,64
3–8. Correspondence and Miscellaneous Papers relating to American Revolution.
9. Correspondence from his Resignation as Commander-in-Chief to his Inauguration as President.
10, 11. Correspondence from the beginning of his Presidency to the end of his Life.
12. Speeches and Messages to Congress; Proclamations and Address.
The same. Boston, 1837. 12 v. 8°. . . . . . . . s.c.
Washington City, Public Schools, Annual Report, 1856. Wash. 1856. 8°. o,1251,2
Smithsonian Institution. See *Smithsonian Institution.*
Washington Sketch-Book. J. P. Varnum. New York, 1864. 12°. v,42
Washington Territory, Three Years in. J. G. Swan. New York, 1857. 12°. v,128
Watch and Wait. W. T. Adams. Boston, 1861. 16°. . . . . j,1467,3
Watch-Making. E. B. Denison. London, 1850. 12°. . . . . . . m,907
Water as applied to Mills. J. Glynn. London, 1853. 12°. . . . m,922
as a Preservative and a Remedy. J. Bell. Philadelphia, 1859. 8°. l,907
Drops of, with the Microscope. A. Catlow. London, 1851. 12°. . o,13
for Locomotive Engines. W. West. London, 1846. 8°. . . n,252,39
Power of, and Wind to turn Mills. J. Smeaton. Lond. 1826. 8°. . n,143
Process for purifying. T. Clark. London, 1841. 8°. . . n,252,22
Das Wasser. E. A. Rossmässler. Leipzig, 1858. 8°. . . . g,709
Water Babies; a Fairy Tale. C. Kingsley. London, 1869. 12°. . . j,1728
Water-bearing Strata around London. J. Prestwich, jr. Lond. 1851. 8°. n,818
Water-Cure Journal and Herald, v. 8–10. New York, 1849–50. 8°. . . l,947
Water-Power of Maine; edited by W. Wells. Augusta, 1869. 8°. . . c,24
Water-Supply of Lancaster, England. E. Sharpe. Lancaster, 1850. 16°. n,252,37
of London. Sir W. Clay. London, 1849. 8°. . . . . . n,252,39
J. L. Tabberner. London, 1847. 8°. . . . . . n,252,39
Water-Witch. J. F. Cooper. New York, 1867. 12°. . . . . k,53
The same. New York, 1860. 8°. . . . . . . . k,83
Water-Works for Cities and Towns. S. Hughes. London, 1856. 12°. . m,940
Waterbury, Ct., Catalogue of the Bronson Library. Waterbury, 1870. 8°. l.r.
History of. H. Bronson. Waterbury, 1858. 8°. . . . . . c,12
Waterdale Neighbors. Leipzig, 1868. 2 v. in 1. 16°. . . . . j,516
Waterhouse, G. R. Pouched Animals. Edinburgh, n. d. 16°. . . n,470,24
Waterloo, Battle of. G. R. Gleig. New York, 1847. 12°. . . . b,86
History of the Campaign of. H. *Baron* de Jomini. N. Y. 1853. 12°. b,204
Stories of. W. H. Maxwell. London, 1835. 16°. . . . . j,637
to the Peninsula. G. A. Sala. London, 1867. 2 v. 8°. . . v,379
Waterton, C. Wanderings in South America. London, 1836. 16°. . . v,230
Watertown, Mass., Family Memorials of. H. Bond. Boston, 1855. 2 v. in 1. 8°. c,56
Wathen, G. H. Golden Colony; or, Victoria in 1854. London, 1855. 12°. v,875
Watson, E. Memoirs of Elkanah Watson. New York, 1857. 12°. . c,1014
Travels, and Reminiscences of the Revolution. New York, 1856. 8°. c,723
Watson, H. C. Camp Fires of the Revolution. New York, 1865. 8°. . b,752
Watson, J. S. Life of William Warburton. London, 1863. 8°. . . d,456
Watson, J. J. W. Electrical Illumination. London, 1853. 8°. . n,252,50
Watson, J. Y. Compendium of British Mining. London, 1843. 8°. . n,252,40
Watson, R., Life of. T. Jackson. New York, 1836. 8°. . . . . . d,33
Life of John Wesley. Cincinnati, 1857. 8°. . . . . . . d,269
Watson, R. Reply to Gibbon and Paine. New York, n. d. 18°. . p,746,14

Watson, R. History of Reign of Philip II., of Spain. London, 1777. 2 v. 4°. B,573
The same. London, 1839. 8° . . . . . . . . B,474
History of the Reign of Philip III., of Spain. London, 1783. 4°. . F,224
Watson, T. J. Illust. Vocabulary for Deaf and Dumb. London, 1857. 4°. O,1268
Watson, W. C. Pioneer History of Champlain Valley. Albany, 1863. 8°. C,122
Watt, A. Electro-Metallurgy. London, 1869. 12°. . . . . . . M,861
Watt, J., Life of. F. Arago. Boston, 1859. 12°. . . . . . . C,498
Life of. J. P. Muirhead. New York, 1859. 12°. . . . . . D,30
S. Smiles. London, 1865. 8°. . . . . . . . . D,59
Mechanical Inventions of. J. P. Muirhead. London, 1854. 3 v. 8°. M,643
Origin and Progress of his Inven. J. P. Muirhead. Lon. 1854. 3v. 4°. M,732
Watt, R. Bibliotheca Britannica. Edinburgh, 1824. 4 v. 4°. . . L.R.
Watts, H. Dictionary of Chemistry. London, 1864-68. 5. v. 8°. . . *N,240
Watts, I. Horæ Lyricæ and Divine Songs. Boston, 1854. 16°. . . I,234
Improvement of the Mind. Boston, n. d. 16°. . . . . . O,638
Works. London, 1812-13. 9 v. 8°. . . . . . . . . P,776

Vol. 1. Memoir of Dr. Watts; Sermons on various Occasions.
2. Sermons; Evangelical Discourses; Essay on the Powers and Contests of Flesh and Spirit; Death and Heaven; Doctrine of the Passions; Love of God.
3. Self-love and Virtue; Humility represented in the Character of St. Paul; Orthodoxy and Charity united; Caveat against Infidelity; Harmony of Religions; Strength and Weakness of Human Reason; Holiness of Times, Places, etc.
4. Foundation of a Christian Church; Civil Power in Things Sacred; Ruin and Recovery of Man; Freedom of Will; Sacrifice of Christ; Attempt towards Revival of Practical Religion.
5. Revival of Religion; Guide to Prayer; Catechisms; Follies of Youth; Scripture Names; Prayers for Children; Scripture History; Questions proper for Students in Divinity.
6. Essay on Charity Schools; Art of reading and writing English; The Trinity.
7. The World to Come; Logic; Education of Children and Youth.
8. Improvement of the Mind; First principles of Geography and Astronomy; Twelve Philosophical Essays; Ontology; Dissuasive from Self-murder.
9. Essay on Psalmody; Psalms and Hymns; Divine Songs for Children; Horæ Lyricæ; Reliquiæ Juveniles; Remnants of Time, or, short Essays; Index.

Wau-Bun, the Early Day. J. H. Kinzie. New York, 1856. 12°. . . C,275
Waverley. Sir W. Scott. Boston, 1857. 2 v. 16°. . . . . . . K,952
The same. Philadelphia, 1869. 8°. . . . . . K,1105
The same. Leipzig, 1845. 16°. . . . . . . . J,452
Waurin, J. de. Ancient Histories of Great Britain, v. 1. Lond. 1864. 8°. W,190
Chroniques de la Grant Bretaigne. London, 1864-68. 2 v. 8°. . W,189
'Way Down East; or, Yankee Life. S. Smith. Philadelphia, 1866. 12°. H,93
Way to do Good. J. Abbott. New York, n. d. 12°. . . . . P,281,3
Way to Prosper, and other Tales. T. S. Arthur. Philadelphia, n. d. 16°. J,619
Wayland, F. Collegiate System in the United States. Boston, 1842. 16°. O,961
Elements of Intellectual Philosophy. Boston, 1858. 12°. . . O,621
Elements of Moral Science. Boston, 1855. 12°. . . . . O,717
Elements of Political Economy. Boston, 1869. 12°. . . . O,512
Memoir of Adoniram Judson. Boston, 1853. 2 v. 12°. . . C,927
Principles and Practices of Baptist Churches. New York, 1867. 12°. P,805
Wayne, A., Life of. J. Armstrong. Boston, 1860. 12°. . . . . C,860,4
Ways of the Hour. J. F. Cooper. New York, 1867. 12°. . . . K,52
The same. New York, 1861. 8°. . . . . . . . . K,84
Wayside Thoughts on Education. D. W. Thompson. Edinburgh, 1868. 8°. O,976
We Girls; a Home Story. A. D. T. Whitney. Boston, 1870. 12°. . . K,394

Weal and Woe in Garveloch. H. Martineau. London, 1859. 16°. . K,551,2
Weale's Rudimentary Series. London, 1851–70. 161 v. 12°. and 4°. viz.:

Abel, C. D. Principles of Machinery. . . . . . . M,825
Atlas to same. . . . . . . . . Q,359
Allen, C. B. Cottage Building. . . . . . . . M,887
Andrews, G. H. Agricultural Engineering. . . . . M,888
Arman, A. Admeasurement of Land. . . . . . M,826
Arman, A. Key to Haddon's Arithmetic. . . . M,844,2
Arman, A. Stepping Stone to Arithmetic and Key. 2 v. . . M,827
Armstrong, R. Steam Boilers. . . . . . . M,889
Baird, J. Guide to Australia. . . . . . . . M,866
Baird, J. Guide to Tasmania and New Zealand. . . . M,867
Baird, J. Management of Health. . . . . . M,828
Baker, T. Elements of Mechanism. . . . . . M,891
Baker, T. Land Engineering and Surveying. . . . . M,890
Baker, T. Mensuration. . . . . . . . . M,892
Baker, T. Statics and Dynamics. . . . . . . M,893
Beaton, A. C. Quantities and Measurements. . . . M,868
Bland, W. Construction of Arches, Piers, etc. . . . M,829
Bland, W. Forms of Ships and Boats. . . . . . M,830
Bond, R. Hand-Book of the Telegraph. . . . . M,831
Brooks, S. H. Erection of Dwelling Houses. . . . . M,869
Burgoyne, Sir J. Blasting and Quarrying. . . . . M,894
Burgoyne, Sir J. Roadmaking; Maintenance of Macadamized Roads. M,870
Burn, R. S. Outlines of Modern Farming. 5 v. . . . M,832
Burnell, G. R. Hydraulic Engineering. 2 v. . . . M,896
Burnell, G. R. Limes, Cements, Concretes, etc. . . . M,898
Bury, T. T. Rudimentary Architecture. . . . . . M,899
Campin, F. W. Law of Patents. . . . . . . M,834
Chattaway, E. D. Railways. . . . . . . . M,900
Costell, G. Ships' Anchors. . . . . . . . M,901
County Court Guide. . . . . . . . . M,871
Cox, H. Integral Calculus. . . . . . . . M,902
Dempsey, G. D. Drainage of Districts and Lands. . . . M,903
Dempsey, G. D. Drainage of Towns. . . . . . M,904
Dempsey, G. D. Locomotive Engines. . . . . . M,905
Atlas to same. . . . . . . . . Q,366
Dempsey, G. D. Tubular Bridges. . . . . . . M,906
Atlas to same. . . . . . . . . Q,148
Denison, E. B. Clock and Watchmaking; with Appendix. . H,907
Dobson, E. Art of Building. . . . . . . . M,908
Dobson, E. Bricks and Tiles. . . . . . . . M,909
Dobson, E. Foundations. . . . . . . . M,910
Dobson, E. Masonry and Stonecutting. . . . . M,911
Donaldson, J. Clay Lands and Loamy Soils. . . . . M,912
Emigrants, General Hints to. . . . . . . . M,836
Emmens, S. H. Selections from Locke on the Understanding. . M,838
Emmens, S. H. Treatise on Logic. . . . . . M,837
Euclid, Elements of; translated by H. Law. . . . M,945
Fenwick, T. and Baker, T. Subterraneous Surveying. . . M,839
Field, G. Grammar of Coloring. . . . . . . M,913
Fownes, G. Rudimentary Chemistry. . . . . . M,914
Frisi, P. Rivers, Torrents, and Canals. . . . . M,840
Fromberg, E. O. Painting on Glass. . . . . . M,915
Garbett, E. L. Design in Architecture. . . . . M,916
Gessert, M. A. Painting on Glass. . . . . . M,917
Gibbons, D. Law of Contracts. . . . . . . M,920
Gibbons, D. Limited Liability Acts. . . . . . M,919
Gibbons, D. and Hesketh, R. Metropolitan Building Act. . . M,921
Glynn, J. Construction of Cranes. . . . . . M,923
Glynn, J. Power of Water. . . . . . . . M,922
Gooding, R. Domestic Medicine. . . . . . . M,841

Weale's Rudimentary Series. *Continued.*

Gordon, G. H., *Earl of Aberdeen.* Grecian Architecture. . . M,843
Graham, W. Brass-Founder's Manual. . . . . . M,842
Grantham, J. Iron Ship-Building. . . . . . . M,924
Atlas to same. . . . . . . . . Q,149
Greenwood, J. Navigation. . . . . . . . M,925
Haddon, J. Algebra, and Key by J. R. Young. 2 v. . . M,926
Haddon, J. Arithmetic, and Key by A. Arman. 2 v. . . M,844
Haddon, J. Book-Keeping and Commercial Phraseology. . . M,872
Haddon, J. Differential Calculus. . . . . . M,927
Halleur, G. C. H. Art of Photography. . . . . M,928
Hann, J. Geometry and Conic Sections. . . . . M,845
Hann, J. Integral Calculus. . . . . . . . M,929
Hann, J. Trigonometry, Plane and Spherical. 2 v. in 1. . . M,930
Harris, W. S. Electricity. . . . . . . . M,932
Harris, W. S. Galvanism. . . . . . . . M,931
Harris, W. S. Magnetism. . . . . . . . M,933
Heather, J. F. Geometry applied to Drawing. . . . M,934
Heather, J. F. Mathematical Instruments. . . . M,935
Hipsley, W. Equational Arithmetic. 2 v. . . . . M,937
Hoare, C. Slide-Rule. . . . . . . . . M,846
Hobbs, A. C. and Mallet, R. Locks and Safes. . . . M,873
Hughes, S. Gas-Works. . . . . . . . . M,939
Hughes, S. Water-Works. . . . . . . . M,940
Hughes, S. and others. Construction of Roofs. . . . M,874
Kipping, R. Masting and Mastmaking. . . . . M,941
Kipping, R. Sails and Sailmaking. . . . . . M,847
Kirkman, T. P. Geometry, Algebra, and Trigonometry. . . M,942
Lamborn, R. H. Metallurgy of Copper, Silver, and Lead. 2 v. . M,848
Lardner, D. Steam Engine. . . . . . . . M,875
Law, H. Civil Engineering. . . . . . . . M,943
Law, H. Constructing and Repairing Roads. . . . M,944
Law, H. Elements of Euclid. . . . . . . . M,945
Law, H. Logarithms. . . . . . . . . M,946
Leeds, W. H. Orders of Architecture. . . . . M,947
M'Carthy, D. F. Engineer's Guide to the Navies. . . . M,849
McGregor, W. Questions on Magnetism, Electricity, and Telegraphy. M,850
Main, R. Rudimentary Astronomy. . . . . . . M,948
Mann, R. J. Guide to Natal. . . . . . . . M,851
Marey, Col. Memoir on Swords, etc. . . . . . M,852
Metropolis Local Management Act. . . . . . M,949
Metropolis Local Management Amendment, 1862. . . . M,876
Monckhoven, D. van. Photography. . . . . . M,853
Murray, R. Marine Engine, Steam Vessels, and the Screw. . M,877
Nuisances Removal Act. . . . . . . . . M,950
Peake, J. Naval Architecture. . . . . . . M,951
Playford, F. Hints for Investing Money. . . . . M,854
Portlock, J. E. Rudiments of Geology. . . . . . M,952
Prideaux, T. S. Economy of Fuel. . . . . . . M,953
Pyne, G. Perspective for Beginners. . . . . . M,954
Ramsay, A. Rudiments of Mineralogy. . . . . . M,855
Raspail, F. V. Domestic Medicine. . . . . . M,955
Ready Reckoner. . . . . . . . . . . M,856
Richardson, T. A. Architectural Modeling in Paper. . . M,936
Robison and Tredgold. Carpentry and Joinery. . . . M,957
Atlas to same. . . . . . . . . . Q,162
Robison, Price, and Tredgold. Carpentry and Joinery of Roofs. . M,956
Atlas to same. . . . . . . . . . Q,174
Rudimentary Dictionary of Terms in Architecture, etc. . . M,973
Sabine, R. History of the Electric Telegraph. . . . M,857
Sewell, J. Steam and Locomotion. . . . . . . M,958
Six Legislative Enactments on Bankruptcy, etc. . . . M,959

Weale's Rudimentary Series. *Continued.*

Smith, T. R. Acoustics in Buildings. . . . . . . M,858
Sommerfeldt, H. A. Construction of Ships. . . . . M,859
Plates to same. . . . . . . . . Q,150
Spencer, C. C. Playing the Pianoforte. . . . . . M,961
Spencer, C. C. Treatise on Music. . . . . . . M,960
Stephenson, R. McD. Railway Construction. . . . . M,964
Stevenson, A. Lighthouses. . . . . . . . M,962
Stevenson, D. Civil Engineering of North America. . . M,963
Swindell, J. G. Well-Digging, Boring, and Pump-Work. . . M,965
Taubert, Capt. Field Artillery. . . . . . . M,966
Tomlinson, C. (Ed.) Construction of Locks . . . . . M,967
Tomlinson, C. Experimental Essays on the Motion of Camphor and Modern Theory of Dew. . . . . . . . . M,878
Tomlinson, C. Mechanics. . . . . . . . M,968
Tomlinson, C. Natural Philosophy. . . . . . . M,969
Tomlinson, C. Pneumatics. . . . . . . . M,970
Tomlinson, C. Warming and Ventilation. . . . . . M,971
Varley, D. Mineralogy. . . . . . . . . M,972
Vitruvius Pollio, M. Architecture; tr. by J. Gwilt. . . . M,860
Watt, A. Electro-Metallurgy. . . . . . . M,861
White, N. Friendly Societies, etc. . . . . . . M,862
Wiggins, J. Embanking Lands from the Sea. . . . . M,974
Williams, C. W. Combustion of Coal. . . . . . M,975
Winton, J. W. Modern Workshop Practice. . . . . M,864
Woodward, S. P. and Tate, R. Mollusca. . . . . M865,
Woolhouse, W. S. B. Differential Calculus. . . . . M,978
Woolhouse, W. S. B. Weights and Measures of all Nations. . . M,979
Young, J. R. Arithmetic. . . . . . . . M,980
Key to the same. . . . . . . . . M,982
Young, J. R. Key to Haddon's Algebra. . . . . M,926,2
Young, J. R. Nautical Astronomy. . . . . . . M,977
Young, J. R. Navigation Tables. . . . . . . M,981

Wealth and Welfare. J. Gotthelf. London, 1866. 2 v. 12°. . . . . G,240
Distribution of. W. Thompson. London, 1869. 8°. . . . . O,560
Guide to. W. Smead. Cincinnati, 1856. 18°. . . . . . . O,466
of Nations, Nature and Causes of. A. Smith. Edinburgh, 1853. 8°. O,521
Science of. A. Walker. Boston, 1866. 8°. . . . . . . O,550
Wearing the Gray; Scenes of the War. J. E. Cooke. New York, 1867. 8°. B,955
Weather, Philosophy of. T. B. Butler. New York, 1856. 12°. . . N,104
Wetter und Wetterprophezeiung. J. Helmes. Hannover, 1858. 8°. . G,723
Weatherly, H. Treatise on Boiling Sugar. Philadelphia, 1865. 12°. . M,646
Weaver, J. Practical Elocution and Rhetorical Gesture. Phil. 1846. 12°. L,591
Weaving, Treatise on the Art of. J. Murphy. Glasgow, 1857. 12°. . . M,656
Webb, T. W. Celestial Objects for the Common Telescope. Lond. 1868. 16°. N,259
Webber, C. W. Gold Mines of the Gila. New York, 1849. 2 v. in 1. 12°. K,308
Weber, G. Allgemeine Weltgeschichte. Leipzig, 1857–66. 6 v. 8°. . E,10
Metrical Romances, 13th–15th Centuries. Edinburgh, 1810. 3 v. 8°. I,468
Outlines of Universal History. Boston, 1853. 8°. . . . . . A,33
and Jameson, R. Illustrations of North. Antiquities. Edinb. 1814. 4°. F,232
Weber, J. Mémoires concernant Marie Antoinette. Paris, 1847. 12°. . D,614
Webster, D., Life of. J. Banvard. Boston, 1853. 16°. . . . . J,1206
Life of. G. T. Curtis. New York, 1870. 2 v. 8°. . . . . C,1030
S. L. Knapp. Boston, 1831. 12°. . . . . . . C,1024
S. P. Lyman. New York, 1853. 2 v. 12°. . . . . . C,675
S. M. Schmucker. Philadelphia, 1859. 8°. . . . . . C,979

Webster, D., Oration on. T. Walker. Cincinnati, 1852. 8°. . . . *H,302,4
Private Correspondence. Boston, 1857. 2 v. 8°. . . . . U,106
Private Life of. C. Lanman. New York, 1853. 12°. . . C,1008
Works; with Memoir by E. Everett. Boston, 1853. 6 v. 8°. . . U,103
Vol. 1, 2. Biographical Memoir; Orations and Speeches.
3, 4. Speeches in Massachusetts Convention, 1820, and in Congress.
5, 6. Legal Arguments; Diplomatic and Official Papers.
Webster, E. Phonographic Teacher. New York, 1852. 16°. . . . L,685
Webster, J. Dramatic Works. London, 1857. 4 v. 16°. . . . I,750
Webster, J. Elements of Chemistry. London, 1811. 8°. . . . N,251
Webster, N. Dictionary of the English Language. Springfield, 1870. 4°. L.R.
The same. Springfield, 1867. 4°. . . . . . . . R.R.
History of the United States. Cincinnati, 1835. 12°. . . . B,684
Papers, Political, Literary, and Moral. New York, 1843. 8°. . . U,109
Webster, T. and Parkes. Encyclopædia of Domes. Economy. N. Y. 1849. 8°. L.R.
Wedderburn, J. W. Naturalist in Bermuda. London, 1859. 12°. . . N,521
Wedgwood, H. Dictionary of English Etymology, v. 1. Lond. 1859. 8°. L.R.
Origin of Language. London, 1866. 8°. . . . . . . L,501
Wedgwood, J., Life of. E. Meteyard. London, 1865–66. 2 v. 8°. . . M,644
Wedgwood, W. B. Questions on Constitution of United States. Phil. 1844. 12°. O,1087
Weeds and Useful Plants, American. W. Darlington. N. Y. 1859. 12°. . N,953
Week on the Concord and Merrimack. H. D. Thoreau. Boston, 1862. 12°. V,24
Weeks, H. C. Ainslee Stories. New York, 1869. 16°. . . . J,1618
Grandpa's House. New York, 1869. 16°. . . . . . J,1370
White and Red; Life among the Indians. New York, 1869. 16°. J,1263
Weeks, J. M. Easy Method of Managing Bees. New York, 1856. 12°. M,533,3
Weems, M. L. Life of Benjamin Franklin. Philadelphia, 1845. 12°. . C,840
Life of Francis Marion. Philadelphia, 1863. 12°. . . . C,1009
Life of George Washington. Philadelphia, 1869. 12°. . . . C,873
Life of William Penn. Philadelphia, 1852. 12°. . . . . D,151
Weidemann, C. F. Papers on Miscellaneous Subjects. London, 1850. 16°. H,391
Weighed in the Balance. S. S. Robbins. New York, 1868. 16°. . J,1666
Weights and Measures, Dictionary of. J. H. Alexander. Baltimore, 1850. 8°. L.R.
Handbuch der. J. C. Nelkenbrecher. Reutlingen, 1834. 12°. E,427
Legal System of. A. L. Lamotte. Philadelphia, 1867. 16°. M,1094
Report upon. J. Q. Adams. Washington, 1821. 8°. . . O,502
A. D. Bache. Washington, 1857. 8°. . . . . . O,500
Measures and Moneys. W. S. B. Woolhouse. London, 1859. 12°. M,979
Weil, G. Bible, Koran, and Talmud. New York, 1855. 16°. . . . P,73
Geschichte der Chalifen. Mannheim, 1846–51. 3 v. 8°. . . . E,25
Mohammed, der Prophet. Stuttgart, 1843. 12°. . . . . . E,242
Weir, A. St. Petersburg and Moscow. London, 1862. 8°. . . . V,1086,2
Weisbach, J. Mechanics of Machinery and Engineering. Lon. 1847–8. 2 v. 8°. M,675
Weiss, C. History of the French Protestant Refugees. N. Y. 1854. 2 v. 12°. B,364
Weiss, J. American Religion. Boston, 1871. 12°. . . . . . . P,583
Life of Theodore Parker. New York, 1864. 2 v. 8°. . . . C,945
Weitling, W. Evangelium der Armen Sünder. New York, 1854. 16°. . E,442
Weitzmann, C. T. Geschichte der Griechischen Musik. Berlin, 1855. 4°. G,737
Welby, A. Poems. New York, 1846. 12°. . . . . . . . I,155
Welcker, F. G. Griechische Götterlehre. Göttingen, 1857–63. 3 v. 8°. E,463
Weld, C. R. History of the Royal Society. London, 1848. 2 v. 8°. . F,164

Weld, C. R. Tour in the United States and Canada. Lond. 1855. 12°. . V,140
Vacation in Brittany. London, 1856. 12°. . . . . . . V,461
Weld, H. H. Life of Benjamin Franklin. Cincinnati, 1854. 8°. . . C,811
Weld, I. jr. Travels in the States and Canada. London, 1799. 4°. . V,151
Well-Digging, Boring, and Pump-Work J. G. Swindell. Lon. 1854. 12°. M,965
Wellesley, Sir A., *Duke of Wellington*, Life of. A. Brialmont. Lon. 1860. 4 v. 8°. D,217
Life of. W. H. Maxwell. London, 1867. p 8°. . . . . . L,154
Memoir of; from The Times. London, 1852. p. 8°. . . I,661,1
Military Memoirs of, by an Old Campaigner. London, 1842. 16°. J,1273
Victories of. W. H. Maxwell. London, 1852. 16°. . . . L,125
Words of; compiled by E. Walford. London, 1869. 16°. . . I,561
Wellesley, R., *Marquis*, Memoirs of. R. R. Pearce. London, 1846. 3 v. 8°. D,35
Wellington, Duke of. See *Wellesley, Sir A.*
Wells, A. Normal School. London, 1849. 16°. . . . . . . O,969
Wells, D. A. (Ed.) Things not generally known. New York, 1859. 12°. H,233
(Ed.) See *Annual of Scientific Discovery.*
Wells, J. G. Every Man his own Lawyer. New York, 1867. 12°. . . U,488
Wells, S. R. Physiognomy; or, Signs of Character. New York, 1866. 8°. N,421
Wells, W., Sketches of. J. McDonald. n. t. p. 12°. . . . . . C,839
Wells, W. (Ed.) Water-Power of Maine. Augusta, 1869. 8°. . . . . C,24
Wells, W. C. Essay on Dew. London, 1866. 8°. . . . . . . N,91
Wells, W. H. Graded School. New York, 1867. 12°. . . . . . O,939
Wells, W. V. Life of Samuel Adams. Boston, 1865. 3 v. 8°. . C,1067
Welsh Dictionary. W. Evans. Carmarthen, 1812. 8°. . . . . . L.R.
Welt als Wille und Vorstellungen. A. Schopenhauer. Leip. 1859. 2 v. 8°. G,574
Wentworth, C. W., *Marquis of Rockingham*, Memoirs of. G. T. Keppel. London, 1852. 2 v. 8°. . . . . . . . . . . . D,431
Wentworth, T., *Earl of Strafford*, Life of. J. Macdiarmid. Lond. 1807. 4°. F,24
Trial of. J. Rushworth. London, 1680. f°. . . . . . . F,41
Wepf, L. Church of God and her Adversaries, v. 1. Chicago, 1871. 12°. P,384
Wept of Wish-ton-Wish. J. F. Cooper. New York, 1867. 12°. . . K,55
The same. New York, 1859. 8°. . . . . . . . K,81
Werne, F. African Wanderings. London, 1852. 12°. . . . . . V,766
The same. London, 1854. p. 8°. . . . . . . I,658,2
Expedition to the White Nile. London, 1849. 2 v. 12°. . . V,770
Wesley, C., Life of. T. Jackson. New York, 1842. 8°. . . . . D,293
seen in his Familiar Poems. New York, 1867. 16°. . . . I,173
Wesley, J. and his Coadjutors. W. C. Larrabee. Cincinnati, 1853. 2 v. 16°. C,1181
and Methodism. I. Taylor. London, 1851. 8°. . . . . . P,829
Compendium of Natural Philosophy. London, 1836. 3 v. 16°. . I,643
Journal. New York, n. d. 2 v. 8°. . . . . . . . D,464
Life of. R. Southey. New York, 1847. 2 v. 12°. . . . . C,1251
The same. London, 1864. p. 8°. . . . . . . L,245
R. Watson. Cincinnati, 1857. 8°. . . . . . . . D,269
J. Whitehead. Auburn, 1852. 8°. . . . . . . C,1201
Works. Bristol, 1771–74. 32 v. 12°. . . . . . . . . P,756

Vol. 1–4. Sermons.
4–6. Duties of Husbands and Wives; Mr. Law on Christian Perfection, and Serious Call to a Holy Life.
7, 8. Mr. Law on the Spirit of Prayer and Love; T. à Kempis on the Christian Pattern.
8. Mr. Norris on Christian Prudence; Fear of Man.

Wesley, J. Works. *Continued.* . . . . . . . . . . . . P,576

9. Manners of Ancient Christians; Doctrine of Salvation, Faith, and Good Works.
10. Earthquake at Lisbon; Forms of Prayer; Address to the Clergy; Deaths of T. Hitchens, S. Hitchens, N. Othen, M. Lee, J. Janeway, and T. Haliburton.
11. Lives of M. de Renty and T. Walsh.
12. Life of David Brainerd.
13. M. Gilbert's Journal; E. Harper's Journal; Accounts of A. Johnson, A. Rogers, M. Langson, and H. Richardson; Letters.
14. Meditations; Letters by J. Cooper; Earnest Appeal to Men of Reason and Religion.
15. Plain account of Methodists; Minutes of Conversations; Character of a Methodist.
16. Advice to the Methodists; Principles of a Methodist; Letters.
17. Distinguishing Marks of a Work of the Spirit of God; Thoughts on the Revival of Religion in New England.
18. Account of the Trial at Gloucester; Modern Christianity; Case of John Nelson; Letters.
19. Letter to a Roman Catholic; Roman Catechism; Preservative against unsettled Notions in Religion; Short and Easy Method with Deists; Treatise on the Godhead of Jesus Christ; Advantage of the Members of the Church of England over those of Rome; Letters; Treatise on Baptism; Thoughts upon Infant Baptism; Thoughts on Godfathers and Godmothers.
20. Scripture Doctrine of Predestination, etc.; Extract from a Short View of the Difference between the Moravian Brethren and Mr. J. and C. Wesley; Dialogue between Antinomian and his Friend; Free-Grace, a Sermon; Serious Considerations on Election and Reprobation; On absolute Predestination; Thoughts on the Perseverance of Saints; Predestination calmly considered; The Consequence proved; Thoughts on the imputed Righteousness of Christ; A Blow at the Root, or, Christ stabbed in the House of his Friends; Answer to the Author of Theron and Aspasio; Conflagration and Renovation of the World.
21. Doctrine of Original Sin.
22. On the present State of Public Affairs; Thoughts upon Liberty; Thoughts concerning the Origin of Power; Remarks on Mr. Hill's Review; On Justification.
23. On Justification; Reasons against a Separation from the Church of England; The Christian Sacrament and Sacrifice; Treatise on Religious Affections; Remarks on Mr. Hill's Farago double-distilled; Short Account of John Dillon.
24. Plain Account of Christian Perfection; Instructions for Christians; Christian Reflections; Thoughts on a Single Life; Letter on Tea; The Desideratum, or, Electricity made easy.
25. Primitive Physic; Advice with respect to Health.
26. Extracts from Dr. Cadogan's Dissertation on the Gout and all Chronic Diseases; Short English Grammar; Punctuation and Gesture; Journals.

27–32. Journals.

Wesley Family, Memoirs of. A. Clarke. New York, 1851. 12°. . C,1186

Wesleyan Preachers, Memoirs of. P. P. Sanford. New York, 1843. 12°. D,438

West, B., Life of. J. Galt. London, 1820. 8°. . . . . . . D,86

West, G. Poetical Works; illustrated by B. Foster. London, 1855. 16°. . I,453

West, J. Management of Woods, Plantations, etc. Newark, 1842. 8°. . M,358

West, N. Complete Analysis of the Holy Bible. New York, 1855. 4°. . P,558

West, W. Methods of preventing or consuming Smoke. London, 1842. 8°. N,252,13

Water for Locomotive Engines. London, 1846. 8°. . . . N,252,39

West, The, Annals of. J. H. Perkins. Cincinnati, 1847. 8°. . . . C,273

Historical Collections of. H. Howe. Cincinnati, 1853. 8°. . . C,277

Incidents and Sketches of the History of. Cincinnati, n. d. 8°. . C,149

its Soil, Surface, and Productions. J. Hall. Cincinnati, 1848. 12°. V,10

Letters from. J. Hall. London, 1828. 8°. . . . . . . V,85

Legends of. J. Hall. New York, 1854. 12°. . . . . . . C,142

Life in. J. Hall. Philadelphia, 1835. 8°. . . . . . . V,5

Life in the Far West. G. F. Ruxton. Edinburgh, 1849. 12°. . V,137

Loyal West in the Rebellion. J.W. Barbour and H. Howe. Cin. 1865. 8°. B,957

New Purchase; or, Seven and a Half Years in. N. Y. 1843. 2 v. 12°. V,156

West, Our New. S. Bowles. Hartford, 1869. 8°. . . . . . . v,111
Pioneer Life in; Autobiography of J. B. Finley. Cin. 1858. 12°. . c,787
Pioneer Women of the. E. F. Ellet. New York, 1852. 12°. . . c,651
Plea for. L. Beecher. Cincinnati, 1835. 12°. . . . . . . o,987
Poetical Literature of. W. D. Gallagher. Cincinnati, 1841. 12°. . H,661
Recollections of Persons, etc., in. H. M. Brackenridge. Phila. 1834. 12°. v,95
The same. Philadelphia, 1868. 12°. . . . . . . v,95
Sketches of. J. Hall. Philadelphia, 1835. 2 v. 12°. . . . v,5
Statistics of. J. Hall. Cincinnati, 1837. 12°. . . . . . v,6
Tour to the Western Country. F. Cuming. Pittsburgh, 1810. 12°. v,96
Travels to the West of Alleghanys. F. A. Michaux. Lond. 1805. 8°. v,73
West-American Review; edited by G. W. L. Bickley. Cincinnati, 1853. 8°. T,16
West Indies and Spanish Main. A. Trollope. Leipzig, 1860. 16°. . . J,507
Emancipation in. J. A. Thome and J. K. Kimball. N.Y. 1838. 12°. v,186
Geography, Hist., and Statistics of. H. C. Carey and Lea. Lond. 1823. 8°. B,621
Impressions of, 1849. R. Baird. Philadelphia, 1850. 16°. . . v,18
Six Months in. H. N. Coleridge. London, 1832. 16°. . . . I,614
West Point, History of. E. C. Boynton. New York, 1864. 8°. . . . C,316
Military Academy. G. W. Cullum. New York, 1868. 2 v. 8°. . C,1031
West Virginia, Early Set. and Indian Wars of. W. De Hass. Wheel. 1851. 8°. C,281
Resources of. J. R. Dodge. Philadelphia, 1865. 12°. . . . C,177
Westbrook Parsonage. H. B. M'Keever. Philadelphia, 1870. 12°. . . K,113
Westcott, B. F. Introduction to the Gospels. Boston, 1869. 12°. . . P,505
Westcott, T. Life of John Fitch. Philadelphia, 1857. 12°. . . . C,925
Weste, R. Booke of Demeanor. London, 1868. 8°. . . . . . L,605,32
Westerhovius, A. H. Hieroglyphica of Merkbeelden der oude Volkeren; en Verbeeld door Romeyn de Hooghe. Amsteldam, 1735. 4°. . *Q,340
Western Academician and Journal of Education, v. 1. Cincin. 1837–38. 8°. T,11
Western Empire, History of. Sir R. Comyn. London, 1851. 2 v. p. 8°. . A,246
Western Gazetteer; or, Emigrant's Directory. S. R. Brown. Auburn, 1817. 8°. C,199
Western History, Romance of. J. Hall. Cincinnati, 1857. 12°. . . C,143
Western Horticultural Review, v. 2. Cincinnati, 1852. 8°. . . . . M,577
Western Literary Institute, Transactions, 1834–40. Cincin. 1835–41. 6 v. 8°. O,1253
Western Literary Journal; edited by E. Z. C. Judson. Cincinnati, 1845. 8°. T,28
Western Literary Magazine; edited by G. Brewster. Columbus, 1853. 8°. T,29
Western Magazines, Miscellaneous, 1827–54. 8°. . . . . . . . *T,18
Western Medical Gazette. Cincinnati, 1833–34. 2 v. 8°. . . . . L,933
Western Miscellanies. 3 v. 8°. . . . . . . . . . . . *T,19
Western Monthly Magazine, v. 1-3, 5, 6. Cincinnati, 1833–37. 5 v. 8°. . T,31
Western Monthly Review, v. 1, 3. Cincinnati, 1828–30. 2 v. 8°. . . T,9
Western Pilot; Ohio and Missis. Rivers. S. Cummings. Cincin. 1836. 8°. M,689
Western Quarterly Reporter. Cincinnati, 1822–23. 2 v. in 1. 8°. . . L,934
Western Quarterly Review, v. 1. Cincinnati, 1849. 8°. . . . . . T,10
Western Reserve, Presb. and Cong. Churches. W. S. Kennedy. Hudson, '56. 12°. C,200
Western Review, v. 1. Columbus, 1846. 8°. . . . . . . . . . T,17
Western Travel, Retrospect of. H. Martineau. London, 1838. 3 v. 12°. V,143
Westminster Abbey, Memorials of. A. P. Stanley. London, 1868. 8°. . B,60
Westminster Assembly, History of. W. M. Hetherington. N. Y. 1856. 12°. P,601
Westminster Review. London, 1824–67. 88 v. 8°. . . . . . . S,16
Weston, H. H. and others. Fairy Egg and what it held. Boston, 1870. 12°. J,1648

Westphal, R. Allgemeine Griechische Metrik. Leipzig, 1865. 8°. . G,596,2
Fragmente der Griechischen Rhythmiker. Leipzig, 1861. 8°. . G,596,4
Harmonik und Melopöie der Griechen. Leipzig, 1863. 8°. . G,596,2
Westward Empire. E. L. Magoon. New York, 1856. 12°. . . . A,30
Westward Ho!; or, Sir Amyas Leigh. C. Kingsley. N. Y. 1866. 2 v. 16°. K,753
The same. Leipzig, 1865. 2 v. in 1. 16°. . . . . . J,245
Westwood, J. O. Arcana Entomologica; Rare Insects. Lond. 1845. 2 v. 8°. O,51
Entomologist's Text-Book. London, 1838. 12°. . . . . . O,15
Heteromera of Tropical Africa. n. t. p. 4°. . . . . . . *Q,114
Insect Architecture. London, 1845. 2 v. 18°. . . . . . . O,1
Insect Transformation. London, n. d. 12°. . . . . . . O,12
Insect Transformations and Architecture. London, 1831–50. 3 v. 16°. L,479
Modern Classification of Insects. London, 1839–40. 2 v. 8°. . . O,46
Nycteribia; Wingless Insects. n. t. p. 4°. . . . . . *Q,114
Sacred Beetles. n. t. p. 4°. . . . . . . . . *Q,114
Wet Days at Edgewood. D. G. Mitchell. New York, 1865. 16°. . . M,551
Wetherell, Elizabeth, *pseud.* See *Warner, S.*
Wetherill, C. M. Manufacture of Vinegar. Philadelphia, 1860. 12°. . M,686
Wetmore, A. Gazetteer of Missouri. St. Louis, 1837. 8°. . . . . C,241
Weyer, G. D. E. Differential Formeln für Cometenbahnen. Berlin, 1852. 8°. G,779
Whale, The. H. Melville. London, 1851. 3 v. 12°. . . . . J,642
Whale-Fishery, Northern, Journal of Voyage to. W. Scoresby. Edinb. '23. 8°. V,181
Whales. R. Hamilton. Edinburgh, 1853. 16°. . . . . . . N,470,26
Whaling and Fishing. C. Nordhoff. Cincinnati, 1856. 16°. . . . K,140
Wharton, C. H., Memoir of. G. W. Doane. Philadelphia, 1834. 2 v. 12°. C,681
Wharton, F. State Trials of the United States. Philadelphia, 1849. 8°. . O,426
Treatise on Theism. Philadelphia, 1859. 12°. . . . . . . P,267
Wharton, Grace and Philip. See *Thomson, K. B.* and *J. C.*
Wharton, T. and others. Essays on Gothic Architecture. London, 1808. 8°. M,208
What Answer? A. E. Dickinson. Boston, 1869. 16°. . . . . K,101
What can Woman do? T. S. Arthur. Philadelphia, n. d. 16°. . . J,620
What I know of Farming. H. Greeley. New York, 1871. 12°. . . M,565
What to Read, and how to Read. C. H. Moore. New York, 1871. 12°. . O,984
What will he do with it? Sir E. B. Lytton. Philadelphia, 1869. 2 v. 12°. K,830
The same. Leipzig, 1853–58. 4 v. 16°. . . . . . J,330
Whately, E. J. Life of Richard Whately. London, 1866. 2 v. 8°. . . D,294
Whately, R. Elements of Logic. Boston, 1860. 12°. . . . . O,727
Elements of Rhetoric. New York, 1853. 12°. . . . . . . L,592
Essays on the Difficulties of St. Paul. London, 1861. 8°. . . P,523
Historic doubts relative to Napoleon I. London, 1859. 8°. . . D,585
History of Religious Worship. London, 1867. 8°. . . . . P,14
Life of. E. J. Whately. London, 1866. 2 v. 8°. . . . . D,294
Logic and Rhetoric. London, 1855. 8°. . . . . . . O,726
Mental Science. London, 1855. 12°. . . . . . . . O,726
Miscellaneous Lectures and Reviews. London, 1861. 8°. . . . H,375
Rise, Progress, and Corruptions of Christianity. New York, 1860. 12°. P,297
Scripture Revelations concerning a Future State. London, 1870. 12°. P,224
Scripture Revelations on Good and Evil Angels. London, 1855. 12°. P,265
Thoughts and Apophthegms. Philadelphia, 1856. 12°. . . . H,613
Thoughts on Secondary Punishments. London, 1832. 8°. . . P,117

Whateley, S. England's Gazetteer, v. 1, 2. London, 1751. 12°. . . v,297
Wheat Plant. J. H. Klippart. Cincinnati, 1860. 12°. . . . . . M,558
Wheatley, C. Illustration of Book of Common Prayer. Lond. 1857. p. 8°. L,247
Wheatley, P. Memoir and Poems. Boston, 1838. 16°. . . . . . I,104
Wheaton, H. Elements of International Law. Boston, 1866. 8°. . . U,507
History of the Northmen. London, 1831. 8°. . . . . . . B,580
Life of William Pinkney. Boston, 1860. 12°. . . . . . C,860,6
Scandinavia, Ancient and Modern. New York, 1856. 2 v. 16°. . B,574
The same. New York, 1854. 2 v. 16°. . . . . . L,429
Wheaton, R., Memoir of. Boston, 1854. 16°. . . . . . . . C,765
Wheel of Fortune. W. J. Bradley. Boston, 1870. 16°. . . . . J,1681
Wheeler, G. Rural Homes. New York, 1868. 12°. . . . . . . M,157
Wheeler, J. H. Historical Sketches of North Carolina. Philad. 1851. 8°. C,192
Wheeler, J. T. History of India, v. 1. London, 1867. 8°. . . . C,405
Life and Travels of Herodotus. New York, 1856. 2 v. 8°. . . D,770
Wheeler, W. A. Dictionary of noted Names of Fiction. Bost. 1866. 16°. L.R.
Wheels and Pulleys, Mechanism of. W. Fairbairn. Philadelphia, 1867. 12°. M,610
Wheildon, W. W. Inauguration of Statue of Jos. Warren. Bost. 1858. 8°. C,23
Memoir of Simon Willard. Boston, 1865. 8°. . . . . . . C,749
Where there's a Will there's a Way. A. B. Haven. New York, 1867. 16°. J,1334
Whewell, W. Astronomy, Physics, and Natural Theology. Lond. 1852. p. 8°. L,277
Elements of Morality. New York, 1845. 2 v. 12°. . . . O,711
English University Education. London, 1838. 8°. . . . . . O,924
History of the Inductive Sciences. New York, 1859. 2 v. 8°. O,697,1
Liberal Education. London, 1850. 8°. . . . . . . . O,910
Philosophy of the Inductive Sciences. London, 1847. 2 v. 8°. . O,698
Plurality of Worlds; edited by E. Hitchcock. Boston, 1861. 12°. . N,273
Which is the Wiser. M. Howitt. New York, 1852. 18°. . . . . J,1172
Whim and its Consequences. G. P. R. James. Leipzig, 1847. 16°. . . J,216
Whincop, T. Scanderbeg; or, Love and Liberty. London, 1747. 8°. . I,742
Whip, Hoe, and Sword; Gulf Dep., 1863. G. H. Hepworth. Bost. 1864. 12°. H,39
Whipple, E. P. Character and Characteristic Men. Boston, 1867. 12°. . H,255
Essays and Reviews. Boston, 1853. 2 v. 16°. . . . . . H,208
Lectures on Literature and Life. Boston, 1853. 16°. . . . H,207
Literature of the Age of Elizabeth. Boston, 1869. 12°. . . . H,702
Whiskey Insurrection in Pennsylvania. H. M. Brackenridge. Pittsb. 1859. 8°. B,861
Whistler; or, the Manly Boy. W. Simonds. Boston, 1859. 16°. . J,1431,4
Whitaker, J. Mary Queen of Scots vindicated. London, 1790. 3 v. 8°. D,112
Whitby, D. Commentary; Gospels and Epistles. Philadelphia, 1848. 8°. P,556
Whitcher, F. M. Widow Bedott Papers. New York, 1867. 12°. . . H,65
Widow Spriggins, Mary Elmer, etc. New York, 1867. 12°. . . H,81
White, A. British Crustacea. London, 1857. 16°. . . . . . . O,6
Popular History of Birds. London, 1855. 16°. . . . . . O,81
Popular History of Mammalia. London, 1850. 16°. . . . N,678
White, E. E. Class-Book of Local Geography. Cleveland, 1860. 16°. . O,899
White, G. S. Memoir of Samuel Slater. Philadelphia, 1836. 8°. . . D,363
White, G. Natural History of Selborne. Edinburgh, 1829. 16°. . . I,519
The same. London, 1851. 12°. . . . . . . . L,164
The same. London, 1851. 8°. . . . . . . . . N,471
The same. New York, 1860. 16°. . . . . . . . . L,437

White, H. Elements of Universal History. Edinburgh, 1853-54. 3 v. 12°. A,6
Massacre of St. Bartholomew. New York, 1868. 8°. . . . . B,366
Outlines of Universal History. Edinburgh, 1855. 16°. . . . . A,17
Sacred History. Edinburgh, 1855. 16°. . . . . . . . . P,561
White, H. K. Poetical Works. Boston, 1854. 16°. . . . . . . I,235
The same. London, 1857. 16°. . . . . . . . . I,464
White, J. Eighteen Christian Centuries. Edinburgh, 1859. 8°. . . . A,320
History of France to 1848. New York, 1859. 8°. . . . . . B,339
White, J. Planters' Plea. London, 1630. See *Force's Tracts*, v. 2.
White, N. Friendly, Loan, etc., Societies. London, 1867. 12°. . . . M,862
White, R. G. Life of Shakespeare, and the English Drama. Bost. 1865. 8°. C,1227
New Gospel of Peace. New York, 1866. 12°. . . . . . . B,891
Shakespeare's Scholar; Studies of his Text, etc. N. Y. 1854. 8°. . I,871
Words and their Uses. New York, 1870. 12°. . . . . . . L,578
White, W. Emanuel Swedenborg; his Life and Writings. Lon. 1867. 2 v. 8°. P,849
White and Red; Life among the Indians. H. C. Weeks. N. Y. 1869. 16°. J,1263
White as Snow. E. and R. Garrett. New York, n. d. 12°. . . . K,138
White Chief; a Legend of North Mexico. M. Reid. N. Y. 1869. 12°. J,1576
White Elephant; or, the Hunters of Ava. W. Dalton. London, 1860. 16°. J,1509
White Gauntlet. M. Reid. New York, 1870. 12°. . . . . . J,1577
White Lies. C. Reade. Boston, 1867. 16°. . . . . . . . K,909
White Mountain Guide. E. C. Eastman. Concord, 1863. 16°. . . . V,26
White Mountain History, Incidents in. R. G. Willey. Boston, 1856. 12°. H,10
White Nile, Expedition to. F. Werne. London, 1867. 12°. . . . V,770
White, Red, Black; American Society. F. and T. Pulszky. N.Y. 1853. 2 v. 12°. V,50
White Rose. G. J. W. Melville. Leipzig, 1868. 2 v. in 1. 16°. . . J,381
White Staff, Secret History of. D. De Foe. London, 1714-5. 3 v. in 1. 8°. U,248
Whitefield, George, Memoirs of. J. Gillies. Philadelphia, 1859. 12°. . D,229
Whitehead, J. Life of John Wesley. Auburn, 1852. 8°. . . . C,1201
Whitehead, W. East Jersey under Proprietary Governments. Newark,'46. 8°. C,107
Whitehead, W. A. Early History of Perth Amboy. New York, 1856. 8°. C,108
Whitelands Institution, Prizes at. B. Coutts. London, n. d. 8°. . O,1200
Whitgift, J., Life and Acts. J. Strype. London, 1822. 3 v. 8°. . . P,691
Whiting, H. Life of Zebulon M. Pike. Boston, 1860. 12°. . . . C,860,15
Whiting, W. War Powers under United States Constitution. Bost. 1871. 8°. U,510
Whitling, H. J. Pictures of Nuremberg. London, 1850. 2 v. 12°. . V,421
Whitman, S. H. Edgar A. Poe and his Critics. New York, 1860. 12°. . H,662
Whitman, W. E. S. and True, C. H. Maine in War for the Union. Lew.'65. 8°. B,950
Whitmore, W. H. Elements of Heraldry. Boston, 1866. 8°. . . . . M,370
Hand-Book of American Genealogy. Albany, 1862. 4°. . . . . F,39
(Ed.) Catalogue of the Prince Library. Boston, 1868. 12°. . . L.R.
Whitney, A. D. T. Faith Gartney's Girlhood. Boston, 1863. 12°. . . K,396
Gayworthys. Boston, 1865. 12°. . . . . . . . . . K,399
Hitherto; a Story of Yesterdays. Boston, 1869. 12°. . . . . K,389
Patience Strong's Outings. Boston, 1869. 12°. . . . . . . K,388
Summer in Leslie Goldthwait's Life. Boston, 1871. 12°. . . . K,395
We Girls; a Home Story. Boston, 1870. 12°. . . . . . K,394
Zerub Throop's Experiment. Boston, 1871. 12°. . . . . . K,384
Whitney, J. D. Geology of California, v. 1. San Francisco, 1865. 4°. . N,741
Metallic Wealth of the United States. Philadelphia, 1854. 8°. . M,723

Whitney, P. History of Worcester County, Mass. Worcester, 1793. 8°. C,51
Whitney, W. D. Compendious German Grammar. New York, 1870. 12°. L,576
Language and the Study of Language. New York, 1867. 8°. . L,514
Whittier, J. G. Among the Hills. Boston, 1869. 16°. . . . . . I,152
In War-Time, and other Poems. Boston, 1864. 16°. . . . I,151
Literary Recreations and Miscellanies. Boston, 1854. 16°. . . H,209
Margaret Smith's Journal. Boston, 1849. 16°. . . . . . H,286
Miriam, and other Poems. Boston, 1871. 16°. . . . . . I,101
Old Portraits and Modern Sketches. Boston, 1850. 16°. . . H,31
Poetical Works. Boston, 1870. 16°. . . . . . . . . I,133
Prose Works. Boston, 1866. 2 v. 12°. . . . . . . . . U,2

Vol. 1. Margaret Smith's Journal; Old Portraits and Modern Sketches.
2. Literary Recreations and Miscellanies.

Snow-Bound; a Winter Idyl. Boston, 1867. 12°. . . . . . I,154
Songs of Labor, and other Poems. Boston, 1856. 16°. . . . I,159
Tent on the Beach, and other Poems. Boston, 1867. 16°. . . I,153
Voices of Freedom; Poems. Philadelphia, 1846. 12°. . . I,150
Whittington, G. D. Ecclesiastical Antiquities of France. London, 1811. . M,174
Whittlesey, C. Ancient Mining on Shores of Lake Superior. Wash. 1863. 4°. Q,324,13
Early History of Cleveland, Ohio. Cleveland, 1867. 8°. . . C,224
Life of John Fitch. Boston, 1860. 12°. . . . . . . C,860,16
Sketch of the Geology of Ohio. Columbus, 1838. 8°. . . . N,874
Whittock, N. Oxford Drawing-Book. London, n. d. 8°. . . . M,142
Who Breaks—Pays. C. Jenkin. Leipzig, 1861. 16°. . . . . J,221
Who shall be greatest. M. Howitt. New York, 1867. 24°. . . . J,1157
Whom to Marry, and how. H. and A. Mayhew. London, n. d. 12°. . J,650
Why did he not die? A. von Volckhausen. Philadelphia, 1871. 12°. . G,170
Why Not? a Book for every Woman. H. R. Storer. Boston, 1868. 16°. L,833
Why Paul Ferroll killed his Wife. C. Clive. Leipzig, 1861. 16°. . . J,69
Whymper, F. Travels in Alaska. London, 1868. 8°. . . . . . V,82
Wickersham, J. P. School Economy. Philadelphia, 1864. 12°. . . O,940
Wickham, H. L. and Cramer. Hannibal's Passage of the Alps. Lond. 1828. 8°. A,159
Wickliff, J., Life of. C. W. Le Bas. London, 1832. 16°. . . . . . D,332
Wide, Wide World. S. Warner. Philadelphia, 1868. 12°. . . . K,375
Widow and the Marquess. T. Hook. London, n. d. 12°. . . . K,723
Widow Bedott Papers. F. M. Whitcher. New York, 1867. 12°. . . H,65
Widow Goldsmith's Daughter. J. P. Smith. Hartford, 1870. 12°. . . K,152
Widow Spriggins, Mary Elmer, etc. F. M. Whitcher. New York, 1867. 12°. H,81
Widow's Son. E. D. E. N. Southworth. Philadelphia, 1870. 12°. . . K,441
Wied-Neuwied, Prinz zu. See *Maximilian.*
Wiegmann, A. F. Entstehung des Torfes. Braunschweig, 1837. 8°. N,252,4
und Polstorff, L. Anorgan. Bestandtheile der Pflanzen. Brschw. '42. 8°. N,252,6
Wieland, C. M. Oberon; ein Romantisches Heldengedicht. Leip. 1867. 12°. E,285
The same; trans. by W. Sotheby. Newport, 1810. 2 v. 12°. G,47
Sämmtliche Werke. Leipzig, 1839–40. 36 v. in 23. 16°. . . E,364

Bd. 1, 2 Abenteuer des Don Sylvio von Rosalva.
3. *Poetische Werke:* Musarion; Die Grazien; Der verklagte Amor; Nadine; Erdenglück; Celia an Damon; Bruchstücke von Psyche; Das Leben ein Traum; Aspasia, oder die platonische Liebe.
4–6. Geschichte des Agathon.
7, 8. Der goldene Spiegel, oder die Könige von Scheschian.
9. Geschichte des weisen Danischmend.

Wieland, C. M. Sämmtliche Werke. *Continued.* . . . . . . . E,364
10. Komische Erzählungen (Poetische): Diana und Endymion; Das Urtheil des Paris; Aurora und Cephalus; Kombabus; Die erste Liebe; Sixt und Clärchen, oder der Mönch und die Nonne auf dem Mädelstein; Gandalin, oder Liebe um Liebe; Schach Lolo, oder das göttliche Recht der Gewalthaber.
11. *Poetische Werke:* Das Wintermährchen; Das Sommermährchen; Geron, der Adelige; Clelia und Sinibald, oder die Bevölkerung von Lampeduse.
12. *Poetische Werke:* Pervonte, oder die Wünsche; Der Vogelsang, oder die drei Lehren; Hann und Gulpenheh; Die Wasserkufe; Gedichte an Olympia; Idris und Zenide.
13, 14. Geschichte der Abderiten.
15. Der neue Amadis.
16, 17. Peregrinus Proteus.
18. Agathodämon.
19. *Poetische Werke:* Nachlass des Diogenes von Sinope; Das Hexameron von Rosenhain.
20. Oberon; Nachrichten von Wieland's Leben.
21. *Poetische Werke:* Menander und Glycerion; Krates und Hipparchia; Koxkox und Kikequetzel.
22–24. Aristipp.
25. *Poetische Werke:* Die Natur der Dinge, oder die vollkommenste Welt; Moralische Briefe in Versen; Der Anti-Ovid; Der Frühling; Erzählungen in Versen: Balsora, Zemin und Gulindy, Serena, Der Unzufriedene, Melinda, Selim und Selima.
26. Briefe von Verstorbenen an hinterlassene Freunde, Poetische; Die Prüfung Abrahams; Hymne auf Gott; Psalmen; Erinnerungen an eine Freundin; Cyrus.
27. Araspes und Panthea; Bonifaz Schleichers Jugendgeschichte; Der Stein der Weisen; Die Salamandrin und die Bildsäule; Göttergespräche; Gespräche im Elysium.
28. *Dramatische Werke:* Lady Johanna Gray; Clementina von Porretta; Die Wahl des Herkules; Alceste; Rosemunde; Pandora; Singgedicht; Das Urtheil des Midas.
29–36. Vermischte Schriften.

Wieland; or, the Transformation. C. B. Brown. Philadelphia, 1870. 12°. K,462
Wiese, L. German Letters on English Education. London, 1854. 16°. . O,1169
Wife of a Vain Man. M. S. Schwartz. Boston, 1871. 8°. . . . . G,229
Wife's Secret. A. S. Stephens. Philadelphia, 1870. 12°. . . . K,453
Wife's Victory. E. D. E. N. Southworth. Philadelphia, 1870. 12°. . K,442
Wigand, A. Metamorphose der Pflanze. Leipzig, 1846. 8°. . . . G,901
Wiggins, J. Embanking Lands from the Sea. London, 1852. 12°. . M,974
Wight, O. W. Philosophy of Sir William Hamilton. New York, 1854. 12°. O,663
Wightman, J. M. Annals of Boston Primary Schools, 1818–55. Bost. 1860. 8°. O,841
Wigwam and the Cabin. W. G. Simms. New York, 1864. 12°. . . K,260
Wilberforce, E. Brazil through a Naval Glass. London, 1856. p. 8°. I,659,1
Wilberforce, S. Hist. of the Prot. Epis. Church in America. Lond. 1844. 12°. P,838
Life of William Wilberforce. London, 1868. 8°. . . . . . C,1192
Wilberforce, W. Correspondence; ed. by his Sons. Phila. 1841. 2 v. 12°. H,839
Life of. S. Wilberforce. London, 1868. 8°. . . . . . . C,1192
Practical view of Christianity. New York, n. d. 18°. . . P,746,2
Wilcken, P. I. Drei Freunde. Hannover, 1861. 2 v. 16°. . . G,515
Wild Flowers. S. Thomson. London, 1866. 16°. . . . . . N,922
Wild Huntress. M. Reid. New York, n. d. 12°. . . . . . J,1578
Wild Life; Adventures on the Frontier. M. Reid. New York, n. d. 12°. J,1579
under the Equator. P. B. Du Chaillu. New York, 1870. 12°. . J,1502
Wild Northern Scenes. S. H. Hammond. Philadelphia, 1869. 12°. . J,1503
Wild Oats. L. Wraxall. Leipzig, 1862. 16°. . . . . . . . J,536
Wild Oats and Dead Leaves. A. Smith. London, 1860. 12°. . . . J,653
Wild Sports in the Far-West. F. Gerstäcker. Boston, 1870. 16°. . . J,1623
of the West. W. H. Maxwell. London, 1838. 12°. . . . V,404
of the World. J. Greenwood. London, 1864. 8°. . . . . . N,636

Wilde, R. R. Conjectures concerning Tasso, v. 2. New York, 1842. 12°. D,730
Wilderspin, S. Early Discipline illustrated. London, 1840. 12°. . . O,1142
Infant System of Education. London, 1840. 16°. . . . . O,1134
System for the Education of the Young. London, 1840. 16°. . O,991
Wilhelm Meister's Apprenticeship. J. W. von Goethe. Boston, 1865. 2 v. 8°. G,189
The same. London, 1855. p. 8°. . . . . . . L,188,3
Wilhem, P. Method of Teaching Singing. J. Hullah. Lond. 1841–42. 2 v. 8°. M,401
Musical Manual; translated by A. Perrot. Philadelphia, 1854. 8°. M,428
Wilken, F. Geschichte der Kreuzzüge. Leipzig, 1807–32. 7 v. 8°. . E,29
Wilkes, C. U. S. Exploring Expedition, 1838–42. Phila. 1850. 5 v. 8°. V,962
Wilkes, J. and Horne, J. Controversial Letters. London, 1771. 8°. . H,856
Wilkie, F. B. Davenport, Iowa, Past and Present. Davenport, 1858. 8°. C,240
Walks about Chicago, and Sketches. Chicago, 1869. 12°. . . H,273
Wilkins, C. (Tr.) Bhâgvât-Gēētā. London, 1785. 4°. . . . . . Q,420
Wilkins, W. W. Political Ballads. London, 1860. 2 v. 12°. . . I,99
Wilkinson, J., Memoir of. Bath, N. Y. 1844. 16°. . . . . . . C,828
Wilkinson, Sir J. G. Account of the Ancient Egyptians. N.Y. 1854. 2 v. 12°. V,775
Dalmatia and Montenegro. London, 1848. 2 v. 8°. . . . V,434
On Color and Taste. London, 1858. 8°. . . . . . . . M,93
Wilkinson, J. J. G. The Human Body. Philadelphia, 1851. 12°. . . L,886
Wilkinson, W. F. Personal Names in the Bible. London, 1865. 12°. . L,557
Will, The. M. Edgeworth. New York, 1860. 12°. . . . . . K,678,2
Will Adams, the First Englishman in Japan. W. Dalton. Lond. 1861. 12°. J,1510
Will Rood's Friendship. W. J. Bradley. Boston, 1870. 16°. . . . J,1678
Willard, S., Memoir of. W. W. Wheildon. Boston, 1865. 8°. . . C,749
Wille in der Natur. A. Schopenhauer. Frankfurt-a.-M. 1854. 8°. . . G,575
Willet, J. E. Wonders of Insect Life. Philadelphia, 1871. 16°. . . O,14
Willey, B. G. Incidents in White Mountain History. Boston, 1856. 12°. H,10
William the Conqueror; a Historical Romance. Sir C. Napier. Lon. 1858. 8°. J,643
History of. J. Abbott. New York, 1869. 16°. . . . . J,1405
William Henry Letters. A. M. Diaz. Boston, 1870. 16°. . . . . J,1504
William III., Letters illustrative of Reign of. J. Vernon. Lond. 1841. 3 v. 8°. A,554
and Louis XIV., Letters; ed. by Paul Grimblot. Lond. 1848. 2 v. 8°. A,555
William of Malmesbury. Chron. of Kings of England. N. Y. 1847. p. 8°. L,27
Gesta Regum Anglorum. London, 1840. 2 v. 8°. . . . . U,618
Kings of England and Modern History. London, 1815. 4°. . . F,278
William of Newbury. Historia Rerum Anglicarum. London, 1856. 2 v. 8°. U,619
William of Palerne; or, William and the Werwolf. London, 1867. 8°. L,604,1
Williams, B. Manual for Teaching Model-Drawing. London, 1852. 8°. . M,170
Williams, C. Dogs and their Ways. London, 1865. 16°. . . . . . N,679
Williams, C. G. Eugenic Acid. London, 1858. 8°. . . . . . N,252,44
Williams, C. W. Combustion of Coal, and Preven. of Smoke. Lond. 1858. 12°. M,975
Heat in Relation to Water and Steam. Philadelphia, 1867. 8°. . N,43
Williams, D. E. Life of Sir Thomas Lawrence. London, 1831. 2 v. 8°. D,428
Williams, E., Identified as the Lost Prince. J. H. Hanson. N.Y. 1854. 12°. D,575
Williams, E. (Ed.) Presidents' Messages from 1789 to 1846. N.Y. 1846. 2v. 8°. O,591
Williams, E. Virginia. London, 1650. See *Force's Tracts*, v. 3.
Williams, F. Lives of the English Cardinals, v. 1, 2. London, 1868. 8°. D,429
Memoirs of Francis Atterbury. London, 1869. 2 v. 8°. . . D,340
Memoirs of Sophia Dorothea. London, 1846. 2 v. 8°. . . . D,676

Williams, H. W. Our Eyes, and how to take care of them. Bost. 1871. 12°. L,958
Recent Advances in Ophthalmic Science. Boston, 1866. 12°. . . L,881
Williams, J. Life and Times of Alexander the Great. London, 1829. 16°. I,623
Life of Julius Cæsar. London, 1854. 8°. . . . . . . . D,714
Williams, J. Life of Alexander Hamilton. New York, 1865. 8°. . B,812,1
Williams, J. Thermometrical Navigation. Philadelphia, 1799. 8°. . M,774
Williams, J. J. Isthmus of Tehuantepec, with maps. N. Y. 1852. 2 v. 8°. V,201
Williams, M. Grammar of the Sanskrit Language. Oxford, 1857. 8°. . L,742
Williams, R. Bloody Tenent of Persecution. Providence, 1868. 4°. . C,84,3
Bloody Tenent yet more bloody. Providence, 1870. 4°. . . . C,84,4
Cotton's Letter examined. Providence, 1866. 4°. . . . . C,84,1
Key into the Indian Language. Providence, 1866. 4°. . . . C,84,1
Letter of John Cotton to. Providence, 1866. 4°. . . . . C,84,1
Life of. W. Gammell. Boston, 1860. 12°. . . . . C,860,14
The same. Boston, 1854. 16°. . . . . C,1187
R. A. Guild. Providence, 1866. 4°. . . . . . C,84,1
Reply to. J. Cotton. Providence, 1867. 4°. . . . . . C,84,2
Williams, S. Natural and Civil History of Vermont. Burling. 1809. 2 v. 8°. C,32
Williams, S. Two Western Campaigns. Cincinnati, 1871. 8°. . . . C,223

1. Brush, Capt. H. Expedition with supplies for General Hull, 1812.
2. Meigs, Gov. R. J. Expedition for the Relief of Fort Meigs, 1813.

Williams, S. W. Middle Kingdom; China. New York, 1857. 2 v. 12°. V,618
The same. New York, 1848. 2 v. 12°. . . . . . . S.C.
Williams, T. and Calvert, J. Fiji and the Fijians. New York, 1859. 8°. V,899
Williams College, History of. C. Durfee. Boston, 1860. 8°. . . . O,807
Williams's Cincinnati Directory, for 1849–71. Cincinnati, 1849–71. 21 v. 8°. P.D.
Williamson, A. W. Chemistry for Students. Oxford, 1865. 16°. . . N,167
Williamson, T. Oriental Field Sports. London, 1819. 2 v. 4°. . Q*,329
Williamson, W. D. History of Maine till 1820. Hallowell, 1832. 2 v. 8°. C,33
Willis, N. P. Death of Edgar A. Poe. New York, 1864. 8°. . . . U,91,1
Famous Persons and Places. New York, 1854. 12°. . . . H,84
Fun-Jottings. Auburn, 1855. 12°. . . . . . . . . H,79
Health-Trip to the Tropics. New York, 1853. 12°. . . . . V,135
Hurry-Graphs; or, Sketches from Life. Boston, 1864. 16°. . . H,83
Life here and there. New York, 1853. 12°. . . . . . . H,78
Out-Doors at Idlewild. New York, 1855. 12°. . . . . . . H,86
Paul Fane. New York, 1857. 12°. . . . . . . . . K,390
Pencilings by the Way in Europe. New York, 1852. 12°. . . V,323
The same. Auburn, 1856. 12°. . . . . . . . H,82
People I have met. New York, 1853. 12°. . . . . . . H,76
Poems. New York, 1865. 12°. . . . . . . . . . I,136
Sacred, Passionate, and Humorous. New York, 1859. 12°. . I,157
Rag-Bag; a Collection of Ephemera. New York, 1855. 12°. . . H,77
Rural Letters. New Orleans, 1854. 12°. . . . . . . . H,80
Sketches of Society and Adventure. Auburn, 1853. 12°. . . . H,78
Summer Cruise in the Mediterranean. New York, 1854. 12°. V,1040
Willis and Sotheran, Sale Catalogue of Books, 1859, 62. Lon. 1859-62. 2 v. 8°. L.R.
Willis, the Pilot. Boston, n. d. 16°. . . . . . . . . . J,1438
Willkomm, E. Frau von Gampenstein; Roman. Leipzig, 1865. 3 v. 16°. G,516
Männer der That. Leipzig, 1861. 4 v. 12°. . . . . . . G,517

Willkomm, E. Rheder und Matrose. Frankfurt-a.-M. 1857. 3 v. 12°. . G,518
Willkomm, M. Deutschlands Laubhölzer in Winter. Dresden, 1864. 4°. Q,116
Wunder des Mikroskops. Leipzig, 1856. 12°. . . . . . . G,729
The same. Leipzig, 1861. 8°. . . . . . . . G,728
Zwei Jahre in Spain und Portugal. Dresden, 1847. 3 v. 12°. . E,195
Willm, J. Education of the People. Glasgow, 1847. 8°. . . . . . O,919
Willmott, R. A. Pleasures, Objects, and Advan. of Literature. Lon. 1857. 16°. H,638
Willoughby, Lady, Diary of. H. M. Rathbone. New York, 1860. 12°. . D,157
Wills, J. Lives of Distinguished Irishmen, v. 2-6. Dublin, 1847. 8°. . D,274
Willson, A. M. Lives of the three Mrs. Judsons. Boston, 1869. 12°. . C,533
Willson, H. Practical Treatise on Composition, Color, etc. Lond. 1851. 8°. Q,163
Willson, M. American History. New York, 1847. 8°. . . . . B,701
History of the United States. New York, 1855. 12°. . . . B,691
Manual of Object Lessons. New York, 1862. 12°. . . . . O,945
Outlines of History. New York, 1869. 8°. . . . . . . A,35
Willy Reilly, and his dear Cooleen Bawn. W. Carleton. Dublin, 1857. 16°. K,601
Wilson, A. American Ornithology. New York, 1828-29. 3 v. 4°. . *Q,2
Plates to the same. New York, 1829. 4°. . . . *Q,78
The same; with synopsis by T. M. Brewer. N. Y. 1854. 8°. O,106
Life of. W. B. O. Peabody. Boston, 1860. 12°. . . . C,860,2
and Bonaparte, C. L. American Ornithology. Edinb. 1831. 4 v. 16°. I,533
The same. Edinburgh, 1831. 4 v. 16°. . . . . . O,80
Wilson, A. J. *A. J. Evans.* Beulah. New York, 1868. 12°. . . . K,105
Inez; a Tale of the Alamo. New York, n. d. 12°. . . . . K,123
Macaria. New York, 1869. 12°. . . . . . . . . K,104
St. Elmo. New York, 1870. 12°. . . . . . . . . K,125
Vashti. New York, 1869. 12°. . . . . . . . . K,106
Wilson, Capt. and Warren, Capt. Recovery of Jerusalem. N. Y. 1871. 8°. V,668
Wilson, D. Oliver Cromwell and the Protectorate. London, 1848. 16°. . D,377
Wilson, E. Healthy Skin. Philadelphia, 1854. 12°. . . . . . L,858
System of Human Anatomy. Philadelphia, 1858. 8°. . . L,1021
Wilson, G. Chemistry of the Stars. London, 1862. p. 8°. . . . . I,666
Dry Gases on Organic Coloring Matter. Edinburgh, 1848. 4°. N,252,42
Early History of the Air-Pump in England. Edinburgh, 1849. 8°. N,252,33
Electricity and the Electric Telegraph. London, 1862. p. 8°. . I,666
Five Gateways of Knowledge. Philadelphia, 1857. 16°. . . H,206
Objects of Technology and Industrial Museums. Edinb. 1856. 4°. N,252,52
Physical Sciences and Technology. Edinburgh, 1857. 8°. . N,252,49
What is Technology? Edinburgh, 1855. 8°. . . . . N,252,49
Wilson, G. Youth's Pocket Companion. London, 1777. 12°. . . O,1104
Wilson, G. F. Process of obtaining and purifying Glycerine. Lon. 1855. 8°. N,252,50
Wilson, H. Anti-Slavery Measures in Congress. Boston, 1865. 12°. . O,403
Wilson, H. Wonderful Characters. Louisville, 1854. 8°. . . . C,579
Wilson, H. B. United States Infantry Tactics. Philadelphia, 1862. 12°. M,746
Wilson, H. H. History of British India. London, 1848. 3 v. 8°. . . C,402
Wilson, James. Capital, Currency, and Banking. London, 1847. 8°. . O,530
Wilson, J. G. Life and Letters of F. G. Halleck. New York, 1869. 12°. C,924
Wilson, John. Dies Boreales; Christopher under Canvas. Phil. 1850. 12°. H,607
Genius and Character of Burns. Philadelphia, 1854. 12°. . . H,703
Memoir of. M. Gordon. New York, 1863. 8°. . . . . D,250

Wilson, John. Noctes Ambrosianæ. New York, 1855. 5 v. 12°. . . H,605
Recreations of Christopher North. Edinburgh, 1857. 2 v. 12°. . H,608
The same. Boston, 1854. 8°. . . . . . . . H,609
Works; edited by Prof. Ferrier, v. 1–8,10,12. Edinb. 1855–58. 8°. U,285
Vol. 1. Noctes Ambrosianæ.
5–8. Essays; Critical and Imaginative.
9. Missing.
10. Recreations of Christopher North, v. 2.
11. Missing.
12. Poems.
and Chambers, R. Land of Burns. Glasgow, 1846. 4°. . . M,283
Wilson, John, Life of, 1588–1667. A. W. M'Clure. Boston, 1870. 12°. . D,8,2
Wilson, John. Treatise on English Punctuation. Boston, 1856. 16°. . L,561
Wilson, John. History of Switzerland. London, 1832. 12°. . . . M,990
Wilson, J. L. Western Africa; its History, etc. New York, 1856. 12°. V,793
Wilson, J. L. *vs.* Beecher, L. Trial before Cin'ti Presbytery. Cin. 1835. 8°. P,765
Wilson, J. M. Earth, Sea, and Sky. London, 1859. 16°. . . . N,257
The Potato; its Diseases, Varieties, etc. Edinburgh, 1850. 16°. . M,437
Rural Cyclopædia. Edinburgh, 1852. 4 v. 8°. . . . . . M,587
Wilson, J. M. Tales of the Borders. Edinburgh, 1857. 10 v. 16°. K,1065
Wilson, M. Memoirs of Harriet, *Duchess of St. Albans.* Lon. 1839. 2 v. 12°. D,416
Wilson, O. M. Digest of Parliamentary Law. Philadelphia, 1869. 8°. . U,491
Wilson, Sir R. Invasion of Russia by Napoleon I. London, 1860. 8°. . B,286
Wilson, R. A. Mexico; Adventures, etc., 1851–54. New York, 1856. 12°. V,194
Wilson, S. Bath Fables in Phonographic Characters. Lundun, 1850. 24°. L,663
Wilson, S. R. Discourse at Dedication of First Presb. Church. Cin. 1851. 8°. T,19,9
Wilson, W. Manual for Infants' Schools. London, 1829. 12°. . O,1181
Wilson, W. Popular Preachers of the Ancient Church. London, n. d. 16°. C,517
Wilson, W. New Dictionary of Music. London, n. d. 12°. . . . M,8
Winch, N. J. Plants of Northumberland, Cumberland, etc. Newc. 1825. 8°. N,252,44
Winchell, A. Sketches of Creation. New York, 1870. 12°. . . . M,771
Winchester College, School Life at. R. B. Mansfield. London, 1870. 12°. O,830
Winckelmann, J. J. History of Ancient Art. Boston, 1856. 2 v. 8°. . M,134
The same. Boston, 1856. 2 v. 8°. . . . . . . S.C.
Wind-Wafted Seed. N. Macleod and T. Guthrie. New York, 1869. 12°. . H,132
Windham, W., Select Speeches of; ed. by R. Walsh. Philadelphia, 1837. 8°. H,806
The same. Philadelphia, 1841. 8°. . . . . . . H,805
Winding of the River of Water of Life. G. B. Cheever. N. Y. 1849. 12°. P,262
Winds, Law of Variable. W. Reid. London, 1849. 8°. . . . . N,110
Windsor Castle; a Romance. W. H. Ainsworth. Leipzig, 1844. 16°. . J,25
Winemaking and Grape Culture. R. Buchanan. Cincinnati, 1835. 12°. M,490
P. B. Mead. New York, 1867. 8°. . . . . . . M,501
Winer, G. B. Grammar of the Idiom of the New Testament. And. 1870. 8°. P,439
Grammar of the New-Testament Diction. Philadelphia, 1849. 2 v. 8°. P,484
Wines, History and Description of Modern. C. Redding. Lond. 1851. p. 8°. L,145
History of Ancient and Modern. A. Henderson. London, 1824. 4°. Q,290
Wines, E. C. Laws of the Ancient Hebrews. New York, 1853. 8°. . A,220
Wing-and-Wing. J. F. Cooper. New York, 1867. 12°. . . . . . K,54
The same. New York, 1860. 8°. . . . . . . . K,85
Winifred Bertram. E. Charles. New York, 1866. 12°. . . . . . K,629
The same. Leipzig, 1869. 12°. . . . . . . . J,67
Winifred's Wooing. G. M. Craik. Leipzig, 1868. 16°. . . . . . J,100

Winkler, K. A. Silbererze. Freiberg, 1848. 8°. . . . . . N,252,30
Freyberger Schmelzhüttenprozesse. Freiberg, 1837. 8°. . N,252,18
Winkles, R. R. Cathedral Churches of Eng. and Wales. Lon. 1860. 3 v. 8°. *M,143
Winkworth, C. Christian Singers of Germany. Philadelphia, n. d. p. 8°. H,648
Winning his Way. C. C. Coffin. Boston, 1866. 16°. . . . . J,1270
Winslow, C. F. Force and Nature; Attraction and Repulsion. Phil. 1869. 8°. N,87
Winslow, F. Obscure Diseases of the Brain and Mind. Phil. 1866. 8°. . L,930
Winslow, H. Elements of Moral Philosophy. New York, 1856. 12°. . O,718
Intellectual Philosophy. Boston, 1850. 12°. . . . . . . O,708
Study of Language. Boston, 1848. 12°. . . . . . . . O,820,18
Winslow, H. L., Memoir of. M. Winslow. New York, n. d. 18°. . P,746,22
Winsor, J. History of Duxbury, Mass. Boston, 1849. 8°. . . . C,82
Winterfeld, A. von. Die Reisen von Bambus und Co. Leip. 1865. 3 v. 16°. G,519
Winthrop, J. History of New England from 1630–49. Bost. 1853. 2 v. 8°. C,6
Life and Letters of. R. C. Winthrop. Boston, 1864–67. 2 v. 8°. . C,1105
Winthrop, J. Two Lectures on Comets. Boston, 1759. 8°. . . . N,291
Winthrop, T. Canoe and the Saddle. Boston, 1863. 12°. . . . . V,4
Cecil Dreeme. Boston, 1868. 16°. . . . . . . . . . K,400
Edwin Brothertoft. Boston, 1865. 12°. . . . . . . . K,401
John Brent. Boston, 1864. 16°. . . . . . . . . . K,402
Life in the Open Air. Boston, 1869. 16°. . . . . . . . H,42
Winthrop, Me., History of, 1764–1855. D. Thurston. Portland, 1855. 12°. C,16
Winthrops, The. New York, 1864. 12°. . . . . . . . . K,403
Wintle, T. Book of Daniel; an Improved Version. London, 1836. 8°. . P,485
Winton, J. G. Modern Workshop Practice. London, 1870. 12°. . . M,864
Wirt, W. Letters of the British Spy. New York, 1848. 12°. . . . H,215
Life of. J. P. Kennedy. Philadelphia, 1854. 2 v. 12°. . . C,766
Life of Patrick Henry. Hartford, 1852. 8°. . . . . . . C,796
Wirth, J. G. A. Geschichte der Deutschen. Stuttgart, 1853. 4 v. 8°. . E,52
Geschichte der Deutschen Staaten, v. 3, 4. Karlsruhe, 1848–50. 2 v. 8°. E,53
Wirth, M. Deutsche Nationaleinheit. Frankfurt-a.-M. 1859. 8°. . . E,72
Wisconsin and its Resources. J. S. Ritchie. Philadelphia, 1858. 12°. . C,242
Common Schools, Reports, 1858–59. Madison, 1858–59. 2 v. 8°. O,1212
Editorial Association, Proceedings. n. t. p. 8°. . . . . . T,34
Geological Survey. J. G. Percival. Madison, 1855. 12°. . . N,869
History of. W. R. Smith, v. 1, 3. Madison, 1854. 2 v. 8°. . C,233,1,3
Iowa and Minnesota, Geological Surv. D. D. Owen. Phila. 1852. 2 v. 4°. *Q,52
Historical Society, Reports and Collections, 1854–8. Mad. '55–9. 4 v. 8°. C,232
Wisdom, Parental. J. Antrobus. London, 1849. 8°. . . . . . O,928
Wit and Whims of Ancient Philosophers. J. Banvard. N. Y. 1855. 12°. H,13
Wise, D. Glen Morris Stories. New York, 1869. 5 v. 16°. . . J,1345

Vol. 1. Guy Carlton. Vol. 3. Jessie Carlton.
2. Dick Duncan. 4. Walter Sherwood.
Vol. 5. Kate Carlton.

Wise Saws; or, Sam Slick. T. C. Haliburton. New York, n. d. 12°. . K,130
Wiseman, N. Essays on various Subjects. London, 1853. 3 v. 8°. . . H,491

Vol. 1. Controversy concerning the Genuineness of I. John, v. 7; Catholic Versions of Scripture; Parables of the New Testament; Miracles of the N. T.; Letters on Popery in Alliance with Heathenism; Authority of the Holy See in South America; Ecclesiastical Organization; Fate of Sacrilege; On Prayer and Prayer-Books; National Holidays; Minor Rites and Offices of the Church; Ancient and Modern Catholicity; Actions of the New Testament.

Wiseman, N. Essays on various Subjects. *Continued.* . . . . . H,491

2. Hampden Controversy; Tracts for the Times; Froude's Remains; High-Church Theory of Dogmatical Authority; Anglican Claims of Apostolical Succession; Catholic and Anglican Churches; Anglican System; Protestanism of the Anglican Church; Unreality of Anglican Belief; High-Church Theory at the close of 1847; Fourth of October.

3. Papers on History, Antiquities, and Art; Pope Boniface VIII.; St. Elizabeth of Hungary; Council at Constantinople, 1166; Writings of St. Ephrem; Recently discovered Inscription: Lady Morgan's statement regarding St. Peter's Chair; The Roman Forum; Christian Art; Spanish and English National Art; Superficial Traveling; Italian Guides and Tourists; Religion in Italy; Italian Gesticulation; Early Italian Academies; Sense *vs.* Science.

Fabiola; or, the Church of the Catacombs. London, 1855. 12°. . K,695
Recollections of the last four Popes. London, 1858. 8°. . . . C,559
Science and Revealed Religion. Andover, 1837. 8°. . . . P,315
Wit and Humor, Cyclopædia of. W. E. Burton. New York, 1866. 2 v. 8°. H,172
Witch-Hill; History of Salem Witchcraft. Z. A. Mudge. N. Y. 1870. 12°. O,325
Witchcraft and Demonology, Letters on. Sir W. Scott. London, 1830. 16°. I,647
The same. New York, 1855. 2 v. 16°. . . . . . . L,344
and Magic, Sketch of. W. E. H. Lecky. New York, 1869. 8°. P,213,1
and Witches, Dialogue on. G. Gifford. London, 1842. 12°. . L,606,8
Astrology and Magic. H. Christmas. London, 1849. 2 v. 12°. . O,322
Delusion of 1692. T. Hutchinson; edit. by W. F. Poole. Bost. 1870. 4°. O,324
Historical Essay on. F. Hutchinson. London, 1718. 8°. . . O,337
in New England; edited by S. G. Drake. Roxbury, 1866. 3 v. 8°. O,432

Vol. 1. Mather, C. Wonders of the Invisible World.
2, 3. Calif, R. More Wonders of the Invisible World; Appendix; Index.

Remarkable Providences concerning. I. Mather. London, 1856. 12°. O,344
Sadducismus Triumphatus; or, Evidence concerning Witches and Apparitions. J. Glanvil. London, 1726. 8°. . . . . O,335
Salem, History of. C. W. Upham. Boston, 1867. 2 v. 8°. . . O,328
Lectures on. C. W. Upham. Boston, 1831. 16°. . . . O,343
Cotton Mather and. W. F. Poole. Boston, 1869. 8°. . . O,341
Mr. Upham his Reply. W. F. Poole. Boston, 1870. 16°. O,323
Records of, from original Documents. Roxbury, 1865. 2 v. 4°. O,338
Ueber Zauberei und Geisterspuk. M. J. Schleiden. Leip. 1855. 8°. G,711
Wonders of the Invisible World. C. Mather. London, 1862. 16°. . O,339
Witches of New York. M. Thomson. Philadelphia, n. d. 12°. . . K,346
Wither, G. Hallelujah; Britain's Second Remembrancer. Lond. 1857. 16°. I,465
Hymns and Songs of the Church. London, 1856. 16°. . . . I,466
Withered Heart. T. S. Arthur. Philadelphia, n. d. 16°. . . . . J,621
Witherspoon, J. Education of Children, and Marriage. Andover, 1817. 12°. O,1157
Works, v. 2–4. Philadelphia, 1802–3. 3 v. 8°. . . . . . P,767
Within an Ace. C. Jenkin. Leipzig, 1869. 16°. . . . . . J,222
Witkowetze, Die. A. Peters. Wien, 1863. 3 v. 24°. . . . . G,503
Wits and Beaux of Society. K. B. and J. C. Thomson. London, 1867. 12°. C,589
The same. New York, 1861. 12°. . . . . . . . C,591
Witzleben, C. A. F. von. Sächsische Schweiz. Leipzig, n. d. 8°. . E,186,1
Wives and Daughters. E. C. Gaskell. New York, 1866. 8°. . . . K,710
The same. Leipzig, 1866. 3 v. 16°. . . . . . . J,182
Wives and Widows. A. S. Stephens. Philadelphia, 1870. 12°. . . K,454
Wives, Biographies of good. L. M. Child. New York, 1859. 12°. . . C,536
Wizard of the Mountain. W. Gilbert. London, 1867. 2 v. 12°. . . K,590

Woburn Abbey, History of. P. F. Robinson and J. Britton. Lond. 1847. f°. L.R.
Woburn, Mass., History of. S. Sewall. Boston, 1868. 8°. . . . . . C,68
Wodrow, R. Sufferings of the Church of Scotland. Glasgow, n. d. 4 v. 8°. P,646
Wöhler, F. Grundriss der Unorganischen Chemie. Berlin, 1837. 8°. N,252,5
Uebungen in der Chemischen Analyse. Göttingen, 1853. 8°. . . G,774
and Siebold, E. von. Arsenik-Vergiftung. Berlin, 1847. 8°. N,252,44
Wolcott, J. Works of Peter Pindar. London, 1794–1801. 5 v. 8°. . J,879
Wolf-Boy in China. W. Dalton. London, n. d. 16°. . . . . J,1511
Wolfe of the Knoll, and other Poems. Mrs. G. P. Marsh. N. Y. 1860. 12°. I,89
Wolfert's Roost. W. Irving. New York, 1868. 16°. . . . . . . U,19
The same. New York, 1867. 12°. . . . . . . . U,31
Wolff, J. Mission to Bokhara, 1843–45. New York, 1845. 8°. . . . V,702
Wollaston, T. V. Variation of Species. London, 1856. 12°. . . . N,506
Wollaston, W. H. New Metal found in Crude Platina. Lond. 1804. 4°. N,252,42
Wollstonecraft, M. Vindication of the Rights of Woman. N. Y. 1856. 12°. O,414
Wolsey, T. *Cardinal*, Life of. J. Galt. London, 1812. 4°. . . . F,27
Life of. A. T. Thomson. London, n. d. 8°. . . . . . . C,581
Woman, Beauty in. A. Walker. London, 1836. 8°. . . . . . *M,106
Biographies of good Wives. L. M. Child. New York, 1859. 12°. C,536
Education des Filles. F. de S. de la M. Fénélon. Paris, 1854. 12°. H,1000
Education of Daughters. F. de S. de la M. Fénélon. Bost. 1820. 24°. O,1110
Excellent, descri. in Proverbs; intr. by W. B. Sprague. Bost. 1852. 12°. J,1281
Die Frauen. G. Klemm. Dresden, 1859. 6 v. 16°. . . . E,380
History of. S. W. Fullom. London, 1855. 16°. . . . . O,367
Homme et Femme, v. 1, 3. J. A. V. L. Lignac. Lille, 1773–74. 2 v. 8°. L,843
in America. A. J. Graves. New York, 1855. 18°. . . . . . L,450
in the Nineteenth Century. M. F. Ossoli. New York, 1869. 12°. . U,97
Ladies' Guide to True Politeness. E. Leslie. Philadelphia, n. d. 12°. H,281
Ladies of the Reformation. J. Anderson. London, 1855. 16°. . C,516
Noble Deeds of. E. Starling. London, 1864. p. 8°. . . . . L,148
Physical Life of. G. H. Napheys. Philadelphia, 1871. 12°. . . L,955
Thoughts on Female Education. A. S. Semple. London, 1812. 12°. O,1179
Vindication of the Rights of. M. Wollstonecraft. N. Y. 1856. 12°. O,414
Why not? a Book for every. H. R. Storer. Boston, 1868. 16°. . L,833
Wrongs of. C. E. Tonna. New York, n. d. 16°. . . . . J,1107
Woman in White. W. Collins. New York, 1867. 8°. . . . . . K,637
The same. Leipzig, 1860. 2 v. in 1. 16°. . . . . . J,81
Woman killed with Kindness. T. Heywood. London, 1850. 8°. . I,885,45
Woman our Angel; a Novel. A. S. Roe. New York, 1867. 12°. . . K,235
Woman who Dared. E. Sargent. New York, 1853. 12°. . . . . . I,122
Woman's Friendship. G. Aguilar. New York, 1867. 12°. . . . K,582
Woman's Journey round the World. I. Pfeiffer. London, n. d. 12°. V,1062
Woman's Kingdom. D. M. Craik. New York, 1868. 8°. . . . . . K,651
The same. Leipzig, 1868. 2 v. in 1. 16°. . . . . . J,102
Woman's Record; Sketches of Distinguished. S. J. Hale. N. Y. 1855. 8°. *C,583
Woman's Relation to Education, Labor, and Law. C. H. Dall. Bos. 1867. 12°. O,386
Woman's Rights Convention, Worcester, October, 1851. Boston, 1851. 8°. B,809,1
Woman's Suffrage; the Reform against Nature. H. Bushnell. N.Y. '69. 12°. O,371
Woman's Thoughts about Women. D. M. Craik. New York, 1864. 12°. O,409
The same. Leipzig, 1860. 16°. . . . . . . . . . J,103

Woman's Work and Culture; edited by J. E. Butler. London, 1869. 8°. O,377
Essays on. B. R. Parkes. London, 1865. 12°. . . . . . O,411
Woman's Worth. New York, 1853. 16°. . . . . . . . . . H,465
Woman's Wrongs; a Counter-Irritant. M. A. Dodge. Boston, 1868. 16°. H,57
Women and Theaters. Olive Logan. New York, 1870. 12°. . . . I,720
Characteristics of. A. Jameson. London, 1858. 2 v. 8°. . *O,388
The same. Boston, 1866. 16°. . . . . . . . . M,18
Employment of, and Educa. of Girls. W. B. Hodgson. Lon. 1869. 12°. O,458
Essays on. E. L. Linton. London, 1869. 16°. . . . . . O,412
Extraordinary. W. Russell. London, 1864. 8°. . . . . . C,493
Friendships of. W. R. Alger. Boston, 1868. 12°. . . . . H,282
Industrial and Social Position of. London, 1857. 8°. . . . O,374
Legends of Good. G. Chaucer. Philadelphia, 1864. 12°. . . I,243
Lives of Celebrated. S. G. Goodrich. Boston, 1855. 12°. . . C,499
Memorable. N. Crosland. Boston, 1857. 12°. . . . . . C,504
Noble Deeds of American. J. Clement. New York, 1856. 12°. . C,739
of the American Revolution. E. F. Ellet. N. Y. 1852–54. 3 v. 12°. C,653
of Christianity. J. Kavanagh. New York, 1852. 12°. . . . P,232
of the French Revolution. J. Michelet. Philadelphia, 1855. 12°. D,627
of Israel. G. Aguilar. New York, 1864. 2 v. 12°. . . . D,766
of Letters, English. J. Kavanagh. Leipzig, 1862. 16°. . . . J,230
French. J. Kavanagh. Leipzig, 1862. 16°. . . . . J,231
of the War. F. Moore. Hartford, 1866. 8°. . . . . . . B,949
Pioneer Women of the West. E. F. Ellet. New York, 1852. 12°. C,651
Portraits of Celebrated. C. A. Sainte-Beuve. Boston, 1868. 16°. . C,494
Present to be given to Teeming. J. Oliver. London, 1669. 16°. . P,339
Pursuits of. F. P. Cobbe. London, n. d. 12°. . . . . . . O,410
Reflex Insanity in. H. R. Storer. Boston, 1871. . . . . . L,938
Subjection of. J. S. Mill. New York, 1869. 12°. . . . . . O,370
True Remedy for the Wrongs of. C. E. Beecher. Boston, 1851. 12°. O,387
Women-Artists in all Ages. E. F. Ellet. New York, 1859. 12°. . . M,12
Wonder-Book for Boys and Girls. N. Hawthorne. Boston, 1868. 12°. U,40,13
The same. Boston, 1869. 16°. . . . . . . . . J,1335
Wonder-Stories told for Children. H. C. Andersen. New York, 1870. 12°. J,1492
Wonderful Characters. H. Wilson. Louisville, 1854. 8°. . . . C,579
Wonderful Escapes. F. Bernard. New York, 1871. 12°. . . . M,1061
Wonderful Inventions. J. Timbs. London, 1868. 8°. . . . . M,682
History of. New York, 1855. 12°. . . . . . . . . . M,606
Wonderful Tales from Denmark. H. C. Andersen. New York, 1869. 16°. J,1661
Wonders, Events, and Discoveries, Book of. J. Timbs. London, n. d. 12°. M,681
Illustrated Library of. See *Library of Wonders.*
of the Deep. M. Schele de Vere. New York, 1870. 12°. . . N,501
of Insect Life. J. E. Willett. Philadelphia, 1871. 16°. . . . O,14
of the Invisible World. C. Mather. London, 1862. 12°. . . O,339
The same; edited by S. G. Drake. Boston, 1860. r. 8°. O,432,1
of Science. H. Mayhew. London, 1856. 12°. . . . . . . D,2
Wood, A. Class-Book of Botany. Claremont, 1851. 12°. . . . . N,977
Wood, G. The Gates wide Open. Boston, 1870. 12°. . . . . . K,404
Wood, G. B. and Bache, F. Dispensatory of United States. Phil. 1869. 8°. *L,987
Wood, Mrs. H. Anne Hereford. Leipzig, 1869. 2 v. in 1. 16°. . . J,517

Wood, Mrs. H. Channings. Leipzig, 1862. 2 v. in 1. 16°. . . . . J,518
East Lynne. New York, n. d. 8°. . . . . . . . . K,1066
The same. Leipzig, 1861. 3 v. 16°. . . . . . . J,519
Elster's Folly. Leipzig, 1866. 2 v. in 1. 16°. . . . . J,520
George Canterbury's Will. Philadelphia, 1870. 8°. . . K,1068
The same. Leipzig, 1870. 2 v. in 1. 16°. . . . . . J,521
Lady Adelaide's Oath. Leipzig, 1867. 2 v. in 1. 16°. . . . J,522
Life's Secret. Leipzig, 1867. 16°. . . . . . . . . . J,523
Lord Oakburn's Daughters. Leipzig, 1864. 2 v. in 1. 16°. . . J,524
Mildred Arkell. Leipzig, 1865. 2 v. in 1. 16°. . . . . . J,525
Mrs. Haliburton's Troubles. Leipzig, 1863. 2 v. in 1. 16°. . . J,526
Orville College. Leipzig, 1867. 16°. . . . . . . . . J,527
Oswald Cray. Leipzig, 1865. 2 v. in 1. 16°. . . . . . . J,528
Red Court Farm. Leipzig, 1868. 2 v. in 1. 16°. . . . . . J,529
Roland Yorke. Leipzig, 1869. 2 v. in 1. 16°. . . . . . J,530
St. Martin's Eve. Leipzig, 1866. 2 v. in 1. 16°. . . . . . J,531
Shadow of Ashlydyat. Leipzig, 1863. 3 v. 16°. . . . . . J,532
Squire Trevlyn's Heir. Philadelphia, 1863. 8°. . . . . K,1067
Trevlyn Hold. Leipzig, 1864. 2 v. in 1. 16°. . . . . . J.523
Verner's Pride. Philadelphia, n. d. 8°. . . . . . . . K,1069
The same. Leipzig, 1863. 3 v. 16°. . . . . . . . J,534
Wood, J. Edinburgh Sessional School. Edinburgh, 1840. 12°. . O,1034
Wood, J. Stories from Greek Mythology. London, 1867. 16°. . . P,342
Wood, J. History of the Administration of John Adams. Phil. 1846. 12°. B,852
Wood, J. G. Animal Traits and Characteristics. London, 1860. 16°. . N,627
Athletic Sports and Recreations. London, 1864. 12°. . . . M,302
Bees; their Habits and Treatment. London, n. d. 16°. . . . M,442
Bible Animals. London, 1869. 8°. . . . . . . . . . N,690
Boy's Own Book of Natural History. London, 1861. 8°. . . N,625
Common Objects of the Country. London, 1858. 8°. . . . N,478
of the Microscope. London, 1866. 16°. . . . . . N,3
of the Sea-Shore. London, 1866. 12°. . . . . . . N,475
Fresh and Salt-Water Aquarium. London, 1868. 16°. . . . N,473
Homes without Hands; Habitations of Animals. New York, 1866. 8°. N,555
Illustrated Natural History. London, 1862–63. 3 v. 8°. . . N,558
The same, abridged. New York, 1854. 12°. . . . N,632
Natural History. Birds. London, 1865. 4°. . . . . . . O,105
Mammalia. London, 1867. 4°. . . . . . . . . N,682
of Man. London, 1870. 8°. . . . . . . . . . N,580
Reptiles, Fishes. London, 1867. 4°. . . . . . . N,700
Our Garden Friends and Foes. London, 1864. 8°. . . . N,647
Sketches of Animal Life. London, 1854. 16°. . . . . . N,621
and others. Boy's Sports and Pastimes. London, 1866. 8°. . . M,300
Wood, M. A. E. (Ed.) Letters of Illustrious Ladies of Gr. Brit. Lon.'46. 3v. 12°. H,837
Wood, N. Furnace and Steam-Jet for Ventilating. Newcastle, 1853. 8°. N,252,56
Inaugural Address, Institute of Mining Engineers. Durham, 1852. 8°. N,252,56
Wood, R. Essay on the Genius of Homer. London, 1824. 8°. . . H,729
Wood, S. V. Monograph of the Crag Mollusca. Lond. 1848–56. 2 v. 4°. Q,24,Q,30
Wood, W. Conchology. London, 1835. 8°. . . . . . . . O,69
Index Entomologicus. London, 1854. 8°. . . . . . . . O,52

Wood, W. New England's Prospect, 1634. Boston, 1865. 4°. . . . C,31
Wood, W. B. Personal Recollections of the Stage. Philadelphia, 1855. 12°. I,724
Wood, W. M. Wandering Sketches in South America. Phila. 1849. 12°. V,241
Wood-Carving, Manual of. W. Bemrose, jr. London, n. d. 4°. . . . M,677
Wood-Engraving, Art of. T. Gilks. London, n. d. 12°. . . . . . M,62
Wood Leighton; or, a Year in the Country. M. Howitt. Lond. 1847. 16°. . . J,1368
Wood-Rangers; or, Trappers of Sonora. M. Reid. New York, n. d. 12°. J,1580
Woods and Waters. A. B. Street. New York, 1860. 12°. . . . . K,97
Plantations, etc., Management of. J. West. Newark, 1842. 8°. . M,358
Woodbridge, W. C. American Annals of Education, v. 4. Boston, 1834. 8°. O,1259
Sketches of Hofwyl. London, 1842. 12°. . . . . . . O,1007
Woodburn Grange. W. Howitt. Philadelphia, n. d. 12°. . . . K,1144
Woodbury, L. Writings; Political, Judicial, and Literary. Bost. 1852. 3 v. 8°. U,115
Woodcraft. W. G. Simms. New York, 1864. 12°. . . . . . . K,262
Woodlands, Heaths, and Hedges. W. S. Coleman. London, 1859. 16°. . N,926
Voices from. M. Roberts. London, 1850. 8°. . . . . . N,913
Woodruff, H. Trotting Horse of America. New York, 1868. 12°. . . M,460
Woodstock. Sir W. Scott. Boston, 1858. 2 v. 16°. . . . . . K,953
The same. Philadelphia, 1860. 8°. . . . . . . . K,975
The same. Philadelphia, 1869. 8°. . . . . . K,1114
Woodville Stories. W. T. Adams. Boston, 1870. 6 v. 16°. . . . J,1467

1. Rich and Humble.
2. In School and Out.
3. Watch and Wait.
4. Work and Win.
5. Hope and Have.
6. Haste and Waste.

Woodward, G. E. and F. W. Country Homes. New York, 1866. 12°. . M,149
Woodward, S. P. Manual of the Mollusca. London, 1868. 12°. . . M,865
Wool, History of. New York, 1845. 8°. . . . . . . . . M,657
Wool-Gathering. M. A. Dodge. Boston, 1867. 16°. . . . . . H,58
Woolhouse, W. S. B. Differential Calculus. London, 1852. 12°. . . M,978
Measures, Weights, and Moneys. London, 1859. 12°. . . . M,979
On Eclipses. London, 1836. 8°. . . . . . . . . N,342
Woolman, J., Journal of the Life of. New York, 1845. 12°. . . . C,679
Woolrych, H. W. Life of Judge George Jeffreys. Philadelphia, 1852. 12°. D,177
Woolsey, T. D. Essay on Divorce and Divorce Legislation. N. Y. 1869. 12°. O,372
Religion of the Present and of the Future. New York, 1871. 12°. P,198
Study of International Law. Boston, 1860. 12°. . . . . . U,492
Worcester, J. E. Dictionary of the English Language. Boston, 1846. r. 8°. L.R.
The same, unabridged. Boston, 1869. 4°. . . . . . R.R.
Worcester, S. Fourth Book of Lessons for Reading. Boston, 1838. 12°. O,874
Worcester County, Mass., History of. P. Whitney. Worcester, 1793. 8°. *C,51
Worcester, England, Sanitary Condition of. H. Austin. Worcester, 1847. 8°. N,252,29
Word of the Spirit to the Church. C. A. Bartol. Boston, 1859. 16°. . P,229
Worde, W. de. Boke of Keruynge. London, 1868. 8°. . . . . L,605,32
Words and Phrases, Thesaurus of English. P. M. Roget. Bost. 1855. 12°. L,567
and Places. I. Taylor. London, 1865. 12°. . . . . . . L,511
and their Uses. R. G. White. New York, 1870. 12°. . . . . L,578
for the Hour. J. W. Howe. Boston, 1857. 16°. . . . . . I,61
Meaning of. A. B. Johnson. New York, 1854. 12°. . . . . L,512
peculiar to the United States. J. Pickering. Boston, 1816. 8°. . L.R.
Rambles among. W. Swinton. New York, 1864. 12°. . . . . L,507
Study of. R. C. Trench. London, 1869. 16°. . . . . . L,509

Wordsworth, C. Discourses on Public Education. London, 1844. 12°. . O,1037
Greece; Pictorial, Descriptive, and Historical. London, 1868. 8°. . A,100
Memoirs of William Wordsworth. Boston, 1851. 2 v. 12°. . . D,392
Wordsworth, W., Memoirs of. G. S. Phillips. London, 1852. 12°. . . C,1225
Memoirs of. C. Wordsworth. Boston, 1851. 2 v. 12°. . . . D,392
Poems; with Essay by H. T. Tuckerman. New York, 1855. 8°. . I,469
Poetical Works. Philadelphia, 1854. 8°. . . . . . . J,885
The same. Boston, 1854. 7 v. 16°. . . . . . . I,236

Vol. 1. Poems written in Youth; The Borderers; Poems referring to Period of Childhood; Poems founded on the Affections.
2. Poems on the naming of Places; Poems of the Fancy; The Wagoner; Poems of the Imagination; Peter Bell; Miscellaneous Sonnets.
3. Memorials of a Tour in Scotland; Poems to National Independence and Liberty; Tour on the Continent; Tour in Italy; River Duddon; Yarrow Revisited, and other Poems.
4. White Doe of Rylstone; Ecclesiastical Sonnets; Evening Voluntaries; Tour in the Summer of 1833; Poems of Sentiment and Reflection; Sonnets to Liberty and Order; Sonnets upon Punishment of Death.
5. Miscellaneous Poems; Inscriptions; Selections from Chaucer, modernized; Poems on Old Age; Epitaphs and Elegiac Pieces.
6. The Excursion.
7. The Prelude; Appendix.

Select Poetical Works. Leipzig, 1864. 2 v. in 1. 16°. . . . J,535
Work and Play. H. Bushnell. New York, 1864. 12°. . . . . H,257
and Wages. M. Howitt. New York, 1852. 18°. . . . . J,1158
and Win. W. T. Adams. Boston, 1869. 16°. . . . . J,1467,4
Working Man's Life, Story of. F. Mason. New York, 1870. 12°. . . C,730
Working Man's Way in the World. C. M. Smith. New York, 1854. 12°. K,758
Workman and the Franchise. F. D. Maurice. London, 1866. 8°. . . B,102
Works of Eminent Masters, in Painting, etc. London, 1854. 2 v. in 1. 8°. *Q,164
Workshop, The, v. 1. New York, 1868. 4°. . . . . . . . Q,365
Workshop Practice, Modern. J. G. Winton. London, 1870. 12°. . M,864
World before the Deluge. L. Figuier. New York, 1867. 8°. . . . N,820
Displayed; Voyages and Travels. Philadelphia, 1795–96. 8 v. 8°. V,1096

Vol. 1. Columbus's four Voyages to America; Discoveries made by other Spaniards, while Columbus was engaged in the third Voyage; Discoveries by the Spaniards from the Death of Columbus to Cortes's Expedition; Conquest of Mexico by Cortes; Discovery of Golden Castile; Conquest of Peru by Pizarro.
2. Settlement of Brazil by the Portuguese; Discoveries of the English in America; Discoveries and Settlements of the French in America; Discoveries and Settlements of the Dutch in America; Discoveries of the Danes in America; Voyage of Sir Francis Drake round the World; Voyage of Schovten and Le Maire round the World; Voyage of Capt. Wm. Dampier round the World.
3. Voyage of Capt. Woodes Rogers round the World; Voyage of Com. Anson round the World; Voyage of Vasco de Gama to India; Voyage of Pedro Alvarez de Cabral to the East Indies; Expedition of Com. Beaulieu to the East Indies; Voyage of Sir Henry Middleton to the East Indies; Voyage of Capt. G. Roberts to the Cape de Verd Islands.
4. Voyage of P. Kolben to the Cape of Good Hope; Voyage of Com. Roggewein for Discovery of Southern Lands; Description of the Maldiva Islands by F. Pirard de Lavel; Voyage of Capt. T. James for Discovery of a North-West Passage to the South-Sea; Voyage of H. Ellis for Discovery of a North-West Passage to the South-Seas; Travels of Henry Maundrell from Aleppo to Jerusalem; Account of the Ruins of Balbec; Travels into Syria and the Holy Land by T. Shaw; Travels of J. Thevenot in the Levant.
5. Travels of R. Pococke through Egypt; Journey to Palmyra, by R. Wood; Description of Aleppo and the adjacent parts, by A. Russel; Travels of the Ambassadors of the Duke of Holstein into Muscovy, Tartary, and Persia; Travels of J. Hanway through Russia, Persia, Germany, and Holland; Account of Denmark, by Lord Molesworth.
6. Travels of Sir John Chardin through Mingrelia and Georgia into Persia; New History of the East Indies; Description of China

World Displayed; Voyages and Travels. *Continued.* . . . . . v,1096

by L. Le Compte and P. Du Halde; Description of Guinea; Travels into the Inland Parts of Africa by F. Moore; Of the Religion of the Mahometans by J. Pitts; Shaw's Travels through Babary; Natural History of Norway by E. Pontoppiddon.

7. Misson's Travels through Germany and Italy; Addison's Travels through Italy and Switzerland; Stevens's Travels through France; Travels through the most Northern parts of Europe; Travels of M. Maupertuis; Description of Spain and Portugal; Description of Sweden; Account of the Pelew Islands by Capt. H. Wilson, and others.

8. Account of Capt. James Cooke; Voyage to the Pacific Ocean.

Encompassed. Sir F. Drake. London, 1854. 8°. . . . . . v,987
External; or Universal Immeterialism. London, 1847. 12°. . . o,689
of Anecdote. E. P. Hood. London, 1870. 12°. . . . . . H,574
of Cartesius, Voyage to. D. De Foe. London, 1692. 8°. . . o,640
of Ice. R. M. Ballantyne. London, 1863. 16°. . . . . J,1718
Organic Remains of a former. J. Parkinson. Lon. 1804-11. 3 v. 4°. N,748
Welt als Wille und Vorstellung. A. Schopenhaur. Leip. 1859. 2 v. 8°. G,574
The, Essays. E. Moore, R. O. Cambridge, etc. Bost. 1866. 3 v. 8°. H,536,22-24
The, a Workshop. T. Ewbank. New York, 1855. 12°. . . . M,759
Worlds, Other, than ours. R. A. Proctor. New York, 1871. 12°. . . N,274
Unity of. B. Powell. London, 1855. 8°. . . . . . . . o,676
Wornum, R. N. Analysis of Ornament. London, 1856. 8°. . . . M,112
Epochs of Painting characterized. London, 1859. 12°. . . . M,31
Life and Works of Hans Holbein. London, 1867. 8°. . . . M,292
Worseley, H. Juvenile Depravity. London, 1849. 12°. . . . . o,353
Worth, G. A. American Bards. West of the Mountains, 1819. 12°. . I,156
Random Recollections of Albany. Albany, 1866. 8°. . . . . C,121
Worthen, A. H. and others. Geological Survey of Illinois. Springfield and Chicago, 1866-68. 3 v. 4°. . . . . . . . . . . *N,742

Vol. 1. Geology. Vol. 2. Palæontology. Vol. 3. Geology and Palæontology.

Worthen, W. E. (Ed.) Cyclopædia of Drawing. New York, 1866. 8°. . M,230
Worthies of England. T. Fuller. London, 1840. 3 v. 8°. . . . B,18
The same. London, 1811. 2 v. 4°. . . . . . . F,156
Wossidlo, P. Structur der Jubæa Spectabilis. Jena, 1861. 4°. . . Q,117
Wotton, Sir Henry, Life of. I. Walton. New York, 1854. 8°. . . . D,404
Poems. London, 1843. 12°. . . . . . . . . . L,606,6
Woven Fabrics, Prüfung der Gewebe. H. Schacht. Berlin, 1853. 8°. . G,766
The same. Berlin, 1853. 8°. . . . . . . . . . G,872
Woven of many Threads. Boston, 1871. 8°. . . . . . . . K,344
Wrangell, F. Expedition to the Polar Sea. New York, 1861. 18°. . . L,438
Wrangham, F. The Pleiad; Evidences of Christianity. Edinb. 1828. 16°. I,508
Wraxell, Sir F. C. L. Backwoodsman; or, Life on Frontier. Bos. 1866. 12°. K,1104
Life in the Sea. London, 1860. 8°. . . . . . . . . . N,505
Wild Oats. Leipzig, 1862. 16°. . . . . . . . . . J,536
Wraxell, Sir N. W. Courts of Berlin, Dresden, etc. Lond. 1799. 2 v. 8°. V,430
Historical Memoirs of my own Time. Philadelphia, 1837. 8°. . D,63
Posthumous Memoirs. Philadelphia, 1836. 8°. . . . . . D,64
Wrecked in Port. E. Yates. Leipzig, 1869. 2 v. in 1. 16°. . . . J,542
Wren, Sir C., Life of. H. B. Ker. London, n. d. 8°. . . . . . C,581
Wright, C. India and its Inhabitants. Cincinnati, 1856. 8°. . . . S.C.
Wright, F. Few days in Athens. London, 1822. 8°. . . . . . V,546

Wright, G. B. Ohio Railroads and Telegraphs. Columbus, 1870. 8°. . P.D.
Wright, J. H. Ocean-Work, Ancient and Modern. New York, 1853. 18°. J,1303
Wright, J. McN. Almost a Nun. Philadelphia, 1868. 16°. . . . . K,407
Almost a Priest. Philadelphia, 1870. 12°. . . . . . . K,408
How could he escape? a Temperance Story. New York, 1870. 16°. K,405
Priest and Nun. Philadelphia, 1869. 12°. . . . . . . K,406
Wright, R. Memoir of James Oglethorpe. London, 1867. 8°. . . D,292
Wright, S., Life of. J. S. Jenkins. Auburn, 1850. 12°. . . . . C,978
Wright, T. Archæological Album. London, n. d. 4°. . . . . B,184
Biographia Britannica Literaria. London, 1846. 8°. . . . D,360
British Fossil Echinodermata, pts. 1, 3. London, 1859. 4°. . . Q,30
Caricature History of the Georges. London, 1867. 8°. . . . A,537
Dictionary of Obsolete and Provincial English. Lond. 1857. 2 v. 12°. L,258
The same. London, 1857. 2 v. 12°. . . . . . . L.R.
History of Caricature and Grotesque. London, 1865. 8°. . . M,80
History of Ireland. London, n. d. 3 v. 8°. . . . . . . F,267
History of Scotland. London, n. d. 3 v. r. 8°. . . . . F,264
and Evans, R. H. Account of Gillray's Caricatures. Lon. 1851. 8°. L.R.
(Ed.) Chester Plays at Whitsuntide. London, 1843–47. 2 v. 8°. I,885,33,34
Latin Stories. London, 1842. 12°. . . . . . . L,606,8
Lyric Poetry of the Time of Edward I. London, 1842. 12°. L,606,4
Political Ballads during the Commonwealth. Lond. 1841. 12°. L,606,3
St. Brandan; a Mediæval Legend of the Sea. Lond. 1844. 12°. L,606,14
Seven Sages, in English Verse. London, 1845. 12°. . L,606,16
Songs and Carols of the 15th Century. London, 1848. 12°. L,606,23
Queen Elizabeth and her Times. London, 1838. 2 v. . 8°. D,356
Wrigley, A. Examples and Problems in Mathematics. London, 1865. 8°. M,1121,1
Companion to the same. Cambridge, 1861. 8°. . . . M,1121,2
Wrongs of Woman. C. F. Tonna. New York, n. d. 16°. . . J,1107
Wurtz, A. History of Chemical Theory. London, 1869. 8°. . . . N,185
Wuthering Hights. E. Brontë. New York, n. d. 12°. . . . . K,610
The same. Leipzig, 1851. 2 v. in 1. 16°. . . . . . J,46
Wyandotte; or, the Hutted Knoll. J. F. Cooper. New York, 1864. 12°. K,56
The same. New York, 1859. 8°. . . . . . . . . K,82
Wyatt, M. D. History and Practice of Illuminating. London, n. d. 12°. M,83
Wyatt, T. History of the Kings of France. Philadelphia, 1846. 12°. . D,558
Wyatt, Sir T. Poetical Works. Boston, 1854. 16°. . . . . . . I,237
The same; with Life; edited by R. Bell. London, 1854. 16°. I,257
Wycherly, W. Dramatic Works. London, 1866. 8°. . . . . . I,728
Wylde, J. Book of Trades. London, 1866. 16°. . . . . . . M,668
Wylder's Hand; a Novel. J. S. Le Fanu. New York, 1866. 12°. . . K,767
Wyman, M. Treatise on Ventilation. Boston, 1846. 12°. . . . . . M,619
Wynne, J. Eminent Literary Men of America. New York, 1850. 12°. C,1045
Wynne, J. H. British Empire in America. London, 1770. 2 v. 8°. . B,696
Wynter, A. Curiosities of Civilization. London, 1860. 8°. . . . H,316
Our Social Bees. London, 1869. 2 v. 12°. . . . . . . H,315
Subtle Brains and Lissom Fingers. London, 1863. 8°. . . . H,318
Wyoming, Poetry and History of. W. L. Stone. Albany, 1864. 12°. . C,174
Wyse, T. Education Reform, v. 1. London, 1836. 8°. . . . . . O,929
Excursion in the Peloponnesus. London, 1865. 2 v. 8°. . . V,576

Wyss, J. R. v. and Montolieu, I. Swiss Family Robinson. Phil. 1865. 12°. J,1444
Wythe, J. H. The Microscopist. Philadelphia, 1853. 12°. . . . . N,6

Xenia Orchidacea, v. 1. H. G. Reichenbach. Leipzig, 1858. 4°. . . *Q,112
Xenophon. Anabasis; recensuit J. F. Macmichæl. New York, 1863. 16°. U,395
Anabasis and Memorabilia of Socrates; tr. J. S. Watson. N. Y. 1868. 12°. A,63
Cyropædia and Hellenics; trans. by Watson and Dale. Lond. 1870. p. 8°. L,90,2
Minor Works; translated by J. S. Watson. London, 1857. p. 8°. . L,90,3
Scripta quæ supersunt; Græce et Latine. Parisiis, 1838. 8°. . . U,559
Werke. Stuttgart, 1827–31. 16 v. in 4. 24°. . . . . . . E,1

Bd. 1–3. Cyropädie; übersetzt von C. Walz.
4. Errinnerungen an Socrates; übersetzt von C. E. Finckh.
5. Errinnerungen an Socrates; Vertheidigung des Socrates; Gastmahl; übersetzt von C. E. Finckh.
6–8. Feldzug des jüngern Cyrus; übersetzt von L. Tafel.
9. Von der Haushaltungskunst; Hiero, oder Herrscherleben; übersetzt von A. H. Christian.
10. Lobrede auf Agesilaus; Staatsverfassung der Lacedämonier; Staatsverfassung der Athener; übersetzt von A. H. Christian.
11. Von den Staatseinkünften der Athener; Von der Reitkunst; Der Reiterbefehlshaber; übersetzt von A. H. Christian.
12. Von der Jagd; Briefe; übersetzt von A. H. Christian.
13–16. Hellenische Geschichte; übersetzt von C. N. Osiander.

Xerxes the Great, History of. J. Abbott. New York, 1850. 16°. . J,1415

Yale, C. Life of Jeremiah Hallock. New York, n. d. 12°. . . . . C,733
Yankee in Canada, etc. H. D. Thoreau. Boston, 1866. 12°. . . . . V,176
Yankee Middy. W. T. Adams. Boston, 1869. 16°. . . . . . J,1536,4
Yankee Travels in Cuba. New York, 1856. 12°. . . . . . V,232
Yarmouth, Great, Sanitary Condition of. C. L. Robertson. Yarm. 1847. 16°. N,252,37
Yarns of an Old Mariner. M. C. Clarke. Boston, 1869. 16°. . . J,1550
Yarrell, W. Athalia Centifoliæ; Insect destructive to Turnips. n. t. p. 4°. Q,114
History of British Fishes. London, 1859. 2 v. 8°. . . . . . N,703
Yates, E. Black Sheep. Leipzig, 1867. 2 v. in 1. 16°. . . . . . J,537
Broken to Harness. Boston, 1866. 12°. . . . . . . K,1073
The same. Leipzig, 1866. 2 v. in 1. 16°. . . . . . J,538
Forlorn Hope. Leipzig, 1867. 2 v. in 1. 16°. . . . . . . J,539
Land at Last. Leipzig, 1866. 2 v. in 1. 16°. . . . . . . J,540
Rock Ahead. Leipzig, 1868. 2 v. in 1. 16°. . . . . . . J,541
Wrecked in Port. Leipzig, 1869. 2 v. in 1. 16°. . . . . . J,542
Yates, R. Proceedings of the Constitutional Convent., 1787. Cincin. 1838. 12°. O,479
Year after Year. C. Clive. Leipzig, 1858. 16°. . . . . . . . J,70
Year-Book of Facts, 1839–71. J. Timbs. London, 1839–71. 33 v. 16°. . M,810
Extra vol. Exhibition of 1851. London, 1861. 16°. . . M,811
Extra vol. Exhibition of 1862. London, 1862. 16°. . . M,812
Year Nine; Tale of the Tyrol. A. Manning. London, 1858. 12°. . . J,646
Year with Maggie and Emma. M. J. McIntosh. New York, 1861. 16°. J,1364
Year's Life. J. R. Lowell. Boston, 1841. 12°. . . . . . . . I,52
Yeast; a Problem. C. Kingsley. New York, 1864. 12°. . . . . K,752
The same. Leipzig, 1851. 16°. . . . . . . . J,246
Yellow Fever in Philadelphia in 1797. B. Rush. Philadelphia, 1798. 8°. L,935

Yellowplush Memoirs. W. M. Thackeray. Boston, 1869. 12°. . . K,1038,2
The same. Leipzig, 1849. 16°. . . . . . . J,484,4
Yemassee, The. W. G. Simms. New York, 1866. 12°. . . . . . K,264
Yesterday, To-day, and Forever. E. H. Bickersteth. New York, 1869. 8°. I,284
Yoakum, H. History of Texas from 1685–1846. New York, 1856. 2 v. 8°. C,188
Yolland, W. Measurement of the Lough Foyle Base. London, 1847. 4°. Q,52
Yonge, C. D. English-Latin, and Latin-English Dictionary. Lond. 1868. 8°. L.R.
France under the Bourbons. London, 1866–67. 4 v. 8°. . . . B,348
History of the British Navy. London, 1863. 2 v. 8°. . . . B,94
Parallel Lives. London, 1858. 12°. . . . . . . . . C,486
Epaminondas and Gustavus Adolphus; Philip of Macedon and Frederick the Great.
Yonge, C. M. Beechcroft. New York, 1856. 12°. . . . . . K,1074
Caged Lion. Leipzig, 1870. 2 v. in 1. 16°. . . . . . . J,543
Cameos from English History. New York, 1869. 12°. . . . A,478
Castle Builders. New York, 1868. 12°. . . . . . K,1075
Chaplet of Pearls. New York, 1869. 8°. . . . . . . K,1076
The same. Leipzig, 1869. 2 v. in 1. 16°. . . . . J,544
Clever Woman of the Family. New York, 1868. 8°. . . . K,1077
The same. Leipzig, 1865. 2 v. in 1. 16°. . . . . J,545
Countess Kate. New York, 1866. 16°. . . . . . . J,1285
Daisy Chain. New York, 1867. 2 v. 12°. . . . . . K,1078
The same. Leipzig, 1856. 2 v. in 1. 16°. . . . . J,546
Danvers Papers; Prince and the Page. Leipzig, 1867. 16°. . . J,547
Dove in the Eagle's Nest. New York, 1867. 12°. . . . K,1072
The same. Leipzig, 1866. 2 v. in 1. 16°. . . . . J,548
Dynevor Terrace. New York, 1866. 2 v. 12°. . . . K,1079
Heartsease. New York, 1866. 2 v. 12°. . . . . . . K,1081
The same. Leipzig, 1855. 2 v. in 1. 16°. . . . . J,549
Heir of Redclyffe. New York, 1868. 2 v. 12°. . . . K,1080
The same. Leipzig, 1855. 2 v. in 1. 16°. . . . . J,550
Hopes and Fears. Leipzig, 1861. 2 v. in 1. 16°. . . . . J,551
Kenneth. New York, 1866. 12°. . . . . . . . K,1082
Lances of Linwood. New York, 1856. 16°. . . . . . J,1354
Landmarks of History. New York, 1867–69. 3 v. 12°. . . . A,230
Pioneers and Founders in the Mission Field. London, n. d. 12°. . C,512
Pupils of St. John, the Divine. London, n. d. 12°. . . . . P,266
Richard the Fearless; or, the Little Duke. New York, 1856. 16°. J,1238
Scripture Readings for Schools and Families. London, 1871. 12°. . P,185
Trial; or, More Links of Daisy Chain. N. Y. 1866. 2 v. in 1. 12°. K,1083
The same. Leipzig, 1864. 2 v. in 1. 16°. . . . . J,552
Two Guardians. New York, 1866. 12°. . . . . . . K,1084
The same. Leipzig, 1869. 16°. . . . . . . . J,553
Young Step-Mother. New York, 1866. 2 v. 12°. . . . K,1085
The same. Leipzig, 1861. 2 v. in 1. 16°. . . . . J,554
York, Eng., Depositions from the Castle of. Durham, 1861. 8°. . F,126,40
Fabric Rolls of York Minster. London, 1859. 8°. . . . F,126,35
Visitation of, 1665. W. Dugdale. Durham, 1859. 8°. . . F,126,36
Yorke, P. *Earl of Hardwicke.* Athenian Letters. London, 1798. 2 v. 4°. F,221
Yorke, S. Oration before the Odd Fellows. Cincinnati, 1833. 8°. . . H,302,4

Yorkshire, Rural Economy of, 1641. H. Best. London, 1857. 8°. . F,126,33
Yo-Semite Valley, Guide to. J. M. Hutchings. New York, 1870. 8°. . V,113
Youatt, W. The Dog. London, 1861. 8°. . . . . . . . . N,689
Sheep; their Management and Diseases. New York, 1857. 8°. . M,477
Structure and Diseases of the Horse. Auburn, 1854. 12°. . . M,471
and Martin, W. C. L. Cattle. New York, 1858. 12°. . . . M,466
Hog; Breeds, Management, etc. New York, 1856. 12°. . M,450
Youmans, E. L. Alcohol and the Constitution of Man. New York, 1854. 12°. L,875
Chemical Atlas. New York, 1855. 4°. . . . . . . . Q,326
Class-Book of Chemistry. New York, 1865. 12°. . . . . N,172
Correlation and Conservation of Forces. New York, 1865. 12°. . N,77
Culture Demanded by Modern Life. New York, 1867. 12°. . . M,627
Hand-Book of Household Science. New York, 1868. 12°. . . M,762
Youmans, W. J. Elements of Physiology and Hygiene. New York, 1868. 12°. L,872
Young, A. Chronicles of the Planters of Massachusetts Bay. Bost. 1846. 8°. C,45
Young, A. Tour in Ireland, 1776–78. Dublin, 1780. 2 v. 8°. . . V,390
Travels in France and Spain, 1787–89. Dublin, 1793. 2 v. 8°. . V,458
Young, A. W. American Statesman. New York, 1855. 8°. . . . O,592
Science of Government. Auburn, 1854. 12°. . . . . . O,473
Young, C. Amazon and Rio Madeira. London, 1862. 8°. . . V,1086,2
Young, C. M., Memoir of. J. C. Young. London, 1871. 12°. . . C,1241
Young, E. Poetical Works. Boston, 1854. 2 v. 16°. . . . . . I,238
Young, J. Autobiography of a Pioneer. Cincinnati, 1859. 8°. . . C,722
Young, J. R. Arithmetic. London, 1857. 12°. . . . . . . M,980
Key to the same. London, 1853. 12°. . . . . . . M,982
Elements of Differential Calculus. London, 1831. 12°. . . M,1145
Elements of Integral Calculus. London, 1831. 12°. . . M,1145
Navigation and Nautical Astronomy. London, 1858. 12°. . . M,977
Tables for the same. London, 1859. 12°. . . . . . M,981
Young, P. History of Mexico. Cincinnati, 1847. 8°. . . . . . C,384
Young, T., Life of. F. Arago. London, n. d. 8°. . . . . . C,498,2
Young, T. J. Duty of Religious Instruction. Charleston, 1841. 8°. O,1251,1
Young America Abroad; 1st Series. W. T. Adams. Boston, 1870. 6 v. 16°. J,1535

Vol. 1. Outward Bound.
2. Shamrock and Thistle.
3. Red Cross.
Vol. 4. Dikes and Ditches.
5. Palace and Cottage.
6. Down the Rhine.

The same; 2d Series. Boston, 1871. 16°. . . . . . J,1544

Vol. 1. Up the Baltic.

Young Americans Abroad. J. O. Choules. Boston, 1864. 16°. . . J,1424
Young Cadet. B. Hofland. Philadelphia, n. d. 18°. . . . . . J,1296
Young Christian. J. Abbott. New York, n. d. 12°. . . . P,746,32
Young Christian Series. J. Abbott. New York, n. d. 4 v. 12°. . . P,281

Vol. 1. Young Christian.
2. Corner-Stone.
Vol. 3. Way to do Good.
4. Hoaryhead and M'Donner.

Young Citizen's Manual. A. Conkling. Albany, 1836. 18°. . . . O,464
Young Crusoe. A. J. Harley. Boston, n. d. 16°. . . . . . J,1477
Young Deliverers of Pleasant Cove. E. Kellogg. Boston, 1871. 16°. J,1475,2
Young Duke. B. Disraeli. New York, 1868. 12°. . . . . . . K,676
Young Fur Traders. R. M. Ballantyne. London, n. d. 16°. . . . J,1239
Young Lady at Home; Home Stories. T. S. Arthur. Philadelphia, n. d. 16°. J,622
Young Lady's Book; edited by H. G. Bohn. London, 1859. p. 8°. . . L,165

Young Lady's Friend. Mrs. J. Farrar. New York, 1860. 12°. . . H,299
Young Lady's Guide. H. Newcomb. New York, 1853. 12°. . . . H,298
Young Lieutenant. W. T. Adams. Boston, 1869. 16°. . . . J,1536,3
Young Man's Friend. D. C. Eddy. Boston, 1866–68. 2 v. 12°. . . H,223
Young Marooners on the Florida Coast. F. R. Goulding. Phil. 1870. 16°. J,1604
Young Mathematician's Guide. J. Ward. Dublin, 1755. 8°. . . M,1119
Young Men, Duties of. E. H. Chapin. Boston, 1849. 18°. . . . H,247
Gift-Book for. W. A. Alcott. Auburn, 1853. 12°. . . . H,254
Lectures to. H. W. Beecher. Boston, 1869. 12°. . . . . H,221
W. G. Eliot, jr. Boston, 1856. 12°. . . . . . . H,263
Three Great Temptations of. S. W. Fisher. Cincinnati, 1859. 12°. H,262
Young Naturalist's Journey. J. W. London. London, 1851. 16°. . . N,620
Young of America, Thoughts for. L. U. Reavis. New York, 1871. 12°. H,17
Young Pilgrim. C. Tucker. London, 1869. 12°. . . . . . . K,577
Young Pioneers of the North-West. C. H. Pearson. Boston, 1871. 16°. J,1613
Young Singleton. T. Gwynne. London, 1856. 2 v. 16°. . . . J,569
Young Step-Mother. C. M. Yonge. New York, 1866. 2 v. 12°. . K,1085
The same. Leipzig, 1861. 2 v. in 1. 16°. . . . . J,554
Young Voyageurs. M. Reid. Boston, 1866. 16°. . . . . . . J,1562
Young Wrecker of the Florida Reef. R. M. Bache. Philadelphia, n. d. 16°. J,1606
Young Women, Duties of. E. H. Chapin. Boston, 1850. 18°. . . H,300
Young Yachtmen. A. Bowman. London, n. d. 16°. . . . . J,1227
Young Yägers. M. Reid. Boston, 1868. 16°. . . . . . . . J,1564
Younger Son, Adventures of. E. J. Trelawney. London, n. d. 16°. . K,693
Youth of the Old Dominion. S. Hopkins. Boston, 1856. 12°. . . K,98
Youth's History of the Rebellion. W. M. Thayer. Boston, 1864–66. 4 v. 12°. J,1280
Contents. See *Thayer, W. M.*
Youth's Pocket Companion. G. Wilson. London, 1777. 12°. . . . O,1041
Yucatan, History of, until 1700. C. St. J. Fancourt. London, 1854. 8°. . C,374
Incidents of Travel in. J. L. Stephens. New York, 1860. 2 v. 12°. V,200
and Central America, Travels in. J. L. Stephens. N. Y. 1853. 2 v. 8°. V,199
Yule-Tide Stories; edited by B. Thorpe. London, 1853. p. 8°. . . L,28

Zambesi, Expedition to, 1858–64. D. and C. Livingstone. N. Y. 1866. 8°. V,867
Zanoni. Sir E. B. Lytton. Philadelphia, 1869. 12°. . . . . K,831
The same. Leipzig, 1842. 16°. . . . . . . . J,331
Záwis von Rosenberg; Historischer Roman. A. Peters. Prag, 1860. 3 v. 24°. G,504
Zech, J. Logarithmen-Tafeln. Leipzig, 1849. 8°. . . . . . . E,436
Zedlitz, J. C. F. von. Gedichte. Stuttgart, 1859. 16°. . . . . E,286
Zeisberger, D. (Tr.) S. Lieberkuhn's History of Our Lord in the Delaware
Indian Language. New York, 1821. 16°. . . . . . . P,382
Zeising, A. Aesthetische Forschungen. Frankfurt-a.-M. 1855. 8°. . . G,576
Zeller, E. Socrates and the Socratic Schools. London, 1868. 12°. . . D,772
Strauss and Renan. London, 1866. 8°. . . . . . . . H,736
Zeluco. J. Moore. London, 1820. 2 v. 12°. . . . . . . . K,543
Zerub Throop's Experiment. A. D. T. Whitney. Boston, 1871. 12°. . K,384
Zillah; a Tale. H. Smith. London, 1828. 4 v. in 2. 12°. . . . K,566
Zimmermann, G. Analyse des Blutes. Berlin, 1847. 8°. . . N,252,32

Zimmermann, T. F. Bilder und Skizzen aus dem Zoologischen Garten zu Hamburg. Hamburg, 1865. 8°. . . . . . . . . . G,932
Zincke, F. B. Last Winter in the United States. London, 1868. 12°. . V,62
School of the Future. London, 1852. 12°. . . . . . O,1146
Zinkeisen, J.W. Gesch. des Osman. Reichs in Europa. Hamb. 1840–59. 7 v. 8°. E,118
Zirkel, F. u. Preyer, W. Reise nach Island im Sommer, 1860. Leip. 1862. 8°. E,174
Zodiacal Light, Observations on. G. Jones. Washington, 1856. 4°. Q,413,3
Das Zodiacallicht. J. F. J. Schmidt. Braunschweig, 1856. 8°. . G,797
Zoe's Brand. Leipzig, 1864. 2 v. in 1. 16°. . . . . . . . J,555
Zoller, K. A. Fibel; oder, erster Unterricht. Reutlingen, 1843. 12°. . O,888
Zoölogical Magazine and Journal of Natural History. London, 1833. 8°. N,667
Zoölogical Notes and Anecdotes. London, 1852. 12°. . . . . N,651
Zoölogical Recreations. W. J. Broderip. London, 1849. 12°. . . . N,656
Zoölogical Science. A. M. Redfield. Hartford, 1867. 12°. . . . N,649
Zoölogical Temperance Convention. E. Hitchcock. Northampton, 1854. 12°. N,624
Zoölogist, The. London, 1843–64. 22 v. 8°. . . . . . . . . R,41
Zoölogist's Text-Book. T. Brown. Glasgow, 1832. 2 v. 16°. . . N,659
Zoölogy; Account of Animal Kingdom. W.B.Carpenter. Lon. 1858. 2v. p. 8°. L,282
Bibliographia Zoölogiæ et Geologiæ. L. Agassiz. Lon. 1854. 4v. 8°. *O,300
Bibliography of, and Taxidermy. W. Swainson. London, 1840. 12°. M,1038
Class-Book of. B. Jaeger. New York, 1860. 16°. . . . . N,622
Forest Creatures. C. Boner. London, 1861. 12°. . . . . N,634
Handbuch der Zoologie. J. van der Hoeven. Leipzig, 1850–56. 2 v. 8°. G,919
F. H. Troschel and J. F. Ruthe. Berlin, 1853. 8°. . . G,916
Lehrbuch der Zoologie. F. S. Voigt. Stutt. 1835–40. 6 v. in 3. 8°. G,812,8–10
Magazine of, v. 1, 2. Edinburgh, 1837–38. 2 v. 8°. . . . R,29
Manual of. S. Tenney. New York, 1866. 8°. . . . . N,654
of a Voyage to the Pacific. F. W. Beechey. London, 1839. 4°. . Q,6
Popular Scripture. M. E. Catlow. London, 1852. 16°. . . . N,623
Principles of. L. Agassiz and A. A. Gould. Boston, 1854. 12°. . N,650
Principes de Philosophie Zoologique. E. Geoffrey Saint-Hilaire. Paris, 1830. 8°. . . . . . . . . . . . . N,252,17
Reports on, for 1843–44. E. Wagner and others. London, 1847. 8°. O,294
Text-Book of. P. H. Gosse. London, 1851. 12°. . . . . N,479
and Botany, Reports on, for 1841–42. Edinburgh, 1845. 8°. . . O,292
Zoöphytes. J. D. Dana. Philadelphia, 1848. 4°. . . . . . *Q,278
Atlas to the same. Philadelphia, 1849. f°. . . . . *Q,352
British. G. Johnston. London, 1847. 2 v. 8°. . . . . . O,66
or Corallines, British. D. Landsborough. London, 1852. 16°. . O,5
Die Macht des Kleinen. P. Harting. Leipzig, 1851. 8°. . . G,833
Zornlin, R. M. Physical Geography. Boston, 1855. 16°. . . . . P,288
Zouch, T. Account of Izaak Walton. New York, 1854. 8°. . . . D,404
Zschokke, J. H. D. Autobiography of. London, 1845. 8°. . . . D,504
Gesammelte Schriften. Aarau, 1854–65. 36 v. 16°. . . . E,367

Bd. 1. Alamontade; Harmonius; Der Eros, oder über die Liebe; Die Hernnhuter-Familie.
2. Diocletian in Salona; Blätter aus dem Tagebuche des armen Pfarr-Vikars von Wiltshire; Die Verklärungen; Kleine Ursachen; Jonathan Frock.
3. Ein Narr des neunzehnten Jahrhunderts; Die weiblichen Stufenjahre; Der Millionär; Der todte Gast; Der Fürstenblick; Das Loch im Aermel.
4. Addrich im Moos.

Zschokke, J. H. D. Gesammelte Schriften. *Continued.* . . . . . E,367

5. Der Freihof von Aarau.
6. Der Flüchtling im Jura; Die Gründung von Maryland; Die Irrfahrt des Philhelenen; Florette, oder die erste Liebe Heinrich IV.; Maryam in der Wüste.
7. Die Prinzessin von Wolfenbüttel; Agathokles, Tyrann von Syrakus; Der Pflanzer in Cuba; Hermingarde.
8. Der Pascha von Buda; Der Creole; Der Feldweibel; Das blaue Wunder.
9. Das Abenteuer der Neujahrsnacht; Die Walpurgisnacht; Der Blondin von Namur; Kriegerische Abenteuer eines Friedfertigen; Die Bohne; Die Nacht in Breczwezmcisl; Das Bein; Es ist sehr möglich!; Erzählungen im Nebel; Die isländischen Briefe.
10. Rückwirkungen, oder wer regiert denn?; Der zerbrochene Krug; Herrn Quint's Verlobung; Hans Dampf in allen Gassen; Tautchen Rosmarin, oder alles verkehrt; Die Reise wider Willen; Der Abend vor der Hochzeit; Das Wirthshaus zu Cransac.
11. Die Rose von Disentis; Die Liebe der Ausgewanderten; Schulze von Celle und Cäcilie.
12. Lyonel Harlington; Die Lampe des Anaxagoras und die russische Fürstin; An Euphrasien über den Nachruhm; Der König von Akim; An Rosais, ueber Ahnungsvermögen und Schutzgeister.
13. *Genfer Novellen:* — Das Pfarrhaus; Die Erbschaft; Ein Buckliger; Julius, oder die zwei Gefangenen; Julius, oder die Bibliothek des Oheims; Julius, oder die Mansarde; Das Thal von Trient; Elisa und Widmer; Der Col d'Anterne; Das Abenteuer am See von Gers.
14. Bilder aus dem häuslichen Leben; Schweizer-Skizzen; Olavides, der neue Belisar; Der Besuch im Marienbade.
15. Wie man lieben muss; Abellino, Schauspiel; Gedichte.
16. Das Goldmacherdorf; Meister Jordan; oder Handwerk hat goldenen Boden; Die Branntweinpest.
17. Spruch und Schwank des Schweizerboten.
18. Selbstschau, erster Theil: Das Schicksal und der Mensch.
19. Selbstschau, zweiter Theil: Welt- und Gottanschauung.
20-29. Stunden der Andacht.
30. Die Sorge der edlern Menscheit für ihre Würde in unsern Tagen; Geschichtliche Darstellung der Ausbreitung des Christenthums auf dem Erdball; Schicksale der Freimaurerei in Europa; Ueber das Verhältniss der Freimaurerei zu Kirche und Staat.
31. Culturgeschichtliches; Biographisches.
32. Biographisches.
33, 34. Geschichtliche Zeitbilder.
35. Geschichtliche Zeitbilder; Klio's Winke.
36. Schweizerland's Geschichte für das Schweizervolk.

and E. History of Switzerland. New York, 1858. 12°. . . . . B,416

Meditations on Death and Eternity. Boston, 1865. 12°. . . . . P,126

Meditations on Life and its Duties. Boston, 1863. 12°. . . . . P,125

Zug um Zug. E. Fritze. Hannover, 1863. 16°. . . . . . G,277,4

Zulus of Natal, Life with. G. H. Mason. London, 1855. p. 8°. . . I,658,1

Zurcher and Margollé. Volcanoes and Earthquakes. London, 1868. 12°. V,1140

Zwei gnädige Frauen. G. von Struensee. Breslau, 1860. 2 v. 16°. . G,501

Zweites Lesebuch. Cincinnati, 1853. 16°. . . . . . . . . . . G,544

Zwölf Zettel. F. W. Hackländer. Stuttgart, 1868. 2 v. 12°. . . . . G,307

www.ingramcontent.com/pod-product-compliance
Lightning Source LLC
LaVergne TN
LVHW021054110826
845150LV00001B/68

* 9 7 8 1 4 2 5 5 6 7 2 6 2 *